American Institute of Certified Public Accountants

Understanding Business Valuation

SECOND EDITION

A Practical Guide to Valuing Small to Medium-Sized Businesses

GARY R. TRUGMAN

CPA/ABV, MCBA, ASA, MVS

Notice to Readers

Understanding Business Valuation: A Practical Guide to Valuing Small to Medium-Sized Businesses, Second Edition, does not represent an official position of the American Institute of Certified Public Accountants, and it is distributed with the understanding that the author and publisher are not rendering legal, accounting, or other professional services in this publication. If legal advice or other expert assistance is required, the services of a competent professional should be sought.

1 2 3 4 5 6 7 8 9 0 CS 0 9 8 7 6 5 4 3 2

ISBN 0-87051-362-1

Dedication

To Linda, my wife and business partner

Everyone who knows us thinks that I am joking when I say that without you none of this would be possible or worthwhile.

Well, it's no joke—it's the truth!!!

Preface

It's hard to believe that this is the second edition. Can you imagine, I was talked into doing this again! I said it the last time, and I will say it again: This is just what we need, another book on business valuation. Years ago, there were only a limited number of books on this topic—mostly finance texts. Today, you cannot read everything that is being published unless you have no life. However, for those of us with a limited life, there are definitely some books on this topic that are worth reading. Some of my favorites include the following:

- *Valuing a Business*, by Shannon Pratt et al.
- *Basic Business Appraisal*, by Raymond Miles
- *Guide to Business Valuations*, by Jay Fishman, Shannon Pratt, et al.
- *Valuing Small Businesses and Professional Practices*, by Shannon Pratt et al.
- *The Advanced Handbook of Business Valuation*, edited by Robert Reilly and Robert Schweihs

So why did I do this again? After spending many years reading, teaching, and practicing in the business valuation field, I have found that there is still quite a bit of confusion among my colleagues when it comes to understanding appraisal theory and applying it to real-world practice. Please don't get me wrong! I may not know as much as many of my colleagues, but I finally realize that there are things in this world we may never understand.

The purpose of this book is to provide some guidance on the theory, as well as on how to apply it in a meaningful fashion. Whether or not I'm successful is up to you. First, some basic ground rules:

1. To get the most out of this book, you *must* read it, not only in its entirety but also in the sequence in which it is written. Don't go to the chapter on capitalization rates without reading the earlier sections of the book. Otherwise, you may not understand what you are capitalizing and why. It is also important to make sure that you read the exhibits and the appendixes at the time they are referenced. The exhibits have been included as an integral part of this book. If you skip over them, or if you go back to them later, you may miss a valuable point that I am trying to make.
2. In general, I do not think in terms of complex mathematical formulas. Therefore, if you really get off on mathematical equations, this book is not for you. Believe it or not, I want readers to understand this stuff! In certain sections of this book, you will see some mathematical formulas. The notation may be different from that found in other books. Concentrate on the concepts and not on the letters and symbols used.
3. I am a firm believer of the KISS theory (keep it simple, stupid). This does not mean, however, that business valuations are simple. Quite the contrary! If you are at all like me, after reading this book you will never feel comfortable doing a business valuation again. This can be an extremely subjective

process. For the accountants out there, this is not at all like accounting, where the debits have to equal the credits. What you will learn is that there is no black-and-white answer. There are a million shades of gray. To quote a good friend of mine, the answer to most questions is, "It depends."

4. The concepts discussed in this book cannot be read and applied as if they were in a vacuum. Many of the items discussed will—directly or indirectly—affect other parts of the valuation process. You must be a big-picture type of person.
5. This book is not intended to present every alternative to every situation. Just because I have included something in this book, *please* do not rely solely on my writings. There may be facts and circumstances that could negate my opinion. You will find that there is no substitute for common sense in this process.
6. In some instances, I will be illustrating points from the negative. Several of the exhibits contain sections of actual valuation reports critiquing someone else's work. Learn from what they may have done wrong.
7. Please don't shoot the messenger! Throughout this book, many topics will be discussed that are controversial. Some may not even have a definitive answer. But you must think about these issues when you do a business valuation.
8. While reading this book, you are going to be exposed to my own form of humor. This is not intended to insult anyone but, rather, to add a little levity to what can be a very dry and technical topic. Although business valuation tends to be extremely complex, let's have some fun while we learn.

With that stuff out of the way, please enjoy my attempt to explain what little I know about business valuation.

Acknowledgments

There are several people whom I must acknowledge for their contributions to this book. These people are not listed in any special order, but they are all very important to me. First and foremost, I would like to thank my business partner and my wife (not necessarily in that order), Linda Trugman, CPA/ABV, CBA, ASA, for her countless hours in assisting me to make this book more readable, logical, and technically accurate. I should also mention her kindness, as administrative manager of our practice, for allowing my billable hours to fall during the period of authorship. We have now stayed married through two editions of this book. It must be love!

Another special thanks goes to several of my staff at Trugman Valuation Associates Inc., who assisted not only in writing various sections of this book, but also in acting as reviewers to make sure that I wrote this technical stuff in English. First, my special thanks to Kyle Garcia for his valuable contributions to the market approach chapters. Next, my gratitude to Fran Goodin for her input into Chapter 4, on research stuff. Fran also made a valuable contribution in the chapter on premiums and discounts. Then there is Anthony Frendo, who assisted me with Chapter 18, on my favorite court cases, as well as reading the entire manuscript to make sure that it was understandable. And finally—get this one—thanks to Manuel Pata, a brand new staff person who was handed my manuscript on his first day on the job and was asked to read it for his input. Believe it or not, he still works for me. All kidding aside, I truly appreciate all of the assistance from these folks, not only for their input into this book, but for their terrific work that continues to allow us to produce the quality product that our clients have come to expect.

Other technical reviewers to whom I owe a great deal of thanks include Robert Schlegel, ASA, MCBA, and Christopher Mellen, ASA, MCBA. No professional publication could truly be considered good without the input from outside reviewers who bust the author's chops. These guys were the best! (Particularly, at busting chops.) I am truly flattered that they agreed to assist me with this project, and I am honored to have them as part of my review team. They are truly some of the smartest people I know in this business.

One more thank-you goes to two different groups of practitioners. The first group consists of the many practitioners I have taught with over the years, who have taught me so much. This list goes on and on, and I just wanted to say thank you. You know who you are. The second group of practitioners consists of all of the students who have attended my classes, participants at conferences who have attended the sessions I have spoken at, and all of my colleagues who have had such flattering things to say to me over the years about my teaching, my writings, and particularly, the first edition of this book. It is hard to make me humble, but you have succeeded. Thank you so very much.

Additional thanks go to the editors and the publications department within the AICPA. You made a kid from the Bronx sound like he is from Manhattan. Actually, more important—you let me keep my Bronx accent! Thanks.

Contents

Introduction . . . . **xvii**
Steps of an Appraisal xviii
Notation System Used in This Book xix

Chapter 1 **Overview of Business Evaluation** **1**
Chapter Goals 1
Introduction 1
A Walk Down Memory Lane 1
Why Are Businesses Appraised? 3
Who Values Businesses? 9
Professional Appraisal Organizations 12
Business Appraisal Standards 14
Conclusion 19

Chapter 2 **Getting Started** **21**
Chapter Goals 21
Introduction 21
Learning About the Engagement 21
Deciding Whether to Accept the Engagement 22
Engagement Letters 32
Five Steps of an Appraisal Assignment 45
The Initial Document Request 45
Conclusion 53

Chapter 3 **Appraisal Principles and Theory** **55**
Chapter Goals 55
Principles of Appraisal 55
Definitions of Value 57
How the Purpose of the Valuation Influences the Standard of Value 64
Internal Revenue Service Influence on Appraisals 64
Conclusion 68

Chapter 4 **Data Gathering** **69**
Chapter Goals 69
What Items Affect Value? 69
Internal Information 69
Financial Information 77
External Information 77
Data Gathering—Mostly Electronic? 90
The On-Site Interview 108
Conclusion 114

Chapter 5 **Data Analysis** **115**
Chapter Goals 115
Introduction 115
Economic Analysis 115
Industry Analysis 118
Subject Company Analysis 124
Financial Analysis 125
Financial Statement Adjustments 139
Conclusion 155

Chapter 6 **The Market Approach—Part I** **157**
Chapter Goals 157
Introduction 157
Guideline Public Company Method 158
Using Valuation Multiples 186
Valuing Invested Capital Instead of Equity 189
Advantages of Using the Guideline Public Company Method 201
Disadvantages of Using the Guideline Public Company Method 201
The Guideline Public Company Method Illustrated 202
Conclusion 219

Chapter 7 **The Market Approach—Part II** **221**
Chapter Goals 221
Overview 221
Transaction (Merger and Acquisition) Method 221
Transaction Analysis—Qualitative and Quantitative 238
Let's Get Back to Theory 253
Internal Transactions 255
Industry Method 255
Conclusion 256

Chapter 8 **The Asset-Based Approach** **257**
Chapter Goals 257
Introduction 257
Common Applications of the Asset-Based Approach 257
Advantages and Disadvantages of the Asset-Based Approach 259
Valuation Methods 259

Working With Other Appraisers 279
How to Locate and Recognize Specialists 279
Conclusion 280

Chapter 9 **The Income Approach 281**
Chapter Goals 281
Introduction 281
Value Is From an Investor's Viewpoint 283
Advantages and Disadvantages of the Income Approach 283
Selecting Benefit Streams 284
Using Pretax or After-Tax Information 285
Debt-Free or After-Debt 286
Using Cash Flow Instead of Earnings 286
Defining Cash Flow 287
Projecting Future Benefit Streams 288
The Acceptance of Forecasts and Projections 293
Income Approach Methods 299
Conclusion 321

Chapter 10 **Discount Rates and Capitalization Rates 323**
Chapter Goals 323
Introduction 323
Discount Rates 324
Capitalization Rates 344
Deriving Discount and Capitalization Rates Applicable to Net Income Directly From the Market 348
Back to the Real World 348
Conclusion 356

Chapter 11 **Premiums and Discounts 357**
Chapter Goals 357
Introduction 357
Control Premium 359
Lack of Control (Minority) Discounts 366
Discount for Lack of Marketability 370
Small Company Discount 391
Discount From Net Asset Value 392
Key Person Discount 400
Application of Discounts and Premiums 401
Other Premiums and Discounts 401
Conclusion 407

Chapter 12 **Revenue Ruling 59-60 . . . . . 409**
Chapter Goals 409
Revenue Ruling 59-60 409
Conclusion 420

Chapter 13 **The Valuation Report** **421**
Chapter Goals 421
Introduction 421
Components of a Valuation Report 421
Types of Valuation Reports 425
Preparing the Business Valuation Report 426
Defending the Business Valuation Report 443
Common Errors in Business Valuation Reports 443
The Reconciliation Process 445
Conclusion 448

Chapter 14 **Estate and Gift Valuations** **449**
Chapter Goals 449
Introduction 449
Revenue Ruling 59-60 449
Chapter 14 Guidelines 450
The Valuation Report 450
The Family Limited Partnership Report 450
Court Cases 489
As Appraisers, Do We Go for the Big Discounts? 503
Conclusion 503

Chapter 15 **Divorce Valuations** **505**
Chapter Goals 505
Introduction 505
The Role of the Appraiser 506
Definition of Value 506
Valuation Dates 509
Valuation Methods 510
Data Gathering and Analysis 511
The Valuation Process 512
Normalizing the Financial Statements 512
More About Valuation Methods 514
Reaching a Conclusion of Value 514
Divorce Valuations of Professional Practices 514
Non-Compete Agreements 518
Valuation of Other Marital Assets 546
Conclusion 548

Chapter 16 **Professional Practice Valuations** **549**
Chapter Goals 549
Overview 549
Why Are Professional Practices Valued? 550
Characteristics of the Professional Practice 550
Professional Practice Versus Other Business Valuations 550
The Valuation Process 557

Valuation Calculations: Unique Aspects . . . 614
Conclusion . . . 619

Chapter 17 **Shareholder Disputes . . . 621**
Chapter Goals . . . 621
Overview . . . 621
Dissenting Shareholder Matters . . . 623
Oppressed Shareholder Matters . . . 624
Fair Value . . . 625
The Valuation Date . . . 628
Fair Value Methodology . . . 633
Conclusion . . . 643

Chapter 18 **My Favorite Court Cases . . . 645**
Chapter Goals . . . 645
Overview . . . 645
Estate of Joyce C. Hall v. Commissioner . . . 645
Estate of Samuel I. Newhouse v. Commissioner . . . 648
Charles S. Foltz v.U.S. News and World Report, Inc. . . . 650
Bernard Mandelbaum et al. v. Commissioner . . . 653
Mad Auto Wrecking Inc. v. Commissioner . . . 657
Conclusion . . . 671

Chapter 19 **Economic Damages . . . 673**
Chapter Goals . . . 673
Introduction . . . 673
Lost Profits . . . 673
The Lost Profits Analysis . . . 676
Conclusion . . . 753

Appendix 1 **AICPA Statement on Consulting Services Standards I . . . 755**
Introduction . . . 755
Definitions . . . 755
Standards for Consulting Services . . . 756
Consulting Services for Attest Clients . . . 757
Effective Date . . . 757

Appendix 2 **IBA Standards . . . 758**
Foreword . . . 758
Founding Standards Committee . . . 758
Preamble . . . 759
Format . . . 759
Standard One: Professional Conduct & Ethics . . . 759
Standard Two: Oral Appraisal Reports . . . 766
Standard Three: Expert Testimony . . . 766
Standard Four: Letter Form Written Appraisal Reports . . . 767
Standard Five: Formal Written Appraisal Reports . . . 768
Standard Six: Preliminary Reports . . . 770

Appendix 3 **ASA Standards** **771**
BVS-I. General Requirements for Developing a Business Valuation 771
BVS-II. Financial Statement Adjustments 773
BVS-III. Asset-Based Approach to Business Valuation 774
BVS-IV. Income Approach to Business Valuation 775
BVS-V. Market Approach to Business Valuation 776
BVS-VI. Reaching a Conclusion of Value 777
BVS-VII. Comprehensive Written Business Valuation Report 778
Definitions 780
SBVS-1. The Guideline Company Valuation Method 783

Appendix 4 **NACVA Professional Standards** **785**
Contents 785
Preamble 786
General Standards 787
Development Standards 787
Reporting Standards 789
Other Guidelines and Requirements 790
Effective Date 791
Appendix I: AICPA Code of Professional Conduct Rules 791

Appendix 5 **International Glossary of Business Valuation Terms** **800**

Appendix 6 **Revenue Ruling 59-60** **806**
Rev. Rul. 59-60, 1959-1 C.B. 237 IRC Sec. 2031 806
Headnote 806
Text 806

Appendix 7 **Revenue Ruling 65-192** **813**
Rev. Rul. 65-192 813
Full Text 813

Appendix 8 **Revenue Ruling 65-193** **817**
Rev. Rul. 65-193, 1965-2 C.B. 370, IRC Sec. 2031 817
Text 817

Appendix 9 **Revenue Procedure 66-49** **818**
Rev. Proc. 66-49 818
Headnote 818
Full Text 818

Appendix 10 **Revenue Ruling 68-609** **821**
Rev. Rul. 68-609, 1968-2 C.B. 327 IRC Sec. 1001 821
Headnote 821
Text 821

Appendix 11 **Revenue Procedure 77-12** **823**
Rev. Proc. 77-12, 1977-1 C.B. 569 823
Text 823

Appendix 12 **Revenue Ruling 77-287** **825**
Rev. Rul. 77-287, 1977-2 C.B. 319 IRC Sec. 2031 825
Headnote 825
Text 825

Appendix 13 **Revenue Ruling 83-120** **830**
Rev. Rul. 83-120, 1983-2 C.B. 170 IRC Sec. 2512 830
Headnote 830
Text 830

Appendix 14 **Revenue Ruling 85-75** **833**
Rev. Rul. 85-75, 1985-1 C.B. 376 IRC Sec. 6659 833
Headnote 833
Text 833

Appendix 15 **Revenue Ruling 93-12** **835**
Rev. Rul. 93-12, 1993-7 I.R.B. 13, 1/26/93 835
Headnote 835
Full Text 835

Appendix 16 **Technical Advice Memorandum 94-36005** **837**
Full Text 837

Appendix 17 **Private Letter Ruling 91-50001** **840**
Full Text 840

Appendix 18 **Equitable Distribution Value of Small, Closely Held Businesses and Professional Practices** **843**
Abstract 843
Contents 843
Introduction 844
History and Review of the Literature 845
Theory and Methods 847
Argument 852
Replies to Opposition 870
Summary and Conclusion 871
Works Cited and Consulted 872

Appendix 19 **Business Valuation Resources** **874**
Books, Periodicals, and More 874
Government Regulatory Material 880
Organizations 880
Sources of Data 881

Index **883**

Introduction

This book has been methodically organized to help you get the most out of it that you possibly can. Each chapter contains lots of new stuff since the last edition, so you might want to go through them all in sequence. The chapters are set up as follows:

- Chapter 1 provides background stuff regarding why businesses are appraised, who appraises them, and the various appraisal organizations and their standards. Although you probably fit into one of the categories discussed, you should be aware of the other types of appraisers and their standards, since you will most likely run across them in your endeavors.
- Chapter 2 gets you started in the appraisal process. In this chapter, I discuss the things that you must know to start an assignment. Chapter 2 includes information about engagement letters, conflicts of interest, internal work programs, and the initial document request.
- Chapter 3 takes you through the basic appraisal principles and theory behind the stuff that we are trying to figure out how to do. We will learn that the term *value* has many different meanings in business valuation, and we will discuss some of the more important meanings. Since so much of the valuation work we do involves taxes, this chapter will also point out the influence of the Internal Revenue Service on what we do.
- Chapter 4 includes a discussion of internal and external sources of information that will be gathered by the appraiser. Numerous references are provided as to where you can locate information. This chapter lists all types of neat sites on the Internet for doing the required research.
- Chapter 5 walks you through the process of what to do with the data that was gathered during the appraisal process. This chapter includes a discussion of economic, industry, company, and financial analysis.
- Chapter 6 presents the first part of market approach to valuation. The underlying theory for the market approach is presented in this chapter. The balance of the chapter concentrates on the guideline public company method, including more detail on how to perform the analysis involving publicly traded companies. You will have to read this chapter to find out about SGLPTL.
- Chapter 7 presents the second half of the market approach. This chapter includes a detailed discussion of the guideline transaction method, including a description of the various databases available to find merger and acquisition information involving closely held businesses. This chapter takes you step by step through the process of using this method. Rules of thumb are also discussed in this chapter.
- Chapter 8 presents the asset-based approach to valuation. Here also, several methods are explored, and there is a discussion of how to find and communicate with other types of appraisers.
- Chapter 9 presents the income approach to valuation. For small and medium-sized businesses, this chapter may be one of the most important. Single-period and multi-period models are presented. Forecasting financial information is also included in this chapter since it is the very essence of this approach to valuation.

- Chapter 10 is the chapter that everyone will want to turn to! Discount rates and capitalization rates are discussed. Since I have been reading about this topic for years, waiting for someone to give me the correct answer, and nobody has, I wrote my own chapter. Lots of theory and, hopefully, practical guidance has been included in this chapter.
- Chapter 11 includes a discussion on valuation premiums and discounts. Learn when to use different premiums and discounts, as well as how to support your opinion. This revised chapter now includes a discussion on some of the more controversial issues still being debated among practitioners.
- Chapter 12 contains an annotated version of Revenue Ruling 59-60. This revenue ruling is so important that I decided to include it as a separate chapter. You can never get enough of a Revenue Ruling that is over 40 years old but has the makings of being the best writing in business valuation of all time (even counting my book).
- Chapter 13 addresses the appraisal report. Learn how to prepare and defend the report, and learn some tips regarding presentation techniques.
- Chapter 14 is brand new. This chapter addresses valuation assignments that are performed for estate and gift tax purposes. Learn about the Chapter 14 (of the Internal Revenue Code) requirements, the adequate disclosure requirements, and family limited partnership valuations.
- Chapter 15 is also brand new. This chapter covers issues involved in divorce valuations. Valuations performed as part of a divorce assignment entail very unique considerations for the appraiser.
- Chapter 16 is also new. This chapter contains a discussion on unique aspects of valuing professional practices. Learn what factors should be considered in valuing different types of professional practices, making these assignments different from valuing an operating company. Also included in this chapter is a detailed analysis on the valuation of work in process for a contingent-fee law firm.
- Chapter 17 is another new one. Shareholder disputes are covered here, including issues involving the fair value standard of value.
- Chapter 18 is a discussion of some of my favorite court cases. In fact, the name of this chapter is "My Favorite Court Cases." Pretty catchy, isn't it? This chapter has a few really good court cases that will help you understand some important issues regarding valuation.
- Chapter 19 is not only a new one, but it contains a discussion about economic damages. Since so many business valuation techniques are used in this type of analysis, I decided to include it in the new edition.
- And finally, the accompanying CD-ROM contains some reports for you to plagiarize. I only hope that you will give our firm proper attribution. Several sample reports are included so that you can see the difference between the different types of reports.

While the material in this book is not necessarily unique, it has been organized in a manner that is intended to provide you with a logical analysis of the appraisal process. Many of the exhibits contain actual sections of appraisal reports, to help emphasize the subject matter. Make sure you read them!

Steps of an Appraisal

This book proceeds in a sequence that resembles the steps of performing an appraisal. The chapters will address these steps in detail. Since you are probably dying to know what these steps are, I list them here:

1. Define the appraisal engagement.
2. Gather the necessary data to perform the engagement.
3. Analyze the data that you gathered.

4. Estimate the value of the interest being appraised.
5. Write the report to communicate the value.

Notation System Used in This Book

A source of confusion for those trying to understand financial theory and methods is the fact that financial writers have not adopted a standard system of notation. While I have attempted to follow the most common notation system, I may have deviated along the way. This should not concern you.

Following are the symbols used in this book:

- Value at a point in time:

  PV = Present value
  FV = Future value

- Cost-of-capital and rate-of-return variables:

  k = Discount rate (generalized)
  k_e = Discount rate for common equity capital (cost of common equity capital); unless otherwise stated, it generally is assumed that this discount rate is applicable to the net cash flow available to common equity
  k_d = Discount rate for debt (*note*: for complex capital structures, there could be more than one class of capital in any of the above categories, in which case expanded subscripts would be required)
  c = Capitalization rate
  C_{pt} = Capitalization rate for a pretax benefit stream
  C_{at} = Capitalization rate for an after-tax benefit stream
  CP = Control premium
  t = Tax rate (expressed as a percentage of pretax income)
  R_f = Rate of return on a risk-free security
  β = Beta (a coefficient, usually used to modify a rate-of-return variable)
  $(R_m - R_f)$ = Risk premium for the "market" (usually used in the context of a market for equity securities such as the NYSE or S&P 500)
  SCA = Specific company adjustment
  SCP = Small company premium
  WACC = Weighted average cost of capital

- Income variables:

  E = Expected economic income (in a generalized sense [i.e., could be dividends], any of several possible definitions of cash flows, net income, and so on; also called a benefit stream)
  EBIT = Earnings before interest and taxes
  EBITDA = Earnings before depreciation, interest, and taxes ("depreciation" in this context usually includes amortization)

- Periods or variables in a series:

i = The *i*th period, or the *i*th variable in a series (may be extended to the *j*th variable, the *k*th variable, and so on)
n = The number of periods or variables in the series, or the last number in the series
∞ = Infinity
0 = Period, the base period, usually the latest year immediately preceding the valuation date

- Weightings:

W = Weight
W_e = Weight (percentage) of common equity in capital structure
W_p = Weight of preferred equity in capital structure
W_d = Weight (percentage) of debt in capital structure

Note: For purposes of computing a weighted average cost of capital (WACC), it is assumed that the above weightings are at market value.

- Growth:

g = Rate of growth

- Mathematical functions:

Σ = Sum of (add up all the variables that follow)

1

Overview of Business Valuation

Chapter Goals

Since starting at the beginning is always a logical place to begin, this chapter is designed to:

1. Give you some history about the valuation profession
2. Explain why businesses are appraised
3. Provide some background about who values businesses
4. Familiarize you with the professional appraisal organizations
5. Provide you with an overview of professional standards relating to business valuations

Introduction

Business valuations are performed for companies of all sizes and types. In addition, business valuations are frequently performed for fractional interests in companies without ever valuing the entire business enterprise. The conceptual principles are the same for companies of different sizes, but very often, the manner in which these principles are applied varies greatly. The level of data available for the appraisal of smaller companies tends to be considerably lower, but more data is available than when the previous edition of this book was released. When there is a lack of data available for the smaller companies, either certain methodologies cannot be used, or the result should be considered less reliable. The appraiser must be even more careful in these circumstances.

The appraiser should understand the business valuation process from the large-company, more theoretical basis, in order to adapt these concepts properly to the smaller business. However, valuing smaller businesses can be extremely challenging, since most of the empirical data that is regularly used by an appraiser applies to larger companies and only tangentially to smaller ones.

A Walk Down Memory Lane

No book would really be complete if it didn't include a history lesson. Unless, of course, that book is a dictionary (I know—bad joke!). Anyway, some of the key events in our history include:

- Oldest known appraisal: Book of Genesis, Chapter 23, Verse 15—"The land is worth 400 shekels." This was a real estate appraisal.
- First century B.C.—"Everything is worth what its purchaser will pay for it."—Publius.

- 1919—Arthur Stone Dewing's first edition of *Financial Policy of Corporations* (the fifth and final edition was issued in 1953)—suggested rates ranging from 10 percent to 100 percent at which to capitalize corporate net income, the rate being dependent on which of seven descriptive categories best characterizes the company.
- 1920—U.S. Treasury Department Appeals & Review Memorandum ARM 34—issued as a result of the Eighteenth Amendment to the U.S. Constitution, which created Prohibition. The intent was to provide a means of valuing the lost intangible value of existing breweries and distilleries. (I'll drink to that!)
- 1925—Ralph A. Badger, *Valuation of Industrial Securities*—an early and frequently quoted treatise that opined on required rates of return by risk classification.
- 1937—James C. Bonbright, *Valuation of Property*—considered to be one of the most classic works ever, it is frequently quoted in court opinions. It includes several chapters on valuation of businesses and securities.
- 1938—John Burr Williams, *The Theory of Investment Value*—this early treatise lays out the foundation for the principle of future benefits, which will be discussed later in this book. The author stands for the proposition that the value of the investment is the cash it will pay out to the owner over the life of the investment, discounted to a present value at a rate that reflects current market conditions and the risk of the investment. Good stuff!
- 1952—American Society of Appraisers formed—multi-disciplinary professional society awarding certification in several areas of appraisal, one of which was "intangible property," which included stock and business ownership.
- 1959—Revenue Ruling 59-60—probably the most widely quoted treatise in valuation history. The intent was to provide guidance on how to value closely held stocks. Sets out the definition of fair market value, offers approaches to valuation, explains the need to apply common sense, and calls valuation a "prophecy as to the future." Also lists the eight factors to consider *at a minimum* when performing a valuation.
- 1964—first publication of University of Chicago Center for Research in Security Prices (CRSP) data on rates of return on the New York Stock Exchange, initially covering the period 1926–1960. This data provides the necessary empirical evidence for development of required rates of return for equities (discount rates). The data is maintained and published annually by Ibbotson Associates in their annual *Stocks, Bonds, Bills & Inflation,* as well as in other publications.
- 1968—Revenue Ruling 68-609—detailed explanation of the "formula" (excess earnings) method of valuing intangibles.
- 1978—formation of The Institute of Business Appraisers. This was the first professional organization in the United States dedicated exclusively to business valuation.
- 1981—establishment of the Business Valuation Committee of the American Society of Appraisers, after they recognized business valuation as a specialty.
- 1981—establishment of the Management Advisory Services Division by the American Institute of CPAs (now known as the Consulting Services Division).
- 1987—establishment of the Appraisal Foundation. This organization was set up by seven real estate organizations and the American Society of Appraisers in response to the growing problem facing the real estate appraisal world. This organization is the creator of the *Uniform Standards of Professional Appraisal Practice* (*USPAP*). The provisions of the *USPAP* include standards 9 and 10, which pertain to business valuations.
- 1989—passage of the Financial Institutions Reform, Recovery, and Enforcement Act of 1989 (FIRREA). Among other provisions, this law requires all who perform real estate appraisals involving a federally related transaction to follow the *USPAP.*
- 1991—formation of the National Association of Certified Valuation Analysts.

- 1997—the American Institute of CPAs Executive Board passes a specialty designation known as "Accredited in Business Valuation" (ABV). The first examination was given in November 1997.
- 1998—the American Institute of CPAs, through great insight and foresight, published the first edition of my book. (Hey, don't laugh—it could not have been that bad—this is the second edition and you bought it!)

Oh, I forgot to mention one other important date in history. In 1953, my mom and dad had me. This profession may never be the same as a result! From the time that I was just an infant, they were calling me a CPA (constant pain in the . . .). I knew I was destined for stardom!

Why Are Businesses Appraised?

Before an appraisal assignment can be started, the appraiser must know the purpose of the valuation, as the purpose can influence the valuation process. This does not mean that if the purpose is a sale and you represent the business owner, you should value this business as highly as possible. However, the purpose of the valuation may influence methods, standards of value, and other factors that are considered to be part of the assignment. For example, certain types of business valuations are guided by specific sets of rules, such as state statutes, IRS regulations, or Department of Labor regulations. Also, if a minority interest is being valued, certain adjustments may not be made to the company's financial statements because the minority interest cannot legally effectuate such adjustments. Valuations performed for divorce purposes may have case law restrictions that must be considered (e.g., separating professional goodwill from the goodwill of the practice). If you have never performed a business valuation, this stuff probably has you wondering what I am talking about. Be patient, this will start to make more sense as we proceed.

Business valuation engagements are performed for a variety of reasons, including the following:

- Mergers, acquisitions, reorganizations, spinoffs, liquidations, and bankruptcy
- Allocation of purchase price
- Estate, gift, and income taxes
- Marital dissolution
- Employee stock ownership plans (ESOPs)
- Buy-sell agreements
- Stockholder disputes
- Financing
- Ad valorem taxes
- Incentive stock option considerations
- Initial public offerings
- Damages litigation
- Insurance claims
- Charitable contributions
- Eminent domain actions
- Fairness opinions

Mergers, Acquisitions, Reorganizations, Spinoffs, Liquidations, and Bankruptcy

Business valuations are frequently performed when one company acquires another company, when a company is targeted for an acquisition, when a company's capital structure is reorganized, when a company splits up, and when a company enters bankruptcy in liquidation or reorganization. The transactions may include entire or partial acquisitions, divestitures, liquidation, or recapitalization. Mergers will generally require both companies to be valued, while an acquisition may require only a single valuation. The terms of the transaction generally include cash, notes, stock, or a combination of these forms of payment. In bankruptcy, in addition to the involvement of the different classes of creditors and the shareholders, the approval of the Bankruptcy Court is usually required.

Closely held companies with two or more definable divisions may be split up or spun off into separate corporations. Reasons for doing this can include estate tax considerations, family conflict, or sale of only part of the total business. Valuations are necessary for tax purposes, financial reporting, and, if applicable, equitable distribution of the assets among family members. In the liquidation of a corporation, the appraiser's allocation of the assets distributed to the stockholders may be required to substantiate subsequent depreciation and other deductions claimed.

Over the past several years, many publicly traded companies have acquired closely held businesses by using restricted stock (Rule 144 stock) as the form of payment. Restricted stock is discussed in Chapter 11. The advantage of using stock as a form of payment is that the acquirer does not have to use cash to make the acquisition. Frequently, the transaction can also provide the seller with a tax-free transaction under Internal Revenue Code (IRC) Section 1031. It also provides the seller with the opportunity to take advantage of the tax-deferred appreciation of owning the acquirer's stock. This can be a good or bad thing. This can also create work for the appraiser.

Allocation of Purchase Price

In prior years, both the purchaser and seller would determine their own values and treat the purchase and sale of the assets differently. The purchaser did not want to buy goodwill, since it was not tax deductible, and the seller wanted to sell goodwill, because it was subject to lower capital gains tax treatment. This created some very interesting allocations between the buyer and the seller. The all-around loser was Uncle Sam. However, the Tax Reform Act of 1986 changed all that. IRC Section 1060 requires that when a business is acquired, a valuation must be performed to support the allocation of the total purchase price to the component parts for income tax purposes. The law requires a uniform allocation of the purchase price based on an appraisal of the underlying assets. The IRS now pays more attention to these transactions to ensure that the purchase price allocation is reasonable and is treated consistently by both the purchaser and the seller. An inappropriate or inconsistent allocation of the purchase price can result in an increased tax liability and, in some instances, penalties.

In 1993 the tax law changed, providing for intangible assets to be amortized over 15 years. This change reduced the necessity for appraisers to allocate the purchase price between different classes of intangible assets that had different amortization periods, or no amortization period (e.g., goodwill), under the old law. Allocation of purchase price continues to be a required service, although the tax law has made it a little easier.

Not all allocations of purchase price are performed for income tax purposes. In some instances, an allocation may be performed when it is necessary to value certain components of a company and not the entire equity of an enterprise. This can be illustrated by the following situation. A company was sold and the value of the transaction was known. However, the $17 million sales price was problematic because our client thought that her husband's business was worth $5 million. After all, he told her this when they settled their divorce action based on this value. To say the least, she was not happy when she found out that the business was sold for $17 million shortly after the divorce. The Court decided that she was entitled to her equitable share of the excess (due to the husband's fraud), but since the divorce was in a state that did not consider personal goodwill or personal covenants not to compete as part of equitable distribution, she was entitled to the non-personal portion.

The appraiser representing the husband allocated a large portion of the purchase price to personal goodwill and/or a personal covenant not to compete. We had to allocate the purchase price to support the value of what our client was entitled to receive. This is an example of a non-tax allocation of purchase price. This concept is discussed in greater detail in Chapter 15.

In addition to allocating the purchase price for tax purposes, generally accepted accounting principles (GAAP) may also require these types of valuations. The appraiser needs to be aware of pronouncements such as Accounting Principle Bulletins (APBs) 16 and 17 as well as pronouncements made by the Financial Accounting Standards Board (FASB) dealing with issues such as the impairment of goodwill.

As this book was being edited, the FASB issued Pronouncements 141 and 142 changing the accounting rules for pooling of interests and impairment of acquired goodwill. Pooling has been eliminated, and treatment of impairment of acquired goodwill will become a new practice area for business valuers. Little guidance is available as of right now on this issue, but the AICPA, in conjunction with CPA2Biz, will be on top of the issues and will be providing information on the subject. Whatever you do, do not ignore the importance of these pronouncements.

Estate, Gift, and Income Taxes

The valuation of a closely held business or business interest is important to estate planners as they consider the impact of the unified estate and gift tax credit on lifetime transfers of property. Although this is not a tax book, appraisers working in this area are urged to consult the appropriate IRC sections and regulations for specifics on the unified estate and gift tax requirements. If you think that finance books on business valuation are fun reading, try the tax code. You will never have so much fun!

IRC Section 2036(c), relating to estate freeze techniques, was repealed and superseded by a new, complex set of rules in Chapter 14 of the IRC (Sections 2701 to 2704). These rules can be advantageous to the client, but the IRC and IRS regulations include strict provisions for compliance. Appraisers therefore should familiarize themselves with these tax provisions. Chapter 14 of this book (oh, what a coincidence!) contains specific information about estate and gift tax valuations.

In addition, the IRC contains special rules for the redemption of stock in a closely held company when the owner dies and the value of the stock represents more than 35 percent of the gross estate. Appraisers need to be aware of the alternatives under IRC Section 303.

At the time of the writing of this book, President Bush managed to get Congress to pass a repeal of the estate tax, a phase-out that begins in 2002 and eliminates the tax completely in 2010. However, it comes back in 2011 if nothing is done to make it permanent. If Congress completely repeals the estate tax, you want to be familiar with these other areas of why businesses are appraised. You may otherwise end up preparing income tax returns again.

Valuations performed for income tax purposes may include S corporation conversions due to the built-in gains tax issues that arise if a sale occurs before the 10-year period required by the Internal Revenue Code. Appraisers should consult applicable sections of the tax law to properly understand the unique requirements of S corporation valuations performed for a conversion.

Marital Dissolution

In a marital dissolution, most of a couple's assets and liabilities are valued, regardless of whether a state follows equitable distribution or community property rules. Frequently, one of the assets included in the marital estate is an interest in a closely held business. It is typical to have the business valued in its entirety if it is a small business, but sometimes only a portion of the business (e.g., a minority interest) is valued in a large business. Usually the business is not divided between the spouses. Instead, one spouse keeps the business and the other receives different assets of equal value. Since marital dissolution laws vary significantly from state to state, the appraiser must be aware of the rules of the state in which the divorce takes place. For example, in some states, goodwill associated with a professional is excludable from distribution, while in other states, it is includable.

Another item that the appraiser must be aware of is the standard of value (covered in Chapter 2) used in the jurisdiction of the marital dissolution. Frequently, fair market value is the discussed standard of value, but the application from state to state varies greatly from the definition found in the tax laws. This can be illustrated by reviewing cases from various states. For example, in Florida, fair market value has been interpreted to be the value of the business, assuming that the business owner walks away without a covenant not to compete. In most instances, fair market value assumes a covenant not to compete. Logically, what willing buyer would purchase a business if the seller could open up next door and compete with him or her? In Pennsylvania, fair market value excludes personal goodwill. Clearly, the appraiser cannot be expected to know every state law, but he or she should ask the client's attorney for information before proceeding in a direction that may have his or her report thrown out for failure to comply with the rules of the jurisdiction. Chapter 15 contains specific information about divorce valuations.

Employee Stock Ownership Plans

An ESOP is an incentive ownership arrangement funded by the employer. In general, employer stock is contributed instead of cash. ESOPs provide capital, liquidity, and certain tax advantages for private companies whose owners do not want to go public. An independent appraiser must value the employer's securities, at least annually, and must determine the price per share supporting transactions with participants, plan contributions, and allocations within the ESOP. Appraisers are urged to become familiar with the rules promulgated by the Department of Labor before they begin an ESOP engagement. A good publication to obtain is *Valuing ESOP Shares*, published by the ESOP Association. They can be reached at (202) 293-2971 or www.the-esop-emplowner.org.

Buy-Sell Agreements

A buy-sell agreement allows a partner or stockholder in a closely held business to acquire the interest of a partner or stockholder who withdraws from the business. The agreement may contain a designated price, or a formula to determine the price, that the remaining owners of the entity will pay to acquire the interest. The price or the formula needs to be updated periodically. Payment terms and conditions of sale are also generally provided. A client may ask an appraiser to assist in determining which valuation method is appropriate in such an agreement.

Buy-sell agreements are also used frequently to establish a value for a transaction between the partners or stockholders in the event of death, disability, or retirement. It is common to see different formulas for each event. The appraiser must be aware of IRC Section 2702 and its impact on valuations when there is a buy-sell agreement in effect.

In working with the client, the appraiser should caution him or her about the use of a single formula. Formulas do not always appropriately consider the economic and financial climate at the valuation date, stand the test of time, or achieve the parties' intentions. Therefore, their usage should be limited. Instead, the basis of a buy-sell agreement should be a valuation. If an extensive valuation is required, it should be performed by a qualified appraiser.

Stockholder Disputes

Stockholder disputes can range from breakups of companies resulting from disagreements between stockholders to stockholder dissent relating to mergers, dissolutions, and similar matters. Since many states allow a corporation to merge, dissolve, or restructure without unanimous stockholder consent, many disputes have arisen over the years because minority stockholders have felt that the action of the majority had a negative impact on them. Dissenting stockholders have filed lawsuits to allow their shares to be valued as if the action never took place.

In such cases, the value of the stockholder's interest is what it was immediately before the change; it does not reflect the effect of the proposed change on the value of the corporation. In these instances, the value is generally determined according to the standard of fair value, based on the case law within the state of incorporation. When an appraiser accepts an engagement relating to a stockholder action, it is advisable for him or her to request the client's legal counsel to clarify the value definition used in the particular state. The appraiser cannot address such issues as control premiums, minority discounts, and discounts for lack of marketability without adequate legal information about the value definition to be used.

Many states also have statutes to protect minority shareholders from being "oppressed" (abused) by the controlling shareholder(s). This is another instance where the appraiser must become familiar with the statutes and case law of the jurisdiction in which the legal action is pending. Chapter 17 contains some specific information about shareholder dispute valuations.

Financing

A valuation of the business may provide lenders or potential investors with information that will help the client obtain additional funds. Financial statements present information about a business based on historical amounts. For a new business, the traditional statement may closely reflect the estimated current value. However, this is generally not the case for an established business that has developed intangible value over the years. Assets with intangible value (such as special trademarks, patents, customer lists, and goodwill) may not be reflected in the financial statements. Furthermore, other assets and liabilities of the business (such as real estate and equipment) may be worth significantly more or less than the book value as recorded under GAAP.

Ad Valorem Taxes

In some jurisdictions, ad valorem taxes are based on the value of property used in a trade or business. Various entities are subject to ad valorem taxation, and therefore, the fair market value of such properties must frequently be determined to ascertain the amount of tax. Regulations and case law differ significantly from jurisdiction to jurisdiction. To determine the appropriate standard of value for these properties, the appraiser needs to consult the client's lawyer.

Incentive Stock Option Considerations

Many large companies provide fringe benefits in the form of incentive stock option plans that allow their employees to purchase the company's stock at a certain point in time and at a stated price. Employees pay no taxes when the incentive stock option is granted or when the stock option is exercised. Employees do pay tax, however, when they sell the stock received through the exercise of the option. To qualify as an incentive stock option, a stock's option price must equal or exceed its fair market value when the option is granted. Accordingly, the valuation of a closely held company has a significant impact on its incentive stock option plan.

Over the past several years, stock options have become a major component of employee compensation packages. This is especially true for start-up companies that may not have the cash flow to pay market rates of compensation to its employees. Instead, the employee works for the company for a lower salary but a very generous stock option plan. The computer industry has produced many millionaires as a result of these programs. Boy, am I jealous!

Initial Public Offerings

A substantial amount of legal and accounting services must be rendered to bring a private business to the public marketplace. From a financial standpoint, the corporation's accounting records and statements are carefully reviewed and amended, if necessary. The capital structure may need enhancement, and executive benefit plans may need revisions. More important, the corporation's stock is valued for the initial offering.

The underwriter must exercise a great deal of judgment about the price the public may be willing to pay for the stock when it is first offered for sale. Such factors as prior years' earnings, potential earnings, general stock market conditions, and the stock prices of comparable or guideline companies need to be considered to determine the final offering price. The client may ask the appraiser to support the offering price by performing a valuation.

Damages Litigation

Many court cases involve damages. Some cases relate to compensation sought for patent infringements, illegal price fixing, breaches of contract, lost profits, or lost business opportunities, while others relate to lender liability, discrimination, and wrongful death actions. The appraiser may also be asked to perform hypothetical valuations of a company to determine the amount of damages resulting from the loss of business value to the stockholders. These types of valuations generally require the appraiser to value the company twice. The first valuation determines the value of the company at the present time. The second valuation is based on what the company would have been worth had a certain action taken place or not taken place. The difference is generally a measure of damages.

Practitioners are cautioned to be aware of such court decisions as *Daubert*[1]and *Kumho Tire*[2] to ensure that the methodologies employed in these and other types of litigation are generally accepted in the literature. Using methods that are not generally accepted can result in the expert's disqualification in a litigation. This is sure to make for unhappy clients and attorneys. Chapter 19 contains specific information pertaining to economic damages.

Insurance Claims

Cases involving risk insurance claims focus on the loss of income because of business interruptions and the value of such separate business assets as inventory and equipment. A valuation may be required to support the owner's position or the insurer's position. The loss of income would be determined based on documentable lost profits. The value of individual business assets, such as inventory and equipment, would be based on the replacement cost of these assets.

Charitable Contributions

Owners of closely held businesses may wish to give all or part of their interest in a business to a favorite charity. Although shares of stock in a closely held business are donated to charity infrequently, this option exists, and the appraiser must be aware of the rules concerning the deductibility of such gifts. Current tax laws encourage charitable donations by permitting a tax deduction equal to the fair market value of certain appreciated capital gains property. For gifts of property in excess of $500, the IRS requires that donors provide documentation to support the deduction for the year in which the gift was given. If the amount of the tax deduction warrants the expense, donors can obtain a valuation of the gift. If the value of the gift exceeds $5,000, an appraisal is required.

---

[1] *William Daubert, et al. v. Merrell Dow Pharmaceuticals, Inc.*, 509 U.S. 579, 113 S. Ct. 2786, 125 L.Ed.2d 469 (1993).

[2] *Kumho Tire Company, Ltd., et al. v. Patrick Carmichael, et al.*, 119 S. Ct. 1167, 143 L.Ed.2d 238 (1999).

Eminent Domain Actions

An eminent domain action takes place when government exercises its right to take over property and must compensate the owner for any resulting reduction in the value of the property. For example, a business may have to forfeit a prime location to accommodate the widening of a street. Although the business can relocate, its value may be adversely affected during the period of the move or as a result of changing locations. An expert opinion on the monetary impact of the condemnation may be necessary to support the business owner's claim or the government's offer.

As part of the business valuation, the appraiser should become familiar with the demographics of the area and should assess the impact of the change in location. In assessing the impact, the business appraiser needs to remember that real estate appraisers have often said that the key to a business's success is "location, location, location."

Projections may be required to calculate the losses. A valuation of the business, both before the condemnation and after the move, may be required. The expenses of the actual move need to be considered in the valuation.

Fairness Opinions

A service that is very closely related to business valuation is the fairness opinion. A fairness opinion is generally required when a publicly traded corporation is involved in a merger, acquisition, or other type of transaction where the board of directors wants to have an independent appraiser give its blessing to the transaction. This is a high-risk type of service, and it should not be performed by an appraiser unless he or she really understands the nuances of the fairness opinion.

This service is frequently provided by investment bankers (with deep pockets). Appraisal firms may also offer this service. In fact, many do. The purpose of the fairness opinion is for the appraiser to opine that the transaction is *fair* to the stockholders. The appraiser does not determine value since there is already an agreed-upon price for the transaction. The appraiser should read many other publications, including actual fairness opinions, before even thinking about doing one. Think liability!

Who Values Businesses?

There is a considerable amount of competition among business valuers. There are a growing number of full-time appraisers in the business, but they are outnumbered by the part-time appraisers, who spend much of their time in other areas. It is important to understand who the other players in the field are, because you will come across them if your practice is anything like mine. Understanding the strengths and weaknesses of your opposition, particularly in a litigation engagement, will allow you to properly assist the attorney with whom you are working so that he or she can cross-examine the other expert more thoroughly.

Among the groups providing business appraisal services are the following:

- Business appraisers
- Accountants (CPAs)
- Business brokers
- College professors (Finance and Economics)
- Commercial real estate appraisers
- Investment bankers

Each group of professionals brings something unique to the practice of business valuation. Each group has its advantages and disadvantages, although the better business appraisers have crossed over boundaries and obtained some of the advantages of the other groups. Each of these groups is discussed in the following sections.

Business Appraisers

Professional business appraisers are those individuals who provide business appraisal services as their main area of focus. They are generally well educated in business valuation, and this includes having an understanding of issues involved in the fields of finance, economics, security analysis, and accounting, among others. Most of these individuals either have received some form of accreditation from a professional appraisal organization or are currently pursuing these credentials (credentials are discussed later in this chapter).

Many of these individuals work in an environment where they are exposed to businesses of a particular type (e.g., professional practices, large companies, small companies, or a particular industry). One difficulty that these individuals may encounter is trying to value a company that is not in their area of specialization. For example, an appraiser who is accustomed to using public stock market information to value large closely held companies may have a difficult time valuing the small paint manufacturer (not Sherwin-Williams!).

Accountants (CPAs)

Over the past decade, the number of accountants performing business valuations has grown exponentially. An accountant's background and training provide both advantages and disadvantages with regard to being a business appraiser.

Accountants have several advantages in rendering business valuation services. They are educated in financial concepts and terminology. This gives the accountant a distinct advantage in understanding financial statements. It also may give the accountant the ability to analyze the financial statements using the same analytical tools (e.g., ratio analysis) that he or she employs to perform other types of accounting services.

Working with numbers is another clear advantage for the accountant. We bean counters can count beans better than anyone else. Accountants are also frequently exposed to revenue rulings and tax laws. This can represent a significant advantage over other types of appraisers, especially when tax-related appraisals are being performed. To illustrate this point, our firm performed a valuation assignment for the Internal Revenue Service (I know, the so-called bad guys! They really are not a bad group to work for once you get to know them) where the subject of the valuation was a 1.6 percent beneficial interest in a trust. The taxpayer's appraiser took a discount for lack of marketability, which we pointed out as being incorrect because of specific IRS regulations that pointed to mortality tables that took this into consideration. Don't try to figure out all of the details; suffice it to say that our awareness of the tax laws gave us a distinct advantage over the non-CPA appraiser.

However, there are disadvantages as well. Accountants are used to working with financial statements and concepts that are either GAAP oriented or tax oriented. These concepts deal with book value rather than market value. Accountants are also frequently uncomfortable working with forecasts of the operating performance of the business being valued. Accountants are historians by nature. Financial statements generally report the past, not the future.

Over the years, accountants have been exposed to an ever-increasing number of malpractice lawsuits, particularly in the audit area. Recently, the lawsuits have gone beyond the audit arena into litigation support engagements. As a result, accountants tend to be concerned with malpractice exposure because of the subjective nature of business valuation. The debits do not equal the credits; therefore, is the answer correct? Accountants also have to be concerned with potential conflicts of interest (e.g., preparing tax returns for the business and then adjusting the officer's compensation in the appraisal as being excessive). Even if there is not a conflict of interest, there can be a perceived bias in certain types of assignments.

Business Brokers

Business brokers have a distinct advantage as business appraisers because they are involved with actual transactions in the marketplace. Since fair market value comes from the market, the business broker is frequently more familiar with the market for the business being appraised.

However, many business brokers do not complete appraisal training. They are generally salespeople, as opposed to appraisers. They will tell you that a similar business sold for $250,000 and that the appraisal subject is therefore also worth $250,000, but they may not understand the impact on value that the terms of the transaction can have. What if the similar business sold with terms of 20 percent down, with the balance being paid off over 10 years with no interest? The present value of this transaction would be quite a bit less than $250,000. Business brokers are generally involved in the investment value standard and often have trouble switching to fair market value due to their lack of appraisal training.

Business brokers are also very quick to value a business based on "rules of thumb." Rules of thumb can be dangerous. They are discussed in Chapter 7. It has also been my experience that some brokers tend to sell the same type of business for the same multiple of earnings, or gross revenues, over and over again, which tends to make them market makers instead of interpreters of the market—which is actually the role of the appraiser. Frequently, the business broker also lacks training in financial statement analysis.

College Professors

Another group of appraisers who are visible in the field are college professors. Many professors are entering this field, since they have time after school, or as a means to supplement their income (not a bad part-time job). Professors with backgrounds in economics and finance are the ones entering the profession. Sometimes these folks even have Ph.D.s. Almost every time I have a Ph.D. on the opposite side of a case, it reminds me that Ph.D. stands for *philosophically different*. Sometimes these guys are out in left field with their theory of the universe.

There is no doubt that the vast majority of these individuals understand the theory, but some (not all) demonstrate two shortcomings: first, they try to apply some very complex formulas to simple little businesses, and second, they cannot explain what they did in language that most jurors can understand. Many of these individuals are very strong in their comprehension of financial modeling and formulas. Although the mathematical formula may be correct, the answer may still be wrong.

Commercial Real Estate Appraisers

In the recent past, we have seen a growing number of commercial real estate appraisers entering the field of business valuation. Included among the students of courses that I have taught are members of this profession who are trying to expand their businesses. Changes in real estate appraisal over the last several years have left many appraisers looking to fill up their work week.

Although real estate appraisers understand the valuation process and principles, they often have a difficult time with the accounting aspects of financial reporting. They also have some difficulty making the transition into business valuation, where the ability to verify comparables is not always possible. Finally, although many real estate appraisals involving a capitalization of income use capitalization rates between 9 percent and 12 percent, real estate appraisers have a difficult time understanding the substantially higher capitalization rates used to appraise small businesses.

Investment Bankers

Investment bankers are frequently employed to perform valuations for a wide variety of assignments, including estate and gift tax valuations, initial public offerings, and going private, as well as for other purposes. More often than not, the investment bankers perform pretty large valuation assignments. Money is usually not an issue regarding the fee. It is much different from the local hardware store owner.

Professional Appraisal Organizations

When one thinks of business valuation, several organizations come to mind:

- The American Institute of Certified Public Accountants
- The American Society of Appraisers
- The Institute of Business Appraisers
- The National Association of Certified Valuation Analysts
- The Association for Investment Management and Research
- The Appraisal Foundation

The American Institute of Certified Public Accountants (AICPA)

The AICPA is not an appraisal organization, but its members probably provide the largest percentage of the appraisals performed because of their sheer numbers. In 1981, the AICPA established a membership section for CPAs who provide management advisory services, recognizing that AICPA members provide services other than audit and tax. Today, that section is known as Consulting Services (CS). The AICPA recognizes business valuation services as an important component of CPA services.

An "accredited in business valuation" (ABV) designation was approved by the AICPA Council in the fall of 1996, and the first examination was given in November 1997. This has been an area of specialization recognized by the accounting profession. At the time that this edition was written, there were 1,310 accredited individuals. To obtain this accreditation, an applicant must pass a fairly rigorous (but fair) written examination. Eligibility to sit for the written examination requires that the candidate be an AICPA member in good standing, hold an unrevoked CPA certificate or license issued by a recognized state authority, and provide evidence of 10 business valuation engagements that demonstrate substantial experience and competence.

After receiving the accreditation, the holder will be required to demonstrate substantial involvement in five business valuation engagements during each subsequent three-year period, as well as complete 60 hours of related continuing education during the same three-year period.

The American Society of Appraisers

The American Society of Appraisers (ASA) is a multi-disciplinary organization specializing in all types of appraisals. The organization was founded in 1936, but by 1981 there was a growing need within the organization (which was primarily a real estate–dominated professional appraisal organization) to recognize business valuation as a specialty. In 1981, ASA established a business valuation committee after recognizing the business valuation discipline as a separate specialization. ASA has approximately 6,000 members, about 817 of whom are in the business valuation discipline. Other specialties bring their designated individuals to just under 3,000.

ASA accredits its members by requiring candidates to pass an extensive series of written examinations, usually given at the end of four 3-day training courses. An alternative to this method of testing is a single, all-day examination that is administered at various times and places. Candidates are also required to submit two appraisal reports that the International Board of Examiners must approve and that demonstrate knowledge and compliance with appraisal theory and standards.

ASA has two levels of accreditation based on the experience of the applicant. First, a designation of "accredited member" (AM) is granted to those individuals who meet the other requirements and have greater than two, but less than five, years of full-time experience. ASA gives credit for partial years for those applicants who do not perform appraisals on a full-time basis. CPAs (and CFAs, discussed below) are given one year of appraisal experience for being a CPA (CFA) for five years. Second, those applicants with five or more years of experience are granted the "accredited senior appraiser" (ASA) designation.

The Institute of Business Appraisers, Inc.

A funny thing happened in 1978. Raymond Miles, an engineer by educational background and a licensed business broker, searched for a professional organization that he could join that was involved solely with the appraisal of businesses. Miles concluded that no such organization existed. So he started his own. This was the start of The Institute of Business Appraisers, Inc. (IBA). Miles got people to join the organization by soliciting membership through a 700-piece mailing. Today, IBA has approximately 3,250 members, of whom approximately 350 have been certified as business appraisers. IBA's primary focus is the small closely held business.

The "certified business appraiser" (CBA) designation is earned after the applicant passes a written examination and submits two appraisal reports, which the Qualifications Review Committee must approve. The requirements have changed since the last edition of this book was written. Previously, there was no experience requirement. Now, in addition to a four-year college degree, the applicant must have successfully completed at least 90 classroom hours of upper-level coursework. At least 24 hours of this coursework must have been obtained from courses given by IBA. The balance can come from any of the other business valuation organizations (including the AICPA). In lieu of the 90-hour requirement, the applicant may demonstrate five years of full-time, active experience as a business appraiser. CBAs are also required to document 24 hours of continuing professional education every two years.

Candidates for the CBA designation may be exempt from the examination if they hold an ASA designation, an ABV designation, a CVA designation (discussed below), or completion of the AICPA's Certificate of Educational Achievement (CEA) program in business valuation.

"Accredited by IBA" (AIBA) is IBA's junior designation, which is awarded to individuals who pass the written examination given at the end of an eight-day workshop, and upon submittal and acceptance of one appraisal report to the Qualifications Review Committee.

IBA also has a Master Certified Business Appraiser (MCBA) designation, which is given to individuals who hold the CBA designation, have 10 or more years of experience, and have been endorsed by senior business appraisers as leading contributors to the profession's body of knowledge. I don't know how, but I am an MCBA.

The National Association of Certified Valuation Analysts

Founded in 1991, the National Association of Certified Valuation Analysts (NACVA) is one of the newest organizations accrediting appraisers. This organization has several designations. To become a Certified Valuation Analyst (CVA), the applicant must hold a valid and unrevoked CPA license (CA in Canada), complete a five-day training workshop, and pass a two-part examination.

NACVA also awards an Accredited Valuation Analyst (AVA) designation for those individuals who are not CPAs but hold a business degree from an accredited university and can demonstrate business valuation experience. Certain credentialed individuals (e.g., CFAs, CMAs) may be exempt from part of the examination.

NACVA also provides the certification of Government Valuation Analyst (GVA) to those individuals who are employed by a government agency, have a level of GS-12 or higher, and have two years of experience in performing business valuations. At the time that this book was written, NACVA had 4,800 members, of whom about 3,900 were designated.

The Association for Investment Management and Research

The Association for Investment Management and Research is not really an appraisal organization. This organization grants the designation "chartered financial analyst" (CFA) after an applicant passes three extensive annual examinations. The CFA designation has more of a public company orientation (mostly portfolio and asset management) than the designations of the appraisal organizations that primarily deal with closely held companies. There is no report requirement, and the experience level needed for one to obtain this designation is three years.

The Appraisal Foundation

Established in 1987, the Appraisal Foundation is not an appraisal organization. This organization was set up by seven real estate organizations and ASA, which was the only multi-disciplinary organization, in response to a growing problem facing the real estate appraisal world. Real estate appraisers lacked standards to provide consistency in their work product. As a result, relying on these real estate appraisals caused bad bank loans to be made, creating severe problems for lending institutions. Facing some form of regulation in the near future, the Appraisal Foundation promulgated a set of standards relative to appraisals.

These standards are known as the *Uniform Standards of Professional Appraisal Practice (USPAP)*. Although these were primarily intended to cover real estate appraisals, ASA used its influence to have standards included for its other disciplines as well: personal property and business valuation. The *USPAP* is discussed in greater detail throughout this book.

As a result of the economic problems suffered by banks and thrifts, the Financial Institutions Reform, Recovery, and Enforcement Act of 1989 (FIRREA) was enacted by Congress and signed into law. FIRREA requires two things. First, it mandates the licensing or certification of real estate appraisers. Second, it requires that the *USPAP* be adhered to whenever a real estate appraisal is performed for a federally related transaction. This topic, too, will be expanded upon later in this book.

Business Appraisal Standards

Different organizations have different standards, and so the question that often arises is: What standards should I follow? Anyone who belongs to a professional organization knows that each organization mandates that its members follow its own set of standards.

The discussion that follows is intended to give some helpful suggestions, but it is up to each individual to make certain that the proper sets of standards are followed. The following standards are discussed:

- AICPA MCS Statement on Consulting Services Standards 1 (and others)
- IBA Standards
- ASA Standards
- *USPAP*
- NACVA Standards

AICPA MCS Statement on Consulting Services Standards 1

The AICPA promulgated the MCS Statement on Consulting Services Standards 1 to cover the broad range of consulting services that its members provide, not just business valuations. This standard is therefore extremely general and deals with such issues as due care and proper staffing for consulting engagements. This standard follows the format of other accounting-oriented standards but cannot be used to provide guidance or direction, other than on a superficial level. This standard is reproduced in Appendix 1.

At the time that this book was being written, the AICPA CS Division's Business Valuation and Appraisal Subcommittee was working on standards strictly pertaining to business valuations assignments. This author expects to see the AICPA promulgate business valuation standards in the near future (how near is like saying beauty is in the eye of the beholder).

In October 1995, the Florida Board of Accountancy passed a rule that requires CPAs performing business valuations to consider AICPA Practice Aid 93-3, entitled *Conducting a Valuation of a Closely Held Business* (authored by yours truly!), as a standard. In certain other engagements, however, AICPA members will be obligated to follow the *USPAP*.

Although the AICPA does not have specific standards that relate to business valuations, it should be noted that there are many other standards requiring AICPA members to perform these assignments properly. Though I did not include them in the first edition of this book (clearly an oversight on my part), they should nevertheless be mentioned here. This list may not be all-inclusive.

AICPA Code of Professional Conduct—Rule 102. CPAs are required to follow the Code of Professional Conduct when performing business valuations. It covers ethical considerations (integrity and objectivity). This rule requires that in the performance of any professional service, a member shall maintain objectivity and integrity, shall be free of conflicts of interest, and shall not knowingly misrepresent facts or subordinate his or her judgment to others. This is an important rule because business valuers should understand the differences between the responsibility of the attorney and the accountant related to conflicts of interest—the attorney is an advocate for the client, while the business valuer (accountant) is *only* an advocate for his or her opinion.

Professional Competence. As stated in the AICPA Consulting Services Practice Aid 93-3, *Conducting a Valuation of a Closely Held Business*:

- 13/115.01—In performing business valuation engagements, practitioners are advised to determine whether the competency provisions of Rule 201, General Standards of the AICPA Code of Professional Conduct, are met. Although accountants have a thorough understanding of financial statements and related matters, they also need to be proficient in the area of appraisals to competently complete an engagement. Usually, being proficient requires an in-depth knowledge of finance, economics, and security analysis and an understanding of appraisal principles and methods.
- 13/115.02—In order for the practitioner to obtain competency required to accept a business valuation engagement, appropriate education is required.

Due Professional Care. As stated in the AICPA Consulting Services Special Report 93-1, *Application of Professional Standards in the Performance of Litigation Services:*

- A practitioner exercises due professional care in the performance of an engagement. Due care requires diligence and critical analysis of all work performed. It also requires that all work be completed in accordance with the provisions of the applicable professional standards of the AICPA, including the Code of Professional Conduct. A practitioner engaged to attest to the results of the services rendered must perform in accordance with the SSAEs (Statement on Standards for Attestation Engagements).

Planning and Supervision. As stated in the AICPA Consulting Services Special Report 93-1, *Application of Professional Standards in the Performance of Litigation Services:*

- A practitioner adequately plans and supervises the performance of professional services. Planning is essential in a litigation engagement both to control costs and to focus the practitioner's work product on the engagement requirements. Planning consists of developing engagement objectives and translating them into the activities necessary for the CPA to form an opinion within the constraints of cost, time, and available information. Planning guides the conduct, supervision, control, and completion of the engagement. As with any professional services, the supervision of assistants helps to ensure quality performance. The extent of the supervision will vary according to the number of assistants, their experience, and the complexity of the engagement. The practitioner, as the potential expert witness or consultant, is responsible for the results of the engagement.

Sufficient Relevant Data. As stated in the AICPA Consulting Services Special Report 93-1, *Application of Professional Standards in the Performance of Litigation Services:*

- A practitioner attempts to obtain relevant data that is sufficient to provide a reasonable basis for conclusions or recommendations for professional services performed. The data-gathering process may include a review of relevant documents, research and analysis, and interview. The nature and extent of the data will vary with each valuation engagement and may include the practitioner's computations and analysis and other information supporting conclusions.

Other portions of the AICPA standards relate to *client interest, understanding with the client,* and *communications with the client.* These sections tell us to do the following:

Client Interest. Serve the client interest by seeking to accomplish the objectives established by the understanding with the client while maintaining integrity and objectivity.

Understanding With the Client. Establish with the client a written or oral understanding about the responsibilities of the parties and the nature, scope, and limitations of services to be performed, and modify the understanding if circumstances require significant change during the engagement.

Communication With the Client. Inform the client of (1) conflicts of interest that may occur pursuant to interpretations of Rule 102 of the Code of Professional Conduct; (2) significant reservations concerning the scope of benefits of the engagement; and (3) significant engagement findings or events.

IBA Standards

The IBA Standards, which are reproduced in Appendix 2, are probably the most comprehensive set of standards that exist for business appraisals. These standards offer guidance and have been written by a committee consisting of full-time appraisers, CPAs, and business brokers.

All members of IBA must adhere to the IBA standards. It is also recommended in these standards that IBA members should follow the *USPAP.* The intent of these standards is that by following either the IBA standards or the *USPAP,* the appraiser will be complying with both.

ASA Standards

The ASA standards, which are reproduced in Appendix 3, are a well-thought-out set of standards and must be followed by members of ASA. These standards do not provide the same level of guidance that is included in the IBA standards, but they are essentially the same. A similar group of individuals, appraisers, CPAs, and brokers strongly influenced the creation of these standards. ASA also has one other requirement imposed on its members that IBA does not have. Since ASA is a sponsoring member of the Appraisal Foundation, all of its members must comply with the *USPAP* in all appraisals. Fortunately, the *USPAP* and the ASA standards do not contradict each other.

Until recently, ASA members had to take a comprehensive, 15-hour *USPAP* course and pass a *USPAP* examination every five years to remain in good standing in the organization. The Board of Governors of ASA recently passed a resolution to adopt the Appraisal Foundation's new position on taking the *USPAP* course. Based on the new policy, real estate appraisers will have to take seven hours of *USPAP* (with exam) every two years. For all other disciplines (including business valuation), only the initial 15-hour *USPAP* course (with exam) is required.

Uniform Standards of Professional Appraisal Practice

The 2002 *USPAP* publication is approximately 225 pages long (75 pages longer than the 1998 edition). The price at the time this book was published was $30. If you wish to obtain a copy (and every appraiser should), this amount should be sent to:

The Appraisal Foundation
Attn.: Publications Dept.
1029 Vermont Avenue N.W., Suite 900
Washington, D.C. 20005-3517

Don't forget to tell them what you want!

In my opinion, if you are considering business valuation assignments, you should not only be familiar with the *USPAP*, but you should also attempt to follow these standards in all your assignments. This is like motherhood and apple pie. The *USPAP* is made up of the following sections:

- Preamble
- Ethics Provision
- Competency Provision
- Departure Provision
- Jurisdictional Exception and Supplemental Standards Section
- Definitions
- Standards 1–6, "Real Estate"
- Standards 7–8, "Personal Property"
- Standards 9–10, "Business Valuation"
- Statements on Appraisal Standards
- Advisory Opinions

Although Standards 9 and 10 pertain to business valuations, various other sections of the *USPAP* also apply. The essence of Standards 9 and 10 is to do your job in a competent manner and communicate it properly.

According to the FIRREA legislation, the *USPAP* must be adhered to when an appraisal is performed in accordance with a "federally related transaction." The legislation, however, never clearly defined what a federally related transaction is. Although the language leans toward real estate, many new interpretations have come about.

In real estate, a federally related transaction has been interpreted to mean that there is federal backing in the financing. Many government agencies have adopted provisions requiring the *USPAP* to be followed for all appraisals performed for their agencies.

More and more courts are becoming familiar with the *USPAP*, and as a result, business appraisers are advised to follow these standards. Better to follow some known standards than none at all. Imagine the litigation engagement that I was involved in a few years ago (fortunately as an expert and not a defendant). My client's attorney had a CPA on the witness stand and was questioning his qualifications and standards for performing the business valuation assignment that he was about to testify to. The questions and answers went something like this:

Q: Are you a CPA?

A: Yes.

Q: Are you an ABV?

A: No.

Q: Are you a CBA?

A: No.

Q: Are you an ASA?

A: No.

Q: Are you a CVA?

A: No.

Q: Do you follow the standards of IBA?

A: No.

Q: Do you follow the standards of ASA?

A: No.

Q: Do you follow the standards of NACVA?

A: No.

After becoming really rattled from the rapid-fire questioning of the attorney, the final question got the answer that you *never* want to blurt out (even by accident):

Q: What standards do you follow?

A: I'm a CPA—I have no standards!

Clearly, as CPAs, we have many standards. This was a terrible example of having not only an inexperienced expert witness, but a CPA who does not do enough of this stuff to be well versed in the standards that exist. Even without membership in an appraisal organization, the *USPAP* could have been followed.

By the way, you should have seen the facial expression on the judge when the CPA gave his final answer. And it was his final answer because the judge found that if he did not follow standards, he could not prove that his work would be acceptable in the valuation community; thus he was disqualified as an expert. This could be your worst nightmare!

NACVA Standards

NACVA has its own set of standards, which have been greatly expanded since the first edition of this book. Most of these standards come from the AICPA and are the very standards that I referred to above. Take the time to read them. In Appendix 4, the NACVA standards are reproduced.

Glossary of Business Valuation Terms

In an attempt to assist users of valuation services at being better able to understand the terminology used by our profession, various organizations came together to form a committee whose purpose was to establish a single set of terminology that is recommended to be used by its members. These organizations include the

AICPA, IBA, ASA, NACVA, and the Canadian Institute of Chartered Business Valuers. The glossary is reproduced as Appendix 5.

Conclusion

Since this was only the first chapter of the book, you are probably starting to doze off. What did you expect? This is introductory stuff. It gets better. By now you are at least familiar with some history of the profession, who appraises businesses, why businesses are appraised, appraisal organizations, and appraisal standards. I know the suspense of the next chapter is probably killing you, so let's move on.

2

Getting Started

Chapter Goals

In this chapter, I will attempt to explain the following:

1. Learning about the engagement
2. Deciding whether to accept the engagement
3. Defining the engagement
4. Engagement letters
5. The initial document request

Introduction

Before we can get to the good stuff, it is important to get some of the preliminary items out of the way. Let's start off with some items that should be addressed at the beginning of this process.

Learning About the Engagement

After the telephone rings, and after the caller tells you that he or she needs the services of a good appraiser, what should you do? Should you find out more about the assignment, automatically accept it, or recommend a good appraiser? Believe it or not, these are serious considerations that you must think about. The beginning of the assignment, or should I say the pre-beginning of the assignment, is the most important part of the valuation process for several reasons.

First and foremost, you need to properly understand the nature of the assignment to determine if you are competent to perform it. Take a step back and ask yourself if you are competent to do the job. We all like to think that we are competent to do every assignment that comes in the door, but, truthfully, we are not. You cannot possibly be competent to take on every assignment that comes your way. If the proper level of competence can be obtained, you can accept the assignment. All the appraisal organizations (and especially the AICPA) have competency standards for their members. Furthermore, the *USPAP* requires the appraiser to disclose to the client any deficiencies in his or her level of competence, as well as what he or she will do to compensate for it. Imagine telling the client, "Although I am incompetent, I really want to do this job for you." If they hire you, they deserve what they get. However, full disclosure to the client is essential. At that point, it is up to the client to decide if he or she is comfortable with you handling the assignment.

After the client has decided to go forward with you as the appraiser, and assuming that you do a good job, there should be no reason for the client to have the opportunity at a later date to question why you didn't tell him or her something. Can you imagine the client, sitting in a courtroom on the witness stand, stating that "the appraiser never told me that this was the first appraisal he had ever done?" Do not feel intimidated because of your inexperience. We all have to start somewhere. Unfortunately, we are in a more litigious society than we were in when I got started, and as a result, we have to be especially careful not to find ourselves a party to the litigation, instead of the expert in it.

If the client is not comfortable with you or your experience level at the start, do not try to oversell yourself to get the assignment. If anything can go wrong, it probably will, and as a result, you are staring a malpractice suit in the eyes. The worst thing you can do is to try to boost your level of experience to impress a potential client. There are serious ethical considerations that go far beyond just the appraisal.

Deciding Whether to Accept the Engagement

Before you accept an assignment, considerations include, but should not be limited to, the following:

- The possibility of a conflict of interest or the appearance of a conflict of interest
- The purpose and function of the engagement
- The amount of time required to do the job
- The scope of the assignment, including the possibility of giving expert testimony
- The type of report to be issued

These items will be addressed over and over again throughout this book, and they must be understood at the start of the assignment, especially since many of these issues will affect your ability to accept the engagement.

Conflicts of Interest

The telephone rings and you are asked to do a business valuation for a litigation that is pending. The attorney asks if you know any of the parties. You say no. The operative word is "you." Does "you" mean you, or does "you" mean someone in your firm, your staff, your partners, your cousin, or your great uncle? You better check for conflicts! Conflicts are a great way to be sued. Sometimes the conflict is immediately apparent. Other times, conflicts are well hidden. The first step in avoiding a problem is to make certain that your firm employs some form of conflict-of-interest verification form for use in all assignments. Ours is reproduced as Exhibit 2.1.

First of all, let me give attribution where it belongs. Our forms (and many of the other forms that you may see in this book) have been adapted using the aids from Practitioners Publishing Company's *Guide to Business Valuations*. There is no reason to start from scratch when we have good tools that we can use as a jumping-off point. Customize them for your firm!

In addition to checking with all professional staff, it is a good idea to make certain that nonprofessional staff do not present a problem. What if it is your secretary's next-door neighbor? Or what if it is your assistant's child's godfather? Oops!

Let's stick with conflicts of interest for a little longer. Checking all staff becomes critically important, especially when you have multiple offices. Imagine your staff in New York being hired against your staff in Chicago. Another oops! Or what happens when you are asked to represent an existing client?

EXHIBIT 2.1

TRUGMAN VALUATION ASSOCIATES INC.
BUSINESS VALUATION ENGAGEMENT ACCEPTANCE FORM
CONFLICT OF INTEREST VERIFICATION

INSTRUCTIONS: This form should be completed for a prospective new client and sent to ALL staff for confirmation that there are no conflicts of interest with any of the parties or entities involved in this matter. If the referral source, attorneys, CPAs, or others associated with these individuals/entities are known, list them also for conflict verification. ALL staff must immediately respond via e-mail to the sender of the original e-mail.

TRUGMAN VALUATION ASSOCIATES INC. has been requested to perform services with respect to the following individuals and/or entities:

	Yes	No
1. Do you know any of these individuals/entities?		
2. Do you have any personal knowledge about these individuals/entities that would cause our firm to have information that another firm would not readily have?		
3. Are we doing any work for any of these individuals/entities currently?		
4. Have we done any work for them in the past?		
5. Have we been approached by any of these individuals/entities to do work for them in the past?		
6. Do you know of any reason that we should not do this assignment?		

If you answered yes to any of these questions, please explain and give details. ______________________

____

____

____

____

____

The appearance of impropriety is almost as bad as the act itself. Litigation services are an area that the SEC has suggested may impair an auditor's independence. Think about the cross-examining attorney who is in front of you, almost salivating, asking you some of the following questions:

- You receive current income from this client for accounting services, don't you?
- This company has been your firm's client for the last 10 years?
- Isn't it true that they paid you about $10,000 in fees last year?

- Do you consider them a good client?
- You wouldn't want to lose this client, would you?
- Do you expect this jury to believe that you can sit on this witness stand and be objective with respect to this client when your opinion in this matter may hurt your client?

Even if you can be objective, you're dead in the water. No juror will believe that you are not acting as an advocate for the client. It is often difficult to prove that, as a paid expert, we are objective even when we are truly independent from the client. The burden becomes that much more difficult when you are the client's accountant.

Even in non-litigation jobs (e.g., estate tax valuation), a perceived conflict can arise. Imagine being the tax return preparer taking a deduction on a return for officer's compensation of $1 million and then adjusting it in the valuation to reflect "reasonable" compensation of $250,000. We all know that the standard for deductible compensation for income tax purposes is very different from the concept of a replacement salary on a prospective basis, but think about the reader of the report who does not know better. If you think that you will educate the reader, think again.

Let's discuss one more conflict that is sure to get you in trouble. As chairman of the ethics committee of one of the appraisal organizations, I see this more often than you can imagine. An accountant's business client is going through a divorce. The accounting firm prepares the corporate tax returns. The accounting firm also prepares the personal tax returns for the stockholders. The accounting firm has been preparing joint income tax returns for the clients, who are about to get divorced. The business client turns to the partner in the firm who handles this account, the trusted business advisor, to perform various divorce-related services, maybe including a business valuation. Since the partner expects the firm to remain the company's accountants, and since the owner is a good client, the partner says, "Sure, we'll do it." Guess what? What about the spouse? The accounting firm has been the spouse's accountant also, since the couple have been preparing joint income tax returns. The accounting firm cannot suddenly say, "Sorry, but we are no longer going to be your accountant, so that we can represent your soon-to-be ex-spouse against you in the divorce."

There is no easy way to avoid appearances of conflict other than to stick with my motto, "perception is reality." If it can in any way be conceived to be a conflict, you probably want to protect yourself. Protection can come in many different forms. First, stay away from the engagement. Second, have the client(s) sign a waiver acknowledging that there may be a conflict and that they have been made aware of it, and despite that, they still want you to proceed.

Let me give you a real example of how to protect yourself. We were retained by a former accounting client to assist him as his expert in a litigation where he was being accused of fraud relating to the sale of a laundromat (a cash business—imagine that!). I was afraid not only of the appearance of conflict of interest, but also that I could be asked on the witness stand why his tax returns had different amounts than the current information sheet he had put together for prospective purchasers (like many clients, he got honest when he went about selling the business). In our retainer agreement (and we will discuss these agreements in much more detail soon), we put in the following language:

> The client also acknowledges that a discussion took place between himself and Gary Trugman regarding the possible appearance of a conflict of interest. The client, by signing this agreement, acknowledges that Gary Trugman has expressed his concern about the appearance of conflict of interest, and despite this, the client has expressed his desire to have Trugman Valuation Associates Inc. perform services in this matter. The client agrees to completely indemnify Trugman Valuation Associates Inc., its officers, its directors, and its shareholders, as well as Trugman & Company CPAs (a partnership) and its partners, Gary and Linda Trugman, from any liability that may arise out of the client's request to these parties or firms involved as a result of this litigation engagement.

Fortunately, the case settled before we had to go to court. Do not expect to be so lucky. Protect yourself.

Sometimes, something as simple as an engagement letter signed by two parties will help. We are often hired as a mutual appraiser by both sides of a litigation. We use the retainer agreement (engagement letter) in Exhibit 2.2, which we have each party sign individually.

EXHIBIT 2.2
Mutually Retained Business Valuation Retainer Agreement

The undersigned acknowledges this engagement of Trugman Valuation Associates Inc., who is mutually retained by the undersigned and Mary Smith, to perform a business valuation of 100 percent of the outstanding common stock of Jack's Automotive, Inc. as of December 31, 1999.

The purpose of this business valuation is to determine the fair market value of the subject property. Said fair market value is defined to be a value at which a willing seller and willing buyer, both being informed of the relevant facts about the business, could reasonably conduct a transaction, neither party acting under any compulsion to do so.

It is understood that Trugman Valuation Associates Inc. is not being engaged to perform an audit as defined by the American Institute of Certified Public Accountants, but rather the necessary tests of the accounting records that will be performed for the purpose of issuing a valuation report and not a statement regarding the fairness of presentation of the financial statements of the above business.

Certain values, derived from reports of others, and which are so designated, will be included in our report. We take no responsibility for those items. Nor do we take responsibility to update the report or disclose any events or circumstances occurring after the date of the report.

In the event sufficient records and/or documentation cannot be supplied to Trugman Valuation Associates Inc., no such valuation report will be issued.

This appraisal will be subject to, at least, the following contingent and limiting conditions, which will be included in the report as an appendix:

1. Information, estimates, and opinions contained in this report are obtained from sources considered reliable; however, Trugman Valuation Associates Inc. has not independently verified such information and no liability for such sources is assumed by this appraiser.
2. All facts and data set forth in the report are true and accurate to the best of the appraiser's knowledge and belief. We have not knowingly withheld or omitted anything from our report affecting our value estimate.
3. Possession of this report, or a copy thereof, does not carry with it the right of publication of all or part of it, nor may it be used for any purpose without the previous written consent of the appraiser, and in any event only with proper authorization. Authorized copies of this report will be signed in blue ink by a partner of Trugman Valuation Associates Inc. Unsigned copies, or copies not signed in blue ink, should be considered to be incomplete.
4. None of the contents of this valuation report shall be conveyed to any third party or to the public through any means without the express written consent of Trugman Valuation Associates Inc.
5. No investigation of titles to property or any claims on ownership of the property by any individuals or company has been undertaken. Unless otherwise stated in our report, title is assumed to be clear and free of encumbrances and as provided to the appraiser.
6. Unless otherwise provided for in writing and agreed to by both parties in advance, the extent of the liability for the completeness or accuracy of the data, opinions, comments, recommendations, and/or conclusions shall not exceed the amount paid to the appraisers for professional fees and, then, only to the party(s) for whom this report was originally prepared.
7. The various estimates of value presented in this report apply to this appraisal only and may not be used out of the context presented herein. Any other use of this report may lead the user to an incorrect conclusion for which Trugman Valuation Associates Inc. assumes no responsibility.
8. The appraisal estimate of fair market value reached in this report is necessarily based on the definition of fair market value as stated in the Introduction Section. An actual transaction in the shares may be concluded at a higher value or lower value, depending on the circumstances surrounding the company, the appraised business interest, and/or the motivations and knowledge of both the buyers and sellers at that time. Trugman Valuation Associates Inc. makes no guarantees as to what values individual buyers and sellers may reach in an actual transaction.
9. It should be specifically noted that the valuation assumes the business will be competently managed and maintained by financially sound owners over the expected period of ownership. This appraisal engagement does not entail an evaluation of management's effectiveness, nor are we responsible for future marketing efforts and other management or ownership actions upon which actual results will depend.

(Continued)

EXHIBIT 2.2 ***(Continued)***

10. No opinion is intended to be expressed for matters that require legal or other specialized expertise, investigation, or knowledge beyond that customarily employed by appraisers valuing businesses.
11. It is assumed that there are no regulations of any government entity to control or restrict the use of the underlying assets unless specifically referred to in the report and that the underlying assets will not operate in violation of any applicable government regulations, codes, ordinances, or statutes.
12. Valuation reports may contain prospective financial information, estimates, or opinions that represent the view of the appraiser about reasonable expectations at a particular point in time, but such information, estimates, or opinions are not offered as predictions or as assurances that a particular level of income or profit will be achieved or that specific events will occur.
13. We assume that there are no hidden or unexpected conditions of the business that would adversely affect value, other than as indicated in this report.
14. Hazardous substances, if present, can introduce an actual or potential liability that will adversely affect the marketability and value of a business. Such liability may be in the form of immediate recognition of existing hazardous conditions, or future liability that could stem from the release of currently nonhazardous contaminants. In the development of the opinion of value, no consideration was given to such liability or its impact on value. We have not taken into account any and all future environmental considerations and potential liability.

It is possible that additional contingent and limiting conditions will be required, and the client agrees that all conditions disclosed by the appraiser will be accepted as incorporated into the appraiser's report.

It is our intention to perform this engagement as quickly and affordably as possible, but these services take a reasonable amount of time to render. We will make certain that the appropriate personnel in our firm render those services that will comply with the level of expertise required by this engagement. In that regard, hourly rates will be charged based on the billing rates in effect at the time that the services are rendered.

Hourly rates are charged portal to portal from our Rockaway office. In addition to these hourly rates, the following charges may be applicable:

a) A minimum fee of four hours will be charged for appearance at depositions and/or court appearances.
b) Any out-of-pocket expenses relating to this valuation. It is expected that we will perform research through computer databases, and that we may be required to purchase research materials relating to this engagement. These and other such costs will be billed to you at our cost.

Payment terms shall be as follows:

The total retainer due in advance, from one or both parties, is $x,xxx. Any amount over the retainer shall be billed monthly. Since it is considered unethical for us to perform these services on a contingency basis, it is important to us that our fees be paid promptly. The appearance of independence is of considerable importance for our firm to maintain our credibility, and therefore, we reserve the right to stop providing services at any time that there is a balance due our firm beyond 30 days. In the event that we continue to provide services, we do not waive our right to stop at a later date.

The client must understand that professional business valuation services are not inexpensive, and unless other arrangements are made, in writing, with our firm, services rendered by our firm will be invoiced regularly and are due upon presentation of our invoice to you.

Balances outstanding beyond 30 days will have a service charge added at the rate of 1.5 percent per month or part thereof. All costs relating to collection of these fees will also be the responsibility of the undersigned, including, but not limited to, attorney fees, collection agency fees, etc. Reasonable attorney fees will be considered to be up to 33.33 percent of the outstanding balance. In the event a collection action is brought against the client, the client acknowledges that the venue will be Morris County, New Jersey.

An additional invoice will be rendered once the appraiser completes the appraisal report. Payment is due in full prior to the release of said report to the client.

The undersigned client agrees to indemnify Trugman Valuation Associates Inc. and its shareholders and employees from any legal expenses incurred as a result of this engagement. This would include, but not be limited to, any legal expenses required to protect the confidentiality of this or any other client who becomes an issue in this matter.

The final report is copyrighted by Trugman Valuation Associates Inc. It shall remain the property of Trugman Valuation Associates Inc. and no copies or reproductions shall be allowed without the written consent of Trugman Valuation Associates Inc. until such time as any outstanding balance is paid.

EXHIBIT 2.2 *(Continued)*

Trugman Valuation Associates Inc. reserves the right to withdraw from this engagement at any time for reasonable cause. It is not our intention to withdraw. In the event there is an outstanding balance, we further reserve the right not to make a court appearance in this matter. All workpapers created by Trugman Valuation Associates Inc. will remain in the possession of Trugman Valuation Associates Inc. In the event of a withdrawal, we would be liable only to return those materials and documents supplied by the client and the unused portion of the retainer.

The undersigned gives Trugman Valuation Associates Inc. the right to discuss this matter with the client's attorney, accountant, other individuals so designated by the client, and any professional colleagues of the appraiser from whom professional information is sought.

If this is acceptable, please sign the acknowledgment below and return a signed copy of this retainer agreement with the requested retainer fee to our office.

TRUGMAN VALUATION ASSOCIATES INC.

Gary R. Trugman
CPA/ABV, MCBA, ASA, MVS

ACKNOWLEDGMENT:

The undersigned accepts the terms of this retainer agreement and guarantees full payment of the fees with respect to this engagement. It is also acknowledged that Mary Smith will be signing a similar retainer agreement with respect to this agreement.

____________________________ ____________
Jack Smith Date

THIS BUSINESS VALUATION RETAINER AGREEMENT CONSISTS OF FIVE (5) PAGES INCLUDING THIS ONE. ALL FIVE (5) PAGES MUST BE RETURNED TO TRUGMAN VALUATION ASSOCIATES INC. AFTER EXECUTION OF THIS DOCUMENT WITH THE REQUESTED RETAINER IN ORDER TO RETAIN OUR FIRM. IF THIS DOCUMENT IS NOT RECEIVED BY TRUGMAN VALUATION ASSOCIATES INC. FULLY EXECUTED BY THE CLIENT WITH THE REQUESTED RETAINER BY (SOME DATE) THE TERMS OF THIS AGREEMENT AND THE OFFER TO PERFORM BUSINESS VALUATION SERVICES PURSUANT TO THIS AGREEMENT WILL BE DEEMED NULL AND VOID BY TRUGMAN VALUATION ASSOCIATES INC.

The same retainer agreement is sent to Mary Smith, with Jack Smith's name replacing hers. This way, each party is retaining us to do the work while acknowledging that he/she is aware that the other party is also retaining us.

Purpose and Function of the Engagement

When you are first approached about an appraisal assignment, it is important to gain a clear understanding of the purpose and function of the engagement. In simple terms, what are you going to be doing and how will it be used? This also raises the question, What is going to be valued? Very often, an entire company will be valued; this is frequently referred to as the "equity" of the company. There are other times when you may be asked to value the entire capital structure of the business; this is referred to as the "invested capital" of the company (this will be discussed in more detail later).

There will also be times when only a portion of the equity will be valued. This may involve valuing a fractional interest in the company (less than 100 percent) or valuing only certain assets and liabilities. For example, you may be approached to value a 40 percent interest in the company. This is not as simple as taking 40 percent of the value of the entire company. A minority interest may be worth less than a pro rata share of the entire company. This will also be discussed later.

Another alternative might be that you are asked to value the company for a sale in which the owner will be keeping certain assets, such as the company car or cash in the bank. Many, if not most, small businesses are sold as "asset" sales as opposed to "stock" sales. This means that the purchaser will generally transfer the assets—and possibly liabilities—that were part of the deal to a new entity. There are several reasons why this is done, but this book is not the forum for that discussion. A proper understanding of the appraisal subject is essential if you are going to do a good job.

Another important consideration is the intended use of your appraisal. The intended use can affect the manner in which the job is performed. For example, if the appraisal assignment is for a divorce litigation in a jurisdiction that does not recognize goodwill, you will have to conduct your valuation in a manner that would meet the requirements of that jurisdiction. However, if the same company is being appraised for a sale, the methodologies employed in the appraisal will most likely be different. Since goodwill is part of the sales price of the company, the valuation result would have to be different. After all, one has goodwill and the other does not.

Amount of Time Required to Do the Job

Knowing how much time is required to do the job properly is an important part of the planning stage for the assignment. Understanding the assignment will provide the appraiser with the ability to budget staff time and meet any deadlines that are imposed on the assignment. The client will also want to know how much the appraisal will cost. Unfortunately, an answer such as "How high is up?" is generally unacceptable. Budgeting time is probably more difficult than the appraisal itself at times, because you never know what type of research problems you may run into. In Chapter 4, I will discuss data gathering and will expand on the research portion of the assignment.

The Scope of the Assignment

Understanding the scope of the assignment, including the possibility of giving expert testimony, will help you determine whether you can accept it. If a client tells you at the beginning that you will have severe scope restrictions but are expected to testify in court, you may want to think twice about taking the assignment. You may end up on the short end of the stick if you allow the client to limit the scope. Clients frequently look to save money and will often ask the appraiser to streamline the process. If expert testimony is anticipated, the judge or jury will remember only that the appraiser did not do a complete job. Regardless of whether you qualify your opinion because of your client's scope restrictions, the appraiser's reputation will be the most damaged element in the litigation. Be selective when you allow scope limitations. Exhibit 2.3 contains another form that may make your life a whole lot easier.

EXHIBIT 2.3

TRUGMAN VALUATION ASSOCIATES INC.
BUSINESS VALUATION ENGAGEMENT ACCEPTANCE FORM

Prospective client: ______________________________

Completed by: ______________________________ Date: __________

INSTRUCTIONS: This form should be completed for a prospective new client or a prospective engagement for an existing client. The person completing this checklist need only complete those parts of the form that apply to the proposed engagement.

Source: Adapted with permission from *Guide to Business Valuations*, Twelfth Edition (January 2002), published by Practitioners Publishing Company, Fort Worth, Texas.

EXHIBIT 2.3 (*Continued*)

I. PROSPECTIVE CLIENT DATA

[The following data should be obtained for the prospective client (the person or company that will be engaging our firm). That client may not be the actual entity being valued. Accordingly, a separate section of the form is designed for documenting information about the entity being valued.]

Prospective Client's Name ____________________ Phone no.: ____________________

Fax no.: ____________________

Business address: ____

____

Referral source: ____

____

Is the prospective client the same entity that is to be valued?

______ Yes Proceed to Section II of this form (Entity to Be Valued). The remaining portion of Section I does not need to be completed.

______ No Complete the remaining portion of Section I before proceeding to Section II.

Briefly explain the prospective client's relationship to the entity to be valued (e.g., the client's ownership interest in the entity, if any; whether the entity is a proposed acquisition candidate of the entity; etc.). ____________________

____

____

____

____

____

II. ENTITY TO BE VALUED

(If the prospective client and the entity to be valued are the same, it is not necessary to repeat the data obtained in the preceding section of this form.)

Name of entity to be valued: ____

Type of legal entity (Corp., S Corp., Partnership, Proprietorship, etc.): ____________________

Business address: ____

____

Phone no.: ____________________ Fax no.: ____________________

Contacts at the entity with whom we would work (state name and title): ____________________

____

____

____

Brief description of the entity's business: ______________________________

____

____

____

(Continued)

EXHIBIT 2.3 *(Continued)*

Entity's accounting firm: ______________________________

Address: ______________________________

Phone no.: ______________ Contact: ______________

Entity's primary attorney: ______________________________

Address: ______________________________

Phone no.: ______________ Contact: ______________

Other contact: ______________________________

Address: ______________________________

Phone no.: ______________

III. SCOPE OF THE ENGAGEMENT

Briefly describe the purpose of the engagement (e.g., determination of a party's interest in a divorce proceeding, valuation of a company for a proposed sale of acquisition, determination of a value for an estate tax return, etc.).

____

____

____

____

Describe the interest to be valued (i.e., the ownership percentage being valued and whether it is a controlling or minority interest).

____

____

____

____

Valuation date(s): ______________ Proposed deadline: ______________

Describe any obvious difficulties that may be associated with the valuation date (e.g., the date may be at an interim period, no financials are available). ______________________________

____

____

____

Do there appear to be enough historical financial statements and tax returns to assess the financial background and trend of the company? Yes ______ No ______

If the answer to the preceding question is "no," explain how this absence will affect the scope of the engagement.

____

____

____

EXHIBIT 2.3 ***(Continued)***

How are the valuation conclusions to be communicated? (check one)

______ oral report ______ comprehensive report ______ abbreviated report ______ letter report

What is the intended distribution of a written report? (check one)

______ It will be restricted to internal use or to use solely by a court of law.

______ It will be distributed to third parties.

Based on your knowledge of the company to be valued, what valuation methods appear to be appropriate for the engagement?

____

____

____

Will an asset appraiser be needed? Yes ______ No ______

Is it likely that we will be asked to provide expert witness testimony? Yes ______ No ______

What will our role be on this proposed engagement? (check one)

______ We will be objective, third-party appraisers.

______ We will be client advisors and, accordingly, will not be able to render an independent valuation conclusion or act as expert witnesses.

IV. ACCEPTANCE CONSIDERATIONS

	Yes	No
1. Are we aware of any independence problems or conflicts of interest?	______	______
2. Are we aware of any potential fee collection problems?	______	______
3. Is the professional competence (expertise) necessary to perform the engagement beyond our capabilities?	______	______
4. Is the staffing commitment required by the engagement beyond our capabilities?	______	______
5. Do the terms of the proposed engagement, including fee arrangements, violate applicable professional standards?	______	______
6. Is the fee arrangement unacceptable given the scope of the engagement?	______	______
7. Is there anything about the engagement that subjects us to undue legal risk or causes us to be uncomfortable about being associated with the engagement?	______	______

COMMENTS—A "yes" answer does not necessarily indicate that the prospective engagement should be rejected. However, for any "yes" answer, explain the steps that we plan to take to mitigate the situation (e.g., closer supervision, a substantial fee deposit before work can start, renegotiation of the fee, or use of specialists).

____

____

____

(Continued)

EXHIBIT 2.3 (Continued)

V. CONCLUSION

We should accept ______ not accept ______ the engagement.

Approved by: ______________________________ Date: ____________

Note: If "yes" was answered to any question in Part IV, an officer other than the original contact must approve acceptance.

The Type of Report to Be Issued

Knowing the type of report that is expected to be issued is important for several reasons. First, long narrative reports take a considerable amount of time to write. This affects not only the fee to be charged, but also your time budget for meeting deadlines. In Chapter 13, I will discuss different types of reports (including the suggested content of each type), as well as their applicability to various types of assignments.

Engagement Letters

Always, and I mean always, have your client sign an engagement letter (sometimes called a "retainer agreement") in order to avoid any potential misunderstanding between you and your client. I cannot emphasize strongly enough the need for a good engagement letter. Exhibit 2.4 contains a sample engagement letter for use in a business valuation assignment. This can be changed to meet the specific needs of each business valuation engagement. A well-constructed engagement letter should be perceived to be the contract that it is. Any modifications to the agreement should be in writing and agreed to by both parties. It may also prove to be a good idea to have an attorney review the engagement letter that you plan to use, so that you are protected legally in your jurisdiction.

EXHIBIT 2.4
Sample Engagement Letter (Retainer Agreement)

The undersigned acknowledges this engagement of Trugman Valuation Associates Inc. to determine the fair market value of 100 percent of the common stock of XYZ Corporation, a New Jersey corporation, as of December 31, 2000, to be used as part of the litigation pending in the Superior Court of New Jersey entitled *Jones v. Smith*, Docket No. 12-3456.

The purpose of this business valuation is to determine the fair market value of the subject property. Said fair market value is defined to be a value at which a willing seller and willing buyer, both being informed of the relevant facts about the business, could reasonably conduct a transaction, neither party acting under any compulsion to do so.

It is understood that Trugman Valuation Associates Inc. is not being engaged to perform an audit as defined by the American Institute of Certified Public Accountants but rather the necessary tests of the accounting records that will be performed for the purpose of issuing a valuation report and not a statement regarding the fairness of presentation of the financial statements of the above business.

Certain values, derived from reports of others and which are so designated, will be included in our report. We take no responsibility for those items. Nor do we take responsibility to update the report or disclose any events or circumstances occurring after the effective date of the appraisal.

In the event sufficient records, documentation, or both cannot be supplied to Trugman Valuation Associates Inc., no such valuation report will be issued. It is expected that a formal valuation report will be issued as part of this assignment.

This appraisal will be subject to, at least, the following contingent and limiting conditions, which will be included in the report as an appendix:

1. Information, estimates, and opinions contained in this report are obtained from sources considered reliable; however, Trugman Valuation Associates Inc. has not independently verified such information, and no liability for such sources is assumed by this appraiser.
2. All facts and data set forth in the report are true and accurate to the best of the appraiser's knowledge and belief. We have not knowingly withheld or omitted anything from our report affecting our value estimate.

EXHIBIT 2.4 *(Continued)*

3. Possession of this report, or a copy thereof, does not carry with it the right of publication of all or part of it, nor may it be used for any purpose without the previous written consent of the appraiser, and in any event only with proper authorization. Authorized copies of this report will be signed by an officer of Trugman Valuation Associates Inc. Unsigned copies should be considered to be incomplete.
4. None of the contents of this valuation report shall be conveyed to any third party or to the public through any means without the express written consent of Trugman Valuation Associates Inc.
5. No investigation of titles to property or any claims on ownership of the property by any individuals or company has been undertaken. Unless otherwise stated in our report, title is assumed to be clear and free of encumbrances and as provided to the appraiser.
6. Unless otherwise provided for in writing and agreed to by both parties in advance, the extent of the liability for the completeness or accuracy of the data, opinions, comments, recommendations, or conclusions shall not exceed the amount paid to the appraisers for professional fees and, then, only to the party or parties for whom this report was originally prepared.
7. The various estimates of value presented in this report apply to this appraisal only and may not be used out of the context presented herein. Any other use of this report may lead the user to an incorrect conclusion for which Trugman Valuation Associates Inc. assumes no responsibility.
8. The appraisal estimate of fair market value reached in this report is necessarily based on the definition of fair market value as stated in the Introduction. An actual transaction in the shares may be concluded at a higher value or lower value depending on the circumstances surrounding the company, the appraised business interest, or the motivations and knowledge of both the buyers and sellers at that time. Trugman Valuation Associates Inc. makes no guarantees as to what values individual buyers and sellers may reach in an actual transaction.
9. It should be specifically noted that the valuation assumes the business will be competently managed and maintained by financially sound owners over the expected period of ownership. This appraisal engagement does not entail an evaluation of management's effectiveness, nor are we responsible for future marketing efforts and other management or ownership actions upon which actual results will depend.
10. No opinion is intended to be expressed for matters that require legal or other specialized expertise, investigation, or knowledge beyond that customarily employed by appraisers valuing businesses.
11. It is assumed that there are no regulations of any government entity to control or restrict the use of the underlying assets, unless specifically referred to in the report, and that the underlying assets will not operate in violation of any applicable government regulations, codes, ordinances, or statutes.
12. Valuation reports may contain prospective financial information, estimates, or opinions that represent the view of the appraiser about reasonable expectations at a particular point in time, but such information, estates, or opinions are not offered as predictions or as assurances that a particular level of income or profit will be achieved or that specific events will occur.
13. We assume that there are no hidden or unexpected conditions of the business that would adversely affect value, other than as indicated in this report.
14. Hazardous substances, if present, can introduce an actual or potential liability that will adversely affect the marketability and value of a business. Such liability may be in the form of immediate recognition of existing hazardous conditions, or future liability that could stem from the release of currently nonhazardous contaminants. In the development of the opinion of value, no consideration was given to such liability or its impact on value. We have not taken into account any and all future environmental considerations and potential liability.

It is possible that additional contingent and limiting conditions will be required, and the client agrees that all conditions disclosed by the appraiser will be accepted as incorporated into the appraiser's report.

It is our intention to perform this engagement as quickly and affordably as possible, but these services take a reasonable amount of time to render. We will make certain that the appropriate personnel in our firm render those services that will comply with the level of expertise required by this engagement. In that regard, hourly rates will be charged based on the billing rates in effect at the time the services are rendered.

Hourly rates are charged portal to portal from our office. In addition to these hourly rates, the following charges may be applicable:

1. A minimum fee of four hours will be charged for appearance at depositions and/or court appearances.
2. Any out-of-pocket expenses relating to this valuation. It is expected that we will perform research through computer databases, and that we may be required to purchase research materials relating to this engagement. These and other such costs will be billed to you at our cost.

(Continued)

EXHIBIT 2.4 *(Continued)*

Payment terms shall be as follows:

$X,XXX due in advance as a retainer. Since it is considered unethical for us to perform these services on a contingency basis, it is important to us that our fees be paid promptly. The appearance of independence is of considerable importance for our firm to maintain our credibility, and therefore, we reserve the right to stop providing services at any time that there is a balance due our firm beyond thirty days. In the event that we continue to provide services, we do not waive our right to stop at a later date.

The client must understand that professional business valuation services are not inexpensive and that unless other arrangements are made, in writing, with our firm, services rendered by our firm will be invoiced regularly and are due upon presentation of our invoice to you.

Balances outstanding beyond thirty days will have a service charge added at the rate of 1.5 percent per month or part thereof. All costs relating to the collection of these fees will also be the responsibility of the undersigned, including, but not limited to, attorney's fees, collection agency fees, etc. Reasonable attorney's fees will be considered to be up to 33.33 percent of the outstanding balance.

An additional invoice will be rendered once the appraiser has completed the appraisal report. Payment in full is due prior to the release of said report, in draft or as a final version.

The final report is copyrighted by Trugman Valuation Associates Inc. It shall remain the property of our firm, and no copies or reproductions shall be allowed without the written consent of Trugman Valuation Associates Inc. until such time as any outstanding balance is paid.

Trugman Valuation Associates Inc. reserves the right to withdraw from this engagement at any time for reasonable cause. It is not our intention to withdraw. In the event there is an outstanding balance, we further reserve the right not to make a court appearance in this matter. All working papers created by Trugman Valuation Associates Inc. will remain in the possession of Trugman Valuation Associates Inc. In the event of a withdrawal, we would be liable to return only those materials and documents supplied by the client and the unused portion of the retainer.

The undersigned gives Trugman Valuation Associates Inc. the right to discuss this matter with the client's attorney, accountant, other individuals so designated by the client, and any professional colleagues of the appraiser from whom professional information is sought.

If this is acceptable, please sign the acknowledgment below and return a signed copy of this retainer with your check in the amount of $X,XXX to our office.

TRUGMAN VALUATION ASSOCIATES INC.

Linda B. Trugman
CPA/ABV, CBA, ASA, MBA

ACKNOWLEDGMENT

The undersigned accepts the terms of this retainer agreement and guarantees full payment of the fees with respect to this engagement.

Client's Signature and Date

THIS BUSINESS VALUATION RETAINER AGREEMENT CONSISTS OF THREE (3) PAGES INCLUDING THIS ONE. ALL THREE (3) PAGES MUST BE RETURNED TO TRUGMAN VALUATION ASSOCIATES INC. AFTER EXECUTION OF THIS DOCUMENT WITH THE REQUESTED RETAINER IN ORDER TO RETAIN OUR FIRM. IF THIS DOCUMENT IS NOT RECEIVED BY TRUGMAN VALUATION ASSOCIATES INC. FULLY EXECUTED BY THE CLIENT WITH THE REQUESTED RETAINER BY (SOME DATE), TRUGMAN VALUATION ASSOCIATES INC. RESERVES THE RIGHT TO DEEM THE TERMS OF THIS AGREEMENT AND THE OFFER TO PERFORM BUSINESS VALUATION SERVICES NULL AND VOID.

If you think our engagement letter is long, you're right. We had an attorney draft it for us, and he charged us by the word. An engagement letter is a written contract between you and the client. As with any legal contract, you should take it seriously. You should be clear on what you will be doing for the client, and in some cases, what the client is expected to do for you. When we have a very tight deadline, we generally will include language that outlines that the client is responsible for getting us the requested information by a certain date, or we cannot be held responsible for a missed deadline. Missed deadlines can have your report excluded from a litigation; they can cause an estate tax return to be filed late, generating penalty and interest; and they can get you sued.

If your engagement is to include forensic accounting work, this should be properly explained in your engagement letter. If the assignment does not include forensics, make sure that it is clear that you will be relying on the information that you are provided with. Look back at limiting condition number 1 in the retainer agreement. This does not mean that we will not perform the necessary due diligence as an appraiser to look for the normalization adjustments, but we certainly are not going to try to find the unreported income as part of this assignment unless it is spelled out. Be careful here also, because if you are mutually retained by both parties, trying to find unreported income may cause you to be working more as an advocate for one of the clients, since any finding may assist the other client in furthering his or her position.

The easiest trap to fall into in a business valuation engagement is when the attorney asks you for a "ballpark." Next thing you know, the ballpark becomes your expert report without you even realizing that it has been submitted to the other side for a litigation. If your engagement letter and report are not crystal clear as to what you will and will not do and as to what restrictions are placed on the use of the report, you are looking for trouble. Your reputation will be the most impaired part of the litigation. When you find yourself in court trying to explain that this report was not intended to be used for the litigation, the only thing that everyone will remember is that the expert did a poor job. Who needs the grief?

Your engagement letter should also include the "as of" date for the valuation. You do not want to start doing your research and analysis as of a certain date, have your client's attorney tell you that you should be using a different date, and then not be able to collect fees from the client because you did your work twice. In some states, valuations for certain types of litigation can be a moving target. For example, in Connecticut, a divorce valuation starts out at the current date but will frequently be updated at the time of the trial. This can cause several valuations to be done as part of the same engagement. Your engagement letter should clearly spell out that the valuation assignment may require additional dates to be used and that the client acknowledges and gives you his/her permission to do whatever needs to be done.

Another way to fall into a trap is the engagement to "critique" the other side's report without being hired to give your own opinion of value, because the client does not want to spend the money to have you do a full appraisal. Besides having your assignment spelled out in the engagement letter—e.g., "we are being retained only to critique the report of XYZ Appraisal Firm, and we are not being hired to opine on the value of the company"—some of the language that goes into our report may look like this:

> Mr. Charles H. Jones
> Smith Jones & Associates, P.A.
> 2 Main Street
> Anytown, NJ 07777
>
> Re: *Jones v. Jones*
>
> Dear Mr. Jones:
>
> Pursuant to your request, I have reviewed the valuation report of Roberts, Green & Co., CPAs (hereafter referred to as "Roberts" or "The Roberts Report") regarding your interest in Smith Jones & Associates, P.A. (hereafter referred to as "SJA"). **The purpose of my review was to determine if I could find any glaring errors in the valuation report. I have not performed an appraisal of your interest, and accordingly, I am not offering an opinion of value in this critique.**

Sometimes, we are asked to perform less than a full appraisal. In many engagements, this service is known as a calculation of value. The engagement letter may look like the one in Exhibit 2.5

EXHIBIT 2.5
Business Valuation Consulting Agreement

The undersigned acknowledges this engagement of Trugman Valuation Associates Inc. to perform consulting services with respect to Jones Advertising Inc. The purpose of this consulting assignment is to estimate a selling price for the business equity based on the most current information that the client can provide to the appraiser.

Although the purpose of this business valuation consulting assignment is to determine the reasonable value of the subject property, the client has requested only limited analyses to be performed. Based on these limitations, Trugman Valuation Associates Inc. will not be rendering an opinion of value based on the standards established by the *Uniform Standards of Appraisal Practice*, the American Society of Appraisers, or The Institute of Business Appraisers.

Trugman Valuation Associates Inc. will perform limited analyses to estimate the negotiable price that can be used by the client in lieu of the more definitive estimate of fair market value of the common stock. Said fair market value is defined to be a value at which a willing seller and willing buyer, both being informed of the relevant facts about the business, could reasonably conduct a transaction, neither party acting under any compulsion to do so.

Trugman Valuation Associates Inc. will provide consulting services in the form of business valuation calculations. Such business valuation calculations are defined by the American Society of Appraisers as:

> The objective of calculations is to provide an approximate indication of value based upon the performance of limited procedures agreed upon by the appraiser and the client.
>
> Calculations have the following qualities:
>
> (1) They may be expressed as a single dollar amount or as a range.
>
> (2) They may be based upon consideration of only limited relevant information.
>
> (3) The appraiser performs limited information collection and analysis procedures.
>
> (4) The calculations may be based upon conceptual approaches as agreed upon with the client.

It is understood that Trugman Valuation Associates Inc. is not being engaged to perform an audit as defined by the American Institute of Certified Public Accountants, but rather the necessary analysis of only those records deemed necessary to perform this consulting assignment.

In the event sufficient records and/or documentation cannot be supplied to Trugman Valuation Associates Inc., no such consulting report will be issued.

This consulting engagement will be subject to, at least, the following contingent and limiting conditions, which will be expressed as part of our report:

1. Information, estimates, and opinions contained in this report are obtained from sources considered reliable; however, Trugman Valuation Associates Inc. has not independently verified such information, and no liability for such sources is assumed by this consultant.
2. Possession of this report, or a copy thereof, does not carry with it the right of publication of all or part of it, nor may it be used for any purpose without the previous written consent of the consultant, and in any event only with proper authorization. Authorized copies of this report will be signed in blue ink by a shareholder of Trugman Valuation Associates Inc. Unsigned copies, or copies not signed in blue ink, should be considered to be incomplete.
3. None of the contents of this consulting report shall be conveyed to any third party or to the public through any means without the express written consent of Trugman Valuation Associates Inc.
4. Any estimate of value presented in this report applies to this consulting assignment only and may not be used out of the context presented herein. Any other use of this report may lead the user to an incorrect conclusion for which Trugman Valuation Associates Inc. assumes no responsibility.
5. It should be specifically noted that any estimate of value assumes the business will be competently managed and maintained by financially sound owners over the expected period of ownership. This consulting engagement does not entail an evaluation of management's effectiveness, nor are we responsible for future marketing efforts and other management or ownership actions upon which actual results will depend.
6. No opinion is intended to be expressed for matters that require legal or other specialized expertise, investigation, or knowledge beyond that customarily employed by consultants/appraisers valuing businesses.
7. It is assumed that there are no regulations of any government entity to control or restrict the use of the underlying assets unless specifically referred to in the report and that the underlying assets will not operate in violation of any applicable government regulations, codes, ordinances, or statutes.
8. We assume that there are no hidden or unexpected conditions of the business that would adversely affect value, other than as indicated in this report.

EXHIBIT 2.5 *(Continued)*

It is possible that additional contingent and limiting conditions will be required, and the client agrees that all conditions disclosed by the consultant will be accepted as incorporated into the consultant's report.

It is our intention to perform this engagement as quickly and affordably as possible, but these services take a reasonable amount of time to render. We will make certain that the appropriate personnel in our firm render those services that will comply with the level of expertise required by this engagement. In that regard, hourly rates will be charged based on the billing rates in effect at the time that the services are rendered.

Hourly rates are charged portal to portal from our Tampa office. In addition to these hourly rates, any out-of-pocket expenses relating to this assignment will be billed to you at our cost. It is expected that we will perform some research through computer databases, and that we may be required to purchase research materials relating to this engagement. We will do everything possible to minimize these expenses, but the client is advised that they most likely will exist.

Payment terms shall be as follows:

> $X,XXX due in advance as a retainer. Any amount over the retainer shall be billed monthly. Since it is considered unethical for us to perform these services on a contingency basis, it is important to us that our fees be paid promptly. The appearance of independence is of considerable importance for our firm to maintain our credibility, and therefore, we reserve the right to stop providing services at any time that there is a balance due our firm beyond 30 days. In the event that we continue to provide services, we do not waive our right to stop at a later date.
>
> The client must understand that these services are not inexpensive, and unless other arrangements are made, in writing, with our firm, services rendered by our firm will be invoiced regularly and are due upon presentation of our invoice to you.
>
> Balances outstanding beyond 30 days will have a service charge added at the rate of 1.5 percent per month or part thereof. All costs relating to collection of these fees will also be the responsibility of the undersigned including, but not limited to, attorney fees, collection agency fees, etc. Reasonable attorney fees will be considered to be up to 33.33 percent of the outstanding balance. In the event a collection action is brought against the client, the client acknowledges that the venue will be Morris County, New Jersey.
>
> An additional invoice will be rendered once the appraiser has completed the appraisal report. Payment in full is due prior to the release of said report to the client.
>
> The undersigned client agrees to indemnify Trugman Valuation Associates Inc. and its shareholders and employees from any legal expenses incurred as a result of this engagement. This would include, but not be limited to, any legal expenses required to protect the confidentiality of this or any other client who becomes an issue in this matter.
>
> The final report is copyrighted by Trugman Valuation Associates Inc. It shall remain the property of Trugman Valuation Associates Inc., and no copies or reproductions shall be allowed without the written consent of Trugman Valuation Associates Inc. until such time as any outstanding balance is paid.

Trugman Valuation Associates Inc. has estimated the cost of this assignment to approximate $X,XXX to $X,XXX plus out-of-pocket costs. Although we cannot guarantee the exact fee, we will do everything reasonably possible to minimize this expense without jeopardizing the quality of the services rendered. In the event that it appears that the fee will deviate upwards by more than 20 percent, we will call it to your attention as soon as we become aware of the extra time required to complete the assignment.

Trugman Valuation Associates Inc. reserves the right to withdraw from this engagement at any time for reasonable cause. It is not our intention to withdraw. All workpapers created by Trugman Valuation Associates Inc. will remain in the possession of Trugman Valuation Associates Inc. In the event of a withdrawal, we would be liable only to return those materials and documents supplied by the client and the unused portion of the retainer.

The undersigned gives Trugman Valuation Associates Inc. the right to discuss this matter with the client's accountant and other individuals so designated by the client and any professional colleagues of the appraiser from whom professional information is sought.

If this is acceptable, please sign the acknowledgment below and return a signed copy of this retainer agreement with your check in the amount of $X,XXX to our office.

TRUGMAN VALUATION ASSOCIATES INC.

Gary R. Trugman
CPA/ABV, MCBA, ASA, MVS

(Continued)

EXHIBIT 2.5 *(Continued)*

ACKNOWLEDGMENT:

The undersigned accepts the terms of this retainer agreement and guarantees full payment of the fees with respect to this engagement.

____

Client's Signature and Date

THIS BUSINESS VALUATION CONSULTING AGREEMENT CONSISTS OF FIVE (5) PAGES INCLUDING THIS ONE. ALL FIVE (5) PAGES MUST BE RETURNED TO TRUGMAN VALUATION ASSOCIATES INC. AFTER EXECUTION OF THIS DOCUMENT WITH THE REQUESTED RETAINER IN ORDER TO RETAIN OUR FIRM. IF THIS DOCUMENT IS NOT RECEIVED BY TRUGMAN VALUATION ASSOCIATES INC. FULLY EXECUTED BY THE CLIENT WITH THE REQUESTED RETAINER BY (SOME DATE) TRUGMAN VALUATION ASSOCIATES INC. RESERVES THE RIGHT TO DEEM THE TERMS OF THIS AGREEMENT AND THE OFFER TO PERFORM BUSINESS VALUATION CONSULTING SERVICES NULL AND VOID.

Other items that should be spelled out in the engagement letter include the standard of value, payment terms, dispute resolution, and indemnification provisions. The standard of value is as important as the date of the valuation. Are you being hired to use fair market value or fair value? This stuff is discussed in Chapter 3. You need the client's attorney to tell you which you should be using. Though we all want to be helpful, some of these items require legal decisions. As an accountant or appraiser, one is generally not qualified (by education and training) to provide legal determinations about standards of value. While we know that fair market value will be used for estate tax issues, different states have different standards of value for shareholder disputes. Sometimes even within the same standard of value, there can be many different jurisdictional interpretations. This is the kind of stuff that can get you in trouble if you use the wrong one. Imagine the judge knocking out your report because you used the wrong standard of value. Hello lawsuit!

Do not forget to put payment terms in the engagement letter, unless you like to work for free. I like to choose what pro bono work our firm does. I try not to let the client decide that we should work for free. Get a retainer. If you notice, our retainer agreements contain a provision that says, "An additional invoice will be rendered once the appraiser has completed the appraisal report. Payment in full is due prior to the release of said report to the client." This means we get paid before we release the report. I do not like to chase fees. In fact, my insurance carrier would probably prefer that I do not chase fees. They say that one of the biggest reasons that clients sue their accountants for malpractice is that the clients are countersuing because of a collection dispute. Get paid before they sue you!

Let me point out some other important stuff about the engagement letter. In the first paragraph, the name of the appraisal firm, not the appraiser, should appear, since it is the firm and not the individual being engaged. This will allow the staffing to be determined by the firm. This will also allow someone else in your firm to step into the assignment if you are unable to complete it. In addition, a good engagement letter should, at a minimum, include:

- A description of the scope of the assignment
- A detailed description of the appraisal subject
- The standard of value that will be used, including the definition of that standard
- The effective date(s) of the valuation
- The type of report that will be issued to communicate the value estimate
- A list of assumptions and limiting conditions that are expected to be part of the report (more about this shortly)
- The responsibilities of the client, in particular, to provide requested documentation on a timely basis

Description of the Scope of the Assignment

This section of the engagement letter describes the purpose and function of the appraisal assignment. The best way to differentiate between the purpose and function of the appraisal is as follows:

Purpose = Type of value (standard of value)
Function = How the appraisal will be used

This is probably a good time to introduce another concept that fits into this section. It is called the "highest and best use" of the business. We also call this the *premise of value*. Whenever you pick up a real estate appraisal, the appraiser discusses the concept of highest and best use. In the *Dictionary of Real Estate Appraisal*, it is described as "the reasonably probable and legal use of vacant land or an improved property, which is physically possible, appropriately supported, financially feasible, and that results in the highest value."[1]

The concept is to value the property in the manner in which it would generate the greatest return to the owner of the property. Logically, if a land purchaser wanted to maximize the return on his or her investment in a vacant lot, the maximum return would be to build an office building, rather than a single-family house, assuming that the zoning (what is legally permissible) allows it to be built. The land becomes worth more because of its allowed usage.

The business appraiser should determine the "highest and best use" of the business enterprise in a manner similar to how the concept is used in real estate appraisal. This is not to say that a hardware store should become a manufacturer of plastics, but rather to pose the question, Is the business to be valued as a going concern or as if in liquidation? Some businesses are clearly worth more dead than alive and, therefore, should be valued based on their highest and best use in order to provide the maximum return to the investors. For example, if a business is losing money each year and there is no turnaround in sight, the owner of the business would maximize his or her return by liquidating the company, rather than losing equity each year by going forward. This assumes, however, that the interest being appraised has the ability to control the direction of the business. A minority interest usually cannot.

The scope section of the engagement letter should also describe the level of service, as well as (in some instances) whatever you will not be doing. In most instances, you will be performing an appraisal, a limited appraisal, or a calculation, which will soon be defined. For CPA appraisers, language relating to financial statement opinions should be included, as I have in the third paragraph of Exhibit 2.4. Non-CPAs who are reading this book do not need to include the section that discusses audits and the AICPA in their engagement letter. Yours truly has those CPA letters after my name, so I worry a little bit more than the typical appraiser that my work is not being misconstrued as an accounting type of service. For CPAs, better to be safe than sorry!

There will be times when you will be requested to perform less than a full appraisal. Considering the fact that we need to make a living and that the spirit of the *USPAP* is to allow less than full appraisals under certain circumstances, it seems acceptable to do less than full appraisals when applicable. What does that mean? You should never do less than a full appraisal if the end result will be misleading or prone to error.

One of the best distinctions between the various types of appraisal services that you might be asked to render was created by the Business Valuation Committee of the ASA, which explains these different levels of service as follows:

> The nature and scope of the assignment must be adequately defined. Acceptable scopes of work would generally be of three types as delineated below. Other scopes of work should be explained and described.

[1]Stephanie Shea Joyce, ed., *Dictionary of Real Estate Appraisal*, 3rd ed. (Chicago: Appraisal Institute, 1993).

1. Appraisal
   a. The objective of an appraisal is to express an unambiguous opinion as to the value of the business, business ownership interest, or security, which is supported by all procedures that the appraiser deems to be relevant to the valuation.
   b. An appraisal has the following qualities:
      (1) It is expressed as a single dollar amount or as a range.
      (2) It considers all relevant information as of the appraisal date available to the appraiser at the time of performance of the valuation.
      (3) The appraiser conducts appropriate procedures to collect and analyze all information expected to be relevant to the valuation.
      (4) The valuation is based upon consideration of all conceptual approaches deemed to be relevant by the appraiser.
2. Limited Appraisal
   a. The objective of a limited appraisal is to express an estimate as to the value of a business, business ownership interest, or security, which lacks the performance of additional procedures that are required in an appraisal.
   b. A limited appraisal has the following qualities:
      (1) It is expressed as a single dollar amount or as a range.
      (2) It is based upon consideration of limited relevant information.
      (3) The appraiser conducts only limited procedures to collect and analyze the information which such appraiser considers necessary to support the conclusion presented.
      (4) The valuation is based upon the conceptual approach(es) deemed by the appraiser to be most appropriate.
3. Calculations
   a. The objective of calculations is to provide an approximate indication of value based upon the performance of limited procedures agreed upon by the appraiser and the client.
   b. Calculations have the following qualities:
      (1) They may be expressed as a single dollar amount or as a range.
      (2) They may be based upon consideration of only limited relevant information.
      (3) The appraiser performs limited information collection and analysis procedures.
      (4) The calculations may be based upon conceptual approaches as agreed upon with the client.[2]

This information should be clearly spelled out in an engagement letter with the client. Limited appraisals and calculations are not part of the *USPAP*. Therefore, caution should be exercised concerning when these types of services should be provided. Sample engagement letters are provided in Exhibit 2.5 and Exhibit 2.6.

EXHIBIT 2.6
Limited Business Valuation Retainer Agreement

The undersigned acknowledges this engagement of Trugman Valuation Associates Inc. to perform a limited business valuation of the common stock of Jones Graphics, Inc., a Connecticut Corporation, as of December 31, 2000.

The purpose of this limited business valuation is to determine the fair market value of the subject property. Said fair market value is defined to be a value at which a willing seller and willing buyer, both being informed of the relevant facts about the business, could reasonably conduct a transaction, neither party acting under any compulsion to do so.

[2] ASA Standards, BVS-I, General Requirements for Developing a Business Valuation, Sec. II.B.

EXHIBIT 2.6 *(Continued)*

According to the standards of the American Society of Appraisers, the objective of a limited appraisal is to express an estimate as to the value of a business, business ownership interest, or security, which lacks the performance of additional procedures that are required in an appraisal. A limited appraisal has the following qualities: (1) It is expressed as a single dollar amount or as a range; (2) It is based upon consideration of limited relevant information; (3) The appraiser conducts only limited procedures to collect and analyze the information which such appraiser considers necessary to support the conclusion presented; and (4) The valuation is based upon the conceptual approach(es) deemed by the appraiser to be most appropriate.

It is understood that Trugman Valuation Associates Inc. is not being engaged to perform an audit as defined by the American Institute of Certified Public Accountants, but rather the necessary tests of the accounting records that will be performed for the purpose of issuing a limited valuation report, and not a statement regarding the fairness of presentation of the financial statements of the above business.

Certain values, derived from reports of others, and which are so designated, will be included in our report. We take no responsibility for those items. Nor do we take responsibility to update the report or disclose any events or circumstances occurring after the date of the report.

In the event sufficient records and/or documentation cannot be supplied to Trugman Valuation Associates Inc., no such valuation report will be issued.

This appraisal will be subject to, at least, the following contingent and limiting conditions, which will be included in the report as an appendix:

1. Information, estimates, and opinions contained in this report are obtained from sources considered reliable; however, Trugman Valuation Associates Inc. has not independently verified such information and no liability for such sources is assumed by this appraiser.
2. All facts and data set forth in the report are true and accurate to the best of the appraiser's knowledge and belief. We have not knowingly withheld or omitted anything from our report affecting our value estimate.
3. Possession of this report, or a copy thereof, does not carry with it the right of publication of all or part of it, nor may it be used for any purpose without the previous written consent of the appraiser, and in any event only with proper authorization. Authorized copies of this report will be signed in blue ink by a partner of Trugman Valuation Associates Inc. Unsigned copies, or copies not signed in blue ink, should be considered to be incomplete.
4. None of the contents of this valuation report shall be conveyed to any third party or to the public through any means without the express written consent of Trugman Valuation Associates Inc.
5. No investigation of titles to property or any claims on ownership of the property by any individuals or company has been undertaken. Unless otherwise stated in our report, title is assumed to be clear and free of encumbrances and as provided to the appraiser.
6. Unless otherwise provided for in writing and agreed to by both parties in advance, the extent of the liability for the completeness or accuracy of the data, opinions, comments, recommendations, and/or conclusions shall not exceed the amount paid to the appraisers for professional fees and, then, only to the party(s) for whom this report was originally prepared.
7. The various estimates of value presented in this report apply to this appraisal only and may not be used out of the context presented herein. Any other use of this report may lead the user to an incorrect conclusion for which Trugman Valuation Associates Inc. assumes no responsibility.
8. The appraisal estimate of fair market value reached in this report is necessarily based on the definition of fair market value as stated in the Introduction Section. An actual transaction in the shares may be concluded at a higher value or lower value, depending on the circumstances surrounding the company, the appraised business interest, and/or the motivations and knowledge of both the buyers and sellers at that time. Trugman Valuation Associates Inc. makes no guarantees as to what values individual buyers and sellers may reach in an actual transaction.
9. It should be specifically noted that the valuation assumes the business will be competently managed and maintained by financially sound owners over the expected period of ownership. This appraisal engagement does not entail an evaluation of management's effectiveness, nor are we responsible for future marketing efforts and other management or ownership actions upon which actual results will depend.
10. No opinion is intended to be expressed for matters that require legal or other specialized expertise, investigation, or knowledge beyond that customarily employed by appraisers valuing businesses.
11. It is assumed that there are no regulations of any government entity to control or restrict the use of the underlying assets unless specifically referred to in the report and that the underlying assets will not operate in violation of any applicable government regulations, codes, ordinances, or statutes.

(Continued)

EXHIBIT 2.6 *(Continued)*

12. Valuation reports may contain prospective financial information, estimates, or opinions that represent the view of the appraiser about reasonable expectations at a particular point in time, but such information, estimates, or opinions are not offered as predictions or as assurances that a particular level of income or profit will be achieved, or that specific events will occur.
13. We assume that there are no hidden or unexpected conditions of the business that would adversely affect value, other than as indicated in this report.
14. Hazardous substances, if present, can introduce an actual or potential liability that will adversely affect the marketability and value of a business. Such liability may be in the form of immediate recognition of existing hazardous conditions, or future liability that could stem from the release of currently nonhazardous contaminants. In the development of the opinion of value, no consideration was given to such liability or its impact on value. We have not taken into account any and all future environmental considerations and potential liability.

It is possible that additional contingent and limiting conditions will be required, and the client agrees that all conditions disclosed by the appraiser will be accepted as incorporated into the appraiser's report.

It is our intention to perform this engagement as quickly and affordably as possible, but these services take a reasonable amount of time to render. We will make certain that the appropriate personnel in our firm render those services that will comply with the level of expertise required by this engagement. In that regard, hourly rates will be charged based on the billing rates in effect at the time that the services are rendered.

Hourly rates are charged portal to portal from our Stamford office. In addition to these hourly rates, the following charges may be applicable:

1. Any out of pocket expenses relating to this valuation. It is expected that we will perform research through computer databases, and that we may be required to purchase research materials relating to this engagement. These and other such costs will be billed to you at our cost.

Payment terms shall be as follows:

$X,XXX due in advance as a retainer. Any amount over the retainer shall be billed monthly. Since it is considered unethical for us to perform these services on a contingency basis, it is important to us that our fees be paid promptly. The appearance of independence is of considerable importance for our firm to maintain our credibility, and therefore, we reserve the right to stop providing services at any time that there is a balance due our firm beyond 30 days. In the event that we continue to provide services, we do not waive our right to stop at a later date.

The client must understand that professional business valuation services are not inexpensive and, unless other arrangements are made, in writing, with our firm, services rendered by our firm will be invoiced regularly, and are due upon presentation of our invoice to you.

Balances outstanding beyond 30 days will have a service charge added at the rate of 1.5 percent per month or part thereof. All costs relating to collection of these fees will also be the responsibility of the undersigned including, but not limited to, attorney fees, collection agency fees, etc. Reasonable attorney fees will be considered to be up to 33.33 percent of the outstanding balance. In the event a collection action is brought against the client, the client acknowledges that the venue will be Morris County, New Jersey.

An additional invoice will be rendered once the appraiser has completed the appraisal report. Payment in full is due prior to the release of said report.

The final report is copyrighted by Trugman Valuation Associates Inc. It shall remain the property of Trugman Valuation Associates Inc. and no copies or reproductions shall be allowed without the written consent of Trugman Valuation Associates Inc. until such time as any outstanding balance is paid.

Trugman Valuation Associates Inc. reserves the right to withdraw from this engagement at any time for reasonable cause. It is not our intention to withdraw. All workpapers created by Trugman Valuation Associates Inc. will remain in the possession of Trugman Valuation Associates Inc. In the event of a withdrawal, we would be liable only to return those materials and documents supplied by the client and the unused portion of the retainer.

Trugman Valuation Associates Inc. *will not* allow this report to be used as a report to be submitted to a court for a legal proceeding. No appraiser will testify as part of this engagement. If testimony will be required, Trugman Valuation Associates Inc. must be retained under a separate retainer agreement permitting the appraiser to perform a comprehensive appraisal without scope limitations.

The undersigned gives Trugman Valuation Associates Inc. the right to discuss this matter with the client's attorney, accountant, other individuals so designated by the client, and any professional colleagues of the appraiser from whom professional information is sought.

EXHIBIT 2.6 (Continued)

If this is acceptable, please sign the acknowledgment below and return a signed copy of this retainer agreement with your check in the amount of $X,XXX to our office.

TRUGMAN VALUATION ASSOCIATES INC.

Gary R. Trugman
CPA/ABV, MCBA, ASA, MVS

ACKNOWLEDGMENT:

The undersigned accepts the terms of this retainer agreement and guarantees full payment of the fees with respect to this engagement.

____

Signature of Client and Date

THIS BUSINESS VALUATION RETAINER AGREEMENT CONSISTS OF FIVE (5) PAGES INCLUDING THIS ONE. ALL FIVE (5) PAGES MUST BE RETURNED TO TRUGMAN VALUATION ASSOCIATES INC. AFTER EXECUTION OF THIS DOCUMENT WITH THE REQUESTED RETAINER IN ORDER TO RETAIN OUR FIRM. IF THIS DOCUMENT IS NOT RECEIVED BY TRUGMAN VALUATION ASSOCIATES INC. FULLY EXECUTED BY THE CLIENT WITH THE REQUESTED RETAINER BY (SOME DATE), TRUGMAN VALUATION ASSOCIATES INC. RESERVES THE RIGHT TO DEEM THE TERMS OF THIS AGREEMENT AND THE OFFER TO PERFORM BUSINESS VALUATION SERVICES NULL AND VOID.

Detailed Description of the Appraisal Subject

To avoid confusion, a detailed description of the appraisal subject should be included in your engagement letter whenever possible. Stating that you are valuing XYZ Corporation is very ambiguous. Are you valuing the common stock of the company? Maybe you are valuing only those assets that will be sold as part of an "asset" sale. Maybe certain liabilities are supposed to be transferred as well. As you can see, a good description is essential for the reader to understand the appraisal report. Putting the description in your engagement letter not only requires you to get a proper understanding of your assignment early in the process, but also prevents the client or the client's attorney from changing the nature of the assignment on you, which changes the amount of time that you will have to bill for.

Defining the property to be appraised includes being very specific about the appraisal subject. If the entity being valued (in whole or in part) is a corporation, you must be precise as to what the appraisal subject is. Is it the common stock, preferred stock, specific assets, specific liabilities, or the invested capital? You must also know if 100 percent of the stock or a fractional interest is being valued. The valuation process will depend on the property being appraised. For partnerships and proprietorships, you will need to know whether you are valuing total capital, specific assets, specific liabilities, or a combination of these.

Good guidance can be obtained from the appraisal standards. These standards tell us what we should consider and what should be included in a valuation report.

Standard of Value That Will Be Used, Including the Definition of That Standard

One of the advantages of being the author of this book is that I get to choose when we cover each topic. Since I do not want to cover the standard of value until Chapter 3, all I will say at this point is that you need to determine the appropriate standard of value as part of defining the assignment. This standard, as well as its definition, should be spelled out in the engagement letter. Be patient! We will discuss everything in due time.

Effective Date(s) of the Valuation

Appraisals are similar to balance sheets in that they are as of a specific point in time. Both internal and external factors affect the value of a company, and therefore, the valuation date is a critical component of the appraisal process. Changing values are easily illustrated in the public stock market. The constant movement of the price of a share of stock illustrates the potential volatility of the value of the stock. In a divorce engagement, we valued an individual's ownership interest in his company at three different dates: 1995, 1999, and 2001. The values were about $14 million, $21 million, and $16 million, respectively. What a difference a date makes!

Type of Report That Will Be Issued to Communicate the Value Estimate

The engagement letter should also include what type of report the appraiser is expected to issue. Our firm's policy is to issue a comprehensive report as part of our standard engagement letter. If something less is requested by the client, we will include the lower level of reporting in our engagement letter. We are particularly concerned when a client wants a lower level of service to save money, but the end result may be less than what is required for those circumstances.

List of Assumptions and Limiting Conditions Expected to Be Part of the Report

Most appraisal standards require the appraiser to include, as part of the report, any limiting conditions and assumptions made during the appraisal process. This allows a reader to understand more fully any limitations and assumptions that could have an impact on the conclusions reached by the appraiser. This section is similar to the "Disclaimer of Opinion" section of an accountant's compilation report, only with a lot more detail.

Many appraisers include the limiting conditions in the report but exclude them from the engagement letter. If you do not have these items in your engagement letter, slapping them on your report will not always work to protect you when your client says that he or she did not agree to accept your work subject to these conditions. I'm not an attorney, but if the client signs your engagement letter with these items included, that seems like an acceptance of these terms to me. (P.S. My attorney thinks so also!)

Client Responsibilities

There is nothing worse than a client who does not cooperate with his or her own appraiser in providing the requested documentation on a timely basis. The attorney calls you and tells you that your report is due in two weeks. You ask your client for the information, and it is delivered to your office at 5 P.M. on the thirteenth day. To prevent this from happening, you may need to put some language in the engagement letter requiring your client to respond to your information requests by a certain date, especially when the turnaround is short.

In a litigation engagement, your problem may be getting the other side to provide you with vital information for you to do your job properly. Although this problem can take up a book by itself, we are not going to discuss it in any great detail. Make sure your engagement letter includes language stating that if you do not get the information requested, you will not be obligated to issue a report.

Method of Determining Fees and the Terms of Payment

Don't forget this stuff. We are not charitable organizations. The manner in which you will be billing the client should be clearly spelled out in your engagement letter. Some of the alternatives that I have seen include the following:

- Straight hourly rates
- Flat fees
- Hourly rates with a ceiling
- Hourly rates with a floor

Regardless of the manner in which the billing takes place, it is customary for out-of-pocket costs to be added to these rates. Furthermore, requesting a retainer of approximately 50 percent of the estimated fee is quite normal. This way, your out-of-pocket costs, and then some, are in the bank. For many litigation assignments, you may want to keep a replenishing retainer, so that the client does not end up behind in paying fees.

Five Steps of an Appraisal Assignment

As you can tell from the engagement letter in Exhibit 2.1, the initial part of the valuation process is not to be taken lightly. In the Introduction, we outlined the five steps of an appraisal assignment. Many of the items for defining the appraisal assignment are required before you begin the job so that you can include this important stuff in your engagement letter.

Engagement Letter Considerations for Litigation Reports

The previous discussion addressed engagement letters for any type of engagement. Those readers who are CPAs are probably more familiar with engagement letters than any other professional group. In a business valuation litigation engagement, it is important that your engagement letter clearly define the type of report that will be expected from you. The different types of reports are discussed in Chapter 13. A formal report is a very time-consuming document to create, and consequently, the client should acknowledge the fact that you are being engaged to render these services.

Many times, a client does not want to spend the money to have you render a long report, and you may be asked to provide an informal or letter report. These types of reports are not always appropriate. An informal business valuation that is used in Tax Court may be tossed out by the judge for not complying with the *Federal Rules of Civil Procedure*. If this is the case, you can count on having a very unhappy client. The client may even sue you for malpractice! To protect yourself, use your engagement letter to avoid this problem.

At our practice, we may render an informal report but restrict its use. Our engagement letter will expressly prohibit the client from using the informal report as an expert report. When the appraiser steps into the courtroom, the only thing that the judge will remember is a poor report. You will not be given time to explain that your client was too cheap to allow you to do your job the right way. Our engagement letter will advise the client that in the event of a litigation, we will have to expand our report so that it will qualify with the *USPAP*. This is generally a good compromise for the client, because he or she does not have to pay for the full report if it is not needed.

The Initial Document Request

Once the appraiser has been retained, the next step is to request information from the client. There are several schools of thought regarding the document request. Many appraisers send out a general request for information, such as the one that appears in Exhibit 2.7. Other appraisers make the initial request much smaller. Depending on the facts of the situation, both of these methodologies make sense.

Using a Standard Checklist

Using a standard checklist is an easy way to request all of the things that you might need to do a business valuation. However, several problems are associated with standard checklists. The appraiser frequently does not know much about the company that is being valued. Sending out a standard checklist may demonstrate a lack of interest on the part of the appraiser if he or she asks for many items that are totally irrelevant to the assignment. Think about how the client might feel if you ask for stockholder agreements when you were told that the business is a partnership or sole proprietorship.

EXHIBIT 2.7
General Document Checklist

XYZ Widgets Company, Inc. Business Valuation
Valuation Date: December 31, 2000

For Trugman Valuation Associates Inc. to render a meaningful opinion relating to the estimate of value of XYZ Widgets Company, Inc., it is important that as much of the following information be supplied as may be available. In the event certain information is not available as of the valuation date, please provide this information for the time period as close to the valuation date as possible.

Financial Statements

1. Annual financial statements for the years ended December 31, 1995 through 2000
2. Interim financial statements for the most recent 12 months
3. A balance sheet as of December 31, 2000 [use this *only if the appraisal date is different from the date of the financial statements above*]
4. Federal income tax returns for the years ended December 31, 1995 through 2000; state income tax returns for the same time period, if applicable
5. Copies of any forecasts or projections
6. List of subsidiaries or other businesses in which the subject company has an ownership interest, together with theft financial statements

Other Financial Data

7. List of cash accounts and any significant cash investments
8. Accounts receivable listing as of December 31, 2000, preferably aged
9. List of items comprising inventory (quantity, description, and cost) and information on inventory accounting policies as of December 31, 2000
10. Fixed-asset register, depreciation schedule, or both, including real estate and equipment lists, date of acquisition, cost, depreciation method, useful life, and accumulated depreciation
11. List of items comprising significant other asset balances as of December 31, 2000
12. Accounts payable listing as of December 31, 2000, preferably aged
13. Analyses of significant accrued liabilities as of December 31, 2000
14. List of notes payable and other interest-bearing debt as of December 31, 2000
15. List of items comprising significant other liability balances as of December 31, 2000
16. Copies of sales, capital, or operating budgets
17. Copies of any business plans
18. Schedule of officers' compensation, owners' compensation, or both

Source: Adapted with permission from *Guide to Business Valuations*, Twelfth Edition (January 2002), published by Practitioners Publishing Company, Fort Worth, Texas.

EXHIBIT 2.7 (Continued)

19. Schedule of key-man life insurance
20. Reports of other professionals:
    (a) Appraisals on specific assets
    (b) Reports of other consultants

Other Operating Data

21. Brochures, price lists, catalogs, or other product information
22. List of stockholders, showing the stock owned by each person
23. Organization chart
24. List of five largest customers over the past three years and the total amount of sales to that customer in each year
25. List of five largest suppliers over the past three years and the total amount purchased from each of those suppliers in each year
26. Details of transactions with related parties

Legal Documents

27. Copies of significant leases or loans, including notes receivable and notes payable
28. Copies of stockholder agreements
29. Minutes of board of directors' meetings
30. Copies of any buy-sell agreements, written often to purchase the entire company or any portion thereof, or both
31. Copies of key managers' employment contracts
32. Copies of any major sale or purchase contracts
33. Details of any litigation, including pending or threatened lawsuits
34. Details of any employee benefit plans, including pension plans, profit-sharing plans, and employee stock option plans
35. Collective bargaining agreement
36. Reports of examination issued by government agencies such as the EPA, OSHA, the IRS, and the EEOC
37. Invoices for all legal fees paid during the last five years

Other Company Data

38. List of any of the following: patents, copyrights, trademarks, or other similar intangibles
39. Detail of any contingent liabilities (such as guarantees or warranties) or off-balance-sheet financing (such as letters of credit) as of December 31, 2000
40. Résumés or a summary of the background and experience of all key personnel
41. Copies of other value indication, such as property tax appraisals

Industry Data

42. List of trade associations
43. List of trade publications
44. Standard industrial classification code
45. Copies of any surveys received as part of a membership in a trade association

Miscellaneous

46. Any other information that is deemed to be pertinent for us to fairly express our opinion of value

Additional information may be requested during the appraisal process. In addition to the information above, there may be some instances in which we will request general ledgers, accounting journals, payroll tax returns, sales tax returns, bank statements, canceled checks, and other such documentation.

Using this type of document in a litigation may also prove to be dangerous. I learned the hard way when an attorney went down my checklist and asked me whether I had received each item of information. This particular assignment was so small that much of the information either did not exist or did not matter. After I said that I had not received about 70 percent of the items on my checklist, he had to ask me only two questions to embarrass me while I was on the witness stand. This is what happened:

Attorney: Mr. Trugman, you must think these items are important in performing a business appraisal if you ask for them as a general rule, do you not?

Trugman: Yes sir, I do.

Attorney: Well then, Mr. Trugman, if you consider these items important to your valuation, and you did not receive them from my client, how can you expect this court to believe that you did a credible job when you were missing about 70 percent of what you asked for?

Trugman: Gulp!

We all make mistakes. I may be one of the few authors who will admit that I am not perfect. (I can't tell you how many times some attorney has tried to use this against me in court!) As you can see, asking for too much information can prove to be as dangerous as not asking for enough. It is important to analyze each situation and act accordingly for that assignment. If you try to standardize this process too much, you are doomed.

As an alternative to sending out a massive document request at the beginning of the assignment, some appraisers prefer to send out an initial request for tax returns and financial statements only. This allows the appraiser to review these documents and get a feel for the financial side of the company. If the company's revenues are $80,000, a massive document request may be overkill. However, do not let the small valuations fool you. Sometimes, as much work goes into these types of assignments as the big ones.

After you have a feel for the company, a second document request might make sense. Before you send out this request, however, you may want to perform a site inspection and interview the management (these steps are discussed further in Chapter 5). Either your fieldwork may streamline your document request, or you may find that additional documentation is required because something came to your attention during the interview.

Setting Up Multiple Checklists

As long as you remember to customize each checklist for the particular assignment, you may find it to be a time-saver to have multiple checklists set up on your word processor for those types of jobs that you do over and over again. Exhibits 2.8, 2.9, and 2.10 provide document checklists for a medical practice, a law practice, and an accounting practice, respectively. These particular checklists are intended for use if the entity being valued is a professional corporation. Our firm has other checklists for sole proprietorships and partnerships. By the way, Chapter 16 includes a discussion of the valuation of professional practices.

You will notice that in the exhibits, the sections that are different are in italics for your convenience. Rather than have to constantly make changes, we find it easier to have a master checklist set up for each of these professional practices since we value many of them.

EXHIBIT 2.8
Document Checklist—Medical Practice

Dr. Smith, P.C.
Business Valuation—Medical Practice
Valuation Date: December 31, 2000

For Trugman Valuation Associates Inc. to render a meaningful opinion relating to the estimate of value of Dr. Smith, P.C., it is important that as much of the following information be supplied as may be available. In the event certain information is not available as of the valuation date, please provide this information for the time period as close to the valuation date as possible.

EXHIBIT 2.8 ***(Continued)***

Financial Statements

1. Annual financial statements for the years ended December 31, 1995 through 2000
2. Interim financial statements for the 12 months ended December 31, 2000
3. A balance sheet as of December 31, 2000 (use this only if the appraisal date is different from the date of the financial statements above)
4. Federal income tax returns for the years ended December 31, 1995 through 2000; state income tax returns, if applicable
5. List of subsidiaries or other businesses in which the subject company has an ownership interest, together with their financial statements

Other Financial Data

6. List of cash accounts and any significant cash investments
7. Aged accounts receivable listing as of December 31, 2000, preferably aged
8. *List of items comprising medical supplies inventory (quantity, description, and cost) as of December 31, 2000*
9. Fixed-asset register, depreciation schedule, or both, including real estate and equipment lists, date of acquisition, cost, depreciation method, useful life, and accumulated depreciation
10. List of items comprising significant other asset balances as of December 31, 2000
11. Accounts payable listing as of December 31, 2000, preferably aged
12. Analyses of significant accrued liabilities as of December 31, 2000
13. List of notes payable and other interest-bearing debt as of December 31, 2000
14. List of items comprising significant other liability balances as of December 31, 2000
15. Schedule of officers' compensation, owners' compensation, or both
16. Schedule of key-man life insurance
17. Reports of other professionals:
    (a) Appraisals on specific assets
    (b) Reports of other consultants

Other Operating Data

18. List of stockholders, showing the amount of stock owned by each person.
19. Details of transactions with related parties
20. *Information relating to accounts receivable submitted to a collection agency or law firm*
21. Copies of significant leases or loans, including notes receivable and notes payable
22. Copies of stockholder agreements
23. Minutes of board of directors' meeting
24. Copies of any buy-sell agreements, written offers to purchase the entire practice or any portion thereof, or both
25. Invoices for all legal fees paid during the last five years

Other Company Data

26. Details of any contingent liabilities (such as guarantees or warranties) or off-balance-sheet financing (such as letters of credit) as of December 31, 2000
27. *List of all personnel broken down by status with the firm, department, etc. For professionals, please indicate specialization, board certifications, medical school, where internship and residency were performed, and fellowships received*
28. Copies of other value indicators, such as property tax appraisals

(Continued)

EXHIBIT 2.8 *(Continued)*

29. *Appointment books for the past three years*
30. *List of all hospital affiliations*
31. *List of all specialties, subspecialties, or both*

Legal Documents

32. Copies of significant leases or loans, including notes receivable and notes payable
33. Copies of stockholder agreements
34. Minutes of board of directors' meetings
35. Copies of any buy-sell agreements, any transactions relating to the stock interests in the firm, or both
36. *Copies of associates' or stockholders' employment contracts*
37. Details of any litigation, including pending or threatened lawsuits
38. Details of any employee benefit plans, including pension plans, profit-sharing plans, and employee stock option plans

Miscellaneous

39. Any other information that is deemed to be pertinent for us to express fairly our opinion of value

Additional information may be requested during the appraisal process. In addition to the information above, there may be some instances in which we will request general ledgers, accounting journals, payroll tax returns, sales tax returns, bank statements, canceled checks, and other such documentation.

EXHIBIT 2.9
Document Checklist—Law Practice

I. Sueyou, P.C.
Business Valuation—Law Practice
Valuation Date: December 31, 2000

For Trugman Valuation Associates Inc. to render a meaningful opinion relating to the estimate of value of I. Sueyou, P.C., it is important that as much of the following information be supplied as may be available. In the event certain information is not available as of the valuation date, please provide this information for the time period as close to the valuation date as possible.

Financial Statements

1. Annual financial statements for the years ended December 31, 1995 through 2000
2. Interim financial statements for the 12 months ended December 31, 2000
3. A balance sheet as of December 31, 2000 (use this only if the appraisal date is different from the date of the financial statements above)
4. Federal income tax returns for the years ended December 31, 1995 through 2000; state income tax returns, if applicable
5. List of subsidiaries or other businesses in which the subject company has an ownership interest, together with their financial statements

Other Financial Data

6. List of cash accounts and any significant cash investments
7. Accounts receivable listing as of December 31, 2000, preferably aged
8. *List of all unbilled work in process as of December 31, 2000*
9. Fixed asset register, depreciation schedule, or both, including real estate and equipment lists, date of acquisition, cost, depreciation method, useful life, and accumulated depreciation

EXHIBIT 2.9 *(Continued)*

10. *Detailed lists of books and services in the law library*
11. List of items comprising significant other asset balances as of December 31, 2000
12. Accounts payable listing as of December 31, 2000, preferably aged
13. Analyses of significant accrued liabilities as of December 31, 2000
14. List of notes payable and other interest-bearing debt as of December 31, 2000
15. List of items comprising significant other liability balances as of December 31, 2000
16. Schedule of officer's compensation, owner's compensation, or both
17. Schedule of key-man life insurance
18. Reports of other professionals:
    (a) Appraisals on specific assets
    (b) Reports of other consultants

Other Operating Data

19. List of stockholders, showing the amount of stock owned by each person
20. *List of ten largest clients over the past three years and the total amount billed and collected from each client in each year*
21. *Schedule of fees billed and collected, broken down by specialty (e.g., criminal, municipal, real estate, and matrimonial) for the past three years*
22. Details of transactions with related parties
23. *A schedule of all contingent fees received since December 31, 2000, for all matters started prior to that date*
24. *A list of all contingent matters that have not been finalized and that were started on or prior to December 31, 2000*
25. *A schedule of all contingent litigation matters for the past three years, indicating fees received, professional hours billed, and costs associated with each suit*
26. *A schedule of all attorney time written off over the past three years*
27. Payroll records for the last three years including, but not limited to, W-2 forms

Legal Documents

28. Copies of significant leases or loans, including notes receivable and notes payable
29. Copies of stockholder agreements
30. Minutes of board of directors' meetings
31. Copies of any buy-sell agreements, any transactions relating to the stock interests in the firm, or both
32. Copies of associates' or stockholders' employment contracts
33. Details of any litigation, including pending or threatened lawsuits
34. Details of any employee benefit plans, including pension plans, profit-sharing plans, and employee stock option plans

Other Company Data

35. Details of any contingent liabilities (such as guarantees or warranties) or off-balance-sheet financing (such as letters of credit) as of December 31, 2000
36. *List of all personnel, broken down by status within the firm, department, etc. For professionals, please indicate specialization and the year they were admitted to the bar*
37. Copies of other value indicators, such as property tax appraisals

Miscellaneous

38. Any other information that is deemed to be pertinent for us to express fairly our opinion of value

Additional information may be requested during the appraisal process. In addition to the information above, there may be some instances in which we will request general ledgers, accounting journals, bank statements, canceled checks, and other such documentation.

EXHIBIT 2.10
Document Checklist—Accounting Practice

We Do Numbers, CPAs, P.C.
Valuation Date: December 31, 2000

In order for Trugman Valuation Associates Inc. to render a meaningful opinion relating to the estimate of value of We Do Numbers, CPAs, P.C., it is important that as much of the following information be supplied as may be available. In the event certain information is not available as of the valuation date, please provide this information for the time period as close to the valuation date as possible.

Financial Statements

1. Annual financial statements for the years December 31, 1995 through 2000
2. Interim financial statements for the 12 months ended December 31, 2000
3. A balance sheet as of December 31, 2000
4. Federal income tax returns for the years December 31, 1995 through 2000; state income tax returns, if applicable
5. Copies of any forecasts or projections
6. List of subsidiaries or other businesses in which the subject company has an ownership interest, together with their financial statements

Other Financial Data

7. List of cash accounts and any significant cash investments
8. Aged accounts receivable listing as of December 31, 2000
9. *Schedule of unbilled work in process as of December 31, 2000*
10. Fixed asset register and/or depreciation schedule including real estate and equipment lists, date of acquisition, cost, depreciation method, useful life, and accumulated depreciation
11. List of items comprising significant other asset balances as of December 31, 2000
12. Accounts payable listing as of December 31, 2000, preferably aged
13. Analyses of significant accrued liabilities as of December 31, 2000
14. List of notes payable and other interest-bearing debt as of December 31, 2000
15. List of items comprising significant other liability balances as of December 31, 2000
16. Copies of operating budgets
17. Schedule of officers' and/or owners' compensation
18. Schedule of key-man life insurance
19. Reports of other professionals:
    (a) Appraisals on specific assets
    (b) Reports of other consultants

Other Operating Data

20. List of stockholders showing the amount of stock owned by each person
21. *List of five largest clients over the past three years and the total amount of fees charged to each client in each year*
22. *Breakdown of fees billed and collected over the past three years between audit, tax, compilation and review, management advisory services, and all other*
23. Details of transactions with related parties

Legal Documents

24. Copies of significant leases or loans, including notes receivable and notes payable
25. Copies of stockholder agreements

EXHIBIT 2.10 *(Continued)*

26. Minutes of Board of Directors' meetings
27. Copies of any buy-sell agreements and/or written offers to purchase the entire practice or any portion thereof
28. Copies of key managers' employment contracts
29. Details of any litigation, including pending or threatened lawsuits
30. Details of any employee benefit plans, including pension plans, profit sharing plans and employee stock option plans

Other Company Data

31. Details of any contingent liabilities (such as guarantees or warranties) or off-balance-sheet financing (such as letters of credit) as of December 31, 2000
32. Résumés or a summary of the background and experience of all key personnel
33. Copies of other value indicators, such as property tax appraisals

Miscellaneous

34. Any other information that is deemed to be pertinent in order for us to fairly express our opinion of value

There may be additional information requested during the appraisal process. In addition to the information above, we will want access to all books of original entry, including but not limited to, cash receipts journals, cash disbursements journals, payroll journals, sales journals, general journals, general ledgers, bank statements, cancelled checks, deposit tickets and other records that may exist.

Conclusion

By now, you should have more of an idea about how to get the job started. Please do not underestimate the importance of the contents of an engagement letter. It is more important to the appraiser than the appraisal report! You should also have an idea of the type of information to request in the initial stages of the valuation assignment.

3

Appraisal Principles and Theory

Chapter Goals

In this chapter, I will attempt to do the following:

1. Explain the principles of appraisal
2. Explain various definitions of value
3. Explain how the purpose of the valuation influences the standard of value
4. Discuss the IRS's influence on appraisals and expose the reader to many of the key revenue rulings

Principles of Appraisal

Three main appraisal principles constitute the foundation of valuation theory. Each of these principles is as important to valuation as the law of supply and demand is to economics. These very important principles are (1) the principle of alternatives, (2) the principle of substitution, and (3) the principle of future benefits.

Principle of Alternatives

The principle of alternatives states that in any contemplated transaction, each party has alternatives to consummating the transaction.[1] This indicates that there are generally alternatives to the investment. This concept is relatively simple and does not need to be belabored. Assume that I want to sell my boat. I have alternatives for whether I sell the boat, how much I sell it for, and to whom I sell it. In *Basic Business Appraisal,* Miles points out:

> Because it is one of the fundamental principles that form the basis of almost all appraisals, including those under circumstances that do not actually involve a contemplated sale or other transaction, the appraiser needs to be aware of its existence.[2]

Principle of Substitution

The principle of substitution is a presupposition of appraisal practice, expressing a generalized prediction concerned with behavior related to an event involving economic choices and values. It predicts how people will normally choose among comparable properties when prices vary.[3] In English, prudent individuals

[1]Raymond C. Miles, *Basic Business Appraisal* (Boynton Beach, Fla.: Institute of Business Appraisers, 1989).

[2]Ibid., 22.

[3]Richard Rickert, *Appraisal and Valuation: An Interdisciplinary Approach* (unpublished textbook from my graduate school days at Lindenwood College, St. Charles, Missouri).

will not pay more for something than they would pay for an equally desirable substitute. To illustrate how the principle of substitution operates to determine value, assume that an individual wants to purchase a hardware store. That person begins looking at various stores that are for sale and narrows down the choice to two of these stores. Both have good inventory, geographic location, and profits and are equally acceptable as purchase alternatives. One is listed for sale for $250,000 and the other is listed for $300,000. Which one do you think that person will most likely buy? This stuff is not rocket science!

The principle of substitution, in essence, states that nobody will pay more for something than he or she would pay for an equally desirable substitute. Logically, if two items are identical except for the price, a willing buyer will gravitate to the item with the lower price.

This is also illustrated in the investment field. If two investments have equal risk, an investor will invest in the item that will provide the greatest return on investment.

Application of the Principle of Substitution. As you will learn in a little while (unless you already know it!), there are three approaches that should be considered when one performs a business valuation. Each of these approaches, when applied, illustrates the principle of substitution.

The market approach estimates the value of the business being appraised from information derived from the market about prices actually paid for other, similar businesses. The asset-based approach simulates the starting of an equivalent business from scratch. In this approach, the value of the business being appraised is determined from the estimated cost of replacing (duplicating) the business asset by asset, liability by liability.

The income approach looks to financial equivalents (not necessarily a business) to estimate the value of the appraisal subject. The value of the business being appraised is estimated by either capitalizing a single-period benefit stream or discounting a multi-period benefit stream. The rates used to capitalize or discount the benefit stream are determined from alternative investments based on the risk factors attributable to the stream being capitalized or discounted. This will begin to make more sense in a little while.

Principle of Future Benefits

The principle of future benefits is the third appraisal principle that is fundamental to the valuation process. This principle states that "economic value reflects anticipated future benefits."[4] This appraisal principle can best be illustrated by assuming that you want to buy a particular business. Would historic earnings be as important as prospective earnings in determining value? Probably not. You would not care what the business did for the prior owner as much as what it can do for you, the purchaser.

There are only three economic reasons that investors will invest in a certain stock: (1) dividends (future cash flows to the investor), (2) capital appreciation (future cash flows to the investor upon sale), or (3) a combination of the two (future cash flows). It should always be remembered that valuation is based on the future outlook of the business.

If you really stop to think about it, this is the foundation for making a financial investment. I will soon discuss standards of value and the approaches to value, but the bottom line is that regardless of how you go about it, economic value should be determined based on the anticipated future cash flow that is expected from an investment. This means that the discounted cash flow methodology that I will discuss in Chapter 9 is theoretically the most sound method, because it measures the present value of the future cash flows to the investor. Unfortunately, you will also see that it is real easy to make a mistake in the application of this method, if you are not careful, so you do not want to hang your hat solely on this method. More of that stuff later.

---

[4]Miles, *Basic Business Appraisal*, 27.

Definitions of Value

A good place to start in any book on appraisal is to define what is meant by an appraisal. An appraisal is a supportable opinion about the worth of something. In this book and in much of the appraisal literature that you will read, the term *appraisal* is used synonymously with the term *valuation*. Therefore, a business appraisal is the same as a business valuation.

It is not enough to state that the appraisal will determine the "value" of what is being appraised. The term *value* has many different meanings in the valuation field. One of the first lessons to be learned relates to what are called "standards of value." These are also called "definitions of value." Before an assignment can be started, it is imperative that the standard of value that will be used in the assignment be clearly defined. In Chapter 2, I recommended that the standard of value, including a definition, be included in your engagement letter. In addition to discussing standards of value, an appraiser must also consider the ownership characteristics of the appraisal subject and the premise of value that will be used.

The ownership characteristics refer to whether the appraisal will be conducted using the actual buyer and seller, versus some hypothetical buyer and seller. Believe it or not, this makes a really big difference. There have been many court battles over this stuff. Using real or hypothetical individuals changes the standard of value.

The premise of value relates to the concept of highest and best use, which I mentioned earlier. Will we be valuing the company as a going concern or as if in liquidation? This, too, is an important concept because there are instances when a business that can be sold for its parts may be worth more than a business that is up and running. Let me give you a quick example. Assume that you have a client that delivers home heating oil. The company has been losing money for the last seven years with no turnaround in sight. The industry has changed, and small independent dealers are struggling because they have these really big trucks that they are sending out to customers half full, due to the lack of volume. The big players in the industry are purchasing the customer lists for substantial multiples of revenue because they feel that they can fill up their trucks and have their drivers stop at a few more customers on the route, and the incremental sales will only cost them the price of the fuel oil. If your client sells the customer list (and everything else, since it will put him or her out of business), the money from the sale could be invested at a profit. This would provide a greater return than running the business at a loss each year. This is the concept of highest and best use.

According to Webster's Dictionary, the definition of *value* is "a fair return or equivalent in goods, services, or money for something exchanged." In business valuation, the following standards of value are the most frequently used:

- Fair market value
- Fair value
- Investment value
- Intrinsic value

Fair Market Value

Probably the most commonly used standard of value is fair market value. Revenue Ruling 59-60 defines fair market value as:

> The amount at which the property would change hands between a willing buyer and a willing seller, when the former is not under any compulsion to buy, and the latter is not under any compulsion to sell, both parties having reasonable knowledge of relevant facts.

This definition implies that the value is the *most probable price* in cash or cash equivalent that would be paid if the property were placed on the open market for a reasonable period and, in all likelihood, assumes the existence of a covenant not to compete. If it did not assume a covenant not to compete, why would a buyer pay anything for the business above the value of the tangible assets? Usually the price is allocated for income tax purposes after the negotiated figure has been agreed to by each party to the transaction. In certain jurisdictions, and for certain types of appraisals, this definition assumes *the highest price* rather than *the most probable price*. The appraiser needs to make sure that the correct definition is used.

The concept of fair market value is frequently misunderstood, and therefore, many errors are committed by the inexperienced appraiser trying to estimate the fair market value of the appraisal subject. To illustrate the concept of fair market value, a real-life example can be used. A number of years ago, I was engaged in a matrimonial matter to determine to what extent an offer to purchase a business, made during the course of negotiating a settlement, was to be considered the fair market value of the business. What rendered this situation especially interesting and unusual was that the offer was made by the wife.

The court had appointed an accountant to value the husband's car wash business. After the accountant arrived at a value, the wife put together a group of potential investors and, during the negotiations, offered the husband $200,000 more than what was, in the court-appointed accountant's opinion, the fair market value of the car wash. The question was whether this offer should have been considered bona fide and representative of the fair market value of the business.

The answers to these questions lay in the definition of fair market value. In the specific facts and context of this case, I concluded that fair market value would probably not be represented by the wife's offer. I say "probably" because I was not asked to determine the fair market value of the car wash per se, only whether the wife's offer could constitute fair market value.

Working from expert reports, courts frequently use fair market value as the basis for property distribution. The most frequently used definition of fair market value is the one I cited previously. A similar definition can be found in Miles's *Basic Business Appraisal*:

> Fair market value is the price, in cash or equivalent, that a buyer could reasonably be expected to pay and a seller could reasonably be expected to accept, if the property were exposed for sale on the open market for a reasonable period of time with buyer and seller being in possession of the pertinent facts, and neither being under any compulsion to act.[5]

Both of these definitions are regularly accepted by the appraisal profession and used interchangeably. These definitions contain the following components: (1) cash or equivalent, (2) exposure for sale on the open market, and (3) neither party under compulsion to act. The concept of fair market value will be understood better through an analysis of these components.

Cash or Equivalent. The appraiser's assignment is to determine the equivalent of cash that would be paid for the item being appraised as of the valuation date. Often, a property may be sold with the seller holding a mortgage at a rate of interest below the market rate, to induce the buyer to enter into the transaction. This situation requires a present-value calculation, because some of the value will not be received until a future date. Appraisal theory is founded on the principle of future benefits, with the value of any property constituted by the sum of the benefits that will be obtained by its owner in the future. No one will buy property if there will be no future benefits, whether in the form of income or the appreciation to be realized upon subsequent resale of the property.

[5]Ibid., 43.

Present-value theory can be illustrated by comparing the sale of two businesses, each for $100,000—one with a five-year payout and the other a seven-year payout. The value of these businesses can be determined using the present-value formula:

$$PV = FV \div (1 + k)^n$$

where

PV = Present value
FV = Future value
k = Rate of return (sometimes called the discount rate)
n = Number of periods into the future for which the compounding is being computed

A discount rate of 10 percent would yield the following present values:

Business 1	***Business 2***
$PV = FV \div (1 + k)^n$	$PV = FV \div (1 + k)^n$
$PV = \$100{,}000 \div (1 + .10)^5$	$PV = \$100{,}000 \div (1 + .10)^7$
$PV = \$62{,}092.13$	$PV = \$51{,}315.81$

The example illustrates that the cash equivalents of these two businesses are quite different in today's dollars. This part of the definition of fair market value is frequently overlooked. For a value to be representative of fair market value, it must be *reasonable*. Simply put, an offer to buy or sell will not represent fair market value if both parties do not feel that the offer is fair. Obviously, a unilateral offer cannot represent the true value of an asset.

> The willing buyer and willing seller are hypothetical persons dealing at arm's length, rather than any particular buyer or seller. In other words, a price would not be considered representative of fair market value if influenced by special motivations not characteristic of a typical buyer or seller.[6]

Exposure for Sale on the Open Market. The concept of "market" is extremely important to the definition of fair market value. In many situations the appraisal subject is not for sale. This is usually the case when property is valued for distribution in a matrimonial case. To estimate fair market value, the appraiser must assume that the property has been placed on the open market.

The appraiser assumes that a number of similar properties are available in the open market under the principle of substitution. This principle, as previously discussed, is based on the theory that no person will pay more for a property than he or she would have to pay for an equally desirable substitute.

This principle can be illustrated by the following scenario. Let's assume that the wife wants to purchase a car wash. In addition to the one that is owned by the husband, five other car washes are for sale in the general area. All of these car washes have similar revenues, similar locations, and the same overall characteristics. The principle of substitution dictates that the wife would purchase the one that is offered for the lowest price. Let's also assume a number of prospective buyers. The interaction of the buyers with the sellers of these car washes will eventually establish the fair market value for this type of business. However, for the price offered to be representative of fair market value, all of the other attributes of fair market value must be present.

The phrase "open market" must also be explored. The market for a $30 billion business would be very small, since there would be few buyers who are willing and able to make such a purchase. There would also be very few "equally desirable substitutes." However, the size of the market does not prevent the appraiser

[6]Shannon P. Pratt, Robert F. Reilly, and Robert P. Schweihs, *Valuing a Business*, 4th ed. (New York: McGraw-Hill, 2000), 29.

from assuming an "open market." Although limited, the appraiser's environment is the hypothetical market, the price at which the property would change ownership if it actually were offered for sale.

The definition of fair market value also assumes that the subject property would be exposed on the open market for a reasonable amount of time. This means that the property should be made available for a time period long enough for all potential purchasers to be aware of its availability, rather than be offered to a select group of prospective purchasers. The property should remain on the market "for a sufficient length of time to allow the action of market forces to . . . have full effect," according to Miles, who adds that this may even be "in contrast to some actual situations in which the property may be on the market only a short time before it is sold, possibly even being sold to the first potential buyer who makes an offer, at a price that may very well be lower than its actual open market value."[7]

Neither Party Under Compulsion to Act. If a seller is under compulsion to sell a business, he or she may accept an offer that represents a "distress sale." Similarly, if, because of overindebtedness, the only way a transaction could occur is if the seller finds a buyer willing to pay more than fair market value for the business, the buyer may also be "under compulsion to act" if he or she needs to acquire a business to earn a living. Under these circumstances, a buyer may overpay.

Returning to the original car wash example, the wife's offer cannot be considered fair market value. Although her offer does constitute value, it is what Pratt, Reilly, and Schweihs refer to as *investment value* or "the specific value of an investment to a particular investor or class of investors based on individual investment requirements; distinguished from market value, which is impersonal and detached."[8] Her offer would establish a price for this business but would not reflect the value of the business.

The distinction between price and value is crucial. In the real world, businesses are bought and sold for a *price*. The appraiser's purpose, though, is to estimate *value*. Compared to the appraisal environment required by the definition of fair market value, the conditions that exist in the real world often influence price without affecting value. According to The Institute of Business Appraisers, "*Price is what you pay; value is what you hope to get.*"[9]

The determination of fair market value is a process where the appraiser is frequently being forced to make a determination as to *fair market value to whom?* An excellent lesson can be learned from court cases dealing with this issue. In Chapter 18, I have included a discussion about one of my favorite court cases, *Estate of Samuel B. Newhouse,*[10] which illustrates that fair market value can result in different values to different classes of investors. Take the time to read this one. It's a dandy!

Fair Value

The definition of fair value in a business valuation context varies from state to state. The definition has been developed from case law, primarily in dissenting and oppressed stockholder actions. This concept is also used in many corporate dissolution statutes, but here also, the definition is an enigma. The appraiser should obtain the definition of value from the client's legal counsel based on the corporate statutes and case law in the jurisdiction in which the litigation will take place.

One of the fundamental differences between fair value and fair market value is that in the former situation there is rarely a "willing" seller. Most courts are concerned with the concept of fairness, and as a result, the valuation is intended to be "equitable" for the disadvantaged party. Some of the differences between fair value and fair market value are illustrated in Exhibit 3.1.

[7]Miles, *Basic Business Appraisal*, 44.

[8]Pratt, Reilly, and Schweihs, *Valuing a Business*, 30.

[9]*The Institute of Business Appraisers Inc. Newsletter* (January 1986).

[10]*Estate of Samuel I. Newhouse v. IRS Commissioner*, 94 T.C. 193 (1990).

EXHIBIT 3.1
Differences Between Fair Market Value and Fair Value

Fair Market Value	*Fair Value*
1. Willing buyer	1. *Not always a* willing buyer
2. Willing seller	2. *Not* a willing seller
3. Neither under compulsion	3. Buyer *not always* compelled; *seller under compulsion*
4. Assumes a typical *hypothetical* buyer and seller	4. The impact of the proposed transaction not considered; the concept of *fairness to the seller* a possible consideration
5. A price *equitable to both*	5. A concept of "fairness" to the seller, considering the inability to keep the stock
6. Assumes buyer and seller have *equal knowledge*	6. *No such assumption*
7. Assumes *reasonable knowledge of both* parties	7. *No such assumption*
8. Applicable to *controlling interests or minority blocks*	8. Applicable to *minority blocks*
9. Applies to *all federal tax valuations*	9. The most common value standard in *state dissenting and oppressed shareholder statutes*

The concept of fair value is driven by case law, and it is ever-evolving. The appraiser should never take it upon him- or herself to take the legal positions regarding the interpretation of the standard or the case law. However, the appraiser needs to be aware of when not to use a standard of value that is incorrect. This can be illustrated by a partial critique of another appraiser's report, which appears as Exhibit 3.2. In this matter, the appraiser used fair market value instead of fair value. This is a definite oops!

EXHIBIT 3.2
Critique of Report With Incorrect Standard of Value

Mr. Jack J. Jackson
123 Main Street
Sometown, NJ 07000
Re: Primary Supply Corp.

Dear Mr. Jackson:

In accordance with your request, I have reviewed various documents sent to me regarding the above-referenced company. You have asked that I review these documents for the purpose of providing you with a critique of the valuation report regarding shares of the above-referenced company, prepared by the Smith Consulting Group, Inc., under cover letter dated October 28, 2000 ("the Smith Report"). This critique is intended to discuss matters involving the valuation of the shares of Primary Supply Corp. ("Primary"), and is not an attack on the author of that report.

After reviewing all of the documents sent to me, I find the Smith Report to be somewhat troublesome. In particular, I believe that incorrect instructions were provided to Smith Consulting regarding the standard of value to be used in the valuation of the shares of Primary, particularly since it states that the purpose was to establish a price for the acquisition of shares from the minority shareholders. The Smith Report clearly indicates, "the objective of this appraisal is to determine the *fair market value* per share of the outstanding common stock of Primary Supply Corporation as of June 30, 2000" (*emphasis added*). Furthermore, the author of this report indicates that the shares are being appraised "on a non-marketable minority ownership basis as of June 30, 2000."

First and foremost, it is obvious from the shareholder meeting notice, as well as the August 3, 2000 correspondence, that the intention was to buy out the minority shareholders from this corporation. New York State Business Corporation Law requires a "fair value" and not "fair market value" to be paid to shareholders in this type of situation. According to Section 910 of the Business Corporation Law in Chapter 4, Article 9, "a shareholder of a domestic corporation shall, subject to and by complying with Section 623, have the right to receive payment of the fair value of his shares, and the other rights and benefits provided by such section . . . ."

(Continued)

EXHIBIT 3.2 *(Continued)*

One of the underlying reasons for the language in this statute is to protect minority shareholders from being placed at a disadvantage when they are being forced to give up their shares of stock. Various case law in New York State clearly indicates that fair value is the correct standard that should be used. Using fair market value as the standard of value would require the minority shareholders to give up their holdings at a lower value per share than the value of the controlling shareholder, which clearly is not the intention of the law. In fact, in the matter of *Selma K. Friedman v. Beway Realty Corp.* (638 N.Y.S.2d 399), the court stated,

> Mandating the imposition of a minority discount in fixing the fair value of the stockholdings of dissenting minority shareholders in a close corporation is inconsistent with the equitable principles developed in New York decisional law on dissenting stockholder statutory appraisal rights (a position shared by the Courts in most other jurisdictions), and the policies underlying the statutory reforms giving minority shareholders the right to withdraw from a corporation and be compensated for the value of their interests when the corporate majority takes significant action deemed inimical to the position of the minority.

In fact, the opinion quotes several other cases (citations omitted), and it states, "fair value requires that the dissenting stockholder be paid for his or her proportionate interest in a going concern, that is, the intrinsic value of the shareholders' economic interest in the corporate enterprise." The decision also states, "determinations of the fair value of a dissenter's shares are governed by the statutory provisions of the Business Corporation Law that require equal treatment of all shares of the same class of stock." There is little reason for me to turn this critique into a legal brief, but most experienced appraisers recognize that shareholder disputes require a fair value determination of the stock, and not fair market value.

If you are not sure about the standard of value, I cannot emphasize strongly enough the need to get advice from legal counsel. In the example in Exhibit 3.2, the appraiser, whom I know, is an accredited individual who should have known better. I have to believe (or at least I hope) that he was given incorrect marching orders in his engagement letter. See, here it is again—the need for a good understanding in the engagement letter. Chapter 17 covers additional issues regarding shareholder disputes.

Investment Value

The investment value of a closely held company is the value to a *particular* buyer, as compared with the *population* of willing buyers, as is the case in fair market value. This is one of those instances where the appraiser will determine the value to a particular person, instead of the hypothetical person. Fair market value deals in the land of make-believe, while investment value deals in reality. This value definition would be applicable when an investor has specific investment criteria that must be fulfilled in an acquisition. For example, a purchaser may decide that, as owner-manager, his or her compensation must be at least $95,000 per year. In addition, the business must have the ability to pay from operating cash flow any indebtedness resulting from the purchase over a period of no longer than five years.

An appraiser will frequently use this standard of value when he or she represents a buyer who wants to know, how much is the business worth to me? The fact that the buyer is specific about the business value to him or her changes the standard of value to investment value, as opposed to fair market value, which may be the value to everyone else.

Investment value is being examined more closely by many of the family courts as the standard of value that is appropriate in divorce situations. In a divorce, the elements of fair market value are rarely present; the owner is not a willing seller, nor will there be a sale. We frequently hear the concept of the "value to the owner" used as an alternative to fair market value. Essentially, "value to the owner" is the investment value to that individual. Make certain that you consult with your client's attorney before using this standard of value. These concepts are discussed in much more detail in Chapter 15, addressing valuations for divorces.

Intrinsic Value

If you have ever heard the expression "Beauty is in the eye of the beholder," you will probably understand the term *intrinsic value*. Although not really a standard of value, this term is frequently used by financial analysts. The intrinsic value of a stock is generally considered to be the value based on all of the facts and circumstances of the business or the investment. Financial analysts in brokerage firms often ignore the fluctuations of the stock market in determining the intrinsic value of a specific stock.

Although I knew what intrinsic value meant, it was not until recently that this definition became more important to a valuation assignment than ever before. The issue was the determination of fair value of a client's interest in a family-owned business. Using the market approach, based on public companies, we estimated the value of the company to be about $75 million. Using the income approach, we estimated the value of the company at about $125 million. After spending a considerable amount of time trying to reconcile these values, we realized that the publicly traded companies were selling at very low multiples, despite having solid growth expectations. The market was undervaluing these companies. In fact, the investment banking firms that follow this industry had *strong buy* recommendations for the public comparables. This means that the intrinsic value of the public companies was greater than the market value. While we were doing a critique of the opposing side's valuation (who only used the market approach to value the business), we reread *Valuing a Business*.

It is truly amazing how much we learn by rereading books that we read on a regular basis. Pratt et al. discuss intrinsic value. On page 31, they indicate the following:

Intrinsic or Fundamental Value[11]

Intrinsic value (sometimes called *fundamental value*) differs from *investment value* in that it represents an analytical judgment of value based on the perceived characteristics inherent in the investment, not tempered by characteristics peculiar to any one investor, but rather tempered by how these perceived characteristics are interpreted by one analyst versus another.

In the analysis of stocks, *intrinsic value* is generally considered the appropriate price for a stock according to a security analyst who has completed a *fundamental analysis* of the company's assets, earning power and other factors.

Intrinsic Value. The amount that an investor considers, on the basis of an evaluation of available fact, to be the "true" or "real" worth of an item, usually an *equity security*. The value that will become the market value when other investors reach the same conclusions. The various approaches to determining intrinsic value of the *finance* literature are based on expectations and discounted cash flows. See *expected value; fundamental analysis; discounted cash flow method.*[12]

Fundamental Analysis. An approach in security analysis which assumes that a security has an "intrinsic value" that can be determined through a rigorous evaluation of relevant variables. Expected earnings is usually the most important variable in this analysis, but many other variables, such as dividends, capital structure, management quality, and so on, may also be studied. An analyst estimates the "intrinsic value" of a security on the basis of those fundamental variables and compares this value with the current market price of this security to arrive at an investment decision.[13]

The purpose of security analysis is to detect differences between the value of a security as determined by the market and a security's "intrinsic value"—that is, the value that the security *ought* to have and will have when other investors have the same insight and knowledge as the analyst.[14]

If the market value is below what the analyst concludes is the intrinsic value, the analyst considers the stock a "buy." If the market value is above the assumed intrinsic value, the analyst suggests selling the stock. (Some analysts also factor market expectations into their fundamental analysis.)

It is important to note that the concept of intrinsic value cannot be entirely divorced from the concept of fair market value, since the actions of buyers and sellers based on their *specific* perceptions of intrinsic value

---

[11]Shannon P. Pratt, Robert F. Reilly, and Robert P. Schweihs, *Valuing a Business*, 4th ed. (New York, NY: McGraw-Hill, ©2000). Reproduced with permission of The McGraw-Hill companies.

[12]W.W. Cooper and Yuri Ijiri, eds., *Kohler's Dictionary for Accountants*, 6th ed. (Englewood Cliffs, N.J.: Prentice Hall, 1983), 285.

[13]Ibid., 228.

[14]James H. Lorie and Mary T. Hamilton, *The Stock Market: Theories and Evidence* (Burr Ridge, Ill.: Irwin, 1973), 114.

> eventually lead to the general consensus market value and to the constant and dynamic changes in market value over time.
>
> Case law often refers to the term *intrinsic value*. However, almost universally such references do not define the term other than by reference to the language in the context in which it appears. Such references to *intrinsic value* can be found both in cases where there is no statutory standard of value and in cases where the statutory standard of value is specified as *fair value* or even *fair market value*. When references to *intrinsic value* appear in the relevant case law, the analyst should heed the notions ascribed to that term as discussed in this section.

As you can see from the above definition, Pratt et al. indicate that "the various approaches to determining intrinsic value in the finance literature are based on expectations and discounted cash flows." Clearly, expected earnings are of critical importance, but other variables such as dividends, capital structure, management quality, and so on, are also considered in a fundamental analysis. What is striking is that Pratt et al. state, "If the market value is below what the analyst concludes is the intrinsic value, the analyst considers the stock a 'buy.'" This is exactly what takes place when an investment banking firm gives a strong buy recommendation on a company's stock. If the market price of these stocks is low enough to warrant this type of recommendation, using multiples (discussed in Chapter 6), without proper adjustment, may undervalue the subject company.

How the Purpose of the Valuation Influences the Standard of Value

There should be little doubt that the purpose and function of an appraisal will have a dramatic influence on the standards of value that may be applicable in a particular assignment. The following table highlights how the purpose and standard of value relate to each other.

Valuation Purpose		*Applicable Standard of Value*
Estate and gift taxes	☞	Fair market value
Inheritance taxes	☞	Fair market value
Ad valorem taxes	☞	Fair market value
ESOPs	☞	Fair market value
Financial acquisitions	☞	Fair market value
Stockholder disputes	☞	Fair value (in most states)
Corporate or partnership dissolutions	☞	Fair value (in most states)
Going private	☞	Fair value (in most states)
Strategic acquisitions	☞	Investment value
Buy-sell agreements	☞	Whatever the parties agree to
Marital dissolutions (divorce)	☞	No standard is specific in most states; look to case law

IMPORTANT

Author's Note: Throughout this book, unless otherwise noted, fair market value will be the standard of value applicable to the valuation methodologies discussed.

Internal Revenue Service Influence on Appraisals

When most people think about the IRS, they think of April 15. Believe it or not, the IRS does more than just pick our pockets at tax time. Since so many appraisals are performed for tax-related matters, the IRS is actively involved in business valuations. Many appraisals are performed that may ultimately be used to defend a position before the IRS. Appraisers need to be familiar with the various IRS promulgations that may also be applicable, by reference, to other types of appraisals.

The following summary of the key IRS revenue rulings and procedures is intentionally brief because the important stuff will be highlighted throughout this book. Many of these rulings and procedures are included in their entirety as appendixes.

Appeals and Review Memorandums 34 and 68

Appeals and Review Memorandums (ARMs) 34 and 68, which discuss the "formula method" for valuing goodwill, have been superseded. However, the importance of these documents should not be overlooked. ARM 34 was issued in 1920 in response to the need for guidance in valuing the intangible value lost by breweries and distilleries as a result of Prohibition. A suggested methodology to perform these valuations was put forth by the Treasury Department, including examples of rates of returns and capitalization rates. ARM 68 was an update to ARM 34. These were superseded by parts of Revenue Rulings 59-60 and 68-609.

Revenue Ruling 59-60

Revenue Ruling 59-60 is probably the greatest treatise ever issued on valuation. It is almost hard to believe that something this good came out of our government. It's even better than the first edition of this book! This ruling started out providing guidance on the minimum factors to consider for one to perform a competent valuation for estate and gift tax purposes. Its application was subsequently expanded to other tax matters. After you read this revenue ruling, reread it! After that, I suggest that you get into the habit of rereading it on a regular basis. This ruling not only contains good stuff, but also really emphasizes what the valuation process is all about.

Revenue Ruling 59-60 has so many important factors that you will see references to it throughout this book. One of the most important points made in the ruling is that "valuation is a prophecy as to the future." Even in 1959, the Treasury Department recognized that a willing buyer purchases the future, not the past. This may seem pretty logical, but there are an awful lot of individuals who regularly rely on history to perform appraisals because they feel that forecasting the future is too speculative. If you believe that history is more important that the future in valuing a business or an investment, can I interest you in buying some stock in Eastern Airlines?

Revenue Ruling 59-60 is also well known in the appraisal field for its discussion of the eight factors to consider, as a minimum, in valuing closely held businesses. Throughout much of this book, I will be discussing the eight factors to consider. If you learn nothing else, you must know and understand these eight factors. Consideration of these factors is required if you are going to perform a competent business valuation. Even though you will see these again and again, let's start the learning process by letting you see these factors for the first time. If you are like me, you need acronyms to help you remember some of this stuff. So, in this book, I am going to give you a few. Let's start here. When determining the fair market value of a business or business interest, the appraiser should consider NEBEDISM:

1. (N) The **n**ature of the business and history of the enterprise since its inception
2. (E) The **e**conomic outlook in general and the condition and outlook of the specific industry in particular
3. (B) The **b**ook value of the stock and the financial condition of the business
4. (E) The **e**arning capacity of the company
5. (D) The **d**ividend-paying capacity of the company
6. (I) Whether the enterprise has goodwill or other **i**ntangible value

7. (S) **S**ales of the stock and the size of the block of stock to be valued
8. (M) The **m**arket price of stocks of corporations engaged in the same or a similar line of business and having their stocks actively traded in a free and open market, either on an exchange or over the counter[15]

The applicability of NEBEDISM will be discussed in many of the methods of valuation that you will read about. I will point them out as we proceed. Chapter 12 contains an annotation of this important document, which is also reproduced in Appendix 6.

Revenue Ruling 65-192

Revenue Ruling 65-192 modifies Revenue Ruling 59-60 by providing that the theory in 59-60 is applicable to income and other taxes, as well as to estate and gift taxes. This revenue ruling also indicates that the formula approach described in ARM 34 and ARM 68 has no valid place in valuing a business or business interest unless the intent is to value the intangibles. The ruling states that even then, the formula approach should not be used if there is a better basis for valuing the intangibles. This revenue ruling was superseded by Revenue Ruling 68-609, which reiterates these points. See Appendix 7.

Revenue Ruling 65-193

Revenue Ruling 65-193 modifies Revenue Ruling 59-60 by deleting several statements about the separation of tangible and intangible assets. See Appendix 8.

Revenue Procedure 66-49

Revenue Procedure 66-49 is to be used as a guideline by all persons making appraisals of donated property for federal income tax purposes. It also provides additional insight into what is expected to be included in a formal appraisal report that is used to support the values determined by the appraiser.

This revenue procedure discusses factors to consider in arriving at the fair market value of the property. It states that "as to the measure of proof in determining the fair market value, all factors bearing on value are relevant including, where pertinent, the cost, or selling price of the item, sales of comparable properties, cost of reproduction, opinion evidence and appraisals. *Fair market value depends upon value in the market* and not on intrinsic worth" (emphasis added). See Appendix 9.

Revenue Ruling 68-609

Revenue Ruling 68-609 covers what is known as the "formula approach" or "excess earnings method" of appraisal. This is the successor to ARM 34 and ARM 68. For most appraisers, this revenue ruling has become our nemesis. It is so frequently misapplied that even the IRS states that this method should not be used if there is a better method to value the intangible assets of the appraisal subject. This is similar to the language found in Revenue Ruling 65-192.

The ruling discusses the return on tangible assets and capitalization rates for intangibles. (Please note that the rates provided in Revenue Ruling 68-609 are examples only and are not intended to be the only rates used in the application of this methodology.) A detailed discussion of this revenue ruling appears in the discussion of the excess earnings method in Chapter 8. See Appendix 10.

---

[15]Rev. Rul. 59-60, 1959-1 C.B. 237, Sec. 4(.01).

Revenue Procedure 77-12

Revenue Procedure 77-12 describes the acceptable methods for allocating a lump-sum purchase price to inventories. This revenue procedure sets forth guidelines for use by taxpayers and IRS personnel "in making fair market value determinations in situations where a corporation purchases the assets of a business containing inventory items for a lump sum, or where a corporation acquires assets including inventory items by the liquidation of a subsidiary pursuant to the provisions of section 332 of the Internal Revenue Code of 1954 and the basis of the inventory received in liquidation is determined under section 334(b)(2)." See Appendix 11.

Revenue Ruling 77-287

Revenue Ruling 77-287 was intended "to provide information and guidance to taxpayers, IRS personnel, and others concerned with the valuation, for Federal tax purposes, of securities that cannot be immediately resold because they are restricted from resale pursuant to Federal security laws." This revenue ruling covers marketability discounts related to restricted stock. It recognizes the reduced value of closely held stocks as a result of not having an active trading market. Reference is made to "restricted securities" and other types of securities that are issued at a discount from their freely traded counterparts. This reduction in value is known as a "discount for lack of marketability" and is discussed further in Chapter 11. See Appendix 12.

Revenue Ruling 83-120

Revenue Ruling 83-120 amplifies Revenue Ruling 59-60 by specifying additional factors that should be considered in valuing the common and preferred stock of a closely held corporation for gift tax and recapitalization purposes. This revenue ruling emphasizes that the value of preferred stock is determined by considering its yield, its dividend coverage, and the protection of its liquidation preference. See Appendix 13.

Revenue Ruling 85-75

Revenue Ruling 85-75 basically provides that the IRS will not be bound to accept values that it accepted for estate tax purposes as the basis for determining depreciation deductions or income taxes on capital gains from a subsequent asset sale. In this particular instance, a taxpayer relied on a valuation of depreciable property that was overstated for estate tax purposes. Since the IRS did not play "gotcha" on the estate tax return, they got their second chance on the beneficiary's individual return. See Appendix 14.

Revenue Ruling 93-12

Revenue Ruling 93-12, which supersedes Revenue Ruling 81-253, allows appropriate minority discounts to be applied when the minority interests of family members in a closely held corporation are valued. Formerly, the IRS looked to family attribution rules as a means to disallow these minority discounts. Revenue Ruling 81-253, which described the IRS's position on the allowance of minority discounts in valuing a closely held family corporation's stock that has been transferred to the donor's children for federal gift tax purposes, was superseded by Revenue Ruling 93-12. Previously, the IRS's long-standing position was that no minority discount should be allowed when a gift of minority shares was passed between family members. It was not a surprise that the IRS finally acquiesced on this point, since they constantly lost this battle in court.

Fair market value assumes any willing buyer, not the actual recipient of a gift. Therefore, even though a gift may be given to a taxpayer's child, the block should be valued without regard to the family relationship. Unfortunately, the IRS did not see things this way until 1993, when they issued Revenue Ruling 93-12.

Revenue Ruling 93-12 was a long time coming in light of the IRS's inability to win cases involving Revenue Ruling 81-253. Do not get too comfortable, however, until you read Technical Advice Memorandum 94-36005. See Appendix 15.

Technical Advice Memorandum 94-36005

In 1994, the Treasury Department issued Technical Advice Memorandum 94-36005, which discusses the concept of applying a "swing premium" in a case where a gift of a minority interest among family members creates a swing vote among the stockholders. This was the Treasury Department's effort to circumvent Revenue Ruling 93-12, in which they finally acquiesced regarding minority discounts among family members. This technical advice memorandum does not have the same weight as a revenue ruling, but it shows that the Treasury Department is looking for ways to circumvent Revenue Ruling 93-12. Nobody really believed that they would give up on Revenue Ruling 81-253 that easily! This memorandum appears in Appendix 16.

Chapter 14 of the IRC

Readers are advised to become familiar with the Chapter 14 requirements of the IRC. Some of the more important provisions are covered in Chapter 14 of this book in the discussion of estate and gift tax valuations.

Conclusion

If I did my job, you now have more of an idea about the principles of appraisal, definitions of value, and the various promulgations of the IRS. By now, you must realize that the IRS has had a significant impact on the valuation process. Although you are bound to follow the mandates of the IRS only for valuation assignments that involve taxes, some of these revenue rulings make enough sense that it is actually good practice to follow them in most valuations.

4

Data Gathering

Chapter Goals

In this chapter, I will attempt to:

1. Explain which items have an impact on value
2. Discuss internal information sources for gathering data
3. Discuss external information sources for gathering data
4. Inform you about some print and electronic data sources

What Items Affect Value?

An important part of the valuation assignment is to determine the proper amount of information necessary to do the job competently. The information-gathering part of the assignment will generally require the appraiser to demonstrate knowledge about the subject company and the factors affecting its value. Both internal and external factors affect the value of a business or business interest. During the information-gathering step of the appraisal process, a variety of information will be requested by the appraiser.

Internal Information

Internal information obtained during the data-gathering process will consist of both nonfinancial and financial information. Each type of information will play an important role in the valuation process. The appraiser must consider the nonfinancial information to be as important as, and in some instances more important than, the financial information. Too often, a telephone call comes in from the attorney who states, "I got you five years of tax returns and financial statements. Can you give me the value?" After you stop laughing, the attorney should be told, "Of course I can give you the value, but not until I get the other 47 things that are on my checklist." Although not every job will require 47 other items, there will always be more information needed.

Nonfinancial Information

Nonfinancial information may be gathered through a document request, a management interview, or independent research by the appraiser. Some of the more important information that the appraiser should gather includes the following:

- The form of organization and ownership of the business
- The products and services

- Markets and marketing
- Physical facilities
- Equipment
- Personnel

Form of Organization and Ownership of the Business. The form of ownership is an important component of the business valuation process because, during the appraisal process, the appraiser will have to consider the comparability of information obtained about either other companies (known as "comparables" or "guideline companies") or industry composite data. Good comparability must be maintained to ensure the quality of the data that will be used for comparison purposes during the appraisal process.

Another reason to know the form of organization is that the legal rights applicable to the interest being valued must be considered by the appraiser for the determination of possible restrictions that apply to the subject company or the owners. For example, a minority owner in a corporation normally does not have the ability to force the liquidation of a corporation. Therefore, that minority interest will most likely be valued using an approach that is not based on the value of the assets. On the other hand, a minority interest in a partnership is controlled by the Uniform Partnership Act, which states that any partner who withdraws from the partnership can cause a winding down and dissolution of the partnership, thus providing him or her with the ability to obtain the proportionate share of the proceeds from the partnership's dissolution.

The ownership of the business is also important, since the appraiser will need to assess considerations such as control, minority, or swing vote issues. This can be illustrated by considering the value of a 2 percent interest in a company. If there are 50 owners with 2 percent interest in the company, each 2 percent interest would probably be worth very little. However, what if the 2 percent interest were to be valued when the other owners each own 49 percent? The 2 percent interest could have swing value, which could be very valuable to one of the other owners since it would give one of them control of the company. This could cause a premium to be associated with the 2 percent interest.

Let me give you another example of a real-life situation where the rights of ownership can impact value. Remember that in Chapter 1, I gave you some details about valuing a 1.6 percent beneficial interest in a trust for the IRS. Well, in that same job the trust owned a 90 percent interest in a closely held investment holding company that owned, among other things, a 47.3 percent block of a thinly traded public company ("thinly traded" means that there are not too many shares trading on the exchange at any one time). Since the stock was thinly traded, the appraiser who represented the taxpayer deducted a blockage discount (this will be discussed in more detail in Chapter 11, but in the meantime, a blockage discount is a reduction in value because it will take a long time to sell). When I first received the assignment, I asked the attorneys for the IRS for a copy of the bylaws of the public corporation so that I could see what rights, if any, are spelled out in this legal document. I was told that they would get the document for me, but until they did, since the public company was incorporated in the state of Delaware, I was told to assume that a simple majority constitutes a controlling interest. By the way, the second largest block of stock (8 percent) was owned by the trustee of the trust that I was valuing an interest in. Got it so far? This is the type of assignment that you either live for or die doing. Anyway, because the 47.3 percent interest in this public company had effective control (all they really had to do was show up to a stockholders meeting and they would carry the vote), and because the trustee owned the next largest block of stock, I took the position that the prudent thing for the board of directors to do was to find someone to purchase the company since it was undervalued according to my intrinsic analysis.

To make a long story short, I added a control premium to the publicly traded value instead of taking a blockage discount. To put things into perspective, the difference in value between myself and the other appraiser for the publicly traded stock alone was $150 million. So where am I going with this story? A week before I was getting ready to testify in Tax Court, I received a phone call from the attorney for the IRS. He said, "I finally tracked down those bylaws that you asked me for (three months ago!). Let me read something to you and see if it changes anything that you have done." I knew I was in trouble. The bylaws were from 1896 and had not been updated. They required an 80 percent supermajority to sell, liquidate, or merge the company. I said, "Settle the case." The rights of the shareholders made a difference of about $150 million in this case.

Products and Services. It is generally a good idea to understand information about the products and services that the appraisal subject sells to its customers. Besides the fact that you need to know this information to select guideline companies, it is also imperative that the appraiser understand information about factors that affect these products and services. For example, how do changes in the economy affect the demand for the products? A rise in interest rates would certainly have an impact on an automobile dealership. It is also important to understand what alternative products are available in the marketplace to assess the future success of the products. If you were appraising a company that sold an electronic rolodex and did not have the ability to sell other personal digital assistants (PDAs, e.g., Palm Pilot), the likelihood that the company would continue to be successful in the future is slim, since everyone and their mothers are buying PDAs.

Markets and Marketing. Part of the valuation process includes understanding the markets served by the appraisal subject. Geographic diversification frequently does not exist for very small businesses. However, understanding the market for the products or services allows the appraiser to assess the degree of risk relevant to the lack of diversification. Understanding the market will also allow the appraiser to determine if there are alternative products in the marketplace that will have an effect on the subject company.

The marketing efforts of the subject company should also be considered, since a large, visible company in the market will frequently attract more new customers than an obscure company that the public has never heard of.

Physical Facilities. Factors to be considered in a business valuation assignment include information about the physical plant. This information would pertain to the plant's size and whether it is owned or rented, as well as to the amount of room available for expansion. The valuation process requires the use of projections, which must consider whether the facilities are large enough to meet the expected production forecasts. If a plant is at full capacity and management provides the appraiser with forecasts that include significant growth, how can that growth be achieved without either expanding the current facilities or relocating to larger quarters? Either way, there will be an additional expense incurred by the company if it is to meet its expansion projections.

Equipment. It is generally a good idea for an appraiser to learn about the equipment that is employed by the business to accomplish its business purposes. Even if an appraisal of the equipment is unnecessary, the appraiser should find out information about the type of equipment used, the age of the equipment, its capacity, its maintenance schedules, the availability of parts, and its approximate replacement cost. The appraiser should also inquire as to whether there is newer technology being used by the competition.

Older equipment usually means higher maintenance costs and a lower level of productive capacity. This could be an essential component of a cash flow forecast, since asset replacement can be costly. Older equipment could mean difficulty in getting parts and service, which could force the replacement of equipment, creating a financial hardship for the company. However, there are many companies that can continue to use older equipment for a long time without a problem. These companies generally have a well-established maintenance schedule, and by examining the equipment you can generally tell whether it is regularly maintained.

The appraiser should ask to review insurance policies to get an idea of the amount of coverage the company is carrying so that the appraiser can "ballpark" the replacement cost of these assets. The appraiser should also make certain that these policies have been kept up to date. Otherwise, the company may be exposed to an additional risk attributable to the replacement of the equipment in the event of a loss.

Personnel. The appraiser should seek information about the personnel requirements of the company. This includes gaining an understanding of the role of key persons in the company. In smaller companies, the owner is frequently the key person. The appraiser must determine what it would take to replace that individual with someone who is capable of getting the job done. Sometimes this may take two or more people. Other times, it may take people with different skills from those the owner has.

For example, in appraising an internal medicine practice, the appraiser may find that the doctor does not trust anyone in his or her office to do the bookkeeping. Therefore, the doctor performs this function in addition to all of the duties of being a doctor. What if the doctor is turning away new patients due to a lack of time because the bookkeeping is taking up 10 hours per week? The appraiser would consider replacing the doctor not only with another doctor but also with a part-time bookkeeper, which would allow the new doctor to spend the additional 10 hours seeing new patients. You are probably asking yourself, What kind of doctor would do this? If I had not seen this in reality, I could not have provided you with this example!

Other Stuff. The appraiser should pay particularly close attention to other items that may exist for the appraisal subject. These may include, but should not be limited to, operating data about the company's products, competitors, suppliers, and customers so that you can demonstrate a clear understanding of the appraisal subject. These items will help you make a determination regarding the risk involved in the subject company's business. For example, few products, many competitors, high employee turnover, few sources of supply, and dependence on key customers add up to a lot of risk. This will affect value.

Other stuff can include information about patents, copyrights, proprietary processes, pending litigation, and environmental exposure. These items will either increase or decrease the value of a company, depending on the competitive advantage or disadvantage that may come with these items. Sometimes an appraiser will find that the competition holds an important patent in the field, and therefore, breaking into the field may be impossible without different technology. All of these situations should be considered during the valuation process.

If the valuation is for an employee stock ownership plan (ESOP), make sure you get a copy of the plan documents so that you fully understand the terms. This will have an impact on marketability discounts, as well as on other factors affecting your valuation. Since most small and medium-sized businesses do not have ESOPs, I have not included a discussion about them in this book.[1]

Legal documentation (including copies of legal contracts and agreements affecting the company) should also be obtained. This will allow the appraiser to determine if there are any restrictions on the operations of the business, any restrictions on the owners, or any commitments that will require the company to perform in a certain manner that can affect operations in the future. You saw what a difference it made in my IRS job. Find out if there are any lawsuits against the company, either pending or threatened. A lawsuit may affect the financial success of the company and should be considered as a risk factor even if it cannot be quantified.

Exhibit 4.1 provides a sample section of a report showing how this information can be used.

EXHIBIT 4.1
History and Nature of the Business

XYZ Computer Corporation ("XYZ" or "the Company") is a computer distributor based in Louisville, Kentucky. The Company distributes new and used mid-range computer systems and peripherals to domestic customers. XYZ provides hardware solutions to their customers. The Company plans to continue increasing its product offerings and maintaining good customer relationships, thus adding value through its quality relationships with customers and equipment providers alike.

Background

The Company was founded by John Smith and began operations in 1979. XYZ was incorporated in the State of Delaware in 1983. The Company operates from its Louisville headquarters, marketing its products to commercial enterprises throughout the United States. XYZ distributes its products from its 25,000-square-foot warehouse facility in Overlook Park, Kansas.

[1]For more information on ESOPs, you can see either Shannon P. Pratt, Robert F. Reilly, and Robert P. Schweihs, *Valuing a Business*, 4th ed. (New York: McGraw-Hill, 2000), 697–740; or James H. Zukin, ed., *Financial Valuation: Business and Business Interests* (New York: Warren Gorham & Lamont, 1990), 8-2–8-33 (updated annually). Or you can take an excellent ESOP course offered by the American Society of Appraisers.

EXHIBIT 4.1 *(Continued)*

The Company originally operated as a mid-range computer reseller. Operations consisted of purchasing used mid-range computers, disassembling them, and selling the parts to maintenance companies. These maintenance companies would use the parts to repair mid-range computers that were in place. According to XYZ President, Chris Garcia, "Prior to 1992, XYZ was basically a used equipment broker in the mid-range market."

In 1992, there were some dramatic changes in the computer resale industry. Louis Gerstner took the reigns of IBM in 1992 and began using distribution channels to get IBM products to customers, whereas prior to this time, IBM sold most of its products directly to customers. IBM began using value-added resellers and distributors, like XYZ, to get their products out in the market. In 1992, the Company formed a strategic alliance with IBM, by which XYZ would distribute IBM terminals (dumb terminals that hook up to mid-range or mainframe machines). This strategic alliance marked the beginning of XYZ's extraordinary growth. By establishing this strategic alliance with IBM, the Company opened a door leading to future opportunities with IBM and its extensive product line.

XYZ began selling dumb terminals in 1992, while at the same time continuing to broker used mid-range computers. As time progressed, opportunities arose to distribute new products. As the salespeople of XYZ established customer contacts and put hardware in place, they began getting requests for more and different hardware. Working with IBM and its customers, XYZ increased product offerings. The Company expanded its product lines to include printers, modems, and controllers utilizing its existing customer base. XYZ was able to increase revenues with the addition of each product line. According to Mr. Garcia, "We went from terminals to printers, and then from printers to modems, and from modems to controllers, and you can see a definite spike (in revenues)."

XYZ and IBM entered into a Business Partner Service Agreement, signed and dated by Mr. Garcia on September 29, 1995. XYZ was given the opportunity to remarket IBM storage systems. Storage products are much more costly than the peripheral hardware distributed by XYZ. Regarding the opportunities available for selling storage, Mr. Garcia noted, "So now, instead of selling things that cost at most $20,000, you're selling something that could cost $1 million." Distributing storage products could dramatically increase the revenues of XYZ, and the addition of this new product could mark the beginning of a strong growth period for the Company. Excerpts from XYZ's storage distributor plan are provided below. The plan lists XYZ's experience in computer equipment distribution and details how the Company plans to distribute storage products.

XYZ Goals

Short Term (0–6 months)

To be able to perform light manufacturing for normal IR (industry remarketer) transactions and MIR (managing industry remarketer) transactions. To have signed up five storage IRAs (industry remarketing agent).

Long Term (7–24 months)

To have 25 storage resellers selling IBM storage products to non-IBM platforms, each selling approximately $1 million of disk and storage.

Marketing Demographics

Target Reseller

The typical storage IRA would be an HP Platform mid-range Unix reseller. The typical sales volume of the IRA would be anywhere from $2 million to $10 million and would be located primarily east of the Rockies. Other resellers would include both PC server and database consultants.

The IRA End User

The end user is typically a medium to large company with no industry specialization. The only common thread among the end users is that they need high-performance transaction database processing. The Company has anywhere from 500 to 45,000 employees and has revenues from $150 million to $1 billion (Fortune 1000).

XYZ's Current Reseller Network

XYZ, at this time, has a limited reseller network consisting of 20 to 30 independent consultants and contractors that act as agents for XYZ Computer. This reseller network has proficiencies in open systems, connectivity, management, and software implementation.

Recruiting Plan for Additional Solution Providers

XYZ has successfully installed more than eight terabytes of SSA on third-party platforms at more than 50 end-user locations. XYZ plans on recruiting the resellers who sold the original third-party platform to these 50 end users.

All in all, the Company has experienced extraordinary growth over the past five years, fueled by the strategic alliance with IBM. XYZ plans to continue growing the Company by working with IBM to increase product lines. The next product that XYZ plans to distribute is storage devices. The addition of this high-dollar product will dramatically increase XYZ's revenues even further.

Products

XYZ operates as a hardware distributor specializing in IBM peripheral equipment. The Company offers IBM terminals, printers, modems, and controllers, and expects to increase its product offering to include IBM storage equipment. In addition to new equipment, XYZ brokers used mid-range computers and computer parts including the RS/6000 and AS/400 machines.

(Continued)

EXHIBIT 4.1 *(Continued)*

Customers

XYZ's customers range from mid-size companies to Fortune 500 corporations. A breakdown of the Company's 12 largest customers for fiscal year end 1995 is shown in Table 1.

TABLE 1

Top Customers
Year Ended August 31, 1995

Customer	Amount
Allstate Ins. Co.	$2,989,372
State of IN Co. offices	1,083,242
Office Depot	716,794
Intel Corporation	645,120
American Gen. Finance	558,531
Crawford & Co.	519,408
Greentree Financial	494,996
Waste Management	465,951
Skelgas, Inc.	447,405
Enterprise Rent-A-Car	427,926
Innovative Computing	419,226
Costco Wholesale	403,702
Total	$9,171,673
% of total revenues	25%

Mr. Garcia has also indicated that XYZ provides hardware through alliances with other value-added resellers that concentrate on selling software solutions that run on IBM hardware. Many of these companies do not have an interest in selling peripheral hardware; therefore, XYZ has developed relationships with certain IBM VARs (value-added resellers) to provide hardware to their customers. This practice of providing hardware solutions to other IBM VAR customers has effectively increased XYZ's client base.

Suppliers

XYZ's major supplier is IBM. IBM equipment accounted for 99 percent of XYZ's sales in 1995. Other suppliers include Citrix, Microsoft, Hewlett-Packard, and Lexmark. IBM supplies the hardware, while other suppliers provide software and products to enhance IBM equipment performance. Notes to the Company's audited financial statements indicate that management is of the opinion that loss of IBM as a supplier would not have a material adverse effect on the operations of the Company.

Competition

The Company's main competition comes from other regional and national IBM distributors, including companies like Computer Marketplace.

Marketing and Sales

According to XYZ's Industry Remarketer Business Plan:

> XYZ, with its additional influx of products and relationships, began undergoing rapid growth. In 1993 XYZ began updating all of its internal systems, increased its office space and sales force, and began formulating new and innovative strategies to increase business while achieving the highest attainable levels of employee, vendor, and customer satisfaction.
>
> Today, XYZ is the recognized leader in network marketing with almost 50,000 contacts, including approximately 37,000 end-user sites, more than 4,800 customers, and over 7,700 IBM Marketing Representatives and Business Partners that turn to XYZ for solutions. XYZ has consistently led the Authorized Distributor channel since its inception and continues to be the number one IBM products and services provider while expanding to accommodate customer needs.

In addition, its established telemarketing resources were described as follows:

> XYZ is a telemarketing and consulting based business staffed with over 60 professionals who field over 2,800 outgoing calls and more than 800 incoming calls per day, promoting the sale and support of IBM hardware peripheral products to mid-range system users.

Management and Employees

The Company has over 60 employees, many of whom are key to the success of the business.

EXHIBIT 4.1 (Continued)

John Smith, Chairman and CEO
Mr. Smith is the founder of XYZ, with over 20 years of experience in the mid-range marketplace. He possesses a deep understanding of the market, customers, products, and services. Over the years, Mr. Smith has developed many contacts that allowed the Company to operate in the used equipment market. Mr. Smith became less active in the Company as the relationship with IBM continued to grow. By late 1995, Mr. Smith was relatively removed from the day-to-day operations of the Company.

Christopher Garcia, President
Mr. Garcia started with the Company in 1985, right out of college. He had interned at IBM over the last two years of his studies and developed an interest in computers. Mr. Garcia started at XYZ as a sales associate and over his tenure has been promoted to Executive Vice President and then to President. Since 1995, he has managed the day-to-day operations of the Company as well as the main customer and supplier relationships. Mr. Garcia was responsible for nurturing XYZ's relationship with IBM and continues to be the main contact between IBM and XYZ. Mr. Garcia's employment contract indicates that his compensation is a result of three components: salary, spread compensation, and profit-sharing spread.

Patrick Ewing, Vice President—Sales
Mr. Ewing has been employed with XYZ for four years, progressing from sales representative to Vice President of Sales. He is responsible for developing and maintaining XYZ's customer base and increasing overall sales. He is also responsible for all sales managers, consultants, and their associated training and development.

Beatrice Camby, Manager of Channel Operations
Ms. Camby has been with XYZ for over six years, overseeing all strategic and tactical operations as they relate to partner alliances. She is responsible for all order processing, contracts, special bids, and business partner promotions.

Steven Spreewell, Vice President of Sales and Information Systems
Mr. Spreewell has over 16 years of research and marketing experience with IBM Corporation. A graduate of Hunter College, New York, Mr. Spreewell was number one in sales while at IBM, averaging over $6 million per year. He has achieved invention achievement awards for six patents and has published 12 technical publications. He is a recognized authority on mid-range hardware and is frequently quoted in national publications.

Mike Johnson, Advanced Product Manager
Mr. Johnson has over 12 years of industry technical experience in the following areas:

- High-performance I/O subsystems
- UNIX System V
- Supercomputing
- Networking

Ownership Structure
As of the valuation date, shares were owned as follows:

	Shares	*% of Outstanding Shares*
John Smith	77,850	90
Christopher Garcia	8,650	10

Per the stockholders' agreement dated May 20, 1993, significant restrictions were to limit the transferability of Mr. Garcia's 10 percent interest. First and foremost, no transfers may be made until Mr. Garcia has left the Company. Sales to third parties are at the discretion of Mr. Smith, who can purchase Mr. Garcia's interest at any time after his employment has ended at fair market value agreed upon by the shareholders. If there has been no agreement on fair market value in the 12 months prior to the buyout, then the fair market value shall be the amount paid for such shares by Mr. Garcia, or 50 percent of the quarterly profit sharing income payable to Mr. Garcia per his employment agreement in excess of $7,500 per quarter for each of the 20 consecutive calendar quarters commencing with July 1, 1992, calendar quarter and terminating at the end of June 30, 1997, calendar quarter, provided that the maximum purchase price pursuant to the following formula shall not exceed $40,000.

(Continued)

EXHIBIT 4.1 *(Continued)*

Strengths and Weaknesses

Strengths

XYZ lists its strengths in its Industry Remarketing Business Plan as follows:

- *Proven track record*—XYZ has proven to be the leader in all endeavors it embarks upon. XYZ is the IBM PC Company's top *Authorized Distributor* of terminal, controller, and modem products, the number one IBM Printing Systems Company *Printer Remarketer*, and IBM's top *RS/6000 Storage Remarketer*. XYZ anticipates quickly rising to the top of the IBM *Industry Remarketer* Channel.
- *Dedicated quality assurance team*—XYZ has a dedicated six-person quality assurance team (QAT) that closely monitors, tracks, and follows up on every order. Additionally, XYZ's QAT adds value by assisting customers with simple configurations and suggestions to leverage the customer's hardware investment.
- *Technical/customer support*—XYZ provides expert pre- and post-sales support. Its support staff represents over 100 years of combined industry and platform experience in both the AS/400 and RS/600 environments.
- *Systems*—XYZ has state-of-the-art information systems that supply all tools necessary to perform a job function directly at the employee's desk. All information is electronically online and not filed on paper, and all systems are fully integrated so that any employee of XYZ may service any customer as though that employee had handled that account from the beginning of time. XYZ has been publicly recognized for its use of in-house technology.
- *Personnel*—XYZ employees want to be a part of the IBM/customer team and not just another vendor. Their professionalism, expertise, training, and attitude express their dedication to providing the highest level of service to their customers, referral sources, and fellow employees.
- *Priority delivery notices*—Every order is confirmed by fax immediately upon shipment. The priority delivery notice (PDN) informs the customer exactly what equipment shipped, the ship-to location, the carrier, the carrier's tracking number, and the carrier's phone number. This eliminates any problems before they occur and gives the customer control, if desired, in tracing lost shipments. Additionally, the PDN contains the XYZ invoice number upon which the shipped equipment will appear.
- *Training*—All XYZ employees undergo continuous and ongoing training in all facets of customer service, sales, management, and product knowledge. Each member of our sales staff is an authority on AS/400 and RS/600 platforms, a sales professional, and an expert in maintaining client satisfaction.
- *Longevity*—XYZ has been in the business of supplying computer peripheral products since 1979. As such, XYZ is a recognized leader in the industry with a strong reputation for excellence. XYZ continues to build upon this reputation with each new transaction and is poised to remain the leader as it progresses into the future.
- *Customer base*—XYZ has over 4,800 dedicated and loyal customers and a database of over 35,000 qualified mid-range accounts with almost 50,000 contacts. These accounts are the lifeblood of XYZ and are treated as such. They are a consistent source of business and referrals.
- *Understanding of IBM relationships*—XYZ recognizes the interdependence of all IBM business partners and marketing reps and has built tremendous loyalty in the IBM community for the services it performs. Likewise, XYZ extends tremendous loyalty to IBM, ensuring that product moves only through authorized channels and eliminating channel conflict through the development of strategic relationships across all IBM channels.

Weakness

- The Company has few weaknesses, but none is more overwhelming than its dependence on a single supplier, which is IBM. XYZ has enjoyed phenomenal growth over the past five years, which was due mainly to its relationship with IBM. When considering the long-term earnings potential of the Company, much consideration must be given to the strength of the relationship between these companies. IBM products account for 99 percent of XYZ's revenues. Although management has indicated that loss of IBM as a supplier would not have a material adverse effect on the Company's operations, the loss could affect profit margins. The Company's reputation and proven track record illustrate the picture of an excellent performer, but this single supplier dependence is a definite weakness for the Company.

Conclusion

The Company has experienced strong growth over the past five years, which was due to its relationship with IBM. Started by Mr. Smith and accelerated by Chris Garcia, XYZ was able to evolve from a used hardware parts broker, generating $5 million in sales, to a $41 million revenue-generating, award-winning IBM hardware remarketer. The Company has continued to grow sales by adding peripheral products such as terminals, printers, modems, and controllers, and hopes to continue this growth by selling high-price-tag storage units. XYZ's sales are highly dependent on its relationship with IBM, which is managed directly by XYZ's President, Chris Garcia. Agreements between IBM and XYZ are relatively short-term (two years), which increases the opportunities that IBM has to break this relationship. However, there is no reason to believe that this is likely to occur. All in all, expectations for future growth are high. The large customer base of the Company indicates excellent opportunities for growth of revenues with additional products, while its experienced sales force and support teams reflect the potential of the Company.

Financial Information

The financial information requested will include annual financial statements for a relevant period of years. Most often, five years of data is obtained, but the appraiser should consider whether to ask for a longer or shorter period of time, if appropriate. This information should be from the most recent years preceding the valuation date. Ideally, you would like to get as many years' financial statements as may be applicable to the subject's business cycle. This way, a more complete picture of the company can be obtained.

You should request tax returns for the same period, so that you can determine if there are any differences between tax and financial reporting that need investigation. Tax returns will also identify any subsidiaries that are part of a consolidated tax return or any other companies that are part of a controlled group of companies, as defined by the Tax Code. This may make the appraiser aware of other companies that may need to be considered during the appraisal process. Even if the appraisal assignment does not include the other companies, there can be transfer-pricing issues, dependence on the other companies, or a splitting of costs that would be discontinued if the appraisal subject was sold.

Interim financial statements should be obtained for the year prior to the valuation date. This provides financial statements that may be closer to the effective date of the valuation, as opposed to the prior year end. Internal financial statements should be more carefully scrutinized, since they may exclude many of the adjustments that the outside accountant makes at the reporting period. External financial statements must also be analyzed to ensure consistency in the reporting between the year-end and interim periods. For example, the interim financial statements may record inventory using the gross profit method, whereas at year end the company takes a physical inventory and values it properly.

Copies of forecasts or projections should be requested for several reasons. First, valuation is a prophecy of the future, and there may be no better indication than management's estimate of what they expect to happen. Second, reviewing prior budgets or projections may provide you with a better understanding of how well management is able to direct the company's activities.

Request supporting information for the balance sheet items that may require fair-market-value adjustments. This is more important in valuing a controlling interest than a minority interest, since the minority interest generally does not have the ability to liquidate the assets to realize the fair market value.

The appraiser should also request supporting information for income statement items that may require normalization adjustments. We will discuss the normalization process in Chapter 5. For now, accept the fact that normalization is the process of removing those items from the financial statements that do not contribute to the economic earnings of the subject company on a prospective basis. This will make more sense in a little while.

External Information

During the appraisal process, the valuer will also be required to perform research to obtain information about the environment in which the business operates. This information is known as "external" information. Some of the more important information that should be looked into includes (1) economic information, (2) industry information, and (3) guideline company information.

Revenue Ruling 59-60 specifically states that one of the factors to be considered in the appraisal of a closely held business is "the economic outlook in general and the condition and outlook of the specific industry in particular." Economic and industry information are key components of a business valuation assignment. Analysis of these items is discussed in the next chapter.

Economic Information

Various economic data should be gathered by the appraiser. This data will allow an assessment of how the subject company will be affected by changes in the economy. For example, rising residential mortgage interest rates may adversely affect a construction company that is primarily engaged in building new houses. Changes in consumer confidence can affect a retail business.

An analysis should be performed to see how the subject company has performed in light of past economic cycles, and the past performance may be used to project how the company is expected to do based on economic forecasts. The analysis should consider all aspects of the economy that directly or indirectly affect the appraisal subject. The appraiser should also think in terms of the factors that might affect the subject company's customers or suppliers. Too often, these factors are overlooked.

A global approach to considering economic data is illustrated in Exhibit 4.2. A broad spectrum of information should be considered with respect to the economy. Starting with the big picture, the appraiser should consider the international economic factors that may affect either the appraisal subject or its customers or suppliers. The availability of supply, exchange rates, fluctuations in economic conditions abroad, and trade restrictions will all impact a global company.

EXHIBIT 4.2

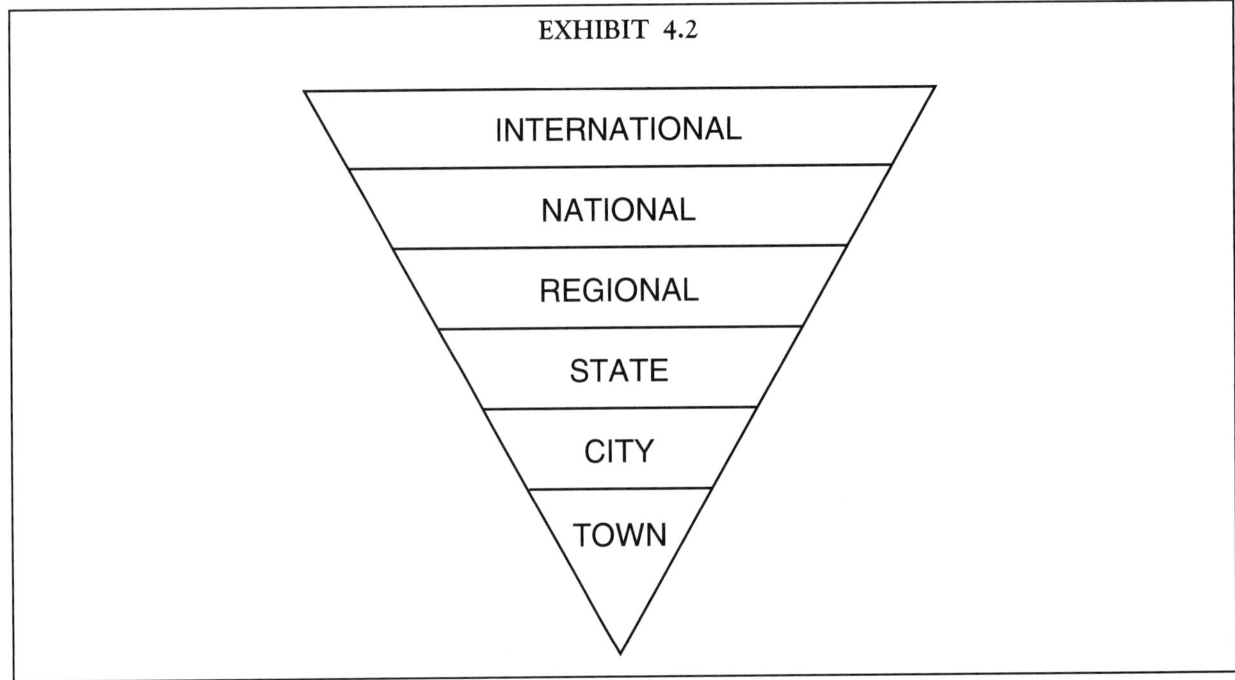

After the global aspects of the economy are considered, the national economy should be next. After that, the geographic regions get smaller and smaller, but even the town in which the business operates could be extremely relevant to the appraisal. What if a company depends on a military base for its business and the government announces a base closure? This can have a devastating effect on the company as well as on the community in which the company operates. The same holds true for communities after a layoff is announced by a major employer. However, this could be good news if the appraisal subject has experienced a shortage of qualified labor and people may now become available to them.

The local economy becomes an important component in the appraisal of a small neighborhood business. Some of the factors that should be considered regarding the local economy include:

- Labor supply
- Local unemployment
- Disposable income
- Wages
- Availability of materials

- Taxes
- Growth trends

Key economic indicators that may be reviewed by the appraiser include, but should not be limited to:

- Foreign trade
- Foreign currency
- Gross domestic product
- Federal deficit
- Inflation—consumer price index
- Unemployment
- Consumer confidence
- Business investment
- Interest rates
- Housing starts
- Building permits
- Demographics
- Health care
- Gross state product

For each of these items, the relevance to the appraisal subject is important. Rarely will all of these factors be included in one appraisal. Do not use a boilerplate discussion of the economy! Clearly, the economic factors that affect a construction company will be substantially different from the economic factors that affect a medical practice. Tough stuff, huh?

To find the economic data that you are looking for, your local librarian could be your greatest asset. Get friendly, be nice, and if all else fails, beg. Although there is a tremendous amount of information available on the Internet, be careful not to get caught in the trap of never leaving your desk. Sometimes you may find the library to be better for finding things than the inside of your computer. For new appraisers who do not have library resources in their offices, the public library or a business college library may turn out to be your home away from home. Whether you have your own library or you use a public library, the following sources should be familiar to the appraiser.

- *Statistical Abstract of the United States*
- *Economic Report of the President*
- *Federal Reserve Bulletin*
- *Survey of Current Business*
- *Annual Metro, City and County Data Book*
- *Business Conditions Digest*
- *Monthly Labor Review*
- *The Wall Street Journal*
- Business magazines
- Trade magazines
- Professional magazines:
    - *Medical Economics*
    - *Electrical World*

- State agency reports:
  - Employment
  - Planning
  - Economic development
  - State Web sites
- Chambers of commerce
- *Blue Chip Economic Indicators*
- *Blue Chip Financial Forecasts*
- *Value Line Investment Survey*
- *Stocks, Bonds, Bills, and Inflation Yearbook*
- *Standard & Poor's Industry Surveys, Trends and Projections*
- *The Complete Economic and Demographic Data Source*

This list should give you some idea of the abundance of information that is available if you look for it. Although most of these resources are print publications, many are also available on the Internet. In fact, the Internet has become such a powerful research tool that I decided to add a separate section devoted to what you can find online with very little trouble. I am not going to discuss those sites that my mother won't let me look at!

Statistical Abstract of the United States. This publication provides statistical data on various subjects, including population, education, the labor force, prices, vital statistics, the environment, income, the gross domestic product (GDP), science, transportation, agriculture, construction and housing, trade, business enterprise, and energy. In addition to statistics, each subject contains a brief explanation of the contents of the data.

The statistical data is presented in various ways (graphs, tables, charts, and maps), depending on what is appropriate for the subject being analyzed. The data is also shown historically as percentage changes computed annually and monthly, and in some cases projections are given. The data is also divided into such classifications as age, race, marital status, sex, and region. This book can be a useful resource tool, since a huge collection of data regarding the nation is compiled into one reference source.

Statistical Abstract of the United States is issued by the U.S. Department of Commerce along with the Economics and Statistics Administration and the Bureau of the Census and is made available for distribution by the U.S. Government Printing Office in Washington, D.C. The publication is updated on an annual basis.

This excellent publication is also available online in PDF (Portable Document Format). Tables of data for all sections for 1995 through 2000 can be found and easily printed a section at a time. You do not have to get them all to get what you need. Find this at www.census.gov/prod/www/statistical-abstract-us.html.

Economic Report of the President. This publication, which includes the *Annual Report of the Council of Economic Advisers*, contains the President's report on the economic condition of the United States to the Speaker of the House of Representatives and the President of the Senate. These reports often focus on interesting topics. For example, the highlight of the report submitted by President Bush in January 2001 was a comprehensive review of the so-called new economy and its effects on the United States.

The Annual Report of the Council of Economic Advisers is an excellent source of various economic information relating to the nation. In this report, the council provides summarizations and corresponding charts on the various aspects of the U.S. economy for a specific time period, as well as the indicators that affect economic growth. Health care reform, income, inflation, monetary policy, trade policy, taxes, employment, economic trends, and the status of the United States in the global marketplace are discussed.

In addition, the book provides tables, charts, and "boxes" (highlighted captions that give further explanations and the views of the U.S. administration) pertaining to the economic condition of the time. The data in these tables and charts gives historical, current, and projected figures and is presented on an annual basis; for more current years, it is also presented on either a monthly or quarterly basis. The *Economic Report of the President* is a useful tool in the search for the economic condition of the nation, as well as for its future outlook and data relating to it.

The Economic Report of the President, including the *Annual Report of the Council of Economic Advisers*, is distributed by the U.S. Government Printing Office in Washington, D.C. It is available free online at www.access.gpo.gov/usbudget/index.html. I like free!

Federal Reserve Bulletin. The monthly issues of the *Federal Reserve Bulletin* focus on aspects of the U.S. economy that impact monetary policy, such as international transactions, production, income, lending, interest rates, and the conditions of U.S. commercial banks, as well as other economic topics. It discusses such subjects as Treasury and Federal Reserve foreign exchange operations and publishes the Fed Chairman's *Monetary Policy Report to Congress*.

Other important topics discussed in the *Federal Reserve Bulletin* are employment conditions, prices, the condition of the economy, and forecasts made by the Fed governors and Federal Reserve Bank presidents. Also presented in the *Federal Reserve Bulletin* are the minutes of the Federal Open Market Committee meetings; new legal developments; announcements relating to new policies, appointments, etc.; and statements made by the chairman of the Board of Governors with regard to current economic conditions.

Each monthly issue has a section entitled "Financial and Business Statistics." In this section, there are helpful tables providing statistical data relating to the U.S. economy and on subjects such as money, stock and bank credit, the GDP, the consumer price index (CPI), unemployment, interest rates, real estate, financial markets, the stock market, securities, production, consumer credit, and income. This data is presented historically, annually, quarterly, monthly, or in combination.

The Federal Reserve Bulletin is published by the Board of Governors of the Federal Reserve System in Washington, D.C., and can be obtained from Publications Services, Board of Governors of the Federal Reserve System, Washington, D.C. Sections of this report are available for free (there's that word again!) online on the Federal Reserve Board's Web site. Find it at www.federalreserve.gov.

Survey of Current Business. This publication contains information from the National Income and Products Accounts (NIPA), which is used to add up GDP. A regular feature of this monthly publication is a description of the business situation, which is done in summary, tabular, and chart form. Economic growth as measured by the GDP, consumption expenditures, investments, interest rates, housing, imports and exports, the gross state product, involvement of the United States in foreign business, and other data that can be of use in analyzing the nation's economy can also be found in this book. Some issues also include special features that report on topics of significance for the specific time period.

Survey of Current Business is issued by the U.S. Department of Commerce, Economics and Statistics Administration, and the Bureau of Economic Analysis, and is distributed by the Superintendent of Documents, U.S. Government Printing Office, Washington, D.C. This monthly publication is also available online at no cost on the BEA Web site at www.bea.gov.

Stocks, Bonds, Bills, and Inflation Yearbook. This publication is an annual yearbook that contains historical data about returns in the capital markets since 1926 and through the current year. It supplies useful investment information and features sections reflecting highlights of the current year's market, major events, and highlights from the previous decade, along with corresponding charts and tables for further explanation.

A section of the book is devoted to returns on stocks and bonds of various types, along with statistical data and formulas, returns for different sizes of firms, and cost of capital and discount rate information. I discuss this publication in greater detail in Chapter 10.

Stocks, Bonds, Bills, and Inflation Yearbook is published in two separate versions annually by Ibbotson Associates, Chicago. One version (the blue book) is a "valuation edition."

Cost of Capital Quarterly. This book is published annually by Ibbotson Associates, with quarterly updates also available. The purpose of the book is to provide additional data that can be used to estimate the cost of capital. It does this by providing cost-of-capital information that is broken down by various industries. Within each of these industries, the data is also broken down by company size.

The information provided includes compound annual equity returns, five-year growth in net sales, and operating income and net income, as well as margins, capital structure ratios, equity valuation ratios, and betas.

Industry Data

Industry data that should be considered by the appraiser will generally include information about the competition, the general outlook for the industry (locally and nationally), and special industry situations, such as technological developments and the effect of regulatory activities. The purpose of obtaining industry data is to allow the appraiser to make an assessment of how the appraisal subject compares with its peers. Determining the strengths and weaknesses of the appraisal subject is an important element in the risk analysis and is necessary for the determination of appropriate pricing multiples for the market approach, or discount and capitalization rates for the income approach.

One of the best places to start in the search for industry information is a trade organization. These organizations frequently publish trade journals, gather statistical data about members of the organization, and are extremely helpful in getting information that the appraiser can use. I have found that people working at trade organizations are generally very helpful.

If you go to your local library, you can look up trade associations in books such as Gale Research's *Encyclopedia of Trade Associations*.[2] Several Internet sources of trade association information are reviewed later. Some of the other sources that you will find helpful for the industry outlook are:

- *U.S. Industry & Trade Outlook*
- Standard & Poor's (S&P) industry surveys
- Brokerage house industry studies
- Regulatory agencies' reports
- Financial publications
- *Predicast's Forecasts*

Data sources for financial information include the following:

- Integra Information's *Business Profiler*
- Trade association surveys
- *Corporation Source Book of Statistics of Income*
- *Partnership Source Book of Statistics of Income*
- *Sole Proprietorship Source Book of Statistics of Income*
- *Almanac of Business and Industrial Financial Ratios*
- *Financial Statement Studies of the Small Business*
- *RMA Annual Statement Studies*
- *S&P Analysts' Handbook*
- *D&B Industry Norms and Key Business Ratios*

Once again, a description of many of these data sources follows. This should help acquaint you with them.

[2]Gale Research, Inc., *Encyclopedia of Trade Associations* (835 Penobscot Building, Detroit, Mich. 48226-4095).

U.S. Industry & Trade Outlook. Beginning in 1997, DRI/McGraw Hill teamed up with Standard & Poor's and the U.S. Department of Commerce to bring back a close equivalent to the old *U.S. Industrial Outlook*, which ceased publication in 1994.

This publication includes a detailed analysis of hundreds of industries, including reviews and forecasts. Each chapter is devoted to an industry sector and includes a discussion of variables that affect it. Graphs are included that show growth trends, market share, U.S. trade and export dependence, import penetration, output, and output per worker. This publication is expected to be available only online beginning in 2002.

Integra Information's Business Profiler. Chapter 5 includes a complete discussion of how to use this database as part of the financial analysis process.

Almanac of Business and Industrial Financial Ratios. This annually updated publication provides current corporate performance facts and figures for a specific accounting period, summarized from tax return data. This information can be used to make comparisons of specific companies to similar ones in the industry. Two types of tables are given for each industry. Both report the operating and financial information for corporations; however, one reports it with and without net income, whereas the other reports it specifically for those corporations that were operating at a profit.

The book divides each industry into categories according to asset size. For each category, ratios are given for the operating factors (cost of operations, repairs, bad debts, etc.), financial ratios (current ratio, quick ratio, asset turnover, etc.), and financial factors (debt ratio, return on assets, return on equity, and return on net worth), which are also defined in the book for reference purposes. The information supplied in the *Almanac of Business and Industrial Financial Ratios* is beneficial in determining how a company compares with its competition and in what areas improvements need to be made or costs need to be cut.

The industrial sectors that are covered in the *Almanac of Business and Industrial Financial Ratios* include construction, agriculture, manufacturing, mining, communications, transportation, banking, insurance, trade, real estate, holding and investment companies, and electric, gas, and sanitary services.

The Almanac of Business and Industrial Financial Ratios is written by Leo Troy, Ph.D., in association with Prentice-Hall, Englewood Cliffs, N.J.

Financial Statement Studies of the Small Business. The purpose of this annually updated publication is to offer a view of the small firm in a perspective that reflects the composition of the small firm. This specific analysis is necessary in making comparisons among firms of a smaller size, as opposed to comparing them with larger firms. This publication focuses solely on small firms that, according to the book, have a total capitalization of less than $1 million.

The data in the book is compiled from more than 30,000 financial statements, as well as contributions made by CPA firms throughout the United States, and is based on fiscal year ends of April 30. The small firms are arranged by common characteristics and the data is expressed in tables. The firms are categorized by asset size and sales volume, the top 25 percent most profitable firms are listed, and five-year trends are analyzed. The tables show income data, operating items, ratios, assets, liabilities, and capital for small firms, and they can be used in making industry comparisons. The industrial sectors analyzed include retailing, manufacturing, professional services, contracting, wholesaling, and other types of services.

Financial Studies of the Small Business is published by Financial Research Associates, Winter Haven, Fla.

RMA Annual Statement Studies. This publication consists of composite financial data on several industries (including agriculture, wholesaling, contracting, services, manufacturing, and retailing), which is categorized by Standard Industrial Classification (SIC) codes. Common-size financial statements and ratios are provided for each industry. Current data for each industry is sorted by sales and by assets, and comparative historical data is provided for both groups. Assets, liabilities, and income data are given with appropriate subdivisions (cash, inventory, payables, sales, etc.), and financial ratios are listed as well. These include liquidity ratios, coverage ratios, leverage ratios, operating ratios, and expense-to-sales ratios. In addition, formulas and explanations of the ratios are provided for a further understanding of their usefulness.

The Risk Management Association, formerly Robert Morris Associates (RMA), the publisher of the book, receives its data from sources that submit it on a voluntary basis, not on a randomly selected basis. These sources include banks that have obtained financial statements from companies that are looking to borrow money. Therefore, the data in this particular publication should not be used as industry guidelines when comparisons are made to other businesses in the industry, since there is a possibility that the data may not include all of the necessary information to make an absolute comparison.

RMA *Annual Statement Studies* is updated yearly, and the data it presents for the more recent years is in terms of fiscal years from April 1 through March 31 (e.g., 2000/2001). Risk Management Association is located in Philadelphia.

Industry Norms & Key Business Ratios. This publication provides financial information on over 800 lines of business and can be used for comparing companies in the same industry. The industries covered in the book are arranged numerically by SIC code. For each SIC code, the specific name of the industry that corresponds to the code is given, along with the number of companies in the industry that were surveyed for the determination of the statistical data. The financial information provided for each industry includes current assets, total assets, current liabilities, total liabilities and net worth, net sales, gross profit, net profit after taxes, and working capital, along with solvency, efficiency, and profitability ratios. The financial ratios are given for companies that fall into the upper quartile, lower quartile, and median.

The figures found in this publication can be used as a guideline in determining the financial condition of comparable companies regardless of whether the company is operating above or below the norms in the industry. In addition to statistical data, the book gives an explanation of the use and meaning of the ratios, along with an explanation of their derivation.

Industry Norms & Key Business Ratios is published by Dun & Bradstreet Information Services, a company of the Dun & Bradstreet Corporation.

Guideline Company Information

Another component of the data-gathering part of the assignment is to locate information about "comparables." These comparables are also known as "guideline companies." The business valuation committee of ASA captioned this terminology as a means of differentiating what the business appraiser does from what the real estate appraiser does in the application of the market approach. Since real estate appraisers can generally find "comparables" that are close enough to the appraisal subject to use in the appraisal process, this terminology seems appropriate. However, business appraisers do not enjoy the same luxury of finding other companies that are close enough to be considered good "comparables." Instead, we use other companies to provide "guidance," and therefore, these companies are termed guideline companies.

Standard Industrial Classification Manual. To find guideline company information, the appraiser has numerous sources to consult. Usually, the starting point of this analysis is to determine the subject company's SIC code. Once the appraiser knows the SIC code for the subject company, he or she can consult various sources that categorize companies in this manner. If the appraiser is not sure which SIC code is appropriate for the subject company, he or she can consult the *SIC Manual*. (Exhibit 4.3 contains a sample from this publication.) The *SIC Manual* classifies business establishments by industry, arranging them by the primary activity in which the company is engaged. The code system is used to assist in comparing similar companies within a specific industry. Each individual industry is classified by a major group number, then further classified by an industry group number, followed by an industry number. The industries are arranged in the book in numeric order and in the back of the book in alphabetical order by business classification. The major group, industry group, and industry numbers are explained, and a listing of industries included under each classification number is also given.

The SIC Manual is published by the Executive Office of the President, Office of Management and Budget, and is provided for sale by National Technical Information Service, Springfield, Va. The publication is revised periodically to reflect the changes within the industrial organization in the economy. The last revision of the *SIC Manual* was in 1987.

If you don't have this book, you can search for an SIC code and its description online at www.osha.gov/oshstats/sicser.html and use keywords to find what you need.

EXHIBIT 4.3
Sample From SIC Manual
Major Group 72—Personal Services
The Major Group as a Whole

This major group includes establishments primarily engaged in providing services generally to individuals, such as laundries, dry-cleaning plants, portrait photographic studios, and beauty and barber shops. Also included are establishments operating as industrial launderers and those primarily engaged in providing linen supply services to commercial and business establishments.

Industry Group No.	*Industry No.*	
721		LAUNDRY, CLEANING, AND GARMENT SERVICES

7211 Power Laundries, Family and Commercial

Establishments primarily engaged in operating mechanical laundries with steam or other power. Establishments primarily engaged in supplying laundered work clothing on a contract or fee basis are classified in Industry 7218.

Laundries, power: family and commercial
Laundry collecting and distributing outlets operated by power laundries
Power laundries, family and commercial

7212 Garment Pressing and Agents for Laundries and Dry Cleaners

Establishments primarily engaged in providing laundry and dry-cleaning services but that have the laundry and dry-cleaning work done by others. Establishments in this industry may do their own pressing or finishing work. Establishments operating their own laundry plants are classified in Industry 7211, and those operating their own dry-cleaning plants are classified in Industry 7216.

Agents, retail: for laundries and dry cleaners
Bobtailers, laundry and dry cleaning
Cleaning and laundry pickup stations, not owned by laundries or cleaners
Press shops for garments
Truck route laundry and dry cleaning, not operated by laundries or cleaners
Valet apparel service

7213 Linen Supply

Establishments primarily engaged in supplying to commercial establishments or household users on a rental basis such laundered items as uniforms, gowns, and coats of the type used by doctors, nurses, barbers, beauticians, and waitresses; and table linens, bed linens, towels and toweling, and similar items. Establishments included in this industry may or may not operate their own laundry facilities. Establishments primarily engaged in providing diaper service are classified in Industry 7219.

Apron supply service
Coat supply service
Continuous towel supply service
Gown supply service, uniform
Linen supply service
Shirt supply service
Table cover supply service
Towel supply service, except wiping
Uniform supply service, except industrial service

(Continued)

EXHIBIT 4.3 ***(Continued)***

Industry No.

7215 Coin-Operated Laundries and Dry-Cleaning

Establishments primarily engaged in the operation of coin-operated or similar self-service laundry and dry-cleaning equipment for use on the premises or in apartments, dormitories, and similar locations.

Coin-operated laundries
Dry-cleaning, coin-operated launderettes
Self-service laundry and dry-cleaning
Laundromats
Laundry machine routes, coin-operated

7216 Dry-Cleaning Plants, Except Rug Cleaning

Establishments primarily engaged in dry-cleaning or dyeing apparel and household fabrics other than rugs. Press shops and agents for dry cleaners are classified in Industry 7212; establishments primarily engaged in cleaning rugs are classified in Industry 7217; and establishments primarily engaged in dyeing fabrics for the trade are classified in Manufacturing, Major Group 22.

Clearing and dyeing plants, except rug cleaning
Collecting and distributing agencies—operated by cleaning plants
Drapery dry-cleaning plants
Dry-cleaning plants, except rug cleaning

7217 Carpet and Upholstery Cleaning

Establishments primarily engaged in cleaning carpets and upholstered furniture at a plant or on customers' premises. Establishments primarily engaged in rug repair are classified in Industry 7699, and those primarily engaged in reupholstering and repairing furniture are classified in Industry 7641.

Carpet cleaning and repairing plants
Carpet cleaning on customers' premises
Furniture cleaning on customers' premises
Rug cleaning, dyeing, and repairing plants
Upholstery cleaning on customers' premises

7218 Industrial Launderers

Establishments primarily engaged in supplying laundered or dry-cleaned industrial work uniforms and related work clothing, such as protective apparel (flame and heat resistant) and clean room apparel; laundered mats and rags; dust control items, such as treated mops, rugs, mats, dust tool covers, and cloths; laundered wiping towels; and other selected items to industrial, commercial, and government users. These items may belong to the industrial launderer and be supplied to users on a rental basis, or they may be the customers' own goods. Establishments included in this industry may or may not operate their own laundry or dry-cleaning facilities.

Clean room apparel supply service
Flame and heat resistant clothing supply service
Industrial launderers
Industrial uniform supply service
Laundered mat and rug supply service
Radiation protective garments supply
Safety glove supply service
Towel supply service, wiping
Treated mats, rugs, mops, dust tool covers, and cloth supply
Wiping towel supply service
Work clothing supply service, industrial

7219 Laundry and Garment Services, Not Elsewhere Classified

Establishments primarily engaged in furnishing laundry and garment services not elsewhere classified, such as the repair, alteration, and storage of clothes for individuals and for the operation of hand laundries. Custom tailors and dressmakers are classified in Retail Trade, Industry 5699; fur shops making fur apparel to custom order are classified in Retail Trade, Industry 5632; and press shops are classified in Industry 7212.

North American Industry Classification System Manual. Since having one classification system was not enough, our government decided to join forces with Canada and Mexico to come up with a new system. Those of us old enough to remember experienced this same disaster with the metric system. I think I still have a metric tool set that does not fit anything because our country never adopted the system. Well, this is another one of those questionable brainstorms.

The NAICS system is similar to the SIC system. (This whole thing makes me sick! Yeah, I know, bad joke.) It is more detailed and *may* eventually take over the SIC system. The manual is published by Bernan

Press and can be ordered at (800) 274-4447, or send an e-mail to info@bernan.com. This publication is available in hardcover, softcover, and CD-ROM versions. Use the principle of substitution and buy the cheapest one.

S&P Register of Corporations. If the appraiser knows of public companies that are in the same industry as the appraisal subject, the appraiser can turn to the *S&P Register of Corporations*. This publication, found in most libraries, lists companies and their SIC codes. Other sources for finding public guideline company information include:

- *SEC Directory*. This directory lists all companies that are required to file annual reports with the SEC.
- *S&P Register—Indexes*. This publication lists both public and private companies according to SIC code.
- *S&P Corporation Records—Index of Companies by SIC Code*. This publication lists public companies only.
- *Moody's Manuals*
- *Value Line Investment Survey*
- Electronic sources

Standard & Poor's Register of Corporations. This publication is the first of the three volumes of *Standard & Poor's Register of Corporations, Directors & Executives*. This book is updated annually and serves as a guide to the business community, providing aid to those making buying decisions.

The publication lists corporations by name and provides such information as its address, telephone number, officers, directors, the exchange the company trades its stock on, its SIC code, and its subsidiaries. The register covers corporations in the United States and Canada, as well as other major international corporations.

Standard & Poor's Register of Corporations is published by Standard & Poor's, a division of McGraw-Hill, Inc., New York.

Standard & Poor's Register of Corporations, Directors & Executives—Indexes is Volume 3 of *Standard & Poor's Register of Corporations, Directors & Executives*. This volume supplies the reader with a breakdown of the major SIC codes, a list of the companies in each grouping, a geographical list of the companies, an index of parent companies and their subsidiaries, obituaries, plus other significant information about the companies. This book is also published annually.

Standard & Poor's Register of Corporations, Directors & Executives—Indexes is published by Standard & Poor's, a division of McGraw-Hill, Inc., New York.

Moody's Manuals. *Moody's Manuals* consists of numerous annual editions of investment manuals, providing credit information on just about every type of debt security issuance and issuer. Among these manuals are the *Industrial, OTC Industrial, Municipal & Government, Transportation, Bank & Finance, Public Utility, International, OTC Unlisted,* and *News Reports*.

The information includes a description of each company's history, the names of any subsidiaries, the names of company officers and directors, and a description of the company's primary operations. The manuals also give significant financial information about each company, including balance sheets, income statements, bond information and ratings, long-term debt, stock information, geographical listings, and SIC codes.

In addition, the manuals provide information on security issues, bond yields, preferred stock yields, the commodity price index, and industrial stocks. They also provide a chronological list of maturing industrial bonds and notes and information on interim earnings and dividends, as well as on corporate bond and preferred-stock ratings.

Moody's Manuals is published and copyrighted by Moody's Investors Service, Inc., a subsidiary of Moody's Corp.

Value Line Investment Survey. This survey is published weekly in three parts: "Summary & Index," "Selection & Opinion," and "Ratings & Reports." The "Summary & Index" section features a listing of companies alphabetized by company name and shows the price, beta, current price/earnings ratio, the estimated dividends for the year, and other stock data for each company. There is also a listing of timely stocks in timely industries and various stock rankings and estimates. In addition, the index to part 3, "Ratings & Reports," lists the industries, the page references to them, and the rankings of each industry's probable performance.

Part 2 of the *Value Line Investment Survey* features articles, graphs, and tables on current economic conditions, the Federal Reserve's actions, stock market conditions, earnings estimates, Federal Reserve data, economic information on the GDP, consumer confidence, home sales and starts, and stock market averages.

Part 3 of the *Value Line Investment Survey* gives an in-depth analysis of each industry listed. Recent developments and actions that have affected the industry are discussed, and statistics and graphs showing both current and historical data are provided. News about the major companies involved in the particular industry is presented, along with stock information, the company's current financial position, quarterly earnings, earnings per share, and dividends. The information provided in the three parts of the *Value Line Investment Survey* can be used in analyzing the economy at specific time periods, analyzing industries, and making comparisons with those companies involved in a particular industry.

The Value Line Investment Survey is published and copyrighted by Value Line Publishing, Inc., New York.

Other financial and descriptive information about public companies can be obtained from Form 10-K, Form 10-Q, and the annual reports of the guideline company, which are available either directly from the guideline company or through commercial vendors.

Sources of forecast financial data include the following:

- Brokerage houses
- The Institutional Brokers Estimate System (I/B/E/S), available through the Thomson Corp.
- *S&P Earnings Guide*
- *Nelson's Earnings Outlook*
- *Zack's Earnings Forecaster*
- *Bloomberg Financial Markets*

In addition to locating specific guideline company information, the appraiser will also be looking for data about mergers and acquisitions in the same or similar industry as the appraisal subject's. I will explain more about this in Chapters 6 and 7, but first let's point out where you can get merger and acquisition information.

Merger and acquisition data can be obtained from the following sources:

- *Acquisition/Divestiture Weekly Report*
- *Mergers and Acquisitions Sourcebook*
- *Mergerstat Review*
- *The Merger Yearbook*
- *Mergerstat Control Premium Study*
- *Predicast's Forecasts*
- Computer databases:
  - The Institute of Business Appraisers, Inc.
  - BizComps
  - Pratt's Stats
  - Done Deals
  - Securities Data Company (a Thomson Company)

Mergerstat Review. This annual publication presents compiled statistics relating to mergers and acquisitions. Data on merger and acquisition announcements and purchase prices are presented annually and quarterly, for the current period and historically. Current transactions that are either completed or pending are also shown, as well as the prices offered and equity interest sought for companies that are in the $100 million category.

The one hundred largest announcements in history are featured, as are the largest by industry. The publication also has announcements on mergers and acquisitions for specific industries, including a ranking of the dollar value offered and the number of transactions in each industry. International transactions, divestitures, a transaction and cancellation roster by industry, and acquisitions of privately owned companies are other areas featured in the book. The information provided in *Mergerstat Review* can be used to identify industry guideline companies that were involved in actual transactions. The most widely used application of *Mergerstat Review* is the reporting of control premium data. This is discussed in greater detail in Chapter 11.

Mergerstat Review is published by Houlihan, Lokey, Howard & Zukin of Los Angeles.

The Merger Yearbook. This yearbook, which comes in two editions (U.S. and international), offers a listing of a particular year's transactions; it also offers corporate acquisitions, mergers, divestitures, and leveraged buyouts. The transactions featured include mergers and acquisitions that have statuses such as pending, fully, or partially completed. The information is arranged by SIC code and provides the target company, its SIC code, the buyer, and the value and type of the transaction. It also gives a brief explanation of the transaction.

The publication is updated annually and can be a useful source in comparing the sales of similar companies. *The Merger Yearbook* is published and copyrighted by Securities Data Company, New York.

Mergerstat Control Premium Study. The *Mergerstat Control Premium Study* offers quarterly information on control premiums and analyzes the mergers and acquisitions of public companies to determine the premium paid to obtain a controlling interest. This information can be used to help quantify premiums and discounts.

A list of the companies that were acquired, in addition to the companies that acquired those companies, is given, along with business descriptions and SIC codes. Numerous tables relating to the acquisition are provided and contain such information as the acquisition announcement and closing dates, the value of the deal, the percentage of common stock held by the acquirer before and after the acquisition, the price of the stock per share for various time frames, selected ratios, the specific stock exchange on which the stock is traded, and the nature of the takeover. The Mergerstat unaffected price is featured (the common stock price per share that has not been affected by the announcement of the acquisition), as is the Mergerstat control premium (found by subtracting the Mergerstat unaffected price from the purchase price, then dividing the difference by the Mergerstat unaffected price).

The book also contains a list of companies (grouped by their SIC codes) that were acquired during a 12-month period. The data provided on these acquisitions is the Mergerstat control premium and the range, median, and mean for each industry. Historical data on control premiums is also provided on a quarterly basis in the form of graphs.

The Mergerstat Control Premium Study is published and copyrighted by Mergerstat LP.

Predicast's Forecasts. This publication is updated quarterly and provides forecasts of the economy, industries, products, and markets, as reported by the experts within the business and trade press. The forecasts are categorized by SIC code and a listing of industries together with their respective SIC codes, which provides assistance in searching. In addition to the SIC code, *Predicast's Forecasts* gives the primary product, annual growth, and long-range forecasts for each company.

This publication can also be useful in the search for forecasts on specific aspects of the economy, such as GDP, employment, industrial production, consumption, investment, and various industries.

Predicast's Forecasts is published quarterly and copyrighted by the Information Access Company, a Thomson Corporation company, Foster City, Calif.

Data Gathering—Mostly Electronic?

Let's face it—the ubiquitous computer has become entrenched as a fixture in our offices. These machines just will not go away, so we may as well use them as much as we can. Computers can make our search for information much easier, whether we use CD-ROMs or the Internet. This entire landscape has changed so much since the first edition of this book that much of this section has been completely revised.

The electronic services mentioned in the following sections are available on CD-ROM and the Internet. The following list is not meant to be comprehensive. Sources that are of particular value to appraisers have been included. The decision on which sources to include was based on many factors, including depth of coverage, cost, ease of access, and availability of support. Although every attempt was made to provide up-to-date information, the nature of this rapidly changing industry makes that virtually impossible. Many of the paid Internet subscription services post their prices on their Web sites. It has been our experience that some Web sites are updated more often than others, so it is best to contact the vendor directly for the most up-to-date pricing. The product will not be available until you become a subscriber or divulge credit card information, so there is no danger of "accidentally" buying something you do not want (like a new washing machine).

These data sources are arranged by business valuation function. The section titled "Sources of Economic Information" focuses on obtaining economic data at the national, regional, and local levels, and also focuses on industry information. Subsequent sections focus on finding information on guideline public companies, merger and acquisition sources, and Tax Court cases, as well as related information. Information about many of the databases and publications discussed in this section, as well as about others that you may want to become familiar with, is included in Appendix 19, "Business Valuation Resources," at the end of this book.

Before I go too much further, let's step back to discuss some basics. In this discussion, I will address the following:

- What is electronic data gathering?
- Data providers and vendors
- The Internet
- Sources of information

What Is Electronic Data Gathering?

Electronic data gathering involves the use of a computer to retrieve data either from a remote computer database or from a compact disk (CD-ROM). As personal computers (PCs) became cheaper and simpler to use and as more and more individuals and businesses have come to rely on them, data providers moved away from print products to CD-ROMs (compact disks—read only memory) as a way to distribute the information they collect. CD-ROMs are more versatile than the traditional print product because they can be updated more cheaply (and thus more frequently) and take up less room on your shelf than a book (except this one, which is a must to own). More importantly, they are often easier to use than the traditional print product. They are capable of holding vast amounts of data, and, with a bit of practice, users can find what they need very quickly.

Like the PC, the Internet has grown in importance in the years since this book was first published. Technological advances in both hardware and software have made it possible to store and retrieve huge amounts of information from remote locations quickly and easily. Data providers have moved from CD-ROMs to the Internet as a way to deliver their products. As a result, it is now possible to completely research economic developments, an industry, or a company at home in your bathrobe and slippers at any hour of the night or day. Vast amounts of data are available—much of it for free—quite literally at your fingertips.

Though I am still not sure whether computers really do make our lives easier, I feel certain that your computer and your Internet connection can make research for your valuation report much easier. The Internet is an immense collection of information, some of it interesting, some of it useful, and some of it a complete waste. To get the most out of your Web research, it is good to have some knowledge of what is available so that you do not spend hours going around in circles. Unless, of course, you like to go around in circles. To that end, this section is devoted to giving you some tools and tricks that can make data gathering on the Internet more efficient and rewarding. Since I am not in a position to teach you how to get around the Web, I am assuming that you can find your own way around—at least I hope you do not get as lost as me!

Data Providers and Vendors

It is important to distinguish between the data providers, companies that are actually compiling the original data, and the vendors, which do not originate content but only distribute it. Some data providers use a third-party vendor to distribute products electronically. These vendors may include enterprises such as Dialog, Dow Jones News Retrieval, or Lexis/Nexis. Vendors seldom offer the entire product line of a data provider. For example, the Standard & Poor's data offered through Dialog is more complete than the S&P data offered on CompuServe but is less extensive than the data purchased directly from S&P. Most data providers now offer products directly to consumers either online or on CD-ROM. Providers such as the U.S. government offer raw data for free, and it is then up to the user to do his or her own analysis and commentary. Some vendors include analysis and commentary as part of their subscription services. This can be worth the additional cost if you are not comfortable with analysis of economic and industry data. Remember to pass along the cost to the client.

The Internet

The Internet is a global network of computers originally conceived by the U.S. Department of Defense as a way to "bomb-proof" vital communications during the cold war, almost 50 years ago. For many years, access was effectively limited to governmental, scientific, and academic organizations because only technically oriented users were willing to learn the complex methods of accessing the system. There were few commercial providers offering access.

The driving force behind the growth of the Internet is the World Wide Web (WWW), a simple yet ingenious system that allows users to interact with documents stored on computers across the Internet as if they were parts of a single hypertext. The Web grew tremendously in popularity after the release of a free browser program, Mosaic, created at the University of Illinois's National Center for Supercomputing Applications (NCSA). NCSA Mosaic provided an easy-to-use graphical interface to the Web that behaved the same on UNIX, Macintosh, and Windows computers. When Mosaic was released in the spring of 1993, there were about 130 Web sites on the Internet. By November 1994, this number had increased to more than 10,000. As of the time this book was written, millions of Web sites exist, and anyone with an ISP can set up a site of their own.

Here is some real basic stuff—mainly definitions that you probably know by now but may want a refresher about. These are a few definitions of some of the most widely used Internet terms. The World Wide Web is the most popular service on the Internet. The Web is an information retrieval system using hypertext links to combine text with graphics, audio, and video. Hypertext links allow users to connect to the data by clicking or jumping from file location to file location in a nonlinear manner.

Web browser software, such as Netscape or Mosaic, allows the user to navigate the Internet and take advantage of all the graphical and sound features of the World Wide Web. The Uniform Resource Locator (URL) is the addressing system that allows users to locate information on the Internet. An example is http://www.census.gov.

A home page is the electronic equivalent of a front door. This is the top level of information at a data provider's Web site. Newsgroups are bulletin-board-like topic groups that allow people with common interests to share information. Telnet is a system that allows users to log in to other computers on the Internet. These are but a few of the topics related to the Internet. There are a number of how-to books available that provide detailed descriptions of the Internet and its components, like the *For Dummies* books. My library is filled with them. After all, they were written and titled with me in mind!

Sources of Economic Information

The federal government collects vast amounts of economic and demographic data for the United States as a whole, as well as for states, counties, and many cities. Data is also collected on various industries. The information is available in print form, on government-produced CD-ROMs, and electronically on the government's many Web sites. Although the government-produced data may be available through other vendors' online services and/or print or electronic products, there is no reason ever to pay for this data, unless what you are looking for is very old. And in that case, you might be better off in the public library.

Every department, bureau, and section of the federal government has a Web site. Every state in the United States has a Web site containing a variety of information about the state. Almost every U.S. county and many U.S. cities have Web sites as well. These may contain information of interest only to a tourist or other visitor, but some may also have economic or business information.

This section deals exclusively with electronic data sources located on the Internet. Let's begin with the U.S. federal government and then review private sources of data. Some of these Web sites are free and others are subscription services, which charge either a flat annual fee or a fee per use or article. Many of these Web sites are so rich that inclusion of the addresses of individual pages would become cumbersome. Therefore, I am only giving you the address of the home page and inviting you to visit the sites and explore them by "clicking" on the links. Do it in your spare time.

The discussion is subdivided into sections as follows:

- Economic information
  - United States
  - State and local
  - Market data (stocks and bonds)
  - International data
- Other information
  - Industry data
  - Access to newspapers and periodicals
  - Search engines

Economic Information

United States

FedStats (www.fedstats.gov). Perhaps the most comprehensive and easy-to-use government Web site, FedStats is the new window on the full range of official statistical information available to the public from the federal government. Use the Internet's powerful linking and searching capabilities to track economic and population trends, health care costs, aviation safety, foreign trade, energy use, farm production, and more. Access official statistics collected and published by more than 70 federal agencies without having to know in advance which agency produces them. All of the statistical information available through FedStats is maintained and updated solely by federal agencies on their own Web servers. And it's all free.

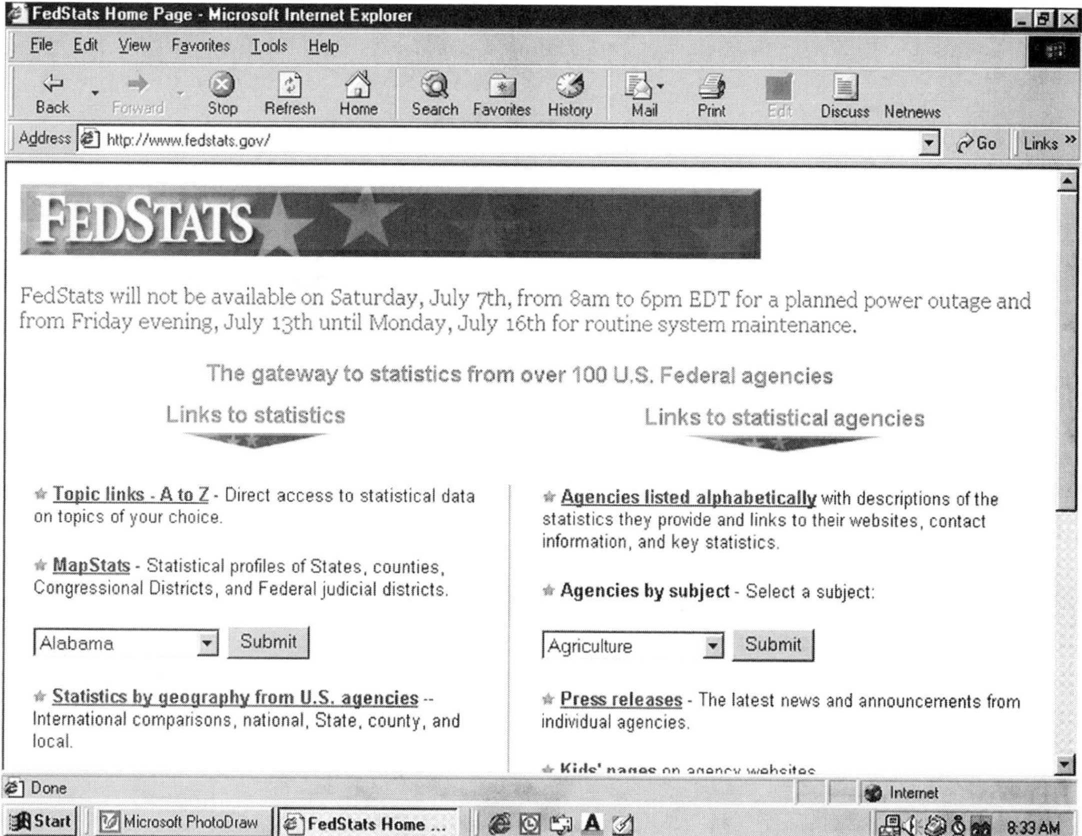

The FedStats home page begins with easy-to-use links to statistics and links to statistical agencies:

- *Topic links—A to Z* (direct access to statistical data on topics of your choice—there are 270 of them)
- *MapStats* (statistical profiles of states, counties, congressional districts, and federal judicial districts)
- *Statistics by geography from U.S. agencies* (international, national, state, county, and local comparisons)
- *Statistical reference shelf* (published collections of statistics available online, including the *Statistical Abstract of the United States*)
- *Search* (across agency Web sites)
- *Agencies listed alphabetically* (with descriptions of the statistics they provide and links to their Web sites, contact information, and key statistics)
- *Agencies by subject* (a dropdown menu is available for selection of subject)
- *Press releases* (the latest news and announcements from individual agencies)
- *Kids' pages* (on agency Web sites)
- *Data access tools* (selected agency online databases)

Three principal statistical agencies gather data on economic activity, demographic trends, and industry developments in the United States, nationally and on the state and local levels. These are:

Bureau of Economic Analysis (BEA) (www.bea.gov). Measures, presents, and interprets gross domestic product, personal income, corporate profits, and related items in the context of the National Income and Product Accounts. BEA also maintains personal income and related measures for states and localities, the U.S. balance of payments accounts, and the foreign direct investments accounts. Data is released monthly in the *Survey of Current Business* (available both in print and on the Web).

Bureau of Labor Statistics (BLS) (www.bls.gov). Produces statistics on employment and unemployment, consumer expenditures, prices and living conditions, wages and employee benefits, productivity and technological changes in U.S. industries, projections of economic growth, the labor force, employment by industry and occupation, and occupational injuries and illnesses.

Bureau of the Census (www.census.gov). Provides information on the number, geographic distribution, and social and economic characteristics of the nation's population. Conducts several periodic censuses every five years, covering the years ending in 2 and 7. The Economic Censuses include censuses of manufacturing, mineral industries, construction industries, retail and wholesale trade, service industries, and transportation and other businesses. The Census of Governments collects state and local data on public finance, public employment, and governmental organization, powers, and activities.

The Census Bureau operates the *Census Information Center* (CIC) program, which is a cooperative effort between the U.S. Census Bureau and 59 national, regional, and local nonprofit organizations (including universities). These are listed on www.census.gov/clo/www/cic.html and can be sources of additional, more specific data. The organizations range from the Arab American Institute to the William C. Velazquez Institute; contact information is available, including e-mail addresses and/or Web sites.

Twelve other statistical agencies collect data on more specific areas of the economy; for example, the Bureau of Transportation Statistics gathers data on the nation's transportation systems, and the Energy Information Administration collects information on energy reserves, production, consumption, etc. Each of these agencies' Web sites can be accessed through FedStats. Most recent years' statistics and contact information are available.

FirstGov (www.firstgov.gov). This is an official U.S. government Web site that allows visitors to browse government by topic and lists 16 topics from Agriculture and Food (farms, food, nutrition) to the United States in the World (defense, trade, immigration). These provide links to the agency involved. There are links to the executive, legislative, and judicial branches of the federal government, as well as links to state and local governments. This site is free.

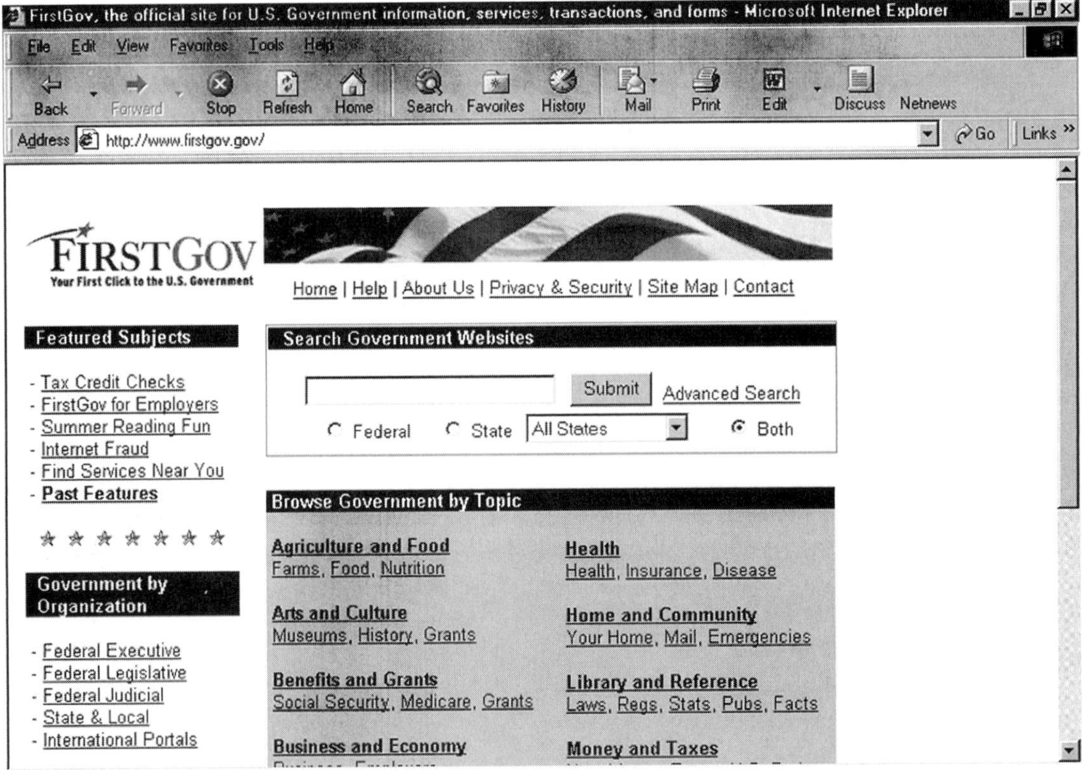

Stat-USA/Internet (www.stat-usa.gov). This is a fee-based subscription service of STAT-USA, U.S. Department of Commerce. To access the information, one must purchase a user name and password. This costs $175 for a year or $75 quarterly. STAT-USA is an agency in the Economics and Statistics Administration of the U.S. Department of Commerce. They deliver economic, business, and international trade information produced by the U.S. government. There are also business leads available for subscribers; these are requests for bids on government procurement items.

This agency states that "by charging a low cost recovery fee, we can look forward to continuing to offer the best service possible with cutting-edge technology, award-winning software, and knowledgeable, professional customer service." This may be so, but the overwhelming majority of the information available here is also available on the free Web sites just mentioned. Why pay for something that you can have for free? I told you before—I like free!

Statistical Resources on the Web (www.lib.umich.edu/libhome/Documents.center/statsnew.html). This is a University of Michigan Web site with links to many different types of statistical information. The topics range from Agriculture (crops and livestock), Business and Industry (employment and production), to Weather (United States and international). There is a section entitled Comprehensive Subjects (directories and multi-topic) that might have some useful information. Not all of these will contain economic or business-related information; some of them contain policy statements, for example. But many of them are useful, and they are all free sites.

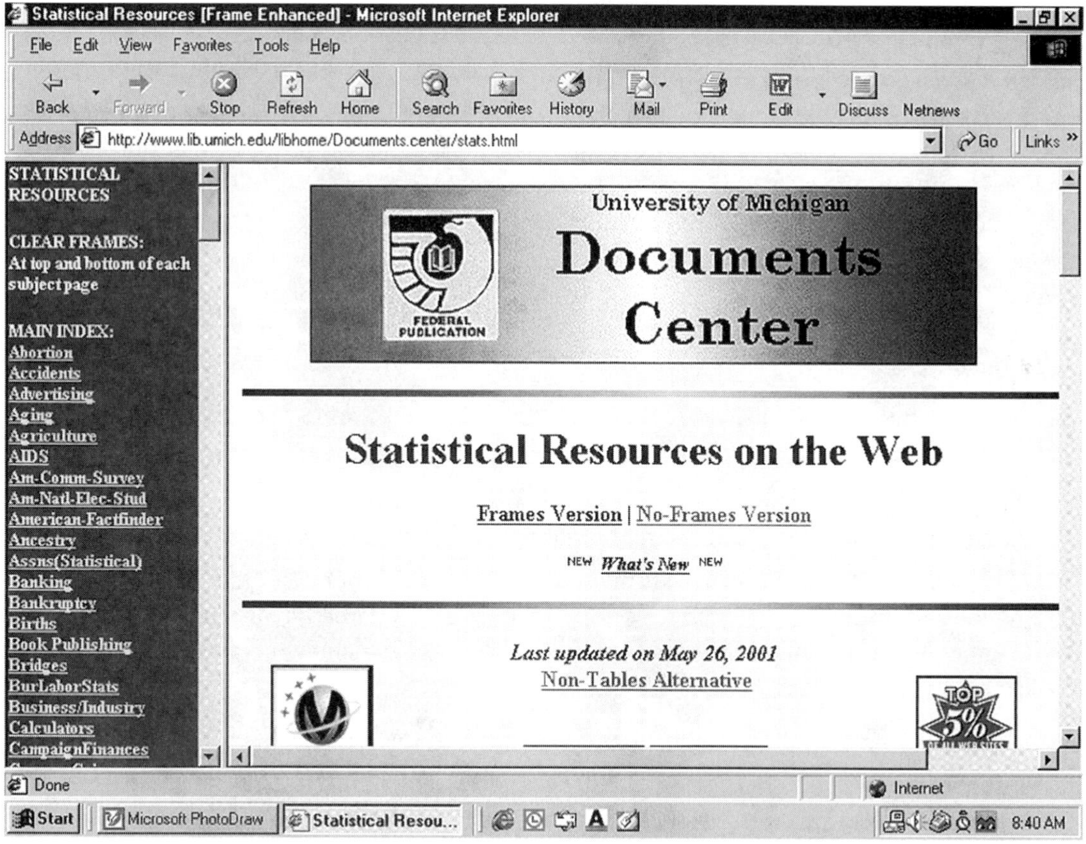

In fact, most university libraries have Web sites, and their collections are generally listed. The Web sites can be searched by subject, title, author, publisher, publication, etc. They are often a good source of industry material.

Federal Reserve Board (www.federalreserve.gov). This is a good source for economic data, interest rates, monetary policy information, and international information. All of the Fed's statistical releases (daily, monthly, quarterly, etc.) are available. Information that is published in the monthly *Federal Reserve Bulletin* is on this Web site, including Federal Open Market Committee meeting minutes, transcripts of testimony before Congress, monetary policy reports, and more. The Fed's "Beige Book" is published on this Web site as well and includes a summary and each District Bank's report.

Links are available to the Bank for International Settlements, the European Central Bank, and other foreign central banks (www.federalreserve.gov/centralbanks.htm). Sixteen foreign central banks are linked to the U.S. Fed, and these sites are all available in English.

There are also links to each of the 12 regional Federal Reserve District Banks (www.federalreserve.gov/otherfrb.htm). Federal Reserve District Banks' Web sites contain district economic activity and other economic research. Many of the research pieces are very academic and technical, but some may be useful in a valuation report. Links to related Web sites, including FirstGov, are included.

The Conference Board (www.conference-board.org). This is a not-for-profit, worldwide research and business membership organization and a leading private source of economic and business intelligence. The Economics Program is a recognized source of business economics research and objective indicators, analyses, and forecasts. Several widely watched economic indicators are published by this program, including: Consumer Confidence, Help-Wanted Advertising, U.S. Leading Economic Indicators, U.S. Regional Performance, and Business Executives' Expectations. U.S. Leading Economic Indicators were once produced by the Bureau of Economic Analysis. Business cycle indicators and general information about the economy are on www.globalindicators.org as a public service. To subscribe to Business Cycle Indicators, access their database; to receive reports and analyses, the cost is $500 per year, with a per-use fee of $15 per U.S. series and $25 per other-country series.

Economagic (www.economagic.com). This is a free service where you can browse over 100,000 data files with charts and Excel files for each. You can browse by region or by source. Most of the data is from U.S. federal statistical agencies, but there are some links to foreign sources and a few trade associations and private companies. For example, at www.economagic.com/cenret.htm, you can access retail sales data for a wide variety of industries and businesses.

According to the Web site, Economagic is meant to be a comprehensive site of free, easy-to-access economic time series data useful for economic research, particularly economic forecasting. The core data sets contain macroeconomic data at the national level; however, much of it is at the local level. All of the data can be downloaded to Excel files.

Economy.com (www.economy.com). This site has sections that are free and others that offer reports for a fee. Some of the areas of this Web site are:

FreeLunch.com (www.freelunch.com). Free access to over 1,000,000 economic time series in Excel file format—easy to use. Who says there is no such thing as a free lunch?

The Dismal Scientist (www.dismal.com). Part of economy.com and covers over 75 economic releases from over 15 countries. The releases are accompanied by a summary and an analysis, which can be quite useful. This Web site is excellent because it includes analyses as well as raw data. But the analyses are for recent releases.

In addition to current releases and analyses, the Web site has a series of archives sorted according to broad subject matter. There is one for Industrial Markets, for example, which includes a series of articles about a variety of industries. These date back to 1997. Each article deals with conditions in the particular industry at the time it was written.

Research@Economy.com. Provides comprehensive reports on conditions in a variety of industries together with both macro- and microeconomic forecasts. These reports are not cheap: individual reports are $200 and subscriptions (one report with two updates) are $500. Free samples are available for all industries, but they are not up-to-the-minute.

Mercer Capital (www.bizval.com). *The National Economic Review*, the only overview of the national economy prepared specifically for the business valuation industry, is available on diskette or on their

Web site. The reports take information from many business publications and government-produced data, are about three or four pages long, and include tables of statistics and references. They are offered on a subscription basis (quarterly issues), and quarterly reports can be obtained by request all the way back to 1992. A one-year subscription costs $259 (two years for $399), and individual quarterly *Reviews* sell for $150 each. The subscriptions may be worth it if you are not comfortable with interpreting the myriad statistics that are released each quarter on the nation's economy.

State and Local

U.S. Census Bureau (www.census.gov). This site gathers data at the state and local level and offers "Geography Quick Reports" by state and by county through the American Fact Finder feature on its home page. These reports list industries in the area, number of establishments, number of employees, annual payroll, and sales. Data comes from the most recent Economics Census (year ending in 2 or 7). Data on population trends, employment, incomes, and other demographics is available at the county level as well.

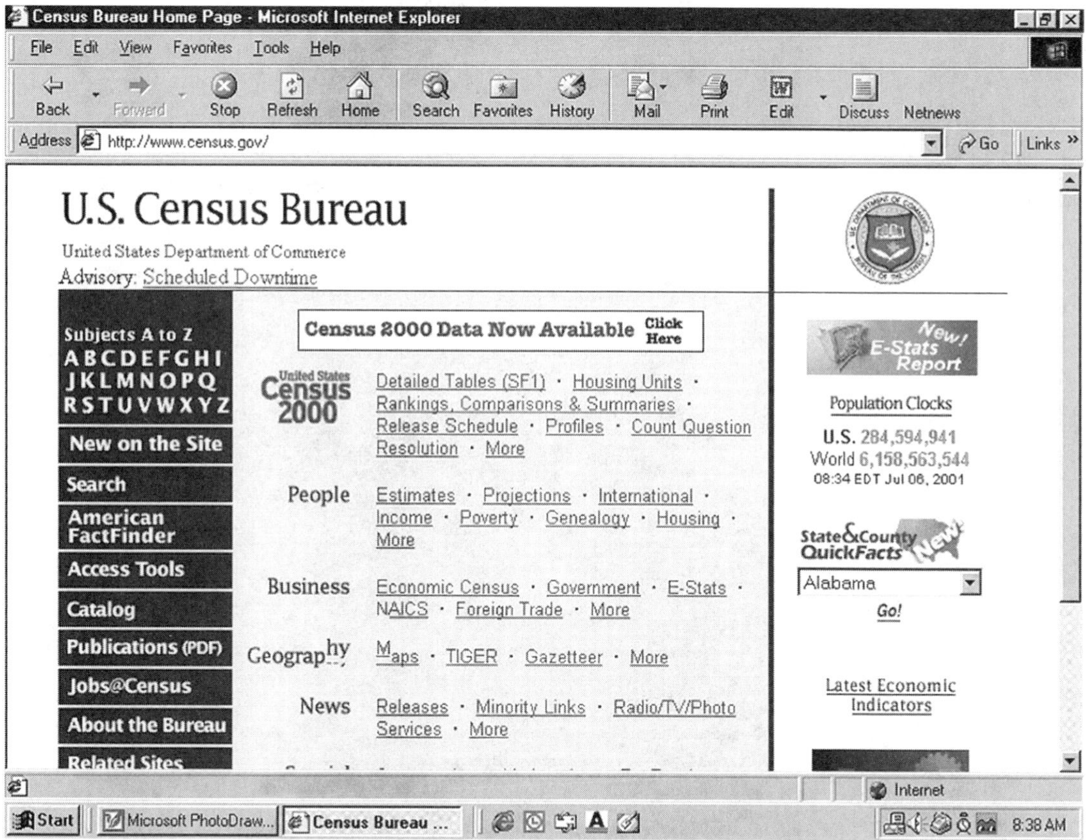

The Census Bureau operates the State Data Center (SDC) program, a cooperative effort between the states and the Census Bureau that was created in 1978 to make data available locally to the public through a network of state agencies, universities, libraries, and regional and local governments. More information about this program and access to links to each SDC are available on www.census.gov/sdc/www/. This Web page has a map of the United States, and one mouse click will bring the visitor to the state of interest. Many states have more than one data center.

Bureau of Economic Analysis (www.bea.gov). Regional accounts data is available at (www.bea.doc.gov/bea/regional/gsp/). In a series of easy-to-use dropdown menus, the user can select various components of gross state product (GSP), state or region, industry, or year and receive either an html-formatted table for viewing or printing, or a comma- and quote-delimited text file format for importing into either a spreadsheet or database application. The data consists of revised estimates of BEA's GSP for 1977–97 and new estimates for 1998, all of which were released in September 2000. The Web sites are updated as new data is released.

State and Local Government on the Net (www.piperinfo.com/state/index.cfm). This is a Piper Resources guide to government-sponsored Internet sites. State and local links are to servers that are controlled and managed by state or local governmental agencies. They *exclude* personal sites, neighborhood pages, political advocacy and campaign pages, promotion and travel sites, and Chamber of Commerce sites. Although the State and Local Government on the Net pages are updated frequently, they are not as up to date as the information contained on individual state and local government servers.

A list of states and other governmental links (www.piperinfo.com/state/index.cfm) is given together with the date when it was last updated. Double-clicking on a state, say Arizona, brings you to a page that gives all of the state agencies, regional commissions, departments, counties, and cities in the state that have Web sites.

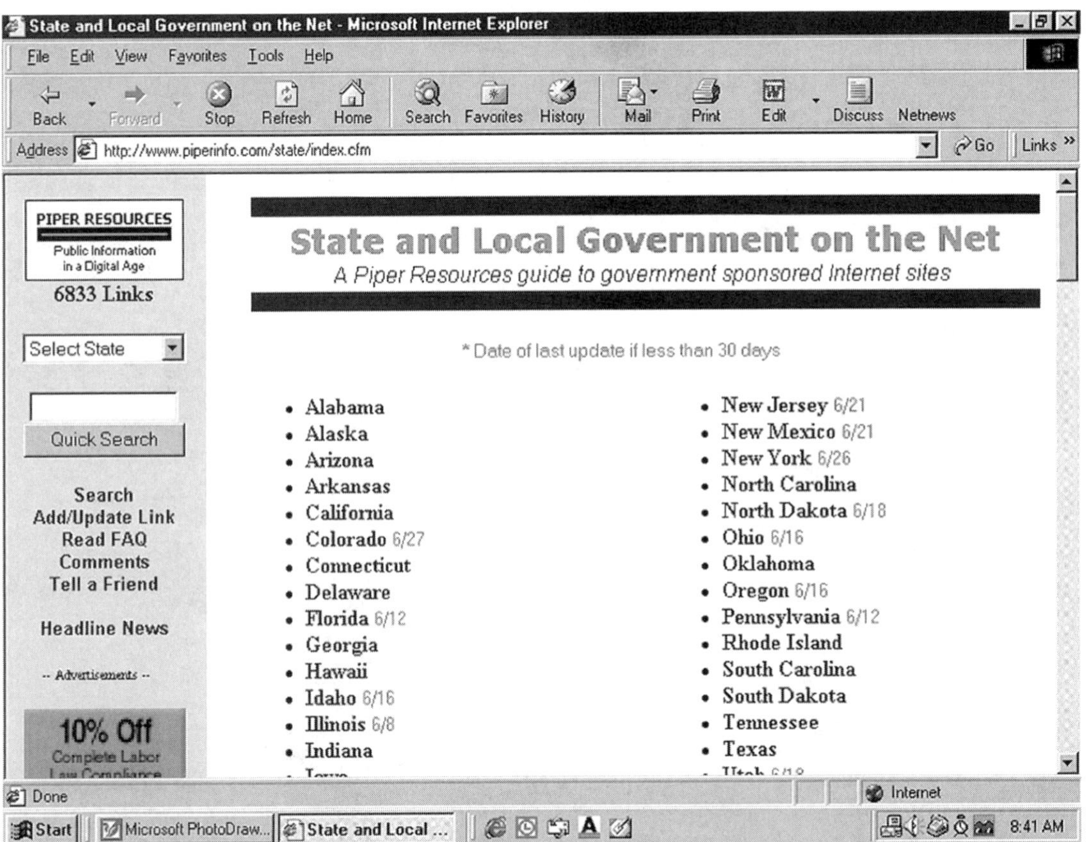

Source: State and Local Government on the Net, a service of Piper Resources.

State and Local Web Sites (www.state.xx.us or www.co.yyyyy.xx.us). Here "xx" is the two-letter state abbreviation, and "yyyyy" is the entire name of the county. So, for example, if you wanted to see the Beaver County, Pennsylvania, Web site, it would be www.co.beaver.pa.us. Piper Resources (see above) makes this easy.

FirstGov (www.firstgov.gov/state_gov/statistics.html). This page has a number of links to various providers of state and local information. Some of these are *American Fact Finder* (www.factfinder.census.gov) from the Census Bureau, *Community 2020* (Department of Housing and Urban Development), *Demographic and Economic Profiles by State and County,* State Exports to Countries and Regions (Department of Commerce), and *State of the Cities* (Department of Housing & Urban Development).

Most of these Web sites provide information on GSP, industry, population trends, income, employment, and other demographic data, geographic information, and the like. Some include broad industry information as well.

Market Data (Stocks and Bonds). There may be times when the value of a market index at some date a few years ago is needed, or you would like to include a discussion of stock market trends in your report. Rather than save all of your old editions of *The Wall Street Journal*, you can get this information online.

Dow Jones Averages (www.indexes.dowjones.com). Historical data on each of the Dow Jones indexes is available for free on this Web site, but one at a time and one date at a time. You can also get the components of each average on any date you select.

S&P500 (www.yahoo.com). The S&P 500 index is not the only market index that can be retrieved from this site. Under the heading "Finance" are links to pages with market indexes (up-to-the-minute as well as historical), individual company stock quotes, mutual fund data, news, interest rates, and much more.

Nasdaq Web Site (www.nasdaq.com). This Web site has data on every stock that trades in the "over-the-counter" market and is listed in the National Association of Securities Dealers Automated Quote (Nasdaq) system. Essentially, these are all of the publicly traded stocks that are not listed on the New York or the American Stock Exchange. Available on the Web site are historical quotes for stocks and mutual funds and dividend information, as well as information about stock splits and the like. Daily, weekly, monthly, and quarterly results are available. There are links to news headlines, global markets, economic releases, and more. The information is all free.

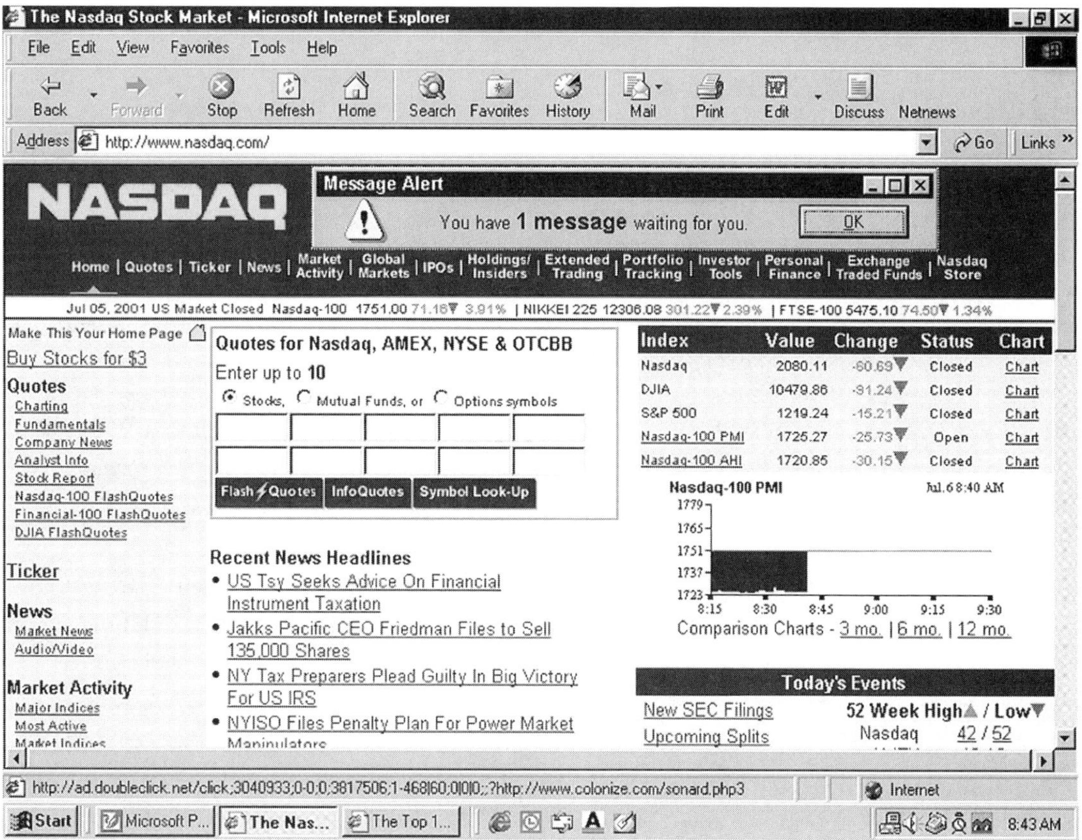

Other Sites. Current and historic stock price information can be obtained from www.bigcharts.com or from www.justquotes.com. There are others as well, but this should at least get you going in the right direction.

International Data. Many of the Web sites I mentioned earlier include international information, as well as U.S. information. Directories such as Yahoo! and CompuServe have global information. The Federal Reserve Board's Web site includes links to foreign central banks, which may have data on conditions in the countries in which they are located.

International Trade Administration (www.ita.com). This site helps U.S. businesses participate fully in the growing global marketplace. The Web site is not as user friendly as other federal Web sites, but with some persistence, trade data can be found. There are links to foreign government Web sites, but most of these are not offered in English.

Organization for Economic Cooperation and Development (OECD) (www.oecd.org). This Web site has economic surveys for all member countries and some non-member countries. Free summaries are available at www.oecd.org/eco/surv/esu.htm in PDF and can be opened with Adobe Acrobat Reader.[3]

Central Intelligence Agency (www.cia.gov/cia/publications/factbook/). *The World Factbook* is produced by the CIA and gives information on every country on the planet. Topics include geography, the people, government, economy, communications, transportation, military, and transnational issues. Some of the information might be a year or two old, but it will give a good overview of the country. *The World Factbook 2000* is available for downloading on the above Web site. It is also available in print.

Countries' Embassies. Every country that has an embassy in the United States has a Web site, and these Web sites have a wealth of good information about the country and, quite often, data on trade with the United States. You can find these using a search engine such as Google. More about search engines later.

Other Information

Industry and Company

Trade Association Web Sites. As mentioned, broad industry data is available from the Census Bureau and the Bureau of Economic Analysis. Additional broad data may be available in the "Beige Book" of the Federal Reserve Board. More specific industry data is available through newspapers, magazines, trade publications, and the like. Almost every human endeavor seems to have a trade organization devoted to it. Many of these are listed in *Gale's Encyclopedia of Associations*.[4] The listing gives addresses, phone numbers, contact information, number of staff, publications, and other information, including a Web site if there is one. Often, a Web site exists even if it is not listed in *Gale's*. Once a Web site is found, you can see what type of information is available through the organization. Sometimes the information is free; often there is a charge for a back issue of a publication or a survey.

Associations on the Net (www.ipl.org/ref/AON/). This site lists associations in the same subject areas listed above except Reference and Associations. This is a feature of the Internet Public Library (www.ipl.org). Under Business & Economics, the subheadings are:

---

[3] Acrobat Reader is a product of Adobe and is available for free on many Web sites. It is easily and quickly downloaded, and once it is on your computer you can forget it's there. But it is essential for opening and reading PDF files.

[4] Available at most public libraries. *Gale's* listings can be found online, but there is a fee for this service.

Accounting	Industry
Banking	Insurance
Business Administration & Management	International Business
Business Directories	Labor & Workplace
Commerce & Trade	Marketing & Advertising
Consumer Issues & Services	Non-Profit Organizations
E-Commerce	Real Estate
Economics	Statistics
Employment	Tax
Finance	Business & Economic News

Under the subheading of Industry are association links in the following industries:

Business and Personal Services	Publishing & Media
Construction	Resource Development
Hotels and Lodging	Retail Trade
Manufacturing	Utilities
Public & Investor Relations	Other Industries

Under each subheading are a large number of links to different industry associations' Web sites. A few mouse clicks should provide you with a great deal of information. The Internet Public Library is a free site.

The Dismal Scientist (www.dismal.com). Articles and analyses are featured on a variety of industries. The Web site includes archives devoted to almost two dozen general topics. Recent articles are on www.dismal.com/thoughts, and archives are on www.dismal.com/thoughts/archive. This Web site is part of Economy.com.

Research@Economy.com. This is a subscription service offering comprehensive industry reports on a variety of industries. Reports include industry conditions, drivers, macro drivers, profitability, long-term outlook, and upside and downside risks. Each report is for a separate industry. A single report costs $200 and a subscription (one report with two updates) costs $500. This Web site is part of Economy.com (www.economy.com).

Encyclopedia Britannica (www.britannica.com). This is the online version of the encyclopedia. There is information on a large variety of subjects, but much of it may require updating if the valuation date is fairly recent. The information is easily located and is free.

Dialog Corporation (www.dialog.com). This resource is a leading provider of Internet-based information. It was acquired by Thomson Corp. when it bought Knight-Ridder. Everything is being bought by Thomson. Products include *Profound, DataStar, DialogWeb*, and others.

Profound gives the subscriber access to over 94,000 research reports, 480,000 analyst reports, economic analyses on 192 countries, financial reports from over 4.5 million companies, breaking news from 27 global newswires, and a news archive that dates back to the 1980s with over 5,000 publications translated from 17 languages. Needless to say, such a service is not free. Subscriptions range from $300 per month to $800 per month, depending on the number of user licenses requested. The minimum is five user licenses. Each news article costs about $3 to $4, depending on the publisher. Market research is priced on a per-line basis and runs about $0.25 to $2.00 per line, depending on who the publisher of the report is. There is a separate *Newsline* product for full text articles, if market research reports are not required.

DialogWeb (www.dialogweb.com) is a search tool that provides access to thousands of authoritative business, scientific, intellectual-property, and technical publications. Among the wealth of information available is worldwide company and industry information, including trends, overviews, market research, and more. Full financial information is available at the company level.

CompuServe (www.compuserve.com). This site provides access to databases managed by ABI/INFORM, *Business & Industry*, *Journal of Commerce*, Knight-Ridder/Tribune Business News, McGraw-Hill Publications, News Product Announcements, PROMT, Newsletter Database, and Trade & Industry Database Full-text. A search can be done by company, record, or publication date. Fees vary depending on the extent of the search. In general, there are three fees associated with each search of these databases: first, for the initial search and display of a group of headings (usually five); second, for each additional group of headings that you wish to view; and third, for each full record that you wish to view. The initial and subsequent searches of many databases are free, with a charge incurred only for viewing a full record. All of the Dun & Bradstreet as well as many foreign databases carry the first two charges. A list of the databases and fees is available on www.iq.telebase.com/cgi-bin/scribe.cgi/pricing.htm.

Access to Newspapers. Many local and regional newspapers publish articles on conditions in an area's economy. Every major city's daily newspaper and many small regional papers now have an Internet site. If the Web address is unknown, here are several Web sites that have links to many publications.

Newspapers.Com (www.newspapers.com). This site offers links to tens of thousands of interesting and useful sites, including newspapers within the United States, international newspapers by country, college newspapers, and business publications. For U.S. newspapers, you can enter the state and get links to all of the newspapers and periodicals published in that state. These cover such a variety of topics that it is difficult to describe them all. I entered New Jersey and got hundreds of links to such publications as *Advanced Coatings & Surface Technology*, *Burlington County Times*, *Bartender Magazine*, *Casino Player*, and *Catholic Advocate*, and I hadn't finished with the C's yet. Included on a separate page are links to the top 10 newspapers published in the United States (www.newspapers.com/top10.html). This site is another one of those freebies.

AJR NewsLink (www.ajrnewslink.org). This site is produced by the American Journalism Review and claims to have the most links to local news sites in the United States by type. There are major metropolitan newspapers, business newspapers, specialty newspapers, and radio and television stations. The publication Web sites that you find may or may not have an archive feature for older articles, and they may or may not charge a retrieval fee for articles. But you can retrieve current news articles from most of them.

The Internet Public Library (www.ipl.org). This site has a comprehensive listing of newspapers that have Web sites located in Africa, Asia, Central America, the Caribbean, Europe, the Middle East, North and South America, the South Pacific, and the United States (by state) at www.ipl.org/reading/news/. One can also browse by title. The Internet Public Library is a public service organization and learning/teaching environment at the University of Michigan School of Information. Their mission is to provide library services to Internet users.

A Reference Center is included at www.ipl.org/ref/ that includes links to Sciences & Technology, Reference, Education, Arts & Humanities, Health & Medical Sciences, Law, Government & Political Science, Computers & Internet, Business & Economics, Social Sciences, Entertainment & Leisure, and Associations.

Dow Jones Interactive (www.nrstg2p.djnr.com/cgi-bin/DJInteractive). This Web site has a Publications Library that gives access to 6,000 newswires, newspapers, magazines, and trade journals. Full text articles are available on a huge assortment of topics. There is a full archive, and articles can be found that date back several years. In fact, when I got back as far as 1975, I gave up looking. That's far enough back in time for me!

After the annual user fee (about $69), full text only articles cost $2.95 each. Articles from *The Wall Street Journal* that contain graphics cost only $2.95 each. However, for other articles with text and graphics, there is an additional charge of $2.00 per article. For article images in PDF format, there is an additional charge of $4.00 per article. There is no charge to search. Each article found includes a headline and lead sentence. The charges begin only when an article is viewed. Once viewed, there is a charge, so you might as well print it out. There is no additional charge to print. One nice thing about this service is that the number of words in each article is given, so you might be able to tell from its length if it is just a summary of an event or an in-depth report.

The articles are on a variety of subjects. Often, even a small privately held company may issue press releases or be mentioned in a story, so it never hurts to enter the name of the small company. There are many articles about a wide variety of industries, places, economics, and more.

Dow Jones Interactive also offers the *Historical Market Data Center*, where you can retrieve histories on securities, dividends, and exchange rates. If you need to know the price of Microsoft stock on a given date, you can get it easily on this part of the Web site. The price is $0.25 for each quote for domestic securities and $0.50 per price for all international securities. So, if your report covered 22 business days worth of quotes, the full price would be $0.25 times 22, or $5.50.

InSite (www.iac-insite.com). A very easy way to do business research, Business InSite features an array of more than 1,000 trade and industry publications, regional business journals, management journals, newswires, and business magazines. Derived from Gale Group's widely used online database, Trade & Industry Database, Business InSite provides coverage of over 65 industries and can help you identify trends, developments, and activities that influence an industry. Company InSite offers key facts about 110,000 U.S. and 30,000 non-U.S. companies and provides links to articles about the companies and other related information.

This service is particularly powerful in the way all of the articles and other information are linked together. A listing in the Company Directory will be linked to industry information by SIC code. Articles are further linked according to subject matter, so that a search can be very easily refined with a click of the mouse. The price of the subscription depends on usage. For example, an average of 250 articles accessed per month will cost $600 monthly. If usage increases, the cost will increase. All databases are available with a subscription.

Search Engines. When I was a kid, I used to play with fire engines. Now that I am a grown-up kid, I play with search engines. Still a kid, but different toys! There is a difference between an Internet site that is strictly a search engine (like Google) and a search tool that is also a directory (like Yahoo!). Both have their uses and appeal. For example, when you use a search engine, all that is necessary is for you to enter a few wisely chosen keywords. A directory offers you many choices of things to click on, as well as an opportunity to enter some well-chosen keywords. Although there are many of these kinds of sites on the Internet, we only have space to name a few.

Not all search tools are created equal. We tried a few and entered the keywords Gross Domestic Product, and got quite a variety of results.

Google (www.google.com). Google returned 543,000 hits in 0.13 seconds and displayed them 10 at a time. The top 5 hits were BEA (link to tables), BEA (national accounts data), St. Louis Fed, USA Today, and OECD.

Yahoo! (www.yahoo.com). Yahoo! returned 256,000 matches and displayed them 20 at a time. The top 5 hits were BEA, St. Louis Fed, OECD, USA Today, and NASA (yep, the space people).

AllTheWeb (www.alltheweb.com). This engine returned 223,740 hits in 0.514 seconds and displayed them 10 at a time. The top 5 were BEA, masonc.home.netcom, gherrity.org, quantideas.com, and aptech resources.

CompuServe (www.compuserve.com). This engine returned 49,661 hits and displayed them 10 at a time. The top 5 were St. Louis Fed, BEA, cftech,[5] USA Today, and Statistik.

About.Com (www.about.com). This returned 47,784 hits and displayed them 10 at a time. The top 5 hits were St. Louis Fed, BEA, USA Today, cftech, and NASA.

AltaVista (www.altavista.com). This resource returned 19,528 hits and displayed them 10 at a time. The top 5 were separate pages in the Iowa State University's economics department database of state economic information links.

Ask Jeeves (www.ask.com). This site displayed hits 10 at a time. It did not say how many it found. The top 5 hits were Boston Fed, Dismal Scientist, St. Louis Fed, cftech, and the Georgia (Russia) parliament.

The point of the exercise was to highlight that using different search tools will give different results, and not all of the results will be optimal. My particular favorites are Google, because it is easy and returns the most pertinent results; Yahoo!, because it gives good results, especially on business-related topics (that is, it is less consumer oriented than other directories); and Ask Jeeves (although it did not appear to perform well in the GDP exercise, requests can be entered in the form of questions, and most of the time, results are on the money).

One can also search the Net using meta search engines such as Mamma.com (mother of all search engines) and Dogpile.com (all results, no mess). These engines search other search engines and return the most relevant site on each search engine they look at.

Additional Industry Data Sources. Investext (now owned by Thomson Financial—surprise, surprise) is a database of brokerage research reports available online via its *Research Bank Web* product on www.tfsd.com. Wilson Business Abstracts, available at www.hwwilson.com as well as in print or on CD-ROM, indexes trade periodicals.

Industry statistics compiled by the federal government are available in print through numerous U.S. Department of Commerce and Census Bureau publications, such as *Business Conditions Digest*. Trade and industry magazines are listed in the standard *Rate and Data Service Directory*. Other print sources that track industry statistics include *Moody's Industry Review, Value Line Investment Survey*, and *Predicast's Basebook*.

Industry Ratio and Compensation Data Sources. Salary Assessor and the Executive Compensation Assessor, two products produced by the Economic Research Institute, contain salary information for more than 3,000 jobs compiled from salary surveys. The information is available online at www.erieri.com. The cost for an annual subscription to these products is $2,845 (Ouch!). This price includes other products that come with the package.

Compensation surveys are frequently done by industry trade groups, either in conjunction with an industry survey or as a stand-alone study. Often a hint of the study will be given on the trade association's Web site. Most of the studies are available to nonmembers for a fee, so it is worth it to check the Web site and perhaps call the association's headquarters to ask.

Integra Information, Inc. offers a terrific online product called *Business Profiler,* which provides detailed information on profiling small businesses and private companies. This resource covers more than 3.5 million firms in more than 950 U.S. industries. It is capable of analyzing any size firm or one of 14 industry size ranges. See Chapter 5 for more details about this product. It is one of my favorites.

Integra gets its information from 31 databases, which makes this product one of the most extensive of its kind. Integra will sell you individual reports by SIC code on their Web site at www.integrainfo.com. This is too good to be ignored! (And no, I do not own the company!)

[5]Cftech came up often enough to be explained. It stands for "Cool Fire Technology," and a set of pages known as the "Brain Bank" gives links to a lot of information, some of which might be worthwhile. They also offer a customized news delivery service.

Finding Publicly Traded Guideline Companies

As will be explained in Chapter 6, the guideline company method of developing an opinion of value involves finding publicly traded companies that are comparable to the one being appraised. Perhaps the easiest way to do this is to find a database that is searchable by SIC code. This section provides some reference sources that might help in your search.

Perhaps the two oldest sources of information on publicly traded companies are Moody's Investors Services and Standard and Poor's (S&P). Moody's offers credit opinions, research, and credit ratings on debt securities and their issuers. S&P is more equity oriented. A search of Moody's Web site did not reveal a database product.

S&P has a product called Compustat that contains data on thousands of active and inactive publicly traded companies, including 20-year historical data if available. This database, together with S&P's Xpressfeed service, delivers a wealth of information to your computer—for a fee, of course.

S&P offers corporate profiles on its Web site (www.standardandpoors.com). Searches are done either by company name or by ticker symbol and produce a two-page report on the condition of the company.

Dialogweb, owned by Thomson Corp., combines the business databases of Dun & Bradstreet, S&P, Frost & Sullivan, Find/SVP, and SEC filings to produce a prodigious amount of information. It is searchable by SIC code, and, among other things, searches can be done for top companies in an industry and for mergers and acquisitions in an industry. Prices vary according to the databases searched and are available on the Web site (www.dialogweb.com).

Disclosure is also owned by Thomson Corp.; it is a database of over 12,000 public U.S. companies, 13,000 global companies, SEC filings, and more. It is searchable by company name or ticker symbol for up-to-date reports on individual companies. SEC filings, annual reports, and financial information are among the things that are available. More information is available on www.disclosure-investor.com.

Nasdaq's Web site (www.nasdaq.com) makes information on publicly traded companies available for free. If a publicly traded company in the industry you are studying is known, it can be entered on the Nasdaq home page to obtain a quote. Below the quotes are links to additional information. One link is called "Fundamentals." By clicking on "Fundamentals" you will find additional information and other links, one of which is called "View Competition." Clicking on "View Competition" will reveal a list of other publicly traded companies in the same industry as the one originally entered. The search cannot be done by SIC code and must begin with a known company. This may not work well in all situations, but it is an overlooked source of a lot of free information about companies in a given industry.

Additional Data Sources. Media General Plus, which is available on Dialog, provides detailed financial and stock price information on companies listed on the New York Stock Exchange, the American Stock Exchange, and Nasdaq. Using Dialog and Media General Plus, you can find companies and industry groups and generate detailed income statements, balance sheets, and reports, consisting of price history, ratios, and comparative industry data. The ability to create customized reports makes this product particularly attractive. For more information, see www.dialogweb.com.

CompuServe (www.compuserve.com) has searchable databases using company name, keywords, ticker symbols, or SIC codes as look-ups. A search by SIC code will reveal records that can be purchased for $20 apiece.

Hoover's Company Database, available at www.hoovers.com, contains a great deal of good information about publicly traded companies as well as industries. Most of it is available through a subscription, but a free search can be done for companies by industry type. The search will produce Company Capsules, Financials, and Company Profiles for each company in the industry. The first two reports are free; the profiles are available to subscribers. Searches by SIC code are also available to subscribers. These searches can turn up both publicly traded and privately held companies.

The most economical method of creating a guideline company group uses the databases available through Nasdaq or Hoover's. Another site with a lot of free information is www.zacks.com/free.html, the free research page of Zack's Investment Research. A company search can be done by industry type, revealing analysts' reports on companies within the industry group. Each report is priced individually, and they range from about $10 each on up. You can choose which ones you want, adding them to a shopping cart as you would at any online store. Earnings estimates are available in most cases for free. At the other end of the pricing spectrum is Standard & Poor's CompuStat product, which contains 20 years of annual financial data on approximately 9,000 companies.

Publicly Traded Guideline Companies—Financial Statement Information

All of the sources listed in the section "Finding Publicly Traded Guideline Companies" also contain financial statement information on public companies. When evaluating sources of financial statement data, be aware that some sources present data "as reported" in the original SEC filings, while others recast the financial statement data into their own customized formats. Recast data is easier to download and manipulate but is more likely to contain errors.

EDGAR. The Electronic Data Gathering Analysis and Retrieval (EDGAR) database allows appraisers to access information that used to cost the client quite a bit of money. Because we were usually in a rush, appraisers had to rely on companies such as Disclosure to provide us with copies of various documents filed with the Securities and Exchange Commission for public companies. Now, this information can be accessed from your computer. EDGAR can be accessed free via the Internet at www.freeedgar.com or online with charges through Global Securities Information, Inc. FreeEDGAR is not altogether free any more. Filings can be viewed and printed out; however, RTF (Rich Text File) formatted versions of filings are no longer downloadable for free. A subscription is available, starting at $9.95 a month, giving users access to a variety of services. Group subscriptions are available. For more information go to www.edgar-online.com.

Publicly traded companies are required to submit filings to the Securities and Exchange Commission electronically through the EDGAR system. All U.S. companies were required to file electronically by 1996. Unfortunately, not every filing is available for every company, and there are no historical filings available. A number of data providers are now offering EDGAR products. EDGAR filings are available for free from www.disclosure-investor.com.

Dialog Select on www.dialog.com contains 10-K information. Several of the databases mentioned here contain earnings estimates. I/B/E/S (recently acquired by Thomson Corp. when it acquired Disclosure, Inc.) earnings estimates are available electronically on its Web site, www.ibes.com, for a cost.

A print version of I/B/E/S is available. Other print sources include the *Standard & Poor's Earnings Guide*, which contains consensus earnings estimates on more than 4,300 stocks. The *Value Line Investment Survey*, mentioned previously, includes at least two years of projected financial statement data for most companies. *Zack's Earnings Forecaster*, *Bloomberg Financial Markets* (Merrill Lynch), and *Nelson's Earnings Outlook* are other print sources. Analysts' reports are available from the major brokerage houses and contain earnings estimates, buy/sell recommendations, and sometimes forecast financial information. *Nelson's Directory of Investment Research* lists the names of analysts and the industries they follow. Some public companies make analysts' reports available to prospective investors.

Publicly Traded Guidelines Companies—Stock Quotes

Since part of the pricing multiples that you may want to use include the prices of the publicly traded guideline companies, I thought that it might also be a good idea to give you some sources for gathering pricing information. Historical and current stock prices for any publicly traded company are available on the Web sites of the New York Stock Exchange and the Nasdaq (which includes the American Stock Exchange prices), as well as on Yahoo! All of these sources are free, so there is no reason ever to pay for this information.

Tradeline. If you insist on paying for something you can get for free, this database is available at www.tradeline.com. Tradeline includes current and historical security pricing for over 145,000 U.S. and Canadian securities, 30,000 international securities, and 1,600 market indexes. It also contains exchange rate, dividend, capitalization, and descriptive information about the companies. This is not a free service. For information about products and prices, visit the Web site mentioned above.

Finding Acquired or Merged Guideline Companies

There is no limit to the amount of information that can be retrieved if you know where to find it. The scary part about what we do for a living is not knowing what is out there.

Securities Data Company. This company offers information about the mergers and acquisitions (M&A) of public and private companies. Even if you do not subscribe directly to this database, you can contact Securities Data Company and they will do the search for you. The search is free, but they charge a minimum of $300 for reports that you get from them.

The Securities Data Company database provides information on a wide array of topics spanning eight major categories: worldwide corporate new issues, municipal new issues, worldwide M&A, joint ventures/strategic alliances, restructurings, corporate governance, venture capital financing, and trading information. The M&A section of this service is a comprehensive listing of deals and deal information and is searchable by SIC code. Over 600 data items are available for more than 100,000 transactions. Though the database does contain some information on private company transactions, pricing data is rarely available. With an Internet connection and the SDC Platinum (IFR Platinum for European companies) software, you can access their databases, perform searches, view results, and create presentation-ready reports. For more information, visit www.tfsd.com.

BizComps. This database is available on disk using the Wiley-ValuSource computer program or as a stand-alone version. The database is updated annually. Compiled by Jack R. Sanders, BizComps contains information on over 5,000 small business sales. Deals are sorted by industry and contain revenue and cash flow multiples. BizComps studies are also available covering various regions of the United States, and, in addition, there is a National Industrial edition containing data only on Manufacturing, Wholesale/Distribution, and Business to Business Service Businesses. Many appraisers who are familiar with the print editions of BizComps will want to check out this electronic version.

Cost of Capital and Betas

Information about cost of capital and betas, topics to be discussed in Chapter 10, is available from ValueScreen Software, sold by Value Line Publishing, Inc. This product contains market data, projections, earnings estimates, and summary financial data for approximately 1,800 public companies. One can use Value Line projections to produce an estimate of expected returns on the market.[6]

Additional data sources include Standard & Poor's CompuStat CD, which is perhaps the best source for betas. *Standard & Poor's Stock Reports*, available in print and on CD-ROM, contains descriptive and summary financial information on hundreds of publicly traded companies as well as on betas. For more information, see www.standardandpoors.com.

Betas for individual companies are available free on the Nasdaq Web site. These betas use the S&P 500 as the underlying index to calculate performance of the market.

I think that I have given you enough to get started. By now, you probably wish you were finished. The sources of information listed in this chapter are some of my favorites. Surely once you log on to the Internet and begin clicking around on things, you will find many of your own favorite sources. Be wary, though. A person can easily get lost in his or her Internet research. It has a way of drawing you in. Good luck and happy clicking!

[6]See David King, "The Equity Risk Premium for Cost of Capital Studies: Alternatives to Ibbotson," *Business Valuation Review* (September 1994), 123–129.

The On-Site Interview

An important part of the data-gathering phase of the appraisal engagement is the on-site interview. It is generally a good idea to see what you are appraising. Interviewing management at the company's facility has several advantages. First, seeing the physical layout of the facility can help you understand such items as the capacity of the plant and the working environment (is the place busy or can you take a nap there?). Management will also feel more comfortable in their own environment. Being at the business location will also make it easier for the appraiser to obtain trade journals and other information that he or she may not have been supplied with yet.

The person or persons whom you choose to interview will vary from job to job, but in general, the following interviewees should be considered:

- Your client
- The company's officers and management
- The company's accountant
- The company's attorney
- The company's banker

The questions that should be raised at the interview(s) will cover such topics as operations, financial performance, the depth of management, competition, the history of the company, personnel, suppliers, customers, marketing, legal issues, and capital requirements. In addition, don't forget to ask your client for any trade journal articles that he or she may be aware of on how to value the client's business. If you don't find it yourself, you may be confronted by your client afterward for not using a particular methodology. Exhibit 4.4 contains a monograph published by The Institute of Business Appraisers, Inc., titled "Questions to Ask When Appraising a Business."

EXHIBIT 4.4
Questions to Ask When Appraising a Business

The answers to the following questions should give the appraiser a good base of information about the business he has been asked to appraise.

Not all of these questions will apply to all businesses, nor to all situations. However, many of them will apply in a given situation, and even those that do not apply directly may suggest other information that the appraiser may wish to obtain.

No list of questions about a business can be exhaustive. However, the following questions cover many of the most important aspects of a business that should be scrutinized when the business is to be appraised.

About the Form of Organization of the Business

Is the business a sole proprietorship, partnership, or corporation?

If a partnership:

- How many partners, and who are they?
- Are they all in favor of selling?
- If not, is this likely to be a serious problem?

If a corporation:

- How many stockholders are there?
- Who are the major stockholders, and what percentage of the total outstanding shares does each of them own?
- Are all of the stockholders in favor of selling?

EXHIBIT 4.4 *(Continued)*

- If not, what percentage of the total outstanding shares is represented by those stockholders who are in favor of selling?
- Are the stockholders who are not in favor of selling likely to be a serious problem?
- Is the stock traded on a market?
- What market?
- What are recent prices for shares traded?

About the Products/Services of the Business

- What are the principal products/services?
- For what length of time has each been sold?
- What has been the sales volume of each, for each of the past five years?
- What are the (a) costs and (b) gross profits for each of these products/services?
- What portion of the total cost is for materials?
- What portion is for labor?
- What portion is for overhead?
- Which of the products/services are proprietary?
- Which products are purchased from others, for resale?
- What is the nature of the agreement(s) with the supplier(s) of these products?
- What features of the business' products/services distinguish them from competition?
- What product/service warranties are given to customers?
- What is the forecast of future sales and profits for each major product/service?
- How do quality and price compare with similar products/services offered by competitors?
- To what extent does the business rely on the services of outside vendors or subcontractors?
- Who are the principal vendors/subcontractors?
- What other products/services could be produced/furnished with the existing facilities?

About Markets and Marketing

- What are the principal applications for each major product/service?
- What are the principal markets for each major product/service?
- To what extent are these markets already established, and to what extent must they still be developed?
- What is the future outlook for growth, or lack of growth, of each of these markets?
- Who are the principal customers?
- What portion of the total sales volume does each of these customers represent?
- Which major potential customers have not yet been secured as actual customers?
- How do sales break down geographically?
- What is the present backlog for each major product/service?
- How has this backlog varied over the past three years?
- Who are the principal competitors?
- What are the relative strengths and weaknesses of each of these competitors?
- What is the estimated sales volume of each of these competitors?
- What is this business's relative position among its competitors with regard to sales volume?

(Continued)

EXHIBIT 4.4 *(Continued)*

- What is its relative position among its competitors with regard to reputation?
- Has the business's past sales growth generally followed the industry trend, or has it been ahead of or behind this trend?
- What is the forecast of future *industry-wide* sales for each of the business's products/services?
- What is the forecast of *this* business's future sales for each major product/service?
- Does the business regularly use the services of any advertising and/or public relations firms?
- Who are they?
- Is the marketing aggressive and skillful?
- Who is responsible for market research?
- Who is responsible for advertising and sales promotion?
- Who is responsible for product applications?
- Who is responsible for exploiting new markets?
- What is the nature of the direct selling organization (supervision, personnel, field offices, salary, and other compensation)?
- What is the nature of the distributor and/or sales representative organization (list of distributors/sales representatives, exclusive or non-exclusive nature of agreements, expiration dates of individual appointments, past performance of each distributor/representative, commission and/or discount rates, contract terms)?
- What is the nature of the service organization (who is responsible for service, installation, maintenance, etc.)?
- Are there any foreign operations?
- Details?
- Does the business use the services of any outside consultants for market research or similar activities?
- Who are they?
- What is their past record of accomplishment?
- How are they compensated?
- Are any of them under contract?

About the Financial Situation of the Business

- What is the sales and earnings record of the business for each of the past five years?
- What salaries/dividends have been paid to owners/stockholders during each of the past five years?
- Are income/expense statements available for each of the past five years?
- Is a current balance sheet available?
- What are the details of the accounts receivable (from whom receivable, amounts, age, etc.)?
- What about inventory?
- What is normal inventory level?
- What is the actual inventory at present?
- How does this inventory break down among raw material, work in process, and finished goods?
- What is the condition (new, obsolete, damaged, etc.) of the existing inventory?
- Is any portion of the inventory on consignment?
- What portion?
- Consigned to whom?
- For how long?
- On what terms?
- What are the details of the accounts payable (to whom payable, amounts, age, any special circumstances, etc.)?

EXHIBIT 4.4 *(Continued)*

- What loans are outstanding, to whom are they payable, and what are the terms of each loan (interest rate, payment schedule, collateral, etc.)?
- What is the amount of accrued expenses payable?
- What items does this include?
- Are all federal and state taxes (including employee withholding taxes) current?
- What is the present book value (net worth; invested capital plus retained earnings) of the business?
- What is the amount of available working capital?
- What is the business's depreciation policy for fixed assets?
- What overhead (burden) rates are used in determining costs?
- What are the various departmental budgets?
- What is the advertising and sales promotion budget?
- What is the total payroll?
- Does the business own equity in any other businesses?
- What liabilities, contingent or otherwise, exist in connection with product/service warranties?
- Are there any existing claims and/or known contingent liabilities of any nature whatsoever?
- Details?
- Are there any contract disputes or renegotiations pending?
- Are there any outstanding stock options, convertible notes, or the like?
- Is there an existing forecast of future sales, profits, and capital requirements?
- What does this forecast show?

About the Physical Facilities

- Is a complete list of physical facilities and equipment available?
- Is the real estate owned or leased?
- If owned, what is the appraised value?
- When was this appraisal made?
- By whom?
- If leased, what are the terms of the lease (period, rental, security deposit, restrictions on use of premises, renewal options, etc.)?
- What are the zoning restrictions?
- Are any of the other physical facilities or equipment leased rather than owned?
- Details?
- Is there any excess or idle capacity?
- How much?

About Personnel and Organization

- Is a complete organization chart available?
- Are position descriptions available?
- What are the functions of key executives and personnel?
- What is the total personnel complement?
- Are there established rates of pay or pay ranges for the various jobs?
- How do these rates compare with those of other employers in the general area?

(Continued)

EXHIBIT 4.4 *(Continued)*

- What is the wage and salary review policy?
- What employee benefits exist (life insurance, hospitalization insurance, vacation, sick leave, pension, profit sharing, etc.)?
- Is the cost of these benefits paid entirely by the business, or do the employees contribute part of the cost?
- What part?
- Are the workers unionized?
- Which ones?
- What are the contract details?
- Have there ever been any unsuccessful attempts to organize the workers?
- Details?
- Have there ever been any strikes?
- Details?
- What has been the experience with respect to employee turnover?
- Are the employees given any formal training for theft jobs?
- Details?
- Is there a house organ, employee bulletin, or newsletter for employees?
- Details?
- Are written personnel policies and/or procedures available?
- What is the general situation in the area with regard to availability of labor?

About Management

- Is an organization chart available?
- What are the backgrounds of key members of management?
- What is the compensation of key members of management?
- Are any members of management (or any other employees) under contract to the business?
- Details?
- Will the sale of the business involve or require any substantial reorganization of management?
- How is it regarded by its banks(s) and by the financial community in general?
- How is it regarded by its employees?
- How is it regarded by the community in which it is located?
- Has the business or any of its principals ever been found guilty or ever entered a plea of no contest or been a party to a consent decree with regard to anti-trust laws, anticipation regulations, securities laws or regulations, or the like?
- Details?
- Has the business complied with applicable requirements of the Occupational Safety and Health Administration (OSHA) to the satisfaction of the cognizant OSHA office?
- What has been the past history of the business with regard to litigation?
- Is the business involved in any joint ventures or similar undertakings?
- Details?
- What are the business's major accomplishments?
- Where has the business failed to an appreciable degree?
- Which members of management can be expected to remain with the business following the sale?
- What are the management capabilities of the persons in charge of each of the key departments?

EXHIBIT 4.4 *(Continued)*

- How well is each of these departments staffed?
- How capable is the second echelon of management?
- Are there any strong differences of opinion among members of management?
- Details?
- Do separate departments cooperate willingly and effectively with each other, or are there cases where cooperation is grudging or non-existent?
- Is management progress-minded and willing to take reasonable risks?
- Who dominates the organization?
- If the business is a corporation, what control do major stockholders exercise over the company's policies and/or activities?
- Are there any proxy fights or attempts by outsiders to take over control of the company?

About the Business in General

- When was the business established?
- For how long has it been owned by the present owner(s)?
- Does success of the business depend to an unusual degree on the capabilities, performance, and/or contacts of one or more key persons?
- Details?
- What potentially dangerous situations exist, or might arise, in connection with the business's management, products, services, markets, finances, facilities, legal obligations, etc.?
- How is this business regarded by its customers?
- How is it regarded by its competitors?
- How is it regarded by its suppliers?
- How is it regarded by cognizant government agencies?
- How is it regarded by its bank(s) and by the financial community in general?
- How is it regarded by its employees?
- How is it regarded by the community in which it is located?
- Has the business or any of its principals ever been found guilty or ever entered a plea of no contest or been a party to a consent decree with regard to anti-trust laws, anti-discrimination regulations, securities laws or regulations, or the like?
- Details?
- Has the business complied with applicable requirements of the Occupational Safety and Health Administration (OSHA) to the satisfaction of the cognizant OSHA office?
- What has been the past history of the business with regard to litigation?
- Is the business involved in any joint ventures or similar undertakings?
- Details?
- What are the business's major accomplishments?
- Where has the business failed to an appreciable degree?

An appraiser will generally find that more information is gathered during the management interview than by reviewing the volumes of documents that are frequently gathered. Financial documents rarely tell the entire story. Management should be able to provide the appraiser with a good history of the company, an understanding of what made the company's financial results appear the way they do, and expectations about where the company is going. The history could even be written by the client. Sometimes, this information can be obtained by going to the company's Web site or by going through the company's brochures.

It's terrible to say, but frequently appraisers must take what their own clients tell them with a grain of salt. For example, if you have a client who is going through a divorce, you are most likely to get a story of doom and gloom. However, if that same client is looking to sell the business, the future always looks great. Do not lose sight of the purpose and function of the appraisal assignment when you conduct your interview.

Another practical consideration is whether the appraisal assignment is impaired if you do not get to speak to management. It is not uncommon in litigation assignments for the appraiser to be prevented from speaking to the company's management. Even if you are allowed to speak to them, they may not be as cooperative as you may like. What do you do then? We are all tempted to teach them a lesson, but it is unprofessional and highly unethical to make your point by becoming adversarial. You also may not want to hit them if they are bigger than you!

In the situation where you are prevented from getting information from management, you must determine if the missing information will prevent you from being able to give an unqualified opinion of value. One of your limiting conditions in the report will be something like this:

> This appraisal was conducted without the benefit of management's cooperation. We were not allowed to interview management. If we had been allowed to interview them, we might have discovered information that would have affected our opinion of value.

This is called, protect thyself! The last thing you want sprung on you are questions like "How come you didn't speak to management?" or "How come you did not know that the company was planning to file for bankruptcy?" or "Wouldn't your answer be different if you knew that 82 percent of the company's sales came from one customer?" Answers like "Of course it would" don't bode well before a judge or jury. Of course, they may laugh inside because they know that you are right.

In litigation engagements, the appraiser can and should request that a deposition of the management personnel be taken if they won't cooperate with you. You can provide your client's attorney with all of the questions that you want asked. Your questions should generally be as detailed as possible in order to get a full response. This is because the person being deposed, if prepared for the deposition, will give a lot of "Yes," "No," and "I don't remember" types of responses. The attorney asking the questions should be provided with an understanding of what you are trying to achieve. If permitted, you may even sit in the room while the deposition is taking place. Then if there are additional questions that must be asked to clarify some of the answers given, you can write them out and hand them to the attorney asking the questions.

Conclusion

Now that you have finished this chapter, you should have more of an idea about the data-gathering process. You should also be more familiar with many of the data sources that will be needed to do the appraisal. At this point, you should also be familiar with the on-site interview. If not, reread this chapter before going any further.

5

Data Analysis

Chapter Goals

In this chapter, I will attempt to explain what to do with all of the data that I told you to get in the previous chapter. This will include a discussion on how to use the data, as well as what it means. Therefore, in this chapter I will discuss the following:

1. Economic analysis
2. Industry analysis
3. Subject company analysis
4. Financial analysis
5. Financial statement adjustments

Introduction

Data analysis is an important component of the valuation process. Since assessment of risk is a goal of the appraiser, the analysis of the information collected must be performed with a view toward the future of the business. In general, we feel more comfortable using historical information for a valuation, but we have to remember that a "willing buyer" is not interested in buying history. As appraisers, it is our role to assess how much the future will resemble the past; only then can we determine the value of the business.

Economic Analysis

Revenue Ruling 59-60 tells us to consider "the economic outlook in general and the condition and outlook of the specific industry in particular." During the analysis of the economy, the appraiser attempts to determine the economic risks associated with the subject business. Questions regarding the demand for the company's goods or services and the sources of supply are frequently asked. The outlook for the general economic trends that might affect supply and demand for the company's goods and services should be thoroughly investigated. This analysis must be relevant to the appraisal subject, not just boilerplate. For example, if the appraisal subject is a construction company, economic factors such as interest rates, housing starts, and building permits may be important. How important might they be if the appraisal subject is a cardiovascular surgeon?

Another component of the economy that should be considered by the appraiser is where in the economic cycle the appraisal subject is at the date of the appraisal. If the economy is in a recession, it will make a big difference whether the recession is just starting or if it is about to end. Depending upon where the company is in the economic cycle, the short-term and long-term projections may be radically different. This would be important to the "willing" buyer, since he or she would have to ride out the balance of the cycle. Since valuation is a prophecy of the future, this is extremely important.

The economic analysis will be used in at least two sections of the appraisal assignment. The economic outlook will be helpful in forecasting the future performance of the subject company. The economic analysis will also help the appraiser in performing an analysis of the economic risk that the company is exposed to. This will be one of the many considerations in the determination of (1) the pricing multiples used in the market approach and (2) the discount or capitalization rates used in the income approach.

During the management interview, the appraiser will want to ask company representatives about how the economy impacts the business. Some businesses are cyclical with the economy, but others may be counter-cyclical; these businesses react opposite to the economy. An example of one such business is a tractor-trailer driving school. When the economy is strong, business is bad. When the economy is weak, business is good. Why? During a good economy, people are working and they are not necessarily looking to be retrained in a new field. During a bad economy, economic layoffs require people to find new employment. The issues for the appraiser to also consider about training schools are: Is available funding for the students (if they are unemployed, they may not want to or may not be able to spend $2,000+ for education), and after the students complete the course, will the economy turn around so that drivers will be needed? Exhibit 5.1 gives you an illustration of a sample economic section from a real report.

EXHIBIT 5.1
Economy Section

Generally, business performance varies in relation to the economy. Just as a strong economy can improve overall business performance and value, a declining economy can have the opposite effect. Businesses can be affected by global, national, and local events. Changes in regulatory environments, political climate, and market and competitive forces can also have a significant impact on business. For these reasons, it is important to analyze and understand the prevailing economic environment when valuing a closely held business. Since the appraisal process is a "prophecy of the future," it is imperative that the appraiser review the economic outlook as it would impact the appraisal subject.

The U.S. economy remained strong in the first half of 1999, although there was some deceleration in growth from 4.8 percent in the first quarter to 1.8 percent in the second period.[1] The data presented in Table 1 shows the trend in several economic indicators annually since 1995, together with performance in the first two quarters of 1999. Note the departure from the trend in the first quarter of 1999 for real business investment and industrial production; both indicators returned to former levels in the second quarter. Job growth was strong; the unemployment rate fell to 4.3 percent. Clearly, the downward movement of the overall economy was concentrated in two areas: the widening of the trade gap and the decline in inventories. Net exports fell from a negative $238 billion in 1998 to a negative $337 billion in the second quarter of 1999, and growth in inventories declined from $63.2 billion in 1997 to only $12.1 billion in 1999's second quarter.

Industrial production registered another large increase in July, partly due to higher electric utility output resulting from the ongoing heat wave, but also because of strong mining and manufacturing activity.[2] Production of motor vehicles and high-tech equipment was up during the summer months, and manufacture of other goods was robust as well. Other measures of economic activity continued to show strength. Consumer spending was still strong because of increased incomes and wealth, and very positive consumer sentiment. Business fixed investment advanced rapidly in the second quarter, although this measure abated somewhat later in the summer.

According to Federal Reserve ("Fed") economists, the U.S. trade deficit in goods and services widened substantially in the second quarter, as the value of imports rose much more than that of exports. The rise in imports was along a broad range of products and the increase in exports was mainly in agricultural goods, automotive products, industrial supplies, computers, and semiconductors. The Fed attributed this change to strengthening economic conditions abroad.[3]

---

[1] *Consensus Forecasts—USA* (September 13, 1999), 1.

[2] U.S. Federal Reserve Board, "Minutes of the Meeting of the Federal Open Market Committee Held on August 24, 1999," *Federal Reserve Bulletin* (December 1999), 822.

[3] Ibid.

EXHIBIT 5.1 *(Continued)*

TABLE 1

Selected Economic Indicators: 1995–2Q1999

	1995	*1996*	*1997*	*1998*	*1Q1999*	*2Q1999*
Real GDP[1]	2.3	3.4	3.9	3.9	4.3	1.8
Nominal GDP*	4.6	5.4	5.9	4.9	6.0	3.4
Real government consumption and investment*	0.2	1.1	1.3	0.9	N.A.	N.A.
Real business investment*	9.6	9.3	10.7	11.8	8.4	11.2
Nominal pretax profits*	17.9	11.6	9.0	0.8	N.A.	N.A.
Change in bus. inventories ($bn)	27.7	30.0	63.2	57.4	38.7	12.1
Real net exports ($bn)	−96.5	−111.0	−136.0	−238.0	−304.0	−337.0
Industrial production*	4.9	4.5	6.0	3.6	1.3	3.8
Producer prices*	1.9	2.7	0.4	–0.9	1.3	2.7
Employment costs*	3.0	2.8	3.0	3.4	N.A.	N.A.
Unemployment rate, %	5.6	5.4	4.9	4.5	4.3	4.3
Current account, $bn	– 114.0	−129.0	−143.0	−221.0	N.A.	N.A.
3-mo. Treasury bill, %, end yr.	5.1	5.2	5.4	4.5	4.5	4.8
10-yr. Treasury bond, %, end yr.	5.6	6.3	5.7	4.7	5.3	5.8

[1]Average % change on previous calendar year.

Source: *Consensus Forecasts* (September 1999).

Prices remained fairly stable overall. Consumer prices rose in mid-1999, mostly due to higher oil prices, although core consumer prices (CPI less food and energy) remained subdued. Core producer prices rose more in the 12-month period ending in July than in the year earlier period, mainly due to sharply higher tobacco prices. Producer prices of crude and intermediate materials other than food and energy had firmed noticeably in recent months. Adding to producers' costs was an increase in the employer cost index for hourly compensation of private industry workers.

In financial markets, short-term interest rates (as measured by the three-month Treasury bill) had fallen from 1998, while long-term rates (20-year constant maturity Treasury bonds) had risen about three quarters of a point in the same period, resulting in a steepening of the yield curve from less than 100 basis points to almost 200 basis points.[4] The Federal Reserve agreed to raise the Federal Funds rate by one-quarter of a point to 5.25 percent because of uncertainty over the future course of inflation. Rising interest rates in general make it more costly for a business to raise capital, all other things being equal.

Government spending began to grow in the fourth quarter of 1998, rising 2.2 percent in that quarter. The government sector is expected to increase as growing budget surpluses weaken restraints on federal outlays. This is true of defense spending as well, which had an uptick in 1999 for the first time in 13 years. Plans call for 4.5 to 5 percent annual growth for modernization outlays.[5]

The outlook for the expansion is positive; a rebound to the economy's long-term potential growth rate is expected by the Fed's economists.[6] *Consensus Forecasts* polls some two dozen private-sector economists each month and publishes their forecasts. Their consensus outlook has not changed in the past month, with 3.8 percent real GDP growth seen for 1999 and 2.7 percent in 2000. Industrial production should rise 2.6 percent in 1999 and 2.9 percent the following year. Inflation is expected to be low with producer prices up only 1.6 percent in 1999 and 1.8 percent in 2000. The trade deficit is expected to widen further.[7]

---

[4]Ibid., Table 1.35, p. A23. A basis point is equal to one-hundredth of a percentage point.

[5]The Wall Street Transcript Publishes Aerospace/Defense Sector Issue," *PR Newswire* (August 4, 1999), 5907.

[6]Ibid., 824. The long-run potential growth rate of the U.S. economy is around 2 percent to 3 percent.

[7]*Consensus Forecasts*, 2.

(Continued)

EXHIBIT 5.1 *(Continued)*

The subject company relies heavily on laborers for production. The Company uses both skilled and unskilled labor from the surrounding area of Camden County. The total population of the county was 502,824 during the 1990 census. The Census Bureau estimates that the population will have grown to 508,300 in the year 2000 and to 514,200 by 2006. The labor force in 1990 was made up of 253,621 people; by 2000 there will be 257,600 laborers, and 271,400 laborers by 2006.[8]

County industry employment projections predict a 10 percent increase in nonfarm payroll employment between 1994 and 2005. Manufacturing employment is expected to decline 13.1 percent or 3,300 jobs. This is slower than the state rate of 18.1 percent.[9] The labor force for the subject company is on the decline. Between 1996 and 2006, a 14.6 percent drop in the number of tool and die makers is expected. Machinist and sheet metal worker employment is expected to decline 7.7 percent and 7.3 percent, respectively.[10]

Even though the population and workforce are growing in the area, employment in this field is declining. As much of the industry has moved abroad, there will be fewer jobs and less incentive to go into the manufacturing sector of the labor market.

[8]www.wnjpin.state.nj.us/onestopcareercenter/labormarketinformation/lmi03/cototal.htm.

[9]*Southern Regional Labor Market Review* (July 1998), www.wnjpin.state.nj.us/onestopcareercenter/labormarketinformation/lmi12/sorlmr.pdf.

[10]www.wnjpin.net/onestopcareercenter/labormarketinformation/lmi04/camfin.htm.

Industry Analysis

The purpose of the industry analysis is to allow a comparison of the appraisal subject with the industry as a whole, as well as to allow the appraiser to use industry forecasts to help predict how the subject company will perform in the future. Questions frequently raised about the industry include the following:

- Who makes up the industry? Are there many companies or are there very few companies that control everything?
- Is it a cyclical industry?
- Is it a new industry with many new companies entering it, or is it a mature industry that has reached its saturation point?
- What are the barriers to entry, if any, into the industry?
- Is this a self-contained industry, or is it dependent on another industry?
- Is the industry dependent on new technology? If so, is the appraisal subject keeping up with the industry?
- Is the industry expected to change? If so, how will that affect the appraisal subject?
- What is the forecast for growth within the industry?

The answers to these questions are important in assessing the future of the subject company when you are considering what is happening around it. If the industry is made up of a few large players and the company being appraised is small, there is little likelihood that the company will influence the industry. A local paint manufacturer with $30 million in sales is most likely not going to be a major factor in an industry dominated by companies such as Sherwin-Williams, with $3 billion in sales.

If an industry is cyclical, as are automobile dealerships, consideration should be given to where in the economic cycle the industry is. If the economy is at the bottom of the cycle, the forecast for the next several years may look good. This will affect the forecast of future operations, as well as the risk component of the market multiples, discount rates, or capitalization rates that will be used.

Another important consideration is whether this industry follows another industry. For example, while appraising a retail furniture store, the appraiser must consider the residential real estate industry. There is approximately a six-month lag between the furniture industry and real estate sales. Logically, if people stop buying homes, there will not be as much of a need for new furniture.

Sometimes, it is necessary to analyze another industry in addition to the appraisal subject's industry. An example is a company that provides goods or services to a particular industry. A company that installs automatic teller machines would be highly dependent on the banking industry. Therefore, an analysis of the banking industry could be an essential part of the industry analysis for a company that is an electrical-mechanical firm.

Exhibit 5.2 provides an industry section of a report that demonstrates the importance of these points.

EXHIBIT 5.2
Industry Section

The appraisal subject is a Lexus auto dealership selling both new and used cars and offering repairs and other services. The Lexus line consists of five car models and two sport utility models, most of which were redesigned in early 1998. These cars range in price from about $31,000 to over $62,000, placing them in the category of "near luxury" vehicles. As such, the Lexus brand competes with such makes as BMW, Cadillac, Infiniti, Jaguar, Mercedes, and Volvo.

The Lexus line is manufactured by Toyota Motor Sales in Japan; none are built in North America. Traditionally, Lexus's market share has been about 1 percent in the United States. Recent redesign and the introduction of the popular sport utility vehicle has spurred sales. According to *Automotive News*, sales of new Lexus products grew 55.1 percent in April 1998, spurred by incentives and the newly designed cars.

To put these sales in perspective, Table 1 presents total car sales for 1994 through 1997 for all makes that are sold in the United States.

TABLE 1
Sales of New North America—Built and Imported Cars

	1993	*1994*	*1995*	*1996*	*1997*
Acura	108,291	112,137	97,151	105,443	106,844
Alfa Romeo	1,325	565	414	—	—
Audi	12,528	12,575	18,124	27,379	34,160
Aston Martin	60	—	—	—	—
BMW	78,010	84,501	93,309	105,761	122,467
Buick	500,691	546,836	471,819	427,350	438,072
Cadillac	204,159	210,686	180,504	170,379	182,624
Chevrolet	1,049,623	1,004,157	1,054,071	1,045,172	980,554
Chrysler division	194,588	197,342	215,164	212,021	188,929
Daihatsu	19	—	—	—	—
Dodge	368,183	354,174	403,839	421,945	372,832
Eagle	71,225	62,495	53,612	28,695	15,352
Ferrari	480	420	700	750	825
Ford division	1,292,227	1,369,268	1,279,096	1,240,928	1,132,540
Honda	608,955	650,105	643,336	680,711	722,536
Hyundai	108,796	126,095	107,378	108,468	113,186
Infiniti	50,547	51,450	58,616	53,984	46,759
Isuzu	1,762	109	16	1	—
Jaguar	12,734	15,195	18,085	17,878	19,503
Kia	692	12,163	16,725	26,366	35,494
Lamborghini	120	120	36	36	34
Lexus	94,677	87,419	79,334	74,001	90,800
Lincoln	173,644	179,166	150,814	141,476	139,540
Lotus	120	120	120	120	118

(Continued)

EXHIBIT 5.2 *(Continued)*

	1993	*1994*	*1995*	*1996*	*1997*
Mazda	259,890	282,799	223,711	180,975	168,540
Mercedes-Benz	61,899	73,002	76,752	90,844	107,696
Mercury	412,278	390,407	361,315	354,848	337,082
Mitsubishi	168,202	201,004	175,267	172,186	150,382
Nissan	431,826	485,710	460,992	446,393	420,741
Oldsmobile	380,563	423,847	371,725	306,486	251,663
Peugeot	3	—	—	—	—
Plymouth	200,136	197,813	113,565	169,972	159,417
Pontiac	544,302	586,343	566,826	529,710	556,662
Porsche	3,729	5,819	5,770	7,150	12,976
Rolls/Bentley	360	263	420	462	454
Saab	18,783	21,679	25,595	28,440	28,450
Saturn	229,356	286,003	285,674	278,574	251,099
Subaru	104,179	100,543	100,372	120,748	133,783
Suzuki	6,608	7,136	8,511	10,388	8,530
Toyota	647,149	677,725	714,640	719,591	731,782
Volkswagen	43,899	92,368	87,045	134,912	136,093
Volvo	72,955	81,788	115,114	88,581	90,894
Total	8,519,573	8,991,347	8,635,557	8,529,124	8,289,413
American Honda	717,246	762,242	740,487	786,154	829,380
Chrysler Corp.	834,132	811,824	786,180	832,633	736,530
Ford Motor Co.	1,878,149	1,938,841	1,791,225	1,737,252	1,609,162
General Motors	2,908,694	3,057,872	2,930,619	2,757,671	2,660,674
Nissan Motor Co.	482,373	537,160	519,608	500,377	467,500
Toyota Motor Co.	741,826	765,144	793,974	793,592	822,582
Volkswagen of Amer.	56,427	104,943	105,169	162,291	170,253

Source: "U.S. North America Built and Imported Sales," *Automotive News* (May 27, 1998), 49.

Sales of Lexus cars increased 22.7 percent in 1997 versus 1996, but market penetration remained at 1.1 percent. BMW had market share of 1.5 percent, Cadillac 2.2 percent, Infiniti 0.6 percent, Mercedes 1.3 percent, and Volvo 1.1 percent in the same year. Note also that the Lexus sales decline from 1993 through 1996 appears to have been arrested in 1997, with the introduction of new designs. The early indications are for continued increases in sales for 1998.

Light trucks have become increasingly popular during the 1990s, despite the fact that many of them are not fuel-efficient. In 1991, light trucks were about 32 percent of new motor vehicle sales of about 12.7 million units. By 1997, light trucks comprised 44 percent of a 15.38 million–unit new motor vehicle market. Most of these trucks are the popular sport utility vehicles, small pickup trucks, and vans.

Lexus offers two vehicles in the light truck category; the RX 300 sport wagon and the LX 470 sport utility vehicle. Both of these models were very popular in the first half of 1998. The RX 300 was launched in late April, with a sales forecast of about 25,000 units in 1998. Early estimates are that sales will exceed this forecast. This car competes with the Mercedes M class, but at a lower price. The LX 470 model competes very successfully with the Range Rover at the high end of the price spectrum.[1]

Overall, Lexus cars have been represented well in industry publications. The Lexus GS series was named *Motor Trend* Import Car of The Year in 1998. In addition, the Lexus LS 400 and ES 300 received the highest marks in the premium luxury car and entry luxury car categories of the J.D. Power Quality Survey. The LS 400 received the highest score of any vehicle in the study, as it has done five out of the last six years.[2] Considering continued demand for its established quality products and the addition of its light trucks, Lexus increased its sales forecast to reflect a growth rate of 40 percent for 1998, which represents a sales increase of 60 percent over the previous two years.[3]

[1]Mark Rechtin, "Lexus: Products Fuel Sizzling Sales," *Automotive News* (October 12, 1998), 3.

[2]"Lexus Remains Benchmark in Revised J.D. Power Quality Survey; LS 400 Tallies Best Score of Any Model," *PR Newswire* (June 3, 1998).

[3]"Lexus Breaks All-Time Sales Record for Second Consecutive Month; Division Announces New Sales Forecast," *PR Newswire* (June 2, 1998).

EXHIBIT 5.2 *(Continued)*

The appraisal subject competes with about 21 new car dealers. There are four franchises in the area that sell near-luxury vehicles: Smith BMW, Jones Mazda Volvo, Green Ford Toyota Saab, and Brown Autos of Newtown, which sells Jaguars. All of these companies have Web sites offering dealership information, and auto inventory with prices and specifications. Customers can make service appointments or get a quote on a new or used car online.

The National Automobile Dealers Association (NADA) maintains a database of information on this industry. This data suggest that the number of franchised new car dealerships in the United States has declined from about 27,900 in 1980 to about 22,700 in 1997. In the same period, retail sales of new passenger cars and light trucks have increased from 11.466 million units in 1980 to about 15.5 million units in 1997.[4] Clearly, more vehicles are being sold at fewer dealerships. This trend is the direct result of the move toward increased consolidation in this industry in recent years. This phenomenon will be reviewed later in this report.

Nationwide, new car dealers employed over 1.0 million people in 1997, rising steadily from around 745,000 in 1980. Payroll has increased as well, from about $11.0 billion in 1980 to over $37.0 billion in 1997. Although the industry employs fewer than one-half of 1 percent of the population, it is clearly one of the largest industries in the United States in terms of sales. According to NADA, the automotive industry as a consumer market generates over $1 trillion in annual revenue. In 1997, this market included about $330 billion of retail sales of new vehicles, $370 billion of retail sales of used vehicles, and $189 billion of retail sales of parts and maintenance/repair service.[5] In other words, the retail automobile industry amounts to almost one-eighth of the $8.0 trillion U.S. economy.

Table 2 presents NADA's Average Dealership Profile for the Middle Atlantic Region, which includes New York, New Jersey, and Pennsylvania, for 1996 and 1997. Note that sales have increased about 3 percent, but gross profit as a percent of sales has fallen slightly. Another interesting thing to note is that the gross profit margin on used cars is much higher than that for new vehicles.

TABLE 2

Average Dealership Profile
Middle Atlantic Region
(New York, New Jersey, Pennsylvania)

	1996	*1997*
Total sales	$ 18,076,596	$ 18,653,538
Total gross profit	$ 2,306,309	$ 2,338,066
As % of total sales	12.8%	12.5%
Total expense	$ 2,071,327	$ 2,143,388
As % of total sales	11.5%	11.5%
Net profit before tax	$ 234,983	$ 194,677
As % of total sales	1.3%	1.0%
New vehicle sales	$ 10,977,172	$ 11,417,716
As % of total sales	60.7%	61.2%
Used vehicle sales	$ 4,867,272	$ 4,996,241
As % of total sales	26.9%	26.8%
Service and parts	$ 2,232,152	$ 2,239,582
As % of total sales	12.3%	12.0%
Advertising expense	$ 172,578	$ 181,599
As % of total sales	0.95%	0.97%
Per new vehicle retailed	$ 373	$ 396
Rent & equivalent	$ 184,035	$ 188,984
As % of total sales	1.02%	1.01%
Per new vehicle retailed	$ 397	$ 412

[4]U.S. Department of Commerce, Census Bureau, *Statistical Abstract of the United States*, 119th ed., 773.

[5]Excerpt from *10-K Annual Report of Republic Industries, Inc.* (March 27, 1998), Ft. Lauderdale, Fla., Section I: Business.

(Continued)

EXHIBIT 5.2 *(Continued)*

	1996	1997
Floor plan interest	$ 63,620	$ 70,004
As % of total sales	0.35%	0.38%
Per new vehicle retailed	$ 137	$ 153
New vehicle selling price	$ 21,680	$ 22,800
Gross as % of selling price	6.30%	6.29%
Retail gross profit	$ 1,366	$ 1,433
Used vehicle selling price	$ 11,454	$ 12,061
Gross as % of selling price	11.92%	11.41%
Retail gross profit	$ 1,365	$ 1,376

There were 1,355 new car dealerships in the subject company's state in 1997, down 45 from the previous year. These employed an average of 39 persons per establishment and had an average annual payroll of $1.23 million.

There are a number of issues facing the automobile retailing industry, many of which have been around for several decades. These include governmental regulation, dealership image, manufacturer success, declining gross margins on new vehicles, the nature of the franchise agreement, manufacturer programs to reduce the numbers of franchises, currency fluctuations, consumer perceptions and tastes, a changing retail environment, and industry consolidation.

Most auto dealerships are subject to federal and state regulations relating to taxing and licensing vehicles, consumer protection, insurance, advertising, used vehicle sales, zoning and land use, and labor issues. In addition, many dealers own and operate underground storage tanks to store gasoline. These are generally subject to federal, state, and local environmental regulations mandating periodic testing, upgrading, closure, and removal of such tanks.

Some industry experts believe that consumers in general are dissatisfied with the service and retail experience offered by automotive retailers. They cite the stress associated with shopping for a new car as the most negative aspect of dealing with new car dealers. People like to think they are getting the best deal possible. Many dealers are working to change consumer perceptions by offering better training for their employees, one-price marketing, and the reduction of high-pressure selling techniques. J.D. Power & Associates annually ranks automakers on how well their dealers satisfy their customers in purchasing or leasing transactions and delivering the new vehicle. Lexus was among the top 10 automakers in customer satisfaction, according to the 1998 survey.[6]

Manufacturer success is critical to dealership success. Toyota Motor Corp.'s sales of vehicles from both its Toyota division and Lexus division have been excellent during 1998 as compared to the same period in 1997. June 1998 sales have been the best ever for this company (see Table 3).

TABLE 3

Toyota Motor Corp. Sales of New Cars and Trucks—1998 (% Change Is From the Same Period in 1997)

	Current Month			Calendar YTD		
	1998	*1997*	*% Chg*	*1998*	*1997*	*% Chg*
Total vehicle sales	117,043	96,046	17.2	635,266	629,238	1.0
Total Toyota div. cars						
Import	14,568	8,635	62.2	70,397	67,991	3.5
North American built	55,078	50,675	4.5	286,504	326,475	212.2
Total Lexus cars	7,916	6,147	23.8	51,700	40,317	28.2
Total SUVs	20,039	17,096	12.7	110,091	105,266	4.6
Lexus SUVs	4,946	628	657.3	16,668	3,951	321.9

Source: "Toyota Announces Best Ever Second Quarter Sales," *PR Newswire* (July 1, 1998).

[6] Ibid

EXHIBIT 5.2 *(Continued)*

The annualized total sales of Lexus cars and light trucks of 136,736 units is a substantial increase over the previous year's performance, giving ample evidence of the success of the brand.

Gross margins for U.S. auto dealers were about 18 percent in 1990, and rose to 19.2 percent in 1995. In 1996, gross profit margins had declined to 18.3 percent.[7] As mentioned earlier, auto dealers in NADA's Middle Atlantic Region tend to be holding steady at about 12.5 percent. Pretax profit as a percentage of sales has declined from a high of 2.2 percent in 1995 to about 1.7 percent in 1998 for all U.S. dealers. Note that Middle Atlantic Region dealers had pretax profits of only 1 percent of sales in 1997.

The number and mix of new cars sent to a franchised dealer by the manufacturer can be determined by provisions in the franchise agreement as well as other factors, such as the size and location of the dealership, the dealer's sales record, and its customer satisfaction rating.

The number of franchises has declined from 53,310 at the beginning of 1997 to 49,240 at January 1, 1998.[8] Most of the loss was the elimination of 4,000 Geo franchises by General Motors. The remaining 70 lost franchises were almost equally divided between the Big Three and the imports. Chrysler and Saturn gained franchises, as did Kia, which is still extending its dealer network in the United States.

For those dealerships selling vehicles that are manufactured outside the United States, changes in the value of the U.S. dollar, relative to other currencies, will affect the value of imports. The Lexus is built in Japan and distributed to U.S. dealerships by Toyota Motor Sales, U.S.A., Inc. of Torrance, California. In general, as the U.S. dollar becomes stronger compared to the Japanese yen, Japanese exports will become cheaper in the United States. From 1995 through mid-1998, the yen declined 39 percent, from about 93.96 yen per dollar in 1995 to 134.9 yen to one dollar in May 1998.

Consumers have more car-buying choices today than they had in the past. Some car dealers offer the traditional price-haggling experience, but more and more dealers are structuring the sales force's pay in such a way as to reduce this type of sales technique. Saturn has eliminated the "haggle" experience altogether. Several nationwide used car superstores also offer "no-haggle" pricing.

Consolidation among auto manufacturers and the suppliers of parts has been going on for some time. But consolidation among auto dealerships is a relatively new occurrence. Generally, the reason for consolidation in any industry is to realize the economies of scale that are inherent in a larger organization. In the case of auto dealerships, these savings can manifest themselves in a lower cost of capital for floor plan inventory financing, cheaper advertising and insurance expense through consolidated purchasing, as well as more efficient administration and information systems.

Retail auto consolidation began with used car stores as companies such as Auto Nation, a division of Republic Industries, and Car Max, owned by Circuit City, bought up used car dealers across the country. These ventures proved successful and forays were made into the arena of new vehicle retailing. The largest of these, Auto Nation, had sales of $6.2 billion in 1997. Many of these so-called consolidators are public companies, but the majority are privately held. They generally maximize the number of new car franchises they hold in order to be able to offer whatever the consumer might want.

Several of these mega-dealers have gone public since 1996. For years, the auto manufacturers had strict policies forbidding outside stock ownership of dealer franchises. This precedent was broken in 1996 when Cross-Continental Auto Retailers of Texas initiated agreements with GM and Nissan that enabled it to complete an IPO.[9] For years Wall Street ignored car dealerships because "they were largely family-owned businesses with limited product lines and geographical territory, which made their performance cyclical."[10] This trend began to change in 1997 as mega-dealers began to tap into public markets for capital. "Valuation paradigms are shifting upwards, as some dealers are realizing they might be worth more on Wall Street than on Main Street."[11]

Carl Spielvogel, former head of United Auto Group of New York City, predicts that the industry will gradually evolve into a three-tier business, with five huge firms at the top. Several other mega-dealers will occupy the middle, and "a group of smaller companies will occupy the bottom rung in this retail market. And, of course, there will be mom and pop stores existing in markets too small to interest the big boys."[12]

---

[7]U.S. Department of Commerce, Bureau of the Census, *Statistical Abstract of the U.S.*, 199th ed. (1999), 773.

[8]Arlena Sawyers, "Dealer Total Slips 76; Import Brands Add Exclusives," Automotive News, no. 5758 (March 23, 1998), 1. Note the number of franchises exceeds the number of dealerships because many dealers are "duals."

[9]Maynard M. Gordon, "Going Public," *Ward's Dealer Business*, vol. 31, no. 4 (December 1996), 40.

[10]Erica Copulsky, "Wall Street Scrambles to Bank the Auto Dealer Market," *Investment Dealers Digest*, vol. 63, no. 10 (March 10, 1997), 16.

[11]Ibid.

[12]Herbert Shuldiner, "Moving Up," *Ward's Dealer Business*, vol. 31, no. 8 (April 1997), 22.

(Continued)

EXHIBIT 5.2 *(Continued)*

The automobile industry in the United States is cyclical in nature. An automobile is a big-ticket item, and consumers will be more disposed to purchase or lease one if certain economic conditions are present. These conditions—employment, incomes, wealth, and general outlook for the future—have all been positive for some time now. As a result, new car and truck sales have risen steadily since the beginning of the 1990s. Clearly, a strong economy has a positive effect on auto sales and auto dealership revenues. If the outlook is for continued strength, car sales should increase from current levels.

The overall decline in interest rates during the 1990s is beneficial to the auto retailer as it has the twin effects of reducing the dealer's cost of financing his inventory, as well as the cost to the consumer of buying or leasing a car. Interest rates are expected to hold fairly steady in the future, boding well for interest-rate-sensitive businesses.

The auto retailing industry is not without its problems, however. Competition among automakers is fierce, resulting in declining margins for new cars. The industry is working through a massive consolidation phase as automakers soften their stance on such issues as multiple-line dealerships and public ownership of auto retailers. Mega-dealerships, offering dozens of nameplates in hundreds of locations nationwide, are growing in number. These huge companies can achieve economies of scale that a small "mom and pop" dealership cannot. Floor-planning will be obtained at lower rates than at a small dealership. Many mega-dealers have captive finance arms to help customers finance purchases.

If mega-dealerships are able to achieve the economies of scale they believe will occur with continued consolidation of the industry, gross margins on new and used cars may soften further. This could make it more difficult for mom and pop operations to be profitable.

In March 1998, Lexus introduced newly designed versions of its SUVs and sedans. Sales of these new models have been strong so far, and if they continue to be popular, market share may increase from the historic 1 percent. The greater popularity of its product notwithstanding, the subject company is operating in an increasingly competitive and dynamic environment. In order to ensure its survival, the subject company must show that it is equal to the challenges before it.

Overall, the outlook for the industry is positive, but clearly not without its problems. The Lexus line of vehicles has proven that it is a quality product, backed by the strong Toyota brand, and should continue to do well in the future.

The industry analysis will vary depending upon the amount of information available, as well as the impact that it may have on the appraisal subject. Obviously, the example in Exhibit 5.2 had a considerable amount of information. But think about this—while valuing a Lexus dealership, didn't this analysis cover everything that you can think of that may have been important? I hope so. Otherwise, we spent a considerable amount of time for no reason.

Subject Company Analysis

Item number one on the Revenue Ruling 59-60 hit parade tells us to consider the "nature of the business and the history of the enterprise from its inception." In other words, where has the company been and how did it get there? In this situation, the appraiser is looking to analyze not only the company's financial statements, but also the entire business operation. Of course, the financial statement analysis is an important component of the process, but at this stage in the valuation process, you are attempting to determine how effectively the company is being run. Also, what risk factors are associated with the company, and how would they affect the rate of return that an investor may require if a transaction was to be consummated?

Some of the more common questions raised here include the following:

- How does the subject company compare with the entire industry? Is it a large player or a small player in the industry? Is it in its infancy, or is it mature?
- Has the company kept up with technology?
- What percentage of market share does the subject company have?
- Does the subject company distribute its products locally, regionally, nationally, or internationally?
- Are there alternative products available in the marketplace that may affect the future of the company's goods and services?
- What is the management structure of the company? Is the business highly dependent on one or a few key people?
- Is there a succession plan for management?

The answers to these questions will serve dual purposes. The first purpose is to demonstrate that the appraiser understands the nature of the business, as well as what makes the business run. The second purpose, once again, is to perform a risk assessment of the subject company. What we are trying to do is determine whether the appraisal subject is similar or dissimilar, or more risky or less risky, than other companies in the industry. Factors that the appraiser will analyze include the products and services offered by the company, customer base, suppliers, management, operations, and ownership structure. A good portion of this information will fit nicely into the history and nature of the company section of the appraisal report. This will also assist the appraiser in developing market multiples, discount rates, and capitalization rates.

Financial Analysis

The purpose of the financial analysis is to review the subject company's performance with respect to other companies, its industry peers, or itself. Comparing the subject company to its peers helps the appraiser assess whether the company is more or less risky in relation to its peer group. Comparing the company to itself allows the appraiser to determine how the company has performed over the past few years. This can help give the appraiser an idea of future trends that may occur.

During the financial analysis, the appraiser attempts to identify unusual items, nonrecurring items, and trends. An attempt should be made to explain what happened and why it happened. If there is a departure from the norms of the industry, this should also be investigated and explained.

The following analytical tools are used by the appraiser:

- Comparative company analysis
- Common-size financial statements
- Financial ratio analysis
- Comparative industry analysis
- Trend analysis

Comparative Company Analysis

Most business appraisers will request at least five years of financial information about the subject company. The amount of data will depend on the facts and circumstances. However, a good rule of thumb is to ask for enough years of data to cover a complete business cycle. This will allow the appraiser to create a spreadsheet looking for trends that may have occurred, as well as inconsistencies in the reported data.

Common-Size Financial Statements

The use of common-size financial statements is an excellent way to analyze the subject company with respect to other companies of different sizes. By presenting the data as percentages, the size differentials are eliminated between the subject company and its peer group. Exhibit 5.3 illustrates a common-size analysis taken from an actual report. In this illustration, industry information was used as a comparison to the appraisal subject.

Common-size statements are also useful in allowing the appraiser to perform an analysis about the company's financial performance over a period of years. Trends can be more readily identified, which will allow the appraiser to make projections or evaluate the budget information provided by management.

EXHIBIT 5.3
Common-Size Financial Analysis

A common-size balance sheet is presented in Table 1. This allows the appraiser to make a comparison of the subject company to the industry composite data. For the purposes of this analysis, we have used comparative industry statistics from Integra Information, Inc.'s *Business Profiler* for Standard Industrial Classifications (SIC) code 5023—Wholesale Trade, Home Furnishings (includes linoleum, carpets, and other floor coverings). The data used by Integra comes from numerous government data sources, including, but not limited to, *IRS Corporate Source Book* Form 10-K and 10-Q Filings for Public Companies, U.S. Census Bureau, and various regional databases. The data was a composite of 18 companies within the $50,000,000 to $99,999,999 annual sales range.

The common-size balance sheet information provided in Table 1 allows us to analyze business trends, as well as make a comparison between the subject company and other companies within the industry.

The Company's level of current assets was lower than the industry composite data for 1994 through 1997. This was due primarily to lower levels of cash and inventory. However, The Company's current assets are comparable to that of the composite data in 1998, primarily due to an increased level of inventory.

TABLE 1
Common-Size Balance Sheet as of December 31

	1995		*1996*		*1997*		*1998*	
	Integra	*Apex*	*Integra*	*Apex*	*Integra*	*Apex*	*Integra*	*Apex*
Assets								
Cash	6.25 %	0.75%	6.29%	4.28%	6.23%	3.89%	6.19%	1.93%
Marketable securities	0.96 %	0.00%	0.94%	0.00%	0.93%	0.00%	0.91%	0.00%
Accounts receivable (net)	30.06 %	30.07%	30.25%	29.36%	29.95%	33.50%	29.74%	30.11%
Inventory	38.85 %	28.06%	39.07%	28.23%	38.73%	33.19%	38.49%	41.48%
Other current assets	3.73 %	0.88%	3.81%	1.01%	3.85%	0.91%	3.96%	0.67%
Total current assets	79.85 %	59.76%	80.36%	62.88%	79.69%	71.49%	79.29%	74.20%
Fixed assets								
Property, plant & equipment	24.62%	70.05%	23.87%	77.74%	24.81%	59.37%	25.19%	55.57%
Accumulated depreciation	−10.66%	−44.44%	−10.30%	−49.96%	−10.63%	−35.71%	−10.57%	−33.21%
Net fixed assets	13.96%	25.62%	13.57%	27.77%	14.18%	23.66%	14.62%	22.36%
Other assets								
Intangible assets (net)	0.62%	0.00%	0.63%	0.00%	0.65%	0.00%	0.67%	0.00%
Investments	4.29%	0.00%	4.10%	0.00%	4.09%	0.00%	3.98%	0.00%
Other assets	1.28%	14.63%	1.34%	9.34%	1.39%	4.85%	1.44%	3.44%
Total other assets	6.19%	14.63%	6.07%	9.34%	6.13%	4.85%	6.09%	3.44%
Total assets	100.00%	100.00%	100.00%	100.00%	100.00%	100.00%	100.00%	100.00%
Liabilities and net worth								
Notes payable—banks	13.30%	2.81%	12.89%	0.87%	12.87%	0.91%	12.55%	2.92%
Accounts payable	25.66%	23.84%	26.51%	24.64%	26.21%	44.47%	26.87%	42.44%
Other current liabilities	9.87%	0.16%	10.21%	0.17%	9.49%	0.11%	9.34%	2.06%
Total current liabilities	48.83%	26.81%	49.61%	25.68%	48.57%	45.49%	48.77%	47.42%

EXHIBIT 5.3 *(Continued)*

	1995		1996		1997		1998	
	Integra	*Apex*	*Integra*	*Apex*	*Integra*	*Apex*	*Integra*	*Apex*
Long-term liabilities								
Long-term debt	14.02%	0.00%	13.92%	1.90%	13.43%	2.00%	13.23%	0.90%
Loans from stockholders	3.66%	0.00%	3.67%	0.00%	3.57%	0.00%	3.54%	0.00%
Other liabilities	1.65%	0.00%	1.72%	0.00%	1.70%	0.00%	1.75%	0.00%
Total long-term liabilities	19.33%	0.00%	19.31%	1.90%	18.70%	2.00%	18.52%	0.90%
Total liabilities	68.17%	26.81%	68.92%	27.58%	67.28%	47.50%	67.29%	48.32%
Total net worth	31.83%	73.19%	31.08%	72.42%	32.72%	52.50%	32.71%	51.68%
Total liabilities net worth	100.00%	100.00%	100.00%	100.00%	100.00%	100.00%	100.00%	100.00%

Note: 1994 was left out of exhibit intentionally. Figures may not add due to rounding.

The Company's fixed assets have been consistently higher than the composite data over the five-year period. As mentioned previously, The Company owns the real estate that it operates in and, as such, this may be contributing to its fixed assets representing a larger portion of its total assets.

The Company's current liabilities were much lower than the composite data for 1994 through 1996, primarily due to its historically low levels of bank and trade debt. In 1997 and 1998, The Company's accounts payable increased dramatically. This was most likely due to increased sales to the main supplier's direct accounts. This increase in accounts payable resulted in total current liabilities that were comparable to the industry data for 1997 and 1998.

As The Company had limited its debt exposure in the past, it has significantly lower long-term obligations as compared to the industry composite data. This results in The Company having a greater level of equity (or net worth) than the industry composite data for the five-year period. In 1994 through 1996, The Company's net worth was well over twice that of the industry composite data. Given the increase in current liabilities, The Company's net worth was approximately 1.5 times the industry data in 1997 and 1998.

Overall, The Company appears to be very healthy from a balance sheet perspective.

The next step in the valuation process is to analyze The Company's income statements. The historic income statements appear as Schedule 2 at the end of this report. This step requires the appraiser to analyze Apex's earnings capacity based on its historic results, as well as what may be produced in the future. Future earnings capacity is critical, as it is an important component of valuation. For this reason, the appraiser analyzes the historic financial statements with an eye toward probable future earnings that can be generated by the subject company.

In order to further analyze The Company's operating performance, a common-size income statement is shown in Table 2.

TABLE 2

Common-Size Income Statement for the Years Ended December 31

	1995		1996		1997		1998	
	Integra	*Apex*	*Integra*	*Apex*	*Integra*	*Apex*	*Integra*	*Apex*
Revenue	100.00%	100.00%	100.00%	100.00%	100.00%	100.00%	100.00%	100.00%
Cost of sales	72.52%	79.61%	72.85%	81.53%	73.08%	80.99%	73.57%	88.12%
Gross margin	27.48%	20.39%	27.15%	18.47%	26.92%	19.01%	26.43%	11.88%
Operating expenses	24.38%	20.58%	24.09%	20.54%	23.87%	19.14%	23.21%	10.84%
Operating income	3.10%	−0.19%	3.06%	−2.07%	3.05%	−0.13%	3.22%	1.04%
Interest expense	−0.88%	−0.15%	−0.81%	−0.07%	−0.79%	−0.06%	−0.78%	−0.15%
Total other income (expenses)	0.11%	0.38%	−0.09%	0.77%	−0.24%	1.55%	−0.54%	−0.15%
Pretax income (loss)	2.33%	0.19%	2.16%	−1.30%	2.02%	1.42%	1.90%	0.90%
Income taxes	−0.89%	−0.01%	−0.82%	0.10%	−0.77%	−0.19%	−0.72%	−0.01%
Net income (loss)	1.44%	0.20%	1.34%	−1.20%	1.25%	1.23%	1.18%	0.88%

Note: 1994 was left out of exhibit intentionally. Figures may not add due to rounding.

(Continued)

EXHIBIT 5.3 ***(Continued)***

The common-size figures provided in Table 2 allow the appraiser to analyze trends in The Company's expenses in relation to revenues and also permit us to compare the expenses and income of the subject company to the industry composite data from Integra.

Cost of sales for the industry has been steadily increasing over the five-year period from 72.2 percent in 1994 to 73.6 percent in 1998. The same trend is exhibited by The Company's cost of sales, which increased from 78.8 percent in 1994 to 81.0 percent in 1997, and more dramatically to 88.1 percent in 1998. As discussed previously, this is due to the fact that The Company's sales mix has been experiencing a shift toward lower profit margin sales to the main supplier's customers. As such, this results in Apex being much less profitable (in terms of gross margin) than the industry composite data in 1998; 11.88 percent gross margin for The Company compared to 26.4 percent for the composite data.

However, The Company has been able to make up some of this difference by minimizing its operating expenses (on a relative basis). In 1998, The Company's operating expenses represented 10.8 percent of sales compared to 23.2 percent for the composite data. This results in an operating margin for The Company of 1.0 percent in 1998, compared to 3.2 percent for its peer group. Again, this is mainly due to the lower profit sales to the main supplier's accounts. In prior years, The Company did not have any operating income, compared with roughly a 3 percent operating margin for the industry composite data.

Financial Ratios

The use of financial ratios allows the appraiser to analyze the performance of the subject company in terms of liquidity, performance, profitability, and leverage. These ratios are compared against industry data, guideline company data, or both, for the assessment of risk.

Different industries sometimes use different financial ratios, but the basic ratio analysis is the same. However, the same financial ratio will have different meanings depending upon the industry being considered. For example, you would expect the inventory turnover ratio for a perishable food business to be greater than that for an automobile dealership. A description of some of the more common ratios follows.

IMPORTANT

NOTE: Some sources use average figures whereas others use year-end data. Make certain that you are consistent in your calculations to ensure that you are using the same basis when comparing with industry sources of ratios. Also, make sure that you use the ratios from the comparative data that best match the time period of the valuation.

Current Ratio = Current Assets ÷ Current Liabilities. The current ratio measures the margin of safety that management maintains to allow for the inevitable unevenness in the flow of funds through the current asset and current liability accounts. A company needs a supply of current funds to be assured of being able to pay its bills when they come due. This ratio shows the company's ability to pay for its ongoing operations in the short term. A company's liquidity is essential to its good credit, its ability to grow with its own funds, and its ability to pay dividends to its owners.

Quick Ratio = (Cash + Marketable Securities + Accounts Receivable) ÷ Current Liabilities. Quick assets include cash, marketable securities, and current accounts receivable. Presumably, these items can be converted into cash quickly at approximately their stated amounts, unlike inventory, which is the principal current asset that is excluded from this calculation. The quick ratio is therefore a measure of the extent to which liquid resources are available to meet current obligations. This ratio tends to be a better measure of the company's short-term liquidity, particularly if cash needs to be generated quickly to pay bills.

Cash to Current Liabilities = Cash ÷ Current Liabilities. Cash and cash equivalents are the most readily available assets with which to pay liabilities. This ratio tells the appraiser whether the subject company has a strong enough cash position to meet its short-term obligations. This ratio can also assist the appraiser in determining whether the subject company is carrying excess cash on its balance sheet. Excess cash may show a poor use of current assets by management. I wish that I had the problem of having excess cash. My kid makes sure that never happens!

Accounts Payable to Inventory = Accounts Payable ÷ Inventory. Businesses generally purchase inventory on credit. The ratio of accounts payable to inventory measures the extent to which a company's inventory is financed by the suppliers of that inventory. A low ratio may indicate that management is not taking advantage of the credit terms available from suppliers. It may also indicate a high level of inventory being carried by the company, when the ratio is used in conjunction with inventory turnover ratios.

Accounts Payable Payout Period = Accounts Payable ÷ (Cost of Goods Sold) Number of Days). The accounts payable payout period measures the timeliness of paying suppliers. This figure is related directly to the normal credit terms of the company's purchases. This ratio allows the appraiser to consider the company's ability to obtain favorable terms from vendors because of good creditworthiness.

Debt to Equity = Total Liabilities ÷ Net Worth. Debt is risky because if creditors are not paid promptly, they can take legal action to obtain payment, which, in extreme cases, can force the company into bankruptcy. The greater the extent to which a company obtains its financing from its owners, the less worry the company has in meeting its fixed obligations. The debt-to-equity ratio shows the balance that management has struck between debt and stockholders' equity. A proper capital structure should include a portion of debt, since debt has a lower cost of capital. Different industries have different debt-to-equity relationships.

EBIT to Total Assets = Earnings Before Interest and Taxes ÷ Total Assets. Earnings before interest and taxes (EBIT) to total assets is an important return-on-investment ratio that provides a profit analysis based on earnings before interest and income taxes. This ratio is best compared with a company's annual interest rate on borrowed funds. If the ratio of a firm's EBIT to total assets is higher than its weighted average cost of capital, the ratio is favorable.

Times Interest Earned = EBIT ÷ Interest. The times interest earned ratio measures the number of times that the earnings before interest and taxes will cover the total interest payments on debt. The result indicates the level to which income can decline without impairing the company's ability to meet its interest payments on liabilities. If the ratio falls below 1.0, the firm is not generating enough earnings to cover the interest due on loans. This ratio indicates the financial risk of the company.

Average Collection Period = Accounts Receivable ÷ (Credit Sales ÷ 365). The average collection period can be evaluated against the credit terms offered by the company. As a rule, the collection period should not exceed $1\frac{1}{3}$ times the regular payment period; that is, if a company's typical terms call for payment in 30 days, the collection period should not exceed 40 days. Changes in the ratio indicate changes in the company's credit policy or changes in its ability to collect receivables.

Inventory Turnover = Cost of Goods Sold ÷ Ending Inventory. Inventory turnover is an indication of the velocity with which merchandise dollars move through the business. An increase in the value of inventory may represent the additional stock required by an expanding business, or it may represent an accumulation of merchandise from a declining sales volume. In the latter case, the inventory turnover will decrease. A decrease in the inventory turnover ratio may therefore be a significant danger signal.

Inventory Holding Period = 365 ÷ Inventory Turnover. Some of the company's products come in and go out in a matter of days; other goods may stay in stock for six months or longer. The holding period differs for different products. Business managers and owners must be concerned with a holding period that is longer than necessary because of the high costs of tying up capital in excess inventory. On the other hand, reducing inventory levels too much could result in lost sales, because certain products are not available when the customer wants them. The cost of carrying inventory has to be balanced against the profit opportunities lost by not having the product in stock, ready for sale.

Other Financial Ratios. There are many other financial ratios that can be considered by the appraiser. Some of the ratios that will be calculated may relate to the company's equity, while others relate to the company's invested capital. Invested capital is considered to be the company's long-term debt or nonworking capital debt plus the equity of the company. Since a proper capital structure will generally include an appropriate mix of debt and equity, some appraisers prefer to value the company in this manner. What this really does is allow the appraiser to value the company on an invested capital basis, eliminating differences in leveraging between the subject company and the guideline companies. This becomes more important in the valuation of larger companies, since the companies being used for comparison purposes may be publicly traded. We will discuss this further in Chapter 6.

The return-on-equity ratio (also known as the *Dupont analysis*) is considered to be one of the most important financial ratios, since it measures profitability, turnover, and leverage all in one ratio. The mathematical breakdown of the return on equity ratio is as follows:

$$\frac{\text{Net income}}{\text{Equity}} = \frac{\text{Net income}}{\text{Sales}} \times \frac{\text{Sales}}{\text{Assets}} \times \frac{\text{Assets}}{\text{Equity}}$$

Another analytical tool used by appraisers is the compound growth rate. Compound growth rates are frequently used by the appraiser in the selection of guideline companies, pricing multiples, discount rates, and capitalization rates. Both revenues and net income (cash flow can be used also) should be analyzed by the appraiser. The mathematical formula for calculating compound growth as a percentage is as follows:

$$\left(\sqrt[(n-1)]{\text{amount}_n \div \text{amount}_1}\right) - 1$$

The compound growth rate is often calculated for historical data to give an indication of future growth. However, keep in mind that the formula considers only the first and last year. Therefore, it does not calculate a change from year to year. Because of this, you must be careful in selecting the first and last years for your calculation. Ideally you want to look at the business cycle (peak to peak or valley to valley) or look at a constant trend.

When looking at growth, the appraiser should also examine the year-to-year change as well as the actual numbers. Over a longer period of time, this is very often more meaningful than the compound growth rate. Let's look at a simple example to illustrate this concept. Assume that Smith Company had sales as follows:

Year	*Amount*
1996	$ 1,350,000
1997	1,675,000
1998	2,100,000
1999	2,200,750
2000	2,450,000

The five-year compound growth rate for Smith Company is 16.1 percent (calculated as the fourth root of $2,450,000 divided by $1,350,000, or 1.1606, then minus 1). A review of the increase in sales on an annual basis indicates that the company experienced constant growth during this five-year period. But what if the sales were as follows:

Year	*Amount*
1996	$ 1,350,000
1997	6,450,000
1998	5,375,000
1999	3,900,000
2000	2,450,000

In this situation, the compound growth rate would be the same 16.1 percent, but look at the difference in the trend. Graphically, these trends look like this:

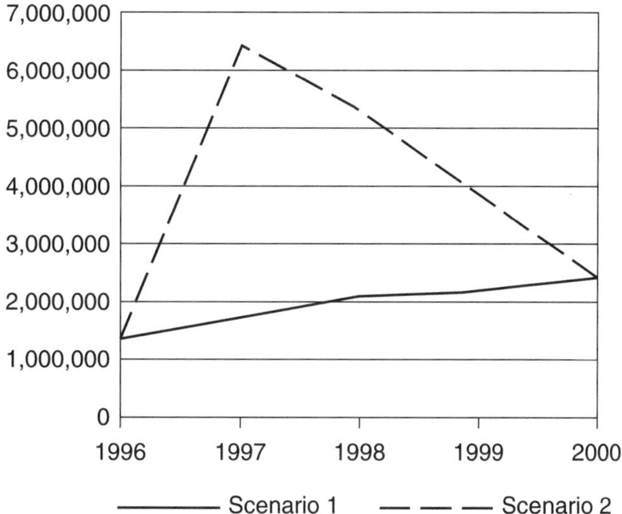

The appraiser needs to pay attention to trends, not just a group of calculations. Remember that the goal is to be able to use this information to forecast the future. In this instance, the appraiser would probably not use compound growth rates, since they would have little relevance. You must pay particular attention to the information and not just go through the motions of doing a series of calculations because you read a book or you have a computer program that will calculate these ratios for you. Analysis means that you must *analyze* the information! Otherwise, financial analysis would be called financial calculation.

Comparative Industry Analysis

The purpose of a comparative analysis is to compare the subject company's operating performance with that of its peer group. This analysis is undertaken to determine the company's position with respect to its peers. Is it more or less risky than its peer group? How well does the company perform as compared with the peer group? Some of the more common sources for comparative data include the following:

- Trade association surveys
- Integra Information's *Business Profiler*

- RMA Annual Statement Studies
- Almanac of Business and Industrial Ratios
- Financial Statement Studies
- D&B Key Business Ratios
- Guideline companies

Comparative analysis is a useful tool for an appraiser to use only if the subject company can be meaningfully compared with either specific guideline companies or industry composite data. Common-size financial statements and financial ratio analyses are much more meaningful if the results can be compared with guideline company results or industry data.

If a company is large enough, there may be publicly traded companies that can be used for this type of analysis. For the smaller companies, and even sometimes for the larger companies, it is generally worthwhile to compare the subject to some form of industry data, whether it is obtained from a trade organization or Integra Information's *Business Profiler.*

Business Profiler. I want to spend some time showing you the type of information that can be obtained and used from this great resource. For many appraisers that value smaller companies, this is the ideal type of information to use as a basis for comparison. Let me show you what I am referring to.

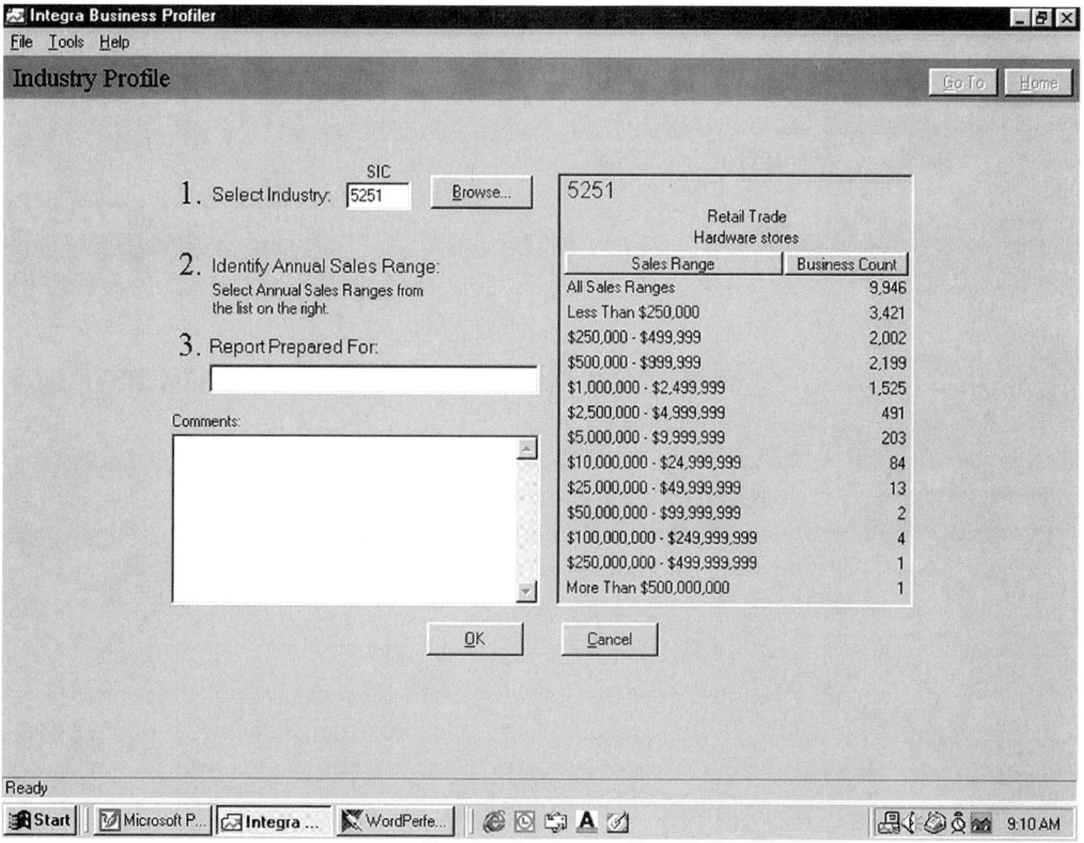

Source: Reprinted with kind permission from Integra Information, a Division of Microbilt Corp.

When you first enter the program, you will have to identify the SIC code for the subject company. Let's use 5251, Retail Hardware Stores. What is of considerable importance to a business appraiser is comparability. *Business Profiler* allows the analyst to choose between different size companies, so that the comparison is more relevant to the appraisal subject.

As you can see, *Business Profiler* has a total of 9,946 companies in the hardware store profile. This is a greater number of items than you will find anywhere else for this type of information. Let's assume that the appraisal subject has sales of $2 million. By selecting the range of $1 million to $2.499 million, we will be working with 1,525 companies.

A quick overview is available for all of the data in our group. It looks like this:

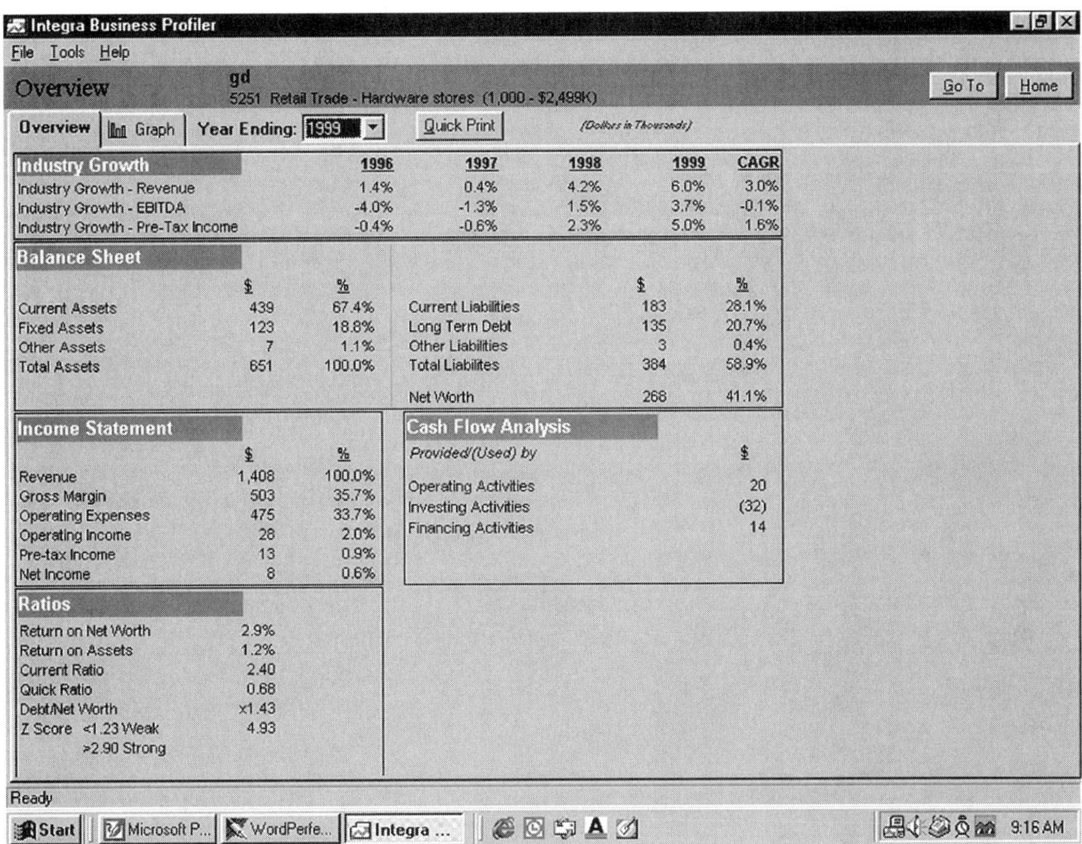

Integra Business Profiler

File Tools Help

Overview — gd — 5251 Retail Trade - Hardware stores (1,000 - $2,499K)

Overview | Graph | Year Ending: 1999 | Quick Print | (Dollars in Thousands) | Go To | Home

Industry Growth	1996	1997	1998	1999	CAGR
Industry Growth - Revenue	1.4%	0.4%	4.2%	6.0%	3.0%
Industry Growth - EBITDA	-4.0%	-1.3%	1.5%	3.7%	-0.1%
Industry Growth - Pre-Tax Income	-0.4%	-0.6%	2.3%	5.0%	1.6%

Balance Sheet	$	%		$	%
Current Assets	439	67.4%	Current Liabilities	183	28.1%
Fixed Assets	123	18.8%	Long Term Debt	135	20.7%
Other Assets	7	1.1%	Other Liabilities	3	0.4%
Total Assets	651	100.0%	Total Liabilites	384	58.9%
			Net Worth	268	41.1%

Income Statement	$	%
Revenue	1,408	100.0%
Gross Margin	503	35.7%
Operating Expenses	475	33.7%
Operating Income	28	2.0%
Pre-tax Income	13	0.9%
Net Income	8	0.6%

Cash Flow Analysis — Provided/(Used) by	$
Operating Activities	20
Investing Activities	(32)
Financing Activities	14

Ratios	
Return on Net Worth	2.9%
Return on Assets	1.2%
Current Ratio	2.40
Quick Ratio	0.68
Debt/Net Worth	x1.43
Z Score <1.23 Weak >2.90 Strong	4.93

Ready

Source: Reprinted with kind permission from Integra Information, a Division of Microbilt Corp.

The summary format provides the appraiser with a concise snapshot of the peer group. The industry growth rates allow you to compare the compound annual growth figures of the appraisal subject to the industry on a year-by-year basis. All of the financial statements can be expanded into larger amounts of information for each of these statements. The financial ratios provided in the detail section give you almost everything that you would need to calculate for an industry comparison. Let's look at the detail.

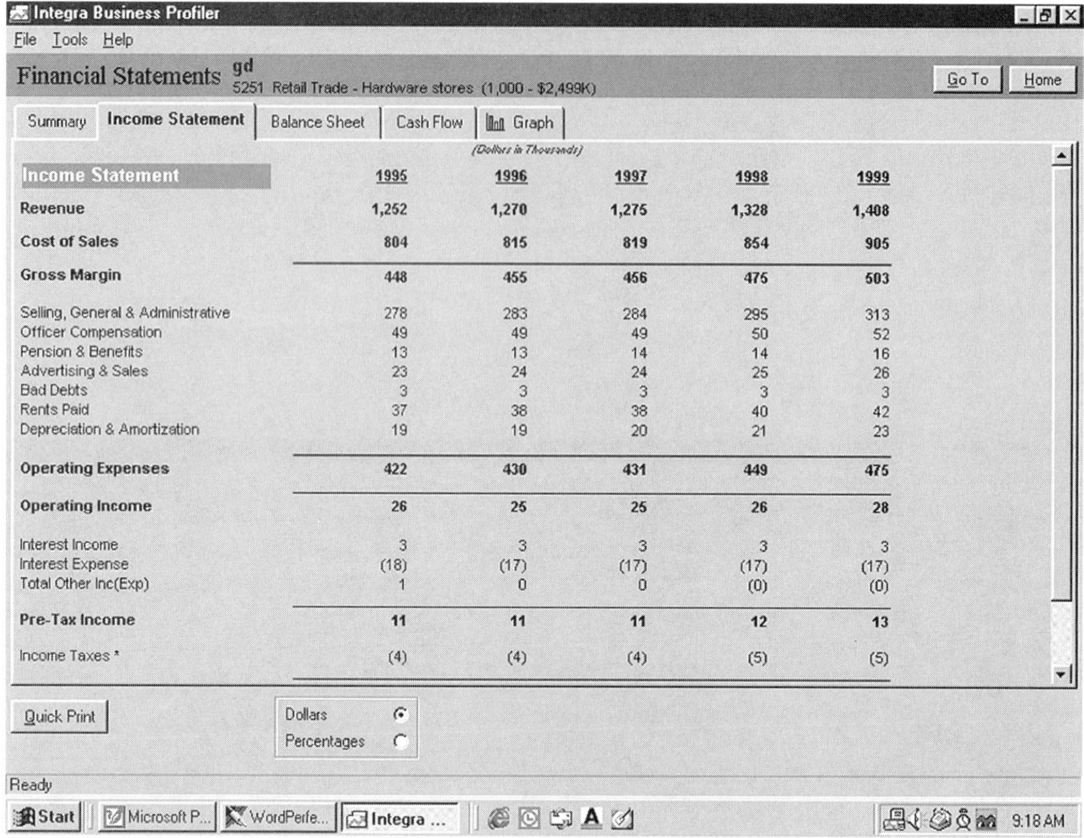

(Dollars in Thousands)

Income Statement	1995	1996	1997	1998	1999
Revenue	1,252	1,270	1,275	1,328	1,408
Cost of Sales	804	815	819	854	905
Gross Margin	448	455	456	475	503
Selling, General & Administrative	278	283	284	295	313
Officer Compensation	49	49	49	50	52
Pension & Benefits	13	13	14	14	16
Advertising & Sales	23	24	24	25	26
Bad Debts	3	3	3	3	3
Rents Paid	37	38	38	40	42
Depreciation & Amortization	19	19	20	21	23
Operating Expenses	422	430	431	449	475
Operating Income	26	25	25	26	28
Interest Income	3	3	3	3	3
Interest Expense	(18)	(17)	(17)	(17)	(17)
Total Other Inc(Exp)	1	0	0	(0)	(0)
Pre-Tax Income	11	11	11	12	13
Income Taxes *	(4)	(4)	(4)	(5)	(5)

Source: Reprinted with kind permission from Integra Information, a Division of Microbilt Corp.

As you can see from the above illustration, the financial statements can be viewed (and printed) in terms of dollars or common-size financial statements. Although we have not discussed this yet, even officer's compensation is provided in these figures. You may need this when you normalize the financial statements (discussed soon). The balance sheet can be accessed both ways as well. The cash flow statement is comparative in dollars for four years.

Financial ratios allow the appraiser to dissect the subject company's industry group the same way that we used to dissect frogs in biology. (My mother said I should have become a doctor, maybe even a brain surgeon!). Look at this breakdown of ratios.

LIQUIDITY/SOLVENCY

- Quick Ratio
- Current Ratio
- Days Accounts Receivables Outstanding
- Days Accounts Payable
- Days Working Capital
- Days Inventory
- Accounts Receivable to Sales
- Accounts Payable to Sales
- Current Liabilities to Net Worth
- Current Liabilities to Inventory
- Cost of Sales to Payables

TURNOVER

- Receivables Turnover

- Cash Turnover
- Inventory Turnover
- Current Asset Turnover
- Working Capital Turnover
- Fixed Asset Turnover
- Total Asset Turnover

DEBT

- Debt Service Coverage—EBITDA
- Debt Service Coverage—Pre-Tax
- Debt Service Coverage— After-Tax
- Interest Coverage
- Current Assets to Short-Term Debt
- Accounts Payable to Total Debt
- Short Term Debt to Total Debt
- Long Term Debt to Total Assets
- Short Term Debt Plus Long-Term Debt to Net Worth
- Total Debt to Assets
- Total Debt to Inventory
- Total Debt to Net Worth

PROFITABILITY

- Gross Margin
- EBITDA to Sales
- Operating Margin
- Operating Cash Flow to Sales
- Pre-Tax Return on Assets
- After-Tax Return on Assets
- Pre-Tax Return on Net Worth
- After-Tax Return on Net Worth
- Pre-Tax Return on Sales
- After-Tax Return on Sales

WORKING CAPITAL

- Working Capital
- Working Capital to Sales
- Net Income to Working Capital
- Inventory to Working Capital
- Short-Term Debt to Working Capital
- Long-Term Debt to Working Capital

OPERATING EFFICIENCY

- Operating Expenses to Gross Margin
- Operating Expenses to Sales
- Depreciation & Amortization to Sales
- Total Assets to Sales
- Sales to Net Worth
- Sales to Fixed Assets

Inventory to Cost of Sales
Intangible Assets to Sales
Capital Expenditures to Sales

RISK

Z Score
Fixed Assets to Net Worth

GROWTH (COMPOUND AVERAGE GROWTH RATE—5 YEARS)

Sales
Operating Income
Pre-Tax Profit
Net Income
Assets
Liabilities
Net Worth

The above list reflects Z *Score* under the risk category. If you are like me, you are probably wondering what this is. The Z Score is a financial distress (or solvency) prediction model. In assessing a company's level of financial distress or solvency, four ratios are used together, and each ratio is weighted. The following weighted averages are used: 6.56 × (working capital to total assets) + 1.05 × (net worth to total debt) + 3.26 × (net worth to total assets) + 6.72 × (operating income to total assets). A score greater than 2.90 is preferred, and a score less than 1.23 indicates significant risk of bankruptcy.

Business Profiler can now be downloaded to Excel from The Internet. The CD-ROM version could be downloaded, but it is now available only online. We set up our valuation model so that we import this information directly from *Business Profiler* into our spreadsheet to perform an analysis against the data without having to input this stuff manually. The end result is this:

Microsoft Excel - Hilltop Holdings, Inc. Valuation

S1 = Five

	B	G	H	I	J	K	L
1							
2							
3							
7	**LIQUIDITY / SOLVENCY**	Five	Six	Seven	Eight	Nine	Ten
8	Quick Ratio	1.67	2.07	3.31	2.18	4.19	2.96
9	Quick Ratio - Integra	-	0.60	0.60	0.60	0.60	0.60
10	Current Ratio	2.67	3.64	5.95	3.96	6.83	5.48
11	Current Ratio - Integra	-	1.12	1.12	1.12	1.12	1.12
12	Days Accounts Receivables Outstanding	25.60	53.71	53.64	54.08	53.70	53.10
13	Days Accounts Receivables Outstanding - Integra	#DIV/0!	49.86	49.86	49.86	49.86	47.22
14	Days Accounts Payable	13.03	21.69	14.28	11.57	14.78	17.52
15	Days Accounts Payable - Integra	#DIV/0!	22.08	44.17	44.17	44.17	41.96
16	Days Working Capital	42.09	92.07	110.39	115.90	125.17	133.63
17	Days Working Capital - Integra	#DIV/0!	#DIV/0!	#DIV/0!	#DIV/0!	#DIV/0!	10.87
18	Days Inventory Sales	32.55	71.82	80.79	83.60	85.84	93.53
19	Days Inventory Sales - Integra	#DIV/0!	57.03	57.03	57.03	57.03	53.68
20	**TURNOVER**						
21	Receivables Turnover	14.26	6.80	6.81	6.75	6.80	6.87
22	Receivables Turnover - Integra	-	7.32	7.32	7.32	7.32	7.73
23	Cash Turnover	32.29	23.90	25.47	20.72	16.10	17.35
24	Cash Turnover - Integra	-	41.11	41.11	41.11	41.11	40.11
25	Inventory Turnover	11.21	5.08	4.52	4.37	4.25	3.90
26	Inventory Turnover - Integra	-	6.40	6.40	6.40	6.40	6.80
27	Current Asset Turnover	5.42	2.69	2.58	2.48	2.35	2.28
28	Current Asset Turnover - Integra	-	3.30	3.30	3.30	3.30	3.22
29	Working Capital Turnover	8.67	3.96	3.31	3.15	2.92	2.73
30	Working Capital Turnover - Integra	-	-	-	-	-	33.58
31	Fixed Asset Turnover	12.25	5.47	4.95	5.43	6.50	8.23
32	Fixed Asset Turnover - Integra	-	5.42	5.42	5.42	5.42	5.57
33	Total Asset Turnover	3.43	1.73	1.68	1.65	1.66	1.67
34	Total Asset Turnover - Integra	-	1.85	1.85	1.85	1.85	1.85
35	Payables Turnover	28.01	16.82	25.56	31.55	24.70	20.83
36	Payables Turnover - Integra	#DIV/0!	16.53	8.26	8.26	8.26	8.70
37	SG&A Expense to Cash	5.77	4.13	4.76	3.72	2.69	2.59
38	SG&A Expense to Cash - Integra	#DIV/0!	14.26	7.13	7.13	7.13	7.46

Assumptions / Reconcile / JFP / Industry / B-S Input / B-S / I-S Input / I

Ready NUM

Source: Reprinted with kind permission from Integra Information, a Division of Microbilt Corp.

The subject company's financial ratios are calculated and presented directly above the Integra *Business Profiler* ratios. This way, we not only get to compare the financial ratios, but we also get to perform a trend analysis (discussed below). Before we move off the topic of financial ratios, one other item needs to be raised. Frequently, financial statements of the subject company have to be normalized (discussed below) for economic adjustments that are necessary to present the subject company from the point of view that the willing buyer would be purchasing. This raises an issue—should the appraiser use the unadjusted or the adjusted figures to perform the financial analysis and compare the results against the industry group? The answer depends on the facts and circumstances of the appraisal, as well as the nature of the adjustments that are made. Sometimes we compare both the unadjusted and the adjusted to the industry group. How is that for being definitive?

Trend Analysis

The purpose of a trend analysis is to compare the subject company's performance over the past several years. The exact number of years used in the analysis depends on the facts and circumstances of each individual case. Although five years is the number commonly used, it is not always the correct number. Ideally, the period of years should cover a normal business cycle for the subject company.

During the trend analysis, the appraiser attempts to identify positive and negative trends affecting the company. The appraiser should review this data with the goal of determining the future prospects of the company based on historical growth patterns and based on the company's normal operations. This is a good time to identify items that are nonrecurring and will be removed during the normalization process and not considered in the forecast of future net earnings or cash flows.

Operational Analysis

The purpose of performing an operational analysis is to determine information regarding the quality and stability of the earnings or cash flow from the business. The appraiser should be mindful that an equity investor is concerned with the ability of the subject company to provide earnings, cash flow, or both so that he or she will obtain a return on investment (e.g., dividends).

Some important components of this process include an analysis of (1) gross profit, (2) discretionary costs, and (3) financial statement consistency.

Gross Profit Analysis. An analysis of the cost of goods sold will provide the appraiser with information about the gross profit that the company has been able to achieve. Since the selling price of the goods is dictated by competition, the company's gross profit should be in line with the industry's. The subject company must produce an adequate volume of sales if it is to cover its operating expenses.

A gross profit analysis is also a useful tool for determining if the inventory is properly valued or if there is unreported income. Although there is a difference between an appraiser and a forensic accountant, there are times when one professional may perform both functions. Let me share with you an example of how this analysis can impact an appraisal. We were valuing a pharmacy that also sold liquor. The store never took a physical inventory, and we found out from one of the owners that there was cash payroll. Our gross profit analysis is reflected in Exhibit 5.4.

EXHIBIT 5.4
Gross Profit Analysis

To account for the significant amounts of cash not recorded by The Company, as well as the ending inventory being calculated based on a gross profit percentage rather than a physical valuation, the appraiser has recalculated gross profit based on industry gross profit percentages. Using these industry averages, we can estimate the amounts of gross revenue and net income that ABC Drug Stores, Inc. should have had each year.

(Continued)

EXHIBIT 5.4 *(Continued)*

In order to reflect the gross profit percentage of ABC Drug Stores, we have relied on industry data from Integra Information. To accurately calculate a gross profit percentage, we utilized data from both the drug store industry (SIC code 5912), and liquor store industry (SIC code 5921). The Integra data consisted of 1,050 drug stores with revenues between $2.5 million and $5 million, and 3,621 liquor stores with revenues between $250,000 and $500,000. The gross profit information appears below.

Integra Gross Margins

	1995	*1996*	*1997*	*1998*	*1999*
Drug stores	28.00%	27.60%	27.30%	27.00%	26.70%
Liquor stores	25.00%	24.60%	24.20%	23.80%	23.40%

The gross margin percentages shown above are then applied to the percent of revenues ABC Drugs received from the sale of drugs or liquor in each year. The breakdown of ABC Drugs' revenues by type appears below.

ABC Drug Revenue Breakdown

	1995	*1996*	*1997*	*1998*	*1999*
Drug revenues	91.10%	88.09%	88.58%	87.20%	86.97%
Liquor revenues	8.90%	11.91%	11.42%	12.80%	13.03%

Multiplying the revenue percentages by the industry gross margin figures in each year results in a weighted margin for drugs and liquor. Totaling the two figures in each year results in a weighted gross margin for ABC Drugs based on industry gross margins, and The Company's revenue breakdown by product type. The margin calculations appear below.

Gross Margin Percentage Calculation

	1995	*1996*	*1997*	*1998*	*1999*
Drug margin subtotal	25.51%	24.31%	24.18%	23.54%	23.22%
Liquor margin subtotal	2.23%	2.93%	2.76%	3.05%	3.05%
Gross margin percent	27.74%	27.24%	26.94%	26.59%	26.27%
Gross margin less 10	24.97%	24.51%	24.25%	23.93%	23.64%

After calculating the gross profit margins relative to ABC Drug Stores, the appraiser applied a 10 percent discount to those figures in order to account for economic and industry-specific risk related to ABC Drug Stores. Based on The Company's operation in a low-income area, which includes a significant amount of customers utilizing government prescription plans such as Medicaid, and the overall competitiveness of the retail pharmacy industry, especially within the metropolitan region in which ABC Drugs operates, a 10 percent discount was determined to be appropriate.

To account for the significant amounts of cash not recorded by The Company, as well as the ending inventory being calculated based on a gross profit percentage rather than a physical valuation, the appraiser has recalculated gross profit based on industry gross profit percentages. Using these industry averages, we can estimate the amounts of gross revenue and net income that ABC Drug Stores, Inc. should have had each year.

Using the calculated weighted gross profit margin percentages, the estimated amounts of cost of goods sold, as a percent of revenues, can be calculated. These figures are as follows:

Cost of Goods Sold Percentage Calculation

	1995	*1996*	*1997*	*1998*	*1999*
Revenue %	100.00%	100.00%	100.00%	100.00%	100.00%
Less: Gross profit %	24.97%	24.51%	24.25%	23.93%	23.64%
COGS %	75.03%	75.44%	75.75%	76.06%	76.36%

The above cost of goods sold percentages are then used to calculate the gross profit adjustment necessary to reflect the approximate amount of revenue that ABC Drug Stores should have achieved in each year. The gross profit adjustment for each year is listed in the income normalization table. With the addition of the gross profit adjustment to annual historic revenues and the cash payroll adjustment, the appraiser has reasonably calculated the annual revenues ABC Drugs attained each year.

Discretionary Costs. Several items included in the company's income statement may be discretionary and should be investigated by the appraiser. Some of the common items to be reviewed are repairs and maintenance (have they been deferred, or are there items that should have been capitalized?), research and development (is the company's policy to continue spending an equal amount on R&D, or is there a measurable payback for past R&D?), and advertising (is the company spending too much for too little?).

An analysis of discretionary costs will almost always be performed by a willing buyer, since that individual will be interested in knowing how much of the company's expense structure can be done away with to produce the maximum return to him or her. Because of the synergies that will be brought to the transaction by the buyer, merger and acquisition appraisals will also look to the level of discretionary costs that can be eliminated.

Financial Statement Consistency. Just as an auditor looks for consistency in financial reporting, the appraiser should analyze the financial statements for consistency from period to period. The appraiser must pay particular attention to the company's accounting policies. If the company has an aggressive capital expenditure expensing policy, the company's balance sheet will be understated for those assets that were expensed rather than capitalized. Not only does this understate the value of the balance sheet, but it also destroys the usefulness of many of the financial ratios calculated, common-size analyses, and cash flow projections.

Consistency should also be investigated during a trend analysis, since a review of a spreadsheet of the past several accounting periods may highlight discrepancies that exist between the reporting periods. For example, during a review of the insurance expense, the appraiser sees that the expense has been as follows:

	2000	*1999*	*1998*	*1997*	*1996*
Insurance expense	$ 47,395	$ 45,977	$ 22,984	$ 62,255	$ 39,888

Reviewing the preceding figures for consistency reveals that something happened in 1997 and 1998 that warrants further explanation. An inquiry by the appraiser determined that in 1997 this "cash basis" company made a $21,000 insurance payment that was for 1998. The owner decided to accelerate the expense into 1997, so that she could reduce her taxes for that year. Let's hear it for the matching principle!

Financial Statement Adjustments

Before the appraiser can determine whether or not there will be the need to adjust the financial statements, he or she will have to assess the quality of the available financial information. While reviewing the historical financial statements, the business appraiser must determine the answers to the following questions:

- Are the financial statements complete with all footnotes and supplemental schedules?
- Is there sufficient detail to make the information usable in the comparative analysis to the industry and market data?
- Are the financial statements prepared under GAAP?

Conversion of Cash or Income Tax Basis to GAAP

In assessing the quality of the company's financial statement information, there may be times when adjustments are necessary to convert the information presented to GAAP. More often than not, this will prove to be an accounting exercise that may not add any value to the appraisal process. A large part of the determination as to the need to make this conversion will depend on the information that the appraiser will be using for comparison purposes. For example, if you are valuing a medical practice that reports on a cash basis, and you are going to compare the practice to other practices reported on a cash basis, why bother going through this exercise?

Most likely, the balance sheet will need to be adjusted for accounts receivable and accounts payable, but the impact on the income statement may be relatively immaterial (I love talking accounting talk!). This will be discussed further in Chapter 16, on the subject of valuing professional practices.

Tax Return Adjustments

There will be many times that an appraiser will work from tax returns and not have the benefit of having financial statements (the client is probably too cheap to pay for this level of service). When this occurs, the appraiser needs to make the necessary adjustments to account for the different treatment of certain expenses between the tax returns and what would have been in the financial statements had they existed. For example, entertainment expenses are only 50 percent deductible on a tax return, but as a legitimate expense, 100 percent should be considered in determining net income.

In order to address these items, the book-tax items, we have modified our valuation model to automatically adjust the appropriate lines from the historical data entry that may have been done from the tax returns. Our model addresses this as follows:

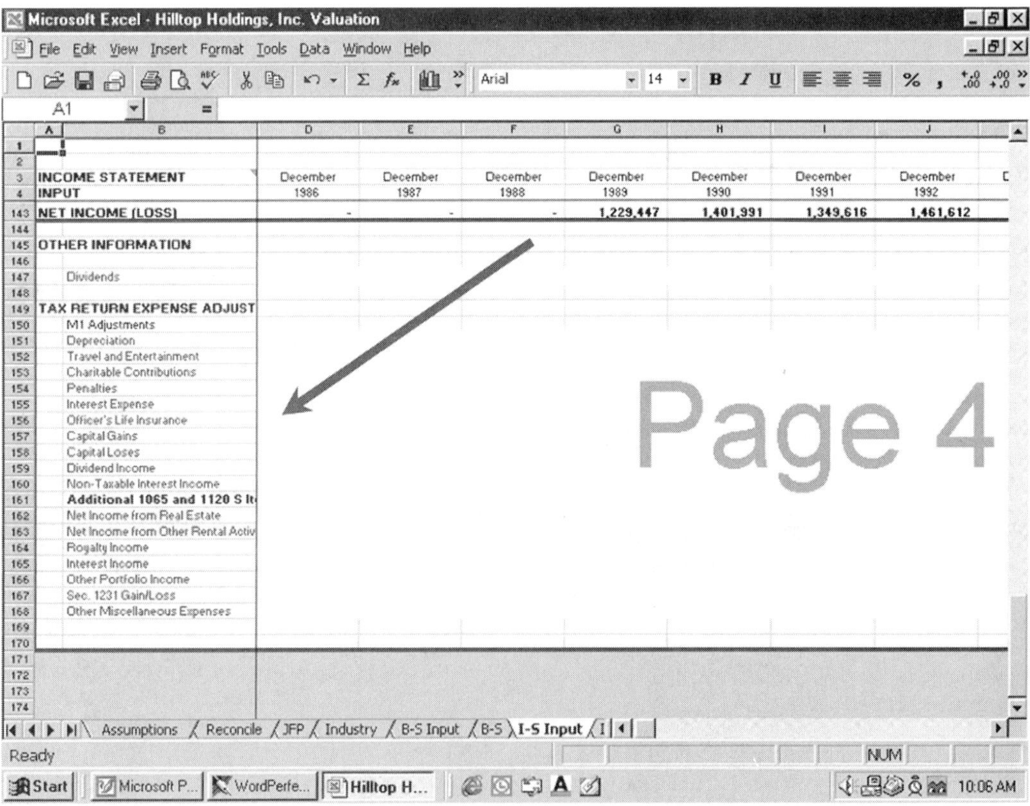

In the event that tax returns are used as the original source document, the template contains certain tax return adjustments that are frequently found in either Schedule K on a partnership or S corporation return, or Schedule M-1 on a regular corporation return. These items should be entered in the area illustrated by the arrow.

Even something like a Schedule C (sole proprietorship) should be adjusted for differences in reporting. Make sure that all material items are accounted for.

Analysis of Historical Balance Sheets

Once the appraiser is pretty sure that all of the data is gathered and input into some form of spreadsheet program, he or she can use all of the analytical tools that I discussed before to try to understand more about the subject company's operations and its industry. Some of the more frequently encountered issues addressed in the historical balance sheet analysis include the following:

- What is the minimum amount of cash or working capital required to operate the company? (See the discussion of Bardahl analysis later in this chapter.)
- What is the status of accounts receivable (i.e., condition, turnover, bad debt experience, reserve, and aging)?
- What are the amounts, terms, and collectibility of officer and employee loans?
- How are inventories valued? How does the company determine inventory quantity and pricing at year end?
- Does inventory cost include material, freight, labor, and overhead where applicable?
- What are the company's operating and nonoperating assets and liabilities?
- What is the policy for capitalization of property and equipment?
- What depreciation methods and lives are used?
- Have write-downs for obsolescence or costs in excess of net realizable value been made?
- What are the terms of all interest-bearing debt?
- What are the trends in payables and turnover ratios?
- What are the terms of all long-term liabilities?
- Are there any preferences for classes of stock, rights, warrants, options, etc.?

Many of these questions can be answered from reading the notes to the financial statements, but many will be answered during the management interview.

Analysis of Historical Income Statements

The income statement analysis is also intended to answer many questions. Some of the more frequent items addressed in the analysis include:

- What is the method of recognizing income and expense?
- What are the company's sources of income?
- What is the breakdown of the revenues in terms of dollars and/or percentages? How have these changed during the last five years?
- Which of the company's products/services are proprietary? Does this impact income?
- Which products are purchased for resale?
- What are the company's main expenses? How have these changed during the last five years?
- How are expenses allocated to inventories?
- Which of the expenses are fixed, semi-fixed, or variable in relation to sales?
- What are the company's gross margins by product/service?
- Are there any deferred charges? If so, do they have any value?

Bardahl Analysis

One of the factors that an appraiser is often faced with is the determination of how much working capital is required in the subject company's operations. Frequently, there may be excess working capital, which becomes a nonoperating asset (explained shortly). There are a number of ways to analyze the working capital needs of the subject company. One such way would be to review industry data on companies or groups of companies, such as from *Business Profiler*. This could give you an idea as to the norm in the industry.

Another way to test the working capital needs came out of a court case entitled *Bardahl Manufacturing Corp.*[1] A formula came out of this court case that is easy to build into a spreadsheet program. Exhibit 5.5 presents the discussion from our training manual on the use of the *Bardahl* formula.

EXHIBIT 5.5
Bardahl Analysis

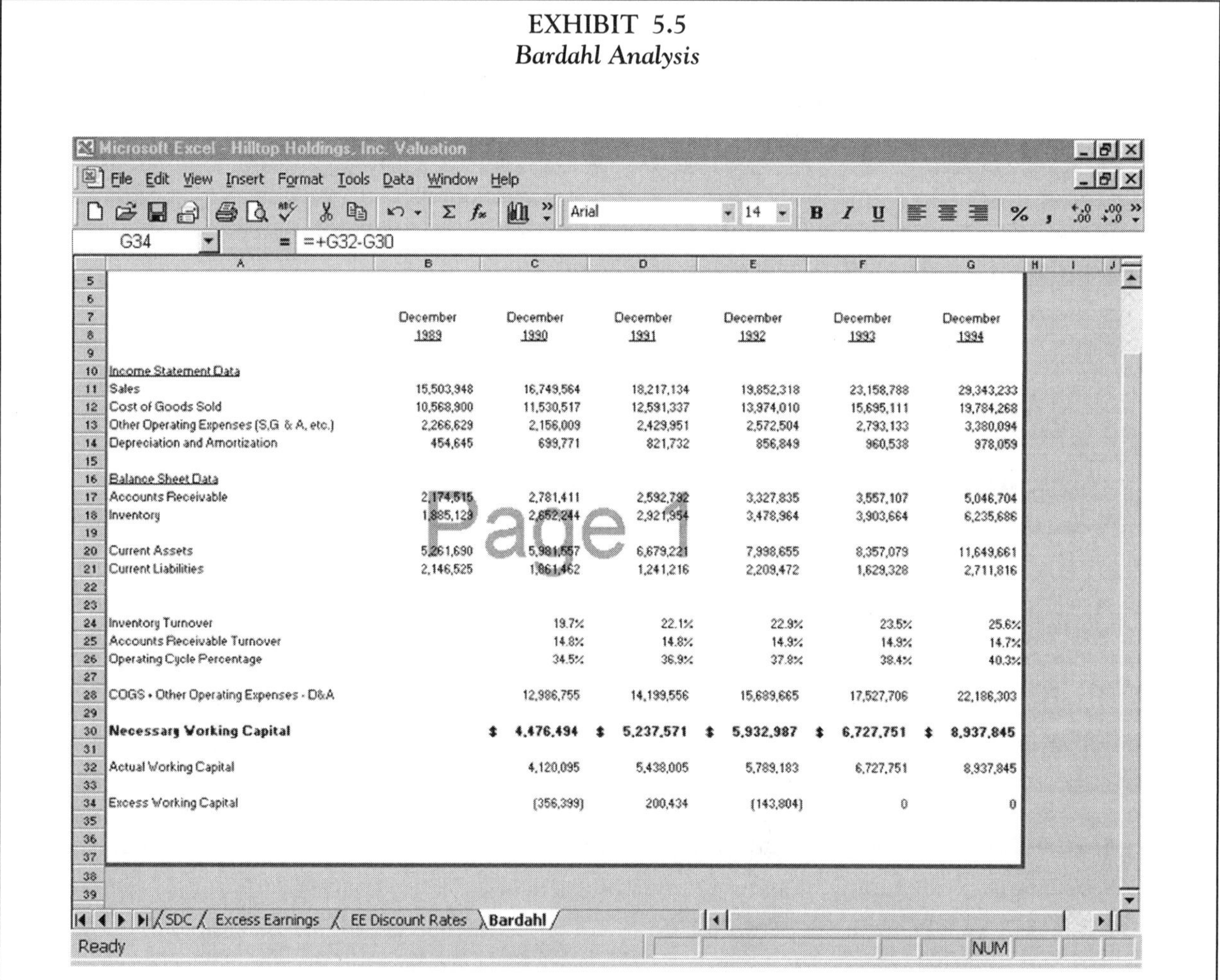

Microsoft Excel - Hilltop Holdings, Inc. Valuation

G34 = =+G32-G30

	December 1989	December 1990	December 1991	December 1992	December 1993	December 1994
Income Statement Data						
Sales	15,503,948	16,749,564	18,217,134	19,852,318	23,158,788	29,343,233
Cost of Goods Sold	10,568,900	11,530,517	12,591,337	13,974,010	15,695,111	19,784,268
Other Operating Expenses (S,G & A, etc.)	2,266,629	2,156,009	2,429,951	2,572,504	2,793,133	3,380,094
Depreciation and Amortization	454,645	699,771	821,732	856,849	960,538	978,059
Balance Sheet Data						
Accounts Receivable	2,174,515	2,781,411	2,592,792	3,327,835	3,557,107	5,046,704
Inventory	1,885,129	2,652,244	2,921,954	3,478,964	3,903,664	6,235,686
Current Assets	5,261,690	5,981,557	6,679,221	7,998,655	8,357,079	11,649,661
Current Liabilities	2,146,525	1,861,462	1,241,216	2,209,472	1,629,328	2,711,816
Inventory Turnover		19.7%	22.1%	22.9%	23.5%	25.6%
Accounts Receivable Turnover		14.8%	14.8%	14.9%	14.9%	14.7%
Operating Cycle Percentage		34.5%	36.9%	37.8%	38.4%	40.3%
COGS + Other Operating Expenses - D&A		12,986,755	14,199,556	15,689,665	17,527,706	22,186,303
Necessary Working Capital		**$ 4,476,494**	**$ 5,237,571**	**$ 5,932,987**	**$ 6,727,751**	**$ 8,937,845**
Actual Working Capital		4,120,095	5,438,005	5,789,183	6,727,751	8,937,845
Excess Working Capital		(356,399)	200,434	(143,804)	0	0

SDC / Excess Earnings / EE Discount Rates / Bardahl

This is the last sheet in the valuation template. It takes data from the Adjusted Income Statement ('I-Sadjd') and the Adjusted Balance Sheet ('B-Sadjd') worksheets for each year in the analysis and calculates three ratios, as well as "necessary," and "excess" working capital.

[1] *Bardahl Manufacturing Corp.* (1965), TC Memo 1965-200, PH TCM 65200, 24 CCH TCM 1030.

EXHIBIT 5.5 *(Continued)*

The following explanation is for each row and applies to all columns until row 24, where ratios are calculated. Since these require the use of a previous year's data, no ratios are available for the firs.t year for which there is data. There is no input for this page.

Row 11, Sales. This row comes from 'I-Sadjd'!G7.

Row 12, Cost of Goods Sold. This row comes from 'I-Sadjd'!G9.

Row 13, Other Operating Expenses. This row comes from 'I-Sadjd'!G13 minus 'I-Sadjd'!G31 (Total Operating Expenses less Depreciation, Amortization)

Row 14, Depreciation and Amortization. This row comes from 'I-Sadjd'!G31.

Row 17, Accounts Receivable. This row comes from 'B-Sadjd'!G10.

Row 18, Inventory. This row comes from 'B-Sadjd'!G12.

Row 20, Current Assets. This row comes from 'B-Sadjd'!G33.

Row 21, Current Liabilities. This row comes from 'B-Sadjd'!G88.

Row 24, Inventory Turnover. This row is calculated as AVERAGE(C18,B18)/C12 or Average Inventory, current and prior years, divided by Cost of Goods Sold, current year.

Row 25, Accounts Receivable Turnover. This row is calculated as AVERAGE(C17,B17)/C11 or Average Accounts Receivable, current and prior years, divided by Sales, current year.

Row 26, Operating Cycle Percentage. This row is calculated as C25 + C24 or Inventory Turnover Ratio plus Accounts Receivable Turnover Ratio.

Row 28, COGS + Other Operating Expenses – Depreciation & Amortization. This row is calculated as C12 + C13 − C14.

Row 30, Necessary Working Capital. This row is calculated as C28 * C26 or (COGS + Other Operating Expenses − Depreciation & Amortization) times Operating Cycle Percentage.

Row 32, Actual Working Capital. This row is calculated as C20 − C21 or Current Assets less Current Liabilities.

Row 34, Excess Working Capital. This row is calculated as C32 − C30 or Necessary Working Capital less Actual Working Capital.

Normalization Adjustments

Once all of the historical financial information has been analyzed, any potential adjustments should be made. Financial statement adjustments, frequently called "normalization adjustments," are intended to place the subject company's financial information on an economic basis. During this process, a "cleansing" of the financial statements takes place. This cleansing is intended to remove those items that the willing buyer would not necessarily take into consideration in assessing the income or cash flow of the company. Another reason for these adjustments is to make the subject company's financial statements more comparable to either other companies that will be used in the analysis or the industry peer group.

The adjustments made to the financial statements will depend on the valuation approach and on whether a controlling interest or a minority interest is being valued. Since a minority interest may not be able to effectuate a change in the company's financial position, it may be inappropriate to make such adjustments. For example, if the minority interest cannot set the compensation for the officers, an adjustment should probably not be made to the income stream.

These adjustments are designed to provide better comparability to similar types of businesses. The normalization process involves adjusting items in the financial statements that are not considered to be normal operating expenses of the subject business. The result should be economic financial statements, rather than those that are GAAP or tax oriented. Most often, the normalization adjustments that are made are categorized as (1) comparability adjustments, (2) non-operating/non-recurring adjustments, or (3) discretionary adjustments. Exhibit 5.6 provides part of an internal form that our firm uses to make certain that the analyst does not overlook the obvious.

Comparability Adjustments

Certain types of adjustments are designed to make the subject company more comparable to the guideline companies or industry group being used as a means of comparison. For example, if the subject company uses last in, first out (LIFO) inventory accounting, a switch to first in, first out (FIFO) may allow the appraiser to compare the balance sheet of the subject company with those of the guideline companies more appropriately, if the guideline companies are using FIFO. Depreciation methods are another type of adjustment that fall into this category.

Non-Operating/Non-Recurring Adjustments

Another type of adjustment is intended to remove those items that appear in the subject company's income statement and are unrelated to the business operations, or those that are not likely to recur in the future. An example of a non-operating income item would be rental income from a condo in Vail, Colo., that is owned by a company in New Jersey that manufactures chemicals. In this instance, the normalization adjustments would be to remove all income and expenses relating to this non-operating asset. A willing buyer of the chemical company would not be buying the condo. Therefore, these items are adjusted, so that what is left would represent the operating income of the company.

Non-operating assets and liabilities are generally removed from the valuation analysis, so that the value reached will be indicative of the operating entity. Afterward, the value of these items is added or subtracted to reach the value of the equity of the company. After all, the buyer may purchase only the operations, but the seller would continue to own the assets that were not sold.

Non-recurring items are also adjusted during the normalization process, since the willing buyer would not expect these income or expense items to be pertinent to him or her in the future. An example of a non-recurring item would be a one-time $1 million contract that resulted in a net profit of $350,000. Since the willing buyer would not expect to realize the benefit of this contract, it should be adjusted.

EXHIBIT 5.6
Partial Internal Checklist

TRUGMAN VALUATION ASSOCIATES INC.
BUSINESS VALUATION INTERNAL CHECKLIST

Company Name: ____________________

Completed by: ____________________ Date Completed: __________

INSTRUCTIONS: This form is to be completed and should become part of the workpapers. It is intended to ensure that important items are not overlooked. Only the information that is relevant to the valuation should be obtained. If the information is not relevant, write N/A in the space opposite the step. If information is missing or incomplete, the analyst should let an officer of the company know BEFORE attempting to prepare a valuation report. The "Comments" section on the last page can be used to document problems that were encountered or to highlight unusual matters for discussion with others.

Balance Sheet Normalization

	Yes	*No*	*N/A*
Cash			
1. Is there excess cash on the balance sheet?	____	____	____
Accounts Receivable			
2. Has accounts receivable been included in the balance sheet? If not, why?	____	____	____
3. Did you tax-effect the accounts receivable?	____	____	____

EXHIBIT 5.6 ***(Continued)***

	Yes	*No*	*N/A*
Inventory			
4. Is inventory included in the balance sheet?	____	____	____
5. Is it reflected on a FIFO basis?	____	____	____
6. Is there any excess inventory?	____	____	____
Marketable Securities			
7. Are these non-operating assets that should be segregated?	____	____	____
8. Have they been reflected at market value as of the val date?	____	____	____
Stockholder Receivables			
9. Are these collectible?	____	____	____
10. Are they legitimate borrowings or just accounting adjustments?	____	____	____
11. Have they been written off?	____	____	____
Fixed Assets			
12. Is there real estate included on the books of the subject company?	____	____	____
13. Is it a non-operating asset?	____	____	____
14. Has it been appraised?	____	____	____
15. Why hasn't it been appraised?	____	____	____
16. Have all corresponding mortgages been treated consistently with the treatment of the real estate?	____	____	____
17. Have all real estate related expenses been segregated on the income statement for possible normalization adjustments along with rent expense?	____	____	____
18. Have machinery & equipment, furniture & fixtures, vehicles, etc. been appraised?	____	____	____
19. If not, did we use our depreciation template to estimate FMV?	____	____	____
20. Do we need to make a depreciation adjustment on the income statement?	____	____	____
21. If there is high appreciation in these assets, have we considered taxes in our analysis?	____	____	____
Other Assets			
22. Did we write off intangible assets that will be revalued?	____	____	____
23. Do we know what all of the assets represent in this category?	____	____	____
Accounts Payable			
24. Did we include accounts payable on the balance sheet?	____	____	____
25. Did we tax-effect it?	____	____	____
26. Notes Payable			
27. Are these notes at market rates of interest?	____	____	____
28. Have non–interest-bearing notes been reflected at FMV?	____	____	____
29. Are any of the notes considered to be non-operating?	____	____	____
30. If notes are high, did we consider using a debt-free approach?	____	____	____
31. Does the debt-equity relationship compare to the industry data to allow a reasonable analysis to be performed?	____	____	____
Stockholder Payables			
32. Are these legitimate?	____	____	____
33. Should they be reclassified as equity?	____	____	____

(Continued)

EXHIBIT 5.6 ***(Continued)***

Income Statement Normalization

1. Was officer's compensation adjusted?
2. If yes, did you consider if any adjustment was required due to retirement plan contributions or payroll taxes?
3. Are there officer's perquisites that need to be adjusted?
4. Are there any nonworking family members on the books?
5. Are there any other payroll adjustments necessary (e.g., maid)?
6. Have you considered the reasonableness of the following:
   (a) Automobile expenses
   (b) Travel
   (c) Entertainment
   (d) Non–arm's-length leases
   (e) Depreciation
   (f) Interest expense
7. Have you added back federal taxes before recalculating taxes on the adjusted income?
8. Have you added back state and local taxes before recalculating taxes on the adjusted income?
9. Have you adjusted all non-operating income/expense items?
10. Have you adjusted all non-recurring income/expense items?
11. Have you made GAAP adjustments to make the statements more comparable to the guideline companies?

Comments. (This section may be used to document problems that were encountered or to highlight unusual matters for discussion with others.)

Discretionary Adjustments

The last group of adjustments that I will discuss are the most common adjustments made for small and medium-sized businesses. Although some of these adjustments may be applicable to larger companies as well, they will more frequently be applicable to the smaller ones. Discretionary adjustments are those items that relate to expenses that are solely at the discretion of management, generally the owners. Some of the more common items include the following:

- Officer's and owner's compensation
- Owner's perquisites
- Entertainment expenses
- Automobile expenses
- Compensation to family members
- Rent expenses (if not an arm's-length lease)
- Interest expense

There also may be other items included in this list, although you will probably find that the preceding items are the most common. Let's discuss each one so that you can gain a better understanding of why we make these adjustments. Remember that most of these adjustments will be appropriate only when controlling interests are being valued. I will discuss this in more detail later.

Officer's and Owner's Compensation. Smaller businesses frequently pay their officers or owners an amount equal to what the officers need to live, or what the businesses' accountants tell them to pay to reduce taxes. A common tax-planning technique used among smaller businesses is to bonus out profit at the end of the year to eliminate taxable income. Sometimes, we see businesses that are doing so poorly that they cannot afford to pay their officers a reasonable wage.

The officer's compensation adjustment is intended to restate the economic income statement of the company to a basis that includes the amount of salary that would be necessary to attract others that are qualified to perform the duties required by the company. I usually put myself in the position of an investor who will have to hire a replacement for the present management. How much will I have to pay to replace management going forward? Many factors should be considered in the determination of reasonable compensation. Consider among others the type of duties, education, experience, the number of hours worked, and the geographical region of the country.

Further guidance for reasonable compensation can be obtained from Tax Court cases in which reasonable compensation was an issue. One of the best constructed judicial opinions in this area can be found in *Mad Auto Wrecking, Inc. v. Commissioner,* T.C. Memo 1995-153, RIA T.C. Memo P. 95153, 69 CCH TCM 2330. This opinion is discussed in greater detail in Chapter 18. In this opinion, Judge Laro addressed, one by one, many points that eventually led to the allowance of what would otherwise seem to be a substantial amount of compensation for the two officers in an auto salvage business that had gross revenues of about $2 million.

Where do you look for reasonable compensation? I can write a book on that subject! Reasonable compensation can be obtained from numerous sources. Some are easier to find than others. I prefer salary surveys that break out the levels of compensation by individual, rather than as a percentage of revenues. As you perform industry research, it is generally a good idea to inquire whether the trade organization has a salary survey. That is always a good starting point. Your best bet will be to compare the officers of the subject company with officers of other companies in the same industry. If the company is large enough, salary disclosure information from the proxy statements of public companies can be used.

If you cannot narrow down this information from the trade associations, another good alternative is other types of salary surveys. For example, the National Institute of Business Management publishes an annual survey entitled *Executive Compensation Survey Analysis*. Another resource is Gale Research's *American Salaries and Wages Survey*. This publication covers much more than executive salaries and has proven to be a useful tool.

Other sources of compensation include business journals, specialized salary surveys published by employment agencies, and employment agencies. Don't be afraid to make telephone calls to executive recruiting firms or "headhunters" to find out what compensation a specific position would command in the marketplace. I generally call two or three firms, so that I can try to get a consensus of opinion. Make sure you carefully document your sources.

As a last resort, I will use publications such as RMA *Annual Statement Studies, Financial Statement Studies of Small Businesses,* and similar publications or I might even go to *Business Profiler*. It is not that they are bad, but they present officer's compensation as a percent of revenues, based on the financial information that they accumulate. It is not possible to answer questions such as How many officers? or What part of the country is the data from? This information can be useful, however, as a means of spot-checking other sources for reasonableness. Exhibit 5.7 shows sections from two reports, from one small company and one large company, that addressed reasonable compensation.

EXHIBIT 5.7
Reasonable Compensation

Report 1—Small Company

Officers' compensation was added back and recalculated at a market rate. The appraiser referenced the National Institute of Business Management's *Executive Compensation Survey Analysis 1999*, Integra's *Business Profiler*, and the New Jersey Department of Labor's *Occupation Employment Statistics Wage Survey*. We used these sources to estimate compensation for two officers for a company in SIC 27, which resulted in the following:

NIBM	$ 239,650
Integra	263,648
NJDOL	193,440
Average	232,246
Rounded	$ 230,000

We decided to use the rounded average of $230,000 as an estimate of the market value of officers' compensation in 1998. This value was deflated by 3 percent for each year prior to 1998. Payroll costs were adjusted in each year to account for the change in officers' compensation. This has been estimated at 15 percent of the change in payroll.

Report 2—Large Company

An estimate of reasonable compensation was made for services rendered by the officers of The Company. In order to estimate this amount, several sources were reviewed.

Public companies that were considered similar to The Company were analyzed to determine the level of compensation being paid to officers. We stratified this data between all of the guideline companies and those with revenues under $150 million. This was intended to get closer to the size of The Company.

Integra data was also reviewed. We broke this data down between SIC Codes and size. We also reviewed information from *RMA Annual Statement Studies* ("RMA") published by Robert Morris Associates.

The data compiled from these sources was as follows:

Public Co. Proxies: Percentage of Revenues (All Companies)	*1993*	*1994*	*1995*
Average	0.53%	0.69%	0.55%
Median	0.39%	0.41%	0.36%
Options (% of companies with options)	53.00%	68.00%	58.00%
Public Co. Proxies: Percentage of Revenues (Under $150 Million)			
Average	1.05%	1.35%	0.94%
Median	0.66%	0.68%	0.65%
Options (% of companies with options)	50.00%	67.00%	40.00%
Local Trucking:			
Integra			
All companies (37,030)			4.00%
100M–250M (23) (avg. rev. $126M)			2.00%
RMA over $25M			n/a
All Companies (349)			4.10%
Except Local Trucking:			
Integra			
All companies (23,920)			2.40%
$50–99 million (45) (average revenues $54 million)			1.30%
Over $500 million (2) (average revenues $1.2 billion)			1.00%
RMA over $25 million (270)			4.10%
All companies (1,165)			3.30%

EXHIBIT 5.7 *(Continued)*

Based on the data compiled, the median salary for officers in public companies was 0.36 percent in 1995. The smaller group was 0.65 percent. However, the officers were given stock options that would effectively increase compensation.

Based on size, the Integra data indicates compensation to be 2 percent and 1.3 percent of sales for local and nonlocal trucking companies, respectively. The companies in the nonlocal group are smaller than The Company. The RMA figures seem higher than the others, but the maximum category is over $25 million in revenues. This group is too small to be useful.

From all of the above, 2 percent of revenues appears to be a reasonable level of compensation. This allows a greater percentage than the public companies and is in line with Integra for companies in this size range.

Owner's Perquisites. During your analysis of the company's financial statements, pay close attention to owner's perquisites. Many business owners will take as much income as they can out of their businesses, whether as salary or as fringe benefits (perqs). These perqs can range from retirement plans, life insurance, disability insurance, and health club memberships to sky boxes at sporting arenas. After all, why own a business if you can't enjoy the fruits of your labor? Well, besides the fact that many of these items are often buried so that our friends at the Internal Revenue Service (one hopes) will not find them, they are also considered to be another form of compensation to the owner of the business.

Part of the normalization process involves removing those items that are considered "discretionary" and would not necessarily have to be paid to someone else who would be hired to replace the owner. If the company has a retirement plan, a health insurance plan, a life and disability insurance plan, or other fringe benefit plans that are offered to all other employees, these items may not be considered a normalization adjustment. However, if the owner is getting a greater benefit than everyone else, a partial adjustment may be required. Whether you add back these expenses may also depend on the salary survey that you use to determine reasonable compensation. Sometimes, the surveys include not only base salary information, but also total compensation, including perqs. Be careful of double counting!

Entertainment Expenses. Entertainment expenses are reasonable and necessary expenses for many businesses. However, we all know that many business owners deduct entertainment expenses that really do not have anything to do with the business. There may be times when the amount of entertainment expense differs significantly from industry data. In this situation, the appraiser must investigate the reason for the differences. Ask yourself, Would the willing buyer have to spend that much on entertainment? If you answer no, you probably need to consider an adjustment. For some reason, I see this happen frequently when we appraise medical practices. Specialists seem to have an incredible amount of entertainment on the books. When was the last time your doctor took you to lunch? Although they have some legitimate meetings with colleagues, many of the entertainment expenses are really perqs.

Automobile Expenses. Once again, be on the lookout for automobile expenses that are not business related. There are many businesses that require a vehicle for business use. However, the adjustments made during the normalization process are intended to remove the expenses related to non-business vehicles (such as the husband's, wife's, son's, daughter's, boyfriend's, aunt's, uncle's, or cousin's). Don't forget to look at other line items on the income statement besides automobile expenses for the total expenses attributable to the vehicle. Automobile insurance may be in insurance expense. Automobile repairs may be in repairs and maintenance. Gasoline may be in utilities. Make believe that you are playing hide and seek!

Sometimes, the automobile will be a necessary business expense, but the type of vehicle may cause the expense to be excessively high. In this situation, the appraiser should try to estimate the normal vehicle expenses for the business. Similar companies can be a good source for this data. My all-time favorite automobile adjustment was during a valuation of a two-doctor neurosurgery practice. Each doctor had a Lamborghini on the books (at an average cost of $155,000). When I questioned the doctors about the need for these expensive cars, they told me that in the event of an emergency, they needed to get to the hospital fast!

Compensation for Family Members. There is nothing wrong with family members working for the business, as long as they really show up and their pay is reasonable for the services that they render. Frequently the spouse is on the books so that a contribution can be made to an individual retirement account, although no services are rendered for the compensation. In other situations, children are on the books as a means to get spending money and college expenses to them in a lower tax bracket. When family members work for the business, the appraiser should check to see if the amount of compensation would be the same if it were paid to a non–family member. If my daughter performs secretarial services for my firm, she should not be compensated as an executive.

Rent Expense. Frequently, closely held businesses operate in a facility that is owned by the stockholders or a related entity and is leased to the business establishment. This is not a problem if the lease is at a market rate of rent. More often than not, the rent being charged is based on the mortgage payment that the owner is required to make. A market rental analysis should be obtained by the appraiser to support the fair rental value of the premises. This can be obtained from a real estate appraiser or a local realtor who is familiar with the market rents in the area for that type of property.

Another factor to consider, although not necessarily a normalization adjustment, is when a business is operating without a lease. Rent may be paid to an unrelated landlord at market rates, which would not require an adjustment to be made, but the risk associated with not having a lease should be built into market multiples, capitalization rates, or discount rates. Also consider the difficulty in selling the business to a willing buyer if a lease cannot be obtained. This could cause the business to be less marketable.

Interest Expense. An adjustment for interest expense may depend on whether the appraiser is valuing the equity of the company or the invested capital of the company. In an equity valuation, the interest expense adjustment may relate only to interest paid on non-operating liabilities. This could be interest on the mortgage of the condo in Vail that we discussed previously. Since the asset was considered to be non-operating, all associated income and expenses, including interest, should be removed during the normalization process.

The appraiser should also pay attention to sizable amounts of interest related to debt used to finance excessive compensation and perquisites. A company may be borrowing for working capital and using the proceeds of the debt to pay the owners. A willing buyer would not be expected to incur this debt, and therefore, it should be removed during the normalization process.

When the appraiser values the invested capital of the company, the interest is added back to determine the earnings available to the invested capital holders. This can be useful when the appraiser values companies that have different capital structures from those of the guideline companies. This is not truly a "discretionary" adjustment, but the discretion is on the part of the appraiser to value the equity or the invested capital. More about this in Chapter 6.

Normalizing the Financial Statements

The starting point of the normalization process is to obtain or prepare historical financial statements for an appropriate period. Although five years is frequently used, it is not always appropriate. These statements are then normalized if the appraiser is estimating the value of a controlling interest in the enterprise. Since in many cases, minority interests have a lack of control over the items being adjusted, the normalization process may not be appropriate. (I have repeated this point several times because it's important!) Exhibit 5.8 contains a sample normalization section of an actual valuation report. Our firm was retained by the husband of the business owner when the two were going through a divorce. This example is an extreme case, with more adjustments than normal. However, it covers all of the adjustments and then some!

The example shown in Exhibit 5.8 is an abnormality in the sense that the owner of the business was so flagrant about her disregard for the tax laws. However, this report section should be viewed as a good learning tool, since it contains almost all of the types of adjustments that were discussed previously.

Once the financial statements have been normalized, the appraiser uses the adjusted information as a basis for the valuation. This information can then be used to forecast the future operating results of the business as well as analyze the economic return to the owner. The appraiser should not use an average of the historical figures *unless* the outcome reflects the anticipated financial results of the appraisal subject. Remember, valuation is a prophecy of the future!

As a general rule, I like to use the adjusted figures in addition to the unadjusted figures in performing my ratio analysis. This gives me not only the unadjusted ratios that can be compared with similar data, but also the adjusted figures that can be used to assess the economic future of the company. This becomes an easy task if you use computer templates that you write yourself.

EXHIBIT 5.8
Sample Normalization of Income Section

In addition to the balance sheet adjustments, the company's income statement needed to be adjusted. The adjustments made are intended to normalize the net income to an economic basis. The "normalization" process removes non-operating, non-recurring, and other items that would not be expected to continue in the hands of the "willing buyer."

In this appraisal, *many* items appear to have been included in the corporate tax returns that are personal in nature. It appears that serious tax fraud is being committed, and many of the adjustments shown in Table 1 reflect these abuses. They are explained in the footnotes to the table.

To review this business as if it were being considered by a "willing buyer," we not only have normalized the income statement, but have also estimated the normalized cash flow of the enterprise. This will be used later in this report to perform valuation calculations.

TABLE 1
Cash Flow Normalization

	2000	*1999*	*1998*	*1997*
Net income (as reported)	$ (3,516)	$ 18,371	$ 19,111	$ 59,833
Officer's salary[1]	82,500	115,005	103,300	68,298
Depreciation[2]	19,935	20,989	24,298	23,203
Outside services[3]	5,200	7,400	—	—
Consulting[4]	2,400	7,000	11,250	—
Education[5]	—	2,000	1,000	1,415
Office supplies[6]	16,501	22,224	—	—
Repairs[7]	984	3,000	8,885	107
Furniture and fixtures[8]	10,000	19,000	5,807	45,694
Office equipment[9]	3,200	2,972	1,000	495
Office expense[10]	2,873	5,263	23,031	13,033
Licenses and fees[11]	—	55	—	—
Auto lease[12]	9,000	7,200	6,452	2,488
Rent[13]	6,100	5,000	3,600	3,600
Entertainment[14]	1,502	300	2,954	621
Retirement plan[15]	30,000	30,000	30,000	17,000
Disability insurance[16]	1,713	1,713	1,709	1,713
Travel[17]	2,317	784	—	598
Maintenance[18]	2,530	2,400	309	2,215
Sundry[19]	67	66	103	755

(Continued)

EXHIBIT 5.8 *(Continued)*

	2000	*1999*	*1998*	*1997*
Contributions[20]	2,489	2,510	1,786	545
Professional fees[21]	5,200	500	2,551	187
Advertising[22]	690	225	—	—
Dues and subscriptions[23]	68	28	75	—
Stockholder loan[24]	5,137	1,000	17,873	14,000
Cash advances[25]	5,895	700	6,750	5,925
Medical supplies[26]	18,263	—	12,641	—
Subcontractors[27]	—	—	632	2,000
Leasehold improvements[28]	3,500	—	—	—
Interest[29]	375	45	769	2,228
Taxes[30]	—	521	—	—
Sharon Brown[31]	—	—	2,000	—
Office salaries[32]	—	—	—	7,425
Postage[33]	—	—	—	84
Automobile[34]	(4,000)	(4,000)	(4,000)	(4,000)
Officer's salary[35]	(110,000)	(103,400)	(97,196)	(91,364)
Gross cash flow	$ 120,923	$ 168,870	$(186,690)	$178,098

[1]Officer's salary, as reflected in the corporate tax return, has been added back in its entirety. Reasonable compensation for the officer will be computed as a separate item at the end of this process.

[2]Depreciation has been added back in its entirety. Since cash flow is being calculated, depreciation expense representing noncash charges must be added back to net income. In addition, most of the assets listed on the depreciation schedule appear to be personal in nature, not business related, so an adjustment would be necessary since the depreciation does not reflect the economic wear and tear of business assets.

[3]Outside services have been adjusted for 1999 and 2000 as a result of payments made to Robert and Bonnie Brown, Ms. Brown's children, as well as payments to Ronald Brown, her husband, and Arnold Pincus, Ms. Brown's brother. These items are not deemed to be valid business expenses, and as such, they are added back to derive the normalized cash flow of the business.

[4]Consulting expenses have been adjusted for payments made to Arnold Pincus and John Williams, an individual affiliated with a company called Unlimited Pleasures, which appear to relate to the redecorating of Ms. Brown's personal residence. Documentation requested regarding these expenses was not provided; however, a significant number of payments were made to Unlimited Pleasures, John Williams, or both, and have been charged to various accounts in an attempt to hide the expenses.

[5]Education expenses have been adjusted to reflect payments made to Arnold Pincus, which are deemed to be personal expenses.

[6]Office supplies have been adjusted for a significant number of items charged on an American Express credit card and various MasterCard credit cards, as well as payments to a company called Room Service, which are all deemed to be personal expenses. These expenses appear to be excessive, considering the type and size of business that is being appraised, and even if they are business-related, they are not reasonable and necessary business expenses.

[7]Repairs have been adjusted to add back items charged on American Express to jewelry stores, payments to Unlimited Pleasures, payments to lawn services, and similar non-business expenses.

[8]As indicated in the discussion of fixed assets on the balance sheet, there are a significant number of personal assets that have been reflected on the depreciation schedule of the company. A substantial number of payments to Unlimited Pleasures, Macy's, Country Workshop, and Room Service have been deemed personal. It appears that Ms. Brown refurnished her home out of the business account.

[9]Payments charged to office equipment include such items as Bernie's Bicycle, Unlimited Pleasures, American Express, Nordstrom, and other such payees, and have been deemed personal.

[10]The office expense has been adjusted for payments to Robert and Bonnie Brown, ShopRite Liquors, K. McDougall, American Express, MasterCard, Unlimited Pleasures, and other such non-business items that have been deemed personal.

[11]Licenses and fees have been adjusted in 1999 to reflect credit card fees. Since such a large portion of the credit card charges is personal in nature, we have added back one payment as being personal.

[12]Automobile lease payments have been added back in their entirety since a provision for reasonable auto expenses will be deducted later in this process.

EXHIBIT 5.8 *(Continued)*

[13]Payments made to the Brown family have been added back since the business rents space outside of the personal residence. There is no justification for the second office. It appears that this second office has been set up to try to justify an extraordinary amount of personal items charged relating to the personal residence, including landscaping, furniture, leasehold improvements, etc.

[14]Certain entertainment expenses were added back, primarily items charged on credit cards, because we were not provided with adequate documentation to show that these were valid business expenses.

[15]Retirement plan contributions have been added back for the portion that relates to Sharon Brown, since this will be calculated as part of reasonable compensation. These are considered to be discretionary expenses, and Sharon Brown's portion has been estimated.

[16]Payments made to the Equitable, representing disability insurance, have been added back as being perquisites that are personal to the shareholder.

[17]Travel expenses have been adjusted for payments to American Express, MasterCard, and similar sources for which we did not obtain adequate documentation to support the validity of the expense.

[18] Maintenance expenses have been adjusted for personal landscaping and lawn care, as well as other similar expenses deemed personal.

[19]Sundry expenses have been adjusted for payment to the Township of East Bonntown Municipal Court in Gaitertown, as well as other items deemed personal.

[20]Contributions have been added back. Although they are not reflected in deductible business expenses in the tax return, they are allocated to the stockholder because of the election to be treated as an S corporation under the tax law. These items are not only discretionary but also do, in fact, require an outflow of cash, and therefore have been added back in determining the gross cash flow of the business.

[21]Professional fees have been adjusted for various payments deemed to be personal. These payments include payments to Gerry Conway, Ms. Brown's former divorce lawyer, Sheldon O'Hara, Ms. Brown's current divorce lawyer, and Skip & Jones, another law firm providing divorce services, as well as payments to Stock & Stock. These items were all deemed personal and have been adjusted accordingly.

[22]Advertising expense has been adjusted. Such items as payments to Neiman Marcus and American Express were deemed personal and therefore adjusted in the normalization process.

[23]Dues and subscriptions have been adjusted to add back various subscriptions to magazines that are deemed personal. Since the nature of a physical therapy business is providing services in the home, as opposed to in an office, these subscriptions have no business purpose and are considered to be discretionary items.

[24]Over the years, various items were paid either to Sharon Brown or on behalf of Sharon Brown and were charged to a stockholder loan account. This stockholder loan was set up at the inception of the corporation when the assets of a sole proprietorship were transferred into the corporation. In fact, the stockholder loan should have been set up as equity in the corporation, and it was purposely set up in this manner so that Ms. Brown could withdraw funds as she had done over the years. Removal of these funds is actually an improper withdrawal, and therefore, they have been added back in determining the cash flow of the business.

[25]The company uses a Merrill Lynch WCMA account as its checkbook. Accordingly, a credit card was issued to the company, which Ms. Brown uses for her own personal purposes. Cash advances were taken at various times over the years, and all of these cash advances have been added back as being personal in nature.

[26]Medical supplies have been adjusted in 1998 and 2000 to reflect payments to Arnold Pincus, Unlimited Pleasures, Room Service, MasterCard, and American Express. Many of these items are the same items that have been charged elsewhere, and without adequate documentation being provided to us to prove that these are valid business expenses, they have been deemed personal in nature and have been adjusted accordingly.

[27]The subcontractor's expense has been adjusted in 1997 and 1998 to reflect payments to Sharon Brown and Arnold Pincus.

[28]In 2000, payments made to Ray Shine and Robert Brown in the amounts of $1,000 and $2,500, respectively, were charged as leasehold improvements. These are deemed personal and have been added back in determining gross cash flow.

[29]Interest expense has been added back in its entirety since there is no valid business reason for interest to be paid by this business. Had Ms. Brown not chosen to use the business account as a personal checkbook, the business would have had adequate cash flow and no interest would have been paid. Furthermore, some of this interest represents payments to Ms. Brown herself or represents accounting adjustments reflecting balances due to Ms. Brown. Since this is not expected to recur in the hands of a "willing buyer," these items have been adjusted.

[30]The tax payment of $521 was added back in 1999, since this payment was made to the Internal Revenue Service and it could not be determined what this payment represented. It is possibly personal in nature, and as such, we have made this assumption and adjusted it in determining gross cash flow.

(Continued)

EXHIBIT 5.8 *(Continued)*

[31]Payments in the amount of $2,000 were paid to Sharon Brown and did not show up in the shareholder loan account. We were unable to ascertain which account this was charged to, but based on the many personal items withdrawn from this business, we have assumed that this does not represent a business expense.

[32]Office salaries have been adjusted in 1997 for payments to Robert Brown and Bonnie Brown that are not considered to be valid business expenses.

[33]Postage has been adjusted for a payment made to Unlimited Pleasures. This is not deemed to be a business expense.

[34]Automobile expenses have been adjusted by factoring in an additional expense of $4,000 per year, representing an additional allowance determined by the appraiser to compensate for either depreciation expense or reasonable wear and tear on a modest business vehicle. The lease payments previously added back relate to luxury vehicles that would not be leased in the normal course of business. However, a reasonable expense allowance should be factored in, since Ms. Brown uses her vehicle to go out to many patients, which is clearly for a valid business reason.

[35]To determine Sharon Brown's reasonable compensation as the manager of Physical Therapy Associates, three sources were consulted:

1. A salary survey prepared by the American Physical Therapy Association (APTA), based on 1999 data
2. The *2001 Survey of Executive Compensation*, prepared by the National Institute of Business Management, based on 2000 data
3. *Basic Statistics About Home Care 2001*, published by the National Association for Home Care (NAHC)

In the survey prepared by APTA the "median gross earned income" of a sole owner of a physical therapy practice in 1999 was $85,000. We spoke to John Smith, Director of Research Services at APTA, to determine how gross earned income was defined. He clarified that gross earned income is income after expenses of the practice and is equivalent to take-home salary.

In addition to the incomes of the sole owners of a physical therapy practice, the survey provided the following median incomes:

By geographic region (Middle Atlantic)	$ 55,800
By primary employment setting (Home health)	$ 54,600
By years of experience (16 or more years)	$ 55,000
By highest earned academic degree	$ 48,755

According to APTA, the median, nonsupervisory salary for physical therapists in private practice was $48,000 in 1999. In the *2000 Active Membership Profile Report*, compiled by APTA, full-time self-employed females had a mean gross earned income of $93,699.

The 2001 Survey of Executive Compensation included companies performing nonfinancial services in SIC code 80-82. The median sales volume of the respondents in the group was $2.4 million, and the largest geographic concentration was the east north central region.

According to the survey, the median total compensation for the chief executive officer was $120,000. This figure includes perquisites as extra compensation.

The final survey used came from the National Association for Home Care, where it was reported that the chief executive officer of Home Health Agencies averaged $64,570 in 2000 and the average compensation of physical therapists was $50,495.

One additional factor should be considered in the determination of reasonable compensation for Sharon Brown. According to Ms. Brown, the amount billed to Visiting Therapists Association in 2000 was $797,556. According to the VTA contract, Physical Therapy Associates was paid $49.80 per visit. This indicates that there were approximately 16,015 visits in 2000. Ms. Brown claims that she performed 3,246 of these visits.

Assuming that total revenues of $917,171 were earned at $49.80 per visit, the total visits in 2000 to all patients would be 18,417. Subcontractors were paid $593,089 in 2000. The per-visit amount paid to subcontractors was as follows:

Total visits	$ 18,417.00
Sharon Brown's visits	3,246.00
Subcontractor visits	15,171.00
Amount paid to subcontractors	$ 593,089.00
Amount per visit	$ 39.09

EXHIBIT 5.8 (Continued)

If Ms. Brown were a subcontractor, her compensation would have been $126,886 (3,246 visits × $39.09). However, a prudent businessperson would consider hiring a full-time salaried physical therapist, or possibly two individuals, to cover the number of visits made by Ms. Brown. Even if one of these people was compensated as a manager, the total payroll would be less than paying a subcontractor for more than 3,000 visits.

After considering all of the information, including Ms. Brown's efforts as a physical therapist, we believe that a reasonable level of compensation would be approximately $110,000. This places the heaviest weight on the self-employed income figures, with an added allowance for Ms. Brown's personal performance of therapy services. This also seems reasonable based on the executive compensation survey since companies with median sales of $2.4 million were paying $120,000 to the chief executive officer.

The prior years' salaries have been calculated using a 6 percent deflation factor.

Conclusion

You should have more of an idea about what to do with the data that you collect. By now, you should be getting the message that the appraiser performs a risk assessment with the data collected. This information can then be used in the determination of market multiples, discount rates, and capitalization rates.

The data collected and analyzed is critical to the valuation process. If you are not comfortable with analyzing the gobs and gobs of data that you will be collecting, you may want to reread some financial statement analysis textbooks. I hope for your sake you are okay with this stuff. These types of textbooks are like watching paint dry on a wall—real excitement!

6

The Market Approach—Part I

Chapter Goals

In this chapter, I will begin to explain the market approach. There is a lot of important information here! After an introduction to the market approach, I will cover the guideline public company method. This discussion will include:

1. The guideline public company method
2. Selecting potential guideline companies
3. Analyzing guideline companies
4. Using valuation multiples
5. Advantages and disadvantages of the guideline public company method
6. Illustrating the guideline company method

Introduction

The market approach is probably the most fundamental approach in a fair market value appraisal. Since fair market value is supposed to come from the "market," it seems natural that this approach should be greatly emphasized. The application of this approach can, at times, be the most difficult approach to use in a business appraisal. In real estate appraisal, the appraiser looks for properties similar to the piece of real estate being appraised in order to compare the similarities and dissimilarities between the properties. After the comparison is made, the real estate appraiser estimates the value of the subject property using the sales price of the "comparable" properties as a starting point.

This concept can be illustrated using the following example. Property A sold for $200,000. It is a single-family house on a busy main road; it is on one acre of land and has three bedrooms, two baths, and a newly renovated family room. Property B sold for $175,000. It is also a single-family residence in the same neighborhood, but it is up the street off the main road on one acre of land, and it has two bedrooms, two baths, and a well-maintained interior. Property C sold for $190,000 on the same block as property B; it is also on one acre, has two bedrooms, has two-and-one-half baths, and is in relatively good shape on the inside. An appraisal of property D is requested. The comparative statistics about the properties are given in the following table.

	Property A	*Property B*	*Property C*	*Property D*
Sales price	$200,000	$175,000	$190,000	Unknown
Acreage	1	1	1	1
Location	Main road	Quiet street	Quiet street	Quiet street
Bedrooms	3	2	2	3
Baths	2	2	2.5	2.5
Interior	New condition	Good condition	Good condition	Good condition
All else	Same	Same	Same	Same

After a comparison of the features of properties A, B, and C with those of property D, it appears that property D most closely resembles property C, except the appraisal subject has an extra bedroom. Therefore, the real estate appraiser concludes that the appraised value of property D is $200,000.

This is a simplistic example and is not intended to make light of the role of the real estate appraiser. However, real estate sales are generally available in public records, and therefore, the real estate appraiser has a definite advantage over the business appraiser. The point being made is that an estimate of fair market value is an interpretation of market data indicating the worth of a property. The role of the appraiser is that of an interpreter, not a market maker. Our job is to use the information available in the market to estimate the value of the appraisal subject. Despite the similarities to real estate appraisal, business valuation methods are a bit different.

The market approach emphasizes the principle of substitution, which was discussed in Chapter 3. This means that given alternative investments, an individual would be expected to gravitate toward the property with the lowest price if all other attributes are the same. This gravitation may frequently involve the personal choices of the purchaser, but "risk" is a key ingredient in the selection process.

The market approach is the most direct approach for establishing the fair market value of a business. The methods that are used most often under this approach are (1) the guideline public company method, (2) the transaction (merger and acquisition) method, and (3) the industry method (sometimes called "rules of thumb"). This chapter will be solely dedicated to the guideline public company method. Chapter 7 will discuss the transaction method and rules of thumb.

Regardless of the method used, the appraiser must consider the sources of market data. Whereas in real estate appraisal the appraiser is able to obtain "good" information about the comparable properties, business appraisers do not always have the same luxury. The data that is available may differ significantly depending on the types and sizes of the companies. The data used will come either from publicly traded companies or from those that are closely held. Both of these sources can present real problems to the business appraiser.

Guideline Public Company Method

Proper application of the guideline public company method is labor intensive and will take time. Following the basic steps laid out in this section will increase your success rate in applying this approach, but remember, valuation is an iterative process, so don't kick yourself if you find that you are repeating these steps. Practice makes perfect.

The guideline public company method of appraisal is based on the premise that pricing multiples (a relationship between the price of a publicly traded stock and some other variable, such as earnings, sales, book value, etc.) of publicly traded companies can be used as a tool to be applied in valuing the closely held appraisal subject. Using multiples of public companies in this manner is suggested in Revenue Ruling 59-60 in the famous eight factors to consider (at a minimum). The Revenue Ruling tells us to consider the "*market price of stocks of corporations engaged in the same or similar line of business having their stocks actively traded in a free and open market either on an exchange or over the counter."*

The mechanics of the method require the appraiser to use the stock price of the public company in conjunction with some other factor (such as earnings, cash flow, or book value), to create a pricing multiple. With certain adjustments, the pricing multiple is applied to the appraisal subject's similar factor to determine an estimate of value for the company. A price-to-earnings multiple would be applied to the company's earnings, a price-to-cash flow multiple would be applied to the company's cash flow, and so forth.

To use this method properly, the publicly traded companies that are used as surrogates must be comparable to the closely held appraisal subject. The comparable companies will not be identical to the appraisal subject but should be similar enough to provide guidance to the appraiser during the appraisal process. The similar companies, formerly known as "comparative companies" or "comparables," a term taken from the real estate appraisal world, are known as "guideline companies" in our world. This terminology was suggested by the Business Valuation Committee of ASA to highlight the fact that no two companies are truly comparable, but rather, that similar companies can provide guidance about other companies in the marketplace.

In business valuation, the requirements for "similarity" are considered from an investment point of view. The factors that will be considered by the appraiser will vary from assignment to assignment. One concise list of factors to consider in determining the similarity of the guideline companies is impossible. However, some of the factors to consider have been included in the writings of Graham, Dodd, and Cottle;[1] Stockdale;[2] and Bolten, Brockardt, and Mard.[3] The following are some of the factors to consider, though not necessarily in any special order:

- Past growth of sales and earnings
- Rate of return on invested capital
- Stability of past earnings
- Dividend rate and record
- Quality of management
- Nature and prospects of the industry
- Competitive position and individual prospects of the company
- Basic nature of the activity
- General types of goods or services produced
- Relative amounts of labor and capital employed
- Extent of materials conversion
- Amount of investment in plant and equipment
- Amount of investment in inventory
- Level of technology employed
- Level of skill required to perform the operation
- Size

[1]B. Graham, D. Dodd, and S. Cottle, *Security Principles and Technique*, 4th ed. (New York: McGraw-Hill, 1962).

[2]John J. Stockdale, "Comparison of Publicly Held Companies With Closely Held Business Entities," *Business Valuation Review* (December 1986), 3–9.

[3]Steven E. Bolten, James W. Brockardt, and Michael J. Mard, "Summary (Built-up) Capitalization Rates for Retailers," *Business Valuation Review* (March 1987), 6–13.

- Financial position
- Liquidity
- Years in business
- Financial market environment
- Quality of earnings
- Marketability of shares
- Operating efficiency
- Geographical diversification

Various writings have created a substantial list of attributes to consider in determining whether the guideline companies are "comparable" enough to be used as good surrogates in an appraisal. In its courses The Institute of Business Appraisers teaches that a guideline company must be "similar" and "relevant" to be used as a surrogate. Comparing the local hardware store with Home Depot may involve similar businesses, but let's face it, where's the relevance? In Chapter 18, I discuss the Tax Court case of *Estate of Joyce C. Hall.* This case has some great stuff in it about choosing guideline companies. When you get to this chapter, read my summary and then get the actual case. This will assist you further in understanding the concept of *same or similar.*

How do we really identify guideline companies? Earlier, I indicated the criteria for determining similarity. In the real world, the search for guideline companies can be accomplished the old-fashioned way, by legwork in the library, or the modern way, sitting at your desk in front of a computer. Those of us who started in this business a long time ago (it seems like when the dinosaurs roamed the earth) did not have a choice. Today, I opt for the latter alternative. It's much faster and a lot less work.

Before we walk through the process of finding guideline companies and figuring out what to do with them once we have found them, take a look at Exhibits 6.1, 6.2, and 6.3. These are the document checklists that we use to help keep track of the basics. We have adapted them from PPC's *Guide to Business Valuations.* I already told you, if it ain't broke, don't fix it. These can be modified (as we have done) for your own use.

EXHIBIT 6.1
Guideline Company Checklist

TRUGMAN VALUATION ASSOCIATES INC.
GUIDELINE PUBLIC COMPANY VALUATION PROCEDURES CHECKLIST

Company Name: ______________________________

Completed by: ______________________________ Date: __________

INSTRUCTIONS: This form lists procedures commonly performed in applying these valuation methods. The exact procedures used are a matter of professional judgment based on the circumstances of each engagement, and this form should be tailored accordingly. The appraiser performing the procedures should initial the space labeled "Completed by" as each step is performed. If a procedure does not apply to a particular engagement, write N/A in the space opposite the step. If additional procedures are needed, document them on a separate page or memo. Use the "Comments" section on the last page to document problems encountered or unusual matters.

Note: This checklist is designed to determine an equity (net-of-debt) value. Modifications may be needed to determine an invested capital (debt-free) value.

Source: Adapted with permission from *Guide to Business Valuations*, Twelfth Edition (January 2002), published by Practitioners Publishing Company, Fort Worth, Texas.

EXHIBIT 6.1 ***(Continued)***

PROCEDURE	*Completed by or N/A*	*Workpaper Reference*
1. Obtain financial statements of the company being valued for a representative period of time. Adjust the financial statements for any GAAP errors or normalization adjustments. Recompute federal and state income taxes based on normalized pretax earnings.		
2. Identify comparative companies by performing the following procedures: ▪ Assemble a list of potentially comparative public companies. The list should normally be compiled in the following manner: ▪ Through discussions with management, identify the company's major competitors. ▪ Determine the company's Standard Industrial Classification (SIC) code and perform a search of published sources for companies with the same or similar code. The company's primary SIC codes are as follows: ____________________ ____________________ ▪ Identify additional companies from other sources, such as trade magazines or stockbrokers. ▪ Obtain financial and other information for each potentially comparative company.		
3. Complete a "Comparative Company Comparison Worksheet" for each potentially comparative company.		
4. If necessary, adjust the financial statements of the comparative companies to make them more comparable to the company being valued.		
5. Decide which multiples are appropriate for the engagement given the unique aspects of the company being valued and the definition of value.		
6. Determine what time period of operations (recent 12 months, recent fiscal year, etc.) should be used in measuring the company's operations.		
7. Compute the selected multiples for each comparative company based on the adjusted financial information. You may use the "Value Multiple Computation Worksheet" to document each value multiple computation. Earnings or cash flow for each comparative company should be measured for the same time period as the company being valued.		
8. Select an appropriate value multiple based on the individual multiples of each comparative company. You may use the "Determination of a Single Value Multiple Worksheet" to document this selection.		
9. Increase or decrease the selected multiple based on differences between the comparatives and the company being valued. Any adjustments should be documented in the SGLPTL analysis.		
10. Multiply the selected multiple by the normalized benefit stream of the company (or ownership interest) being valued to arrive at the estimate of value.		
11. If more than one type of value multiple (price/earnings, price/revenue, etc.) was used on the engagement, determine the relative weighting to be given to each type of multiple.		

(Continued)

EXHIBIT 6.1 *(Continued)*

12. Apply sanity checks on the values computed in Step 10 to determine the reasonableness of those values.		
13. If there were any adjustments made in Step 1 to the financial statements of the company being valued for any non-operating or excess assets, determine an appropriate value for those assets. Add the value of those assets to the values computed in Step 10. If asset shortages were identified in Step 1, determine if the value estimate should be reduced to reflect the value of such shortages. If the normalized income statement was adjusted to reflect the impact of identified asset shortages, it is not necessary to further reduce the value estimate.		
14. Determine whether the estimated values of the company that were determined in Step 13 should be adjusted for marketability discounts, control premiums, lack of control (minority) discounts, or other premiums and/or discounts.		
Comments. (This section may be used to document problems encountered or unusual matters.) __________ __________ __________ __________ __________		

EXHIBIT 6.2
Guideline Public Company Comparison Worksheet

TRUGMAN VALUATION ASSOCIATES INC.
GUIDELINE PUBLIC COMPANY COMPARISON WORKSHEET

Company ____________________ Valuation Date: __________

Prepared by: ____________________ Date: __________

INSTRUCTIONS: This form should be completed for each potentially comparative company. The form is a guide to the key factors that should be considered in determining how similar each potentially comparative company is to the company being valued. It is not necessarily a complete listing of all factors that might be considered—specific engagement circumstances may require additional considerations.

1. Potentially Comparative Company Data

Name of potentially comparative company: ____________________

How was this company identified as a potentially comparative company? ____________________

____

Briefly describe the operations of the potentially comparative company, including its products, customers, geographic markets, and apparent strengths and weaknesses. Indicate the source of this information. __________

____

____

Source: Adapted with permission from *Guide to Business Valuations*, Twelfth Edition (January 2002), published by Practitioners Publishing Company, Fort Worth, Texas.

EXHIBIT 6.2 *(Continued)*

2. Trading Activity

Test for market activity in the guideline company's stock using data obtained from **Dow Jones** (adjusted for capital changes) **(do not use Yahoo as trading volume is unadjusted!)** and the comparative company's current outstanding shares. This is done by downloading monthly stock pricing reports for the 12 months prior to the valuation date. Calculate the average trading volume for 6 and 12 months prior to the valuation date. Trading activity is equal to the calculated averages divided by current shares outstanding. This should be formatted as a percentage. See W/P reference __________ for a printout of this information. If the shares are too thinly traded, go to Part D of this form.

3. Comparisons to the Company Being Valued

Compare the potentially comparative company to the company being valued in the following areas. Highlight significant differences and similarities.

1. Product similarity: ____

____

____

____

____

2. Similarity of customer services: ____

____

____

____

____

3. Competitive advantages and disadvantages: ____

____

____

____

____

4. Historical trends (including growth rates): ____

____

____

____

____

5. Financial risk (capital structure, credit status, liquidity, etc.): ____

____

____

____

____

(Continued)

EXHIBIT 6.2 *(Continued)*

6. Size, including geographic diversification: ______________________

____

____

____

____

7. Management depth: ______________________

____

____

____

____

8. Other factors: ______________________

____

____

____

____

4. Conclusion

Check one of the following conclusions:

_______ The company is comparable to the company being valued in many material respects.

_______ The company is insufficiently comparable to the company being valued and will therefore not be used.

(Explain.) ______________________

____

____

____

_______ The company's stock is too thinly traded to be usable as a guideline company.

EXHIBIT 6.3
Value Multiple Computation Worksheet

TRUGMAN VALUATION ASSOCIATES INC.
VALUE MULTIPLE COMPUTATION WORKSHEET

Company: ______________________ Valuation Date: __________

Prepared by: ______________________ Date: __________

Source: Adapted with permission from *Guide to Business Valuations*, Twelfth Edition (January 2002), published by Practitioners Publishing Company, Fort Worth, Texas.

EXHIBIT 6.3 *(Continued)*

INSTRUCTIONS: The appraiser should complete one of these forms for each guideline company. The form is a guide to the key factors that affect the numerator and the denominator of the value multiple computation.

1. General Information

Name of guideline company: ______________________________

Check the value multiple that will be computed for this engagement:

Measures of operations for the period ended: ______________.[a]

______ Price/earnings ______ Price/gross cash flow

______ Price/dividends ______ Price/revenues

Measures as of a single point in time ______

______ Price/book value ______ Price/net asset value

If a measure of operations for a given period of time is selected above, indicate how the period will be determined:

______ Most recent 12 months (or 4 quarters) ______ Most recent fiscal year

______ Projected operations ______ Historical average

______ Five-year ______ Three-year

______ Simple ______ Weighted

______ Other (Describe) ______________

Indicate the type of value the value multiple will be used to determine.

______ Minority interest ______ Controlling interest

______ Equity ______ Invested Capital

______ Marketable ______ Nonmarketable

2. Numerator of the Value Multiple

Indicate the stock price of the guideline company. ______________________________

Note: This could also be the company price if it is based on a merger or acquisition transaction.

What is the source of this stock price?

Wall Street Journal dated ______________________________

Other (describe): ______________________________

[a]Note: The time period used for each comparative company should match exactly, or as closely as possible, the time period over which the same variable is measured for the company being valued.

(Continued)

EXHIBIT 6.3 *(Continued)*

3. Denominator of the Value Multiple

Indicate the company's earnings (or other measure). ______________________

Note: This measure should be in total or per share, depending on how the stock price is measured.

Should the earnings (or other measure) be adjusted in any way? If so, describe the nature of each adjustment and how the amount of each adjustment was determined. ______________________

____

____

____

____

Note: Such adjustments are sometimes needed to make the comparative company more similar to the company being valued.

Indicate the adjusted earnings (or other measure) of the comparative company. ______________________

4. Computation of the Value Multiple

Compute the value multiple by dividing the stock price of the comparative company from Section B by its adjusted earnings (or other measure) from Section C. ______________________

Your procedures for employing the guideline public company method may go something like the following.

Creating a List of Potential Guideline Companies

The first step of each guideline public company analysis is to generate a list of potential guideline companies. It is important to consider as many potential guideline companies as possible, and that means that you must perform a thorough and comprehensive search to locate as many as possible. I suggest that you consider, at a minimum, these four sources for learning about or finding potential guideline companies.

- Management
- SIC code search
- Online databases
- Industry research

Management. A management interview is a useful part of every valuation assignment. While you are asking management about all the stuff that was on your questionnaire, make sure to specifically ask about any publicly traded competitors. Good managers have a real handle on their competitive environment and will know who their public competitors are. This is a good starting point for each guideline company search. This will also be very helpful because many databases that classify companies by SIC code use different codes for the same company. If you perform a search of a database (which will soon be explained) and you do not come up with a company that management told you about, see what SIC code that company is categorized under and expand your search. You may find other companies there as well.

SIC Code Search. An intuitive starting point when you are back at your computer is an SIC code search. If you do not know the SIC code for the subject or are not sure if your subject is correctly

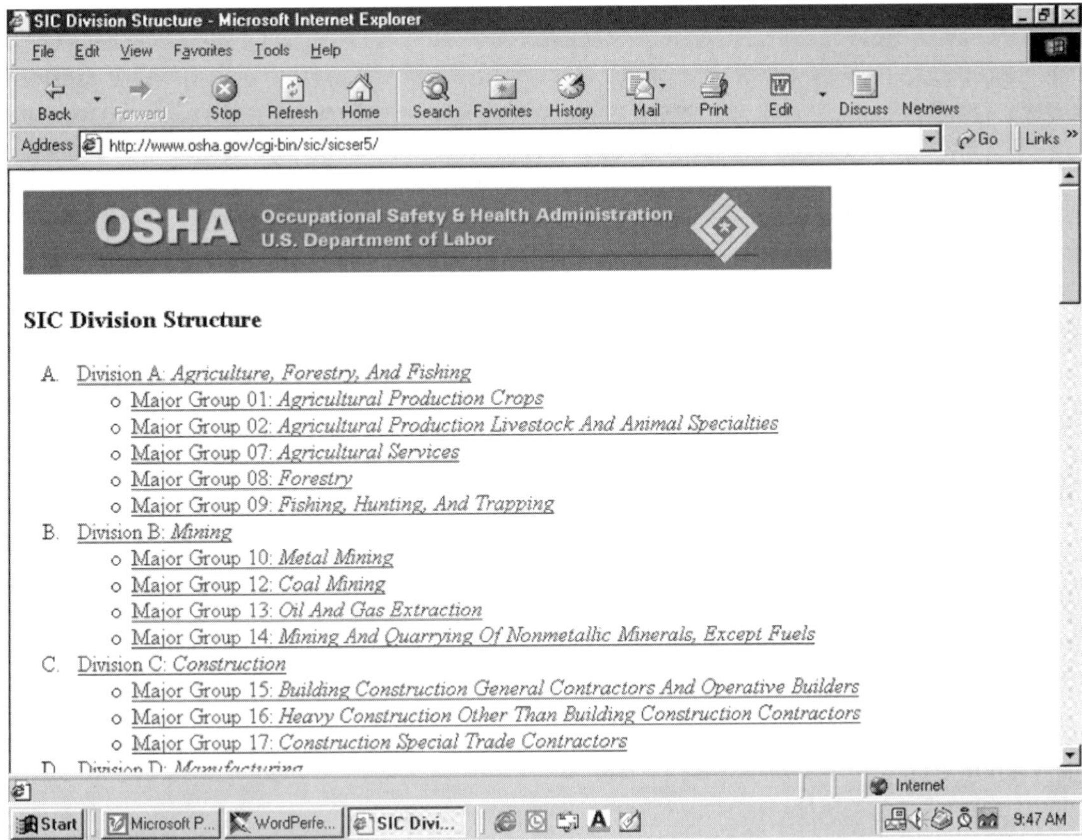

Figure 6.1: OSHA Web Site

defined, there are many sources for SIC code information. The Organizational Safety and Health Administration (OSHA) Web site lists all SIC codes, as shown in Figure 6.1. This Web site allows you to review two-, three-, and four-digit SIC code descriptions, which is helpful in determining the subject's SIC code.

Remember that the goal of this exercise is to locate companies that are in a *same or similar* industry as the subject company. Using the information available on this site, you can research other SIC codes to determine if you could possibly use multiple codes to search for guideline companies.

A useful tool on this page is the "SIC Search." This search allows a user to search SIC codes by keyword. If the subject manufactures metal pipe, for instance, you may want to search on "metal pipe," the results of which are shown in Figure 6.2. In addition to the subject company's SIC code, you have codes for all businesses that deal with metal pipe.

This tool allows a user to quickly and easily expand a guideline company search by performing a simple text search.

Now that you have an SIC code or group of SIC codes, you can use one of many search engines to find companies by industry code. The question becomes which one to use. There are many free Web sites that allow you to get information about guideline companies. There are also many fee-based Web sites that charge without mercy. Basically, it works out that the higher the fees, the more services you sometimes get. The free sites have most of the same information; it's just not packaged as well. I discussed some of these sites in Chapter 4. For free (or almost free) public company information, you can try out some of these sites:

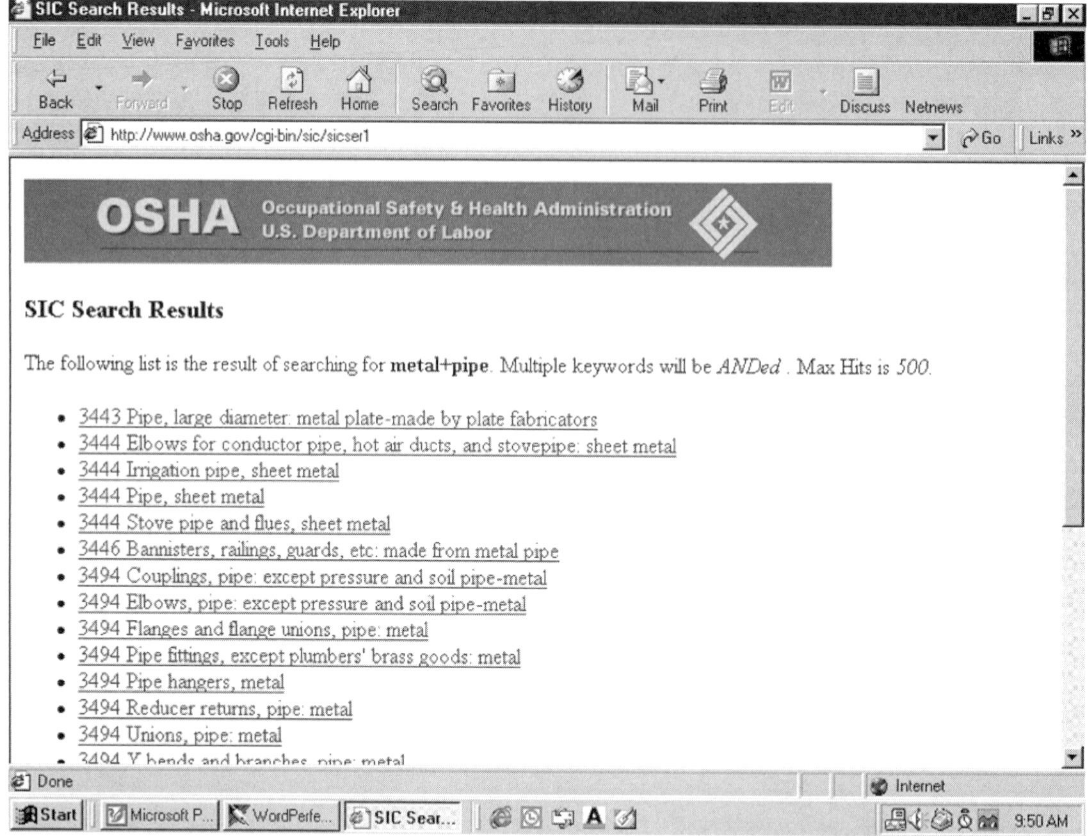

Figure 6.2: Search by Keyword

- Securities Exchange Commission (www.sec.gov/cgi-bin/srch-edgar)
- FreeEDGAR (www.freeedgar.com)
- 10K Wizard (www.10kwizard.com)

Each of these sites provides EDGAR filings with minimal or no charge, but only FreeEDGAR and 10K Wizard allow a user to search by SIC code. While I will attempt to help you get through some of these sites, you need to be aware of the fact that they change regularly. Don't get frustrated if you try to follow this book and find that the directions have changed. Our firm runs into this problem on a regular basis. We have created our own internal manuals to help staff muddle through this stuff, and updating the manual has become a full-time job.

The initial search screen for FreeEDGAR appears in Figure 6.3. This main search page allows you to search by company name, ticker symbol, or SIC code.

Simply plugging SIC code(s) into this search engine results in a list of companies in the subject's classification. Figure 6.4 reflects a FreeEDGAR SIC code search on code 3317.

It is always a good idea to print your search so that your work file includes sufficient documentation to support your work. You can print the screens as you go along.

An alternative to using FreeEDGAR is the 10K Wizard. Its screen is shown in Figure 6.5.

In addition to searching by SIC code, 10K Wizard allows you to search by industry categorization.

The SIC code search takes only a few minutes and allows the analyst to quickly and easily develop a list of potential guideline companies. Previously, this search could take hours in the library. The companies that show up

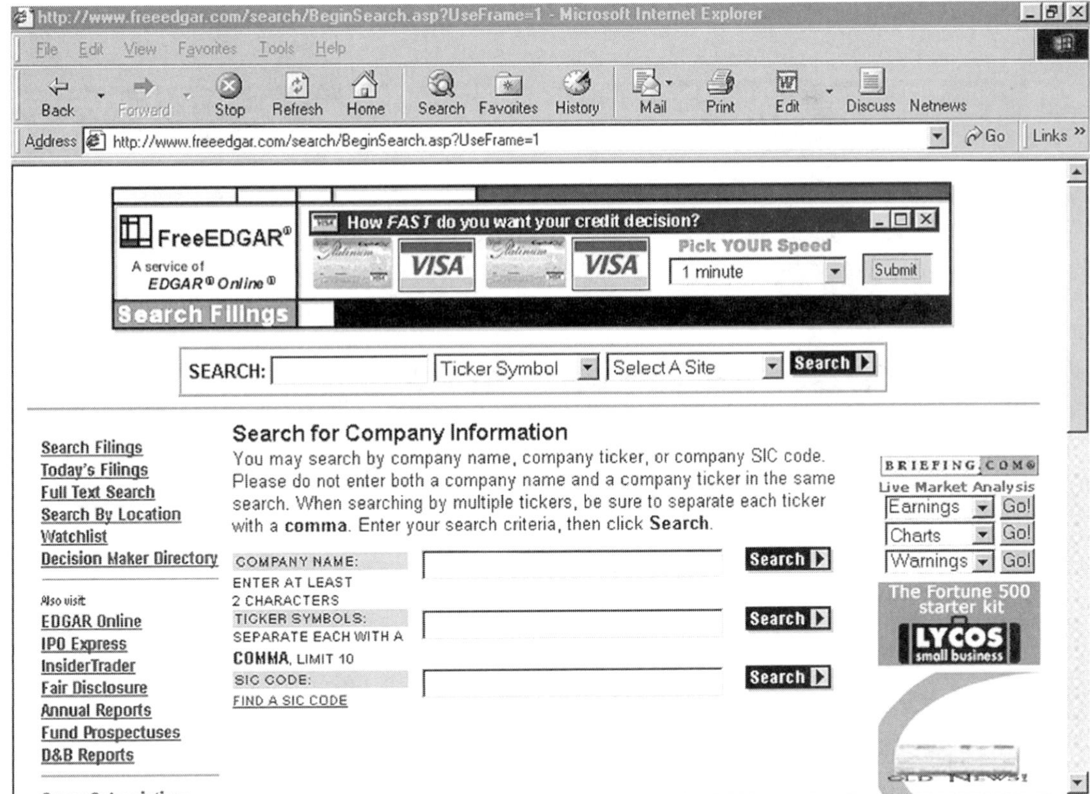

Source: EDGAR Online, Inc. (http://www.edgar-online.com)

Figure 6.3: FreeEDGAR Company Search

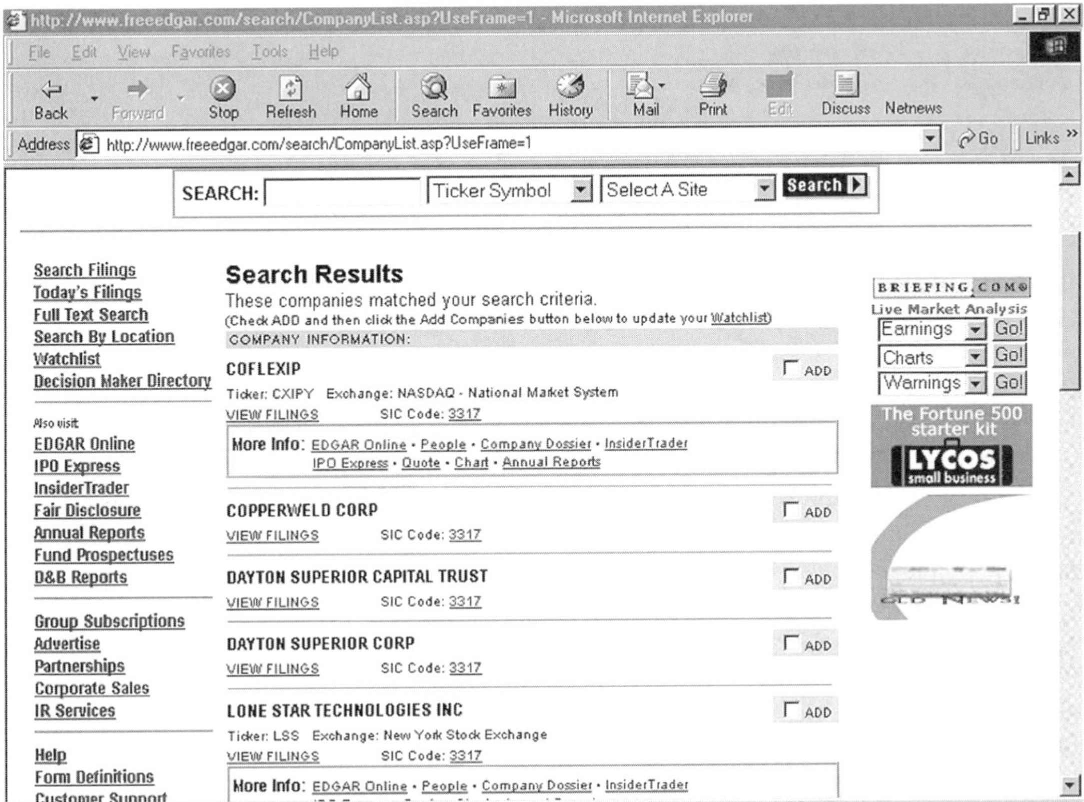

Source: EDGAR Online, Inc. (http://www.edgar-online.com)

Figure 6.4: FreeEDGAR SIC Code Search

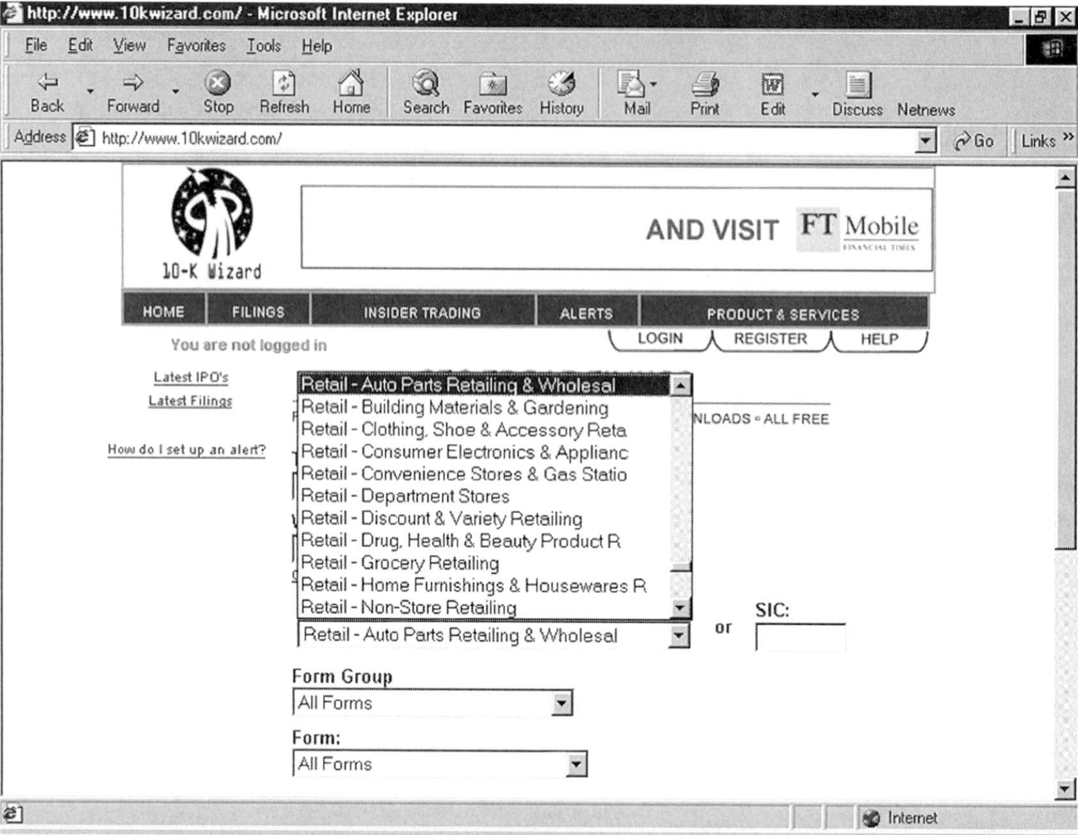

Figure 6.5: 10K Wizard

in your search will be based on the SIC code that is listed in the documents filed by the public company with the SEC. Other databases may classify these companies under a different SIC code. This is part of the frustrating exercise that we call business valuation. It is also the reason for checking multiple Web sites and multiple SIC codes.

Online Databases. There are a multitude of financial advice Web pages in existence that provide some type of industry analysis. These tools should not be substituted for performing a thorough industry analysis, but they can serve as a useful tool in locating guideline companies. For instance, Hoover's Online (www.hoovers.com) provides free industry lists on its Web site. However, these industry lists are nothing more than company names. I would not depend on these types of services as a sole source for locating guideline companies, but they do help to expand a potential guideline companies list. An example is shown in Figure 6.6.

Some of the more sophisticated databases allow you to put in more search criteria than those that I just described. For example, using a database such as Standard & Poor's or Disclosure, you can enter your search criteria, which may include the SIC code, country of location, and maximum sales volume. I will explain the maximum sales volume criteria in a little while.

Industry Research. As previously discussed, an analyst should have a thorough understanding of the valuation subject and its industry. In performing your industry analysis, you will frequently become aware of publicly traded companies in the subject company's industry. Trade journals and published industry reports are excellent tools for locating potential guideline companies. Another great source of information is industry experts. Business brokers, financial analysts, accountants, and industry consultants can be excellent sources of information; you just need to find them.

Figure 6.6: Hoover's Online Industry Snapshots (Courtesy of Hoover's, Inc.)

Get the Business Description

After the possible guideline companies are identified by the initial set of criteria, we used to examine the corporate description included in databases such as Standard & Poor's. Now, we look at the business descriptions that are included in the company's Form 10-K. Since access to the 10-K is free, we can view a more in-depth description than we used to do by looking at the databases. This allows us to look at the narrative about the possible guideline company to further determine if the company appears to be similar enough to use in our analysis. See Figure 6.7.

From this description, you can find out the business purpose, products, market segments, and many other significant pieces of information. You can use this information to perform a qualitative analysis of the potential guideline company.

Search engines can also prove a valuable tool in finding information. Figure 6.8 shows the search results from a search on the Google search engine. A quick search on a company name can turn up valuable information that may not have been picked up by a major news service. In addition to getting the 10-K, we generally will visit the company's Web site.

Size Criteria

If you value small companies, you are probably asking yourself, Why is the author going through all of this stuff about the public market? I know I will not find any guideline companies because the subject company is too small! I hear that nonsense all of the time. Believe it or not, you can still use public company data

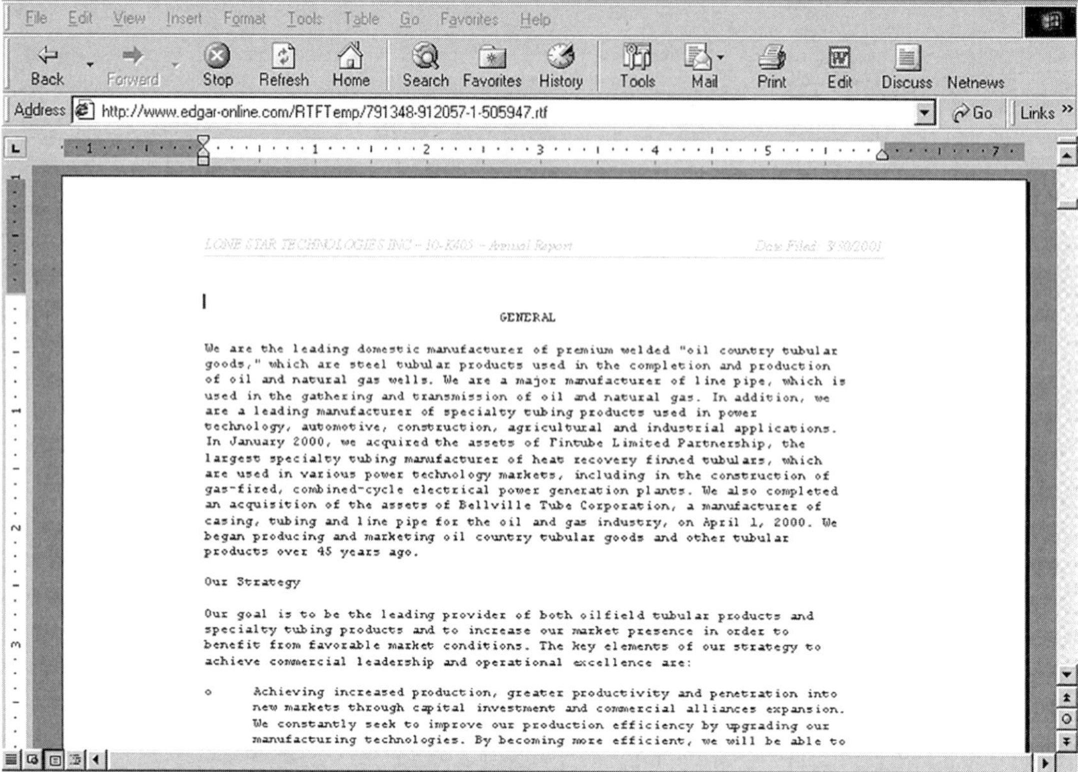

GENERAL

We are the leading domestic manufacturer of premium welded "oil country tubular goods," which are steel tubular products used in the completion and production of oil and natural gas wells. We are a major manufacturer of line pipe, which is used in the gathering and transmission of oil and natural gas. In addition, we are a leading manufacturer of specialty tubing products used in power technology, automotive, construction, agricultural and industrial applications. In January 2000, we acquired the assets of Fintube Limited Partnership, the largest specialty tubing manufacturer of heat recovery finned tubulars, which are used in various power technology markets, including in the construction of gas-fired, combined-cycle electrical power generation plants. We also completed an acquisition of the assets of Bellville Tube Corporation, a manufacturer of casing, tubing and line pipe for the oil and gas industry, on April 1, 2000. We began producing and marketing oil country tubular goods and other tubular products over 45 years ago.

Our Strategy

Our goal is to be the leading provider of both oilfield tubular products and specialty tubing products and to increase our market presence in order to benefit from favorable market conditions. The key elements of our strategy to achieve commercial leadership and operational excellence are:

o Achieving increased production, greater productivity and penetration into new markets through capital investment and commercial alliances expansion. We constantly seek to improve our production efficiency by upgrading our manufacturing technologies. By becoming more efficient, we will be able to

Source: EDGAR Online, Inc. (http://www.edgar-online.com)

Figure 6.7: Lone Star Industries, Inc. Business Description

Figure 6.8: Google Search on Lone Star Technologies, Inc. (Google, Inc.)

when applying the market approach to smaller companies. In addition to the selection criteria used for your search of guideline companies, it is generally a good idea to place a size restriction of no more than 10 to 25 times the sales volume of the appraisal subject. Shannon Pratt had indicated in an earlier edition of *Valuing a Business* that a magnitude of 10 times is a good upper limit. Our firm has found that going to a magnitude of 25 times the appraisal subject's sales volume sometimes works. There are many appraisers who believe that no size restriction should be placed on the guideline company search criteria. The size differential should be made up in the multiple because of the risk factors relative to the size differential. I have a difficult time comparing IBM with the local computer manufacturer. Here also, common sense must be applied. If the guideline companies are too big, they lose relevance to the appraisal subject.

Individuals who disagree with the use of public company data for small, closely held companies generally state that the size differentials are often so great that the result is meaningless. I disagree. First, there are many public companies that are small. I have found many companies traded over the counter with sales volumes below $10 million. In addition, when you look closely at these publicly traded companies, you will find that other than their financial ability to go public, they are not run much differently than many of our appraisal subjects. Granted, there are differences; for example, fewer perquisites for the owners, more reliable financial statements, little management depth, and not much ability to raise additional capital.

Active Trading and Penny Stocks. Once you have located possible guideline companies, it is generally a good idea to test these companies to see if their stocks are actively traded, and while you're at it, make sure that these stocks are not penny stocks. According to Revenue Ruling 59-60, guideline companies should have their stock actively traded in the market. Active trading is essential if the market forces are to interact in the manner necessary to reach the equilibrium point in the market known as fair market value. Greater market activity increases the possibility that fair market value will be achieved because many of the personal motivations of particular buyers and sellers would have been eliminated by offsetting their unique situations in arriving at the equilibrium point.

The question is, What does active trading mean? I have never seen a definition in any of the appraisal textbooks, so I am going to give you one. We consider active trading to mean that at least 5 percent of the company's outstanding stock trades over the six-month period prior to the valuation date. Like everything else in valuation, 5 percent is not a hard and fast rule. There are times that we will use a guideline company with less than 5 percent trading activity, but obviously, more is better.

Stock Pricing Reports. Before selecting guideline companies from the pool of businesses that made our initial list, we check the stock price and trading activity of each. A monthly stock pricing report from Dow Jones Interactive is depicted in Figure 6.9.

A pricing report such as this can tell you many important things about a company. From this report you can see if a business has a very low stock price and would be classified as a *penny stock*. There is often speculation in the market for penny stocks, which may limit the quality of your pricing multiples. We generally prefer to use guideline companies when the stock is selling for at least $5 per share. This gets rid of the speculators that violate the requirement that a willing seller be typically motivated. Speculation is not typical motivation. Here also, there are times that we will use a stock below $5. However, it is rare that we will go below $3.

Stock price volatility is another factor that can be seen on a stock pricing history. Highly volatile stocks, or stocks that have high swings in stock value, at a minimum will let you know that you should take a closer look at that company. Large price swings could indicate changes in the economy, industry, or company, and you will need to understand these factors to properly apply guideline company multiples.

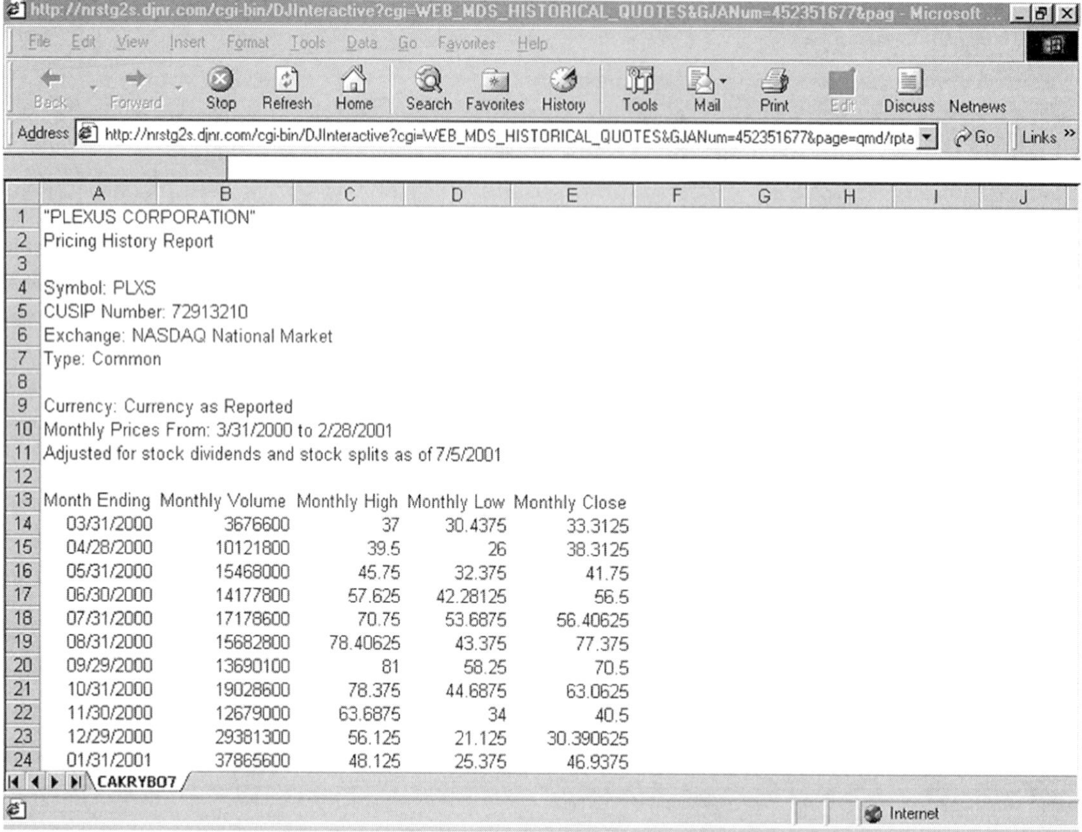

"PLEXUS CORPORATION"
Pricing History Report

Symbol: PLXS
CUSIP Number: 72913210
Exchange: NASDAQ National Market
Type: Common

Currency: Currency as Reported
Monthly Prices From: 3/31/2000 to 2/28/2001
Adjusted for stock dividends and stock splits as of 7/5/2001

Month Ending	Monthly Volume	Monthly High	Monthly Low	Monthly Close
03/31/2000	3676600	37	30.4375	33.3125
04/28/2000	10121800	39.5	26	38.3125
05/31/2000	15468000	45.75	32.375	41.75
06/30/2000	14177800	57.625	42.28125	56.5
07/31/2000	17178600	70.75	53.6875	56.40625
08/31/2000	15682800	78.40625	43.375	77.375
09/29/2000	13690100	81	58.25	70.5
10/31/2000	19028600	78.375	44.6875	63.0625
11/30/2000	12679000	63.6875	34	40.5
12/29/2000	29381300	56.125	21.125	30.390625
01/31/2001	37865600	48.125	25.375	46.9375

Figure 6.9: Dow Jones Pricing History Report

Trading activity can also be calculated from a stock pricing report. Calculating the average trading over a certain period will allow the analyst to see if the stock is trading regularly, or if it is thinly traded. A trading activity analysis is shown in Figure 6.10. As seen in this analysis, we have divided the average monthly trading volume of the potential guideline companies by their respective shares outstanding to calculate a percentage of outstanding shares traded, which can be used as a criterion for thin trading.

Many of the small public companies are relatively "thinly traded." Little activity makes it a bit more uncomfortable for the appraiser, but it does not mean that the company cannot be used. After all, what is the alternative? In general, thinly traded data can be used, albeit cautiously, if the appraiser can determine adequate information about the thin trading. In order to learn more about a company's trading activity, we will search the public documents filed with the SEC, look for press releases and other announcements, and even go as far as to call the investor relations people in the company to inquire whether there is anything special about the stock transactions that would disqualify the activity from being used in this analysis. Often, the thin trading takes place among insiders. This information can be used if it is determined that the logical market for the appraisal subject is insiders.

Let's talk about insiders for a moment. There are many times when an appraiser must struggle to decide who the logical players in the market are. A fractional interest in a closely held business may be worth more in the hands of an insider than in those of an outside investor. As a matter of fact, there are many times when there may not be a market for a minority interest in a closely held business, other than for the other shareholders of the company. Swing votes and insider knowledge may create value for the insiders that an outsider would not be privy to. Remember, one of the components of fair market value is that the willing buyer and willing seller must have knowledge about the subject property.

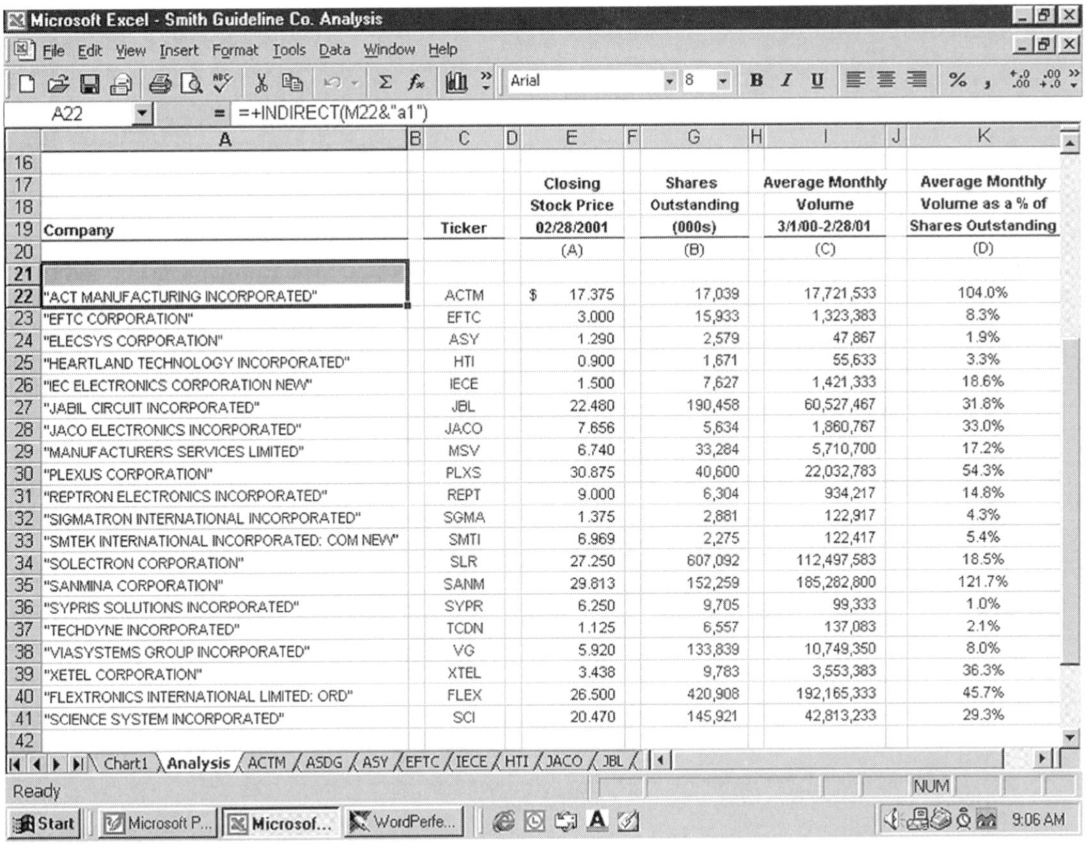

Microsoft Excel - Smith Guideline Co. Analysis

A22 = =+INDIRECT(M22&"a1")

	Company	Ticker	Closing Stock Price 02/28/2001 (A)	Shares Outstanding (000s) (B)	Average Monthly Volume 3/1/00-2/28/01 (C)	Average Monthly Volume as a % of Shares Outstanding (D)
22	"ACT MANUFACTURING INCORPORATED"	ACTM	$ 17.375	17,039	17,721,533	104.0%
23	"EFTC CORPORATION"	EFTC	3.000	15,933	1,323,383	8.3%
24	"ELECSYS CORPORATION"	ASY	1.290	2,579	47,867	1.9%
25	"HEARTLAND TECHNOLOGY INCORPORATED"	HTI	0.900	1,671	55,633	3.3%
26	"IEC ELECTRONICS CORPORATION NEW"	IECE	1.500	7,627	1,421,333	18.6%
27	"JABIL CIRCUIT INCORPORATED"	JBL	22.480	190,458	60,527,467	31.8%
28	"JACO ELECTRONICS INCORPORATED"	JACO	7.656	5,634	1,860,767	33.0%
29	"MANUFACTURERS SERVICES LIMITED"	MSV	6.740	33,284	5,710,700	17.2%
30	"PLEXUS CORPORATION"	PLXS	30.875	40,600	22,032,783	54.3%
31	"REPTRON ELECTRONICS INCORPORATED"	REPT	9.000	6,304	934,217	14.8%
32	"SIGMATRON INTERNATIONAL INCORPORATED"	SGMA	1.375	2,881	122,917	4.3%
33	"SMTEK INTERNATIONAL INCORPORATED: COM NEW"	SMTI	6.969	2,275	122,417	5.4%
34	"SOLECTRON CORPORATION"	SLR	27.250	607,092	112,497,583	18.5%
35	"SANMINA CORPORATION"	SANM	29.813	152,259	185,282,800	121.7%
36	"SYPRIS SOLUTIONS INCORPORATED"	SYPR	6.250	9,705	99,333	1.0%
37	"TECHDYNE INCORPORATED"	TCDN	1.125	6,557	137,083	2.1%
38	"VIASYSTEMS GROUP INCORPORATED"	VG	5.920	133,839	10,749,350	8.0%
39	"XETEL CORPORATION"	XTEL	3.438	9,783	3,553,383	36.3%
40	"FLEXTRONICS INTERNATIONAL LIMITED: ORD"	FLEX	26.500	420,908	192,165,333	45.7%
41	"SCIENCE SYSTEM INCORPORATED"	SCI	20.470	145,921	42,813,233	29.3%

Chart1 | Analysis | ACTM | ASDG | ASY | EFTC | IECE | HTI | JACO | JBL

Figure 6.10: Trading Activity Analysis

For Those That Pass Muster . . .

For those companies that pass muster, we now download financial information that is included as part of the Form 10-K filed in EDGAR or a similar database. In fact, we will generally download the entire Form 10-K so that we can gain a thorough understanding about the public company. This will allow us to take a much more detailed look at the company to determine its level of comparability to the appraisal subject. This can be accomplished by comparing financial ratios and other attributes of the guideline companies with those of the appraisal subject. Before we can do this, certain adjustments may be necessary to the guideline company data.

Analyzing Publicly Traded Information. Part of using public company information in the valuation process requires the appraiser to obtain and analyze the financial and operating data of the guideline companies. The appraiser will use this information to ensure that the appraisal subject can be properly compared with these other companies. Sometimes, there will be differences in the manner in which the publicly traded company reports its financial results, or nonrecurring events may have taken place that require the appraiser to recompute the multiples used after adjusting the public company data. These adjustments are made to compare the appraisal subject more appropriately with the guideline companies.

The appraiser should always keep in mind that there are limits to what can be done with the information that is obtained. Exact comparability will most likely never be achieved. Don't let this upset you. The adjustments that will be made will generally be similar to the normalization adjustments discussed in Chapter 5, particularly the comparability adjustments and the nonrecurring adjustments. Rarely will you have to make a discretionary adjustment. The stockholders of the public company would go bonkers! Besides, the CEO's nephew being on the books would be an insignificant adjustment.

Some of the adjustments that are frequently encountered as a result of the differences between public companies and closely held companies are for (1) inventory accounting such as LIFO-FIFO, (2) items that are nonrecurring, and (3) items that are extraordinary.

If the public company reports its results using the LIFO method of inventory valuation and the appraisal subject uses FIFO, an adjustment is generally made to the public company data in order to compare these companies properly. It would be silly, and probably impossible, for the appraiser to convert the appraisal subject to LIFO. Accountants reading this book will understand this better than anyone. The information necessary to perform a LIFO calculation is not available in any of the documents obtained by an appraiser. For the non-accounting types, LIFO inventory valuation is relatively complicated and requires more than a few words to explain it properly. Since this book is a valuation text and not a book on LIFO, you will have to trust me.

The number of adjustments that an appraiser will make to the public company information is usually small. The adjustments are intended to achieve consistency. For right now, recognize the importance of being consistent in your analysis. You need to compare apples with apples, oranges with oranges, and pears with pears. Otherwise, your valuation will take on the characteristics of a fruit salad: a little of this and a little of that.

Exhibit 6.4 takes you through a series of screen shots demonstrating the adjustments made to a public company in an analysis that we did.

EXHIBIT 6.4
Adjustments to the Guideline Company

First, we input the historic information as reported by the public company into our valuation template.

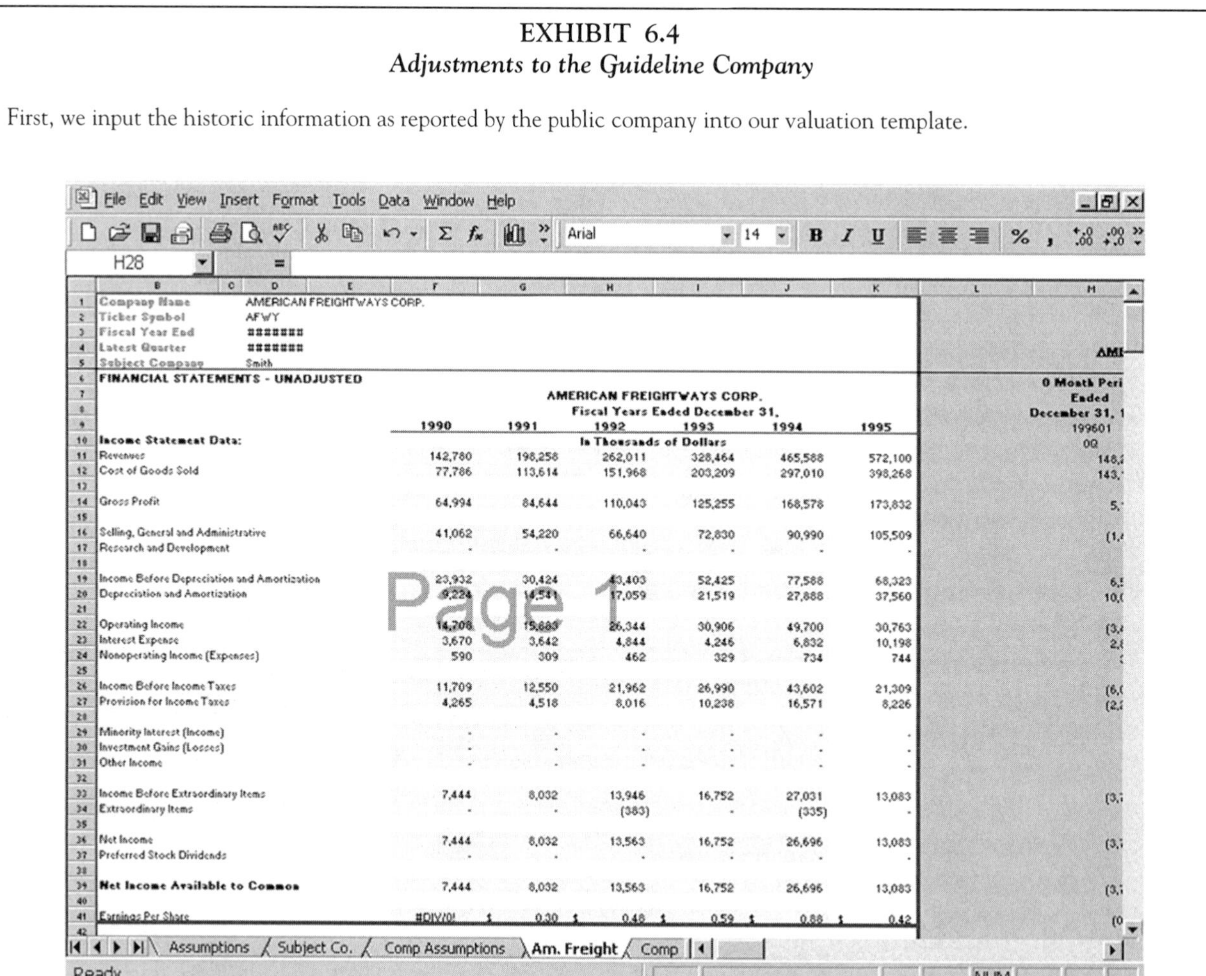

Company Name	AMERICAN FREIGHTWAYS CORP.
Ticker Symbol	AFWY
Fiscal Year End	#######
Latest Quarter	#######
Subject Company	Smith

FINANCIAL STATEMENTS - UNADJUSTED

AMERICAN FREIGHTWAYS CORP.
Fiscal Years Ended December 31,

	1990	1991	1992	1993	1994	1995
Income Statement Data:			In Thousands of Dollars			
Revenues	142,780	198,258	262,011	328,464	465,588	572,100
Cost of Goods Sold	77,786	113,614	151,968	203,209	297,010	398,268
Gross Profit	64,994	84,644	110,043	125,255	168,578	173,832
Selling, General and Administrative	41,062	54,220	66,640	72,830	90,990	105,509
Research and Development	-	-	-	-	-	-
Income Before Depreciation and Amortization	23,932	30,424	43,403	52,425	77,588	68,323
Depreciation and Amortization	9,224	14,541	17,059	21,519	27,888	37,560
Operating Income	14,708	15,883	26,344	30,906	49,700	30,763
Interest Expense	3,670	3,642	4,844	4,246	6,832	10,198
Nonoperating Income (Expenses)	590	309	462	329	734	744
Income Before Income Taxes	11,709	12,550	21,962	26,990	43,602	21,309
Provision for Income Taxes	4,265	4,518	8,016	10,238	16,571	8,226
Minority Interest (Income)	-	-	-	-	-	-
Investment Gains (Losses)	-	-	-	-	-	-
Other Income	-	-	-	-	-	-
Income Before Extraordinary Items	7,444	8,032	13,946	16,752	27,031	13,083
Extraordinary Items	-	-	(383)	-	(335)	-
Net Income	7,444	8,032	13,563	16,752	26,696	13,083
Preferred Stock Dividends	-	-	-	-	-	-
Net Income Available to Common	7,444	8,032	13,563	16,752	26,696	13,083
Earnings Per Share	#DIV/0!	$ 0.30	$ 0.48	$ 0.59	$ 0.88	$ 0.42

Then we adjust those items that are nonrecurring, extraordinary, etc. that would impact the pricing multiples that we might be using in the valuation. We also want to ensure that the financial ratios that will be calculated allow a better comparison to the subject company.

EXHIBIT 6.4 *(Continued)*

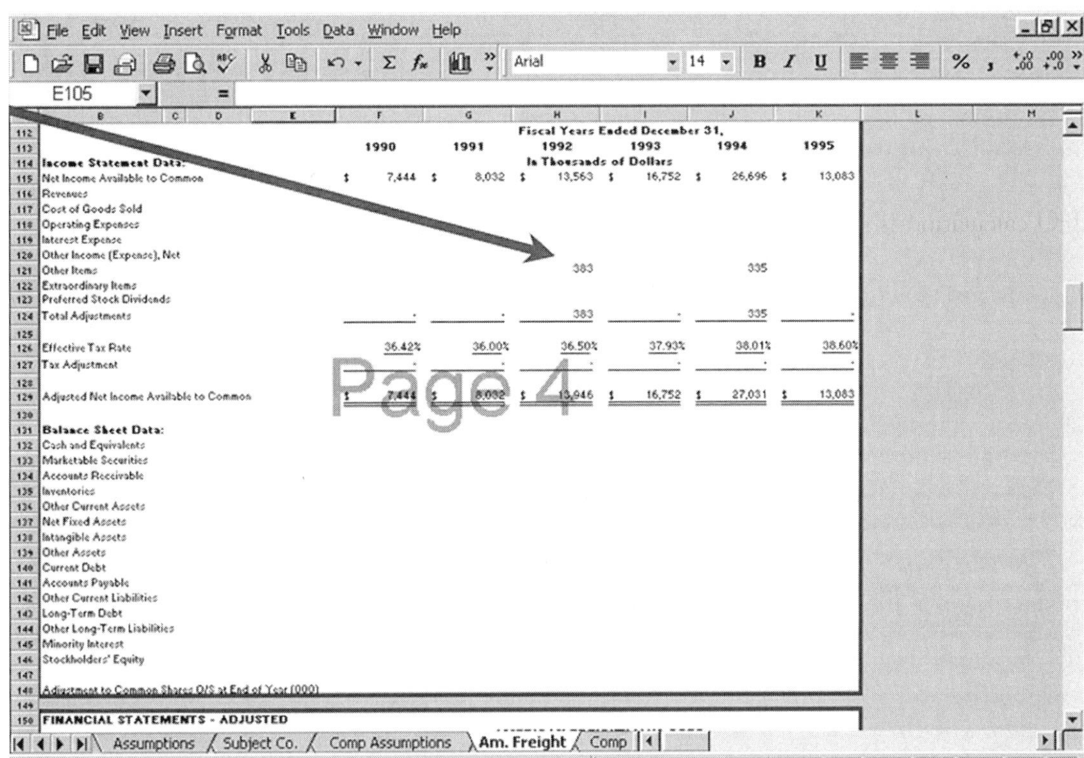

	1990	1991	1992	1993	1994	1995
			Fiscal Years Ended December 31,			
Income Statement Data:			In Thousands of Dollars			
Net Income Available to Common	$ 7,444	$ 8,032	$ 13,563	$ 16,752	$ 26,696	$ 13,083
Revenues						
Cost of Goods Sold						
Operating Expenses						
Interest Expense						
Other Income (Expense), Net						
Other Items			383		335	
Extraordinary Items						
Preferred Stock Dividends						
Total Adjustments	-	-	383	-	335	-
Effective Tax Rate	36.42%	36.00%	36.50%	37.93%	38.01%	38.60%
Tax Adjustment	-	-	-	-	-	-
Adjusted Net Income Available to Common	$ 7,444	$ 8,032	$ 13,946	$ 16,752	$ 27,031	$ 13,083
Balance Sheet Data:						
Cash and Equivalents						
Marketable Securities						
Accounts Receivable						
Inventories						
Other Current Assets						
Net Fixed Assets						
Intangible Assets						
Other Assets						
Current Debt						
Accounts Payable						
Other Current Liabilities						
Long-Term Debt						
Other Long-Term Liabilities						
Minority Interest						
Stockholders' Equity						
Adjustment to Common Shares O/S at End of Year (000)						

After the adjustments are input, the historic information is recalculated with the adjustments that have been made. We then reproduce the adjusted financial statements for the purpose of performing our financial analysis and calculating our multiples.

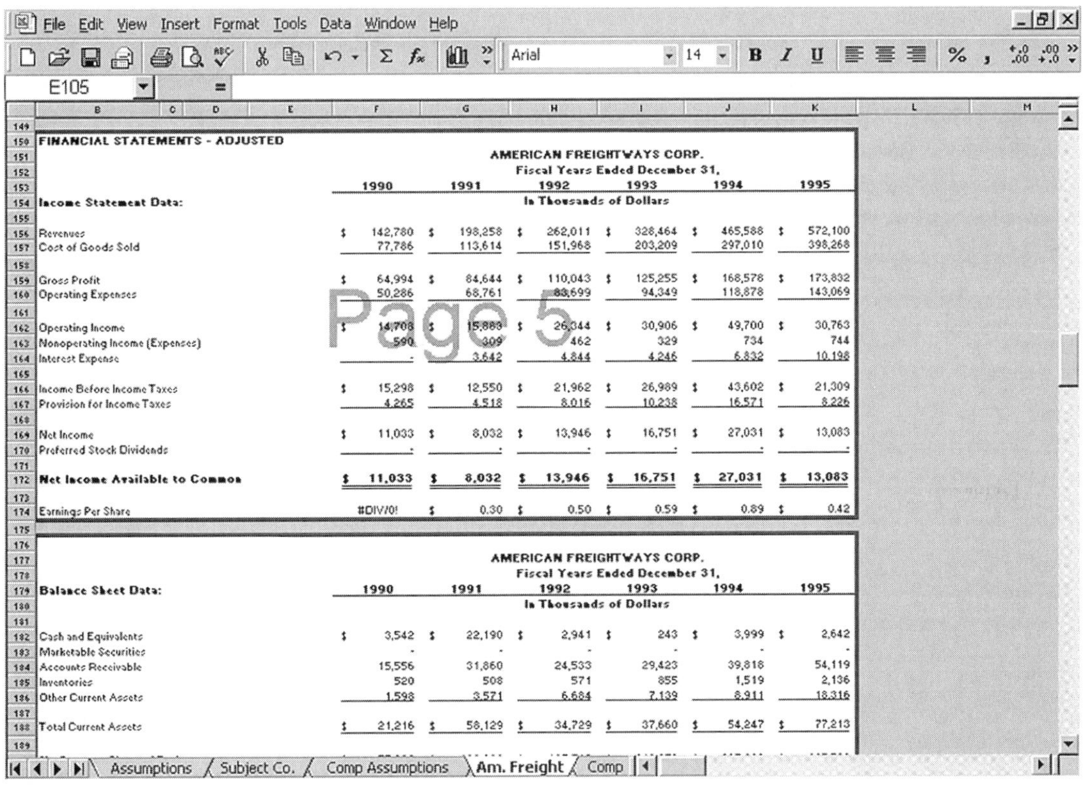

FINANCIAL STATEMENTS - ADJUSTED

AMERICAN FREIGHTWAYS CORP.
Fiscal Years Ended December 31,

Income Statement Data:	1990	1991	1992	1993	1994	1995
			In Thousands of Dollars			
Revenues	$ 142,780	$ 198,258	$ 262,011	$ 328,464	$ 465,588	$ 572,100
Cost of Goods Sold	77,786	113,614	151,968	203,209	297,010	398,268
Gross Profit	$ 64,994	$ 84,644	$ 110,043	$ 125,255	$ 168,578	$ 173,832
Operating Expenses	50,286	68,761	83,699	94,349	118,878	143,069
Operating Income	$ 14,708	$ 15,883	$ 26,344	$ 30,906	$ 49,700	$ 30,763
Nonoperating Income (Expenses)	590	309	462	329	734	744
Interest Expense	-	3,642	4,844	4,246	6,832	10,198
Income Before Income Taxes	$ 15,298	$ 12,550	$ 21,962	$ 26,989	$ 43,602	$ 21,309
Provision for Income Taxes	4,265	4,518	8,016	10,238	16,571	8,226
Net Income	$ 11,033	$ 8,032	$ 13,946	$ 16,751	$ 27,031	$ 13,083
Preferred Stock Dividends	-	-	-	-	-	-
Net Income Available to Common	**$ 11,033**	**$ 8,032**	**$ 13,946**	**$ 16,751**	**$ 27,031**	**$ 13,083**
Earnings Per Share	#DIV/0!	$ 0.30	$ 0.50	$ 0.59	$ 0.89	$ 0.42

AMERICAN FREIGHTWAYS CORP.
Fiscal Years Ended December 31,

Balance Sheet Data:	1990	1991	1992	1993	1994	1995
			In Thousands of Dollars			
Cash and Equivalents	$ 3,542	$ 22,190	$ 2,941	$ 243	$ 3,999	$ 2,642
Marketable Securities	-	-	-	-	-	-
Accounts Receivable	15,556	31,860	24,533	29,423	39,818	54,119
Inventories	520	508	571	855	1,519	2,136
Other Current Assets	1,598	3,571	6,684	7,139	8,911	18,316
Total Current Assets	$ 21,216	$ 58,129	$ 34,729	$ 37,660	$ 54,247	$ 77,213

Before we go to the next step, let's discuss one other item. When searching for publicly traded company financial information, you want to get as close to the date of the valuation as possible. Many times, this will mean calculating the latest 12 months' financial results. Whenever possible, we will use this information. Let me give you an example.

Tables 6.1 and 6.2 reflect financial statements for Plexus Corp. Notice in this analysis we have performed a latest-12-months calculation for the last period on the income statement. This is done using quarterly statements. For instance, Plexus Corp.'s year end is September 30, but the valuation date is March 1. The market is pricing companies based on all available information, including the December 31 quarterly earnings. To estimate revenues for the latest 12 months, we would perform the following calculation:

December 31, 2000, quarterly revenues
\+ September 31, 2000, annual revenues
− December 31, 1999, quarterly revenues
= December 31, 2000, LTM revenues

This calculation may be repeated for all line items, and the result is an income statement reflecting all known financial information as of the valuation date. The result looks like Table 6.1.

TABLE 6.1

Plexus Corp. Income Statement for Years Ended

	September 30,		*LTM Dec. 31,*
	1998	*1999*	*2000*
	(In Thousands of Dollars)		
Revenues	$466,795	$492,414	$876,642
Cost of goods sold	406,648	426,005	751,437
Gross profit	$ 60,147	$ 66,409	$125,205
Operating expenses	23,754	31,981	45,039
Operating income	$ 36,393	$ 34,428	$ 80,166
Other income	975	1,995	1,765
Interest expense	86	274	4,404
Income before income taxes	$ 37,282	$ 36,149	$ 77,527
Provision for income taxes	14,345	15,838	32,372
Net income	**$ 22,937**	**$ 20,311**	**$ 45,155**
Earnings per share	$ 0.68	$ 0.59	$ 1.12

The last column of the balance sheet reflects the balance sheet of the latest quarter prior to the valuation date.

We typically present financial statements for the guideline companies for periods similar to those that we have for the subject. Doing so allows us to look at trends in operating performance of the guideline companies over as much time as possible. These trends, among other things, will indicate a level of comparability. For instance, if all of the guideline companies experience a sales decline, but the subject company's sales do not, it may indicate that the subject company is not sensitive to similar economic factors. Another tool that will help us in this analysis is a financial ratio analysis. Comparative financial ratio analysis allows us to look at what some businesses do better, or worse, than others and gives us a quantitative basis to compare subject to guidelines.

TABLE 6.2
Plexus Corp. Balance Sheet

	September 30,		Dec. 31,
	1998	1999	2000
	(In Thousands of Dollars)		
Cash and equivalents	$ 24,106	$ 15,906	$ 77,426
Marketable securities	5,517	17,224	—
Accounts receivable	61,622	69,318	110,468
Inventories	57,321	79,017	221,417
Other current assets	7,278	9,932	16,174
Total current assets	$ 155,844	$ 191,397	$ 425,485
Net property, plant, and equipment	26,517	35,868	108,506
Intangible assets	—	408	50,363
Deposits and other assets	1,993	1,963	3,325
Total assets	**$184,354**	**$229,636**	**$587,689**
Current portion of interest-bearing debt	$ 672	$ 10	$ 8,091
Accounts payable	41,272	55,928	95,046
Other current liabilities	22,741	25,048	43,920
Total current liabilities	$ 64,685	$ 80,986	$ 147,057
Long-term interest-bearing debt	$ 2,587	$ 142	$ 45,146
Other long-term liabilities	1,219	2,105	3,914
Total long-term liabilities	$ 3,806	$ 2,247	$ 49,060
Total liabilities	$ 68,491	$ 83,233	$ 196,117
Stockholders' equity	115,863	146,403	391,562
Total liabilities and equity	**$184,354**	**$229,636**	**$587,679**
Common shares outstanding at end of year	33,688	34,646	40,290

It is a good idea to set up a spreadsheet that will automatically calculate ratios based on the input financial statements. This can be done on a historic basis as well as on an adjusted basis. Tools such as this are helpful in speeding up the analysis for a business, and by setting it up in advance (and checking the formulas), you may limit errors that result from creating the spreadsheet. I respect the work that my staff does, but we have password-protected the majority of our spreadsheet template to avoid someone making the mistake of changing a formula. Better to be safe than sorry.

A sample ratio analysis of some guideline companies with the narrative that accompanied it in a report appears in Exhibit 6.5.

EXHIBIT 6.5
Financial Ratio Analysis With Guideline Companies

The next step in the analysis is to compare The Triad Entities' financial results with its public counterparts. Select financial ratios appear in Table 1. These ratios have been analyzed in order to make quantitative and qualitative assessments regarding the similarities and dissimilarities between the companies.

(Continued)

EXHIBIT 6.5 *(Continued)*

TABLE 1
Adjusted Financial Ratios

	AFWY	ABFS	AIND	TRUKQ	HTLD	JBHT	MSCA	OTR	SWFT	TCAM	XPRSA	WERN	TRIAD
Liquidity/solvency													
Quick ratio	1.08	0.67	1.14	0.38	1.63	0.80	0.67	0.35	0.96	0.47	1.03	1.37	0.92
Current ratio	1.47	1.06	1.41	0.84	1.97	1.01	1.01	0.40	1.11	0.78	1.47	1.86	1.05
Days accounts receivable	29.97	39.80	32.91	29.61	33.81	37.96	33.41	42.75	42.20	30.58	44.48	34.98	30.54
Days working capital	11.03	(2.34)	22.70	(2.84)	41.29	0.78	16.14	(55.85)	8.26	(5.20)	19.52	24.62	3.14
Turnover													
Receivables turnover	12.18	9.17	11.09	12.33	10.80	9.61	10.93	8.54	8.65	11.93	8.21	10.44	11.95
Cash turnover	172.29	140.89	22.52	4,907.24	6.82	422.44	21.29	1,726.70	137.59	38.28	71.17	41.31	13.74
Current asset turnover	8.70	5.66	4.90	5.74	3.02	7.34	5.71	7.62	6.92	6.31	5.27	6.09	5.46
Working capital turnover	33.10	(155.79)	16.08	(128.59)	8.84	467.01	22.61	(6.54)	44.17	(70.21)	18.70	14.83	116.32
Fixed asset turnover	1.64	4.62	1.79	1.58	2.33	1.69	1.54	1.36	2.11	2.30	2.86	1.49	4.14
Total asset turnover	1.37	2.40	1.30	1.22	1.30	1.35	1.20	1.15	1.61	1.64	1.83	1.20	2.31
Debt													
Times interest earned	3.09	(1.68)	NM	1.00	385.46	1.56	4.72	0.89	6.96	6.26	1.92	26.74	3.70
Total liabilities to total assets	0.59	0.98	0.32	0.93	0.38	0.65	0.46	0.81	0.58	0.63	0.71	0.39	0.82
Total liabilities to equity	1.44	(31.13)	0.46	12.69	0.60	1.85	0.84	4.34	1.40	1.74	2.48	0.64	4.57
Short-term debt to equity	0.04	(1.60)	0.10	1.97	0.01	0.08	0.11	1.53	0.18	0.35	0.27	—	0.75
Long-term debt to equity	0.97	(16.14)	0.03	8.94	—	0.95	0.31	2.28	0.55	0.67	1.33	0.13	2.61
Total interest-bearing debt to equity	1.01	(17.75)	0.12	10.92	0.01	1.03	0.42	3.80	0.73	1.02	1.60	0.13	3.36
Total assets to equity	2.44	(31.68)	1.46	13.69	1.60	2.85	1.84	5.34	2.40	2.74	3.48	1.64	5.57
Total liabilities to invested capital	0.72	1.86	0.41	1.06	0.60	0.91	0.59	0.90	0.81	0.86	0.95	0.57	1.05
Net fixed assets/equity	2.03	(16.47)	1.14	10.82	0.75	2.27	1.53	4.59	1.85	2.05	2.18	1.32	3.43

EXHIBIT 6.5 (*Continued*)

	AFWY	ABFS	AIND	TRUKQ	HTLD	JBHT	MSCA	OTR	SWFT	TCAM	XPRSA	WERN	TRIAD
Profitability													
EBITDA return on total assets	14.46%	2.30%	28.58%	16.12%	30.77%	16.61%	23.29%	17.48%	25.97%	23.15%%	16.10%	24.26%	28.70%
EBIT return on assets	6.59%	−3.66%	18.64%	6.01%	20.72%	3.80%	9.31%	4.15%	15.48%	12.82%	5.54%	12.20%	17.09%
Pretax return on assets	4.46%	−5.83%	18.64%	0.00%	20.66%	1.36%	7.34%	−0.52%	13.25%	10.77%	2.66%	11.75%	12.47%
After-tax return on assets	2.74%	−4.02%	11.87%	0.39%	13.02%	0.86%	4.70%	−0.32%	7.62%	6.14%	1.66%	7.17%	7.49%
EBITDA return on net sales	12.07%	1.25%	22.25%	14.04%	25.41%	12.49%	19.58%	17.37%	17.14%	15.96%	9.74%	21.38%	14.59%
EBIT return on net sales	5.51%	−1.99%	14.51%	5.23%	17.11%	2.86%	7.82%	4.13%	10.21%	8.84%	3.36%	10.76%	8.69%
Pre-tax return on net sales	3.72%	−3.18%	14.51%	0.00%	17.06%	1.02%	6.17%	−0.51%	8.75%	7.43%	1.61%	10.35%	6.34%
After-tax return on net sales	2.29%	−2.19%	9.24%	0.34%	10.75%	0.65%	3.95%	−0.32%	5.03%	4.23%	1.00%	6.32%	3.81%
EBITDA return on invested capital	17.57%	4.34%	37.25%	18.52%	48.99%	23.26%	30.11%	19.44%	36.08%	31.35%	21.55%	35.28%	36.64%
EBIT return on invested capital	8.02%	−6.92%	24.29%	6.90%	32.98%	5.32%	12.03%	4.62%	21.50%	17.36%	7.42%	17.75%	21.82%
Pretax return on invested capital	5.42%	−11.03%	24.29%	0.00%	32.90%	1.91%	9.48%	−0.58%	18.41%	14.59%	3.56%	17.09%	15.92%
Return on invested capital	3.33%	−7.61%	15.47%	0.45%	20.72%	1.20%	6.07%	−0.36%	10.59%	8.31%	2.22%	10.42%	9.56%
Working capital													
Working capital ($000)	24,699	19,148	16,219	(9,161)	40,781	2,479	575	(10,389)	6,735	(6,298)	19,424	46,804	944
Short-term debt to working capital	0.34	2.07	1.03	(3.97)	0.02	12.23	28.98	(1.34)	3.38	(2.02)	0.68	—	7.97
Long-term debt to working capital	7.66	20.85	0.31	(17.99)	—	136.75	82.39	(2.01)	10.24	(3.88)	3.36	0.85	27.72
Other													
Size of revenues ($000)	572,100	1,437,279	330,136	289,527	191,507	1,352,225	333,070	49,211	458,165	144,254	282,468	576,022	109,812
Earnings ($000)	13,083	(31,495)	30,501	982	20,586	8,725	13,152	(157)	23,040	6,106	2,837	36,380	4,179
3 year compound growth rate earnings	−11.62%	NM	1.00%	−43.18%	29.86%	−52.22%	−1.66%	NM	37.01%	61.40%	−35.08%	10.19%	−2.43%
3 year compound growth rate revenues	31.98%	19.30%	10.03%	7.61%	−9.92%	15.09%	21.74%	26.72%	28.61%	17.49%	16.75%	17.35%	3.46%

(*Continued*)

EXHIBIT 6.5 *(Continued)*

Looking at the ratios in totality reveals many differences between the Triad Entities and the guideline companies. In order to do a more comprehensive analysis, we analyzed specific figures and ratios by ranking the information contained in Table 1 from highest to lowest to determine how the Triad Entities stack up against the 12 guideline companies.

The first area looked at is the size of the company from both a revenue and an earnings standpoint.

Size of Revenues ($000)		*Size of Earnings ($000)*	
ABFS	$1,437,279	WERN	$ 36,380
JBHT	1,352,225	AIND	30,501
WERN	576,022	SWFT	23,040
AFWY	572,100	HTLD	20,586
SWFT	458,165	MSCA	13,152
MSCA	333,070	AFWY	13,083
AIND	330,136	JBHT	8,725
TRUKQ	289,527	TCAM	6,106
XPRSA	282,468	**TRIAD**	**4,179**
HTLD	191,507	XPRSA	2,837
TCAM	144,254	TRUKQ	982
TRIAD	**109,812**	OTR	(157)
OTR	49,211	ABFS	(31,495)

The Triad Entities are smaller than all of the companies except OTR; most of the companies fall within five times the Company's revenues, although ABFS and JBHT are 13 and 12 times revenues, respectively. The Company has less earnings than most of the guideline companies. This does not necessarily mean that the Triad Entities are less profitable though. This will be discussed when we look at profitability ratios.

In conjunction with the size of revenues and earnings are compound annual growth rates. Three-year rates are shown below.

3 Year CAGR— Revenues %		*3 Year CAGR— Earnings %*	
AFWY	31.98%	ABFS	NM
SWFT	28.61%	OTR	NM
OTR	26.72%	TCAM	61.40%
MSCA	21.74%	SWFT	37.01%
ABFS	19.30%	HTLD	29.86%
TCAM	17.49%	WERN	10.19%
WERN	17.35%	AIND	1.00%
XPRSA	16.75%	MSCA	−1.66%
JBHT	15.09%	**TRIAD**	**−2.43%**
AIND	10.03%	AFWY	−11.62%
TRUKQ	7.61%	XPRSA	−35.08%
TRIAD	**3.46%**	TRUKQ	−43.18%
HTLD	−9.92%	JBHT	−52.22%

Three-year compound annual growth in revenues indicates that the Triad Entities' revenues have been growing more slowly than all of the guideline companies except one. Looking at earnings growth reveals that the Triad Entities fall about midway between the faster earnings growth and the faster earnings losses. As previously discussed, the economy faltered somewhat in 1995, resulting in a "down" year for the industry. Analysts who follow these companies have indicated that they expect better results in 1996.

EXHIBIT 6.5 (Continued)

Current Ratio		*Quick Ratio*	
HTLD	1.97	HTLD	1.63
WERN	1.86	WERN	1.37
AFWY	1.47	AIND	1.14
XPRSA	1.47	AFWY	1.08
AIND	1.41	XPRSA	1.03
SWFT	1.11	SWFT	0.96
ABFS	1.06	**TRIAD**	**0.92**
TRIAD	**1.05**	JBHT	0.80
MSCA	1.01	ABFS	0.67
JBHT	1.01	MSCA	0.67
TRUKQ	0.84	TCAM	0.47
TCAM	0.78	TRUKQ	0.38
OTR	0.40	OTR	0.35

In looking at these ratios, the Triad Entities are closest to JBHT, despite the difference in the companies' sizes. From a current ratio and quick ratio standpoint, the Triad Entities fall right in the middle.

Two other liquidity ratios, days accounts receivable and days working capital, appear to contradict one another somewhat.

Days Account Receivables		*Days Working Capital*	
XPRSA	44.48	HTLD	41.29
OTR	42.75	WERN	24.62
SWFT	42.20	AIND	22.70
ABFS	39.80	XPRSA	19.52
JBHT	37.96	MSCA	16.14
WERN	34.98	AFWY	11.03
HTLD	33.81	SWFT	8.26
MSCA	33.41	**TRIAD**	**3.14**
AIND	32.91	JBHT	0.78
TCAM	30.58	ABFS	(2.34)
TRIAD	**30.54**	TRUKQ	(2.84)
AFWY	29.97	TCAM	(5.20)
TRUKQ	29.61	OTR	(55.85)

Although the Triad Entities collect their accounts receivable faster than most of the guideline companies, they only have approximately three days of working capital available. Despite this, a number of the guideline companies appear to be even weaker in this area.

Turnover ratios measure how effectively a company utilizes its assets.

Current Asset Turnover		*Fixed Asset Turnover*		*Total Asset Turnover*	
AFWY	8.70	ABFS	4.62	ABFS	2.40
OTR	7.62	**TRIAD**	**4.14**	**TRIAD**	**2.31**
JBHT	7.34	XPRSA	2.86	XPRSA	1.83
SWFT	6.92	HTLD	2.33	TCAM	1.64

(Continued)

EXHIBIT 6.5 *(Continued)*

Current Asset Turnover		*Fixed Asset Turnover*		*Total Asset Turnover*	
TCAM	6.31	TCAM	2.30	SWFT	1.61
WERN	6.09	SWFT	2.11	AFWY	1.37
TRUKQ	5.74	AIND	1.79	JBHT	1.35
MSCA	5.71	JBHT	1.69	AIND	1.30
ABFS	5.66	AFWY	1.64	HTLD	1.30
TRIAD	**5.46**	TRUKQ	1.58	TRUKQ	1.22
XPRSA	5.27	MSCA	1.54	WERN	1.20
AIND	4.90	WERN	1.49	MSCA	1.20
HTLD	3.02	OTR	1.36	OTR	1.15

Overall, the Triad Entities are stronger in utilizing their assets than the guideline companies. Any weakness that exists is in their current asset turnover, which confirms their liquidity ratios. Although the Triad Entities utilize their asset base more efficiently, their liabilities are high, which adds weakness.

The debt ratios indicate that although the Triad Entities are more than able to service their debt, they utilize more debt than most of the guideline companies. This is depicted in the following rankings:

Times Interest Earned		*Total Liabilities to Total Assets*		*Total Liabilities to Equity*	
AIND	NM	ABFS	0.98	TRUKQ	12.69
HTLD	385.46	TRUKQ	0.93	**TRIAD**	**4.57**
WERN	26.74	**TRIAD**	**0.82**	OTR	4.34
SWFT	6.96	OTR	0.81	XPRSA	2.48
TCAM	6.26	XPRSA	0.71	JBHT	1.85
MSCA	4.72	JBHT	0.65	TCAM	1.74
TRIAD	**3.70**	TCAM	0.63	AFWY	1.44
AFWY	3.09	AFWY	0.59	SWFT	1.40
XPRSA	1.92	SWFT	0.58	MSCA	0.84
JBHT	1.56	MSCA	0.46	WERN	0.64
TRUKQ	1.00	WERN	0.39	HTLD	0.60
OTR	0.89	HTLD	0.38	AIND	0.46
ABFS	(1.68)	AIND	0.32	ABFS	(31.13)

With respect to profitability, the Triad Entities fall in the middle of the grouping.

EBITDA Return on Net Sales		*After-Tax Return on Net Sales*	
HTLD	25.41%	HTLD	10.75%
AIND	22.25%	AIND	9.24%
WERN	21.38%	WERN	6.32%
MSCA	19.58%	SWFT	5.03%
OTR	17.37%	TCAM	4.23%
SWFT	17.14%	MSCA	3.95%
TCAM	15.96%	**TRIAD**	**3.81%**

EXHIBIT 6.5 *(Continued)*

EBITDA Return on Net Sales		*After-Tax Return on Net Sales*	
TRIAD	**14.59%**	AFWY	2.29%
TRUKQ	14.04%	XPRSA	1.00%
JBHT	12.49%	JBHT	0.65%
AFWY	12.07%	TRUKQ	0.34%
XPRSA	9.74%	OTR	−0.32%
ABFS	1.25%	ABFS	−2.19%

When looking at after-tax income, the Company is closest to MSCA, which is slightly more profitable. Of the 12 guideline companies, 6 are more profitable and 6 are less profitable. This is influenced greatly by debt structure, age of the fixed assets, and tax rates. Therefore, another comparison utilized is EBITDA (earnings before interest, taxes, depreciation, and amortization) to sales. In utilizing this category, the Triad Entities fall in the middle of the group, with seven companies showing more profitability.

One final profitability measurement is the EBITDA return on invested capital, which reflects the amount of profits generated to a company's capital holders. Here, the Triad Entities are at the high end of the ranking. This could be the result of the Company's reduced equity due to financial difficulties in the past.

EBITDA Return on Invested Capital	
HTLD	48.99%
AIND	37.25%
TRIAD	**36.64%**
SWFT	36.08%
WERN	35.28%
TCAM	31.35%
MSCA	30.11%
JBHT	23.26%
XPRSA	21.55%
OTR	19.44%
TRUKQ	18.52%
AFWY	17.57%
ABFS	4.34%

The next step in our analysis was to compare the Triad Entities to each of the guideline companies, looking for similarities and differences that can be used to aid us in the determination of the proper multiples.

American Freightways (AFWY): AFWY is five times the size of the Triad Entities, with faster growing revenues but weaker earnings growth. Whereas the Triad Entities have low liquidity ratios and working capital, AFWY is highly liquid. AFWY also operates with considerably less debt. Despite all of these factors, the Triad Entities were more profitable in 1995.

Arkansas Best Corp. (ABFS): ABFS is 13 times the size of the Triad Entities and has revenues that are growing considerably faster. Despite this, earnings have been growing at a negative rate over the past three years, and ABFS showed a substantial loss in 1995. Looking at liquidity and turnover indicates that each company has strengths and weaknesses, and these are neutral factors. After removing non-operating assets from ABFS' balance sheet, the company shows negative equity. Therefore, we looked at the company's historic debt-to-equity ratio, which is 2.39 and is considerably lower than the Triad Entities'. Finally, due to ABFS' 1995 loss, the profitability ratios indicate that the Triad Entities are stronger.

Arnold Industries (AIND): AIND is approximately three times the size of the Triad Entities and is experiencing faster revenue growth. Earnings growth has been flat, which is positive as many companies have experienced negative earnings. The Triad Entities appear to have weaker liquidity and profitability than AIND and utilize considerably more leverage. Overall, despite the similarity in size, the Triad Entities appear to be weaker than AIND.

(Continued)

EXHIBIT 6.5 *(Continued)*

Builders Transport (TRUKQ): TRUKQ is slightly less than three times the size of the Triad Entities in revenues. Revenues have grown a little faster over the past three years and were flat in the most recent year; earnings, on the other hand, decreased considerably over the last three years, particularly in 1995. TRUKQ utilizes considerably more debt than the Triad Entities and was less profitable. Finally, its liquidity was extremely weak. Overall, TRUKQ is a very weak company, and the Triad Entities are considerably stronger.

Heartland Express (HTLD): HTLD is only two times the revenue size of the Triad Entities. Overall, its growth, liquidity, and profitability are all stronger than those of the Triad Entities, and HTLD utilizes much less debt. The only weak portion of HTLD is that the company experienced negative revenue growth over the last three years. In spite of this, the company has experienced 30 percent earnings growth over the past three years. Overall, despite its smaller size, HTLD appears to be a strong, well-run company.

J.B. Hunt Transport Services (JBHT): JBHT is more than 12 times the size of the Triad Entities. Despite 15 percent growth in revenues over the last three years, JBHT's earnings have declined significantly. The company's utilization of debt is considerably lower than that of the Triad Entities, making it stronger in this area, yet JBHT is still less profitable, and its liquidity ratios do not indicate strength. Overall, despite JBHT's size, the company appears weak financially.

M.S. Carriers (MSCA): MSCA is approximately three times the size of the Triad Entities but has experienced revenue growth of approximately 22 percent and relatively flat earnings. MSCA utilizes very little debt, yet despite this does not show stronger liquidity or profitability than the Triad Entities.

OTR Express (OTR): OTR is approximately two times the size of the Triad Entities and has experienced substantial revenue growth over the past three years. The company's earnings had been increasing over the period 1991 to 1994, but the company experienced a loss in 1995. OTR utilizes less debt than the Triad Entities but has very weak liquidity; the company's working capital deficit has been growing and was in excess of $10 million at the end of 1995. Due to OTR's loss in 1995, its profitability ratios were also weaker than those of the Triad Entities.

Swift Transportation (SWFT): SWFT is approximately four times the size of the Triad Entities, with revenues and earnings growth of 28.6 and 37 percent, respectively. SWFT utilizes less debt and is more liquid and more profitable than the Triad Entities, and overall appears to be stronger.

Transport Corp. of America (TCAM): TCAM is approximately the same size as the Triad Entities; in 1995, its revenues were only about 30 percent higher. TCAM has been growing very quickly, however; earnings and revenues have experienced annual compound growth of 61.4 and 17.5 percent, respectively. This fast growth has created liquidity problems, however, and at the end of 1995, TCAM had a working capital deficit of $6.2 million. The company has a very strong leverage structure, however, and could possibly borrow money to meet its current obligations. Along with the growth in earnings, TCAM has also been fairly profitable. Overall, TCAM is stronger than the Triad Entities.

US Xpress Enterprises (XPRSA): XPRSA is approximately two times the size of the Triad Entities and despite increasing revenues is suffering from decreasing earnings. Despite this, XPRSA has built up $19 million in working capital and has stronger liquidity ratios than the Triad Entities. XPRSA utilizes less debt than the Triad Entities but appears to be less profitable. XPRSA does not appear to be substantially stronger or weaker than the Triad Entities.

Werner Enterprises (WERN): WERN is more than five times the size of the Triad Entities. Despite flat earnings from 1994 to 1995, WERN has experienced both earnings and revenue growth over the past three years. Overall, WERN is more liquid and more profitable than the Triad Entities and operates with less debt. It appears to be stronger overall than the Triad Entities.

As you can see from Exhibit 6.5, there can be a tremendous amount of analysis required in the application of the guideline company method. The more guideline companies that you end up with, the more time you will spend. Make sure you leave an adequate amount of time built into your budget when you quote fees! What you just saw is an analysis that was done to determine the true level of comparability between the subject company and each of the guideline companies. This analysis will allow us to select the best companies for our subject and ultimately perform our SGLPTL analysis. What is SGLPTL? If you read the checklist earlier in this chapter, you saw it there. How come you didn't ask about it then? Well, it stands for size growth leverage profitability turnover liquidity. We call it SGLPTL (pronounced single-pittle).

SGLPTL is a great analytical tool for comparing the subject and guideline companies. These are the six categories of factors that assist the appraiser in determining comparability as well as justifying the multiples that are selected. I will discuss this part of the analysis later.

Using Valuation Multiples

Valuation multiples are considered to be usable if the appraiser has good information about companies that are "similar enough" to the appraisal subject and if the engagement is to value the equity of the appraisal subject.

The multiples used frequently result in a minority, marketable estimate of value, since the pricing multiples are determined from the public market. As we will discuss in a short while, this is not always the case.

Once the multiples are derived from the marketplace, they must be adjusted for the differences between the valuation subject and the guideline companies. The multiple that will ultimately be used for the appraisal subject will probably not be exactly the same as that which was derived from the guideline companies. Risk and other characteristics generally play an important part in the process of adjusting the multiples. For example, if the publicly traded guideline companies have price-to-earnings multiples of 15 (assume an incredible coincidence and that all companies were the same), and the closely held company that is being appraised is considered to be more risky, the logical conclusion is that the closely held company would be worth less. Therefore, a lower multiple would be used.

Following are some of the more commonly used equity multiples:

- Price to net earnings
- Price to pretax earnings
- Price to cash flow
- Price to operating income
- Price to book value
- Price to dividend-paying capacity or dividend yield
- Price to gross profit

The price represented in the above multiples is the equity price of the common stock of the public company. This is used when the appraiser chooses to value the equity directly. There will be times when the appraiser chooses to value the invested capital of the company. This is usually done when there are significant differences in the financial leverage between the subject and guideline companies. Be patient and I will demonstrate this point in a little while.

When the appraiser values invested capital, some of the multiples that are common include:

- MVIC to revenues
- MVIC to EBIT
- MVIC to EBITDA
- MVIC to tangible book value and debt

In these instances, MVIC represents the *market value of invested capital*, defined as the market value of equity and debt.

Those appraisers who value small and medium-sized companies often lose sight of the reason why certain multiples are used rather than others. Comparability is probably the single most important factor in choosing a particular multiple. Sometimes, the choice of multiples depends on the availability of good data. Avoid choosing your favorite multiple and using it in every appraisal. Chances are if you stick with the same multiple all of the time, you will be wrong a good portion of the time.

Price to Net Earnings

The appropriate situation for using a price-to-net earnings multiple is (1) when the appraisal subject has relatively high income compared to its depreciation and amortization, or when depreciation represents actual or economic physical wear and tear, and (2) when the appraisal subject has normal tax rates. If a company has higher net income compared to depreciation and amortization, a price-to-earnings multiple is considered to be the appropriate multiple to use. However, this considers the fact that the depreciation and amortization must be a good representation of the actual wear and tear of the assets, so that replacements are being accounted for properly. If book or tax depreciation is used, rather than economic depreciation, the company may need to replace these assets either more quickly or more slowly than the manner in which depreciation is being recorded. Capital expenditures can greatly affect the cash flow of the company and, therefore, have an impact on its value. In that case, a cash flow rather than an earnings multiple would be more appropriate.

A company with normal tax rates allows comparison to publicly traded guideline company data that is reported on an after-tax basis. If the company has a unique tax structure (S corporation, limited liability corporation, IC DISC, etc.), better comparability may be achieved by using pretax earnings. Of course, an appraiser could also tax-effect the subject company's earnings to make them consistent with those of the guideline companies. Tax-effecting pretax earnings means that a provision for income taxes is subtracted as if the company paid these taxes in the normal course of business.

Price to Pretax Earnings

A price-to-pretax earnings multiple should be used when the subject company (1) has a relatively high income compared to its depreciation and amortization, or when depreciation represents actual physical wear and tear, but (2) has abnormal tax rates. Once again, the same rules apply for the first two items. Pretax earnings should be used when taxes are different from those of the guideline companies. I generally prefer to use pretax earnings for smaller companies since they frequently pay no taxes. Most smaller companies (and professional practices) conduct business in a manner that minimizes taxes, as opposed to maximizing shareholder wealth. Comparing these companies with similar companies or industry composite data (not large public companies) will frequently be more meaningful if it is performed on a pretax basis (you know, apples with apples, oranges with oranges).

Price to Cash Flow

A price-to-cash flow multiple is generally used when the appraisal subject has a relatively low level of income compared to its depreciation and amortization, or when depreciation represents a low level of physical, functional, or economic obsolescence. Low levels of physical, functional, or economic depreciation generally mean that the assets will not have to be replaced in the near term. Many profitable businesses go out of business because of insufficient cash flow. On the other hand, many businesses that have high levels of depreciation and amortization are cash machines, generating very high levels of cash for the owners in comparison to low earnings. These are typical situations in which a cash flow multiple makes sense.

Many experienced business appraisers are of the belief that "cash is king." Let's face it, the more cash you have, the more you can buy. Therefore, it seems logical that a great emphasis should be placed on cash flow. In many small companies, there is little difference between cash flow and earnings.

Price to Sales

A price-to-sales multiple is generally appropriate in two situations. The first situation is when the appraisal subject is "homogeneous" to the guideline companies in terms of operating expenses. The second situation in which this multiple may be appropriate is when smaller businesses, particularly cash businesses, are appraised. Service companies and companies that are light in tangible assets are considered to be candidates for application of a price-to-sales multiple.

Price to Dividend or Dividend-Paying Capacity

A price-to-dividend multiple is probably best utilized when the appraisal subject actually pays dividends. It can also be useful when the company has the ability to pay dividends, even if it does not actually pay them. Of course, dividend-paying capacity can be measured only after the appraiser considers the appraisal subject's ability to finance its operations and growth. Revenue Ruling 59-60 tells us to consider "the dividend-paying capacity of the company." But even the Revenue Ruling suggests that this is not as important as the other factors to consider.

In a valuation of a minority interest, actual dividends are more important than the dividend-paying capacity, since the minority interest cannot force dividends to be paid. Sometimes you may find that actual dividends paid are disguised as excess compensation. For example, assume you are appraising a 45 percent interest in GRT Corp. The company has two stockholders: one owns 55 percent of the stock, and the interest that you are appraising owns the balance. Compensation and bonuses are taken in proportion to the stockholdings. The salaries were $55,000 and $45,000, respectively, and the stockholders-officers received bonuses of $110,000 and $90,000. The minority stockholder received a total compensation of $135,000.

Some professionals may argue that if the minority interest is truly a minority, the compensation should not be adjusted, since that individual cannot change the policy of the company, nor can he or she force dividends to be paid. However, if you look at the relationship between the two individuals in my example, you may find that they run the company together, they have been friends and business partners for quite a while, and all major decisions are made jointly. In this situation, you may also find that reasonable compensation—defined as what it would take to replace the individual with someone of sufficient talent, experience, etc. to do the job that is currently being done—will be less than the sum of the salary and the bonus. If reasonable compensation is deemed to be $75,000, a dividend was actually paid ($135,000 − $75,000 = $60,000). In this instance, a multiple of dividends may allow you to value the minority interest directly by using multiples from the public market and adjusting them for risk.

Another consideration in determining the dividend-paying capacity for minority shareholder valuations is whether the minority shareholder would be considered "oppressed" under state statutes. *Oppression* is a legal term, and the appraiser should not try to make a determination without input from legal counsel. If a company has the ability to pay dividends but the controlling shareholder refuses to do so, the minority shareholders may have recourse against the controlling shareholder under the oppressed shareholder statute in that jurisdiction. This could result in a mandatory buyout at fair value, or dividends may have to be paid. What all of this means is that a minority shareholder may have legal rights, at the expense of litigation, to force dividends. This could make this multiple feasible even when dividends are not actually being paid. There is a discussion about stockholder litigation in Chapter 17.

Price to Book Value

A price-to-book value multiple may be appropriate when the appraisal subject is in an industry that has a meaningful relationship between the book value and the price of the company's stock. This would require guideline companies to be used. In the determination of the book value, smaller companies would use the sales price of the entire company as the "price" and only those assets that were actually to be sold. The appraiser can use return on equity to assist in the adjustment of the price-to-book value ratio to compensate for differences in quality between the company being appraised and the guideline companies being used to assist in the development of the multiple.

Valuing Invested Capital Instead of Equity

As indicated previously, there may be circumstances in which it makes more sense to value the invested capital of the appraisal subject instead of the equity. One of the questions often posed in a valuation assignment is when to use invested capital methods. If the appraisal subject's capital structure is significantly different from those of the publicly traded guideline companies, consider using a debt-free method. For example, if the appraisal subject is highly leveraged (or operating with all equity) but the industry has a very different debt-to-equity relationship, it could make sense to eliminate the effects of leveraging to make a more meaningful comparison. This does not eliminate the financial risk of the subject company. This assumes, however, that the interest being appraised has the ability to change the capital structure of the business. A minority interest does not, and accordingly, the capital structure will generally not be altered in the valuation.

Smaller closely held companies frequently have debt on their balance sheets that may have been used for either non-operating purposes (a mortgage on a ski resort in Vail, Colorado, when the company is a manufacturer in New Jersey) or to finance the owner's perqs (the owner would not have to borrow if an excessive salary was not being taken, or if a Ford was the company car instead of a Lotus). Using valuation multiples that include the non-operating debt, or even operating debt that is out of line with the industry, would result in an incorrect estimate of the value of the company. A willing buyer will rearrange the debt-to-equity relationship as necessary to optimize the value of the company, if that is prudent.

When an invested capital method is used, the appraiser will determine the value of the company's total invested capital (equity plus debt) rather than just the equity. When an appraiser values a company based on the total invested capital, some modifications are generally made during the valuation process. Some of these modifications include the following steps:

1. Add the market value of the publicly traded guideline company's equity (price per share times the number of shares outstanding) to the guideline company's market value of the interest-paying debt. The sum of these two items takes the place of the "price" in the various multiples previously discussed.
2. Interest expense reflected on the income statement is added back to the earnings (or cash flow) used in the denominator of the various multiples. If the appraiser is using an after-tax basis, interest expense is added back to earnings or cash flow, net of taxes, since there is a tax benefit that is derived from the deductibility of interest expense.
3. Once an estimate of value has been reached on a total-invested-capital basis, the appraiser then deducts the fair market value of the appraisal subject's debt to determine the value of the company's equity.

If you can be patient for a little bit longer, I will illustrate these computations with an example. But before I illustrate the invested capital computations, I want you to feel more comfortable with the concept of using multiples. Let's go over a little more theory, and then you will be ready for some number crunching.

Adjusting Public Company Multiples for Risk

Once valuation multiples are determined for the guideline companies, it becomes necessary for the appraiser to adjust these multiples for the qualitative differences between the guideline companies and the appraisal subject. These qualitative differences will most likely relate to such factors as expected growth and the risks attributable to the appraisal subject that are different from those of the guideline companies.

Different risk factors considered by the appraiser will generally include, but will not be limited to, the following:

- Economic risk
- Business risk
- Operating risk
- Financial risk
- Asset risk
- Product risk
- Market risk
- Technological risk

- Regulatory risk
- Legal risk

There are many other risk factors to be considered as well, but these are some of the more important items that an appraiser must think about in the application of not only the market approach, but also (as you will see in Chapter 9) the income approach. Each of these risk factors should be analyzed from the point of view of how the appraisal subject differs from the guideline companies. Most of the information about risk will be obtained from sources other than the financial statements (imagine that: there is more to business valuation than number crunching!). Let's discuss the risk factors.

Economic Risk. Economic risk is analyzed as part of the economic analysis performed by the appraiser. Revenue Ruling 59-60 suggests that consideration be given to "the economic outlook in general and the condition and outlook of the specific industry in particular." The appraiser must determine how the subject company will be affected by changes in the economic environment in which it operates. Economic conditions at the valuation date and how they affect the company must also be considered. For example, if you were appraising an automobile dealership, consideration would have to be given to the impact that interest rates have on auto loans. If the economic forecast was that interest rates were expected to go up, one would think that car sales may be affected if people could not afford to borrow at the higher rates.

To the extent that the guideline companies selected are good "comparables," economic risk will be incorporated in the pricing multiples. The adjustments to be made will more likely compensate for differences between the guideline company and the appraisal subject that are due to factors such as regional or local economic risk. The appraisal subject may operate in an area that is different from that of the guideline companies.

Business Risk. Business risk involves the analysis of the appraisal subject's business. Once again, we are interested in how the subject company differs from the guideline companies. The appraiser analyzes the company in terms of the risk associated with factors such as sales volatility and the volatility of the company's growth. If a company has revenues that fluctuate widely, a greater risk exists than if the company is somewhat stable. Volatile growth is obviously a greater risk as well, when you consider the cash flow needs of a growing company. If growth is volatile, it may be difficult for the company to raise the necessary capital to foster that growth. The banks may be reluctant to lend money to a company that may not be able to repay its debt next year if a reversing trend takes place.

Operating Risk. The operating risks associated with a business include such factors as the fixed versus variable cost structure of the appraisal subject. The appraiser must analyze the cost structure of the appraisal subject to determine how much risk the company is exposed to as a result of the commitments and costs associated with the business operations. If a company has a high level of fixed costs, that may not bode well in times when revenues decrease. Obviously, if two companies are the same except that one company has higher fixed costs than the other, the company with the higher level of fixed costs would be considered to be more risky and, therefore, worth less.

Financial Risk. The financial risks associated with a company pertain to the amount of leverage the company uses and the company's ability to cover its debt payments. The appraiser must pay particular attention to the capital structure of similar companies to analyze the appraisal subject. Companies that were heavily leveraged in the late 1980s found themselves in trouble when the recession hit the United States. Bankruptcy filings were at an all-time high, indicating that too much debt was dangerous. To determine the level of risk of the appraisal subject, different debt structures should be analyzed when one performs the appraisal.

Proper capital structure plays an important part in the financial success of a business. Companies that are overcapitalized or undercapitalized are not necessarily "comparable" to companies that have a normal capital structure. A normal capital structure is one that is similar to that of other companies in the same industry. If the appraisal subject is heavily leveraged, the appraiser may want to consider using an invested capital approach using EBIT or EBITDA in the pricing multiples.

In many instances, smaller companies that are heavily indebted are structured in that manner as a result of the owner of the business choosing to finance his or her perqs, and therefore, the interest and the liability should be treated as a non-operating item, since they do not affect the business operations of the company.

Asset Risk. Asset risk relates to the age and condition of the company's assets. Older assets represent a higher degree of risk for a company in terms of higher maintenance costs, a lower level of productivity, and functional and technological differences in available production. Not only do these items increase the level of expenditures for the company, but the future cash flow needs may also be greater due to replacement needs, which further increases the risk of the enterprise.

Product Risk. Product risk relates to a company that has little diversification in its product line or has a product line that may become extinct with the introduction of a newer product by a different company. An example of this is the effect that the fax machine had on the teletype machine.

Market Risk. Market risk relates to how geographically diversified the company is. If the company operates within a local marketplace, it can be greatly affected by changes in that local area. A more diversified market reduces the risk associated with a company. An illustration of market risk is a local restaurant that operates in a community that is dependent on a military base for business. If the government decides to close the military base, what do you think will happen to the restaurant's business?

Technological Risk. New technology can adversely affect a company if it does not have the ability to keep up with other companies in the appraisal subject's industry. For example, within the printing industry, four-color printing presses provide a capability that does not exist for companies without these types of machines. A commercial printing operation that does not have a particular type of press is at a competitive disadvantage, which increases the risk of the company.

Regulatory Risk. Regulatory agencies can also adversely affect a business. Environmental regulations are probably one of the best examples of the risks that a company faces. A chemical manufacturing company can be put out of business in a very short time by the Department of Environmental Protection. (What about gas stations?) This increased risk will generally cause a willing buyer to pay less for a business, since he or she must be able to generate a faster return on the investment to compensate for the possible impact of new regulations. Obviously, only those regulations that can be reasonably forecast can be considered in this analysis. Do not forget about possible cleanup costs if a problem is discovered. An appraiser may not be able to quantify these costs, but the increased risk will affect market multiples, discount rates, and capitalization rates.

Legal Risk. The cost of litigation in today's society can mean the end of any successful business. Even if successful, litigation can create such a financial burden on a business that it can be greatly exposed to the risk of being put out of business. Product liability claims, employee discrimination claims, antitrust litigation, and a host of other types of claims will, at times, significantly affect the value of a business enterprise.

Valuation Considerations

Since valuation is premised on investment theory, the appraiser must perform a comparative analysis of qualitative and quantitative similarities and differences between the guideline companies and the appraisal subject to assess the investment attributes of the guideline companies relative to the appraisal subject. Not all pricing multiples will be appropriate for each guideline company. Therefore, the appraiser should use only those multiples that are deemed to be appropriate based on the underlying financial data of each guideline company. Financial ratios for the guideline companies, as well as the comparative analysis of the qualitative and quantitative factors regarding the differences between the guideline companies and the appraisal subject, should be used together to determine the appropriate valuation multiples to apply to the appraisal subject.

Various valuation multiples may be selected for application to the appraisal subject, and this results in several value estimates. In arriving at the valuation conclusion, the appraiser should consider the quality of the information that is available for the determination of each multiple.

Another consideration is the time period to be covered in the application of pricing multiples. The following are some of the more common time periods that are used:

- Pro forma period
- Latest 12 months
- Last fiscal year
- Year ahead
- Average (mean) over number of years
- Weighted average over number of years

Regardless of which time period an appraiser uses, Revenue Ruling 59-60 makes it clear that "valuation is a prophecy as to the future." Whether a three-year average, a five-year average, or pro forma earnings are used in the application of these multiples, the ultimate decision on which period will be used is a subjective one on the part of the appraiser. Which time period is most representative of what is expected to occur in the future?

The factors to consider in selecting the time period and the method of calculating the earnings base will depend on the appraiser's (or management's) ability to forecast the future. For example, if the company has cyclical earnings, the appraiser may want to consider an arithmetic average. This has the tendency to smooth out the effect of the periodic cycles of the business. If the past five years, on average, are expected to resemble the next five years, plus or minus some growth, using an arithmetic average as a base and adding or subtracting some growth may be perfectly acceptable.

If the appraisal subject is experiencing modest growth, the appraiser should consider weighted average earnings, the earnings for the latest 12 months, or pro forma earnings. In high-growth companies, the appraiser should consider a discounted future benefits method (this will be discussed in Chapter 9). Since the intention of the valuation process is to arrive at a "prophecy of the future," caution must be exercised when one uses a weighted average, particularly when the company is growing. The result of the weighted average will rarely, if ever, reflect "probable future earnings" (this is the future concept discussed in Revenue Ruling 68-609). The danger in using a weighted average is illustrated in Exhibit 6.6.

EXHIBIT 6.6
Danger of a Weighted Average

Assume that a company's earnings grew from $1,000 to $25,000 over a five-year period. If the earnings were as indicated in the table, the weighted average would be calculated as follows:

Year	*Earnings*		*Factor*		*Extension*
2000	$ 25,000	×	5	=	$ 125,000
1999	15,000	×	4	=	60,000
1998	10,000	×	3	=	30,000
1997	5,000	×	2	=	10,000
1996	1,000	×	1	=	1,000
			15		$ 226,000

$226,000 ÷ 15 = $15,066

In the foregoing example, the weighted average earnings would be $15,066. Clearly, the company's growth would not justify a forecast of earnings of $15,066 in the subsequent period. The growth would warrant a forecast of earnings greater than $25,000, all other factors remaining constant. Therefore, applying a pricing multiple to the weighted average earnings would result in a value that is not truly representative of what a willing buyer would use to assess an investment decision, unless the guideline companies have similar trends, which may cause their price-to-five-year weighted average earnings multiple to be pretty high. This same concept applies in the application of the income approach. Using a weighted average is appropriate only if the result reflects the "probable future earnings" of the appraisal subject or if the earnings trends are the same for the guideline companies.

If the company's earnings are relatively stable, it does not matter what earnings base is used as long as it reflects the facts of your engagement. If the historic stable earnings are a reasonable representation of the future, by all means use them. It is not too often that an appraiser will get lucky enough to have this portion of the assignment made easy. Forecasting is like using a crystal ball. Good luck!

If the company's earnings are declining, the appraiser may want to consider weighted average earnings, the latest 12 months earnings, or pro forma earnings, assuming that a turnaround is expected to take place. If it is not, declining earnings may also require the appraiser to consider a liquidation method if the decline appears to be long-term or permanent. Applying the concept of "highest and best use" requires the appraiser to consider whether the shareholder's value would be maximized by liquidating at the date of the valuation. Continuing to operate could cause the company's equity to decline. Obviously, this is a consideration only if the interest being valued has the ability to liquidate the company.

If the appraisal assignment involves a company whose earnings are volatile, use common sense and good judgment. Experts in the appraisal field who are much smarter than yours truly could not give you better advice. A company with erratic earnings is one of the most difficult appraisal subjects. Other than applying common sense to valuation methodologies and trying to support your assumptions with good reasoning, the appraisal assignment in this situation is almost impossible. After you write your report in this type of case, it is more important than ever to have another appraisal professional review your work to see if your logic holds together. Make believe your doctor just told you that you need a serious operation. Get a second opinion!

What Price Do We Use in the Multiples?

Once the earnings base is determined, the next step is to determine the price to be used in the determination of the multiples. For public companies, the price of the stock on the appraisal date will be used in most instances. The average of the "high" and "low" prices for the day may be preferred to the "close" price; this eliminates any last-minute price run-ups that may have taken place on the appraisal date. However, price run-ups may reflect the market; these various prices are generally pretty close to each other. If they are not, that may indicate that the public company may be thinly traded and lacks liquidity.

There may be times when the appraiser will choose to use an average of the high and low prices over some time period other than the appraisal date in order to compensate for unusual peaks and valleys in the market. For example, an appraiser may wish to compensate for stock prices on October 19, 1987, when there was a 500-point drop in the Dow Jones Industrial Average. These types of unusual stock market corrections can cause the pricing multiples to be skewed.

Regression Analysis

One of the tools that appraisers frequently find useful is the statistical technique known as regression analysis. If you are a statistical nerd like me, you hate this stuff. However, like it or not, you better know how to use it. So, I am going to give you the benefit of my little knowledge about this stuff, hopefully in plain English.

First, what is regression analysis? Simply stated, regression analysis is a statistical tool that compares two variables, such as price and earnings. If you are lucky, you will be able to prove that there is a relationship between these two variables. Let's skip the heavy-duty theory and talk about the mechanics of how to do this stuff. This is accomplished by performing the following steps:

1. Set up an Excel spreadsheet.
2. Input earnings in the first column.
3. Input the price per share in the second column.
4. Make sure that the price and the earnings for the same company end up on the same line.
5. Using your mouse, highlight all of the numbers that you just input.
6. Click Insert in the Excel menu.
7. Choose Chart from this menu. This will bring up the chart wizard (no, it's not the same as the Wizard of Oz).
8. Select XY (Scatter) as your chart type.
9. Click Finish and you get a graph.
10. Click one of the data points on the graph and they will all highlight.
11. Right-click and choose Add trend line.
12. Click Linear.
13. Click the Options tab.
14. Click the Equation and R^2 boxes, and click OK. Then you get this:

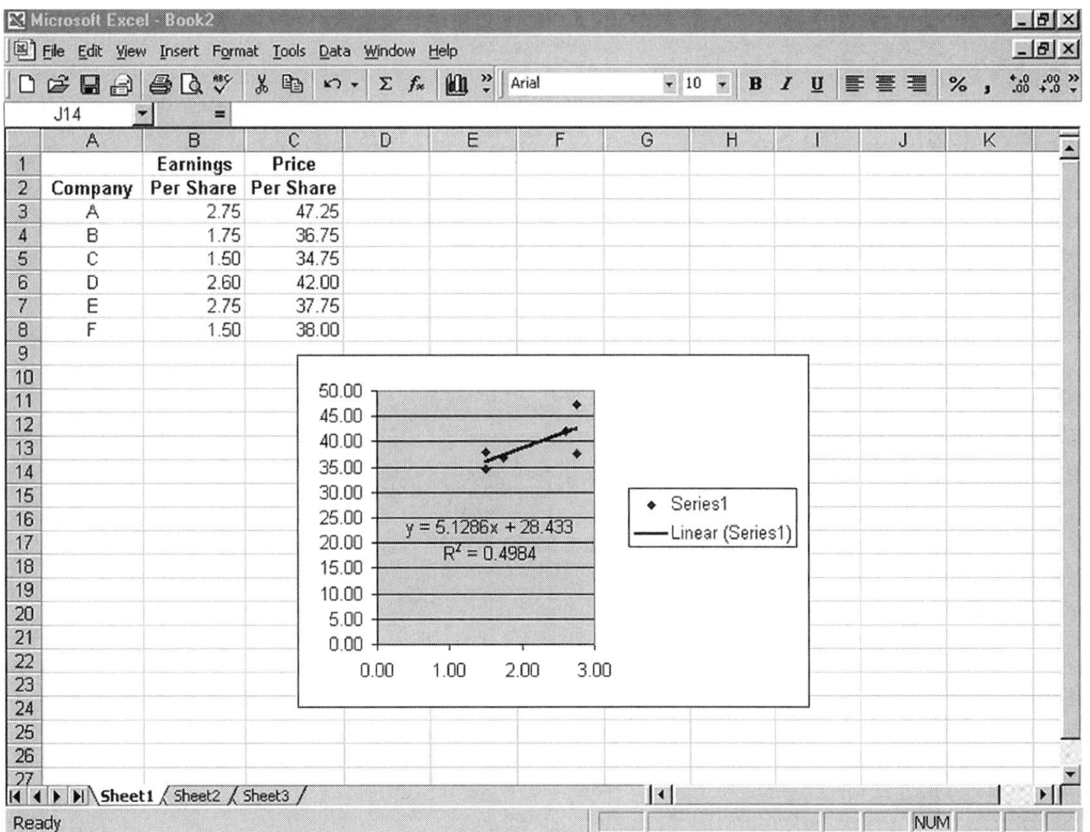

Company	Earnings Per Share	Price Per Share
A	2.75	47.25
B	1.75	36.75
C	1.50	34.75
D	2.60	42.00
E	2.75	37.75
F	1.50	38.00

Let me tell you the little bit that I know about this graph. The price per share appears on the *Y* axis (the one that goes up and down), and the earnings per share (I bet you can figure out all by yourself) is on the *X* axis (the one that you would lay down on to take a nap).

Next, let's talk about the data points. Each point reflects the point where the price per share meets the earnings per share. The objective of this exercise is to see if there is a relationship between the price and the earnings of the guideline companies. If there is, this may be a good relationship to use when you choose a multiple.

Now, the line. The trend line represents the relationship between the price and the earnings for all of these companies. Linear regression is a *best-fit* relationship that illustrates the price to earnings fit for the entire group in aggregate. Let's keep it simple. The R^2 needs to be high in order for there to be a good fit. What is high? The sky is high. But in this case, a number such as 0.5 tells us that there is some relationship between the variables. The closer you get to 1.0, the better the relationship.

Remember that the purpose of this exercise is to figure out what the market evidence shows about the relationship between these factors. The market may have better evidence about how the public prices the stocks. Choose those multiples that have the best correlation, i.e., an R^2 close to 1.0. For more information about this nonsense, buy a "Statistics for Dummies" book! God knows I need one.

Adjusting Multiples Based on SGLPTL

So what's the deal with this SGLPTL stuff? This is a technique that I learned from several co-instructors when I was teaching for one of the appraisal organizations. It is one of the most logical, well-organized concepts that I have seen. For appraisers, one of the most difficult parts of applying the guideline public company method is figuring out how to get from the public company multiples to an appropriate multiple for the subject company. The purpose of the SGLPTL worksheet is to help the analyst do just that.

For each pricing multiple that is chosen to be appropriate in the valuation assignment, we create a separate worksheet. The worksheet in Exhibit 6.7 is for a price-to-revenue analysis. The public company multiples are listed across the top of the worksheet. The analyst will then consider each of the six elements of SGLPTL and the similarities or dissimilarities between the public company and the subject company. The question asked is whether the subject company is stronger, weaker, or the same as the public company with regard to each attribute. If the subject is stronger, the analyst knows that the multiple should be higher than the public company multiple and puts a + on the appropriate line. A weakness gets −, and the same gets a +/−.

Then the analyst has to decide which of the six factors are the most important in the view of investors. Typically, growth drives the public market. The really high multiples that we see are created because the investors are paying for anticipated growth. Usually, the higher the growth, the higher the multiples. Our analysts will perform a regression analysis using the guideline company data to see what the investor seems to be putting the most weight on. For example, is the multiple more highly correlated with a return on equity, return on invested capital, profitability, etc.? The analyst must then use his or her subjective judgment to determine the appropriate multiple for the subject company compared to that one guideline company. The same process is then performed for each guideline company.

The result of the analysis is that the analyst has considered the differences between each public company, individually, compared to the subject and has chosen what is believed to be an appropriate multiple. Take a look at Exhibit 6.7.

Based on the analysis that was performed, the analyst concluded a range of possible multiples for the subject company from 0.15 to 0.25, fitting well within the range of the mean and median guideline company

EXHIBIT 6.7
***SGLPTL* Analysis**
Guideline Company Valuation Multiple Analysis

Price to Revenues Analysis

		ATEC	*MTMC*	*SVTG*	*SYCM*	*Mean*	*Median*
	Multiple	0.21	0.26	0.25	0.09	0.2	0.2
Ratio Comparison	Size[1]	–	+	–	+		
	Growth[2]	–	+/–	–	+		
	Liquidity[3]	–	–	+	–		
	Profitability[4]	+	+	+	+		
	Turnover[5]	–	+	–	+		
	Leverage[6]	+/–	+/–	–	–		
	GPCM multiple*	0.2	0.25	0.2	0.15	0.2	0.2

"+" Indicates that the subject company ratios are higher than those of the guideline company.
"–" Indicates that the subject company ratios are lower than those of the guideline company.
"+/–" Indicates that the subject company ratios are similar to those of the guideline company.
"NA" Indicates that the subject company and guideline company ratios are not comparable.

*Guideline public company method
[1]Size was based on revenues for 1999.
[2]Growth was based on three- and five-year compound average growth of revenues, unless otherwise noted.
[3]Liquidity was based on the current and quick ratios.
[4]Profitability was based on the return on sales.
[5]Turnover was based on the working capital turnover.
[6]Leverage was based on the long-term debt–to–equity ratio.

multiples. In this case, a multiple of 0.2 was chosen. If you notice, this multiple is better than some of the guideline companies and worse than others. The narrative that would appear in the workpapers and eventually the report would be similar to the example that you saw in Exhibit 6.5.

There is no doubt that the valuation process requires the appraiser to exercise subjective judgment. We cannot merely apply a mathematical formula to do this. If we could, none of our clients would pay us the kind of fees that we get for this stuff. While you cannot *quantify* every aspect of the assignment, you can at least attempt to *qualify* the judgment calls. This will allow you to explain to the reader of your report the thought process that went into selecting the multiples. Hopefully, there is a thought process behind it! Is it perfect? Of course not. That is why we try to use several different pricing multiples in our analysis, as well as why we consider other approaches to valuation as well. Until we have a chance to reconcile all of the approaches and methods, and then perform additional *sanity checks* to test the reasonableness of the result, we cannot possibly know if we are in the ballpark.

Exhibit 6.8 provides you with a simple example illustrating the application of the market approach using guideline company information. At the end of the chapter, there is an exhibit with a real example. Be patient! As you review Exhibit 6.8, there are several points to keep in mind. First, the selection of the guideline companies would have come from a careful review of many of the items discussed previously that makes these companies similar to the appraisal subject. Another consideration is that the median multiple rather than the arithmetic average is calculated. This is because the median is often a better statistical measurement, since it eliminates highs and lows that may skew the average.

EXHIBIT 6.8
Example of the Guideline Public Company Method

Guideline Company Information

	Date	Price/Earnings Ratio	Percent of Sales	Multiple of Book Value
ABC Toy Company, Inc.	12/31/00	8.70	55.30%	2.85
XYZ Funtime, Inc.	10/31/00	9.30	47.43%	4.65
Toys, Inc.	12/31/00	8.50	35.25%	3.65
Games Corp.	12/31/00	6.60	54.80%	3.90
Fun Corp.	11/30/00	7.80	48.20%	4.25
	Median multiple	8.50	48.20%	3.90
	Selected multiple	6.20	44.00%	2.50

The selected multiples are now applied against the figures of the appraisal subject.

	Price/Earnings	Price/Sales	Price/Book Value
After-tax earnings	$ 959,446		
Gross sales		$ 13,983,541	
Book value (without non-operating items)			$ 2,415,822
Multiple	× 6.20	× 44.00%	× 2.50
Operating entity value	$ 5,948,565	$ 6,152,758	$ 6,039,555
Net non-operating assets	+ 250,000	+ 250,000	+ 250,000
Total entity value	$ 6,198,565	$ 6,402,758	$ 6,289,555
Rounded	$ 6,200,000	$ 6,400,000	$ 6,300,000

This example intentionally omits any calculation of valuation discounts or premiums, which are discussed in Chapter 11.

The question that you are probably asking yourself is how the selected multiples were chosen. This is accomplished by comparing the appraisal subject to the guideline companies. We would have performed a SGLPTL analysis. Growth is frequently the most important factor to consider. After performing a financial analysis, the appraiser felt that the multiples selected were reasonable.

The results, as presented in Exhibit 6.8, represent the value of the company on a marketable, minority basis, since the pricing multiples come from the public stock market. This also assumes that discretionary normalization adjustments were not made for the appraisal subject. Stock market activity consists primarily of minority shareholders who trade in a free and active market. This derives a minority basis value. The value indication stays on a minority basis if the appraiser does not make "control" normalization adjustments. If adjustments are made, the result is a hybrid of minority and control, and a reasonable control premium may be added to derive a full control value. Many appraisers believe that the public market is not truly a minority value. Temporarily accept the theory, and I will discuss this more in Chapter 11.

Furthermore, these shareholders have the ability to call their stockbrokers to sell these shares, and they will generally have their money within three business days. This makes these shares marketable. If a controlling interest was being valued, you might add a control premium. If the shares being valued represented a minority interest, no such premium would be necessary. Regardless of which type of interest (control or minority) is being valued, a discount for lack of marketability would probably be required if a minority interest is being appraised, and it might be required for a controlling interest, since a closely held stock is not as marketable as its publicly traded counterpart.

The selection of the multiple is a subjective process based on the analysis that the appraiser performs throughout the valuation assignment. This process considers the risk elements, as well as the differences between the guideline companies and the appraisal subject with respect to growth expectations, size, financial performance, and everything else that makes these companies different. Unfortunately, if you bought this book looking for the answer to the mysterious multiple question, you're out of luck. Seriously, the differential in the multiples has to consider the differences between the companies under analysis, and you have to test your conclusion to see if it makes sense. There are no magic tables that you can turn to for help. Remember, our job is to opine on value, not develop multiples. If your value conclusion makes sense, your multiples are probably reasonable.

You will also notice that the multiplication of the base amount by the multiple results in the value of the operating entity. This amount includes all the operating assets and liabilities of the company (assuming that you are valuing the equity). The non-operating assets and liabilities are added or subtracted from the value of the operating entity to reach the final entity value. However, this assumes that the non-operating income and expenses were adjusted in the first place. Most appraisers round out the conclusion, since the valuation process is not an exact science and precision is not possible.

Now that we have the basic concept under control (ha ha!), let's go back to our discussion about valuing the invested capital of the appraisal subject. As indicated previously, there are several different steps that the appraiser must take to accomplish this. Let's use one of the guideline companies from Exhibit 6.8 for our example. ABC Toy Company, Inc. had a price-to-earnings ratio of 8.70 on December 31, 2000. If the price of ABC's stock was $47.50 on this date, this means that ABC's earnings would have to have been $5.46 per share. The price-to-earnings ratio would be calculated as follows:

Price/earnings = Multiple
$47.50/$5.46 = 8.70

To convert the price-to-earnings ratio from an equity multiple to an invested capital multiple, we need to adjust both the price and the earnings. First, the price. To determine the market value of the company's equity, we would multiply the price per share by the number of outstanding shares. The outstanding shares can be obtained from the annual report. Let's assume that there were one million shares outstanding. This would make the market value of ABC's equity $47.5 million (1,000,000 shares × $47.50 per share).

ABC's balance sheet reflects interest-bearing debt in the amount of $5 million. Assume that this debt is at a market rate of interest (this way, the market value of the debt is equal to the face amount). Therefore, the market value of the company's invested capital is $52.5 million, or $52.50 per share. This becomes the new price in the price-to-earnings ratio. The price is now referred to as MVIC (market value of invested capital).

Now we need to adjust the earnings. The earnings previously calculated for ABC were $5.46 per share. This means that the net income, after taxes, was $5.46 million ($5.46 × 1,000,000 shares). Upon review of the company's income statement, you find that the interest expense was $500,000 for the year. The adjustment to the earnings in the price-to-earnings ratio would be as follows:

Net income after taxes		$5,460,000
Add: Interest expense (net of taxes)		
Interest expense	$500,000	
Effective tax rate	× 40%	
Tax benefit	$200,000	300,000
Debt-free net income		$5,760,000

ABC's earnings have now been adjusted to an invested capital basis of $5.76 million, or $5.76 per share. The new ratio for the market value of invested capital to debt-free net income (MVIC/DFNI) would be:

$$\$52.50/\$5.76 = 9.11$$

This same calculation would be performed for each of the guideline companies. The appraiser then selects the appropriate multiple to apply to the appraisal subject's debt-free net income. In this situation, our appraisal subject had an after-tax net income of $959,446. Its interest expense, net of taxes, would be added back to get to the debt-free net income. It would be this figure against which a multiple would be applied. Let's recalculate the price-to-earnings portion of Exhibit 6.8 and do the new calculations. For simplicity, Exhibit 6.9 already has the new price-to-earnings multiples for the guideline companies on an invested capital basis.

EXHIBIT 6.9
Guideline Public Company Method Using Invested Capital

Guideline Company Information

Guideline Companies	*Date*	*Price/Earnings Ratio*
ABC Toy Company, Inc.	12/31/00	9.11
XYZ Funtime, Inc.	10/31/00	10.15
Toys, Inc.	12/31/00	9.45
Games Corp.	12/31/00	7.30
Fun Corp.	11/30/00	8.90
	Median multiple	9.45
	Selected multiple	6.90

The selected multiples are now applied against the figures of the appraisal subject.

	Price/Earnings
After-tax earnings	$ 959,446
Add: Interest (net of taxes)[1]	90,000
Debt-free net income	$ 1,049,446
Multiple	× 6.90
Value of operating invested capital[2]	$ 7,241,177
Net non-operating assets	+ 250,000
Total value of invested capital	$ 7,491,177
Rounded	$ 7,500,000

[1]Interest expense for the year was $150,000. Effective tax rate was 40 percent.

[2]We have once again intentionally omitted valuation discounts or premiums from this example.

Exhibit 6.9 illustrates the use of the invested capital pricing multiple. If you look at the multiples for the guideline companies, you will see that they were higher on an invested capital basis. This makes sense, since the result is the value of the companies' invested capital. The result is that the multiple used for the appraisal subject was also higher (6.90 instead of 6.20). A similar type of analysis of the qualitative differences between the guideline companies and the appraisal subject would have been performed to derive the selected multiple.

There should always be a correlation between the multiples that you select, regardless of what earnings base you apply them to. In the example in Exhibit 6.9, the appraiser can test the validity of the selection process by subtracting the interest-bearing debt from the value of the invested capital of the appraisal subject. If the appraisal subject's balance sheet reflects debt in the amount of $1.3 million, the value of the equity would have been calculated as follows:

Value of invested capital	$7,500,000
Less: Interest-bearing debt	1,300,000
Value of equity	$6,200,000

The value of the equity is similar to the values illustrated in Exhibit 6.8. Rarely will they be exactly the same.

Advantages of Using the Guideline Public Company Method

Different approaches and methods have distinct advantages and disadvantages in the valuation process. Not all methods will be appropriate every time, but it is up to the appraiser to determine the best methods to be used based on the facts and circumstances of each situation. The use of information from the public stock market is considered by many appraisers to be an objective source of data. The stock prices of public companies are set by many transactions involving relatively few buyers and sellers. Therefore, the result is considered to be objective. However, there are some skeptics who believe that factors such as institutional computer trading remove a considerable amount of the objectivity. Others believe that the public marketplace is efficient. For those of us who remember the "efficient market hypothesis" from our finance courses, one has to wonder if the creators of this hypothesis could have ever dreamed that computers would be trading stocks on Wall Street (there goes that theory!).

Many studies of the public marketplace have been performed, analyzing the activity that has taken place in the market. These studies assist the appraiser in the determination of risk and value. Control premium studies, restricted stock studies, initial public offering studies, and a group of proprietary studies have been performed and published as a basis of empirical data that can be used by an appraiser. These items are discussed in Chapter 11.

Appraisals of larger closely held companies can be performed using these methods, since larger companies frequently take on many of the characteristics of their publicly traded counterparts. Therefore, comparing larger closely held companies with publicly traded guideline companies is an effective method of valuation (remember: fair market value comes from the market!).

Disadvantages of Using the Guideline Public Company Method

Despite the fact that the public market affords certain advantages to an appraiser, many appraisers feel that there is a lack of comparability between publicly traded guideline companies and a closely held appraisal subject. Although the concept of using publicly traded guideline companies as surrogates is intended to be based on comparability, no two companies are ever so closely alike that they make perfect comparables. Sometimes, particularly if the appraisal subject is a small or mid-size company, there are so many differences between the appraisal subject and the publicly traded companies (e.g., size, depth of management, capital structure, ability to borrow, product diversification, and geographical diversification) that a meaningful comparison cannot be made without making extraordinary leaps of faith.

In addition, the public stock market has an emotional aspect to it. This is evidenced by the fact that announcements made by companies, the government, or both create peaks and valleys in the stock market. As I was writing this section of the book, Cisco Systems stock swung from $20 per share to $15 per share in a two-week period. If the Federal Reserve Board raises interest rates, the stock market tends to react based on the expectation that future growth will be limited because of less borrowing and the increased costs of borrowing. There can be no doubt that emotion plays a considerable role in the market's performance.

Another disadvantage of using publicly traded methods is that it is frequently difficult to interpret and understand the stock market data that is disseminated. Despite the amount of information available about public companies, there is often a considerable amount of information that is not available about public companies. This makes it difficult to truly compare the companies. The information that can be obtained about a public company appears in annual reports, 10-Ks, other SEC filings, and proxy statements, as well as information that is published in financial periodicals, trade publications, and the like. Since the appraiser is rarely given the opportunity to speak with the long-range planning group, management, or anyone else in the public company, the only information that can be obtained is what the public company wants the appraiser to know.

For those appraisers who value entire companies, there is also the difficulty of translating the minority, marketable value that is derived using these methods into a control, nonmarketable value (you know, small portions of companies with almost instant liquidity versus full companies with no liquidity). Ten shares of IBM stock have very different characteristics from 100 percent of the stock of closely held XYZ Computer, Inc.

The Guideline Public Company Method Illustrated

Exhibit 6.10 contains an entire guideline public company method analysis from a report of a smaller company. My previous examples in this chapter were based on some larger companies, but there is no reason you cannot do this stuff for smaller companies as well.

EXHIBIT 6.10
Guideline Company Method Section of Report

The last factor discussed in Revenue Ruling 59-60 is "the market price of stocks of corporations engaged in the same or similar line of business having their stocks actively traded in a free and open market either on an exchange or over the counter." This is usually referred to as the market approach to valuation.

Under this approach, there are two methodologies that can be applied, the guideline public company method and the transaction method. Both require the search for and utilization of data from outside sources. This section of the report discusses our search for appropriate data and our analysis of it.

Guideline Companies

In order to apply the market approach, this appraiser performed a computerized search in the *Global Researcher* database compiled by Disclosure, looking for guideline companies that could be considered "comparable" to PDQ. Comparability is generally difficult to achieve in business valuations, as privately owned businesses tend to adapt to the management of the company. Smaller companies often take on the personality of the individual owner, and it is not until the company is considerably larger and becomes managed by a team of professional managers who are responsible to multiple owners rather than just one or two that it becomes comparable.

In order to locate guideline companies, this appraiser used the following search criteria:

1. The prospective guideline company's three-digit SIC code had to be 346 (Metal Forging and Stampings), 349 (Miscellaneous Fabricated Metal Products), or 3621 (which includes the manufacture of rotors and stators).
2. The company had to operate in the United States.
3. The maximum sales volume should be no greater than $240 million, approximately 20 times PDQ's annual sales.

EXHIBIT 6.10 *(Continued)*

Based on these criteria, nine companies were located. In addition, we performed a text search of all SEC documents listed in the Disclosure database. We searched for companies that listed "Stamping" in their business descriptions. We located one more company through this search criterion.

We then analyzed the trading activity of the 10 companies selected. Some of these companies were eliminated because the stocks were not traded actively, which limits the quality of their valuation multiples.

Next, we obtained annual statements for each of the companies and performed a more thorough analysis of the business descriptions to determine if the remaining companies were reasonable guideline companies. Companies were disqualified if the major product lines were not related to PDQ's.

The following companies remained after this initial screening:

1. Autocam Corp.
2. Kollmorgen Corp.
3. Oilgear Co.
4. SIFCO Industries, Inc.
5. SEMX Corp.
6. WSI Industries, Inc.

A description of each of these companies follows. The information provided is primarily from The Company's Form 10-K that is filed with the Securities and Exchange Commission.

Autocam Corp.

Autocam designs and manufactures close-tolerance, specialty metal alloy components sold to the transportation and medical device industries. These components are used primarily in gasoline and diesel fuel, power steering and braking systems, and devices for surgical procedures. The Company's production equipment consists of high-precision, automatic cam-driven turning machines and computer numerically controlled turning, milling, and grinding machines capable of high-volume production while maintaining close tolerances.

The Company currently sells its products in the transportation and medical devices industries.

Select financial data is found in Tables 1 and 2. Adjustments have been made to the income statements to account for income from extraordinary items that would not be expected to recur as part of the operating business.

TABLE 1

Autocam Corp. Income Statement for the Years Ended June 30,

	1995	*1996*	*1997*	*1998*	*1999*
			(In Thousands)		
Revenues	$ 54,304	$ 57,711	$ 61,986	$ 90,361	$179,726
Cost of goods sold	41,693	44,231	48,618	69,436	150,742
Gross profit	$ 12,610	$ 13,480	$ 13,369	$ 20,925	$ 28,984
Operating expenses	3,236	3,581	3,785	6,086	10,208
Operating income	$ 9,374	$ 9,899	$ 9,584	$ 14,839	$ 18,776
Interest expense	—	—	—	2,719	8,104
Other income (expenses)	(1,420)	(1,396)	(1,346)	(166)	(645)
Income before income taxes	$ 7,954	$ 8,503	$ 8,238	$ 11,954	$ 10,027
Provision for income taxes	2,720	2,914	2,827	4,213	3,757
Net income	$ 5,233	$ 5,589	$ 5,411	$ 7,741	$ 6,270
Earnings per share	$ 1.02	$ 1.03	$ 0.86	$ 1.22	$ 0.99

Note: Figures may not add due to rounding.

(Continued)

EXHIBIT 6.10 *(Continued)*

TABLE 2

Autocam Corp. Balance Sheet as of June 30,

	1995	1996	1997	1998	1999
			(In Thousands of Dollars)		
Cash and equivalents	$ 44	$ 1,467	$ 2,511	$ 1,644	$ 3,654
Accounts receivable	6,840	7,468	8,842	11,680	40,781
Inventories	3,809	4,171	5,444	6,389	15,237
Other current assets	621	662	722	1,088	2,103
Total current assets	$ 11,313	$ 13,768	$ 17,518	$ 20,801	$ 61,775
Net property, plant and equipment	38,307	42,555	55,934	64,421	129,744
Intangible assets	—	—	6,443	14,366	28,376
Investment and advances to subsidiaries	—	—	—	—	534
Deposits and other assets	3,370	3,489	3,742	13,861	9,062
Total Assets	**$52,990**	**$59,812**	**$83,638**	**$113,449**	**$229,491**
Current portion of long-term debt	$ 3,872	$ 3,739	$ 5,906	$ 6,554	$ 4,478
Accounts payable	3,811	4,124	4,398	7,830	22,130
Accrued expenses	1,480	1,378	2,912	3,291	13,063
Total current liabilities	$ 9,163	9,241	$ 13,216	$ 17,675	$ 39,671
Long-term debt	13,334	12,086	25,192	37,851	109,560
Deferred charges	5,274	7,199	8,616	10,051	31,045
Other long-term liabilities	—	—	—	561	—
Total liabilities	$ 27,772	$ 28,526	$ 47,023	$ 66,138	$ 180,276
Minority interests	—	—	—	2,250	2,813
Stockholders' equity	25,218	31,286	36,615	45,061	46,402
Total liabilities and equity	**$52,990**	**$59,812**	**$83,638**	**$113,449**	**$229,491**
Common shares outstanding at end of year (000)	5,141	5,428	6,289	6,342	6,352

Note: Figures may not add due to rounding.

Kollmorgen Corp.

Kollmorgen Corporation incorporated in the State of New York in 1916. It is one of the major worldwide manufacturers of high-performance electronic motion control products and systems and has operations in two industry segments: (1) industrial and commercial and (2) aerospace and defense.

Industrial and Commercial Group

Kollmorgen's products and services in this segment include (1) a number of different types of permanent magnet motors, associated electronic amplifiers and feedback components, and controls and related systems for a variety of applications; and (2) specialized engineering services to the electric utility industry. Kollmorgen's line of servo motors and related drive electronics are used in many types of industrial automation, process control, machine tool, underwater equipment, and robotic applications. Its torque motors and tachometer generators are used worldwide in medical, machine tool, and process control applications.

Kollmorgen's stepper motors and brushless motors are used for office and factory automation, instrumentation, and medical applications. Its Commack, New York, facility designs, manufactures, and sells a line of low-inertia, high-speed-of-response dc motors and associated electronics used primarily in industrial automation and medical applications. Kollmorgen also manufactures and sells linear motors for various industrial applications.

Aerospace and Defense Group

Kollmorgen's motion control products and subsystems in this segment are primarily manufactured by Kollmorgen Artus, a wholly owned French subsidiary; the Inland Motor Division, located in Radford, Virginia; and its Electro-Optical Division, located in Northampton, Massachusetts.

EXHIBIT 6.10 *(Continued)*

Kollmorgen Artus manufactures and sells generators, special motors, electromechanical actuators, and drive electronics, synchros, and resolvers, which are sold worldwide into the defense and aerospace market. After the successful test flight of its proprietary ac/dc regulated power management system for the Bell-Boeing V-22 Osprey tiltrotor aircraft in 1997, Kollmorgen Artus began production of that system in 1998. This business also has a motor facility in Bien Hoa, Vietnam, for the manufacture of resolvers, subassemblies, and motors. Kollmorgen Artus also manufactures and sells calibration systems for air traffic control navigation aids.

The specialty dc torque motors, tachometer generators, and electromechanical actuators and related electronics are used worldwide in a variety of aerospace and defense applications, including missiles, commercial and military aircraft, and sophisticated guidance tracking systems.

Select financial data is located in Tables 3 and 4.

TABLE 3

Kollmorgen Corp. Income Statement for Years Ended

	December 31,				LTM June 30,
	1995	1996	1997	1998	1999
	(In Thousands of Dollars)				
Revenues	$228,655	$230,424	$222,246	$243,939	$246,199
Cost of goods sold	152,614	152,928	152,276	167,501	171,324
Gross profit	$ 76,041	$ 77,496	$ 69,970	$ 76,438	$ 74,875
Operating expenses	65,025	64,061	65,758	59,776	63,008
Operating income	$ 11,016	$ 13,435	$ 4,212	$ 16,662	$ 11,867
Other income (expenses)	148	761	(2,979)	11,626	(66)
Interest expense	4,007	5,806	4,650	3,387	3,615
Income before income taxes	$ 7,157	$ 8,390	$ (3,417)	$ 24,901	$ 8,186
Provision for income taxes	—	—	2,838	10,085	2,366
Net income	**$ 7,157**	**$ 8,390**	**$ (6,255)**	**$ 14,816**	**$ 5,820**
Earnings per share	$ 0.74	$ 0.86	$ (0.63)	$ 1.47	$ 0.57

Note: Figures may not add due to rounding.
LTM indicates latest 12 months.

TABLE 4

Kollmorgen Corp. Balance Sheet as of

	December 31,				June 30,
	1995	1996	1997	1998	1999
	(In Thousands of Dollars)				
Cash and equivalents	$ 17,789	$ 13,445	$ 14,854	$ 13,086	$ 8,951
Accounts receivable	40,831	43,189	39,528	48,927	42,427
Inventories	26,210	22,450	25,162	27,838	29,914
Other current assets	13,673	6,618	7,803	$ 4,482	7,558
Total current assets	$ 98,503	$ 85,702	$ 87,347	$ 94,333	$ 88,850
Net property, plant and equipment	28,803	25,147	26,673	30,809	29,535
Intangible assets	5,631	5,649	14,343	20,420	31,443
Deposits and other assets	14,537	24,832	17,081	23,071	23,865
Total assets	**$147,474**	**$141,330**	**$145,444**	**$168,633**	**$173,693**

(Continued)

EXHIBIT 6.10 *(Continued)*

	December 31,				*June 30,*
	1995	*1996*	*1997*	*1998*	*1999*
	(In Thousands of Dollars)				
Current portion of interest-bearing debt	$ 12,920	$ 12,487	$ 7,244	$ 11,689	$ 11,476
Accounts payable	24,969	21,765	18,467	14,336	13,875
Other current liabilities	33,149	26,756	32,953	34,843	28,988
Total current liabilities	$ 71,038	$ 61,008	$ 58,664	$ 60,868	$ 54,339
Long-term interest-bearing debt	$ 36,888	$ 53,054	$ 36,379	$ 36,120	$ 49,764
Other long-term liabilities	5,501	5,202	8,673	14,943	13,984
Total long-term liabilities	$ 42,389	$ 58,256	$ 45,052	$ 51,063	$ 63,748
Total liabilities	$ 113,427	$ 119,264	$ 103,716	$ 111,931	$ 118,087
Minority interests	—	287	136	175	—
Stockholders' equity	34,047	21,779	41,592	56,527	55,606
Total liabilities and equity	**$147,474**	**$141,330**	**$145,444**	**$168,633**	**$173,693**
Common shares outstanding at end of year (000)	9,693	9,732	9,875	10,082	10,185

Note: Figures may not add due to rounding.

OilGear Co.

OilGear's products primarily involve the flow, pressure, condition, control, and measurement of liquids, which OilGear refers to as fluid power. OilGear provides advanced technology in the design and production of fluid power components, systems, and electronic controls. Its product line includes hydraulic pumps, high-pressure intensifier pumps, valves, controls, cylinders, motors, and fluid meters. OilGear manufactures both radial and axial piston type hydraulic pumps in sizes delivering from approximately 4 gallons per minute to approximately 230 gallons per minute at pressures ranging up to 15,000 pounds per square inch. The intensifier pumps are reciprocating pumps operating at pressures up to 120,000 pounds per square inch. The valves manufactured are pressure control, directional control, servo, and prefill valves for pressures up to 15,000 pounds per square inch. OilGear's pumps and valves are controlled through the actions of manual, hydraulic, pneumatic, electric, and electrohydraulic controls or control systems. The cylinders manufactured are heavy-duty special-purpose cylinders operating at up to 3,500 pounds per square inch. The Company's bent axis and axial piston motors are produced in sizes ranging from 0.85 cubic inch per revolution to 44 cubic inches per revolution.

OilGear offers an engineering and manufacturing team capable of providing advanced technology in the design and production of unique fluid power components, systems, and electronic controls. OilGear's global involvement focuses its expertise on markets in which customers demand top quality, prompt delivery, high performance, and responsive aftermarket support. Its piston pumps, motors, valves, controls, manifolds, electronic systems and components, cylinders, reservoirs, skids, meters, and other products are utilized in many industries such as the primary metals, machine tool, automobile, petroleum, construction equipment, chemical, plastic, glass, lumber, rubber, and food industries. OilGear strives to serve those markets requiring high technology and expertise where reliability, top performance, and longer service life are needed. The products are sold as individual components or integrated into high-performance systems. A portion of OilGear's business comes from responsive, high-quality aftermarket sales and flexible rebuilding services that include exchange, factory rebuild, and field repair service.

Select financial data appears in Tables 5 and 6.

TABLE 5

OilGear Co. Income Statement for Years Ended

	December 31,				*LTM June 30,*
	1995	*1996*	*1997*	*1998*	*1999*
	(In Thousands of Dollars)				
Revenues	$82,157	$89,621	$90,904	$96,455	$ 94,972
Cost of goods sold	55,858	62,061	63,127	71,635	70,842
Gross profit	$26,299	$27,560	$27,777	$24,820	$ 24,130
Operating expenses	21,817	22,355	23,017	21,913	21,550

EXHIBIT 6.10 *(Continued)*

	December 31,				LTM June 30,
	1995	1996	1997	1998	1999
	(In Thousands of Dollars)				
Operating income	$ 4,482	$ 5,205	$ 4,760	$ 2,907	$ 2,580
Other income (expenses)	278	144	253	531	462
Interest expense	1,690	1,728	1,650	2,154	2,029
Income before income taxes	$ 3,070	$ 3,621	$ 3,363	$ 1,284	$ 1,013
Provision for income taxes	878	1,050	600	677	630
Net income	**$ 2,192**	**$ 2,571**	**$ 2,763**	**$ 607**	**$ 383**
Earnings per share	$ 1.26	$ 1.42	$ 1.46	$ 0.31	$ 0.19

Note: Figures may not add due to rounding.

TABLE 6
OilGear Co. Balance Sheet as of

	December 31,				June 30,
	1995	1996	1997	1998	1999
	(In Thousands of Dollars)				
Cash and equivalents	$ 2,779	$ 2,368	$ 3,011	$ 4,059	$ 5,005
Accounts receivable	16,384	14,894	18,678	17,639	18,197
Inventories	26,596	26,230	26,397	30,084	25,541
Other current assets	824	1,067	1,551	2,782	3,158
Total current assets	$ 46,583	$ 44,559	$ 49,637	$ 54,564	$ 51,901
Net property, plant and equipment	27,108	28,854	31,379	29,480	27,720
Intangible assets	700	600	500	350	350
Deposits and other assets	3,512	3,826	7,682	6,464	6,341
Total assets	**$77,903**	**$77,839**	**$89,198**	**$90,858**	**$86,312**
Current portion of interest-bearing debt	$ 3,824	$ 2,296	$ 5,566	$ 2,142	$ 2,096
Accounts payable	7,922	5,728	8,167	7,785	5,724
Other current liabilities	8,002	7,871	8,477	8,791	8,413
Total current liabilities	$ 19,748	$ 15,895	$ 22,210	$ 18,718	$ 16,233
Long-term interest-bearing debt	$ 16,075	$ 16,155	$ 20,792	$ 24,558	$ 23,508
Other long-term liabilities	19,307	18,123	13,865	14,103	13,841
Total long-term liabilities	$ 35,382	$ 34,278	$ 34,657	$ 38,661	$ 37,349
Total liabilities	$ 55,130	$ 50,173	$ 56,867	$ 57,379	$ 53,582
Minority interests	—	348	502	632	667
Stockholders' equity	22,772	27,317	31,828	32,847	32,063
Total liabilities and equity	**$77,902**	**$77,838**	**$89,197**	**$90,858**	**$86,312**
Common shares outstanding at end of year (000)	1,740	1,807	1,896	1,944	1,977

Note: Figures may not add due to rounding.

(Continued)

EXHIBIT 6.10 *(Continued)*

SIFCO Industries, Inc.

SIFCO is engaged in the production and sale of a variety of metalworking processes, services, and products produced primarily to the specific design requirements of its customers. The processes include forging, heat treating, coating, welding, machining, and electroplating; and the products include forgings, machined forgings and other machined metal parts, remanufactured component parts for turbine engines, and electroplating solutions and equipment. SIFCO's operations are conducted in two segments: (1) turbine component services and repair and (2) aerospace component manufacturing.

Select financial information appears in Tables 7 and 8.

TABLE 7

SIFCO Industries Inc. Income Statement for the Years Ended

	September 30,				*LTM June 30,*
	1995	*1996*	*1997*	*1998*	*1999*
	(In Thousands of Dollars)				
Revenues	$68,134	$85,420	$108,790	$123,175	$120,712
Cost of goods sold	54,898	67,714	85,049	97,587	100,641
Gross profit	$13,236	$17,706	$ 23,741	$ 25,588	$ 20,071
Operating expenses	11,106	12,335	14,224	13,240	13,136
Operating income	$ 2,130	$ 5,371	$ 9,517	$ 12,348	$ 6,935
Other income (expenses)	2,028	464	747	566	641
Interest expense	1,091	1,141	1,141	1,305	1,380
Income before income taxes	$ 3,067	$ 4,694	$ 9,123	$ 11,609	$ 6,196
Provision for income taxes	255	(914)	2,047	2,324	958
Net income	**$ 2,812**	**$ 5,608**	**$ 7,076**	**$ 9,285**	**$ 5,238**
Earnings per share	$ 0.55	$ 1.10	$ 1.38	$ 1.80	$ 1.01

Note: Figures may not add due to rounding.

TABLE 8

SIFCO Industries Inc. Balance Sheet as of

	September 30,				*June 30,*
	1995	*1996*	*1997*	*1998*	*1999*
	(In Thousands of Dollars)				
Cash and equivalents	$ 1,469	$ 2,130	$ 2,998	$ 3,503	$ 3,056
Accounts receivable	15,121	17,929	20,516	20,073	22,586
Inventories	13,285	17,789	19,846	27,639	24,434
Other current assets	545	820	689	552	1,385
Total current assets	$ 30,420	$ 38,668	$ 44,049	$ 51,767	$ 51,461
Net property, plant and equipment	23,460	23,200	24,714	32,582	30,691
Intangible assets	4,097	3,980	3,864	3,748	3,661
Deposits and other assets	2,705	2,122	1,817	2,787	2,176
Total assets	**$60,682**	**$67,970**	**$74,444**	**$90,884**	**$87,989**

EXHIBIT 6.10 *(Continued)*

	September 30,				June 30,
	1995	1996	1997	1998	1999
		(In Thousands of Dollars)			
Current portion of interest-bearing debt	$ 2,300	$ 2,500	$ 1,256	$ 1,400	$ 1,400
Accounts payable	6,664	9,402	10,497	12,192	9,871
Other current liabilities	4,785	5,906	7,776	7,923	8,011
Total current liabilities	$ 13,749	$ 17,808	$ 19,529	$ 21,515	$ 19,282
Long-term interest-bearing debt	$ 10,875	$ 10,575	$ 11,716	$ 16,500	$ 17,100
Other long-term liabilities	5,253	3,630	2,631	2,979	2,966
Total long-term liabilities	$ 16,128	$ 14,205	$ 14,347	$ 19,479	$ 20,066
Total liabilities	$ 29,877	$ 32,013	$ 33,876	$ 40,994	$ 39,348
Stockholders' equity	30,805	35,957	40,568	49,890	48,641
Total liabilities and equity	**$60,682**	**$67,970**	**$74,444**	**$90,884**	**$87,989**
Common shares outstanding at end of year (000)	5,092	5,112	5,141	5,164	5,177

Note: Figures may not add due to rounding.

SEMX Corp.

SEMX Corporation, formerly Semiconductor Packaging Materials Co., Inc., consists of a Delaware corporation and its wholly owned and majority-owned subsidiaries. SEMX provides specialty materials and services to the microelectronic and semiconductor industries on a worldwide basis.

At the end of the fiscal year, the SEMX Materials Group consisted of the operating division of the parent company (SPM) and its subsidiaries, Polese Company, Inc. (Polese) and Retconn Incorporated (Retconn) and its subsidiary, S.T. Electronics, Inc. (S.T.). The materials group primarily designs, develops, manufactures, and markets customized fine wire and metal ribbon, precision metal stampings, aluminum silicon carbide stamping, powdered metal copper/tungsten heat dissipation products, seal frames, RF coaxial contacts and connectors, and cable and cable harness assemblies, which are used in the assembly of microelectronic packages. Such products are incorporated into electronic components used for industrial and commercial applications, primarily to conduct electrical currents or signals, solder electronic circuitry, provide electrical interconnects, house electronic components, mount components, or dissipate heat.

In 1997, SEMX entered the recreational products market by supplying a proprietary copper/tungsten sole weight to Taylor Made Golf for use in its Titanium Bubble 2(TM) irons. In 1998, SEMX further expanded its product offering of sole weights to additional customers in the recreational products marketplace. SEMX products are sold through internal sales personnel and a network of independent sales representatives, principally to manufacturers and assemblers of electronic devices who service the aerospace, automotive, communications, computer, medical, military, and semiconductor industries. SEMX completed the sale of its Retconn and S.T. businesses in February 1999, and as of that date no longer designs, develops, or manufacturers RF coaxial contacts, connectors, and cable and cable harness assemblies.

The SEMX service group consists of its American Silicon Products, Inc. (ASP) subsidiary and a jointly owned Singapore corporation, International Semiconductor Products Pte Ltd (ISP). Each provides silicon wafer polishing and reclaiming services to the semiconductor industry. Reclaimed wafers are used in the evaluation and testing of equipment and processes in semiconductor fabrication. ISP is 50.1 percent owned by The Company, 39.9 percent owned by Semiconductor Alliance Pte Ltd., and 10 percent owned by EDB Ventures 2 Pte Ltd. ISP began operations in the third quarter of 1997.

Select financial information appears in Tables 9 and 10.

(Continued)

EXHIBIT 6.10 *(Continued)*

TABLE 9

SEMX Corp. Income Statement for the Years Ended

	December 31,				LTM June 30,
	1995	1996	1997	1998	1999
	(In Thousands of Dollars)				
Revenues	$28,064	$46,027	$71,076	$65,903	$ 61,953
Cost of goods sold	17,681	30,717	50,699	47,943	44,084
Gross profit	$10,383	$15,310	$20,377	$17,960	$ 17,869
Operating expenses	6,146	8,203	11,992	20,970	20,110
Operating income	$ 4,237	$ 7,107	$ 8,385	$ (3,010)	$ (2,241)
Interest expense	989	920	2,601	3,475	2,978
Income before income taxes	$ 3,248	$ 6,187	$ 5,784	$ (6,485)	$ (5,219)
Provision for income taxes	722	2,445	2,214	(5,500)	147
Net income	**$ 2,526**	**$ 3,742**	**$ 3,570**	**$ (985)**	**$(5,366)**
Earnings per share	$ 0.53	$ 0.63	$ 0.59	$ (0.16)	$ (0.89)

Note: Figures may not add due to rounding.

TABLE 10

SEMX Corp. Balance Sheet as of

	December 31,				June 30,
	1995	1996	1997	1998	1999
	(In Thousands of Dollars)				
Cash and equivalents	$ 4,244	$ 3,531	$ 2,260	$ 1,141	$ 1,265
Accounts receivable	3,581	5,637	10,789	8,007	7,228
Inventories	4,736	9,078	12,369	10,447	4,835
Other current assets	561	886	2,079	6,591	1,240
Total current assets	$ 13,122	$ 19,132	$ 27,497	$ 26,186	$ 14,568
Net property, plant and equipment	11,043	20,701	42,031	38,352	35,363
Intangible assets	11,530	15,566	20,865	16,901	9,468
Deposits and other assets	376	1,090	1,472	885	783
Total assets	**$36,070**	**$56,489**	**$91,865**	**$82,324**	**$60,182**
Current portion of interest-bearing debt	$ 931	$ 2,723	$ 8,086	$ 32,041	$ 9,339
Accounts payable	1,479	3,462	7,322	5,262	3,285
Other current liabilities	1,536	2,001	2,602	2,947	3,232
Total current liabilities	$ 3,946	$ 8,186	$ 18,010	$ 40,250	$ 15,856
Long-term interest-bearing debt	$ 2,299	$ 10,961	$ 32,717	$ 13,055	$ 11,191
Other long-term liabilities	563	1,470	2,143	2,329	1,745
Total long-term liabilities	$ 2,862	$ 12,431	$ 34,860	$ 15,384	$ 12,936

EXHIBIT 6.10 *(Continued)*

	December 31,				*June 30,*
	1995	*1996*	*1997*	*1998*	*1999*
	(In Thousands of Dollars)				
Total liabilities	$ 6,808	$ 20,617	$ 52,870	$ 55,634	$ 28,792
Minority interests	—	1,932	1,537	1,319	1,177
Stockholders' equity	29,261	33,940	37,458	25,371	30,213
Total liabilities and equity	**$36,070**	**$56,489**	**$91,865**	**$82,324**	**$60,182**
Common shares outstanding at end of year (000)	4,784	5,968	6,070	6,054	6,044

Note: Figures may not add due to rounding.

WSI Industries, Inc.

WSI manufactures metal components in medium to high volumes requiring tolerances as close as one ten-thousandth (0.0001) of an inch. These components are manufactured in accordance with customer specifications using materials generally purchased by WSI but occasionally supplied by the customer. The major markets served by WSI have changed in the past several years because of declining requirements in several mature computer programs and WSI's effort to diversify its customer and market base. WSI's sales to the computer industry amounted to 34 percent, 14 percent, and 5 percent of total sales in fiscal 1995, 1996, and 1997, respectively. WSI expects that in fiscal 1998, a major portion of its sales will be to the agricultural industry and it will continue diversification efforts to broaden its customer and industry base.

WSI has a reputation as a dependable supplier, one capable of meeting stringent specifications to produce quality components at high production rates. WSI has demonstrated an ability to develop sophisticated manufacturing processes and controls essential to produce precision and reliability in its products.

Select financial information appears in Tables 11 and 12.

TABLE 11

WSI Industries, Inc. Income Statement for the Years Ended

	August 31,				*LTM May 31,*
	1995	*1996*	*1997*	*1998*	*1999*
	(In Thousands of Dollars)				
Revenues	$30,409	$20,174	$ 24,153	$23,948	$ 21,681
Cost of goods sold	27,535	18,555	20,495	18,431	17,245
Gross profit	$ 2,874	$ 1,619	$ 3,658	$ 5,517	$ 4,436
Operating expenses	2,560	2,145	2,329	3,568	3,791
Operating income	$ 314	$ (526)	$ 1,329	$ 1,949	$ 645
Other income	1,254	658	583	162	217
Interest expense	645	492	287	190	356
Income before income taxes	$ 923	$ (360)	$ 1,625	$ 1,921	$ 506
Provision for income taxes	(22)	6	42	46	31
Net income	**$ 945**	**$ (366)**	**$ 1,583**	**$ 1,875**	**$ 475**
Earnings per share	$ 0.38	$ (0.15)	$ 0.65	$ 0.77	$ 0.19

Note: Figures may not add due to rounding.

(Continued)

EXHIBIT 6.10 *(Continued)*

TABLE 12

WSI Industries, Inc. Balance Sheet as of

	August 31, 1995	*August 31,* 1996	*August 31,* 1997	*August 31,* 1998	*May 31,* 1999
	(In Thousands of Dollars)				
Cash and equivalents	$ 1,260	$ 1,643	$ 2,848	$ 2,697	$ —
Accounts receivable	3,735	1,869	2,545	2,853	2,447
Inventories	624	1,099	1,356	919	3,399
Other current assets	411	123	90	207	108
Total current assets	$ 6,030	$ 4,734	$ 6,839	$ 6,676	$ 5,954
Net property, plant and equipment	7,233	6,839	5,952	6,939	9,159
Intangible assets	—	—	—	—	2,573
Deposits and other assets	1	1	—	—	—
Total assets	**$13,264**	**$11,574**	**$12,791**	**$13,615**	**$17,746**
Current portion of interest-bearing debt	$ 839	$ 954	$ 1,001	$ 709	$ 1,120
Accounts payable	1,280	786	1,154	1,535	1,014
Other current liabilities	1,172	798	1,443	1,193	1,162
Total current liabilities	$ 3,291	$ 2,538	$ 3,598	$ 3,437	$ 3,296
Long-term interest-bearing debt	$ 4,852	$ 4,124	$ 2,671	$ 1,802	$ 6,117
Other long-term liabilities	411	459	467	380	357
Total long-term liabilities	$ 5,263	$ 4,583	$ 3,138	$ 2,182	$ 6,474
Total liabilities	$ 8,554	$ 7,121	$ 6,736	$ 5,619	$ 9,776
Stockholders' equity	4,711	4,453	6,055	7,995	7,916
Total liabilities and equity	**$13,264**	**$11,574**	**$12,791**	**$13,615**	**$17,686**
Common shares outstanding at end of year (000)	2,482	2,411	2,425	2,434	2,453

Note: Figures may not add due to rounding.

An analysis of these guideline companies has been performed in order to compare PDQ's financial results with its public counterparts. Select financial ratios appear in Table 13. These ratios have been analyzed in order to make qualitative assessments about the similarities and dissimilarities between the companies.

TABLE 13

Adjusted Financial Ratios

	ACAM	*KOL*	*OLGR*	*SIF*	*SEMX*	*WSCI*	*PDQ*
Liquidity/solvency							
Quick ratio	1.12	0.95	1.43	1.33	0.54	0.74	1.11
Current ratio	1.56	1.64	3.20	2.67	0.92	1.81	2.10
Days accounts receivables outstanding	53.27	67.72	68.86	64.49	44.88	44.61	69.35
Days accounts payable	36.27	30.05	34.80	40.01	35.38	26.98	60.87
Turnover							
Receivables turnover	6.85	5.39	5.30	5.66	8.13	8.18	5.26
Cash turnover	67.85	22.34	20.96	36.81	51.50	16.08	20.87
Inventory turnover	13.94	5.93	2.55	3.87	5.77	7.99	4.81

EXHIBIT 6.10 ***(Continued)***

	ACAM	KOL	OLGR	SIF	SEMX	WSCI	PDQ
Current asset turnover	4.35	2.69	1.78	2.34	3.04	3.43	2.41
Working capital turnover	14.25	7.24	2.66	3.87	(8.07)	7.35	4.65
Fixed asset turnover	1.85	8.16	3.32	3.82	1.68	2.69	4.48
Total asset turnover	1.05	1.44	1.07	1.35	0.87	1.39	1.51
Payables turnover	10.06	12.15	10.49	9.12	10.32	13.53	6.00
Debt							
Times interest earned	2.24	3.26	1.50	5.49	(0.75)	2.42	5.39
Short-term debt to equity	0.10	0.21	0.07	0.03	0.31	0.14	0.07
Long-term debt to equity	2.36	0.89	0.73	0.35	0.37	0.77	0.37
Total interest-bearing debt to equity	2.46	1.10	0.80	0.38	0.68	0.91	0.44
Total liabilities to invested capital	1.12	1.01	0.93	0.59	0.57	0.64	0.76
Profitability							
EBITDA return on total assets	7.91%	11.41%	7.87%	13.53%	6.18%	12.35%	11.89%
EBIT return on assets	7.91%	6.79%	3.52%	8.61%	–3.72%	4.87%	7.37%
EBITDA return on net sales	10.09%	8.05%	7.15%	9.86%	6.01%	10.08%	8.39%
EBIT return on net sales	10.09%	4.79%	3.20%	6.28%	–3.62%	3.98%	5.20%
EBITDA return on invested capital	13.73%	23.22%	11.84%	18.76%	9.02%	17.37%	17.28%
EBIT return on invested capital	13.73%	13.82%	5.31%	11.93%	–5.43%	6.85%	10.71%
Pretax return on invested capital	7.59%	9.59%	1.77%	9.76%	12.64%	4.02%	8.93%
Return on invested capital	4.75%	6.81%	0.67%	8.25%	13.00%	3.78%	5.23%
Working Capital							
Working capital (000)	22,104	34,511	35,668	32,179	(1,288)	2,658	2,857
Short-term debt to working capital	0.20	0.33	0.06	0.04	(7.25)	0.42	0.09
Long-term debt to working capital	4.96	1.44	0.66	0.53	(8.69)	2.30	0.53
Operating efficiency							
Operating expense to sales	5.68%	25.59%	22.69%	10.88%	32.46%	17.49%	13.25%
Depreciation & amortization to sales	0.00%	3.26%	3.95%	3.59%	9.62%	6.10%	3.19%
Capital expenditures to sales	–13.88%	3.86%	–0.17%	5.34%	0.62%	31.17%	3.32%
Growth (CAGR—5 years)							
Sales	34.88%	2.13%	4.23%	16.48%	25.39%	–8.63%	7.83%
Operating income	18.96%	2.15%	–14.60%	37.00%	NM	21.16%	24.01%
EBT	5.96%	3.91%	–27.15%	20.63%	NM	– 14.81%	33.90%
Net income	4.61%	–5.74%	–39.25%	18.04%	NM	– 16.76%	26.94%
	179,726	246,199%	94,972%	120,712	61,953	21,681	12,108%
Other							
Revenues ($000)	179,726	246,199	94,972	120,712	61,953	21,681	12,108
Earnings ($000)	6,270	5,820	383	5,238	(5,366)	475	308

NM = not meaningful.

(Continued)

EXHIBIT 6.10 ***(Continued)***

A financial analysis was performed by the appraiser comparing PDQ to the publicly traded companies.

PDQ is by far the smallest company of the group. Ranking the companies by size of revenues indicates the following:

	Size of Revenues ($000)
KOL	$246,199
ACAM	179,726
SIF	120,712
OLGR	94,972
SEMX	61,953
WSCI	21,681
PDQ	**12,108**

As can be seen from the figures above, PDQ has revenues that are less than 56 percent of those of the smallest guideline company and less than 5 percent of those of the largest company in the group. Since smaller companies tend to sell for lower multiples, this will impact the selection of the appropriate multiples in our analysis. While PDQ is closest to WSCI, there is still a considerable difference between their revenues.

Comparing some of the key liquidity ratios ranks PDQ closest to ACAM with respect to the quick ratio and slightly stronger than WSCI with respect to its current ratio. Our ranking analysis indicates the following:

Quick Ratio		*Current Ratio*	
OLGR	1.43	OLGR	3.20
SIF	1.33	SIF	2.67
ACAM	1.12	**PDQ**	**2.10**
PDQ	**1.11**	WSCI	1.81
KOL	0.95	KOL	1.64
WSCI	0.74	ACAM	1.56
SEMX	0.54	SEMX	0.92

An analysis was conducted comparing PDQ to the guideline companies with respect to its turnover ratios. With respect to the working capital turnover ratio, PDQ is slightly stronger than SIF, but considerably weaker than KOL. PDQ's fixed asset turnover ratio is among the highest in this peer group. While it is considerably lower than KOL's turnover in this category, it is stronger than all other guideline companies. The ranking analysis appears as follows:

Working Capital Turnover		*Fixed Asset Turnover*	
ACAM	14.25	KOL	8.16
WSCI	7.35	**PDQ**	**4.48**
KOL	7.24	SIF	3.82
PDQ	**4.65**	OLGR	3.32
SIF	3.87	WSCI	2.69
OLGR	2.66	ACAM	1.85
SEMX	(8.07)	SEMX	1.68

With respect to profitability ratios, PDQ is stronger than ACAM, WSCI, OLGR, and SEMX but considerably weaker than KOL and SIF based on a comparison of its return on invested capital. Comparing earnings before interest, taxes, depreciation, and amortization as a return on invested capital, PDQ is slightly weaker than WSCI but stronger than ACAM, OLGR, and SEMX. The ranking in this category appears as follows:

EXHIBIT 6.10 ***(Continued)***

Return on Invested Capital		*EBITDA Return on Invested Capital*	
SIF	8.25%	KOL	23.22%
KOL	6.81%	SIF	18.7%6
PDQ	**53.23%**	WSCI	17.37%
ACAM	4.75%	**PDQ**	**17.28%**
WSCI	3.78%	ACAM	13.73%
OLGR	0.67%	OLGR	11.84%
SEMX	−13.00%	SEMX	9.02%

Analyzing the leverage ratios, once again, tells a bit of a mixed story. PDQ is weaker than SIF but stronger than all of the other guideline companies with respect to its times interest earned ratio. This is the ratio that is based on The Company's profitability and indicates how well it would be expected to cover its interest expense. With respect to its long-term debt–to–equity ratio, PDQ reflects one of the lowest percentages of long-term debt to equity. While having less leverage could indicate less risk, it also indicates management's unwillingness to leverage The Company in order to maximize its growth potential and return to the equity holders. PDQ has the second lowest ratio, slightly above SIF and the same as SEMX. All of the companies in this category tend to have more leverage on their balance sheets. These rankings appear as follows:

Times Interest Earned		*Long-Term Debt to Equity*	
SIF	5.49	ACAM	2.36
PDQ	**5.39**	KOL	0.89
KOL	3.26	WSCI	0.77
WSCI	2.42	OLGR	0.73
ACAM	2.24	**PDQ**	**0.37**
OLGR	1.50	SEMX	0.37
SEMX	(0.75)	SIF	0.35

By far, the factor that probably impacts multiples in the public market the most are growth rates. Various growth rates have been calculated by the appraiser. These growth rates appear in our ranking analysis as follows:

5-Year CAGR Sales		*3-Year CAGR Sales*	
ACAM	34.88%	ACAM	70.28%
SEMX	25.39%	KOL	7.06%
SIF	16.48%	SIF	6.12%
PDQ	**7.83%**	OLGR	2.96%
OLGR	4.23%	**PDQ**	**(4.04)%**
KOL	2.13%	WSCI	(5.98)%
WSCI	(8.63)%	SEMX	(8.75)%

N/M = Not meaningful.

(Continued)

EXHIBIT 6.10 *(Continued)*

5-Year Operating Income		*5-Year Net Income*	
SIF	37.00%	**PDQ**	**26.94%**
PDQ	**24.01%**	SIF	18.04%
WSCI	21.16%	ACAM	4.61%
ACAM	18.96%	KOL	(5.74)%
KOL	2.15%	WSCI	(16.76)%
OLGR	(14.60)%	OLGR	(39.25)%
SEMX	N/M	SEMX	N/M

N/M = Not meaningful.

PDQ is in the middle of the range with respect to five-year compound annual growth rate in sales, while it has demonstrated greater growth than OLGR, KOL, and WSCI, whose growth was actually negative during this time period. However, PDQ is far inferior with respect to sales growth in comparison to ACAM, SEMX, and SIF. Over the last three years, PDQ has experienced negative growth, slightly lower than WSCI and SEMX, while ACAM, KOL, SIF, and OLGR have experienced positive growth during this same time frame. With respect to sales growth, ACAM is certainly the strongest of the group of companies.

Compound growth rates with respect to operating income places PDQ among the highest performers during the last five years, being exceeded only by SIF; however, PDQ outperformed SIF with respect to its five-year net income compound annual growth rate, as it was the strongest among the companies.

The public market, however, looks more to the future than to the past with respect to how stocks are priced. Companies that experience higher rates of growth historically are sometimes penalized because the expectation of that repeated growth cannot be ensured in the future. Certainly, reviewing the forecast for PDQ indicates that while growth is expected to be somewhat modest, it is certainly not expected to result in the type of growth rates with respect to profitability witnessed over the last five years.

Table 14 reflects selected market multiples that the appraiser deemed appropriate for this analysis.

TABLE 14

Market Multiples[1]

Company	*MVIC to Revenues*	*MVIC to EBITDA*	*MVIC to EBIT*	*MVIC to Debt-Free Net Income*	*MVIC to Tangible Book Value and Debt*
ACAM	2.00	16.17	16.17	25.28	2.47
KOL	0.78	8.94	13.46	20.24	2.32
OLGR	0.42	5.24	10.30	17.16	0.68
SIF	0.47	3.84	5.34	6.65	0.93
SEMX	0.88	8.70	56.13	72.87	1.12
WSCI	0.81	6.47	11.51	11.88	1.71
Mean	0.89	8.23	18.82	25.68	1.54
Median	0.79	7.58	12.48	18.70	1.42
Selected multiple	0.40	3.50	4.50	7.00	0.70

[1]All market multiples are calculated using three-year averages of the benefit stream (revenues, EBITDA, etc.)

The market multiples displayed in Table 14 reflect the investing public's perception as to the value of the stock of these public companies. The market price of a publicly traded stock reflects a marketable, minority interest since public companies generally have many owners, all of whom are deemed to be minority owners due to the lack of control that they can exercise over the corporate entity. These shares are considered to be marketable because one only has to contact his or her stockbroker to turn the investment into cash within a three-day period.

EXHIBIT 6.10 *(Continued)*

The guideline company method attempts to use these market multiples to determine the value of the appraisal subject. Once the appraiser analyzes the differences between the subject company and the guideline companies, appropriate adjustments are made to the market multiples of the public companies in order to reflect the difference in risk between the entities.

In reviewing the guideline company multiples, we have utilized the previous ratio analysis. The public market favors certain factors over others in valuing public companies. The three factors most significantly affecting valuation multiples include size, growth, and profitability. We have analyzed each multiple on a company-by-company basis according to these factors and have selected the multiples that we believe to be applicable to PDQ.

A review of the market multiples calculated in Table 14 for the guideline companies reflects the market perception based on the price of the stock at the valuation date. The market clearly perceives the greatest growth potential for ACAM, resulting in a much greater multiple in almost all categories. SEMX reflects higher multiples, particularly because it has been ranked so poorly on a historic basis that the market's perception is clearly that of a company that will turn around. With respect to size, PDQ is much closer to WSCI, and The Company is much closer to OLGR with respect to the five-year and three-year compound growth rates. If anything, PDQ exhibited negative growth with respect to the three-year compound annual growth rate, making it inferior to OLGR. With respect to leverage ratios, PDQ comes closest to SIF, and The Company is also closest with respect to the five-year compound annual growth rates of operating income and net income to SIF. The multiples selected for PDQ attempt to take all of these comparisons into consideration, recognizing that PDQ is considerably smaller than all of the public counterparts, which also reduces the selected multiples. These multiples will be utilized in the valuation calculations performed next.

We now calculate the value of PDQ based on the selected multiples. We have used three-year average multiples and earnings streams as we feel that an average of the prior three years best reflects the value of The Company going forward.

MVIC to Revenues

The three-year average revenues from PDQ's financial statements are $13,325,323. Therefore, the value of PDQ on a minority, marketable basis is calculated as follows:

Revenues	$13,325,323
Multiple	× 0.40
Minority, marketable value	$ 5,330,129

This value represents the total value of invested capital as of the valuation date. To calculate the value of PDQ's equity, we subtracted the value of The Company's debt as follows:

Minority, marketable invested capital	$ 5,330,129
Less: Interest-bearing debt	(1,788,531)
Minority, marketable equity	$ 3,541,598

Our assignment is to determine the value of PDQ on a control, nonmarketable basis. To convert the calculated minority, marketable value to a control, nonmarketable value requires two steps. The first step is the application of a control premium. We applied a premium of 20 percent to convert the calculated value to a control, marketable value (see section of report entitled "Premiums and Discounts" for a discussion of this item). The calculation was as follows:

Minority, marketable value	$ 3,541,598
Control premium (20%)	708,320
Control, marketable value	**$4,249,918**

The second step of the conversion is the application of a discount for lack of marketability. The discount for lack of marketability adjusts the value to account for the fact that PDQ is privately held. We applied a 10 percent discount (see section of report entitled "Premiums and Discounts" for a discussion of this item) for lack of marketability to convert the control, marketable value to a control, nonmarketable value. The calculation was performed as follows:

Control, marketable value	$ 4,249,918
Discount for lack of marketability (10%)	(424,992)
Control, nonmarketable value	$ 3,824,926
Rounded	**$3,825,000**

(Continued)

EXHIBIT 6.10 *(Continued)*

MVIC to EBITDA

The three-year average EBITDA was calculated from PDQ's financial statements as $1,589,932. Therefore, the value of PDQ on a control, nonmarketable basis is calculated as follows:

EBITDA	$ 1,589,932
Multiple	× 3.50
Minority, marketable value-invested capital	$ 5,564,762
Less: Interest-bearing debt	(1,788,531)
Minority marketable value-equity	$ 3,776,231
Control premium (20%)	755,246
Control, marketable value	4,531,477
Discount for lack of marketability (10%)	(453,148)
Control, nonmarketable value	$ 4,078,329
Rounded	**$4,078,000**

MVIC to EBIT

According to the adjusted financial statements of PDQ, average EBIT for the most recent three years is $1,340,121. Therefore, the value of PDQ on a control, nonmarketable basis is:

EBIT	$ 1,340,121
Multiple	× 4.50
Minority, marketable value	$ 6,030,546
Less: Interest-bearing debt	(1,788,531)
Minority marketable value-equity	$ 4,242,015
Control premium (20%)	848,403
Control, marketable value	$ 5,090,418
Discount for lack of marketability (10%)	(509,042)
Control, nonmarketable value	$ 4,581,376
Rounded	**$4,581,000**

MVIC to Debt-Free Net Income

According to the adjusted financial statements of PDQ, average debt-free net income for the most recent three years is $804,877. Therefore, the value of PDQ on a control, nonmarketable basis is calculated as follows:

Debt-free net income	$ 804,877
Multiple	× 7.0
Minority, marketable value-invested capital	$ 5,634,138
Less: Interest-bearing debt	(1,788,531)
Minority marketable value-equity	$ 3,845,607
Control premium (20%)	769,121
Control, marketable value	$ 4,614,728
Discount for lack of marketability (10%)	(461,473)
Control, nonmarketable value	$ 4,153,256
Rounded	**$4,153,000**

EXHIBIT 6.10 ***(Continued)***

MVIC to Tangible Book Value and Debt

According to the adjusted financial statements of The Company, average tangible book value and debt over the prior three years is $8,369,083. Therefore, the value of PDQ on a control, nonmarketable basis is calculated as follows:

Net free cash flow	$ 8,369,083
Multiple	× 0.70
Minority, marketable value-invested capital	$ 5,858,358
Less: Interest-bearing debt	(1,788,531)
Minority marketable value-equity	$ 4,069,827
Control premium (20%)	813,966
Control, marketable value	$ 4,883,793
Discount for lack of marketability (10%)	(488,379)
Control, nonmarketable value	$ 4,395,414
Rounded	**$4,395,000**

Notice the values in Exhibit 6.10. They were:

MVIC to revenues	$3,825,000
MVIC to EBITDA	4,078,000
MVIC to EBIT	4,581,000
MVIC to debt-free net income	4,153,000
MVIC to tangible book value	4,395,000

While the upper and lower limits range from $3.8 million to $4.5 million, these indications of value have a reasonableness to them that gives me a warm, fuzzy feeling, especially when the transaction method (discussed in Chapter 7) and the income approach (discussed in Chapter 9) came in at about $4.3 million. When we have this many indications of value within a relatively small range, it tells me something—either we are right, or we are consistently wrong!

Conclusion

By now, either you should be very excited and ready to forge ahead, or you may be suffering from an anxiety attack. The guideline public company methodology can be overwhelming if you have never done this stuff before. In fact, if you have done it before, it still can be overwhelming. We discussed the methodology, the selection of multiples, the assessment of risk, and the advantages and disadvantages of the methods. I hope you realize that the guideline public company method can be applied to small and medium-sized companies. Sometimes it may be difficult to apply, but that does not excuse you from using it. In the next chapter, we get to apply the spirit of this same approach, but at the entity level. Let's do it!

7

The Market Approach—Part II

Chapter Goals

In this chapter, I will finish explaining the market approach. Since the last chapter discussed the theory behind the market approach, it will not be repeated (too much) here. This chapter will include:

1. A discussion about the transaction method
2. Highlights of different private transaction databases
3. The practical application of the transaction method
4. Internal transactions
5. Rules of thumb (count your fingers because here it comes!)

Overview

After the last chapter you are probably thinking that since you value small businesses, you will never use the market approach. So now I am going to shift gears to show you how the market approach will change your life. The guideline public company method will not be applicable in all assignments, particularly if the subject company is very small, but the appraiser has alternatives. The transaction method allows the appraiser to locate sales of businesses in the *same or a similar* industry for the purpose of applying the market approach.

Although rules of thumb should never be used as a valuation method, the appraiser needs to be aware of them. Just sit back, grab a drink, and let's discuss the market approach some more.

Transaction (Merger and Acquisition) Method

The spirit of Revenue Ruling 59-60 is frequently applied by the use of the transaction (or merger and acquisition) method of appraisal. In this method, transaction data is used in a manner similar to that in the guideline public company method previously described. Instead of selecting individual guideline companies, actual transactions involving companies *similar* to the appraisal subject are used to determine pricing multiples. In this instance, the price is that of the entire company instead of a share of stock.

The transaction method can be applied by using either public company or private company data. Since the entire company has been sold, the transaction is considered by most appraisers to result in a control value. If public companies are used to develop the multiples, the results are control, marketable values. If private companies are used instead, the result is a control, nonmarketable value.

Before we go too far, let's discuss this concept of *control, nonmarketable*. This tends to confuse a lot of people. The *control* portion of that phrase should not be the problem. Obviously, if an entire company is sold, it represents a controlling interest. But how can it be nonmarketable if it has been sold? Here is where the confusion sets in. Chapter 11 will cover this stuff in more detail, but a preview is in order. An interest in a privately held company is often considered to be less marketable than an interest in a publicly traded company. If you own shares of a public company, you can call your broker, sell the stock, and usually receive cash in about three days. You cannot do that with closely held stock. That is why the private company is considered to be nonmarketable compared to the public stock.

Since selling a privately held company takes more than three days, it too is considered to be nonmarketable. This does not mean that it cannot be sold. It only means that it lacks the liquidity of shares of publicly traded stock. There is a debate in the appraisal profession about this entire topic, and I discuss it in much greater detail in Chapter 11. However, for the purpose of this chapter, and until you decide which side of the battle you want to defend, sales of closely held companies are considered to be nonmarketable. Sales of entire publicly traded companies are considered to be marketable. This should give you enough for the time being, but here's something to tuck away in the back of your head (if it isn't already spinning from this stuff): Can an entire company really be sold in three days, and if not, does the closely held company, taken as a whole, really have any less liquidity than the public company sold as an entire unit?

Sources of data about acquired or merged companies were discussed in Chapter 4. At this point, the manner in which you proceed depends on whether you are using transaction data from the public or private marketplace. Let's discuss each separately.

- *Public market*. Once you have identified transaction data from the public market, an analysis must be performed similar to what was suggested under the guideline public company method. Once the target companies are determined to be similar enough to the appraisal subject, pricing multiples can be calculated for the transactions. These multiples can then be adjusted for the differences between the appraisal subject and the target companies and then applied to the appraisal subject's figures. Since this process is so closely related to the guideline public company method, there is little need to elaborate further.
- *Closely held market*. The real difference in the transaction method comes when one uses closely held company transaction data. This type of data is frequently available with limited amounts of details. Some authors believe that if you cannot verify each and every transaction, you cannot use this data. I believe that some data may be better than no data. As long as the appraiser recognizes the potential deficiencies in the application of this method, it remains a viable alternative. In fact, sometimes I would rather use this method than any other for small businesses.

Getting away from the public sector moves our discussion to compilations of actual transactions in the closely held world. Our firm has found six main sources to be somewhat useful in our quest for transaction data for the closely held business. They are:

1. The Institute of Business Appraisers (IBA) Market Data Base
2. BizComps
3. Pratt's Stats
4. Done Deals
5. Thomson Financial Securities Data
6. Business brokers

These databases are presented in order of increasing complexity of the data and size of transactions contained in each. One of the first things that the appraiser must do if these databases are going to be used is to learn the various definitions used by each one. The terminology used in these databases varies, and therefore, it is very easy to apply a multiple to the wrong level of earnings, or other benefit stream, if you are not careful. Some of the more important variations of the terminology will be detailed in this discussion. Recognizing that each of these sources of information has certain deficiencies, the appraiser is faced with using common sense and sanity tests to ensure the reasonableness of the results. This is not any different from everything else that we do in this business.

IBA Market Data Base

Available only to IBA members,[1] this database is the largest known source of market transactions of small closely held businesses. It has been compiled over the years from IBA members and other professionals associated with the sales of businesses. The IBA Market Data Base includes about 20,000 transactions in 680 SIC codes. Many SIC categories have so many transactions that a highly supportable statistical inference can be drawn from this data. Most of the transactions included in the database are for businesses that had a sales volume below $1 million. The last time that someone summarized the transactions in the IBA database by sales volume, the breakdown of the data looked like this:

$0–$500,000 in annual sales	8,918	(74.0%)
$500,001–1,000,000 in annual sales	1,241	(10.3%)
$1,000,001–$5,000,000 in annual sales	1,021	(8.5%)
$5,000,001–$10,000,000 in annual sales	234	(1.9%)
Greater than $10,000,000 in annual sales	635	(5.3%)

Obviously, the number of transactions above does not total 20,000. In fact, it totals only 12,049. This is for the benefit of the accountant who is reading this book and feels the urge to foot a column of numbers (for the non-accountants, "foot" means add). I have been told that the newer transactions fall in about the same proportions as the old ones.

As you can see, the database is geared toward transactions of the very small business. Small businesses typically are sold as *asset sales* as opposed to *stock sales*. An asset sale is a transaction where only certain assets (and maybe liabilities) are transferred to a new owner who will effectively become the new owner of the business. More often than not, only the operating assets of the business are transferred to the buyer. This type of transaction is common for smaller businesses. It is also very different from a stock sale, which is typical of larger business transactions. In a stock sale, the stock (all assets and liabilities) is transferred to a buyer. This transfer represents the entire equity of the company. The transaction type is a critical point to understand when considering multiples, and it will be addressed in length later in this chapter.

Exhibit 7.1 contains a sample of what you get when you request information from IBA. It is in Excel format.

[1]The annual cost of membership in the IBA is approximately $350. Access to the database is free for members. All that a member has to do is call IBA headquarters at (954) 584-1184 (or send an e-mail) and ask for the SIC code or codes to be covered in the search, and the information is generally mailed to the member within 48 hours. This information is also sent via e-mail in an Excel format.

EXHIBIT 7.1
IBA Market Data Base—SIC Code 6531

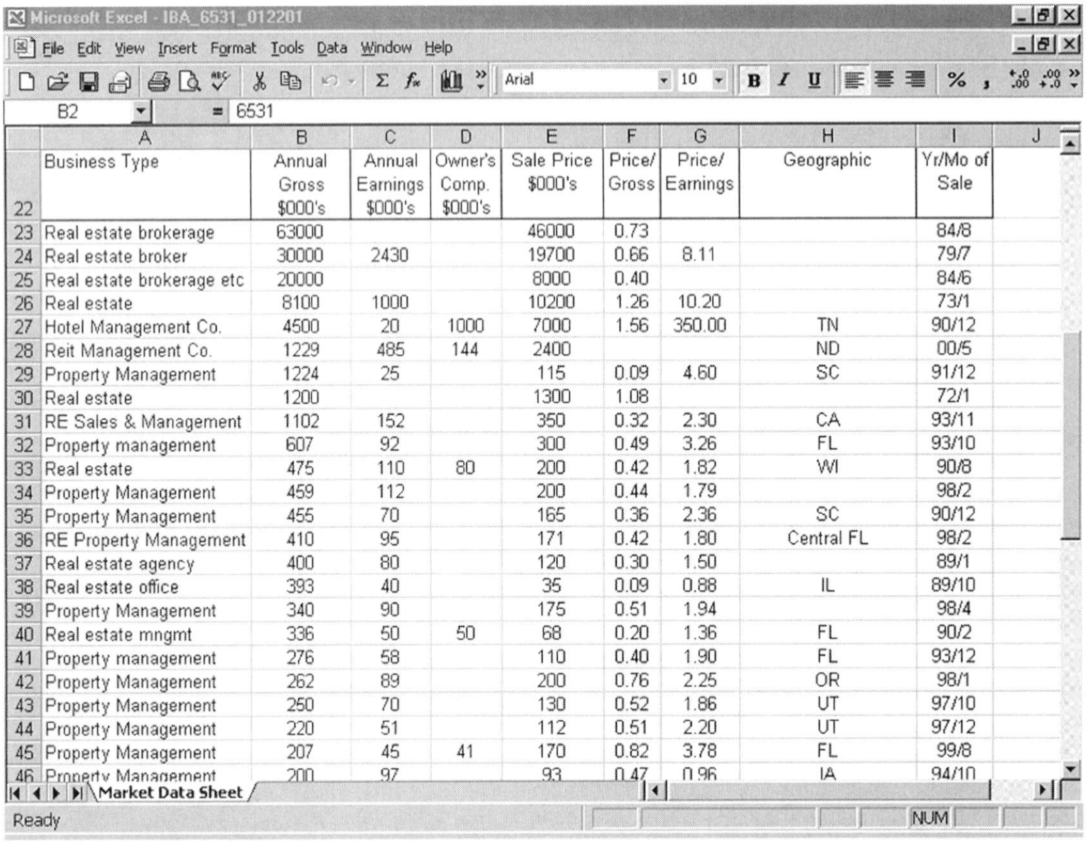

Microsoft Excel - IBA_6531_012201

File Edit View Insert Format Tools Data Window Help

Arial 10

B2 = 6531

	A	B	C	D	E	F	G	H	I	J
22	Business Type	Annual Gross $000's	Annual Earnings $000's	Owner's Comp. $000's	Sale Price $000's	Price/ Gross	Price/ Earnings	Geographic	Yr/Mo of Sale	
23	Real estate brokerage	63000			46000	0.73			84/8	
24	Real estate broker	30000	2430		19700	0.66	8.11		79/7	
25	Real estate brokerage etc	20000			8000	0.40			84/6	
26	Real estate	8100	1000		10200	1.26	10.20		73/1	
27	Hotel Management Co.	4500	20	1000	7000	1.56	350.00	TN	90/12	
28	Reit Management Co.	1229	485	144	2400			ND	00/5	
29	Property Management	1224	25		115	0.09	4.60	SC	91/12	
30	Real estate	1200			1300	1.08			72/1	
31	RE Sales & Management	1102	152		350	0.32	2.30	CA	93/11	
32	Property management	607	92		300	0.49	3.26	FL	93/10	
33	Real estate	475	110	80	200	0.42	1.82	WI	90/8	
34	Property Management	459	112		200	0.44	1.79		98/2	
35	Property Management	455	70		165	0.36	2.36	SC	90/12	
36	RE Property Management	410	95		171	0.42	1.80	Central FL	98/2	
37	Real estate agency	400	80		120	0.30	1.50		89/1	
38	Real estate office	393	40		35	0.09	0.88	IL	89/10	
39	Property Management	340	90		175	0.51	1.94		98/4	
40	Real estate mngmt	336	50	50	68	0.20	1.36	FL	90/2	
41	Property management	276	58		110	0.40	1.90	FL	93/12	
42	Property Management	262	89		200	0.76	2.25	OR	98/1	
43	Property Management	250	70		130	0.52	1.86	UT	97/10	
44	Property Management	220	51		112	0.51	2.20	UT	97/12	
45	Property Management	207	45	41	170	0.82	3.78	FL	99/8	
46	Property Management	200	97		93	0.47	0.96	IA	94/10	

Market Data Sheet

Ready NUM

Now that you have a feel for what the data looks like, you may want to know what the data represents. Exhibit 7.2 lists the fields contained in the IBA database, along with a definition of each item.

EXHIBIT 7.2
IBA Data and Definitions

Business type	Principal line of business
SIC code	Principal Standard Industrial Classification number applicable to the business sold
Annual gross	Reported annual sales volume of business sold
Annual earnings	Reported annual earnings before owner's compensation, interest, and taxes
Owner's comp.	Reported owner's compensation
Sale price	Total reported consideration, i.e., cash, liabilities assumed, etc., excluding real estate
Price/gross	Ratio of total consideration to reported annual gross
Price/earnings	Ratio of total consideration to reported annual earnings
Yr./mo. of sale	Year and month during which transaction was consummated

In reviewing Exhibit 7.2, there are a few things that may come to your attention. The first is that the database lists only the principal line of business, which is typically two or three words. Not much information is given about the target company (the one that was acquired) that will aid an appraiser in determining comparability. One of the major drawbacks of this database is that it contains little qualitative information about each business.

Annual earnings is reported as earnings before owner's compensation, interest, and taxes, which reflects the total compensation of an investor in a small business (assuming that the owner will be the operator of that business; it also assumes only one owner). As discussed throughout this book, an appraiser must take care to apply a multiple to the correct level of earnings. When applying an IBA multiple to earnings, make sure that the earnings stream is defined and calculated as indicated in Exhibit 7.2.

Another question that may arise when using this data is about the sales price, which is reported as a dollar figure. Terms of the deal (typically including some type of seller financing) are not disclosed. As every good student knows, a dollar today is more valuable than a dollar 10 years from now. Since fair market value is considered to be a cash or cash equivalent value, knowing the terms of the deal could make a difference. If you do not know the terms of a deal, the IBA listed price may not be its cash equivalent value.

In an attempt to better understand the significance of the transaction data included in the database, an empirical study was undertaken by Raymond Miles, the founder and past Executive Director of IBA, and his results were presented at an IBA national conference. Mr. Miles concluded the following:

- The price-to-earnings and price–to–gross revenues multiples are almost equally valid criteria for estimating the market value of businesses. This conflicts with the conventional wisdom that the price-to-earnings ratio is the most significant performance criterion of a business.
- In practice, the price–to–gross revenue multiple is especially useful for appraising closely held businesses, because price–to–gross revenue multiples are available for all sales in the IBA Market Data Base, while price-to-earnings multiples are only available for some sales.
- Empirical data for all business categories, in aggregate, does not show any significant change in business value as a function of time. This is contrary to the conventional wisdom that only recent sales should be considered when choosing guideline ("comparable") companies.
- The data shows no significant correlation between the selling price and the percentage down payment. This differs from the conventional wisdom that a business sold for cash should bring a lower total price than one sold for "terms."
- As expected, business values as measured by price to earnings and price to gross multiples differ from one kind of business to another. However, this difference is not as large as might have been expected. This suggests that the search for guideline companies does not need to be limited to businesses in the same SIC category as the business being appraised. Thus, the search for guideline companies can reasonably include SIC categories other than the category assigned to the business being appraised.
- Empirical evidence indicates that the "most probable price" for a business is significantly different from the average price of businesses that have been sold. Thus, when the standard of value is "most probable price," use of the average selling price of guideline companies can lead to a value estimate that is in error by a significant amount.[2]

Being the accountant that I am, and being suspicious of people who publish information that could be deemed to be self-serving, I was provided with the opportunity to review Mr. Miles's study in this area. His findings were accurate. In fact, what really blew my mind was the fact that transactions that were 10 and 15 years old, in most industries, are still valid today. The multiples across most industries, for these small businesses, have not changed materially, if at all. Even geographically, the multiples were not materially different. Now of course, you want to test the data before you use it, but this database gives the appraiser a methodology that can be applied to small businesses. You must also use your head when using this or any other database to ensure that you have enough transactions to be statistically reasonable.

As you can see, there are many things to consider when using this data. Answers to many of the issues discussed above, as well as others that may not have been addressed, can be found in publications available from IBA on their Web site (www.go-iba.com). IBA even offers a free data analyzer (I like that word) on its

[2]Raymond C. Miles, "Business Appraising in the Real World—Evidence From the IBA Market Database" (document presented at the IBA National Conference, Orlando, Fla., February 7, 1992).

Web site that allows the user to analyze market data (the IBA market analyzer is available for download at www.go-iba.com/benefits.asp). Use of this analyzer, as well as a more detailed discussion of transaction data analysis, is included later in this chapter.

BizComps

The BizComps publication includes sales information by SIC category as accumulated by Jack Sanders. Each year, this regional, and now national, publication expands the number and size of the transactions included in it. The 2001 edition contains transaction information on 5,000 actual businesses sold totaling over $1 billion dollars. It is available online (www.bizcomps.com) or on CD-ROM (order online or call (858) 457-0366).

Here also is a lot of useful data, but the appraiser should be careful to understand what is included in each item. Much like the IBA database, BizComps reports seller's discretionary cash flow as a measure of earnings, but this definition includes depreciation, amortization, and all other non-cash and non-operating expenses. To better illustrate the contents of this database, as well as what the contents include, I have included a listing of the BizComps 2001 fields in Exhibit 7.3.

EXHIBIT 7.3
BizComps 2001 Field Definitions

% down	Down payment as a percentage of the actual sales price.
Ann. rev.	Annual revenues (normally net of sales tax).
Area	Region or geographical location of the business (C = Central, W = West, E = East).
Ask price	The price that the seller was initially asking for the business. This price does not include inventory.
Business type	Best description of subject business.
Days on market	Number of days the business was available for sale.
FF&E	Estimate of the value of the business's furniture, fixtures, and equipment.
Franchise royalty	Franchise royalty, if any, paid by the business.
Inventory	Amount of inventory at the time of the sale (shown for informational purposes only).
Location	Geographic region in which the business is located.
NAICS #	The North American Industry Classification System (NAICS) is replacing the U.S. Standard Industrial Classification (SIC) system. It was developed jointly by the United States, Canada, and Mexico to provide comparability in statistics about business activity across North America.
Rent %	Rent expense as a percentage of annual revenues.
Sales date	The actual date of sale.
Sales price	Actual sales price excluding inventory.
SDCF	Seller's Discretionary Cash Flow, which is defined as net profit before taxes plus all owner's compensation plus amortization, depreciation, interest, other non-cash expenses, and non–business related expenses (normally to one working owner).
SIC #	The business's primary four-digit SIC (Standard Industrial Classification) code. For a complete listing of all SIC codes, see the *Industrial Classification Manual*, 1987, published by the National Institute of Technical Services. Or you can purchase this SIC code manual database directly from Wiley-ValuSource by calling (800) 825-8763.
SDCF/rev	Seller's discretionary cash flow divided by annual revenues. Simple profit measure that allows the transactions to be compared against each other.
SP/rev	Actual sales price (excluding inventory) divided by annual revenues.
SP/SDCF	Actual sales price (excluding inventory) divided by seller's discretionary cash flow.
Terms	Terms of new or assumed encumbrance.

There are many useful data points in the BizComps database that the IBA database does not have. BizComps has the asking price as well as the sales price, which can give an appraiser a better idea of what is really going on in the market. Two important pieces of information included in BizComps are the percent down payment and terms of financing. Although the Miles study claims that the down payment does not matter, the terms of financing certainly do. This will allow an appraiser to estimate the cash equivalent value of the transaction price. An example of a BizComps transaction is shown in Exhibit 7.4.

EXHIBIT 7.4
BizComps Transaction

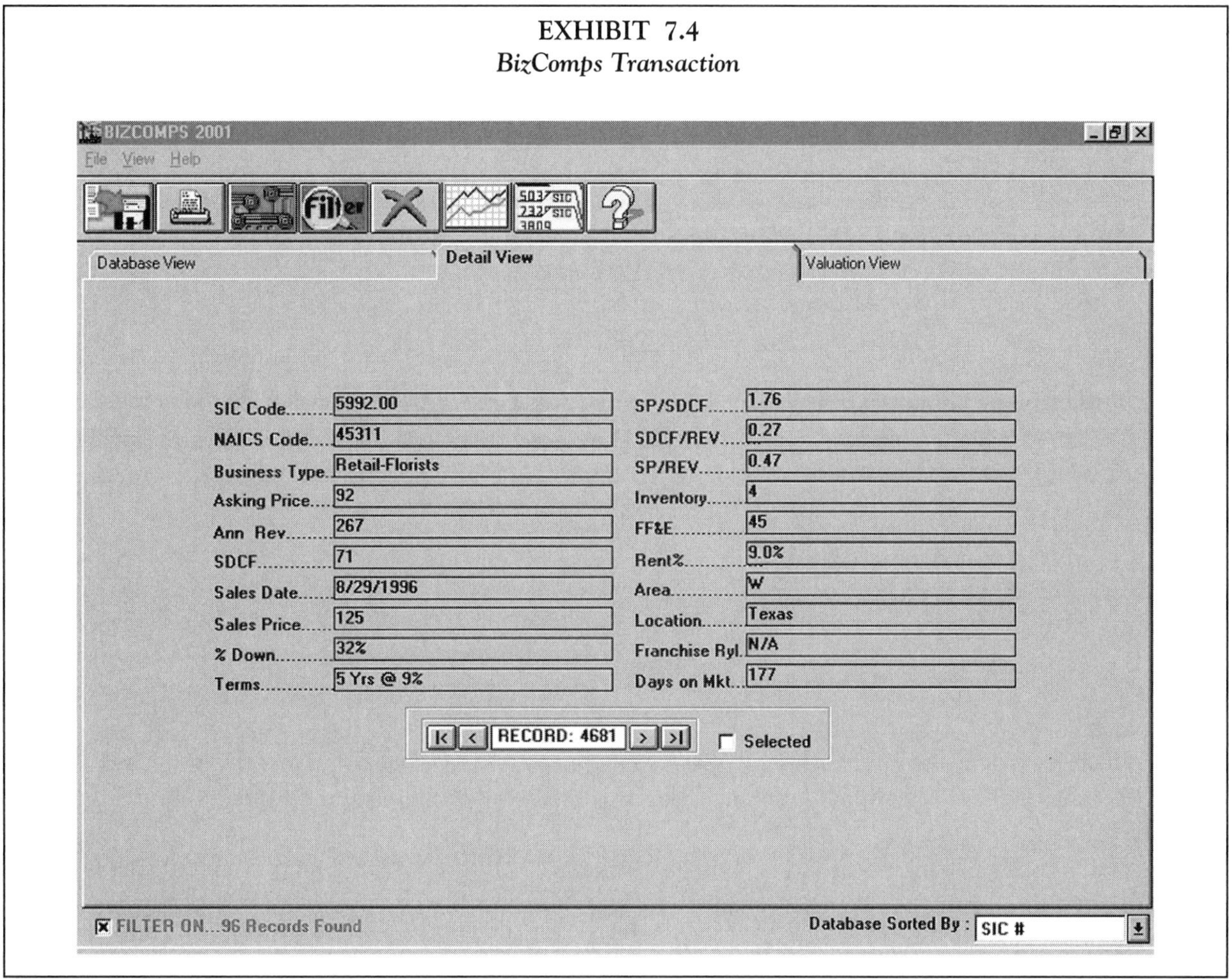

As seen in Exhibit 7.4, this particular transaction was closed at a sales price of $125,000, with a 32 percent down payment and the remainder financed over five years at an interest rate of 9 percent. As of the date of the sale, prime rate was 8.25 percent. For argument's sake, let's assume that a typical buyer of this type of business could only get financing at prime rate plus 3 percent, or 11.25 percent. What this means is that this buyer was able to obtain below-market-rate financing, which adds value to the buyer, but the price listed is not indicative of a cash equivalent value.

To calculate the cash equivalent value, the analyst must forecast all cash flows from the loan and discount them to the present value at the date of the transaction using the market rate of debt as the discount factor. For illustration purposes, let's assume that the loan is paid out in equal installments over a five-year period. The cash equivalent value would be calculated as follows:

Sale price	125,000
Down payment	40,000
Amount financed	85,000
Financing period	5
Interest rate	9.00%
Market interest rate	11.25%

Year	1	2	3	4	5
Loan balance	85,000	68,000	51,000	34,000	17,000
Principal payment	17,000	17,000	17,000	17,000	17,000
Interest payment	7,650	6,120	4,590	3,060	1,530
Total payment	24,650	23,120	21,590	20,060	18,530
Present value of total payment	22,157	18,680	15,680	13,096	10,874

Total present value	80,487
Plus: Down payment	40,000
Cash value	120,487

This example demonstrates that the cash equivalent value of this deal was only $120,487, almost $4,500 below the reported transaction price. In this same example, the annual revenues of the business were $267,000. If the appraiser were to calculate the multiple of sales price to annual revenues, this would be the result:

	As Reported	*Cash Equivalent Value*
Annual revenues	$ 267,000	$ 267,000
Deal value	$ 125,000	$ 120,487
Multiple	0.47	0.45

If the appraiser uses the cash equivalent multiple for the subject company, the result will be different. This example has only a small difference, but imagine how far off you could be depending on the financing terms.

Also stated separately in this database are inventory and fixed assets. As with the IBA Market Data Base, the BizComps transactions are asset sales, which means that only the operating assets are transferred to the purchaser. The $125,000 sales price, by definition in the database, excludes $4,000 of inventory. However, it would include the fixed assets (these are the operating assets). Therefore, even though it is not given in the database, the intangible assets that were part of the transaction can be calculated by subtracting the fixed assets from the transaction price ($125,000 − $45,000 = $80,000). By including the operating assets in the database, BizComps gives the user the ability to estimate the intangible value that was part of the deal.

BizComps lists rent and franchise royalties as a percent of sales so that a user of the database can get a better idea of the fixed costs of the business. It also provides the number of days that the business was on the market before the sale closed. This piece of information is very interesting. One of the issues that analysts encounter with every assignment is the level of marketability of the subject business and a corresponding discount for lack of marketability (discussed in Chapter 11) if it is applicable. Although using a sales price–to–earnings stream multiple yields a control, nonmarketable value, this information gives the user some basis to support a discount for lack of marketability for another approach (let's say that you capitalized earnings—discussed in Chapter 9).

Overall, BizComps gives more data fields than the IBA Market Data Base, but as discussed, it has much fewer transactions (5,000 as compared with 20,000). The electronic version of the database comes with software that enables quick and easy analysis of selected transactions and gives a user the ability to value subject companies based on sets of transaction multiples. The analysis performed is by no means all-inclusive, but it provides an easy way to do a quick analysis. Analysis of transaction data will be discussed in more detail later in this chapter.

Pratt's Stats

Pratt's Stats is a resource for small/medium to large closely held company sale information. The database tracks sales of privately held companies with selling prices of up to $100,000,000 (65 percent of the selling prices range from $1 to $30 million). It also includes some public company transactions. This database, started by Shannon Pratt, is an excellent source for transaction data, and it has taken small business transaction reporting to the next level. Pratt's Stats data is available online at www.bvmarketdata.com. Other useful stuff is available online as well.

Pratt's Stats currently has 3,800 private transactions and 250 public transactions, and new transactions are added monthly. Its search feature allows you to specify your search criteria, which can include the industry SIC or NAICS code, company description, city and state location, revenue range, text searches, and many other key data fields for each transaction. The ability to further select specific deals from the initial search, recalculate the summary statistics, and print or export to Excel spreadsheet formats are some of the features found here. Currently, you can download up to over 80 fields of information for each transaction from the database (although, as you may have noticed with IBA and BizComps, not all information is available for each transaction). Exhibit 7.5 reflects a Pratt's Stats transaction report for a gas station/convenience store.

EXHIBIT 7.5

Pratt's Stats™ Transaction Report
Prepared 1/31/02 11:20:55 AM

Transaction Details

Intermediary Name	Janke Harold A.
Firm Name	Janke & Associates, Inc.
SIC Code	5541 Gasoline Service Stations
NAICS Code	44711 Gasoline stations with convenience stores
Business Description	Gas Minimart and Car Wash
Company Name	N/A
Sale Location	Esconida, CA
Years In Business	4
Number Employees	17
Report Date	35472

Income Data		Asset Data		Transaction Data	
Data is "Latest Full Year" Reported	Yes	Data is "Latest Full Year" Reported	Yes	Income Statement Date	12/31/95
				Balance Sheet Date	12/31/95
Data is Restated (see Notes for any explanation)	No	Data is "Purchase Price Allocation agreed upon by Buyer and Seller"	No	Date Sale Initiated	6/1/96

(Continued)

EXHIBIT 7.5 ***(Continued)***

Income Data		Asset Data		Transaction Data	
				Date of Sale	12/1/96
Net Sales	$7,240,000	Cash Equivalents	$0		
				Asking Price	$2,600,000
COGS	N/A	Trade Receivables	$0	Selling Price	$1,800,000
Gross Profit	N/A	Inventory	$44,000	Amount of Down Payment	$800,000
Yearly Rent	$19,200	Other Current Assets	N/A	Deal Price	$2,200,000
Owner's Compensation	N/A	Total Current Assets	N/A	Stock or Asset Sale	Asset
Other Operating Expenses	N/A	Fixed Assets	$600,000	Company Type	C Corporation
Noncash Charges	N/A	Real Estate	$0		
Total Operating Expenses	N/A	Intangibles	N/A	Was there an Employment/Consulting Agreement?	Yes
Operating Profit	$460,000	Other Noncurrent Assets	N/A		
Interest Expenses	$0	Total Assets	$900,000		
EBT	$460,000	Liabilities Assumed	$400,000	Was there an Assumed Lease in the sale?	Yes
Taxes	$0	Employment Agreement Value	$0		
Net Income	$460,000	Noncompete Value	$300,000	Was there a Renewal Option with the Lease?	Yes

Additional Transaction Information

Was there a Note in the consideration paid?	Yes
Was there a personal guarantee on the Note?	No
Terms	9%, 120 Months
Balance of Assumed Lease (Months)	N/A
Terms of Lease	Two 5 Year Options
Noncompete Length (Months)	60
Noncompete Description	N/A
Employment/Consulting Agreement Description	30 Days training, seller available for 6 Months as consultant
Additional Notes	4,800,000 annual gallonage ending 12/31/96

Valuation Multiples

Equity/Net Sales	0.25	Deal Price/Net Sales	0.3
Equity/Gross Cash Flow	N/A	Deal Price/EBITDA	N/A
Equity/EBT	3.91	Deal Price/EBIT	4.78
Equity/Net Income	3.91	Deal Price/Discretionary Earnings	N/A

N/A = Not Available

Source: Pratt's Stats™ (Portland OR: Business Valuation Resources, LLC). Reprinted with permission.

As illustrated in Exhibit 7.5, Pratt's Stats has many more data points for each transaction than IBA or BizComps. For instance, look at the first item on the page, titled intermediary name. As previously discussed, the first two databases had limited data to determine comparability, whereas Pratt's Stats has taken the next step and given the user the name of the intermediary who participated in the transaction. Just from this one field, you have the opportunity to verify the listed transaction with the broker. There are many other useful data points listed in Pratt's Stats, and full definitions for all fields are available on the Web site under Pratt's Stats FAQ, which is shown in Exhibit 7.6.

EXHIBIT 7.6
Pratt's Stats™ Field Definitions

What is the legend for Pratt's Stats™ Income data?

Reports	*Definition*
Net sales	Annual gross sales, net of returns and discounts allowed, if any
COGS	(Cost of goods sold)—the cost of the inventory items sold during the year, net of any discounts, returns, or write-offs
Gross profit	Net sales minus COGS
Yearly rent	Annual cost of occupying all space necessary for operation of the business
Owner's comp	Annual income, salary, or wage paid to business owner(s) plus any incidental payment, benefit, privilege, or advantage over and above the income, salary, or wage
Other operating expense	All selling and general and administrative expenses, excluding rent, owner's compensation, and noncash charges
Noncash charges	Annual decrease in value due to wear and tear, decay, or decline in the price of tangible and/or intangible fixed assets (depreciation and amortization)
Total operating expenses	Sum of yearly rent plus owner's compensation plus noncash charges plus other operating expenses
Operating profit	Gross profit minus total operating expenses
Interest expense	Cost of borrowing expressed as an annual dollar amount
EBT (earnings before taxes)	Operating profit minus interest expense
Taxes	Annual value of taxes
Net income	EBT minus taxes

"As restated" indicates that income data is reported without nonrecurring and exceptional items that will not affect future financial statements (e.g., items not transferred with the sale of the business).

What is the legend for Pratt's Stats™ Asset data?

Reports	*Definition*
Purchase price allocation	Asset data reflects the agreed-upon allocation price between buyer and seller.
Cash and equivalents	All cash, marketable securities, and other near-cash items. Excludes sinking funds. Cash equivalents (NOW accounts and money market funds) must be available upon demand in order to justify inclusion.
Trade receivables	All accounts from trade, net of allowance for doubtful accounts, that will result in the collection of cash.
Inventory	Anything constituting inventory for the firm, including raw material, work in progress, and finished goods. Those items of tangible property that are held for sale in the normal course of business, are in the process of being produced for such purposes, or are to be used in the production of such items.
Other current assets	Any other current assets, excluding cash and equivalents, trade receivables, and inventory.
Total current assets	Cash and equivalents plus trade receivables plus inventory plus other current assets.
Fixed assets	All property, plant, leasehold improvements, and equipment, net of accumulated depreciation or depletion.
Real estate	Dollar value placed on any real estate associated with the sale of the business.
Intangibles	Assets with uncertain or hard-to-measure benefits, such as brand names, trademarks, patents or copyrights, a trained workforce, special know-how, and customer or supplier relationships, that make the company a viable competitor and give it earning power. These values are net of accumulated amortization.

(Continued)

EXHIBIT 7.6 (Continued)

Reports	*Definition*
Other noncurrent assets	Any other noncurrent assets, excluding real estate, fixed assets, intangibles, noncompete agreements and employment/consulting agreements.
Total assets	Total current assets plus real estate plus fixed assets plus intangibles plus other noncurrent assets.
Liabilities assumed	Those long-term financial liabilities that the buyer assumes upon the purchase of the company.
Employment/consulting agreement	Dollar value placed on an agreement between the buyer and seller for the seller's personal services to be provided to the buyer either as an employee or consultant after the sale of the business.
Noncompete agreement	Dollar value placed on an agreement with the selling party not to compete with the purchaser, usually for a certain period of time and usually in a specified geographic area.

What is the legend for Pratt's Stats™ other data?

Reports	*Definition*
Latest full year report date	Date of last full-year or partial-year financial report. In the case of partial-year financial statements, the period covered or date of report is indicated in the notes field.
Date sale initiated	Date on which business was listed for sale.
Date of sale	Date on which sale of business was closed.
Length of time on market	In months.
Asking price	Price desired by seller at time of listing.
Equity price	Dollar value of consideration paid for the equity of the business sold. Equity price does not include long-term liabilities assumed, noncompete agreements, and employment/consulting agreements. Equity price includes all current assets, noncurrent assets, and current liabilities (unless otherwise noted in the notes field). Equity price does not include noncurrent (long-term) liabilities.
Amount down	Dollar value of consideration given to close the business sale transaction.

What is the legend for Pratt's Stats™ business type data?

Reports	*Definition*
C corp	A corporation acting as a separate entity for income tax purposes.
S corp	A corporation with restrictions on equity ownership.
LLC	A limited liability company is one wherein the members have limited legal liability and may participate in the management of the organization.
Partnership	A business composed of two entities, either created as a general partnership or limited partnership.

What is the legend for Pratt's Stats™ calculations?

Reports	*Definition*
Equity price	Reported selling price (not including long-term liabilities assumed, noncompete agreements, and employment/consulting agreements)
Deal price	Equity price + long-term liabilities assumed
Discretionary earnings	([Net income] + [Taxes] + [Interest expense] + [Owner's compensation] + [Noncash charges])

EXHIBIT 7.6 (Continued)

Reports	*Definition*
Equity price/Net sales	[Equity price] / [Net sales]
Equity price/Gross cash flow	[Equity price] / ([Net income] + [Noncash charges])
Equity price/EBT	[Equity price] / ([Net income] + [Taxes])
Equity price/Net income	[Equity price] / [Net income]
Deal price/Discretionary earnings	Deal price / ([Net income] + [Taxes] + [Interest expense] + [Owner's compensation] + [Noncash charges])
Deal price/Net sales	[Equity price + Long-term liabilities assumed] / [Net sales]
Deal price/EBITDA	[Equity price + Long-term liabilities assumed] / ([Net income] + [Interest expense] + [Taxes] + [Noncash charges])
Deal price/EBIT	[Equity price + Long-term liabilities assumed] / ([Net income] + [Interest expense] + [Taxes])

What are the assumptions for Pratt's Stats™ data?

- A blank field indicates that the data in question was not available.
- A dollar value of zero has been expressly specified as zero.
- Interest on the noncompete agreement value is not included unless expressly stated.
- If there are no reported liabilities assumed, the assumption is made that there are either zero liabilities assumed or that there are insignificant liabilities assumed such that they would not make a material difference in the calculation of a deal price (equity price + liabilities assumed). Therefore, when there are no reported liabilities assumed, we report the deal price to be equal to the equity price.

Source: Pratt's Stats™ (Portland OR: Business Valuation Resources, LLC). Reprinted with permission.

Each transaction does not have information in every data field, but this database does a good job at increasing the amount of information that is available for small company transactions. The more information that is available, the better the decision-making process will be. This will lead to better valuation opinions. Pratt's Stats provides up to eight different valuation multiples including equity and invested capital (deal price) multiples. These include:

1. Equity price/net sales
2. Equity price/net income
3. Equity price/gross cash flow
4. Equity price/EBT
5. Deal price/discretionary earnings
6. Deal price/EBITDA
7. Deal price/EBIT
8. Deal price/net sales

In addition, the database gives the user information to calculate other multiples (e.g., equity price to book value). With so much data available, the possibilities are endless, but be careful that you understand what is listed in each field before you go crazy making up multiples.

Another important item that you must consider is that Pratt's Stats reports two different transaction types. BizComps and IBA report only asset sales. In addition to asset sales, Pratt's Stats also reports stock sales.

Stock sales are transactions in which a business transfers its equity to the acquirer, or in other words, transfers *all* of its assets and liabilities. Based on the transaction type, price will most likely reflect different assets and/or liabilities that were transferred as part of the deal. This becomes very important in comparing and applying multiples. I will demonstrate this shortly.

Pratt's Stats' Web site automatically calculates statistics on selected transaction data, and these are displayed on the subscriber results page. Users can limit the data set to include certain transactions and may recalculate statistics such as count, range, mean, median, and coefficient of variation for each data set. These statistics can be useful in performing transaction searches, as well as multiple selection. Discussion of transaction analysis is included later in this chapter.

Done Deals

The Done Deals database contains slightly larger transactions than the databases discussed previously, with purchase prices ranging between $1 and $100 million. Done Deals focuses on the smallest acquisitions reported to the Securities Exchange Commission (SEC), and most of its data comes from company financial reports filed with the SEC. The financial data is typically presented in accordance with GAAP. Done Deals is available over the Internet at www.donedeals.com.

There are over 4,000 completed transactions included in this database, and up to 250 new transactions are added each quarter, depending upon the transaction activity among mid-market sized companies. Approximately 60 percent of the companies sold in the Done Deals database were privately owned, and 10 percent of the companies sold were subsidiaries of public companies. Search results for Done Deals transactions are shown in Exhibit 7.7.

Done Deals does not list as many data points as Pratt's Stats, but it is still significantly more detailed than BizComps or the IBA Market Data Base. Similar to Pratt's Stats, Done Deals lists asset and stock transactions. You can perform much of the same analysis that you can with Pratt's Stats, although Done Deals does not differentiate between equity price and deal price. To illustrate this point, here is the definition of price taken from the Done Deals Frequently Asked Questions (FAQ) Web page:

> Price is the summation of each part of the consideration paid by the buyer to the seller as listed in the "Terms" field. For "Stock Sales" the price is an Equity Price, or the price paid for the seller's equity. Approximately 70 percent of the Done Deals transactions are stock sales. For "Asset Sales," about 30 percent of Done Deals, the price indicated is a Deal Price and is equal to the price paid for the equity acquired plus the value of any liabilities assumed. In Done Deals the assets acquired are listed in the "Terms" field, when known, as is the value of any liabilities assumed by the buyer. Where there is no debt assumed, as is the case in the majority of asset sales, the Deal Price is equal to the Equity Price.[3]

As I said before, be careful in the application of these multiples. Analysis of this data can be performed similarly to Pratt's Stats.

One very nice tool available through Done Deals is the "Multi-Database Transaction Search," which should appear as soon as you log on. This search engine allows the user to search for transactions in Done Deals, BizComps, and the IBA Market Data Base simultaneously. Searches may be conducted by SIC code, transaction date, revenue, and/or sales price. This is a quick and easy way to get an idea of how many transactions are out there.

Done Deals' Web site automatically calculates statistics on selected transaction data, which is displayed on the search results page. Users can limit the data set to include certain transactions and may recalculate

---

[3]Done Deals Frequently Asked Questions (http://www.donedeals.com/faq.html)

EXHIBIT 7.7
Done Deals Search Results

DONE DEALS DATA
Search Results

Closing Date: 1/3/00 **SIC:** 7361 Look up SIC Code **Price:** $1.1 (MM)

Buyer	**Seller**
HeadHunter.NET, Inc. 6410 Atlantic Blvd., Suite 160 Norcross, GA 30071 Mark W. Partin, CFO 770-349-2400	Chicago Computer Guide, Inc. and All In One Submit (IL)

Seller Description
Provides TECHNICAL LITERATURE to subscribers throughout the U.S. and an on-line job-posting company based in Chicago, Illinois

Seller Type: Private

Terms
$250M cash + $356M in HHNT com. stk. + $494M potential earnout

Sale Type: Stock

Seller's Financials & Ratios

Amounts expressed in $MM	**Amount**	**Months**	**Comments**		
Assets:	0.105	N/A	10/99	**P/A:**	10.5
Stockholder's Equity	0.066	N/A	10/99	**P/SE:**	16.7
Revenue	0.145	12	end 10/99	**P/R:**	7.6
Net Income (Loss):	0.066	12	end 10/99	**P/E:**	16.7
Cash Flow:	0.073	12	end 10/99	**P/CF:**	15.1
EBITDA:				**P/EBITDA:**	

Close This Window

statistics such as range, mean, median, and standard deviation for each data set. Discussion of transaction analysis is included later in this chapter.

Overall, the Done Deals database is most applicable if you are valuing large companies. The only companies included in the database are those that are large enough to be public companies, or at least large enough to be purchased by a public company. If you are valuing a small business, much of the information contained in this database will not be applicable to your subject business.

Thomson Financial Securities Data[4] (TFSD)

The TFSD database contains information about public company mergers and acquisitions of public and private companies. There is also other neat stuff in the database. Although it typically covers very large transactions, it is another resource worth mentioning. Our firm uses the Worldwide Mergers, Acquisitions, and Alliances database of TFSD Platinum. The database contains 116,100 domestic merger and acquisition transactions beginning in 1979 and is updated daily. TFSD transactions are typically larger than those available in the other transaction databases. TFSD contains 273,000 transactions and offers more than 1,400 detailed information elements (and you thought Pratt's had a lot). This database can be quite costly and is really only applicable for valuing very large businesses.

This database can be accessed in two different manners. You can call the company and they will perform a search for you. If you use the data from the search, it will cost a minimum of $300. They charge by the data field with a $300 minimum. The other alternative is to purchase their software, which allows you to do your own search. Each search costs $50, and then you pay for the data fields used. Using their software gives you much greater flexibility, and frequently reduces the cost.

Since this book is primarily geared to the small to medium-sized business, I am not going to spend any more time on this database. However, you can find out more information about this product at www.tfsd.com. I strongly suggest that you get professional help (training on the database and/or therapy, your choice—maybe both) before you attempt to use it.

Business Brokers

Business brokers can also be an excellent source of market transaction data. The local business broker is frequently involved in many transactions. He or she has access to information about many similar businesses that have been bought and sold in the geographical region of the appraisal subject. The major problem with business broker information is twofold: First, the broker may not have access to fully reliable financial information about the company that was sold; the seller frequently provides the figures to the broker without any verification. Second, the seller, the buyer, or both are generally going to require the broker to respect their confidentiality, which would prohibit the broker from opening the file to the appraiser.

On occasion, enough data can be obtained from a business broker to allow some empirical data to be used in applying the market approach. There may be times when a reliable broker will be allowed to verify the transactions and the other party, assuming a litigation, will stipulate to confidentiality, since their expert will want to do the same. This is exactly what happened in the report excerpted in Exhibit 7.8.

EXHIBIT 7.8
Business Broker Information

This valuation method uses information that comes from the actual sales transactions of similar properties to determine a ratio of the sales price to the net profit from the property (commonly known as a multiple), which is then applied against the appraisal subject's net profit. This is probably the most widely used ratio in valuation methodologies today. Two important components of this method are the net profit (for this appraisal, net profit is defined as the amount available to the owner after normal business expenses but before taxes, loan payments, and owner's compensation; this is sometimes called owner's discretionary cash flow) and the appropriate multiple to be used.

XYZ Products, Inc. had an average net profit for the past three years of $110,500. The multiple applied to the net profit must reflect the appropriate amount of risk that is associated with the net profit as calculated. In this instance, a multiple of 1.81 has been deemed appropriate, as explained in a later section of this report.

[4]The database formerly known as Securities Data Company (SDC).

EXHIBIT 7.8 *(Continued)*

Therefore, the value of the intangible assets of XYZ Products, Inc. is calculated as follows:

Average net profit	$ 110,500
Multiple	× 1.81
Estimate of value	$ 200,005
Rounded	$ 200,000

The Market Price of the Sales of Closely Held Food Routes

To assess the market price of sales of routes comparable to XYZ Products, Inc., we consulted with John Smith, President of Busbroke, Inc. and a business broker who specializes in the sale of food route businesses. Mr. Smith provided us with the actual sales transactions of 10 routes that were used as "guideline companies." (A guideline company is used in a business valuation in a manner that is similar to the way "comparables" are used in valuing real estate. It is recognized that closely held businesses can be used as guidelines in the determination of value, even though they are not truly comparable.) Table 1 provides financial data regarding the 10 guideline companies. All 10 routes relate to either dairy, cheese, or yogurt product lines. Table 1 provides ratios based on the relationship of the purchase price of the route to the net profits of the selling company.

TABLE 1

Summary of Food Route Sales[1]

Route	Gross Type	Net Sales ($)	Purchase Profit ($)	Gross Profit ($)	Price/Net Price ($)	Profit (%)	Multiple[2]
1465	Cheese	390,000	50,700	44,200	100,000	13.00	2.26
1474	Dairy	520,000	78,000	68,380	125,000	15.00	1.83
1514	Yogurt	650,000	110,500	85,800	248,000	17.00	2.89
1543	Yogurt	610,000	118,950	85,700	200,000	19.50	2.33
1546	Yogurt	478,400	119,600	91,780	205,000	25.00	2.23
1571	Yogurt	442,000	88,400	80,600	165,000	20.00	2.05
1726	Yogurt	338,000	60,840	54,860	155,000	18.00	2.83
1773	Cheese	936,000	112,320	90,740	200,000	12.00	2.20
1784	Dairy	327,600	88,400	82,160	120,000	26.98	1.46
1818	Dairy	468,000	93,600	70,980	85,000	20.00	1.20
						Average	2.13

[1]Supplied by Busbroke, Inc.

[2]Calculated by the appraiser.

Some additional information should be highlighted about these transactions. The sale of food routes generally involves an individual purchasing a food route with the intention of working the route; in essence, the individual is "purchasing" his employment. This is in contrast to the potential investor, who would buy a route and then pay someone to service the route. As a result, an individual purchasing these food routes tends to be motivated and frequently bases the amount that he or she is willing to pay on a figure that is considered to be net profit but, in fact, excludes owner's compensation.

The cash flow generated by the food route must be adequate not only to allow the owner to make a living, but also to pay down the debt service that comes about as a result of the purchasing of the route itself. To determine the fair market value of a food route business, reasonable compensation should be considered, to avoid confusing a true return on investment with the owner receiving compensation for working the business. Logically, value is generally measured by the return received in excess of reasonable compensation; otherwise, employees would be paying their employer for the opportunity to work.

In comparing XYZ Dairy Products, Inc. with the routes listed in Table 1, the following items should be noted:

1. The guideline companies reflect a gross profit (sales less direct cost of sales) of 12 percent to 26.98 percent, whereas XYZ Dairy Products, Inc. has averaged only 10.35 percent over the last five years.
2. Many of the guideline companies reflect a net profit to the owners of $85,000 to $90,000 based on sales of $300,000 to $600,000, whereas XYZ Dairy Products, Inc. reflects an average net profit of $105,771 based on average net sales of approximately $3,373,000.

(Continued)

EXHIBIT 7.8 *(Continued)*

In addition to the above, a price–to–net profit ratio was calculated by the appraiser for each actual transaction, resulting in ratios of 1.20 to 2.89, with an average ratio actually paid of 2.13 times the net profit. In fact, a multiple of 2.13 is equivalent to a capitalization rate of 46.9 percent, indicating an extremely high rate of return required by the buyers in the food route marketplace. This is the same as saying that the willing buyers expect to recoup their investments in a little over two years, in addition to their labor.

Another important factor that must be considered in reaching a value conclusion about intangible assets is risk. The level of risk associated with an investment generally determines the required rate of return for an investor. This is why, for example, certificates of deposit may pay 5 percent, while corporate bonds pay 8 percent and junk bonds pay 16 percent. The higher the level of risk, the higher the required rate of return must be in order to attract an investor.

Almost every closely held business is extremely risky. XYZ Dairy Products, Inc. is certainly no exception. The willing buyer of a customer list is not assured that customers will continue with that company. In fact, unless there were contracts guaranteeing volume, a substantial discount would normally be applied in the value of the company. In the real world, buyers and sellers address this contingency through sales contracts, because if a customer were lost, no payment would be required. This is almost like buying a business on a royalty basis. If the business volume continues as anticipated, the willing buyer will pay the willing seller.

Some of the more pertinent risk factors that a willing buyer would consider are the following:

1. Brand X represented approximately 90 percent of XYZ Dairy Products, Inc.'s business.
2. XYZ Dairy Products, Inc. had no contract with Brand X indicating that business would continue at any point in the future. The fact that the company had been delivering Brand X products for a number of years could not by itself be relied upon for continuity to take place in the future.
3. In the early 1980s PQZ became a broker for Brand X. PQZ represented Brand X in stores and supermarket headquarters and actively worked with the supermarkets through central billing. At that point XYZ Dairy Products, Inc. started billing with Brand X invoices, and Brand X collected the money directly. PQZ also began handling the promotional aspects with the supermarket to further change the role of the company.
4. In approximately 1984, Roberts Foods, Inc. purchased Brand X. According to the deposition of Sam Jones, when Roberts took over Brand X, many distributors were concerned about Brand X "going warehouse" (i.e., distributing through a central warehouse instead of directly to the supermarkets).
5. Compared to the guideline companies, XYZ Dairy Products, Inc. was considerably less profitable despite a larger sales volume. The company's gross profit on sales was lower than all 10 guideline companies.
6. XYZ Dairy Products, Inc. had no control over the billing, distribution, and collections associated with Brand X products. The company was primarily a one-company distribution agent with little diversification.

In addition to the above, a financial analysis was performed by the valuer using *RMA Annual Statement Studies*, published by Robert Morris Associates (RMA). This publication contains statistical data broken down by Standard Industrial Classification (SIC) code based on information submitted in financial statements to RMA member banks. In this instance, SIC code 5143, "Wholesalers of Dairy Products," was used.

In our opinion, XYZ Dairy Products, Inc. appears to be weaker than the industry group, due primarily to its lower profitability. As a result, we believe that a 15 percent discount is appropriate from the average guideline company multiple. This indicates that an appropriate multiple to be used for XYZ Dairy Products, Inc. is 1.81, to be applied against the net profit available to the owner.

Business brokers can be an excellent source of market data. Sometimes, you may find it helpful to offer the broker compensation for his or her time (brokers just love me!). Another excellent way to gain cooperation is to refer some sales his or her way. Since brokers are involved in the market, it is only natural that they should be able to provide good market information in the appraiser's local area.

Transaction Analysis—Qualitative and Quantitative

Get ready. Here comes the good stuff! Now that you know where to find transaction data, I will shed some light on how to use it. The fact of the matter is that the transaction method has some major limitations because most of the transactions retrieved through database services cannot be independently verified, and there is a limited amount of information for each transaction. Real estate appraisers verify each transaction, whereas in this situation, business appraisers must rely on someone else's work, which is composed of limited information about the target companies.

However, fear not! Although an appraiser may have limited data, it can still be used. Actually, this method is often the most direct and applicable method for valuing a small company (just don't use it by itself as the only method). There is a wide array of tools and techniques that can help you analyze transaction data. Before we start in on the analysis, I want to clearly define what the appraiser is really trying to do. An appraiser needs to fully understand the purpose of this exercise to perform the task correctly. When we get a data set (transaction data), be it from IBA, BizComps, Pratt's Stats, or any other transaction information, we attempt to determine:

- If the transactions appear to be usable transactions (qualitative analysis)
- What multiple, if any, should be applied to the subject company (quantitative analysis)

An appraiser can utilize qualitative and quantitative analysis, much the same as was done in applying the guideline public company method to build a meaningful and supportable indication of value for the subject company.

Qualitative Analysis

Qualitative analysis refers to the soft stuff, or the nonnumerical information, known about the transactions. As discussed, we know very little about the transactions, as compared to real estate appraisers, who can get all sorts of information on their comparables. However, we have to work with what we've got. For instance, the business descriptions listed in the IBA and BizComps databases may be brief (often one or two words), but they still serve as a good indicator for what a business does. Analyzing business descriptions, particularly in large data sets, can prove to be an invaluable asset to an analyst. Exhibit 7.9 reflects an analysis of IBA transactions performed for an Italian restaurant/pizzeria located in a mall.

EXHIBIT 7.9
IBA Business Description Analysis

This database was searched for transactions involving companies in SIC code 5812—Retail Trade, Eating Places. Our search located approximately 1,500 transactions in this SIC code containing all types of restaurants whose revenues ranged from $13,000 to in excess of $200,000,000. In order to more appropriately utilize this information, we stratified this data into several more applicable categories.

The first category consisted of small Italian restaurants and pizzerias. This data is presented in Table 1.

TABLE 1
IBA Market Comparison Data
Italian Restaurants/Pizzerias

Business Type	*Annual Gross ($000)*	*Sales Price ($000)*	*Price/Gross*	*Geographic*	*Yr./Mo. of Sale*
Deli with pizza	89	28	0.31	CA	86/04
Fast food—pizza	227	55	0.24	GA	93/07
Fast food—pizza	230	49	0.21	CA	94/12
Restr—pizza	306	120	0.39	CA	90/05
Restr—Italian	310	29	0.09	CA	95/08
Restr—pizza	317	81	0.26	TX	91/04
Restr—Italian	324	75	0.23	FL	94/05
Restr—Italian	390	53	0.14	CA	95/07
Restr—pizza	477	397	0.83	ID	95/04
Restr—Italian	516	212	0.41	CA	95/08
Restr—Italian	653	89	0.14	CA	95/02
Mean			0.30		
Median			0.24		

(Continued)

EXHIBIT 7.9 *(Continued)*

As indicated, there were 11 transactions in this category, indicating an average price-to-revenue multiple of 0.30 and a median of 0.24.

The second category consisted of 55 restaurants categorized as fast food restaurants. This information is shown in Table 2.

TABLE 2
IBA Market Comparison Data
Fast Food Restaurants

Business Type	*Annual Gross ($000)*	*Sales Price ($000)*	*Price/Gross*	*Geographic*	*Yr./Mo. of Sale*
Fast food/coffee shop	58	23	0.40	FL	96/02
Fast food—yogurt	65	24	0.37	LA	93/12
Fast food/coffee shop	74	60	0.81	FL	96/06
Fast food—smoothies	80	40	0.50	LA	95/02
Fast food—yogurt	86	27	0.31	LA	93/04
Fast food/coffee shop	90	20	0.22	FL	95/09
Sandwich shop, fast food	90	34	0.38	Midwest	86/07
Fast food/coffee shop	100	32	0.32	FL	94/10
Fast food/coffee shop	108	50	0.46	FL	93/12
Fast food rest	111	20	0.18	Midwest	87/02
Fast food—chicken	120	68	0.57	FL	94/04
Fast food—yogurt	120	52	0.43	FL	94/08
Fast food—chicken	120	40	0.33	FL	95/01
Fast food/coffee shop	120	40	0.33	FL	95/02
Fast food—yogurt	120	38	0.32	TX	92/02
Restr-mall fast food	120	48	0.40	FL	91/03
Fast food/coffee shop	120	56	0.47	FL	94/08
Fast food/coffee shop	132	27	0.20	FL	95/08
Fast food—chicken	132	25	0.19	FL	95/07
Deli, fast food	132	55	0.42	NJ	91/
Fast food—yogurt	135	70	0.52	Midwest	93/03
Fast food—yogurt	136	100	0.74	ID	92/07
Fast food/coffee shop	140	85	0.61	FL	94/07
Fast food/coffee shop	147	85	0.58	FL	94/08
Fast food/coffee shop	150	65	0.43	FL	96/01
Fast food—baked potatoes	152	43	0.28	MN	94/11
Fast food—yogurt	160	80	0.50	CA	92/01
Deli, fast food	175	76	0.43	MA	90/09
Fast food/coffee shop	175	70	0.40	FL	96/10
Fast food—Dairy Queen	185	25	0.14	NM	92/09
Fast food—Dairy Queen	186	20	0.11	NM	91/10
Fast food/bakery/coffee	200	95	0.48	FL	95/03
Fast food/coffee shop	200	65	0.33	FL	96/11
Deli, fast food	200	70	0.35	MA	90/08
Fast food—Dairy Queen	220	99	0.45	Midwest	93/09
Fast food (mall store)	220	90	0.41	NC	96/10
Fast food—Mexican	222	88	0.40	OR	95/03

EXHIBIT 7.9 *(Continued)*

Business Type	*Annual Gross ($000)*	*Sales Price ($000)*	*Price/Gross*	*Geographic*	*Yr./Mo. of Sale*
Fast food—pizza	227	55	0.24	GA	93/07
Fast food—pizza	230	49	0.21	CA	94/12
Fast food—hamburgers	237	140	0.59	CA	91/08
Fast food/coffee shop	250	128	0.51	FL	95/05
Fast food—Dairy Queen	275	57	0.21	NM	91/07
Deli, fast food	285	83	0.29	FL	91/11
Fast food/coffee shop	300	70	0.23	FL	97/05
Fast food—take out	300	161	0.54	ID	95/09
Fast food—Dairy Queen	312	117	0.38	NM	91/07
Fast food—Dairy Queen	324	40	0.12	Midwest	94/01
Fast food/coffee shop	346	150	0.43	FL	95/03
Fast food/coffee shop	346	100	0.29	FL	95/06
Sub shop/fast food sand.	354	205	0.58	IL	89/
Fast food—ice cream	354	185	0.52	CA	95/07
Fast food—roast beef	398	93	0.23	CA	94/11
Fast food—fried chicken	540	248	0.46	TX	94/08
Fast food/coffee shop	832	200	0.24	FL	94/11
Fast food—hamburgers	832	200	0.24	FL	94/10
Fast food—hamburger	936	665	0.71	NV	90/07
Mean			0.39		
Median			0.40		

This category indicated an average multiple of 0.39 and a median of 0.40.

The final category consisted of restaurants with sales in the range of $400,000 to $700,000, regardless of type, as this range more appropriately reflects the revenues of the subject company. There were 168 transactions in this category shown in Table 3.

TABLE 3

IBA Market Comparison Data
Revenues of $400,000 to $700,000

Business Type	*Annual Gross ($000)*	*Sales Price ($000)*	*Price/Gross*	*Geographic*	*Yr./Mo. of Sale*
Bagel shop	400	190	0.48	L I New York	90/03
Restaurant	400	125	0.31		84/02
Bagel restaurant	400	160	0.40	FL	95/01
Bagel restaurant	400	150	0.38	FL	95/04
Deli bakery—retail	425	125	0.29	NJ	93/08
Restaurant	426	20	0.05	Texas	86/03
Restaurant in office bldg	430	175	0.41	CT	90/
Café	430	175	0.41	Texas	92/
Restaurant	433	145	0.33	HI	92/03
Restaurant/lounge	435	142	0.33		93/
Café, gourmet	435	105	0.24	FL	95/09

(Continued)

EXHIBIT 7.9 *(Continued)*

Business Type	*Annual Gross ($000)*	*Sales Price ($000)*	*Price/Gross*	*Geographic*	*Yr./Mo. of Sale*
Delicatessen & stationery	438	275	0.63		84/10
Restaurant—Ital. café	638	275	0.43	CA	96/08
Restaurant w/ice cream	639	215	0.34	IL	91/
Restaurant/ice cream	639	215	0.34	IL	91/
Yogurt, franchise store	640	400	0.63	PA	90/
Restaurant, full service	643	175	0.27	WA	90/
Restaur./dinner only	644	190	0.30	FL	96/01
Restr—family	650	250	0.38	TN	89/01
Restr—Italian	653	89	0.14	CA	95/02
Restaurant Function Ctr.	654	125	0.19	NH	96/03
Restaurant	669	90	0.13	AL	93/
Restaurant—Dinnerhouse	672	158	0.24	FL	92/08
Restaurant, family style	678	152	0.22		89/12
Restaurant	679	275	0.41		88/09
Restaurant, full line	680	325	0.48	NC	93/
Restaurant	693	205	0.30	WA	90/
Restr—Dinnerhouse	700	140	0.20	MA	92/10
Dunkin Donuts	700	400	0.57	East	90/01
Diner	700	235	0.34	FL	93/12
Mean			0.36		
Median			0.34		

Many transactions were omitted from this exhibit to save space.

This category indicates an average price-to-revenue multiple of 0.36 and a median multiple of 0.34.

The price-to-revenue multiple was analyzed, as this is typically the way that small businesses sell. This is because owners of very small companies tend to adjust expenses in order to minimize taxes, and therefore, a willing buyer looks at the revenues he or she will be able to generate, believing that there will be certain costs that will be eliminated when he or she takes over the running of the business.

For each category, a mean and median price-to-revenue multiple was calculated. Statistically, the median is more appropriate than the mean because an average can be skewed by data that are outliers in the sample. The median is the point of central tendency when all of the values are arranged by size. Therefore, the median multiple was utilized.

The three median multiples derived result in an average price-to-revenues multiple of 0.33. This is the multiple that will be applied to the appropriate revenue stream.

An analysis of historic and adjusted revenues was performed in the financial analysis section of the report. This analysis indicated that revenues increased from 1993 through 1995 and then declined again. Since there appears to be no consistent growth pattern over the last five years, it appears that average adjusted revenues over the period should be used to reflect the future. This amounts to $703,067.

The values derived using the IBA database include any assets that the buyer will receive, such as equipment, but do not include the assets that the seller will keep, such as cash, accounts receivable, and accounts payable. Therefore, the value of these assets and liabilities must be added or subtracted from the sales value to determine the value of the operating entity.

Therefore, the calculation of value on a control, nonmarketable basis utilizing the data from The Institute of Business Appraisers is as follows:

Average revenues	$ 703,067
Price-to-revenue multiple	× 0.33
Value	$ 232,012
Plus: Inventory	6,250
Less: Current liabilities	(63,460)
Value of operating entity	$ 174,802
Rounded	$ 175,000

Exhibit 7.9 illustrates how the appraiser can "slice and dice" the transaction data to attempt to get various cross sections of data that may be considered to be similar enough to provide guidance about pricing multiples. Other useful analysis can be done considering geography or any of the other descriptive factors found in the different databases. Stratification analysis based on qualitative factors can be an extremely useful tool in understanding how businesses are sold.

If more data is available, then why not use it? As I mentioned before, Pratt's Stats database has many more data points, many of which can be very useful. Pratt's Stats provides the appraiser with a business name and location, which can add a little meat to any analysis. Knowing who the company is allows the appraiser to perform additional research about the company and the transaction itself. Exhibit 7.10 contains a section of a report where there were many transactions in the SIC code of the subject company, but the subject was in a different sector of the industry, which would cause the multiples to be very different. In this instance we used the Google.com search engine to find information about each transaction.

EXHIBIT 7.10
Analysis of Transaction Data Qualitative Factors

The appraiser was retained by DEBT Mortgage Corporation (hereafter referred to as DEBT or The Company) to appraise the common stock owned by the estate of Mr. Smith as of December 31, 1999. We conducted a search for transactions of privately held companies that might be used in the application of the transaction method. We searched the following databases:

- BA Market Data Base
- BizComps
- Pratt's Stats
- Done Deals

The IBA Market Data base and BizComps had no usable transactions. Pratt's Stats had a number of transactions, but upon closer scrutiny of the available information, these could not be used. For example, several of the transactions involved the seller getting the purchaser's stock as part of the consideration in the deal. Without knowing the basis for the valuation of the stock, it would be too easy to draw false conclusions about the value of the deal. Stock subject to restrictive agreements is worth considerably less than stock without restrictions.

Some of the transactions also had earn-out provisions, and no details were disclosed. Some of the transactions involved employment contracts, and others had restrictive covenants. Without adequate knowledge about these transactions, an appraiser would easily draw inaccurate inferences about the transaction.

Research was performed about these transactions, and the following bullet points further justify the exclusion of this data from this report:

- In July 1999, Altiva Financial Corp. of Atlanta signed an agreement to purchase The Money Centre, Inc. of Charlotte, North Carolina, for $20 million. The Money Centre is a retail and wholesale subprime mortgage company that does business in 15 states. In 1998, it had a loan volume in excess of $400 million. In an announcement in *The Business Journal*, it was expected that Altiva would keep all 200 employees of The Money Centre. Altiva is a publicly traded company that announced on April 19 that it would be closing its wholly owned subsidiary, The Money Centre, in Charlotte. The Company was unable to obtain enough cash to continue operations.
- Jupiter Mortgage Corporation was sold in August 1999 to Americas Senior Financial Services. Jupiter Mortgage Corporation is primarily a residential lender for buying, building, or refinancing. This transaction involved partial cash consideration and part common stock of the purchaser, including employment agreements where the terms were not disclosed.
- First American Mortgage Corporation was purchased by AmeriResource Technologies, Inc. in August 1998. First American Mortgage was a residential lender that provided mortgages, home loans, refinancing, debt consolidation, and similar loans.
- Bloomfield Acceptance Company was merged into publicly held Bingham Financial Services Corp. in March 1998. Bloomfield Acceptance Company has been providing capital to the owners of manufactured home communities for over 15 years and is one of the country's largest lenders to that industry. The Company was also a direct lender on a nationwide basis, specializing in fixed- and floating-rate financing for most commercial property types.

(Continued)

EXHIBIT 7.10 ***(Continued)***

- Hartger & Willard Mortgage Associates, Inc. was acquired by Bingham Financial Services Corp. on July 1, 1999, by exchanging 66,667 shares of Bingham stock. Integrating this company into Bingham Financial Services Corporation allowed Bingham to increase its commercial loan servicing portfolio to nearly $1 billion.
- Salt Lake Mortgage was purchased by Celtic Investment Inc. in January 1997. Salt Lake Mortgage was a full-service, residential mortgage broker. Salt Lake Mortgage Associates was acquired by Conning Corp. in August 1998. Little information was available regarding the seller, but the purchaser, Conning Corp., is a publicly traded company, strong in asset management.
- First Bankers Mortgage Service was acquired by Equitex, Inc. in August 1999. Equitex is a publicly traded company. The transaction was structured with Equitex's common stock, and a commitment of working capital being infused into First Bankers Mortgage Service.
- Mortgage Credit Services Inc. was acquired by Factual Data Corp. in December 1998. Factual Data Corp. had acquired eight companies within the last six months of 1998, rolling up a total of $15 million in additional business. Factual Data Corp. is a leading national provider of customized information services to the mortgaging, consumer lending, employment, and real estate rental markets. Mortgage Credit Services Inc. was acquired in order to remain at its current location and became Factual Data's south Texas processing center.
- The Leader Mortgage Company was purchased by First Defiance Financial Corp. in July 1998. Leader Mortgage is primarily a residential, real estate lender.
- Bankers Mutual was acquired by Franchise Mortgage Acceptance in April 1998. Bankers Mutual is a resource available for multi-family financing needs. Bankers Mutual is a nationally recognized industry leader in providing full-service multi-family financing. The Company joined Berkshire Mortgage Finance, and with the combination, the companies formed one of the largest privately owned mortgage banking companies in the industry.
- American National Mortgage Corp. was acquired by IMN Financial Corp. in December 1997. American National Mortgage Corp. was a residential lender.
- The Accent Group, Inc. was acquired by Lahaina Acquisitions Inc. in August 1999. The Accent Group brought 113 net branches for mortgages to Lahaina. Accent Mortgage had a mortgage banking division, as well as a real estate development operation. The transaction involved the issuance of in excess of 14 million shares of common stock, subject to Rule 144 of the Securities and Exchange Act. As a result, the true value of the transaction could not be determined without performing a valuation of the restricted stock of this public company.
- Spectra Precision Credit Corp. was acquired by Linc Capital Inc. in June 1998. Linc is a publicly traded company that considers itself to be a specialty finance company. Spectra Precision Credit Corp. had a $34 million lease portfolio that was part of the transaction.
- Midland Financial Holdings, Inc. was acquired by Municipal Mortgage & Equity, LLC, a publicly traded company, in October 1999. Midland Financial Holdings was a holding company of several entities.
- NewState Capital Company, Ltd. was acquired by Racom Systems Inc. in July 1999. NewState Capital Company is a Korean company that started in the business of factoring, auto loans, lease financing, and accounts receivable financing.
- LRS, Inc. was acquired by Trans National Financial Network in July 1999. The focus of LRS, Inc. is to develop and deliver information technology solutions, and it appears to be in an unrelated industry.

As a result of our analysis, we have determined that the market approach cannot be applied in this valuation because none of the transactional information would be beneficial in providing guidance to the appraiser as to the appropriate multiple that would pertain to the subject company.

Beyond company name, Exhibit 7.10 illustrates how the qualitative information listed in the databases can be used to analyze data. A point of interest is how we went about finding information on small businesses such as those listed in Exhibit 7.10. The Internet is a very powerful tool, and search engines have the ability to locate all sorts of publications ranging from business and finance publications to local newspapers. It has given us the ability to access stores of information that were previously unobtainable or the cost associated with the research was unjustifiable. Next time you use a database that lists the target company's name, try typing it into your favorite search engine and see what you get.

The qualitative analysis of transaction data allows an appraiser to get a better feeling for the quality of the information that exists within the data that has been located. It also allows him or her to make certain decisions regarding which data should be included or excluded from the information that will be used to determine value. All in all, this type of analysis will increase an appraiser's understanding of this "unverifiable" data and allow the appraiser to begin to develop a much more supportable opinion on which to base an indication of value.

Quantitative Analysis

Once you have performed a qualitative analysis of a transaction set, and you are comfortable (ha ha!) with the remaining transactions, then it is time to figure out how to use the selected transactions to indicate values. There are important questions to answer, including the following:

1. Are multiples calculated from a transaction set meaningful?
2. Which multiple(s) should be used to indicate value?
3. What multiple should be applied to the subject company?

These three questions should come to mind when looking at any set of pricing multiples, but the final, and often confusing, question is how to go about answering the first three.

As indicated above, all of the databases offer some type of statistical toolbox to analyze transactions. The reason for this is that statistics is one of the few means that we have to glean information from a transaction data set. In the last chapter, I gave you a taste for statistics. I'm going to try again.

According to *Webster's*, statistics is defined as follows:

> *Statistics*, n. Facts or data of a numerical kind, assembled, classified and tabulated so as to present significant information about a given subject.[5]

Statistics provides us with an excellent set of tools to use to develop an opinion on how a market is pricing a certain type of business. If you are like me, the word *statistics* alone is enough to put you to sleep. Numbers and graphs and natural logarithms—it can be overwhelming. Like it or not, statistics provides an analytical toolbox that does what we need to do, which, as indicated in the transaction data described previously, is to pull significant information out of a data set.

It is easy enough to take an average of multiples and not think about it anymore, but that can get you into a lot of trouble. Years ago, many of us did just that. If we really got crazy, we would use a median instead. However, to properly apply these ideas and techniques, you must be somewhat comfortable with the theory. A course in statistics is beyond the scope of this book, but there are a few basic tools (believe me, no rocket science) that we need to address. Exhibit 7.11 lists and defines certain statistical tools that every appraiser should get to know and love, if they have not already done so.

Exhibit 7.11 reflects one grain of sand in the universe of statistical theory, but you do not need much more than this for what we are trying to accomplish here. Since we are attempting to figure out what multiple to use, the mean and the median reflect measures of central tendency. These are proxies for the most probable observation in a data set. If you have a set of multiples and you want to figure out what multiple to use, the mean or median approximates the most likely one. Whether you use a mean or median is based on professional judgment. Some prefer one to the other. Means can be skewed dramatically by outliers, whereas medians have less reliability as the size of a data set decreases. Like everything else, which one to use is based on the facts and circumstances of the assignment.

So which multiples do you use? Measures of dispersion and location both yield insight as to the spread of a data set. A very disperse data set is not as meaningful as one that is not. For example, think of two data sets of price-to-revenues multiples. The first one contains multiples of 0.3 and 0.7, and the second one contains

---

[5] *Webster's New World Dictionary of the American Language*, College Edition (New York: World Publishing Company, 1968), 1425.

EXHIBIT 7.11
Statistics—Terms and Definitions[1]

Measures of Central Tendency—The purpose of a measure of central tendency is to determine the "center" of a distribution of data values or possibly the "most typical" data value. Mean, median, and mode are measures of central tendency.

Mean (Arithmetic)—Calculated by adding together all the observations and dividing by the number of observations.

Median—The middle observation of a data set of ordered observations if the number of observations is odd; the average of the middle pair if the number of observations is even.

Mode—The number that appears most often within the data set. This is probably the least useful to the appraiser.

Measures of Dispersion—The purpose of measures of dispersion is to develop an understanding of the dispersion, or spread, of a data set.

Dispersion—The degree to which numerical data tend to spread around an average value.[2]

Variance—The variance is equal to the sum of the squared deviations between each observation and the mean value.

Standard Deviation—The square root of the variance.

Coefficient of Variation—1. The ratio of the standard deviation to the mean. 2. The measure of relative dispersion[3] (observations relative to the mean).

Measures of Relative Position—These describe the relative position of an observation in a data set.

Percentiles (Decile and Quartile)—1. Give valuable information about the rank of an observation. 2. If a set of data is arranged in order of magnitude, the middle value that divides the data set into two equal parts is the median. By extending this idea we can think of those values that divide the data set into four equal parts (quartiles). . . . Similarly the values that divide the data into ten equal parts are called deciles.[4]

Author's note: I am going to spare you from the formulas because they get really ugly! Most of this stuff can be calculated in Excel or a similar spreadsheet program. Learn how to use it—or at least make sure one of your staff knows how to use it. You just need to understand what it means.

[1]Cheng F. Lee, *Statistics for Business and Financial Economics* (Lexington, Mass.: D.C. Heath and Company, 1993), 92–106.

[2]Murray R. Spiegel, *Schaum's Outline Series, Statistics* (New York: McGraw-Hill, 1961), 69.

[3]Ibid., 73.

[4]Ibid., 49.

multiples of 0.4 and 0.5. Which set would you feel more comfortable with in a valuation assignment? Of course, none of us would rely heavily on a multiple with only two observations, but obviously, the second data set appears to be more meaningful since we have no further information. The second data set has the lower dispersion of the two and, all other things being equal, is more meaningful.

Measures of location can give us an idea of where transactions fit into a data set. The most common example of this is class rank. Were you in the top 10 percent of your class? Thinking along these lines, we can numerically stratify a data set. Using such information can allow an analyst to determine the position of a multiple.

Another very valuable tool is linear reg ression. Linear regression is used to determine the relationship between two variables. A common example that we see is the relationship between the weight and height of human beings. As people get taller, they tend to weigh more (I must be eight feet tall). We can use this same logic to help us in our attempt to value businesses. As revenues increase, similar businesses tend to sell for higher prices. Can you say that for your data set? Maybe, maybe not. There is a simple way to figure this out and that is to perform a regression analysis. An example of a linear regression of price to revenues is shown in Exhibit 7.12.

If you are like me, when you look at Exhibit 7.12 all you see is a big group of dots. However, each dot reflects the intersection of a price and revenues for a single transaction from one of the databases. The line

EXHIBIT 7.12
Linear Regression

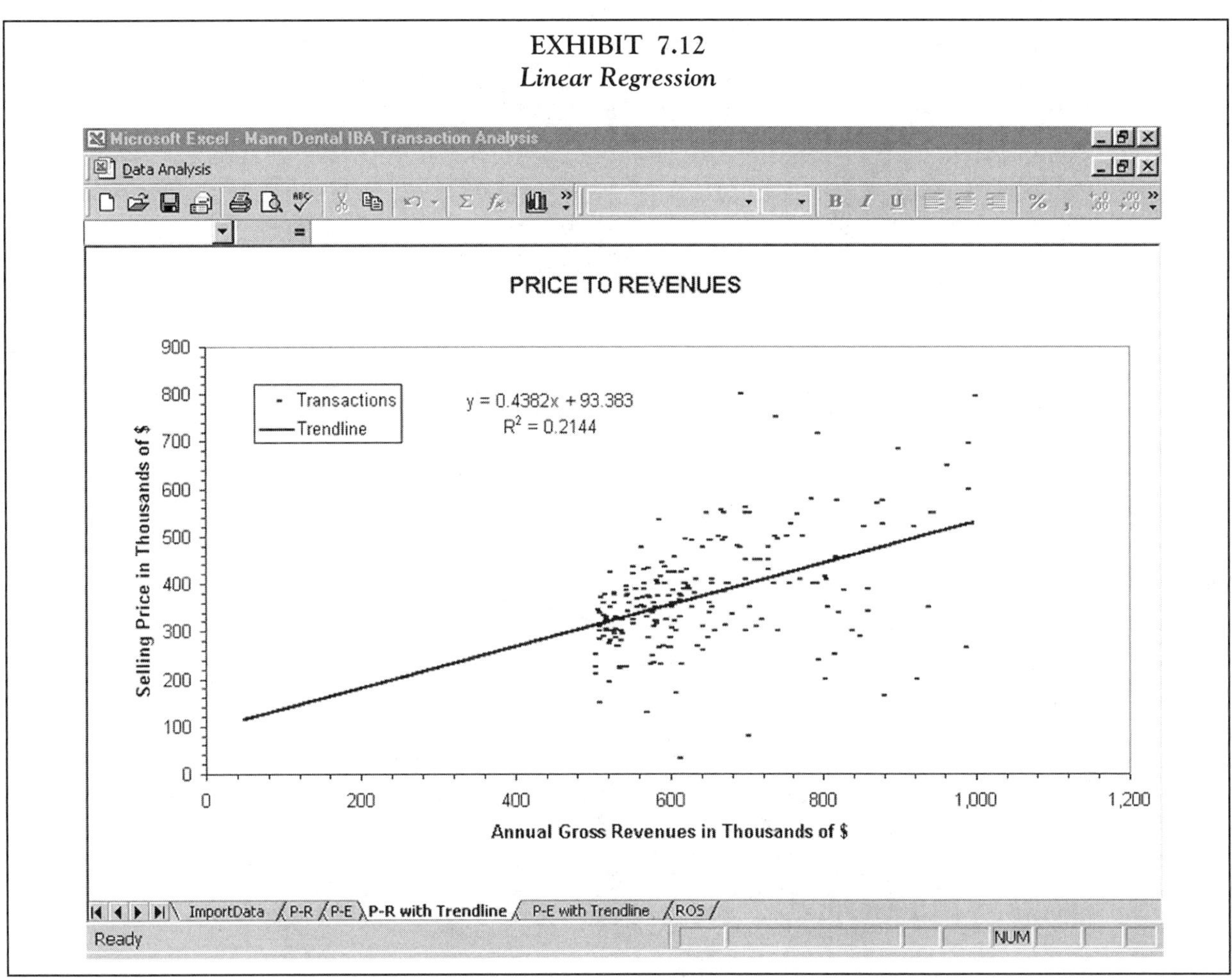

going through the dots is an illustration of a regression line through the data. The line is estimated using *least squares* regression. Remember back in Exhibit 7.11, when we discussed variation and standard deviation? Well, this is where it comes into play. The equation on the line is calculated by minimizing the distance (dispersion) between each data point and the line. When it is properly applied, it reflects the linear relationship between the observations. This equation is shown in Exhibit 7.12. Notice that next to the equation for this line is a value titled R^2. R^2 indicates the fit of the line. Remember from Chapter 6, an R^2 of 1.0 indicates that the line goes right through all data points (perfect correlation), whereas an R^2 of less than 0.5 indicates that there is not much of a relationship between the line and the plotted transaction multiples. In this case, the R^2 equals 0.21, which indicates that there is not much of a relationship between the data points. Exhibit 7.13 illustrates a regression with a stronger relationship.

As seen in Exhibit 7.13, the R^2 value is 0.66, indicating a much stronger relationship between price and revenues for the second data set. Just looking at the data points in the data set can give you an appreciation for the lower spread in the transactions. If you had to choose an average price-to-revenues multiple from these two data sets, which one would you choose? All other things being equal, I would feel better about using a multiple based on the data in Exhibit 7.13 over that in Exhibit 7.12. The stronger relationship between price and revenues in Exhibit 7.13 indicates that this multiple is more meaningful. Just keep in mind that with all of this statistics stuff, you cannot rely on one set of relationships alone. Although there is a correlation between the price and revenues, you need to consider all of the other factors that might make the subject company stronger or weaker than the average group of companies assumed to be part of this data.

EXHIBIT 7.13
Linear Regression (Better Relationship)

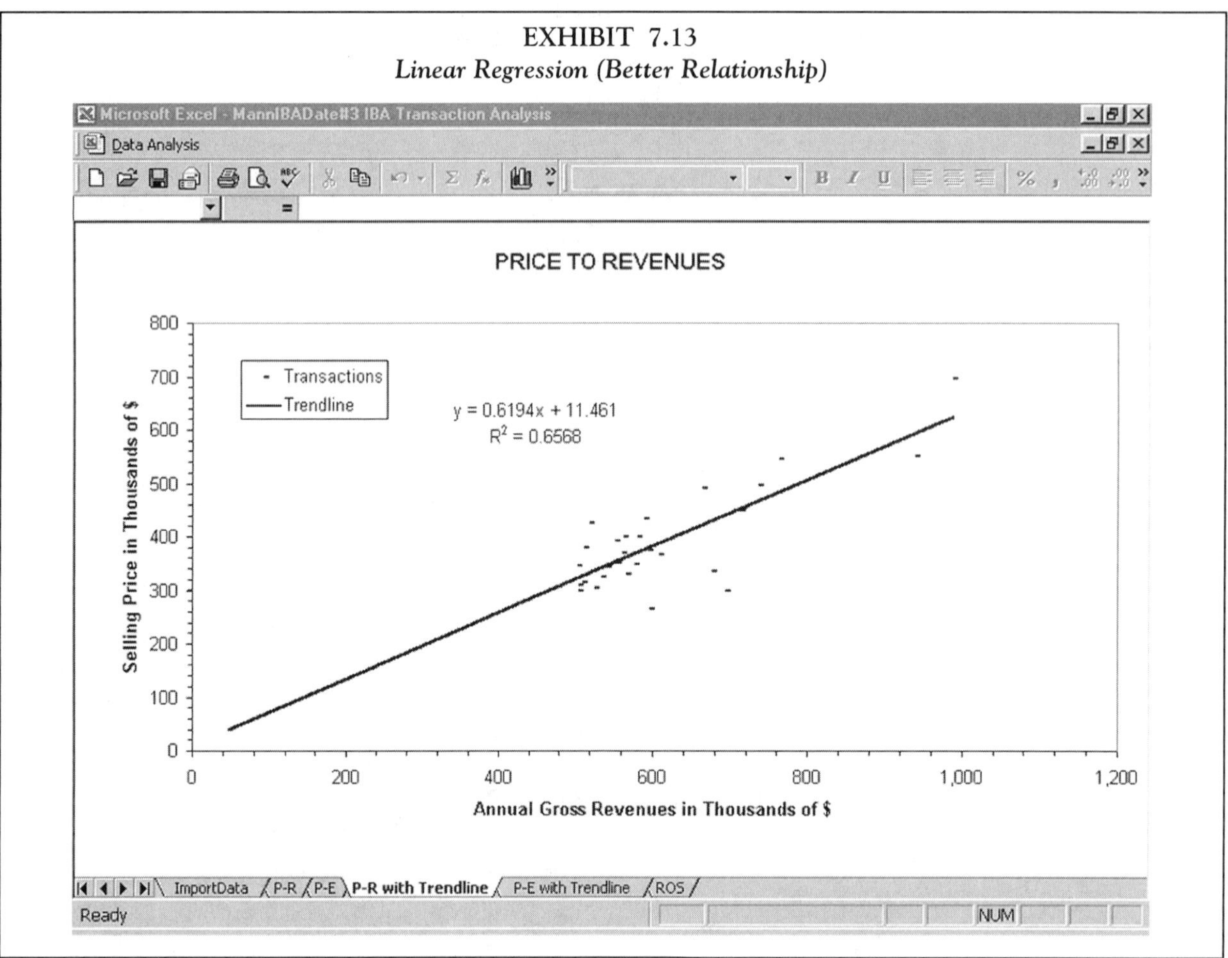

Another tool touched upon in Exhibit 7.11 is measures of relative position. We also use these to get an idea of how the data is spread. Exhibit 7.14 reflects a price-to-earnings chart, but this time the lines on the chart reflect measures of relative position.

The transactions are marked with dots in Exhibit 7.14. The lines reflect the lowest decile, the lowest quartile, the median, the upper quartile, and the highest decile. As you can see, the data points are well spread around the median. One of the questions that I posed previously was whether to use the mean or the median. A simple way to decide this is to construct a plot, like this one, with a median line and an average line. Look at the data and determine for yourself which one best represents the data set. Charts like these are included in our workpapers and are often incorporated into our reports to illustrate these relationships. Pictures are worth a thousand words; save a tree.

As I said before, all of the databases have some sort of statistical toolbox, so get comfortable with the different databases. If you are a part-time appraiser, these may be your best bet. For those of you who do this full time, it may be worthwhile to construct your own spreadsheet templates that can automate this process. As mentioned, the IBA has an analyzer available on its Web site. We have developed one that can import data from any of the databases listed above and generate statistical reports on the imported data. We have more freedom to analyze all of the data we want and are more comfortable performing all of our own multiple calculations since we know what was programmed.

So how far do you take this analysis? I say all the way, but sometimes too much analysis is just that. We typically will chart price (equity and invested capital) versus all applicable earnings streams. This gives us an idea of which multiples to use. If we have a high R^2 value for revenues but a low one for earnings, we would tend to put more weight on the price-to-revenues multiple in our valuation.

EXHIBIT 7.14
Measures of Relative Position

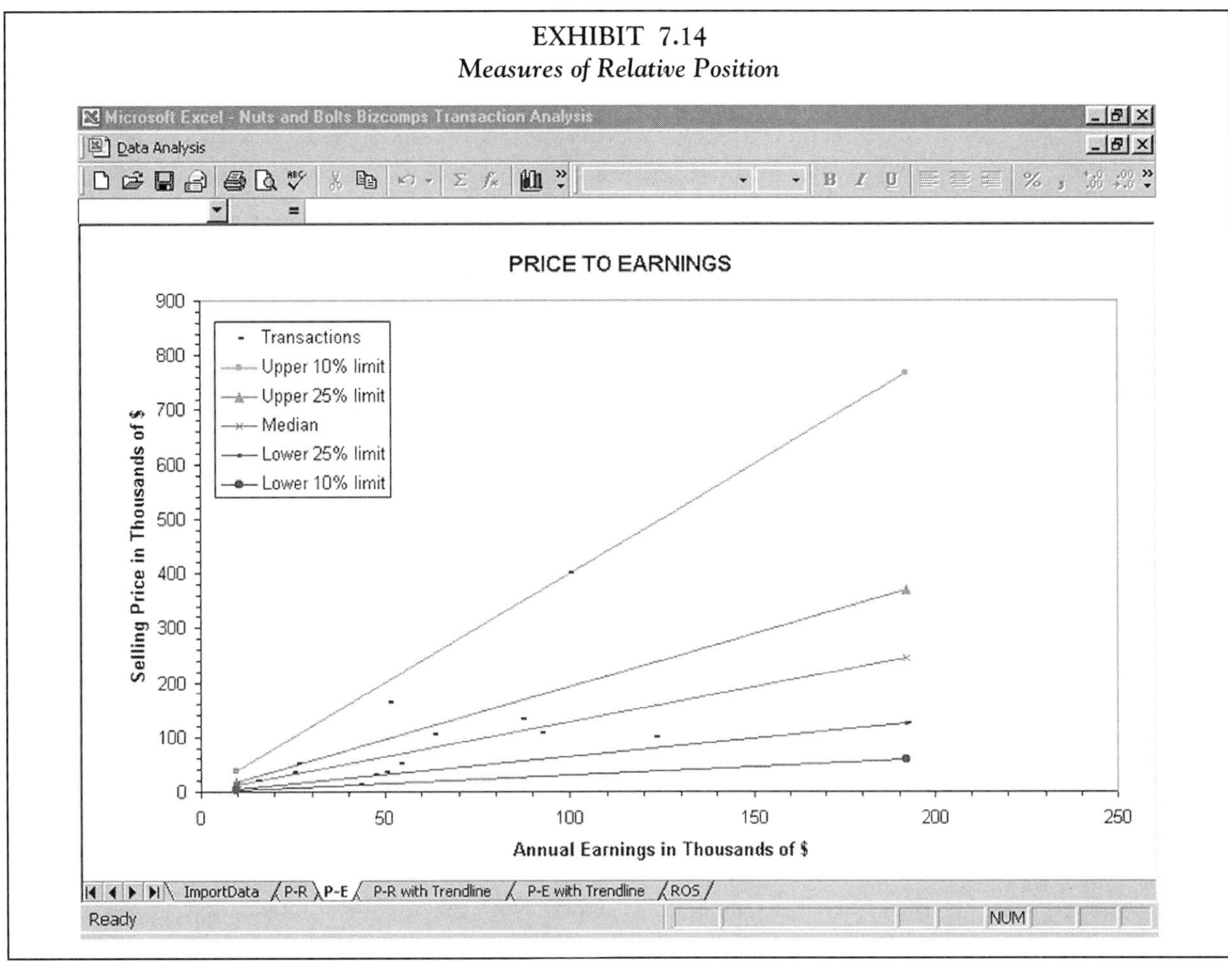

One thing that we always try to keep in focus is that businesses often sell based on operating performance (profitability). Revenues, assets, and book value do not reflect a level of operating performance, so in addition to our price charts, we plot price to revenues and asset and equity multiples with their corresponding returns (return on revenues, etc.). One such chart is shown in Exhibit 7.15.

In my experience, these charts tend to be more meaningful for larger companies. Small companies are often bought based on sales, regardless of profitability. People buy jobs. Some of us also believe in the *bigger fool theory*. Some bigger fool will come along and overpay for a business, thinking that he or she will do a better job of running the business than the seller. Sometimes the bigger fool can even be a large company. Think about when Quaker Oats bought Snapple. Who was the bigger fool?

We have built these types of charts into our statistical analysis templates, so they come up automatically. Once you have constructed such spreadsheets, it does not take any additional time to perform these statistical exercises, as the calculations are done automatically as you add new data.

The charts give us a feeling of which multiples are similar, but how do you choose a single multiple to apply to an earnings stream? One intuitive comment is, "If you have a regression through a good data set with high correlation, then use the equation of the line to estimate price." This seems very logical, and sometimes it may be the best way, but think about what you are doing. A chart reflects how price varies with one variable. Thinking back to the SGLPTL analysis in Chapter 6, there are many factors that affect the value of a business. For example, let's suppose that there is a high correlation between price and revenues in the selected data set. Now, consider that the subject company has very high debt and is having problems meeting its obligations. Can you simply apply a revenues multiple to it? You must consider other

EXHIBIT 7.15
Price to Revenues to Return on Sales

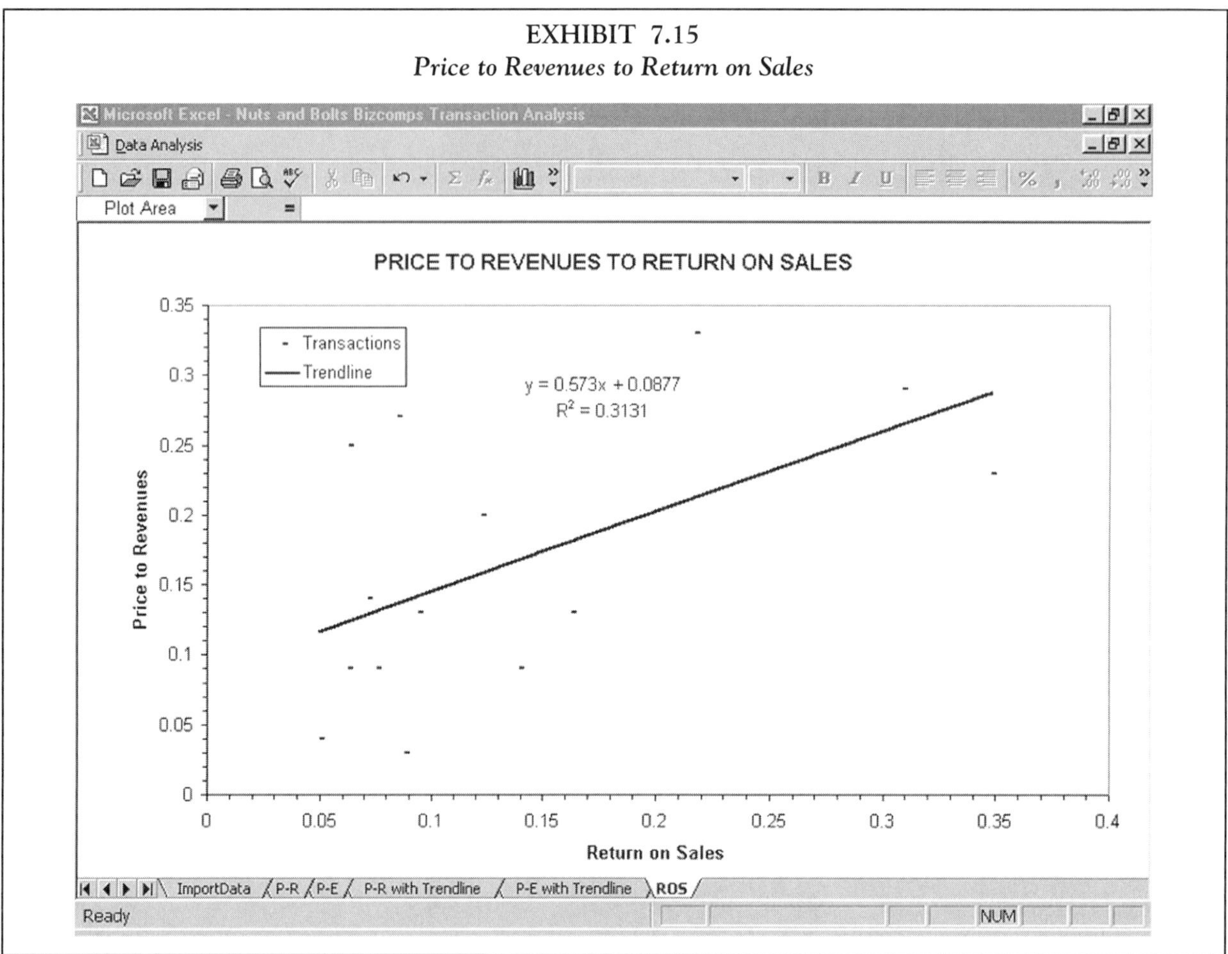

pertinent factors, including the SGLPTL factors when performing a transaction method. In the case of IBA or BizComps, you will not get enough information to do much analysis, but you do have price-to-revenues information. BizComps has a little more information, but when you get to Pratt's Stats you have a lot of financial information. There is no reason not to perform SGLPTL analysis for data derived from the larger databases.

In addition to the charts, we calculate means, medians, standard deviations, and percentiles on the price to multiple data sets. This gives us a basis on which to estimate an applicable multiple. We base our analysis on all information available for the subject company, as well as that available for the transactions. Weighing the strengths and weakness of each transaction and the guideline transactions can prove an invaluable tool for developing a meaningful and supportable analysis. Exhibit 7.16 reflects an analysis of Pratt's Stats transactions for an automobile dealership.

EXHIBIT 7.16
Pratt's Stats Analysis

We searched the Pratt's Stats database for all transactions of businesses in SIC code 5511 with annual sales less than 20 times the subject company's latest-12-months (LTM) sales. We then separated the transactions by type, stock or asset sale. In a stock transaction, the operating assets and liabilities are transferred to the new owner. In an asset transaction, only certain assets are transferred, and therefore, to establish the value of the equity, an additional adjustment is required for those assets and liabilities not included in the transaction. The two transaction types result in very different multiples. Therefore, they were analyzed separately. The resultant transactions from this database are shown in Tables 1 and 2.

EXHIBIT 7.16 (Continued)

TABLE 1
Pratt's Stats™ Asset Transactions

Business Name	Business Type	Sale Date	Selling Price	Revenues	EBT	Net Income	Total Assets	Equity Price to: Sales	Equity Price to: Earnings Before Taxes	Equity Price to: Net Income	Equity Price to: Total Assets
Shannon Automotive Ltd.	Auto dealers	03/06/97	$ 8,400,000	$ 96,962,172	$ 3,122,682	$ 3,122,682	$13,333,038	$0.09	2.69	2.69	0.63
Clearwater Dealership	Automobile dealer	03/24/98	15,000,000	121,899,000	2,191,000	2,191,000	22,265,000	0.12	6.85	6.85	0.67
Hatfield Automotive Group	Automobile dealer	06/09/98	48,600,000	275,280,000	(24,000)	(24,000)	61,335,000	0.18	(2,025.00)	(2,025.00)	0.79
Bowers Dealerships	Owns and operates auto dealerships	10/01/97	33,500,000	127,115,799	830,658	769,808	63,006,557	0.26	40.33	43.52	0.53
De la Cruz Auto Group	Owns and operates four franchised auto dealerships	07/01/97	40,000,000	191,858,273	3,232,713	3,232,713	55,970,375	0.21	12.37	12.37	0.71
Pierce Automotive Group	Retail and commercial sale of new and used autos	06/01/97	48,000,000	138,636,000	6,322,000	6,322,000	24,953,000	0.35	7.59	7.59	1.92
	Retail automobile dealership, Chevrolet and Pontiac	01/15/98	1,114,506	4,024,311	(33,886)	(33,886)	789,271	0.28	(32.89)	(32.89)	1.41
						Mean		0.22	(97.38)	(96.72)	0.91
						90th percentile		0.28	39.61	40.54	1.45
						75th percentile		0.24	16.54	16.54	1.07
						Median		0.19	8.23	10.24	0.76
						25th percentile		0.16	0.99	0.99	0.63
						10th percentile		0.12	(55.07)	(55.07)	0.61

Some data intentionally left out of this exhibit.

Source: Pratt's Stats™ (Portland, OR: Business Valuation Resources, LLC). Reprinted with permission.

(Continued)

EXHIBIT 7.16 (Continued)

TABLE 2
Pratt's Stats™ Stock Purchases

Business Name	Business Type	Sale Date	Selling Price	Revenues	EBT	Net Income	Total Assets	Equity Price to: Sales	Equity Price to: Earnings Before Taxes	Equity Price to: Net Income	Equity Price to: Total Assets
B & B Enterprises Inc.	Auto dealer, retail	08/29/97	$ 2,977,549	$ 24,473,010	$ (1,331,200)	$ (1,331,200)	$ 2,878,465	0.12	(2.24)	(2.24)	1.03
Young Automotive Group	Operates 18 automobile franchises	02/06/98	68,600,000	410,298,000	11,933,000	11,933,000	84,307,000	0.17	5.75	5.75	0.81
Gene Reed Automotive Group	Auto dealers	05/31/97	34,000,000	138,040,000	4,731,000	4,731,000	27,310,000	0.25	7.19	7.19	1.24
Grubb Automotive	Owns and operates five franchised auto dealerships	01/01/97	100,000,000	397,810,000	3,259,000	3,259,000	72,338,000	0.25	30.68	30.68	1.38
Ken Marks Ford, Inc.	New and used automobile dealership	07/01/97	25,500,000	144,467,067	766,327	465,597	17,012,813	0.18	33.28	54.77	1.50
Bledsoe Dodge, Inc.	Owns and operates three franchised automobile dealerships	05/31/97	42,000,000	154,046,407	4,415,225	4,216,940	28,016,445	0.27	9.51	9.96	1.50
						Mean		0.21	12.66	14.04	1.08
						90th percentile		0.27	30.94	31.24	1.52
						75th percentile		0.25	14.18	14.31	1.28
						Median		0.19	9.84	10.24	1.05
						25th percentile		0.16	5.73	5.73	0.85
						10th percentile		0.14	4.91	4.91	0.64

Some data intentionally left out of this exhibit.

Source: Pratt's Stats™ (Portland, OR: Business Valuation Resources, LLC). Reprinted with permission.

EXHIBIT 7.16 ***(Continued)***

We performed a regression analysis on these transactions in an attempt to better understand these multiples. We found that price-to-revenues and price–to–total asset multiples had strong relationships, whereas there was little relationship between the profitability multiples. Due to the statistical relationship between these multiples, we chose the median as best representing the data set.

Pratt's Stats Asset Transactions

Two different multiples were used from this database. The control, nonmarketable values have been estimated as follows:

	Revenues	*Total Assets*
Base	$ 20,571,235	$ 2,984,772
Multiple	× 0.19	× 0.76
Indication of value	$ 3,908,535	$ 2,268,427
Net retained assets	392,167	392,167
Value of equity	$ 4,300,702	$ 2,660,594

In an asset transaction, a seller retains certain assets and liabilities. In this case, a seller would retain cash, accounts receivable, and marketable securities, as well as all liabilities except for floor plan financing. The floor plan financing is associated with the inventory, and therefore, would most likely accompany the inventory to the purchaser. Net retained assets would be calculated as follows:

Cash	$ 749,505
Marketable securities	6,286
Accounts receivable	520,976
Total liabilities less floor plan	(884,600)
	$ 392,167

Pratt's Stats Stock Transactions

The transaction data from the stock transactions resulted in the following estimates of control, nonmarketable values.

	Revenues	*Total Assets*
Base	$ 20,571,235	$ 2,984,772
Multiple	× 0.19	× 1.05
Indication of value	$ 3,908,535	$ 3,134,011

Let's Get Back to Theory

As with any valuation methodology, the transaction method has both advantages and disadvantages. Let's discuss them in case you have not figured them out yet for yourself.

Advantages of Using Transaction Data Methods

Acquisition methods are those that value a company based on transactions involving a large portion of the company or its entirety. The most readily determinable advantage of using this methodology is that the appraiser is able to estimate the value of the appraisal subject based on the prices of entire companies that changed hands. Since most closely held transactions involve entire companies, this method is a logical application of the market approach.

The acquisition transactions used in this method are considered to be an objective source of information, since they come from the market. Market transactions are assumed to be between informed buyers and sellers, and therefore, a good representation of fair market value occurs if there are enough transactions to be statistically meaningful. The problem becomes how to determine the number of transactions required for them to be statistically valid. Who said it would be easy?

Disadvantages of Using Transaction Data Methods

Although the acquisition method is logical and inherently makes sense, it is difficult to find similar companies that have been acquired. It would be great if we had access to the same type of data that the real estate appraisers have, but unfortunately we do not. Although public company information is sometimes available, there are generally not enough of these transactions to help the appraiser adequately. For a meaningful analysis to be performed, there have to be enough transactions to enable you to reach a conclusion (if you just asked yourself how many is enough, you are getting the hang of this stuff!).

An experienced appraiser recognizes that appraisers do not work in a perfect world and, frequently, are forced to use less than perfect information. Although a greater amount of detail is generally available about public companies that are acquired, there are frequently times when an appraiser turns to closely held data. Private company transactions are difficult to locate, particularly since the owners of these businesses do not feel that they are anyone's business, and if a transaction is located, the details of the transaction are rarely available. For the deal to be consummated, the terms of the deal are frequently an important part of small company transactions. Hearing about two businesses that sold for $200,000 could lead you to believe that they were of similar value if you did not know the terms of the transaction. If one sold for all cash and the other sold for $20,000 down, with the balance due over 10 years with no interest, the value of these two transactions would be very different. This is because of the time value of money.

Another problem with this method is that once the transaction is located, it is generally difficult to find out anything other than the financial terms of the transaction. Of considerable importance would be whether the transaction was an asset or a stock sale. Acquisitions frequently involve specific buyers who pay a premium for special or unique considerations, such as the synergies between the two companies. This also makes it difficult to know if the price paid for the business truly represents the value of the business.

Another disadvantage of this method is that since the values derived under these methods result in a control value, it is difficult to translate the estimated value into a minority interest value. If the appraisal subject is a minority interest in a closely held business, the results of acquisition methods will have to be discounted for the minority interest. The problems with these discounts will be discussed later.

Words of Advice (I would call this words of wisdom, but you know better)

Before we conclude our discussion of the transaction method, I need to give you a few words of caution. First and foremost, know as much about the provided information as possible. If you are working in a litigation environment, you can expect that the other side will do their homework. Know how each data point is defined so that you can properly apply multiples to your subject company.

Second, you may not want to mix and match data from different databases. Even though you know how information is defined, it may not be input under the same assumptions or using the same conventions. I am not telling you not to do this—that is your judgment—but you must weigh the facts and consider the quality of the value that you calculate.

Third, beware of duplicates. Duplicate transactions appear in some of these databases. If it looks like a flower and smells like a flower, it's probably a flower. Duplicates will mess up any statistical analysis.

And finally, combine suggestions 2 and 3. If you bite the bullet and decide to combine databases, be very, very careful of duplicates. The databases get their data from business brokers, who may submit the same data to more than one database. It's not uncommon to find very similar deals in the above-referenced databases, so carefully review transaction data.

Internal Transactions

Another variation of the market approach comes from Revenue Ruling 59-60. This ruling suggests that the appraiser consider any sales of the company's own stock. These internal transactions may provide the appraiser with useful information for use in the market approach. If internal transactions are located, the next step will be to determine whether these transactions were consummated at arm's length.

Internal transactions are very useful if the appraiser has many transactions, rather than just a few. Professional practices, where partners come and go on a regular basis, may be a good example of when to use this data. In these instances, partnership agreements often are used as a road map as to how partners come and go. This concept is discussed further and illustrated in Chapter 16.

Industry Method

Sometimes called "rules of thumb," the industry method can prove to be a valuable tool but should never be relied on by itself for the valuation of an appraisal subject. Industry methods are an important part of the valuation process. If an industry uses a particular method to determine the value of a business, the appraiser should pay close attention to that method. If enough transactions take place using a particular method, the end result is that there is market data that will support the use of that method. However, if these formulas are the only methods used, an inappropriate valuation may result.

Sources of rules of thumb include published compilations, industry sources, business brokers, trade associations, and industry members. The advantage of industry methods is that they generally provide a sanity check on other valuation methods. The disadvantages of industry methods are as follows:

- Different sources may provide different rules of thumb for the same industry.
- The application of an uninformed rule of thumb may result in an incorrect estimate of value.
- While they are simplistic in their applications, rules of thumb may ignore the economic reality of the situation.
- Information (profit margins, capital structure, etc.) about the companies that made up the rules of thumb transactions is not known.

Rules of thumb are sometimes used in the application of the market approach, but care must be exercised by the appraiser. Rules of thumb *should not be used alone* since appraisers frequently lack the information required to adjust the rule of thumb for particular questions, such as the following:

- Was the transaction based on an asset or equity purchase?
- Did the buyer pay cash, or were there terms that would affect the purchase price?
- Was there a continuation of employment by the seller or a covenant not to compete?
- Was the business profitable?

Clearly, if used incorrectly, a rule of thumb can be dangerous. However, it serves a useful purpose in some smaller appraisals when all else fails. Just be careful! In Exhibit 7.17, the potential uses and dangers of rules of thumbs are discussed. This exhibit is based on excerpts from actual reports.

EXHIBIT 7.17
Rules of Thumb

A very popular but often abused method of valuation for professional practices is the multiple-of-revenue method. This method is also referred to as the "industry rule of thumb" method. There are many disadvantages to this method. The major disadvantage is the number of different multiples that are used for the same type of practice. A classic example of the danger in applying this method is the rule of thumb for an accounting practice. Over the years, accounting practices are said to have been sold for an amount that ranges between 50 percent and 150 percent of gross billings. This means that an accounting practice with gross billings of $1 million could be valued anywhere from $500,000 to $1.5 million. This is clearly too wide a spread to be meaningful. Disparities such as this take place all of the time and must be considered before applying *unsupported* rules of thumb.

The major advantage of this method is that it is easily understood by all parties: buyer, seller, financier, and appraiser. According to Ronald Klein, CPA, "a particular multiplier may, in fact, be self-serving, used because it is so widely quoted." In New Jersey, the multiplier of 3 became popular because of its application in *Dugan v. Dugan*. Since 1983, this multiplier has been used over and over again, regardless of the facts and circumstances of the current appraisal subject.

Some appraisers have extended the use of *Dugan* and have applied the *Dugan* multiplier to different types of professional practices. Mr. Dugan was an attorney. Even an appraisal of another law practice may not result in an appropriate multiple of 3. Qualitative factors (such as the type of practice, the type of clients, and profitability) must be considered in the development of an appropriate multiplier.

Looking for rules of thumb for our valuation subject (a dental practice), we found several methods. In *Valuing Professional Practices*, published by CCH International, James L. Horvath, CA, CBV, ASA, suggests two different methods: (1) fair market value of furniture, fixtures, and equipment plus 20 to 60 percent of annual revenues; and (2) net asset value plus one year's pretax earnings before owner's compensation. Using method 1 results in a range of values from $307,655 to $802,615, whereas method 2 yields a value of $730,489.

The 1993 Business Brokers Reference Guide, published by Business Brokerage Press, lists four different methods. These methods, with their calculated range of values, are as follows:

1. 1 to 1.5 times annual adjusted earnings plus fixtures, equipment, and inventory: $212,073 to $286,272
2. Net assets plus 25 to 30 percent of gross annual revenues: $567,935 to $629,805
3. 20 to 60 percent of annual fee revenues plus fixtures, equipment, and inventory: $311,155 to $806,115
4. One year's pretax earnings before owners' salary, plus fixtures, equipment, and inventory: $535,579

In *Handbook of Small Business Valuation Formulas and Rules of Thumb*, published by Valuation Press, Glenn M. Desmond, ASA, MAI, suggests two additional methods: (1) monthly revenues times 8 to 12, plus net asset value, less fixed assets, which yields values of $1,023,343 to $1,435,810; and (2) monthly revenues times 2.5 to 5, plus net asset value, yielding a range of $516,377 to $774,168.

Finally, in *Valuing Small Businesses and Professional Practices*, Shannon P. Pratt mentions two additional methods: (1) equipment and fixtures plus 25 to 35 percent of revenue, resulting in a range of $369,525 to $493,263; or (2) equipment and fixtures plus 50 to 100 percent of earnings available to the doctor, yielding values of $29,127 to $532,079.

Although some of the methods discussed previously are similar, there are 10 different methods that yield values for the practice ranging from $212,000 to $1.4 million.

Conclusion

By now, either you should be very excited and ready to forge ahead, or you may be suffering from an anxiety attack. The market approach chapters contained a lot of stuff. We discussed methodologies, the selection of multiples, the assessment of risk, and the advantages and disadvantages of these methods. We even discussed statistics. Wow, if my mother could see me now! I hope you realize that the market approach can be applied to small and medium-sized companies. Sometimes it may be difficult to apply, but that does not excuse you from using it.

8

The Asset-Based Approach

Chapter Goals

In this chapter, I will attempt to explain the following:

1. When to use the asset-based approach
2. The advantages and disadvantages of the asset-based approach
3. The adjusted book value method
4. How to communicate with other appraisers
5. How to find other appraisers
6. The liquidation value method
7. The cost to create method

Introduction

The asset-based approach is also commonly known as the "cost approach" or the "replacement-cost approach." Sometimes you may even see this approach called the "asset accumulation approach." In this approach, each component of the business is valued separately. This also includes liabilities. The asset values are totaled, and the total of the liabilities is subtracted to derive the total value of the enterprise.

The appraiser estimates value by adjusting the asset values of the individual assets and liabilities of the business to fair market value. Some appraisers will use this approach for the tangible assets only and consider it to be complete. In fact, I used to do this. However, as we get older, we get wiser. This approach, like the market and income approaches, is intended to value the entire company. This means that the tangible assets, as well as the intangible assets, should be valued and the liabilities subtracted. You may have to use other approaches to value the intangible assets, but I will discuss that later. If you value only the tangible assets and liabilities, this approach is generally considered to be a "floor" value for an enterprise being valued as a going concern.

Common Applications of the Asset-Based Approach

The asset-based approach is most commonly applied to the following types of business valuations:

- Not-for-profit organizations
- Holding companies

- Manufacturing companies
- Asset-intensive companies
- Controlling interests that have the ability to liquidate assets

In all of these instances, the valuation subject will have most, if not all, of its value in its tangible assets or identifiable intangible assets, such as copyrights, patents, or trademarks. Intangible assets, such as goodwill, will not play an important role in the value of the enterprise. If goodwill or another type of intangible value exists, it will be added to the value.

This approach is generally not used for the following types of business valuation assignments:

- Service businesses
- Asset-light businesses
- Operating companies with intangible value
- Minority interests, which have no control over the sale of the assets

Service businesses and asset-light businesses generally get the bulk of their value from intangible assets. Therefore, it seems logical that the asset-based approach would not be an effective means of valuing these types of entities. Operating companies are generally valued based on the ability of the company to generate earnings and cash flow and, therefore, rely on a market or income approach for the determination of their value. If you recall, Revenue Ruling 59-60 indicates the following in Section 5:

> *Weight to Be Accorded Various Factors.* The valuation of closely held corporate stock entails the consideration of all relevant factors as stated in section 4. Depending upon the circumstances in each case, certain factors may carry more weight than others because of the nature of the company's business. To illustrate:
>
> (a) Earnings may be the most important criterion of value in some cases whereas asset value will receive primary consideration in others. In general, the appraiser will accord primary consideration to earnings when valuing stocks of companies which sell products or services to the public; conversely, in the investment or holding type of company, the appraiser may accord the greatest weight to the assets underlying the security to be valued.
>
> (b) The value of the stock of a closely held investment or real estate holding company, whether or not family owned, is closely related to the value of the assets underlying the stock. For companies of this type the appraiser should determine the fair market values of the assets of the company. Operating expenses of such a company and the cost of liquidating it, if any, merit consideration when appraising the relative values of the stock and the underlying assets. The market values of the underlying assets give due weight to potential earnings and dividends of the particular items of property underlying the stock, capitalized at rates deemed proper by the investing public at the date of appraisal. A current appraisal by the investing public should be superior to the retrospective opinion of an individual. For these reasons, adjusted net worth should be accorded greater weight in valuing the stock of a closely held investment or real estate holding company, whether or not family owned, than any of the other customary yardsticks of appraisal, such as earnings and dividend paying capacity.

Minority interests will usually not be valued using an asset-based approach, since the minority shareholder does not have the ability to liquidate the assets. However, do not take this as a hard and fast rule. In Chapter 14, I discuss valuing limited partnership interests in family limited partnerships, which is similar in many respects to valuing minority interests. All of this stuff will be explained further in my discussion about adjusting the balance sheet and in the later chapter. Meanwhile, as a general rule, if the shareholder cannot get to the cash flow that will be generated by selling off the assets, this approach will not get to the value of the cash flow to the minority shareholder. After all, value is based on the future benefits stream that will flow to the investor.

Advantages and Disadvantages of the Asset-Based Approach

The asset-based approach has both advantages and disadvantages. Some of the advantages include the following:

- Net tangible assets can be valued more reliably under this approach than under the other two approaches.
- This approach creates a better reflection of the economic balance sheet of the appraisal subject.
- Net tangible assets can generally be seen and felt, giving the user of the appraisal a "warmer feeling" about the value.
- On a control basis, this approach generally provides a "floor" value for a business enterprise if only the tangible assets are appraised.

The disadvantages of using an asset-based approach include the following:

- This approach is most readily applicable only to tangible assets, liabilities, and identifiable intangible assets; therefore, it may not recognize the full earning power or cash-generating power of a total business enterprise.
- The asset-based approach provides the appraiser with the cost of duplicating the business being appraised, but it may not necessarily result in the most economically sound method of finding a substitute for the business.
- This approach is frequently more time consuming (and sometimes costly) to apply than the other approaches, particularly for smaller businesses for which market data about the assets and liabilities may not be readily available. In this case, an income approach can be used.

The asset values derived using this approach allow an appraiser to test the reasonableness of the concept of highest and best use when he or she compares the results with other methodologies in the income or market approach. If these other approaches yield a value considerably less than the value of the entity's assets, liquidation may be a viable alternative if the interest being appraised has the ability to effect a liquidation.

Valuation Methods

Included in the asset-based approach are the following valuation methods: (1) the adjusted book value method, (2) the liquidation value method, and (3) the cost to create method.

Adjusted Book Value Method

The adjusted book value method finds its theoretical basis in the principle of substitution, which was discussed in Chapter 3. In the adjusted book value method, all of the assets and liabilities (including all intangible assets) are adjusted to reflect their fair market value. The fair market value of the subject company's equity will be the fair market value of the assets less the fair market value of the liabilities.

The adjusted book value method is primarily used in the appraisal of asset-intensive businesses in the valuation of a controlling interest. Just as a reminder, a control valuation is one in which the owner of the interest being appraised has the ability to throw his or her weight around. This is to be distinguished from a minority interest valuation.

The mechanics of the adjusted book value method are to convert the book value of the assets and liabilities shown or not shown on the appraisal subject's balance sheet to a market-oriented basis. This will generally involve adjusting the appraisal subject's balance sheet to fair market value. Certain values are easily ascertained by the business appraiser, but others are not. There will be times when the business appraiser will look to other appraisers (such as real estate or machinery and equipment) to provide the values of certain assets.

Adjusting the Balance Sheet. The adjustments made to the balance sheet will depend on the purpose and function of the appraisal assignment. If the assignment is to value the equity of the company, every asset and liability should be reviewed for possible adjustment to fair market value. If specific assets, liabilities, or both are the subject of the valuation, only those assets or liabilities should be valued.

Balance sheet adjustments should generally be made only if the interest being valued has the ability to liquidate the assets and liabilities of the company. If a minority interest does not have the ability to sell off the assets to realize the fair market value of these assets, it makes little sense to revalue them in a fair market value appraisal. Sometimes, appraisers will adjust the values to fair market value and then apply a discount for lack of control. I find this to be a time-consuming and costly exercise. However, if fair value is the definition of value being used, the minority shareholder is sometimes put in a position to receive the benefit of the appreciated net assets of the company.

In the *U.S. News & World Report* case,[1] this point was a much-disputed part of the litigation. Retiring employee-shareholders were being bought out based on an annual appraisal performed by one of the large appraisal firms. The stock was being valued on a minority, nonmarketable basis (as if closely held). The company had amassed a large portfolio of highly appreciated real estate that was not valued at fair market value, since the assignment called for a minority valuation. A short while after a buyout of some employee-shareholders, the company was sold for a considerably larger amount than the appraised value. Disgruntled former employees sued the appraisal firm and the company, claiming that their shares had been undervalued at the time that they were bought out. The court found otherwise. In the opinion, Judge Barrington D. Parker stated:

> In a minority valuation . . . assets may or may not play an important part in arriving at a per-share figure, because a minority shareholder cannot reach those assets. . . . Generally speaking, if the valuation being undertaken is of a business, such as *U.S. News*, that produces goods or services, primary consideration will be given to the earnings of the company and the resultant return on a shareholder's investment.

This was a good opinion and can be used as instruction for all appraisers. Get a copy of this case! It is worth having in your library.

The balance sheet should be adjusted as follows:

- *Cash and equivalents*. Cash and equivalents usually require no adjustment. On occasion, excess cash may be considered non-operating and should be segregated from that which is used for working capital. This is done for analysis purposes only since it will not affect the value.
- *Marketable securities*. Marketable securities should be adjusted to their fair market value. Frequently, an average of the high and low prices on the valuation date will be used to accomplish this.
- *Accounts receivable*. Accounts receivable should be reviewed to see what is collectible. Older receivables may require a present-value adjustment. A comparison of the ratio of receivables to revenues with industry composite data should be made to determine if there are any significant differences.

[1]*Charles S. Foltz et al. v. U.S. News & World Report, Inc., et al.* and *David B. Richardson et al. v. U.S. News & World Report, Inc., et al.*, U.S. District Court, District of Columbia, Civil Actions Nos. 84-0447 and 85-2195 (June 22, 1987).

For cash-basis taxpayers, accounts receivable will generally have to be added to the balance sheet. Professional practices frequently have an additional subset of accounts receivable, namely, work in progress.

- *Inventory*. Inventory should be adjusted to reflect fair market value, which is generally the current cost to replace salable inventory. However, inventory valuations for income tax purposes must consider Revenue Procedure 77-12. An appraiser may want to consider the following procedures with respect to inventory:

    - Determine the method used to value the inventory carried on the books of the appraisal subject (FIFO, LIFO, etc.).
    - Determine if the inventory can be sold, and if it cannot, adjust the book value accordingly.
    - If the company uses the LIFO method, adjust the value to reflect the current cost to replace the inventory. Although LIFO provides better matching on the income statement, FIFO provides a better balance sheet valuation.
    - If the company does not maintain proper inventory records, consider if there are any necessary adjustments to management's estimate to compensate for possible errors in the valuation of the inventory. If the effective date of the valuation is relatively recent, suggest a physical inventory. A physical inventory that was taken long ago may prove to be meaningless (what's long ago?).

- *Prepaid expenses*. Prepaid expenses should be reviewed to determine whether the balance reflected on the balance sheet reflects fair market value. Prepaid insurance may be subject to short ratings by the insurance company and, as such, may be worth less than its face value. Many cash-basis professional practices write off insurance when it is paid, although it may have value on the balance sheet as a prepaid asset. This is particularly true with medical practices, for which the malpractice insurance premiums can be substantial.
- *Land*. Land should be appraised at fair market value and adjusted accordingly. This will generally require the services of a real estate appraiser.
- *Buildings*. Buildings should also be valued at fair market value, which is generally considered to be the estimated depreciated replacement cost, considering such factors as age and economic depreciation. The alternative is to value the property using an income or market approach. This will also generally require the services of a real estate appraiser.
- *Machinery and equipment*. Machinery and equipment should be adjusted to reflect their estimated fair market value in use. Assets owned by the business that are not being used can be valued as if those assets will be sold. We will discuss some definitions later in this chapter.

  A visit to the business premises will often disclose assets that may be fully depreciated, expensed, or both and that do not appear on fixed asset schedules. These assets may have significant value to the enterprise and must be considered in the valuation. The services of a machinery and equipment appraiser will frequently be required.
- *Leasehold improvements*. Leasehold improvements may have a fair market value greater than what is shown on the balance sheet, if the expected life of the improvements is greater than the term of the lease and if the probability of a renewal of the lease is high. In certain situations, the value of the leasehold improvements may be practically nil, particularly when these improvements will shortly revert to the property owner.
- *Leasehold interests*. Leasehold interests may have value to the lessee if the lease is transferable and the lease calls for favorable rental payments based on the current market conditions for that type of property.

The fair market value of the lease is usually determined as the discounted present value of the future benefits to the lessee. This is the difference between the market rent and the actual rent being paid. An unfavorable lease could be a liability for the company, and if it is not treated in that manner, it will affect profitability and make the company worth less.

- *Identifiable intangible assets*. Identifiable intangible assets may require the services of a specialist in the appraisal of a particular type of asset. Whether or not a specialist is employed, an estimate of the remaining useful economic life of the asset is essential. All three approaches to value may be used, depending on the type of asset being valued. A market approach may be difficult to apply in many cases due to the lack of information about comparable sales of similar intangible assets, but it should not be overlooked. It may be applicable for such assets as customer lists. A cost approach may be used for such assets as an assembled workforce, architectural drawings, or computer software, whereas an income approach may be appropriate for patents, copyrights, and trademarks.

  Since the first edition of this book, a terrific new book has been published on the subject of intangible assets. It is *Valuing Intangible Assets* by Robert Reilly and Robert Schweihs (Pratt's co-authors of *Valuing A Business*). This is an essential part of any valuation library. The authors did a great job. In fact, they did such a good job on issues about intangible assets (and a subset known as intellectual property) that I am not going to even try to cover this topic in this edition of my book. Get theirs! And no, I am not getting a commission!

- *Contracts*. Contracts that provide future income to the business, such as royalty agreements, often have a determinable value. Other types of contracts may require the business to actually make payments, but by the very nature of the contract (for example, a covenant not to compete), these contracts may also have value. However, there may also be the need to recognize a corresponding liability in some instances.

- *Accounts payable*. Accounts payable should be reviewed to determine if these items would actually be paid. If the payable has been on the company's books for a long time, the appraiser may want to discount the liability based on when it might actually be paid. Cash-basis taxpayers may need to have accounts payable added to the balance sheet, since this item is frequently omitted. This is similar to accounts receivable.

- *Notes payable*. Notes payable, particularly the current portion, should be reviewed to determine not only whether the liability is valid but also whether it is properly classified as short-term. The appraiser uses this information in the financial analysis portion of the assignment. Therefore, incorrect classification will result in the use of incorrect ratios when comparison is made with guideline company data or industry composite data.

  Working capital credit lines must be carefully analyzed to determine whether this form of debt is temporary or permanent in nature. A credit line that is used and paid down on a regular basis should be considered as short-term debt. However, some companies use the credit line as a form of permanent financing that keeps growing as the company grows, with no principal reductions taking place. This may be considered long-term financing or a form of invested capital.

  Long-term debt should be analyzed similarly to the current portion. All notes payable should be adjusted to fair market value if the interest rate does not reflect the market rate of interest.

- *Deferred taxes*. Deferred taxes can be valued by estimating their market value and adjusting the book value of the deferred taxes account to its market value. Deferred taxes caused by temporary timing differences are similar to zero percent government financing, and as such, they are essentially the same as an interest-free loan. The appraiser should calculate the present value using a discount rate based on the current market rate of interest. If the liability can be permanently deferred (this may be possible if the company is growing and the asset base grows while the tax rates do not change), the appraiser may be able to exclude this item from the economic balance sheet.

- *Stockholder loans.* Stockholder loans frequently show up on the company's books and records. More often than not, the subject company, particularly a smaller business, is undercapitalized and the "loans" are actually a form of paid-in capital. In these instances, the loans should not be considered a valid liability of the business but rather equity. In other situations, the stockholder loan shows up as a receivable because the stockholder is either disguising compensation in this manner or because the stockholder is using the company's checkbook as his or her personal checkbook. Since the likelihood of repayment is slim, the value of these loans would be zero. A legitimate stockholder loan should be treated as a bank loan and valued accordingly if it is in lieu of bank financing.

  The final acid test would be to determine if these loans would have to be repaid if the business were sold.

Tax-Effecting the Balance Sheet. Tax-effecting of the balance sheet adjustments will often depend on the purpose and function of the appraisal assignment. The Treasury Department indicated in Private Letter Ruling 91-50001 that capital gains taxes should not be considered when one determines fair market value if there is no plan of liquidation. However, in recent years, the Tax Court allowed built-in gains taxes to be considered as part of the discount for lack of marketability. I will discuss this in greater detail in Chapter 11.

Before the *Tax Reform Act of 1986*, a tax-free liquidation of a corporation could have been accomplished under the General Utilities Doctrine.[2] The former position of the Tax Court was that if there was no plan for liquidation, the taxpayer should not be allowed to value an asset as if it were going to be liquidated. However, as the tax law changed, the prevailing wisdom presented to the Tax Court by an IRS appraiser was that the willing buyer and the willing seller would consider taxes, even if there were no plan for liquidation. Quite frankly, a willing buyer is not going to pay the market value for an asset without considering the impact of a large built-in gains tax on the asset.

In the first edition of this book, I said that in my opinion, Private Letter Ruling 91-50001 was problematic. At that time, I said:

> It defies the concept of what a willing buyer would pay a willing seller if all of the facts are known. In some instances, the potential built-in gains tax could be so great that the purchaser would not purchase the corporate stock at all. The real estate would be sold as an asset sale, and the taxes would be paid at the corporate level. In the *Estate of William Luton*,[3] the Tax Court did not permit a discount for the costs in selling the stock in a real estate holding company, nor was the potential capital gains tax at the corporate level taken into account. The Internal Revenue Service has recently settled several cases that have allowed some discount for the built-in taxes.

Do not think that built-in gains taxes are an automatic deduction from the value of the assets. The case law has not always allowed a full deduction for the amount of taxes that would be paid by the purchaser of these assets. In fact, as you read the case law, the rationale in which the taxes were calculated is extremely unclear, since they were buried into the discount for lack of marketability. Exhibit 8.1 presents selected sections of a real valuation situation that we were involved in before the most recent cases allowing the discount. Exhibit 8.2 presents selected sections of a real valuation situation after the recent cases.

[2]See old IRC Sections 336 and 337, as amended by Section 631 of the *Tax Reform Act of 1986*.

[3]T.C. Memo. 1994-539, RIA T.C. Memo. 94539, 68 CCH T.C.M. 1044 (1994).

EXHIBIT 8.1
Real Estate Holding Company Valuation

Valuation Calculations

In this instance, there is only one valuation method that is appropriate. Section 5, paragraph b of Revenue Ruling 59-60 states the following:

> The value of the stock of a closely held investment or real estate holding company, whether or not family owned, is closely related to the value of the assets underlying the stock. For companies of this type the appraiser should determine the fair market values of the assets of the company. Operating expenses of such a company and the cost of liquidating it, if any, merit consideration when appraising relative values of the stock and the underlying assets. The market values of the underlying assets give due weight to potential earnings and dividends of the particular items of property underlying the stock, capitalized at rates deemed proper by the investing public at the date of appraisal. A current appraisal by the investing public should be superior to the retrospective opinion of an individual. For these reasons, adjusted net worth should be accorded greater weight in valuing the stock of a closely held investment or real estate holding company, whether or not family owned, than any of the other customary yardsticks of appraisal, such as earnings and dividend paying capacity.

Clearly, the value of the underlying assets must be considered. This is the analysis that follows.

Table 1 reflects the balance sheet of the corporation at December 31, 1993, per the corporate tax return. Certain adjustments have been made to reflect the fair market value (FMV) of the underlying assets.

TABLE 1
Balance Sheet Analysis

	Book Value (12/31/93)	*FMV Adjustments*	*Adjusted Book Value (12/31/93)*
Cash	$ 81,081	$ —	$ 81,081
Stockholder loan	184,783	—	184,783
Fixed assets	111,266	814,309	925,575
Net worth	$ 377,130	$ 814,309	$ 1,191,439

Fixed assets consist of the real estate and a 1990 Oldsmobile Cutlass Sierra automobile. The real estate was appraised for $920,000 by ABC Appraisal Company. The automobile is valued at $5,575 based on the *N.A.D.A. Used Car Guide*, January 1994 edition, published by the N.A.D.A. Used Car Guide Co. The adjustment brings these assets to fair market value.

Based on the above, the enterprise value of Smith Holding Co, Inc. as of December 31, 1993, is estimated to be $1,191,439 before applicable premiums or discounts.

Premiums and Discounts

Discount for Lack of Marketability/Discount from Net Asset Value

A discount for lack of marketability (DLOM) is used to compensate for the difficulty of selling shares of stock that are not traded on a stock exchange compared with those that are traded publicly. A DLOM may also be appropriate when the interests have either legal or contractual restrictions placed upon them (for example, restricted stock, buy-sell agreements, and bank loan restrictions). Even when a 100 percent interest of a subject is being valued, a DLOM may be appropriate if the owner cannot change the restrictions on the stock or readily liquidate the investment.

A control value may reflect a DLOM, although it probably would be smaller than a DLOM attributable to minority shares. Since a minority interest is more difficult to sell than a controlling interest, the DLOM is usually larger for minority interests.

Sources of data about the DLOM include the *SEC Institutional Investor Study* and studies by Maher, Moroney, Gelman, and others.

A "Real World" Consideration

Establishing the appropriate discount for a closely held business is a subjective process. There is no doubt that the size of the various discounts has been a constantly controversial topic in the courts.

However, it is difficult to ignore the real world. Discounts attributable to the lack of marketability, or the illiquidity of an investment, are a reality and must be considered. Many times, these discounts are taken from the net asset value and reflect not only a lack of marketability and the illiquidity of the investment, but also a profit factor for the purchaser, who looks for a reasonable rate of return to justify the investment.

EXHIBIT 8.1 *(Continued)*

In *IRS Valuation Guide for Income, Estate and Gift Taxes—Valuation Training for Appeals Officers*, published by Commerce Clearing House, Inc. (January 1994), the concept of "highest and best use" is discussed with respect to real estate. In the *Dictionary of Real Estate Appraisal*, highest and best use is defined as follows:

> The most important concept on which the final estimate of value is based is the "highest and best use" of the property being appraised. This may be defined as "the reasonably probable and legal use of vacant land or an improved property, which is physically possible, appropriately supported, financially feasible, and that results in the highest value."

The *IRS Valuation Guide* points out that the four criteria the highest and best use test must meet are: (1) legal permissibility, (2) physical possibility, (3) financial feasibility, and (4) maximum profitability. Also pointed out in the guide is that "the existing use may not be the highest and best use."

The principles of business valuation come from the real estate world. We consider similar concepts but apply them differently because of the differences in the appraisal subjects.

The concept of highest and best use is not unique to real estate. It has an application in business valuation. Regardless of the discipline, the question becomes, in what capacity is the property going to provide the maximum financial benefits to the owner(s)?

In real estate, the concept might be to value the property for a commercial office building or a single-family house. In business valuation, the concept might be, should the business be valued as a going concern or as if in liquidation? The bottom line is that some businesses are worth more dead than alive.

Although earnings and cash flow are considered of primary importance as a going concern, there are also instances (such as holding companies) in which the value of the underlying assets can provide the company's value without liquidation being considered. However, investors in the real world generally make a financial investment in a business for three reasons: (1) income distributions (dividends), (2) capital appreciation (growth), and (3) a combination of dividends and growth.

According to the real estate appraisal that was performed:

> During the mid 1980s, Jackson County's strong attraction and appeal led to tremendous price increases and corresponding increases in new development.
>
> Price escalations were experienced in some years in excess of 30% per year, which were significantly sustained through 1984 to 1987. Such growth in price coincided with the national and regional expansion of the economy. Property appreciation seen in most, if not all, sectors of the market resulted in a significant increase in new construction, which produced enormous supply.
>
> As a result, the years 1988 through 1992 have displayed dramatic decreases in potential rents and market values in most segments of the real estate market. This is partially due to the increasing prices, which exceeded the rise in real income of the area and were further exacerbated by the increased supply. The market had stabilized as of the first half of 1992 and has been relatively stable with no discernible value changes since this period.
>
> Due to the lack of speculative construction in recent years, vacancy rates, potential rents, and values should begin to improve slightly over the next several years. However, significant improvement in these areas is not expected in the foreseeable future even as the economy moves through its usual cycle.

Pursuant to the foregoing comments, it does not appear as if growth will take place in the "foreseeable future." Therefore, an investor in the subject company would most likely look for income.

According to the real estate appraisal, the net operating income from this property was estimated to be approximately $100,000. The net operating income from the real estate should be reduced by the other expenses incurred at the corporate level, which is not considered a part of the value of the real estate. Other than legal and accounting expenses, estimated at $5,000 annually, the company's only other expense would appear to be income taxes.

Income taxes are estimated to be $27,000, resulting in a corporate net income of about $68,000. This would be the amount available to a "willing buyer" for a return on investment. If the buyer paid $1,191,439 for this business, the return on investment would be about 5.7 percent. Logically, this does not make sense. At December 31, 1993, 30-year U.S. Treasury bonds were paying about 6.3 percent, higher than an investor could earn by investing in Smith Holding. Furthermore, the investment in the bonds would be virtually risk-free.

A willing buyer with little prospects for growth and, with a choice of a safe U.S. Treasury bond investment or a riskier income from a real estate venture, could not be induced to invest in the latter based on these figures. A discount from the net asset value would be required to produce a reasonable return to the buyer. A differentiation must be made, however, to distinguish between risk and illiquidity.

Risk of loss has been considered in the discount rates used to value the underlying real estate. There is also an element of liquidity loss in this rate as well, according to the ABC appraisal. However, the valuation subject is not the real estate but, rather, common stock in a closely held corporation that owns the real estate.

Owning appreciated real estate inside a corporate entity has some tax problems associated with it. In this instance, a sale of the real estate would trigger a gain of approximately $800,000 and a corresponding tax of $320,000. Tax Court cases have frequently taken the position that prospective capital gains taxes are speculative and not includable in a valuation. This was made clear in *Estate of Piper*, 72 T.C. 1062; *Estate of Cruikshank*, 9 T.C. 162; and *Estate of Robinson*, 69 T.C. 222.

Despite prior case law, changes in the tax code by the Tax Reform Act of 1986 have now made capital gains taxes a reality, as opposed to speculation. After the repeal of the General Utilities Doctrine, a C corporation is no longer allowed to liquidate tax-free. Therefore, a tax liability could exist if the appreciated property were sold.

(Continued)

EXHIBIT 8.1 *(Continued)*

Another issue that has been addressed by various cases is whether liquidation was being contemplated. The Internal Revenue Service has taken the position, and the Tax Court has concurred, that if liquidation was not being contemplated, associated costs should not be permitted.

However, this violates the concept of highest and best use. If the highest and best use of a property was as if in liquidation, the property should be so valued. A poor decision on the part of the property's owner should not affect the value of the property to a willing buyer. If that were the case, Smith Holding would be worth considerably less based on the actual average historical annual income of about $15,900, as opposed to $100,000 in the real estate appraisal.

The purchaser of Smith Holding would most likely continue to use the company for what it is currently intended to do, namely, generate net rental income. Therefore, liquidation would probably not occur. However, that same purchaser would require a higher rate of return to make the investment worthwhile.

At the valuation date, the rates of return on various types of investments were as follows:

U.S. Treasury bonds	
5-year	5.14%
10-year	5.77%
20-year	6.41%
30-year	6.28%
Corporate bonds (seasoned issues)	7.28%
Corporate bonds	
Aaa	6.94%
Aa	7.15%
A	7.33%
Baa	7.71%

Considering the increased risk of illiquidity, an investor would not be unreasonable to expect a 10 percent return on his or her investment based on alternative rates of return available in the marketplace. The result is that the maximum price paid for this investment would be about $680,000 ($68,000 ÷ 10%). This would indicate a discount of approximately 43 percent.

Although this method of justifying a discount from net asset value is a bit unconventional, the result ends up within a reasonable range when one considers the previously discussed studies on discounts for lack of marketability. This also results in an estimate of value that makes sense.

Final Value

In our opinion, the value of 100 percent of the common stock of Smith Holding, after appropriate discounts, is approximately $680,000. The decedent's pro rata share, representing a 62.5 percent interest, is estimated to be $425,000 ($680,000 × 62.5%).

EXHIBIT 8.2
After the Recent Cases

Description of the Assignment

Trugman Valuation Associates Inc. has been retained by Tony Korn, Executor on behalf of the Estate of Jack Jones, to determine the fair market value of the decedent's 100 percent interest in the common stock of XYZ Corp. The date of death in the matter is March 10, 1999, and will be used as the effective date for this appraisal. The purpose of this appraisal is for utilization in the preparation of the estate tax returns.

Brief Description of Business

XYZ Corp., a New York State corporation, holds a leasehold interest in a New York City property located at 123456 First Avenue. There are approximately 40 years to run on the lease. The Company subleases this space, as it has no other operations. The decedent, Jack Jones, was the sole shareholder of the company. This appraiser has been informed that as of the valuation date, the subject company is a "C" corporation. Previously, The Company had been an "S" corporation.

At the valuation date, there was a contract for sale of the leasehold interest. However, there were numerous problems, involving lawsuits and the inability to obtain a Certificate of Occupancy from the City of New York that would permit a legal transfer of this leasehold interest. As a result, there was great uncertainty as to whether the sale would be consummated. It was expected that a significant sum of money would have to be expended to cure the various problems, before such a sale could take place.

EXHIBIT 8.2 *(Continued)*

Book Value and Financial Condition of The Company

The balance sheet of XYZ Corp, as reflected on Form 1120S, U.S. Federal Return for an S Corporation, was as follows:

TABLE 1

Balance Sheet as of December 31,

	1998	*1997*	*1996*
Assets			
Cash	$ 26,641	$ 3,167	$ 1,572
Loans receivable	12,868	8,378	8,378
Loans to shareholders	241,548	43,012	30,149
Security deposits	10,872	10,872	10,872
Total assets	**$ 291,929**	**$ 65,429**	**$ 50,971**
Liabilities			
Loans payable	$ (561)	$ (18,665)	$ 7,885
Security deposits payable	43,877	43,877	43,877
Loans from shareholders	(27,097)	(26,052)	(25,302)
Capital stock	500	500	500
Retained earnings	275,210	65,769	24,011
Total liabilities & stockholder's equity	**$ 291,929**	**$ 65,429**	**$ 50,971**

Stockholder's equity was $275,710 as of the end of the fiscal year closest to the valuation date.

The Earning Capacity of the Company

The earning capacity of XYZ Corp., as a real estate (lease) holding company, is meaningful only in the context of the earnings that can be converted to cash flow available for distribution to the shareholder. The reported earnings for these periods were as follows:

Net rental income	**$ 209,441**	**$ 41,758**	**$ 9,079**

The Company has become substantially more profitable as time has gone on. Profitability from the sublease arrangement is expected to continue. It is described in more detail in the real estate appraisal performed by Thomas B. Smith & Associates Inc.

Valuation Calculations

Asset Approach—Adjusted Book Value Method

Revenue Ruling 59-60 states in Section 5, paragraph (b) that:

> The value of the stock of a closely held investment or real estate holding company, whether or not family owned, is closely related to the value of the assets underlying the stock. For companies of this type the appraiser should determine the fair market values of the assets of the company. Operating expenses of such a company and the cost of liquidating it, if any, merit consideration when appraising relative values of the stock and the underlying assets. The market values of the underlying assets give due weight to potential earnings and dividends of the particular items of property underlying the stock capitalized at rates deemed proper by the investing public at the date of appraisal. A current appraisal by the investing public should be superior to the retrospective opinion of an individual. For these reasons, adjusted net worth should be accorded greater weight in valuing the stock of a closely held investment or real estate holding company, whether or not family owned, than any of the other customary yardsticks of appraisal, such as earnings and dividend paying capacity.

(Continued)

EXHIBIT 8.2 *(Continued)*

Clearly, the value of the underlying assets must be considered. The primary asset of XYZ Corp. is a leasehold interest. According to the real estate appraisal report prepared by Thomas B. Smith & Associates Inc., the market value of this leasehold interest is $2,750,000 as of March 10, 1999. In order to apply the adjusted book value method, we must also add any other assets to and deduct any liabilities from the value of the leasehold. The balance sheet at December 31, 1998, is the balance sheet that is closest to the valuation date. The adjusted book value is calculated as follows:

Appraised value of leasehold	$ 2,750,000
Plus other assets/liabilities	
Cash	26,641
Loans receivable	12,868
Security deposits	10,872
Loans payable	(561)
Security deposits payable	(43,877)
Net asset value	**$2,755,943**
Net asset value (rounded)	**$2,760,000**

Loans from stockholders and loans to stockholders were removed from the balance sheet in determining the adjusted book value of XYZ Corp. These loans are considered to be distributions to the estate.

Based on the adjusted book value method, the net asset value of XYZ Corp. is estimated to be $2,760,000 before applicable premiums and discounts. After the application of the appropriate discounts, the value is as follows:

Net asset value	$ 2,760,000
Discount for lack of marketability	1,742,116
Value after discount	$ 1,017,884
Rounded	**$1,018,000**

Please see the section of this report titled "Premiums and Discounts" for a detailed explanation of the discount for lack of marketability.

Income Approach

The capitalization of benefits method is premised on the concept that value is based on a stabilized income stream that is capitalized by an appropriate capitalization rate to reflect the risk associated with the income stream. The use of this method requires an estimate of income to be made for the subject business. In order to apply this method, we are estimating future income to be equal to the most recent period, or $209,441. The next portion of the application of this method requires the determination of the appropriate capitalization rate to be used for this level of income.

In order to estimate an appropriate capitalization rate, the appraiser researched the composite dividend yield for equity interests in publicly traded Real Estate Investment Trusts (REITs) as of the valuation date. This information was obtained from the March 1999 edition of *Global Research Review* published by Merrill Lynch. This publication listed a dividend yield composite of 10.3 percent. However, the publicly traded REITs are more diversified, considerably larger, and professionally managed. In our opinion, an investment in the subject company would be considerably more risky. Therefore, we believe that a capitalization rate of 15 percent is appropriate. The calculation for capitalizing income is as follows:

Latest-year net income	$ 209,441
Capitalization rate	÷ 0.15
Capitalized value	$ 1,396,273
Rounded	**$1,400,000**

Therefore, based on the income approach, XYZ Corp. has a value of $1,400,000 before any applicable premiums and discounts. After discounts, we believe it should be valued as follows:

Capitalized value	$ 1,400,000
Discount for lack of marketability	490,000
Value after discount	$ 910,000
Rounded	**$ 910,000**

EXHIBIT 8.2 *(Continued)*

Please see the section of this report titled "Premiums and Discounts" for a detailed explanation of the discount for lack of marketability.

Reconciliation of Value

The asset and income approaches were used to estimate the value of XYZ Corp. The results are summarized as follows:

Asset approach	$ 1,018,000
Income approach	910,000

Weighting the estimates 75 percent/25 percent results in the value of XYZ Corp. being estimated as $991,000.

Premiums and Discounts

The final value reached in the appraisal of a closely held business may be more or less than the values that were calculated using the various methods of appraisal that are available. The type and size of the discount(s) or premium(s) will vary depending on the starting point. The starting point will depend on which methods of valuation were used during the appraisal as well as other factors such as the sources of the information used to derive multiples or discount rates, and normalization adjustments.

The valuation subject in this report was a controlling interest that was valued on a control basis. Therefore, control premiums and discounts for lack of control are not applicable in this appraisal.

Discount for Lack of Marketability

A discount for lack of marketability (DLOM) is used to compensate for the difficulty of selling shares of stock that are not traded on a stock exchange compared with those that can be traded publicly. If an investor owns shares in a public company, he or she can pick up the telephone, call a broker, and generally convert the investment into cash within three days. That is not the case with an investment in a closely held business. Therefore, publicly traded stocks have an element of liquidity that closely held shares do not have. This is the reason that a DLOM will be applied. It is intended to reflect the market's perceived reduction in value for not providing liquidity to the shareholder.

A DLOM may also be appropriate when the shares have either legal or contractual restrictions placed upon them. This may be the result of restricted stock, buy-sell agreements, bank loan restrictions, or other types of contracts that restrict the sale of the shares. Even when a 100 percent interest is the valuation subject, a DLOM may be appropriate if the owner cannot change the restrictions on the stock.

The most commonly used sources of data for determining an appropriate level of a DLOM are studies involving restricted stock purchases or initial public offerings. Revenue Ruling 77-287 references the Institutional Investor Study,[1] which addresses restricted stock issues. Many studies have updated this one.

Restricted stock (or letter stock as it is sometimes called) is stock issued by a corporation that is not registered with the Securities and Exchange Commission (SEC) and cannot be readily sold into the public market. The stock is usually issued when a corporation is first going public, making an acquisition, or raising capital. The main reasons that corporations issue restricted stock, rather than tradable stock, are to avoid dilution of their stock price with an excessive number of shares available for sale at any one time and to avoid the costs of registering the securities with the SEC.

The registration exemption on restricted stocks is granted under Section 4(2) of the 1933 Securities Act. The intent of Section 4(2) is to allow "small" corporations the ability to raise capital without incurring the costs of a public offering. Regulation D, a safe harbor regulation, which became effective in 1982, falls under section 4(2) of the code and provides uniformity in federal and state securities laws regarding private placements of securities. Securities bought under Regulation D are subject to restrictions, the most important being that the securities cannot be resold without either registration under the Act, or an exemption.[2] The exemptions for these securities are granted under Rule 144.

> Rule 144 allows the limited resale of unregistered securities after a minimum holding period of two years. Resale is limited to the higher of 1 percent of outstanding stock or average weekly volume over a four-week period prior to the sale, during any three-month period. There is no quantity limitation after a four-year holding period.[3]

[1] "Discounts Involved in Purchases of Common Stock (1966–1969)," *Institutional Investor Study Report of the Securities and Exchange Commission*, H.R. Doc. No. 64, Part 5, 92d Cong., 1st Sess., 1971, 2444–2456.

[2] Kasim L. Alli, Ph.D., and Donald J. Thompson, Ph.D., "The Value of the Resale Limitation on Restricted Stock: An Option Theory Approach," American Society of Appraisers: *Valuation* (March 1991), 22–23.

[3] Ibid.

(Continued)

EXHIBIT 8.2 *(Continued)*

Therefore, a holder of restricted stock must either register the securities with the SEC or qualify for a 144 exemption in order to sell the stock on the public market. A holder of restricted stock can, however, trade the stock in a private transaction. Historically, when traded privately, the restricted stock transaction was usually required to be registered with the SEC. However, in 1990, the SEC adopted Rule 144a, which relaxed the SEC filing restrictions on private transactions. The rule allows qualified institutional investors to trade unregistered securities among themselves without filing registration statements.[4] Effective April 1997, the two-year holding period was reduced to one year.

The overall effect of these regulations on restricted stock is that when issued, the corporation is not required to disclose a price and, on some occasions, even when traded, the value of restricted securities is still not a matter of public record.

Table 2 is a summary of more familiar studies regarding restricted stock.

TABLE 2

Restricted Stock Studies

Study	*Years Covered in Study*	*Average Discount (%)*
SEC overall average[1]	1966–1969	25.8
SEC non-reporting OTC companies[1]	1966–1969	32.6
Gelman[2]	1968–1970	33.0
Trout[3]	1968–1972	33.5[9]
Moroney[4]	[8]	35.6
Maher[5]	1969–1973	35.4
Standard Research Consultants[6]	1978–1982	45.0[9]
Willamette Management Associates[7]	1981–1984	31.2[10]
Silber study	1981–1989	34.0[10]
FMV study	1979–April 1992	23.0[11]
Management Planning, Inc.	1980–1995	27.7[12]

[1]From "Discounts Involved in Purchases of Common Stock (1966–1969)," *Institutional Investor Study Report of the Securities and Exchange Commission.* H.R. Doc. No. 64, Part 5, 92d Cong., 1st Sess. 1971, 2444–2456.

[2]From Milton Gelman, "An Economist-Financial Analyst's Approach to Valuing Stock of a Closely Held Company," *Journal of Taxation* (June 1972), 353–354.

[3]From Robert R. Trout, "Estimation of the Discount Associated with the Transfer of Restricted Securities," *Taxes* (June 1977), 381–385.

[4]From Robert E. Moroney, "Most Courts Overvalue Closely Held Stock," *Taxes* (March 1973), 144–154.

[5]From J. Michael Maher, "Discounts for Lack of Marketability for Closely Held Business Interests," *Taxes* (September 1976), 562–571.

[6]From "Revenue Ruling 77-287 Revisited," *SRC Quarterly Reports* (Spring 1983), 1–3.

[7]From Willamette Management Associates study (unpublished).

[8]Although the years covered in this study are likely to be 1969–1972, no specific years were given in the published account.

[9]Median discounts.

[10]From William L. Silber, "Discounts on Restricted Stock: The Impact of Illiquidity on Stock Prices," *Financial Analysts Journal* (July–August 1991), 60–64.

[11]Lance S. Hall and Timothy C. Polacek, "Strategies for Obtaining the Largest Discount," *Estate Planning* (January/February 1994), 38–44. In spite of the long time period covered, this study analyzed only a little over 100 transactions involving companies that were generally not the smallest capitalization companies. It supported the findings of the SEC *Institutional Investor Study* in finding that the discount for lack of marketability was higher for smaller capitalization companies.

[4]Richard A. Brealey and Steward C. Myers, "How Corporations Issue Securities," Chapter 14, *Principles of Corporate Finance*, 5th ed. (New York:

EXHIBIT 8.2 *(Continued)*

[12]Management Planning, Inc. Analysis of Restricted Stocks of Public Companies: 1980–1995. Published in *Quantifying Marketability Discounts—Developing and Supporting Marketability Discounts in the Appraisal of Closely Held Business Interests* by Z. Christopher Mercer (Memphis: Peabody Publishing, LP, 1997), 345–370. Also available on *Business Valuation Update Online*, http://www.nvst.com/bvu.

Source: *Guide to Business Valuations* (Fort Worth Tex.: Practitioners Publishing Co., 2000).

Other Considerations

Another consideration in determining a discount for lack of marketability is the cost of flotation of a public offering. These costs are generally significant and will frequently include payments to attorneys, accountants, and investment bankers. The costs associated with smaller offerings can be as much as 25 to 30 percent of a small company's equity.

As far back as 1977, through Revenue Ruling 77-287, the Internal Revenue Service recognized the effectiveness of restricted stock study data in providing useful information for the quantification of discounts for lack of marketability. The Baird and Willamette studies of transactions in closely held stocks did not exist at that time, but the IRS and the courts have been receptive to using this data to assist in quantifying discounts for lack of marketability.

The IPO studies are proof that larger discounts can be justified than those quoted from the restricted stock studies. One of the best explanations of why a DLOM varies from case to case was included in an article published by Robert E. Moroney titled "Why 25% Discount for Nonmarketability in One Valuation, 100% in Another?"[5] In Moroney's article, he points out 11 factors that should be considered in the application of a DLOM. (*Author's note:* These factors are discussed in Chapter 11.)

The discount for lack of marketability for XYZ Corp. comprises three factors: the present value of litigation costs, the present value of income taxes on the sale of the leasehold interest, and the risk inherent in holding the business as an investment prior to sale.

At the valuation date, XYZ Corp. was already entangled in litigation with tenants and already experiencing problems with its Certificate of Occupancy. The contract for sale of the leasehold was for $3,000,000, but there was great uncertainty as to whether that contract price would ever be realized. In fact, there was already some renegotiating being pursued by the purchaser. In the meantime, XYZ Corp. was incurring litigation expenses that would continue until all of the problems were resolved. Based on a discussion with legal counsel and the real estate broker who assisted in the deal, these litigation expenses could easily reach $300,000 to $400,000. We have therefore assumed $350,000 to be part of the discount necessary to achieve liquidity.

The next factor considered as part of the DLOM is the amount of income taxes that would be incurred on the sale of the leasehold interest by XYZ Corp. If the leasehold interest had been sold as of March 10, 1999, the seller would incur significant income taxes on the sale. A willing buyer could not ignore these taxes as they would be substantial. The notion of built-in gains taxes as part of a DLOM has been allowed in various modern-day cases, such as *Estate of Artemus D. Davis v. Commissioner* (110 T.C. 530), *Irene Eisenberg v. Commissioner* (82 AFTR 2d 98-5757, 155 F.3d 50), and *Estate of Welch v. Commissioner* (85 AFTR 2d 2000-1200, 208 F.3d 213).

Under such precedent, we have considered taxes in the DLOM for XYZ Corp. The sale of the leasehold interest would trigger an immediate tax to the corporation. We have estimated the expected taxes to be paid based on the appraised value of the leasehold and discounted these taxes one year to approximate the timing of when the sale and resulting taxes might take place. This calculation takes place in Table 3.

TABLE 3

C Corp. Tax Calculation

Federal	$ 768,765
New York State	254,372
New York City	200,105
Total taxes to be paid	**$ 1,223,242**
Present value factor	
Interest rate = prime (7.75%) + 2%	**÷ 1.0950**
Present value of taxes	**$ 1,117,116**

As indicated above, the willing buyer of the XYZ Corp. stock would be faced with a corporate tax liability of approximately $1,117,116 on a present value basis if the leasehold interest was sold on March 10, 1999. The best that the buyer could end up with is the net amount after taxes are paid.

[5]Robert E. Moroney, "Why 25% Discount for Nonmarketability in One Valuation, 100% in Another?" *Taxes* (May 1977), 316–320.

(Continued)

EXHIBIT 8.2 *(Continued)*

The final component of the DLOM is the holding risk, as the seller attempts to sell the stock of XYZ Corp. The real estate market faces many ups and downs as the economy goes through its various cycles. At the date of death, the market was well on its way to the top of the current cycle. Therefore, the risk of holding the investment in a downturn could impact liquidity. Also unknown at this date is how much of a concession will have to be reached with the purchaser of the leasehold interest, clearly the largest owned asset, before a sale is ultimately consummated. Taking all of this into consideration, we have added an additional 10 percent to the discount.

Therefore, the DLOM for XYZ Corp. has been estimated as follows:

Litigation and occupancy costs	$ 350,000
Income taxes	1,117,116
Holding risk	275,000
Total	**$1,742,116**

The DLOM applied to the asset approach of $1,742,116 is not the same DLOM that should be applied to the income approach. Although there is a large built-in gains tax, if an investor purchases The Company based on its lower income-producing capacity, we believe that the intention would be to hold the investment and not incur the income tax from selling the leasehold interest. In this instance, we believe the litigation and occupancy expenses would still have to be incurred, which was not factored into the income stream capitalized, and there would still be a holding period risk (10 percent of the capitalized value), resulting in a DLOM of $490,000.

Exhibit 8.2 demonstrates, among other things, that the income taxes that might be paid should probably be estimated based on when the taxes might be paid. This allows a present value calculation to be made, reducing the income taxes to their net present value. The obvious difficulty arises when you have no idea as to when the sale might take place. Another question that arises in the negotiation process between the willing buyer and willing seller is, would the full amount of taxes be part of the deal? The answer is probably no. However, as appraisers we have to figure out the most likely situation.

The situation in Exhibit 8.2 was that an actual sale had taken place, but under the fair market value standard we could consider only that which was known or knowable at the appraisal date. The knowledge was that there was a contract for sale, but there were some problems with ongoing litigation that delayed the expected closing. Here also, we had to check with legal counsel.

Tax-effecting the balance sheet has been the subject of much controversy in the appraisal profession and has not been fully resolved. However, most experienced appraisers believe that accounts receivable and accounts payable should be tax-effected when going from cash basis to accrual basis, if there is a likelihood that taxes would be paid by the entity. Be careful not to get caught in the trap of automatically tax-effecting these items. The purpose and function of the assignment must be considered here. If the accounts receivable are the same at the beginning and end of the accounting period and revenues have been flat, taxes will probably not be paid in the immediate future. In addition, many professional practices bonus out profit, eliminating any tax. If it is assumed that the hypothetical willing buyer will do the same, there may not be tax here either.

If an asset, such as inventory, is sold as a normal part of the business, the adjustment should be tax-effected *if* there is a likelihood that taxes would be paid by the entity. This relates to income taxes, as opposed to capital gains taxes. Therefore, it appears that a reasonable argument can be made for making this type of adjustment.

Changes from LIFO to FIFO will frequently require a tax adjustment. Here also, the income tax implications are being considered. Clearly, there are no hard and fast rules about tax-effecting. Why should this be any different from everything else that we have discussed? Common sense must be used to justify tax-effecting. There is no substitute for using your head to support your position.

When All Adjustments Have Been Made. After all of the adjustments have been made, the difference between the value of the adjusted assets and the value of the adjusted liabilities equals the value of the adjusted equity of the enterprise. If *all* assets, both tangible and intangible, have been considered, the value should be in the same ballpark as the value estimates reached in the other approaches. However, if the unidentifiable intangible assets (i.e., goodwill) are excluded, the result may be considered to be the "floor" value in a valuation of a controlling interest (without any discounts at this point). This "floor" value is probably greater than what the company would realize in liquidation.

Most likely, the appraiser will have to value the unidentifiable intangible assets using a different methodology and add the result to the adjusted book value estimate of all of the other assets and liabilities. A frequently used method to accomplish this is the *excess earnings method.* The problem with this method is that it should not be used unless *there is no better basis for determining the value of the intangibles.* If you don't believe me, re-read Revenue Ruling 68-609. I will discuss the mechanics of the excess earnings method in the next chapter, so be patient.

Communication Among Appraisers. Communication among appraisers is an important component of the valuation process. The business appraiser should be thought of as the team's quarterback. He or she will be responsible for making sure that the other appraisers provide information that will be useful in the business valuation. This means that the business appraiser must have a clear understanding of the terminology used by appraisers in other disciplines (real estate, machinery, etc.) to ensure that the same premise of value (going concern or liquidation) is consistently applied throughout the appraisal. This is more of a problem when the client hands you an appraisal that was done for a different purpose than the assignment that you are involved in. For example, an insurance appraisal may end up with a very different standard of value than an appraisal for estate tax purposes.

To keep the lines of communication open and clear, the business appraiser should be familiar with certain terminology used by these other professional appraisers. Let's discuss some of the important terms:

- *Replacement cost new.* This has been defined by machinery and equipment appraisers as "the current cost of a similar new item having the nearest equivalent utility as the item being appraised."[4] As the term implies, "replacement cost new" is the cost of replacing a piece of equipment that is similar (not exact) in functional usage to the item being appraised. Since technology and models change, this term recognizes the fact that an exact duplicate may not be used as a replacement for an old piece of equipment. Why would anyone want to replace a 57-year-old machine with 57-year-old technology when the new and improved models are so much more efficient?
- *Depreciated replacement cost new.* This is the current cost of replacement of an item less the physical deterioration, and functional and economic obsolescence. This term takes into account the loss of value of the existing item as a result of age, deterioration (wear and tear), obsolescence (functional or economic), or a combination of the three. This value may include the costs of getting the asset delivered, installed, and debugged.

  "Depreciated replacement cost new" takes into consideration the fact that the piece of equipment being appraised is not new and, as such, the replacement should be appraised in roughly the same condition as the appraisal subject. In most business appraisals, this concept makes sense. Unless you are forecasting the cash flow needs that will result from the replacement of the existing plant, a willing buyer will not pay the new price of an asset if it is in used condition.
- *Reproduction cost new.* This represents the current cost of duplicating an identical new item. Rarely will this concept be used in practice. Other than for special-purpose equipment, this concept would not

[4]John Alico, ed., *Appraising Machinery and Equipment* (New York: McGraw-Hill, 1989) (sponsored by the American Society of Appraisers).

necessarily be feasible. Reproducing the exact same item could be considerably more expensive than replacing it with a new and improved model.

- *Fair market value in place in use*. This term assumes that the asset will be used for the same purpose and in the same place as it is in the hands of the current owner. The value is determined based on the economic contribution of the asset being valued. It is the cost of replacing the existing item with a similar item of equivalent utility. This definition also includes all of the costs of getting the asset ready for use.
- *Fair market value in exchange*. For this term, the assumption is made that the asset will be sold. Rather than valuing the asset based on the economic contribution that it makes to the company, the appraiser values the asset as if a sale will take place to a willing buyer of only that asset or a group of assets. This concept is frequently used when one values non-operating assets, since they, by definition, do not make a contribution to the business operations of the appraisal subject.

The Adjusted Book Value Method Illustrated. In Exhibit 8.3, the adjusted book value method is illustrated. The example in Exhibit 8.3 was part of an appraisal that was being used by the client for a divorce litigation.

EXHIBIT 8.3
Adjusted Book Value Method

The next step in our analysis was to normalize the financial statements. The process of normalization is intended to restate The Company's financial statements on an economic basis; in other words, restate the financial statements to reflect the financial condition and operating income that the willing buyer would anticipate. The balance sheet is normalized in Table 1.

TABLE 1
Balance Sheet Normalization

	September 1999	*Adjustments*	*Adjusted 1999*
Current assets			
Cash	$ 46,794	$ —	$ 46,794
Accounts receivable	140,879	—	140,879
Inventories	69,619	—	69,619
Prepaid expenses	11,136	—	11,136
Prepaid insurance	879	—	879
Total current assets	$ 269,307	$ —	$ 269,307
Fixed assets			
Land[1]	$ 24,770	$ (24,770)	$ —
Building & improvements[1]	532,628	374,372	907,000
Machinery & equipment[2]	285,672	(188,672)	97,000
Land improvements[1]	18,942	(18,942)	—
Gross fixed assets	$ 862,012	$ 141,988	$ 1,004,000
Accumulated depreciation[3]	292,648	(292,648)	—
Net fixed assets	$ 569,364	$ 434,636	$ 1,004,000
Other assets			
Patent costs (net)[4]	$ 7,044	$ (7,044)	$ —
Deferred loan costs[5]	3,700	(3,700)	—
Total other assets	$ 10,744	$ (10,744)	$ —
Total assets	**$ 849,415**	**$ 423,892**	**$1,273,307**

EXHIBIT 8.3 *(Continued)*

	September 1999	*Adjustments*	*Adjusted 1999*
Current liabilities			
Accounts payable	$ 45,295	$ —	$ 45,295
Long-term debt—current portion	24,610	—	24,610
Total current liabilities	$ 69,905	$	$ 69,905
Long-term liabilities			
Long-term debt	$ 598,231	$ —	$ 598,231
Deferred taxes[6]	—	95,620	95,620
Total long-term liabilities	$ 598,231	$ 95,620	$ 693,851
Total liabilities	$ 668,136	$ 95,620	$ 763,756
Stockholder's equity			
Common stock	$ 500	$ —	$ 500
Paid-in capital	25,625	—	25,625
Retained earnings[7]	155,154	328,272	483,426
Total stockholder's equity	$ 181,279	$ 328,272	$ 509,551
Total liabilities and stockholder's equity	**$ 849,415**	**$ 423,892**	**$1,273,307**

[1]Real estate, including land, building and improvements, and land improvements, has been adjusted to $907,000 as estimated by real estate appraiser Calvin L. Brown, IFAS, CREA. [The real estate appraisal would be attached to this report as an exhibit.]

[2]The Company's machinery and equipment have been appraised by G. Murphy & Associates as of October 7, 1999. The fair market value in continued use of the company's machinery and equipment was estimated at $97,000. [The appraisal report would be attached to this report as an exhibit.]

[3]Accumulated depreciation has been adjusted to zero, as the appraised values reflect the economic value of the fixed assets.

[4]Patent costs have been normalized from the balance sheet, as these capitalized costs would not be transferred to a willing buyer.

[5]Deferred loan costs have been normalized from the balance sheet, as this asset would not be transferred in the event of a sale.

[6]Deferred taxes reflect the tax liability incurred due to the difference in the economic value of the fixed assets and book value. In the event of sale, The Company would owe tax on the appreciation of these assets, which was calculated as follows:

Fair market value	$1,004,000
Book value	(569,364)
Appreciation	434,636
Tax rate	0.22
Tax liability	$ 95,620

The tax rate has been calculated based on applicable state and federal capital gain tax rates as of the valuation date.

[7]Stockholder's equity has been adjusted to reflect the previous adjustments to the balance sheet.

(*Author's note:* There was no intangible value in this assignment, so the value before a discount for lack of marketability was $509,551.)

Liquidation Value Method

Before we can discuss the liquidation value method, let's first define liquidation value. Liquidation value is the net amount expected to be left over after the assets are sold off and the proceeds are used to satisfy existing liabilities. The types of liquidation value generally include orderly liquidation and forced liquidation. Orderly liquidation value is defined as the value given a reasonable amount of time to find a purchaser of the assets. The reasonable amount of time will differ based on the facts and circumstances at the time of the appraisal, as well as on the type of assets involved; in general, the time is three to six months or longer. The values used in an orderly liquidation are based on the price that the market would pay for an asset in a similar, depreciated condition.

In a forced liquidation, there is generally a lack of adequate time to find a purchaser for the assets. A fire sale value will generally apply. This is a case in which the assets are disposed of as quickly as possible, generally in less than three months. A forced liquidation will generally take place when someone other than the owners of the business "forces" the liquidation. Obviously, an owner will want to maximize the amount derived from a liquidation. Thus, a plan of liquidation, combined with an adequate amount of time to get the best price in the market, will accomplish this task. This does not happen in a forced liquidation.

When considering the liquidation value method, all costs of liquidation should be deducted. Some of the following liquidation costs may apply:

- Commissions
- Administrative costs and losses that may continue during the period of liquidation
- Legal and accounting costs
- Taxes on the disposal of assets as a result of the liquidation

The time value of money should also be considered, since it may take time to liquidate the company. It is rare that a business owner can liquidate the assets quickly. For example, if the company is no longer servicing its customers, it may take longer to collect the accounts receivable. Furthermore, during the winding-down stage of the business, the company may not be able to dispose of certain assets that may be required until the very end. Depending on the time frame involved, the appraiser may feel that a present value adjustment is in order.

When would you use the liquidation value method? The most obvious use of the liquidation method is when an actual liquidation of the business is contemplated. In this situation, the appraiser is aware that a liquidation will take place and will generally have the ability to discuss the plan of liquidation with the management of the company. This is the cleanest manner in which to deal with liquidation.

What do you do, however, if a liquidation is not actually planned? The liquidation methodology should also be considered when the highest and best use of the property is to liquidate, as opposed to valuing the entity as a going concern, if the interest being valued has the right to liquidate.

Let's make sure that you are clear on what I just stated. Even though a business may not plan to liquidate, the appraiser may be required to value the company on a liquidation basis if the value estimate is higher than it would be as a going concern.

> **Example:** XYZ Fuel Oil Corp. is a well-established, old-time home heating oil business that delivers home heating oil and repairs furnaces. The company's financial statements reflect losses for the last seven years. A turnaround in profitability looks doubtful, but the owner of the company wants to continue the business so that it can provide a job for his son, who is employed by the company as a repairer of customers' furnaces.
>
> The value of the net tangible assets of the company is $350,000. Economic and industry research reflects several important factors that affect the appraiser's valuation. First, many customers have converted from home heating oil to natural gas, which explains why the company's sales gallonage has fallen off over the last several years.

Second, the large companies in the industry are making acquisitions of smaller local companies to utilize the excess capacity on their delivery trucks. Many of these companies are sending out trucks with a capacity of 2,800 gallons, but they are only half full. The management of these companies realize that it costs them only the price of the extra fuel oil to fill up the trucks and have their driver stop at additional locations along their routes. Therefore, the acquisition of additional customers, through the purchase of smaller independent dealers, is a good business decision.

If larger companies are making these types of acquisitions, the value of the customer list probably has a premium attached to it. However, the customer list is not worth much as an intangible to XYZ on a going-concern basis if the company cannot generate profits. In the real world, the customer list can be sold to another fuel oil company for a significant amount of money. If the customer list is sold, XYZ is effectively out of business. Therefore, the sale of the customer list would be part of a liquidation, if the owner of the company wanted to truly maximize his or her value.

This is a classic situation in which the company is worth more dead than alive. The highest and best use of the company's assets is in liquidation. The only way that the shareholders of XYZ can gain the benefit of value of the customer list is to sell it, especially since the company has been losing money each year.

At a minimum, this method can be used to set the lower limit of the range of possible fair market values of a controlling interest in a going concern. Remember, you do not want to use this method if the interest that you are valuing does not have the ability to liquidate the company (for example, a minority interest).

If the appraisal is for tax purposes, be careful to follow, or at least consider, the case law. The Internal Revenue Service and, particularly, the Tax Courts have frowned on a liquidation methodology unless a plan of liquidation is in place.

Exhibit 8.4 highlights a liquidation analysis section of an appraisal report that included an equipment appraisal. This assignment required the concept of highest and best use to be applied in the fair market value determination of a going concern.

EXHIBIT 8.4
Liquidation Value Method

The value of a business should be determined in accordance with the concept of its highest and best use.

In *Basic Business Appraisal*, by Raymond C. Miles, *highest and best use* is defined as "the legally permissible and reasonably feasible present use, or series of future uses, that will result in the greatest economic benefit to the owner of the property." Applying this concept to Southeast Explosives and Southeast Equipment requires a determination of whether the business's highest and best use is as a going concern or as if in liquidation.

Miles also states:

> In extreme cases, an appraiser may sometimes be asked to appraise a business which, though profitable, is only marginally so, and rather than continuing as an operating business, might better be liquidated. The business would be discontinued, its assets being sold individually for whatever price they might bring, and the liabilities of the business would then be satisfied from the proceeds of the sale of assets.

Southeast Explosives and Southeast Equipment are not even marginally profitable and are not expected to be profitable in the future. A going-concern value assumes the company will continue in business and looks to its earning power and cash generation capabilities as indications of fair market value. In this case, the business does not exhibit these characteristics. It has been experiencing losses, and this is expected to continue into the future.

Therefore, the highest and best use, resulting in the greatest economic benefit to the owners, would be in liquidation and not as a going concern. Since we have concluded that the highest value would be produced from a liquidation valuation, we have not applied a market or income approach typically used in valuing a going concern.

However, an asset-based appraisal is in order. To prepare a liquidation analysis of Southeast Explosives and Southeast Equipment, a listing must be made of all of the companies' assets and liabilities, both tangible and intangible. Appropriate sale or liquidation values must then be determined for each item in the listing. The balance sheets at June 30, 1999, as prepared by the companies' accountant, are the starting point for the analysis. The following table details the calculation of the net proceeds to be received upon liquidation.

(Continued)

EXHIBIT 8.4 *(Continued)*

Net Proceeds from Liquidation
Historical Value June 30, 1999

	Southeast Equipment	*Southeast Explosives*	*Adjustments*	*Liquidation Values*
Tangible assets				
Cash[1]	$ 12,798	$ 24,078	$ —	$ 36,876
Money market fund[2]	—	127,753	—	127,753
Due from Southeast Equipment[2]	—	41,381	(41,381)	—
Accounts receivable[3]	1,302	—	5,040	6,342
Fixed assets[4]	4,875	2,113	96,012	103,000
Proceeds from asset sales	$ 18,975	$ 195,325	$ 59,671	$ 273,971
Identifiable liabilities				
Payroll taxes payable[5]	—	2,606	459	3,065
Accrued payroll[6]	—	—	1,800	1,800
Accounts payable[7]	—	—	4,174	4,174
Union benefits payable[8]	—	—	3,497	3,497
Due to Southeast Explosives[2]	41,381	—	(41,381)	—
Loan to shareholder	1,500	—	—	1,500
Total liabilities	$ 42,881	$ 2,606	$(31,451)	$ 14,036
Net proceeds before liquidation expenses				$ 259,935
Liquidation expenses				
Legal and accounting				$ 5,000
Overhead				1,000
Income taxes				—
Total liquidation expenses				$ 6,000
Net proceeds from liquidation				$ 253,935
Rounded				$ 254,000

[1]Cash in bank accounts and the money market account has not been adjusted, since the balances at June 30, 1999, are indicators of the cash balances at July 22, 1999. According to Bill Jones, there were no significant changes in cash between June 30, 1999, and July 22, 1999.

[2]The inter-company receivable/payable due from one of the companies to the other has been eliminated, since if the companies were liquidated together, the amounts would not be paid by one company to the other.

[3]Since the companies maintain their books on a cash basis, accounts receivable are generally not reflected on the balance sheet. However, on June 30, 1999, there was a small balance on the books of Southeast Equipment. This appraiser reviewed documentation at the valuation date indicating that total accounts receivable for both companies were $6,676 at that time. Not all of it has been collected. Allowing for the time to collect and possible bad debts, this appraiser has reduced the accounts receivable by 5 percent. Therefore, the accounts receivable at July 22, 1999, are $6,342.

[4]The value of the majority of the fixed assets has been determined through an equipment appraisal performed by Brown Appraisal Associates. Their appraisal resulted in a fair market value in exchange of $103,000 for three drill systems, an air compressor, a 1994 truck, a 1992 truck, and various other items. Fair market value in exchange is the fair market value of the equipment after a deduction for sales and marketing expenses. This value is higher than an auction value, which was estimated by Brown to be $84,000. This, however, represents a forced liquidation value and is not appropriate for this appraisal.

[5]Payroll taxes payable of $3,065 were due at the valuation date.

[6]Accrued payroll of $1,800 is payroll due for Messrs. Jones and Masterson for work performed prior to the valuation date.

[7]Accounts payable of $4,174 were verified as of the valuation date.

[8]Union benefits payable of $3,497 were verified as of the valuation date.

EXHIBIT 8.4 (Continued)

Upon liquidation, the net proceeds before any liquidation expenses would be $259,935. However, the costs associated with the liquidation must also be considered. As mentioned previously, Shannon Pratt, author of *Valuing A Business*, states that "it is essential to recognize all costs associated with the enterprise's liquidation. These costs normally include commissions, the administrative cost of keeping the company alive until the liquidation is completed, taxes and legal and accounting costs."

Brokerage commissions have already been deducted in the determination of the fair market value in exchange of the fixed assets. Legal and accounting costs that will be incurred are estimated to be $5,000. The overhead costs that will continue to be incurred while the companies are in the process of liquidating are estimated to be minimal. There may be some miscellaneous amounts due for items such as insurance and some administrative costs. Salaries will not be paid, since no additional jobs will be performed. Therefore, these overhead costs are estimated to be $1,000.

There will be realized gains from sales of the fixed assets in liquidation; however, there are significant net operating loss carry-forwards available, which would offset these gains. Therefore, we have estimated that there will be no taxes due upon liquidation of the assets.

In certain cases, the net liquidation proceeds are discounted, since time is needed to sell the assets. The liquidation proceeds will not be received until some time after the valuation date; therefore, the proceeds are worth less at the valuation date than when they are actually received. In this case, the liquidation proceeds available as computed represent the value at the valuation date, since the cash and accounts receivable are readily liquidated. In addition, the equipment appraiser has considered the time needed to sell the fixed assets in the valuation. Therefore, it is not necessary to discount the estimated net proceeds.

Therefore, the final value of these companies, on a combined basis, is estimated to be $253,935, or $254,000 rounded.

Cost to Create Method

The cost to create method is similar to the adjusted book value method. The main difference is that under this method, in addition to valuing the net tangible assets, the appraiser values the intangible assets as well. This method requires the appraiser to estimate how much it would cost to recreate the enterprise being valued. This would also include trying to estimate the time, effort, and monetary contribution necessary to recreate the intangible assets of the business.

The cost to create method will often result in a value estimate that is higher than the cost to reestablish a business enterprise, much in the same manner I discussed earlier in this chapter when I defined "reproduction cost new." There is rarely a situation in which the business would be rebuilt from scratch in the same fashion as had been done previously. However, the cost to create method can be useful for valuing intangibles such as customer lists.

Working With Other Appraisers

One of the first steps in working with other appraisers is to properly define the type of value that you will require as part of your business valuation. Very often, you may ask a machinery and equipment appraiser to give you two or more estimates of value for the equipment. This may include the value in place, the value if sold, and a liquidation value. Do not leave it up to the other appraiser to give you a value, since the result may be totally inconsistent with the appraisal approaches and methodologies that are chosen to value the equity of the company. For example, a machinery and equipment appraiser may value the assets as if they were in place in use, whereas the business appraiser has determined that the highest and best use of the business requires a liquidation methodology. Sometimes it may be necessary to have the machinery valued using two or more concepts.

How to Locate and Recognize Specialists

There are various organizations that designate appraisers. Some of the more common designations in real estate are granted by the American Society of Appraisers, the Appraisal Institute, and the National Association of Independent Fee Appraisers. These designations are as follows:

- The American Society of Appraisers
    - AM: This designation is granted in various disciplines to individuals who have qualified with at least two years of experience.

  - ASA: This designation is granted in various disciplines to individuals who have qualified with at least five years of experience.

  The various disciplines of the American Society of Appraisers include business valuation, gems and jewelry (with subspecialties in diamonds and unmounted colored gemstones, contemporary jewelry, art and designer jewelry, Native American or other collectible ethnic jewelry, antique and period jewelry, gemstones rough, gemstone carvings, and mineral specimens), machinery and technical valuation (with subspecialties in agricultural chattels, aircraft, arboriculture, computers and high-tech personal property, cost surveys, industrials, machinery and equipment, marine survey, mines and quarries, natural resources, oil and gas, and public utilities), personal property (with subspecialties in antique and collectible glass, antique and decorative arts, antique firearms, armor and militaria, antique furniture, Asian art, automatic musical instruments, automotive specialties, books, equines, ethnographic art, fine arts, fine arts photography, furs, Native American art, numismatics, oriental rugs, pre-Columbian art, residential contents, silver and metal ware, stamps, violins, and fine and rare wines), and real property (with subspecialties in urban real property, residential real property, rural real property, ad valorem real property, and timber and timberlands).

- The Appraisal Institute
  - MAI: This is the highest-level designation held by members who are experienced in the valuation and analysis of commercial, industrial, residential, and other types of properties and are qualified to advise clients on real estate investment decisions.
  - SRPA: This designation is held by members who are experienced in the valuation of commercial, industrial, and residential property, as well as other types of properties.
  - SREA: This designation is held by members who are experienced in the valuation and analysis of commercial, industrial, and residential property, as well as other types of properties, and are qualified to advise clients on real estate investment decisions.
  - SRA: This designation is held by members who are experienced in the valuation of single-family homes, townhouses, and residential income properties up to and including four units.
  - RM: This designation is held by members who are experienced in the valuation of single-family homes, townhouses, and two- to four-unit residential income properties.
- The National Association of Independent Fee Appraisers
  - IFA (member)
  - IFAA (agricultural member)
  - IFAS (senior member)
  - IFAC (appraiser-counselor)

By now, you must feel like alphabet soup. Your local *Yellow Pages* will assist you in finding many of these types of individuals. Many of the appraisal organizations also have directories, which you can obtain by calling them. Another alternative is to call equipment dealers, but be careful using the information that you get from them. Problems similar to those discussed earlier can arise from getting information from business brokers. Some pieces of information are going to be better than others.

Conclusion

Fortunately, this chapter was easier than the last one. By now, you should know when to use the asset-based approach, how to apply the methods, and the advantages and disadvantages of each of them. So let's move on.

9

The Income Approach

Chapter Goals

In this chapter, I will attempt to explain the following:

1. When to use the income approach
2. Advantages and disadvantages of using the income approach
3. Using pretax or after-tax information
4. Using debt-free methods
5. The capitalization of benefits method
6. The discounted future benefits method
7. The excess earnings method
8. Common errors in applying the income approach

Introduction

Revenue Ruling 59-60 suggests that an appraiser should consider the earning capacity of the business in the determination of fair market value. *Earning capacity* or *income*, as applied in the methods about to be discussed, may be defined in a number of different ways. Some of the more common definitions include:

- Net income after tax
- Net income before taxes (pretax income)
- Cash flow (gross or net)
- Debt-free income
- Debt-free cash flow (gross or net)
- Earnings before interest and taxes (EBIT)
- Earnings before interest, taxes, depreciation, and amortization (EBITDA)

These income streams, also known as benefit streams, are converted into estimates of the value of the appraisal subject. The two processes that are used in the income approach are known as capitalization and discounting:

- *Capitalization*. A single-period valuation model that converts a benefits stream into value by dividing the benefits stream by a rate of return that is adjusted for growth. A common variation of this theme is the reciprocal of the market multiple price/earnings, which would be earnings/price. An earnings/price ratio is a capitalization rate.

- *Discounting.* A multiple-period valuation model that converts a future series of benefit streams into value by discounting them to present value at a rate of return that reflects the risk inherent in the benefits stream.

Viewing these two models as pictures, these processes look like this:

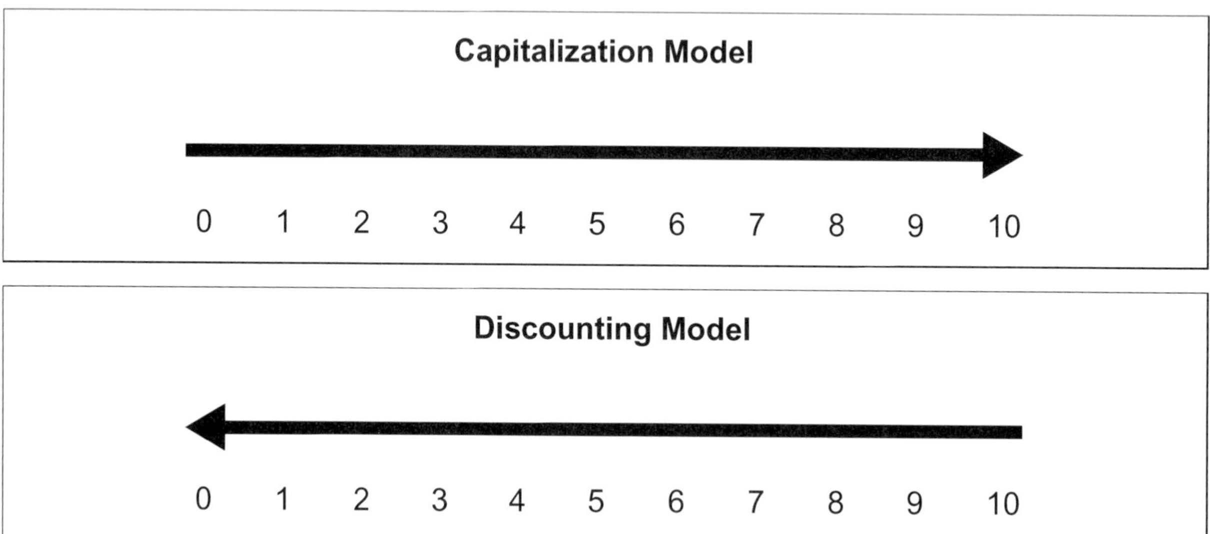

A capitalization model uses a current benefit stream and assumes that the particular stream of income will be received into perpetuity. A discounting model uses a forecast benefit stream and then discounts that stream back to present value. While the pictures look like backward arrows at this point, stay with me on this for a while, and it will all start to make sense (hopefully).

In general, the capitalization rates and discount rates used for various benefit streams will be different in each situation. Capitalization and discount rates are discussed in Chapter 10.

The fundamental theory behind the income approach to valuing a business interest is that *the value of an investment is equal to the sum of the present values of the future benefits it is expected to produce for the owner of the interest*. The present value of the future benefits is determined through the application of a rate of return (discount rate), which reflects the time value of money, the relevant investment characteristics, and the degree of risk perceived by the market. The application of the income approach results in an estimate of the fair market value of the normalized net operating assets. In simple terms, the income stream that is capitalized or discounted is produced by using the net assets of the business. Therefore, the value that results from these net assets is included in the income of the company as a going concern. If the income being produced is lower than it should be, there may be a sign of economic depreciation that is applicable to the value of the assets. The assets alone have value only if they can be sold or exchanged (value in exchange sound familiar?). If the owner sold these assets, the business could no longer generate income, and therefore, the value would be sold with the assets.

After the value of the net operating assets is determined, the value of the net non-operating assets is added to the result to obtain the value of the equity. In the debt-free versions of the income approach, the estimate of the value derived results in the value of the invested capital of the enterprise.

Value Is From an Investor's Viewpoint

The income approach is generally used in determining the value of the appraisal subject from the viewpoint of an investor. In many of the older textbooks, we see the income approach referred to as the "investment value approach." This can become confusing, since *investment value* is a standard of value and not an approach to valuation. Although the appraiser will most likely understand the difference in these terms, he or she should avoid using the older terminology for the income approach so that the users of this information will not be confused.

The income approach is based on the assumption that an investor could invest in a property with similar investment characteristics, but not necessarily the same business. This approach looks to the earnings power, or cash generation capabilities, of the enterprise being appraised.

Very often, closely held businesses are so unique that the appraiser cannot find good information about market multiples or capitalization rates to apply to the company's benefit stream. Instead, the appraiser tries to compare the risk associated with the benefit stream to alternative types of investments in the marketplace. This becomes another form of the principle of substitution at work. The appraiser will go a long way by having knowledge about the rates of return available in the marketplace.

Although this method can be difficult to apply at times, it is frequently the best approach for estimating the value of a business. Intuitively, if you can put together a reasonable forecast and you can determine a reasonable rate of return from other, similar investment alternatives, the estimate of value may be a much more reasonable approach than attempting to find guideline companies that may or may not be similar enough to the subject company to make a good comparison. If you are lucky enough to find good guideline companies, you then have the feat of subjectively choosing how to adjust the multiples that will be applied to the subject company. While the income approach also has its own degree of subjectivity, a well-grounded forecast is sometimes easier to achieve. Some appraisers reading this may not agree with me, but if you really start to think about companies that are acquiring other companies, most of them are using some form of discounting model (usually cash flow) as a primary method of determining the value of the target company. Of course, they may not ignore the market multiples, but it will usually come down to the forecast cash flow.

Advantages and Disadvantages of the Income Approach

As to be expected, the income approach has both advantages and disadvantages. By now you should realize that this valuation stuff is not perfect. Let's discuss the good, the bad, and the ugly!

Advantages of the Income Approach

The income approach has some definite advantages, including the following:

- It values an enterprise based on its earnings or cash flow generating abilities. Therefore, there is a relationship between the value of the enterprise and the earnings or cash flow it produces.
- It requires a simple mathematical application that is frequently performed more quickly relative to the other approaches.
- At times, it is the only approach that can be used to value intangible assets.
- Financial markets frequently use the income approach in the decision-making process.

Disadvantages of the Income Approach

As you would expect, there are also disadvantages to the income approach:

- It is frequently difficult to determine the correct level of the sustainable benefits stream that will be used in the application of this approach. This is especially true for most smaller companies (some of our clients are lucky if they can file their current year's tax returns, let alone forecast the future!).

- It is extremely difficult to choose the correct capitalization or discount rate that will be used to capitalize or discount the benefit stream. This requires the appraiser to exercise judgment, which is subjective. At times (most), it is a difficult number to defend on its own merits.

Selecting Benefit Streams

The benefit stream(s) to be used in the application of the income approach depend on many factors. These factors are somewhat similar to those factors that were discussed in Chapter 6 in determining pricing multiples. Special attention should be paid to the following factors: (1) the nature of the business and its capital structure, (2) the purpose and function of the appraisal, and (3) the particular subject of the valuation (e.g., whether the valuation involves a controlling interest or a minority interest).

The Nature of the Business and Its Capital Structure

The benefits stream used by the appraiser will frequently depend on the nature of the business and its capital structure. For example, net income (after-tax) may be the appropriate income stream in certain valuation assignments involving larger companies. Net income may be used to achieve comparability with the guideline companies that report their earnings on an after-tax basis. A pretax income stream may be warranted for smaller appraisal subjects that operate the business to minimize taxes. Chances are that the willing buyer will operate the business in a manner similar to that of the willing seller.

The capital structure of the subject business will also be a factor in the determination of the benefit stream to be used by the appraiser. Companies that are heavily leveraged, compared with guideline companies or industry composite figures, may be more appropriately valued on a debt-free basis. Earnings before interest and taxes may prove to be a more meaningful comparison than net income. Of course, if the goal is to value equity, the liabilities will be subtracted from the value of the invested capital.

The Purpose and Function of the Appraisal

The purpose and function of the appraisal assignment will also play a role in the benefit stream that the appraiser will select. As a refresher, the purpose and function of the appraisal relates to why you are doing the job and what it will be used for. An appraisal assignment for a merger or acquisition will most likely have more of an emphasis on pro forma earnings than on historic earnings. If the appraiser is representing the buyer, the investment value to that buyer may require certain adjustments to be made that would not normally exist in a fair market value appraisal (for example, removal of certain expenses that will go away because of the synergies between the companies).

In certain jurisdictions, particularly for divorce assignments, future earnings are not allowed to be used in valuations submitted to the courts. In these jurisdictions, the primary emphasis becomes the historic figures. Since when does a willing buyer purchase history? These jurisdictions may be misguided.

The Particular Subject of the Valuation

The particular subject of the valuation makes a big difference in the benefit stream that can be used in an appraisal. When an appraiser values a controlling interest, adjustments are commonly made, as discussed in Chapter 5. For minority appraisals, however, many of the adjustments that would have been made for control are not made. The appraiser will use a normalized benefit stream for both valuations, but the minority valuation will most likely not contain the adjustments related to discretionary items.

Another consideration in this process is the fact that the minority shareholder cannot control the balance sheet of the company. Therefore, valuing the minority shares by assuming a normalized debt-to-equity relationship would not make sense. A small closely held company with a considerable amount of debt on the balance sheet is going to be paying a lot of interest expense. Valuing this company for the minority shareholder on a debt-free basis would result in an overvaluation of the company's true worth to that individual. The fact that the controlling shareholder has elected to put the company in debt reduces the value of the company.

Using Pretax or After-Tax Information

In general, it should not really matter whether the appraiser is working with pretax or after-tax information. The key is to be consistent. The use of either pretax or after-tax information has advantages and disadvantages. Remember that you are trying to perform an analysis using "comparable" information from either guideline companies or industry information. You must be able to compare similar information to reach a meaningful conclusion concerning value.

Following are some of the advantages of using pretax information:

- The form of ownership of the appraisal subject will not make a difference. This will allow you to compare C corporations with S corporations with partnerships with sole proprietorships. Varying tax rates will affect neither your analysis nor its conclusion.[1]
- Non-corporate entities can be valued without considering the tax impact of itemized deductions, personal exemptions, etc.
- Small businesses generally operate to minimize income taxes. The willing buyer would probably run the business in a similar manner as the willing seller in that regard. Since "comparable" data will rarely be found, you will find yourself using industry composite data, which is often made up of companies such as the one you are appraising.

There is also something to be said for using after-tax information. Following are some of the advantages:

- Most data derived from the public market is reported on an after-tax basis. This makes the comparison more meaningful if guideline companies from the public market are used.
- After-tax information more appropriately reflects the amount that is available to the stockholders for dividends. Other items affecting cash flow are also considered.
- Larger company valuations will frequently be performed this way for mergers and acquisitions, ESOPs, and initial public offerings because of the available information being reported in this manner.

There is a big controversy in the appraisal field regarding the valuation of non–tax-paying entities such as S corporations and limited liability companies. One school of thought is that since these entities do not pay taxes, the reported results are already after-tax. This would increase the cash flow available to the stockholders and make these companies more valuable. This school of thought seems to create an unfair arbitrage situation for the S corporation. The other school of thought is that all of these entities should be tax-effected based on the premise that the willing buyer may not be eligible to continue the tax election of

[1]It is also acceptable to tax-effect pass-through entities and value these entities on an after-tax basis. In these circumstances, many appraisers will use the corporation tax rates for C corporations on the premise that the willing buyer could be a C corporation. This will also avoid getting involved with personal income tax rates, itemized deductions, personal exemptions, the self-employment tax, and other items that vary greatly between taxpayers. For more information on valuing pass-through entities, you can turn to Pratt's *Valuing a Business*.

the seller and that the population of willing buyers would be too restricted to meet the definition of fair market value. A corporation is frequently the purchaser of another entity. If the seller was an S corporation, the willing C corporation buyer could not qualify to be a stockholder under current law. If you want to read more on this subject written by yours truly, read McGraw-Hill's *The Handbook of Advanced Business Valuation*. I contributed a chapter dealing specifically with valuing S corporations. There is no point in rewriting a masterpiece (only kidding!).

For the nonaccountants reading this book, a C corporation is a typical tax-paying corporation. An S corporation is a legal corporation that, for tax purposes, is treated like a partnership. This means that the shareholders pay personal taxes on the profit instead of corporate taxes being paid by the entity.

The Internal Revenue Service has frequently taken the position that pass-through entities should be tax-effected. However, at the time that I was working on this edition, we were all anxiously awaiting an appeal decision in *Walter L. Gross Jr., et al. v. Commissioner*.[2] In this decision, Judge Halpern allowed the IRS expert to commit the cardinal sin in business valuation of mixing apples and oranges. An after-tax discount rate was applied to a pretax income stream. Most appraisers believe that this was a bad decision. (While I was editing this chapter, the appeal decision was released and Judge Halpern was upheld. However, from reading the opinion, it seems that this issue was never addressed in the appeal. What were they thinking?) More of this stuff will be discussed in the next chapter. In the meantime, as long as the discount or capitalization rates that are used are consistent with the benefit stream being discounted or capitalized, the answer will be the same. Even in a tax-related valuation, pretax information can be used.

Debt-Free or After-Debt

This is like Shakespeare. "To be or not to be. . . ." Should the appraiser consider using a debt-free or an after-debt benefit stream? The same rules apply as we discussed under the market approach (invested capital, remember?). Regardless of which you use, the answer should ultimately be the same. The choice of one over the other will frequently be based on comparability with the guideline companies, industry composite data, or the source of the capitalization or discount rates used in the application of this approach.

Using Cash Flow Instead of Earnings

An appraiser will frequently find that using cash flow is a better measure of the company's earnings capacity. This is particularly true when a more realistic picture is being sought of the amount of money that will be available to pay to the owners of the business as a return on their investment. Many profitable companies go out of business, but it is rare that we see a business with solid cash flow go under. Therefore, cash flow is the name of the game. Similar to pricing multiples (discussed in Chapter 6), cash flow, as opposed to earnings, may be a better measure for the business when the net earnings are low compared with depreciation and amortization. The use of cash flow will depend on the facts and circumstances of each case.

If the valuation subject is a controlling interest, it can be assumed that the controlling interest is able to effectuate changes in the balance sheet of a company. Management must decide what they want to do with respect to the company's cash flow. They can distribute all of the available cash and have no funds for growth, or they may reinvest all or part of the available cash into the company and provide for growth.

An operating business must have a sufficient amount of net working capital, a reasonable amount of fixed asset reinvestment, and available cash flow to pay its long-term obligations as they come due. The growth of the company results from investing more than is required to just maintain the existing assets.

[2]*Walter L. Gross Jr., et al. v. Commissioner*, T.C. Memo. 1999-254.

Growth may generally be funded from internally generated cash flow, new equity, new debt, or a combination of these items.

Defining Cash Flow

The definition of cash flow, as used in a valuation context, differs from the traditional accounting definitions as described in the FASB's *Statement of Financial Accounting Standards No. 95*. Understanding valuation terminology is an important part of the education process so that the appraiser can be conversant in business valuation jargon. The following definitions of cash flow have been used by professional appraisers, and therefore, users of business valuation services may already be familiar with the terminology. Even if the users are not terribly familiar with this terminology, there is no point in recreating the wheel with another set of terminology. The basic net cash flow model is as follows:

	Normalized net income
+	Normalized noncash charges
=	Gross cash flow
−	Anticipated capital expenditures
− or +	Working capital necessary to support growth (or generated due to negative growth)
− or +	Debt borrowings or repayments
−	Preferred stock dividends
=	Net cash flow

In the foregoing model, the net cash flow would be the amount that is available to the common stockholders of the company. This could be thought of as the dividend-paying capacity. It is the amount that is left over after the company reinvests in itself to continue its operations while allowing for growth. After investing in capital expenditures, reinvesting the amount of working capital to allow the company to grow, and taking care of changes in debt, the company is in a position to begin making distributions to the stockholders or owners. Granted, small businesses do not generally pay dividends, but this would be the amount that would be available if they did.

Gross cash flow is the measure of cash flow that we often see in the pricing multiples in the guideline company method. Net cash flow can't be used in that situation because it is rare that an appraiser will have access to the public company's working capital requirements, fixed asset requirements, and other assorted information needed to get from gross cash flow to net cash flow. However, the income approach concentrates on the subject company's cash generation ability. The more information included in deriving the cash flow available to the stockholders, the less risky the cash flow is usually perceived as being since more factors went into its derivation. Of course, this could also result in more errors regarding these factors. It's not a perfect world!

The manner in which net cash flow is derived will depend on whether the appraiser is valuing the equity or the invested capital of the company. As a reminder, valuing the invested capital involves appraising the company on a debt-free basis. The net cash flow model illustrated previously is used by an appraiser when he or she is valuing the equity of the company. If the goal is to value the invested capital of the company, certain modifications must be made to get there. Interest expense is added back, net of taxes, to restate the net income on a debt-free basis. Since interest expense gives rise to a tax benefit, the add-back must be reduced by the corresponding tax benefit.

Another modification is that there will be no addition or subtraction for new borrowings or repayment of old borrowings. Logically, if we are attempting to derive a debt-free result, debt should be eliminated from the model. This results in the following net cash flow model for invested capital:

	Normalized net income
+	Interest expense (net of taxes)
+	Normalized noncash charges
=	Gross cash flow
−	Anticipated capital expenditures
− or +	Working capital necessary to support growth (or generated due to negative growth)
−	Preferred stock dividends
=	Net cash flow

Net cash flow to the equity owner is defined as the gross cash flow generated by the business operations, adjusted for:

- Amounts required for working capital that are needed to meet the growth expectations of the appraisal subject
- Amounts required by the business for the fixed assets needed to maintain the productive capacity necessary to meet the increasing demands of the business
- Amounts that will be used to repay long-term debt principal
- Amounts representing additional long-term debt borrowings
- Amounts for dividends paid to senior equity securities (e.g., preferred stock dividends)

There must be a clear distinction made between short-term cash flow, specific to a particular year, and long-term sustainable cash flow. It is the long-term sustainable cash flow that generally is of interest to the business appraiser. Short-term cash flows may be the result of peaks or valleys in the business cycle or the manner in which management operates the business. The projected net cash flow should be a normalized cash flow. It assumes a required reinvestment into the business each year in an amount sufficient to finance projected operations, as opposed to a discretionary short-term excess reinvestment or deficiency that is not sustainable in the long run. This also implies that the willing buyer would have control of the cash flow. If a minority valuation is being performed, the appraiser will generally not make changes to what the minority investor cannot control. By now, I have emphasized this point enough times that you should realize that it is important!

Projecting Future Benefit Streams

One of the most important parts of the valuation process is the projection of the future benefits stream that will be used in the income approach. Since cash flow is frequently used in business valuation, the discussion about the projection of benefit streams will primarily concentrate on net cash flow, unless otherwise indicated.

The starting point of the projection process is that historical income statements must be analyzed and adjusted (normalized if you are valuing a controlling interest) to reflect the economic income of the business being appraised. Some of the more common adjustments that have been previously discussed are as follows:

- The inventory accounting method may be adjusted to conform to industry practice or expected future treatment. This could include a change in inventory accounting from LIFO to FIFO.
- Depreciation may be adjusted to reflect current economic write-offs more accurately, based on the value determined by the machinery and equipment appraisers or real estate appraisers.
- Non-recurring items should be removed.
- Non-operating income or expense items may be eliminated, if appropriate.
- The effect of the non-operating assets on the income statement must be removed if a control position is being appraised and the assets are to be separately treated in the valuation.
- Related-party transactions may need to be adjusted if the results are other than those that would be negotiated at arm's length.

Some of the normalization adjustments will be made regardless of whether the appraisal subject is a controlling interest or a minority interest. These types of adjustments would be those that affect the future benefit stream, particularly when the historical operations are expected to be different from the future operations. For example, a company may have incurred a hurricane loss in the past year that would not be expected to occur again in the foreseeable future. Certainly, as an appraiser, we do not want to start trying to forecast hurricanes. However, in certain parts of the world, this may be somewhat predictable.

Historical operating results should also be analyzed to gain an understanding of the quality of the earnings reported. This includes asking and answering at least the following questions:

- Are sales concentrated in few customers (risky) or are they spread out among many customers?
- Is the business trendy? Is its popularity only temporary, or is the business expected to be around for a while?
- To what extent is the business able to control its own destiny? Is it dependent on another industry? For example, the retail furniture industry has about a six-month lag behind the residential housing market. If new home sales go down, retail furniture will follow soon thereafter.
- Is the business subject to seasonal or cyclical fluctuations? If so, where in the cycle is the business?
- Does the company have any problem with its suppliers or source of supply? What if the company imports a product from a particular country and the government imposes a trade restriction?
- Is the business dependent on technology, and if so, is the company keeping up with the industry?

The appraiser should also look for trends that may help predict the future with respect to the direction in which the company is headed. These trends may indicate growing, declining, flat, or volatile income streams. If a company has been growing at an exceptionally high rate, the likelihood is slim that the same rate will continue into the future. Since this rate cannot be maintained, the appraiser must compensate in the projection by reducing the growth going forward.

If the company is in a declining mode, the terminal value may be calculated on the basis of liquidation, as opposed to that of a going concern. If a decline is forecast indefinitely into the future, the appraiser should consider whether the highest and best use of the business is in liquidation. If so, the business should be valued in this manner.

If the company's future appears to be flat, there is no reason to use a multi-period valuation model; in this situation, a single-period capitalization model will suffice. When a company's results are erratic, projections become extremely difficult and may have little value in the appraisal process. An averaging of history may prove to be beneficial, but this should be done only as a last resort.

Don't forget to use other information that was gathered from the company or through your own research. Customer contracts can help you forecast expected changes as a result of a customer's growth. For example, if you were valuing a trucking firm that had major contracts with large retail customers, your economic and industry analysis would become important in helping to forecast the trucking firm's growth. Exhibit 9.1 illustrates a section of an economy/industry report that we created and relied on to assist in the forecast of a trucking firm's revenues.

EXHIBIT 9.1
Economy/Industry Section for a Trucking Firm

The appraisal subject transports apparel and other consumer goods for several large, multi-store retailers in the eastern United States, to some extent the Midwest, and in California. Since The Company relies on the retail sector for most of its business, it is important to review the outlook for this sector of the economy.

Consumer spending drives the U.S. economy. In 1995, personal consumption expenditures (PCE) were 68 percent of total GDP. PCE is further divided into spending on durable goods (12 percent in 1995), nondurable goods (30 percent), and spending for services (58 percent). Table 1 presents information on recent consumer spending habits.

TABLE 1
Selected Spending Statistics

	Percentage Change	
	1993–1994	*3Q94–3Q95*
Real personal consumption expenditures	3.0	2.6
Durable goods	7.3	4.8
Furniture and household equipment	10.6	9.7
Video and audio products, computing equipment, and musical instruments	21.9	n/a
Nondurable goods	3.1	2.0
Clothing and shoes	6.0	4.0
Other	3.7	1.2
Services (ex food and energy)	2.1	2.4
Real disposable personal income	2.4	2.8
		1994–1995
Retail sales	10.4	4.2

Source: Survey of Current Business, *Federal Reserve Bulletin*.

Although real disposable personal income rose a bit in the period between the third quarter of 1994 and the third quarter of 1995, spending did not rise because consumer debt burdens were at very high levels. According to *Business Week*, "consumers' non-mortgage debt-to-income ratio hit an all-time high of 19 percent in late 1995." In spite of high consumer confidence and a soaring stock market, spending slowed as consumers paid down some of this debt.

According to this same analyst, retail sales are expected to rise about 4.5 percent in 1996, with clothing sales growing 3.5 percent, and "consumer-electronics stores . . . expected to have another hot year, as shoppers snap up computers and related items."

The outlook for retailing in the second half of the 1990s is not as good as it was in the previous decade, but it is not all gloom. Value Line retail analyst David R. Cohen stated in late 1995, "It is generally agreed that the country is overstored, so successful operators are the ones taking market share from others." Like the trucking industry, retailing is experiencing a period of consolidation, as stronger companies acquire weaker ones. This should be healthy for the industry. Department stores should continue to consolidate, discount retailers should see sales gains, and specialty stores may see a mixed outlook depending on the merchandise mix.

EXHIBIT 9.1 *(Continued)*

Table 2 presents selected statistics for six major retailers that are customers of the subject company. These six companies will have estimated sales totaling almost $100 million in 1995 according to Value Line. The same companies combined operated more than 16,000 stores during the same year. Combined sales are forecast to grow to almost $108 million in 1996 (up 9.2 percent for the year) and about $137 million by 2000, an increase of 27 percent. The total number of stores is expected to grow about 22 percent to 19,580 stores by 2000.

TABLE 2
Retailers' Selected Statistics: 1985–2000

	1985A	*1990A*	*1995E*	*1996F*	*1998–2000F**
Melville Corp.					
Number of stores	5,574	7,754	7,200	7,345	7,790
Sales ($ mln)	4,775	8,687	11,885	12,720	15,290
% Change—sales (AGR)		12.71%	6.47%	7.03%	20.20%
Kmart Corp.					
Number of stores	3,848	4,180	2,480	2,475	2,550
Sales ($ mln)	22,420	32,070	34,140	35,500	40,000
% Change—sales (AGR)		7.42%	1.26%	3.98%	12.68%
Federated Department					
Number of stores		244	440	415	440
Sales ($ mln)		7,142	14,720	16,700	19,900
% Change—sales (AGR)		n/a	15.56%	13.45%	19.16%
The Limited, Inc.					
Number of stores	2,353	3,864	4,867	5,345	7,000
Sales ($ mln)	2,387	5,254	7,321	7,950	12,500
% Change—sales (AGR)		17.09%	6.86%	8.59%	57.23%
Dayton Hudson					
Number of stores	1,206	708	1,050	1,125	1,350
Sales ($ mln)	8,793	14,739	23,100	25,000	31,500
% Change—sales (AGR)		10.88%	9.40%	8.23%	26.00%
Best Buy					
Number of stores	12	73	250	290	450
Sales ($ mln)	113	665	7,600	9,990	18,000
% Change—sales (AGR)		42.54%	62.78%	31.45%	80.18%

A = Actual, E = Estimated, F = Forecast.
*Percentage change is 1996–2000 total.

Source: *Value Line Investment Survey,* November 24, 1995.

At the end of a major restructuring, Melville Corp. will operate CVS Drug Stores, Bob's apparel stores, Kay-Bee Toys, and Linens-n-Things household furnishings stores. The changes should ultimately enhance the earnings power of its remaining businesses. Value Line believes the company "has speculative appeal on a long-term basis."

Kmart Corp. has been hurt by intense competition from other general discount merchandise retailers, but is in the process of dealing with its cash flow problems. Although the company's shares "have ill-defined prospects to 1998–2000" according to Value Line, further cost reductions and store closings should improve cash flow. Kmart is the third largest retailer in the world.

(Continued)

EXHIBIT 9.1 ***(Continued)***

Federated Department Stores operates Macy's, Bloomingdale's, Stern's, Rich's, Burdine's, and The Bon Marche department stores. Data prior to 1992 is not available because the company operated under Chapter XI protection in 1990–91. According to Value Line, "The Company plans to utilize Macy's renowned strength in private-label merchandising to increase its private-label sales from the current 7 percent level (excluding Macy's stores) to about 15 percent by the latter part of fiscal 1996."

The Limited, Inc. operates stores under the names Limited, Express, Lerner, Lane Bryant, Victoria's Secret Stores, Henri Bendel, Abercrombie & Fitch, Structure, Limited Too, Cacique, Bath & Body Works, and Penhaligon's. Value Line's assessment: "The sluggish women's apparel area has hurt earnings this year. . . . Looking ahead three to five years however, the issue has attractive appreciation potential based on the dominant position of several of its lines in specialty retailing."

Dayton Hudson Corp. operates three retail divisions: upscale discount (Target), soft goods (Mervyn's), and department stores (Hudson's, Dayton's, and Marshall Field's). Although the latter two divisions have had disappointing results recently, the former has seen operating profits jump 37 percent in the past two fiscal years. "Next year the company plans to spend about 80 percent of its $1.4 billion budget to expand Target's store base by 65 to 75 units, about a 10 percent increase." Target is entering the Northeast in fiscal 1995 and plans to develop a major presence in that area of the country by 2000.

Best Buy sells consumer electronics, major appliances, home office equipment, entertainment software, and photographic equipment in superstores in 27 states. Total sales have grown rapidly due to strong demand for computers and peripherals. Value Line believes The Company's shares "have superior prospects to 1998–2000."

Retailing closely follows economic activity. As the economy comes out of its slowdown in 1996, retailing should follow. Overall, bankers and analysts are cautiously optimistic on the outlook for retailing in the second half of 1996. They claim that consolidation will continue since economies of scale will be necessary for survival in the sluggish environment. The market should shake itself out by the end of 1996.

Long-term moderate economic growth accompanied by low inflation and unemployment offers an excellent environment for business to thrive. Stability provides an excellent arena for long-term planning, and low interest rates make inexpensive financing available. This steady growth environment should produce sufficient goods to be moved by all players in the transportation sector.

As has been seen, trucking's share of freight, especially general, higher-cost goods, should increase well into the next century. Industry consolidation during 1995 and early 1996 would remove the excess capacity. Strong, well-managed carriers, providing excellent service, will be the survivors. These companies will be well positioned to enjoy double-digit growth rates into the 21st century.

The assignment in Exhibit 9.1 had a valuation date of January 31, 1996. The growth of retail customers was an essential part of the forecasting process for the trucking company that was the subject of the appraisal. The customer contracts in place assisted us in forecasting the growth used in our appraisal.

The next question that the appraiser asks is, how far out into the future should the projections go? The projections should go out far enough into the future that they represent sustainable future levels of income for the company. If the company has been showing losses, the projections should go out far enough to allow the company to return to a level of normal sustainable profitability. The same is true if the company has been making large profits. Go out far enough to reflect the normal conditions for the company. The overall idea is to go out beyond periods that contain the peaks and valleys that may be short-term. The willing buyer is going to be looking for the income stream that he or she can count on beyond the near term.

Another consideration related to the projection period is that the projections should go out far enough so that the business can get through a period of significant plant construction or expansion. If new products are being introduced, the projections should extend to the point that the results of the new product's introduction can be understood. If a merger or acquisition is expected to take place or is in the process of taking place, the projections should extend to the period after the combination is completed.

The anticipated rate of growth is the primary factor to be considered in how far the projections should be continued. Stabilization is the goal to be achieved in the projection period. This is frequently much more difficult than it seems. You will have to conduct a thorough analysis of the subject company, the economy, and the industry if you hope to get reasonably close. Keep in mind that during the earlier years of the projection, year-to-year growth can exceed the discount rate selected, but that cannot continue beyond the terminal year since the discount rate minus growth (capitalization rate) cannot logically be less than zero. Can you imagine a willing seller paying the willing buyer to take the business off his or her hands? A negative discount rate would create this result. This is explained more fully in Chapter 10.

A common error made among inexperienced appraisers who rely on computer software to assist with (or do) the projections is to allow these programs to determine the period to be used in the projection. Most software programs allow either a 5-year or a 10-year period to be used for a projection. This may not be the correct period for a particular appraisal assignment. The facts and circumstances of each situation will be different and require a different projection period. Do not depend on a software program to make decisions that require judgment!

In practice, the most common projection period is five years. Some appraisers consider this period to be a normal business cycle, while others focus on Revenue Rulings 59-60 and 68-609, which suggest five years. There is no magic about five years. The period used can be two years, three years, seven years, or even longer. It is almost always difficult to forecast the future, especially if the future is many years forward.

The Acceptance of Forecasts and Projections

In tax-related appraisals, Revenue Ruling 59-60 discusses the fact that "valuation is a prophecy of the future." This is an indication that the future is an important component of the valuation process. In *Central Trust v. United States*,[3] the court found that "past earnings are important only insofar as they reasonably forecast the future earnings." In the *Estate of Kirkpatrick*,[4] the court emphasized the fact that a potential investor would analyze the business enterprise from the viewpoint of its prospects as a money-making enterprise. In some non–tax-related appraisals (divorce appraisals), the courts are still uncertain about using forecasts. However, more and more courts are beginning to accept this methodology if a well-thought-out and well-presented forecast is used in an appraisal. Some judges are uncomfortable with projections and discount their value.

It is up to the appraiser to be able to explain the importance of the future in the context of an appraisal. Who buys history? Many divorce-related appraisals refer to Revenue Rulings 59-60 and 68-609, in which case the appraiser should remember that these rulings emphasize "probable future earnings." The problem is that the judge gets an uncomfortable feeling because the projections are usually poorly done. This makes the projections seem highly speculative. Performing a forecast is not a guarantee that the company will actually achieve the forecast results, but not doing a forecast is like not really doing an appraisal. Even if you use historical data, you are effectively saying that the future is expected to resemble the past.

The key to having your forecast accepted is to document your assumptions. Do not just blindly ask your client for a forecast and accept it as if it is objective. Clients have desired end results, and despite what they say about not understanding the business valuation process, they almost always know if they need a good forecast or a doom and gloom forecast. Don't get caught up in being an advocate for your client, particularly

[3] 305 E.2d 383 (1962).

[4] T.C. Memo. 1975-344.

in a litigation assignment, because it will come back to get you in your tail. Exhibit 9.2 reflects a forecast from an actual assignment. The client was a mid-sized company with operations around the world. While this may be larger than some of the companies that you may appraise on a regular basis, the principles are the same.

EXHIBIT 9.2
Sample Forecast Section

The Earning Capacity of the Company

ABC's comparative statement of income reflected economic net income for the years ended December 31, 1996, through December 31, 1998, and annualized results for 1999 as follows:

1996	$ 5,031,635
1997	6,486,433
1998	11,990,797
1999	14,191,540

As can be seen, ABC's earnings have grown significantly during this period. For the entire period, earnings grew at a compound average annual rate of 36 percent. This is a relatively high rate of growth.

In order to determine the earning capacity of The Company, we used management's forecasts for the business. Management provided the appraiser with a five-year forecast for worldwide operations. This forecast appeared to be fairly aggressive, and as such, the appraiser met with company personnel, as well as the firm's U.S. auditors to discuss these projections. As a result of our meeting, the appraiser has adjusted management's forecast to a more reasonable level. The forecast appears in Table 1.

TABLE 1
Adjusted Management's Forecast

	1999[1]	*2000*	*2001*	*2002*	*2003*	*2004*
Sales	$40,617,255	$ 50,429,925	$ 60,548,243	$ 70,957,326	$ 80,998,393	$ 93,294,701
Cost of goods sold	9,958,735	13,616,080	17,256,249	21,287,198	25,514,494	30,787,251
Gross profit	$30,658,520	$ 36,813,845	$ 43,291,994	$ 49,670,128	$ 55,483,899	$ 62,507,450
Operating expenses	13,691,488	15,633,277	17,196,605	18,916,265	20,807,892	22,888,681
Earnings before depreciation, interest, and taxes	$16,967,032	$ 21,180,568	$ 26,095,389	$ 30,753,863	$ 34,676,007	$ 39,618,769
Depreciation and amortization	1,832,107	2,488,000	2,947,000	3,499,800	4,005,000	4,591,600
Earnings before interest and taxes	$15,134,925	$ 18,692,568	$ 23,148,389	$ 27,254,063	$ 30,671,007	$ 35,027,169
Interest expense	307,613	220,000	240,700	264,300	288,000	316,000
Interest income	(1,000,720)	(500,000)	(500,000)	(500,000)	(500,000)	(500,000)
Earnings before taxes	$15,828,032	$ 18,972,568	$ 23,407,689	$ 27,489,763	$ 30,883,007	$ 35,211,169
Taxes	6,321,716	7,589,027	9,363,076	10,995,905	12,353,203	14,084,468
Net income	**$9,506,316**	**$11,383,541**	**$14,044,613**	**$16,493,858**	**$18,529,804**	**$21,126,701**

[1]Actual presented on a normalized basis.

The following adjustments were made to management's forecast:

1. Net revenue was reduced by 10 percent per year in order to recognize that The Company probably could not continue to grow at the rate that it has grown over the past several years. The revised compound growth rate amounts to 23.5 percent over the next five years, which although less than the 36 percent over the past four years, certainly reflects a continuing rate of growth far in excess of the 8 percent forecast for the industry by Integra.

EXHIBIT 9.2 *(Continued)*

2. Cost of sales has been adjusted in the forecast to reflect higher costs and a slimming of the gross profit percentage available to The Company due to competitive demands, and demands by the customer for rebates. Management's original forecast had cost of sales ranging from 29 percent to 32 percent. In order to make a reasonable adjustment, we reviewed the 1999 annualized financial statement, which reflected a 24.5 percent cost of sales. Based on this presentation, an increase from 24.5 percent to 29 percent seemed considerably high during one year. We have adjusted the forecast to reflect cost of sales as follows:

2000	27.0%
2001	28.5%
2002	30.0%
2003	31.5%
2004	33.0%

3. Operating expenses had been forecast by The Company but did not seem to reflect a logical increase that would be necessary in order to accommodate the rapid growth in revenues expected. As such, we reviewed the operating expenses of The Company as a percentage of sales, removing variable expenses and certain other expenses that are being treated separately, in order to determine what percent of revenue these expenses typically amount to for The Company. Based on our analysis, it appears that fixed operating expenses are approximately 31 percent of revenue. Therefore, we have adjusted the operating expenses to agree with this percentage for the year 2000. Thereafter, we have increased the dollar amount by 10 percent per year, allowing for inflation and some level of real growth in the expenses that will be needed to accommodate a larger company.
4. Taxes have also been adjusted, as we have calculated taxes based on U.S. corporation tax rates.

In addition to forecasting the operations of The Company, management also provided us with a forecast balance sheet (Table 2). As a result of the changes that were made to the forecast income statement, as well as the historical balance sheet, we have made various adjustments to the forecast balance sheet in order to keep it consistent with The Company's forecast operations.

TABLE 2
Adjusted Management's Forecast

	2000	*2001*	*2002*	*2003*	*2004*
Current assets					
Cash	$ 3,000,000	$ 3,000,000	$ 3,000,000	$ 3,000,000	$ 3,000,000
Accounts receivable	7,691,507	9,234,740	10,822,320	12,353,771	14,229,188
Inventory	57,200	72,492	89,426	107,185	129,335
Other current assets	3,764,959	4,141,455	4,555,601	5,011,161	5,512,277
Total current assets	$ 14,513,666	$ 16,448,687	$ 18,467,347	$ 20,472,117	$ 22,870,800
Gross fixed assets	$ 10,303,000	$ 15,762,000	$ 21,025,000	$ 26,281,000	$ 32,027,000
Capital expenditures	5,459,000	5,263,000	5,256,000	5,746,000	6,370,000
Accumulated depreciation	(5,640,000)	(8,587,000)	(12,087,000)	(16,092,000)	(20,684,000)
Net fixed assets	$ 10,122,000	$ 12,438,000	$ 14,194,000	$ 15,935,000	$ 17,713,000
Total other assets	$ 1,465,605	$ 1,612,166	$ 1,773,383	$ 1,950,721	$ 2,145,793
Total assets	**$26,101,271**	**$30,498,853**	**$34,434,730**	**$38,357,838**	**$42,729,593**
Current liabilities					
Accounts payable	$ 1,855,766	$ 2,351,892	$ 2,901,279	$ 3,477,427	$ 4,196,063
Income taxes payable	1,897,257	2,340,769	2,748,976	3,088,301	3,521,117
Other current liabilities	713,635	784,999	863,498	949,848	1,044,833
Current portion of long-term debt	1,187,000	1,200,000	1,067,000	1,075,000	858,000
Total current liabilities	$ 5,653,658	$ 6,677,660	$ 7,580,753	$ 8,590,576	$ 9,620,013

(Continued)

EXHIBIT 9.2 *(Continued)*

	2000	*2001*	*2002*	*2003*	*2004*
Long-term debt	$ 1,731,000	$ 1,400,000	$ 1,050,000	$ 925,000	$ 550,000
Other liabilities	651,470	651,470	651,470	651,470	651,470
Total long-term liabilities	$ 2,382,470	$ 2,051,470	$ 1,701,470	$ 1,576,470	$ 1,201,470
Total liabilities	$ 8,036,128	$ 8,729,130	$ 9,282,223	$ 10,167,046	$ 10,821,483
Equity					
Capital stock	$ 1,373,500	$ 1,373,500	$ 1,373,500	$ 1,373,500	$ 1,373,500
Retained earnings	16,691,643	20,396,223	23,779,007	26,817,291	30,534,610
Total equity	$ 18,065,143	$ 21,769,723	$ 25,152,507	$ 28,190,791	$ 31,908,110
Total liabilities and equity	**$26,101,271**	**$30,498,853**	**$34,434,730**	**$38,357,838**	**$42,729,593**

The adjustments made to the balance sheet were as follows:

1. Inventory has been reflected based on the financial ratio calculated for 1999.
2. Accounts receivable has been calculated based on the number of days of outstanding sales for 1999.
3. Cash has been maintained at a $3 million level, which provides more than adequate liquidity to The Company, and in that regard, all excess cash is assumed to be available for distribution to the "willing buyer."
4. Income taxes payable have been assumed to be 25 percent of the year's tax liability assuming that quarterly estimated tax payments would be paid.
5. Deferred taxes have been adjusted and kept constant throughout the period.

In order to review the forecast financial statements for reasonableness, we prepared a forecast common-size income statement, which is reflected in Table 3.

TABLE 3

Forecast Common-Size Income Statement

	2000	*2001*	*2002*	*2003*	*2004*
Sales	100.00%	100.00%	100.00%	100.00%	100.00%
Cost of goods sold	27.00%	28.50%	30.00%	31.50%	33.00%
Gross profit	73.00%	71.50%	70.00%	68.50%	67.00%
Operating expenses	31.00%	28.40%	26.66%	25.69%	24.53%
Earnings before depreciation, interest, and taxes (EBITDA)	42.00%	43.10%	43.34%	42.81%	42.47%
Depreciation	4.93%	4.87%	4.93%	4.94%	4.92%
Earnings before interest and taxes (EBIT)	37.07%	38.23%	38.41%	37.87%	37.54%
Interest expense	0.44%	0.40%	0.37%	0.36%	0.34%
Interest income	(0.99%)	(0.83%)	(0.70%)	(0.62%)	(0.54%)
Earnings before taxes	37.62%	38.66%	38.74%	38.13%	37.74%
Taxes	15.05%	15.46%	15.50%	15.25%	15.10%
Net income	**22.57%**	**23.20%**	**23.24%**	**22.88%**	**22.65%**

Note: Figures may not add due to rounding

EXHIBIT 9.2 *(Continued)*

In addition to the common-size forecast income statement, we also prepared a growth analysis in order to reflect the period-to-period changes as a result of the forecast. This appears in Table 4. In our opinion, we believe as adjusted, the forecast financial statements reflect the earning capacity of ABC.

TABLE 4

Growth Analysis for Forecast Income Statement

	2000	2001	2002	2003	2004
Sales	24.16%	20.06%	17.19%	14.15%	15.18%
Cost of goods sold	36.73%	26.73%	23.36%	19.86%	20.67%
Gross profit	20.08%	17.60%	14.73%	11.70%	12.66%
Operating expenses	14.18%	10.00%	10.00%	10.00%	10.00%
Earnings before depreciation, interest, and taxes (EBITDA)	24.83%	23.20%	17.85%	12.75%	14.25%
Depreciation	35.80%	18.45%	18.76%	14.44%	14.65%
Earnings before interest and taxes (EBIT)	23.51%	23.84%	17.74%	12.54%	14.20%
Interest expense	(28.48%)	9.41%	9.80%	8.97%	9.72%
Interest income	(50.04%)	0.00%	0.00%	0.00%	0.00%
Earnings before taxes	19.87%	23.38%	17.44%	12.34%	14.01%
Taxes	20.05%	23.38%	17.44%	12.34%	14.01%
Net income	**19.75%**	**23.38%**	**17.44%**	**12.34%**	**14.01%**

What if the forecast is incorrect? *You can be absolutely certain that your valuation will be wrong!* But don't worry, potential investors are frequently wrong also. If I were right every time that I made an investment, I would probably be writing this book from a lounge chair from my private beach resort somewhere warm! The concept of fair market value requires the appraiser to put himself or herself in the position of the willing buyer on the valuation date and to make an informed judgment, based on all information known at that time, on what the future will be like. That is what is really being purchased. But don't forget about the willing seller also. Any knowledge that the willing seller has would also be known and factored into the selling price.

One of the real-world difficulties that will take place regarding your projections, especially if the appraiser is testifying in a court proceeding, is when the opposing attorney gives the appraiser subsequent financial data beyond the valuation date to prove that the forecast was wrong. This is where the cross-examining attorney tries to be a hero and says, "Gotcha."

The appraiser should emphasize that the concept of fair market value would be violated if subsequent information were used. A willing buyer cannot know what is in store for the future, other than by performing the same level of due diligence that the appraiser attempts to perform. The analysis of the company's historical results, economy and industry forecasts, and other similar information should be used to project the future results of the appraisal subject. All of the information gathered during this analysis will assist the appraiser in making reasonable forecasts. Work with management to get the forecast to a reasonable level.[5] Understand, however, that what management wants to accomplish with the appraisal may be a factor in the type of information that you will be given.

[5]Unlike any other class of appraisers, the CPA must consider the standards promulgated by the AICPA on prospective financial reporting. See the AICPA *Statements on Standards for Accounting and Review Services*.

The appraiser frequently obtains projections from the company's management. If these projections are to be used, the appraiser should attempt to compare previous projections against actual results (even budget versus actual). This will give the appraiser a comfort level regarding management's ability to project the future of the business. If the appraiser is not comfortable with management's projections, there are several options on how to proceed. The following are some of them:

- Discuss with management any items that might need to be changed.
- Adjust the discount rate for the additional element of risk by increasing the rate used.
- Do not use the multi-period benefit stream discounting method in favor of the single-period income capitalization method or other valuation approaches suitable to the circumstances of the particular assignment.
- Withdraw from the engagement. Although most appraisers do not wish to turn away an assignment, there are times when the projection is so critical in the valuation process that it becomes impossible to proceed with the job. An example would be when the valuation is being performed for the purpose of obtaining financing.
- If the projected operations are expected to be stable, do not use a multi-period model if a single-period model will suffice. A single-period model is easier to understand and there are fewer variables to be attacked, especially if the valuation might be used in a litigation.

Avoid accepting management's forecast without doing a reasonableness check. I have seen the following scenario too often. The subject business has normalized earnings for the last five years as follows:

1996	$178,000
1997	170,000
1998	180,000
1999	175,000
2000	200,000

Now, the client helps us with the projection. Going through a divorce, the client projects that business is terrible, the industry is falling apart, and the business will never be the same. Therefore, the next five years look like this:

2001	$180,000
2002	170,000
2003	150,000
2004	135,000
2005	125,000

That poor, poor client! Now let's look at the information that the same client might give us if he or she were trying to sell the business. In this case, the projections might be the following:

2001	$225,000
2002	250,000
2003	275,000
2004	300,000
2005	350,000

Don't you just love this business? Where else can the same client give you such nonsense? Part of the role of being a good appraiser is to maintain an objective attitude, which includes recognizing that your own client may try to help you get to his or her desired end result by giving you bad numbers. Sometimes you will not be able to use this information, and you will be required to consider other valuation methods. However, don't roll over and play dead just because the job is difficult. That is why they pay us the big bucks!

Income Approach Methods

The value derived under the income approach is the value of the operating assets less liabilities of the enterprise. The value of the non-operating assets less the non-operating liabilities is then added to the value of the operating entity to obtain the value of the total enterprise. The valuation methods included in the income approach are (1) the capitalization of benefits method and (2) the discounted future benefits method. Although not truly an income approach method, I am also going to cover the excess earnings method in this group of methods. As you will see, the excess earnings method is really a method used to determine the value of the unidentifiable intangible assets (goodwill). When added to the adjusted book value method, the result is really closer to an asset approach than an income approach. However, since capitalization of a benefit stream is required in this method, I chose to cover it here. After all, it's my book!

Capitalization of Benefits Method

The theoretical value of a business is the present value of all of the benefits that can reasonably be expected to be generated to the owners in the future. This concept can be mathematically displayed. If you are anything like me, you will not be happy trying to remember all of the mathematics of finance that you took in school and forgot shortly thereafter. But this stuff is important, so I am going to give you what I consider to be the minimum of math to demonstrate what we will be doing in the application of these models. The mathematical model to express this concept is as follows:

$$PV = \frac{E_1}{(1+k)^1} + \frac{E_2}{(1+k)^2} + \frac{E_3}{(1+k)^3} + \frac{E_\infty}{(1+k)^\infty}$$

where

E = Benefit stream
k = Discount rate

If you do not like long equations, this one can be reduced to the following:

$$PV = \sum_{n=1}^{n=\infty} \frac{E_n}{(1+k)^n}$$

where

E = Benefit stream
k = Discount rate
n = Time period (1 to infinity)

For those mathematical neophytes (like myself), the symbol $\sum$ stands for "summation." Therefore, this formula means the sum of the expected benefit streams from period 1 to period infinity, discounted to present value. Even more simply stated, it is the sum of the present values of the forecast benefit streams going out for a long, long time (you can't get much longer than infinity).

If the growth of the benefit stream (the numerator) is assumed to be constant over time, the equation can be reduced again to the following:

$$PV = \frac{E_1}{k - g}$$

where

E = Benefit stream expected in the next period
k = Discount rate
g = Growth rate from time $t = 0$ to time t = infinity

Now that we got the math stuff out of the way, let's restate what we just did in English. The equation for the single-period benefit stream capitalization method is:

Value = Benefit stream ÷ Capitalization rate

If you think about what we just did, you will realize that we took the growth out of the numerator (we assumed it to be constant) and we removed the growth from the discount rate ($k - g$). Since this capitalization model assumes a continued benefit stream into perpetuity, the growth that is removed from the discount rate must be the long-term sustainable growth. We will cover this in more detail in the next chapter. The mathematics, however, can be demonstrated with a simple example. Let's assume that the following information is available to you:

This year's cash flow	$ 909
Next year's forecast cash flow	$1,000
Forecast growth	10%
Required rate of return	35%

Forecasting the future cash flows and discounting them back to present value would result in the following calculation:

Forecast	*Present Value*	*Forecast*	*Present Value*
1,000	741	5,5610	19
1,100	604	6,116	15
1,210	492	6,727	12
1,331	401	7,400	10
1,464	327	8,140	8
1,611	266	8,954	7
1,772	217	9,850	5
1,949	177	10,835	4
2,144	144	11,918	4
2,358	117	13,110	3
2,594	96	14,421	2
2,853	78	15,863	2
3,138	63	17,449	2
3,452	52	19,194	1
3,797	42	21,114	1
4,177	34	23,225	1
4,595	28	25,548	1
5,054	23	Total	4,000 (rounded)

Instead of forecasting constant growth in each period and discounting it for the 35 periods in the table above, the mathematics of removing growth from the numerator and the denominator of the equation allows us to capitalize a single stream as follows:

$$\$1,000 \div (.35 - .10) = \$4,000$$

Much easier, isn't it? What this example actually proves is that the single-period capitalization model should derive the same answer as the multi-period discounting model if you have constant growth. I will explain further in a little while, but the reason for using one model as opposed to the other has to do with the stability of the income stream that is being forecast.

To apply the single-period capitalization of benefits model correctly, the benefit stream to be capitalized must be from stabilized operating conditions. Combining this with anticipated growth, the stabilized benefit stream should reflect the future expectations of the business or of the investment. Each benefit stream calls for a different capitalization rate. The risk associated with a particular benefit stream will cause the difference in the rates. Exhibit 9.3 illustrates this point.

EXHIBIT 9.3

Matching the Benefit Stream With Capitalization Rates: An Example

Let's assume that Doodles, Inc. was valued by an appraiser as having an equity value of $1 million. Based on Doodles's income statement used for the valuation, the following capitalization rates would apply:

	Benefit Stream		*Cap. Rate*		*Value ($)*
Revenues	$10,000,000	÷	1,000%	=	1,000,000
Cost of sales	9,000,000				
Gross profit	$ 1,000,000	÷	100%	=	1,000,000
Operating expenses	600,000				
EBIT	$ 400,000	÷	40%	=	1,000,000
Interest expense	50,000				
Pretax income	$ 350,000	÷	35%	=	1,000,000
Taxes	100,000				
Net income	$ 250,000	÷	25%	=	1,000,000

For right now, don't worry about how I calculated the capitalization rates. Obviously, a capitalization rate of 1,000 percent does not make sense. However, the point of this example is that regardless of the benefit stream that is capitalized, the answer should be the same. This does not mean that you can come up with the answer using one benefit stream and force all of the other elements to fit. That would be cheating!

The benefit stream will be capitalized by a rate that reflects the risk of the benefit stream being capitalized. The appraiser should apply a sensitivity analysis to the capitalization process since relatively minor variations in either the benefit stream or the capitalization rate being considered can result in significant differences in the end result. This can be illustrated as follows:

Benefit Stream ($)	*Cap. Rate (%)*	*Value ($)*
100,000	20	500,000
100,000	25	400,000
100,000	30	333,333
100,000	35	285,714
100,000	40	250,000

Alternatively, this can be shown as follows:

Benefit Stream ($)	*Cap. Rate (%)*	*Value ($)*
100,000	25	400,000
120,000	25	480,000
140,000	25	560,000
160,000	25	640,000
180,000	25	720,000
200,000	25	800,000

Relatively small changes in the capitalization rate or benefit stream can have a major impact on the conclusion. Now if the benefit stream is wrong and the capitalization rate is wrong but you got the right answer, count your blessings. Also, pay your malpractice premiums, since you may not be that lucky the next time.

The objective in a single-period capitalization method is to determine through analysis—and if necessary, adjustments—the level of benefits that are reflective of a *sustainable* level for the appraisal subject. As discussed previously, the purpose and function of the appraisal influence the nature of the benefit stream to be capitalized.

In valuing a minority interest in a closely held business, the appraiser generally does not make discretionary adjustments to the benefit stream. Non-recurring items and GAAP adjustments might be made when these items are considered to affect the benefit stream available to the minority interest in the future. Since the minority interest does not have the ability to effectuate change in the discretionary items, it is generally considered to be inappropriate to modify the benefit stream for items that cannot be changed by the minority.

In certain instances, adjustments to the benefit stream may be required, even in a minority situation. Adjustments may be appropriate when there are non-recurring items or when the controlling party is abusing control to the detriment of the minority owner (in this instance, an oppressed-shareholder action may be lurking in the wings). Another situation where you may need to make certain adjustments is when you are valuing a family business, particularly for estate and gift tax purposes. Although the standard is the hypothetical willing buyer and willing seller, a reality check needs to be made when the parent is taking an above-market salary or perquisites in comparison to the minority interest being valued. Use discretion and do the right thing. If the business is expected to be sold, pro forma earnings or cash flow will be more important to the willing buyer. Appropriate adjustments should be made to accommodate this situation.

One of the most fundamental concepts to consider when one does a business appraisal is that there must be a consistent matching of the capitalization rate with the benefit stream being capitalized. Even if the capitalization rate is developed from information from the public stock market (which primarily relates to minority shares), adjustments may be made to the benefit stream being capitalized. The benefit stream (not the capitalization rate!) will determine whether the valuation result is control or minority. There is probably a valid argument that can be made to support the premise that capitalization rates (or discount rates) that are derived from the public stock market contain an element of minority interest in them. Therefore, if you believe that these discount and capitalization rates are applicable to minority interests[6] but you apply them to an income stream that reflects control, the appraiser can probably justify a slightly smaller minority discount if the subject of the appraisal is a minority interest. But if the appraisal subject is a minority interest, why would the appraiser make control adjustments to the income stream?

[6]Numerous articles that discuss this subject in detail have appeared in *Business Valuation Review*. Some authors believe that publicly traded stocks trade at a value close to the control value and there is no true distinction between a control and minority discount rate. After all, why should the required rate of return be different for the same investment? Others believe the opposite is true. I discuss some of this in Chapter 11.

Service businesses with few fixed assets are generally valued based on net income (pretax or after-tax) or sometimes on a multiple of revenues. The multiple is another form of capitalization rate. Mathematically, a capitalization rate is the inverse of a multiple (a multiple of 5 equals a capitalization rate of 1/5, or 20 percent).

If a business tends to be cyclical in nature, an average of historical data is sometimes used to approximate the stable earnings base that can be capitalized. Once again, as a reminder, any time that historical data is used, it should represent probable future earnings. Do not rely purely on historical data! Willing buyers do not buy history!

When a business is growing, a multi-period method (soon to be discussed) should be considered, since the benefit stream is not expected to be stable. A weighted average of historical data—or more preferably, forecast data—should be used as a basis for discounting. When a business's operations have changed, the appraiser should ignore the historical data that is no longer representative of the current business. This means that even though the revenue rulings suggest that a period of five or more years be used as the basis of the valuation, it is perfectly acceptable to ignore the historical information if the future is expected to be different. (Don't worry about not following the revenue rulings. You will still be in compliance with the intent of these rulings.)

Adjustments made to the benefit stream to be capitalized are generally made only when a majority/control interest in the business is being appraised. In the real world, just before the closing, willing sellers and willing buyers will adjust the sales or purchase price for certain items that may be known. Additional adjustments can be made for any of the following items:

- *An excess or deficiency of net working capital*. An abundance of working capital may be considered to be a non-operating asset and may be added to the ending value determined for the operations. In addition, if a willing buyer is aware that he or she will have to infuse additional capital into the business immediately, a reduction in the sales price is likely to occur. For example, assume that a willing buyer knows that the widget machine must immediately be replaced upon purchase to keep the business running. What is the likelihood that the price will not be adjusted if the cash flow used to calculate value did not have the replacement of this asset in it?
- *The existence of non-operating assets*. The value of these assets, net of non-operating liabilities, will be added to the operating value of the enterprise.
- *Evidence of underutilized capacity*. Underutilized capacity has value if the buyer has the ability to use it properly. The business may be worth more in someone else's hands than in the hands of the current owner for this reason. Although a willing buyer will not want to pay for what he or she will bring to the company after the acquisition, the willing seller will want compensation for the ability to increase capacity. Negotiations will probably result in a compromise value. This is frequently a very tough adjustment to make, since it requires the valuation of the company to be made based on a different set of assumptions than the business actually operates under. If the calculations are performed as if in the hands of a particular buyer, the result may be investment value and not fair market value. However, if all willing buyers would most likely make the same changes, it may be fair market value after all.
- *The need to invest in additional productive capacity to meet future operational demands*. This should be considered in the cash flow requirements of the business.
- *Insufficient management or employee skills or capacity*. Poor management increases the risk of the business and, therefore, decreases its value. More often, this is reflected in poor earnings capacity or a higher discount or capitalization rate due to the increased risk of having a buffoon run the company. Just don't double-count and put it in both places.

On occasion, but not always, there may be times when adjustments that will affect both the balance sheet and the income statement are required. For example, a balance sheet adjustment from LIFO to FIFO inventory does not necessarily require a corresponding adjustment to the cost of goods sold, since a better matching has been accomplished in the income statement. On the other hand, an adjustment to the value of the fixed assets on the balance sheet may require a corresponding adjustment to the depreciation expense on the income statement. This is the part that drives many accountants nuts! The debits do not equal the credits.

Revenue Ruling 59-60 states that "determination of the proper capitalization rate presents one of the most difficult problems in valuation" (no kidding!). Capitalization of the total benefit stream results in an indication of value for the entire operating enterprise (shareholder's equity or invested capital); partial benefit streams can also be capitalized to estimate the value of portions of the enterprise (excess earnings can be used to estimate the value of the intangibles).

Exhibit 9.4 shows the mechanics of the capitalization of benefits method without valuation discounts or premiums.

EXHIBIT 9.4

Example of Single-Period Capitalization Method

Adjusted net income	$ 1,000,000
Forecast growth	× 1.05
Estimated future income	$ 1,050,000
Capitalization rate	÷ 25.0%
Indicated value from operations	$ 4,200,000
Add: Net non-operating assets	350,000
Total enterprise value	$ 4,550,000

In this example, you will notice that the estimated future income is being capitalized. Discount rates and capitalization rates that are determined from the market are considered to be prospective in nature. To match the income stream and the capitalization rate appropriately, both must be on a prospective basis. Historical income and rates could have been used as well, but it is not preferable. If historical data were used, the results would look like this:

Adjusted net income	$ 1,000,000
Capitalization rate (25.0 ÷ 1.05 = 23.81)	÷ 23.81%
Indicated value from operations (rounded)	$ 4,200,000
Add: Net non-operating assets	350,000
Total enterprise value	$ 4,550,000

In this instance, the capitalization rate has been adjusted by the anticipated growth into the next year (5 percent). By removing the growth, an historical capitalization rate can be applied to the adjusted historical net income. Note that the answer is the same in both examples.

Discounted Future Benefits Method

Founded on the principle of future benefits, the value of a business is the present value of all of the "benefits" it can reasonably be expected to generate in the future. These "benefits" are generally considered to be the future cash flows available to the owners from the business or investment (dividends and ultimate sale). In theory, if the holding period is expected to go into perpetuity, the future dividend stream discounted to the appraisal date, at an appropriate discount rate, should represent the value of the investment. Since investments rarely go to perpetuity, a long time horizon is generally substituted as the holding period for most investments in closely held businesses.

Although distributions to the owners are the main consideration, the application of this method can also be applied to earnings, cash flow (gross or net), and other benefit streams. Regardless of the benefit stream being discounted, the basic concept is the same. This methodology generally involves two steps: First, calculate the sum of the present values of the benefit stream for each of a number of periods (normally years) in the future, and second, add to that amount the present value of a "terminal" value.

The terminal value is generally calculated under a benefit stream residual method or an asset residual method, soon to be discussed. The benefit stream residual method assumes that the benefit stream being discounted will eventually stabilize and, therefore, the stabilized benefit stream can then be capitalized into perpetuity and discounted back to the valuation date. The asset residual method assumes that the benefit stream being discounted will stop at some point in the future as a result of the business coming to an end and being disposed of either through a sale or a liquidation. This method tends to be popular if the business is expected to have a limited life.

What did I just say? The terminal value assumes that the benefit stream of the business will eventually stabilize. This is similar to the assumption about single-period capitalization models. Don't panic; later, I hope to clear this up for you with some examples.

Since we had so much fun with the last mathematical equations, I thought that we should do it again. The mathematical equation for multi-period discounting is derived as follows:

$$\sum_{n=1}^{n=\infty} \frac{E_n}{(1 + k)^n}$$

where

E = Benefits stream
k = Discount rate
n = Time period (1 to infinity)

The equation just illustrated can be changed. If we use a definite period of time instead of infinity, we can add another component to the equation that would represent the "terminal" value. Let's change n to a finite period of time ending with period t. Let's also allow for the inclusion of all future value beyond the end of period t as a terminal value. The equation then becomes:

$$\sum_{n=0}^{n=\infty} \frac{E_n}{(1 + k)^n} + \frac{FV_{t+1}}{(1 + k)^t}$$

where

E = Benefits stream
k = Discount rate
n = Time period (0 through t)
FV = Future value or terminal period benefits stream

In simple language, value is estimated as the sum of the present values of the benefit stream for the projection period plus the present value of the terminal value. The terminal value will be the present value of the stabilized benefit stream capitalized into the future. The terminal value may also be the present value of the sale or liquidation proceeds of the company. Use one or the other, but not both!

Exhibit 9.5 illustrates the mechanics of the discounted future benefits method. In the example in Exhibit 9.5, it is assumed that the first five years of the projection are "unstable" and that stability takes place at the end of year 5. Two calculations require an explanation. The first is the calculation of the terminal value (TV) of $350,000. This is achieved by starting with the year 5 forecast net income of $70,000 and growing it by the next year's rate of growth that will result in the stable income stream of the company into the future (in this case, we assumed 5 percent). This means that the next year's (year 6) net income is assumed to be $73,500 ($70,000 × 1.05).

EXHIBIT 9.5
Example of the Discounted Future Benefits Method

Year	*Forecast Cash Flow*		*26% Present Value Factors*		*Present Value Future Cash Flow*
2001	$ 40,000	×	.79365	=	$ 31,746
2002	49,000	×	.62988	=	30,864
2003	57,500	×	.49991	=	28,745
2004	64,300	×	.39675	=	25,511
2005	70,000	×	.31488	=	22,042
TV	350,000	×	.31488*	=	110,208
			Total		$ 249,116

*The terminal value is usually discounted at the same rate as in the final year of the projection.

The next step is to capitalize the stable benefit stream by using a capitalization rate equal to the discount rate used in the present value computations and subtracting the assumed long-term growth rate (in this case, 5 percent). Therefore, the capitalization rate in this example would be 21 percent (0.26 – 0.05). (*Note:* Don't worry yet about where these rates come from because we will spend more time on this subject later in this book.)

The TV is therefore calculated as follows:

$$\$73{,}500 \div 0.21 = \$350{,}000$$

The second item needing an explanation is the fact that the discount factor used to discount the terminal value is the same factor that was applied to the year 5 forecast net income. Since stability is reached at the end of year 5, we are capitalizing the future income (year 5 plus growth), but it is being done at the end of year 5. Since year 5 is used for both the forecast net income for that year and the terminal value, both years should have the same present value factor used. This is assuming that the income stream is being received on the last day of the year during the forecast period, say December 31. Then, the terminal period begins on the first day of the next year, January 1. This is the reason why we use the same present value factor.

This example assumes that discounting is being performed at the end of each year. If a mid-year convention is assumed, the present value factor that would be used for the terminal value might not be the same as the factor used for year 5. There is a debate in the appraisal profession on whether the year 5 factor should be used in a mid-year model. A mid-year convention would change the basic formula to the following:

$$V = \frac{E_1}{(1+k)^{0.5}} + \frac{E_2}{(1+k)^{1.5}} + \frac{E_3}{(1+k)^{2.5}} + \frac{E_4}{(1+k)^{3.5}} + \frac{E_5}{(1+k)^{4.5}} + \frac{TV_5 \div (k-g)}{(1+k)^{4.5}}$$

where

$$E = \text{Benefit stream}$$
$$TV = \text{Terminal value}$$
$$k = \text{Discount rate}$$
$$g = \text{Rate of growth}$$

The difference between these two formulas is the period used to discount the terminal value back to present value. There is one school of thought that indicates that the same factor should be used for the final forecast period and the terminal period. I used to disagree. Another school of thought says that since the terminal period is intended to begin on the first day after the forecast period, the factor should be as of the first day of that terminal period or, conversely, the last day of the forecast period. Using 4.5 instead of 5 in the preceding formula would move the income stream up six months. This would result in a higher value. I now agree with the first school of thought that the same factor should be used. The income stream is considered to be a continuous stream, and therefore, there really is no gap at the end of a forecast period and the beginning of the terminal period. However, you are entitled to your own opinion, but mathematically the same period can be proven to be correct.

There may not be one correct answer for which model the appraiser should use, but the model chosen should be properly explained. Keep in mind that a mid-month convention could be used if you really want that income stream to be more representative of how the income stream is received throughout the year. This would close the gap to only one-half of one month.

Some additional considerations about the terminal value are worth pointing out. If no growth is anticipated after the projection period, the capitalization rate used will be the same as the discount rate. Many finance textbooks estimate that long-term growth for most businesses tends to be somewhat modest, generally in the 3 to 5 percent range (inflation and population growth). Since capitalization into perpetuity is a long time into the future, sustainable growth may not reflect too much more than the rate of inflation. However, the facts of each valuation may warrant different growth rates to be used. If a company has a greater rate of growth in the near term, the present value of the future growth can easily exceed the 3 to 5 percent range.

Calculating the Terminal Value. In the discounted future benefits method, the terminal value can represent a significant portion of the overall value of the business, and therefore, care must be exercised in its derivation. The terminal value should represent the fair market value at the point in time in which the business is in a stabilized and sustainable condition. It is frequently calculated using a single-period capitalization methodology. The benefit stream capitalized is the projected stream for the year after stabilization (time period $t + 1$). The capitalization rate used to convert the benefit stream into an indication of the fair market value of the business at that point is calculated by subtracting the long-term sustainable growth rate from the discount rate used to discount the annual projections.

Other acceptable methods to determine a capitalization rate may also be used for the derivation of the terminal value, but there should be some correlation between the discount rate used and the capitalization rate applied to the terminal benefit stream. After the terminal benefit stream is capitalized, it must then be discounted to its present value (at the valuation date). Exhibit 9.5 demonstrates the basic mechanics of this methodology. Exhibit 9.6 contains a portion of an actual valuation using this methodology. In this valuation, the subject company manufactured a product that started being marketed by two very large public companies that virtually took away that component of the subject company's sales. After our analysis of the historical financial information, we requested that management provide us with a forecast for the business. We actually received a pretty reasonable forecast. The exhibit illustrates what we did with it.

EXHIBIT 9.6
Discounted Future Benefits Method—Report Excerpt

The next step in this analysis is to determine how the historic performance of the company will compare with what is expected in the future. At the request of the appraiser, management has provided an estimate of what it expects future sales to be. This forecast appears in the following table.

Management's Forecast ($000)

	Historic		Forecast		
	1996	*1997*	*1998*	*1999*	*2000*
Total company					
Sales	$2,498	$1,614	$ 910	$ 700	$ 800
Cost of sales	1,174	697	320	196	224
Gross profit	$1,324	$ 917	$ 590	$ 504	$ 576
Expenses	1,206	934	500	500	500
Operating profit	$ 118	$ (17)	$ 90	$ 4	$ 76
Normalized profit	$ 767	$ 341	$ 90	$ 4	$ 76
Product A					
Sales	$2,054	$1,149	$ 310	$ 0	$ 0
Cost of sales	1,050	567	152	0	0
Gross profit	$1,004	$ 582	$ 158	$ 0	$ 0
Other products					
Sales	$ 444	$ 465	$ 600	$ 700	$ 800
Cost of sales	124	130	168	196	224
Gross profit	$ 320	$ 335	$ 432	$ 504	$ 576

The table reflects the decreased sales in the product A business while the sales of other products increase. Management recognizes the fact that they must make a concerted effort to increase the sales of the other products of the company to compensate for the loss of the product A business. Based on our discussions with management, this forecast appears reasonable. Although we cannot guarantee that the actual results will be achieved, the underlying assumptions are consistent and are well thought out. Projected income is significantly reduced from the 1996 and 1997 banner years. Even when allowing for a compound growth rate of about 20 percent in the continuing segment of the business, profits in 1998 through 2000 are projected to average $57,000 per year. This forecast also includes a reduction in expenses, which appears to bring the company's historic expenses in line with those on a normalized basis.

A willing buyer will clearly be much more concerned with the expectation of future profitability than with historic results. Historic results are generally used as a basis of forecasting the future, but reliance purely on history will generally result in an incorrect conclusion of value. Revenue Ruling 59-60 discusses the future in at least 15 different instances, and it is clear from the guidance provided in this treatise that the future is of greater importance than the past. This will be discussed further in the following section.

Valuation Calculations—Discounted Future Earnings Method

The discounted future earnings method is one of the most theoretically correct methods of appraisal. It is premised on the concept that value is based on the present value of all future benefits that flow to an owner of a property. These future benefits can consist of current income distributions, appreciation in the property, or a combination of the two. The formula for the discounted future earnings method is as follows:

$$\sum_{n=1}^{n=t} \frac{E_n}{(1+k)^n} + \frac{FV_{t+1}}{(1+k)^t}$$

EXHIBIT 9.6 *(Continued)*

where

E = Forecast income
n = Year in which the income is achieved
k = Required rate of return
FV = Terminal value, which is the estimated income during a stabilized period
t = Year of stabilization

The formula appears much more complicated than it is. In essence, this valuation method requires a forecast to be made of future earnings, going out far enough into the future until an assumed stabilization occurs for the property being appraised. In this instance, XYZ Company, Inc. is expected to incur a substantial fluctuation in its earnings over the short term due to the change in the company's product mix.

The previously discussed table shows an operating profit for this business estimated at $90,000 in 1998, $4,000 in 1999, and $76,000 in 2000. When a fluctuation of this type takes place, a multi-period model, such as this one, is generally deemed appropriate for valuing the entity. A single-period capitalization method such as the capitalization of earnings method would be appropriate only if projected earnings are relatively stable and predictable into the future.

The company should experience modest growth, but over the long term the company is not expected to grow at much more than the rate of inflation. Factoring in the maturity of the company and the shifting of the product mix, the high end of inflation, or 5 percent, will be used for the calculation of the terminal value.

The earnings stream being discounted in this model represents the return on investment to the stockholders. In this instance, there are employment contracts with two non-owner employees that require the company to pay them each 2 percent of all dividends that are paid to the company's shareholders. In this valuation, we have assumed that the company will not be paying dividends, and therefore, no reduction will be made to the earnings stream reflected in the table.

Once the earnings stream has been forecast, the selection of a proper discount rate becomes necessary. Since the income being estimated will not occur until some time in the future, the future income must be discounted to its present value. In this instance, a discount rate of 32 percent has been deemed applicable. This results in the value estimate of XYZ Company, Inc. being calculated as follows:

$$PV = \frac{90{,}000}{(1+.32)^1} + \frac{4{,}000}{(1+.32)^2} + \frac{76{,}000}{(1+.32)^3} + \frac{FV}{(1+.32)^3}$$

In this instance, the terminal value is determined by growing the last year's forecast income by a stabilized growth rate. The result is then capitalized and discounted to its present value. Once again, this appears to be much more complicated than necessary, but it is consistent with the Gordon Growth Model used in the securities market. Although long-term growth is forecast to be no greater than the long-term rate of inflation, the growth from 2000 to 2001 is still expected to be a bit higher than that rate in the short term. Therefore, a 10 percent growth rate has been used to determine the stabilized income after 1996. The capitalization rate applied in this instance is based on the selected discount rate less long-term growth, as opposed to next year's growth. The terminal value is therefore calculated as follows:

$$FV = \frac{76{,}000 \times 1.10}{.32 - .05} = \frac{83{,}600}{.32 - .05}$$

$$FV = \$309{,}630$$

The insertion of the terminal value into the equation indicated results in the present value of the future earnings of XYZ Company, Inc. to be determined as follows:

$$PV = \frac{90{,}000}{(1+.32)^1} + \frac{4{,}000}{(1+.32)^2} + \frac{76{,}000}{(1+.32)^3} + \frac{309{,}630}{(1+.32)^3}$$

$$PV = 68{,}182 + 2{,}299 + 33{,}043 + 134{,}622$$

$$PV = \frac{90{,}000}{1.32} + \frac{4{,}000}{1.74} + \frac{76{,}000}{2.30} + \frac{309{,}630}{2.30}$$

$$PV = \$238{,}146$$

The present value of the future benefits of XYZ Company, Inc. results in an estimate of value of $238,146, or $238,000 rounded.

The Excess Earnings ("Formula") Method

An argument can easily be made that the excess earnings method is more of an asset-based approach than it is an income approach. Actually, it is a hybrid of both approaches. The excess earnings method, which is also known as the formula approach, is probably the most widely used method of appraisal, particularly for small businesses and professional practices. This hybrid of the asset-based approach and the income approach is based on Revenue Ruling 68-609, which provides a method for valuing intangible assets. Note that I said "valuing intangible assets," not entire companies.

The excess earnings method involves valuing the subject company's tangible assets and liabilities at fair market value using the adjusted book value method, which was discussed in Chapter 8. The capitalization of excess earnings is used to value the intangibles. This is a single-period capitalization model that is similar to what was discussed at the beginning of this chapter.

Excess earnings—rather than net income, cash flow, EBIT, EBITDA, etc.—becomes the numerator in the capitalization model. These excess earnings are derived by forecasting the normalized annual net income (after-tax or pretax) for the entity in the same manner as in the other income approach methods. Then, a reasonable return on the net tangible assets is subtracted from the normalized net income to determine the excess earnings. These excess earnings are then capitalized to arrive at the intangible value of the enterprise.

The underlying theory behind this method is logical, but is often misapplied. The theory is that a company's earnings stream results from the company's investment in both tangible and intangible assets. All of those machines that make widgets allow the company to have products to sell. Combined with the other operating assets and liabilities, a return on investment is produced that is attributable to those net assets. If you subtract this return on the net assets from the total earnings stream produced by the company, the balance would be attributable to the intangible assets of the company. Logical, isn't it?

Pictorially, it looks like this:

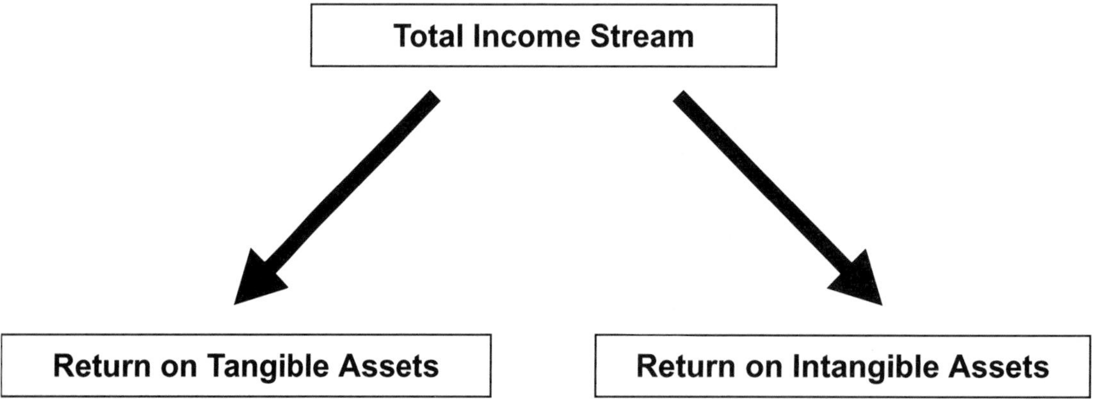

The appraiser needs to understand the theoretical basis of this method to avoid many of the common errors that are made in practice. The following are important guidelines for using this method:

- Since valuation is a "prophecy of the future," the appraiser should estimate the normalized future annual income. A common error is to calculate a weighted average net income for the five prior years, or some measure of historical data. The revenue rulings emphasize that using a weighted average of history is incorrect unless it reasonably reflects "probable future earnings."
- The reasonable return on the net tangible assets should be based on the level of risk associated with these assets, as well as on the returns available in the market. The theory behind this assumption is that if a business owner invested in an investment other than the business assets, a return would be

received. Therefore, the investment in assets should also generate a return on investment that is unrelated to the intangible value of the enterprise.

- The return on investment can be determined by reviewing what other investments are paying. For example, if an investor can buy government securities and receive a 6 percent return, the return on accounts receivable, fixed assets, etc. should be higher to reflect the amount of risk related to an investment in these assets. Obviously, a balance sheet with all cash would be considerably less risky than a balance sheet that contains only highly technical specialty machinery.
- A common error is to consider the return of 8 percent to 10 percent given as an example in Revenue Ruling 68-609 as gospel. The rate must reflect risk and will generally differ from the rate in the revenue ruling, which was promulgated in 1968. Even the revenue ruling states that "the above rates are used as examples and are not appropriate in all cases. In applying the 'formula' approach, the average earnings period and the capitalization rates are dependent upon the facts pertinent thereto in each case."
- The capitalization rate chosen must reflect the appropriate amount of risk relating to intangible assets. The example of 15 percent to 20 percent in Revenue Ruling 68-609 will, in most cases, be far too low for the average business's intangible assets. Recognizing the riskiness of the intangible assets will be one of the most difficult jobs for the appraiser. The capitalization rate chosen will depend on how much of the earnings stream is attributable to the tangibles versus the intangibles. This will be explained further in Chapter 10.
- The excess earnings method should be used only if no better method is available to determine the value of the intangibles. The enterprise can frequently be valued using other methodologies. This is not just my opinion. Reread the revenue ruling! Exhibit 9.7 shows the basic calculations of the excess earnings method. The mechanics are simple, which is probably why judges like this method so much. Unfortunately, this method is frequently applied incorrectly, and the result is a poor valuation.

EXHIBIT 9.7

Capitalization of Excess Earnings

Non-operating assets are usually excluded from this calculation so that the total entity value reflects the value of the operations of the subject company. Any net non-operating assets are added to the end result to value the total equity of the subject.

Estimated future income (normalized)	\$ 1,000,000
Less: Return on net tangible assets ($800,000 × 15%)	120,000
Excess earnings	\$ 880,000
Capitalization rate	÷ 40%
Intangible value	\$ 2,200,000
Plus: Adjusted book value	800,000
Total entity value	\$ 3,000,000

In using the excess earnings method, rules similar to those discussed in the single-period capitalization model apply. Since a single income stream is being used, that income stream should reflect "stability." If the forecast earnings are not expected to be relatively stable, a different method should be used. Furthermore, since the assets and liabilities are adjusted to their fair market values, this method implies a control valuation. This method may not be appropriate for minority interests since they cannot liquidate the assets. Of course, you can always subtract a discount for lack of control (discussed in Chapter 11) from the control value to get to a minority value. Quite frankly, I would rather use a different method.

There are frequently better methods to use in valuing businesses, and therefore, the excess earnings method is not always appropriate. Still, it continues to be used by many appraisers. As mentioned previously, the excess earnings method is commonly applied in the valuation of professional practices and small owner-operated businesses. In essence, the valuation of these entities is an asset-based approach, with the goodwill (unidentifiable intangibles) being valued this way.

To use the excess earnings method for intangibles, all of the operating assets and liabilities of the business must first be appraised. This is frequently accomplished using the adjusted book value method. There are many appraisers who believe that since small companies and professional practices are usually sold as *asset sales* as opposed to *stock sales*, a more appropriate way to apply this method is on a debt-free basis. This would change the rates of return used in the method from equity rates to weighted average costs of capital or invested capital rates (this will make more sense after you read the next chapter). Personally, I like to apply this method the old-fashioned way, based on equity. If you do it correctly, you should get similar answers (particularly if you are lucky!).

The next step is to calculate the normalized sustainable (stable) earnings of the business. Be careful to remove any non-operating income or expenses during the normalization process. Also remove any items on the balance sheet that may be attributable to non-operating assets or liabilities. The appraiser must then determine the appropriate rates of return on the net operating tangible assets (other than goodwill) owned by the company.

Required Rate of Return on Net Tangible Assets. There are several acceptable ways to determine the required rate of return on the net tangible assets of the business. There are no hard and fast rules, but there is no substitute for common sense in choosing appropriate rates. One method of determining the rate of return on the net tangible assets is to review the assets and liabilities that make up the balance sheet to assess the amount of risk attributable to these assets. I said it before, and I will say it again: A balance sheet with all cash would be considerably less risky than a balance sheet that is heavy in special technology equipment. The difference in the rates in this instance would be the difference between what a certificate of deposit pays, as opposed to the cost of leasing the equipment. The principle of substitution should be considered in weighing alternative returns.

Another method used to determine the rate of return on the net tangible assets is to calculate a weighted average rate based on the borrowing power of the company. This calculation appears in Exhibit 9.8. The idea behind this calculation is that the return should be based, in one part, as a return on the equity investment and, in another part, as a return on the borrowed funds. The return on the debt portion will generally be lower than the return on equity since the latter is considered to be more risky.

EXHIBIT 9.8
Return on Net Tangible Assets

Tangible Assets	*FMV*		*Loan %*		*Loan Amount*
Accounts receivable	$ 150,000	×	80%	=	$ 120,000
Inventory	$ 80,000	×	60%	=	$ 48,000
Fixed assets	$ 200,000	×	50%	=	$ 100,000
Borrowing capacity	$ 430,000		62.3%		$ 68,000
Existing debt					$ 100,000
Remaining capacity	$ 430,000		39.0%		$ 168,000
Market borrowing rate	10%				
1 – Effective tax rate	65%				
After-tax borrowing rate	6.5%		39%		2.54%
Required equity rate of return on tangible assets	28%[1]		61%		17.08%
Required rate of return on net tangible assets					19.62%

[1]Net earnings discount rate.

Another source of rates of return on net tangible assets is the market itself. The appraiser cannot necessarily use public companies because the returns measured also include intangible assets, but sources such as trade associations, Integra Information's *Business Profiler,* and Risk Management Association's *Annual Statement Studies* may help provide information about returns on tangible net worth. The problem with using this data is that the returns presented are based on book value and not fair market value. Regardless of which method is used to determine the reasonable return on the net tangible assets, it is generally accepted in the appraisal community that this rate should not be below the subject company's cost of borrowing money.

The return on the net assets is then subtracted from the normalized earnings, resulting in "excess earnings" subject to capitalization. The capitalization rate applied to the excess earnings must be sufficiently high, since the excess earnings represent the return from intangibles, which are considered to be more risky. Logically, if the rate of return on tangible assets is 15 percent, and the required rate of return on the company's earnings (which includes a return on the net tangible and intangible assets) was determined to be 33 percent, then the rate of return for only the intangibles has to be higher than 33 percent, so that on a weighted basis, the 15 percent plus the intangibles return equals 33 percent. This concept is illustrated in Exhibit 9.9.

EXHIBIT 9.9
Excess Earnings Method—Rates of Return Comparison

Assume that the following calculation was deemed appropriate by the appraiser.

Estimated future income (normalized)	$1,000,000
Less: Return on net tangible assets ($800,000 × 15%)	120,000
Excess earnings	$ 880,000
Capitalization rate	÷ 40%
Intangible value	$2,200,000
Plus: Adjusted book value	800,000
Total entity value	$3,000,000

The capitalization of benefits method applied to the estimated future income, instead of the excess earnings, would necessitate a capitalization rate as follows:

$1,000,000 income ÷ $3,000,000 value = 33.33% capitalization rate

This means that the appraiser would have had to determine a capitalization rate of 33.33 percent for a single-period model to be consistent with the results of the excess earnings method. The mathematical proof is the weighted average return on the tangible and intangible components of the value as follows:

Tangible component	$800,000/$3,000,000	×	15%	=	4.00
Intangible component	$2,200,000/$3,000,000	×	40%	=	29.33
Weighted average capitalization rate					33.33

The example in Exhibit 9.9 demonstrates that on a weighted average basis, the returns on the tangible and intangible portions of the income stream must result in the return for the entire income stream. This makes sense if you think about it. However, the proof requires circular logic, because you need to know the value of the enterprise in order to perform the mathematical calculation. If we know the value, why would we go any further? This is an excellent sanity check on the soundness of the rates of return used in the various methods.

Background and Drawbacks. If used correctly, the excess earnings method can be a good method to use. However, the answer is only as good as the information that the appraiser uses to calculate it. There are many negatives with regard to the excess earnings method. The discussion that follows is intended to provide you with more background about this method, as well as show the problems that can result by using it incorrectly.

The excess earnings method was promulgated in Appellate Review Memorandum (ARM) 34 in 1920. The purpose of ARM 34 was to provide a formula to be used in determining the proper amount of compensation for the owners of breweries and distilleries for the loss of goodwill that resulted from Prohibition. To assist in this task, ARM 34 included rates of return on the investment in assets employed in these types of businesses. This was supposed to allow a separation of the tangible and intangible portion of the taxpayer's income stream to be used in the formula. As the formula method became more popular and started being used for other types of businesses, it became apparent that the rates included in the memorandum may not have been appropriate in every situation or appropriate over time.

Revenue Ruling 68-609 was issued to correct the misinterpretations regarding the use of the excess earnings method in the valuation of goodwill. This revenue ruling suggested higher rates of return but also led appraisers to the belief that this methodology is appropriate for all types of businesses. As time went by, the Internal Revenue Service began to recognize that the excess earnings approach was being misapplied in practice. It had been used to value entire businesses, when it was intended to value only the intangible assets.

In Revenue Ruling 68-609, the IRS has gone on record to state, "The (excess earnings) approach may be used *only* if there is no better basis available for estimating the value of intangible assets." There are frequently better methods to use in valuing businesses, and therefore, the excess earnings method is not always appropriate. Still, it continues to be used by many appraisers.

The basic formula in applying this methodology is to restate the balance sheet at fair market value. The next step is to calculate the probable future earnings of the business. A reasonable return on the net tangible assets is subtracted from the probable future earnings, resulting in the excess earnings that are attributable to the intangible value of the entity. The excess earnings are then capitalized to determine the value of the intangibles.

The problems with this methodology are plentiful. The most basic problem is the false assumption that the earnings of a business can easily be divided between the amounts attributable to the tangibles and intangibles. The appraiser must determine the appropriate rates of return on the net tangible assets (other than goodwill) owned by the company. There is no empirical data to support these rates of return.

Errors are also frequently committed because of a lack of understanding of the theoretical background and application of the method. Therefore, since this method is so easily misapplied, it is not widely favored by experienced appraisers.

In *Business Valuation News*, Shannon Pratt states:

> The excess earnings method of valuation actually is another version of a capitalized earnings approach. It is the most widely used and misused of all methods for valuing small businesses and professional practices. It is widely written about, and more than half the business and professional practice brokers that I know use some version of it. It is widely used in divorce proceedings by courts for determining the value of goodwill in professional practices. Yet the Internal Revenue Service, who spawned the method back in 1920, now roundly denounces it.[7]

Discussing the methodology further, Pratt quotes *How to Buy or Sell a Business: Small Business Reporter Series*, in which it is stated that because each business and sales transaction is different, the formula should be used only to indicate some of the major considerations in pricing a business.[8]

In an article titled "Closely Held Business Valuations: The Uninformed Use of the 'Excess Earnings/Formula' Method," Jeffrey Fox, ASA, indicates that "to mechanically cite the excess earnings/formula method as the authority for a closely held business valuation will leave an appraiser very vulnerable to criticism."[9]

---

[7]Shannon Pratt, "The Excess Earnings Method," *Business Valuation News* (September 1985), 4–12 (now known *as Business Valuation Review*, published by the Business Valuation Committee of the American Society of Appraisers).

[8]Ibid. (quoting Bank of America, *How to Buy or Sell a Small Business: Small Business Reporter Series* [San Francisco: Bank of America, 1982], 8–9).

[9]*Business Valuation News* (September 1984).

Fox indicates that this method should be used only as a last resort. All of the difficulties in the application of this method are discussed in the article, but the author sums up the use of this method when he states, "the utility of the excess earnings/formula method is definitely in doubt when the creator of the method has its own questions concerning its validity."

Despite the overall dislike of the excess earnings method, it has its use in business valuation. For professional practices and small owner-operated businesses, information is difficult, if not impossible, to obtain, and the appraiser has no other choice of method. Care must be exercised in its application, however, because the end result does not always make sense. A blind application of this method without sanity checks and tests for reasonableness will frequently result in a serious misstatement of the value of the subject business.

Although there is wide acceptance of the excess earnings methodology, the mechanics of the method make it a method of last resort. First and foremost among its many deficiencies is that unless the appraiser is extremely lucky, the excess earnings method will rarely reflect the market. In a fair market value appraisal, there is nothing more important than the market. Exhibit 9.10 contains a discussion of an actual case (as well as an excerpt from the valuation report) demonstrating the magnitude of error that can result for even a small business.

EXHIBIT 9.10
Excess Earnings Method—A Problematic Result

As part of a divorce litigation, the business owner's accountant, who represented our client's husband, performed an excess earnings calculation for his auto parts client as follows:

Average annual earnings	$ 29,145
Adjustments:	
Reasonable compensation	40,000
Adjusted earnings	$(10,855)
Return on tangible assets ($222,635 × 8%)	17,811
Excess earnings	negative

Since there were no excess earnings, the conclusion was that there was no intangible value above the $222,635 of net tangible assets. Therefore the conclusion was $223,000 for the business.

As part of our analysis, it was determined that there was an additional $150,000 of unreported income. Factoring this amount into the other side's excess earnings calculation resulted in the following revised valuation for this company:

Average annual earnings	$ 179,145
Adjustments:	
Reasonable compensation	40,000
Adjusted earnings	$ 139,145
Return on tangible assets ($222,635 × 8%)	17,811
Excess earnings	$ 121,344
Capitalization rate	÷ .30
Intangible value	$ 404,480
Tangibles (net)	+ 222,635
Value of business	$ 627,115
Rounded	$ 627,000

(Continued)

EXHIBIT 9.10 *(Continued)*

The revised calculation yields a value estimate for the entire business of $627,000 and utilized the excess earnings method to calculate the intangible value. The problem is that this calculation totally ignores the real world.

In the real world, businesses such as this one are bought and sold every day. Buyers pay more than book value for these types of businesses. During our market analysis, we located transaction data for businesses similar to the one being appraised. A selected portion of the discussion in our appraisal report follows. There is obviously a considerable amount of additional analysis than what is illustrated, but the intention is clear that the excess earnings method does not reflect the market.

XYZ Auto Parts Distributors, Inc.

Based on the information analyzed, it appears that XYZ's pretax earnings should be adjusted to reflect owner's discretionary cash flow as follows:

	1999
Reported net income	$ 21,930
Gross profit adjustment	150,000
Officer's compensation	49,725
Owner's discretionary cash flow	$221,655

A common method utilizing owner's discretionary cash flow in the valuation of small, closely held businesses is to apply a multiplier to the cash flow. This result represents the intangible value of the business plus the assets (such as equipment and fixtures) that are normally included in the sales price. This is added to the other assets and liabilities of the company in determining the overall value of the company. The most common multipliers range from 1 to 5, depending on the risk of the business.

To assist in determining the appropriate multiple, we contacted The Institute of Business Appraisers, Inc., a professional appraisal organization that maintains a proprietary database of actual transactions of closely held businesses all over the United States. As a result of our search, 28 such transactions were located under Standard Industrial Classification code 5013, "Wholesaler of Auto Parts." Of these 28 transactions, 13 were eliminated based on the description of the business, as they appeared to be something other than auto parts wholesalers. For example, some of the entries eliminated included auto parts importers, auto battery distributors, and truck electronic equipment distributors. The remaining transactions are presented in the table that follows.

Data for Market Comparison

Business Type	*Annual Gross ($000)*	*Annual Earnings ($000*)*	*Sale Price ($000)*	*SalePrice/ Gross*	*Price/ Annual Earnings*	*Geographic Location*	*Year/ Month of Sale*
Auto parts, dist.	42	—	75	1.79	—	FL	98/07
Motor vehicle supplies	93	2	37	0.40	18.50	OR	97/05
Auto parts, dist.	193	43	75	0.39	1.74	FL	98/07
Auto parts, dist.	209	42	30	0.14	0.71	FL	98/07
Auto parts, wholesale	399	—	134	0.34	—	—	94/01
Product dist.	400	120	222	0.56	1.85	CA	99/12
Auto parts, wholesale	650	—	33	0.05	—	CA	96/05
Auto parts, wholesale	670	110	230	0.34	2.09	TN	96/03
Automotive supply	724	96	155	0.21	1.61	CA	92/12
Auto parts, dist.	730	15	350	0.47	23.33	MIDATL	90/03
Automotive supplies, dist.	937	120	350	0.37	2.92	CA	96/08
Motor parts/supplies	1,200	167	495	0.41	2.96	FL	98/09
Auto parts, wholesale	2,000	125	656	0.33	5.25	OH	97/04
Auto parts dist.	3,251	264	1,200	0.37	4.55	—	89/05
Auto parts, wholesale	11,200	1,124	5,417	0.48	4.82	PA	99/10

*Reported annual earnings before owner's compensation, interest, and taxes.

EXHIBIT 9.10 *(Continued)*

Several items should be noted about the data presented above. The information is submitted by members of The Institute of Business Appraisers who have been involved in actual transactions. As the geographical location indicates, these transactions have taken place across the United States. As the "Year/Month of Sale" column indicates, they have also taken place during a variety of time periods. A review of the data demonstrates that there is little correlation to the multiples calculated based on various geographical locations in the country. Therefore, it does not appear that these transactions are sensitive to geographic location.

With respect to the date of sale, it is common to hear arguments about old data. Raymond C. Miles, CBA, ASA, executive director of The Institute of Business Appraisers, published a paper titled "Defense of Stale Comparables," in which he examined the almost 14,000 entries in the database and demonstrated that most industries are unaffected by the date of the transaction when smaller businesses are involved. Miles performed a study that examined the multiples across various industries and time periods to see if, in fact, the multiples changed. The conclusion reached was that the multiples do not appear to be time-sensitive; inflation affects not only the sales price but also the gross and net earnings of the business. Therefore, this information can be used to provide actual market data.

A cross section of this data was analyzed to determine the potential statistical significance of sales price–to–gross and price–to–annual earnings multiples. These are presented and broken down by total transactions of Mid-Atlantic/Pennsylvania transactions and businesses whose annual gross sales exceed $1 million. We attempted to calculate mean and median statistical measurements determined in these transactions. This is presented as follows.

	Sales Price/ Gross	*Sales Price/ Net*
Total		
Mean	0.44	5.86
Median	0.37	2.96
Mid-Atlantic/PA		
Mean	0.48	14.08
Median	0.48	14.08
Over $1M gross		
Mean	0.40	4.40
Median	0.39	4.69

To assist in the determination of the value of XYZ, we have applied these multiples to the annualized sales and owner's discretionary cash of XYZ. This appears in the next table.

	Sales Price/Gross	*Sales Price/Net*	*Sales*	*Net*	*Value*	*Value*
Total transactions						
Mean	0.44	5.86	2,678,718	221,655	1,178,636	1,298,898
Median	0.37	2.96	2,678,718	221,655	991,126	656,099
Mid-Atlantic/PA						
Mean	0.48	14.08	2,678,718	221,655	1,285,785	3,120,902
Median	0.48	14.08	2,678,718	221,655	1,285,785	3,120,902
Over $1M gross						
Mean	0.40	4.40	2,678,718	221,655	1,071,487	975,282
Median	0.39	4.69	2,678,718	221,655	1,044,700	1,029,562

According to the information calculated above, there appears to be a significant correlation in the value estimates reached based on actual transactions. Applying gross sales multipliers, as well as applying net multipliers representing owner's discretionary cash, the values reached range from approximately $950,000 to $1.3 million. The only clear outliers from this range are the multipliers of owner's discretionary cash for the Mid-Atlantic region. This is clearly attributable to a multiple of 23.33 times in an actual transaction from this region. Since this multiple appears to be an anomaly, it should be discarded from this valuation.

(Continued)

EXHIBIT 9.10 ***(Continued)***

What the data presented above demonstrates is that actual transactions—regardless of the region of the country, year of sale, or size of the company—correlate well and can be used as a statistical measurement of the value of XYZ. A closer review of this information shows the value of the intangible and fixed assets to be approximately $1.2 million. The value of the other assets and liabilities should then be added to this value to determine the enterprise value of the company.

In this instance, the balance sheet at October 31, 2000, reflects stockholders' equity in the amount of $118,706. Included in the determination of this amount, however, is a liability to the stockholders of XYZ. However, this company was undercapitalized, and in essence, this loan reflects an equity investment in the company. In addition, the net fixed assets in the amount of $18,272 should be subtracted since their value is included in the $1.2 million figure. Therefore, the correct tangible stockholder's equity of the company should be $222,635.

Adding this amount to the $1.2 million value determined previously results in an estimate of value for the enterprise of approximately $1.42 million.

The information in Exhibit 9.10 indicates that the value concluded by the other side ($627,000) was substantially lower than what was derived from market transactions ($1.42 million). For the other side's conclusion to have been close to ours, the value of the intangibles would have to have been $1.2 million, which would have meant a pretax capitalization rate of approximately 8.2 percent. I do not think that I need to belabor how ridiculous this would be!

The automobile parts distributorship case in this exhibit was a slam dunk when we got to court. The judge ruled in our client's favor and found the excess earnings method to be flawed.

Another problem with the excess earnings method is having to determine two rates of return (return on net tangibles and capitalization rate for excess earnings) instead of one. We have enough trouble supporting our capitalization rates for small businesses because of the lack of empirical data, and now proponents of the excess earnings method have to determine a capitalization rate for excess earnings, for which there is absolutely no empirical data.

As we will discuss in Chapter 10, we are taught as appraisers to build up a capitalization rate by starting with a discount rate developed for cash flow (assuming we use Ibbotson data). We add a subjective element called the specific company risk premium, to reflect the added element of risk that is associated with the appraisal subject as compared to other companies or with industry data that we obtain. Now we are being asked to add an additional subjective element for only the unidentifiable intangibles portion of the income stream. Where is this supposed to come from? Is this one of those "leaps of faith" that experienced appraisers refer to as a common error in many valuation reports?

Another reason to avoid the excess earnings method is that it violates the spirit of Revenue Ruling 59-60, in which the IRS has stated:

> In general, the appraiser will accord primary consideration to earnings when valuing stocks of companies which sell products or services to the public; conversely, in the investment or holding type of company, the appraiser may accord the greatest weight to the assets underlying the security to be valued.

It is commonly accepted in the appraisal community that a business valued as a going concern will generally be appraised based on the earnings or cash flow capacity of the business. Only in limited circumstances would primary weight be afforded to an asset-based approach. The excess earnings method places a great emphasis on net asset values to determine the value of the intangibles. This is contradictory.

If a company had to be valued by separately stating the tangible and intangible assets, the excess earnings method could possibly be used in limited situations. However, the subtraction method can also be used to determine the value of the intangibles. Using this method, the company is valued in its entirety, and then the appraiser subtracts the value of the net tangibles to determine the value of the remainder, the intangibles.

Now let's look at the modern-day thinking of the IRS. According to the IRS *Valuation Guide for Income, Estate and Gift Taxes*,[10]

---

[10]January 1994 edition.

Intangibles, for purposes of valuation, are divided into two categories.

1. Intangibles with a determinable useful life, and
2. Intangibles with a nondeterminable useful life.

This publication points out that for a taxpayer to be entitled to a depreciation deduction under Section 167, three requirements must be met:

1. The assets must be separate from goodwill and/or going-concern value.
2. The assets must be susceptible to valuation.
3. The assets must have a determinable, limited useful life.

Discussing separability, the IRS notes:

> The qualities that make intangibles so attractive to a buyer, such as providing a competitive advantage and/or the ability to achieve excess earnings, are the same qualities that make the intangible assets so difficult to identify and value. As noted by Nicholas Fiore in the article "Valuing Intangibles," intangibles may be so interrelated that they are viewed as a single, indivisible asset, rather than in terms of separate parts.[11] The mass asset doctrine, in the case of indivisible intangibles, treats all intangible assets as goodwill. This indivisible asset ensures that intangible assets in the nature of goodwill, with indeterminable lives, will not be depreciated.

Several court cases dealing with intangibles are discussed, but the conclusion is the following:

> The Courts continue to hold, however, that the burden of proof remains upon the taxpayer to provide sufficient and reasonable evidence to support a claim that an acquired intangible asset exists, has *value separate and distinct* from goodwill, and a *limited useful life*.

The discussion about the capitalization method of valuing intangibles states the following:

> The capitalization method supposes that the value of the business is based on its ability to generate profits.
>
> This method is computed as follows:
>
> 1. Determine net value of tangible assets.
> 2. Determine a capitalization period and whether to use a straight line or weighted average.
> 3. Determine a capitalization rate and apply it to the average determined above.
> 4. If the earnings, once capitalized, are greater than the net tangible assets, the difference represents goodwill.

Since goodwill has generally been described in terms of earning capacity, one method to calculate its existence is based on a capitalization of earnings approach. One of the early attempts to arrive at the value of goodwill by capitalizing earnings was set forth by the IRS in ARM 34. An example of the form of the computation prescribed by ARM 34 is as follows:

> Welch Company, a low-risk company, had net tangible assets as of the appraisal date of $100,000. In addition, its earnings record was as follows:

Preceding Years' Earnings	
1st yr. earnings	$ 20,000
2nd yr. earnings	30,000
3rd yr. earnings	15,000
4th yr. earnings	40,000
5th yr. earnings	25,000
Total	$130,000

[11]Nicholas Fiore, "Valuing Intangibles," *Journal of Accountancy* 162 (September 1986), 12.

Average annual earnings for five preceding years:

$$\frac{130{,}000}{5 \text{ years}} = \$26{,}000$$

ARM 34 uses a rate of return for low-risk companies of 8 percent. In this case, the earnings attributable to tangible assets is 8 percent of the net tangible asset value:

$$\$100{,}000 \times .08 = \$8{,}000$$

The balance of earnings attributable to intangible assets is:

Average earnings	$26,000
Less: Earnings attributable to tangible assets	8,000
Earnings attributable to intangible assets	$18,000

ARM 34 then recommends, for low-risk companies, a capitalization rate of 15 percent. The value of the intangible assets is as follows:

Earnings attributable to intangible assets	$ 18,000
Divided by: Capitalization rate	÷ .15
Value of intangible assets	$ 120,000

Initially, this formula was interpreted as providing set rates of return on tangible and intangible assets. This resulted in many improper valuations since the use of arbitrary capitalization rates has no relationship to the financial marketplace at the time of valuation. The IRS has clarified its position by stating that the appropriate average earnings period and capitalization rates are dependent upon pertinent facts of each case.

In making the calculation, the following factors should be considered:

1. The period of past earnings should fairly represent probable future earnings. Ordinarily this will not be less than five years.
2. Abnormal years, whether above or below average, should be eliminated.

Factors that influence the capitalization rate include:

1. nature of the business
2. risk involved, and
3. stability or irregularity of earnings.

The formula approach may be used for determining the fair market value of intangible assets of a business only if there is not better basis [sic] *available* [emphasis added]. A recent Tax Court decision used the formula approach to calculate going-concern value in a situation where it was determined that no goodwill existed.

The valuation guide indicates that even though the excess earnings method is discussed in Revenue Ruling 68-609:

- The Service has stated that a taxpayer may use the capitalization of excess earnings method only if there is no better basis for determining the value of intangibles.
- The Tax Court has, on occasion, rejected the taxpayer's use of the capitalization of excess earnings method for valuing intangible assets (e.g., core deposit intangible in *Banc One*, 84 T.C. 506).

- The Court, in *Banc One*, criticized the basic assumptions made in the capitalization of excess earnings method, noting that the "[d]etermination of the 'normal' earnings of business, the 'average' return on the tangible assets, and the 'appropriate' capitalization rate is a highly subjective task."
- The Court even rejected the theory supporting the capitalization of excess earnings method, finding that "there is no goodwill unless there is also an expectancy of continuing excess earnings capacity," and noted also that goodwill may be present in the absence of excess earnings capacity.

To make a long story short, the promulgator of the methodology is not too thrilled with its own invention. Clearly, fair market value is supposed to come from the market. It is not to be conceived from formula methodologies that often fail to reflect the market value of a business. Since good appraisal practice dictates that the appraiser should use multiple methods of valuation in any assignment, and there are other methods of valuation that can be used in any given assignment, we should learn from the IRS when they tell us, "The formula approach may be used for determining the fair market value of intangible assets of a business only if there is not a better basis available." Any experienced appraiser should understand that there is always a better basis for valuing an entire enterprise and almost always a better method for valuing only the intangibles.

As you probably realize, the foregoing discussion was extremely critical of the excess earnings method. I would have liked to highlight a positive side of this method, but I could not think of one. The excess earnings method should be used only if all else fails. You can use this method when you know that you are going in front of a judge who will throw your report out of court if you do not use it. Whatever you do, do not use this method only. Use other methods that may be applicable to the assignment at hand, so that you can have a feeling of comfort about the estimate of value that you come up with.

Conclusion

I hope that you now understand the income approach. You should have learned various methodologies, the advantages and disadvantages of each method, various pretax or after-tax considerations, and the derivation of net cash flow from the appraisal point of view.

10

Discount Rates and Capitalization Rates

Chapter Goals

In this chapter, I will attempt to explain:

1. Discount and capitalization rates in general
2. The use of pretax or after-tax rates
3. Discount rates
4. The factors that affect the selection of a discount rate
5. The components of a discount rate
6. The build up model
7. The capital asset pricing model (in English, no subtitles)
8. Alternatives to the build up and capital asset pricing models
9. Capitalization rates
10. The factors that affect the selection of a capitalization rate
11. The data sources for discount and capitalization rates

Pretty optimistic, huh?

Introduction

Here comes the good stuff! This is the chapter that you have been waiting for. If you are dangling on the edge, this is the chapter that is sure to push you over. Hold on tight because here we go! One of the most difficult tasks that the appraiser faces is selecting an appropriate discount or capitalization rate. For many years, I went to seminars waiting for some business valuation guru to give me the formula for developing the "right" discount rate. When I realized that no one could do it, I started writing about this stuff myself.

The theory behind discount rates is quite simple. The amount of risk that is perceived by the market must generally be balanced by the rate of return that is offered for the investment in order to entice investors to take the risk of making the investment. Stated differently, if a willing buyer wants to make an investment in a closely held company, the rate of return being offered, based on the price to be paid for the investment, must be high enough to justify taking the risk with his or her money.

As long as we are still in the introduction section, let's get another goodie out of the way up front. Discount and capitalization rates are not the same. A discount rate is a required rate of return, a yield rate used to convert expected future receipts into present value. The rate of return represents the *total rate of return* expected by the market, the rate necessary to attract capital to the subject investment.

A capitalization rate is not a rate of return; it is a divisor used to convert a future return into an indication of value. The capitalization rate *plus* the long-term sustainable rate of growth in the selected return combine to provide the rate of return. The rate of return is *market driven*. It is the rate determined to be available on alternative investments of comparable risk and with similar characteristics—an opportunity cost. And of course, risk represents uncertainty. If there is no uncertainty, there is no risk. Therefore, risk is the degree of uncertainty associated with a given investment.

The discount and capitalization rates used will depend on what is being discounted or capitalized. Some possibilities include the following:

- Net income (after-tax)
- Net income (pretax)
- Gross cash flow
- Net cash flow
- Excess earnings
- Dividends/dividend-paying capacity
- EBIT
- EBITDA

The determination of which benefit stream will be discounted or capitalized will depend on various factors, including the availability and reliability of data. This data can relate either to market information about discount or capitalization rates or to the subject company's information. The appraiser may have better information to work with in certain assignments and may not feel comfortable with financial information in others (cash businesses). The amount of risk associated with the valuation subject should be a major consideration in determining an appropriate rate. The appraiser also considers alternative rates of return on comparable investments available to the "willing buyer." This is the principle of substitution at work.

Discount Rates

If this were a finance text, I would probably include a rather complex explanation of discount rates. Fortunately for both of us, it is not a finance text. In simple terms, a discount rate is the required rate of return that an investor would demand—based on the risks associated with the benefit stream under consideration—to induce him or her to make the investment. What do I mean by risk? Risk is uncertainty. The greater the amount of uncertainty, the greater amount of risk. The greater the risk, the less someone is willing to pay for something. The lower purchase price is used to provide a greater potential return to the buyer. For example, assume that ABC Company has an expected income of $100,000 that is sustainable into the future. To keep the example simple, let's assume there is no growth anticipated. This would make the discount rate and the capitalization rate equal to each other. If the required rate of return was 20 percent, the value of ABC would be calculated as follows:

$$\$100{,}000 \div .20 = \$500{,}000$$

If the perceived risk was greater than what would warrant a 20 percent rate of return, the buyer might offer only $400,000 for ABC. This would provide a 25 percent rate of return to the buyer, calculated as follows:

$$\$100{,}000 \div \$400{,}000 = .25$$

Lowering the price provides a greater return for the buyer. However, if the risk related to an investment in ABC is really lower, the seller would insist on a greater price for the business. A $600,000 price would provide the buyer with a lower rate of return. In the real world, a negotiation will go forward between the buyer and the seller based on the perceived risk of the investment. The buyer will think it is very risky and the seller will tell the buyer that there is no risk. Who would ever figure this could happen?

The discount rate represents the rate of return that an investor requires to justify his or her investment in an asset, depending on the amount of risk associated with the investment. For example, an investor may expect a 5 percent return on a certificate of deposit from a bank, a 10 percent return on a corporate bond, and a 20 percent return on junk bonds. Usually, the higher the risk, the higher the required rate of return. The discount rate is the basis for present value factors, which are used to discount a stream of future benefits to their present value.

On occasion, appraisers use other terms of art (such as *opportunity cost of capital, alternative cost of capital,* or *weighted average cost of capital)* instead of the term *discount rate*. Regardless of what term is used, discount rates are supposed to reflect the required rate of return on the benefit stream being discounted given the risks associated with the benefit stream. One such risk element is the ability of the investor to receive the benefit stream that is being forecast as part of the valuation. A company with a steady track record of earnings and distributions will generally be considered less risky than a company that has had a volatile past.

Discount rates are determined by the market. They will vary with time, even for the same investment. This is easily illustrated through an explanation of why the interest rates paid on 30-year Treasury bonds vary. Discount rates take into consideration the inflationary expectations of the future benefit stream being used. If *constant dollar* projections are made, the discount rate should not include an inflationary element. The appraiser must be consistent!

Discount rates take into consideration the risks in the marketplace and must also include an element that is specific to the appraisal subject. These rates are based on the yields available for alternative investments. If an investor can get a 16 percent rate of return on a type of investment that is less risky than the appraisal subject, why would he or she accept less than 16 percent? Logically, the investor would not. The discount rate will also depend on the nature of the future benefit stream being reduced to the present value.

Factors That Affect the Selection of a Discount Rate

Factors that affect the selection of a discount rate are considered to be external (noncontrollable) and internal (controllable) to the appraisal subject. The external factors are those over which the owners or managers of the business have no control. For example, general economic conditions and the economic outlook at the valuation date are considered to be external factors that affect the selection of the appropriate rate. The nature and economic condition of the industry within which the business operates, as well as the market served by the enterprise, are also considered to be external factors.

Market perceptions regarding similar investment opportunities are another example of external factors that are beyond the control of the owners. The sources and availability of capital to finance operations are other examples. These items are important to the willing buyer and, therefore, should be considered by the appraiser.

Internal factors are those that the owner or owners of the business have some control over. The financial condition of the appraisal subject is one example. The earning capacity of the company is another. This includes the level and quality of the earnings or cash flow of the company. The ability of the company to obtain the goods and services it needs to produce its products is also considered an internal factor; this is clearly within the control of management. The ability to bring the products to an available market is also a burden that rests with management. The quality of the management team running the company is another factor that should be considered by the appraiser.

Another internal factor is the quality of the available data. High-quality data is usually the result of a good accounting system with proper controls. The ability of management to meet its budgets, forecasts, and projections reflects on the quality of management.

Regardless of internal or external factors, discount rates are driven by risk. In the discussion that is about to take place, I will be telling you more about discount rates. Keep one important point in mind—discount rates are derived from the market based on the risk associated with comparable types of investments. You can apply all of the fancy formulas or methodologies that I will discuss, and even others, but the bottom line is that the result has to make sense. If you are a finance nerd, you may choose to use some extravagant formulas from a finance textbook and calculate the discount rate properly but end up with the wrong answer. Don't try to impress your client, the attorney, or the judge with your ability to develop discount rates. It's the value that counts!

Components of a Discount Rate

There are many different ways to derive a discount rate. In this book I will attempt to address several of them, but you must recognize that *these are not all-inclusive*. In some instances (when the long-term growth rate is known), the discount rate can be derived from a capitalization rate.

The formula most often seen in the literature for the derivation of a capitalization rate is the following:

$$c = k - g$$

where

c = Capitalization rate

k = Discount rate (Many textbooks use k as the notation for a discount rate. That is like spelling cat with a "k." *D* is for discount rate and k is for kat, but I am going to use the common notation to avoid confusing you more than you might be already.)

g = Long-term sustainable growth

By moving the formula around, the appraiser can determine a discount rate as follows:

$$k = c + g$$

Every discount rate, regardless of how it is derived, includes the following basic components: (1) the risk-free rate of return, (2) the equity risk premium, and (3) the specific company risk premium. Sometimes the specific company risk premium is broken down into many smaller premiums. Exhibit 10.1 provides an example of the components of a discount rate.

EXHIBIT 10.1
Components of a Discount Rate

Risk-free rate	6.0%
Equity risk premium	7.0%
Specific company risk premium	5.0%
Discount rate	18.0%

Risk-Free Rate of Return. The risk-free rate of return is sometimes known as the "safe rate" or the "cost of money." In theory, this is the minimum return that an investor would accept for an investment that is virtually risk-free. It is the pure cost of money plus the rate of inflation anticipated by those who deal in these types of transactions. What this really represents is the minimum rate of return that an investor should accept, since he or she can earn this amount with reasonable safety instead of risking an investment in a closely held company.

Sources of risk-free rates of return include U.S. Treasury bonds. More often than not, long-term rates are used to simulate the long-term holding period of a closely held business. The 20-year bond (actually, it is a composite rate for bonds that have 20 years to maturity) is frequently used, although the 30-year bond has been used as well. Depending on the yield curves, the difference is pretty small (for 20- versus

30-year bonds). The 20-year bond has become popular among appraisers because of the fact that many appraisers use the equity risk premium data provided by Ibbotson Associates, and these are based on 20-year bonds. I will explain more about this in a little while.

Other sources of risk-free rates can be used as well, although few can give the true feeling of being risk-free. Making the assumption that our government is risk-free is as much of a leap of faith as I am generally willing to take. As a matter of fact, as I was writing this section of the original book, our government announced that it would be closing down due to its inability to borrow more money. Some appraisers believe that they can use high-quality corporate bonds as a risk-free rate, but they are usually not considered to be as good as Treasury bonds.

Intermediate-term rates (from 1 to 10 years) are sometimes used when the expected holding period of the investment is short. Treasury notes can be used in this instance. Others prefer short-term rates (1 year or less), such as those on U.S. Treasury bills. These are considered to be the safest of the investments, since the nature of a short-term vehicle is that it is less affected by inflationary expectations and the risk associated with the investment. However, short-term rates tend to have a greater degree of volatility than long-term investments. If you really want more of an explanation about this stuff, read a finance textbook. It is guaranteed to put you to sleep at night!

The selection of a long-term, intermediate-term, or short-term rate will depend on the investment horizon implicit in the asset being appraised. Closely held businesses are generally purchased with the intent of a longer holding period and, therefore, should involve longer-term rates in deriving the discount rate. On the other hand, a contract right with a life of three years must be properly matched with the proper risk-free rate.

Equity Risk Premium. The equity risk premium is sometimes called the "general risk premium." This component of the discount rate takes into consideration market perceptions and the expectations of a broad measure of the market. For example, if the appraisal subject's industry is returning 17 percent on equity, an investor in the subject company would expect to receive the same 17 percent, all other factors being equal. After all, why would someone be willing to accept less than what they could get from an equally desirable substitute? We have already discussed this point, so let's keep going.

Appraisers have been attempting to develop alternative ways to determine the equity risk premium. Some methods look at the entire market, while others look at only segments of the market. Standard & Poor's industry studies include indexes that show how different industries have performed. These and other studies are being used to differentiate between returns on equity, which are calculated based on the book value of companies (primarily tangible assets), and hypothetical returns, as if the intangible value of the companies were included in the calculation. Direct market comparison methods are used to suggest that other investments in the marketplace may provide an indication of the risk associated with a closely held business. Some appraisers believe that comparing low-quality bonds with stocks may better equate the risk of a closely held stock.

The equity risk premium for corporate equity securities can be obtained from various sources. By far the most commonly used source is the *Stocks, Bonds, Bills and Inflation Yearbook* (the *SBBI Yearbook*), published by Ibbotson Associates of Chicago. Ibbotson data is a compilation of investment returns, begun in 1926, for several types of financial assets. Business appraisers are generally interested in the information relating to risk-free returns, market equity returns, small company stock premiums, and the calculated differentials between them.

The Ibbotson studies are considered to be the most comprehensive compilation of data relating to the equity risk premium. In addition to the overall equity risk premium, the appraiser also considers the small company risk premium. This is frequently considered to be part of the specific company risk premium but is very often separately stated. The Ibbotson data provides information about returns for small company stocks. Ibbotson breaks down the premium based on the market capitalization of public companies. To put things into perspective for you, Ibbotson's 2001 *SBBI Yearbook* indicates that the size of the micro capitalization stock premium is represented by companies with market capitalizations of under $84,521,000. In fact, Ibbotson uses a breakdown of the tenth decile reflecting a size premium of 2.78 percent for the larger half of the decile and 8.42 percent[1] for the smaller half of the same decile. This demonstrates the very sizable impact of companies that have market capitalizations ranging from about $84.5 million to $48.3 million. These companies fall in a range that is still a lot larger than most of the companies we will value on a regular basis. Can you imagine the size impact for a company that is valued at $1 million?

The Ibbotson data indicates that the returns for these smaller companies have been higher than those of the larger companies. This means that an investment in a smaller company should yield a higher return based on this market data. Size may have something to do with it. Obviously, there are many other factors that cause smaller companies to be at greater risk than larger companies.

The size premium is usually considered to be part of the subject company's specific company risk premium, whether stated separately or on a combined basis. It is a good idea to make certain that the size premium is treated separately from the equity risk premium because it will make a difference in the calculation of discount rates under certain methods of calculating the rates.

Another series of size premium studies has been performed by Pricewaterhouse Coopers (PWC). These have been published in *Business Valuation Review* and as an appendix to PPC's *Guide to Business Valuations*. The PWC studies have expanded the Ibbotson analysis into more subsets of the market. Let's discuss some of the differences between these studies.

Comparison of the Ibbotson and Pricewaterhouse Coopers Studies

Ibbotson	*Pricewaterhouse Coopers*
▪ Addresses returns on investments in publicly traded securities based on size	▪ Addresses returns on investments in publicly traded securities based on size
▪ Segments NYSE securities[1] into deciles based on equity capitalization	▪ 25 size groups
▪ Analyzes arithmetic returns, betas, and real returns in excess of risk-free rate	▪ Utilizes NYSE, AMEX, and NASDAQ data[2] starting in 1963
▪ Concludes size premiums over risk-free rate and CAPM	▪ "High financial risk" securities analyzed in a separate portfolio
	▪ Seven size metrics in addition to equity capitalization
	▪ Concludes size premiums over risk-free rate

[1]NYSE companies back to 1926 excluding closed-end mutual funds, American Depository Notes, unit investment trusts, and Americus trusts.
[2]Excludes American Depository Notes and non-operating holding companies.

According to the PWC study, "high financial risk" is defined as companies:

1. In bankruptcy or liquidation,
2. That have five-year average net income less than zero,
3. That have negative book value of equity, or
4. That have a debt–to–total capital ratio greater than 80 percent.

PWC segregates the returns from this group of companies in an attempt to better reflect the market.

Rather than solely relying on market capitalization as Ibbotson does, PWC breaks down its analysis by the following metrics:

1. Book value of invested capital
2. Five-year average EBITDA
3. Sales

[1]Ibbotson Associates, *Stocks, Bonds, Bills and Inflation, Valuation Edition* (Chicago: Ibbotson, 2001), Chapter 6, 123.

4. Number of employees
5. Market value of equity
6. Book value of equity
7. Five-year average net income
8. Market value of invested capital

Another difference between the Ibbotson and PWC studies is that in the PWC study the premiums have not been adjusted to remove beta risk (as in the Ibbotson study). This is relatively advanced stuff, and if you are not familiar with beta risk, you are probably confused. This has to do with the capital asset pricing model (CAPM), which we have not discussed yet. For now, just accept the fact that PWC does not recommend multiplying these equity risk premiums by a CAPM beta. A more appropriate use would be a simple "build-up" approach. (CAPM and beta will be explained soon!)

So where are we with these two studies? Here is where we have come to thus far:

Ibbotson	*Pricewaterhouse Coopers*
▪ NYSE equity from 1926	▪ NYSE, AMEX, and NASDAQ from 1963
▪ One measure of size	▪ Eight measures of size
▪ 10 size groups	▪ 25 size groups
▪ Premiums inversely proportional to size	▪ Premiums inversely proportional to size
▪ Beta-adjusted premiums	▪ Premiums not beta adjusted

Probably one of the most interesting parts of these studies is the fact that even with PWC breaking down the equity risk premium into smaller groups than Ibbotson, there really is a very small difference in the equity risk premium overall. To put things into perspective, look at the results:

Decile	*Ibbotson*
1	6.93%
2	8.34%
3	8.71%
4	9.35%
5	10.08%
6	10.24%

PWC	*Group*
5.21%	1
3.94%	2
3.53%	3
6.16%	4
4.20%	5
6.26%	6
6.74%	7
7.52%	8
6.16%	9
7.94%	10
8.01%	11
8.55%	12
7.53%	13
8.79%	14
8.60%	15

Decile	*Ibbotson*
7	10.54%
8	11.60%
9	12.38%
10	15.52%

PWC	*Group*
9.25%	16
8.07%	17
10.56%	18
9.21%	19
9.21%	20
11.32%	21
10.34%	22
12.10%	23
12.45%	24
15.83%	25

The trend line of the Ibbotson and PWC equity risk premiums look fairly similar. They clearly move in the same direction, indicating that smaller companies have larger premiums. Even if all of the other metrics in the PWC study are graphed, the trend is in the same direction.

The high-risk companies' equity risk premiums are relatively consistent as well. The range approximates 14.5 percent. Once again, remember that the equity risk premium is the portion of the return that is above the risk-free rate. This means that these high-risk companies have returned about 20 percent.

PWC did a nice job of dissecting the public market data a little further than Ibbotson, but it is amazing how close the premiums are, regardless of which study you look at. More data is better, particularly when the data is being relied on to make judgment calls about the rates of return that should be applicable to a company that does not have a ready market.

More data is becoming available every year, providing the appraiser with better breakdowns about size. However, when the subject company is a small or medium-sized closely held company, all of these studies may not be very helpful. They make interesting reading, but how do they help us value the local shoe store? They may not. But if you think about the principle of substitution, an argument can be made that an investment in the public market place may be an equally desirable substitute for the subject company. Another argument can be made that most individuals who buy small to medium-sized companies are buying jobs and not investments. So, there goes another theory!

The rates of return appearing in Ibbotson are after-tax with respect to the corporate entities but pretax to the investor. I am not sure why, but this seems to confuse an awful lot of appraisers. Since public companies report their results on an after-tax basis, Ibbotson data is logically after-tax to the corporations. However, what should we consider the Treasury bonds to be? These returns are actually pretax to the government, or after-tax when you consider that the government does not pay taxes. A source of confusion is that the rates of return are pretax to the investor. Since we are normally being asked to value the business enterprise, personal taxes have no relevance.

The data used in the Ibbotson studies in previous years was not specific to a particular industry. It applied to the overall market. However, Ibbotson has recently started to include industry risk premium data in summary form. When using Ibbotson data, the appraiser should be aware that the rates of return may not be truly comparable to the appraisal subject. Certainly, rates of return for the overall market are not going to be as meaningful as rates of return for the appraisal subject's industry. Then you must be able to differentiate the risk profiles of the public companies included within this data from the appraisal subject. This is accomplished (or at least, we attempt to accomplish this) by performing financial analysis and risk assessment (remember Chapters 5 and 6?).

The information contained in the Ibbotson studies also spans a very long time period. Many appraisers argue that a shorter time horizon should be used in calculating the equity risk premium. The problem lies in defining an appropriate time period so that the data makes sense. During any of the decades covered by this data, there were aberrations in the data that may make the data invalid at any specific point in time. It would be difficult to choose a time period without something weird happening. Interest rates at the beginning of the 1980s were at an all-time high. Black Monday occurred in October 1987, when the stock market dropped 500 points in one day. And let's not forget the 1986 Tax Reform Act, which made my real estate limited partnerships worth pennies on the dollar (another great investment for yours truly!). By the mid-1990s the stock market started to erupt, but by 2000, investors were erupting instead of their stocks.

Total stock returns, as used in the Ibbotson data, are defined as dividends plus unrecognized capital gains. The unrecognized capital gains are measured from the beginning of the year to the end of the year. Therefore, the returns reflected by Ibbotson are considered to be cash returns. Ibbotson data used in determining discount rates should be applied to net cash flow rather than earnings. An adjustment would be required to derive the appropriate discount rate to use for earnings. The reason for this adjustment is that earnings are considered to be more risky than cash flow, since other factors (capital expenditures, working capital needs, and net borrowings) are not taken into consideration.

Although Ibbotson data is the most widely used source for the equity risk premium, it may not be applicable for small closely held companies. Since the Ibbotson data comes from the public marketplace, the companies included are significantly larger than many of the businesses that will be appraised by most of us. The return data also considers the marketability of the public company, which does not exist for the closely held company.

Since many of us value small companies, don't lose sight of the fact that Ibbotson data comes from the public market. The risk factors driving public and private companies are frequently very different. However, this does not always mean that the closely held business is more risky. I'll match our firm with many of the dot-coms any day of the week. At least we sometimes show a profit!

Specific Company Risk Premium. This component of the discount rate provides for the specific risk characteristics of the appraisal subject. These risk elements are not covered by the equity risk premium. The specific company risk premium can increase considerably depending on the risk associated with the appraisal subject. The specific company risk premium can also be negative. This occurs if the appraisal subject is considered to be less risky than its peer group.

This is another part of the book that makes auditors cringe. There is no objective source of data to properly reflect or quantify the specific company risk premium. It is a matter of judgment and experience. There are no mystical tables that an appraiser can turn to, nor can the appraiser be totally comfortable with this portion of the assignment.

Many of the risk factors that are considered in determining an appropriate discount rate are the same factors that an appraiser uses to adjust multiples from guideline companies under the market approach. Although they are a little different, a review is worthwhile. Once valuation multiples are determined for the guideline companies, it becomes necessary for the appraiser to adjust these multiples for the qualitative differences between the guideline companies and the appraisal subject. These qualitative differences will most likely relate to factors such as expected growth and different risks attributable to the appraisal subject as compared with the guideline companies. Remember this stuff from a few chapters ago?

Different risk factors considered by the appraiser will generally include, but will not be limited to, the following:

- Economic risk
- Business risk
- Operating risk

- Financial risk
- Asset risk
- Product risk
- Market risk
- Technological risk
- Regulatory risk
- Legal risk

There are many other risk factors to be considered as well, but these are some of the more important items that an appraiser must think about in the application not only of the market approach but of the income approach as well. In the market approach, each of these risk factors should be analyzed from the point of view of how the appraisal subject differs from the guideline companies. In the income approach, these factors are considered in relationship to the source of the market-derived rates, as opposed to specific guideline companies. For example, since guideline companies tend to be in the same industry as the appraisal subject, an economic risk such as rising interest rates will probably have the same impact on the appraisal subject as the guideline companies. But if the appraisal subject operates in a smaller geographic area, the risk could be different if that part of the country is doing better or worse than the rest of the country, since a larger, more diversified company could reduce its risk by not being concentrated in one area.

Comparing the Subject Company

Being an appraiser is similar to being a risk assessor. Since business valuation theory is so closely related to risk-reward theory, an appraiser must spend a considerable amount of time analyzing the subject company to determine how much risk the income stream is subject to. Whether a single-period capitalization model or a multi-period discounting model is going to be used in the valuation assignment, the appraiser must determine the degree of risk for the earnings, cash flow, or other income stream being considered.

How does the appraiser do this? The answer is simple. He or she compares the subject company to either guideline companies or, in their absence, other forms of industry or investment information. For example, if good guideline companies do not allow the market approach to be used, the income approach is frequently the alternative. Sometimes, the income approach is the preferred approach. Trade association data or industry composite data, such as information available in *Business Profiler*, can be used for this comparison. Information in this type of product allows the appraiser to perform a financial analysis of the subject company and compare the results against industry information. This comparison allows the appraiser to determine whether the subject company is stronger or weaker than the industry group.

The financial analysis is probably the easier part of the analysis. Frequently, the nonfinancial analysis is the more difficult part of the assignment. Factors contributing to this difficulty include, among other things:

- Economic conditions
- Industry conditions
- Location of business
- Competition
- Depth of management
- Quality of management
- Barriers to entry into market

Most of these factors should not come as any great surprise. There must be a reason why every appraisal textbook and educational course suggests that an appraiser look into these items. Revenue Ruling 59-60 addresses many of these items.

Economic Conditions. I previously discussed economic risk, so there is little reason to repeat the discussion. However, Revenue Ruling 59-60 emphasizes the economic conditions by discussing the risk associated with "boom" economies. The outlook for the economy should be considered, as it will affect most businesses in one way or another.

Industry Conditions. Industry conditions are also important since the subject company will probably be affected by changes in their industry. This is easily understood by considering the changes that have taken place, and continue to take place, in the health care industry. Valuing a medical practice is not the same as it used to be. In fact, depending upon the type of medical practice, the outlook may not be so good.

Location of Business. In real estate appraisal, the value of property is greatly affected by the three "L's": location, location, location. Certain businesses are highly dependent on their location, while others are not. Imagine valuing a retail business that is located on a road about to undergo major construction and that this construction is expected to last several years. Because of the construction, traffic flow will be diverted away from that road. How does the location of the business impact its value?

Competition. At a management interview, appraisers always ask for information about the company's competitors. The reason for this is obvious. If a business suffers from the risk of competition, value is impacted. If you were valuing a local hardware store and found out that The Home Depot was about to move in less than a mile down the road, wouldn't this suggest that the appraisal subject has a great risk of lost business?

Depth of Management. Certainly, most smaller businesses have no depth in management. In fact, they are usually highly dependent on one key person. Revenue Ruling 59-60 discusses the possible loss of a key person as being a risk element. Several questions need to be considered by the appraiser. What is the likelihood of the loss of the key person? Sometimes the key person may not be the owner of the business. It may be a key salesperson. If the key person is lost, can a replacement be found? How long would it take to replace this person? At what cost? For many small businesses, the business may die with the owner. Frequently, we see businesses where the owner is also the highly technical person whose knowledge is in his or her head.

Quality of Management. Along with the depth in management the analyst must consider the quality of management. Does the business have adequate management to properly achieve the business goals, or does management have no control over its own destiny? What if the business is being run by a good technical person, but that individual cannot manage people? Or what if the management cannot see what the future has in store for the company?

Barriers to Entry Into Market. Another risk element is the difficulty that others may encounter in entering into the market. If the barriers to entry are nonexistent, competition may become fierce, creating serious risk. If it is difficult to enter the market, the company may be in a better position. This can hold true in situations where the company holds patents, copyrights, and other types of intangibles.

The Bottom Line. The bottom line in the determination of the specific company risk premium is to consider what the total rate of return would have to be, given the risk of the income stream being discounted. Though we use various methods to help quantify a discount rate, these are only tools in our toolbox; these methods do not help us quantify these rates. If nothing else, the final answer has to make sense. Remember, an appraiser's responsibility is to determine an estimate of value that makes sense. It is not to develop rates of return.

An appraiser can look to market evidence to support the specific company risk premium, but the process becomes somewhat circular in logic. For example, a few years ago, we appraised a business and determined that the discount rate should be 80 percent. Everyone involved in the litigation thought exactly what you are now thinking—we must be crazy. I began to testify at the trial and started describing all of the factors that we have been discussing in this book. Obviously, I could not quantify every one of these factors, but I explained that the risk was substantial, and I felt that a rate higher than venture capital returns was appropriate.

Over lunch, the client, the attorney, and I were discussing the testimony, preparing me to go back on the witness stand after lunch. The conversation led to the client telling me that business was really pretty tough. In fact, the only thing that was keeping him alive was the fact that his major supplier was financing his payables for 90 days at 19 percent interest. In fact, I think he called the guy a shylock (actually, some of the other words could not be printed in this book). Since 19 percent for 90 days adds up to approximately 76 percent for the year, I went back to the courtroom feeling pretty good about my 80 percent rate. In this instance, the proof of the rate of return for an unsecured creditor justified the rate used in the valuation assignment. Thereafter, we regularly ask the business owner if there is any kind of financing other than the conventional type.

Logically, if we can determine a rate of return using outside empirical evidence, why would we need to determine a specific company rate? Any time that you can avoid having to quantify the unquantifiable, I would suggest that you do it.

When All Else Fails, Go Back to the Theory

When you get to the point where you cannot get as lucky as I was when I found out that there was another way to determine a rate of return for the subject company, you need to go back to good old appraisal theory. Let's spend some time discussing some of the more popular methods for calculating discount rates. This discussion will include the following:

- The build up method
- The capital asset pricing model
- Price/earnings reciprocal plus growth
- Factor rating method
- Weighted average cost of capital (a method of calculating a discount rate for invested capital, which may include the other methods just mentioned)

The Build up Method

Many appraisers, especially those who work with smaller privately held companies, use a "build up" method of developing a discount rate. The build up method embodies all of the elements of the discount rate previously described, including (1) a risk-free rate, (2) an equity risk premium, and (3) a specific company risk premium. The equity risk premium will normally be developed from the total market, as opposed to industry-specific data.

The appraiser frequently cannot get specific industry data to use in the development of the equity risk premium. Instead, the equity risk premium will be developed from the Ibbotson data for the overall market. In this instance, the specific company risk premium must include a risk factor relating to the difference between the industry and the overall market. All this means is that the specific company risk premium may be slightly higher if the industry is more risky than the entire market. Exhibit 10.2 contains a demonstration of the build up method.

EXHIBIT 10.2
The Build up Method

There are various methods of determining discount rates. Using the build up method of determining the discount rate results in a discount rate as follows:

	%
"Safe" rate	6.59[1]
Equity risk premium	7.80[2]
Small company risk premium	4.30[3]
Specific company risk premium	3.00[4]
Discount rate	21.69

[1]*Federal Reserve Bulletin*—20-year Treasury bonds, week ended May 19, 2000.

[2]Ibbotson Associates—*Stocks, Bonds, Bills and Inflation* 2000 Yearbook: difference between total returns on common stocks and total returns on long-term government bonds from 1926 to 1999 (13.3–5.5).

[3]Ibbotson Associates—*Stocks, Bonds, Bills and Inflation 2000 Yearbook*: difference between total returns on small company stocks and total returns on common stocks from 1926 to 1999 (13.3).

[4]Appraiser's judgment based on the analysis discussed throughout this report relative to the risk associated with the company's ability to perform in the future based on the economy, industry, and financial, technological, management, and other business risks.

A discount rate has been derived above. The components of the discount rate include a safe rate, which indicates the fact that any investor would receive, at a bare minimum, an equivalent rate for a safe investment. In this particular instance, U.S. Treasury bonds are used as an indication of a safe rate.

Added to the safe rate is an equity risk premium, which represents the premium that common stockholders require in the public marketplace over investors in long-term government bonds. This indicates that since equity securities are considered to be more risky by the investor, a higher rate of return has been required over the period of time indicated in the calculation of this premium.

The third component of the discount rate is a small company risk premium. This is a risk premium that is measured in the public marketplace for companies that are in the ninth and tenth deciles, indicating that smaller companies require a larger return due to the risk associated with size. The ninth and tenth deciles of the public marketplace have been measured based on companies that are capitalized at an average capitalization of $94 million, which is considerably larger than the appraisal subject.

For this reason, a fourth component, known as the specific company risk premium, has been added to determine an appropriate discount rate. This specific company risk premium takes into consideration the detailed analysis performed by the appraiser, including the company's performance, the company's management structure, the size of the company, the ability of the company to raise capital, and the many other factors that must be considered in assessing the risk relating to an investment in XYZ Company.

Capital Asset Pricing Model

The capital asset pricing model (CAPM) is a method of determining a discount rate that is commonly used in the appraisal of larger companies. It has little, if any, applicability to small and medium-sized businesses, but no discussion about discount rates would be complete without mentioning its existence. If the appraiser uses the CAPM to develop a discount rate to be used in the valuation of a smaller business, the appraiser has probably lost his or her mind. At any rate, if the CAPM is used in this situation, the premium must be great enough to accommodate the difference between the return on the entire market and the return that applies to smaller companies. This data is available in the Ibbotson study.

As an appraiser, you should be familiar with all of the tools available in the profession, since there is a good possibility that CAPM will be used against you at some point in the future. That's how I found out about it! The discussion that follows is not intended to be a highly technical discussion about CAPM, but rather, it is intended to explain, in English, what this model is all about. Finance textbooks can be consulted if you want to learn more about this subject.

The theoretical basis for the CAPM comes from the application of the "efficient market" theory. In short, this states that the expected returns on investment portfolios are related to the expected risk of the investments included in the portfolios. The relationship between risk and reward becomes apparent in its truest form under the efficient market theory. Since investors are said to be risk averse, portfolios are structured to diversify away the risk. Right away, you should realize the limited applicability of this method for smaller companies, since the owners do not have diversified portfolios and can't diversify away the enormous risk associated with owning the closely held business.

The theory behind the CAPM is that we assume that in the marketplace there are a fixed number of securities in which we can invest. Each of the securities has its own expected return (based on its level of risk) and standard deviation. The investor will select the security that offers the highest return and the lowest standard deviation. What does this mean? Investors don't like to take chances if they can avoid them! They look to minimize their risk and, at the same time, maximize the return available to them.

I hate to do this to you, but the mathematical equation for the CAPM is as follows:

$$k = R_f + [\beta(R_m - R_f)]$$

where

k = Expected return (also known as the discount rate for equity)
R_f = Risk-free rate
β = Systematic risk (volatility explained in the following section)
$(R_m - R_f)$ = Long-term average risk premium of the market as a whole minus the long-term average risk-free rate (also known as the equity risk premium)

The CAPM provides a discount rate that is applicable to the equity of the company (not invested capital). The formula looks a lot worse than it really is because the CAPM is similar to the build up method, which is more commonly used by appraisers of smaller businesses. Always keep in mind that the three main components of a discount rate include a risk-free rate, an equity risk premium, and a specific company risk premium. In the discussion that follows, I will demonstrate that the CAPM has similarities with this much simpler method (the build up method).

Components of the CAPM. There are two different methods that are commonly used to determine the risk-free rate. Long-term U.S. Treasury bond rates are generally used, as discussed earlier in this chapter. The other method is more technically consistent with the CAPM assumption. In this approach, the risk-free rate is determined by taking the long-term Treasury bond rate minus Ibbotson's horizon premium. The horizon premium represents maturity risk. This compensates for the fact that longer-term Treasury securities are considered to be more risky because of their long-term nature.

The systematic risk, beta, is the measure of the volatility of the stock market as a whole. It is a measurement that predicts how a stock will react to the movement of the stock market. The purpose of using a beta is to measure the expected return of the market based on the volatility that takes place when one uses guideline companies as a surrogate for the appraisal subject. Since this is the expected return for a diversified portfolio, it is assumed that there is no specific risk relative to the company being appraised. What this means is that a company's beta will predict what will happen to the price of the stock as the stock market goes up and down. A beta of 1 indicates that a company will move with the market (market up 10 percent, company up 10 percent). The use of public guideline data allows the appraiser to compare the median beta of these similar companies in order to predict the volatility of the appraisal subject if it were a public company.

Various sources can be used to determine betas. First of all, a beta can be calculated by the analyst (this procedure will not be discussed in this book, but more information can be found in Pratt's *Valuing a Business* or *Cost of Capital*). The most common sources for finding betas are Standard & Poor's Tear Sheets, the Media General Computer database, *Value Line*, and Wilshire Associates.

IMPORTANT

Different sources of betas vary in the manner in which they are calculated. It is important that the appraiser be consistent when he or she uses published betas. It is preferable to get them all from the same source or calculate your own.

Since betas are calculated with respect to the entire market, the general risk premium ($R_m - R_f$) should be calculated using an R_m that is representative of the return from the entire market. Some appraisers mistakenly use only the bottom part of the market to compensate for the size of the appraisal subject. The fundamental assumption in the CAPM is that the risk premium portion of the expected return of a security is a function of that security's systematic risk. Capital market theory assumes that investors hold or can hold common stocks in large, well-diversified portfolios. Therefore, unsystematic risk is eliminated because of the diversification in the portfolio (can you believe this stuff?).

The *SBBI Yearbook* is the most commonly used source for R_m. It is derived from a study of long-term returns from the stock market. It is incorrect to include the return on small stocks in the R_m term in the CAPM equation. Since betas are calculated with regard to the entire market, R_m must be the return on the entire market, not just that portion in the bottom of the market. When beta equals 1.0 in the CAPM equation, the indicated return is the return on the market as a whole.

It should also be noted that the R_f at the beginning of the equation is the risk-free rate at the appraisal date, whereas the R_f in parentheses is a long-term average R_f. The beta is generally chosen by examining a list of guideline companies. Although R_f is assumed to be the rate of return on a long-term U.S. Treasury bond, the rate on a short-term Treasury note might make more sense in certain instances. This may be the case when a shorter holding period (such as a self-liquidating investment of 10 years) is expected.

The equity risk premium, which can also be considered the general risk premium (as discussed previously), can be determined from a number of different sources. One of the more common sources is Ibbotson's *SBBI Yearbook*. The equity risk premium is based on the historical average. If R_f is based on Treasury bonds, the equity risk premium should be measured by the difference between stocks and Treasury bonds. If R_f is based on Treasury bonds minus a horizon premium, the equity risk premium should be measured by the difference between stocks and Treasury bills. All we want to do is to be consistent in using this data.

Another source for equity risk premiums is *Quantitative Analysis*, published by Merrill Lynch. This is a source of estimated forward-looking equity risk premiums. Other forward-looking sources include *Global Investor's Digest* and *DRI/McGraw-Hill*. Another source is *Cost of Capital Quarterly*, published by

Ibbotson Associates. Although this publication is a bit pricey ($995 a year), it contains some really good stuff.

There have been several articles written about the merits of using forward-looking equity risk premiums over a reliance on the historical data published by Ibbotson. It seems logical to use forward-looking data, since valuation is a prospective process. The real question to ask yourself over and over again is: How will this get us to be more accurate in determining the value of the subject company? If you believe that the forward-looking equity risk premiums will allow you to do a better job, then use them. I have found that the small businesses that we appraise are relatively unaffected by all of this stuff. Rarely, if ever, will the CAPM be applicable to small companies. (Can you imagine trying to explain this stuff to a jury?) In reality, betas cannot be calculated for the small closely held company for which guideline company information is unavailable. The CAPM assumes that the market is efficient (talk about big assumptions!). An inefficient market will create distortions in the model. Computerized trading and insider information (among other factors) can cause the market to be less efficient than it could be.

The CAPM is used to derive an equity discount rate that is attributable to net cash flow. It is not intended to be applied to invested capital (debt and equity), nor is it intended to be applied to earnings. Since future returns and betas cannot be measured, historical data must be used as a surrogate.

To add a little bit more uncertainty to your life, betas can be unlevered and relevered. Since public companies may have different capital structures than the private company being appraised, better comparability can be achieved by jumping through hoops. This is done for reasons similar to why we value invested capital rather than equity. In case you are going through withdrawal and need a formula fix, you can unlever a beta as follows:

$$\beta_U = \beta_L / [1 + (1 - t)(d/e)]$$

where

β_U = Beta unlevered
β_L = Beta levered
t = Marginal tax rate
d = Debt
e = Equity
d/e = Debt-to-equity ratio (based on fair market value)

Since little of this stuff makes sense without an example, let's do one. XYZ Corp. has revenues of $15 million and its common equity is estimated to be worth between $7 million and $12 million. Interest-bearing debt represents 25 percent of the market value of invested capital for the company. The primary competition in the public world has levered betas that average 1.2. Their average debt-to-equity relationship (considered optimal) is 0.6. Each of the public companies has common equity worth about $70 million. The unlevered beta can be calculated as follows:

$$\beta_U = 1.2/[1 + (1 - 0.40)(0.6)]$$
$$\beta_U = 1.2/[1 + 0.36]$$
$$\beta_U = 0.88$$

Now that we have unlevered the beta, the next step is to relever the beta. Why do we do this? We relever the beta to capture the debt-to-equity relationship of the subject company. This allows a better calculation of the volatility risk (beta) taken from the public guideline companies by incorporating the closely held company's capital structure into the determination of the discount rate. Relevering the beta for the subject company is done as follows:

$$\beta_U = \beta_L/[1 + (1 - 0.40)(.25/.75)]$$
$$0.88 = \beta_L/1.2$$
$$\beta_L = 0.88 \times 1.2$$
$$\beta_L = 1.06$$

Now, hold that thought and we will use this stuff some more when we finish talking about WACC (weighted average cost of capital).

Adapting CAPM for the Closely Held Business. Getting back to the real world requires an appraiser to modify the CAPM if it is to be used for the valuation of a closely held company. Remember that this model was developed for use in portfolio analysis and not business valuation. The assumption of a well-diversified portfolio that eliminates unsystematic risk is a poor assumption. The owner of a closely held company can rarely diversify away the risk element of the closely held business being the major investment in his or her portfolio. Therefore, the CAPM formula is generally modified for the valuation of closely held companies as follows:

$$k = R_f + \beta(R_m - R_f) + \alpha$$

where

α = Alpha, unsystematic risk (specific company)

The alpha may be a specific company risk adjustment, an adjustment for a small company risk premium, or both. Since the CAPM assumes a diversified portfolio, an additional factor that is specific to the investor in a closely held company should be considered. For that investor, the closely held company may be the largest investment of his or her lifetime, and there may not be any diversification. Therefore, unsystematic risk, which was assumed to be diversified away in the original CAPM equation, may be a factor in the discount rates of closely held companies.

The CAPM is frequently expanded to include the unsystematic risk by splitting the alpha into additional components, changing the CAPM formula to the following:

$$k = R_f + \beta(R_m - R_f) + \text{SCP} + \text{SCA}$$

where

SCP = Small company premium
SCA = Specific company adjustment

SCP and SCA constitute the alpha factors.

The small company risk premium should vary depending upon the size of the appraisal subject. The discount rates for small companies are generally higher than those for large ones, despite the fact that the betas of smaller companies are often lower than those of larger companies. Smaller companies tend to trade less often, which ultimately leads to lower betas. However, many smaller companies can have tremendous illiquidity premiums.

The specific company adjustment is based on the appraiser's judgment. The factors used to make this adjustment are similar to those that are used for selecting market multiples. The difficulty with this adjustment is determining how much weight to put on the risk of achieving the forecasted growth. In the market approach, you can at least look at the guideline companies' earnings estimates to get an idea of short-term growth rates. In the derivation of a discount rate, particularly from the overall market, it is considerably more difficult.

It is generally considered unacceptable to have the SCP or SCA inside of the equity risk premium, that is, affected by the beta factor. Beta must be applied only to the "normal" equity risk premium. The following table is an adaptation from PPC's *Guide to Business Valuations*.

$$R_f + \beta(R_m - R_f) + SCP + SCA$$

	Risk-free rate
+	Equity risk premium × Median comparative company beta
=	Comparative company return
+	Specific company risk premium (SCA + SCP)
=	Net cash flow discount rate
+	Incremental adjustment for earnings
=	Net earnings discount rate
−	Long-term growth rate
=	Net earnings cap rate for next year
÷	1 + Growth rate
=	Net earnings cap rate for current year

This illustrates the proper use of the CAPM, but it also demonstrates how to adjust discount rates for cash flow to discount rates for earnings and then to a capitalization rate for next year's earnings as well as the current year's earnings. This table also shows the relationship between these items.

Other Methods for Estimating a Discount Rate

There are many alternatives to the build up and CAPM methods. Although this book cannot possibly cover every alternative, I want to discuss some of the more common methods of deriving a discount rate. More often than not, the same methods are used to develop capitalization rates. Remember that the difference between discount rates and capitalization rates is the long-term sustainable growth factor. Some of the alternatives include the following:

- Price/earnings reciprocal plus growth
- Factor rating method
- Weighted average cost of capital

Price/Earnings Reciprocal Plus Growth. One of the methods used to calculate a discount rate is to take the reciprocal of an industry-specific price/earnings ratio from the market (this provides a capitalization rate) and add the expected growth rate of the returns attributable to the guideline companies. This is said to be a market-derived rate, since the price/earning ratios will be determined from guideline companies. Since an earnings/price ratio is the same as a capitalization rate, the long-term sustainable growth must be added to the result to move from a capitalization rate to a discount rate (remember that $k - g = c$; therefore, $c + g = k$). If the appraiser uses this method, please remember that the result is a discount rate that is applicable to net income and not cash flow. Since the price-to-earnings ratio uses *earnings* and not cash flow, the result will be an earnings-based capitalization rate that is then converted to an earnings-based discount rate. Be careful to remain consistent (apples to apples, not apples to bananas—we do not want a fruit salad).

The difficulty in this method is figuring out what the market's expectations are for long-term sustainable growth and how they are reflected in the market price of the stocks. This is not published anywhere. Some appraisers will turn to industry data to come up with this expected growth rate. In practice, I have found that the rates published for industries are short-term (maybe a few years), not long-term. This makes this method difficult to use.

Let me give you an example. Let's assume you find public companies that are in the industry of the subject company. The average or median (for those who want to be statistically better) price-to-earnings multiple of these companies is 50 to 1. This means that these public companies are currently trading at 50 times earnings. The mathematical inverse, or capitalization rate, implied by the market can be stated as follows:

$$1/50 = .02 \text{ or } 2\%$$

If you refer to Ibbotson's *Cost of Capital Quarterly* you can find out what they have reported as the median discount rate for the specific two- or three-digit Standard Industrial Classification code based on the different methods they use to calculate it. More often than not, the discount rate for equity will fall in the range of ±15 percent. If this were the case, the implied growth rate, which would be the difference between the discount rate and the capitalization rate, would be about 13 percent. The problem with this picture is a simple one. A company cannot possibly grow at a 13 percent rate into perpetuity or it will eventually exceed the Gross Domestic Product of the world. Long-term sustainable growth cannot exceed the rate of inflation and population growth. Even if short-term growth is high, the present value of this growth into perpetuity cannot be that high.

Factor Rating Method. Another way of determining a discount rate is known as the factor rating method. This has become more popular among business brokers than among appraisers. However, this method is not much different from the build up method. In the factor rating method, the specific company risk premium is broken down into numerous factors. Each factor is given a weighting. These weightings will vary depending upon the appraiser, but they generally range from 0 to 3. The factors may include the location of the business, financial performance, management, liquidity, and so forth. In case you have not recognized these factors, they are all of the items that the appraiser should be considering in the risk analysis of the company.

Instead of deriving a specific risk premium of 20, the appraiser may derive 10 different risk factors of 2 each. Guess what—same result! Quite frankly, I would rather defend a single figure than 10 different figures. The same analysis goes into the thought process, but if you are performing the appraisal for a litigation, why would you want to give the cross-examining attorney the opportunity to try to rip you apart 10 times? Once is generally bad enough!

There is nothing empirical about the 0 to 3 range for the factors. There is nothing empirical about the specific company risk premium. It is judgment. That's right, judgment. As a matter of fact, it is subjective judgment. As appraisers, it is our job to be "objectively subjective."

Weighted Average Cost of Capital. The next method for determining a discount rate is known as the weighted average cost of capital (WACC). (Now you know why this business is so wacky! I know, bad joke!) The WACC is a combination of (1) the required rate of return on the equity of the company and (2) the required rate of return on the debt of the company. The WACC is used when the appraiser uses a debt-free method to determine the value of the invested capital of the appraisal subject (invested capital = debt plus equity).

The theory behind a WACC is simple. Since a company is financed partly with debt and partly with equity, the return on investment should consider the risk of each element. Since the business owner is not directly responsible for the debt (assume no personal guarantee), the bank, not the business owner, is the one that is at risk for that portion of the invested capital. Therefore, if the benefit stream comprises part debt and part equity, it would seem logical that the risk is reduced on the overall capital for the investors.

However, the business owner is completely at risk for the money that he or she invests in the business. This money should command a higher return because of the increased risk associated with that portion of the invested capital. So what does this all mean?

The WACC is determined using the following formula:

$$(k_e \times W_e) + (k_d[1 - t] \times W_d)$$

where

k_e = Required rate of return for the company's equity capital (discount rate)
k_d = Company's cost of debt capital (borrowing)
W_e = Percentage of equity capital in the company's capital structure
W_d = Percentage of debt capital in the company's capital structure
t = Company's effective income tax rate

Pretty ugly, isn't it? Once again, this looks more complicated than it really is. Exhibit 10.3 contains a demonstration of the calculations.

EXHIBIT 10.3
Application of the WACC

Assume that after the appraiser analyzes the company, its industry, and other pertinent factors, it is determined that the company's required rate of return on equity is 20 percent. The company is borrowing money from its bank at 9 percent. The company's effective tax rate is 40 percent. The company's condensed balance sheet looks like this:

Assets		*Liabilities and Equity*	
Current assets	$ 500,000	Current liabilities	$ 200,000
Fixed assets (net)	725,000	Long-term debt[1]	300,000
Other assets	175,000	Equity	900,000
Total	$ 1,400,000	Total	$ 1,400,000

[1]Long-term debt contains all of the debt on the balance sheet. The short-term portion of the long-term debt would also be included in the calculation below.

Based on these facts, the WACC would be calculated as follows:

$$(k_e \times W_e) + (k_d[1 - t] \times W_d)$$
$$(.20 \times .75) + (.09[1 - .40] \times .25)$$
$$.15 + .01 = .16$$

Capital structure:

Debt: $300,000 + Equity: $900,000 = Total: $1,200,000

Exhibit 10.3 contains a technical error. The WACC calculation is generally based on the market value of the debt and equity. For closely held companies, we are generally valuing the equity. We need to know the answer to get the answer! For the WACC to truly work, the theory indicates that we should allocate the cost of capital for the invested capital based on the market value of the debt and equity. If we knew the answer to these questions, why would we need to do any other calculations? We would already have the value of the subject company. For guideline companies, this works. For closely held companies, we make assumptions.

Although I have no intention of discussing preferred stock and its impact on the WACC, the appraiser should recognize that if the subject company has preferred stock, it must be addressed as part of the capital structure. The basic formula for the WACC should be expanded for each different class of stock. That should suffice for now since most of the companies that we appraise do not have a complex capital structure.

Regardless of the number of classes and types of stock in the capital structure, one of the questions that arises time and time again is, what capital structure should be used in the WACC equation? Should it be the actual capital structure of the subject company, or should it be the "normal" capital structure of the industry? There are valid arguments for both alternatives if the interest being valued is a controlling interest. A minority interest cannot change the capital structure of the business, whereas the controlling interest can. This means that consideration should be given to the ability of the willing buyer to change things.

In a smaller business, it is not unusual to see much more debt as a percentage of the capital structure. This is usually because the small company is undercapitalized and depends on debt to make up the difference. However, the small business owner frequently must guarantee this debt and must possibly use his or her residence or other belongings as additional security for the lender. In this instance, the debt starts to take on the attributes of equity because of the risk of personal loss to the owner. This could be justification for using a discount rate that is higher than the conventional WACC but lower than the discount rate for pure equity. Once again, common sense and good judgment must be applied on a case-by-case basis.

Since I promised you that we would use the levering and unlevering example again, let's do it. Assume that the controlling stockholder of XYZ Corp. is planning to gift a minority interest to his child. Let's calculate a WACC using CAPM with the information from the previous example along with the following: 20-year risk-free rate = 6%; equity risk premium = 7%; size premium = 5%; tax rate = 40%; borrowing rate = 10%; company-specific risk = 4%.

$$(k_e \times W_e) + (k_d[1 - t] \times W_d)$$

Let's calculate the discount rate (k_e) = 6% + (7% × 1.06) + 5% + 4% = 22.42%. The 1.06 is the levered beta from before. A minority interest cannot change the capital structure, so the actual levered beta is used along with the actual capital structure for XYZ Corp., which provides a WACC as follows:

$$(22.42 \times 75\%) + (10\%[1 - .40] \times 25\%)$$
$$16.82 + 1.5 = 18.32\%$$

The weights of 75 percent and 25 percent were based on the company's actual capital structure, which was given as 25 percent interest-bearing debt. If a control buyer came along, the WACC would be calculated as follows:

$$(22.42 \times 40\%) + (10\%[1 - .40] \times 60\%)$$
$$8.97 + 3.60 = 12.57\%$$

The weights given to the debt and equity are now based on the optimal capital structure that was given earlier based on the guideline companies.

Other Methods. Another method of determining a discount rate is to create a blending of the rates of return that would be required on the various assets employed in the business (cash, accounts receivable, inventory, plant property and equipment, intangible assets, etc.). Liabilities would have to be considered as well in this analysis. The concept is similar to the WACC.

Investment return requirements can also be used, but generally by inference only. An example of this would be what a venture capitalist may require in a given situation. Venture capitalists base their rates on the risk associated with the venture capital, but they generally also consider an exit strategy in a reasonable number of years. This exit strategy may include a public offering or a management buyout.

Other methods that result in a discount rate for net cash flow include the arbitrage pricing model and the dividend yield plus growth model. Since neither of these models will be used in the valuation of small and medium-sized businesses, this discussion ends here.

Regardless of the rate of return selected, it must be correlated with the risk inherent in the subject and, most important, produce a result that makes sense.

Capitalization Rates

A capitalization rate is the rate used to convert a benefit stream for a single period into an indication of the fair market value of the property that is its source. This rate is the required rate of return for an income-generating asset from which anticipated growth has been subtracted. As discussed previously, a capitalization rate is a discount rate minus growth. This is expressed as follows:

$$c = k - g$$

In this equation g represents long-term sustainable growth (not next year's growth). Capitalization rates, similar to discount rates, are determined by the market based on the duration and risk of the investment. They vary with time, even for the same investment, and are sensitive to, and incorporate, long-term inflationary expectations.

Capitalization rates also consider the risk that generally resides in the market, and they must be adjusted to allow for the risk that is specific to the appraisal subject. Capitalization rates are founded on the principle of substitution, since they are based on the yields available on alternative investments. They will also depend on the nature of the benefit stream being capitalized (operating income, income before taxes, net income after taxes, dividends, or cash flow).

A capitalization rate is frequently derived from the appraisal subject's discount rate. It is used primarily as a divisor to determine value. The basis of the relationship between the discount rate and the capitalization rate is the assumption that the business has a perpetual life and its annual growth will be constant. The relationship is expressed as follows:

$$\text{Discount rate} - \text{Growth rate} = \text{Capitalization rate}$$

Mathematically, the discount and capitalization rates used in the multi-period and single-period models discussed in Chapter 9 will result in the same conclusion. What is effectively being done in these models is the removal of growth from the numerator (top) and denominator (bottom) of the equations. I discussed this math stuff in the last chapter, as well.

A simple mathematical proof follows. Assume that during an appraisal, the forecast benefit stream for next year was $110 and was expected to grow each year by 10 percent. Assume a 25 percent discount rate. A multi-period model would result in the present value being calculated for the earlier years as follows:

$$PV = \frac{110}{(1+.25)^1} + \frac{\left(\frac{110 \times 1.10}{.25-.10}\right)}{(1+.25)^1}$$

$$PV = 88 + 645$$

$$PV = 733$$

As a reminder, the terminal value grows the last year of the forecast period to the following year (110 × 1.10). This result is then capitalized by the discount rate minus long-term sustainable growth (.25 − .10). That result is then discounted to present value using the same present value factor as the last year of the forecast period $(1 + .25)^1$. (Assume end-of-year convention.)

If the 10 percent sustainable growth were taken out of the numerator and the denominator, we would have a single-period capitalization model, as follows:

$$PV = \frac{110}{.15}$$

$$PV = 733$$

Capitalization rates can also be directly derived from the market without calculating a discount rate. Methods of calculating this rate will be discussed later in this chapter. For the time being, let's concentrate on the basic formula. The appraiser must use informed judgment in selecting the appropriate growth rate. The company's historical growth, the projected growth of the industry, and many other factors (including, but not limited to, management goals, the ability to achieve desired growth, and borrowing power) should be considered in the determination of the growth rate. The rate should reflect long-term, sustainable growth rather than what is projected for the short term.

The appraiser needs to apply good judgment in selecting a growth rate for the company.An exceptionally high growth rate may not be achievable over the long run. Experts in finance generally expect the long-term growth of a company to average from 3 percent to 5 percent, generally not much more than the rate of inflation. I always enjoy seeing inexperienced appraisers use an incredibly high growth rate for a business without thinking of the implications of the use of a high growth rate. Imagine a company growing so fast that it eventually takes over the Gross Domestic Product of the United States, and maybe the world. A company can only grow so much. However, the long-term growth rate should reflect the present value of the growth. This means that if short-term growth is expected to be higher, the long-term growth rate's present value may be greater than the 3 percent to 5 percent in the books. In fact, it frequently is.

Let's spend a little more time on the growth rate. This is a part of the appraisal that requires the appraiser to tie several other parts of the valuation assignment together. The appraiser should consider the economic environment and industry outlook in determining the impact of the macro environment of the company on future growth, in addition to historic growth and management's expectations of future growth. Finally, do not forget that a company can only grow so much before competitive forces enter to "share" in the future growth.

Factors Affecting the Selection of the Capitalization Rate

The factors considered for the determination of capitalization rates should be similar to those considered for the determination of discount rates. These include the external factors (those that management has no control over) and the internal factors (those that management has the ability to control). There is little need to go over these factors again. However, do not minimize their importance.

Since capitalization rates are used in a single-period model, the rate of growth assumed must be one that could reasonably be expected to be sustained indefinitely. The investment horizon for a closely held business is generally presumed to be long-term in nature, and therefore, the assumption to be made is that the single benefit stream being capitalized will continue forever. What is the likelihood of a business growing at 25 percent per year indefinitely? Pretty slim! A small business would become a large business in no time at all if that were the case. With such rapid growth, the local hardware store would become The Home Depot. I don't think so! All businesses are subject to cycles, as is life (rapid growth, slow growth, stagnation, and death). Therefore, the growth rate assumed in any valuation must take into consideration the existing state of "maturity" of the subject company.

Sources of Data on Capitalization Rates

The ideal source for data on capitalization rates is the public (or private) market for corporate securities. However, if the appraiser is able to locate transactions that can be used in the determination of capitalization rates, the market approach, and not the income approach, would be used. For example, assume that the following transactions were located from the public market:

	ABC Corp.	*XYZ Corp.*	*PDQ Corp.*
Sales price	$ 10,000,000	$ 5,000,000	$ 20,000,000
Net income	2,500,000	750,000	4,000,000
Cash flow (net)	2,000,000	500,000	3,000,000
Revenues	20,000,000	15,000,000	48,000,000

This information could be used to calculate the implied capitalization rates that were the results of actual transactions. This makes merger and acquisition data useful. The implied capitalization rate is as follows:

Net income	25%	15%	20%
Cash flow (net)	20%	10%	15%
Revenues	200%	300%	240%

In Chapter 7, I discussed the calculation of pricing multiples using this data, which can also be used in the determination of capitalization rates for the income approach. However, merger and acquisition transaction data must be carefully scrutinized, since it may embody elements of control as a result of the acquisition. The prices paid for the acquisition may also include a premium based on the expected synergies for the acquirer.

The transaction data derived from the public market is generally an indication of the value of stockholders' equity. This means that capitalization rates for use with debt-free income streams must incorporate assumptions regarding typical capital structures (debt and equity), not necessarily the actual structure of the subject company, since the public companies are more likely to have a better debt-to-equity relationship than the smaller, closely held company. This could require the appraiser to make certain adjustments to compensate for the different risk of the appraisal subject because of its particular capital structure. This problem is reduced if the merger and acquisition data come from private company transactions of similarly sized companies.

On occasion, the appraiser will locate transactions in an industry that has a considerable amount of merger and acquisition activity. When transactions occur in an industry that is "hot," the capitalization rates reflected in the prices paid may have limited applicability. There may be so much anticipated growth in this industry that the capitalization rates may not make any sense. For example, if high price-to-earnings multiples are being paid for companies (say, 103 times earnings), the implied capitalization rate would be less than 1 percent. We could rarely, if ever, use this type of information for the closely held company.

The opinions of authors, experts, and others with special insight into the market may be used to develop capitalization rates. This is a dangerous practice, however, since the rates referred to in the writings are usually based on the individuals' own experiences. Without knowing the facts and circumstances of the particular situations, it is impossible to rely on someone else's experience.

The appraiser should also be aware of current and evolving case law, particularly if the appraisal will be used in a litigation. However, it is a common error to try to apply an old case to a current situation (sort of like putting a square peg in a round hole), since the times and facts are different. In my home state (New Jersey), a common error seen in matrimonial valuations is when the appraiser refers to the *Dugan* case and implies that the appropriate capitalization rate is 33⅓ percent because a multiple of 3 was discussed in the judge's opinion. A case in 1982, when interest rates were 16 percent, can be expected to vary from a case in

2001, when interest rates were about 5 percent. Furthermore, many valuation issues end up being litigated because the positions of the opposing experts are too diverse and, in many cases, indefensible.

The information maintained in the market data file of The Institute of Business Appraisers, BizComps, Pratt's Stats, Done Deals, and even possibly Thomson Financial Securities Data are other sources for determining capitalization rates. This information can allow the appraiser to determine the capitalization rates for various levels of benefit streams based on the available information in the databases. The same caution must be applied as was discussed in Chapter 7, but this information is considerably better than trying to create your own capitalization rate from scratch.

Other, less sophisticated methods for determining capitalization rates include variations on the build up method. These methods assign a factor to various risk elements in order to derive a capitalization rate. This is similar to the factor rating method discussed previously.

The capitalization rate must be derived by a method that matches it to the benefit stream being used. Depending upon the method used to derive the capitalization rate, the result will be applicable to a particular benefit stream. For example, if the CAPM is used, the discount rate is applicable to net cash flow. Subtracting long-term sustainable growth would result in a capitalization rate that is applicable to net cash flow.

The build up method will result in either a discount rate or a capitalization rate for numerous benefit streams, depending upon the source of the information used to perform the build up. Other benefit streams (such as net income) may be used, but the discount rate must be adjusted from what was derived by the cash flow methods. This is accomplished by adding a premium (not to be confused with a control premium) to the rate derived for cash flow in order to compensate for the additional risk related to the other benefit stream. A capitalization rate for earnings *does not equal* a capitalization rate for net cash flow, because earnings do not generally equal net cash flow.

The relationship of the discount rate derived for different benefit streams is based on the amount of risk that is implied in the benefit stream being used by the appraiser. In theory, net cash flow is the cash available to the common stockholders; therefore, it has taken into consideration items such as working capital needs, fixed asset requirements, and long-term debt repayments and borrowings. The more confidence the appraiser has after considering all of these factors, the lower the discount rate.

Many experienced appraisers have written that the range most often seen in practice between the rate used for net cash flow and net earnings is approximately 3 to 6 percent. This does not mean, however, that this range is an absolute and should always be used. In a master's thesis titled "Empirical Research Study of Rates of Return on Earnings and Cash Flow,"[2] Joseph A. Agiato, C.P.A., C.B.A., A.S.A., indicates that his study confirms the 3 to 6 percent rule of thumb.

In general, the higher the net cash flow discount rate, the higher the net income discount rate premium, assuming all other factors are the same. A high cash flow discount rate indicates that there is a degree of risk driving the rate up. Since earnings consider fewer factors than cash flow does, there is a normal tendency to believe that the rate for earnings should be higher. The higher the forecast growth rate, the higher the net income discount rate premium, assuming all other factors are the same.

High growth reflects its own element of risk in the subject company's ability to remain profitable as it incurs new levels of fixed and variable costs that are attributable to growth. If the appraiser has derived a high net cash flow discount rate at the same time that there is expected high growth, then the net income discount rate premium would be pushed higher than the 3 to 6 percent range mentioned previously (sometimes much higher). Low growth would keep the net income discount rate premium above zero, but at the lower end of the 3 to 6 percent range.

[2]This thesis is on file at Lindenwood College, St. Charles, Mo.

Deriving Discount and Capitalization Rates Applicable to Net Income Directly From the Market

The inverse of the price-to-earnings ratio is the earnings-to-price ratio, which is a capitalization rate applicable to net income (where "earnings" are defined as "net income"). To get a discount rate, the appraiser must approximate growth and add that growth to the earnings/price ratio. The difficult part is establishing the proper amount of growth based on the market price-to-earnings multiples. Rarely in the financial information about the guideline companies selected do we find growth rates other than those being forecast by the analysts. We would need the actual growth implicit in the price of the stock in order to be more accurate. Assuming that we could figure out the growth that is implied in the price-to-earnings multiples of the guideline companies, discount rates would be easier to calculate.

The earnings/price ratio is directly observable in the market, which provides the appraiser with solid empirical evidence about the capitalization rate, but we must still estimate the growth rates to achieve a discount rate for those same earnings. Expected growth rates for specific public companies appear in *Value Line Investment Survey*, but they are short-term growth rates. We need a long-term sustainable growth rate, which means that the *Value Line* growth rates will probably be of limited help.

A possible alternative to derive growth for the public companies requires us to assume that over the long term, the dividend payout equals the total cash return on an equity investment. This means that dividends would be growing at the same rate as earnings, indicating a constant payout ratio. In this instance, the capitalization rate for net cash flow would be equal to the dividend yield. If this were the case, the discount rate for net cash flow minus growth would equal dividend yield. Therefore, the discount rate for net cash flow based on the dividend yield would be available in newspapers.

Back to the Real World

In case you need a touch of reality, capitalization rates, like discount rates, are market driven. However, there is really very little information available to help appraisers determine the "correct" rate in valuing smaller companies. Let's keep in mind that our role as appraisers is not to determine discount and capitalization rates, but rather to give an opinion on the valuation of the appraisal subject. Regardless of the method used to derive these rates, the answer has to make sense. The principle of substitution alerts appraisers to the fact that the rates should be relevant to other rates in the marketplace, given the risk of the appraisal subject. But there are no tables, charts, or gurus to help ensure a correct rate.

What we do know is that the discount or capitalization rate selected by the appraiser should match the benefit stream being discounted or capitalized. It is theoretically incorrect to use the same rate for different streams, since each stream will have a different degree of risk. We also know that the rate will be risk driven. This means that a small closely held company with no depth in management, in poor financial condition, with no borrowing capacity, and with a high degree of dependence on a single customer has enough risk that the appropriate rate should be way up there.

As I have examined the transactions for smaller closely held companies, the general range of multiples that I have seen in the majority of cases is from one to three times the owners' discretionary cash flow. Discretionary cash flow is the amount of money that the owner of the business has available for him or her before a deduction is made for owner's compensation. This equates to a capitalization rate ranging from 33⅓ percent to 100 percent for this income stream. Therefore, if this is the market, shouldn't we, as appraisers, use this information? Subtracting a reasonable level of owner's compensation (and possibly either depreciation or a reserve for the replacement of assets) would result in a pretax income stream. This pretax stream would be capitalized at a rate that is less than the multiple used for the owner's discretionary cash flow, since the risk of the amount being capitalized is reduced by subtracting one or two additional items in deriving the pretax income. This is similar to the net cash flow model discussed in Chapter 9. Exhibit 10.4 illustrates this concept.

EXHIBIT 10.4
Discount and Capitalization Rates

Assume that ABC Corporation has the following forecast net cash flow:

Normalized net income	$	150,000
Plus: Non-cash charges	+	25,000
Minus: Fixed asset additions	−	65,000
Minus: Working capital additions	−	10,000
Plus: Change in debt	+	20,000
Net cash flow	**$**	**120,000**

Now assume that the discount rate for the equity of ABC Corporation was determined to be 24 percent using the build up method, based on Ibbotson data. Also assume that the long-term sustainable growth rate is assumed to be 5 percent. What is the discount rate for net cash flow? What is the capitalization rate for net cash flow? What about for net income?

Discount rate for net cash flow	24%*
Less: Long-term growth	5%
Capitalization rate for net cash flow	19%

To convert the discount and capitalization rates for use with earnings instead of cash flow, the following mathematical calculations can be performed:

Normalized net income ÷ Net cash flow (150,000 ÷ 120,000) = 1.25
Discount rate for earnings (24% × 1.25 = 30%)
Capitalization rate for earnings (19% × 1.25 = 23.75%)

*Using Ibbotson data results in a discount rate for net cash flow since the total return (dividends and capital appreciation) is measured in the Ibbotson equity risk premium.

A few observations can be made about the example in Exhibit 10.4. The first observation is that there is supposed to be a relationship between the rates used for the benefit streams capitalized or discounted. In this example, the discount rate for net cash flow was used as a basis to calculate the discount rate for net income. The mathematical relationship between these two elements was used to adjust the original rate that was determined. Wouldn't it be just grand if the world was this simple? Unfortunately, it is not.

The mathematical relationship does not always work in practice. If a multi-period model is going to be used by the appraiser, each year's net income and cash flow would have to be used to calculate a different discount rate for each year. Can you imagine making a discounting model more complicated than it already is? This example also does not work for the calculation of a capitalization rate for excess earnings. I know this because I have tried to use it!

The second observation is that the capitalization rate for net income was calculated by multiplying the mathematical factor against the capitalization rate for net cash flow. Those of you who really read this book are probably wondering why I did not just subtract the 5 percent long-term growth from the discount rate for earnings (30 percent), resulting in a capitalization rate of 25 percent. This is because the long-term growth rate must also change based on which benefit stream is being used. The 5 percent growth rate is applied to net cash flow, not net income. This is why the capitalization rate for net income was 23.75 percent instead of 25 percent.

Once again, what I am saying is that the process is not perfect. There are only two factors that you can use to determine the appropriate rates in any valuation: common sense and good judgment!

Using Pretax or After-Tax Rates

Although the issue of whether to use pretax or after-tax income streams and capitalization rates is one of the points that creates much confusion among lawyers and judges, the resulting value for the appraisal subject should be the same regardless of whether pretax or after-tax income is used in the valuation. The capitalization rate will be adjusted depending on which income stream is used. Exhibit 10.5 contains an example that should illustrate this point.

EXHIBIT 10.5
Pretax or After-Tax?

Assume that the value of Smith Corporation is being determined using a capitalization of income method. Smith has a forecast pretax income of $100,000 and an after-tax income of $65,000 (assumes a 35 percent tax rate). If the appraiser has determined that the appropriate capitalization rate based on pretax information in the market was 20 percent, the valuation calculation would be as follows:

	Pretax	*After-Tax*
Forecast income	$ 100,000	$ 65,000
Capitalization rate	÷ .20	÷ .13
Estimated value	$ 500,000	$ 500,000

If the value of the business was estimated to be $500,000 using a 20 percent capitalization rate derived from the market on a pretax basis, then the value on an after-tax basis should be the same. If the numerator is changed from $100,000 (pretax) to $65,000 (after-tax), the denominator (capitalization rate) must be changed by the same methodology. Mathematically, this can be explained by the following formula:

$$C_p \times (1 - t) = C_A$$

where

C_p = Pretax capitalization rate
t = Effective tax rate
C_A = After-tax capitalization rate

This results in the following:

$$20\% \times (1 - .35) = 13\%$$

The example in Exhibit 10.6 should help you to understand the fact that it does not matter if pretax or after-tax income is used as long as the capitalization rate correlates to the type of income being capitalized. This same premise holds true for cash flow, EBIT, EBITDA, or any other stream being capitalized or discounted. The capitalization rate or discount rate must correlate to the stream of income that is being capitalized or discounted.

There will be times that you will capitalize a benefit stream other than cash flow or earnings. In fact, there are times when you will use an income approach for a real estate holding company that makes distributions. The same may hold true when you value family limited partnerships that have securities and/or real estate. On occasion, you may even choose to capitalize dividends in an operating company for a minority interest where there is a track record of payments being made. Exhibits 10.6, 10.7, 10.8, and 10.9 should provide you with some more ideas for your future reports. These sections came from actual reports.

EXHIBIT 10.6
Capitalization Rate—Real Estate Holdings

Section 6 of Revenue Ruling 59-60 states:

> In the application of certain fundamental valuation factors, such as earnings and dividends, it is necessary to capitalize the average or current results at some appropriate rate. A determination of the proper capitalization rate presents one of the most difficult problems in valuation.

In the text of Revenue Ruling 68-609, capitalization rates of 15 percent to 20 percent were mentioned as an example. Many appraisers are under the misconception that the capitalization rate must stay within this range. In reality, the capitalization rate must be consistent with the rate of return currently needed to attract capital to the type of investment in question.

There are various methods of determining discount and capitalization rates. In this appraisal, we looked at the marketplace for rates of return paid on similar types of investments. The most similar investment to Jacksons LLC are Real Estate Investment Trusts (REIT). A number of brokerage firms report this data, and *Realty Stock Review* (June 16, 2000) publishes summaries of it.

We looked at pricing multiples in the REIT marketplace to determine a capitalization rate to apply to our benefit stream. The inverse of a price-to-dividends multiple is a capitalization rate. Table 1 includes this pricing information.

TABLE 1
Equity REITs Price to Dividends

Company	*Price 6/16/00*	*Equity MarketCap*	*Annual Dividend*	*Dividend Yield*	*Price to Dividend*	*Cap Rate*
Shopping Centers						
Bradley Real Estate Inc.	$ 21.31	$ 543.5	$ 1.52	7.1%	14.02	7.1%
Burnham Pac Pptys Inc.	7.00	236.6	1.05	15.0%	6.67	15.0%
Center Trust Retail Prop.	5.13	204.0	0.84	16.4%	6.10	16.4%
Developers Diversified Rlty.	14.81	1,010.2	1.44	9.7%	10.28	9.7%
Federal Realty Invt Tr.	21.38	979.0	1.80	8.4%	11.88	8.4%
IRT Ppty Co.	8.44	304.6	0.94	11.1%	8.94	11.2%
JDN Rlty Corp.	11.19	371.4	1.20	10.7%	9.33	10.7%
Kimco Realty Corp.	41.13	2,615.6	2.64	6.4%	15.58	6.4%
Konover Property Trust	4.5	156.2	0.50	11.1%	9.00	11.1%
New Plan Excel Rlty Trust	15.38	1,528.3	1.65	10.7%	9.32	10.7%
Regency Rlty Corp.	22.25	1,408.4	1.92	8.6%	11.59	8.6%
Saul Ctrs Inc.	15.94	280.5	1.56	9.8%	10.22	9.8%
Weingarten Rlty Invs.	40.75	1,104.3	3.00	7.4%	13.58	7.4%
Western Prop. Trust	11.50	225.4	1.12	9.7%	10.27	9.7%
Shopping center sector average		782.79		10.15%	10.48	10.16%
Shopping center sector median		452.95		9.75%	10.25	9.75%

(Continued)

EXHIBIT 10.6 *(Continued)*

Company	Price 6/16/00	Equity MarketCap	Annual Dividend	Dividend Yield	Price to Dividend	Cap Rate
Regional Malls						
CBL & Assoc Pptys Inc.	$ 25.1	$ 914.8	$ 2.0	8.1%	12.28	8.1%
Crown Amern Rlty Tr	5.13	185.3	0.83	16.2%	6.18	16.2%
General Growth Pptys Inc.	31.50	2,252.3	2.04	6.5%	15.44	6.5%
Glimcher Rlty Tr	14.25	349.1	1.92	13.5%	7.42	13.5%
JP Realty Inc.	17.75	378.1	1.92	10.8%	9.24	10.8%
Macerich Co.	21.88	1,224.7	2.04	9.3%	10.73	9.3%
Mills Corp.	18.44	733.8	2.07	11.2%	8.91	11.2%
Rouse Co.	24.88	1,930.3	1.32	5.3%	18.85	5.3%
Simon Property Group	24.50	6,186.3	2.02	8.2%	12.13	8.2%
Taubman Ctrs Inc.	10.75	910.5	0.98	9.1%	10.97	9.1%
Urban Shopping Centers	34.00	1,162.8	2.36	6.9%	14.41	6.9%
Westfield America Inc.	14.44	1,569.4	1.48	10.3%	9.76	10.2%
Regional malls sector average		1483.1		9.60%	11.36	9.6%
Regional malls sector median		1038.8		9.20%	10.85	9.2%

Source: *Realty Stock Review*, June 16, 2000.

A review of the information in Table 1 indicates that these entities are substantially larger than Jacksons LLC, which indicates that they are much more diversified. This lack of size and diversification makes an investment in Jacksons LLC riskier than an investment in one of these REITs.

On the other hand, the Company has almost no debt, whereas all of the REITs are highly leveraged. In addition, the Company's distribution yield is substantially higher than the REITs, averaging in excess of 50 percent. This makes an investment in Jacksons LLC more attractive, which would result in a lower desired rate.

Given these strengths and weaknesses of the Company versus the publicly traded REITs, we selected a capitalization rate of 9 percent as appropriate.

EXHIBIT 10.7
Capitalization Rate—Mixed Holdings

Section 6 of Revenue Ruling 59-60 states:

> In the application of certain fundamental valuation factors, such as earnings and dividends, it is necessary to capitalize the average or current results at some appropriate rate. A determination of the proper capitalization rate presents one of the most difficult problems in valuation.

When using the income approach to value, the estimated future income stream generated by the ongoing operations of the Partnership must be discounted at an appropriate risk rate to arrive at the present value of the future benefits of ownership. The discount factor or capitalization rate used to determine the present value of the future cash flow streams reflects both the business and financial risks of an investment in the Partnership.

We have calculated a blended capitalization rate that reflects the risk inherent in the types of securities in the Partnership's portfolio. The rate thus derived is adjusted to reflect the risks associated with the Partnership itself. The blended capitalization rate calculation is presented in Table 1.

EXHIBIT 10.7 *(Continued)*

TABLE 1

Capitalization Rate

Type of Security	*Dividend Yield*	*% of Portfolio*	*Weighted Amount*
Cash[1]	6.25%	3.00%	0.19%
Equities[2]	2.13%	71.70%	1.53%
Bonds[3]	20.40%	16.00%	3.26%
Real estates[4]	9.00%	9.30%	0.84%
Total blended rate			5.82%
Rounded			6.00%

[1]Average of rates in the money market published in the *Wall Street Journal* prior to the valuation date: one-month certificates of deposit, 6.6 percent; 13-week Treasury bills, 5.83 percent; overnight repurchase rate, 6.62 percent; Merrill Lynch Ready Asset Trust (a money market mutual fund), 5.94 percent.

[2]Weighted average dividend yield on the equities in the Partnership's portfolio. Dividend yields are from Merrill Lynch *Global Research Review,* July 2000, and compared with the dividend yield on the Dow Jones Industrial Average of 1.7 percent on June 22, 2000.

[3]Weighted average current yield on the bonds held in the Partnership's portfolio including corporate issues, many of which are in default. Current yield is the bond's coupon divided by its dollar price.

[4]Average dividend yield for Equity REITs/REOCs at June 16, 2000, was 8.8 percent; these ranged from 5.2 percent to 18.4 percent. Average dividend yield for the Morgan Stanley REIT Index at June 30, 2000, was 9.0 percent; these ranged from 0 percent to 16.6 percent.

Some upward adjustment must be made to the capitalization rate calculated in Table 1 to reflect the uncertainty surrounding the outlook for equities in the next 12 months. In addition, the dividend yield attributed to the real estate portion of the Partnership's portfolio is low considering that this real estate constitutes a one-third ownership in a property that produces no income. In this regard, a capitalization rate of 6 percent would appear to be reasonable.

EXHIBIT 10.8

Capitalization Rate—Dividend Yield

Section 6 of Revenue Ruling 59-60 states:

> In the application of certain fundamental valuation factors, such as earnings and dividends, it is necessary to capitalize the average or current results at some appropriate rate. A determination of the proper capitalization rate presents one of the most difficult problems in valuation.

As previously discussed, capitalization rates are determined by the market. Using the capitalization of benefits method, the mathematical formula previously discussed was:

Value = Benefits stream ÷ Capitalization rate

By changing the variables in this formula, a capitalization rate can be determined by the following formula:

Capitalization rate = Benefits stream ÷ Value

In reviewing documentation from the public stock market, two of the variables above can be readily determined, and, therefore, can assist the appraiser in determining the third variable. The benefit stream analyzed was the actual dividends paid by public companies. The value indicated in the formula above can be the price per share of the publicly traded stocks.

(Continued)

EXHIBIT 10.8 *(Continued)*

The capitalization rate determined in this manner reflects the market rate of return for these companies. Since fair market value is supposed to come from the market, there is no better method for determining a capitalization rate.

In order to determine an appropriate capitalization rate for dividends, several sources were reviewed. According to *Value Line*, the dividend yield for the 12-month estimate at October 28, 1994, was 2.8 percent. At approximately the same date, the actual dividend yield of the Standard & Poor's 500 was 2.9 percent.

There are considerable differences between the dividends paid to shareholders in public companies as opposed to those of private companies. The emotional side of the stock market and the public perception creates pressure on public companies to continue to pay dividends to its stockholders, even at times when there are losses.

The public stock market also contains companies that are considerably larger than many private companies and are subject to the continuing scrutiny of the Securities and Exchange Commission.

Dividend yields in the public market are calculated by comparing the dividend per share and the price per share of each company. As the price per share increases, the dividend yield will decrease. This explains why the dividend yields of these large companies are so low. As the price moves up, as the market has been doing, the yield has been declining. Companies do not generally increase dividend payouts in any manner that correlates with the price per share. If anything, the price may go up as a result of the dividend being increased.

Using dividend yields of public companies as a starting point allows the appraiser to understand the lowest rates that would be expected by the investor if the same degree of risk is involved with the appraisal subject.

Jansen's has had a fairly solid track record with respect to its profitability. However, the company has experienced some liquidity problems. Payables are much higher than the industry norm, resulting in poor liquidity ratios and a low turnover ratio. These are significant negative factors.

Furthermore, the company has limited growth potential, not only because of the market, but because of the lead time that it takes for the company to produce its product. Jansen's would require a significant capital infusion to expand its production capacity by opening another location. This would restrict cash flow even more and possibly cause the company to stop paying dividends at all.

At the valuation date, yields on various instruments in the money and capital markets were as follows:

6-month certificates of deposit	5.9%
U.S. Treasuries	
1-year	6.2%
5-year	7.6%
10-year	7.9%
20-year	8.2%
30-year	8.0%
Corporate bonds	
Aaa	8.7%
Aa	8.8%
A	8.9%
Baa	9.3%

After considering the size, liquidity, and other available returns in the market, we believe that a reasonable capitalization rate for dividends should be no less than 12 percent. Anything less would indicate that an investor should purchase U.S. Treasury bonds, which are a much safer investment.

EXHIBIT 10.9
Discount and Capitalization Rates—All in One

Section 6 of Revenue Ruling 59-60 states:

> In the application of certain fundamental valuation factors, such as earnings and dividends, it is necessary to capitalize the average or current results at some appropriate rate. A determination of the proper capitalization rate presents one of the most difficult problems in valuation.

In the text of Revenue Ruling 68-609, capitalization rates of 15 percent to 20 percent were mentioned as an example. Many appraisers are under the misconception that the capitalization rate must stay within this range. In reality, the capitalization rate must be consistent with the rate of return currently needed to attract capital to the type of investment in question.

EXHIBIT 10.9 (Continued)

There are various methods of determining capitalization rates. Using the build up method of determining the capitalization rate results in a capitalization rate as follows:

"Safe" rate	5.95%[1]
Equity risk premium	7.00%[2]
Small company risk premium	3.30%[3]
Specific company risk premium	−1.00%[4]
Discount rate	16.05%
Less: Long-term growth	6.00%
Capitalization rate	10.05%
Rounded	10.00%

[1]Information obtained from the Federal Reserve Board's World Wide Web page located at www.bog.frb.us.

[2]*Stocks, Bonds, Bills and Inflation 1998 Yearbook*, Ibbotson Associates, difference between total returns on common stocks and long-term government bonds from 1926 to 1997.

[3]*Stocks, Bonds, Bills and Inflation 1998 Yearbook*, Ibbotson Associates, difference between total returns on small company stocks and common stocks from 1926 to 1997.

[4]Appraiser's judgment based on the analysis discussed throughout this report.

A capitalization rate has been derived from a discount rate, which has been calculated above. The components of the discount rate include a safe rate, which indicates that any investor would receive, at a bare minimum, an equivalent rate for a safe investment. In this particular instance, U.S. Treasury bonds are used as an indication of a safe rate.

An equity risk premium is added to the safe rate, which represents the premium that common stockholders required in the public marketplace over investors in long-term government bonds. This indicates that since equity securities are considered to be more risky by the investor, a higher rate of return has been required over the period of time indicated in the calculation of this premium.

The third component of the discount rate is a small company risk premium. This is a risk premium that is measured in the public marketplace for companies that are in the ninth and tenth deciles, indicating that smaller companies require a larger return due to the risk associated with size. The tenth decile of the public marketplace has been measured by companies that are capitalized at an average capitalization of $68,400,000.

A fourth component, known as a specific company risk premium, has been considered to determine an appropriate discount rate. This specific company risk premium takes into consideration the detailed analysis performed by the appraiser, including the company's performance, the company's management structure, the size of the company, the ability of the company to raise capital, and the many other factors that must be considered in assessing the risk relating to an investment in PDQ. In this instance, we have subtracted 1 percent from our build up because, as mentioned in the section of this report titled "Financial Analysis," PDQ is very strong financially and has produced excellent returns to shareholders. This is in stark contrast to the returns generated by small public companies in PDQ's industry. According to Ibbotson Associates, equity returns over the last five years for SIC code 2834 were negative 21.5 percent.[1] This fact is partially offset by PDQ's lack of succession planning and its heavy reliance on two products for its sales.

In addition to the build up rate, we have looked at industry-specific rates of return for SIC code 2834. Based on our review, cost of equity capital for the industry has been 15.9 percent and 21.94 percent for small companies.[2] As discussed previously, PDQ has produced much better returns than the small companies in the industry. Therefore, we have chosen to use the industry composite of 15.9 percent, rounded to 16.00 percent, as our discount rate even though PDQ is much smaller than many of these companies.

[1]*Cost of Capital Quarterly 1997 Yearbook*, Ibbotson Associates, 2–44.

[2]Ibid.

(Continued)

EXHIBIT 10.9 ***(Continued)***

Subtracting a long-term growth rate of 6 percent results in a capitalization rate of 10 percent.

Dividend Capitalization Rate

To estimate a dividend capitalization rate, we again went to Ibbotson Associates for industry-specific information. For companies in SIC code 2834, the five-year average dividend yield was 2.65 percent.[3] Since we have estimated that PDQ will grow at rates slower than the industry, and dividend growth has been low, we have added a small company specific risk premium of 0.35 percent, resulting in a capitalization rate for dividends of 3.00 percent.

[3]Ibid

Conclusion

If I didn't do a very good job, you are probably totally confused. If I did an okay job, you are still confused. I'm sorry. I never promised you a rose garden. I hope that despite the uncertainty, you now have more of an idea about discount rates and capitalization rates. What you have really learned is that these rates come from the market. An appraiser has a poor chance of getting them right without some luck. Better to be lucky than smart!

11

Premiums and Discounts

Chapter Goals

In this chapter, I will attempt to explain:

1. Valuation premiums and discounts in general
2. Control premiums
3. Lack of control (minority) discounts
4. Discounts for lack of marketability
5. Small company discounts
6. Discounts from net asset value
7. Key person discounts
8. Other discounts and premiums

Introduction

The final value reached in the appraisal of a closely held business may be more or less than the value that was calculated using the methods previously discussed in this book. Valuation discounts, premiums, or both may or may not be appropriate in every business valuation. The type and size of the discount(s) or premium(s) will vary depending on the starting point. The starting point will depend on which methods of valuation were used during the appraisal, as well as on other factors, such as normalization adjustments and the sources of the information used to derive multiples or discount rates.

The following are some of the common discounts and premiums that we see in business valuations:

- Control premium
- Lack of control (minority) discount
- Discount for lack of marketability
- Small company discount
- Discount from net asset value
- Key person discount

Exhibit 11.1 shows the type of value derived from the various methods discussed throughout this book. The appraiser needs to understand the type of value estimate that each of these methods yields in order to know what type of discounts and premiums may be appropriate in any given situation. For example, if the guideline company method is used to value a controlling interest in a closely held company, the appraiser must consider that the result from this method is generally considered to be a marketable, minority interest. This means that a control premium may be added to bring the minority value to a control value. Then the appraiser might take a discount for lack of marketability to bring the value from a marketable control value to a nonmarketable control value. It's not as bad as it seems!

EXHIBIT 11.1
Types of Value

Method	Control/Minority	Marketable/Nonmarketable
Market Approach		
Guideline public company method	Minority[1]	Marketable
Acquisition method—public cos.	Control	Marketable
Acquisition method—private cos.	Control	Nonmarketable
Asset-Based Approach		
Adjusted book value method	Control	Marketable
Liquidation method	Control	Marketable
Cost to create method	Control	Marketable
Excess earnings method	Control	Marketable or nonmarketable
Income Approach		
Capitalization of benefits method	Control or minority	Marketable or nonmarketable
Discounted future benefits method	Control or minority	Marketable or nonmarketable

[1]There are many appraisers who believe that the guideline public company method yields a control value. The old conventional wisdom is being challenged more and more as time goes on.

Many appraisers look to court decisions to support the premiums or discounts that are used in their appraisals. These are not a form of market evidence. Court decisions are generally subjective decisions of a particular court in a particular case. Appraisers must apply correct methodology, whether it is supported by court decisions or not. The benefit of looking at court decisions is to learn when you will have more of a burden of proof, because the position being taken is outside the range of prior court decisions. Judge David Laro of the United States Tax Court suggested to the participants at the 1999 AICPA Business Valuation Conference that they read his opinions before coming into his court so that they would understand what he expects from the appraiser. Court decisions generally follow the conclusions that appraisers reach from their own valuation research, but often with time delay. Therefore, by using court decisions, we are generally following decisions that were made in the past.

Court decisions are very useful in understanding how the courts have dealt with certain issues. If you plan to deviate from a position taken by the court, I strongly suggest that you do the following:

- Acknowledge in your report (and testimony) the decision of the court.
- Explain why you believe the court's position is not applicable in the case at hand. Do not say that the court made a mistake!
- Provide strong support for your position in order to demonstrate why your position is more theoretically correct than the court precedent.
- Make sure that your client's attorney is aware (and blesses) the fact that you are deviating from the case law.

- Make certain that the client understands that you are taking a contrary position to the position in the case law and that you have the attorney's blessing.
- Pray a lot.

Don't get me wrong. I am not suggesting that you cannot deviate from case law. I am saying that you need a strong argument that is well supported, because if a judge is going to go against legal precedent, the case may be appealed to a higher court. The higher court will need strong evidence (usually testimony, since most reports are not admitted as evidence) to base its opinion upon.

Control Premium

The pro rata value of a controlling interest in a closely held company is said to be worth more than the value of a minority interest because of the prerogatives of control that generally follow the controlling shares. An investor will generally pay more (a premium) for the rights that are considered to be part of the controlling interest. Shannon Pratt recognized these prerogatives of control in his earlier writings, and they continue to hold true today. In the later writings, the list grew. These rights must be considered in assessing the size of the control premium, and they include the right to:

1. Appoint or change operational management
2. Appoint or change members of the board of directors
3. Determine management compensation and perquisites
4. Set operational and strategic policy and change the course of the business
5. Acquire, lease, or liquidate business assets, including plant, property, and equipment
6. Select suppliers, vendors, and subcontractors to do business with and award contracts to
7. Negotiate and consummate mergers and acquisitions
8. Liquidate, dissolve, sell out, or recapitalize the company
9. Sell or acquire treasury shares
10. Register the company's equity securities for an initial or secondary public offering
11. Register the company's debt securities for an initial or secondary public offering
12. Declare and pay cash and/or stock dividends
13. Change the articles of incorporation or bylaws
14. Set one's own compensation (and perquisites) and the compensation (and perquisites) of related-party employees
15. Select joint ventures and enter into joint venture and partnership agreements
16. Decide what products and/or services to offer and how to price those products/services
17. Decide what markets and locations to serve, to enter into, and to discontinue serving
18. Decide which customer categories to market to and which not to market to
19. Enter into inbound and outbound license or sharing agreements regarding intellectual properties
20. Block any or all of the above actions[1]

A control premium is the opposite of the minority discount. The control premium is used to determine the control value of a closely held business when its freely traded minority value has been determined. This

[1] Shannon P. Pratt, Robert F. Reilly, and Robert P. Schweihs, *Valuing a Business*, 4th ed. (New York: McGraw-Hill, 2000), 365–366. Reprinted with permission.

is generally true when the appraiser uses information from the public stock market as the starting point of the valuation.

A control premium may be appropriate for an interest that is less than 100 percent. In this instance, the size of the premium will depend on various factors relating to the amount of control available to the controlling interest. Some of these factors include the following:

- Cumulative versus noncumulative voting rights
- Contractual restrictions (stockholder agreements)
- The financial condition of the business
- State statutes
- The distribution of ownership

Let me give you an illustration of where less than a 50 percent interest could have a control premium associated with it. Part of an assignment that we were involved in required us to value a 47.3 percent block of a public company. We determined that this block should have a premium attached to it. Exhibit 11.2 reflects a portion of our report.

EXHIBIT 11.2
Selected Portion of Control Premium Discussion

The valuation of John Q. Smith & Company, an investment holding company, is based on the value of the underlying assets held in the investment portfolio. The methodology employed will be similar to that used by Adam's Trust Company, as outlined in a memo dated January 14, 1993, from Chuck Jackson to Rebecca Harding. This memo outlined the procedure as:

> To establish the fair market value of Smith & Company's stock holdings, we generally utilized the average price of the individual securities on December 16, 1992 (as determined by referencing the *Wall Street Journal*). An exception to this is the value established for the Company's equity position in the Public Corporation.

According to the Jackson Memo, the condensed balance sheet of John Q. Smith & Company as of November 30, 1992, was as follows:

John Q. Smith & Co.
Condensed Balance Sheet
As of November 30, 1992

Assets		
Current assets		
Cash & equivalents	$ 271,583	
Short-term investments	2,387,627	
Receivables	3,838	
Total current assets		$2,663,048
Investments in capital stock		
Public corp.	$ 876,726	
Others	2,157,886	
Total stock		3,034,612
Investments in oil & gas interests (net)		18,061
Total assets		$5,715,721
Liabilities	$ 218,266	
Stockholders' equity	$5,497,455	
Total liabilities & stockholders' equity		$5,715,721

EXHIBIT 11.2 *(Continued)*

According to the Jackson Memo, the adjusted net asset value of John Q. Smith & Company as of December 16, 1992, was $202,983,073. The other party to the litigation accepted the methodology used to value most of the underlying assets, and, therefore, we will also accept the asset values that were agreed to by the parties as the starting point in our valuation. The major point of contention between the parties is the value of the interest in Public Corporation. We will value this asset separately. Accordingly, subtracting the value of this stock from the total results in the following:

Net asset value	$202,983,073
Public corporation stock	160,721,253
All other assets & liabilities	$ 42,261,820

On December 16, 1992, John Q. Smith & Company owned 5,337,360 shares of Public Corporation common stock. This represents approximately 47 percent of the outstanding shares of Public Corp. The underlying asset values did not present a problem for the valuation of the Public stock because the high and low valuation as of the valuation date is proper. However, consideration must be given to the fact that a 47 percent block of stock of a publicly traded corporation frequently constitutes a control position in the stock.

In our opinion, a 35 percent premium is appropriate in determining the value of the Public holdings of John Q. Smith & Company. The pro rata value of a controlling interest in a company is said to be worth more than the value of a minority interest, due to the prerogatives of control that generally follow the controlling shares. An investor will generally pay more (a premium) for the rights that are considered to be part of the controlling interest. Valuation professionals recognize these prerogatives of control and consider them in the assessment of control premiums. Some of the prerogatives include:

- Elect the board of directors
- Appoint the management team
- Determine compensation and perquisites
- Set business policy
- Acquire or liquidate assets
- Make acquisitions or divestitures
- Sell or acquire treasury stock
- Declare dividends
- Change the articles of incorporation or bylaws of the corporation

Control is demonstrated in the public market as publicly traded companies are purchased at prices above the value at which the shares are trading in the open market. Empirical data is available about these transactions, and measuring the control premium allows the appraiser to use this data as a benchmark in the valuation of other companies.

Generally, the issue that the appraiser faces is the valuation of a closely held company. In this instance, the valuation subject is a controlling interest in a publicly traded company, Public Corp. Control premium data is tracked by several sources. The most widely used source is *Mergerstat Review,* which was published annually by Merrill Lynch Business Brokerage and Valuation, Schaumburg, IL (today, it is published by Houlihan, Lokey, Howard and Zukin, an investment banking firm in Los Angeles, California). Another widely used source is *Control Premium Study,* published by Houlihan, Lokey, Howard and Zukin. (*Author's note:* This is now known as the *Mergerstat Control Premium Study.*)

A summary of the *Mergerstat Review* data appears in Table 1.

TABLE 1

Percent Premium Paid Over Market Price

Year of Buyout	*Number of Transactions*	*Average Premium Paid Over Market (%)*	*Median Premium Paid (%)*
1980	169	49.9	44.6
1981	166	48.0	41.9
1982	176	47.4	43.5

(Continued)

EXHIBIT 11.2 *(Continued)*

Year of Buyout	*Number of Transactions*	*Average Premium Paid Over Market (%)*	*Median Premium Paid (%)*
1983	168	37.7	34.0
1984	199	37.9	34.4
1985	331	37.1	27.7
1986	333	38.2	29.9
1987	237	38.3	30.8
1988	410	41.9	30.9
1989	303	41.0	29.0
1990	175	42.0	32.0
1991	137	35.1	29.4
1992	142	41.0	34.7
Mean		41.2	34.1
Median		41.0	32.0

The mean and median premiums since 1980 have varied with the economy and stock market activity. In the early 1980s, interest rates were at an all-time high, possibly pushing the control premiums paid for companies even higher. As rates came down in the mid-1980s, the premiums followed. By 1992, the year of the valuation, the average and median control premiums were 41.0 percent and 34.7 percent, respectively, for the entire market.

In order to more closely assess the applicability of this data to the control premium that is warranted for the Public holdings, we further analyzed the *Mergerstat Review* data. Information summarized from this publication appears below.

Average premium offered	**41.00%**
Controlling interest	41.30%
Minority interest	38.30%
Industry classification of seller	
Chemicals, paints, & coatings	34.00%
Median premium offered	**34.70%**
Purchase price $100 million or more	39.00%
Method of payment	
Cash	29.60%
Stock	36.80%
Combination	41.90%
Seller's market price five days before announcement	
Over $25.00 through $50.00	25.80%
Seller's P/E ratio five days before announcement	
Over 15.0	34.00%

Dissecting the information included in *Mergerstat Review* illustrates that while the average control premium offered in 1992 was 41.0 percent, the average for controlling interests was slightly higher, at 41.3 percent. However, even minority interests were being bought at a premium of about 38.3 percent. Attempting to get more industry specific, we reviewed the data for transactions in the *Chemicals, paints, & coatings* category. The average control premium in this industry was 34.0 percent.

In addition to the averages, the median premiums paid were also reviewed. The median tends to provide a better indication than the average because the average can be skewed by extremely high or low data. The median is the central point when ranked by size.

EXHIBIT 11.2 *(Continued)*

The median premium offered was 34.7 percent during 1992. When the purchase price was $100 million or more, the premium jumped to 39.0 percent. This is consistent with current studies that indicate larger companies frequently sell for higher multiples. Combination deals involving stock and cash resulted in a premium of 41.9 percent, but even when the deal was all cash, the premium was still 29.6 percent.

Reviewing this data based on the per-share price of the Public stock indicates that companies whose shares were trading between $25 and $50 sold at the lowest control premium of only 25.8 percent. Finally, companies whose price-to-earnings multiples were over 15 reflected premiums of 34.0 percent.

Additional analysis was performed of the data appearing in the *Control Premium Study*. The major difference in this study from *Mergerstat Review* is that the premiums are measured differently. Furthermore, this study only includes cash transactions. Data observed from this study includes the following:

By industry (SIC) (trailing 12 months)	
SIC 28 (Chemicals and Allied Products) (2 transactions)	
Median	70.50%
Mean	70.50%
SIC 38 (Controlling Instruments; etc.) (3 transactions)	
Median	27.00%
Mean	45.50%
Domestic transactions—4th quarter (18 total transactions)	
Median	44.50%
Mean	47.40%
12-month figures (1/1/92–12/31/92) (94 total transactions)	
Median	42.40%
Mean	50.40%
3-month median premium	
First quarter	34.60%
Second quarter	42.40%
Third quarter	49.20%
Fourth quarter	33.50%
12-month median premium	
First quarter	45.30%
Second quarter	45.10%
Third quarter	44.30%
Fourth quarter	42.40%

The data presented above divides the control premiums differently than the data presented from *Mergerstat Review*. This information reflects that the control premiums paid within SIC category 28 were 70.5 percent, while the mean and median premiums for SIC category 38 were 45.5 percent and 27.00 percent, respectively.

However, this data reflects considerably greater premiums for the transactions that are tracked. The specific data for the industry includes only two transactions and therefore is considered to be of little significance. These two transactions reflect control premiums of 12.9 percent and 128.1 percent, too large a spread to be meaningful.

A review of the additional control premium data broken down by domestic transactions and by time periods tends to provide premium data in the range of the mid-40s. During 1992, the median of the 94 transactions tracked by this study was 42.4 percent. Although slightly higher than the *Mergerstat* data, a conclusion can be reached that the median premium during 1992 was approximately 35 percent to 40 percent.

The question to be addressed by the appraiser concerns the appropriate level of premium to be applied to the Public holdings. The economic and industry mood should also be considered when looking at this issue.

(Continued)

EXHIBIT 11.2 *(Continued)*

In the early 1990s, the U.S. economy was in the midst of a recession. The Persian Gulf War added to the problems and was followed by the election of President Clinton. It was during this period that unemployment levels began to rise, consumer spending declined, and consumer confidence drifted downward. During 1992, the state of the economy in the nation began to show some signs of improvement, as the real Gross Domestic Product grew by 2.9 percent. However, the unemployment rate increased from 6.8 percent in 1991 to 7.5 percent in 1992. The sluggishness of the economy at the conclusion of the Bush administration's term was expected to improve in the year ahead with the election of a Democratic president. The feeling in the nation at the end of 1992 was that:

> 1993, it seemed, could not come fast enough.
>
> Wall Street investors know the feeling well. For much of 1992, their sights have been fixed firmly on what the next 12 months may bring. There is, of course, nothing unusual about stock markets anticipating the future. But the presidential election, dominated by its cries of change and transition, and the turning point reached in the domestic economic cycle, have given investors a fixation with tomorrow's joys, obscuring the drearier realities of today.

America had been through tough economic times during the early stages of the decade, resulting in mixed feelings for the nation's consumers, employees, and investors. Optimism about the economy began to lift toward the end of 1992, with the consumer confidence index gaining 12.7 points in December, as reported by the New York–based Conference Board. The real estate market in the United States also began to show some signs of improvement, which indicated a positive attitude about the economy. However, fears of interest rate hikes were also apparent.

Investors, on the other hand, had mixed feelings about the future of the nation's economy.

> This spate of encouraging economic data failed to translate into a traditional year-end rally on Wall Street, largely because investors were also trying to anticipate the tax changes which may take effect in 1993. The Clinton administration, runs the thinking, will almost certainly increase the income tax burden on high-earning individuals. Accordingly, such investors had every incentive to lock into stock market profits before 1992 ended.
>
> Tax-centered concerns have already led to the early payments of bonuses by some Wall Street investment firms. Last week, these told on share prices, as dealers reported confusing "cross-currents" in trading activity. Some investment clients, they suggested, were still buying on the economic news, but others were busily selling on tax fears.

Furthermore, the nation's unsettled economy had an effect on the mood of investors. *Chemical Week*'s monthly stock report made the following statement regarding investors:

> Investor confidence was also hurt by disappointing economic data, leading analysts to trim earnings projections for the second half of this year, and for 1993. Although selling pressure centered on industrial cyclical groups like autos, airlines, and steels, none of the S&P 500 composite's 88 industry groups eked out a gain. The S&P 500 fell 2.4% in August, giving back more than half its July rise, while the more cyclically oriented DJIA sank 4%.

Aside from reporting on the overall stock market, *Chemical Week* also reports on the performance of chemical stocks. During the third quarter of 1992, major chemical firms' earnings declined, while the outlook for specialty chemicals looked bright. Unlike the major chemical firms, specialty chemical companies do not depend on commodity chemicals, as they generally produce "smaller batches of a wider variety of chemicals that command premium prices. These companies as a group are likely to see year over year quarterly earnings increases of about 10% to 15%," claims Jeffrey Cianci, a securities analyst with Bear, Stearns & Co.

While there are some reports of a positive outlook for the specialty chemical industry, a market report of the specialties segment by *Chemical Week* magazine paints a contrasting picture.

> In the specialties sector, losers outpaced winners by a three-to-one margin. Only the Dexter Corp. touched a new 12-month high. Seven issues advanced, with thinly traded LeaRonal, up 9%, posting the biggest rise. Among the biggest losers were Public, –10%; M.A. Hanna, –9%; and Ferro, –9%.

Overall, however, the specialty segment performed better than the large chemical companies. "The S&P chemicals and diversified chemicals indexes fell 6% and 5.8%, respectively, while the specialty chemicals index dropped only 1%." During the third quarter of 1992, specialty chemical makers saw higher returns, despite the weak U.S. economy.

Looking at the performance of specialty chemical firms during 1992, the industry displayed mixed results. During the first half of 1992, major chemical company stock prices increased 11 percent, while specialty chemical company prices fell 1 percent. Despite the differences in the performance of the two chemical sectors, specialty chemical stocks appear to be attractive investments.

> The major, or commodity, chemical companies are highly sensitive to the economic cycle. To judge by the strong performance of these and other cyclical stocks, investors are expecting a sharp recovery. They are likely to be disappointed. Restructuring in the service sector, restrained fiscal policy, high real long-term interest rates, and the slowdown in Japan and Europe are all working against a strong recovery. Real growth of 5% to 6% has been typical of recoveries in the postwar period. The current cycle is more likely to show growth of 2.5% to 3%.
>
> In this sluggish environment, specialty chemical companies look particularly attractive. They have some cyclical exposure but are not dependent on a strong recovery. In the best of times, the major chemical companies price their products on a cost-plus basis, expecting, or rather hoping, to cover production costs, with a little profit left over. These are highly competitive businesses where price is virtually all that distinguishes one company's product from another's. Profit growth is dependent on sales increases and high capacity utilization rates.

EXHIBIT 11.2 (Continued)

> The dynamics of the markets for specialty chemicals are quite different. Prices are driven by the added value each product brings to its customer. A significant amount of research goes into each product, and companies expend considerable resources on marketing.
>
> Not surprisingly, specialty chemical firms tend to be smaller than commodity chemical companies. They typically dominate the markets in which they operate, and they enjoy wider profit margins, stronger growth, and higher returns on equity.
>
> There are at least 70 good-size, publicly traded specialty chemical companies. Broadly speaking, these firms produce chemical solutions to a host of different problems.

Public's primary business operations are in the specialty chemicals industry. The three major product groupings within this segment include oil field chemicals, industrial chemicals, and industrial polymers and waxes.

The chemical industry in the United States is highly competitive. During the early 1990s, the industry experienced market erosion.

> Merger and acquisition activity has also become increasingly important in the oil field chemical industry in recent years due mainly to the declining U.S. market. Consolidation has continued to be a way that companies survive in the increasingly competitive industry. Baker Hughes became the leading U.S. producer and a major worldwide producer of oil field chemicals by making several important acquisitions in the early 1990s. These purchases, which also made Baker Hughes a more balanced chemical supplier, included ChemLink Incorporated (specialty production chemicals), BP's OFRIC business (UK oil field chemicals), the oil field chemical operations of CEDA Reactor in Canada, and the environmental chemical operations of Wen-Don Incorporated.

During the early 1990s, specialty chemical companies took steps toward increasing their market share. "For example, Public Corporation, a leading producer of specialty production chemicals, is working to increase the company's market share by emphasizing technology and value-added services." While Public was taking measures toward improving their market share and future position in the market during the early 1990s, the oil field chemical industry had been experiencing declining sales during the previous two years. "Due to industry consolidation there are also fewer customers for these products."

Within the oil field chemical industry are numerous product segments. Public is concentrated in the area of production chemicals. There are five companies within this segment, which accounted for over 75 percent of the market share. The five companies are Public, Baker Performance Chemicals, Nalco, Exxon, and Champion Technologies.

Aside from the increase in competition, environmental concerns throughout the global economy placed even more pressure on the $200 billion–per–year industry, which has "matured considerably during the past 10 years." The increased awareness of the protection of the environment has resulted in increased costs of operations for specialty chemical producers. Due to the rising costs of operations, many of the industry's small players have been acquired by larger companies. While environmental pressures have had an effect on the cost of doing business, some industry participants view the pressures as an opportunity to capitalize on a new environmentally conscious market.

The industry has seen many changes during the late 1980s and early 1990s, due in part to environmental pressures. The financial aspect of the industry has also changed. Chem Listner, senior V.P. at Kline, stated, "What has been described as a frenzy of purchases in the 1980s has settled down to a period of extreme caution. Deals are made strictly on the basis of strategic synergies with existing business units." It is the consolidation that occurred during the 1980s that has increased competition so dramatically.

Toward the close of 1992 and looking forward to 1993, productivity appears to be the focus of chemical firms.

> The economic chorus praises the U.S. chemical industry as well positioned for a productivity-driven future. The restructuring charges for layoffs and plant closures in the U.S. were taken in 1992, and the benefits will be seen on bottom lines in 1993, although some further charges are likely in Europe and will affect the profits of U.S. based multinationals in 1993. "The restructuring is over," says Amoco's Eck. "Everyone has done a tremendous job of cutting costs. We're ready to grow, and grow profitably." "The chemical industry has a very high value-added," Professor Smith concurs. "If the whole country were in the shape the chemical industry is in," he says, "George Bush would be the one being inaugurated on Jan. 20."

According to Form 10-K filed with the Securities and Exchange Commission for the year ended October 31, 1992, Public was about to acquire Target, Inc., a subsidiary of AAA Chemical Company. This is a positive sign for the company. Making acquisitions of this type is one of the prerogatives of control discussed previously.

Public is a leader in their niche of the market. This factor, along with a favorable outlook for the specialty chemical industry, makes the Company more likely to be acquired at a higher premium. In fact, because of the consolidation occurring in the industry, Public could be postured for a sale to an attractive suitor.

Considering the size of the premiums being paid in the marketplace, the industry outlook for Public, and the niche position that Public has filled in the industry, we believe that a control premium of 35 percent is appropriate.

By the way, the Public Company was acquired. It is definitely better to be lucky than good. In preparing to further explain why a control premium was applicable, we performed a simple analysis. Only 300,000 shares of stock were required for ownership greater than 50 percent. If the management bought these shares at a reasonable premium, control of the entire company would have provided them with an asset that was worth much more money. Also, when a 47 percent shareholder shows up at the annual shareholder meeting, does anyone believe that he or she would not control the vote? What is the likelihood of all of the other stockholders of this public company showing up at the annual meeting to vote? Not likely—the remaining shares were very small blocks in the hands of a lot of other shareholders.

Since I may not have made this statement enough already, be careful to avoid double counting! Certain valuation methods result in a control value for the company. Adding a control premium would result in double counting and should be avoided. For example, using merger and acquisition data would result in a control valuation, since the merger and acquisition data generally comes from the sale of entire companies. The excess earnings method is also considered to be a control valuation method since the appraiser is required to adjust the balance sheet items to fair market value. Minority interests could not benefit from this since they cannot sell off these assets.

Control premium studies, such as the ones discussed in Exhibit 11.2, are regularly used to assist the appraiser in determining the premium that is paid in the marketplace for control. I will discuss these studies in more detail shortly. However, are companies on Wall Street really buying control? Part of what they are buying is control, but there are many motivational factors that extend far beyond the control issue and that cause acquirers to pay considerably more for a company. When IBM purchased Lotus Development Corp. for about $66 per share, Lotus's shares were trading at $33. This would be a 100 percent premium! What about when MFS Communications bought UU Net? The acquired company had $94.5 million in revenues, a $63 million net loss, and negative $21 million in cash flow, but it sold for $2 billion (that's right, billion with a *b*).

Large companies purchase other companies for a variety of reasons besides control. Some of these reasons may include the synergies between the two companies, the ability of the acquirer to enter a new market without starting from scratch, or the ability of the acquirer to enter a completely new line of business that it had not been in before and that complements its existing business. Sometimes, it may just be to eliminate a competitor. In fact, if you examine many of the Wall Street megadeals of the past several years, the acquirer frequently begins selling off parts of the target company immediately to help pay for the acquisition. How does this factor into the control premium studies? It doesn't! So much for the perfect world!

Assume that a company reports a deal for $57 per share. However, after the acquisition is completed, certain subsidiaries are sold and the acquirer gets back the equivalent of $2 per share. The control premium studies would measure the premium as $57 over the trading price. Wouldn't it be more accurate to reflect $55, since that is the net number? Unfortunately, this is the best that we have to work with. It also explains why the courts are not willing to accept a blind application of these studies. The appraiser must think through and support the conclusions reached.

Lack of Control (Minority) Discounts

A lack of control discount is a reduction in the control value of the appraisal subject that is intended to reflect the fact that a minority stockholder cannot control the daily activities or policy decisions of an enterprise, leading to a reduction in value. The size of the discount will depend on the size of the interest being appraised, the amount of control, the stockholder's ability to liquidate the company, and other factors.

A lack of control discount is basically the opposite of a premium for control. This type of discount is used to obtain the value of a noncontrolling interest in the appraisal subject when a control value is the starting point. Conversely, a control premium is used to determine the control value when the freely traded minority value is the starting point. The starting point is determined based on the method of valuation, the normalization adjustments made, and the source of the discount or capitalization rates.

Lack of control discounts can be mathematically determined using control premiums that are measured in the public market. The formula to determine the minority interest is as follows:

$$1 - \left(\frac{1}{1 + \text{Control premium}}\right)$$

Exhibit 11.3 illustrates this concept.

EXHIBIT 11.3
Calculating the Lack of Control Discount

If the control value equals $120 per share and the control premium equals 20 percent, the minority value would be calculated as follows:

$$1 - [1 \div (1 + 0.2)] = 16.67\% \text{ lack of control discount}$$

The 16.67 percent lack of control discount would be subtracted from the control value to derive the freely traded minority value. This is calculated as follows:

$$\$120 \times 16.67\% = \$20 \text{ discount}$$

$$\$120 - \$20 = \$100 \text{ freely traded minority value}$$

If you have ever done this stuff before, you probably know that an appraiser is supposed to be able to support the size of the discount taken. If you have never done this before, you know now. A discount does not get plucked from the air (or maybe I should say that the discount *should not* be plucked from the air). In addition to supporting discount rates, capitalization rates, and forecasts, the greatest problem that an appraiser faces is supporting the size of the valuation discounts and premiums. It is really pretty humorous to see an appraiser write a 100-page valuation report in which he or she spends all of one paragraph to "whack" the value by 35 percent for various discounts. So, where does one go to look for support for the minority discount?

Before we discuss specific sources that are used as a starting point in the process, let's discuss what a minority discount really is. This might best be shown with an example. This is also a good time to illustrate the concept of allowing the normalization adjustments to assist the appraiser in determining control or minority values. Let's assume that ABC Company has a reported net income of $100,000. Let's also assume that the only normalization adjustment for control is officer's compensation, requiring a $50,000 adjustment. To keep things simple, let's ignore taxes. Assuming a capitalization rate of 20 percent, value can be estimated as follows:

	Control	*Minority*
Reported net income	$100,000	$100,000
Normalization		
Officer's compensation	$ 50,000	
Adjusted net income	$150,000	$100,000
Capitalization rate	÷ 20%	÷ 20%
Estimated value	$750,000	$500,000

The difference in value of $250,000 is effectively the lack of control discount. By having control, an owner could create an additional $250,000 of value by adjusting the officer's compensation to market levels. Conversely, the minority owner loses this value by not being able to make *control* adjustments.

The implied lack of control discount in this example is 33⅓ percent ($250,000 ÷ $750,000). The nice part about valuing the minority interest in this fashion is that the appraiser does not have to support a lack of control discount, which is difficult to do.

There is a problem, however, in relying solely on the normalization adjustments to represent the difference in value between control and minority. There are certain attributes of control that may add value but may not impact measurable cash flow or earnings. For example, having the ability to sell the company is an attribute of control that adds value. However, just having a right, which intuitively should add value, may not be measurable. What about the well-run company with no normalization adjustments? Clearly, I would rather have control, even if the cash flow is the same. The question is how much is that right worth?

A couple of the more common sources of information used to measure the lack of control discount include *Mergerstat Review* and *Mergerstat Control Premium Study* (formerly known as the *HLHZ Premium for Control Study*). Each of these sources is referenced in Chapter 4 and measures control premiums. Since the control premiums are used to calculate the lack of control discount, these sources are the most widely used. Unfortunately, there are no sources that measure lack of control discounts directly. One of the problems the appraiser faces is that these studies measure the control premiums differently, and therefore, the implied lack of control discount may be different depending on the source used to calculate the discount.

Mergerstat Review always uses the public price five days prior to a takeover announcement. The benefit of this method is that it is a consistent and objective way of measuring the premium. The drawback of this method is that the public price may have already started to climb based on rumors of a deal, which may understate the premium.

The *Mergerstat Control Premium Study* starts with 1986 data and analyzes the prices of the target company's stock further away from the transaction date. The analysts who publish this study attempt to select a price unaffected by pre-announcement speculation of the transaction. There is a lot to be said for tracking the price changes and daily trading volume as far back as necessary until an apparently "unaffected" minority price is reached, since it eliminates most of the price climb resulting from acquisition rumors. The drawbacks are twofold: First, it can be a subjective standard of measurement, subject to bias, unless price change and volume data are consistently analyzed; and second, if the unaffected price is too far back in time, other factors in the stock market, and not the specific transaction, could have caused the changes.

Another problem that exists in using the control premium data is that we cannot determine if there is a true premium being paid for control or if the acquiring company is paying for synergies that cannot be separately measured. We also do not know how many of the Wall Street megadeals resulted in spin-offs after the acquisition. If a company makes an acquisition for $100 million but intends to sell a subsidiary as soon after the acquisition as possible—for, let's say, $10 million—isn't this really a $90 million net acquisition? However, the control premium data used by the studies would be based on the $100 million. Unfortunately, it is the best that we have to work with.

In case you are not nervous about this yet, one of the difficulties in properly measuring the control premium that was paid is that it must be in a cash equivalent price to help the appraiser determine the fair market value of the appraisal subject. Business transactions are frequently consummated using various payment options, including all cash, cash and noncash, or all noncash consideration.

It is essential to know the value of the noncash consideration in relation to the face amount of the consideration. Most control premium studies that include purchases using noncash consideration report only the price calculated using the face value of the noncash consideration, not its cash equivalent.

Exhibit 11.4 illustrates how the control premium data can be used in the calculation of the lack of control discount.

EXHIBIT 11.4
Percent Premium Paid Over Market Price

Year of Buyout	*Number of Transactions*	*Average Premium Paid Over Market (%)*[1]	*Median Premium Paid (%)*	*Implied Lack of Control Discount (%)*[2]
1980	169	49.9	44.6	30.8
1981	166	48.0	41.9	29.5
1982	176	47.4	43.5	30.3
1983	168	37.7	34.0	25.4
1984	199	37.9	34.4	25.6
1985	331	37.1	27.7	21.7
1986	333	38.2	29.9	23.0
1987	237	38.3	30.8	23.5
1988	410	41.9	30.9	23.6
1989	303	41.0	29.0	22.5
1990	175	42.0	32.0	24.2
1991	137	35.1	29.4	22.7
1992	142	41.0	34.7	25.8
1993	173	38.7	33.0	24.8
1994	260	41.9	35.0	25.9
1995	324	44.7	29.2	22.6
1996	381	36.6	27.3	21.5
1997	487	35.7	27.5	21.6
1998	512	40.7	30.1	23.1
1999	723	43.3	34.6	25.7
2000	574	49.2	41.1	29.1

[1]The premium paid over market is a percentage based on the buyout price over the market price of the seller's stock five business days prior to the announcement date.

[2]Formula: $1 - [1 \div (1 + \text{Median premium paid})]$

Source: *Mergerstat Review 2001* (Los Angeles: Houlihan, Lokey, Howard & Zukin). Discount calculated by Trugman Valuation Associates Inc.

Exhibit 11.4 reflects the table that many of us have seen over and over again, being adjusted for one year at a time. What many of us ignored is the fact that the *Mergerstat* data includes only positive premiums. However, companies are not purchased only at a premium. Sometimes companies are purchased at a discount from the market price.

Our firm performed an analysis using *Mergerstat* data located on the BVmarketdata.com Web site taking into consideration the negative premiums in addition to the positive ones. The results were frightening. Using only target companies from the United States, the results of the average and median premiums from 1998 to 2001[2] are presented below.

[2]Data is taken through September 30, 2001.

Based on Average Premiums

	Positive Premiums Only		Positive and Negative Premiums	
Year of Buyout	*Premium Paid Over Market (%)*	*Implied Lack of Control Discount (%)*	*Premium Paid Over Market (%)*	*Implied Lack of Control Discount (%)*
1998	44.09	30.60	31.60	24.01
1999	47.22	32.07	40.33	28.74
2000	52.54	34.44	36.95	26.98
2001	59.92	37.47	44.18	30.64

Based on Median Premiums

	Positive Premiums Only		Positive and Negative Premiums	
Year of Buyout	*Premium Paid Over Market (%)*	*Implied Lack of Control Discount (%)*	*Premium Paid Over Market (%)*	*Implied Lack of Control Discount (%)*
1998	29.00	22.48	21.00	17.36
1999	33.00	24.81	30.00	23.08
2000	42.50	29.82	33.00	24.81
2001	45.00	31.03	34.50	25.65

Putting this data into perspective, if an appraiser were to base the control premium or discount for lack of control merely on the data included in the table that we are used to seeing, this data would be significantly overstated. This means that the control premium that might be added to the freely traded value would result in the value of the company being too high. Conversely, if a discount for lack of control were calculated from the normally used data, the discount would be overstated and also result in the minority interest being overvalued. So what does all of this mean? It means that we have to be aware of the data that we use and its impact on our conclusions. Merely accepting data without understanding what is included in it is a bad practice.

Discount for Lack of Marketability

A discount for lack of marketability (DLOM) is used to compensate for the difficulty of selling shares of stock that are not traded on a stock exchange compared with those that can be traded publicly. If an investor owns shares in a public company, he or she can pick up the telephone, call a broker, and generally convert the investment into cash within three days. That is not the case with an investment in a closely held business. Therefore, publicly traded stocks frequently have an element of liquidity that closely held shares do not. This is the reason that a DLOM may be applied. It is intended to reflect the market's perceived reduction in value for not providing liquidity to the shareholder.

A DLOM may also be appropriate when the shares have either legal or contractual restrictions placed upon them. These may be in the form of restricted stock, restrictions resulting from buy-sell agreements, bank loan restrictions, or other types of contracts that restrict the sale of the shares. Even when the valuation subject is a 100 percent interest, a DLOM may be appropriate if the owner cannot change the restrictions on the stock. However, most appraisers agree that a DLOM for a controlling interest will generally be lower than a DLOM for a minority interest.

The most common sources of data for determining an appropriate level of a DLOM are studies involving restricted stock purchases or initial public offerings. Revenue Ruling 77-287 refers to the *Institutional*

Investor Study Report of the Securities and Exchange Commission, which addresses restricted stock issues.[3] Many studies have updated this one.

Restricted stock (or "letter stock," as it is sometimes called) is stock issued by a corporation that is not registered with the Securities and Exchange Commission (SEC) and cannot be readily sold into the public market. The stock is usually issued when a corporation is first going public, making an acquisition, or raising capital. Corporations issue restricted stock rather than tradable stock mainly (1) to avoid dilution of their stock price when an excessive number of shares are available for sale at any one time, and (2) to avoid the costs of registering the securities with the SEC.

The registration exemption on restricted stocks is granted under Section 4(2) of the 1933 Securities Act. The intent of Section 4(2) is to provide "small" corporations with the ability to raise capital without incurring the costs of a public offering. Regulation D, a safe-harbor regulation that became effective in 1982, falls under Section 4(2) of the Securities Act and provides uniformity in federal and state securities laws regarding private placements of securities. Securities bought under Regulation D are subject to restrictions, the most important being that the securities cannot be resold without either registration under the act or an exemption.[4] The exemptions for these securities are granted under Rule 144.

> Rule 144 (17C.F.R. 230.144 1980) allows the limited resale of unregistered securities after a minimum holding period of two years. Resale is limited to the higher of 1 percent of outstanding stock or average weekly volume over a 4 week period prior to the sale, during any three month period. There is no quantity limitation after a four year holding period.[5]

Therefore, to sell their stock on the public market, holders of restricted stock must either register their securities with the SEC or qualify for a Rule 144 exemption. A holder of restricted stock can, however, trade the stock in a private transaction. Historically, when traded privately, the restricted stock transaction was usually required to be registered with the SEC. However, in 1990 the SEC adopted Rule 144a, which relaxed the SEC filing restrictions on private transactions. The rule allows qualified institutional investors to trade unregistered securities among themselves without filing registration statements.[6] In 1997 this rule was changed again, shortening the required holding period for these stocks to one year. The overall effect of these regulations on restricted stock is that when the stocks are issued, the corporation is not required to disclose a price, and on some occasions, even when they are traded, the value of restricted securities is still not a matter of public record.

Various studies have been performed relating to restricted stocks. Each of these studies attempts to quantify the discount taken against the freely traded price of minority shares in the public market. The following are some of the more frequently cited studies:

- SEC *Institutional Investor Study*
- Gelman study
- Moroney study
- Maher study
- Trout study

[3]"Discounts Involved in Purchases of Common Stock (1966–1969)," *Institutional Investor Study Report of the Securities and Exchange Commission*, H.R. Doc. No. 64, pt. 5, 92d Cong., 1st Sess. 1971, 2444–2456.

[4]Kasim L. Alli and Donald J. Thompson, "The Value of the Resale Limitation on Restricted Stock: An Option Theory Approach," *Valuation* (March 1991), 22–33 (published by the American Society of Appraisers).

[5]Ibid., 23.

[6]Richard A. Brealey and Stewart C. Myers, "How Corporations Issue Securities," in Richard A. Brealey and Stewart C. Myers, eds., *Principles of Corporate Finance*, 4th ed. (New York: McGraw-Hill, 1991), 354–356.

- Standard Research Consultants study
- Willamette Management Associates study
- Silber study
- FMV study
- Management planning study

Let's discuss some of these studies. Too often, appraisers use the average discounts that are cited in business valuation publications and textbooks without reading the actual studies. This is both dangerous and negligent. You should understand these studies before using them.

SEC *Institutional Investor Study*

As part of a major study of institutional investor actions performed by the SEC, the amount of discount at which transactions in restricted stock take place, compared with the prices of otherwise identical but unrestricted stock on the open market, was addressed. The report introduced the study with the following discussion about restricted stock:

> Restricted securities are usually sold at a discount from their coeval market price, if any, primarily because of the restrictions on their resale. With the information supplied by the respondents on the purchase prices of the common stock and the dates of transaction, the Study computed the implied discounts in all cases in which it was able to locate a market price for the respective security on the date of the transaction.[7]

Exhibit 11.5 contains a reproduction of Table XIV-45 of the SEC *Institutional Investor Study*, which shows the size of the discounts at which restricted stock transactions took place compared with the prices, as of the same date, of the freely traded but otherwise identical stocks. The table shows that about half of the transactions (in terms of real dollars) took place at discounts ranging from 20 percent to 40 percent.

EXHIBIT 11.5
SEC Institutional Investor Study

	Discount							
	−15.0% to 0.0%		0.1% to 10.0%		10.1% to 20.0%		20.1% to 30.0%	
Trading Market	*No. of Transactions*	*Value of Purchases*	*No. of Transactions*	*Value of Purchases*	*No. of Transactions*	*Value of Purchases*	*No. of Transactions*	*Value of Purchases*
Unknown	1	$ 1,500,000	2	$ 2,496,583	1	$ 205,000	0	$ 0
New York Stock Exchange	7	3,760,663	13	15,111,798	13	24,503,988	10	17,954,085
American Stock Exchange	2	7,263,060	4	15,850,000	11	14,548,750	20	46,200,677
Over-the-counter (reporting companies)	11	13,828,757	39	13,613,676	35	38,585,259	30	35,479,946
Over-the-counter (nonreporting companies)	5	8,329,369	9	5,265,925	18	25,122,024	17	11,229,155
Total	26	$34,681,849	67	$52,337,982	78	$102,965,021	77	$110,863,863

[7] *Institutional Investor Study Report of the Securities and Exchange Commission*, 2444.

EXHIBIT 11.5 (Continued)

	Discount							
	30.1% to 40.0%		40.1% to 50.0%		50.1% to 80.0%		Total	
Trading Market	*No. of Transactions*	*Value of Purchases*	*No. of Transactions*	*Value of Purchases*	*No. of Transactions*	*Value of Purchases*	*No. of Transactions*	*Value of Purchases*
Unknown	2	$ 3,332.000	0	$ 0	1	$ 1,259,995	7	$ 8,793,578
New York Stock Exchange	3	11,102,501	1	1,400,000	4	5,005,068	51	78,838,103
American Stock Exchange	7	21,074,298	1	44,250	4	4,802,404	49	109,783,439
Over-the-counter (reporting companies)	30	58,689,328	13	9,284,047	21	8,996,406	179	178,477,419
Over-the-counter (nonreporting companies)	25	29,423,584	20	11,377,431	18	13,505,545	112	104,253,033
Total	67	$123,621,711	35	$22,105,728	48	$33,569,418	398	$480,145,572

Source: *Institutional Investor Study Report of the Securities and Exchange Commission*, H.R. Doc. No. 64, Part 5, 92nd Cong., 1st Session 1971, Table XIV-45.

The discounts were lowest for those stocks that would be tradable when the restrictions expired on the New York Stock Exchange, and were highest for those stocks that could be traded in the over-the-counter market when the restrictions expired. The overall average discount in this study was 25.8 percent. For stocks whose market would be nonreporting over-the-counter companies when the restrictions expired, the average discount was approximately 32.6 percent. Think about the closely held company whose shares have no prospect of any market. The discount would have to be higher.

The research from the SEC *Institutional Investor Study* was the foundation for SEC Accounting Series Release No. 113 (October 13, 1969) and No. 1-18 (December 23, 1970), which require investment companies registered under the Investment Company Act of 1940 to disclose their policies about the cost and valuation of their restricted securities. As a result of the study, there is now an ongoing body of data about the relationship between restricted stock prices and their freely tradable counterparts. This body of data can provide empirical benchmarks for quantifying marketability discounts.

Gelman Study

In 1972, Milton Gelman of National Economic Research Associates, Inc., published the results of his study of the prices paid for restricted securities by four closed-end investment companies specializing in restricted securities investments.[8] Gelman used data from 89 transactions between 1968 and 1970, and found that both the average and median discounts were 33 percent and that almost 60 percent of the purchases were at discounts of 30 percent and higher. This data is consistent with the SEC study.

Moroney Study

An article by Robert E. Moroney of the investment banking firm Moroney, Beissner & Co. contained the results of a study of the prices paid for restricted securities by 10 registered investment companies.[9] The study included

[8]Milton Gelman, "An Economist–Financial Analyst's Approach to Valuing Stock of a Closely Held Company," *Journal of Taxation* (June 1972), 353–354.

[9]Robert E. Moroney, "Most Courts Overvalue Closely Held Stocks," *Taxes* (March 1973), 144–154.

146 purchases at discounts ranging from 3 percent to 90 percent. The average discount was approximately 35.6 percent. Despite the pretty broad range, the average discount was, once again, in line with the other studies.

In this article, Moroney compared the evidence of actual cash transactions with the lower, average discounts for lack of marketability determined in some previous estate and gift tax cases. He stated that at the times of these other cases, there was no available evidence about the prices of restricted stocks that could have been used as a benchmark to help quantify these discounts. However, he suggested that higher discounts for lack of marketability should be allowed in the future as more relevant data becomes available. He stated:

> Obviously the courts in the past have overvalued minority interests in closely held companies for federal tax purposes. But most (probably all) of those decisions were handed down without benefit of the facts of life recently made available for all to see. Some appraisers have for years had a strong gut feeling that they should use far greater discounts for non-marketability than the courts had allowed. From now on those appraisers need not stop at 35 percent merely because it's perhaps the largest discount clearly approved in a court decision. Appraisers can now cite a number of known arm's-length transactions in which the discount ranged up to 90 percent.[10]

Approximately four years later, Moroney wrote another article in which he stated that courts had started to recognize higher discounts for lack of marketability:

> The thousands and thousands of minority holders in closely held corporations throughout the United States have good reason to rejoice because the courts in recent years have upheld illiquidity discounts in the 50 percent area.[11]

Despite Moroney's writings, the courts have not willingly accepted large discounts. We have witnessed some discounts that were larger than the average, but overall, the courts are still somewhat reluctant to recognize the difficulty in liquidating an illiquid asset.

Maher Study

J. Michael Maher of Connecticut General Life Insurance Co. conducted another interesting study on lack of marketability discounts for closely held business interests.[12] The results of this well-documented study were published in the September 1976 issue of *Taxes*. Using an approach similar to Moroney's, Maher compared the prices paid for restricted stocks with the market prices of their unrestricted counterparts. The data covered the five-year period from 1969 through 1973. The study showed that "the mean discount for lack of marketability for the years 1969 to 1973 amounted to 35.43 percent."[13] In an attempt to eliminate abnormally high and low discounts, Maher eliminated the top and bottom 10 percent of the purchases. Guess what? The resulting average discount was 34.73 percent, almost the exact same discount that was derived without the top and bottom items removed.

Maher's remarks are a good learning tool, since he distinguishes between a discount for lack of marketability and a lack of control discount:

> The result I have reached is that most appraisers underestimate the proper discount for lack of marketability. The results seem to indicate that this discount should be about 35 percent. Perhaps this makes sense because by committing funds to restricted common stock, the willing buyer (a) would be denied the opportunity to take

---

[10]Ibid., 154.

[11]Robert E. Moroney, "Why 25% Discount for Nonmarketability in One Valuation, 100% in Another," *Taxes* (May 1977), 316–320. *Edwin A. Gallun*, 33 T.C.M. 1316 (1974), allowed 55 percent. *Estate of Maurice Gustave Heckscher*, 63 T.C. 485 (1975), allowed 48 percent. Although *Estate of Ernest E. Kirkpatrick*, 34 T.C.M. 1490 (1975), found per-share values without mentioning discount, expert witnesses for both sides used 50 percent the first time a government witness recommended 50 percent. A historic event, indeed!

[12]J. Michael Maher, "Discounts for Lack of Marketability for Closely Held Business Interests," *Taxes* (September 1976), 562–571.

[13]Ibid., 571.

> advantage of other investments, and (b) would continue to have his investment at the risk of the business until the shares could be offered to the public or another buyer is found.
>
> The 35 percent discount would not contain elements of a discount for a minority interest because it is measured against the current fair market value of securities actively traded (other minority interests). Consequently, appraisers should also consider a discount for a minority interest in those closely held corporations where a discount is applicable.[14]

Now the plot thickens. Not only are we seeing larger discounts, but we are now starting to see opinions, other than mine, that more than one discount could be applicable. This could mean that smaller, closely held company values should be discounted quite a bit when they are compared with publicly traded guideline companies.

Trout Study

The next study that we learned about was performed by Robert R. Trout.[15] Trout was with the Graduate School of Administration, University of California–Irvine, and Trout, Shulman & Associates. Trout's study of restricted stocks covered the period 1968 to 1972 and addressed the purchases of these securities by mutual funds. Trout attempted to construct a financial model that would provide an estimate of the discount appropriate for a private company's stock. Creating a multiple regression model involving 60 purchases, Trout measured an average discount of 33.45 percent for restricted stock from freely traded stock. Either this was quite a coincidence, or these guys were in cahoots!

Standard Research Consultants Study

In 1983 Standard Research Consultants analyzed private placements of common stock to test the current applicability of the SEC *Institutional Investor Study*.[16] Standard Research studied 28 private placements of restricted common stock from October 1978 through June 1982. The discounts ranged from 7 to 91 percent, with a median of 45 percent, a bit higher than seen in the other studies. During this period, however, the economy experienced extraordinarily high interest rates.

Only 4 of the 28 companies studied had unrestricted common shares traded on either the American Stock Exchange or the New York Stock Exchange, and their discounts ranged from 25 percent to 58 percent with a median of 47 percent—not significantly different from the 45 percent median of the remaining companies that traded in the over-the-counter market.

Willamette Management Associates, Inc. Study

Willamette Management Associates (Shannon Pratt's former firm) analyzed private placements of restricted stocks for the period of January 1, 1981, through May 31, 1984.[17] In discussing this unpublished study, Willamette states that the early part of it overlapped with the last part of the Standard Research study, but there were very few transactions that took place during the period of overlap. According to the discussion of the study in Pratt, Reilly, and Schweihs's *Valuing a Business*, most of the transactions in the study took place in 1983.

---

[14]Ibid.

[15]Robert R. Trout, "Estimation of the Discount Associated With the Transfer of Restricted Securities," *Taxes* (June 1977), 381–385.

[16]"Revenue Ruling 77-287 Revisited," *SRC Quarterly Reports* (Spring 1983), 1–3.

[17]The Willamette Management Associates study is unpublished but is discussed in Shannon P. Pratt, Robert E. Reilly, and Robert P. Schweihs, *Valuing a Business*, 4th ed. (New York: McGraw Hill, 2000), 400.

For this time period, Willamette identified 33 transactions that could be classified with reasonable confidence as arm's-length transactions and for which the price of the restricted shares could be compared directly with the price of trades in otherwise identical but unrestricted shares of the same company at the same time. The median discount for the 33 restricted stock transactions compared with the prices of their freely tradable counterparts was 31.2 percent, a little bit lower than the other studies but substantially lower than the study by Standard Research.

In *Valuing a Business*, Pratt et al. attribute the slightly lower average percentage discounts for private placements during this time to the somewhat depressed prices in the public stock market, which in turn were in response to the recessionary economic conditions prevalent during most of the period of the study (remember a prime rate of 21.5 percent?). Taking this into consideration, the study basically supports the long-term average discount of 35 percent for transactions in restricted stock compared with the prices of their freely tradable counterparts.

Silber Study

In 1991, another study of restricted stock was published, but it included transactions during the period of 1981 through 1988. This study, by William L. Silber, substantiated the earlier restricted stock studies and found an average price discount of 33.75 percent.[18] Silber identified 69 private placements involving the common stock of publicly traded companies. The restricted stock in this study could be sold under Rule 144 after a two-year holding period. Similar to Trout, Silber tried to develop a statistical model to explain the price differences between securities that differ in resale provisions. Silber concluded that the discount on restricted stock varies directly with the size of the block of restricted stock relative to the amount of publicly traded stock issued by the company. He found that the discounts were larger when the block of restricted stock was large compared with the total number of shares outstanding. Silber also noted that the size of the discount was inversely related to the creditworthiness of the issuing company.

FMV Study

FMV Opinions, Inc. conducted a study from 1979 through April 1992.[19] In spite of the long time period covered, this study analyzed only a little over 100 transactions involving companies that were generally not the smallest capitalization companies. It supported the findings of the SEC *Institutional Investor Study* in finding that the DLOM was higher for smaller capitalization companies. This study, however, found an average discount of only about 23 percent.

Management Planning Study

The last study that covered the period before the Rule 144a changes that took place in April 1997 was conducted by Management Planning, Inc. This study is discussed in *Quantifying Marketability Discounts*, by Z. Christopher Mercer, A.S.A., C.F.A. The Management Planning study includes restricted stock transactions for the period from 1980 to 1995.

The primary focus for the Management Planning study was to identify companies that had made private placements of unregistered common shares that would, except for the restrictions on trading, have similar characteristics to that company's publicly traded shares. Companies included in the study had to have in excess of $3 million in annual sales and be profitable for the year immediately prior to the private placement. It was required that the company be a domestic corporation and not considered to be in "a development stage," and the common stock of the issuing company sell for at least $2 per share.

[18]William L. Silber, "Discounts on Restricted Stock: The Impact of Illiquidity on Stock Prices," *Financial Analysts Journal* (July–August 1991), 60–64.

[19]Lance S. Hall and Timothy C. Polacek, "Strategies for Obtaining the Largest Discount," *Estate Planning* (January/February 1994), 38–44.

Management Planning analyzed 200 private transactions involving companies with publicly traded shares. Of the 200, 49 met the base criteria described. Of these, the average mean discount was 27.7 percent, while the average median discount was 28.8 percent.[20]

A more detailed analysis of the Management Planning Study indicated a large range of discounts relative to the sample companies due to varying degrees of revenues, earnings, market share, price stability, and earnings stability. The average revenues for the companies selected for review were $47.5 million; however, the median revenue figure was $29.8 million, indicating that the average sales figure was impacted by a few companies that were significantly larger than the others studied. The average discount for companies with revenues under $10 million was 32.9 percent.

Likewise, the average reported earnings of the study group were skewed by 20 companies in the study whose earnings exceeded $1 million and that in fact had a median earnings figure of $2.9 million. Twenty-nine of the companies studied earned less than $1 million, while the median earnings of all of the companies in the sample was $0.7 million. The following chart indicates that fourth-quartile companies reflected private placement median discounts to the shares traded in the open markets ranging from 34.6 percent to 44.8 percent, based on the factors considered. The average discount of sample companies in the fourth quartile for the five factors considered was 39.3 percent.

Factors Considered in the Analysis		*First Quartile*	*Second Quartile*	*Third Quartile*	*Fourth Quartile*	*Original Expectations Re: Discounts*
		Restricted Stock Discounts				
Revenues	Median	18.7%	22.2%	31.5%	36.6%	Higher revenues, lower discounts
	Mean	21.8%	23.9%	31.9%	34.7%	
Earnings	Median	16.1%	30.5%	32.7%	39.4%	Higher earnings, lower discounts
	Mean	18.0%	30.0%	30.1%	34.1%	
Market price/share	Median	23.3%	22.2%	29.5%	41.0%	Higher prices, lower discounts
	Mean	23.3%	24.5%	27.3%	37.3%	
Price stability	Median	34.6%	31.6%	9.2 %	19.4%	Lower stability, higher discounts
	Mean	34.8%	33.3%	21.0%	22.0%	
Earnings stability	Median	14.1%	26.2%	30.8%	44.8%	Higher earnings stability, lower discounts
	Mean	16.4%	28.8%	27.8%	39.7%	

More About the DLOM

All of the studies about restricted stock generally deal with minority blocks of stock in public companies. Therefore, the restricted stock studies may be a useful guide in assessing a DLOM for a minority interest. However, a control value may also need to reflect a DLOM, although it probably would be smaller than a DLOM attributable to minority shares. Since a minority interest is more difficult to sell than a controlling interest, the DLOM is usually larger for minority interests. The average DLOM ranges between 25 percent and 45 percent based on the studies previously discussed. Larger discounts may be appropriate if the starting point is a marketable, minority interest value based on public guideline company methods.

It is important to point out that the time periods covered by the various studies that have been discussed range from 1966 to 1995. Quite frankly, this is old stuff. These studies would certainly be impacted by the holding period relating to the restrictions that were applicable at the time of those transactions. However, today, the restrictions have been cut in half. This does not mean that the discount should automatically be cut in half, but intuitively, it would seem that the DLOM should be lower, if all else is equal.

[20]Z. Christopher Mercer, *Quantifying Marketability Discounts*, (Memphis: Peabody Publishing L.P., 1997), 345–363.

A newer, unpublished study is discussed in Shannon Pratt's *Business Valuation Update*, May 2000 edition. This study was conducted by Columbia Financial Advisors. Exhibit 11.6 provides a section of a real report addressing both the new and the old studies. In this instance, the appraiser on the other side of the litigation used only the old stuff.

EXHIBIT 11.6
Old and New DLOM Studies Used in Report

Since a private company's stock does not have the ready marketability of a stock that is traded in the public market, a discount for lack of marketability is generally considered to be appropriate. The Smith report begins with a discussion of studies regarding the lack of marketability discounts. The studies discussed all relate to restricted shares under Rule 144a of the Securities and Exchange Act. The time periods covered in these studies were as follows:

SEC *Institutional Investor Study*	1966–1969
SEC nonreporting OTC companies	1966–1969
Gelman study	1968–1970
Trout study	1968–1972
Moroney study	1969–1972
Maher study	1969–1973
Standard Research Consultants study	1978–1982
Willamette Management study	1981–1984

All of the studies presented in the Smith report are old. In fact, Rule 144a changed effective April 1997, further antiquating the discounts reflected in these studies. The two-year holding period was reduced to one year, and as a result, logic says shareholders would gain more liquidity and one would expect to see the discounts fall. In fact, the only study that I have seen published to date was discussed in the May 2000 edition of Shannon Pratt's *Business Valuation Update*. In an article titled, "Restricted Stock Discounts Decline as a Result of 1-Year Holding Period: Studies After 1990 No Longer Relevant for Lack of Marketability Discounts," a study performed by Columbia Financial Advisors, Inc., a business appraisal and financial advisory firm headquartered in Portland, Oregon, was discussed. The Columbia Financial Advisor's study examined private common equity placements over the period from January 1, 1996, through April 30, 1997. According to this study, discounts after April 29, 1997, ranged from 13 percent to 15 percent. The article also reflects discounts after 1990, when Rule 144a was amended, but prior to the reduction in the required holding periods. The findings from various studies covering this period of time ranged from 16 percent to 28 percent. Therefore, the drop to 13 percent to 15 percent should not be unexpected. These ranges certainly reflect lower discounts than the studies covered in the Smith report, which covered the years from 1966 to 1984. There is no relevance to using these considerably older studies in light of new empirical information present.

The next item discussed in the Smith report is the Tax Court case of *Bernard Mandelbaum v. Commissioner*. The author discusses the nonexclusive list of factors that the court pointed out as being relevant in the determination of a marketability discount. There is much debate in the business valuation community regarding the factors considered in the decision issued by the court in *Mandelbaum*. Many of the factors discussed in the judicial opinion relate to risk and not necessarily liquidity. Considering the factors relative to ABC Company, I agree that the new financial leverage should be considered. Though the company's dividend history has been nonexistent, and its leverage may limit the possibility of future dividends, the expectation of increasing shareholder value would nevertheless be a mitigating factor regarding marketability. Not all companies pay dividends. Strong financial performance would certainly enhance marketability.

It seems ironic that Smith chose to use the fact that Mr. Jones is a key executive as an issue that could increase the marketability discount, because ironically, the strong management team would seem to be a mitigating factor to the minority discount that they overestimated previously. It seems obvious from the prospectus that the investment banking firm that took the company private thought a considerable amount of Mr. Jones, as well as the other executives, and it would seem that the only reason for the departure of management would be if the company were not performing well. Otherwise there does not seem to be any justification for taking this position to impact marketability.

As a result of all of the factors discussed in the Smith report, they conclude that a 35 percent discount would be reasonable. However, one of the lessons to be learned from the *Mandelbaum* case is that in the concept of fair market value, the appraiser must consider the view of marketability not only from the standpoint of the willing buyer, but also from that of the willing seller. In fact, this was the major lesson to be learned from this case, as Judge David Laro did not accept the taxpayer's expert's analysis because it was too buyer oriented. Considering the more recent restricted stock studies and the additional financial leverage taken on by the company, as well as Mr. Jones's position with the company as an important part of the management team, controlling the destiny of the financial position of the company, it is my opinion that the marketability discount should be no greater than 20 percent.

Now don't get me wrong; using the older studies as benchmarks is still going to be required, since we do not have enough current empirical data to rely on. If you think about the time period covered by the Columbia Financial Advisors study (1997–1999), the stock market was going strong. Is it possible that some of these much smaller discounts were attributable to the fact that investor expectations were that the market was going to continue to go up, thereby reducing the holding period risk for these securities? Clearly, we will need more work in this area. I know the folks at Columbia personally, and they are a well-respected, talented group of appraisers. I hope that they will update and publish their study.

Another manner in which the business appraisal community and users of its services determine DLOMs is through the use of closely held companies that underwent an initial public offering (IPO) of their stock. In these instances, the value of the closely held stock is measured before and after the company went public.

John Emory, formerly of Robert Baird & Co., has conducted 10 studies over time periods ranging from 1980 through June 2000, comparing the prices in closely held stock transactions, when no public market existed, with the prices of subsequent IPOs in the same stocks. The study consisted of an analysis of 4,088 prospectuses in an attempt to determine the relationship between the IPO price and the price at which the latest private transaction occurred up to five months before the company went public. The average discount in these studies ranged between 42 percent and 60 percent, with the higher discounts occurring at the time that interest rates were high and low. The median discounts ranged from 40 percent to 66 percent. The results are presented in Exhibit 11.7.

EXHIBIT 11.7

The Value of Marketability as Illustrated in Initial Public Offerings of Common Stock

Study	*# of IPO Prospectuses Reviewed*	*# of Qualifying Transactions*	Discount	
			Mean	*Median*
1997–2000[1]	1847	283	50%	52%
1997–2000[2]	1847	36	48%	44%
1997–2000[3]	NA	53	54%	54%
1995–1997	732	91	43%	42%
1994–1995	318	46	45%	45%
1992–1993	443	54	45%	44%
1990–1992	266	35	42%	40%
1989–1990	157	23	45%	40%
1987–1989	98	27	45%	45%
1985–1986	130	21	43%	43%
1980–1981	97	13	60%	66%
Total	4,088	593	47%	48%

[1]Expanded study.

[2]Limited study.

[3]Dot-Com study.

Source: John D. Emory, Sr., F.R. Dengel III, and John D. Emory, Jr., "Expanded Study of the Value of Marketability as Illustrated in Initial Public Offerings of Common Stock," *Business Valuation Review* (December 2001).

Although these discounts seem slightly higher than those of the restricted stock studies, don't jump for joy yet. There are several thoughts that should enter your mind. Were many of the purchases that took place before the IPO (you know—make sure that Uncle Harry, Aunt Millie, and Cousin Gerry all end up with stock before the IPO) truly at arm's length? Furthermore, if the purchaser was aware of the IPO, he or she would also realize that there would soon be liquidity and, because of the new infusion of capital that would be coming into the company, the IPO price might be higher than it would have been had the company not gone public. All of these factors could have affected the IPO price, as well as the price that the purchaser was willing to pay for the shares. Therefore, these discounts may be overstated.

A similar private, unpublished study has been performed by Willamette Management Associates. Pratt explains the differences between the Baird studies and the Willamette studies and emphasizes that one of the main differences is that Willamette tried to identify only those transactions that were at arm's length.[21] Willamette also attempted to adjust the data for changes in market conditions. The median discounts in the Willamette studies were considerably higher than the others, ranging from 31.8 percent to 73.1 percent. Their results are in the data presented in Exhibit 11.8.

EXHIBIT 11.8
Summary of Discounts for Private-Transaction P/E Multiples Compared to Public-Offering P/E Multiples Adjusted for Changes in Industry P/E Multiples

Time Period	*Number of Companies Analyzed*	*Number of Transactions Analyzed*	*Standard Mean Discount*	*Trimmed Mean Discount**	*Median Discount*	*Standard Deviation*
1975–78	17	31	34.0%	43.4%	52.5%	58.6%
1979	9	17	55.6%	56.8%	62.7%	30.2%
1980–82	58	113	48.0%	51.9%	56.5%	29.8%
1983	85	214	50.1%	55.2%	60.7%	34.7%
1984	20	33	43.2%	52.9%	73.1%	63.9%
1985	18	25	41.3%	47.3%	42.6%	43.5%
1986	47	74	38.5%	44.7%	47.4%	44.2%
1987	25	40	36.9%	44.9%	43.8%	49.9%
1988	13	19	41.5%	42.5%	51.8%	29.5%
1989	9	19	47.3%	46.9%	50.3%	18.6%
1990	17	23	30.5%	33.0%	48.5%	42.7%
1991	27	34	24.2%	28.9%	31.8%	37.7%
1992	36	75	41.9%	47.0%	51.7%	42.6%
1993	51	110	46.9%	49.9%	53.3%	33.9%
1994	31	48	31.9%	38.4%	42.0%	49.6%
1995	42	66	32.2%	47.4%	58.7%	76.4%

*Excludes the highest and lowest deciles of indicated discounts.

Source: Willamette Management Associates, as appearing in Shannon P. Pratt, Robert E. Reilly, and Robert P. Schweihs, *Valuing a Business*, 4th ed. (New York, McGraw-Hill, 2000), 410. Reproduced with permission of The McGraw-Hill Companies.

[21]See *Valuing a Business*, 408.

In *Valuing a Business*, the authors respond to several of the criticisms that they have heard over the years regarding the use of their IPO studies. They state the following:

Criticisms of Willamette Management Associates Study

Over the years that Willamette Management Associates has used the pre-IPO study in support of the estimation of the lack of marketability discount, the work has been the subject of certain criticisms. In the following discussion, we will attempt to respond to some of these criticisms.

1. *The results are impossible to verify because Willamette Management Associates will not provide the underlying data or calculation*. The analyses are performed in response to individual client situations at great expense and are proprietary. However, (1) they are based entirely on publicly available data, and (2) all the calculations can be replicated when needed, as the methodology is set forth in detail in several books and articles published by Willamette Management Associates professional staff.
2. *There is a self-selection bias in the determination of "qualifying transactions," resulting in an overestimation of the discount for lack of marketability by excluding "troubled" companies*. The Willamette Management Associates study excludes, by definition, companies that fail, or fail to go public. This is obvious because only companies that go public create a benchmark of liquidity for minority ownership interest shares. Conversely, companies that do not go public are useless for the purpose of deriving a marketable stock price. In order to estimate the lack of marketability discount, one should have a benchmark for comparison (i.e., a marketable price to compare with the nonmarketable price).

   The fact that the Willamette Management Associates study includes only "successful" companies may actually bias the lack of marketability discount downward. One would expect a "troubled" company to be less liquid than a "successful" company, with fewer options for liquidity resulting in a greater lack of marketability discount.

   An argument has been made that the less successful company may trade at a price below the price realized in an earlier transaction (presumably resulting in a premium, or negative lack of marketability discount). This may be true at first glance. However, since we adjust the pricing for changes in the price/earnings multiple, the resulting lack of marketability discount is more reliable. In other words, the exclusion of "troubled" companies, while necessary and logical, does not necessarily lead to an overestimation of the lack of marketability discount.
3. *Many of the transactions are not arm's-length transactions*. A comprehensive effort is made to eliminate non–arm's-length transactions. Each of the transactions included in the database has also passed the scrutiny of the SEC. Although the level of effort we put forth to verify the validity of the arm's-length nature of the pre-IPO transaction is subject to challenge, the number of non–arm's-length transactions that may arguably have been included would not skew the results.[22]

Clearly, the authors seem to respond with an argument that makes sense. Just be careful. Whenever you rely on someone else's work, you should try to understand the underlying data. If other articles are published, for example, try to get them. It will not hurt when you have to defend your position.

Another consideration in determining a DLOM is the cost of flotation of a public offering. These costs are generally significant and will frequently include payments to attorneys, accountants, and investment bankers. The costs associated with smaller offerings can be as much as 25 percent to 30 percent of a small company's equity, but these costs will probably be much less applicable to the small and medium-sized companies that are appraised, since many of these companies, because of their financial condition (among other reasons), could not go public. Exhibit 11.9 contains some older information that may still be useful to you in this regard. On occasion, we reference it in our reports.

[22]Shannon P. Pratt, Robert E. Reilly, and Robert P. Schweihs, *Valuing a Business*, 4th ed. (New York, McGraw-Hill, 2000), 410. Reproduced with permission of The McGraw-Hill Companies.

EXHIBIT 11.9
Costs of Flotation

The methods of liquidating an entire company are to execute an IPO of the stock or to sell the stock in a private transaction. There are several costs associated with executing an IPO, which include:

1. Auditing and accounting fees, to provide potential buyers or underwriters with the financial information and assurances they demand.
2. Legal costs, at a minimum to draft all of the necessary documents, and often to clear away potential perceived contingent liabilities and/or to negotiate warranties.
3. Administrative costs on the part of management to deal with the accountants, lawyers, potential buyers, and/or their representatives.
4. Transaction and brokerage costs, if a business broker, investment banker, or other transactional intermediary is involved.

One of the most comprehensive studies on the costs of public flotation was published by the SEC in December 1974. It covered 1,599 initial public offerings. The breakdown of the study is presented in the following table.

SEC Study on the Costs of Flotation

Size of Issue (Millions)	*Number*	*Compensation (Percent of Gross Proceeds)*	*Other Expense (Percent of Gross Proceeds)*
Under 0.5	43	13.24%	10.35%
0.5–0.99	227	12.48%	8.26%
1.0–1.99	271	10.50%	5.87%
2.0–4.99	450	8.19%	3.71%
5.0–9.99	287	6.70%	2.03%
10.0–19.99	170	5.52%	1.11%
20.0–49.99	109	4.41%	0.62%
50.0–99.99	30	3.94%	0.31%
100.0–499.99	12	3.03%	0.16%
Over 500.00	0	—	—
Total/averages	**1,599**	**8.41%**	**4.02%**

Source: *Cost of Flotation of Registered Issues 1971–72* (Washington, D.C.: Securities and Exchange Commission, 1974), 9.

The data shows a significant decline in the level of expense relative to the size of the issue as the size of the issue increases. Offerings under $1 million can have expenses as high as 23.6 percent of the offering. In contrast, offerings over $500 million on average have expenses equal to only 3.2 percent of the offering.

A second study on the subject was published by Jay R. Ritter in 1987. The results are presented in the following table.

Direct Expenses of Going Public as a Percentage of Gross Proceeds (1977–1982)

Gross Proceeds[1] ($)	*Number of Offers*	*Underwriting Discount[2] (%)*	*Other Expenses[3] (%)*	*Total Cash Expenses (%)*
		Firm Commitment Offers		
100,000–1,999,999	68	9.84%	9.64%	19.48%
2,000,000–3,999,999	165	9.83%	7.60%	17.43%
4,000,000–5,999,999	133	9.10%	5.67%	14.77%
6,000,000–9,999,999	122	8.03%	4.31%	12.34%
10,000,000–120,174,195	176	7.24%	2.10%	9.34%
All offers	664	8.67%	5.36%	14.03%

EXHIBIT 11.9 *(Continued)*

Gross Proceeds[1] *($)*	*Number of Offers*	*Underwriting Discount*[2] *(%)*	*Other Expenses*[3] *(%)*	*Total Cash Expenses (%)*
Best-Efforts Offers				
100,000–1,999,999	175	10.63%	9.52%	20.15%
2,000,000–3,999,999	146	10.00%	6.21%	16.21%
4,000,000–5,999,999	23	9.86%	3.71%	13.57%
6,000,000–9,999,999	15	9.80%	3.42%	13.22%
10,000,000–120,174,195	5	8.03%	2.40%	10.43%
All offers	364	10.26%	7.48%	17.74%

[1]Gross proceeds categories are nominal; no price level adjustments have been made.

[2]The underwriting discount is the commission paid by the issuing firm; this is listed on the front page of the firm's prospectus.

[3]The "other expenses" figure comprises accountable and nonaccountable fees of the underwriters, cash expenses of the issuing firm for legal, printing, and auditing fees, and other out-of-pocket costs. These other expenses are described in footnotes on the front page of the issuing firm's prospectus. None of the expense categories includes the value of warrants granted to the underwriter, a practice that is common with best-efforts offers.

Source: Reprinted from *Journal of Financial Economics* (January 1987), Jay R. Ritter, "The Costs of Going Public," p. 272, Copyright 1987, with permission from Elsevier Science.

This study again shows a relationship between the size of the offering and the expenses as a percentage of the offering. It is clear that smaller deals incur significantly larger costs as a percentage of gross proceeds.

As far back as 1977, in Revenue Ruling 77-287, the IRS recognized the effectiveness of restricted stock study data in providing useful information on the quantification of DLOMs. The Baird and Willamette studies of transactions in closely held stocks did not exist at that time, but the IRS and the courts have been receptive to this data for assisting in quantifying DLOMs.

In Chapter 18, I discuss one of the Tax Court cases that I believe can serve as a good learning tool for all appraisers (even me!). This case is *Bernard Mandelbaum et al. v. Commissioner.*[23] Despite the appraiser's research and logical argument, the court in *Mandelbaum* did not allow the 70 percent and 75 percent discounts deducted in the appraisal.[24] The court, however, was extremely methodical in its opinion, and although the decision has its faults, it can be used as a guide for appraisers, particularly in the tax arena. For more information regarding published court decisions, I recommend *Federal Tax Valuation Digest*[25] and *Marketability Discounts in the Courts, 1991–1996.*[26] While the former publication strictly addresses court cases involving tax matters, the latter publication addresses all types of court cases, including family dissolution and shareholder disputes.

The IPO studies and court cases are proof that discounts that tend to be larger than those quoted from the restricted stock studies can be justified. Think about the appropriateness of the discounts that can be applicable to interests in companies that are not large enough to go public! One of the best explanations of why a DLOM varies from case to case was written by Robert E. Moroney in an article titled "Why 25%

[23]*Bernard Mandelbaum et al. v. Commissioner*, T.C. Memo. 1995-255.

[24]Ibid.

[25]Edited by Idelle A. Howitt (New York: Warren, Gorham & Lamont, annual).

[26]Written by Janet Hamilton as a supplement to Shannon Pratt's *Business Valuation Update* (March 1997).

Discount for Nonmarketability in One Valuation, 100% in Another?"[27] In this article, Moroney points out 11 factors that should be considered in the application of a DLOM:

1. *High dividend yield*. Companies that pay dividends tend to be more marketable than companies that do not.
2. *Bright growth prospects*. Companies that have bright growth prospects are easier to sell than companies that do not. This makes them more marketable.
3. *Swing value*. If a block of stock has swing value, it may be more marketable than the typical small block of stock. This swing value could include a premium. This can be emphasized when a 2 percent interest exists with two 49 percent interests. The 2 percent interest can be worth quite a bit to either 49 percent interest if it will give that interest control of the company.
4. *Restrictions on transfer*. Restrictions on transfer make the stocks less marketable because of the difficulty in selling them.
5. *Buy-sell agreements*. Buy-sell agreements can go either way. The agreement can create a market for the stock, making it more marketable, or the agreement can restrict the sale, making it less marketable.
6. *Stock's quality grade*. The better the quality of the stock, the more marketable it will be. This can be evidenced by comparing the subject company with others for supporting strengths and weaknesses.
7. *Controlling shareholder's honesty*. The integrity of the controlling shareholder can make a big difference with regard to the ability to sell a partial interest in a company. If the controlling shareholder tends to deal with the other shareholders honestly, the other interests in that company tend to be more marketable.
8. *Controlling shareholder's friendliness*. Similar to the degree of that shareholder's honesty, the manner in which he or she deals with others can make the stock more marketable.
9. *Prospects for the corporation*. If a corporation has good prospects for the future, it will generally be more marketable.
10. *Prospects for the industry*. A company that is in an industry with good prospects will also generally be more marketable.
11. *Mood of the investing public*. When the investing public are bullish, they are more readily willing to make an investment. This can increase the stock's marketability.

A discussion of how each of these factors relates to the appraisal subject is a good way to support the size of the discount. Obviously, these items can be used to determine if more or less of a discount is warranted, but they will not help you quantify the discount in terms of percentages.

Using all of the information discussed in this chapter should get you to a reasonable DLOM. The answer must make sense. Controlling interests will almost always be easier to sell than minority interests. As a matter of fact, most minority interests in closely held companies cannot be sold. In reality, this makes them virtually worthless. A well-thought-out discussion of all factors to be considered can help support large discounts.

There have been many writings about discounts for lack of marketability for controlling interests, but the appraisal profession does not have a definitive recommendation as to whether there should be one, and if so, how big it should be. In preparation for a recent presentation that I gave at The Institute of Business

[27] *Taxes* (May 1977), 316–320.

Appraisers' National Conference, I asked my staff to summarize the literature regarding the topic of DLOMs for controlling interests. This is what I got:

Discounts for Lack of Marketability—Should They Be Applied to Controlling Interests?

This controversy has been going on for about 10 years. Chris Mercer appears to be the lone holdout against applying a discount for lack of marketability to controlling interests in privately held companies.

The controversy may have begun with Eric Nath's article in *Business Valuation Review (BVR)* in June 1990. In this article, Nath says:

1. Premiums are paid for takeover candidates because:
   a. A company may be undervalued by the market because it is mismanaged.
   b. A company may be well run, but undervalued by the market because management does not communicate well with shareholders.
   c. A company may be well run and communicate well with shareholders but have strategic value to the acquirer.
   d. Once in a while, somebody just pays too much for a company.
2. If a public company doesn't meet any of the above requirements, it will not be taken over.
3. If (2) is correct, and a company is not in "play," it has no control premium. Its share price will reflect its takeover value.
4. Therefore, a valuation of a private company based on non-takeover comparatives will be a "majority interest" valuation, not a "minority interest" valuation.
5. Furthermore, use of discount and capitalization rates obtained from market rates of return will result in a "majority interest" valuation, not a "minority interest" valuation.
6. Control premiums should not be applied to majority interest valuations obtained using market data.
7. Values obtained using either publicly traded market comparables or the DCF method can be discounted uniformly for lack of control or liquidity.
8. A discount for lack of liquidity might be considered when valuing a controlling interest to account for the greater difficulty of selling a private company versus a public company.

It is this last point that generated the ongoing controversy.

Chris Mercer answers (*BVR* 12/90) and disagrees. His argument is not particularly persuasive. He says:

1. Nath claims appraisers overvalue companies when they use information from the public markets and therefore must apply discounts for lack of control and/or lack of liquidity/marketability.
2. Either Nath is right, or something else must account for the overvaluation problem.
3. Mercer believes that if a company is overvalued using the market approach, the problem does not lie with market-derived information, but with either an underestimation of the risk profile or an overestimation of the growth potential of a closely held company.

Mercer continues his argument regarding the DLOM for a controlling interest in a private company by saying, "We suspect the market for *entire companies* [his emphasis] is not quite as 'efficient' as Nath suggests. Companies simply do not 'trade' like small minority blocks trade. They are cumbersome to deal with, expensive of time, management resources and out-of-pocket costs. In reality, only a small portion of *all* [his emphasis] companies, whether public or private, trade each year" (p. 124).

In *Valuing Financial Institutions* (Val. Fin. Inst.), Mercer says, "I know of no objective evidence supporting marketability discounts to be applied to controlling interest values" (p. 204). He says the reason companies offered for sale don't sell right away is because they are priced too high, not because they are inherently illiquid or lack marketability.

Mike Bolotsky continues the discussion (*BVR* 9/91) by making an assessment of both "Prevailing Wisdom" and the "Nath Hypotheses," and concludes:

1. There is merit to many of Nath's basic arguments.
2. Nath's most important conclusion is flawed because of its logical framework, not because "prevailing wisdom" is necessarily correct.
3. Prevailing wisdom may not adequately describe the differences between publicly held minority interests, non–publicly held minority interests, and 100% ownership interests.
4. Prevailing wisdom may tend to *overvalue* both 100% ownership interests and non–publicly held minority interests when value premise is FMV. Reasons for this do not imply Nath hypotheses are correct.
5. Additional thinking and research are necessary to:
   a. Finalize a framework that better describes differences in various types of ownership interests.
   b. Determine a more complete list of key variables to explain the value differentials between different ownership interests.
   c. Find market-based sources that more adequately measure the value effect of differences in these key variables.

He reviews the arguments and conclusions of both the Nath hypotheses and the prevailing wisdom and presents an analytical framework for assessing both. He presents four shareholder-level attributes that create value differences between the different types of interests. These are:

1. Ownership rights or the factors that comprise control or lack thereof
2. Liquidity, which he does not define precisely except to discuss the time it might take to unload an investment
3. Information access
4. Information reliability

With respect to information, he wonders how these attributes are accounted for in one DLOM unless the starting point is a hypothetical price of an actively traded share of a company that has no information available and no reliability of any information that might become available. He describes these attributes from the perspective of both sellers and buyers on page 100.

He summarizes the three types of ownership interests in light of the four attributes in a table like the one below:

	Private Co. 100% Control	*Public Minority*	*Private Co. Minority*
Ownership rights	Total	Very limited	Very limited
Liquidity	Limited	Nearly total	Nearly none
Information access	(S): Total	(S): Extensive	(S): Very limited
	(B): Varies	(B): Extensive	(B): Even more limited
Information reliability	(S): Completely	(S): Generally	(S): Little assurance
	(B): Varies	(B): Generally	(B): Even less assurance

(S): Indicates "seller"
(B): Indicates "buyer"

In other words, ownership rights, for example, are total if one owns 100 percent of a private company but very limited with ownership of a minority interest in either a public or private company. The information attributes vary with buyers and sellers, with sellers (owners) of private companies generally having better access and more reliability of information.

Value should reflect these four attributes of ownership. The next table illustrates the changes in the four attributes when going from one premise of value to another. For example, when going from a Public Minority Value to a Private Company with 100 percent Control Value, ownership rights change from very limited rights to total rights and value should increase. The rest of the table should be self-explanatory.

	Going From:	*To:*
	Public Minority Value	*Private Company 100% Control Value*
Value Should:	*For Difference Between:*	
Increase	Very limited ownership rights	Total ownership rights
Decrease	Nearly total liquidity	Limited total liquidity
Increase	Extensive information access	Total information access
Increase	General reliable information	Complete information reliability

	Going From:	*To:*
	Public Minority Value	*Private Minority Value*
Value Should:	*For Difference Between:*	
No adjustment	Very limited ownership rights	Very limited ownership rights
Decrease	Nearly total liquidity	Virtually no liquidity
Decrease	Extensive information access	Very limited information access
Decrease	Generally reliable information	Little information reliability

	Going From:	*To:*
	Private 100% Control Value	*Private Minority Value*
Value Should:	*For Difference Between:*	
Decrease	Total ownership rights	Very limited ownership rights
Decrease	Limited total liquidity	Virtually no liquidity
Decrease	Total information access	Very limited information access
Decrease	Complete information reliability	Little information reliability

All of the criticisms of either the "prevailing wisdom" or the "Nath hypotheses" rely on these four attributes of ownership.

If there is no difference between the ownership attributes in moving from one ownership premise to another, there should be no difference in price, and no discounts or premiums should be necessary.

In essence, he adds another level of complexity. Prevailing wisdom gives us discounts or premiums for minority/control issues and discounts for lack of liquidity/marketability. Bolotsky adds the issue of information access and reliability.

He says (p. 103) that "the closer we get to seller-buyer information parity, the higher the price that will be negotiated. . . . Holding all other company-level and shareholder-level attributes equal, there is an inherent tendency for public company acquisition prices to be higher than similar private company acquisition prices."

Recall Nath said that public minority prices represented control values because no tender offer has been made for these companies. Bolotsky says that the value of the two types of interest would be the same when the net of the differences in the four key shareholder-level attributes is zero.

Bolotsky takes the middle of the road by saying that there are a large number of companies for which the control perception of value is higher than the public price, but not enough higher to make a tender offer worthwhile. Most of the public companies would command a modest but positive premium over the public price to derive a 100 percent control value. This value won't be in evidence by many actual transactions because it won't be high enough to induce a sufficient number of public shareholders to sell.

Pratt (*Valuing Small Businesses and Professional Practices*) adds his voice to the controversy for perhaps the first time in the second edition of his book. On page 529, he adds a small note to a chart showing the relationships between the various premiums and discounts. The note says:

> Control shares in a privately held company may also be subject to some discount for lack of marketability, but usually not nearly as much as minority shares.

Chaffee (*BVR* 12/93) says that the main economic factor causing a discount for lack of marketability is the increased risk caused by an inability to quickly and efficiently return the investment to a cash position.

The cost of a put option represents all of the discount to be taken from the marketable price to price the nonmarketable shares.

If an investor holds restricted stock and buys an option to sell (put) those shares at a free market price, the holder has purchased marketability for the shares. The price of the put is the DLOM.

Fowler (*BVR* 12/93), Associate Editor of *BVR*, asks for opinions. He says that for a lot of tiny businesses there will never be sufficient investor interest to take them public. This would imply that a discount for lack of marketability for a controlling interest would be appropriate.

The inability to cash out of an investment is key. It is inappropriate to say that lack of marketability is not a factor when control positions are being valued.

Mercer (*BVR* 6/94) is back. He does not think a DLOM should be applied to controlling interests of private companies.

If a discount is to be applied for lack of liquidity of a controlling interest, it can't be the same discount that is used to move from marketable minority to nonmarketable minority levels of value. A marketability discount for controlling interests is different than a marketability discount for minority interests.

Privately held companies don't trade in the same kind of markets as publicly traded shares. They sometimes take months to trade. This time to trade is incorporated into the price of the company.

Public company data suggests that public companies trade at higher P/Es than private companies. Mercer thinks it's more like *large* companies trade at higher P/Es than *smaller* companies.

A DLOM applied to a controlling interest implies that there is such a thing as a freely traded value of entire companies. These freely tradable controlling interests would trade in a hypothetical market for controlling interests, with investors buying and selling entire companies and achieving liquidity in five days. [*Author's note:* Five days is currently three days.] This is not observable; this market does not exist, thus you can't have a concept of a DLOM for controlling interests in private companies.

This discount would be difficult to quantify.

Taub (*BVR* 9/94): A DLOM for controlling private interests is appropriate because:

1. In a given case, we may have five or six guideline companies covering a range of selling time periods.
2. As time passed, many sellers probably lowered their selling prices. This lowering of price probably can be viewed as indicative of a lack of marketability.
3. There is a risk that the value of a company or market conditions may change adversely between the time a company is put up for sale and it is actually sold.
4. When someone puts his company up for sale, he presumably needs or wants to have cash for it right away. The fact that he is forced to wait constitutes iliquidity.

Summarizing:

When using non–publicly traded guideline company data, the DLOM is already factored in, and it would be incorrect to apply it again.

When reconciling values, the appropriate discounts should be taken on each separate value and then the reconciliation effected.

Abrams (*BVR* 9/94): there is a hierarchy of marketability discounts:

Letter stock has the smallest discount—this is the minimum DLOM.

Control interests in a private firm are less marketable than letter stock because of the high transaction costs of selling a private business and the control shareholder has no guarantee that he can sell his or her business.

Therefore, a control interest in a private firm should contain a DLOM equal to that of letter stock plus additional discounts to cover the transaction costs and uncertainty of sale.

Minority interests in private companies should contain the greatest DLOM.

He offers some formulas for computing these discounts, but they are arbitrary.

His responses to Mercer's arguments:

Argument 1: The time it takes to complete a sale of a private company is factored into the price.

Answer: It is not incorporated into the transaction price without a specific DLOM (uses an example using DCF method). The only place to incorporate the illiquidity of control ownership of a private firm is by explicitly taking a DLOM.

Argument 2: Buyers of companies have different time horizons than typical stock market investors and these are factored into their pricing decisions.

Answer: All equity investments have the same infinite time horizon.

Argument 3: Control shareholder has current cash flow (during the time the company is up for sale); therefore there is no need for a marketability discount.

Answer: There is a difference between access to cash flow and access to the value of the firm. If the owner needs more cash than cash flow permits, he might have to wait some time even to borrow against the value of the business. Prudent investors require a higher return for lack of liquidity. Long-term bondholders do it in the form of a horizon premium; investors in private firms do it in the form of a DLOM.

Peters (*BVR* 9/95) analyzes *Mergerstat Review* data broken down by size and finds that public companies sell for slightly higher P/Es than private companies.

Phillips & Freeman (*BVR* 9/95): Private controlling interests did not sell for less than controlling interests in public companies. Differences in size, industry, and profitability explain much of the difference between the P/E multiples of different companies.

They regressed Enterprise Value on several variables: Cash Flow/Sales, Cap Rate, Size, Industry, and whether or not it was a private company. They found that Net Margin, Cap Rate, Size, and Industry were significant in explaining Enterprise Value at a 5 percent level in the *Mergerstat* data. Securities Data Corp.'s data results were different. Neither study showed that whether or not it was a private company was significant to explain Enterprise Value. They found no evidence that such discounts exist among tested sales of controlling interests.

Pratt (*Val. a Bus.*) on page 350 discusses a DLOM for controlling interests to reflect the time, costs, and risks attendant to achieving a sale of a business. He says that selling a controlling interest in a closely held company is a lengthy, expensive, and uncertain undertaking. He speaks of costs of going public.

Possible bases for a DLOM on a controlling interest are: (1) the price one might get in an IPO, or (2) the price achievable in a private sale of the entire closely held company.

Data indicates that valuation multiples for acquisitions of private companies tend to be less. Pratt cites *Mergerstat* data.

Smaller companies are more risky. Private companies reported in *Mergerstat* are smaller than public companies reported in *Mergerstat*. Pratt believes that public/private explains the lower P/Es more than size. He concludes:

> Empirical data clearly suggest that a valuation discount is appropriate for controlling interests (and, for that matter, 100 percent ownership interests) in closely held businesses. And this lack of marketability discount (or illiquidity discount) applies—although to varying degrees—regardless of whether the subject company is valued by reference to publicly traded guideline companies, consummated guideline acquisitions, or discounted economic income analyses.

Mercer (*Quantifying DLOMs*, Ch. 1) defines marketability and liquidity. The business valuation profession says "cash in three days"; Mercer's definition of DLOM (p. 28):

> Theoretically, the marketability discount is that discount necessary to generate a sufficient increment in return to the [prospective] purchaser of a minority interest of an entity's closely held shares to induce the purchaser to make this particular investment rather than an alternative investment identical in all respects save marketability. Stated alternatively, if predictable and observable returns can be obtained from two investments—one in a marketable stock and the other in a nonmarketable stock—other things being equal, a rational investor will pay somewhat less for the nonmarketable shares than for the freely tradable shares.

(*Quant. DLOM*, Ch. 11): Mercer devotes a chapter to marketability discounts and the controlling interest level of value by reprinting his first article in *BVR* and, in a reprise, says:

> If there is such a thing as a "marketability discount" applicable to controlling interests in companies, it is *not* the same thing as the marketability discount that has been the primary subject of this book.

Mercer has not relented. He sums up his position as follows:

1. The marketability discount applicable to minority interests is clearly different than any "illiquidity discount" or "marketability discount" applicable to controlling interests.
2. These two discounts (if, in fact, the latter exists) are applicable to different valuation bases.
3. By obvious inference, market evidence applicable to minority interests, which comes from publicly traded minority interests, would not be relevant in assessing the magnitude of any "illiquidity discount" or "marketability discount" applicable to controlling interest transactions, which occur in a different market entirely than the public securities markets.

Nath is back (*BVR* 12/97). He tosses out the three levels of value model in favor of a model with two levels of value. This model recognizes two types of sellers in a private company: control sellers and non-control sellers. He eliminates the middle (as–if–freely tradable minority interest) level of value. He determines which buyers would align with these two levels of sellers and explains how valuation would be done:

1. Valuation of the 100 percent control seller's position may be done directly through analysis of the three buyers available to the control owner: the public through an IPO, M&A market buyers, or asset buyers in a liquidation.
2. Valuation of a minority seller's position may be done either directly or indirectly:
   a. Directly—based on prior transactions, capitalizing net income or dividends if there is a reasonable basis for doing so, or through a discounted future benefits model
   b. Indirectly—through valuation of the company as a whole (i.e., the 100 percent control seller's enterprise value), then applying appropriate discounts for lack of control, lack of marketability, lack of liquidity, and possibly other discounts

Using this two-level value model eliminates a lot of the complexity and confusion that is added when the third "as–if–freely tradable" level is included. He concludes:

> It highlights the continuing need to better understand the value of control in a private company setting; we are still nowhere near understanding this issue.

Phillips & Freeman (*BVR* 3/99) looked at *Mergerstat* data and found no difference between the acquisition multiples of public and private companies and no evidence that a marketability discount exists for controlling interests, defined as it is for minority interests.

Do you feel like the Energizer Bunny? This controversy just goes on and on and on and on. If all of these really smart people cannot agree on this stuff, you and I are in trouble!

A Real-World Consideration

Since this book pertains to the valuation of small and medium-sized businesses, let's discuss the real world of DLOMs. The purpose of this discount is to recognize the lack of liquidity of a company's stock or ownership equity. One of the main reasons that smaller companies have difficulty selling is that there are risks associated with them. Risk is supposed to be captured in the discount and capitalization rates or pricing multiples. (Remember that we discussed this in the previous few chapters.) So, if we have a high enough discount rate or low enough multiples, do we really need a DLOM? Maybe!

If valued properly (whatever that means!), smaller companies will generally have risks built into the selling price. If you ask a business broker how long it takes to sell the typical business, the answer rarely is longer than six months. Of course, there are exceptions. However, this shows that a small, closely held company can frequently be sold in a reasonable time period. What is the added holding period worth in terms of lack of liquidity? If the company is profitable, the owner will continue to get a return on his or her investment even during the period in which the owner is trying to sell the company. This would reduce the discount substantially. Conversely, if the company is losing money or has no available cash flow to be distributed to the owner, the period of sale could seem like an eternity. This could justify a larger discount.

What am I trying to say? There is no easy answer to this problem. Each situation will have to be based on the facts and circumstances of that case. The size of the discounts will have to be well thought out and well supported. There are many reasons that a company may take time to sell, but we have to be careful not to double-count when determining the specific company risk premium in the discount or capitalization rates. More often than not, appraisers do not place enough emphasis on many of the risk factors (such as dependence on a key person or reliance on a single customer) and do not adequately provide for these factors in determining the value of the company before discounts. The appraiser also needs to concern himself or herself with the market for the property. If large corporate acquirers are looming out there and the company is in a "hot" industry, a sale may be fast. A quick sale may also take place if the business is one in which the owner is actually buying a job, such as a food delivery route.

Keep one other point in mind. It probably takes longer to complete a sale of an entire publicly traded company than it does to sell a closely held business. Getting regulatory approval takes time. Therefore, comparing the public market to the closely held world may be like comparing apples and oranges.

Small Company Discount

The small company discount is similar to the DLOM. In fact, this discount is the same as the DLOM, except that it is purely size related. The appraiser must again be careful not to double-count when considering this type of discount. Size factors may have already been considered in the selection of multiples or capitalization rates. Data in publications such as *Mergerstat Review* seems to indicate that the acquisition prices for entire private companies tend to be lower than tender offer prices for public companies. One possible explanation for this is that entire private companies tend to be smaller than many of the public companies involved in tender offers.

There are other reasons for a small company discount. Closely held companies do not make as much reliable information available to the willing buyer as public companies do, and this may cause acquirers to view the private company as riskier than its public counterpart. The closely held company may also be less marketable than the public company because of the lack of an institutional following. Another reason for the possible discount is that the majority or single shareholder or owner may have all of his or her investment in one business, and, therefore, he or she has liquidity needs that are very different from those of diversified shareholders in public companies.

Although *Mergerstat Review* documents that the entire private company tends to sell at a lower price than that for tender offers of public companies, it does not indicate whether it took longer to sell the privately held company. This may also be justification for the discount. Most of the *Mergerstat* data results from buyer-initiated transactions. It would be interesting, and probably useful, to know the difference, if any, between published prices of completed transactions in which the seller may have initiated the negotiations and those that were initiated by the buyer. This could help the appraiser understand if the parties' motivations could have affected the transaction price.

Completed transactions in which the buyer initiated the transaction would be applicable for valuations used to establish an estimated sale price for planning or negotiating purposes or to perform an allocation of the purchase price when the transaction has already taken place. Completed transactions in which the seller initiated the transaction would be more applicable for estate and gift tax purposes than for other purposes in which the amount of time and effort required to complete the sale is relevant to the value concluded. The sales of closely held businesses are generally seller initiated since the owners decide to sell their business, and the ultimate sales price already reflects a DLOM. If the business was priced too high, interim reductions in the selling price that would already reflect the DLOM may have taken place during the marketing period. In reality, these reductions may have also corrected the selling price from the seller's "great expectations" to a more reasonable level of market value.

An analysis performed by Raymond Miles and based on data from The Institute of Business Appraisers' (IBA) market database further supports the premise that small companies sell for lower multiples than large companies. Miles included the following table, "Correlation Between Company Size and Price-to-Earnings Multiples," in an article titled "Price/Earnings Ratios and Company Size Data for Small Businesses," published in the September 1992 issue of *Business Valuation Review*:

Correlation Between Company Size and Price-to-Earnings Multiples

Range of Company Size, in Thousands of Dollars	*Mean P/E*
0 to 49	1.66
50 to 99	2.11
100 to 149	2.44
150 to 199	2.74
200 to 249	3.06
250 to 499	3.44
500 to 1,000	4.26

Miles's study of the IBA database indicates that the price–to–annual earnings multiple increases as a company's size increases. Other studies regarding the size of companies in the public marketplace have been published in *Business Valuation Review*; the results are consistent.

Discount From Net Asset Value

A discount from net asset value is commonly applied in the valuation of real estate investment companies, holding companies, and oil and gas interests. This discount is generally appropriate for the valuation of asset-intensive companies and is used to derive a freely traded value. A discount from net asset value is determined by reviewing the prices of the shares of publicly traded guideline companies with respect to their published net asset values. Exhibit 11.10 demonstrates the applicability of a discount from net asset value as it was applied in the valuation of a minority interest in a family limited partnership.

EXHIBIT 11.10
Discount From Net Asset Value—Part of the Minority Discount

The pro rata value of a controlling interest in a limited partnership is said to be worth more than the value of a minority interest, due to the prerogatives of control that generally follow the controlling interest. An investor will generally pay more (a premium) for the rights that are considered to be part of the controlling interest. Valuation professionals recognize these prerogatives of control, and they continue to hold true today. These rights are considered in assessing the size of a control premium. They include:

1. Appoint or change operational management
2. Appoint or change members of the board of directors
3. Determine management compensation and perquisites

EXHIBIT 11.10 *(Continued)*

4. Set operational and strategic policy and change the course of the business
5. Acquire, lease, or liquidate business assets, including plant, property, and equipment
6. Select suppliers, vendors, and subcontractors with whom to do business and award contracts
7. Negotiate and consummate mergers and acquisitions
8. Liquidate, dissolve, sell out, or recapitalize the company
9. Sell or acquire Treasury shares
10. Register the company's equity securities for an initial or secondary public offering
11. Register the company's debt securities for an initial or secondary public offering
12. Declare and pay cash and/or stock dividends
13. Change the articles of incorporation or bylaws
14. Set one's own compensation (and perquisites) and the compensation (and perquisites) of related-party employees
15. Select joint ventures and enter into joint venture and partnership agreements
16. Decide what products and/or services to offer and how to price those products/services
17. Decide what markets and locations to serve, to enter into, and to discontinue serving
18. Decide which customer categories to market to and which not to market to
19. Enter into inbound and outbound license or sharing agreements regarding intellectual properties
20. Block any or all of the above actions[1]

A control premium is the opposite of a lack of control (minority) discount. The control premium is used to determine the control value of a closely held business when its freely traded minority value has been determined. This is generally the case when the appraiser uses information from the public stock market as the starting point of the valuation. In this case, a limited partnership interest, regardless of how large, does not constitute a controlling interest. Control of the day-to-day management of the Limited Partnership is held by the management committee of the LP. This committee has exclusive authority and power to manage, operate, and control the business of the LP without consent of any partner or assignee. Therefore, a discount for lack of control is appropriate for this appraisal.

A lack of control discount is a reduction in the control value of the appraisal subject that is intended to reflect the fact that a minority owner cannot control the daily activities or policy decisions of an enterprise, thus reducing its value. The size of the discount will depend on the size of the interest being appraised, the amount of control, the owner's ability to liquidate the company, and other items provided in the previous list.

Lack of control discounts can be mathematically determined using control premiums that are measured in the public market. The formula to determine the lack of control discount is as follows:

$$1 - [1 \div (1 + CP)]$$

where CP indicates the control premium.

Data on control premiums is generally not available for closely held businesses, so the appraiser often uses transactions from the public stock market to act as a gauge regarding the amount of premium paid in transactions involving buyouts. This data is tracked by several sources. The most widely used is *Mergerstat Review*, which is published annually by Houlihan, Lokey, Howard and Zukin, an investment banking firm in Los Angeles, California. The publication has reflected implied discounts ranging from 21.6 percent to 30.8 percent from 1980 to 1999.

This data is for transactions of large companies in the public marketplace and is not relevant to a limited partnership that is as small as the Limited Partnership.

There are many factors that might impact the degree of control a partial (minority) owner has over the operations of a company. Whenever the control elements are not available to the ownership interest being valued, the value is reduced accordingly. Table 1 (written for corporations, yet applicable to limited partnership interests) summarizes some of the factors that tend to influence the value of minority shares relative to control shares.

[1]Shannon P. Pratt, Robert E. Reilly, and Robert P. Schweihs, *Valuing a Business*, 4th ed. (New York: McGraw-Hill, 2000), 365–366. Reprinted with permission.

(Continued)

EXHIBIT 11.10 *(Continued)*

TABLE 1

Factors Affecting the Degree of Control

Factors That May Increase a Lack of Control Discount or Control Premium

- The presence of voting stock
- An extreme lack of consideration for the interests of minority shareholders on the part of the Company's management, board of directors, or majority owners

Factors That May Decrease a Lack of Control Discount or Control Premium

- The presence of enough minority interest votes to elect or have meaningful input on electing one or more directors in a company with cumulative voting
- The presence of enough minority votes to block certain actions
- The presence of state statutes granting certain minority stockholder rights

Factors That May Increase or Decrease a Lack of Control Discount or a Control Premium

- The distribution of other shares (e.g., 2 shares when 2 others own 49 shares each are more valuable than 2 shares when 49 others own 2 shares each)

Source: *Guide to Business Valuations* (Practitioners Publishing Company, 1999), 8–18, 803.16.

The net asset value of the LP was used to determine the control value of the entire company. However, to realize this value, an investor would need to be able to gain access to, and liquidate, the underlying assets of the LP. If limited partners were afforded this level of control, limited partnership interests might well be worth a pro rata share of the partnership's net asset value. However, this is not the case.

A 1 percent minority interest is the valuation subject; however, the agreement specifically vests all decision making solely in the management committee. The basis for lack of control adjustments for limited partnership interests arises from a range of factors, which include the following:

- Limited partners generally cannot control the day-to-day management or operation of the LP.
- Limited partners generally cannot control the amount or timing of income distributions to partners.
- Limited partners do not have specific claims on the underlying assets of the LP, and they usually cannot compel the dissolution of a partnership or the liquidation of its underlying assets.
- It is usually very difficult for limited partners to remove management.
- It is usually very difficult for limited partners to amend a partnership agreement.

The net asset value method develops a freely traded control value of the LP's net assets of $2,806,221.56 on January 2, 2001, and does not, therefore, provide a meaningful indication of value for a minority interest in the LP. A minority interest discount is appropriate here because an interest in the LP represents an indirect ownership interest in the underlying assets held by the LP partners.

One approach to determining an appropriate minority interest discount is to compare the LP interest under appraisal to published control premium studies. This can be accomplished using publications such as *Mergerstat Review*, cited previously.

As an additional method of estimating the appropriate minority interest discount for the Limited Partnership, we drew a parallel of the LP portfolio to closed-end mutual funds (CEFs). Hundreds of closed-end funds are available for numerous specialized investment options. Prices paid for publicly traded shares in a CEF represent minority interests in fully marketable securities. Therefore, if the net asset value of a CEF can be determined and compared with the freely traded price of the fund, it can be determined when and under what conditions the market affords a discount (or premium) to the net asset value of a minority interest.

Unlike open-end mutual funds, CEFs issue a fixed number of shares. Therefore, investors must buy shares from other investors, not the fund itself. These CEFs mirror the motivations of buyers and sellers and offer empirical evidence for determination of the appropriate magnitude of the minority interest discount to be applied.

The Limited Partnership has a portfolio mixture of equity mutual funds, equities, municipal bonds, and municipal bond funds. To help assess the appropriate discount, we researched general equity funds, specialized equity funds, and national municipal funds appearing in the *Wall Street Journal* on January 2, 2001. The data on these funds is dated December 29, 2000, and is presented in Tables 2, 3, and 4.

EXHIBIT 11.10 ***(Continued)***

TABLE 2

General Equity Funds

Fund Name	*NAV*	*Market Price*	*Prem/Disc*
Adams Express (ADX)	23.71	21.00	–11.4
Alliance All-Mkt (AMO)	29.57	31.31	5.9
Avalon Capital (MIST)	18.79	18.13	–3.5
Bergstrom Cap (BEM)	226.55	224.00	–1.1
Blue Chip Value Fd (BLU)	8.17	7.56	–7.6
Boulder Tot Rtn (BTF)	15.94	12.69	–20.4
Central Secs (CET)	32.94	28.25	–14.2
Engex (EGX)	18.36	20.00	8.9
Equus II (EQS)	15.49	8.81	–43.1
Gabelli Equity Tr (GAB)	10.90	11.44	5.0
General American (GAM)	39.94	36.00	–9.9
Librty AllStr Eq (USA)	13.63	12.38	–9.2
Librty AllStr Gr (ASG)	10.87	9.44	–13.2
MFS Special Value (MFV)	10.63	14.00	31.7
Morgan FunShares (MFUN)	8.19	7.00	–14.5
Morgan Gr Sm Cap (MGC)	13.40	11.75	–12.3
NAIC Growth (GRF)	12.05	11.00	–8.7
Royce Focus Trust (FUND)	6.77	5.69	–16.0
Royce Micro-Cap Tr (OTCM)	10.14	8.63	–14.9
Royce Value Trust (RVT)	16.56	14.44	–12.8
Salomon Brothers (SBF)	16.27	16.25	–0.1
Source Capital (SOR)	48.61	52.69	8.4
Tri-Continental (TY)	25.87	21.19	–18.1
Zweig (ZF)	10.32	9.81	–4.9
Average premium/discount			**–7.3**
Median premium/discount			**–9.6**

TABLE 3

Specialized Equity Funds

Fund Name	*NAV*	*Market Price*	*Prem/Disc*
ASA Limited (ASA)	20.11	15.31	–23.9
C&S Realty Inc (RIF)	7.52	6.94	–7.7
Centrl Fd Canada (CEF)	3.52	3.19	–9.5
Cohen&Steers TotRet (RFI)	12.34	11.88	–3.7
Duff&Ph Util Inc (DNP)	10.50	10.50	0.0
First Financial (FF)	11.84	11.84	–17.7
Gabelli Gl MltiMed (GGT)	12.21	12.21	–15.6
Gabelli Utility (GUT)	8.21	8.21	6.6

(Continued)

EXHIBIT 11.10 *(Continued)*

Fund Name	*NAV*	*Market Price*	*Prem/Disc*
H&Q Health Inv (HQH)	34.00	34.00	–27.9
H&Q Life Sci Inv (HQL)	28.88	28.88	–24.9
INVESCO GloblHlth (GHS)	19.18	19.18	–9.1
J Han Bank (BTO)	9.93	9.93	–10.6
LCM Internet Gro (FND)	5.91	5.91	–13.2
Petroleum & Res (PEO)	32.69	32.69	–16.5
SthEastrn Thrift (STBF)	16.58	13.69	–17.4
Tuxis Corp (TUX)	13.29	11.50	–13.5
meVC DFJ Fd I (MVC)	18.59	12.25	–34.1
Average premium/discount			**–14.0**
Median premium/discount			**–13.5**

TABLE 4

National Muni Bond Funds

Fund Name	*NAV*	*Market Price*	*Prem/Disc*
ACM Muni Sec Incm (AMU)	11.79	13.00	10.3
Amer Muni Income (XAA)	14.37	12.50	–13.0
Amer Muni Tm II (BXT)	10.79	10.44	–3.2
Amer Muni Tm III (CXT)	10.96	10.44	–4.7
Amer Muni Tm Tr (AXT)	10.39	10.25	–1.4
Apex Muni Fd (APX)	9.26	8.00	–13.6
BlckRk Ins 2008 (BRM)	16.62	14.88	–10.5
BlckRk Ins Muni (BMT)	10.85	10.44	–3.8
BlckRk Inv Q Mun (BKN)	14.75	12.94	–12.3
BlckRk Muni Tgt (BMN)	10.67	9.94	–6.8
BlckRk Str Muni (BSD)	14.75	13.69	–7.2
Colonial Hi Inc (CXE)	7.02	6.19	–11.8
Colonial Ins Mun (CFX)	15.22	13.00	–14.6
Colonial Inv Gr (CXH)	11.05	9.41	–14.9
Colonial Mu Inc (CMU)	6.15	5.31	–13.7
Dreyfus Income (DMF)	9.18	8.00	–12.9
Dreyfus St Munis (LEO)	9.57	8.63	–9.8
Dreyfus Str Muni (DSM)	8.76	8.50	–3.0
Duff&Ph Util TF (DTF)	16.18	13.22	–18.3
EV Muni Inc Tr (EVN)	12.59	12.00	–4.7
Ins Muni Income (PIF)	15.16	12.81	–15.5
Inv Grd Muni Inc (PPM)	16.02	14.31	–10.7
Kemper Muni Inc (KTF)	11.66	10.44	–10.5
Kemper Strat Mun (KSM)	11.66	11.19	–4.0

EXHIBIT 11.10 ***(Continued)***

Fund Name	*NAV*	*Market Price*	*Prem/Disc*
MFS Muni Inco (MFM)	7.75	7.31	–5.7
MSDW Ins Bd (IMB)	15.23	13.56	–11.0
MSDW Ins Mun Inc (IIM)	14.99	13.38	–10.7
MSDW Ins Sec (IMS)	15.56	14.13	–9.2
MSDW Ins Tr (IMT)	15.33	15.19	–0.9
MSDW Muni Inc (TFA)	9.99	9.75	–2.4
MSDW Muni Inc II (TFB)	10.00	9.75	–2.5
MSDW Muni Inc III (TFC)	9.81	9.56	–2.6
MSDW Muni Op (OIA)	8.03	8.06	0.4
MSDW Muni Op II (OIB)	8.48	7.44	–12.3
MSDW Muni Op III (OIC)	9.45	8.50	–10.1
MSDW Muni Prem (PIA)	9.97	8.63	–13.4
MSDW Qual Inc (IQI)	15.50	14.06	–9.3
MSDW Qual Inv (IQT)	15.05	14.00	–7.0
MSDW Qual Sec (IQM)	14.82	12.88	–13.1
Managed Munis (MMU)	11.88	9.94	–16.3
Managed Munis 2 (MTU)	11.73	9.94	–15.3
MnHldgs Fd (MHD)	14.03	11.88	–15.3
MnHldgs Fd II (MUH)	12.83	11.50	–10.4
MunHldgsIn (MUS)	13.69	11.56	–15.6
MunHldgsIn II (MUE)	13.64	11.38	–16.7
Muni Partners (MNP)	14.25	12.06	–15.4
Muni Partners II (MPT)	13.94	12.00	–13.9
MuniAssets Fd (MUA)	12.80	12.44	–2.8
MuniEnhancedFd (MEN)	11.35	10.31	–9.2
MuniInsured (MIF)	9.64	8.38	–13.1
MuniVest Fd (MVF)	9.42	8.50	–9.8
MuniVest Fd II (MVT)	13.90	12.31	–11.4
MuniYield Fd (MYD)	13.20	13.13	–0.5
MuniYield Ins Fd (MYI)	14.84	13.69	–7.8
MuniYieldQlty Fd (MQY)	14.80	12.81	–13.4
MuniYieldQlty Fd II (MQT)	12.76	11.38	–10.8
Municipal Adv (MAF)	14.36	12.13	–15.5
Municipal High (MHF)	8.78	8.38	–4.6
Nuveen Div Advtg (NAD)	14.29	13.94	–2.5
Nuveen Ins Opp (NIO)	15.26	13.56	–11.1
Nuveen Ins Pr 2 (NPX)	13.56	12.00	–11.5
Nuveen Ins Qual (NQI)	15.17	13.75	–9.4
Nuveen Inv Qual (NQM)	15.34	13.44	–12.4
Nuveen Muni Adv (NMA)	15.13	13.25	–12.4

(Continued)

EXHIBIT 11.10 ***(Continued)***

Fund Name	*NAV*	*Market Price*	*Prem/Disc*
Nuveen Muni Inc (NMI)	11.12	11.69	5.1
Nuveen Muni Mkt (NMO)	15.00	13.50	–10.0
Nuveen Muni Val (NUV)	9.97	8.75	–12.2
Nuveen Perf Plus (NPP)	15.06	13.19	–12.4
Nuveen Pr (NPI)	14.85	12.94	–12.9
Nuveen Pr 2 (NPM)	15.12	13.63	–9.9
Nuveen Pr 4 (NPT)	13.94	13.00	–6.7
Nuveen Pr Ins (NIF)	15.17	14.19	–6.5
Nuveen Pr Mun (NPF)	14.95	14.19	–5.1
Nuveen Qual (NQU)	15.01	13.75	–8.4
Nuveen Sel Mat (NIM)	11.37	10.50	–7.7
Nuveen Sel Qual (NQS)	15.02	13.50	–10.1
Nuveen Sel TF (NXP)	14.98	14.75	–1.5
Nuveen Sel TF 2 (NXQ)	14.81	14.00	–5.5
Nuveen Sel TF 3 (NXR)	14.46	13.56	–6.2
Putnam Hi Yld (PYM)	8.19	7.69	–6.1
Putnam Inv Gr (PGM)	11.03	10.19	–7.6
Putnam Inv Gr II (PMG)	13.13	11.38	–13.3
Putnam Inv Gr III (PML)	12.70	11.38	–10.4
Putnam Mgd Inc (PMM)	8.49	8.00	–5.8
Putnam Muni Opp (PMO)	13.12	13.00	–0.9
Putnam TxFr Hlth (PMH)	13.51	12.69	–6.1
SB Intmdt Muni (SBI)	10.20	8.81	–13.6
Seligman Quality (SQF)	14.01	11.94	–14.8
Seligman Select (SEL)	11.65	9.88	–15.2
VK Adv Muni (VKA)	16.17	13.38	–17.3
VK Adv Muni II (VKI)	14.13	11.88	–15.9
VK Inv Gr Muni (VIG)	9.81	8.19	–16.4
VK Muni Inc Tr (VMT)	9.67	8.38	–13.3
VK Muni Opp II (VOT)	14.27	12.38	–13.2
VK Muni Opp Tr (VMO)	17.05	14.63	–14.2
VK Muni Trust (VKQ)	15.47	13.06	–15.6
VK Sel Sect (VKL)	13.50	11.31	–16.2
VK Strat Sec (VKS)	14.31	11.81	–17.5
VK Tr Ins Muni (VIM)	16.52	14.25	–13.7
VK Tr Inv Grd (VGM)	17.00	14.16	–16.7
VK Value Muni (VKV)	15.09	12.63	–16.3
Average premium/discount			**–9.8**
Median premium/discount			**–10.7**

The median discounts at which these funds trade from their net asset values are 9.6 percent for general equity funds, 13.5 percent for specialized equity funds, and 10.7 percent for national muni funds. This data can be weighted by the relative amounts of each of these investments in the LP portfolio in order to construct a blended discount. A blended discount will reflect the mixed nature of the Limited Partnership's assets.

EXHIBIT 11.10 *(Continued)*

Table 5 presents the calculation of the blended discount rate.

TABLE 5

Calculation of Blended Discount Rate

Type of Investment	*% of Portfolio*	*Discount From NAV*	*Weighting*
General equities	62.16	–9.6	5.97%
Specialized funds	5.10	–13.5	0.69%
Municipal bonds	26.95	–10.7	2.88%
Cash	5.79	0.0	0.00%
			9.54%

All of the mutual funds listed above are larger and more diversified than the Limited Partnership. They all have professional portfolio managers selecting the investments and have access to sophisticated research and market data that the LP does not have. In addition, according to the agreement, transferred interests in the LP are not partnership interests; they are assignee interests. The difference is that limited partners have voting rights on any partnership issue requiring a vote. Assignee interests, on the other hand, have voting rights only in two limited circumstances that would affect their economic rights. These matters are changes to the agreement regarding liquidation or changes regarding distributions. Therefore, assignee interests have even less control than a limited partnership interest. To reflect this increased lack of control, we have increased the discount by one-third, to 13 percent.

The discount from net asset value may also have applicability in the valuation of smaller, closely held businesses in certain situations. This discount may be applicable when a company is valued as a going concern but the earnings do not support the value of the underlying assets. Liquidation may not necessarily be the highest and best use of the property, since there may be contractual obligations that make liquidation a poor alternative. Exhibit 11.11 contains a section of a valuation report that addresses this issue.

EXHIBIT 11.11

Discount From Net Asset Value—Reconciliation of Values

Throughout this appraisal, several acceptable methods were used to estimate the fair market value of Jackson Engineering. The results were as follows:

Adjusted book value	$352,303
Liquidation value	247,908
Excess earnings	341,532

A willing buyer of Jackson Engineering would be purchasing a group of assets and employment. The business does not generate any excess cash flow that would be available to the buyer. This is further indicated by the $71,000 loan from the stockholder, which has been reclassified as an equity contribution.

Since a return on investment appears to be out of the question, a buyer would be willing to purchase Jackson Engineering based on a discounted net asset value. There are many companies bought and sold in this manner. The reason for a discount to be taken against the value of the net asset value is so that the purchaser is able to obtain a return on investment. Why would someone buy an investment for $10 if he or she would only receive a $10 return? The buyer would be better off putting the money in a savings account and earning a rate of return.

(Continued)

EXHIBIT 11.11 ***(Continued)***

The discount taken from the net asset value would depend on the risk associated with the assets purchased. Cash obviously has no risk and would therefore only warrant a small discount, enough to provide a return to the buyer. Other assets are more risky. This appraiser has estimated the discount on a line-by-line basis to determine the value of Jackson Engineering to a willing buyer. The results are as follows:

	Adjusted Book Value (July 16, 1996)	*Market Value Discount*	*Fair Market Value (July 16, 1996)*
Cash	$ 52,407	0%	$ 52,407
Accounts receivable	296,264	25%	222,198
Fixed assets	31,032	25%	23,274
Accounts payable	(11,600)	0%	(11,600)
Payroll taxes payable	(6,865)	0%	(6,865)
Accrued payroll	(8,935)	0%	(8,935)
Net asset value	$ 352,303		$ 270,479

Based on the facts and circumstances of this appraisal and the analysis performed as part of this process, it is my opinion that the fair market value of Jackson Engineering was approximately $270,000 on July 16, 1996.

Key Person Discount

A key person discount is frequently seen in the valuation of a closely held business when the "key" person is no longer going to be part of the business. This is often the case when the valuation is being performed for an estate of which the decedent was the key person in the business. One way to determine the appropriate discount is to review the case law for the size of discounts allowed in the past and try to associate the facts of a particular case with the assignment at hand. Be careful not to let case law drive your valuation.

A better way to handle this discount may be to build the effect of the loss of the key person into the forecast of future operations or to add an additional risk component to the discount rate. If the loss of the key person is a true loss, the business will probably suffer. The amount of the loss will be based on the importance of the key person, and on how long it may take to find a replacement and bring that replacement up to the level where the key person had been.

Before you automatically take a discount for the key person, consider whether the company is the beneficiary of an insurance policy on the the key person's life (assuming the reason for the loss of the key person is death). Life insurance proceeds can act to offset a discount if they provide the company with the required funds to replace the key individual.

Not all owners of businesses are key persons. Do not take a discount unless you have the appropriate support for the loss attributable to that person. This can be illustrated in a case that our firm was involved in several years ago. The executor of an estate hired another appraiser to value a controlling interest in a company that made baked goods. The appraiser took a 20 percent discount due to the loss of the key person. We were subsequently brought into the case by a beneficiary who challenged the valuation. What we found out was that the so-called key person was not so key after all. In fact, this individual was so conservative that the company's growth was being stunted. His children took over the running of the company after his death, and the company started to grow in a way that it had never experienced in the past. (I wonder if the IRS would assess a key person premium?)

Adding a key person discount may also increase the possibility that the client will be audited by the IRS. If the other discounts total 35 percent, you may or may not get the audit notice. However, add an additional 15 percent to the 35 percent already taken, and the 50 percent discount will very conceivably be looked at. That is not to say that you will not get it through the IRS if it is well supported. Just be ready for the audit!

Application of Discounts and Premiums

The proper application of discounts and premiums requires the appraiser to understand their impact. Some discounts and premiums are additive, while others are multiplicative. For example, the application of lack of control discounts and DLOMs is multiplicative, not additive. This can be illustrated as follows. Assume a lack of control discount of 25 percent and a DLOM of 35 percent. If these discounts were additive, the appraiser would add them together and apply a 60 percent discount from the control value. However, the total discount to be taken from the control value is calculated as follows:

$$1 - [(1 - .25)(1 - .35)] = .5125$$

For those of you who, like me, are not into mathematical equations, this same example can be demonstrated as follows:

Value on a control, marketable basis	$100.00
Less lack of control discount (25%)	25.00
Value on a minority, marketable basis	$ 75.00
Less DLOM (35%)	26.25
Value (cumulative discount 51.25%)	$ 48.75

The application of a DLOM and discounts for legal restrictions, environmental restrictions, and litigation discounts may overlap. Therefore, be aware of the possibility of double counting. Small company discounts that relate to the sale of an entire business—as opposed to the DLOM relating the control value to public prices—are mutually exclusive.

The small company discount that is determinable from the *Mergerstat Review* data and other sources may be caused by several factors, including, but not limited to, lack of marketability. The DLOM is exactly what it is meant to be, and to add it to the small company discount when you value an entire closely held company would result in a double counting of the DLOM.

The discount from net asset value and the lack of control discount are mutually exclusive. When a discount from net asset value is applied, a lack of control discount is generally inappropriate. However, the discount from net asset value may apply to the subject company or to the underlying assets. This could result in discounts being applied at both the asset level and the entity level. This is the concept that is being used to value minority interests in family limited partnerships. If the appraisal subject is a minority block of shares in a closely held investment, holding, or asset-intensive company, the discount from net asset value, used to obtain the freely traded value, and the DLOM are both applicable and are always multiplicative.

Other Premiums and Discounts

There will be times when other premiums and discounts will be appropriate. Some of these occasions may involve swing vote premiums, blockage discounts, or litigation uncertainties. A swing vote premium is the increased value that a minority interest may have due to the ability to swing the control in the entity to one of the other shareholders. A 2 percent owner may have a valuable asset if the other shareholders each own 49 percent.

A blockage discount is another type of discount, although it applies only to publicly traded companies. This discount may occur when a large block of stock is placed on the market at one time. The large block hitting the market all at once may cause the price per share to fall in order for all of the shares to be sold. The tax courts have been pretty clear on the point that a blockage discount cannot be taken on closely held shares. Exhibit 11.12 demonstrates the analysis entering into a blockage discount. In this assignment, we were retained to determine whether there should be a blockage discount, and if so, how much it should be.

EXHIBIT 11.12
Blockage Discount

Trugman Valuation Associates Inc. was engaged by the court to establish the fair market value of seven million shares of Wal-Mart Stores, Inc. stock as of November 1, 1995. The purpose of this appraisal is to determine the fair market value of these shares for inclusion in a gift tax return.

Background of the Assignment

On November 1, 1995, a donor gave each of her daughters a gift of 7,000,000 shares of common stock in Wal-Mart Stores, Inc. On that date, Wal-Mart Stores, Inc. was actively traded on the New York Stock Exchange. Its price was as follows:

High/Ask	Low/Bid	Close/Bid	Average
22¼	21⅝	22¼	21.9375

The value of the seven million share block, before discounts, was $153,562,500. Trugman Valuation Associates was hired to determine the value of these shares on November 1,1995, including the applicable blockage discount.

According to Research Institute of America:

> Where stock is actively traded in, and the turnover is substantial enough, it will yield a representative price picture for valuing smaller blocks but furnish no adequate basis for the valuation of abnormally large blocks. In valuing abnormally large blocks, there has been a definite and flowing recognition by the courts, and reluctantly by IRS, of the blockage rule.
>
> The blockage rule attributes to the unit of a large block a lower value than the market value per unit as found for small lots. It must be shown that the existing market is clearly not broad enough to absorb the large block without decline of the price level. This rule is a concession to the obvious fact that sudden unloading of a large quantity of a commodity tends to drive the price down. It has been applied by the courts for estate, gift and income tax purposes.[1]

The issue in this matter is whether or not a discount for blockage is applicable, and if so, what is the appropriate size of the discount?

History of Wal-Mart Stores, Inc.

Wal-Mart Stores began in 1945, when Sam Walton began a franchise Ben Franklin Variety Store in Newport, Arkansas. Sam's brother, James, began a similar venture in Missouri in 1946. These operations continued until 1962, when the operation was incorporated in Delaware under the Wal-Mart Stores, Inc. name. In 1984, the company opened its first three Sam's Clubs, and in 1988, its first Wal-Mart Supercenter.

By the end of 1995, Wal-Mart Stores, Inc. owned and operated 1,995 Wal-Mart Stores, 433 Sam's Clubs, and 239 Wal-Mart Supercenters in the United States. The company also has operations in Mexico, Puerto Rico, Canada, Brazil, Argentina, and Indonesia.

By October 31, 1995, Wal-Mart was expanding the number of locations in which it was operating, as well as increasing the size of many of its locations. The result was an increase in sales, which increased the company's net income as well. Net income for the nine months ended October 31, 1995, was up almost 9 percent over the same figure from a year earlier.

In August 1995, the company introduced a Web site on the World Wide Web; its main purpose is as a marketing tool. At the company's annual meeting in June 1995, management revealed expected revenues in excess of $90 billion dollars. This was not as high as previously expected, but still substantially higher than the year before.[2]

[1] "Basis and Valuation of Property," *Federal Tax Coordinator 2d* (Research Institute of America), P-6233.

[2] "Wal-Mart Still Growing but Not as Explosively; $100B Maybe in 1996," *Women's Wear Daily*, vol. 169, no. 107 (June 5, 1995), 1.

EXHIBIT 11.12 *(Continued)*

In August 1995, retail stocks including Wal-Mart's were considered to be bargains. "Retail stocks have been beaten down to where they are bargains, and should be helped by the recent drop in interest rates. Recommended stocks include Wal-Mart Stores."[3] Mr. Wyatt explains that despite the slump in retail stocks, Wal-Mart Stores' stock price had increased 22.3 percent during 1995 and was expected to continue rising for another year. This type of article in the press helps to generate interest in a stock such as Wal-Mart Stores.

Valuation Calculations

The subject of this valuation is shares in a publicly traded company. Treasury Regulation 20.2031-2(b)(1) states:

> In general, if there is a market for stocks or bonds, on a stock exchange, in an over-the-counter market, or other, the mean between the highest and lowest quoted selling prices on the valuation date is the fair market value per share or bond.

In Section 25.2512-2(3), the regulation states:

> In certain exceptional cases, the size of the block of stock to be valued in relation to the number of shares changing hands in sales may be relevant in determining whether selling prices reflect the fair market value of the block of stock to be valued. If the executor can show that the block of stock to be valued is so large in relation to the actual sales on the existing market that it could not be liquidated in a reasonable time without depressing the market, the price at which the block could be sold as such outside the usual market, as through an underwriter, may be a more accurate indication of value than market quotations.

The theory behind this is that by attempting to sell a large block of stock, one of two things occurs: The supply of the stock goes up by a large percentage and the demand is not there; and/or it takes such a long time to sell the shares that the present value of money received is less than the market value on a given day. Therefore, a discount might be deemed appropriate to compensate for either the depressive effect of "dumping" a large block of shares into the market or for the time value of not having use of the proceeds of the sale at the valuation date.

The stock exchanges denote a block trade as a trade of 10,000 shares or more. A New York Stock Exchange (NYSE) working paper from 1994 explained that 54 percent of the NYSE's volume was from block trades.[4]

A block trade can be executed in two ways.

> A block trade can be sent directly to "downstairs" markets comprising the continuous intra day market and batch markets such as the after-hours crossing sessions at the NYSE. Alternatively, a block trade may first be directed to the "upstairs" market where a brokerage firm (or block broker) facilitates the trading process by locating counterparties to the trade before sending it to the downstairs market. Although downstairs markets offer anonymity and a high degree of immediacy, these characteristics may result in significant adverse selection costs for large trades. By contrast, upstairs intermediation reduces the price impact of a large trade but is associated with additional costs in the form of potential information leakage during the process, lack of immediacy, and higher brokerage fees.[5]

Stock traded on an active market generally represents the price for a small block or blocks of the stock; there is no mechanism for determining the price of a large block. Although a 7,000,000-share block of Wal-Mart represents only a small percentage of the total share holdings, it is a larger number of shares than is traded on an average day.

However, court cases have specifically stated that the value of a block is not determined by what it would bring if dumped as a whole on the market at one time.

> Determining a reasonable period of time "depends on all the facts and circumstances." Periods of up to a year have been found to be reasonable, although the periods may be much shorter if factors such as market volatility and time limitations so dictate.[6]

Some specific examples of determining a reasonable time frame are:

- A blockage discount was allowed for decedent's 159,000 shares when the average weekly shares traded on the NYSE was 3,600 shares (*Estate of Sophia P. Brownell*, T.C. Memo. 1982-632).
- A blockage discount was not allowed for a block of 32,000 shares when average monthly trading was 10,000 shares per month because the total number of shares being appraised was well below one year's total trading volume (*Richard O. Wheeler*, T.C. Memo 1978-208).

[3] John Wyatt, "Discount Days Are Here for Retailers," *Fortune*, vol. 132, no. 3 (August 7, 1995), 260.

[4] Minder Cheng and Ananth Madhavan, "In Search of Liquidity: Block Trades in the Upstairs and Downstairs Markets," NYSE Working Paper 94-02.

[5] Ibid.

[6] *Estate of Dorothy B. Foote v. Commissioner*, T.C. Memo 1999-37.

(Continued)

EXHIBIT 11.12 *(Continued)*

- A blockage discount was disallowed on two blocks of decedent's shares where the size of the block was approximately 1 percent to 2 percent of the total number of shares traded in the year of death. The justification for the discount was that all of the shares would be sold at one time. The court stated:

> In valuing a block of stock, we are not required to assume that the block was dumped on the market at one time on the valuation date. Rather, the inquiry must be directed to the effect upon the market based on the assumption that the block was being fed out into the market during a reasonable period of time (*Estate of Myrtle M. Sawade*, T.C. Memo 1984-626).

The court follows this up by referencing *Bankers Trust Co. v. United States*, which states, "the courts which have considered the blockage issue have concluded that the problem should be treated in terms of whether the market could have absorbed the shares within a reasonable period of time."

Clearly the courts have ruled that the determination of a reasonable period of time is a facts-and-circumstances test.

According to Wal-Mart's July 31,1995, Form 10-Q filed with the Securities and Exchange Commission, Wal-Mart Stores, Inc. had 2,295,757,065 shares of common stock outstanding. The subject block is 0.3 percent of the total outstanding shares.

Trading activity and stock prices for the year prior to the gift are as follows:

Wal-Mart Stores, Inc. Trading Volume

Date	*Volume*	*High/Ask*	*Low/Bid*	*Close/Bid*
11/1/94	1,174,000	23.75	23.375	23.625
11/2/94	2,917,000	24.125	23.50	23.875
11/3/94	3,009,000	23.75	23.375	23.50
11/4/94	3,114,000	24.125	23.50	23.75
11/7/94	1,718,000	24.125	23.50	23.875
11/8/94	1,712,000	24.125	23.75	23.875
11/9/94	4,184,000	24.375	23.875	24
11/10/94	1,924,000	24.50	24	24.125
10/17/95	7,038,000	22.75	22.125	22.75
10/18/95	5,470,000	23	22.50	22.75
10/19/95	4,758,000	22.875	22.375	22.875
10/20/95	6,559,000	23.125	22.625	23
10/23/95	5,230,000	23	22.50	22.625
10/24/95	3,055,000	22.875	22.50	22.50
10/25/95	3,781,000	22.75	22.25	22.50
10/26/95	3,341,000	22.50	21.75	21.875
10/27/95	3,134,000	22.125	21.75	22.125
10/30/95	2,795,000	22.375	21.75	21.875
10/31/95	5,302,000	22.25	21.50	21.625
11/1/95	4,256,000	22.25	21.625	22.25

Data intentionally left out of this exhibit. It was for an entire year in the original report.

Based on this data, the average daily trading volume was 3,167,730 shares, with average ask, bid, and close prices of $24.50, $23.98, and $24.28, respectively.

Over this period, the price traded in a fairly narrow range from $21¼ to $27½, a spread of $6¼, or approximately 30 percent. Over the one year period, the price rose until July 1995 and then declined again. This appeared to be related to a weakness in retail stocks in general, but Wal-Mart's stock price was predicted to rise.

The question becomes: How long would it take to "trickle" 7,000,000 shares into the marketplace, and what effect would this have on the price? The courts have clearly determined that it is unreasonable to base a blockage discount on the expectation that all of the shares would be put on the market at one time.

One of the issues that the court has addressed in determining the applicability of a blockage discount is the size of the block being valued in relation to the total number of shares traded in the year. According to the trading data previously listed, total shares traded in the period November 1, 1994, to 1995 amounted to 804,603,400. A 7,000,000-share block is less than 1 percent of the annual trading volume. This figure in conjunction with prior court cases seems to indicate that a blockage discount would not be applicable.

EXHIBIT 11.12 *(Continued)*

The second issue revolves around large daily trades in the stock itself. The table that follows excerpts certain days' trading activities. As previously mentioned, average daily trading in Wal-Mart Stores stock is approximately 3.2 million shares. The data in this table shows trading activity for those days when the number of shares traded exceeded 5 million shares. There were 20 such days. It should be noted that we were unable to determine if the additional shares traded were in large blocks. Also provided in this table is the closing price for the day prior to the large-trading-volume days with the percentage change in the closing price.

Large-Trading-Volume Days

Date	*Volume*	*High/Ask*	*Low/Bid*	*Close/Bid*	*Prior Closing*	*% Price Change*
11/17/94	6,512,000	23.5	22.50	22.625	23.375	–3.21%
11/18/94	5,870,000	23.125	22.625	22.75	22.625	0.55%
12/9/94	7,512,000	21.625	21.125	21.50	21.375	0.58%
12/16/94	9,485,000	23	22.25	23	22.625	1.66%
2/28/95	5,310,000	24.25	23.625	23.75	23.375	1.60%
3/28/95	5,678,000	25.125	24.375	24.875	24.50	1.53%
3/29/95	6,047,000	25.75	24.875	25.50	24.875	2.51%
5/12/95	6,291,000	25.50	24.25	25.25	24.375	3.59%
6/13/95	6,307,000	26.125	25.625	26.125	25.50	2.45%
6/14/95	5,282,000	26.625	26	26.50	26.125	1.44%
6/16/95	6,667,000	26.50	26.125	26.50	26.25	0.95%
8/30/95	9,504,000	25.375	24.75	25	25.125	–0.50%
9/15/95	5,989,000	25.875	25.50	25.625	25.375	0.99%
10/11/95	5,909,000	23.875	22.8125	23	23.875	–3.66%
10/12/95	6,791,000	23.50	22.875	22.875	23	–0.54%
10/13/95	7,796,000	23.25	22.875	23.125	22.875	1.09%
10/16/95	5,790,000	23.125	22.125	22.50	23.125	–2.70%
10/17/95	7,038,000	22.75	22.125	22.75	22.50	1.11%
10/18/95	5,470,000	23	22.50	22.75	22.75	0.00%
10/20/95	6,559,000	23.125	22.625	23	22.875	0.55%
				Mean % price change		**0.50%**

Several facts can be observed from this data.

1. There is no consistency in the price change size or direction when a larger number of shares are traded.
2. There is an active market for large blocks of stock to be bought and sold.

Overall, when large blocks of Wal-Mart Stores' stock are placed on the market, the average price change is approximately 0.50 percent. This indicates that a block of 7,000,000 shares could be sold within a matter of days (two to three) and the sale of this block would not affect the price. Therefore, in our opinion, a blockage discount would not be applicable.

Conclusion
The fair market value of 7,000,000 shares of Wal-Mart Stores, Inc. as of November 1, 1995, is $153,562,500, and no blockage discount is applicable.

Discounts come in all shapes and sizes. During an estate valuation, our firm applied a discount because of the uncertainty of an ongoing litigation, which made the marketability of the decedent's shares less desirable. Exhibit 11.13 contains a section from one of our reports. The IRS signed off on this valuation. This should serve as further proof that a well-thought-out discussion can assist the appraiser in obtaining larger discounts than those in the published studies. In this instance, the business was owned equally by three family factions. One of the families filed suit against the others to force a buyout of this interest and several others in related entities. At the last minute, a proposed settlement fell apart. During this time, a second family faction decided they would hold the remaining faction hostage by trying to coerce a buyout of their interests as well. This family was anything but close.

Using the uncertainty of litigation in an appraisal of another entity that was related to the subject in Exhibit 11.13, we could not justify a 100 percent discount, but we used the information that we had to quantify the size of the discount in dollars instead of as a percentage. Exhibit 11.14 contains the section of our report dealing with this issue. The examples in Exhibits 11.13 and 11.14 were part of seven valuation reports that were prepared for a decedent's estate tax return. The cumulative discount taken for the decedent's minority interests was 75 percent. When the IRS audited this estate, it began the negotiations by allowing a 45 percent combined discount. This told us that we had a very strong case for our discounts. The case finally settled, allowing a 52 percent combined discount. The only reason that the case settled at this level was that the IRS threatened to open up the 25 real estate and machinery appraisals that were used by us in determining the value of the various business interests. Power is a wonderful leverage tool!

Some appraisers handle these miscellaneous discounts differently. Some adjust income streams, some adjust discount rates or multiples, and some choose to ignore these factors completely. Short of ignoring them completely, there is no definitive method of handling these items. The appraiser should use common sense. The manner in which the appraiser chooses to handle these situations may depend on the purpose and function of the appraisal assignment. In certain types of litigations, such as divorce, certain jurisdictions seem to be against discounts because they feel that the non–business owner spouse is "getting the shaft." In actuality, that spouse will probably receive a windfall if no discounts are provided for. However, use your head. If you know that your jurisdiction is against discounts, build it into the balance of your valuation. However, if you are working on a job that is governed by statute, you must perform your appraisal in accordance with the law. Remember, you are supposed to be giving your objective opinion about the value of the interest being appraised. If you get a good, supportable number, these types of cosmetics may help you advocate your own opinion!

EXHIBIT 11.13
Discount for Uncertainty of Litigation

At April 11, 1993, the date of the decedent's death, the Jones family litigation was still ongoing. Despite a possible settlement in September 1992, a four-year litigation continued to shadow the Jones's entities. A willing buyer would have to consider the risks associated with this litigation, since it was not finalized until August 1993, four months after the decedent's death.

At the date of death, the proposed settlement had fallen apart. A willing buyer of the decedent's one-third interest in the partnership was looking at a best-case scenario, in which the one-third interest would become a one-half interest, with the remaining one-half interest being owned by a "nonfriendly" partner. At the conclusion of the litigation, it became obvious that the defendants were not necessarily on the same side.

Obtaining the additional interest would force the partnership to commit to a payout of $913,772. In addition, the following parcels of real estate, having the following appraised values, would no longer be owned by the partnership:

Smith Township	$1,165,000
Jones, lot 1	8,000
Jones, lot 2	150,000
Brown Township	3,800
Greene	800,000
Total	$2,126,800

The total settlement amount of approximately $3 million is greater than the enterprise value.

EXHIBIT 11.13 (Continued)

The willing buyer would also expend additional legal fees to resolve the issue, since the settlement was not definite. Why would anyone want to obligate himself or herself in that way? No prudent investor would purchase this 33.3 percent interest knowing that the best-case scenario would render the company insolvent. Furthermore, part of the overall settlement included an indemnification relating to environmental liability, which is a serious problem for this entity.

This litigation would render this partnership interest virtually worthless due to the contingencies associated with it. A settlement was able to take place because the other Jones entities involved in the litigation interacted, and other companies or individuals were able to generate available funds without depending on Jones Inc.'s financial success. Therefore, the amount paid in settlement of the litigation was clearly in excess of the fair market value of the decedent's interest in Jones Inc. This appraiser feels that a discount of 100 percent is justified in this instance.

EXHIBIT 11.14
Discount for Uncertainty of Litigation

On April 11, 1993, the Jones family litigation was still ongoing. Despite a possible settlement in September 1992, a four-year litigation continued to shadow the Jones's entities. A willing buyer would have to consider the risks associated with this litigation, since it was not finalized until August 1993, four months after the decedent's death.

At the date of death, the proposed settlement had fallen apart. A willing buyer would have to acquire the decedent's interest subject to the ongoing litigation. The best-case scenario for the willing buyer would be that the September 1992 tentative settlement is reached and 37.5 shares are redeemed for $250,921. This would turn the 33.3 percent interest into a 50 percent interest, with the balance of the stock owned by an "unfriendly" stockholder group.

The company would also be obligated to disburse $250,921 for the settlement plus the final costs of settling the litigation. Therefore, the best-case scenario would require the willing buyer to assume the interest subject to this obligation. Since the effective pro rata obligation of the decedent's interest would be 50 percent of $250,921, or $125,461, an equivalent discount is appropriate.

Conclusion

By now you realize that supporting valuation premiums and discounts is as much fun as going to the dentist. Although there are empirical studies for control premium data and DLOMs, the application of these and other discounts to small and medium-sized businesses or business interests is a very subjective task.

12

Revenue Ruling 59-60

Chapter Goals

In this chapter, I will attempt to review Revenue Ruling 59-60 in more detail than you have seen throughout this book. In fact, it will probably be in more detail than you have ever seen before, especially for newcomers to business valuation. You should also be able to use this chapter as a review of most of the appraisal concepts that we have covered. If you bought the first edition of this book, this chapter will serve as a good refresher for you. Not much has changed; since it ain't broke, why fix it?

Revenue Ruling 59-60

This chapter contains an annotated version of Revenue Ruling 59-60. The revenue ruling appears in italics, and the sections of this ruling that are in bold italic print are intended to emphasize a particular point. The author, not the Internal Revenue Service, has done the boldfacing. This ruling is so important to business valuation that I was tempted to boldface the entire document. (Relax, I didn't!)

Revenue Ruling 59-60 is said to be one of the greatest business valuation treatises ever written. This ruling is quoted more often than any other source in the valuation field. Although the ruling was written to provide guidance on the valuation of closely held stocks for estate and gift tax purposes, the IRS expanded its applicability to income taxes. Because of its wide acceptance, many other authorities have looked to this ruling for guidance in valuing closely held stocks and other types of entities for many reasons other than taxes.

Despite having read this document more than 200 times (it was 100 in the last edition), I continue to find elements that I had not seen before. As we go over the ruling, I will attempt to point out the intent of the ruling and illustrate its compliance with modern appraisal theory. The essence of this chapter will be to determine what this revenue ruling really says.

> ***Section 1. Purpose. The purpose of this Revenue Ruling is to outline and review in general the approach, methods and factors to be considered in valuing shares of the capital stock of closely held corporations*** *for estate tax and gift tax purposes. The methods discussed herein will apply likewise to the valuation of corporate stocks on which market quotations are either unavailable or are of such scarcity that they do not reflect the fair market value.*

Although the main focus of this revenue ruling is the valuation of closely held stocks, Revenue Ruling 59-60 has equal applicability to other types of entities. Whether the valuation subject is a partnership, sole proprietorship, or a limited liability company, the factors discussed in this ruling can generally be applied.

In addition to the fact that this ruling is applicable to other types of entities, Revenue Ruling 65-192 expanded it to include income taxes, estate and gift taxes, and other taxes.

> ***Section 2. Background and Definitions. .01 All valuations must be made in accordance with the applicable provisions of the Internal Revenue Code of 1954 and the Federal Estate Tax and Gift Tax Regulations.*** *Sections 2031(a), 2032, and 2512(a) of the 1954 Code (sections 811 and 1005 of the 1939 Code) require that the property to be included in the gross estate, or made the subject of a gift, shall be taxed on the basis of the* ***value of the property at the time of death of the decedent, the alternate date if so elected, or the date of gift.***

Two important points are made right off the bat. First, any valuation that is going to be performed for tax purposes must follow the provisions of the Internal Revenue Code and Regulations. The next point is that the valuation is date specific. The property is to be valued at the date of death, the alternate valuation date, or the date of the gift. This is consistent with the discussion in the section of Chapter 2 titled "Effective Date(s) of the Valuation."

> *.02 Section 20.2031-1(b) of the Estate Tax Regulations (section 81.10 of the Estate Tax Regulations 105) and section 25.2512-1 of the Gift Tax Regulations (section 86.19 of Gift Tax Regulations 108)* ***define fair market value,*** *in effect,* ***as the price at which the property would change hands between a willing buyer and a willing seller when the former is not under any compulsion to buy and the latter is not under any compulsion to sell, both parties having reasonable knowledge of relevant facts. Court decisions frequently state in addition that the hypothetical buyer and seller are assumed to be able, as well as willing, to trade and to be well informed about the property and concerning the market for such property.***

The definition included in this ruling is one of the most commonly used definitions of fair market value. To make the definition complete, it is important to understand and include the statement about court decisions (the last sentence of the previous quotation).

For a "true" fair market value to be estimated, the following situations must apply:

1. *There must be a willing buyer.* Not only does the buyer have to be willing, but he or she must also be able to make the purchase. It would not matter if I wanted to buy a company such as Microsoft or IBM if I do not have the ability to consummate the deal. (Maybe next year if I sell enough of these books!)
2. *There must be a willing seller.* This concept seems easier than it really is when it comes to smaller businesses. The business owner frequently has certain obligations that may prohibit the sale of the property. For example, imagine a nonassignable lease with 10 years left on it at an above-market rent. This could prevent the willing seller from being able to sell the business, unless the price is lowered substantially so that the willing buyer can pay the higher-than-market rent. This would indicate that the fair market value of the property is reduced due to the unfavorable lease situation.

   Considering a market or income approach, cash flow would be reduced because of the higher rent, resulting in a lower value. This could also make the business less marketable. Using an asset-based approach, the appraiser would end up with a liability for an unfavorable leasehold. Although the willing seller may not want to sell the property at a reduced price, the economic reality is that the business is worth less.
3. *Neither the willing buyer nor the willing seller should be under any compulsion to buy or sell (no duress).* Since fair market value assumes a reasonable period of exposure on the market, the buyer and seller cannot be compelled to consummate a transaction. The seller should be able to wait for the "market" price and not end up with a fire sale situation. The buyer should not be in a position where he or she has to purchase this business. If the buyer had been unemployed for a while and purchasing his or her employment was the only way to keep from running out of money, the temptation would be to overpay for the "opportunity" to get back to work.

4. *Both buyer and seller must be reasonably knowledgeable about the property (including the market for the property).* Fair market value is not achieved if the parties to the transaction do not know what the business is worth compared with similar businesses in the market. Just as buyers are likely to overpay for the business, sellers may, at times, give the business away for too little. This situation should occur only if the buyer or seller fails to call us to do an appraisal.

Although this point is not separately stated, fair market value also assumes a covenant not to compete between the willing buyer and seller. If there were no such covenant, why would anyone purchase a business if the seller could open up next door? This point is somewhat controversial. Many appraisers believe that a covenant not to compete is not included in fair market value, but let's face reality. When a small business is sold, there is frequently a covenant not to compete. However, its value is rarely determined. More often than not, a negotiation takes place to include something for tax purposes, but this is usually taken off the purchase price. It is included in the sales price that we hear when we are told that the business sold.

> *.03* ***Closely held corporations*** *are those corporations the shares of which are* ***owned*** *by a* ***relatively limited number of stockholders.*** *Often the entire stock issue is held by one family.* ***The result of this situation is that little, if any, trading in the shares takes place. There is, therefore, no established market for the stock and such sales as occur at irregular intervals seldom reflect all of the elements of a representative transaction as defined by the term "fair market value."***

In this section of the Revenue Ruling, the IRS concedes that there is no established market for closely held stocks. This admission indicates that fair market value cannot truly be achieved, since there is virtually no market. This concept begins the recognition of the lack of marketability in a closely held company. Revenue Ruling 77-287 addresses the issue of discounts for lack of marketability as it relates to restricted stock. However, if a property cannot be sold due to lack of a market, how can it be worth something other than its value to the current owner? Marketability issues were discussed in great detail in Chapter 11. Revenue Ruling 77-287 is reproduced in Appendix 12.

> ***Section 3. Approach to Valuation*** *.01* ***A determination of fair market value,*** *being a question of fact,* ***will depend upon the circumstances in each case. No formula can be devised*** *that will be generally applicable to the multitude of different valuation issues arising in estate and gift tax cases. Often, an appraiser will find wide differences of opinion as to the fair market value of a particular stock. In resolving such differences, he should maintain a reasonable attitude in recognition of the fact that* ***valuation is not an exact science. A sound valuation will be based upon all the relevant facts, but the elements of common sense, informed judgment, and reasonableness must enter into the process of weighing those facts and determining their aggregate significance.***

Some very important points are raised in this section. First, the circumstances of each case must be considered individually. This means that you cannot treat each valuation the same. This holds true even if the appraisal subject is the same type of business that you have valued previously. No two businesses are truly alike. Consider all of the facts before you come to an opinion.

Another important concept is that no formula can be devised (not even the formula method from Revenue Ruling 68-609) that can be applied to every appraisal. You must consider the facts and circumstances of each assignment to establish which valuation methodologies are appropriate in each situation. Don't rely on a mechanical application.

Now comes one of my favorite parts: Valuation is not an exact science. No kidding! If you can accept this concept, you are on your way to becoming an appraiser. If you are looking for black-and-white, you have come to the wrong place. By now you should recognize that there is no black-and-white, only a million shades of gray.

The ruling points out the importance of using *common sense*, *informed judgment*, and *reasonableness* in performing the assignment. There are no substitutes for these items. Common sense plays a big role in the valuation process because the decisions that are made by an appraiser are often subjective. Since we do not always have the best information to work with, common sense frequently gets us through the assignment.

Along with common sense, informed judgment is important. Since the valuation process is so subjective, the appraiser needs to be well informed to make the various choices that have to be made. Using economic, industry, and company information to analyze risk as it pertains to multiples or to discount and capitalization rates can only assist the appraiser in making an informed judgment.

.02 ***The fair market value of specific shares of stock will vary as general economic conditions change*** *from "normal" to "boom" or "depression," that is,* ***according to the degree of optimism or pessimism with which the investing public regards the future at the required date of appraisal. Uncertainty as to the stability or continuity of the future income from a property decreases its value by increasing the risk of loss of earnings and value in the future.*** *The value of shares of stock of a company with very uncertain future prospects is highly speculative.* ***The appraiser must exercise his judgment as to the degree of risk attaching to the business of the corporation which issued the stock, but that judgment must be related to all of the other factors affecting value.***

Economic analysis is necessary at the valuation date in order to determine how the investing public feels about *the future* income of the property. Uncertainty about *future* income increases risk and affects the value in *the future*. Judgment is related to all factors in the valuation process, not just some. Each analysis that the appraiser performs—whether it is on the economy, the industry, or the finances of the company—cannot be done in a vacuum. All of these items must be considered for the appraiser to assess risk properly. The risk assessment will be used to adjust the multiples derived from guideline companies (comparables) or to adjust discount and capitalization rates.

Risk analysis is discussed in Chapter 5. Multiples are discussed in Chapters 6 and 7. Discount and capitalization rates are discussed in Chapter 10.

.03 ***Valuation of securities is, in essence, a prophesy as to the future and must be based on facts available at the required date of appraisal.*** *As a generalization, the* ***prices of stocks which are traded in volume in a free and active market by informed persons best reflect the consensus of the investing public*** *as to what the future holds for the corporations and industries represented.* ***When a stock is closely held, is traded infrequently, or is traded in an erratic market, some other measure of value must be used.*** *In many instances,* ***the next best measure may be found in the prices at which the stocks of companies engaged in the same or a similar line of business are selling in a free and open market.***

The most important lesson learned in this section of the ruling is that valuation is based on the future (the principle of future benefits is discussed in Chapter 3). Relying on history alone to perform appraisals is clearly wrong. The only time history can be used is if it represents what is expected to happen in the future.

The ruling also points out that the market is the best source of value. Publicly traded stocks are a good consensus on the market, since these stocks are actively traded in a free and open market. However, since this information is not available for closely held businesses, the appraiser should use the actively traded stocks of companies that are in the same or a similar line of business. "Use the market approach" is the message that is being sent. Even if the guideline company method cannot be used with public companies, the market approach should continue to be a viable alternative. See Chapter 6 or 7 for alternative applications of the market approach.

Section 4. Factors to Consider. *.01 It is advisable to emphasize that in the valuation of the stock of closely held corporations or the stock of corporations where market quotations are either lacking or too scarce to be recognized,* ***all available financial data, as well as all relevant factors affecting the fair market value, should be considered. The following factors, although not all-inclusive, are fundamental and require careful analysis in each case:***

a. The nature of the business and the history of the enterprise from its inception.

b. The economic outlook in general and the condition and outlook of the specific industry in particular.

c. The book value of the stock and the financial condition of the business.

d. The earning capacity of the company.

e. The dividend-paying capacity.

f. Whether or not the enterprise has goodwill or other intangible value.

g. Sales of the stock and the size of the block of stock to be valued.

h. The market price of stocks of corporations engaged in the same or a similar line of business having their stocks actively traded in a free and open market, either on an exchange or over-the-counter.

What can I say? Here it is again. By now, you know the importance of each one of these items. If you don't, you may want to reread the first 11 chapters of this book. If you have read business valuation books, the eight factors outlined in Revenue Ruling 59-60 appear over and over again. These items should be self-explanatory. If they are not, I suggest that you start this book again.

.02 The following is a brief discussion of each of the foregoing factors:

(a) The ***history*** *of a corporate enterprise* ***will show its past stability or instability, its growth or lack of growth, the diversity or lack of diversity of its operations, and other facts needed to form an opinion of the degree of risk involved in the business.*** *For an enterprise which changed its form of organization but carried on the same or closely similar operations of its predecessor, the history of the former enterprise should be considered.* ***The detail to be considered should increase with approach to the required date of appraisal, since recent events are of greatest help in predicting the future; but a study of gross and net income, and of dividends covering a long prior period, is highly desirable.*** *The history to be studied should include, but need not be limited to, the nature of the business, its products or services, its operating and investment assets, capital structure, plant facilities, sales records and management, all of which should be considered as of the date of the appraisal, with due regard for recent significant changes.* ***Events of the past that are unlikely to recur in the future should be discounted, since value has a close relation to future expectancy.***

Revenue Ruling 59-60 discusses the fact that the appraiser has to know where the company has been to predict where it is going. History is an important element in any business valuation exercise, since it allows the appraiser to assess items such as growth, business diversification, and the other elements of risk that pertain to the appraisal subject. This information ultimately helps support the multiples, discount rates, and capitalization rates used in the assignment. You will also want to use history as a basis for forecasting future operations, if that is appropriate in the given assignment.

The appraiser should obtain a thorough understanding of the company. This goes far beyond just gathering numbers. You need to understand the evolution of the business, including information regarding the company's product lines, competition, employees, and management, and also a considerable amount of additional information that is gathered in the early part of the assignment. These items are discussed in Chapter 4.

Revenue Ruling 59-60 also indicates that events of the past that are not expected to recur in the future should be disregarded, since the future is more important than the past. These past nonrecurring items will be adjusted during the normalization process. The normalization process is intended to restate the financial information provided by the company to an economic basis (see Chapter 5).

(b) ***A sound appraisal*** *of a closely held stock* ***must consider current and prospective economic conditions as of the date of appraisal,*** *both* ***in the national economy and in the industry*** *or industries with which the corporation is allied.* ***It is important to know that the company is more or less successful than its competitors in the same industry, or that it is maintaining a stable position with respect to competitors.*** *Equal or even greater significance may attach to the ability of the industry with which the company is allied to compete with other industries.* ***Prospective competition which has not been a factor in prior years should be given careful attention.*** *For example, high profits due to the novelty of its product and the lack of competition often lead to increasing competition.* ***The public's appraisal of the future prospects of competitive industries or of competitors within an industry***

> ***may be indicated by price trends in the markets for commodities and for securities. The loss of the manager of a so-called "one-man" business may have a depressing effect upon the value of the stock of such business,*** *particularly if there is a lack of trained personnel capable of succeeding to the management of the enterprise. In valuing the stock of this type of business, therefore,* ***the effect of the loss of the manager on the future expectancy of the business, and the absence of management-succession potentialities are pertinent factors to be taken into consideration.*** *On the other hand, there may be factors which offset, in whole or in part, the loss of the manager's services. For instance, the nature of the business and of its assets may be such that they will not be impaired by the loss of the manager. Furthermore,* ***the loss may be adequately covered by life insurance, or competent management might be employed on the basis of the consideration paid for the former manager's services.*** *These, or other offsetting factors, if found to exist, should be carefully weighed against the loss of the manager's services in valuing the stock of the enterprise.*

This section of the ruling covers several different topics for consideration. It first tells us to consider current and prospective economic and industry information at the date of the appraisal. To assess economic and industry risk properly, the appraiser must consider the impact of the economy and the industry on the appraisal subject. For example, if the appraisal subject is a building contractor that primarily builds residential housing, and mortgage interest rates at the date of the appraisal are very high but are forecast to go down substantially, a conclusion could be drawn that the current operations, which probably have slowed down considerably because of the high rates, will most likely pick up again in the future with the falling rates. This can affect the forecast of "probable future earnings" and the amount of risk built into your multiples, discount rates, or capitalization rates. Be careful not to double-count by adjusting in both places!

The industry in which the appraisal subject operates is to be considered as well. If the entire computer industry were changing to small personal computers, and the appraisal subject were continuing to build mainframe computers for the same market, there might be a problem with the future sales of the company's products. This would obviously affect the company's value.

The ruling also tells the appraiser to consider the possible impact of competition on the appraisal subject. If you are valuing a company with a product that is highly profitable and extremely "hot," there is a good chance that competition will come into the market, even if it was not there before. If you get the feeling that the situation is too good to be true, it probably is!

The next area covered by the ruling discusses the mood of the investing public. Fair market value comes from the market. You cannot ignore the market if an industry has become so much in favor that investor perception is driving prices up. If investors are willing to pay higher prices for similar types of companies, the appraisal subject may be going along for the ride, if all else is equal.

Finally, this section discusses the impact of the loss of a key person. (The ruling actually refers to a "one-man" business. Ladies, on behalf of the Treasury Department, I apologize. We all know that this is politically incorrect!) The loss of a key person will frequently have an impact on a small company, more so than on a large company that has a management team in place. The loss of a key individual can have an adverse effect on the future operations of any business, but the appraiser must consider whether that individual can be replaced and how much time it would take to replace him or her.

There may be a slight downturn for the business in the short term until a replacement is found, but it may, in fact, be only short-term. The company may be able to find an adequate replacement who, given a reasonable amount of time, could put the company back on track. There may even be life insurance proceeds to protect the company so that adequate funds are available to handle this problem. The ruling is pretty clear on the fact that the appraiser should consider items that offset the loss of the key person, as well as the impact of the loss of the key person.

> *(c)* ***Balance sheets should be obtained, preferably in the form of comparative annual statements for two or more years immediately preceding the date of appraisal,*** *together with a balance sheet at the end of the month preceding that date, if corporate accounting will permit. Any balance sheet descriptions that are not self-explanatory, and*

balance sheet items comprehending diverse assets or liabilities, should be clarified in essential detail by supporting supplemental schedules. ***These statements usually will disclose to the appraiser (1) liquid position (ratio of current assets to current liabilities); (2) gross and net book value of principal classes of fixed assets; (3) working capital; (4) long-term indebtedness; (5) capital structure; and (6) net worth. Consideration also should be given to any assets not essential to the operation of the business, such as investments in securities, real estate, etc.*** *In general, such non-operating assets will command a lower rate of return than do the operating assets, although in exceptional cases the reverse may be true.* ***In computing the book value per share of stock, assets of the investment type should be revalued on the basis of their market price and the book value adjusted accordingly. Comparison of the company's balance sheets*** *over several years* ***may reveal,*** *among other facts, such developments as the* ***acquisition of additional production facilities or subsidiary companies, improvement in financial position, and details as to recapitalizations and other changes in the capital structure of the corporation.*** *If the corporation has more than one class of stock outstanding,* ***the charter or certificate of incorporation should be examined to ascertain the explicit rights and privileges of the various stock issues including: (1) voting powers, (2) preference as to dividends, and (3) preference as to assets in the event of liquidation.***

Here, the ruling tells the appraiser to obtain at least two years of balance sheets for the appraisal subject so that a comparison can be performed. In practice, most appraisers look for more years of data (generally five or more). The idea is to spot changes in the company's makeup that will help the appraiser understand how the company has arrived at its current financial position. A review of the comparative balance sheets will help the appraiser understand if the company has made any major acquisitions of other companies (look for intangibles) or productive capacity (look for large increases in fixed assets) or other items that may be necessary to forecast future operations.

Particularly if a proper comparison is to be made to guideline companies, changes to the capital structure should also be considered, assuming that the interest has the ability to change it. This may affect the appraiser's decision of whether to value equity or invested capital. Changes in the capital structure may also affect many of the financial ratios that the appraiser uses as analytical tools.

Revenue Ruling 59-60 suggests that the appraiser review differences in the rights of the different classes of stock that may exist, and that the appraiser pay particularly close attention to voting differences, dividend preferences, and rights in liquidation. These items will affect the level of control that is afforded the stockholders. For example, if a stockholder has voting stock as opposed to non-voting stock, there is more of an ability to shape the direction of the company (assuming there is enough stock to do this). Therefore, there may be a larger control premium or, conversely, a smaller discount for lack of control (minority).

(d) ***Detailed profit-and-loss statements should be obtained and considered for a representative period immediately prior to the required date of appraisal, preferably five or more years.*** *Such statements should show (1) gross income by principal items; (2) principal deductions from gross income including major prior items of operating expenses, interest, and other expenses on each item of long-term debt, depreciation and depletion if such deductions are made, officers' salaries, in total if they appear to be reasonable or in detail if they seem to be excessive, contributions (whether or not deductible for tax purposes) that the nature of its business and its community position require the corporation to make, and taxes by principal items, including income and excess profits taxes; (3) net income available for dividends; (4) rates and amounts of dividends paid on each class of stock; (5) remaining amount carried to surplus; and (6) adjustments to, and reconciliation with, surplus as stated on the balance sheet. With profit and loss statements of this character available,* ***the appraiser should be able to separate recurrent from nonrecurrent items of income and expense, to distinguish between operating income and investment income, and to ascertain whether or not any line of business in which the company is engaged is operated consistently at a loss and might be abandoned with benefit to the company.*** *The percentage of earnings retained for business expansion should be noted when dividend-paying capacity is considered.* ***Potential future income is a major factor in many valuations of closely held stocks, and all information concerning past income which will be helpful in predicting the future should be secured. Prior earnings records usually are the most reliable guide as to the future expectancy, but resort to arbitrary five- or ten-year averages without regard to current trends or future prospects will not produce a realistic valuation.*** *If, for instance, a record of progressively increasing or decreasing net income is found, then greater*

weight may be accorded the most recent years' profits in estimating earning power. It will be helpful, in judging risk and the extent to which a business is a marginal operator, to consider deductions from income and net income in terms of percentage of sales. Major categories of cost and expense to be so analyzed include the consumption of raw materials and supplies in the case of manufacturers, processors, and fabricators; the cost of purchased merchandise in the case of merchants; utility services; insurance; taxes; depletion or depreciation; and interest.

This section of the ruling tells the appraiser to obtain at least five years of income statement data in sufficient detail so that the appraiser can properly understand the data's components. Five years is not automatically the correct number. There will be times when a company's business cycle is longer or shorter, and the appraiser must use judgment to determine the appropriate time period to use for that particular assignment. Adjustments should be made to past earnings (reasonable compensation), if appropriate.

The ruling also tells the appraiser to consider operating and non-operating income and expense items separately. Since most of the valuation methods are designed to produce the value of the operating assets and liabilities, it is logical to remove the non-operating income and expense items from the stream of income that is used.

Potential future income is discussed in the ruling and is said to be of major importance in valuation. This is the entire valuation process! Nobody buys history. The potential future income, whether in the form of dividends, capital appreciation, or a combination of the two, is what the willing buyer is purchasing. History is used to help predict the future. The ruling emphasizes that the appraiser cannot resort to an arbitrary use of history to value a company if it is not reflective of "probable future earnings." Current trends and future prospects *must* be taken into consideration in the valuation process.

(e) Primary consideration should be given to the dividend-paying capacity of the company rather than to dividends actually paid in the past. Recognition must be given to the necessity of retaining a reasonable portion of profits in a company to meet competition. Dividend-paying capacity is a factor that must be considered in an appraisal, but dividends actually paid in the past may not have any relation to dividend-paying capacity. Specifically, the dividends paid by a closely held family company may be measured by the income needs of the stockholders or by their desire to avoid taxes on dividend receipts, instead of by the ability of the company to pay dividends. ***Where an actual or effective controlling interest in a corporation is to be valued, the dividend factor is not a material element, since the payment of such dividends is discretionary with the controlling stockholders.*** *The individual or group in control can substitute salaries and bonuses for dividends, thus reducing net income and understating the dividend-paying capacity of the company. It follows, therefore, that dividends are a less reliable criterion of fair market value than other applicable factors.*

The use of dividend-paying capacity, as opposed to the actual dividends paid for a controlling interest, should be considered in an appraisal, since the controlling shareholders have the ability to control the level of dividends actually disbursed. In fact, most closely held companies do not pay dividends, since they are not tax deductible. More often than not, dividends are paid as additional compensation to create a tax-deductible expense. The dividend-paying capacity will be determined by normalizing the income statement and by using the normalized earnings to derive the net cash flow available to the stockholders. The net cash flow model (discussed in Chapter 9) demonstrates this process.

For business valuations of minority interests, the actual dividends paid are more important than the dividend-paying capacity. Since the minority interest cannot control the level of dividends to be paid, the capacity does not mean as much as the actual dividends paid. There may be some situations in which the minority stockholders have the right to receive dividends despite nonpayment. This situation may lead to an oppressed shareholder action, and therefore, capacity should not be ignored. The appraiser may need to consult with legal counsel in those situations in which dividends are not being paid although there is the capacity to do so.

(f) In the final analysis, goodwill is based upon earning capacity. The presence of goodwill and its value, therefore, rests upon the excess of net earnings over and above a fair return on the net tangible assets. *While the element of goodwill may be based primarily on earnings, such factors as the prestige and renown of the business, the* *ownership of a trade or brand name, and a record of successful operation over a prolonged period in a particular locality, also may furnish support for the inclusion of intangible value.* ***In some instances it may not be possible to make a separate appraisal of the tangible and intangible assets of the business. The enterprise has a value as an entity. Whatever intangible value there is, which is supportable by the facts, may be measured by the amount by which the appraised value of the tangible assets exceeds the net book value of such assets.***

In this section, the ruling indicates that goodwill is based on the company's earning capacity. However, the ruling also seems to indicate that there are other factors (such as prestige or the brand name) that may add to the value and that also should be considered. In essence, the ruling indicates that the appraiser should value the entire company, and it is the excess over the value of the net tangible assets that becomes the intangible value. The ruling is a bit ambiguous in this section because it starts off by discussing goodwill and concludes by addressing other intangibles as well.

Most appraisers recognize the ruling as suggesting that the value of the entire company will include all intangibles, not just goodwill.

(g) ***Sales of stock of a closely held corporation should be carefully investigated to determine whether they represent transactions at arm's length. Forced or distress sales do not ordinarily reflect fair market value, nor do isolated sales in small amounts necessarily control as the measure of value.*** *This is especially true in the valuation of a controlling interest in a corporation.* ***Since, in the case of closely held stocks, no*** *prevailing market* ***prices are available, there is no basis for making an adjustment for blockage.*** *It follows, therefore, that such stocks should be valued upon a consideration of all the evidence affecting the fair market value.* ***The size of the block of stock itself is a relevant factor to be considered. Although it is true that a minority interest in an unlisted corporation's stock is more difficult to sell than a similar block of listed stock, it is equally true that control of a corporation, either actual or in effect, representing as it does an added element of value, may justify a higher value for a specific block of stock.***

Revenue Ruling 59-60 suggests that the appraiser review past transactions in the subject company's own stock to determine if it can be used as an indication of value. This can be the case only if the stock was transferred in an arm's-length manner meeting all of the requirements of the definition of fair market value. In particular, distress sales and sales of small blocks of stock will generally be a poor indicator of value. The smaller blocks may be used if the appraiser is valuing a small block of stock, but may be very inappropriate for a controlling block.

This ruling also indicates that a blockage discount is inappropriate for large blocks of stock of a closely held corporation. The sale of a large block of stock of a closely held company will generally not have the same impact as the possible depressing effect (supply may be greater than demand) that a large block of stock may have on the public market. However, the ruling recognizes that it is more difficult to sell a minority interest in a closely held company than to sell the same interest in a public company (marketability), but also that controlling interests may have elements giving them more value (control is worth more than minority, and control is more marketable than minority).

(h) Section 2031(b) of the Code states, in effect, that ***in valuing unlisted securities the value of stock or securities of corporations engaged in the same or a similar line of business which are listed on an exchange should be taken into consideration along with all other factors.*** *An important consideration is that the corporations to be used for comparisons have capital stocks which are* ***actively traded*** *by the public. In accordance with section 2031(b) of the Code, stocks listed on an exchange are to be considered first. However, if sufficient comparable companies whose stocks are listed on an exchange cannot be found, other comparable companies which have stocks actively traded on the over-the-counter market also may be used. The essential factor is that whether the stocks are sold on an exchange or over-the-counter, there is evidence of an active, free public market for the stock as of the valuation date.* ***In selecting corporations for comparative purposes, care should be taken to use only comparable companies.*** *Although the only restrictive requirement as to comparable corporations specified in the statute is that their lines of business be the same or similar, it is obvious that consideration must be given to other relevant factors in order that the most valid comparison possible will be obtained. For illustration, a corporation having one or more issues of*

preferred stock, bonds, or debentures in addition to its common stock should not be considered to be directly comparable to one having only common stock outstanding. In like manner, a company with a declining business and decreasing markets is not comparable to one with a record of current progress and market expansion.

Here is the reason that appraisers employ the guideline company method of appraisal. Revenue Ruling 59-60 tells the appraiser to consider using comparative (guideline) companies to determine the value of the subject company. The ruling also points out that care should be exercised in selecting guideline companies. "Comparability" must relate to numerous factors and not be restricted to companies in the same or similar line of business. Review the items discussed in Chapter 6 for suggested factors to consider when you determine comparability.

Another factor discussed is that the publicly traded guideline companies must be actively traded to be used in this analysis. This should eliminate any of the special motivations that buyers and sellers may have had in the market and that are not representative of fair market value (insiders trading shares of a thinly traded issue).

Section 5. Weight to Be Accorded Various Factors. *The valuation of closely held corporate stock entails the consideration of all relevant factors as stated in section 4. Depending upon the circumstances in each case, certain factors may carry more weight than others because of the nature of the company's business. To illustrate:*

(a) ***Earnings may be the most important criterion of value in some cases whereas asset value will receive primary consideration in others.*** *In general, the appraiser will accord* ***primary consideration to earnings when valuing stocks of companies which sell products or services to the public; conversely, in the investment or holding type of company, the appraiser may accord the greatest weight to the assets underlying the security to be valued.***

(b) ***The value of the stock of a closely held investment or real estate holding company, whether or not family owned, is closely related to the value of the assets underlying the stock.*** *For companies of this type the appraiser should determine the fair market values of the assets of the company.* ***Operating expenses of such a company and the cost of liquidating it, if any, merit consideration when appraising the relative values of the stock and the underlying assets. The market values of the underlying assets give due weight to potential earnings and dividends*** *of the particular items of property underlying the stock, capitalized at rates deemed proper by the investing public at the date of appraisal.* ***A current appraisal by the investing public should be superior to the retrospective opinion of an individual.*** *For these reasons, adjusted net worth should be accorded greater weight in valuing the stock of a closely held investment or real estate holding company, whether or not family owned, than any of the other customary yardsticks of appraisal, such as earnings and dividend-paying capacity.*

In Section 5 of the ruling, the weight to be assigned to the different approaches used in business valuation is discussed. For companies that sell products or services to the public, earnings are to be afforded the greatest weight during the valuation process. For companies that are asset intensive, earnings may not be as meaningful. The ruling is consistent with modern-day valuation theory, since an asset-based approach is rarely used for businesses that have an intangible value beyond the valuation of the underlying assets. Obviously, an asset-based approach is available if the intangible assets are valued separately and added to the result.

While discussing the valuation of the underlying assets, Revenue Ruling 59-60 suggests that the expenses of liquidation be considered in the determination of value. The irony of this section is that Private Letter Ruling 9150001 specifically frowns on the application of capital gains taxes attributable to the selling off of assets. The courts had also taken the position that, unless liquidation is imminent, the effect of capital gains taxes is considered too speculative to be factored into the valuation. This was particularly true prior to the repeal of the General Utilities Doctrine, which was associated with Section 337 liquidations.[1] Now, however, capital gains taxes have been permitted as part of the discount for lack of marketability in

[1]The General Utilities Doctrine was repealed as part of the Tax Reform Act of 1986. Previously, it would have been possible to liquidate a corporation and avoid a corporate-level tax. The Tax Reform Act of 1986 removed this escape hatch and created double taxation to the corporation and shareholders on the liquidation.

cases such as *Davis* and *Eisenberg*. This has created a favorable argument for corporate-level taxpayers since they can no longer escape the corporate-level tax.

Finally, this section reiterates the importance of a market valuation as opposed to what is performed by an appraiser. The ruling indicates that the investing public's opinion should be given more weight than a retrospective assessment by an individual. This confirms the importance of having the underlying assets appraised in the determination of the adjusted net worth of a company, particularly when the underlying assets are real estate or investments, which are regularly valued by the market.

> **Section 6. Capitalization Rates.** *In the application of certain fundamental valuation factors, such as earnings and dividends, it is necessary to capitalize the average or current results at some appropriate rate.* ***A determination of the proper capitalization rate presents one of the most difficult problems in valuation. That there is no ready or simple solution*** *will become apparent by a cursory check of the rates of return and dividend yields in terms of the selling prices of corporate shares listed on the major exchanges of the country.* ***Wide variations will be found even for companies in the same industry.*** *Moreover, the ratio will fluctuate from year to year depending upon economic conditions. Thus,* ***no standard tables of capitalization rates applicable to closely held corporations can be formulated. Among the more important factors to be taken into consideration in deciding upon a capitalization rate in a particular case are: (1) the nature of the business; (2) the risk involved; and (3) the stability or irregularity of earnings.***

This section says it all! Determining the appropriate capitalization rate is one of the most difficult parts of the valuation process. The important part of this section is that there are no easy answers, there are no standard tables, and the appraiser needs to consider, *at a minimum*, the nature of the business, the risk involved, and the stability or irregularity of earnings.

> **Section 7. Average of Factors.** *Because valuations cannot be made on the basis of a prescribed formula, there is no means whereby the various applicable factors in a particular case can be assigned mathematical weights in deriving the fair market value.* ***For this reason, no useful purpose is served by taking an average of several factors (for example, book value, capitalized earnings and capitalized dividends) and basing the valuation on the result.*** *Such a process excludes active consideration of other pertinent factors, and the end result cannot be supported by a realistic application of the significant facts in the case except by mere chance.*

Section 7 of the ruling states that while one attempts to reconcile the final value estimate, there is no formula available to reconcile the various valuation methods that may be applicable to a given appraisal. Each valuation assignment consists of a unique set of circumstances that will require the appraiser to analyze the results of the different valuation methods used to derive a final estimate of value. Even between similar assignments, the information that the appraiser may obtain will provide more or less confidence in the application of certain methods. Companies have different balance sheet compositions, which could affect the weight to be afforded to the net worth of the company.

In simple terms, do not take an average of all of the valuation methods that you decided were appropriate because the answer will no doubt be incorrect, unless you are extremely lucky.

> **Section 8. Restrictive Agreements.** *Frequently, in the valuation of closely held stock for estate and gift tax purposes, it will be found that the stock is subject to an agreement restricting its sale or transfer.* ***Where shares of stock were acquired by a decedent subject to an option reserved by the issuing corporation to repurchase at a certain price, the option price is usually accepted as the fair market value for estate tax purposes.*** *See Rev. Rul. 54-76, C.B. 1954-1, 194. However, in such case* ***the option price is not determinative of fair market value for gift tax purposes.*** *Where the option, or buy and sell agreement, is the result of voluntary action by the stockholders and is binding during the life as well as at the death of the stockholders, such agreement may or may not, depending upon the circumstances of each case, fix the value for estate tax purposes. However,* ***such agreement is a factor to be considered, with other relevant factors, in determining fair market value.*** *Where the stockholder is free to dispose of his shares during life and the option is to become effective only upon his death, the fair market value is not limited to the option price.*

It is always necessary to consider the relationship of the parties, the relative number of shares held by the decedent, and other material facts, to determine whether the agreement represents a bona fide business arrangement or is a device to pass the decedent's shares to the natural objects of his bounty for less than an adequate and full consideration in money or money's worth. In this connection see Rev. Rul. 157, C.B. 1953-2, 255, and Rev. Rul. 189, C.B. 1953-2, 294.

Revenue Ruling 59-60 reiterates that buy-sell agreements may be binding for estate tax purposes but may not be binding for gift tax purposes. Factors surrounding the buy-sell agreement must be considered by the appraiser to determine that the agreement represents an arm's-length agreement and not one that is designed to avoid taxes. Consideration must clearly be given to special situations, such as related shareholders, but that is one of many factors to be considered.

The IRS will also scrutinize a situation in which shareholders arbitrarily determine the value for their buy-sell agreement, as opposed to a provision that calls for an independent appraisal by a qualified appraiser. The general feeling is that there is too much room for manipulation if the determination of this value is left to the shareholders alone.

Section 9. Effect on Other Documents. *Revenue Ruling 54-77, C.B. 1954-1, 187, is hereby superseded.*

Conclusion

By now, you should have more of an understanding of Revenue Ruling 59-60. Considering that the ruling was promulgated in 1959, it has stood the test of time. Business valuation theory corresponds to the factors set forth in this ruling. For the most part, this Revenue Ruling is like motherhood and apple pie. It just makes sense! Regardless of the set of standards followed in performing a business valuation (*Uniform Standards of Professional Appraisal Practice* or standards issued by the American Society of Appraisers, The Institute of Business Appraisers, NACVA, or someday the AICPA), they all send the same message: Consider the factors set forth in Revenue Ruling 59-60. I hope that the next time you read this Revenue Ruling, you will see the valuation process in a different light. Valuation has not really changed. We just get smarter as time goes by.

13

The Valuation Report

Chapter Goals

In this chapter, I will explain the following:

1. The components of a valuation report
2. The types of valuation reports
3. The preparation of the business valuation report
4. The defense of the business valuation report
5. Common errors in business valuation reports

Introduction

Appraisal reports will vary depending upon the assignment. The different types of reports generated will be based on the needs of the client and will frequently be cost driven. A full, formal report may be too expensive for a client, although it may be required because of the nature of the assignment. This is a problem the appraiser constantly faces.

Components of a Valuation Report

In addition to being covered by the *USPAP*, appraisers are covered by the standards of the appraisal organizations to which they belong. CPAs are covered by various standards promulgated by the AICPA for consulting services, the presentation of historical financial statements, and the presentation of prospective financial information. Non-CPAs do not have the same level of standards to contend with when financial information is included in the business valuation report. Regardless of whether the appraiser is a CPA, Standard 10 of the *USPAP*, as well as the rest of the *USPAP*, must be followed for all FIRREA engagements, which are engagements that involve a federally related transaction. Many government agencies are now requiring that the *USPAP* be followed. In the first edition of this book, I stated that "in my opinion, it will only be a matter of time before the IRS and the Securities and Exchange Commission will also require the *USPAP* to be followed." I am not so sure of this anymore. However, whatever standards become applicable, they will sure look like the *USPAP*.

Since the *USPAP* is so important, Standard 10 is worth reviewing. According to the standard, each analysis, opinion, and conclusion reached should be communicated in a manner that is not misleading (no kidding!). The report should be clearly and accurately presented. It should also contain enough information to allow the reader to properly understand the contents, the sources of information used by the appraiser to draw certain conclusions, and the basis for the conclusions reached. The appraiser should also disclose any unusual assumption or limiting condition that directly affects the appraisal and should explain its effect on value.

The intent of the *USPAP* is to ensure that the appraiser properly communicates his or her findings in a thorough manner that will be helpful to the reader of the report. To accomplish this task, the *USPAP* lists certain items that *must* be in a report. For example, a definition of value must be in a report. If it is not, how will the reader properly understand the context in which the analysis has been done?

In my opinion, a good appraisal report should contain at least the required disclosures from the *USPAP,* which include the following:

- Letter of transmittal
- Description of the assignment
- Sources of information used in the appraisal
- Assumptions and limiting conditions
- Economic data
- Industry information
- Subject company information
- Financial statement analysis
- Valuation section
- Appendixes, schedules, and exhibits
- Appraisal certification (required by Standard 10-3 of the *USPAP)*

Letter of Transmittal

The letter of transmittal is the cover letter in which you basically tell your client, "Here it is, but if you want to know more, see the attached report." A sample transmittal letter appears on the CD-ROM accompanying this book.

Description of the Assignment

Consider this section of the report as the introduction. This is the part of the report that spells out what your assignment was. It should include a complete description of the appraisal subject—for example, "35 shares of the common stock of XYZ Corp., a New Jersey Corporation, which represents a 43.5 percent minority interest in that corporation owned by John Smith." This section should also provide the reader with the effective date of the appraisal. This is the date at which the business or business interest has been appraised. The appraiser should also disclose the purpose and function of the appraisal. The purpose may be to determine the fair market value of the company, while the function may be to describe how it will be used (for gift tax purposes, estate tax purposes, divorce litigation, etc.).

The description section will generally disclose the identity of the client. The client may not be the same individual to whom the transmittal letter is addressed. We are frequently retained by parties going through litigation who instruct us to send the report to the attorney.

Finally, this section of the report should include the definition of value being used in the report. Most of the time, it will be fair market value. If a different standard of value is used, it should be very clearly defined.

Sources of Information Used in the Appraisal

Appraisal reports are supposed to be replicable by any qualified reader. Therefore, an appraisal report should include all of the sources considered by the appraiser in providing an opinion of value. This allows a qualified reader to independently review the various sources used by the appraiser in order to draw a similar conclusion (or at least understand how the appraiser derived his or her conclusion). (Some appraisers prefer to put this section in an appendix to the report rather than in the report itself.) It is advisable to list all the items that were reviewed, but most important, list those items that had an impact on your opinion. Do not include items that have no relevance to the assignment at hand. For example, if you are valuing a corporate interest for a divorce, do not list the personal tax returns of the parties unless they had some relevance in the assignment.

Assumptions and Limiting Conditions

This is one of the most important sections of the report. It contains the appraiser's assumptions covering the entire report, such as the assumption that the information being provided by the client is valid without independent verification. This should be considered the appraiser's disclaimer. The accounting profession knows all about disclaimers.

Appraisers are a little more subtle about the way they disclaim certain items. Instead of the typical accountant's assumptions, which hit the reader between the eyes on page 1 of the accountant's report, the appraiser's assumptions are placed more subtly within the report. Some appraisers prefer to put this section in an appendix at the back of the report. It does not matter where in the report this goes, as long as it is included. This is called covering your posterior!

Certain assumptions and limiting conditions are standard for all engagements. These should be included in your engagement letter with the client, so that there is no misunderstanding about the client's acceptance of your report subject to at least those assumptions and limiting conditions. There may be others that end up in your report as well. (See Chapter 2 for the discussion of engagement letters.) Some of the more common assumptions and limiting conditions are illustrated in the sample reports on the CD-ROM that came with this book.

Economic Data

The appraisal report should contain a discussion of the economy, concentrating on how it affects the appraisal subject (see Chapter 4 for a detailed discussion about the economic analysis that should be done). Remember to make this section relevant to the appraisal subject. Some commercial vendors sell an analysis of the economy that can be inserted into an appraisal report. The problem with using such an analysis is that it assumes that every appraisal subject is affected by the same economic factors. This is not necessarily true. Although a construction contractor may be affected by rising interest rates, a brain surgeon probably is not. Including a long discussion about interest rates in a valuation report for a brain surgery practice will be not only boring, but also out of place.

Industry Information

The report should also contain a discussion of the appraisal subject's industry. The discussion should be detailed enough to demonstrate how the appraisal subject fits into the industry; how the industry is affected by the economy; whether the industry is mature, stable, or cyclical; and anything else that may be pertinent to the appraisal. The discussion may also cover industries that affect the appraisal subject, even though the appraisal subject is not in that industry. For example, our firm appraised a printing business that was specialized; it serviced only the pharmaceutical industry. Our report contained a discussion of the changes in the pharmaceutical industry, since they had a major effect on the appraisal subject's business. For more information about industry analysis, see Chapter 4.

Subject Company Information

Revenue Ruling 59-60 suggests that one of the eight factors to be considered in performing an appraisal is "the nature of the business and the history of the enterprise from its inception." This section of the report will frequently include a discussion of the following areas:

- History of the business
- Form of organization
- Restrictions on the sale of the subject interest
- Subsidiaries and affiliates
- Ownership and control
- Management
- Product lines
- Subject industry
- Competition
- Location

This section of the report will allow the appraiser to demonstrate his or her knowledge of the subject company. One of the greatest faults that I find in other appraisers' reports is that they either skip this section or write a one-paragraph description of the company. How can anyone understand what makes the company have value if this information is omitted? This information adds to the risk assessment that we discussed previously. It helps justify discount rates, capitalization rates, minority discounts, and control premiums. These items are discussed in detail in Chapter 4.

Financial Statement Analysis

This is the section of the appraisal report that includes the trend and ratio analysis of the subject company. With regard to its performance, the subject company should generally be compared not only with itself but also with either guideline companies or industry composite data. This section of the report also includes the financial projections or forecast for the company, including operational expectations (revenues, net profits, and cash flow). This is a critical section of the report, because not only do you need this information to perform the valuation calculations, but you also need it in assessing risk, which will be used to adjust either the multiples used in guideline company methodologies or the component of the discount rate pertaining to the specific company risk premium.

Valuation Section

All of the methods that were considered as part of the appraisal should be discussed in the valuation section of the report. This section should also contain a discussion about the search for publicly traded guideline companies. The discussion should include the parameters of the search, the reason that certain companies were considered but eliminated, and the companies used as guideline companies. Some appraisers include an adjusted balance sheet and a normalized income statement in this section of the report, along with an appropriate discussion of the adjustments that were made. Other appraisers will include this information in the financial statement analysis section of the report.

After the discussion of the selected methods of valuation and the calculations of value under each method, a reconciliation should be included in the report, and it should lead to a conclusion of value. This is also the section in which some appraisers discuss premiums and discounts and include a detailed justification for those that were applied in the report, as well as a justification for the size of those premiums or discounts.

Appendixes, Schedules, and Exhibits

This section of the report will generally include the backup documentation that supports the appraisal. Some appraisers include a comparative balance sheet and income statement in this section; others may also include all of the valuation calculations. To me, there is nothing worse than reading an appraisal report in which the appraiser makes me constantly jump from the narrative to schedules in the back of the report to follow the story that is being told. I would rather see the financial information included in the body of the narrative. This may be more difficult for your word-processing person to do, but it is more courteous to the reader. Keep in mind that the reader is frequently the one who will be paying your fee!

Types of Valuation Reports

During a typical business valuation engagement, the appraiser may be asked to issue one type of report or several different types. These may include (1) formal reports, (2) informal reports, (3) letter reports, and (4) oral reports.

Regardless of which report format you use, every business valuation engagement requires you to do all of the work that is necessary to formulate a supportable opinion of value about the appraisal subject. The business valuation report is nothing more than the mechanism that is used to communicate your opinion. The report, however, can be a dynamic tool to convince the reader that you have done a good job in deriving your opinion of value.

Each of the report types serves a different purpose in a valuation engagement. The type of assignment can affect the content of your report, and therefore, a clear understanding of the engagement is essential before you can do your job. Before going too much further, let's define each of these report types.

Formal Reports

A formal report is covered by Standard 10 of the *USPAP*. These are also sometimes known as *self-contained reports*. A formal business valuation report is the highest-level report that you can provide to your client. The contents of the report will generally contain all of the information covered earlier in this chapter. A formal business valuation report can range from 40 to 80 pages or more (400 pages is our record).

Since the last edition of this book was published, the *USPAP* has been changed to allow the business appraiser almost as much latitude as the real estate appraiser has. Standard 2, covering real estate reports, allows three types of reports: a self-contained appraisal report, a summary appraisal report, and a restricted appraisal report.

The differences among the three options stem from the use and application of the terms *describe*, *summarize*, and *state*. *Describe* is used to connote a comprehensive level of detail in the presentation of information. *Summarize* is used to connote a more concise presentation of information. *State* is used to connote the minimal presentation of information.

Standard 10-2 uses the terms *state*, *summarize*, and *explain*, but it does not use the word *describe*. The *USPAP* standard applicable to business appraisers seems to be saying:

> When intended users include parties other than the client, an Appraisal Report must be provided. When the only intended user is the client, a Restricted Use Appraisal Report may be provided. . . . An appraiser may use any other label in addition to, but not in place of, the label set forth in this standard for the type of report provided.

Informal Reports

Less-than-formal reports are frequently requested and are perfectly acceptable in certain situations in which the user of the report is informed that much of the detail is excluded from the report. These reports are sometimes known as *summary reports*. Sometimes, based on the needs of the client, he or she may not want to pay the appraiser to include a section in the report that describes the company. This is especially true if the appraisal is for planning purposes. However, this description would be important to a third party who is not familiar with the appraisal subject.

An informal report contains considerably less information than a formal report. This type of report frequently contains little more than valuation calculations. Most of the narrative is excluded, and many sections of the report are brief. This can sometimes be thought of as an "agreed-upon procedures" report. The appraiser limits the discussion to the explanation of the financial schedules attached to the report. This type of report can range from 5 to 25 pages.

Letter Reports

Just as the name implies, a letter report is nothing more than a letter stating the opinion of value. Reference is generally made to all of the work that has been done, including the fact that your working papers contain all of the supporting documentation for your opinion. This type of report can range from one paragraph to several pages. It is also possible to issue fairly long letters.

Some attorneys ask me what the difference is between a formal report and a letter report. My standard answer is "about $3,000." Writing a long, narrative report takes time. Although I'm not going to discuss in this book how to charge for your time, consider the amount of time that it will take you to write an 80-page report.

Oral Reports

Oral reports are also acceptable, although not advisable. Some attorneys prefer oral reports in litigation as a strategy for keeping the other side guessing. The Federal Rules of Civil Procedure have changed the use of oral reports. This "trial by ambush" approach is now frowned on in many courts.

This type of report is generally accomplished through testimony, either at a deposition or a trial. On occasion, your client may just want a verbal opinion as to what his or her business should sell for.

Preparing the Business Valuation Report

Now that we have discussed the types of reports, the next step is to understand when to use each type of report. Personally, I prefer issuing formal valuation reports. This type of report allows me to demonstrate not only that I did my job well, but also the fact that I know valuation theory. For those business appraisers who belong to appraisal organizations, standards exist that must be followed. The CPA business appraiser should be familiar with these standards. They can be followed by the CPA and will generally result in a good work product. Knowledge of these standards can also help you play an important litigation support role by assisting your client's attorney in impeaching the other side's expert for not following the standards of the organizations to which the expert belongs.

The standards have been discussed earlier in this book, so there is no need to repeat the discussion here. However, if you did not read about the standards when you encountered them, now would be a good chance to do so (you thought you could skip them and get away with it, huh?). By this point in the book, you should also have awoken from your nap and ordered your own copy of the *USPAP*.

Federal Rules of Civil Procedure

This book is not a legal treatise, nor is it intended to address the Federal Rules of Civil Procedure (FRCP), but there have been some changes made to the rules, and they affect expert testimony; therefore they may also affect the business valuation reports that we issue in litigation engagements. The changes impose stricter rules regarding the disclosure and timing requirements for expert opinions.

FRCP 26(a)(2)(B) requires that a testifying expert submit a formal written report and that it be signed by the expert personally. The expert's report must contain a complete statement of all opinions to be expressed. If the statement is not in the report, the expert will be precluded from offering the opinion in a deposition or a trial. The expert must also disclose all information considered in formulating his or her opinion.

These new rules should eliminate the "trial by ambush" technique that certain states have allowed previously. Working with a New York law firm, we were once asked to render our opinion by telephone. The other side could have then deposed us, and unless they asked the correct questions, they might never have known what we did or what we relied on. Let's face it, that type of law was counterproductive! Maybe with full disclosure, such a case would have settled.

Using Your Report as a Selling Tool

All of us who serve as expert witnesses know that we should be objective if we are to be credible. Those of us who belong to appraisal organizations are ethically bound not to be advocates for our client. However, this does not mean that we cannot be advocates of our own opinions. The accounting profession has rules on objectivity and integrity. A business valuation report is the perfect forum for selling your opinion of the value of the appraisal subject.

Once you have performed all of the required steps to reach an opinion of value, the next step is to communicate it in such a way that the reader of your report will have no alternative but to realize that you are correct. The manner in which you write and present your report can help you convince the reader that you have reached the appropriate conclusion. I generally want my reports to tell a story. The beginning of my story includes a discussion of the theory of how to value a business or business interest. Keep in mind that the story will change depending on whether you are valuing a controlling interest or a minority interest.

The middle of my story includes the application of the appraisal theory, discussed in the beginning of my story, to the appraisal subject. This is the guts of the valuation. It includes the analysis (financial, economic, and industry) and the valuation calculations. This section of the report is intended to show the reader how the theory applies to this appraisal. After being presented with the approaches and methods in the beginning section, the reader now sees them with numbers.

The final section of the story is my conclusion, which ties together the first two sections of the report. Here is the theory; here is how it is applied; therefore, my conclusion must be correct if I followed the theory. This may seem pretty basic, but it has proven to be an effective tool in the courtroom, regardless of whether it was a bench trial or a jury trial.

The business valuation report should contain a thorough analysis that demonstrates how much you know about the appraisal subject, its industry, and the other items that will affect its value. Too often, reports have all of the correct components, but each section is so skimpy that it fails to demonstrate that the appraiser did any more than the minimum amount of work in that assignment. For example, a common error is to include financial ratios in the report but fail to discuss what they mean.

Your appraisal report is your opportunity to demonstrate your knowledge. If you include items in your report, they should be explained well. Don't be afraid to quote other sources. Use recognized sources in your report to support your work. Quoting sources such as the government (the IRS, Revenue Rulings, the Bureau of Labor and Statistics, and so on) makes your work hard to dispute. Judges and juries show a great deal of respect for information taken from authoritative sources. Quoting other experts in the field also works. I like to include quotes from Pratt. Most of the attorneys who have been involved in business valuation litigation know of his work. You can even quote Trugman! I can't, but you can.

Another way to use your report as a selling tool is to emphasize a particular section, especially if it covers a subjective portion of the process (such as capitalization rates). For example, you can include extra wording in the report if the capitalization rate that you have selected is 75 percent. If you had selected 15 percent to 20 percent, you would still have to justify your rate, but clearly not as much as if the rate is out of the range that people are used to seeing.

In one particular valuation, we included a discussion of the rates of return required by venture capital firms so that we could support a very high capitalization rate (78 percent). We quoted an article published in *Business Valuation Review* that addressed venture capital returns. The author of this article described different rates of return depending on which stage of the business life cycle the subject was in and related this to the appraisal subject. We showed that the appraisal subject could not even qualify for venture capital financing, which supported our assessment of the riskiness of an investment in this company. By quoting another source, we strengthened our argument to the point that the judge found in our favor. Some of the supporting language from our report included the following:

> Further support for these high capitalization rates comes from an examination of the venture capital market. "Professional venture capitalism requires a minimum of 40 to 50 percent rates of return on the small company 'superstars' of tomorrow," according to Bradley A. Fowler, Esq. in an article published in *Business Valuation Review*, June 1989. Rates have not changed materially, and as such, this article lends some excellent insight into required rates of return.
>
> According to the article, venture capitalists who are financing seed or start-up companies were looking for 50 *percent or more* compound rates of return. Quoting a Price Waterhouse article, the author states, "depending upon the perceived risk, the venture firm is going to want a rate of annual return of 40% to 80% or more. And they will also want the ability to liquidate theft investment, usually within five years."
>
> Smith Company is clearly not a "superstar." With negative book value, a history of losses, little depth in management, and heavy short-term liabilities, a venture capitalist would not be interested in the company. This should warrant an exceptionally high required rate of return.

Another selling tool is the use of graphs. The personal computer has given the appraiser a greater capability of demonstrating important points with the use of pictures. Bar charts, pie charts, and trend lines are great tools for driving a point home. Let's assume that the company being appraised has had a decreasing sales volume over the period covered by the appraisal. Look at the impact of a picture:

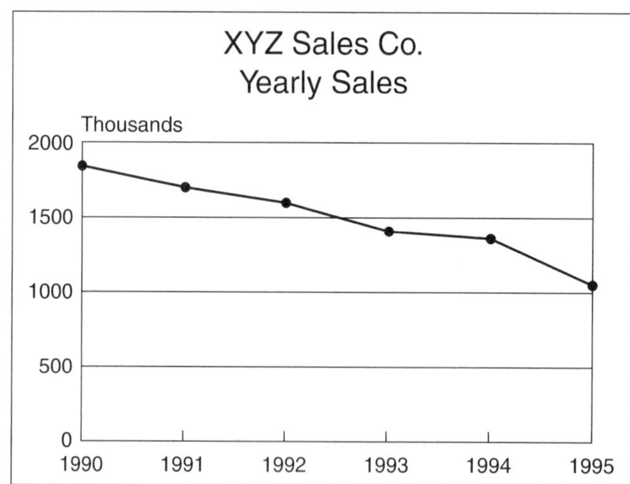

Do you really need to say much more? The downward slope of the graph makes it pretty obvious that the trend was not good. The use of graphs is especially effective when the appraiser is called on to testify. Pointing the judge to a picture in your report will be much more effective than expecting the judge to read a lengthy text.

No matter how much the appraiser points out that a company incurs risk for having most of its sales come from a few customers or from a particular type of service, it can also be effective to present a chart in conjunction with tables to demonstrate this effectively. Exhibit 13.1 illustrates this point.

EXHIBIT 13.1
Using Tables and Charts

A breakdown of revenues by type of service for 1995 appears in Table 1.

TABLE 1
1995 Revenue Breakdown by Type of Service
($000)

	Consolidation	*LTL*	*Truckload*	*Fleet Management*	*Total Revenue*
Revenues	$5,966	$39,293	$31,740	$41,346	$118,345
Percent of total	5%	33%	27%	35%	100%

Graphically, the allocation of the Company's revenues appears as follows:

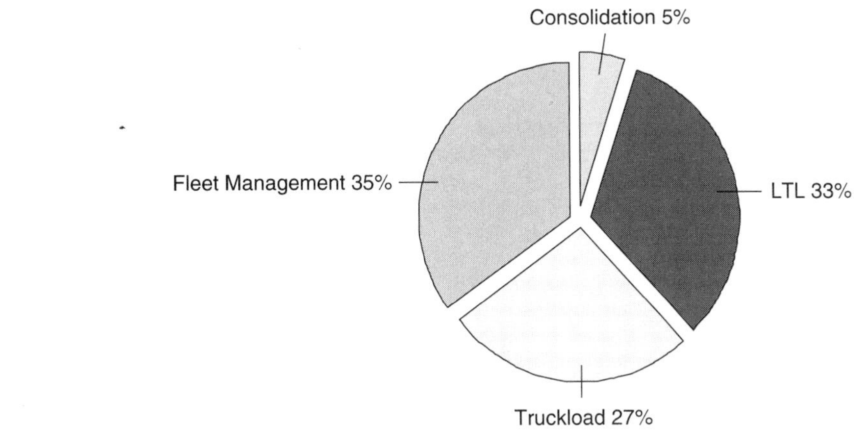

The use of color printers not only dresses up your report, but it also highlights the story even better than black-and-white. A good network-compatible color printer now costs under $5,000. The profit from your next appraisal report can buy you one (or it can pay the rent).

Another selling tool for appraisal reports is the manner in which they are presented. At our firm, we like to bind our reports in our firm's report covers and to include labeled dividers between the sections. We do not use preprinted dividers, since our reports tend to vary. Instead, we use plain dividers and print whatever needs to be on the divider on clear labels. The appearance of an appraisal report can also help sell the report. If it is cosmetically attractive, the reader will believe that a great deal of time went into the work product. We have found that many judges will not read the report but will comment on the fact that it appears to be a well-constructed document.

If you have prepared your business valuation report in a comprehensive manner, that will also help you prepare for trial. I will use my report to refresh my memory in preparation for testimony. I find that I put so much information in my report that I spend more time reading it than I do going over working paper files. At trial, I will use it as a refresher if I am asked a question that I do not remember the answer to. This is a time saver compared to sitting on the witness stand and going through files.

Using the Other Side's Report to Help Sell Your Opinion

In a litigation assignment, wouldn't it be great if we were always lucky enough to get the other side's report before we had to do ours? Unfortunately, this does not happen often enough. However, when it does happen, you might as well take advantage of it. The other side's report can help the appraiser structure his or her report to point out the flaws in the methodologies and conclusions of the other appraiser. Having the other side's report in advance frequently allows the appraiser to emphasize those areas that are known to be a point of contention in the litigation battle of the experts.

Sometimes, critiquing the other side's report before preparing our own points out the many problems that we need to address in our report. We will use whatever information we can to our advantage. The best way to illustrate this point is to use some real examples. Exhibit 13.2 contains an excerpt of a critique that our firm prepared in the past. I will explain how we addressed the problem if it is not evident from the critique itself.

EXHIBIT 13.2
Using the Other Side's Report

Trugman Valuation Associates Inc. has been asked to perform a critique of the valuation report issued in this matter by Levine & Company (hereafter referred to as "the Levine Report") under cover letter dated December 13, 1999.

In order to make this critique easy to follow, we have made page references to the Levine Report.

According to Section 3.01 of Revenue Ruling 59-60:

> A sound valuation will be based upon all relevant facts, but the elements of common sense, informed judgment and reasonableness must enter into the process of weighing those facts and determining their aggregate significance.

This statement lays the foundation for much of the critique presented herein. One of the most critical aspects of business valuation is that the appraiser approach the assignment objectively and use common sense and sound judgment. As the following critique indicates, this does not appear to be the case with the Levine Report.

Page 4. Beginning on page 4 of the Levine Report, the appraisers begin a detailed discussion of the Company and the nature of its operations. The majority of the information used to form the basis for the appraisers' understanding of the Company was taken from a proposal prepared by the Company for the purposes of securing the Regional Distribution Center (RDC) contract from BIG MAJOR SUPPLIER (hereafter referred to as "the Proposal").

In discussions with management, much of the information used to prepare the Proposal was based on future plans. On page 1 of the Proposal, the Company calls the Proposal "hypothetical." In general, the Proposal was a tool used by the Company to acquire what they thought to be a very positive relationship with BIG MAJOR SUPPLIER. Accordingly, it was written to highlight the positives of the relationship and minimize its potential pitfalls and negatives. As indicated in the section of this report titled "History and Nature of the Business," the relationship with BIG MAJOR SUPPLIER (in everyday dealings) was extremely difficult to manage and required a great deal of time and energy from key individuals at the Company. In addition to the amount of work involved in maintaining the BIG MAJOR SUPPLIER relationship, there are a lot of real business risks involved with the BIG MAJOR SUPPLIER agreements.

Regarding the history and future (including the BIG MAJOR SUPPLIER relationship), the Levine Report states:

The Company was founded in 1950 by David Johnson (grandfather of John Johnson). In 1982, Richard Johnson (son of David and father of John) secured the BIG MAJOR SUPPLIER relationship. Since 1995, John Johnson has filled the leadership role and carried the title of President. The expressed intentions are to continue to expand the Company and to carry it from its current third generation into a fourth generation of family in this business. Expectations as expressed in this Proposal were favorable for long-term continued success. In particular, the Proposal expressed expectations of the Company being able to flourish into the next generation because of Mr. Johnson's children, as well as "a fine assortment of nieces and nephews to draw upon." The Proposal went on to describe the continuation of the Company (and by inference its continued success) as "almost a certainty."

Though the complete excerpt from the Report is lengthy, it serves to illustrate the lack of in-depth knowledge the appraisers possessed regarding the Company, the appraisal subject. One important note on the excerpt above is the fact that the BIG MAJOR SUPPLIER relationship was initiated in 1982 (and by no means was it secured). Although this is only a single word, it gives us additional insight into the lack of knowledge of the evolution of the BIG MAJOR SUPPLIER relationship on their part.

Although the Proposal points out that the Company's goals are to be successful and that part of its ability to be successful in the future depends on management succession, these appraisers assume that because the Company has management succession plans, it will undoubtedly be successful. The Proposal states the following:

> With his soon-to-be three children and a fine assortment of nieces and nephews to draw upon, the expectation of The Company being driven into the future by a fourth generation Johnson is almost a certainty.

EXHIBIT 13.2 *(Continued)*

It is quite clear from this excerpt that the Proposal is speaking only to the certainty of a fourth generation and not inferring its guaranteed success. A successful distribution business requires many different factors in order to achieve success. Management has to believe it will be successful, but success is never guaranteed, especially in an industry that is migrating toward an environment with increasing pricing pressure as a result of increased competition and industry consolidation.

Although the points mentioned above may not appear to have a significant impact on the valuation of the Company, the implications of not having a complete understanding of an appraisal subject are significant, as an incorrect outlook can lead to an estimate of value that is unrealistic given the true risks of the subject company.

The appraisers are experienced Certified Public Accountants who are well aware of the fact that a proposal of this type is intended to "sell" the company. Rather than taking a realistic look at the Company, they chose to ignore the facts in order to benefit their client. They chose to not use objectivity in their analysis.

Pages 5 Through 6. The Appraisers go on to explain the Company's top management, key personnel, and sales force. Although we understand that much of this information was taken directly from the Proposal, many of the individuals described on pages 5 and 6 were future hires and were not in place as of the writing of the Proposal. Even after the Company secured the RDC program, several of these individuals either did not take the job offered to them or quit after a short period of time. In addition to the personnel, the sales force members listed on page 6 of the Levine Report were also merely plans, and only 2 of the 11 people listed in the table actually ended up in those positions (again, these individuals either never took the job, quit, or were fired).

Although many of these types of issues do not impact the financial history of the Company, the information was used by the appraisers to form an opinion as to the risk (or lack of risk) inherent in the Company's business. Accordingly, since they clearly did not have a complete understanding of the business they were appraising, there is a great amount of uncertainty as to the accuracy of the estimates they used to derive an estimate of value of the Company.

On the bottom of page 6, the appraisers explain some of the costs that went along with securing the BIG MAJOR SUPPLIER distributorship. Below are the paragraphs (in their entirety) from the Levine Report explaining these costs.

> Recognizing that if it succeeded in securing this distributorship (which it did), the Company would experience very significant and very near term explosive growth, it also addressed in the Proposal the matter of various staffing and capital needs. In particular, in referencing handling inside sales and outside service, the Proposal stated, "The increased order volume will not affect these standards. Sufficient staff will be employed to maintain our service levels." Reference to "these standards" apparently specifically refers to inside sales standards of all calls being picked up by the fourth ring and all calls being processed with 100 percent accuracy.

The Proposal went on to further indicate the Company's plans and efforts to expand its facility's capabilities, including reconfiguration of the warehouse (including improvements to the loading docks, improving warehouse office capabilities, increasing racking, expanding the parking lot, adding equipment, and adding an estimated 24 people). This part of the Proposal went on to indicate the Company's expectation of adding six tractors, 14 trailers, and two straight trucks, as well as increasing loading crew activity from one to three shifts. No concerns were expressed as to the Company's ability to handle the anticipated growth and to continue that sales level and to grow it.

In discussions with management, it has been found that some of these improvements/enhancements have been completed, but the majority have not. Furthermore, many of these initial plans have been altered or eliminated. The point we are trying to make (and this is confirmed in our discussions with management) is that there are a lot of costs associated with the RDC program that the Company has undertaken. These costs (or capital expenditures) should be used as an offset in the calculation of the net cash flows of the Company in the future. However, the Levine Report did not consider the cost of these capital expenditures in their calculation. They mention them in the text part of the Levine Report (as it seems to help them support all the great things the Company will do in the future), but fail to incorporate the impact of these cash outlays into their estimate of value of the Company.

Page 7. On page 7, the appraisers discuss the Company's growth projections given in the Proposal. They also include a discussion of how sales increased once they secured the BIG MAJOR SUPPLIER distributorship. However, the Appraisers do not spend any time discussing the fact that the profitability of the Company (although management would have liked to increase as dramatically as sales did from the increasing volume) did not increase substantially as a result of the increased volume from the RDC program. In 1997, the Company had sales and a normalized net loss of approximately $27 million and $184,000, respectively. However, in 1998, the Company had sales and a normalized net income of approximately $58 million and $34,000, respectively. Accordingly, with an increase in sales of more than $30 million, the Company was able to increase profits by only approximately $218,000. As this indicates, the increased business has proven to result in very little profitability (although more than in the past). Again, the concept presented above deals with the reasonableness of the projections used by these appraisers to value the Company.

Page 8. In the "Industry Outlook" section of the Levine Report, the appraisers state the following:

> According to most recent sales figures, there has been increased demand for hard floor coverings such as hardwood and ceramic flooring, which both increased 5.6 percent and 5.3 percent, respectively, from 1994 to 1995. Carpet and area rug sales decreased by 1.7 percent and vinyl sheet and floor tiles decreased by 2.4 percent during the same period.

(Continued)

EXHIBIT 13.2 *(Continued)*

> Popularity of hardwood and ceramic flooring continues to increase along with laminate flooring. Ceramic tile is gaining specifically in commercial markets where durability, scratch resistance, ease of cleaning, and cost-effectiveness are essential. Though laminate flooring is not as sturdy, it is estimated that this segment nearly doubled between 1996 and 1997.

The appraisers' statements regarding the outlook of the flooring industry should have helped them arrive at the conclusion that the market for the Company's main product lines (vinyl sheet and tile flooring and related products) is decreasing. Even if the Company is able to capture additional market share (which they are trying aggressively to do), the best they will end up with is a bigger piece of a smaller pie. The reality of this shrinking market share was confirmed in our discussions with the Company management and its lack of sales growth in 1999. All they had to do was ask the right questions during discovery, and they would have realized that their analysis was flawed.

Page 9. On page 9, the Levine Report explains the impact of industry fragmentation as follows:

> Due to industry fragmentation competition being strong, customer service is often a means for wholesalers and retailers to differentiate themselves. Included in customer service is product availability, range of floor covering products, and breadth of services offered (design, installation, financing, etc.). Pricing remains the primary competitive factor.

Again, they touch on some critical issues in the floor covering distribution industry, but fail to incorporate these realities into the valuation of the Company. With increasing competition and industry consolidation, industry participants are going to have to provide more service to their customers at a lower price. It is pretty clear that this has to have some negative effect on profitability. Again, this selective lack of follow-through on their part confirms that they did not consider all relevant factors in evaluating the future of the Company (and ultimately its value).

Regarding increasing competition from home centers, they state the following:

> Floor covering wholesalers and retailers are facing increasing competition from home centers. For instance, industry leader Home Depot has reportedly pledged to focus more on the floor covering industry. Many small and medium-sized contractors already purchase from home centers because of competitive pricing of floor coverings as well as for their one-stop shopping environment. Experts predict more builders will turn to home centers in the future.

As the above statement indicates, home centers are grabbing market share from the more traditional wholesale and retail sources. It is unclear whether or not they deemed this element of the floor covering industry to be negative or positive with respect to its impact on the Company. In discussions with management, we verified that this trend is, in fact, a reality. The result of this trend (by their own admission) is turning the Company's traditionally higher-margin sales into higher-volume, lower-margin sales. The Company has BIG MAJOR SUPPLIER squeezing them on one side and Home Depot squeezing them on the other. The Company has to work extremely hard to turn a profit on these sales (with continued superior customer service) as well as its other lines of business. The net result is a less profitable business.

Page 10. An essential aspect of any valuation is an in-depth look into the economy affecting the appraisal subject at the time of the appraisal. In addition to the national economy, a thorough appraisal investigates the effects of the regional economy on the appraisal subject. In the case of the Company, the majority of its business occurs within an 80-mile radius of its headquarters. Accordingly, an in-depth analysis of the economic conditions of the metropolitan area is essential. This will give the overall picture of the major forces that will be acting upon the Company in the future.

Pages 13 Through 15. On these pages, the appraisers calculate adjusted net income using various adjustments to the reported earnings of the Company. This process is called "normalization" and is intended to reflect what a willing buyer would be buying on a prospective basis. The appraisers have chosen to use a debt-free approach that will determine the total operating value of the Company: equity plus interest-bearing debt. Although we agree with the methodology used to normalize the Company's income statements, we disagree with some of the specific adjustments made by them. Given that they used 1998 as the basis for deriving an estimate of value using a discounted-cash-flow (DCF) analysis, it is very important to understand the adjustments made to this base year.

Real Estate Taxes and Building Depreciation. Although we agree that the depreciation expense for the building and improvements should be added back, real estate taxes are an expense normally incurred by a tenant and should not be added back.

Other Income. As discussed, rental income is nonrecurring and, as such, should have been deducted for all the years under review.

Travel and Entertainment. Although we agree with considering the sporting event ticket sales as a non-operating expense in 1998, they should have also considered the income received in prior years.

Fair Market Rent. Though we agree that a fair market rental should be considered in the appraisal, the Levine Report includes a rental figure that is in conflict with the real estate appraisal that they relied upon. We could not tell what caused this inconsistency.

Pages 16 Through 18. The verbiage included in these pages of the Levine Report is excellent. Since this is the exact wording from the sample report included in *Understanding Business Valuation*, authored by Gary R. Trugman, CPA, ABV, MCBA, ASA, MVS, the officer technically responsible for this report should have given proper attribution to the author instead of plagiarizing the work as his own. We are glad, however, that they believe that Gary Trugman is an authority on this subject.

EXHIBIT 13.2 (Continued)

Pages 19 Through 21. *Discounted Cash Flow (DCF) Valuation.* Using the normalized income stream for 1998 derived on page 13 of the Levine Report as a starting point, the appraiser attempted to derive an estimate of value for the Company using a DCF approach to valuation. In order to do this, the appraiser projected each of the individual expense categories for the years 1999 through 2002. As indicated in the "As Adjusted 1998" column, the appraiser determined how each expense was to be projected (1) as a percentage of sales based on the adjusted 1998 income statement, (2) increasing each year at a constant rate based on the adjusted 1998 income statement, or (3) as a percentage of salaries (for payroll taxes only).

Again, although the methodology appears to be sound, the overall results do not make sense. In order to simplify our critique, we will address each of the items in the projection individually in the order in which they are presented on page 19 of the Levine Report.

Sales. Although the overall estimate of 8.5 percent growth for 1999 through 2002 is not that unreasonable, their basis for determining this growth is formed solely from the Proposal. As such, they did not perform any diligence on these sales growth estimates. Furthermore, although they use actual results from 1999 on page 20 of the Levine Report to confirm their estimate of projected gross profit margins of 13 percent, they failed to mention that sales for the nine months ended September 30, 1999, were flat, as compared to the same period in 1998 ($43,974,169 in sales for the nine-month period ended September 30, 1999, compared to $43,324,340 for the same period in 1998). Discussions with management confirmed that year-end 1999 sales will most likely be flat compared to 1998. Based on issues like these, the appraisers did not use sound judgment and reasonableness in some of their assumptions.

Cost of Sales. In projecting cost of sales for the Company, the appraisers used 1998 actual results as the basis for their projections. Although this accurately represents history, future trends for cost of sales may change. Based on discussions with management, as well as common sense, the trend of increasing lower margin sales is expected to continue in the future.

Operating Expenses. In order to put the projections used by the appraisers into some kind of perspective, we looked at total operating expenses as a percentage of sales for the years 1998 (as adjusted) through 2002 (projected). They are as follows:

Year	*Sales*	*Operating Expenses*	*Operating Expenses as a % of Sales*
1998A	$ 58,388,296	$ 6,632,761	11.36%
1999	63,351,301	7,032,547	11.10%
2000	68,736,162	7,494,875	10.90%
2001	74,578,736	7,992,706	10.72%
2002	80,917,928	8,528,921	10.54%

As the table above indicates, the appraiser has projected the operating expenses of the Company to consistently decrease over the period under review. Although this does not seem like a significant amount on a percentage basis, it is very significant when you apply these percentages to the increasing sales in each year. For example, if we compare the difference in profit (before taxes) by holding relative operating expenses constant and using the projections above, the result is a drastic increase in profitability (and value). These results are summarized below:

Year	*Operating Expenses—as Projected*	*Operating Expenses—Constant*	*Difference (%)*	*Sales*	*Difference ($)*
1998A	11.36%	11.36%	0.00%	$ 58,388,296	$ —
1999	11.10%	11.36%	0.26%	63,351,301	163,999
2000	10.90%	11.36%	0.46%	68,736,162	313,377
2001	10.72%	11.36%	0.64%	74,578,736	479,248
2002	10.54%	11.36%	0.82%	80,917,928	663,149

As the table above indicates, income is extremely sensitive to operating expense projections. Furthermore, the appraiser does not provide any support for the reduction in expenses over the period under review. As the projections on page 19 of the Levine Report indicate, the appraiser determined that the majority of the expenses are projected to increase independent of the sales achieved by the Company. As discussed earlier in this report, the Company is going to have a difficult time maintaining its current level of expenses. To assume that they will be able to decrease expenses year after year is not realistic and is further evidence of the lack of diligence performed by the appraisers.

(Continued)

EXHIBIT 13.2 ***(Continued)***

Now that we have touched upon the overall reasonableness of the projected operating expenses used in the Levine Report, we have a few points on some individual expenses which need to be mentioned.

Fair Rental. The fair market rent for the property owned by the Company has been projected to increase at only 1 percent each year for the periods under review. This is less than the rate of inflation. It just does not make sense.

Depreciation/Replacement Cost. The appraiser does not forecast future depreciation expense based on projected capital expenditures and existing fixed assets, but rather projected depreciation as a percentage of sales. This can lead to inaccurate results if depreciation does not follow the same growth pattern as sales. Accordingly, this should be calculated using specific capital expenditure projections and expected future depreciation of existing fixed assets. These appraisers never considered the capital requirements of the Company in their forecast. Since they are significant, the Levine Report contains a fatal flaw in this area.

Debt-free Income. Even if we assume that the adjustments made to 1998 are reasonable, the projected benefit stream (debt-free income) is not. Although no single operating expense projection appears to be unreasonable on its own, the end result (in this case, debt-free income) appears to be very unreasonable.

The concepts of "common sense" and "reasonableness" become very applicable in dealing with a DCF analysis in that the resulting projections have a material impact on the final value of the appraisal subject. Accordingly, they must make sense and be reasonable. According to the projections used by the appraiser to value the Company, projected debt-free income (which is the starting point for the net cash flow calculation) for the years 1998 adjusted through 2002 are as follows:

Year	*Debt-free Income*	*Year-to-Year Growth*
1998	$ 182,486	
1999	721,873	295.58%
2000	864,495	19.76%
2001	1,021,519	18.16%
2002	1,194,247	16.91%

As the table above indicates, the appraisers have projected debt-free net income to nearly quadruple in the first year of the projection period and continue with 20 percent, 18 percent, and 17 percent year-to-year growth during 2000, 2001, and 2002, respectively. Furthermore, the compound annual growth rate (CAGR) for debt-free income is 59.9 percent from 1998 to 2002 and 18.3 percent from 1999 to 2002.

Another way to consider the projected debt-free income is to look at debt-free income as a percentage of sales. The following table does this:

Year	*Sales*	*Debt-free Income*	*Debt-free Income as a % of Sales*
1998A	$ 58,388,296	$ 182,486	0.31%
1999	63,351,301	721,873	1.14%
2000	68,736,162	864,495	1.26%
2001	74,578,736	1,021,519	1.37%
2002	80,917,928	1,194,247	1.48%

As the preceding table indicates, debt-free income as a percentage of sales has been projected to consistently increase over the forecast period. Again, the appraiser does not offer an explanation as to the reasonableness of being able to achieve this dramatic increase in profitability. In the appraisers' explanation of how the projections were derived, the focus was on sales growth rather than income growth. Even though the appraisers acknowledge that the increased volume from BIG MAJOR SUPPLIER would lead to a lower gross profit margin, they fail to follow through with this thought into the projections. They do not explain how the Company is going to be able to cut costs as drastically as has been projected. As such, we believe this projected income stream is not reasonable and has major implications on the value derived using this method.

EXHIBIT 13.2 *(Continued)*

Several adjustments are required to debt-free income in order to arrive at net cash flow. Typically, net cash flow (applicable to invested capital) is defined as follows:

Invested capital net cash flow = Debt-free net income
+ Non-cash charges (D&A, deferred taxes, etc.)
− Capital expenditures
− Increases in net working capital (or + Decreases in net working capital)

Although we agree with the methodology used by the appraisers to arrive at debt-free income, they fail to make the appropriate adjustments in order to arrive at a correct estimate of net cash flow. The following is an explanation of the mistakes made by the appraisers in calculating the projected net cash flows on page 19 of the Levine Report.

Changes in Working Capital. On the bottom of page 20, the appraisers show an analysis of historical working capital (current assets less current liabilities) as a percentage of sales. However, the impact that working capital has on cash flow is related to the increase or decrease from period to period (i.e., Change in working capital = Working capital (period $n - 1$) − Working capital (period n)).

Their assumption of 4 percent of sales for projected changes in working capital does not take into account the actual increase or decrease in cash from year to year. Using the historical working capital figures presented on the bottom of page 20 of their report, we calculated the change in working capital from 1995 to 1998. The results of this analysis are as follows:

Year	*Working Capital*	*(Increase)/Decrease in Working Capital*
1998	$2,229,918	$ 77,044
1997	2,306,962	(427,048)
1996	1,879,914	171,915
1995	2,051,829	(74,016)
1994	1,977,813	

The results shown above illustrate the corresponding sources (as indicated by a positive number) and uses (indicated by a negative number) of cash from changes in working capital for the respective periods. The appraiser should have considered these values—and not just working capital—in the development of net cash flow for a given period. As the preceding table indicates, there does not appear to be any identifiable trend in the changes in working capital on a historical basis. As such, a more detailed analysis would be required.

In order to fully understand the future changes in working capital for the Company, an appraiser should make a reasonable attempt at forecasting the current assets and current liabilities of the subject company. This is done by analyzing each asset or liability and how the appraiser expects it to change in the future (i.e., days receivable, days payable, days inventory, etc.). They chose to take the shortcut approach rather than the more accurate one.

Although the effects of projecting changes in working capital as was done by the appraiser may have actually reduced the projected net cash flow, the use of incorrect methodology is not acceptable. Furthermore, it casts a great deal of doubt on the other assumptions and estimates made in the Levine Report.

Capital Expenditures/Depreciation. According to the projections on page 19 of the Levine Report, the appraisers did not account for the addition of non-cash charges (i.e., depreciation) and the deduction of capital expenditures in their net cash flow projections. Although appraisers may estimate depreciation and capital expenditures to be equal in the future for small, closely held companies (and thus would offset each other), the appraisers have failed to explain the reasoning behind the omission of these items from the cash flow projections. Furthermore, given the Company's high level of expected future capital expenditures (which they discussed earlier in their report), this type of assumption (without a thorough investigation and analysis) led them to inaccurate results. Again, this leads us to believe that they have not been diligent in developing a reasonable estimate of future net cash flows for the Company.

A normal procedure for estimating these adjustments is to estimate future capital expenditures based on the growth and expansion plans of the Company. Since some plans were discussed in the information used by them to develop the projections, one could reasonably expect that capital would be required in the early years of the forecast period in order to align themselves with the future plans of their main supplier (BIG MAJOR SUPPLIER) and the RDC program. Had they chosen to ask the right questions in discovery, they would have been aware of the significant expenditures that the Company is facing in the next several years (if they can put it off that long).

(Continued)

EXHIBIT 13.2 *(Continued)*

Page 21. Once the appraiser calculates debt-free cash flow, an estimate for the discount rate needs to be made.

Equity Discount Rate. The appraisers appear to be using the concept of the build-up method in that they compare the subject company to the overall returns of small companies.

However, the build-up method must begin with a "safe" rate as of the valuation date (typically long-term government bonds). To this safe rate, the returns of large company stocks are added to arrive at a total market return applicable to the valuation date. To the total market return, a small company risk premium is added (if applicable). This increment reflects the additional returns required by an investor to invest in small company stocks. In addition to the small company risk, an additional premium may be added to account for the additional risks involved with an investment in a closely held company. Although this is a very subjective adjustment, some of these risks include industry, financial, management, and supplier, as well as other business risks. They have ignored all of the risks of the Company and have chosen to use a required rate of return as if this company were larger and safer.

Weighting. The appraisers use a 30/70 percent debt-to-equity weighting in their calculation of the weighted average cost of capital. As with some of the other elements of the appraisers' calculations, this is stated without any basis or explanation. As discussed previously in this report, we utilized *Cost of Capital Quarterly* (CCQ) for SIC 50 to estimate a reasonable debt-to-equity ratio. In reviewing the data contained in CCQ, we noticed that the smaller companies in the data had a lower percentage of debt than the larger companies. This is evidenced by the following table of data taken from CCQ:

Percentile	*1997 Sales ($ Millions)*	*Total Capital ($ Millions)*	*Debt/Total Capital*
75th	$647	$ 427	48.46%
Median	215	118	28.37%
25th	40	24	11.78%

Given that the Company is a smaller company, one would expect that it would exhibit the same debt–to–total capital ratios of similar-size companies in the same industry (distribution). By putting greater weight on the debt portion of the capital structure, a lower discount rate is derived, resulting in a higher estimate of value. Once again, this appears to be advocacy instead of objective analysis.

In addition to the methodology used to derive a discount rate (in this case, the WACC), the appraiser must check results for reasonableness. In this case, we believe that a 17 percent discount rate (or WACC) is too low for the Company's risk profile. The build-up method (if applied correctly) provides only a basis for establishing an appropriate discount rate. As such, the appraiser still needs to put the assignment into perspective, and think about how the specific risks of the subject company impact the riskiness of the future benefits being discounted.

Perpetuity Growth Rate. In the DCF analysis on page 19 of the Levine Report, they use a perpetuity growth rate of 5 percent (the perpetuity growth rate is the expected sustainable future growth rate of the appraisal subject after the discrete forecast period). Although we do not have a problem with 5 percent as a perpetuity growth rate, the underlying assumption of a DCF analysis is that the appraisal subject has reached a steady state by the end of the forecast period (in this case 2002). It is clear that, according to the net cash flow projections used by them, this is not the case. Although this is not a major issue (given that there were so many other issues with the Levine Report), it further supports our point that they failed to apply sound financial theory in this valuation. Accordingly, the results cannot provide a useful basis for estimating the value of the Company.

Built-in Capital Gains. As an offset to the fair market value of the non-operating assets used to calculate the total value of the Company, the potential tax liability resulting from capital gains should be considered. Ms. Johnson would receive a windfall if she were to receive a share of the property with the remaining shareholder left to pay all of the capital gains tax.

Discount for Lack of Marketability. Although the methodology and support used to derive the discount for lack of marketability (DLOM) is suspect, the end result of a 20 percent DLOM appears to be reasonable. Accordingly, there are a few points in this section of the Levine Report that we want to highlight to further illustrate their lack of regard for the underlying issues of the Company.

The appraisers state the following regarding the application of these DLOM studies.

> The range of marketability discounts indicated from a review of these data sources tends to be between 15 percent and 50 percent (it should be noted that *these studies are based upon minority blocks of stocks* in privately held companies).

The majority of the studies used as the basis for the DLOM generally deal with minority blocks of stock of publicly held companies, not privately held companies.

EXHIBIT 13.2 (Continued)

Regarding one of the factors to consider when determining a DLOM for a specific appraisal subject, they state:

Whether there are any restrictions governing the sale of the stock to interested third parties [*None known*]. (Emphasis added.)

On page 4, paragraph 23 of the Commercial Flooring Products Distributorship Agreement with BIG MAJOR SUPPLIER, it states the following:

This Agreement is not assignable or otherwise transferable by Distributor without the written consent of BIG MAJOR SUPPLIER. "Assignment" or "transfer" includes any change in ownership or control of Distributor which BIG MAJOR SUPPLIER in its sole discretion deems substantial.

As the preceding excerpt indicates, this limitation (as well as many others in the agreements with BIG MAJOR SUPPLIER) clearly states that BIG MAJOR SUPPLIER can terminate the distributorship at its sole discretion upon change of ownership or control. Although this does not appear to have influenced the choice of a DLOM, it leads us to believe that they probably did not even read the BIG MAJOR SUPPLIER agreements (because if they did, they should have mentioned a lot of the limiting conditions in support of their DLOM). It seems that they should have a higher discount based on the facts.

In Exhibit 13.2, the subject business was a floor covering distributor that was being valued for a shareholder dispute. The minority shareholder was claiming oppression even though there was none. The expert on the other side could not find any signs of it. Obviously, we were not happy with the other side's report. The best way to demonstrate what the report should have looked like is to provide it to you. This report is presented in its entirety on the CD-ROM accompanying this book

Exhibit 13.3 shows a different valuation assignment. In this instance, we were retained to prepare a limited valuation report. The limitation was that we were asked to value a minority stockholder's interest by doing a critique of the other side's report without performing a complete appraisal of our own. Key sections of this report should help demonstrate how we used the other side's report to help our position. In this valuation, the other expert was retained by the estate of a deceased shareholder to value the minority interest. The other expert's value for the minority interest was $210,000.

EXHIBIT 13.3

***Responding to the Other Side's Report*[1]**

Limited Valuation Report

Trugman Valuation Associates, Inc. was retained by Acme Building Maintenance, Inc. to critique the valuation study of Acme Building Maintenance, Inc. prepared by Smith and Company, CPAs, and to appraise the one-third stock ownership interest of John Jones (deceased) in Acme Building Maintenance, Inc.

The format of this critique follows the order of the Smith report. There are numerous errors in the Smith report, both factual and based on the application of the Revenue Rulings referred to in their report. This will be evident as we proceed.

It is our understanding that Mr. Jones died on May 19, 1998, not May 20, 1998, as indicated on page 1 of the Smith report.

This may seem like a minor point, but the more of these small inaccuracies that can be pointed out, the more doubtful the trier of fact will feel about the other side's report.

In the "History and Background Information" section of this report, Smith indicates that Mr. Jones was the "office manager" for the business. It is our understanding that there were no office employees. Therefore, whom did he manage? Also, the business paperwork was done by Jeffrey Johnston and Paula Roberts, the other two owners of the company.

The Smith report omits a detailed discussion of the duties of the officers, the background of the officers, the evolution and demise of the customer base, and, most important, that almost all work is obtained through the bidding process. Our review of the records indicates that 90.4 percent of the recurring monthly business comes from banking institutions; four customers comprise 79.4 percent of the total monthly business.

Since risk plays an important part of any business valuation analysis, we took the opportunity to point out a major factor that was omitted from the other side's report.

In the section titled "Economic Outlook for the Industry and in General," Smith has an almost nonexistent discussion of the banking industry. They ignore the fact that some of the company's larger customers were in financial difficulty, and they state, "The company under study, however, has 'weathered' this turmoil in the industry and has demonstrated its ability to 'hold' a sufficient client base."

[1]Sections in bold are the author's annotations.

(Continued)

EXHIBIT 13.3 *(Continued)*

Since Acme Building Maintenance, Inc.'s business comes from the competitive bidding process, the company's only weathering has been that some of their customers have yet to be taken over by the regulators. The banking industry is in serious trouble, and there is no certainty of continued patronage through the bidding process. Most bids carry a 30-day cancellation provision that can be exercised at any time.

Another factor that has been completely ignored is the relationship of the customers with Jeffrey Johnston. If Mr. Johnston leaves this business or if his contact at a bank leaves the customer, Acme Building Maintenance, Inc. may be significantly affected. This business is highly dependent on one individual who maintains the contacts that allow the company to bid on and win contracts. Despite these high risk factors, Smith concludes, "The outlook, therefore, for the company under study is excellent." *The conclusion reached is contradicted by the facts in this situation.*

In the section titled "Book Value of the Stock and the Financial Condition of the Business," the Smith report indicates that they "adjusted the balance sheet for accounts receivable and accounts payable at December 31, 1998." Although they analyzed the January 1993 disbursements to come up with their estimate of $10,000 for accounts payable, *two significant items were omitted from their analysis.*

The company's payroll is paid twice a month. The payroll for the period December 16 to December 31, 1998, was paid on January 2, 1999. Therefore, a liability should have been included in the Smith report in an amount equal to the gross payroll for that period, or $23,647.

Also omitted is the liability for worker's compensation insurance. The premium adjustment for the period March 1, 1998, to March 1, 1999, was $7,884. An estimated 10/12 of this amount, or $6,570, would have been a liability on December 31, 1998.

The next item that should be disputed in the Smith report is the revaluation of the equipment to an insurance value. First of all, the revaluation of assets is totally inappropriate in the valuation of a minority interest, unless the minority shareholder has the right to liquidate these assets. This is not the case here. Second, even if the revaluation were proper, the value in use on a depreciated basis would be considerably less than the replacement cost used for insurance purposes. Smith uses an incorrect standard of value in this analysis.

Based on our analysis, Exhibit B of the Smith report should be as follows:

Book value	$ (7,289)
Plus: Accounts receivable	165,516
Less: Accounts payable	(10,000)
Payroll payable	(23,647)
W/C insurance payable	(6,570)
Adjusted net book value	$ 118,010

In the section titled "Earning Capacity of the Company," Smith relies on Revenue Rulings 59-60 and 68-609 to perform their calculations. One of the key theoretical components missed by Smith is the fact that these Revenue Rulings result in a value of a controlling interest, not that of a minority interest. The minority shareholder does not have the right to control the daily operations of the business, determine compensation, make decisions about the business, or declare dividends. This is not to be confused with an oppression situation, in which the minority shareholder may have certain rights under the appropriate statute.

The earning capacity discussion should therefore be limited to the earning capacity of the minority stockholder. The adjustments made in Exhibit D of the Smith report are inappropriate, as well as incorrect.

Assuming that this valuation was performed on a control basis, there are errors in Smith's adjustments. Adjustment 1 assumes that the conversion from cash basis to accrual basis is evenly distributed over all five years. This is highly unlikely, since the business was growing during this period.

Furthermore, the spreading of $155,516 is incorrect because Smith failed to include the other payables for the company. Even if we accept their methodology, this adjustment would be $25,050 rather than $31,103.

Adjustment 2 is also incorrect. The Smith report adds back automobile usage for personal commuting purposes estimated at 30 miles per day per officer for 230 work days per year. Smith ignores the fact that two of the officers commute approximately 1.5 miles each way, and Mr. Jones's commute was approximately 20 miles. Besides using incorrect mileage, the use of the IRS mileage allowances is inappropriate because this amount takes into consideration items such as depreciation and car insurance, which the company does not pay.

Granted, there is a minor amount of personal automobile expense included in the figures, but the adjustment is so minor that it should be treated as insignificant. This would get lost in the final rounding in the conclusion of overall value.

The third adjustment removes personal accounting services relating to the manner in which the officers were compensated. This will not be discussed.

For sports fans, this is known as giving up a single. Once in a while, it is better to concede a point than to fight what the other side has done. The result of this was so minor that it had virtually no effect on the conclusion reached.

The fourth adjustment, however, adds back the total expense called "consulting services," which includes officers' compensation, in addition to other compensation. Even if this add-back was proper, the Smith report has included an add-back for compensation for more than just the officers of the company.

The breakdown of consulting services that we reviewed included $7,500 in 1998 for Bob Jobes (a salesman), and $823 in 1995 and $8,818 in 1996 for Don Weiner (a salesman). These add-backs are improper.

EXHIBIT 13.3 *(Continued)*

No mention is made in the Smith report about the fact that payments to Tom and Paula Roberts, who both work for the company, are included in the consulting services expense. This becomes important when compensation is subtracted in the next step because of the manner in which Smith determines reasonable compensation.

The Smith report refers to several salary surveys that are dated from 1994 to 1996. To begin with, these surveys are out of date. **[This illustrates that the appraiser did not even take the time in the assignment to get current information. This demonstrates a quick, sloppy job!]** Next, no consideration is given to the role that each officer plays in the company, the number of hours worked, or the fact that there are four people, not three.

The Smith report indicates that "we believe $55,647 is reasonable compensation for the officers of 'Acme Building Maintenance Inc.' for 1998." We find this level of compensation to be significantly lower than what would be required to replace these individuals, based on their respective duties.

Since Jeffrey Johnston is the chief executive officer responsible for sales, financial aspects of the business, and the overall direction of the company, it is our opinion that he could not be replaced for less than $100,000.

Tom Jacobson is responsible for the janitors and logistical operations, and works, on average, 70 to 75 hours per week. His reasonable compensation is estimated to be $75,000 annually.

Paula Roberts performs various duties, including sales, and handles paperwork for the company. She owned her own business prior to Acme Building Maintenance, Inc., which was merged with Jeffrey Johnston's former company. She could not be replaced for less than $50,000.

John Jones, deceased, was responsible for preparing the work schedule for three night people, answered telephones, and acted as the "inside" office person. Based on our understanding of Mr. Jones's duties, as well as his salary background when he was an employee of Mr. Johnston's company, we have considered $50,000 to be reasonable compensation for him. Therefore, reasonable compensation would be $275,000, not $139,118.

One other important factor must be brought to your attention about the Smith report: All of the calculations are flawed because their 1995 figures are for a six-month period. In 1995, the company changed its fiscal year end from June 30 to December 31. The Smith report includes figures for the six months ending December 31, 1995, rather than for a full year.

This is one of the worst errors that could have been made. All that had to be done was to look at the figures as compared with the other periods, and it would have been obvious that something was wrong. They never looked!

In the section titled "Dividend-Paying Capacity," Smith states that "dividends are not a reliable criterion of value with Acme Building Maintenance, Inc." This is only partially true. We agree that dividend-paying capacity should not be used for determining the enterprise value, but the valuation of a minority interest is the matter at hand. A minority stockholder in a closely held corporation realizes only value based on the dividends paid, the appreciation in the stock being held, or a combination of the two.

Appreciation of a minority interest is relatively insignificant in a company such as Acme Building Maintenance, Inc., since there is virtually no market for the stock. The only measure of value would be the dividends to be paid to the stockholder. In this instance, Mr. Jones received dividends in the form of excess compensation based on the amount he was paid for his labor.

Although Mr. Jones received dividends through his compensation, the other stockholders were compensated for their labor without excess. A review of the reasonable compensation entitlement compared with the actual salary paid indicates an excess of approximately $36,000 annually.

Since Mr. Jones's work responsibilities were redistributed either to the other stockholders or to new employees, the compensation portion of Mr. Jones's entitlement is unavailable for future dividends. However, $36,000 is available to be paid to the stockholders as dividends. Each stockholder would be entitled to a proportionate share based on common stock ownership.

Mr. Jones's minority stockholding would be entitled to a dividend based on the capacity to pay approximately $12,000 annually. To determine the value of this stock, the value of this anticipated benefits stream can be discounted by an appropriate rate of return, indicative of the risk of the investment. Using a discount rate of 25 percent, based on a 10-year holding period, an income stream of $12,000 paid annually would be worth approximately $43,000.

In the section of the Smith report titled "Goodwill," Smith incorrectly applies Revenue Ruling 68-609. Smith indicates that they consider Acme Building Maintenance, Inc. a "high-risk" business, then claims that they "have used the relevant 'high risk' capitalization rate." They also use a 10 percent rate of return on the tangible assets to further recognize "the risk of the venture." Justifying their rate, Smith states, "Risk-free rates of return are currently much less than 10 percent."

The Smith report demonstrates a basic lack of knowledge about this Revenue Ruling. First, Revenue Ruling 68-609, as indicated previously, is a control premise methodology. Second, Revenue Ruling 68-609 states that this approach "should not be used if there is better evidence available from which the value of intangibles can be determined." The ruling continues by stating that "if the assets of a going business are sold upon the basis of a rate of capitalization that can be substantiated as being realistic though it is not within the range of figures here as the ones ordinarily to be adopted, the same rate of capitalization should be used in determining the value of the intangibles."

This Revenue Ruling is frequently misapplied by individuals without proper education in valuation. The ruling makes a reference to capitalization rates of 15 percent to 20 percent and to rates of return on tangible assets at 8 percent to 10 percent, depending upon the risk involved.

This ruling also states that "*the above rates are used as examples and are not appropriate in all cases*" (emphasis added). Many inexperienced valuers make this mistake when they do not fully understand the financial theory behind these rates. These rates are intended to reflect the rate of return required by the marketplace for an investor to invest in an asset with the degree of risk residing therein.

(Continued)

EXHIBIT 13.3 *(Continued)*

At the end of 1998, risk-free securities, generally measured by long-term government bonds, were paying approximately 6.12 percent. Investors in equity securities of small companies in the public stock market have received, on average, a 17 percent return over the period 1926 to 1998, according to Ibbotson & Associates in *Stocks, Bonds, Bills and Inflation 1999 Yearbook*. Small companies are defined in this publication as those that are in the lowest 20 percent of the stock market (average capitalization of $94 million).

Clearly, if an investor can expect a 17 percent return from a diversified portfolio of companies with an average capitalization of $94 million, an investor would require a much higher rate of return to invest in Acme Building Maintenance, Inc. Furthermore, Revenue Ruling 68-609 is used to value the intangible assets, which alone are more risky than the entire enterprise. This would warrant an even higher rate of return.

Another indication of how far off the Smith report is with respect to these rates is that according to *RMA Annual Statement Studies 1998*, published by Robert Morris Associates, the mean return on tangible net worth was 35.1 percent for companies with assets of less than $500,000 in Standard Industrial Classification code 7349, described as "Services—Cleaning & Maintenance—Building." No prudent investor would require less than they could get elsewhere for the same type of investment.

In addition to the errors regarding the rates, the Smith report used weighted average earnings in order to perform the calculation of goodwill. This, too, is incorrect. Revenue Ruling 68-609 states that "the past earnings to which the formula is applied should fairly reflect the probable future earnings." In a growing company, a weighted average will never reflect probable future earnings. Therefore, based on the foregoing comments, we believe that the methodology employed by Smith is incorrect, and even if it was considered correct, it was incorrectly applied.

In the next section of the Smith report, titled "Sales of Stock and the Size of the Block of the Stock to Be Valued," Smith discusses a minority discount. The report also mentions that "studies of inheritance tax case law have shown discounts ranging from 0 percent to 33 percent of value." They conclude a 25 percent discount. This is acceptable.

Smith does not discuss the discount for lack of marketability of the closely held stock. This additional discount is clearly indicated, since it will be extremely difficult to sell a closely held company stock, especially a minority position in the company. Numerous Tax Court cases have allowed total discounts ranging from 0 percent to 80 percent.

Discounts for lack of marketability have been studied through analyses of restricted stock transactions. The summary listed in the following table appeared in the *Guide to Business Valuations*, published by Practitioners Publishing Company.

Summary of Restricted Stock Studies

Study	*Years Covered in Study*	*Average Discount (%)*
SEC overall average[a]	1966–1969	25.8
SEC nonreporting OTC companies[a]	1966–1969	32.6
Gelman[b]	1968–1970	33.0
Trout[c]	1968–1972	33.5[?]
Moroney[d]	—[?]	35.6
Maher[e]	1969–1973	35.4
Standard Research Consultants[f]	1978–1982	45.0[?]
Willamette Management Associates[g]	1981–1984	31.2[?]

[a]From "Discounts Involved in Purchases of Common Stock (1966–1969)," *Institutional Investor Study Report of the Securities and Exchange Commission*, H.R. Doc. No. 64, pt. 5, 92d Cong., 1st Sess., 1971, 2444–2456.

[b]From Milton Gelman, "An Economist-Financial Analyst's Approach to Valuing Stock of a Closely Held Company," *Journal of Taxation* (June 1972), 353–354.

[c]From Robert R. Trout, "Estimation of the Discount Associated With the Transfer of Restricted Securities," *Taxes* (June 1977), 381–385.

[d]From Robert E. Moroney, "Most Courts Overvalue Closely Held Stocks," *Taxes* (March 1973), 144–154.

[e]From J. Michael Maher, "Discounts for Lack of Marketability for Closely-Held Business Interests," *Taxes* (September 1976), 562–571.

[f]From Standard Research Consultants, "Revenue Ruling 77-287 Revisited," *SRC Quarterly Reports* (Spring 1983), 1–3.

[g]From an unpublished Willamette Management Associates study covering the period from January 1, 1981, through May 31, 1984.

Although the years covered in this study are likely to be 1969–1972, no specific years were given in the published account.

Median discounts.

EXHIBIT 13.3 *(Continued)*

The minority discounts and the discount for lack of marketability must be factored into the valuation of Mr. Jones's minority interest, since it is virtually impossible to sell a minority interest in a closely held business, such as Acme Building Maintenance, Inc. In reality, a discount of 100 percent could probably be justified.

There is no clear indication of the correct amount of discount to be applied, although common sense dictates that it should be high. Factoring into the determination is the size of Acme Building Maintenance, Inc. compared with the public market transactions that provided average discounts of approximately 25 percent and 35 percent for minority and lack of marketability, respectively.

Since these discounts are multiplicative rather than additive, the discount must be at least 53 percent. The size and inability of Acme Building Maintenance, Inc. to guarantee a return to an investor would increase these discounts to approximately 70 percent.

The final section of this report is intended to substitute what we feel is a more realistic value of Acme Building Maintenance, Inc. than what was calculated by Smith. The janitorial services industry has developed valuation methodologies that are used to consummate transactions. These should be given more weight than any other methodology, since they are industry specific.

In the *Business Broker's Handbook*, published by Business Brokerage Press, experienced business brokers compiled the methodologies used to sell these types of businesses. Sales are generally made based on a multiple of monthly recurring revenue. The range of the multiple has varied from 1 to 4. The result represents the value of the intangibles.

This is our opportunity to use a rule of thumb as a reasonableness check and, at the same time, use a published source in order to be authoritative. Would we use this as a method of valuation by itself? No.

As of December 31, 1998, Acme Building Maintenance, Inc. had monthly recurring revenues of $85,776. Based on the high concentration of income from a few customers, we believe that the highest multiple should not be used. However, since most of Acme Building Maintenance, Inc.'s customer contracts have a 30-day termination clause, the "willing buyer" would have one month guaranteed. In addition, the customer would probably pay for at least one more month, representing the initial month. This would justify a multiple of at least two months. Since many of the customers are banks and they are known to be slow in reacting to certain situations, another month could go by, justifying a multiple of 3.

The value of the enterprise would therefore be calculated as follows:

Monthly recurring revenue	$ 85,776
Multiple	× 3
Value of intangibles	$257,328
Value of tangibles	118,010
Value of Acme Building Maintenance, Inc.	$375,338
Rounded	$375,000

The value of Mr. Jones's one-third interest would therefore be calculated as follows:

Value of Acme Building Maintenance, Inc.	$375,000
Mr. Jones's interest (33.3%)	× 33.3%
Value before discounts	$125,000
Discount percentage	× 70%
Amount of discount	$ 87,500
Value of Mr. Jones's interest	$ 37,500

Whether the valuation of Mr. Jones's minority interest is performed using the industry methodology for the enterprise, discounted appropriately, or discounted on the basis of dividend-paying capacity, the value of the interest is approximately $40,000.

Besides making plenty of errors, the other side's expert never took into consideration the fact that the valuation was of a minority interest. In this instance, when the other side realized that they were in trouble, the case settled before getting to court.

Understanding the Weaknesses in the Valuation Process

There are generally two schools of thought when it comes to preparing a valuation report, particularly for litigation. The first is to never admit to having weaknesses in your report. Many attorneys feel that if an appraiser includes a discussion about weaknesses in his or her report, or if the appraiser points out weaknesses, he or she is giving the opposition too much ammunition with which to attack the report. On the other hand, admitting that valuation is not an exact science and that the process sometimes requires an appraiser to use information that is potentially flawed can help demonstrate the level of knowledge of the business appraiser, not to mention the objectivity.

Therefore, the other school of thought is to take the wind out of the opponent's sail and address each area that the appraiser expects to be subject to an attack upon cross-examination. If the appraiser addresses those areas that he or she knows will be attacked, the appraiser will not allow the opposing attorney the opportunity to raise these issues as if they are a surprise. Attorneys love to make a judge or jury think that they have caught the expert doing something deceitful. If the appraiser admits that there are shortcomings with the report, there is little surprise and it becomes no big deal. For example, if the appraiser uses industry composite data from RMA *Annual Statement Studies* and the appraisal subject is not a "great" match for that Standard Industrial Classification code, the appraiser can acknowledge that the information should be used with caution.

Any experienced business appraiser knows that he or she can be attacked because of the weaknesses in certain parts of his or her reports. Think about defending a capitalization rate. Unless the appraiser has excellent market data, he or she probably cannot totally support the rate selection. This is a subjective process that is frequently attacked.

The experienced appraiser recognizes that a capitalization rate can be justified only by comparing the rate used with other rates available in the marketplace or by testing the conclusion reached for reasonableness. Admitting the subjectivity of the process is not going to be harmful if the appraiser proves that the answer makes sense. I frequently testify that I am hired not to determine a capitalization rate but, rather, to opine on the value of the business. Quite frankly, if the value makes sense, who cares how I got there? If you concentrate on supporting your overall opinion, the component parts of how you got there are not as important.

Appraiser, Protect Yourself!

When preparing any type of business valuation report, the appraiser must be thinking about the potential liability that can arise from this type of engagement. Unlike many of the conventional accounting engagements that a CPA is asked to perform, a business valuation assignment is calling for an *opinion* of value. A disclaimer on page 1 of the report will not get the appraiser too many jobs. Imagine how the client would feel getting a 100-page report that starts out by stating, "I am not responsible for the opinion that I am about to give."

The appraiser must pay careful attention to each assignment. If I am a CPA-appraiser, the last thing that I want a client to think is that a business valuation is an audit. In fact, our engagement letter specifically indicates that we are not doing an audit. In addition, so many of our litigation jobs involve forensic accounting (you know, playing hide-and-seek with unreported income in a divorce) that we must be very careful in that type of engagement.

Since valuation is a prophecy of the future, forecasts and projections are frequently included in our reports. Appraisers should include some language to indicate clearly that they are not guaranteeing the outcome, nor have they audited the projections, unless they have. We will accept the forecast or projections from management, perform some due diligence purely with respect to the appraisal assignment, and put any and all caveats in our report.

It is also a good idea to restrict the use of your appraisal report. The limiting conditions of our firm make it clear that the report can be used only for the purpose that is outlined in the introduction section. The report also states that only the definition of value defined in the report is the applicable standard of value for that assignment. This prevents your client from taking a report that was performed for estate planning and turning it into an offering memorandum for potential investors.

A final suggestion in this regard. If you issue a less-than-complete report, put in restrictive language such as this:

> This report does not contain all of the required disclosures of a comprehensive appraisal report. Therefore, only those individuals who have complete knowledge about the appraisal subject may be aware of all of the facts and circumstances that are not contained herein. This report should therefore not be used by others, since they may be misled by its incomplete contents.

If that does not scare them away, make them read your report when it is tied around the neck of a Bengal tiger.

Defending the Business Valuation Report

In any assignment, the appraiser may be called upon to defend the business valuation report. For litigation engagements, this may take place at depositions or in the courtroom. At depositions, the usual rules apply. Do not volunteer anything. The appraiser cannot score any points in a deposition, and there is little reason to try to defend the report at this stage of the proceedings. At the deposition, the opposing attorney is generally trying to find out what the appraiser did, why he or she did it, and how it was done. Our firm's experience is that a well-written report often means a short deposition. When we issue a formal valuation report, there is little left to the imagination. Other than wanting to review our underlying documentation and possibly question us about our assumptions, the other side does not have many questions.

Once we have explained what we did in the report, how we did it, and why we did it, there is little left that can be asked. Always discuss your deposition technique with your client's attorney beforehand. Most attorneys will tell you to give the other side nothing. Others, on rare occasions, will tell you to give them everything in the hopes that your knowledge and thoroughness will help the parties settle the case. Never take the latter for granted! That is not your job.

At the time of the trial, you, the expert, will once again have an opportunity to defend the report. The testimony will generally be divided between the direct examination and the cross-examination. On direct examination, I like to use my report as a selling tool. Although the report is rarely entered into evidence, the judge in a bench trial will usually accept a copy of the report to help him or her follow along with my testimony. In these cases, the use of clear tables and graphs is an exceptional way to educate the judge.

Your report's appearance is important. It should look as professional as the job you did. A nice cover, dividers, and good presentation will help. Window dressing works wonders! During your direct examination, take the opportunity to invite the judge to follow along with the chart on page 10, the graph on page 21, or anything else that will give the judge a reason to review this well-structured document. Even if the judge does not read the report, the appearance will indicate your professionalism, as long as your testimony does not negate it.

When preparing for trial with a client's attorney, I ask the attorney to allow me to testify according to the sequence of my report. Since the report is written to tell a story, my testimony follows the same pattern. It is much easier to follow a familiar format than having to learn a new routine just before trial.

Cross-examination can also be used by the expert to defend his or her report. I like to refer to my report before answering certain questions. First, it acts as a refresher of what I have done, and second, it allows me to think about the question and about the answer that I am about to give.

Using the appraisal report during cross-examination can also be an effective demonstration of the appraiser's thoroughness. When the attorney states, "You didn't consider this in your analysis, did you?" it gives you a great opportunity to respond, "With all due respect, if you turn to page 39 of my report, you will see that I did consider that very issue." Needless to say, a well-prepared attorney will rarely give you the opportunity to embarrass him or her that way. Don't be surprised, however, if you are given this opportunity, and be prepared to take advantage of it.

Common Errors in Business Valuation Reports

After reviewing numerous business valuation reports, both those in actual engagements as well as those that have been submitted by applicants who have applied for accreditation to some of the appraisal organizations, I have compiled a list of what not to do in an appraisal report. You have seen many of these items throughout the book when I showed you the other side's work product. These are the most common errors that I have seen (not necessarily in any special order).

1. *Definition of value*. Frequently, appraisal reports refer to a particular standard of value (i.e., fair market value) but the definition is missing from the report. The definition of fair market value has varied considerably in different jurisdictions and must be clearly defined so that the reader can be certain of its meaning.

   Another common error regarding the definition of value occurs when the appraiser defines the standard of value that was supposed to be used in the assignment but applies a different standard of value during the appraisal process.

2. *Choice of appraisal method(s)*. One of the common errors seen in appraisal reports is the use of only one or two appraisal methods in the assignment, as opposed to all appropriate methodologies. Considering all the appropriate appraisal methods acts as a good check on each of the methods used and should always be part of a full appraisal.

   Relying on a "favorite" method is another common error made by inexperienced appraisers. Some individuals take a liking to a particular method and always use it. The excess earnings method is one of the favorite methods. This practice should be avoided. The correct appraisal methods should be based on the availability of information and the facts and circumstances of the appraisal.

   Another common error is using methods that contradict each other. For example, the capitalization of income method is generally used if the income in the numerator is stable, whereas the discounted future earnings method is used when the income being forecast is unstable. The use of each of these methods in the same appraisal is an indication that the income stream is both stable and unstable. How can that be?

3. *Market data*. A major flaw in many appraisals occurs when the appraiser is so sure that market data cannot be located that he or she never bothers to look for it. This is absolutely wrong! Market data should be looked for in every valuation.

4. *Selection of guideline companies*. Many problematic reports include guideline companies that are poor comparables: the guideline companies chosen are not similar and relevant enough to the appraisal subject to make them good companies to use in the appraisal. This often occurs when the appraiser uses guideline companies that are so much larger than the appraisal subject that a true comparison cannot be made. As I mentioned in Chapter 5, imagine comparing a paint manufacturer, with sales of $30 million, to Sherwin-Williams, with $3 billion in sales.

   Another problem with the selection process occurs when the appraiser does not look far enough to find good guideline companies. A company does not necessarily have to be in the same Standard Industrial Classification code to be a good guideline company. Revenue Ruling 59-60 suggests "same or similar."

5. *Financial Analysis*. This is often missing from appraisal reports. Other than using historical financial information for the valuation calculations, some individuals forget to perform a trend or comparative company analysis to make the appropriate determinations of risk.

   Another common error is the inclusion of financial ratios in the appraisal report without any discussion about the meaning or relevance of the ratios. We also frequently see normalization adjustments made in reports that are not adequately explained. There should be an explanation for all adjustments made. Avoid arbitrary adjustments that cannot be properly supported.

6. *Discount and capitalization rates*. The problem in this area could fill up an entire book on valuation. The general problem in this part of the report is usually that there is an inadequate amount of support for the determination of the rates used. The risk analysis may be inadequate to support the appraiser's conclusion of the appropriate rates.

   Another problem is applying a rate for a particular benefits stream to another benefits stream (e.g., applying a discount rate for cash flow to earnings, or applying a pretax rate to an after-tax stream).

   A frequent error is the use of the 15 percent to 20 percent capitalization rates from Revenue Ruling 68-609 regardless of the risk associated with the benefits stream, particularly the excess earnings attributable to intangibles.

7. *Premiums and discounts*. Similar to discount and capitalization rates, the biggest problem is that the report does not include enough support for these items. The percentages used should be supported by a well-thought-out analysis of the factors that affect premiums and discounts.
8. *Typographical errors*. There is nothing worse than seeing an appraiser charge a client thousands of dollars and not take the time to proofread the report properly. Typos are an indication of carelessness and should be avoided whenever possible. Spelling errors are unacceptable, especially in light of the spell-check features of most word-processing software packages.
9. *Illogical conclusion*. Another error, and the most fatal, is reaching a conclusion that does not make sense; the appraiser does not perform any sanity tests, and the end result defies logic. Often, we see that the value conclusion is so high that the cash flow from the business could never support a purchase price in a transaction. My favorite example of this is the time when our client's attorney cross-examined the other side's expert and asked, "Mr. Smith, would you pay that much for this business?" Mr. Smith responded, "Why no, never." How can an appraiser expect anyone to believe in the estimate of value if he or she does not?

The Reconciliation Process

At the end of the appraisal process, the appraiser must choose a value based on the various methodologies that were used. In a perfect world, all of the methods used would result in the same value, making the choice easy. Unfortunately, we do not live in a perfect world. The likelihood of all of the values even coming close to one another is slim.

This is the part of the assignment that will determine if the appraiser understands valuation. The pros and cons of each method should be considered. For example, the adjusted book value method may not have considered any intangibles that the business may have, and therefore may result in an understatement of the value. On the other hand, the Picasso painting is not generating any cash flow, but may have a market value of $42 million.

Each method should be carefully scrutinized for areas that could have resulted in an error (or less confidence), and a determination should be made as to how much weight will be placed on the method in light of the other methods used in the appraisal.

One example of the weighting process follows:

Method	*Value*	*Weight*	*Calculated Value*
Market approach			
Price/earnings	$4,400,000	30%	$1,320,000
Percent of sales	$4,700,000	10%	$ 470,000
Multiple of book value	$4,400,000	30%	$1,320,000
Dividend payout ratio	$4,200,000	10%	$ 420,000
Asset-based approach			
Adjusted book value	$1,200,000	0%	$ 0
Liquidation value	$ 430,000	0%	$ 0
Income approach			
Capitalization of benefits method	$4,800,000	20%	$ 960,000
Estimate of value			$4,490,000
Rounded			$4,500,000

There is no magical formula to the weighting process. It is entirely up to the appraiser's good judgment as to where the final value estimate will come in. Some appraisers do not like to show the computations above, while others do. Either way is acceptable as long as you can explain your conclusion.

Avoid a common error, which is to take a straight mathematical average of all methods. Most often, your result will be incorrect. In fact, Revenue Ruling 59-60 specifically tells us not to just average the numbers.

Make sure you round your conclusion. The number of places to round will depend on the materiality of the conclusion. Rounding to the nearest $1,000 may be appropriate for smaller appraisals, whereas rounding to the nearest $100,000 may be appropriate in others. Rounding the conclusion illustrates to the reader that valuation is not an exact science. Though you want to be accurate, you do not have to be precise.

After you reach your conclusion, don't forget to test it for reasonableness. Ask yourself two key questions:

- If I were the buyer, would I pay this much for the business?
- If I were the seller, would I sell it for that much?

If the answer to either of these questions is no, go back to the drawing board and see where you went wrong.

Another test that works particularly well for the income approach, and should be considered for the market approach as well, is known as the "justification for purchase test." A good friend of mine, Ken McKenzie, former co–executive director of The Institute of Business Appraisers, taught me this test at the first business appraisal seminar that I attended, almost 20 years ago. This is also known as the "business broker's method" since it is used by business brokers to price a business for sale.

The justification for purchase test is designed to determine if the cash flow that is forecast to be generated by the business will be adequate to cover the debt payments that will result from the acquisition of the business, assuming normal business terms. Exhibit 13.4 demonstrates this test as it was included in a valuation report.

EXHIBIT 13.4
Justification for Purchase Test

Reconciliation of Values

During the appraisal, several methods were used to determine the value of the equity of ABC Punch & Die Corp. The values derived in this appraisal are as follows:

Market approach	
M&A transactions	
IBA price to revenues	668,000
BizComps price to revenues	689,000
BizComps price to earnings	381,000
Asset approach	
Adjusted book value	278,000
Income approach	
Single-period capitalization method	372,000

The market approach is normally afforded the greatest amount of weight for a going concern, since fair market value is determined by the market, and it is the appraiser's role to interpret the market. The values derived under the market approach indicate that the values derived using a price to revenues multiple far exceed the values derived using the earnings. Although a buyer would be more concerned with revenues, he or she would also want to be sure that there are earnings available. Therefore, we have put 60 percent of our weighting on the market approach, in an equal amount to each method.

In a going-concern valuation, the asset-based approach does not necessarily reflect the value of the intangible assets. Therefore, the value derived using the approach is generally a floor or minimum value. In this instance, we believe that the market and income approaches capture this intangible value, and therefore, we are putting no weight on the adjusted book value method.

The income approach utilizes the Company's cash flows to derive a value for ABC. Cash flow is important because it must be available to pay any acquisition debt that may be incurred by the hypothetical buyer. In this case, there is a considerable amount of cash flow available. The problem with this method is the subjective nature of the derivation of the capitalization rate. Considering these strengths and weaknesses, we put 40 percent of the weight on this method.

EXHIBIT 13.4 *(Continued)*

Therefore, the operating value of ABC Punch & Die Corp. on a control, nonmarketable basis is calculated as follows:

Approach	*Value*	*Weight*	*Weighted Value*
Income approach			
Single-period capitalization method	$372,000	.40	$148,800
Market approach			
IBA price to revenues	668,000	.20	133,600
BizComps price to revenues	689,000	.20	137,800
BizComps price to earnings	381,000	.20	76,200
Value of operating entity			$496,400
Rounded			$496,000

As previously stated, the Company has $200,000 in non-operating assets. In order to determine the value of the equity of the Company, we must add the value of these assets to the value of the operating entity. Therefore, the value of the equity of ABC Punch & Die Corp. as of January 8, 2000, is as follows:

Operating entity	$496,000
Non-operating assets	200,000
Value of equity	$696,000

Justification for Purchase Test

Valuation is not the process of developing capitalization rates or multiples. It is, however, the process of providing the user of the appraisal with an estimate of value within a reasonable range. Recognizing that valuation is not an exact science, a test was performed to substantiate the amount of indebtedness that could be undertaken, using a five-year payback period, based on the normalized economic income that would be available to a "willing buyer."

Assuming typical terms for a business transaction of this kind, a purchaser would use approximately one-third equity and two-thirds debt to acquire a business of this type. This means that the pretax income would have to carry debt service and taxes. The appraiser decided to use the 1999 adjusted pretax income as indicative of future pretax income that would be available to service the debt incurred by the prospective buyer when purchasing the Company. The tax rate has been assumed to be 40 percent. Using a 10.50 percent interest rate (prime rate as of the valuation date plus 2 percent) and a $496,000 purchase price results in the following:

	Year 1	*Year 2*	*Year 3*	*Year 4*	*Year 5*
Annual payments	$ 85,288	$ 85,288	$ 85,288	$ 85,288	$ 85,288
Interest	32,214	26,365	19,872	12,663	4,658
Principal	$ 53,074	$ 58,923	$ 65,416	$ 72,625	$ 80,630
Cash flow					
Pretax income	$110,060	$110,060	$110,060	$110,060	$110,060
Interest expense	32,214	26,365	19,872	12,663	4,658
Taxable income	$ 77,846	$ 83,695	$ 90,188	$ 97,397	$105,402
Tax	31,138	33,478	36,075	38,959	42,161
Net income	$ 46,708	$ 50,217	$ 54,113	$ 58,438	$ 63,241
Principal payments	53,074	58,923	65,416	72,625	80,630
Cash flow	$ (6,366)	$ (8,706)	$(11,303)	$(14,187)	$(17,389)
Return on down payment	(3.85)%	(5.27)%	(6.84)%	(8.58)%	(10.52)%

(Continued)

EXHIBIT 13.4 *(Continued)*

This table indicates that the purchaser of the Company would have to generate slightly more revenues in order to cover the costs of servicing the acquisition debt. It also assumes that there will be no growth in cash flows. Of course, revenues, income, and cash flows were lower in 1999 than in 1997 and 1998. All valuation calculations were based on averages of these figures, as we anticipate that revenues will fluctuate within a $200,000 range and income and cash flow will fluctuate as well. Therefore, the scenario that was presented was a "worst-case" scenario; we believe that the willing buyer would be able to increase cash flows slightly to cover the anticipated debt service, and therefore, we believe that $496,000 reflects a reasonable value of the operating entity.

Exhibit 13.4 illustrates a simple test that is designed to determine whether the buyer could afford to pay for the business based on the value that was determined by the appraiser. Most small to medium-sized businesses do not have the ability to use creative financing techniques to pay for the acquisition. The two major concerns of the buyer consist of making payroll at the end of the week and being able to pay off the debt service that exists as a result of the acquisition. In fact, if the cash flow of the business is not adequate to pay down the debt, most of these types of transactions cannot take place.

Some appraisers (and some software programs) suggest that there needs to be a cash-on-cash return (return on the down payment) in order for the test to work properly. This is incorrect since the appraiser's role is to determine a cash equivalent value initially. If there is a cash return on the down payment, the seller is allowing the buyer to have an extra return above the required rate of return that entered into the initial determination of value. This means that the seller is leaving too much money on the table as part of the transaction. The optimal situation is for the cash return to be a break-even, or at least reasonably close to it.

The justification for purchase test should attempt to simulate a real transaction using a realistic down payment, interest rate, and term for the financing. Certain businesses require larger down payments than others. Speak to a business broker, and he or she can probably give you some guidance. The interest rate that we use is generally anywhere from prime rate to 3 points above the prime rate depending on the risk of the business. The term rarely goes out more than five or six years. Don't do something silly like using a 15-year payback. The buyer cannot get that type of financing. The results should make sense.

Conclusion

At this point, you now have more of an idea about the appraisal report. The enclosed CD-ROM contains three sample reports. Now you even have some samples that you can plagiarize. How do you think we all get started? Thank you, Dr. Pratt, for that great sample report in your first book! Just remember that there is only a small amount of boilerplate and that the rest will have to be created from scratch each time. Also remember that a good report will be understandable to the reader. With all of that in mind, I'll see you in court!

14

Estate and Gift Valuations

Chapter Goals

In this chapter, I will attempt to explain:

1. Valuation rules for estate and gift tax purposes
2. Valuing family limited partnerships (and similar entities) for gift tax purposes
3. Court cases that you need to be aware of
4. How to do your job properly

Introduction

As I was writing this chapter, President Bush was getting Congress to pass his $1.3 trillion tax bill that would eliminate the estate tax (maybe) over the next 10 years. So why write this chapter? For at least the next 10 years (and probably two or three more editions of this book), the estate and gift tax will be a major tax affecting millions of taxpayers. Currently, with tax rates as high as 55 percent, the opportunities for the business appraiser are great. If you are going to work in this arena, however, you must know the rules. And there are definitely rules.

Business valuation assignments performed for estate and gift tax purposes are subject to the laws found within the Internal Revenue Code and Regulations. This is not optional. It is the law. But as with all laws, there always seem to be interpretations that are questioned. Though it is not my intent to turn this book into a tax treatise, the business valuer needs to be aware of the rules. If you are not an accountant, work with an accountant, a tax attorney, or someone who knows the rules.

Besides the Internal Revenue Code and Regulations, it is also a pretty good idea for you to be familiar with Revenue Rulings, Private Letter Rulings, Tax Court decisions, and all types of other stuff that relates to this area. You also need to know that there are various tax penalties built into the tax law that penalize taxpayers and sometimes appraisers for substantially understating a tax liability. Besides the malpractice issues that I addressed earlier in this book, you certainly do not want to find yourself in a position where you or your firm is laying out money in the form of penalties.

Now that I have sufficiently scared you, let's discuss valuations for estate and gift tax purposes.

Revenue Ruling 59-60

All valuations that are performed for estate and gift tax purposes are subject to Revenue Ruling 59-60. Not only have I discussed this ruling throughout the book, but Chapter 12 was devoted solely to it. You also have a copy of it in Appendix 6. I am not going to repeat all of that stuff here. Just reread it.

Chapter 14 Guidelines

Chapter 14 of the Internal Revenue Code (Sections 2701 through 2704) is an important part of the tax law to know if you are doing this type of work. The rules are very complex and confusing. I will try to explain the more important provisions to you as we go along.

The Valuation Report

Preparing a business valuation report for estate and gift tax purposes should really be no different from preparing a well-written report for other purposes where fair market value is the standard of value. If you follow the guidance that I have tried to give you throughout this book, you should do fine. Since the rules relating to "adequate disclosure," particularly in gift tax situations, changed in December 1999, let's discuss reports being prepared for gift tax purposes. These days, one of the most common types of reports is for a gift of an interest in a family limited partnership.

The Family Limited Partnership Report

Family limited partnerships (FLPs) have grown in popularity during the 1990s as an estate planning tool and a way to depress transfer tax values. Although this discussion refers to family limited partnerships, many of the concepts discussed also apply to family limited liability companies created primarily as asset-holding companies. Business valuation experts should be aware of the issues involved in valuing FLP interests and how to prepare a report that is less likely to be challenged by the IRS, or, if challenged, one that will more likely allow the challenge to be resolved in favor of the taxpayer.

Appraisers need to do more than focus on what discounts they can use to reduce the value of a FLP interest. After all, this is usually the main fight with the IRS (see Chapter 11 for a discussion on discounts). The FLP agreement and other partnership documents must be thoroughly analyzed before the appraiser can begin to render an opinion of value. The final report must at least contain certain information about the assignment—the nature of the interest being valued, the terms of the partnership agreement, and the financial condition of the entity.

This discussion is designed as an overview of the FLP valuation process and the items to consider. It is designed to help you prepare valuation reports more effectively and perhaps minimize the opportunity for the IRS to challenge your opinion of value.

What Is a FLP?

Simply stated, a FLP is a nontaxable entity that is created and governed by statute and whose partners (both general and limited) and assignees consist *mainly* of family members.

It is nontaxable because, as a partnership, it is a "pass-through entity." Unlike a corporation, which is subject to corporate-level income tax, a partnership does not pay any income taxes at the entity level. Partners will be liable for income taxes on their proportionate share of any partnership income, whether it is distributed in the form of cash or not.

A limited partnership is created under and governed by the Revised Uniform Limited Partnership Act (RULPA) of the state in which it is formed. Though they are similar in many respects, each state's Limited Partnership Act contains features that are different (although some states' acts are the same).

The FLP is also affected by various sections of the Internal Revenue Code (IRC), as is the valuation of interests in a FLP.

Even the term "family members" is carefully defined in IRS regulations. Members of the family are defined as the transferor or the transferor's spouse, the transferor's or spouse's lineal descendants, and their spouses. This definition includes adopted children or offspring of the transferor's children but does not include aunts, uncles, cousins, and the like.

Many of the issues that arise in appraising FLPs become legal interpretations of the partnership agreement, rather than "pure" valuation issues. Although as appraisers it is important that we know and understand the issues, it is imperative that we leave the "lawyering" to the lawyers. You have heard me say that over and over again. If there is any doubt in the appraiser's mind regarding the nature of the assignment or the terms of the partnership agreement, the client's attorney should be the one to explain it to the appraiser, not the other way around.

Why Are FLPs Attractive?

FLPs are particularly attractive as estate planning tools because, through the creation of a FLP:

1. Parents or grandparents have the ability to indirectly transfer interests in family-owned assets without losing control of them.
2. A high degree of protection against creditors can be achieved. This is because a partner's creditor is legally unable to gain access to the assets in the partnership.
3. The assets can be kept in the family, which is an objective of many families. This can be achieved by placing restrictions on the transfer of partnership interests, especially in the event of divorce, bankruptcy, or death of a partner.
4. Problems pertaining to undivided or fractionalized interests when a property is gifted to several individuals can be avoided. This can be especially important in the case of real estate properties.
5. When family-owned assets are placed in a partnership, advantages can arise through economies of scale and diversification.
6. A great deal of flexibility can be achieved through the partnership agreement, which can provide broad investment and business powers. These can be amended as the family's needs change, as long as all partners are in agreement.
7. As mentioned earlier, the partnership is a pass-through entity and does not pay income taxes.
8. The gifting or transfer of an ownership interest in a limited partnership may be made at a lower value than that interest's pro rata share of net asset value. The reason for this is that a limited partnership interest is likely to be both noncontrolling and nonmarketable.

Valuation Issues

This is not an estate planning review, but a discussion of valuation techniques, so we will concentrate on item 8 of the previous list. Individuals can, and often do, prepare their own estimate of the value of interests in their FLP. There is no requirement that a taxpayer engage the services of a professional appraiser to do this.

However, Section 6662 of the IRC imposes penalties for the undervaluation of estate and gift assets. These Section 6662 penalties are triggered by asset undervaluation and computed as a percentage of the tax underpayment. The IRS may decide not to apply any penalties if the reported value was made in good faith and had a reasonable basis. A qualified appraisal prepared by a competent valuation analyst may constitute part of the establishment of a "reasonable basis."

You must be warned that applying discounts too enthusiastically can backfire. Section 6701 of the IRC imposes civil penalties on valuation analysts of $1,000 for "aiding and abetting an understatement of tax liability." The IRS could also impose an administrative sanction barring the appraiser from submitting probative evidence in future IRS proceedings. For these reasons, the report must be prepared judiciously, and every statement must be carefully documented and presented in such a way that the valuation conclusion can be replicated and understood by those for whom it is intended.

What Exactly Is the Assignment?

As stated early in this book, the appraiser should obtain a retainer agreement (and a retainer) from the client, which should spell out the precise nature of the assignment the analyst is going to perform. The importance of having a clear understanding of what the valuation assignment is cannot be overemphasized. It is important that the following parameters of the assignment become a part of the appraisal report:

1. The name of the client (i.e., the person who engaged the appraiser). The client is responsible for identifying the nature of the interest to be appraised.
2. The nature of the interest being appraised (e.g., general partner interest, limited partner interest, or assignee interest). It is important to note here that the thing being appraised is *not* a percentage interest in any or all of the assets owned by the partnership, but rather an *interest in the partnership itself*.
3. The size of the interest being valued. Size can be represented by a percentage interest amount, the number of units or shares, or even a dollar amount.
4. The valuation date and the purpose for which the valuation is being performed, i.e., whether it is for estate planning (gifting) or estate valuation purposes.
5. The standard of value. The retainer agreement should provide a definition of the standard of value that will be determined in the appraisal. These standards are defined in the following tax regulations:

   Estate planning (gifting)—Treasury Regulation 25.2512-1

   Estate valuation (after death)—Treasury Regulation 20.2031-1(b)

   Both of these sections define the standard of *fair market value* as follows:

   > The fair market value (of the property being valued) is the price at which the property would change hands between a willing buyer and a willing seller, neither being under any compulsion to buy or sell and both having reasonable knowledge of relevant facts.

   This definition should appear in the report as well.

What Documents Are Needed to Prepare the Appraisal Report?

The analyst should obtain the following documents before beginning the assignment:

1. The Agreement of Partnership (or other type of business agreement depending upon the form of the entity), as well as a copy of the Certificate of Limited Partnership that has been filed with the state where the partnership was created. The certificate is an important document because it gives notice of the formation of the limited partnership and the limited liability of the limited partners, and discloses some of the terms of the partnership agreement. Without this document, the possibility exists that the FLP will not be recognized by the IRS.

   If the appraiser is not familiar with the Limited Partnership Act of the state of formation, he or she should also obtain a copy of it.
2. A list of the assets that were initially contributed to the partnership, as well as documentation of any assets that were contributed after the formation of the FLP.

3. Valuations of real estate and other assets held by the partnership as of the valuation date (for example, market values of marketable securities). If the partnership owns interests in other closely held businesses or partnerships, these interests must be separately appraised before the value of the LP interest can be determined.
4. Financial statements and/or tax returns for the partnership for a reasonable number of years, or since inception. If it is a new partnership, these will not exist.
5. The general partner's anticipated policies regarding distributions or a Section 754 election. The Section 754 election will be covered later.
6. If the FLP is ongoing; a history of distributions, if any, made to partners.

Information such as minutes of meetings of partners or other documents, if they exist, may give the analyst some insight into the intent of the donor at the time of formation of the partnership.

How Does Revenue Ruling 59-60 Help?

Revenue Ruling 59-60 provides basic guidelines for appraising shares of closely held corporations. It is also a valuable guide to appraising FLPs. Every valuation report of a family limited partnership interest should closely follow Section 4 of Revenue Ruling 59-60, which enumerates the factors the appraiser should consider in his or her valuation.

Most of the information necessary to describe the nature of the FLP and its history can be found in the Partnership Agreement and the Certificate of Partnership. This section of the report is often overlooked, as many analysts prefer to concentrate on the valuation calculations and the discounts selected. However, it is important to make a thorough review of the Partnership Agreement and to include a list of the pertinent aspects of it in the report.

Remember, our assignment is to determine the fair market value of a FLP interest, not the fair market value of the underlying assets. That is what the appraiser should be concentrating on in his or her report.

What Is Chapter 14?

Chapter 14 of the IRC was enacted in October 1990 and outlines the special valuation rules that must be adhered to when valuing interests in closely held companies and partnerships. The basic premise behind this section is that when valuing business interests that are to be transferred between family members, the appraiser should ignore restrictions that would not exist if the transaction were between unrelated third parties.

This chapter consists of only four sections; three of which actually relate to family limited partnerships. If the partnership does not comply with the provisions of this chapter, the IRS may determine that the partnership does not exist for tax purposes and value the underlying assets directly in calculating the applicable gift or estate tax.

The provisions of the Partnership Agreement should comply with the sections of Chapter 14; the major items contained in a FLP agreement are listed below, with the applicable sections of Chapter 14.

Provision	*Chapter 14 Section*
Formation	2703
Purpose	2703
Term	2704(b)
Management	2704(a)
Capital contributions	2703
Allocations of profit and loss	2701
Distributions	2701
Transfer restrictions	2703 and 2704(b)
Dissolution	2703 and 2704(b)

Section 2701 addresses special valuation rules used for lifetime gifts when a junior equity interest (corporate, partnership, or LLC) is transferred from one family member to another and the transferor retains a senior equity interest in the company. In this instance, "senior" and "junior" interests refer to interests that are not equal economically, such as preferred stock versus common stock. They do not refer to "general" or "limited" partners as such, because general and limited partners are often economically the same. Although they have disproportionate liability and management responsibilities, this alone does not make a general partner interest "senior" to a limited partner interest.

For this reason, the special valuation rules contained in IRC Section 2701 *do not apply* to a gift of a partnership interest where *all items of income and loss are shared in the same proportions by all partnership interests.* A reading of the Partnership Agreement will determine whether or not the FLP is a "pro rata" partnership, where the only differences between the general partner interest and the limited partner interest are management rights and the extent of liability exposure.

Section 2703 deals with restrictions placed on the rights of the transferee in the partnership interest. This section provides that the value of any property is to be determined *without regard to:*

1. Any option, agreement, or right to acquire or use the property at a price less than fair market value
2. Any restriction on the right to sell or use the property

These rules do not apply when:

1. There is a bona fide business arrangement.
2. It is not a device to transfer the property for full and adequate consideration.
3. Its terms are comparable to similar arrangements entered into by persons in arm's-length transactions.

What is the significance of Section 2703? The term "property" in Section 2703 does not mean the assets contributed to the FLP by the partners, because those assets are 100 percent owned by the FLP. Once the assets have been contributed to the FLP, no partner or assignee has a right to receive, possess, or use the assets. What they do have a right to possess is their general and/or limited partner interests. Since it is the interest in the FLP that is the property for purposes of IRC Section 2703, whether this section applies depends upon the restrictions placed on the rights of the transferees in the partnership interest.

Whether or not Section 2703 applies is for the client or client's attorney to decide, not the appraisal analyst. The appraiser is retained to determine an opinion of value for a partnership interest (not a partnership asset). At most, the appraiser can be alert for provisions in the agreement and contact the client if anything appears questionable.

Under this code section, the IRS will argue that the restrictions in the agreement are more onerous than the restrictions would be between two unrelated parties, and as a result, the agreement is not valid. If the IRS wins this argument, then a partnership does not exist, and the actual gift made was the actual underlying assets, rather than an interest in a family limited partnership.

Section 2704 deals with lapsed voting and liquidation rights.

Section 2704(a) treats certain lapsed voting or liquidation rights in a FLP as "deemed transfers" and they become subject to gift or estate tax. Generally, this code section becomes applicable if there is only one general partner and this partner is an individual. Voting rights lapse if at the time of death this general partnership interest becomes a limited partnership interest, and the general partner's rights to liquidate the partnership lapse as a result. The issue becomes how to measure that loss in "rights."

Many experts conclude that the best way to avoid triggering Section 2704(a) is to have a general partner that is a corporation or other entity. In the alternative, a FLP could have more than one general partner if the partners are individuals and there is a provision for succession from one to another should one die. These provisions must be spelled out in the Partnership Agreement.

Section 2704(b) disallows consideration of certain restrictions (called the "applicable restrictions") on liquidation rights in valuing the transfer of an interest in a family-controlled entity.

An "applicable restriction" is any limitation on the ability to liquidate the entity in whole or in part that is more restrictive than the limitations that would apply under the state law, if the restriction did not exist in the agreement.

If the liquidation restrictions in an agreement are more restrictive than state law, under Section 2704(b), the appraiser should value the interest utilizing state law provisions, rather than the more restrictive rights in the agreement.

There are a number of states that have changed their Limited Partnership Act to state that the provisions of the Partnership Agreement control liquidation restrictions, and therefore, many LPs are formed in these states. For this reason, it is imperative for the appraiser to understand the appropriate state law.

How Does All This Affect the Valuation Assignment?

Many appraisers are concerned with the size of the discounts taken in a FLP valuation, as they believe that this is the biggest concern to the IRS. Although the IRS is concerned with excessive discounts, much of the recent case law has centered on the issue of whether the partnership "truly" exists. The IRS has raised this issue by either attacking the reason for the formation of the partnership or raising Chapter 14 issues, specifically Sections 2703 and 2704.

Remember, if the IRS can win on these issues, then the FLP is not seen as a valid entity, and therefore, the gifts become gifts of the underlying assets directly, rather than partnership interests (in other words, no discounts).

Some recently decided cases that dealt with these issues are:

- *Baine P. Kerr, et ux. v. Commissioner,* 113 T.C. 449
- *Estate of Albert Strangi v. Commissioner,* 115 T.C. 35
- *Ina F. Knight v. Commissioner, et vir v. Commissioner,* 115 T.C. 36
- *Church v. United States,* 85 AFTR 2d 2000-804

This is not intended to be an exhaustive list; it is merely an example of some of the issues that the IRS has brought up on audit that have been decided by the courts. I am also providing only brief synopses of portions of the cases for illustrative purposes. You should read each entire case so that nothing is taken out of context.

***Baine P. Kerr, et ux. v. Commissioner,* 113 T.C. 449.** The IRS contended that the FLP agreement contained restrictions on the liquidation of the partnership that constituted "applicable restrictions" within the meaning of Section 2704(b), and that these restrictions should be disregarded in valuing the transferred interests.

In its decision, the court determined that the agreement was not more restrictive and therefore did not contradict applicable restrictions. The court stated:

> We reach this conclusion because Texas law provides for the dissolution and liquidation of a limited partnership pursuant to the occurrence of events specified in the partnership agreement or upon the written consent of all the partners and the restrictions contained in section 10.01 of the partnership agreement are no more restrictive than the limitations that generally would apply to the partnerships under Texas law.

***Estate of Albert Strangi v. Commissioner,* 115 T.C. 35.** The IRS took the position that under the business purpose and economic substance doctrines, the FLP should be disregarded in valuing the assets in the decedent's estate. The estate contended that there were clear and compelling non-tax motives for creating the partnership, including the provision of a flexible and efficient means by which to manage and protect the decedent's assets. They also gave the following arguments: "(1) to reduce executor and attorney's fees payable at the death of decedent, (2) to insulate decedent from an anticipated tort claim and the estate from a will contest, and (3) to provide a joint investment vehicle for management of decedent's assets."

The court was skeptical of the business purposes claimed by the estate and concluded that no active business was conducted by the FLP after its formation. Despite that, the court stated the following:

> FLP was validly formed under State law. The formalities were followed, and the proverbial "i's were dotted" and "t's were crossed." The partnership, as a legal matter, changed the relationships between decedent and his heirs and decedent and actual and potential creditors. Regardless of subjective intentions, the partnership had sufficient substance to be recognized for tax purposes. Its existence would not be disregarded by potential purchasers of decedent's assets, and we do not disregard it in this case.

***Ina F. Knight v. Commissioner, et vir v. Commissioner,* 115 T.C. 36.** The IRS contended that the partnership lacked economic substance and failed to qualify as a partnership under federal law. The petitioners contended that their rights and legal relationships and those of their children changed significantly when the partnership was formed, assets were transferred to it, and interests were transferred to the children's trusts, and that the partnership must be recognized for federal gift tax purposes.

The court agreed with the petitioners that the partnership must be recognized for federal gift tax purposes. It stated the following:

> State law determines the nature of property rights, and Federal law determines the appropriate tax treatment of those rights.
>
> The parties stipulated that the steps followed in the creation of the partnership satisfied all requirements under Texas law, and that the partnership has been a limited partnership under Texas law since it was created. Thus, the transferred interests are interests in a partnership under Texas law. Petitioners have burdened the partnership with restrictions that apparently are valid and enforceable under Texas Law.

***Church v. United States,* 85 AFTR 2d 2000-804.** The estate was entitled to an estate tax refund based on its expert's valuation of the decedent's family partnership interest. The partnership was valid under law in Texas, where it was formed to preserve the family ranching enterprise, consolidate undivided ranch interests, and raise cattle; the decedent effectively conveyed securities held in a brokerage account to the partnership before death, and the partnership agreement showed her intent to relinquish beneficial interest.

Also, conveyance was not a taxable gift on the partnership's formation; the fact that the securities' value exceeded the decedent's partnership interest did not render the transfer gratuitous where the partnership did not confer financial benefit on any partner. Sections 2036 and 2038 did not apply.

In addition, Section 2703's term "property" did not refer to pre-death contributions; and statutory language and legislative history showed that the statute did not cover the term or the partnership agreement's sale restrictions, thus reducing the partnership interest's value.

Although court cases need to be reviewed on a pretty regular basis, I have provided a section at the end of this chapter on some of the more recent court cases that impact this area. Just remember that these were current when this book was written. There may be newer cases that you need to consider when you are doing your job!

Things to Consider in the Appraisal Process

The basic characteristics of the transferred interest in the FLP, combined with specific provisions in the FLP agreement and state law, form the foundation for the valuation adjustments used in arriving at the fair market value of the transferred interest in the FLP. Some of the factors to be considered in determining appropriate valuation adjustments may come as a result of provisions in the partnership agreement. Some of these are:

- A provision (term-of-years provision) in the partnership agreement that the partnership shall continue to exist for a definite term of years, unless it is dissolved or liquidated prior to this date
- No *guarantee* by the managing general partner or general partners of the return of any partner's capital contributions, nor any allocations of profits or losses, nor any distributions of distributable cash (not even enough to cover the annual taxes of the partners)
- Approval rights of limited partners required for certain major decisions; otherwise limited partners and assignees are excluded from participation in management
- How the election of new managing general partners is accomplished
- A provision that distances the limited partners and assignees from the assets of the FLP
- The right of the managing general partner(s) or general partner(s) to determine distributable cash
- Capital call provision obligating partners and assignees
- Limitations on the voluntary and involuntary transferability of general partner, limited partner, and assignee interests
- The presence of rights of first refusal
- Consent of all partners required for a transferee or assignee of an interest in the partnership to become a substituted limited partner
- Whether the managing general partners or general partners are required to make an IRC Section 754 election
- Limitations on the "right" of the general partner to withdraw from the partnership prior to the expiration of its stated term and provision that, should the general partner exercise his or her power to withdraw early, his or her general partner interest shall become a limited partner interest and he or she may also be subject to damages for breach
- Limitations on the right of a limited partner and assignee to withdraw from the partnership prior to the expiration of its stated term
- Provisions for dissolution of the partnership mirroring state law

Some factors that need to be considered but may not be found in the partnership agreement include:

- The reputation, integrity, and perceived competence of the partnership management/general partner(s)
- The number of investors in the partnership
- The type of assets owned by the partnership
- Whether or not the assets of the partnership are well diversified
- The amount of financial leverage inherent in the partnership's capital structure
- The caliber of the information flow from the partnership and the general partner(s)
- The current and historical amount of cash actually distributed to partners and assignees
- Underlying cash flow coverage of yearly distributions made to partners and assignees
- The size of the interest
- The universe of interest buyers
- The "default rules" under state law

What About Methodology?

What is the best approach for valuing a FLP interest? Which methods can and should be used? Section 4 of Revenue Ruling 59-60 states:

> (a) . . . in general, the appraiser will accord primary consideration to earnings when valuing stocks of companies which sell products or services to the public; conversely, in the investment or holding type of company, the appraiser may accord the greatest weight to the assets underlying the security to be valued.
>
> (b) The value of the stock of a closely held investment or real estate holding company, whether or not family owned, is closely related to the value of the assets underlying the stock. For companies of this type the appraiser should determine the fair market values of the assets of the company. Operating expenses of such a company and the cost of liquidating it, if any, merit consideration when appraising the relative values of the stock and the underlying assets. The market values of the underlying assets give due weight to potential earnings and dividends of the particular items of property underlying the stock, capitalized at rates deemed proper by the investing public at the date of appraisal. A current appraisal by the investing public should be superior to the retrospective opinion of an individual. For these reasons, adjusted net worth should be accorded greater weight in valuing the stock of a closely held investment or real estate holding company, whether or not family owned, than any of the other customary yardsticks of appraisal, such as earnings and dividend paying capacity.

This seems to imply that some type of asset-based approach would be the most appropriate and, indeed, the only approach to appraising a FLP interest. Whereas an asset-based approach might be a frequently used approach to valuing such an interest, it is by no means the only one. Often an income approach may be used as well. The approach to be used may be determined based on the underlying assets of the FLP or whether or not there is a history of distributions to the partners and how extensive and consistent the distributions were. Depending on the assets held by the partnership, a market approach could also be utilized. Depending on the circumstances of the case, more than one method may be appropriate.

In *Estate of Etta H. Weinberg, et al. v. Commissioner* (T.C. Memo 2000-51), the court accepted both an income approach and an asset-based approach for determining the value of the decedent's minority interest in a limited partnership that owned and operated an apartment complex. The court found that the taxpayer's use of the net asset value method under the asset-based approach was warranted since the property would retain most of its inherent value regardless of rental income production. Furthermore, the court found that the capitalization of the three-year average of distributions under the income approach was also appropriate. The findings of the court illustrate that the reliance on one approach (particularly the asset-based approach) for the valuation of FLPs is not always sufficient or relevant.

In deciding on the methodology to apply to the valuation of partnership interests, the following applies:

> When valuation consultants use an asset-based approach to value a FLP interest, the restrictions in the partnership agreement are often the sole justification for the amount of the discounts. In these cases, the IRS attempts to disregard the restrictions for valuation purposes by demonstrating that the terms of the partnership agreement are onerous and not comparable to arm's-length transactions. If the restrictions are disregarded, the IRS then argues to invalidate the partnership agreement for valuation purposes, resulting in a significant increase in the value of the limited partnership interest.
>
> While this rationale has not been proven in tax court, the IRS has used it to successfully negotiate with taxpayers for an increase in the amount of gift and estate taxes that would have otherwise been paid. If the valuation is determined using the income and market approaches and does not rely solely on the restrictions in the partnership agreement, it is more difficult for the IRS to dispute the valuation.[1]

[1] Jay E. Fishman et al., *Guide to Business Valuations*, 10th ed. (Fortworth, Tex: Practitioners Publishing Company, 2000), 14-11.

Asset-Based Approach. Obtain fair market value of all assets and liabilities on the balance sheet and apply appropriate discounts (for lack of control and marketability).

Income Approach. Determine cash flow available to partners and capitalize or discount as appropriate.[2] Apply discount for lack of marketability (no discount for lack of control necessary as cash flow capitalized or discounted is the amount available to the minority owner and, therefore, the result is a minority value).

Market Approach. Determine valuation multiples by looking for comparable publicly traded interests. The appropriate multiple could be price to NAV (net asset value), adjusted for the risks associated with your specific valuation assignment.[3] Since this data is based on trades of minority interests, the result is a minority value. Therefore, only a discount for lack of marketability needs to be applied.

Valuation Adjustments

Valuation adjustments are supposed to reflect the lack of control inherent in limited partnership interests and the lack of marketability any type of closely held partnership interest endures. These are two separate issues that usually result in two separate adjustments or discounts. The courts recognize the necessity for these discounts but often disagree about how much of a discount may be allowed.

Fair market value is determined by the nature of the interest transferred. Unless the partners agree to admit the transferred interest as a partner, it is an "assignee interest." Therefore, the hypothetical willing buyer would consider as significant whether or not the other partners would admit him or her as a partner with all the rights that go with being a partner.

An assignee interest has only an economic interest in the partnership. That is, he or she has a right to receive distributions, if any, and a right to distributions on liquidation. An assignee interest has fewer rights than a limited partner.

A limited partner, like a minority shareholder, does not have the ability to "get at" the partnership assets to either manage them or dispose of them. A limited partner may have little or no say in partnership management issues. And, like a minority shareholder, a limited partner does not control distributions. These are all prerogatives of management or, in the case of the limited partnership, the general partner or the general partner who has been designated as the managing partner.

The hypothetical willing buyer most likely would not pay liquidation price (pro rata of the underlying assets) for a limited partner or assignee interest in a limited partnership. What a willing buyer would pay would be something less than liquidation value in order to receive a return on his or her investment. This is the basis for valuation adjustments or discounts.

The analyst must read the partnership agreement carefully to determine what the rights and duties of both types of partners are. The voting rights of the limited partners should be determined. These are the types of things that will contribute to the size of the discount for lack of control.

Discount for Lack of Control

Although I provided you with some of this stuff in Chapter 11, it is important enough to repeat. The types of assets owned by the partnership must be considered in finding a starting point for this discount. As previously discussed, the appraiser may not need a discount for lack of control if he or she utilizes an income or

[2]Sources of rates of return include the *Wall Street Journal*, Ibbotson Associates, and National Association of Real Estate Investment Trusts (NAREIT).

[3]Sources for comparable (guideline) data are "Closed End Mutual Funds" (the *Wall Street Journal*, Morningstar) and *Partnership Spectrum* (published by Partnership Profiles, Inc.).

market approach for this type of assignment. Although a FLP could hold almost any type of asset, most FLPs own either marketable securities, real estate, or some combination of the two.

Marketable Securities. A logical reference point in valuing such a FLP is a closed-end investment company. It is best to use closed-end investment companies (mutual funds) that hold publicly traded securities similar to the securities held by the FLP, such as domestic stocks, foreign stocks, speciality funds, corporate bonds, municipal bonds, or government bonds. There are many other types of funds.

Typically, these funds trade at discounts to their net asset values (NAVs). Statistical efforts to determine a definitive explanation for these discounts have failed to explain why these discounts occur. In any event, the discounts (and premiums) observed in the marketplace serve as a proxy for the lack of control discount. The reason that they serve as a proxy is that holders of closed-end funds have the same lack of control over the underlying assets that a limited partner in a FLP has. It is presumed that these discounts represent the market's decrease in value for not having access to the assets and not having any control over them.

Whether the appraiser adjusts these discounts before applying them to his or her FLP interest is a question of specific facts and circumstances of your particular valuation. If you believe that the interest you are appraising has less control, then you might increase the discount, and vice versa. Another issue relates to the similarities of the portfolios. The appraiser might believe that his or her portfolio would trade at a higher or lower discount. Whatever position the appraiser takes, the discussion should include all the reasoning behind the adjustments.

This discount pertains only to the issue of lack of control. It has nothing to do with marketability factors. The perceived riskiness of any individual security in the FLP's portfolio will be reflected in the market value of that security. Any adjustments the analyst might be tempted to make because the partnership interest is not as easily traded as a share in a closed-end mutual fund should be avoided. That is a different discount.

There are several factors that might be considered in making adjustments to the starting point for the discount for lack of control. Remember that adjustments should be reasonable and reflect the facts of the particular FLP interests.

- *Professional management*. Many FLPs do not have professional management, whereas closed-end funds do. This would drive the discount higher.
- *Regulation*. Closed-end funds are regulated by the SEC; the FLP investor enjoys no such protection.
- *Diversification and size*. The FLP portfolio may not have the same level of diversification as a closed-end fund. As a comparison, one can look at specialized funds that invest in one industry. FLPs are often very tiny compared to closed-end funds. This might increase the discount.
- *Investment objective*. A FLP portfolio may reflect no defined investment policy or objectives. This may be due to a lack of professional management.
- *Quality: speculative versus investment grade*. Recall that the security's market price should reflect the market's opinion as to its overall quality. Avoid double counting in the discount.
- *Performance*. If the FLP has been in existence for a while, its total return might be compared with that of various similar closed-end funds.
- *Average maturity*. For fixed-income portfolios, the average maturity of the bonds will affect their market values. Again, this factor should be addressed in the price of the security.
- *Real estate*. Very often, a FLP will hold one or more pieces of real property. These might range from the family home to vacation property, vacant land, a farm, or some income-producing real property, such

as apartments, retail space, or office space. The analyst should review these assets carefully in order to determine the nature of each, as this will affect the selection of discounts.

A starting point for determining lack of control discounts for FLPs owning real estate would be real estate limited partnerships (RELPs). These partnerships have been in existence for a number of years, and a body of data has been accumulated on many aspects of them. A fairly liquid secondary market for RELPs exists. It is nowhere near as liquid as a stock exchange, but enough transactions take place that there is good data on the discounts at which these securities trade to their NAVs.

Data on this market has been gathered by Partnership Profiles, Inc. since 1990. Partnership Profiles issues a bimonthly publication titled *Partnership Spectrum*, which offers general commentary about the secondary market for RELPs. Operating data for five years is provided where available, including information on cost of properties owned, percentage of leverage, gross revenues, net income, cash flow, working capital, and a history of distributions to partners.

The May/June issue of *Partnership Spectrum* contains the results of their annual study of market discounts from NAVs. This issue can give the analyst valuable information concerning a starting point for a discount for lack of control for the FLP interest. The following factors can influence the price of a RELP in the secondary market. These factors can be considered by the analyst in determining a value for the FLP interest:

1. The type of real estate assets owned by the partnership
2. The amount of financial leverage inherent in the partnership's capital structure
3. Underlying cash flow coverage of yearly distributions made to partners
4. The caliber of the information flow from the partnership and the general partner
5. Whether or not the assets of the partnership are well diversified
6. The reputation, integrity, and perceived competence of the management/general partner
7. Liquidity factors such as: how often a partnership interest trades, the number of investors in the partnership, the time period until liquidation, the universe of interested buyers, whether the partnership is publicly or privately syndicated, and the presence of rights of first refusal

Whether or not a FLP has a history of making distributions is an important consideration in determining the discount. Generally, partnerships that make distributions trade at smaller discounts than their NAVs, all other things being equal. The amount of debt is important as well. If the appraisal FLP has no debt, it should be compared to partnerships that have little or no debt.

Consider as many comparable partnerships from this study as possible. Courts have maintained that more comparables are better than fewer, and certainly better than only one.

As with a discount obtained using closed-end funds, this discount for real estate limited partnerships is also a starting point. It may be adjusted—either upward or downward—by factors that differentiate the appraisal FLP from the comparable real estate limited partnership. These are similar to the ones enumerated under the marketable securities section.

Discount for Lack of Marketability

An additional adjustment is often made to account for the fact that there is no secondary market for FLP interests, nor is one ever likely to develop. These interests lack marketability; that is, they cannot be liquidated or converted to cash quickly. If one owns shares of a publicly traded corporation, one may call a broker, sell the shares, and have the cash proceeds within a few business days. Not so with FLP interests, and this is the basis for the discount for lack of marketability, or DLOM.

In addition to the lack of a secondary market for FLP interests, certain provisions are often written into FLP agreements restricting the transfer of interests, especially to individuals or entities outside the family circle. These restrictions create an additional lack of marketability factor. Some of them are:

1. With some exceptions, a general partner, limited partner, or an assignee may not transfer all or any part of his or her interest without the prior written consent of the general partners, which consent may be given or withheld at the discretion of the general partners.
2. A transferee of an interest in a FLP shall be entitled to the rights of an assignee only unless the consent of all general partners and a majority in interest of the limited partners is given to make the transferee a substitute limited partner.
3. No partner or assignee shall have the right to withdraw from the FLP prior to its dissolution and liquidation.
4. No partner or assignee may withdraw or reduce his or her capital contribution or capital account without the consent of the general partner.

Other Provisions Affecting Marketability. In addition to provisions in the agreement that restrict transfer, a history of little or no dividends or distributions from the FLP to the partners is a factor that affects marketability. A willing buyer might be more inclined to ignore restrictions on transfer of his or her interest in exchange for a stream of cash benefits. However, little or no distribution history is common with FLPs, which often retain income and gains in order to fulfill the long-term investment goals of the partnership.

Another factor that might affect the marketability of a FLP interest is the "754 election." This is an election that the partnership *might* make under IRC Section 754, which provides that the partnership may elect to adjust the inside basis of the partnership's underlying assets. In other words, the partnership can adjust its internal books to show that a new partner paid a higher price for assets that are worth more at the time of the purchase (transfer). This election would not affect the existing partners, but it would have positive tax consequences for a new partner.

If there is nothing in the agreement that addresses the 754 election, it does not mean that the partnership cannot make the election. It still can. However, a willing buyer might wish to have assurance that such an election will be made. This is especially critical if the appraised fair market value of the underlying assets of the partnership have increased in value over their original basis. Since there is considerable record keeping involved once this election is made, a FLP may be reluctant to make the election.

When valuing a general partner interest, some consideration may be given to an additional marketability factor that reflects the liability exposure assumed by the general partner. Under many states' partnership statutes, a majority of the limited partners may remove a general partner who assigns all of his or her interest in a FLP to a third party. Here, the analyst must read the Partnership Agreement carefully to determine the circumstances under which a general partner interest may be transferred or whether, after withdrawal of a general partner, that general partner interest becomes a limited partner interest. In this case, the DLOM might be increased.

A FLP can require additional capital from the partners in order to meet operating expenses and have extra capital for partnership requirements. This type of provision is not included in every FLP agreement, but its presence may warrant an additional lack-of-marketability factor. Capital calls might require that an interest holder remain liquid in order to meet them, rather than place funds in a higher-yielding but less liquid investment. A willing buyer would consider this additional liability exposure and potential loss of a more favorable investment rate of interest in determining value, and so does the business appraiser when valuing the interest in the FLP.

Sources of Marketability Discounts. The sources for discounts for lack of marketability for FLP assignments are the same as for all valuation assignments: restricted stock studies and IPO transactions. The appraiser starts with these studies and then needs to address the facts and circumstances of the specific valuation assignment to determine the adjustments to the "benchmark" discount that will be utilized in the assignment at hand. Several lists of factors to consider have been published. The first list comes from *Guide to Business Valuations* (p. 14-34):

Some of the factors that would cause an interest to trade at a low marketability discount include—

a. Minimal volatility in the value of the underlying assets.
b. Above-average expectations for future yield.
c. A proven and stabilized history of income.
d. Certainty of distributions or expectation of capital appreciation.
e. Limited time period on restriction of ability to sell the interest.
f. Favorable outlook for future growth of the entity.

Factors that would cause an interest to trade at a higher discount include—

a. High degree of volatility in the value of the underlying assets.
b. Questionable ability to generate a satisfactory return on assets.
c. Inability to generate sufficient earnings for distributions or to support future growth in operations.
d. Small size in relation to other investments and lack of diversification.
e. Involvement in industries or activities viewed unfavorably by the investing public.

The second list comes from an article published by Robert E. Moroney titled "Why 25% Discount for Nonmarketability in One Valuation, 100% in Another?" I gave you this stuff in Chapter 11.

Other Potential Adjustments

There are several other adjustments that may be included in determining a final value. Some of these adjustments may apply to the value of the underlying assets, rather than to the value of a FLP interest.

Fractional Interest Adjustment. The fair market value of an undivided ownership interest in real property is worth something less than the percentage of ownership multiplied by the fair market value of the real property as a whole. Fractional interest adjustments should not be limited to undivided interests in real property, but should be considered any time a fractional interest is held in any type of property. Some of the factors considered by the willing buyer in arriving at a fractional interest adjustment are:

1. Lack of control associated with a minority interest in the property
2. Lack of marketability of a fractional interest
3. Procedural burdens, possible delays, and costs involved in severance proceedings
4. Lack of certainty as to what portion of the property would be awarded to each party upon severance
5. The nature of the property
6. The difficulty of obtaining mortgage financing for the purchase of a fractional interest
7. Declining economic conditions
8. Loss of a major tenant

Since some real estate appraisers apply these fractional interest discounts as a matter of course, the appraiser should check the real estate appraisal, if there is one, to see if this has already been done. This will help the appraiser avoid double discounting.

Portfolio Adjustment. The basis for a portfolio adjustment is a FLP with a nondiversified portfolio of marketable securities. In applying a willing buyer–willing seller test, the appraiser must decide if a willing buyer might not be interested in a portfolio with a specific asset mix, rather than a diversified portfolio. A portfolio containing one or two holdings might be considered more risky than one that is well diversified. See *Estate of Piper v. Commissioner*, 72 T.C. 1062 (Sept. 13, 1979).

Restricted Securities Adjustment. Restricted securities are those that are acquired from an issuer in a transaction exempt from registration requirements of federal and state securities laws (known as "private placements"). There are also restrictions imposed by the SEC on resales of these restricted securities. Several court cases have upheld additional discounts to account for restricted securities, but if the price of the security already reflects such a discount, it should not be taken twice.

Blockage Adjustment. This adjustment accounts for the depressive effect of suddenly placing a large block of stock on the market. This adjustment is expressly recognized by Treasury Regulation Sections 20.2031-2(e) and 25.2512-2(e). Adjustments of this type are limited to blocks of publicly traded stock. It is helpful to fully document trading and volume activity in a stock for a period of time prior to the valuation date in order to justify such an adjustment.

Market Absorption Adjustment. This is an expansion of the blockage adjustment to take into account other assets besides stock, such as real estate, works of art, sheet music, manuscripts, books, animal mounts, and animal trophies. The basis of this adjustment reflects the lack of time in which to make an orderly disposition of these types of assets. It is possible that the sale of all of the property at once or within a short space of time might result in an abrupt increase in supply, which, with no change in demand, might reduce the price the properties could bring. The analyst should consider the number and type of assets being considered and whether or not such an adjustment has been included in any professional appraisal of these assets.

Adjustment for Built-in Capital Gains Tax. Under the willing buyer–willing seller test, an adjustment may be made for the fact that the underlying assets may have a market value greater than their book value and that there may be a built-in capital gain with respect to those assets. If so, a willing buyer might become responsible for capital gains tax when the assets are sold. A hypothetical willing buyer would take this into consideration when evaluating a FLP interest. This issue is also related to the Section 754 election.

Adjustment to Present Value. This type of adjustment was permitted in valuing a FLP's underlying assets that were winnings from a lottery ticket to be paid to the FLP over a period of time. The adjustment would not necessarily be applied to the FLP interest itself.

The FLP Written Report

Now that you have been presented with issues to consider, how do you go about presenting these findings in the report? One useful way is to set up your report following the eight factors of Revenue Ruling 59-60. Remember, the ultimate "user" of your report is the IRS. By laying out your report in the order of the eight factors, you are showing the IRS that you are considering each of the factors laid out in their ruling. In addition, you should include sections relating to capitalization and discount rates, if appropriate, as well as discounts and premiums.

Follow the Internal Revenue Service's adequate disclosure rules as laid out in Regulation Section 301.6501. These are included as Exhibit 14.1.

EXHIBIT 14.1
IRS Adequate Disclosure Rules

Reg. § 301.6501(c)-1. Exceptions to General Period of Limitations on Assessment and Collection
Caution: The Treasury has not yet amended Reg. § 301.6501(c)-1 to reflect changes made by P.L. 105-34.

301.6501(c)-1(a). False return. In the case of a false or fraudulent return with intent to evade any tax, the tax may be assessed, or a proceeding in court for the collection of such tax may be begun without assessment, at any time after such false or fraudulent return is filed.

301.6501(c)-1(b). Willful attempt to evade tax. In the case of a willful attempt in any manner to defeat or evade any tax imposed by the Code (other than a tax imposed by subtitle A or B, relating to income, estate, or gift taxes), the tax may be assessed, or a proceeding in court for the collection of such tax may be begun without assessment, at any time.

301.6501(c)-1(c). No return. In the case of a failure to file a return, the tax may be assessed, or a proceeding in court for the collection of such tax may be begun without assessment, at any time after the date prescribed for filing the return. For special rules relating to filing a return for Chapter 42 and similar taxes, see §§301.6501(n)-1, 301.6501(n)-2, and 301.6501(n)-3.

301.6501(c)-1(d). Extension by agreement. The time prescribed by Section 6501 for the assessment of any tax (other than the estate tax imposed by Chapter 11 of the Code) may, prior to the expiration of such time, be extended for any period of time agreed upon in writing by the taxpayer and the district director or an assistant regional commissioner. The extension shall become effective when the agreement has been executed by both parties. The period agreed upon may be extended by subsequent agreements in writing made before the expiration of the period previously agreed upon.

301.6501(c)-1(e). Gifts subject to Chapter 14 of the Internal Revenue Code not adequately disclosed on the return.

301.6501(c)-1(e)(1). In general. If any transfer of property subject to the special valuation rules of Section 2701 or Section 2702, or if the occurrence of any taxable event described in §25.2701-4 of this chapter, is not adequately shown on a return of tax imposed by Chapter 12 of subtitle B of the Internal Revenue Code (without regard to Section 2503(b)), any tax imposed by Chapter 12 of subtitle B of the Code on the transfer or resulting from the taxable event may be assessed, or a proceeding in court for the collection of the appropriate tax may be begun without assessment, at any time.

301.6501(c)-1(e)(2). Adequately shown. A transfer of property valued under the rules of Section 2701 or Section 2702 or any taxable event described in §25.2701-4 of this chapter will be considered adequately shown on a return of tax imposed by Chapter 12 of subtitle B of the Internal Revenue Code only if, with respect to the entire transaction of series of transactions (including any transaction that affected the transferred interest) of which the transfer (or taxable event) was a part, the return provides:

301.6501(c)-1(e)(2)(i). A description of the transactions, including a description of transferred and retained interests and the method (or methods) used to value each;

301.6501(c)-1(e)(2)(ii). The identity of, and relationship between, the transferor, transferee, all other persons participating in the transactions, and all parties related to the transferor holding an equity interest in any entity involved in the transactions; and

301.6501(c)-1(e)(2)(iii). A detailed description (including all actuarial factors and discount rates used) of the method used to determine the amount of the gift arising from the transfer (or taxable event), including, in the case of an equity interest that is not actively traded, the financial and other data used in determining value. Financial data should generally include balance sheets and statements of net earnings, operating results, and dividends paid for each of the five years immediately before the valuation date.

301.6501(c)-1(e)(3). Effective date. The provisions of this paragraph (e) are effective as of January 28, 1992. In determining whether a transfer or taxable event is adequately shown on a gift tax return filed prior to that date, taxpayers may rely on any reasonable interpretation of the statutory provisions. For these purposes, the provisions of the proposed regulations and the final regulations are considered a reasonable interpretation of the statutory provisions.

301.6501(c)-1(f). Gifts made after December 31, 1996, not adequately disclosed on the return.

301.6501(c)-1(f)(1). In general. If a transfer of property, other than a transfer described in paragraph (e) of this section, is not adequately disclosed on a gift tax return (Form 709, "United States Gift (and Generation-Skipping Transfer) Tax Return"), or in a statement attached to the return, filed for the calendar period in which the transfer occurs, then any gift tax imposed by Chapter 12 of subtitle B of the Internal Revenue Code on the transfer may be assessed, or a proceeding in court for the collection of the appropriate tax may be begun without assessment, at any time.

(Continued)

EXHIBIT 14.1 *(Continued)*

301.6501(c)-1(f)(2). Adequate disclosure of transfers of property reported as gifts. A transfer will be adequately disclosed on the return only if it is reported in a manner adequate to apprise the IRS of the nature of the gift and the basis for the value so reported. Transfers reported on the gift tax return as transfers of property by gift will be considered adequately disclosed under this paragraph (f)(2) if the return (or a statement attached to the return) provides the following information:

301.6501(c)-1(f)(2)(i). A description of the transferred property and any consideration received by the transferor;

301.6501(c)-1(f)(2)(ii). The identity of, and relationship between, the transferor and each transferee;

301.6501(c)-1(f)(2)(iii). If the property is transferred in trust, the trust's tax identification number and a brief description of the terms of the trust, or in lieu of a brief description of the trust terms, a copy of the trust instrument;

301.6501(c)-1(f)(2)(iv). Except as provided in §301.6501-1(f)(3), a detailed description of the method used to determine the fair market value of property transferred, including any financial data (for example, balance sheets, etc. with explanations of any adjustments) that were utilized in determining the value of the interest, any restrictions on the transferred property that were considered in determining the fair market value of the property, and a description of any discounts, such as discounts for blockage, minority or fractional interests, and lack of marketability, claimed in valuing the property. In the case of a transfer of an interest that is actively traded on an established exchange, such as the New York Stock Exchange, the American Stock Exchange, the NASDAQ National Market, or a regional exchange in which quotations are published on a daily basis, including recognized foreign exchanges, recitation of the exchange where the interest is listed, the CUSIP number of the security, and the mean between the highest and lowest quoted selling prices on the applicable valuation date will satisfy all of the requirements of this paragraph (f)(2)(iv). In the case of the transfer of an interest in an entity (for example, a corporation or partnership) that is not actively traded, a description must be provided of any discount claimed in valuing the interests in the entity or any assets owned by such entity. In addition, if the value of the entity or of the interests in the entity is properly determined based on the net value of the assets held by the entity, a statement must be provided regarding the fair market value of 100 percent of the entity (determined without regard to any discounts in valuing the entity or any assets owned by the entity), the pro rata portion of the entity subject to the transfer, and the fair market value of the transferred interest as reported on the return. If 100 percent of the value of the entity is not disclosed, the taxpayer bears the burden of demonstrating that the fair market value of the entity is properly determined by a method other than a method based on the net value of the assets held by the entity. If the entity that is the subject of the transfer owns an interest in another non-actively traded entity (either directly or through ownership of an entity), the information required in this paragraph (f)(2)(iv) must be provided for each entity if the information is relevant and material in determining the value of the interest; and

301.6501(c)-1(f)(2)(v). A statement describing any position taken that is contrary to any proposed, temporary, or final Treasury regulations or revenue rulings published at the time of the transfer (see §601.601(d)(2) of this chapter).

301.6501(c)-1(f)(3). Submission of appraisals in lieu of the information required under paragraph (f)(2)(iv) of this section. The requirements of paragraph (f)(2)(iv) of this section will be satisfied if the donor submits an appraisal of the transferred property that meets the following requirements:

301.6501(c)-1(f)(3)(i). The appraisal is prepared by an appraiser who satisfies all of the following requirements:

301.6501(c)-1(f)(3)(i)(A). The appraiser is an individual who holds himself or herself out to the public as an appraiser or performs appraisals on a regular basis;

301.6501(c)-1(f)(3)(i)(B). Because of the appraiser's qualifications, as described in the appraisal that details the appraiser's background, experience, education, and membership, if any, in professional appraisal associations, the appraiser is qualified to make appraisals of the type of property being valued;

301.6501(c)-1(f)(3)(i)(C). The appraiser is not the donor or the donee of the property or a member of the family of the donor or donee, as defined in Section 2032A(e)(2), or any person employed by the donor, the donee, or a member of the family of either; and

301.6501(c)-1(f)(3)(ii). The appraisal contains all of the following:

301.6501(c)-1(f)(3)(ii)(A). The date of the transfer, the date on which the transferred property was appraised, and the purpose of the appraisal;

301.6501(c)-1(f)(3)(ii)(B). A description of the property;

301.6501(c)-1(f)(3)(ii)(C). A description of the appraisal process employed;

EXHIBIT 14.1 *(Continued)*

301.6501(c)-1(f)(3)(ii)(D). A description of the assumptions, hypothetical conditions, and any limiting conditions and restrictions on the transferred property that affect the analyses, opinions, and conclusions;

301.6501(c)-1(f)(3)(ii)(E). The information considered in determining the appraised value, including in the case of an ownership interest in a business, all financial data that was used in determining the value of the interest that is sufficiently detailed so that another person can replicate the process and arrive at the appraised value;

301.6501(c)-1(f)(3)(ii)(F). The appraisal procedures followed, and the reasoning that supports the analyses, opinions, and conclusions;

301.6501(c)-1(f)(3)(ii)(G). The valuation method utilized, the rationale for the valuation method, and the procedure used in determining the fair market value of the asset transferred; and

301.6501(c)-1(f)(3)(ii)(H). The specific basis for the valuation, such as specific comparable sales or transactions, sales of similar interests, asset-based approaches, merger-acquisition transactions, etc.

301.6501(c)-1(f)(4). Adequate disclosure of non-gift completed transfers or transactions. Completed transfers to members of the transferor's family, as defined in Section 2032A(e)(2), that are made in the ordinary course of operating a business are deemed to be adequately disclosed under paragraph (f)(2) of this section, even if the transfer is not reported on a gift tax return, provided the transfer is properly reported by all parties for income tax purposes. For example, in the case of salary paid to a family member employed in a family owned business, the transfer will be treated as adequately disclosed for gift tax purposes if the item is properly reported by the business and the family member on their income tax returns. For purposes of this paragraph (f)(4), any other completed transfer that is reported, in its entirety, as not constituting a transfer by gift will be considered adequately disclosed under paragraph (f)(2) of this section only if the following information is provided on, or attached to, the return:

301.6501(c)-1(f)(4)(i). The information required for adequate disclosure under paragraphs (f)(2)(i), (ii), (iii), and (v) of this section; and

301.6501(c)-1(f)(4)(ii). An explanation as to why the transfer is not a transfer by gift under Chapter 12 of the Internal Revenue Code.

301.6501(c)-1(f)(5). Adequate disclosure of incomplete transfers. Adequate disclosure of a transfer that is reported as a completed gift on the gift tax return will commence the running of the period of limitations for assessment of gift tax on the transfer, even if the transfer is ultimately determined to be an incomplete gift for purposes of §25.2511-2 of this chapter. For example, if an incomplete gift is reported as a completed gift on the gift tax return and is adequately disclosed, the period for assessment of the gift tax will begin to run when the return is filed, as determined under Section 6501(b). Further, once the period of assessment for gift tax expires, the transfer will be subject to inclusion in the donor's gross estate for estate tax purposes only to the extent that a completed gift would be so included. On the other hand, if the transfer is reported as an incomplete gift whether or not adequately disclosed, the period for assessing a gift tax with respect to the transfer will not commence to run even if the transfer is ultimately determined to be a completed gift. In that situation, the gift tax with respect to the transfer may be assessed at any time, up until three years after the donor files a return reporting the transfer as a completed gift with adequate disclosure.

301.6501(c)-1(f)(6). Treatment of split gifts. If a husband and wife elect under Section 2513 to treat a gift made to a third party as made one-half by each spouse, the requirements of this paragraph (f) will be satisfied with respect to the gift deemed made by the consenting spouse if the return filed by the donor spouse (the spouse that transferred the property) satisfies the requirements of this paragraph (f) with respect to that gift.

301.6501(c)-1(f)(7). Examples. The following examples illustrate the rules of this paragraph (f):

Example (1). (i) Facts. In 2001, A transfers 100 shares of common stock of XYZ Corporation to A's child. The common stock of XYZ Corporation is actively traded on a major stock exchange. For gift tax purposes, the fair market value of one share of XYZ common stock on the date of the transfer, determined in accordance with §25.2512-2(b) of this Chapter (based on the mean between the highest and lowest quoted selling prices), is $150.00. On A's Federal gift tax return, Form 709, for the 2001 calendar year, A reports the gift to A's child of 100 shares of common stock of XYZ Corporation with a value for gift tax purposes of $15,000. A specifies the date of the transfer, recites that the stock is publicly traded, identifies the stock exchange on which the stock is traded, lists the stock's CUSIP number, and lists the mean between the highest and lowest quoted selling prices for the date of transfer.

(ii) Application of the adequate disclosure standard. A has adequately disclosed the transfer. Therefore, the period of assessment for the transfer under Section 6501 will run from the time the return is filed (as determined under Section 6501(b)).

(Continued)

EXHIBIT 14.1 ***(Continued)***

Example (2). (i) Facts. On December 30, 2001, A transfers closely held stock to B, A's child. A determined that the value of the transferred stock on December 30, 2001, was $9,000. A made no other transfers to B, or any other donee, during 2001. On A's federal gift tax return, Form 709, for the 2001 calendar year, A provides the information required under paragraph (f)(2) of this section such that the transfer is adequately disclosed. A claims an annual exclusion under Section 2503(b) for the transfer.

(ii) Application of the adequate disclosure standard. Because the transfer is adequately disclosed under paragraph (f)(2) of this section, the period of assessment for the transfer will expire as prescribed by Section 6501(b), notwithstanding that if A's valuation of the closely held stock was correct, A was not required to file a gift tax return reporting the transfer under Section 6019. After the period of assessment has expired on the transfer, the IRS is precluded from redetermining the amount of the gift for purposes of assessing gift tax or for purposes of determining the estate tax liability. Therefore, the amount of the gift as reported on A's 2001 federal gift tax return may not be redetermined for purposes of determining A's prior taxable gifts (for gift tax purposes) or A's adjusted taxable gifts (for estate tax purposes).

Example (3). (i) Facts. A owns 100 percent of the common stock of X, a closely held corporation. X does not hold an interest in any other entity that is not actively traded. In 2001, A transfers 20 percent of the X stock to B and C, A's children, in a transfer that is not subject to the special valuation rules of Section 2701. The transfer is made outright with no restrictions on ownership rights, including voting rights and the right to transfer the stock. Based on generally applicable valuation principles, the value of X would be determined based on the net value of the assets owned by X. The reported value of the transferred stock incorporates the use of minority discounts and lack of marketability discounts. No other discounts were used in arriving at the fair market value of the transferred stock or any assets owned by X. On A's federal gift tax return, Form 709, for the 2001 calendar year, A provides the information required under paragraph (f)(2) of this section, including a statement reporting the fair market value of 100 percent of X (before taking into account any discounts), the pro rata portion of X subject to the transfer, and the reported value of the transfer. A also attaches a statement regarding the determination of value that includes a discussion of the discounts claimed and how the discounts were determined.

(ii) Application of the adequate disclosure standard. A has provided sufficient information such that the transfer will be considered adequately disclosed and the period of assessment for the transfer under Section 6501 will run from the time the return is filed (as determined under Section 6501(b)).

Example (4). (i) Facts. A owns a 70 percent limited partnership interest in PS. PS owns 40 percent of the stock in X, a closely held corporation. The assets of X include a 50 percent general partnership interest in PB. PB owns an interest in commercial real property. None of the entities (PS, X, or PB) is actively traded and, based on generally applicable valuation principles, the value of each entity would be determined based on the net value of the assets owned by each entity. In 2001, A transfers a 25 percent limited partnership interest in PS to B, A's child. On the federal gift tax return, Form 709, for the 2001 calendar year, A reports the transfer of the 25 percent limited partnership interest in PS and that the fair market value of 100 percent of PS is $y and that the value of 25 percent of PS is $z, reflecting marketability and minority discounts with respect to the 25 percent interest. However, A does not disclose that PS owns 40 percent of X, and that X owns 50 percent of PB and that, in arriving at the $y fair market value of 100 percent of PS, discounts were claimed in valuing PS's interest in X, X's interest in PB, and PB's interest in the commercial real property.

(ii) Application of the adequate disclosure standard. The information on the lower tiered entities is relevant and material in determining the value of the transferred interest in PS. Accordingly, because A has failed to comply with requirements of paragraph (f)(2)(iv) of this section regarding PS's interest in X, X's interest in PB, and PB's interest in the commercial real property, the transfer will not be considered adequately disclosed and the period of assessment for the transfer under Section 6501 will remain open indefinitely.

Example (5). The facts are the same as in Example 4 except that A submits, with the federal tax return, an appraisal of the 25 percent limited partnership interest in PS that satisfies the requirements of paragraph (f)(3) of this section in lieu of the information required in paragraph (f)(2)(iv) of this section. Assuming the other requirements of paragraph (f)(2) of this section are satisfied, the transfer is considered adequately disclosed and the period for assessment for the transfer under Section 6501 will run from the time the return is filed (as determined under Section 6501(b) of this chapter).

Example (6). A owns 100 percent of the stock of X Corporation, a company actively engaged in a manufacturing business. B, A's child, is an employee of X and receives an annual salary paid in the ordinary course of operating X Corporation. B reports the annual salary as income on B's income tax returns. In 2001, A transfers property to family members and files a federal gift tax return reporting the transfers. However, A does not disclose the 2001 salary payments made to B. Because the salary payments were reported as income on B's income tax return, the salary payments are deemed to be adequately disclosed. The transfer of property to family members, other than the salary payments to B, reported on the gift tax return must satisfy the adequate disclosure requirements under paragraph (f)(2) of this section in order for the period of assessment under Section 6501 to commence to run with respect to those transfers.

301.6501(c)-1(f)(8). Effective date. This paragraph (f) is applicable to gifts made after December 31, 1996, for which the gift tax return for such calendar year is filed after December 3, 1999.

Essentially, the IRS is telling the appraiser that to "pass muster," we must present a fully supported and documented report. This is not substantially different from all of the standards discussed earlier in this book—do your work and report it properly.

Do not make the reader of the report guess about your methodology, discounts, or conclusions. For example, you do not want to state, "The studies indicate 25 to 45 percent; therefore, we selected 35 percent." This is not supported. There are numerous court cases that disallow discounts strictly because the appraiser did something similar to this. You should select a benchmark discount and then adjust it (up or down) based on specific items that you discussed in detail in your report.

Exhibit 14.2 provides a sample FLP report.

EXHIBIT 14.2
Sample FLP Report

Description of the Assignment

Trugman Valuation Associates Inc. was retained by Roberts and Roberts, P.A., Attorneys at Law, to appraise a 1 percent interest in Rock n Roll, Ltd., a Florida Limited Partnership, as of December 23, 1999.

The purpose of this appraisal is to determine the fair market value of this interest to be used for estate planning purposes.

Definition of Fair Market Value

Section 25.2512-1(b) of the Federal Gift Tax Regulations defines fair market value as:

> . . . the price at which the property would change hands between a willing buyer and a willing seller when the former is not under any compulsion to buy and the latter is not under any compulsion to sell, both parties having reasonable knowledge of relevant facts.

This definition of fair market value is the most widely used in valuation practice. Also implied in this definition is that the value is to be stated in cash or cash equivalents and that the property would have been exposed on the open market for a long enough period of time to allow market forces to interact to establish the value.

Valuation Methodologies

There are two fundamental bases on which a company may be valued:

1. As a going concern
2. As if in liquidation

The value of a company is deemed to be the higher of the two values determined under a going-concern or a liquidation premise. This approach is consistent with the appraisal concept of highest and best use, which requires an appraiser to consider the optimal use of the assets being appraised under current market conditions. If a business will command a higher price as a going concern, then it should be valued as such. Conversely, if a business will command a higher price if it is liquidated, then it should be valued as if in orderly liquidation.

Going-Concern Valuation

Going-concern value assumes that the company will continue in business and looks to the enterprise's earnings power and cash generation capabilities as indicators of its fair market value. There are many acceptable methods used in business valuation today. The foundation for business valuation arises from what has been used in valuing real estate for many years. The three basic approaches that must be considered by the appraiser are:

1. The market approach
2. The asset-based approach
3. The income approach

Within each of these approaches there are many acceptable valuation methods available for use by the appraiser. Appraisal standards suggest that an appraiser test as many methods as may be applicable to the facts and circumstances of the property being appraised. It is then up to the appraiser's informed judgment as to how these values will be reconciled in deriving a final estimate of value.

(Continued)

EXHIBIT 14.2 *(Continued)*

The Market Approach. The market approach is fundamental to valuation, as fair market value is determined by the market. Under this approach, the appraiser attempts to find guideline companies traded on a public stock exchange in a same or similar industry as the appraisal subject, which allows a comparison to be made between the pricing multiples that the public company trades at and the multiple that is deemed appropriate for the appraisal subject.

Another common variation of this approach is to locate entire companies that have been bought and sold in the marketplace, publicly traded or closely held, which allows the appraiser to determine the multiples that resulted from the transactions. These multiples can then be applied, with or without adjustment, depending on the circumstances, to the appraisal subject.

The Asset-Based Approach. The asset-based approach, sometimes referred to as the cost approach, is an asset-oriented approach rather than a market-oriented approach. The components of a business are valued separately and summed up to derive the total value of the enterprise.

The appraiser estimates value using this approach by estimating the cost of duplicating or replacing the individual elements of the business property being appraised, item by item, asset by asset.

The tangible assets of the business are valued using this approach, although it cannot be used alone, as many businesses have intangible value as well, to which this approach cannot easily be applied.

The Income Approach. The income approach, sometimes referred to as the investment value approach, is an income-oriented approach rather than an asset- or market-oriented approach. This approach assumes that an investor could invest in a property with similar investment characteristics, although not necessarily the same business.

The computations using the income approach generally determine that the value of the business is equal to the present value of the future benefit stream to the owners. This is generally accomplished by either capitalizing a single-period income stream or by discounting a series of income streams based on a multi-period forecast.

Since estimating the future income of a business is at times considered to be speculative, historic data is generally used as a starting point in several of the acceptable methods under the premise that history will repeat itself. The future cannot be ignored, however, since valuation is a prophecy of the future.

Liquidation Valuation

Liquidation value assumes that a business has greater value if its individual assets are sold to the highest bidder and the company ceases to be a going concern.

Shannon Pratt, a well-known authority in business appraisal, states:

> Liquidation value is, in essence, the antithesis of going-concern value. Liquidation value means the net amount the owner can realize if the business is terminated and the assets sold off in piecemeal.[1]

He adds:

> It is essential to recognize all costs associated with the enterprise's liquidation. These costs normally include commissions, the administrative cost of keeping the company alive until the liquidation is completed, taxes and legal and accounting costs. Also, in computing the present value of a business on a liquidation basis, it is necessary to discount the estimated net proceeds at a rate reflecting the risk involved, from the time the net proceeds are expected to be received, back to the valuation date.[2]

Pratt concludes by stating:

> For these reasons, the liquidation value of the business as a whole is normally less than the sum of the liquidation proceeds of the underlying assets.[3]

Revenue Ruling 59-60—Valuation of Closely Held Stocks

Among other factors, this appraiser considered all elements listed in IRS Ruling 59-60, which provides guidelines for the valuation of closely held stocks. Revenue Ruling 59-60 states that all relevant factors should be taken into consideration, including the following:

1. The nature of the business and the history of the enterprise from its inception
2. The economic outlook in general and the condition and outlook of the specific industry in particular
3. The book value of the stock and financial condition of the business
4. The earning capacity of the company
5. The dividend-paying capacity of the company
6. Whether or not the enterprise has goodwill or other intangible value

---

[1]Shannon Pratt, *Valuing a Business: The Analysis and Appraisal of Closely Held Companies*, 2nd ed. (Homewood, Ill.: Dow Jones–Irwin, 1989), 29.

[2]Ibid.

[3]Ibid.

EXHIBIT 14.2 *(Continued)*

7. Sales of the stock and the size of the block of stock to be valued
8. The market price of stocks of corporations engaged in the same or similar line of business having their stocks actively traded in a free and open market either on an exchange or over the counter

Revenue Ruling 65-192 expanded the applicability of Revenue Ruling 59-60 by stating:

> The general approach, methods, and factors outlined in Revenue Ruling 59-60, C.B. 1959-1, 237, for use in valuing closely held corporate stocks for estate and gift tax purposes are equally applicable to valuations thereof for income and other tax purposes *and also in determinations of the fair market values of business interests of any type* and of intangible assets for all tax purposes [emphasis added].

Since determining the fair market value of an interest in a limited partnership is the question at issue, one must understand the circumstances of each individual case. There is no set formula to the approach to be used that will be applicable to the different valuation issues that arise. Often, an appraiser will find wide differences of opinion as to the fair market value of a particular limited partnership or limited partnership interest. In resolving such differences, one should recognize that valuation is not an exact science. Revenue Ruling 59-60 states that "a sound valuation will be based on all relevant facts, but the elements of common sense, informed judgment, and reasonableness must enter into the process of weighing those facts and determining their aggregate significance."

The fair market value of specific shares of stock in an unlisted corporation will vary as general economic conditions change. Uncertainty as to the stability or continuity of the future income from the business decreases its value by increasing the risk of loss in the future. The valuation of shares of stock of a company with uncertain future prospects is a highly speculative procedure. The judgment must be related to all of the factors affecting the value.

There is no single formula acceptable for determining the fair market value of a closely held business, and therefore, the appraiser must look to all relevant factors in order to establish the true business fair market value as of a given date.

Section 5 of Revenue Ruling 59-60 states:

> The valuation of closely held corporate stock entails the consideration of all relevant factors as stated in Section 4. Depending upon the circumstances in each case, certain factors may carry more weight than others because of the nature of the Company's business. To illustrate:
>
> (a) Earnings may be the most important criterion of value in some cases whereas asset value will receive primary consideration in others. In general, the appraiser will accord primary consideration to earnings when valuing stocks of companies which sell products or services to the public; conversely, in the investment or holding type of company, the appraiser may accord the greatest weight to the assets underlying the security to be valued.
>
> (b) The value of the stock of a closely held investment or real estate holding company, whether or not family owned, is closely related to the value of the assets underlying the stock. For companies of this type the appraiser should determine the fair market values of the assets of the Company. Operating expenses of such a company and the cost of liquidating it, if any, merit consideration when appraising the relative values of the stock and the underlying assets. The market values of the underlying assets give due weight to potential earnings and dividends of the particular items of property underlying the stock, capitalized at rates deemed proper by the investing public at the date of appraisal. A current appraisal by the investing public should be superior to the retrospective opinion of an individual. For these reasons, adjusted net worth should be accorded greater weight in valuing the stock of a closely held investment or real estate holding company, whether or not family owned, than any of the other customary yardsticks of appraisal, such as earnings and dividend-paying capacity.

In this appraisal, both earnings and underlying asset values will be considered, as both appear to be relevant. We will then determine how much reliance, if any, will be placed on each methodology.

The Nature of the Business and the History of the Enterprise from Its Inception

Formation of the Partnership

Rock n Roll, Ltd. ("Rock n Roll Ltd." or "the Partnership"), a limited partnership organized under the laws of the State of Florida, was formed on December 23, 1997.

The original ownership of the Partnership was as follows:

General partners	*% Interest*
Charles E. Brown, Jr.	0.9
Wm. Frederick Brown	0.1
Limited partners	
Charles E. Brown, Jr.	49.5
Peggy Brown	49.5

(Continued)

EXHIBIT 14.2 *(Continued)*

Purpose of the Partnership

According to the Articles of Limited Partnership, the purpose of Rock n Roll Ltd. is "to hold investments and maximize the current return and future appreciation of such investments, and in furtherance of this purpose, to engage in any lawful business activities." In addition to investment and management of certain assets, the Partnership shall also provide "a method of distribution of assets to [the] children" of Charles E. Brown, Jr., and Peggy Brown.

Term of the Partnership

The initial term of the Partnership is 20 years from the date it was formed. Thereafter, it will continue from calendar year to calendar year until it is terminated as called for in the Articles of Limited Partnership.

The managing general partner has the power to dissolve the Partnership. If the managing general partner withdraws for any of the reasons outlined in Article XI of the Articles of Partnership, the Partnership will be dissolved.

Management

Rock n Roll Ltd. shall be managed by the managing general partner, who shall be responsible for the administration and management of the Partnership. Although two general partners were named in the Articles of Incorporation, at the valuation date there is only one managing general partner. The general partner who is not the managing general partner "shall not be responsible for the management of the Partnership, shall not have the authority to bind the Partnership, and agrees not to take any action to bind the Partnership."

The managing general partner can do all things necessary to carry out the purpose of the Partnership, including disposal and acquisition of assets, opening and closing of bank accounts, borrowing funds, voting stock owned by the Partnership, entering into contracts, and incurring expenses. Additional powers of the managing general partner are:

1. To admit additional limited partners to the Partnership
2. To dissolve the Partnership at the complete discretion of the managing general partner

The initial managing general partner is Charles E. Brown, Jr. In the event that Charles E. Brown, Jr., is unable to serve as managing general partner, the Articles of Partnership provide that the successor managing general partner will be William Frederick Brown.

Capital Contributions

Capital in the form of cash and marketable securities was contributed to the Partnership by Charles E. Brown, Jr., and his wife, Peggy Brown. Family members may make additional contributions from time to time. The book value of the capital contributed to the Partnership as of December 31,1997, was $1,561,396.

Rock n Roll Ltd. also owns real property as follows:

1. A one-half undivided interest in two noncontiguous, undeveloped parcels of land within Merry Acres Farm located in Polk County, Florida, containing approximately 43 acres.
2. A 100 percent interest in 2.4 acres of undeveloped real property located in Jackson County, North Carolina, purchased in mid-1999.

Allocation of Profits and Losses

The managing general partner has sole discretion over the allocation of profits and losses. Each partner's percentage interest in the Partnership determines his or her share of income, gain, loss, deduction, and credit, as well as his or her share of distributions of property upon dissolution of the Partnership.

Distributions

All distributions are made at the discretion of the managing general partner. If any distribution is made, 1 percent shall go to the general partners, pro rata, and 99 percent shall go ratably to the limited partners. No limited partners may force the managing general partner to distribute the earnings of the Partnership.

Since inception, the following distributions have been made:

1997	$ 64,946
1998	631,259
1999	112,812

EXHIBIT 14.2 *(Continued)*

Transfer Restrictions

Very strict transfer restrictions are placed upon shares of the Partnership in Article VI of the Articles of Partnership. If a limited partner wishes to sell his or her interest in the Partnership, he or she must first offer it to the remaining partners, who then have 30 days to decide to purchase. If no remaining partners purchase the shares, then they may be offered to family members who are approved by the managing general partner. If no approved family member purchases the interest, it must then be offered to the Partnership itself.

The Articles of Partnership specify how the purchase price is to be calculated:

> The sale price of the Offering Limited Partner's interest . . . shall be determined by applying minority interest and lack of marketability discounts to the market value of such interest. The managing general partner shall choose a certified public accountant ("CPA") to value the interest.

No other transfer of partnership interests will be accepted, and the "Partnership shall not be required to recognize the interest of any transferee who has obtained the purported interest as the result of ownership that is not authorized" under Article VI of the Articles of Partnership.

Dissolution and Liquidation

Although the term of the Partnership is 20 years, the managing general partner may elect to dissolve it. It may be dissolved if its business is terminated or if a managing general partner withdraws in a way that is not approved by the Articles of Partnership or by bankruptcy, dissolution, or death of a managing general partner.

Dissolution and Liquidation

Although the term of the Partnership is 20 years, the managing general partner may elect to dissolve it. It may be dissolved if its business is terminated or if a managing general partner withdraws in a way that is not approved by the Articles of Partnership or by bankruptcy, dissolution, or death of a managing general partner.

Ownership

The Partnership was initially conceived so that there would be a 1 percent general partner interest and a 99 percent limited partner interest.

Additional family members[4] may be admitted as new limited partners as the managing general partner permits. Since the inception of the Partnership, partnership interests were gifted to various family members by both Charles E. Brown, Jr., and Peggy Brown. At the valuation date, the ownership structure was:

	Interest
General partners	
Charles E. Brown, Jr.	0.90%
William Frederick Brown	0.10%
Limited partners	
Charles E. Brown, Jr.	42.56%
Peggy V. Brown Revocable Trust	42.56%
Catherine Brown	2.33%
Charles E. Brown, III	2.33%
Bretta Brown Arthur	2.33%
Bruce B. Brown	2.33%
Scott Brown	2.33%
William Frederick Brown	2.23%
Total	100.00%

[4]Defined by the agreement as (i) C.E. Brown and P. Brown; (ii) a descendant of C.E. Brown or P. Brown; (iii) a spouse or surviving spouse; (iv) any estate, trust, guardianship, custodianship, or other fiduciary arrangement for the primary benefit of one or more individuals described; and (v) any corporation, partnership, limited liability company, or other business organization controlled by and substantially all of the interests which are owned, directly or indirectly, by any one or more individuals named or described.

(Continued)

EXHIBIT 14.2 *(Continued)*

The Economic Outlook in General and the Condition and Outlook of the Specific Industry in Particular

Generally, business performance varies in relation to the economy. Just as a strong economy can improve overall business performance and value, a declining economy can have the opposite effect. Businesses can be affected by global, national, and local events. Changes in regulatory environments, political climate, and market and competitive forces can also have a significant impact on business. For these reasons, it is important to analyze and understand the prevailing economic environment when valuing a closely held business. Since the appraisal process is a "prophecy of the future," it is imperative that the appraiser review the economic outlook as it would impact the appraisal subject.

In the third quarter of 1999, the economic expansion caused a renewed upturn, and it appears that the fourth quarter has continued in a similar manner. There has been some indication of a weaker industrial sector; however, the bullish stock market trend is supporting strong consumer confidence and spending. This, along with a tight labor market, has raised the prospect of a continuing consumer boom.

Overall, the third quarter has turned out to be stronger than earlier estimates had suggested; upward revisions to personal spending, net exports, and inventories have pushed GDP growth estimates to over 5.0 percent. Consumer confidence jumped in October, and retailers are expecting a tremendous holiday shopping season. Although retail sales weakened in October, they are widely expected to end the year strongly, and although personal consumption growth is still expected to slow down next year, the 2000 forecasts have again been upgraded. The Federal Reserve Board's (Fed) recent rate increase was supported by the strength of domestic demand during the second half of this year. This demand, combined with higher oil prices, is threatening the inflation picture; as a result the federal funds rate was increased by .25 percent last month. Forecasters have suggested that there is a strong prospect of moderate growth and low inflation continuing.[5]

The expansion that the United States is currently enjoying has been ongoing since the early 1990s. It has been characterized by low unemployment, low inflation, low interest rates, and high industrial production. Consumers have been confident in the economy and, therefore, continue to spend. Table 1 shows indicator growth rates for the last several years:

TABLE 1
Historic Growth Rate Data

	1995	*1996*	*1997*	*1998*
Real GDP*	2.7	3.7	4.5	4.3
Real disposable personal income*	2.7	2.6	3.6	4.1
Real personal consumption*	3.1	3.3	3.7	4.9
Real business investment*	9.8	10.0	10.7	12.7
Nominal pretax profits*	16.7	12.8	11.1	1.0
Industrial production*	4.9	4.4	6.4	4.2
Consumer prices*	2.8	2.9	2.3	1.6
Producer prices*	1.9	2.7	0.4	(0.9)
Unemployment rate, percent	5.6	5.4	4.9	4.5
3-mo. T-bill, % end year	5.1	5.2	5.4	4.5
10-yr. T-bond, % end year	5.6	6.3	5.7	4.7

*Average percent change on previous calendar year.
Source: *Consensus Forecasts* (December 6, 1999).

A considerable portion of the Partnership's assets are invested in equity securities, so a review of the stock market and a brief discussion of the outlook for the equities markets is useful.

For the past five years, the U.S. stock market has continued to push higher and set new records. This is due to healthy economic growth, low inflation, increasing corporate profits, and falling interest rates. These conditions encourage investors to place more funds in equities. Interest rates rose in 1999, but the stock market rose as well, while prices of bonds fell. It is not usually the case that stock prices rise with interest rates; however, during 1999, investors were confident that these increases in interest rates would slow the economy just enough to wring out any signs of incipient inflation.

[5]"Ongoing Strength Behind Upgraded 2000 Outlook," *Consensus Forecasts—USA*, Consensus Economics, Inc., December 6, 1999, 1–2.

EXHIBIT 14.2 (*Continued*)

The Dow Jones Industrial Average passed two 1,000-point milestones in 1999, rising 20.8 percent from 9274.64 on December 30, 1998, to 11,203.6 on December 22, 1999. This was after a similar percentage increase in 1998.[6] Other market indexes showed similar strength; the Nasdaq soared by 80 percent, buoyed by the boom in technology stocks, and the broadest market index, the New York Stock Exchange Composite Index, rose 9.6 percent in the 12 months ended December 22, 1999. Volume on the New York Stock Exchange rose to an average of 884,141,000 shares traded each day in December 1999. Volume is a strong indicator of market exuberance and has increased almost 33 percent from a daily average of 666,534 shares in all of 1998.[7] Table 2 presents stock market performance during the year, as well as for the week just prior to the valuation date.

TABLE 2
Stock Market Indices

	12/16/99	*12/22/99*	*% Change 1 Week*	*% Change 12 Months*
Dow Jones Industrial Average	11,244.89	11,203.60	−0.4%	+23.9%
Standard & Poor's 500	1418.78	1436.13	+1.2%	+19.3%
N.Y. Stock Exchange Composite	631.76	634.16	+0.4%	+9.6%
NASDAQ OTC Composite	3715.06	3937.30	+6.0%	+85.6%
Russell 2000	465.26	477.94	+2.7%	+19.4%

Source: *Value Line Investment Survey*, December 31, 1999.

The outlook for 2000 is quite favorable in terms of economic growth, inflation, and profits. According to *Value Line*, the Dow Jones Industrial Average should average 11,800, 5 percent over current levels.[8]

The Partnership also owns vacant land in Polk County, Florida, and in Jackson County, North Carolina. It is important to understand the economies of these areas to help assess their values.

Population growth gives a clue to development potential in an area. Polk[9] County's population of 940,484 is up 12.8 percent since 1990, compared to 16.8 percent for the state. There is a slightly higher proportion of college-educated individuals in Polk County (20.2 percent versus 18.3 percent) than in the state of Florida, indicating higher income levels. Median household income is $32,650 in the county, compared to $29,998 for the state. Higher education and income levels usually go hand in hand with higher home ownership rates and spending levels. Thus, the economic activity in the area is greater, leading to higher levels of development.

According to the real estate appraisal of the Florida property, Polk County is in the process of being developed. To the north of the Partnership's vacant land, a single-family subdivision has been proposed, and retail, office, hotel, and multi-family projects are all on the drawing board for areas to the west of the Partnership's property.

Jackson County, North Carolina, has a population of 30,260. Between 1990 and 1999, it grew 12.8 percent. More than 68 percent of the population has high school diplomas, and over 19 percent has college degrees. The median household income is $27,912, which is below the state level of $31,987. The poverty level is higher than the state average, at 17.3 percent versus 13.1 percent. The county has only 874 private non-farm establishments; this is a 36.3 percent growth rate between 1990 and 1997, and non-farm employment increased by 25.6 percent.[10] Real wages increased 3.7 percent between 1997 and 1998. The business failure rate is 2 percentage points below the state average, but the employment rate was slightly above the state average.[11]

In conclusion, the U.S. economy continued its expansion in 1999. GDP had a strong growth rate, inflation was low, and interest rates increased only moderately. Stock market performance exceeded all expectations with record gains in many indices and is widely expected to be strong into the new year.

[6] *Value Line Investment Survey*, Selection and Opinioary 15, 1999 and January 7, 2000.

[7] U.S. Federal Reserve Board, *Federal Reserve Bulletin*, March 2000, A24.

[8] Ibid.

[9] *Author's note*: The name of the county has been changed to disguise the location of the property. Do not use this information in an actual report!

[10] U.S. Census Bureau, *State and County Quick Facts*, Jackson County, North Carolina, quickfacts.census.gov/cgi-bin/county?cnty = 37099.

[11] North Carolina Department of Commerce, *1999 County and Regional Scans*, Jackson County.

(Continued)

EXHIBIT 14.2 *(Continued)*

Book Value of the Stock and the Financial Condition of the Partnership

An analysis of the Partnership was performed by the appraiser as of December 23, 1999, the date of the appraisal, using tax returns that are summarized in Schedules 1 and 2 at the end of this report.

The book value of Rock n Roll Ltd. as of the valuation date was $1,628,081. This value does not reflect the market value of the Partnership's assets on the appraisal date. This value is presented in Table 3.

TABLE 3
Market Value of Assets

Cash[1]	$ 363,455	8.9%
Securities[1]	3,316,064	77.0%
Real Estate	571,300	14.0%
Total Market Value[2]	$ 4,070,819	100.0%

[1]Market values for the securities portfolio as of December 23, 1999, were supplied by Prudential Securities and Bank of America.

[2]Market value for the Florida real estate was determined by Lee Summerford, Inc., Real Estate Appraiser, in its appraisal dated October 13, 2000. Market value for the vacant North Carolina property was determined via telephone consultation with the Jackson County, N.C., Tax Assessor's Office on October 25, 2000. This office indicated that the assessed value of the property is equal to 100 percent of its market value.

The value of net intangible assets, totaling $1,107, is not included, as this asset has no value on a going-concern basis.

As of the end of December 1999, the Partnership had no debt or other liabilities on its books. Expenses were very low and consisted only of fees involved in the management of the securities portfolio and taxes. This appears to have been the case since inception; one small liability appearing in 1998 was extinguished during 1999.

The Earning Capacity of the Company

The income statements for the Partnership are presented in Schedule 2 at the back of this report. Future earnings capacity is important, as it is a major component of the valuation process. An analysis of the historic income statements reveals that the Partnership's assets are capable of generating earnings in excess of its expenses.

The largest proportion of assets consists of marketable securities, many of which pay interest or dividends. This is expected to continue for as long as the Partnership exists. Although it is true that occasionally a company may miss a dividend or interest payment, indicating some degree of risk associated with any securities portfolio, the Partnership's assets are sufficiently diversified so as to mitigate much of this risk. Table 4 presents a breakdown of the Partnership's marketable security portfolio.

TABLE 4
Portfolio Analysis

Industry Sector	*% of Total Equities*
Cash apparel/fabrics/textiles	10.38
Communications	12.07
Consumer foods	1.28
Consumer goods	1.20
Diversified industrial/minerals	0.28
Energy	2.39
Engineering/construction	0.15
Farm products	1.27
Fats/oils	0.54
Financial services	42.07

EXHIBIT 14.2 *(Continued)*

Industry Sector	*% of Total Equities*
Investments	0.34
Landscape nurseries	0.32
Machinery	0.02
Mining	0.37
Paperboard mills	1.37
Real estate	1.16
Restaurant	0.95
Technology	18.47
Telecommunications	0.46
Tobacco	3.96
Mutual funds	0.55

A variety of industries are represented. The portfolio is heavily weighted in the financial services, communications, and technology sectors. The financial services portion of the portfolio consists of three major banks and two large insurance/financial conglomerates; communications is represented by CBS Corp., a household name in communications; and the technology sector includes IBM, Apple Computer, MAI Systems, and NCR. There are no "dotcoms" included in the portfolio. In fact, the equities portfolio is made up for the most part of large, well-known U.S. corporations with unquestioned ability to maintain dividends.

As shown in Schedule 2 at the back of this report, a large portion of the earnings of the Partnership results from gains on the sales of the assets. In 1998 and 1999, this made up 72.8 percent and 74.6 percent of income, respectively. Therefore, although earnings capacity exists, the annual amount will depend largely on the trading activity that takes place in any given year.

The Dividend-Paying Capacity of the Company[12]

There is no requirement regarding distributions to partners in the Agreement of Limited Partnership of Rock n Roll Ltd. A publicly traded company often disburses dividends as a means to entice investors to invest in a company, but in this instance, distributions are not required and are solely at the discretion of the managing general partner.

Nevertheless, Rock n Roll Ltd. has made regular distributions to its members as follows:

TABLE 5

Distributions

Year	*Net Income*	*Cash Distributions*	*% Yield*
1997	$ 66	$ 64,946	n.a.[1]
1998	470,121	631,259	134.28
1999	313,708	112,812	35.96

Note: Although the 1999 totals were not determined until after the valuation date, all distributions and most of the income was derived prior to that date. Therefore, they are being considered in our analysis.

[1]Partnership net income for 1997 is for only eight days (December 23–31). The percentage yield would not be meaningful for this year.

Revenue Ruling 59-60 addresses the dividend-paying capacity of an enterprise and explains that a controlling shareholder has the ability to determine the payment or nonpayment of dividends. When the assignment is to appraise a minority interest, as it is in this case, the dividends that were actually paid is the more relevant issue, since a limited partner cannot force the Partnership to pay distributions even if the Partnership has the capacity to pay them.

[12]In this appraisal, the terms "dividends" and "cash distributions" are used interchangeably.

(Continued)

EXHIBIT 14.2 ***(Continued)***

As the data in Table 5 indicates, cash distributions of varying amounts have been paid. The payouts have ranged from 36 percent of income to 134 percent and may be higher or lower in future years. There is clearly a history, since distributions have been paid each year since the Partnership's inception. Therefore, we believe that dividend-paying capacity, as well as the dividends actually paid, are both relevant in this appraisal.

Whether or Not the Enterprise Has Goodwill or Other Intangible Value

Goodwill is a term applied to an intangible asset and may be defined as "those elements of a business that cause customers to return, and that usually enable the business to generate profit in excess of a reasonable return on all other assets of a business." It may also include workforce in place value, information base, noncompete agreement, know-how, and licenses. Our examination sought to identify goodwill as it existed on the valuation date.

We have considered the elements of goodwill including those of a personal, as well as entity, nature. In the valuation of Rock n Roll Ltd., a tangible asset such as real estate generally does not create goodwill. However, there is one small intangible asset on the books of the Partnership. This asset arose because the Partnership incurred certain costs when it was initially formed. These are currently being amortized over five years and will be eliminated in 2002. The amount on the books at December 31, 1999, is $1,107. This asset has no value in and of itself and is immaterial in comparison to the balance of the portfolio. Therefore, it has been removed from the balance sheet and will not be included in the remainder of our analysis.

Sales of the Stock and the Size of the Block of Stock to Be Valued

Revenue Ruling 59-60 suggests that the appraiser consider whether there have been any previous sales of the Partnership and the size of the block being valued. During the life of the Partnership, interests were transferred to the limited partners by Charles E. Brown, Jr., and Peggy Brown, but we were unable to determine how the values of the interests were calculated. Therefore, we have not utilized these prior transfers in our analysis.

This appraisal is to value a 1 percent limited partnership interest in Rock n Roll Ltd. This is considered to be a minority interest, and the valuation methods used take that into consideration.

The Market Price of Stocks of Corporations Actively Traded in the Public Market

The final factor of the eight listed in Revenue Ruling 59-60 is a market comparison between the appraisal subject and other companies in the same or a similar line of business that are traded on public stock exchanges. This is the basis for the market approach to valuation.

In order to apply this methodology, we performed a computerized search of the Morningstar *Principia Pro* for Closed End Mutual Funds database, for closed-end mutual funds investing in equities of both large and medium capitalization companies. All of the funds we looked at invested in a blend of value and growth stocks of domestic companies. These types of funds were selected because we feel they are more representative of the subject company's portfolio. Further, closed-end funds are more comparable to the Partnership because, like the Partnership, they have a limited number of shares available. The search of the Morningstar database revealed eight funds:

Fund Name	*Net Assets ($ Millions)*
Adams Express	$ 1,757
Gabelli Equity	1,371
General American Investors	1,036
Liberty All-Star Equity	1,326
Liberty All-Star Growth	187
NAIC Growth	20
Renaissance Growth & Inc. III	42
Tri-Continental	3,953

Since Rock n Roll Ltd. also owns undeveloped land, we looked for closed-end mutual funds investing in real estate. We found two and, although not directly comparable, they are presented below.

	Total Assets ($ Millions)
Cohen & Steers Realty Income	22.8
Cohen & Steers Total Return	91.4

EXHIBIT 14.2 *(Continued)*

All of these funds were eliminated as possible guideline companies, chiefly because of their size. The smallest, at $19.5 million in assets, is over five times the size of Rock n Roll Ltd. Funds of this size have the ability to diversify assets, especially real estate holdings, as the Partnership cannot. These companies have professional management that is well versed in the intricacies of the equities and real estate markets. Based on this information, we eliminated these companies as potential guidelines.

Valuation Calculations

As mentioned earlier, the three approaches to valuation considered in any appraisal are:

1. The market approach
2. The asset-based approach
3. The income approach

Each of these methods was described in the introduction section of this report.

Market Approach

The market approach was not used for this appraisal because we were unable to locate publicly traded or privately held companies that would have been useful in making comparisons with the Partnership. In the previous section, we discussed the search for closed-end mutual funds whose shares were actively traded on a public exchange. The search did not reveal any useful comparisons.

Asset-Based Approach

Adjusted Book Value Method. Revenue Ruling 59-60 states, "The value of the stock of a closely held investment or real estate holding company, whether or not family owned, is closely related to the value of the assets underlying the stock." Therefore, the asset-based approach, specifically the adjusted book value method, was applied to value a minority interest in Rock n Roll Ltd.

It has previously been determined that the adjusted book value of the Partnership is $4,070,819. This reflects the value of the Partnership on a control, marketable basis.

We were engaged to determine the value of a minority interest in the Partnership on a minority, nonmarketable basis. In order to derive this value, we must apply a lack of control or minority discount, as well as a discount for lack of marketability. These discounts are discussed in the "Premiums and Discounts" section of this report.

Applying these discounts results in the following calculation of value:

Total enterprise value	$4,070,819
Less: Discount for lack of control (20%)	(814,164)
Minority marketable value	$3,256,655
Less: Discount for lack of marketability (25%)	(814,164)
Value—Minority, non-marketable	$2,442,491
	× 1 %
1 percent interest	$ 24,425
Rounded	$ 24,400

Income Approach

As stated earlier, the income approach is accomplished by either capitalizing a single-period income stream or by discounting a series of income streams based on a multi-period forecast. The latter calculation is performed in cases where income growth has not yet stabilized, as often happens in new companies or rapidly growing companies.

In this instance, Rock n Roll Ltd. has a history of making cash distributions to its partners. This is equivalent to a dividend payment in a corporation; it is the partners' return on investment. A limited partner cannot force management to distribute all or any portion of the Partnership's net income or cash flow. Therefore, he or she is more concerned with the funds that are actually distributed to him or her.

(Continued)

EXHIBIT 14.2 ***(Continued)***

The earning capacity and dividend-paying capacity sections of this report indicate that earnings and distributions exist, but since the inception of the Partnership, the amounts have been erratic. Due to the short history of the Partnership and the erratic nature of its earnings and cash distributions history, we could not quantify a projected income amount. Therefore, we were unable to utilize an income approach.

Premiums and Discounts

Valuation Premiums and Discounts in General

The final value reached in the appraisal of a closely held business or limited partnership ("LP") may be more or less than the value that was calculated using the various methods of appraisal that are available. The type and size of the premium(s) or discount(s) will vary depending on the starting point. The starting point will depend on which methods of valuation were used during the appraisal as well as other factors, such as the sources of the information used to derive multiples or discount rates, and normalization adjustments.

Control Premium

The pro rata value of a controlling interest in a closely held company or LP is said to be worth more than the value of a minority interest, due to the prerogatives of control that generally follow the controlling shares. An investor will generally pay more (a premium) for the rights that are considered to be part of the controlling interest. Valuation professionals recognize these prerogatives of control, and they continue to hold true today. These rights are considered in assessing the size of a control premium. They include:

1. Electing the board of directors
2. Appointing the management team
3. Determining compensation and perquisites
4. Setting business policy
5. Acquiring or liquidating assets
6. Making acquisitions or divestitures
7. Selling or acquiring treasury stock
8. Registering the stock for an IPO
9. Declaring dividends
10. Changing the articles of incorporation or bylaws of the corporation

A control premium is the opposite of a minority discount. The control premium is used to determine the control value of a closely held business when its freely traded minority value has been determined. This is generally the case when the appraiser uses information from the public stock market as the starting point of the valuation.

Minority (Lack of Control) Discount

A minority discount is a reduction in the control value of the appraisal subject that is intended to reflect the fact that a minority stockholder or limited partner cannot control the daily activities or policy decisions of an enterprise, thus reducing its value. The size of the discount will depend on the size of the interest being appraised, the amount of control, the stockholder's ability to liquidate the company, and other factors.

A minority discount is basically the opposite of a premium for control. This type of discount is used to obtain the value of a noncontrolling interest in the appraisal subject when a control value is the starting point. The starting point is determined based on the method of valuation, the normalization adjustments made, and the source of the discount or capitalization rates.

Minority discounts can be mathematically determined using control premiums that are measured in the public market. The formula to determine the minority interest is as follows:

$$1 - [1 \div (1 + CP)]$$

where CP equals the control premium.

Data on control premiums is generally not available for closely held businesses, so the appraiser uses transactions from the public stock market to act as a gauge as to the amount of premium paid in transactions involving buyouts. This data is tracked by several sources. The most widely used is *Mergerstat Review*, which is published annually by Houlihan, Lokey, Howard, and Zukin, an investment banking firm in Los Angeles, California.

EXHIBIT 14.2 (Continued)

A summary of the *Mergerstat Review* data appears in Table 6.

TABLE 6

Percent Premium Paid Over Market Price

Year of Buyout	*Number of Transactions*	*Average Premium Paid Over Market (%)*	*Median Premium Paid (%)*	*Implied Minority Interest Discount*
1990	175	42.0	32.0	24.2
1991	137	35.1	29.4	22.7
1992	142	41.0	34.7	25.8
1993	173	38.7	33.0	24.8
1994	260	41.9	35.0	25.9
1995	324	44.7	29.2	22.6
1996	381	36.6	27.3	21.5
1997	487	35.7	27.5	21.6
1998	512	40.7	30.1	23.1

Source: *Mergerstat Review 1999*, (Los Angeles: Houlihan, Lokey, Howard & Zukin). Discount calculated by the appraiser.

In this instance, the minority interest being appraised is a 1 percent limited partnership interest in Rock n Roll Ltd. The limited partner does not have the ability to appoint management or determine compensation or business policy. The limited partner cannot liquidate assets or force the sale of the company to a third party, although no sale is expected to take place.

The limited partner cannot register Rock n Roll Ltd. for sale in a secondary market or declare dividends. The limited partner also cannot change the Articles of Partnership.

The bottom line is that a limited partner is disadvantaged due to the legal rights that correspond to his or her partnership interest. There is little that a limited partner can do to control his or her investment in the Partnership. Therefore, a lack of control discount is deemed proper. Furthermore, application of a lack of control discount is called for by Article 6.2(g) of the Articles of Partnership.

Many factors impact the degree of control a partial (minority) owner has over the operations of the Partnership. Whenever the control elements are not available to the ownership interest being valued, the value is typically reduced accordingly. Table 7 summarizes some of the factors that influence the value of minority interests relative to controlling interests:

TABLE 7

Factors Affecting the Degree of Control[1]

Factors That May Increase a Lack of Control Discount or Control Premium

- The presence of voting stock
- An extreme lack of consideration for the interests of minority shareholders on the part of the Company's management, board of directors, or majority owners

Factors That May Decrease a Lack of Control Discount or Control Premium

- The presence of enough minority interest votes to elect or have meaningful input on electing one or more directors in a company with cumulative voting
- The presence of enough minority votes to block certain actions
- The presence of state statutes granting certain minority stockholder rights

Factors That May Increase or Decrease a Lack of Control Discount or a Control Premium

- The distribution of other shares (e.g., 2 shares when 2 others own 49 shares each are more valuable than 2 shares when 49 others own 2 shares each)

[1]*Guide to Business Valuations* (Practitioners Publishing Company, 1999), 8–18, 803.16.

(Continued)

EXHIBIT 14.2 *(Continued)*

In this appraisal, the net asset value of the Partnership was used to determine the control value of the entire company. However, to realize this value, an investor would need to be able to gain access to, and liquidate the underlying assets of the Partnership. If limited partners were afforded this level of control, an interest might well be worth a pro rata share of the Partnership's net asset value. However, this is not the case.

A lack of control discount is appropriate when a minority shareholder or limited partner cannot control day-to-day or long-range managerial decisions, impact future earnings, control the direction or growth, or control the return on investment. Additionally, a lack of control discount is appropriate if the minority owner lacks control over the payment of distributions and cannot compel a liquidation of partnership assets. All of the preceding factors are characteristics of control.

In this appraisal, the valuation subject is a 1 percent limited partnership interest, which is a minority interest. The Articles of Partnership specifically limit control by vesting all decision making in the managing general partner. The basis for lack of control adjustments for minority interests arises from a range of factors, including:

- Limited partners cannot control the day-to-day management or operation of the Partnership.
- Limited partners generally cannot control the amount or timing of income distributions to partners.
- Limited partners do not have specific claims on the underlying assets of the Partnership, and they cannot compel the dissolution of the Partnership or the liquidation of its underlying assets.
- It is usually very difficult for limited partners to remove management.
- It is usually very difficult for limited partners to amend the Articles of Partnership.

The net asset value method develops a freely traded control value of the Partnership's net assets of $4,070,819 at December 23, 1999, and does not provide a meaningful indication of value for a minority interest in the Partnership. A lack of control discount is appropriate here because a minority interest in the Partnership represents an indirect ownership interest in the underlying assets held by the Partnership.

One approach to determining an appropriate lack of control discount is to compare the minority interest under appraisal to published control premium studies. This can be accomplished by using publications such as *Mergerstat Review,* cited previously.

Another method of estimating the appropriate lack of control discount for Rock n Roll Ltd. would be to parallel the Partnership's portfolio to closed-end mutual funds (CEFs). Hundreds of closed-end funds are available for numerous specialized investment options. Prices paid for publicly traded shares in a CEF represent minority interests in a variety of assets. Therefore, if the net asset value of a CEF can be determined and compared with the freely traded price of the fund, it can be determined when and under what conditions the market affords a discount (or premium) to the net asset value of a minority interest.

This is appropriate because the owner of a share in a CEF cannot gain access to the assets held by the CEF, force liquidation of these assets, or insist on the payment of distributions. As a result, the shares of these funds generally trade at a discount to net asset value (NAV). This discount can serve as a proxy for a lack of control or minority discount.

Unlike open-end mutual funds, CEFs issue a fixed number of shares. Therefore, investors must buy shares from other investors, not the fund itself. These CEFs mirror the motivations of buyers and sellers, and offer empirical evidence for the determination of the appropriate magnitude for the lack of control discount to be applied.

In the valuation of Rock n Roll Ltd., we researched and reviewed closed end domestic stock funds as of December 23, 1999, in order to attempt to determine an appropriate discount to apply to the marketable securities portfolio. Information was obtained from the *Wall Street Journal* on December 23, 1999. Twenty-six funds were listed under the heading of General Equity. These are listed in Table 8.

TABLE 8

General Equity Funds

	NAV	*Market Price*	*Prem/Disc*
Adams Express	39.91	32.44	–18.7
Alliance All-Market	50.85	43.88	–13.7
Avalon Capital	17.79	14.00	–21.3
Baker Fentress	14.72	14.13	–4.0
Bergstrom Capital	272.93	22.60	–17.2
Blue Chip Value Fund	9.76	9.56	–2.1
Boulder Total Return	12.86	9.63	–25.1
Central Securities	33.74	27.06	–19.8
Corp Renaissance	12.86	10.38	–19.3

EXHIBIT 14.2 *(Continued)*

	NAV	Market Price	Prem/Disc
Engex	16.33	17.13	4.9
Equus II	15.31	10.44	–31.8
Gabelli Equity Trust	12.47	11.94	–4.3
General American	40.72	35.75	–12.2
Liberty Allstar Equity	13.83	10.94	–20.9
Liberty Allstar Growth	13.2	10.44	–20.9
MFS Special Value	13.58	15.00	10.5
Morgan FunShares	7.3	6.75	–7.5
Morgan Growth Small Cap	15.28	13.00	–14.9
NAIC Growth	13.11	10.50	–19.9
Royce Focus Trust	5.75	4.75	–17.4
Royce Micro-Cap Trust	10.57	8.91	–15.7
Royce Value Trust	15.25	12.81	–16.0
Salomon SBF	19.12	20.25	5.9
Source Capital	48.76	48.25	–1.1
Tri-Continental	32.75	27.63	–15.6
Zweig	12.01	10.06	–16.2
Mean			**–12.9**
Median			**–15.9**

The median discount from net asset value (NAV) for this group of funds is 15.9 percent as of the valuation date. The median is a better indicator of the central point in the sample as it eliminates outliers that can skew the results. This will be the starting point of our discount analysis.

For the real estate portion of the portfolio, we reviewed information about real estate limited partnerships found in *Partnership Spectrum*, a publication of Partnership Profiles, Inc. Each year, in its May/June issue, *Partnership Spectrum* publishes its annual study of partnership resale discounts. This study looks at sales of interests in publicly traded limited partnerships investing in real estate and compares the prices at which they trade to their unit values. This is similar to the comparison made between the market prices of CEFs to their NAVs cited earlier.

The study summarizes the universe of limited partnerships into six categories, one of which is partnerships investing in undeveloped land. The study has this to say about this category.

> **Undeveloped Land (Average Discount: 46%)**
>
> The four partnerships in this group were formed to invest in undeveloped land on an all-cash basis. The objective of these partnerships is to enhance the value of their land holdings through pre-development activities such as re-zoning, annexation, and land planning. The partnerships pay cash distributions as parcels are sold to developers, assuming such proceeds are not needed to fund pre-development costs at other parcels such as utility access, installation of roads and other infrastructure.
>
> While with only four partnerships this makes for a very small sample group, the average price-to-value discounts for these partnerships fall in a very tight range of 45 percent to 48 percent, with an overall average discount of 46 percent.[13]

Note that this average discount of 46 percent represents the discount from unit value that a publicly registered limited partnership interest would trade in the secondary market. It remains to determine how much of this discount represents a discount for lack of control and how much of it represents a discount for lack of marketability. Both public and private partnerships such as Rock n Roll Ltd. are alike in that "limited partners have no role in their partnership's day-to-day management decisions and are at the mercy of their general partner when it comes to major decisions such as paying distributions or when to liquidate their partnership."[14]

[13]"Partnership Re-Sale Discounts Holding Their Own," *Partnership Spectrum* (May/June 1999), 4–5.

[14]Ibid., 8.

(Continued)

EXHIBIT 14.2 ***(Continued)***

It makes no difference whether the Partnership is private, like Rock n Roll Ltd., or publicly registered; the lack of control issues are the same for all limited partnership interests. The *Partnership Spectrum* study puts it very well:

> Limited partners are purely passive investors who . . . have granted the general partner with almost unlimited discretion to make decisions regarding most every aspect of the partnership's operations. *This lack of control position accounts for most of the price-to-value discount* sought by buyers of partnership units [emphasis added].[15]

The precise proportion of the price-to-value discount attributable to lack of control issues versus marketability issues is difficult to quantify. The secondary market for publicly registered limited partnerships has grown over the years. Though it is not as liquid as an established stock exchange, it is the case that a buyer can be readily found for virtually any publicly registered partnership, and that secondary market volume has increased. Some portion of the overall discount is for lack of marketability, but "lack of control/minority interest considerations play a larger role in the composition of the total discount."[16]

For purposes of calculating an overall discount for lack of control, we have applied a 40 percent discount to the real estate portion of the Partnership's portfolio. No discount is attributable to the cash portion. Therefore, the blended discount for lack of control is calculated as follows.

	% of Market Value		*Discount*		*Weighted Discounts*
Cash	8.9	×	0.0	=	0.0%
Equities	77	×	0.159	=	12.243%
Real estate	14.1	×	0.400	=	5.640%
Blended minority discount					17.883%
Rounded					**18.0%**

There are significant differences between Rock n Roll Ltd. and closed-end mutual funds and publicly registered limited partnerships. The latter investment companies are much larger, have more diversified portfolios, and professional management. Rock n Roll Ltd.'s securities portfolio is small relative to even the smallest publicly traded mutual fund and there are only two parcels of real property. A 1 percent limited partner interest in Rock n Roll Ltd. would have no ability to control a vote on any matter that might be placed before the limited partners, and based on the Agreement of Limited Partnership, there are almost no issues that the limited partners have the right to vote on. For these reasons, we believe that a limited partnership interest in Rock n Roll Ltd. has even less control than a stockholder in a closed-end fund, and we have deemed the appropriate minority discount to be 20 percent.

Discount for Lack of Marketability

A discount for lack of marketability (DLOM) is used to compensate for the difficulty of selling shares of stock that are not traded on a stock exchange compared with those that can be traded publicly. If an investor owns shares in a public company, he or she can pick up the telephone, call a broker, and generally convert the investment into cash within three days. That is not the case with an investment in a closely held limited partnership. Therefore, publicly traded stocks have an element of liquidity that closely held shares do not have.

This is the reason that a DLOM will be applied. It is intended to reflect the market's perceived reduction in value for not providing liquidity to the limited partner.

A DLOM may also be appropriate when closely held interests have either legal or contractual restrictions placed upon them. This may be the result of restricted stock, buy-sell agreements, bank loan restrictions, or other types of contracts that restrict the sale of the shares or interests. Even when a 100 percent interest is the valuation subject, a DLOM may be appropriate if the owner cannot change the restrictions.

The most commonly used sources of data for determining an appropriate level of a DLOM are studies involving restricted stock purchases or initial public offerings. Revenue Ruling 77-287 references the *Institutional Investor Study*,[17] which addresses restricted stock issues. Many studies have updated this one.

[15]Ibid., 8.

[16]Ibid., 9.

[17]From "Discounts Involved in Purchases of Common Stock (1966–1969)," *Institutional Investor Study Report of the Securities and Exchange Commission*, H.R. Doc. No. 64, Part 5, 92d Cong., 1st Sess. 1971, 2444–2456.

EXHIBIT 14.2 *(Continued)*

Restricted Stock Studies. Restricted stock (or letter stock as it is sometimes called) is stock issued by a corporation that is not registered with the Securities and Exchange Commission (SEC) and cannot be readily sold into the public market. The stock is usually issued when a corporation is first going public, making an acquisition, or raising capital. The main reasons that corporations issue restricted stock, rather than tradable stock, are to avoid dilution of their stock price when an excessive number of shares available are for sale at any one time and to avoid the costs of registering the securities with the SEC.

The registration exemption on restricted stocks is granted under Section 4(2) of the 1933 Securities Act. The intent of Section 4(2) is to provide "small" corporations with the ability to raise capital without incurring the costs of a public offering. Regulation D, a safe harbor regulation, which became effective in 1982, falls under Section 4(2) of the code and provides uniformity in federal and state securities laws regarding private placements of securities. Securities bought under Regulation D are subject to restrictions, the most important being that the securities cannot be resold without either registration under the Act, or an exemption.[18] The exemptions for these securities are granted under Rule 144.

> Rule 144 allows the limited resale of unregistered securities after a minimum holding period of two years. Resale is limited to the higher of 1 percent of outstanding stock or average weekly volume over a 4 week period prior to the sale, during any three month period. There is no quantity limitation after a four year holding period.[19]

Therefore, holders of restricted stock must either register their securities with the SEC or qualify for a 144 exemption in order to sell their stock on the public market. A holder of restricted stock can, however, trade the stock in a private transaction. Historically, when traded privately, the restricted stock transaction was usually required to be registered with the SEC. However, in 1990, the SEC adopted Rule 144a, which relaxed the SEC filing restrictions on private transactions. The rule allows qualified institutional investors to trade unregistered securities among themselves without filing registration statements.[20] Effective April 1997, the two-year holding period was reduced to one year.

The overall effect of these regulations on restricted stock is that when issued, the corporation is not required to disclose a price and, on some occasions, even when traded, the value of restricted securities is still not a matter of public record.

Table 9 is a summary of the more familiar studies regarding restricted stock.

TABLE 9

Restricted Stock Studies

Study	*Years Covered in Study*	*Average Discount (%)*
SEC overall average[a]	1966–1969	25.8
SEC non-reporting OTC companies[a]	1966–1969	32.6
Gelman[b]	1968–1970	33.0
Trout[c]	1968–1972	33.5[i]
Moroney[d]	[h]	35.6
Maher[e]	1969–1973	35.4
Standard Research Consultants[f]	1978–1982	45.0[i]
Willamette Management Associates[g]	1981–1984	31.2[j]
Silber Study	1981–1989	34.0[j]
FMV Study	1979–April 1992	23.0[k]
Management Planning, Inc.	1980–1995	27.7[l]

[a]From "Discounts Involved in Purchases of Common Stock (1966–1969)," *Institutional Investor Study Report of the Securities and Exchange Commission*, H.R. Doc. No. 64, Part 5, 92d Cong., 1st Sess. 1971, 2444–2456.

[18]Kasim L. Alli, Ph.D., and Donald J. Thompson, Ph.D., "The Value of the Resale Limitation on Restricted Stock: An Option Theory Approach," American Society of Appraisers: *Valuation* (March 1991), 22–23.

[19]Ibid.

[20]Richard A. Brealey and Steward C. Myers, "How Corporations Issue Securities," *Principles of Corporate Finance*, 5th ed. (New York: McGraw-Hill, 1996), 399–401.

(Continued)

EXHIBIT 14.2 (Continued)

[b]From Milton Gelman, "An Economist-Financial Analyst's Approach to Valuing Stock of a Closely Held Company," *Journal of Taxation* (June 1972), 353–354.

[c]From Robert R. Trout, "Estimation of the Discount Associated with the Transfer of Restricted Securities," *Taxes* (June 1977), 381–385.

[d]From Robert E. Moroney, "Most Courts Overvalue Closely Held Stock," *Taxes* (March 1973), 144–154.

[e]From J. Michael Maher, "Discounts for Lack of Marketability for Closely-Held Business Interests," *Taxes* (September 1976), 562–571.

[f]From "Revenue Ruling 77-287 Revisited," *SRC Quarterly Reports* (Spring 1983), 1–3.

[g]From Williamette Management Associates study (unpublished).

[h]Although the years covered in this study are likely to be 1969–1972, no specific years were given in the published account.

[i]Median discounts.

[j]From William L. Silber, "Discounts on Restricted Stock: The Impact of Illiquidity on Stock Prices," *Financial Analysts Journal* (July–August 1991), 60–64.

[k]Lance S. Hall and Timothy C. Polacek, "Strategies for Obtaining the Largest Discount," *Estate Planning* (January/February 1994), 38–44. In spite of the long time period covered, this study analyzed only a little over 100 transactions involving companies that were generally not the smallest capitalization companies. It supported the findings of the SEC *Institutional Investor Study* in finding that the discount for lack of marketability was higher for smaller capitalization companies.

[l]Management Planning, Inc. "Analysis of Restricted Stocks of Public Companies: 1980–1995." Published in *Quantifying Marketability Discounts—Developing and Supporting Marketability Discounts in the Appraisal of Closely Held Business Interests* by Z. Christopher Mercer (Memphis: Peabody Publishing, LP, 1997) 345–370. Also available on *Business Valuation Update Online*, http://www.nvst.com/bvu.

Source: *Guide to Business Valuations* (Fort Worth, Tex.: Practitioners Publishing Co., 2000).

All of the studies concerning restricted stock generally deal with minority blocks of stock in public companies. Therefore, the restricted stock studies may be a useful guide in assessing a discount for lack of marketability to a minority interest. However, a control value may also need to reflect a DLOM, although it probably would be smaller than a DLOM attributable to minority shares. Since a minority interest is more difficult to sell than a controlling interest, the DLOM is usually larger for minority interests. The average DLOM ranges between 25 percent and 45 percent based on the studies discussed previously. Larger discounts may be appropriate if the starting point is a marketable, minority interest value based on public guideline company methods.

Revenue Ruling 77-287. In 1977, in Revenue Ruling 77-287, the IRS specifically recognized the relevance of the data on discounts for restricted stocks. The purpose of the ruling was "to provide information and guidance to taxpayers, Internal Revenue Service personnel and others concerned with the valuation, for Federal tax purposes, of securities that cannot be immediately resold because they are restricted from resale pursuant to Federal security laws."[21] The ruling specifically acknowledges the conclusions of the SEC *Institutional Investor Study* and the values of restricted securities purchased by investment companies as part of the "relevant facts and circumstances that bear upon the worth of restricted stock."

Initial Public Offering Studies. Another manner in which the business appraisal community and users of its services determine discounts for lack of marketability is with the use of closely held companies that underwent an initial public offering (IPO) of their stock. In these instances, the value of the closely held stock is measured before and after the company went public.

Robert W. Baird & Co., a regional investment banking firm, conducted seven studies over time periods ranging from 1980 through June 1997, comparing the prices in closely held stock transactions when no public market existed with the prices of subsequent IPOs in the same stocks. The results are presented in Table 10.

[21]Revenue Ruling 77-287 (1977-2 C.B. 319), Section I.

EXHIBIT 14.2 *(Continued)*

TABLE 10

The Value of Marketability as Illustrated in Initial Public Offerings of Common Stock

Study	# of IPO Prospectuses Reviewed	# of Qualifying Transactions	Discount Mean	Discount Median
1995–1997	732	91	43%	42%
1994–1995	318	46	45%	45%
1992–1993	443	54	45%	44%
1990–1992	266	35	42%	40%
1989–1990	157	23	45%	40%
1987–1989	98	27	45%	45%
1985–1986	130	21	43%	43%
1980–1981	97	13	60%	66%
Total	2,241	301	44%	43%

Source: John O. Emory, "The Value of Marketability as Illustrated in Initial Public Offerings of Common Stock," *Business Valuation Review* (September 1997).

A similar private, unpublished study has been performed by Willamette Management Associates. Their results are presented in Table 11.

TABLE 11

Summary of Discounts for Private Transaction P/E Ratios Compared With Public Offering P/E Ratios Adjusted for Changes in Industry P/E Ratios

Time Period	Number of Companies Analyzed	Number of Transactions Analyzed	Median Discount (%)
1975–1978	17	31	54.7
1979	9	17	62.9
1980–1982	58	113	55.5
1984	20	33	74.4
1985	18	25	43.2
1986	47	74	47.5
1987	25	40	43.8
1988	13	19	51.8
1989	9	19	50.4
1990	17	23	48.5
1991	27	34	31.8
1992	36	75	52.4

Source: Williamette Management Associates, as appearing in Shannon P. Pratt, Robert F. Reilly, and Robert P. Schweihs, *Valuing a Business*, 3rd ed.

(Continued)

EXHIBIT 14.2 *(Continued)*

Other Considerations. Another consideration in determining a discount for lack of marketability is the cost of flotation of a public offering. These costs are generally significant and will frequently include payments to attorneys, accountants, and investment banker fees. The costs associated with smaller offerings can be as much as 25 percent to 30 percent of a small company's equity.

As far back as 1977, through Revenue Ruling 77-287, the IRS recognized the effectiveness of restricted stock study data in providing useful information for the quantification of discounts for lack of marketability. The Baird and Willamette studies of transactions in closely held stocks did not exist at that time, but the IRS and the courts have been receptive to using this data to assist in quantifying discounts for lack of marketability.

The IPO studies are proof that larger discounts can be justified than those quoted from the restricted stock studies. One of the best explanations of why a DLOM varies from case to case was included in an article published by Robert E. Moroney titled "Why 25% Discount for Nonmarketability in One Valuation, 100% in Another?"[22] In Moroney's article, he points out 11 different factors that should be considered in the application of a DLOM. These factors are as follows:

1. *High dividend yield:* Companies that pay dividends tend to be more marketable than companies that do not.
2. *Bright growth prospects:* Companies that have bright growth prospects are easier to sell than companies that do not. This makes them more marketable.
3. *Swing value:* If a block of stock has swing value, it may be more marketable than the typical small block of stock. This swing value could include a premium. This can be emphasized where a 2 percent interest exists with two 49 percent interests. The 2 percent interest can be worth quite a bit to either 49 percent interest if it will give that interest control of the company.
4. *Restrictions on transfer:* Restrictions on transfer make the stock less marketable due to the difficulty in selling them.
5. *Buy-sell agreements:* Buy-sell agreements can go either way. The agreement can create a market for the stock, making it more marketable, or the agreement can restrict the sale, making it less marketable.
6. *Stock's quality grade:* The higher the quality of the stock, the more marketable it will be. This can be evidenced by comparing the subject company to others for supporting strengths and weaknesses.
7. *Controlling shareholder's honesty:* The integrity of the controlling shareholder can make a big difference regarding the ability to sell a partial interest in a company. If the controlling shareholder tends to deal with the other shareholders honestly, the other interests in that company tend to be more marketable.
8. *Controlling shareholder's friendliness:* Similar to the shareholder's honesty, the manner in which he or she deals with others can make the stock more marketable.
9. *Prospects for the corporation:* If a corporation has good prospects for the future, it will generally be more marketable.
10. *Prospects for the industry:* A company that is in an industry with good prospects will also generally be more marketable.
11. *Mood of the investing public:* When the investing public is bullish, they are more readily willing to make an investment. This can increase the marketability.

In this assignment, we are appraising a minority interest that has no control in the Partnership. Most of the marketability studies just discussed have supported discounts of 35 percent to 40 percent. These studies relate to minority interests in companies that are either public, with restrictions under Rule 144, or private but about to go public. Therefore, an argument can easily be made to support a higher discount for an interest in a closely held company that is not going public. The points that we have taken into consideration with respect to the Moroney factors include the following:

Dividend yield: The assets of Rock n Roll Ltd. have generated steady income for distributions since the Partnership's inception. Although distributions are under the control of the managing general partner, there is no reason to expect that the Partnership will discontinue distributions in the future.

Growth prospects: The securities portfolio is expected to grow in value in accordance with expectations for the stock market. The long-range outlooks for real estate in Florida, as well as North Carolina, are good.

Degree of control: All of the Partnership's operations are controlled by the managing general partner. Also, a 1 percent interest has no swing value.

Restrictions on transfer: The restrictions on transfer of partnership interests have been reviewed. These provisions have the effect of limiting the market for these interests to approved family members, or the Partnership.

Buy-sell agreements: There are no buy-sell agreements involving the Partnership.

[22] *Taxes* (May 1977).

EXHIBIT 14.2 *(Continued)*

Stock quality grade: If this partnership was publicly traded, it would be considered a high-quality portfolio and be expected to generate a reasonable return on its assets. The only caveat is the undeveloped land in the portfolio, which would require some expenditures for predevelopment before a return could be expected. This land represents a small portion of the portfolio, however.

Controlling shareholder's honesty: This is not considered to be an issue in this appraisal.

Controlling shareholder's friendliness: This is not considered to be an issue in this appraisal, although family members must first be approved by the managing general partner in order to join the Partnership.

Prospects for the Partnership: The Partnership is expected to continue for its full term and its assets to grow.

Prospects for the industry: The outlook for the stock market in the coming year is quite good, which should bode well for the Partnership.

Mood of the investing public: According to reports, the investing public appears to be quite optimistic regarding the outlook for the equities markets.

Overall, the factors affecting the liquidity of an interest in the Partnership are positive. The assets are growing, cash is being distributed, and considering the size of the portfolio, these are positive factors that would reduce the discount.

There is one factor that could increase the discount. This is the restriction on transfer. According to the partnership agreement, only certain "family members" can buy the interest, and if no family member is interested, then the only potential buyer is the Partnership. Although the agreement states that, "the Partnership shall purchase such interest for the sale price as determined . . . ," it does not provide for an immediate purchase, or purchase terms. It only provides a description of how the price will be determined. Although this factor increases the illiquidity of the interest, as long as distributions are being made, the limited partner is being compensated, and therefore any potential loss of liquidity dealing with the time to sell is mitigated somewhat by the receipt of distributions, which have been in excess of market rates.

Therefore, considering the facts and circumstances of this interest, a discount for lack of marketability of 25 percent is deemed appropriate.

Court Cases

Since I promised you some court cases, I figure that I have to deliver the goods. I am summarizing *some* of the cases that I believe may be applicable to this topic. Read the entire case if you are going to make any judgment calls. Do not rely solely on my summaries.

Estate of Frank M. DiSanto et al. v. Commissioner, T.C. Memo 1999-421

Tax Court Memorandum decision rendered by Judge Colvin on December 27, 1999.

Issue: (1) Fair market value of 186,777 shares of stock as of November 26, 1992; and (2) fair market value of some of these shares as of June 4, 1993.

Facts. Mr. DiSanto died on November 26, 1992, owning 186,177 shares in Morganton Dyeing & Finishing Corp. (MD&F). Prior to the completion of the administration of his estate, Mrs. DiSanto died. None of Mr. DiSanto's stock had been transferred to Mrs. DiSanto prior to her death.

MD&F had been in existence since 1954 and operating in North Carolina since 1961. The company dyed and finished fabric for clothing and performed its services on a commission basis.

Mr. DiSanto's son began working for the Company in the late 1980s, and a nephew, Jason Yates, was a member of management by 1990. Most of the stock in the corporation was owned by family members.

Prior to 1992, the company had net profit margins of 8 percent to 10 percent. After 1991, profit margins decreased to less than 5 percent due to the financial troubles of many of the company's customers. Prior to Mr. DiSanto's death, the City of Morganton proposed doubling the company's water rates; had this occurred, it would have increased the company's expenses by $750,000 per year, which was almost twice the profits in 1992. In addition, the company had sued a customer for nonpayment of $300,000, and the customer turned around and sued MD&F for damages exceeding $2 million. The lawsuit was settled for an undisclosed amount and the waiver of the unpaid invoices.

Mr. DiSanto left his estate to a trust for the benefit of his wife and children. Prior to her death, Mrs. DiSanto disclaimed her right to inherit a certain amount of the MD&F stock based on the value reported in Mr. DiSanto's estate tax return. This would have resulted in Mrs. DiSanto receiving a minority block of MD&F stock.

Mr. DiSanto's estate reported the value of Mr. DiSanto's stock at $25.80 per share as of the date of his death. The same appraiser then valued Mrs. DiSanto's minority block at $15.53 per share.

In 1995, the company redeemed Mr. DiSanto's shares at a price of $26.81 per share. Although the price appeared to exceed fair market value, the transaction was concluded to assist family members. In addition to the purchase of the stock, certain noncompete agreements were executed as well.

The company filed for bankruptcy protection on November 4, 1997.

The issue before the court was the value of Mr. DiSanto's shares.

Tax Court Opinion. In addition to the original value determined for the estate tax return, the estate hired another appraiser, who determined the per-share value to be $23.50. Despite the two appraisals, the estate contended that the actual fair market value of the stock was $12.16 per share. They based this on three factors:

1. Neither of the appraisers considered the fact that the company was not profitable after 1991.
2. The effect on the company of the death of Mr. DiSanto and the pending lawsuit.
3. The potential for water rate increases.

In addition, the estate believed that the 1995 redemption should not be considered because it was unforeseeable in 1992 and 1993, and the price exceeded fair market value. Finally, the estate argued that the IRS's expert only critiqued the estate's experts; it did not perform an independent analysis and appraisal.

The IRS proposed a per-share value of $30 based on the 1995 redemption price plus the cost of the non-compete agreements. In addition, the IRS did not believe that the 1997 bankruptcy was foreseeable. Finally, the IRS contended that the guideline companies used by the estate's experts were not similar to MD&F, the earnings were improperly weighted, and that too much weight was placed on the importance of Mr. DiSanto.

The court disagreed with the IRS regarding the use of the 1995 transaction because it did not agree that this was an arm's-length transaction. The court believed that emotional factors led to the payment of an excessive redemption price. In addition, the court did not consider the 1997 bankruptcy.

Despite submission of reports by two experts, the estate did not want the court to consider either of the appraisals. The estate did not believe that either appraiser considered the negative financial aspects of the company at the appraisal date, and therefore believed that both experts had overvalued the company.

The court, on the other hand, reviewed the work done by all of the appraisers, and considered the estate's second expert's report to be reasonable and credible. The court stated, "It is cogent and persuasive evidence that the $25.80 per share value reported on Mr. DiSanto's estate tax return is overstated. Respondent offered no evidence of the value of MD&F stock other than the redemption price in 1995, which we do not consider." The court valued Mr. DiSanto's stock at $23.50 per share, the same price that the estate's second appraiser determined.

After a similar discussion regarding the value of Mrs. DiSanto's shares, the court concluded that this same appraiser's analysis was reasonable and utilized their per-share value for Mrs. DiSanto's shares as well.

Estate of Eileen K. Brocato v. Commissioner, T.C. Memo 1999-424

Tax Court Memorandum decision rendered by Judge Vasquez on December 29, 1999.

Issue: The determination of the proper amount of blockage and fractional interest discounts to be applied to petitioner's nine real properties.

Facts. At the time of the decedent's death, she owned interests in nine pieces of real property, all of which were located in the Marina District of San Francisco. The parties stipulated to the values of these properties prior to the application of appropriate discounts. Six of the properties were owned outright, while three were 50 percent interests.

On the estate tax return, the estate utilized a 20 percent blockage discount, as well as a 20 percent fractional interest discount on those properties that the estate owned a fractional interest in. These discounts were based on a real estate appraisal that had been performed for the estate. Subsequently, the estate continued to claim a fractional interest discount of 20 percent but reduced its blockage discount to 12.5 percent and applied it to only eight of the properties.

In its notice of deficiency, the IRS allowed a blockage discount of 1.92 percent on seven of the properties and a fractional interest discount based on partition costs.

Tax Court Opinion. The court started its opinion with the following:

> A determination of the fair market value of a group of items includes a consideration of how many of the items would be available for sale at any one time and the length of time necessary to liquidate the entire inventory. Where the addition of a group of similar items into the market within a short period of time depresses the price of the items, a blockage discount is appropriate.
>
> When dealing with fractional interests in real property, courts have held that the sum of all fractional interests can be less than the whole and have used fractional interest discounts to value undivided interests.

The court then discussed the qualifications of the appraisers. Although both were accepted as experts in real estate appraisal, the court felt that the IRS's expert had limited experience with blockage and fractional interest discounts. As a result, the court accepted the estate's expert's report as best representing fair market value but then went on to make some adjustments.

Regarding the blockage discount, the court believed that it was appropriate to only seven of the properties. It stated, "Based on the number of properties in the same market in 1993, the San Francisco economy at that time, and the limited pool of investors, we believe that the introduction of seven new properties, 3.5 properties each 6 months, warrants an 11-percent blockage factor."

Regarding the fractional interest discount, the court believed that the estate's appraiser had done a more thorough job of considering the factors that would affect this discount and concluded that his discount of 20 percent was appropriate.

Estate of Beatrice Ellen Jones Dunn v. Commissioner, T.C. Memo 2000-12

Tax Court Memorandum decision rendered by Judge Gale on January 12, 2000.

Issue: To determine the fair market value of 492,610 shares of stock in Dunn Equipment, Inc., owned by Beatrice Ellen Jones as of June 8, 1991, the date of death.

Facts. The deceased owned 62.96 percent of the total outstanding shares in Dunn Equipment, Inc. at the time of her death. The company was a family-owned and operated company incorporated and located in Texas. The primary business was the renting of heavy equipment such as cranes, air compressors, backhoes, man lifts, sanders, and grinders, as well as providing operators for such equipment. Crane rentals accounted for more than 50 percent of the revenues of the company. In addition to the equipment, the company owned several parcels of industrial real estate, as well as a townhouse.

The company had been operating for more than 40 years and was the largest heavy equipment rental business in the area. It held a substantial share of the market and was able to command premium rates. Forty-five percent of its rentals came from the petrochemical industry, and the economy and industry were strong at the valuation date. Revenues increased over the period analyzed, but the rental industry was becoming more competitive and Dunn Equipment had not raised its rental rates for 10 years. In addition, the company was replacing its equipment to remain competitive and was spending $2 million per year. Expenses were increasing each year, and the company had not paid dividends in five years.

Tax Court Opinion. The major issue in the determination of value appeared to be how to reconcile the value of a company in which the asset-based and earnings-based values are widely divergent. The taxpayer's expert argued that the value should be based on a 50-50 weighting of the asset-based and earnings-based values. The IRS argued that the value should be a pro rata of the net asset value, minus an appropriate discount for lack of marketability and lack of super-majority control.

The taxpayer had two experts; the IRS had one. The taxpayer's first expert valued the stock and the other two experts critiqued reports; they did not independently value the stock.

The taxpayer's expert used a capitalization of net income method and an asset-based value using liquidation value. The IRS argued that if an earnings method is deemed appropriate, the capitalization of net cash flow is the appropriate methodology to use. The court determined that the taxpayer put too much emphasis on liquidation and that the IRS put too much emphasis on the fair market value of the assets. It was determined that the value is "best represented by a combination of an earnings-based value using capitalization of net cash flow and an asset-based value using fair market value of assets, with an appropriate discount for lack of marketability and lack of super-majority control."

The IRS argued that because of the disparity between the two values, earnings should be disregarded. The IRS also argued that net asset value should represent the minimum value of the company. The court disagreed because this would disregard the operational aspects of the company. In addition, the court noted that the IRS's expert was not an appraiser, and that she had not performed an independent appraisal of the stock. The court stated, "We evaluate the opinion evidence of an expert in light of the qualifications of the expert." In conclusion, the court stated, "In light of the significant operational aspects of Dunn Equipment, the size of the block of stock in issue, the identity and attitudes of the remaining shareholders and directors, and the costs associated with liquidation, we conclude that the hypothetical investor would give earnings value substantial weight."

The court then looked at the taxpayer's weighting. The court found that the taxpayer's expert put too much emphasis on liquidation. Texas law requires a super-majority (two-thirds) vote for liquidation, and testimony indicated that the other stockholders would not have agreed to liquidation. The belief was that this business was cyclical, that it was currently in the low part of the cycle, and that the other stockholders believed that the operating results would increase as the economy and industry rebounded. The court stated:

> In allocating weight among the values determined under each approach, we have considered the degree to which Dunn Equipment was actively engaged in producing income, the nature of the business, market conditions, the economic outlook, the company's history, its financial and business experiences and situation, the size of the block of stock in issue, and the identity, attitudes, and intentions of the remaining shareholders. Due to other factors relevant to value such as low profitability, volatility of earnings, high debt, limited customer base, and dependence upon one industry, we give net asset value the greater significance. Based upon the foregoing, we find that fair market value is best represented by an allocation of 65 percent to net asset value and 35 percent to earnings value.

Estate of Etta H. Weinberg et al. v. Commissioner, T.C. Memo 2000-51

Tax Court Memorandum decision rendered by Judge Whalen on February 15, 2000.

Issue: The fair market value of a limited partnership interest over which the decedent had a general power of appointment on the date of her death, December 15, 1992.

Facts. At the time of her death, the decedent possessed a general power of appointment over a marital trust that held a 25.235 percent interest in the Hill House limited partnership. The partnership owned and operated a building that contained 188 apartments, an office suite, a parking garage, and a swimming pool. At the date of death, only three apartments were vacant; there was less than $500,000 due on the mortgage (which was due by April 1, 1993), and the parties agreed that the fair market value of the real estate was $10,050,000.

Hill House LP operates under a partnership agreement that gives the general partner sole discretion to determine when distributions are made. This agreement also governs the transferability of partnership interests and gives all partners the right of first refusal. The agreement also gives the general partner the discretion to accept or deny the substitution of a limited partner, unless the purchaser is already a partner.

The estate appraised the interest at a value of $1,075,000 on the estate tax return and subsequently amended the amount to $971,838. The IRS originally estimated the value at $2,422,500; it was amended to $1,770,103.

Tax Court Opinion. The estate's expert utilized a capitalization of income approach, as well as a net asset value approach. In the income approach, he utilized a three-year average cash distribution amount as the income stream (ignoring the fact that the final mortgage payment would have to be made) and derived a capitalization rate based on seven publicly registered real estate partnerships that he considered comparable.

For his net asset approach, he applied a 51 percent discount, which was identified as the discount from net asset value for a specific publicly traded real estate venture that he felt was comparable. He then combined the values by applying a weighting of 75 percent to the income approach and 25 percent to the net asset value method. The basis of this weighting was that the capitalization approach was the more important approach for this partnership interest.

The appraiser than applied a 35 percent discount for lack of marketability to the value based on market studies of illiquid securities.

The IRS's expert relied entirely on the capitalization of income approach. He believed that the net asset value approach was inappropriate because Hill House LP's asset was income-producing real estate. In addition, he argued that the net asset value is irrelevant because a hypothetical buyer cannot control the sale of the underlying property or the liquidation of the partnership.

The IRS's expert approached the calculation of a capitalization rate in a similar fashion as the estate's expert. He used a 1993 version of the same source instead of the 1992 version used by the estate. Based on his selection of the correct comparable data, he selected a return of 10.45 percent. He then adjusted this rate down to 9.7 percent by adjusting for a lack of diversity (the partnership owned only one property), the fact that the general partner was also a limited partner (this would ensure cash distributions), and the fact that comparable data might include distressed sales. For his income stream, the expert selected 1992 cash distributions. He felt that distributions were bound to go up in succeeding years when the mortgage was paid off, and this was the minimum amount of distributions an investor would expect.

The IRS's expert then utilized the Quantitative Marketability Discount Model (QMDM) put forth by Z. Christopher Mercer to quantify his discount for lack of marketability. Based on this model, he produced a discount of 15 percent.

The court found it interesting that neither appraiser actually determined a minority discount. It then set forth its calculations of what those discounts would be, based on each expert's analysis. The court determined that the estate's expert implied a 42.6 percent minority discount and a 35 percent illiquidity discount, for a combined discount of 62.7 percent. The IRS's expert implied a 20.1 percent minority discount and a 15 percent illiquidity discount for a combined discount of 32.1 percent. The court did not agree with either expert.

The court did agree with the estate that both the asset and income approaches needed to be considered and agreed that a weighting of 75 percent for the capitalization method and 25 percent for the asset method was appropriate for this partnership. In disagreeing with the IRS's expert, the court stated, "The net asset value should still be considered because the value of the underlying real estate will retain most of its inherent value even if the corporation is not efficient in securing a stream of rental income. Thus, weight must be given to the net asset value of the partnership's underlying assets even though a hypothetical buyer of the subject limited partnership interest would have no ability to directly realize the value by forcing liquidation."

Additional discussion of the appraisers' reports revealed the following:

1. The court agreed with the estate's use of three-year average cash flow, since discretion lies with the general partner and there is no guarantee that past distributions will reflect future distributions.
2. The court agreed with the IRS's expert regarding the use of a number of comparables to determine the capitalization rate, rather than only one, as the estate's expert did.
3. The court derived a discount from these comparables to apply to a net asset value utilizing the IRS's expert's methodology of selecting a capitalization rate.
4. The court disagreed with the discounts for lack of marketability selected by both experts. The court did not agree with the use of the QMDM because slight variations in assumptions result in large variations in the discount. The court disagreed with the estate's expert because it did not believe that sufficient analysis of the appropriate factors had been considered. The court selected a discount of 20 percent but did not discuss how it was derived.

Estate of Emily F. Klauss v. Commissioner, T.C. Memo 2000-191

Tax Court Memorandum decision rendered by Judge Colvin on June 27, 2000.

Issue: Is the fair market value of 184 shares of Green Light Chemical Co., Inc., owned by the decedent on February 1, 1993, equal to the amount that the estate contends ($1,810,000) or the amount that the IRS contends ($2,150,000)?

Facts. The company was founded in 1946. It has always been a closely held family-operated company that has never paid dividends. There are 460 outstanding shares. The company formulates and markets (but does not manufacture) insecticides, weed killers, fungicides, plant foods, and other products for home and garden use. The company sells its products to distributors who sell them to retailers. The company's sales vary according to weather conditions and the planting season. Most products are shipped in December and January, and most revenues are received in May and June. Seventy-one percent of the company's sales are to five customers.

The company had been informed that its facility was contaminated in 1991, although it denies this claim and has not submitted a clean-up plan. In addition, the company was a defendant in at least six product liability lawsuits and had a potential uninsured liability of more than $100 million at the trial date.

Tax Court Opinion. All experts utilized an income capitalization and market or public guideline company method to value the interest in the company. The experts used the same guideline companies. They primarily disagreed as to whether or not to apply a small stock premium and whether or not to adjust the multiple for the growth rates of the subject company and the guideline companies.

The estate utilized a small stock premium of 5.2 percent based on data from Ibbotson Associates, whereas the IRS indicated that it was not appropriate because large capitalization stocks have been outperforming small capitalization stocks. The IRS's expert attempted to utilize only portions of the Ibbotson data for a more recent period of time, rather than using their long-term averages. The court agreed with the estate's analysis and felt that the small stock premium was appropriate.

In analyzing growth rates, the estate's expert utilized a 5 percent growth rate for Green Light, while utilizing growth rates of 14.3 percent to 15.5 percent for the guideline companies. The IRS's expert believed that the estate underestimated the subject company's growth rate because management believed that the company would grow 5 percent to 10 percent in 1993.

Overall, the court primarily agreed with the estate's analysis because the IRS's expert did not adequately consider the differences between the subject company and the guideline company that he believed was most similar.

Another issue brought up by the court was the IRS's use of CAPM. The court did not believe that the CAPM was appropriate because the company had little possibility of going public. In addition, it disagreed with the selected beta of 0.70 because an investment in Green Light would not be 30 percent less risky than an investment in the S&P 500, and the beta selected was not supported.

The court also agreed with both experts that a discount for litigation and environmental claims was appropriate and selected the estate's analysis of this amount.

Overall, other than the selected growth rate for one guideline company, the court agreed with the estate's expert's analysis and conclusion as it was considered to be more "persuasive."

Estate of Morton B. Harper v. Commissioner, T.C. Memo 2000-202

Tax Court Memorandum decision rendered by Judge Wells on June 30, 2000.

Issue: Pursuant to Section 2704(b), should restrictions on the right to liquidate certain limited partnership interests in Harper Financial Co., L.P. be disregarded to the extent that such restrictions are more restrictive than the default provisions of California law?

Facts. On January 1, 1994, a California limited partnership was created. The decedent owned a 0.4 percent general partnership interest, and a trust consisting of marketable securities, mutual funds, and a note receivable that the decedent had a life estate in was the sole limited partner.

On July 1, 1994, an agreement was amended to create two classes of limited partnership interests; a Class A interest of 39 percent, which the trust retained, and a Class B interest of 60 percent, which was assigned to the two general partners.

The partnership agreement provided for dissolution of the partnership under specific circumstances but also stated, "No General Partner shall have the right to withdraw from the Partnership without the consent of the Limited Partners."

The decedent died on February 1, 1995, and reported a 39 percent Class A limited partnership interest (he had previously gifted all of his other interests).

Tax Court Opinion. In rendering its decision, the court relied on its opinion in *Kerr v. Commissioner,* 113 T.C. 449. The court stated:

> We held that provisions in a partnership agreement substantially similar to those in issue in the instant case were not more restrictive than the requirements of the applicable limited partnership law of the State of Texas. Respondent does not dispute the provisions of the limited partnership agreement in the instant case

are substantially similar to those at issue in Kerr. Moreover, respondent does not dispute that there is no substantial difference between California and Texas law with respect to the liquidation of a limited partnership. Unable to distinguish the facts or the law at issue in Kerr, respondent urges this Court to reconsider our opinion in that case. Because the facts of the instant case are indistinguishable from those in issue in Kerr, we need not reiterate our analysis, undertaken in Kerr, which we adopt in this opinion.

Accordingly, we hold that the limitations on liquidation contained in the partnership agreement are not applicable restrictions within the meaning of section 2704(b) and, consequently, must be taken into account in valuing the limited partnership interests in issue in the instant case.

Estate of Pauline Welch, Deceased; Newton G. Welch, Jr.; Lois Welch McGowan, Co-Executors, Petitioners-Appellants v. Commissioner of Internal Revenue, Respondent-Appellee. 85 AFTR 2d 2000-1200 (208 F.3d 213)

Case appealed from the Tax Court. Heard by U.S. Court of Appeals, Sixth Circuit. Decision for taxpayers on March 2, 2000; Tax Court decision was reversed and remanded.

Valuation issue: Built-in capital gains tax liability on condemned property.

Facts. The taxpayer died on March 18, 1993, owning minority interests in two closely held corporations: Electric Service, Inc. ("ESI") and Industrial Sales Company ("ISC").

The appraiser for the estate valued the companies by utilizing the net asset valuation method. Certain properties were excluded from the valuation because it was believed that they had been targeted by the city for eminent domain actions. Since these properties were not included, no discount for a built-in capital gains tax liability was reflected.

In filing the estate tax return, the petitioners utilized the appraiser's figures, but also included the excluded properties and applied discounts to reflect the built-in capital gains tax liability on these properties.

In 1996, the IRS notified the estate of a deficiency in its estate tax return. The IRS accepted a discount for minority interest ownership, but disallowed a discount for the built-in capital gains tax liability. The estate filed a petition in Tax Court challenging this deficiency. On May 6, 1998, The Tax Court ruled that the estate was not entitled to discount the value of the corporate stock for the real estate built-in gains tax liability. The estate appealed this decision to the U.S. Court of Appeals.

Tax Court Decision. The IRS set forth three arguments to the Tax Court:

1. The estate had not established that a liquidation of the corporations or the sale of the corporations' assets was likely to occur.
2. The discount was not warranted where only the real estate, and not the corporations, was subject to condemnation.
3. The discount was not warranted because the corporations "could avoid, and did indeed avoid, the recognition of gain under section 1033."

The Tax Court denied the estate's petition on two factors:

1. Consistent with prior decisions of the Tax Court, the taxpayer, to obtain the reduction in the value of the stock due to built-in capital gains liability, had to show that a liquidation of the corporation or sale of the corporations' assets was likely to occur.
2. As an alternative, assuming that the condemnation of the corporations' real estate was foreseeable as of the valuation date, and consequently that there was a requisite likelihood that the corporations would sell the properties, a Section 1033 election was available to the corporations, and therefore, no reduction in the value of the stock should be allowed for the corporations' built-in capital gains tax.

Since the Tax Court determined that no discount was warranted, it did not discuss or decide the sufficiency of the estate's evidence regarding the amount of such a discount.

Appeal. The major issues raised on the appeal appeared to be resolved by the IRS's acquiescence to the *Eisenberg v. Commissioner* case, which concluded that taxpayers can now discount the value of corporate stock to reflect the built-in capital gains tax liability. Instead, the Commissioner, in an attempt to have the Tax Court decision affirmed, argued the following:

> The Tax Court's determination that the estate may not reduce the value of the shares of stock at issue to take into account the potential 'built-in' capital gains tax liability should be affirmed because (1) the estate is clearly not entitled to a reduction for the full amount of the potential capital gains tax, and (2) the estate, which had the burden of proof, did not provide the court with any basis for arriving at a discount of any particular lesser amount.

The Commissioner did not make an argument for the possibility of a Section 1033 election, but the U.S. Court of Appeals discussed the issue due to its consideration by the Tax Court. The decision of the U.S. Court of Appeals concentrated on the decisions in the *Eisenberg* and *Davis* cases. In effect, the court looked at the factors that the hypothetical willing buyer and seller would look at, including the possibility of a sale or liquidation of the property, and the hypothetical tax consequences that would result. The court concluded that these issues would be factors that the hypothetical willing buyer and seller would consider in deriving a final opinion of value. The court stated:

> In short, the question is what would a hypothetical buyer of the corporations' stock on March 18, 1993 pay for this stock knowing all of the corporations' circumstances, including the threatened condemnation of the real estate and the availability of a section 1033 election when that condemnation occurs. This is a factual issue to be determined from the evidence.

As a result, the judgment of the Tax Court was reversed and the case was remanded for a hearing on the issue, "never determined by the Tax Court, of the market value of the corporations' stock on the date of the decedent's death based on what a hypothetical willing buyer would likely pay for the stock on that date considering all the facts and circumstances at that time, including the built-in capital gains tax on the corporations' real estate and the availability of a section 1033 election."

Estate of Mary T. Maggos et ux. v. Commissioner, T.C. Memo 2000-129

Tax Court memorandum decision rendered by Judge Ruwe on April 11, 2000.

Issue: To determine whether a transaction in which Mary D. Maggos's shares of stock in a family-owned company were redeemed constitutes a taxable gift by Mary D. Maggos for purposes of Section 2512.

Facts. In 1987, the decedent and her son entered into an agreement where the decedent was to sell her controlling interest in PCAB to the corporation for a $3 million promissory note. The result of the transaction would be that her son, Nikita Maggos, would become the sole owner of PCAB. This transaction was designed to be an "estate freeze." The purpose of an estate freeze is to minimize taxes. The price was determined because Mr. Maggos's attorney believed that he could support this value for gift tax purposes.

However, around the same time, Mr. Maggos's accountants contacted an appraisal firm to review the company's financial statements as of October 31, 1986, to derive a value of PCAB for estate planning purposes. They determined that the value of the entire company was between $9.8 and $13.2 million.

The IRS contends that PCAB redeemed Mary Maggos's shares for less than their fair market value and that this transaction resulted in a gift to Nikita Maggos that is subject to gift tax. The IRS asserts that the measure of the gift is the difference between the fair market value of decedent's stock and the redemption price of $3 million.

Tax Court Opinion. After a number of legal issues were argued, the court determined that the transaction was legitimate, and in order to determine if a gift had been made, it had to determine the value of the shares that were subject to the 1987 transaction. It then turned to the valuation issues.

The expert for the IRS determined that the value of the Company was $14 million. This was determined by utilizing a discounted cash flow, a guideline company, a market transaction, and an acquisition analysis. The court analyzed each method individually and had problems with the methodologies as follows:

1. *Discounted cash flow:* The appraiser calculated the terminal value in 10 years and utilized both CAPM and WACC, which the court does not believe are the proper tools for appraising closely held companies.

   The appraiser used a beta of 0.76, which the court objected to because it was not persuaded by the selection of the guideline companies used in the beta calculation. Also, the court disagreed with the debt return as it was 2 points below a government bond rate. The appraiser did not justify his failure to use a small company risk premium in the determination of the rate, and finally, the appraiser did not calculate the value of the non-operating assets properly.
2. *Guideline company and market transaction analysis:* Two of the companies selected were Pepsi-Cola, Inc. and Coca-Cola, Inc., which were totally irrelevant to the value of a Pepsi bottling company. The court did not like the other two companies selected due to their dissimilarity to the subject company. In analyzing the transactions, the court noted that there was nothing in the appraiser's analysis to demonstrate that the companies selected were similar to the subject company and therefore disregarded this analysis.
3. *Acquisition analysis:* The subject company was sold two years after the valuation date. The IRS's expert disregarded it due to the time lag between the valuation date and the sale.

The court then analyzed the petitioner's expert's testimony. This expert used a capitalization of cash flow method as a primary method and utilized a guideline company method as a reasonableness test. This expert rejected a discounted cash flow method as well as the use of multiples from other sales. The court adjusted reasonable compensation as the petitioner's expert considered it to be reasonable and the court did not. It also made some adjustments for non-operating assets.

The court concluded that the adjusted values derived by the DCF and capitalization of cash flow methods were similar and calculated a value of $8,250,000; they also added non-operating assets, resulting in a value of $11 million for 100 percent of the equity.

The court then addressed the issue of a discount for lack of marketability. The taxpayers put forth an argument for a 25 percent to 30 percent discount, whereas the IRS believed that no discount was warranted. The court was more persuaded by the taxpayers' experts and stated, "The facts that PCAB was a small family company and the shares in the company could not be sold without the approval of Pepsi-Cola, Inc. favor the conclusion that some discount is appropriate." They concluded that the appropriate discount was 25 percent.

The final issue was the appropriateness of a control premium. There was little discussion about this premium, although the court stated, "The transfer of 56.7 percent of the shares would allow day-to-day control to the purchaser. Considering the level of control transferred, we find that a control premium of 25 percent, rather than 34 to 38 percent that petitioner's expert calculated, would be more appropriate."

Estate of Charles A. Borgatello et al. v. Commissioner, T.C. Memo 2000-264

Tax Court Memorandum decision rendered by Judge Wells on August 8, 2000.

Issue: To determine the fair market value of an 82.76 percent interest in Valley Improvement Co., Inc. (VIC) as of January 12, 1994, the alternate valuation date.

Facts. VIC owned two shopping centers, Montecito Village North (MVN) and Montecito Village South (MVS), along with several other assets. Other than the values of MVN and MVS, all other asset and liability values had been stipulated to. The estate contends that the value of the combined assets are $13,375,000, whereas the IRS contends that the assets' values are $15,799,000.

Tax Court Opinion. Much of this decision discusses the underlying values of MVN and MVS. After analyzing the various reports submitted by the real estate appraisers, the court determined that the values of MVN and MVS were $9,600,000 and $5,680,000, respectively. The court then turned to the value of Mr. Borgatello's 82.76 percent stock interest in VIC under the standard of fair market value.

The court felt that the best way to value VIC and an interest in VIC was by valuing the company's utilizing its net asset value and then discounting for various factors that affect marketability. "Principal factors affecting the discount in the instant case are the tax liability inherent in the built-in gain assets of VIC and the lack of marketability due to the difficulty of selling stock in a small closely held corporation such as VIC."

The taxpayer's expert determined that the appropriate discount was 35 percent. He presented a general discussion of various factors, but did not quantify the individual factors. The largest part of his discount appeared to be the built-in gains tax liability. This expert calculated the appropriate tax rate to be 31.2 percent and assumed that the property would be sold immediately. Although the court agreed with the application of a deduction for the tax, they quantified a 32.3 percent tax rate, but reduced it because they did not feel that it was appropriate to assume that a sale of the property would take place immediately.

The IRS's expert, on the other hand, attempted to quantify certain items, including dividends, economy, management continuity, potential corporate gains tax, restrictions on stock transfer, and transaction costs. He derived a discount of 27 percent. The court agreed with parts of his analysis and disagreed with other parts of it. The court concluded a discount of 33 percent. It factored in 24 percent for the built-in capital gains discount. This was a compromise between the IRS's expert opinion that the property would not be sold for 10 years, and the estate's expert opinion that the tax would be payable immediately. In addition, the court provided for a 3 percent discount due to the terms of the stock purchase agreement that existed and 6 percent for transaction costs.

Estate of James J. Renier et al. v. Commissioner, T.C. Memo 2000-298

Tax Court memorandum decision rendered by Judge Gale on September 25, 2000.

Issue: To determine the fair market value of 22,100 shares of stock in the Renier Company owned by James J. Renier as of April 10, 1994, the date of death.

Facts. The Renier family has conducted a retail business in Dubuque, Iowa, since 1899, primarily selling televisions, stereo equipment, and VCRs. Industry data indicated that the compound annual growth rate for the company's product mix was 4.15 percent from 1989 through 1993 and that the company's sales had increased at an annual growth rate of 8.3 percent during this period; primarily from July 1, 1992, through June 30, 1993, due to a flood in the area. Eliminating this period results in compound growth of 3.8 percent.

The company operates one 7,200-square-foot store in Dubuque. The area's population has decreased by 7 percent since 1980 and is not expected to grow rapidly. The decedent was actively involved in the day-to-day operations of the business until September 1993. At that time, he stopped working on the sales floor, but remained involved in advertising and finances.

The company's competition consisted of national retail chains (WalMart, Kmart, Target), as well as local businesses that sold consumer electronics. The larger chains were causing the retail environment to become more competitive because they could provide larger product offerings and lower prices. The company was able to be somewhat competitive by purchasing through a buying cooperative. In addition, the company was not highly leveraged and was able to take advantage of purchase discounts.

The estate filed a tax return that included a value of $729,742 for Mr. Renier's stock. The IRS's value was $1,633,000.

Tax Court Opinion. The IRS presented one expert's testimony. This expert utilized the market, income, and asset approaches. He determined that the capitalization of future earnings method was most appropriate and derived his value by putting all of his weight on this method.

The estate's first expert used all three approaches (this was not the expert whose value was included on the estate tax return) and concluded that the value should be based on an average of the market and income approaches. His conclusion of value was approximately $815,000.

The estate's second expert utilized a market approach by using data from The Institute of Business Appraisers' (IBA) database and four rules of thumb. He derived values ranging from $946,000 to $1,100,000 and took a key man discount of 10 percent. His conclusion was approximately $852,000. The court completely disregarded this expert's opinion. It stated, "His report contains no explanation of, or analytical support for, the various 'rules of thumb' employed in reaching several of its valuation estimates. Thus, we are largely unable to assess the merits of the conclusions." In addition, since several of this expert's opinions were based on a percentage of revenues multiple, the court stated, "This raises doubts about the basis for his conclusions, given that Renier's profitability was high in relation to the industry average."

Both of the other experts agreed that the asset approach did not reflect the goodwill inherent in the business as a going concern, so the court restricted its analysis to the income and market approaches.

Both experts determined that the Company had non-operating assets. They both removed those assets from the core operating business, valued the operating entity using a capitalization of future earnings method, and then added the value of the non-operating assets. The experts' reports had many similarities as to methodologies, but the experts differed greatly with respect to normalization adjustments and capitalization rates.

The court addressed the various normalization issues. On some issues, it agreed with the taxpayer's expert. On other issues, it agreed with the IRS's expert. And on still other issues, it disagreed with both and substituted its own judgement.

The court then addressed the issue of the proper capitalization rate. The estate used an equity rate of 22 percent, whereas the IRS used a weighted average cost of capital (WACC) of 10 percent. The estate's expert used a return that it believed a hypothetical buyer would want to receive, whereas the IRS's expert assumed that a buyer would change the capital structure of the business to take on additional debt. In addition to this issue, the experts disagreed with the estimate of the rate of growth of the Company's future earnings that should be taken into account.

The equity rates of return calculated by the experts were similar: 24.76 percent by the IRS and 24.9 percent by the estate, with growth of 6 percent and 3 percent, respectively, subtracted to derive the capitalization rate. The difference between these two rates was that the IRS expert used a 30-year risk-free rate, while the estate used a 20-year risk free rate. The court affirmed the use of the 20-year rate as the appropriate rate to use with data from Ibbotson.

The court rejected the use of a WACC. In its opinion, it enumerated a number of recent Tax Court cases that rejected this method in valuing an equity interest in a closely held company. It was not persuaded by the expert's arguments and presented a number of reasons why it believed that a WACC was not appropriate.

The court finally looked at the experts' long-term growth estimate. It was not persuaded by either expert and performed its own analysis to determine the growth estimate.

The IRS's expert had considered a market approach and rejected it. The court then analyzed the taxpayer's consideration of a business broker method. It did not rely on this method because it believed that the expert had provided no justification for the multiple that was derived. Therefore, the court put all of its weight on the income approach for the value of the operating entity, and the asset approach for the non-operating assets.

J. C. Shepherd v. Commissioner, 115 T.C. No. 30

Full Tax Court decision rendered by Judge Thornton on October 26, 2000.

Issues: (1)The characterization, for gift tax purposes, of petitioner's transfers of certain real estate and stock into a family partnership of which petitioner is 50 percent owner and his two sons are each 25 percent owners; (2) the fair market value of the transferred real estate interests; and (3) the amount, if any, of discounts for fractional or minority interests and lack of marketability that should be recognized in valuing the transferred interests in the real estate and stock.

Facts. Certain facts of the case were stipulated to by the parties. On August 1, 1991, J.C. Shepherd (the petitioner) executed the Shepherd Family Partnership Agreement, which was then executed by his sons on August 2, 1991. The partnership was set up with J.C. Shepherd as a 50 percent owner and each of his sons as 25 percent owners in net income and loss, capital, and partnership property. Mr. Shepherd contributed initial capital of $10; each of his sons contributed $5. Mr. Shepherd was designated as managing partner.

On August 1, 1991, Mr. Shepherd and his wife executed deeds that transferred certain leased land to the partnership. These deeds were recorded on August 30, 1991. On September 9, 1991, Mr. Shepherd transferred some of his stock in three banks into the partnership as well. The parties to this action stipulated to the value of the bank stocks prior to any partnership adjustments.

J.C. Shepherd filed a gift tax return for 1991 reporting gifts to his sons of interests in the leased land and the bank stock. He valued the leased land at $400,000, and the bank stock at $932,219 (stipulated value) less a 15 percent minority discount. The value of each gift was 25 percent of the total assets (after 15 percent discount on the bank stock). The IRS in its notice of deficiency valued a 50 percent interest in the land at $1,278,600 and made no adjustment to the value of the bank stock.

Tax Court Opinion. The first issue that the Tax Court looked at was the characterization of the gifts. The parties agreed that the partnership came into existence on August 2, 1991, when the sons executed the partnership agreement. When the gifts were made, the issue was: were they undivided interests in the real estate or were they gifts of minority partnership interests?

The Tax Court looked to Alabama law to determine the definition of a partnership. Based on Alabama law, a partnership does not exist until all parties to the agreement sign the partnership agreement. This did not happen until August 2, 1991. Therefore:

> In these circumstances, we conclude and hold that petitioner's transfers to the partnership represent indirect gifts to each of his sons, John and William, or undivided 25-percent interests in the leased land and in the bank stock. In reaching this conclusion, we have effectively aggregated petitioner's two separate, same-day transfers to the partnership of undivided 50-percent interests in the leased land to reflect the economic substance of petitioner's conveyance to the partnership of his entire interest in the leased land. We have not, however, aggregated the separate indirect gifts to his sons, John and William.

The second issue considered was the value of the transferred real estate interests. Here, the Tax Court relied on expert testimony presented. The taxpayer utilized three experts, whereas the IRS presented one. The court stated, "the parties are in substantial agreement that the leased land should be valued as of the time the subject gift was made as the sum of: (a) The present value of the projected annual rental income from the lease, plus (b) the present value of the reversion. The parties disagree, however, about numerous assumptions made by the experts at each step of the valuation methodology." The court analyzed the various experts' testimonies and derived a value that considered parts of each expert's report.

The final issue was the quantification of discounts for lack of marketability and lack of control. The Tax Court redetermined discounts specific to the individual assets (land and bank stock), rather than a discount for a minority interest in a partnership.

In regard to the real estate, the court considered each appraiser's testimony. One of the petitioner's experts had included marketability issues in his discount rate. Since the court could not distinguish the factors, it disregarded this expert's testimony. The court also disregarded the IRS's expert because it was felt that he did not consider all of the appropriate factors. The court determined that the taxpayer's other expert's use of a 15 percent discount was appropriate where he specifically accounted for operational, dispositional, and partitioning factors.

As to the lack of control discount for the bank stock, the court accepted the taxpayer's expert's discount of 15 percent since no argument was put forth against it.

Ina F. Knight v. Commissioner, 115 T.C. No. 36

Full Tax Court decision rendered by Judge Colvin on November 30, 2000.

Issues: (1) Whether or not the family limited partnership should be disregarded for federal gift tax purposes, and (2) the appropriate discounts to be applied to the portfolio.

Facts. On December 6, 1994, the petitioner opened an investment account in the name of the petitioner's family limited partnership and transferred Treasury notes to it. On December 12, 1994, a checking account was opened in the name of the partnership and $10,000 was transferred from a personal bank account. On December 15, 1994, $558,939.43 of a municipal bond fund was transferred.

On December 28, 1994, the petitioners signed the documents that created the partnership; they conveyed real property to the partnership; they created a management trust, which would become the partnership's general partner; they each transferred a one-half unit of the partnership to the trust and maintained a 49.5 percent limited partnership interest; they created additional trusts and signed codicils to their wills; and they transferred a 22.3 percent partnership interest to each of the new trusts.

The IRS contends that the partnership lacks economic substance and fails to qualify as a partnership under federal law. The petitioners contend that their rights and legal relationships and those of their children changed significantly when the partnership was formed, assets were transferred to it, and interests were transferred to the trusts for their children, and that the partnership must be recognized for federal gift tax purposes.

Tax Court Opinion. The court agreed with the petitioners that the partnership must be recognized for federal gift tax purposes. It stated the following:

> State law determines the nature of property rights, and Federal law determines the appropriate tax treatment of those rights.
>
> The parties stipulated that the steps followed in the creation of the partnership satisfied all requirements under Texas law, and that the partnership has been a limited partnership under Texas law since it was created. Thus, the transferred interests are interests in a partnership under Texas law. Petitioners have burdened the partnership with restrictions that apparently are valid and enforceable under Texas Law.
>
> We do not disregard the partnership because we have no reason to conclude from this record that a hypothetical buyer or seller would disregard it.

The court then turned to the issue of the appropriate level of discounts. The petitioners applied portfolio, minority, and marketability discounts totaling 44 percent (10 percent, 10 percent, and 30 percent, respectively). The court disallowed the portfolio discount because the appraiser gave no convincing evidence that the partnership's mix of assets would be unattractive to a buyer.

Although the court disagreed with the funds that the appraiser used to determine the minority discount, they agreed that a discount based on an analogy to a closed-end fund was appropriate. The court also disallowed the 30 percent discount for lack of marketability as being unsupported.

The court concluded the following:

> We conclude that Conklin[4] was acting as an advocate and that his testimony was not objective. However, despite the flaws in petitioners' expert's testimony, we believe that some discount is proper, in part to take into account material in the record relating to closed-end bond funds. We hold that the fair market value of an interest in the Knight family partnership is the pro rata net asset value of the partnership less a discount totaling 15 percent for minority interest and lack of marketability.

As Appraisers, Do We Go for the Big Discounts?

You should now have a better idea about our role as valuators. It is important that the appraiser not cross the line from being an independent appraiser to being an advocate of bigger and bigger discounts. This can happen, especially if a client requests that we review a partnership document with an eye to adding restrictions and provisions that might increase the discounts. This is not our role as business appraisers, since we must be unbiased and not lose our objectivity. In addition, by acquiescing in such requests, we move beyond the realm of our own expertise.

This does not excuse business appraisers from being aware of the law, especially state laws regarding limited partnerships, and limited liability companies. Key questions to review with the partnership's attorney might include:

1. What restrictions in the partnership documents are more restrictive than state law?
2. What is the state law? Get a copy of the state's limited partnership act and read it thoroughly.
3. Does a limited partner have a right of withdrawal from the partnership and on what basis?

As we have seen, these issues can impact the valuation opinion.

It is important for the analyst to remember that his or her assignment is the determination of fair market value. This means the consideration of both a hypothetical willing buyer, as well as a hypothetical willing seller. Your final opinion of value must be reasonable. Remember, the buyer might buy for that low a price, but as an independent analyst, you must also ask yourself the question, if I were the seller, would I sell that low?

Conclusion

If I have done my job, you should now have a much better understanding about estate and gift valuations. If I have not, you'd better buy another book if you are going to do this stuff!

[4]The petitioner's expert.

15

Divorce Valuations

Chapter Goals

In this chapter, I will attempt to explain the following:

1. The role of the appraiser
2. Standards of value and their unique aspects in divorce assignments
3. Different valuation dates used in these assignments
4. How the normalization process differs in divorce assignments
5. Valuing professional practices for divorce assignments
6. How non-compete agreements impact values in the distribution of marital property

Introduction

Many valuation assignments are performed for divorce purposes. Regardless of whether the jurisdiction falls under the *equitable distribution* rules or the *community property* rules, a marital business will usually have to be valued so that the parties can allocate the value with the other marital property. Over the last two decades, business valuation assignments related to divorce proceedings have become a growing part of the appraiser's practice. Since closely held businesses are considered to be marital assets and therefore subject to distribution, there is a need to value this asset as part of the marital estate. In this book, closely held businesses include professional practices. However, the unique aspects of valuing professional practices are covered in Chapter 16.

A business valuation for divorce purposes is unlike any other type of business valuation assignment that the practitioner may get involved in. Sometimes, I feel like I could have used a degree in psychology instead of accounting. These types of assignments are not for everyone. Let me illustrate this point. Our firm represented a male psychologist, who got his aerobics instructor pregnant, in a divorce. His wife was a psychiatrist and lost her medical license for sexually molesting a female patient. Not only were these two of the nuttiest people that I have ever met, but the thought that they both counseled others scared the daylights out of me.

In addition to understanding the many nuances of business valuation, case law in the jurisdiction of the divorce must be considered. The appraiser must be aware of the local case law in order to avoid fatal errors in the valuation. For example, in certain jurisdictions, the valuer cannot consider any income that extends beyond the valuation date. Using a discounted cash flow methodology, which requires a forecast to be used to estimate value, may be a futile exercise, since the court may not allow the subsequent figures to be used. This makes the divorce valuation even more challenging since we are sometimes being asked to value a company without considering the future (who buys history?).

The Role of the Appraiser

The appraiser may be engaged to perform business valuation services for a variety of clients. These clients may be:

- The husband
- The wife
- Both parties
- An attorney
- The court

Most often, the appraiser will be engaged by one of the parties to the divorce, although not always. More and more often, litigants are finding the cost of the divorce so prohibitively expensive that they are seeking to retain only one business valuer. However, when the appraiser is hired by only one party, the other party may also engage an appraiser. Sometimes, each party may pick an appraiser, and the two appraisers may choose a third appraiser to act as a neutral appraiser for both parties.

The appraiser may also be court appointed. Certain jurisdictions will appoint an appraiser in order to avoid a battle of the experts. This will not always work, however, because each party will continue to have the right to hire his or her own expert to challenge the court-appointed appraiser. The court-appointed appraiser will generally be looked upon by the judge as the only neutral party in the entire process, other than the judge him- or herself (it may even be a jury in some jurisdictions).

Definition of Value

Early in the valuation process, an appraiser must determine what the definition of value will be for the assignment at hand. In case that you have already forgotten what was discussed in the earlier chapters of this book, re-read Chapter 3, where the different standards (definitions) of value were defined. In the divorce arena, these definitions are frequently twisted, mangled, commingled, and redefined (and that is the easy part of the assignment).

Appraisers are accustomed to the concept of fair market value because of their experience in working with the income tax laws and regulations. However, in divorce-related valuations, the definition of value is usually dictated by the court that has jurisdiction over the matter. The two most common definitions of value used by the courts seem to be:

- Fair market value
- Intrinsic (investment) value[1]

Fair Market Value

Fair market value is by far the most commonly used definition of value in the business valuation arena. However, fair market value seems to vary by jurisdiction. Frequently, the definition of fair market value is quoted from Revenue Ruling 59-60 as:

> the amount at which the property would change hands between a willing buyer and a willing seller when the former is not under compulsion to buy and the latter is not under any compulsion to sell, both parties having reasonable knowledge of the relevant facts.

This definition assumes a hypothetical arm's-length sale without regard to a specific buyer or seller.

[1]Intrinsic value and investment value, in a divorce context, are frequently described as *the value to the owner of the business*. Conventional valuation definitions treat these separately.

Intrinsic Value

"Beauty is in the eye of the beholder." This is probably the easiest way to describe intrinsic value. Although certain jurisdictions use this concept, and momentum is actually building in many others to use it, the term is ambiguous. Intrinsic value is frequently referred to as the investment value to the owner of the business.

Intrinsic value recognizes the fact that a business owner who is going through a divorce will not be selling the business and, therefore, there will be no hypothetical transaction, as in a fair market value appraisal. Instead, the owner will continue to receive the benefits of ownership into the future. In this instance, the value of the business may be worth more or less to the owner than the market as a whole.

While finishing up my master's degree, I wrote a master's thesis entitled *The Equitable Distribution Value of Small Closely Held Businesses and Professional Practices*, which is on file at my alma mater, Lindenwood College, St. Charles, Missouri. I addressed this concept by pointing out the many deficiencies in the leading case law in the state of New Jersey, my home state. Although this was an academic exercise, restricted to attacking the case law in New Jersey, all appraisers can learn a lesson from it, since many other states have similar case law that is equally as bad. A copy of the thesis is included as Appendix 18 in case you have insomnia.

What Do the Definitions Really Mean in a Divorce Context?

If there were a written definition of what the different value concepts mean in a divorce engagement, many of us would have considerably less work to do. Much of the litigation that takes place arises partially because of the various interpretations of the value concepts. Although fair market value and intrinsic value are not strangers to the experienced business valuation professional, case law and state statutes govern the division of property between the parties in a divorce. Unfortunately, most of the state statutes use the term *value* without any precise definition.

The appraiser using the fair market value concept generally assumes a hypothetical transaction. This also means that the valuation of a minority interest should probably include a lack of control discount. However, this may not work in every jurisdiction. The appraiser must be familiar with the local case law. He or she should look for assistance from the client's attorney. Don't be surprised, however, if the attorney asks for your opinion. Be careful not to practice law without a license!

Intrinsic value, rather than fair market value, is sometimes used in the valuation of professional practices for divorce purposes. Shannon Pratt discussed the California case of *Lopez v. Lopez*[2] in an early edition of *Valuing A Business*. In valuing professional goodwill, the court indicated that the following factors should be considered:

- The age and health of the professional
- The professional's demonstrated past earning power
- The professional's reputation in the community for judgment, skill, and knowledge
- The professional's comparative business success
- The nature and duration of the professional's practice, either as a sole proprietor or as a contributing member of a partnership or professional corporation

---

[2] *In re Marriage of Lopez*, 113 Cal. Rptr. 58 [38 Cal App. 3d 1044 (1974)].

Some authors feel that a professional's age, health, judgment, skill, and other factors mentioned by the court are indications of intrinsic value. However, many of these factors may also be considered in a fair market value appraisal. The intrinsic value argument takes the position that since the professional will be staying with the practice, it is important to consider the personal attributes of the individual. Since fair market value assumes *any willing buyer* rather than *a specific buyer* or *the owner*, consideration of personal attributes violates the spirit of fair market value. The fair market value argument states that the willing buyer must be able to carry on the practice in a similar manner as the willing seller, and thus must have a similar level of ability (judgment and skill, or in the case of a surgeon, the hands) to maintain the practice in a manner that has value. Clearly, this can be argued both ways.

Intrinsic value may also be applied to other types of closely held businesses. In a Wyoming case, *Neuman v. Neuman*,[3] one of the highly contested issues involved whether a discount for lack of marketability should be applied to the business value since the owner would not be selling the business. Fair market value assumes a sale, and therefore, a discount would have to be taken, if appropriate. The trial court, and later the Supreme Court of Wyoming, found in favor of not applying a discount, creating a difference between the value of a business to a *willing buyer* and the value of a business to *the owner* for purposes of divorce. My home state, New Jersey, has one judge who never allows a discount for lack of marketability. In fact, on at least two separate occasions, he gave my client more equitable distribution than the client should have received.

Another major issue arises as a result of each jurisdiction's determination of how these concepts should be applied. One of the controversial issues that should be considered by the appraiser is whether a covenant not to compete is to be included as part of a fair market value appraisal. While many appraisers have interpreted fair market value to have an implied covenant, not all do. Logically, a willing buyer would not buy the practice, particularly the goodwill, if the seller has the right to open up across the street. However, in the *Thelien*[4] case in Missouri, the court assigned no value to the intangibles since there was no evidence presented to indicate that Dr. Thelien could sell his share of the dental practice without a covenant not to compete and receive an amount greater than his share of the tangible assets.

Carrying some of these value concepts to an extreme, court cases have expanded accepted standards of value. For example, New Jersey case law typically refers to fair market value. However, in an attempt to bring *fairness* to the litigation, a judge followed the intrinsic standard of value and ruled that celebrity goodwill was a marital asset.[5]

As this book was getting ready to go to press, a judicial decision was handed down from the New Jersey Appellate Division that further illustrates the confusion in this area. In *Brown v. Brown*[6] the standard of value was modified by the Court from fair market value to a standard that is closer to fair value. The Court determined that the value should be determined similarly to the findings in two shareholder cases (one a dissenting stockholder lawsuit and the other an oppressed stockholder suit) using the fair value standard.

This case is important because it stands for the proposition that a closely held minority interest should be valued, for divorce purposes, without discounts for lack of control and lack of marketability. The worst part of this opinion is that the Court felt that the appraiser can use the capitalization rate to reflect the lack of marketability because that is what one of the appraisers did in this case. This violates everything that I have been trying to teach you in this book! Appraisal theory tells us to separate rates of return, addressing risk, and lack of marketability, addressing liquidity issues, but the judicial system has

---

[3]*Neuman v. Neuman*, 842 P.2d 580 (Wyo. 1992).

[4]*Thelien v. Thelien*, 847 S.W.2d 116 (Mo. App. 1992).

[5]*Piscopo v. Piscopo*, 231 N.J. Super. 576 (Ch. Div. 1988), *aff'd* 232 N.J. Super. 559 (App. Div. 1989).

[6]*Ellen Brown v. James Brown*, A-985-00T5, 2002 N.J. Super., LEXIS 105.

now spoken by saying, "Damn the theory, full speed ahead!" This should make divorce practice in New Jersey even more interesting than it was before.

Valuation Dates

Valuation dates in business valuations for divorce purposes should be provided to the appraiser by the clients and/or their attorneys. The correct valuation date may depend on numerous factors, and as a result, the client's attorney will usually be in the best position to provide the date or dates that should be used. Business interests and business assets may be valued at numerous dates. This will frequently depend on the jurisdiction, whether the asset is considered active or passive, particular case-sensitive factors, or the like. Therefore, the valuation date in a divorce engagement may be one, or more, of the following dates:

- Date of the marriage
- Date of a gift or inheritance
- Date of the separation
- Date of the divorce complaint
- A date agreed to by the parties
- Date of the trial

Date of the Marriage

The date of the marriage will generally not be used for valuing the marital business unless there is a claim that part or all of the business is premarital, and therefore separate property. Business assets that are acquired or commingled during the marriage become marital property in most, if not all, jurisdictions. This may require the business to be valued at the date of the marriage, as well as a subsequent date, to measure any incremental appreciation that is considered to be subject to distribution.

Date of a Gift or Inheritance

Property acquired by gift or inheritance frequently is considered to be separate property. When this is the case, valuation may not be necessary, since it is to be excluded from distribution. However, many arguments have been raised that the separate property becomes commingled into marital property. Sometimes only some of the business ownership was inherited or gifted, making the balance subject to distribution. Also, the value of the gift or inheritance is often understated for tax purposes. When this occurs, the appraiser may wish to examine estate or gift tax returns to determine the manner in which the values were derived. This assumes, of course, that estate or gift tax returns were filed. It also assumes that the full disclosure rules (discussed in Chapter 14) were followed so that you can figure out what was done to determine value. Guidance may be required from the attorney as to the extent of the valuation services to be provided in these cases.

Date of the Separation

In certain jurisdictions, the date of the separation of the parties is considered to be the date that the marriage is over. Other jurisdictions consider the date of separation as the time that each party no longer contributes to the marital estate, but not necessarily the date to be used for the valuation. In other jurisdictions, everything is includable until a divorce complaint is filed. If the date of separation is the applicable date, a business valuation may be necessary as of that date.

Date of the Divorce Complaint

For those jurisdictions that consider the date of the divorce complaint to be the applicable date, a business will generally be valued at that date. Many jurisdictions start off with this date but provide the judge with the latitude to change the date if the facts and circumstances warrant it. Sometimes the parties separate and no formal complaint is filed with the court for many years. Some attorneys may argue that the marriage really ended when the parties separated. In certain jurisdictions, this could require two appraisals to be performed, one at separation and one at the complaint date. Speak to your client's attorney for proper direction.

Date Agreed to by the Parties

On occasion, the parties, with the help of their attorneys, may agree to a date to be used for the business valuation. Circumstances surrounding the particular divorce may encourage agreement on the date. For example, suppose a fairly well-known individual is going to be divorced. As soon as a divorce complaint is filed, it becomes public record, subject to media attention. The attorneys and the clients may agree to value all of the assets, come to a written settlement, and take care of all aspects of the divorce before filing the actual complaint. After everything is taken care of, a complaint is filed, but the parties are immediately divorced in an uncontested action. This saves the clients from the media harassment during the months or years that it takes to get divorced under normal circumstances.

Date of the Trial

This is always tricky for the business appraiser, since we all know that it takes quite a bit of time to accumulate the information and analyze it for the purpose of opining on the value of a business. As a result, valuing the asset at the time of trial becomes difficult, particularly since trial dates are frequently postponed, and we do not know the actual date until the last minute. However, many courts are specifying that assets in a marital dissolution be valued as of the date of the divorce trial. This not only makes it difficult for the appraiser to value the asset, but it makes an early settlement of the case even more difficult for the parties. Frequently, a date may be agreed upon by the parties so that the process does not have to be held up until trial.

Valuation Methods

In most business valuation assignments, two or more valuation methods will be used. The number of methods to use, as well as which methods, depend on the purpose of the assignment, the definition of value to be used, the type of business, and the availability of information. The appraiser should apply similar criteria in divorce assignments as in other types of assignments unless the local jurisdiction provides otherwise (in the statute or case law). You also should be aware of any methods that the judge particularly likes or dislikes. If the judge likes the excess earnings method, for example, you really should do everything possible to include it in your valuation.

By the way, there is one method I have seen used by the courts that has not been mentioned in the book yet. It is the *HFB method*. This is the valuation method where the judge hears how much the marital house is worth, and since the non–business owner spouse will get the house, the value of the business ends up coming in at around the same amount. HFB stands for *house for business*. Only kidding!!!! (Well—maybe not.)

Valuation as of a Specific Date

A business valuation is similar to a balance sheet, as it is a picture of the business at a specific moment in time. Values change as factors around the business change. This is especially evidenced in the public stock market. Therefore, the information used in performing a business valuation should be only that information that was known or knowable as of the valuation date. This can best be illustrated by a real situation that I encountered. A valuation of a bicycle shop was to be performed as of June 10, 1992, the date of the divorce complaint. The business burned down on March 14, 1993. In this instance, the value as of June 10, 1992, was the real issue. An appraiser cannot forecast a fire nine months after the valuation date. Several other issues come to light with this example:

- If the business was overinsured, collected a large settlement, and increased in worth, should the court take this into consideration in awarding distribution of the marital estate?
- If the business was underinsured (or co-insured), collected less than the inventory and business was worth, and was truly hurt by the fire, should the court take this into consideration in awarding distribution of the marital estate?

Since most divorce proceedings take place in a *court of equity*, the concept of fairness will often be the driving factor for the courts. The appraiser will have to get guidance from the client's attorney as to which date the valuation should be performed as of, as well as what information can be considered based on the litigation position that will be taken in court. In my real example, it turned out that the business owner was overinsured, and the owner received an unbelievable insurance settlement that allowed him to rebuild a mega-store worth far more than the previous store. The court, however, required the valuation to be as of the earlier date, ignoring the insurance settlement—because the non-owner spouse was convicted of arson. You have to love this business!

Data Gathering and Analysis

The data gathering and analysis phase of a business valuation assignment is very important in providing the appraiser with the ability to render a meaningful and well-informed opinion of value about a business. The procedures and information will be the same regardless of the purpose of the assignment. However, a divorce valuation frequently requires additional documentation to be gathered and analyzed. There also may be other procedures that will be applied for divorce assignments.

Depending on the methods used, the appraiser should gather sufficient information about the company being valued, including, but not limited to, financial data, economy data, industry data, market data, as well as information about the history and nature of the company, its legal status, and its management.

Some practitioners send out massive document requests asking for the sun, the moon, and the stars. Although we would like to obtain as much of this information as possible, some of this data may not exist. If the missing data is important to the assignment, the appraiser may need to use alternative procedures to obtain this information. For example, if an accounts payable listing is requested as of March 4, 1999, and the business does not maintain one, the appraiser can discuss the payment terms for vendor invoices with management, and perform a review of the checkbook to create such a listing based on the checks that were written after that date. This is one instance where being an accountant as well as an appraiser really pays off.

The appraiser must be aware of the difference between information that is not available versus information that is intentionally not provided by the business owner. The latter happens frequently in litigation assignments, divorce or otherwise. If information is being intentionally withheld, the appraiser can try to perform forensic procedures to work around the missing data (either by the appraiser or by a forensic accountant), but the client's attorney will often have to get involved by petitioning the court to compel cooperation. This situation happens all too often and makes it very difficult for the appraiser to complete the assignment on a timely basis, if at all.

Since data gathering is such an important part of the valuation process, and since the nature of a litigation assignment is such that the appraiser may not get everything that is requested, the appraiser must keep good records regarding the documents that have been requested. The initial document request is frequently accomplished by having the client's attorney send the appraiser's document request to the other attorney. The appraiser will generally send written communications to the client's attorney regarding missing information. If the attorney decides to take appropriate legal action, it can be accomplished by attaching the letters received from the appraiser.

Gathering Financial Data

Most appraisers ask for about five years of financial information when performing a business valuation. However, there is no magic to the five-year period. Sometimes more information is needed, sometimes less. Rarely will the valuation date for most divorce valuations be on the year end of the company being valued. Accordingly, the appraiser should request interim financial statements. Other financial information such as tax returns, forecasts, budgets, and projections maintained by the company should also be requested. Analyses of the underlying assets, liabilities, income, and expense accounts may also be needed. These items should not be anything unusual for the appraiser who performs other types of business valuations.

The Valuation Process

The balance of the valuation process is the same as for other types of valuation assignments. However, the nature of a divorce litigation makes it more difficult to follow all of the normal steps that would be performed in a typical assignment. For example, if the non-client spouse is actively involved in managing the business, he or she may be reluctant to allow the appraiser to visit the company's facilities. This individual may be trying to hide information from the appraiser that could be discovered during a site inspection (such as expensive artwork on the walls). Alternatively, confidentiality may be the concern; the individual may not want the employees to know that a divorce is in progress. Sometimes, the business owner is just afraid that the employees will think that the business is going to be sold and they may leave unnecessarily. The appraiser should always request a site visit. If a site visit cannot be arranged, the appraiser should assess the impact of this on the valuation engagement. A qualification should also be put in the report such as:

> We requested the opportunity to perform a physical inspection of the business premises but were denied access. Information gathered during such an inspection may have had an impact on the outcome of our analysis. Had we been allowed to inspect the premises, our conclusions may have been different.

If possible, the appraiser should conduct management interviews during the site inspection. The appraiser should ask all of the questions that are necessary to supplement the written documentation received, as well as to obtain a further understanding of the company's history, customer base, product mix, and financial results. If the appraiser has also been hired to perform forensic examination of the company's records, any additional questions that are important to that examination should also be asked during these interviews.

Normalizing the Financial Statements

The normalization process is intended to restate the reported earnings of the business to an economic basis that a prospective purchaser would receive. In divorce valuations, the restating of the income is also considered in the business owner's ability to pay support (or the amount of support needed). These adjustments become even more important for that reason. Adjustments are generally made either pertaining to GAAP, nonrecurring items, non-operating items, or discretionary items that are under the control of management. Frequently, the discretionary items become part of the business owner's ability to pay support or reduce the need to receive support. In Connecticut, for example, the amount of reasonable compensation used by the appraiser in the valuation of the marital business is often used as the amount that will be considered in the support part of the litigation. This eliminates the situation where the business owner gets double-dipped from the value and support. See my thesis for more of an explanation about double-dipping. It has nothing to do with ice cream cones.

Normalization adjustments are generally made to the income statement to present the results of the company's operations as they might have been in the hands of the prospective buyer of the company. Income statement adjustments are normally made only if a controlling interest is being valued. This is because a minority stockholder is generally unable to influence operations, and therefore would not receive the adjusted income as dividends. However, in most divorce valuations, a minority interest in a family-owned business will be treated as if the minority stockholder has control. The normalization adjustments are the same ones that were discussed previously.

Unreported Revenues

In an attempt to hide income from the government and the business owner's spouse, the issue of unreported income frequently arises in divorce valuations. This is especially true when support is an issue. Forensic procedures can be performed by those appraisers with proper training. This book, however, is not intended to teach you how to play hide-and-seek.

When unreported revenues are located, the appraiser should advise the client's attorney immediately. The attorney may want to use this information to help negotiate a settlement before a report is written and a trial becomes necessary. In many states, the judge has a responsibility to turn over income tax fraud cases to the IRS and/or the local prosecutor if evidence is presented in the courtroom that supports the allegation. If a settlement is not reached, and it becomes necessary to complete the valuation, most appraisers agree that the unreported revenue should be treated as a normalization/GAAP adjustment. You do not do your client a true service if you kill the goose that lays the golden egg. If the spouse goes to jail, where do you think the support will come from?

Stockholder Loans

A common balance sheet normalization adjustment involves the treatment of *stockholder loans*. Very often, an asset may appear on the books representing monies taken by the owner in lieu of compensation. The treatment of this asset will depend on the collectibility of the loan. Since most businesses will be valued based on cash flow or earnings capacity, the appraiser should ignore this balance sheet item as a non-operating asset. If this item is going to be considered as part of the individual's current earnings for support purposes, it seems unfair to also treat it as an asset of the business. Chances are that it will not be repaid in the future. If the balance has been accumulated over many years, only the current increment may end up being treated as income available for support purposes. Therefore, part of this asset *may* be considered as a non-operating asset of the business.

When stockholder loans are recorded as liabilities of the company, the appraiser should assess whether the loan is for legitimate business purposes. For example, if the business owner has sufficient capital to act as a bank for the business, and adequate capitalization of the business is demonstrated, the stockholder loan should be treated as a true business liability. This is especially true when the business would have borrowed from a bank and repayment terms, notes, and other indicia of an obligation are present.

Stockholder loans that do not meet the conditions above should be treated as capital of the business. Undercapitalized businesses are set up frequently. The owner treats the infusion of monies as loans so that the money can be repaid, with or without interest, at the discretion of the owner. In most instances, these loans are paid in capital and should be treated as such. For *cash*-type businesses, the appraiser should investigate the source of these loans, as they may come from unreported revenues.

Income Taxes

Income taxes are probably one of the most confusing adjustments that arise in divorce, and other valuation, assignments. Some valuers prefer to value a company on a pretax basis, while others prefer an after-tax basis. Regardless of which is used, the answer should be the same. Whether the appraiser uses a pretax basis or an after-tax basis, the discount or capitalization rates will change accordingly. By now, you know this!

When appraisers are engaged to value sole proprietorships, partnerships, S corporations, or limited liability companies (non–tax-paying entities), a pretax or an after-tax earnings stream can be used. There is no definitive rule about these entities. Many valuers will use corporate tax rates; others will use individual rates. Individual rates get a bit cloudy because of itemized deductions, personal exemptions, and self-employment taxes. The appraiser can use either set of rates but should be prepared to discuss the merits of the rates used.

More About Valuation Methods

Unless prohibited by local statute or case law, the methods used in a divorce engagement are the same methods used in other types of valuation assignments. Since the nature of divorce valuations are adversarial, the valuation report will often become a source of controversy and come under attack by the opposition. An experienced appraiser will always assume that expert testimony will become necessary. For that reason, it is imperative that the judge and/or jury understand the valuation process and how the estimate of value was determined.

Frequently, the opposing attorney will attempt to destroy an expert's credibility by attacking the contents of the valuation report. It is not uncommon to see an attorney begin to ask an expert an abundance of questions in an attempt to confuse the judge and/or jury. Since most judges do not have a background in business valuation, it becomes easy to confuse some of them. Another favorite tactic used by attorneys is to attack forecasts and projections by sticking a copy of a subsequent financial statement in front of the expert and saying, "Isn't it true that your forecast was wrong?" Of course the forecast ended up different from the actual results. All that an expert can say to this type of question is "At the time the forecast was prepared, we used all of the information that was available to us. This is the same information that a willing buyer would have known about as well. I really cannot say why the actual results were different. I would have to perform an extensive analysis to figure it out. This would take far more time than we have available at the trial."

Reaching a Conclusion of Value

After applying various methods of valuation to the subject company, the appraiser will have to determine the appropriate estimate of value. This is accomplished in the same fashion as for every other type of valuation. However, different jurisdictions vary greatly when it comes to applying valuation premiums and discounts. The appraiser should speak with the client's attorney about local case law.

Divorce Valuations of Professional Practices

Professional practices are generally valued in the same manner as other types of businesses. However, there are definite distinctions between professional practices and other types of businesses. Some of the unique characteristics of the professional practice make them subject to special considerations in valuations, particularly for divorce.

Professional Practices Versus Regular Business Enterprises

Professional practices are generally service businesses. Most of the value in a professional practice will be intangible in nature. The composition of the typical professional practice is such that it does not have a significant investment in tangible assets compared to its investment in people. However, some professional practices may have a sizable investment in equipment. For example, a radiology practice may own MRI and X-ray equipment.

Professionals, such as doctors, lawyers, accountants, and in some cases appraisers and others, are generally licensed by a state licensing body. Therefore, in most circumstances, professional practices can be sold only to similarly licensed professionals. Professional licenses are not transferable between individuals. Therefore, the market value of a license is nonexistent, if consideration is given to the true definition of that concept.

Logic states that if something cannot be sold, it cannot have value. However, a license provides the professional with the ability to make a living, and therefore, it has intrinsic value to the individual licensee. In New York, the value of a license is a marital asset. I'm surprised that they don't value "green cards" since they provide the opportunity for a non-U.S. resident to earn a living! New York is a funny place—they will value almost anything.

Professional practices generally provide specialized services, which requires the owners, and frequently their employees, to possess special levels of knowledge. Because of this, the value of the practice is highly dependent on the skills, reputation, and efforts of individual professionals. Therefore, some of the value of the practice is attributable to the personal reputation or skill of the owner and may not be transferable to a buyer. For example, a skilled heart surgeon cannot transfer his or her skilled hands to a willing buyer. This is known as *professional goodwill*. In some instances, professional goodwill has no value to a prospective purchaser. *Practice goodwill*, or the commercial goodwill of the practice, is generally a component of most professional practice valuation estimates.

Because professional practices are built on specialized services, the nature of the particular practice being valued needs to be considered. This means that one type of medical practice will be valued differently than another type of practice. For example, the nature of a general medical practice would be that referrals come from numerous sources, including existing patients. The patients also tend to return to the same general practitioner. A brain surgeon, however, probably gets most of his or her referrals from other doctors. Hopefully, for the sake of the patient, this type of practice does not have many recurring patients.

Divorce Valuations and the Market Can Be Very Different

The divorce courts have created many precedents regarding the valuation of professional practices. The precedents, however, vary from jurisdiction to jurisdiction, and they do not always make sense from an appraisal point of view. The appraiser must become familiar with the case law in this area. For example, in New Jersey, attorneys were prohibited from selling their law practices. However, in *Dugan v. Dugan*[7] the court found that the attorney's goodwill was a marital asset subject to equitable distribution. This case is cited in many other states. Therefore, for divorce purposes, we need to value that which cannot be sold. Now, let's look at how a law practice could be sold.

Suppose Joe Lawyer brought in an associate who worked with him for two or three years. Joe retires, and the associate takes over the practice and pays Joe a "retirement pension." This type of sale can take place, and does in the other professions pretty regularly. However, from a valuation standpoint, the appraiser should consider a discounted cash flow analysis to include the additional expense of having the associate

[7] *Dugan v. Dugan*, 92 N.J. 423 (1983).

work (an added expense) for the period of time that it may take to transition the practice over to him or her. An income expected to be generated by the associate should also be considered, but the point is that the transition may take a number of years.

Sometimes government regulation affects certain professional practices. For example, through Medicare and Medicaid, health care services become subject to price schedules. When valuing a medical practice, the appraiser should be familiar with the government's regulatory role in the practice's industry.

Financial Information

Most professional practices maintain their books and records using the cash basis of accounting. Therefore, the appraiser should investigate whether an accrual basis of accounting would impact the valuation. This may be easier for accountants who perform appraisals than for other categories of appraisers. For a mature practice that is consistent from year to year, the method of accounting may not make that much difference. However, some practices can be greatly affected by growth, decline, or timing of receipts. This can be true for a personal injury law practice.

Adjustments to Financial Information. Financial statements of professional practices must usually be adjusted for all of the GAAP and normalization items of other types of businesses. In addition, the following additional items are often important for valuing professional practices:

- Cash versus accrual accounting
- Work in process
- Contingent work in process
- Deferred revenues
- Contingencies

Professional Versus Practice Goodwill

The distinction between *professional goodwill* (sometimes called *personal goodwill*) and *practice goodwill* (sometimes called *business* or *commercial goodwill*) is that professional goodwill is associated primarily with the individual whereas practice goodwill is associated primarily with the entity. This can be demonstrated by assuming John Smith, CPA, is a partner at PricewaterhouseCoopers. If a new client calls the firm specifically requesting John Smith, then there may be personal goodwill associated with the individual. However, if the client wants a "big five" name on the financial statements, contacts PricewaterhouseCoopers, and ends up with John Smith, there is probably practice goodwill involved. Sometimes, the two types of goodwill will overlap.

The existence of professional goodwill is based on the fact that clients come to the individual, as opposed to the firm. This may be based on the individual's skills, knowledge, reputation, personality, and other factors. The implied assumption is that if this individual moved to another firm, the clients would go with him or her. Professional goodwill is more difficult to transfer to a new owner, but not impossible. Generally, the professional will assist in a smooth transition to a new owner in order to obtain the maximum price for the practice.

Goodwill in a Professional Practice. The issue of personal versus professional goodwill arises most often during the divorce valuation of professional practices. In most instances, there is little reason to separate the two concepts. However, some courts have determined that a sole practitioner in any profession can only have personal goodwill since he or she *is* the practice. A sole practitioner's practice can easily have both forms of goodwill.

To illustrate this point, let's assume that Sarah Jackson, attorney at law, is a personal-injury specialist. Her trial skills have allowed her clients to get jury verdicts that begin at $1,000,000. Her law practice has a book value of $85,000 and contingent work in progress of $700,000. Gross revenues for the firm are $8,000,000. Ms. Jackson draws a salary of $3,000,000 annually (she's my hero!). The question becomes whether Ms. Jackson's goodwill—her reputation and trial skills—can be transferred to another lawyer. If so, we might have many lawyers earning a lot of money. This illustrates personal goodwill.

Let's illustrate practice goodwill. Now assume that Mary Brown, attorney at law, belongs to a prepaid legal services plan, from which she gets client referrals. Due to the fact that the law firm is signed up with the legal services plan, referrals come to the practice regardless of her reputation and skills. This is practice goodwill. However, assuming that Ms. Brown does a good job for these clients, referrals may come directly to her in the future, which would be an element of personal goodwill.

The standard of value to be applied and the case law regarding goodwill will vary depending on the jurisdiction of the trial. The appraiser should ask the client's attorney early in the process about the proper standard of value to be used. In fact, it is a good practice to have the standard of value spelled out in the engagement letter with the client. The appraiser should also make certain that the case law regarding goodwill is understood in the jurisdiction of the divorce.

Most courts have found that goodwill is an asset to be included in the marital estate of a professional for divorce purposes. In many states, professional goodwill is considered to be marital property even though it is not transferable. In such cases, the standard of value is not fair market value, but rather intrinsic value to the owner. Several states have taken the position that professional goodwill is not a marital asset subject to division, but practice goodwill is. A good source for keeping up with the cases around the country is Shannon Pratt's *Business Valuation Update*.

As I pointed out before, one of the most widely cited cases detailing the factors to consider when valuing professional goodwill in a divorce is a California case, *Lopez v. Lopez*.[8] The factors listed in that case, which are worth repeating, include the following:

- The age and health of the professional
- The professional's demonstrated past earning power
- The professional's reputation in the community for judgment, skill, and knowledge
- The professional's comparative professional success
- The nature and duration of the professional's practice, either as a sole proprietor or as a contributing member of a partnership or professional corporation

As illustrated previously, it is frequently difficult to distinguish between professional goodwill and practice goodwill. In a Florida case, *Williams v. Williams*,[9] the trial court ruled that the value of Mr. Williams's accounting practice included $43,200 in practice goodwill. On appeal, the trial court's finding was reversed. In its opinion, the appellate court stated:

> The goodwill of [a] professional practice can be a marital asset subject to division in a dissolution proceeding, if it exists and if it was developed during the marriage. . . . However,. . . for goodwill to be a marital asset, it must exist separate and apart from the reputation or continued presence of the marital litigant. . . . When attempting to determine whether goodwill exists in a practice such as this, the evidence should show recent actual sales of a similarly situated practice, or expert testimony as to the existence of goodwill in a similar practice in the relevant market. . . . Moreover, the husband's expert, who testified the practice had no goodwill, stated that no one would buy the practice without a noncompete clause. This is telling evidence of a lack of goodwill.

---

[8] *In re Marriage of Lopez*, 113 Cal. Rptr. 58 [38 Cal. App. 3d 1044 (1974)].

[9] *Williams v. Williams*, No. 95-00577, 1996 WL 47675 (Fla. Dist. Ct. App. Feb. 7, 1996).

Clearly, the non-compete clause was the issue in the court's strict interpretation of fair market value. The inconsistency of the various cases throughout the country make this a challenging field. In a little while, you can read an exhibit that deals with the valuation of a non-compete clause.

Probably because of the number of divorces each year, it should be of little surprise that California has more reported cases dealing with the valuation of professional practices than any other state. State courts will frequently look to other courts when they do not have a precedent of their own. The appraiser can be helpful to the attorney by being familiar with the cases, but it is the attorney's job to determine what case law should be followed.

The ongoing problem of the different court rulings can be further demonstrated in *Beasley v. Beasley*[10] and *Dugan v. Dugan.*[11] In *Beasley*, the court ruled that the sole proprietorship law practice cannot have goodwill since goodwill constitutes the present value of future earnings, which stem from the future postmarital efforts of the attorney spouse. In this situation, the court basically felt that the cut-off date for the valuation is the date of the divorce. By using the future earnings of the attorney to calculate goodwill, the same dollars would be used to calculate both value and support. This would be double-dipping.

In *Dugan*, it was decided that an individual's law practice, even though it was a professional corporation, can have goodwill that is transferable. The court stated:

> Goodwill is to be differentiated from earnings capacity. It reflects not simply a possibility of future earnings, but a probability based on existing circumstances. . . . Moreover, unlike the license and the degree, goodwill is transferable and marketable. . . . An individual practitioner's inability to sell a law practice does not eliminate the existence of goodwill and its value of an asset to be considered in equitable distribution. Obviously, equitable distribution does not require conveyance or transfer of any particular asset.

The irony of the *Dugan* case is that the same Supreme Court in New Jersey found that earnings capacity is not a marital asset in *Stern v. Stern.*[12] Earnings capacity was not a marital asset subject to distribution, but probable future earnings is now a factor in determining whether there is goodwill that is subject to distribution. The words are so subtle that it would be easy for the untrained individual to misinterpret these cases. This is just one more reason for the appraiser to rely on the client's attorney for guidance with these matters. By the way, have you noticed that many of the really contested divorce cases involve attorneys as one of the litigants? They are the only ones that are crazy enough to take these issues all the way to the top court in the state. This is a very expensive process.

Non-Compete Agreements

Many appraisers believe that implicit in the definition of fair market value is a covenant not to compete. If the seller has a right to open up next door, why would a willing buyer ever purchase a business or professional practice? Separating the value of the intangible assets (goodwill) from the value of the non-compete agreement is frequently a difficult task. In *Monaghan v. Monaghan,*[13] the business under scrutiny was a dental practice. The court determined that if the practice were sold, the non–business owner spouse would receive 50 percent of the gross proceeds received in excess of $80,000.

---

[10]*Beasley v. Beasley*, 518 A.2d 545 (Pa. Super. 1986).

[11]*Dugan v. Dugan*, 92 N.J. 423 (1983).

[12]*Stern v. Stern*, 66 N.J. Super. 1975.

[13]*In re Delores A. Monaghan and Robert D. Monaghan*, 78 Wash. App. 918, 899 P.2d 841 (Aug. 9, 1995).

The practice was subsequently sold for $160,000. The sales contract allocated the purchase price as follows:

Inventory and supplies	$ 20,000
Patient list	15,000
Goodwill	16,000
Covenant not to compete	109,000
Total	$160,000

A claim was made in this case that the practice actually sold for less than $80,000 and the non–business owner was not entitled to a share in the proceeds. The claim was based on the premise that the non-compete covenant was a personal asset and not part of the practice. Obviously, the opposite position was that the covenant was part of the goodwill of the practice.

The Washington appellate court did not have its own case law regarding the treatment of a non-compete covenant in a divorce case. Relying on other jurisdictions, the appellate court cited cases from other western states. In these jurisdictions, the covenant not to compete was considered personal property belonging to the professional. These other courts reviewed the relationship of the non-compete to the other assets to rule whether or not it seemed fair (like $109,000 out of $160,000). If the allocation was unreasonable in relation to the other assets, then a more fair and objective allocation would be required.

The appellate court remanded the case to the trial court to separate the value of the practice from the value of the covenant not to compete based on all of the evidence. Different jurisdictions treat non-compete agreements differently. Before the appraiser can address issues involving a non-compete agreement, advice should be obtained from the client's attorney as to how the courts in that particular jurisdiction treat this issue. Exhibit 15.1 illustrates valuation issues dealing with a covenant not to compete. This is a really long exhibit, but be patient. It is intended to cover a lot of points about valuing covenants, personal goodwill, intangible assets, and how to document all of this stuff for a litigation report.

EXHIBIT 15.1
Valuing the Covenant Not to Compete
(Many sections of the actual report have been omitted for space.)

Description of the Assignment

Trugman Valuation Associates Inc. was retained by Joan Carnes to determine the equitable distribution value of Carnes Respiratory Services, Inc. ("CRS" or the "Company") as of March 9, 1995, as well as to determine the value of the covenant not to compete that was part of an actual transaction involving certain assets of the Company. We have also been requested to opine on whether the value ascribed to the covenant not to compete is corporate, personal, or a combination of the two.

In order to accomplish the assignment at hand, the following steps were taken by the appraiser:

1. Determine the fair market value of CRS.
2. Determine the fair market value of the tangible assets of CRS.
3. Determine the fair market value of the identifiable intangible assets of CRS.
4. Subtract the fair market value of the tangible and identifiable intangible assets of CRS from the fair market value of the total enterprise.

The result of this process will be to determine the residual, or unidentifiable intangible value that makes up the balance of the fair market value of the enterprise.

Definition of Equitable Distribution Value

For this matter, equitable distribution value of the equity of CRS has been determined as a result of an actual transaction involving certain assets of the Company. Other assets were kept by the sole shareholder. The equitable distribution value has been determined and is referenced in the "Order on Motion to Vacate Final Judgment of Dissolution of Marriage" signed by the Honorable John L. Brown on July 24, 1996. The value established in paragraph (8) of this order is $16,900,000.

(Continued)

EXHIBIT 15.1 *(Continued)*

[By the way—I forgot to explain what happened here. Mr. Carnes went to his wife during the divorce process and said, "Sweetheart, let's not fight. My business is worth $5 million and I am prepared to give you half of the value along with the other assets that you are entitled to. I just don't want to fight with you." Nice guy, right? Wrong!!! Two weeks after the divorce was put through by the court, Mrs. Carnes found out that Mr. Carnes had sold his company for $15+ million. When she called him with not-so-nice things to say, he said, "Tough luck." The court found that fraud was committed and reopened up the issue of equitable distribution. Mr. Carnes hired an appraiser who determined that out of the almost $17 million (sales price plus assets not part of the deal), $5 million was a personal covenant not to compete and should not be considered as a marital asset for equitable distribution purposes. In comes Trugman Valuation Associates to the rescue!]

Nature and History of the Company

Carnes Respiratory Services, Inc. was incorporated on June 10, 1981. The Company began operations in City A, State, providing durable medical equipment and respiratory therapy products to patients referred to the Company by their doctors. Products were sold primarily to elderly patients through Medicare, Medicaid, or private insurance.

As time went on, CRS opened three additional locations, in City B, City C, and City D, State. Each of these locations was opened after Mr. Carnes and his marketing team determined that the location was viable, based on its demographics. Each of the CRS facilities was owned by Mr. Carnes personally, and leased to the Company.

At the valuation date, CRS was operating in various counties, selling items such as beds, wheelchairs, walkers, and respiratory therapy products. Sixty percent of CRS's sales came from respiratory therapy products, 30 percent from durable medical equipment, and 10 percent from miscellaneous products. Management estimated that 70 percent of its revenues resulted from rentals, and 30 percent from sales.

CRS developed a reputation for delivering high-quality service to its patients. Services included guaranteed one-hour delivery, 24-hours-a-day service, and educating patients in the use of their equipment. This was very important in differentiating CRS from the rest of the market. Other companies in the durable medical equipment market competed with CRS. In City A, competitors included Respitch, Inc. and Lincare. In City B, CRS's competition included MediHealth, Inc.; Lincare; Americare, Inc.; and State Oxygen, Inc. Competition in City C consisted of Coast, Inc. and Lincare. In City D, Lincare; Sunshine, Inc.; Medicaid, Inc.; and Homedco, Inc. competed with CRS. As will be discussed later in this report, although these companies participated in the same markets as CRS, Mr. Carnes did not believe that any of these companies offered a significant, competitive threat to CRS.

As of the valuation date, the Company had approximately 50 employees. Responsibility for overall management was shared between Mr. Carnes and Ms. Lori Rodgers. Their duties included day-to-day operations, training, marketing, and ensuring that whatever needed to be done was accomplished. They also shared the responsibilities for managing the City A facility, which was both a retail and billing operation. Each of the other three stores had a manager responsible for the store's operations. The Company had four marketing representatives whose primary responsibilities were to maintain existing referral sources and establish new ones. CRS also had a delivery manager, who was responsible for coordinating drivers and the delivery of products to patients. Additional employees included customer service representatives, drivers, accounts receivable clerks, office staff, warehouse staff, and a dispatcher.

Excess Assets

From our analysis of CRS's financial statements, it appears that CRS has excess assets. Excess assets, sometimes referred to as non-operating assets, are assets that a business owns that are not necessary for the operations of the business.

CRS had two categories of assets that are considered to be excess, current assets and fixed assets. At the valuation date, CRS's balance sheet indicates that the Company had $1,136,933 of current assets and $9,977 of current liabilities. This does not include the $550,000 of accounts receivable sold to Public Company Purchaser. The reason for this is that CRS's financial statements are prepared on a cash basis, which does not include accounts receivable. Taking this into consideration, CRS had current assets of $1,686,933. Subtracting CRS's current liabilities from this figure results in the calculation of CRS's working capital of $1,676,956 ($1,686,933 − $9,977 = $1,676,956).

To check the reasonableness of this position, we reviewed Integra's *Business Profiler* for working capital industry norms for durable medical equipment providers. For 1995, Integra reported that median working capital, as a percentage of sales, was 7 percent. Applying this to CRS's revenues for the 12 months ended February 28, 1995, results in the following calculation of working capital:

Revenues	$ 5,930,480
Integra working capital as a percent of revenues	× 7%
Required working capital	$ 415,134

This indicates that CRS had excess current assets of $1,261,822.

EXHIBIT 15.1 *(Continued)*

Public Company Purchaser and CRS allocated $550,000 of the purchase price to accounts receivable. Public Company Purchaser assumed no other current assets, and $35,000 of accrued current liabilities were not recorded as of February 28, 1995. This results in working capital of $515,000. This represents 8.68 percent of CRS's revenues in the latest 12 months. Although slightly above the median, this figure is still within industry norms. As a result, we have determined that CRS has excess current assets of $1,136,933. This figure represents all of CRS's current assets other than the accounts receivable.

CRS owned certain vehicles that we believe were non-operating assets. These vehicles were as follows:

1992 Mercedes	$125,603
1992 Mercedes	61,158
1989 Jaguar	58,332
1993 Jeep	17,176
	$262,269

In our opinion, these vehicles were not necessary for the operation of CRS. They are luxury automobiles that represented perquisites to Mr. Carnes. In addition, Mr. Carnes retained these vehicles after the asset sale to Public Company Purchaser. As a result, we have determined these vehicles are non-operating assets. Their value has been estimated to be approximately $200,000.

Valuation of Carnes Respiratory Services, Inc.

As indicated previously, the valuation of a closely held company can be accomplished using the three approaches to value. One might ask why the transaction that transpired could not be used as the best indication of fair market value. Our analysis indicates that the price that was paid by Public Company Purchaser, Inc. represents a value that was greater than the fair market value of CRS.

In the actual transaction that took place, Public Company Purchaser purchased certain net assets of CRS at a price of $15,035,000. According to the allocation included in the Asset Purchase Agreement dated March 9, 1995, the following was purchased:

Accounts receivable	$ 550,000
Inventory	40,000
Fixed assets	712,000
Covenants	100,000
Goodwill/customer list	13,633,000
Total	**$15,035,000**

The price paid is greater than the fair market value of the assets purchased. Since the definition of fair market value is based on "the most probable price," a review of other factors brought to our attention in this matter, make us believe that the most probable price is lower than this amount. In addition, we believe that Public Company Purchaser had special motivations in consummating this deal that would cause the definition of fair market value to be violated.

In the deposition transcript of Steve Rice, a principal of Richard Associates, the business broker engaged by Mr. Carnes to assist in the sale of CRS, several statements are made that assist us in substantiating our position. Mr. Rice's responses are relevant in that they reflect the knowledge and expectations of the seller. In the course of Mr. Rice's deposition, he asserts that Public Company Purchaser overpaid for CRS, supporting his opinion with several pieces of information. Other than Public Company Purchaser, Mr. Rice indicated there were four offers made to purchase CRS. The companies and their offers are as follows:

Home Medical	$11 million
Abey Home Healthcare	12 million
Homedco	11 million
Continuem Care	Undisclosed

Mr. Rice was then asked about the first Public Company Purchaser offer of $13.5 million for CRS. This was an all-cash offer, and Mr. Rice thought after presenting the offer to Mr. Carnes "our deal was done." Mr. Rice's opinion is explained in the ensuing dialogue.

(Continued)

EXHIBIT 15.1 *(Continued)*

"I felt that no one would turn that down and we just felt it was—at the time we believed it to be the highest price Public Company Purchaser had ever paid for a company. In fact, we could almost assure that it was the highest price they ever paid for a company." Mr. Rice was then asked, "the highest price in dollar amount or the highest price compared to profits?" To this, Mr. Rice responded:

> It's the highest price compared to gross revenues. Public Company Purchaser's never—they pay between 1.75 and 1.2 times gross revenue and that's just—we thought that was outstanding.
>
> That offer we took to Mr. Carnes, to John, and it never hit his desk before he threw it back at us and I'm telling you the truth. This thing never hit his desk. He wouldn't even look at it. He wouldn't talk to us.

Q. Did he say why he was turning it down?

A. Yes.

Q. Why?

A. Two provisions that we told him about, that most of his employees would be fired and he had no tenant for two of his properties. So after that point we let Public Company Purchaser sit out on a fence and I took that offer to all the other players and they all said let Public Company Purchaser buy it. That went on for about a month and we never had—we probably had some contact, but most of the contact with Public Company Purchaser was coming in the front door. They were calling us, what's going on?

Finally, the last player who hadn't given up was Continuem Care. Continuem Care kept fooling around, fooling around. Public Company Purchaser was getting nervous. They thought they were going to lose the deal. And we went back to them and said, make—give it one best shot. Go ahead. You're still way off the mark. We never told them what the other offers were. We just said, you're way off the mark. With the suggestion that they keep all the employees in the billing center and take all the leases on the property and it did. I mean, I had really nothing to—well, I guess it had a lot to do with me. I pushed it.

Q. You persuaded Public Company Purchaser?

A. I held their hand to the fire because they thought they were going to lose this deal in their own backyard and it would look very, very bad for a public company to do that.

It is clear Mr. Carnes's advisors thought this was a tremendous deal, and it exceeded their expectations. The offer was not rejected by Mr. Carnes because of the price. According to Mr. Rice, the offer was rejected by Mr. Carnes because most of CRS's employees would be fired, and he would not have a tenant for two of his properties. It was Mr. Rice who obtained the higher offer from Public Company Purchaser, along with the accommodation of Mr. Carnes's concerns. He did this by letting Public Company Purchaser "sit out on a fence" and by telling Public Company Purchaser that they were "way off the mark," even though it was by far the best offer he had received for CRS. What allowed Mr. Rice to do this was a non-financial concern on the part of Public Company Purchaser, namely that the deal was in Public Company Purchaser's "own backyard" and losing it would be embarrassing to Public Company Purchaser. From Mr. Rice's statements, it appears that Mr. Carnes would have accepted the $13.5 million dollar offer if his two conditions regarding his employees and tenancy had been met.

In fact, the dialogue comes back to this issue:

Q. All right. Did Mr. Carnes ever tell you what changed his mind regarding deciding to sell his business? He kept turning you down and later he—

A. The key issue was that as soon as we locked the employees in place and no one was to be terminated is when he said that's worth all the money in the world to me and that's exactly what he said, it's worth all the money in the world, these people having a job.

Again, according to Mr. Rice, Mr. Carnes's issues were not related to price, but other non-price factors. Mr. Rice further explains the actions of Public Company Purchaser by stating:

A. They're buying earnings. Earnings drive the price of their stock. John had a lot of earnings for the size of business that he had. And whether they paid 15 million dollars or 12 million dollars or 13 million dollars, at that time it didn't matter. They got rid of a competitor and they got the best—and they got people there that they don't—that are better than any people that they have, so they took everything into—I'd like to say we had a lot to do with getting 15 million dollars for this company.

This further highlights his beliefs that Public Company Purchaser's motivation was beyond financial, and that Mr. Carnes's reasons for rejecting the first Public Company Purchaser offer were unrelated to the purchase price. Mr. Rice's comments raise the issue of whether Public Company Purchaser paid fair market value for CRS, or paid above fair market value for synergistic and public image reasons. As discussed earlier in this report, fair market value is established between a willing buyer and willing seller, neither party being under compulsion and both having reasonable knowledge of the relevant facts. It appears from the comments of Mr. Rice that he believed that Public Company Purchaser was under compulsion, and that he could exploit that compulsion to the advantage of John Carnes.

EXHIBIT 15.1 *(Continued)*

This brings about the possibility of a buyer's premium. A buyer's premium is concerned with elements of investment value. According to Pratt, investment value is defined as "value to a particular investor based on individual investment requirements, as distinguished from the concept of market value, which is impersonal and detached."

As Pratt states, investment value is different for different buyers. There are many factors that can influence investment value, such as estimates of earning capacity, perceptions of risk, tax statutes, and synergies. Stated differently, the investment value of a closely held company is the value to a particular buyer, as compared to the population of willing buyers, as is the case in fair market value. This value definition would be applicable, when an investor might have specific investment criteria that must be fulfilled in an acquisition.

An appraiser will frequently use this standard of value when he or she represents a buyer who wants to know, "How much is the business worth to me?" The fact that the buyer is specific about the business value to him or her changes the standard of value to investment value, as opposed to fair market value, which may be the value to everyone else.

Under such a definition of investment value, certain elements can be quantified numerically in an income stream, and differences between fair market value and investment value can be calculated. Others, like Public Company Purchaser's desire not to let other major competitors into its "backyard" cannot be calculated from an income stream. Typical market data does not allow us to calculate such a premium.

However, one study has provided us with an insight into this type of a premium by comparing the multiples of earnings before interest and tax ("EBIT") paid by financial buyers and strategic buyers. The study consisted of a poll of 35 professional investment bankers, lenders, and the managing partners of buyout firms, and covered the manufacturing, retail, communications, services, and health care industries, in particular.

As discussed above, hard data is difficult to obtain for such a survey. Accordingly, the study is based on the respondents "feel for the industry based on their experiences in both proprietary deals and auction settings. At times, their answers were categorized as a broad interpretation of the diversity within a sector." Table 1 presents the multiples obtained by the survey for 1989, 1993, and 1995, and calculates the premium that strategic buyers are paying over financial buyers.

TABLE 1
Trends in Acquisition Multiples

	1989	*1993*	*1995*
Strategic buyers	7.76	6.11	7.24
Financial buyers	7.41	5.40	6.50
Premium	4.72%	13.15%	11.38%

Source: Jennifer Lea Reed, "Purchase Multiple Press to Rarefield Heights," *Buyouts* (February 20, 1995), 1.

As can be seen in the data in Table 1, the premium for 1995 was 11.38 percent. To apply a buyer's premium to the sale of CRS, the premium is applied to Public Company Purchaser's initial offer of $13.5 million. The justification for this is twofold. First, Public Company Purchaser's offer appears to already have included some elements of investment value, as it was significantly greater than the other offers for CRS. Second, Mr. Carnes's reasons for not accepting the offer were unrelated to the purchase price, but rather were related to the nonfinancial terms of the agreement.

We have applied this premium to Public Company Purchaser's $13.5 million offer to test our hypothesis. The results are presented in Table 2.

TABLE 2
Application of a Buyer's Premium

Initial offer from Public Company Purchaser	$13,500,000
Times one plus strategic premium	× 1.1138
Price with buyer's premium	$15,036,300
Final purchase price	$15,035,000
Difference	$ 1,300

(Continued)

EXHIBIT 15.1 *(Continued)*

This strongly supports the assertion that Public Company Purchaser was a strategic buyer in its acquisition of CRS, and the assertions made by Mr. Rice in his deposition. To verify this against other known data, we relied on the deposition of Mr. Davidson, Public Company Purchaser's national acquisition program manager. Mr. Davidson indicated that Public Company Purchaser's acquisitions typically occur at 3.5 to 4.0 times free cash flow for the trailing 12 months. Based on Public Company Purchaser's estimate of free cash flow for the trailing 12 months of $3.5 million, the price–to–free cash flow multiple paid for CRS using a value of $13,500,000 was 3.86 ($13,500,000 ÷ $3,500,000 = 3.8571, or 3.86 rounded). Based on this data and the information presented in Mr. Rice's deposition, we conclude that the fair market value of the operating business of Carnes Respiratory Services was $13,500,000 at March 9, 1995, based on the actual market transaction that was consummated.

In order to test the conclusion reached in the market approach, we then applied an income approach methodology in our analysis. To implement the income approach, we have selected the discounted future benefits method. The discounted future benefits method is one of the most theoretically correct methods of appraisal. It is premised on the concept that value is based on the present value of all future benefits that flow to an owner of a property. These future benefits can consist of current income distributions, appreciation in the property, or a combination of both.

In order to apply this methodology, we began the analysis with a forecast of expected future operating cash flows for CRS. Table 3 presents the forecast income statement for CRS for the years ended March 9, 1996, through 2000.

TABLE 3

Forecast Income Statement and Cash Flow for the Years Ended March 9, 1996, through 2000

	1996	*1997*	*1998*	*1999*	*2000*
Net sales[1]	$ 6,500,000	$ 7,345,000	$ 8,299,850	$ 9,378,830	$10,504,290
Less: Cost of sales[2]	916,500	1,035,645	1,170,279	1,322,415	1,481,105
Equals: Gross profit	$ 5,583,500	$ 6,309,355	$ 7,129,571	$ 8,056,415	$ 9,023,185
Less: Operating expenses[3]	2,723,500	3,077,555	3,477,637	3,929,730	4,401,297
Equals: Net operating income	$ 2,860,000	$ 3,231,800	$ 3,651,934	$ 4,126,685	$ 4,621,888
Less: Taxes[4]	1,144,000	1,292,720	1,460,774	1,650,674	1,848,755
Net income	**$1,716,000**	**$1,939,080**	**$2,191,160**	**$2,476,011**	**$2,773,133**

[1]Revenues for the trailing 12 months in 1995 are based on the Public Company Purchaser pro forma included in this report as Exhibit 2. Revenues are grown thereafter to generate a compound annual growth rate for the entire forecast period of 12.7 percent. This is the approximate rate of growth projected for the industry, as previously discussed.

[2]Cost of sales is forecast as 14.1 percent of sales for each year in the forecast period. This is based on the historical average for the period analyzed.

[3]The historic average operating expenses for the period ended May 30, 1991, through May 30, 1994, and the latest 12 months ended December 31, 1994, were 45.1 percent of sales. For fiscal 1994, operating expenses were 41.9 percent of sales, which we used in each year of the forecast period. The most recent fiscal year's figure was selected over the average, based on the downward trend in operating expenses as a percentage of sales during the historic period analyzed.

[4]We have assumed a combined federal and state tax rate of 40 percent.

Using the forecast income statements presented in Table 3, combined with an analysis of the balance sheet of CRS, we have prepared a forecast of the net cash flow for the years ended March 9, 1996, through 2000. This appears in Table 4.

TABLE 4

Forecast Net Cash Flow for the Years Ended March 9, 1996, through 2000

	1996	*1997*	*1998*	*1999*	*2000*
Net income (Table 3)	$ 1,716,000	$ 1,939,080	$ 2,191,160	$ 2,476,011	$ 2,773,133
Add: Depreciation[1]	548,422	743,589	964,128	1,213,337	1,492,451
Gross cash flow	$ 2,264,422	$ 2,682,669	$ 3,155,288	$ 3,689,348	$ 4,265,584
Less: Capital expenditures[2]	1,209,000	1,366,170	1,543,772	1,744,462	1,953,798
Less: Increase in net working capital[3]	43,506	59,150	66,839	75,529	78,782
Net cash flow	**$1,011,916**	**$1,257,349**	**$1,544,677**	**$1,869,357**	**$2,233,004**

EXHIBIT 15.1 *(Continued)*

[1]Depreciation is based on two factors: first, depreciating the existing fixed assets as of February 28, 1995, of $1,878,538 over a remaining useful life of five years, and second, depreciating future fixed asset additions over a useful life of seven years.

[2]Capital expenditures are calculated as 18.6 percent of sales. This is based on capital expenditures as a percentage of sales in fiscal 1994. The calculation is as follows:

Net fixed assets at May 31, 1995	$ 1,771,669
Less: Net fixed assets at May 31, 1994	(1,214,949)
1994 fixed asset additions	$ 932,435
Divided by 1994 sales	$ 5,018,896
1994 fixed assets as a percent of sales	18.6%

[3]The increase in working capital is based on the median for medical equipment rental and leasing companies with $3 to $5 million in sales, which was 7 percent. Therefore, we have used this figure times the increase in sales to estimate increases in working capital for each year in the projection period.

Our review of prior years' capital expenditures revealed 15.9 percent and 19.3 percent, for 1992 and 1993, respectively. We felt that the 1994 capital expenditures were reasonable under the circumstances.

Once the cash flow has been forecast, the selection of a proper discount rate becomes necessary. Since the benefit stream being estimated will not occur until some time in the future, the future benefits must be discounted to their present value. In this instance, a discount rate of 19.2 percent has been deemed applicable. This results in the value estimate of CRS being calculated as follows:

Year	*Forecast Cash Flow*	×	*19.2% Present Value Factors*	=	*Present Value Future Cash Flow*
1996	$ 1,011,916		0.8389		$ 848,896
1997	1,257,349		0.7038		884,922
1998	1,544,677		0.5904		911,977
1999	1,869,357		0.4953		925,893
2000	2,233,004		0.4155		927,813
TV	21,636,450		0.4155		8,989,945
Total					**$ 13,489,446**

In this instance, the terminal value is determined by growing the last year's forecast net income by a stabilized growth rate. Net income is then converted to cash flow as follows:

Terminal value net income	$ 2,939,521
Plus: Depreciation[1]	2,000,000
Less: Capital expenditures[1]	2,000,000
Less: Increase in working capital[2]	83,509
Terminal value cash flow	**$2,856,011**

[1]Depreciation and capital expenditures are set equal in the terminal year.

[2]The increase in working capital is calculated as the increase in 2000, times 1 plus the long-term growth rate of 6 percent.

Adding the terminal value to the present value of the anticipated interim benefit stream results in the present value of the future benefits of CRS to be $13,496,690, or $13,500,000 rounded.

Another reasonableness check was performed based on the deposition transcript of Howard Davidson, Executive Vice President and General Counsel of Public Company Purchaser. As he states in his deposition, Mr. Davidson managed "the acquisition function for the company nationwide." The following excerpt from his deposition gives an overview of how Public Company Purchaser analyzes potential acquisitions, including CRS.

(Continued)

EXHIBIT 15.1 *(Continued)*

Q. Okay. Could you tell me what criteria was used by Public Company Purchaser for the purpose of establishing this $13,500,000 value?

A. When we value businesses, we typically look at a number of elements, some financial related, others not specifically financial related. We look at the sales revenue. We look at the earnings on a historical basis of the business. We look at the earnings of what we believe to be a pro forma basis after acquisition. We look at the geographic area that the business serves. We look at the product mix that business has in terms of its respiratory and nonrespiratory components. We look at the scope of their business in terms of geography and referral sources. Those would be the principal criteria that we look at.

Q. Well, is there a rule of thumb that you apply to earnings for the purpose of getting some preliminary feeling as to what a company would be worth to Public Company Purchaser in connection with an acquisition?

A. It's flexible. And those criteria determine whether or not our interest level is higher or lower and our valuation level is higher or lower with respect to a particular business. If it's got a better geographic situation for us, if there are more synergies, if it's a higher respiratory mix, those would be conditions which would put the value at the higher end of the spectrum. If those situations either singularly or in combination are less desirable compared to what we're looking for, then the business—then a particular business is at the lower end of the spectrum.

Mr. Davidson further describes the process and the interest Public Company Purchaser had in CRS:

A. Well, as I said earlier, we look at the financial performance both historically and what it would be on a go-forward basis. And we then look at other elements to determine, you know, whether or not our interest level is at the higher end of the spectrum or the lower end of the spectrum. In this particular case, because of the locations because of the respiratory content, because of the reputation that the company had in the community it was at the higher end of the spectrum.

The key element of this statement is the reasons for Public Company Purchaser's interest in CRS: good locations, high respiratory therapy content, and good company reputation. Mr. Davidson indicates that Mr. Byrnes put together a pro forma income statement based on what he believed Public Company Purchaser would expect to occur at the CRS locations in the 12 months after acquisition by Public Company Purchaser. Mr. Davidson then used this pro forma to derive a value for CRS. Mr. Davidson describes the valuation:

A. The only thing I can tell is that if you look across the broad range of acquisitions we've done, that based on a pro forma basis, the cash flow and reconciling that with historical performance, and looking at it at our operating center level, not at the corporate level on a consolidated basis, but at that center level, businesses typically tend to fall at about the three and a half to four times cash flow basis depending upon various and intangible factors, some higher and some lower.

Q. And some of them you've described here earlier today. And you've also indicated that because of the mix of product, the particular area where respiratory—Carnes Respiratory was operating, the reputation of the company, using the higher end of the spectrum to the extent that that rule of thumb has applicability at all would have been what was—would have been Public Company Purchaser's approach in this situation.

A. I don't have specific recall as to what the pro forma, if any, was done for this reflected. So I don't know what the multiple is in this particular case. But based on the quality of the business and its size and its location, I think it's a fair statement to say that this is at the very high end of the spectrum.

Although Mr. Davidson did not recall the exact pro forma in his deposition, we have been provided a copy of it and it is presented as Exhibit 2 to this report. The pro forma indicated that Public Company Purchaser expected $6.5 million in revenues, earnings before interest, tax depreciation and amortization ("EBITDA") of $3.75 million, and free cash flow of $3.5 million. Free cash flow is defined as EBITDA less capital expenditures. Dividing the purchase price of $15,035,000 by $3,500,000 results in a multiple of price to free cash flow of 4.30. Following Mr. Davidson's testimony, if we divide $13,500,000 by free cash flow of $3,500,000, the result is a multiple of 3.86. This is very much in line with the range of 3.5 to 4.0 times cash flow testified to by Mr. Davidson.

This confirms the reasonableness of establishing the fair market value of the operating assets of CRS at $13.5 million.

Valuation of the Tangible Assets

The next step in our analysis is to value the tangible assets of CRS to be used in the allocation of the purchase price. As previously discussed, Public Company Purchaser and CRS negotiated a transaction that included an allocation of the price to different classes of assets. In this instance, we are accepting the allocation of the tangible assets as being reasonable. This results in the tangible assets being valued as follows:

Accounts receivable	$ 550,000
Inventory	40,000
Fixed assets	712,000
Total	**$1,302,000**

EXHIBIT 15.1 *(Continued)*

Valuation of the Identifiable Intangible Assets

The approaches to the valuation of intangible assets are similar to the approaches used to value a business enterprise: market, asset-based, and income. Each of these approaches is discussed briefly below.

The Market Approach

The market approach, also referred to as the sales comparison approach, entails researching and identifying similar intangible assets to the subject intangibles that have been transacted in the marketplace. These transactions are then used as guidelines in developing the value of the subject intangible asset.

The Asset-Based Approach

The asset based or cost approach attempts to ascertain the value of the asset by determining its cost. Cost typically can have several definitions. The most common definitions of cost are reproduction cost, the cost to reproduce an exact copy of the asset; replacement cost, the cost to purchase an identical asset, or the cost to replace the functionality or utility of the asset; creation cost, the original cost to create the asset; and re-creation cost, what it would cost to re-create or duplicate an existing asset. In many circumstances, the definition of cost also includes the concept of obsolescence, or deterioration in value. Obsolescence can result from physical deterioration of the asset, functional obsolescence, technical obsolescence, or economic obsolescence. Although not all intangible assets suffer from obsolescence, the identification of obsolescence is important to the cost approach.

The Income Approach

As in the case of the valuation of the business enterprise, the income approach for intangible asset valuation determines the present value of the future benefits that will accrue to the owner of the asset. This is generally accomplished by either capitalizing a single period income stream or discounting a series of income streams, based on a multi-period forecast.

Identifiable Intangible Assets

In this appraisal, several intangible assets could be separately identified and valued. These assets include the following:

- Trademark
- Patient records
- Covenant not to compete

Although other intangible assets could be identified as existing in CRS, namely trained employee workforce, procedure manuals, etc., they could not be separately valued. Therefore, these assets are valued under the residual method in the next section of this report.

The Income Approach

To value the identifiable intangible assets and the goodwill of CRS, we have used the income approach. To implement the income approach, we have used the residual cash flow methodology. The residual method allocates the cash flows of the business to its component assets. This includes both tangible and identifiable intangible assets. This is accomplished for assets whose values are known by calculating returns to those assets and subtracting the returns from the forecast cash flows of the business. The cash flow of a business is the product of combining all of the assets of the business in their productive capacities to generate returns to the shareholders. The cash flow that remains after returns to all of the identified assets are subtracted is the cash flow attributable to the unidentified intangible assets.

We started by analyzing the returns being generated by the tangible assets of the business. Since we have previously determined that excess assets existed in CRS at the valuation date, returns to these assets have not been computed, as this analysis focuses on the operating assets of the business. At the valuation date, the tangible operating assets have been valued in addendum 3.4 to the asset purchase and sale agreement between Public Company Purchaser and CRS. The addendum has been attached as Exhibit 3 to this report. As per Exhibit 3, the value of the tangible assets at the valuation date was as follows:

Accounts receivable	$ 550,000
Inventory	40,000
Fixed assets	712,000
Total	**$1,302,000**

To compute returns from these assets, we have developed rates of returns for each, and applied them to the asset values. The starting point to estimate returns on these assets is the prime rate that banks charged at the valuation date. According to the Federal Reserve Board, the average prime rate for all U.S. commercial banks was 9 percent on March 9, 1995. The prime rate represents the rate of interest banks charge their best customers on the most secure types of loans.

(Continued)

EXHIBIT 15.1 *(Continued)*

For this analysis, we have added a premium to the prime rate for each of the different classes of assets to arrive at the following rates of return:

Asset Class	*Return*	*After-Tax Return*
Accounts receivable	11%	6.6%
Inventory	12%	7.2%
Fixed assets	14%	8.4%

Accounts receivable are the most liquid of the three asset classes, making them less risky than the inventory or fixed assets. Yet banks would still charge CRS a premium to lend against the receivables because it still presents risk to the bank. The inventory is less liquid than the accounts receivable and thus presents more risk to the bank. Therefore, we have added an additional 1 percent premium to the inventory rate. The fixed assets of the business are even less liquid than the inventory, and present a greater risk to a bank that is considering lending against the fixed assets of a business. As such, we have added an additional 2 percent over and above the return to inventory.

All of the returns calculated are pretax returns. Since our objective is to allocate after-tax cash flow to these assets, we need to tax effect the returns to put them on an after-tax basis. To accomplish this, we have assumed the tax rate to be 40 percent and multiplied the pretax returns by 1 minus the tax rate, or 60 percent (1 − 40% = 60%). It should be noted that the returns calculated here are minimum returns. The premise used here is that companies would require a rate of return equal to the cost to finance the asset. In fact, companies want to make profits on their assets and would want to earn an incremental return over and above their financing cost.

To calculate the cash flow that is allocable to each asset, the value of the asset is multiplied by the after-tax return. The calculations are presented in Table 5.

TABLE 5
Calculation of Returns to Tangible Assets

Asset	*Value*	*After-Tax Rate of Return*	*Return*
Accounts receivable	$550,000	6.6%	$36,600
Inventory	40,000	7.2%	2,880
Fixed assets	712,000	8.4%	59,808

Once the returns from the tangible assets have been determined, we can subtract these returns from the cash flow of the business to obtain the cash flow allocable to all of the intangible assets. This is shown in Table 6.

TABLE 6
Cash Flows From Intangible Assets

	1996	*1997*	*1998*	*1999*	*2000*
Cash flow (Table 4)	$1,011,916	$ 1,257,349	$ 1,544,677	$ 1,869,357	$ 2,233,004
Less: Returns on:					
Accounts receivable (Table 5)	36,300	36,300	36,300	36,300	36,300
Inventory (Table 5)	2,880	2,880	2,880	2,880	2,880
Fixed assets (Table 5)	59,808	59,808	59,808	59,808	59,808
Cash flows from intangible assets	**$ 912,928**	**$1,158,361**	**$1,445,689**	**$1,770,369**	**$2,134,016**

Trademark

A trademark, or trade name as it is sometimes referred to, is one of the most common types of intangible assets. The trademark is the name that the company is recognized by in the marketplace. This is the reason trademarks have value, because they are recognized by customers and referral sources. Typically in an acquisition, the use of the trademark by the seller is prohibited to protect the value of the assets purchased by the buyer.

EXHIBIT 15.1 *(Continued)*

The valuation of a trademark is based on the present value of a stream of royalties that would be paid for the use of the trademark. Royalty rates for such purposes are typically defined as a percentage of sales. To obtain the actual rates, one must observe similar transactions in the marketplace.

A few companies keep databases of royalty rate data. For the purposes of this assignment, we used the database of ASU Consulting and Trademark Licensing Associates. These databases were searched for companies in the medical equipment and respiratory therapy industries and related fields. The searches did not identify any transaction that would be appropriate to the valuation of CRS' trademark.

Our research and discussions with individuals at ASU Consulting and Trademark Licensing Associates leads us to believe that royalty rates typically range between 1 percent and 10 percent across markets and industries. Considering the low level of technology involved in CRS, as well as the company's strength and reputation, we have selected a royalty rate of 4 percent.

Estimating that the trademark has a relatively long term holding period, we have calculated the cash flow for a 25-year life. The strength of the CRS name becomes more and more apparent when the historic sales growth is examined. Table 7 reflects our calculation.

TABLE 7
Cash Flow Allocable to Trademark

Year	*Sale*	*Rate*	*Cash Flow*
1996	6,500,000	4.0%	260,000
1997	7,345,000	4.0%	293,800
1998	8,299,850	4.0%	331,994
1999	9,378,831	4.0%	375,153
2000	10,504,290	4.0%	420,172
2001	11,134,548	4.0%	445,382
2002	11,802,620	4.0%	472,105
2003	12,510,778	4.0%	500,431
2004	13,261,424	4.0%	530,457
2005	14,057,110	4.0%	562,284
2006	14,900,536	4.0%	596,021
2007	15,794,569	4.0%	631,783
2008	16,742,243	4.0%	669,690
2009	17,746,777	4.0%	709,871
2010	18,811,584	4.0%	752,463
2011	19,940,279	4.0%	797,611
2012	21,136,696	4.0%	845,468
2013	22,404,897	4.0%	896,196
2014	23,749,191	4.0%	949,968
2015	25,174,143	4.0%	1,006,966
2016	26,684,591	4.0%	1,067,384
2017	28,285,667	4.0%	1,131,427
2018	29,982,807	4.0%	1,199,312
2019	31,781,775	4.0%	1,271,271
2020	33,688,682	4.0%	1,347,547

Once the cash flow has been forecast, the selection of a proper discount rate becomes necessary. Since the cash flow stream being estimated will not occur until some time in the future, the future cash flow must be discounted to its present value.

(Continued)

EXHIBIT 15.1 *(Continued)*

The CRS trademark is well established in its local markets. The Company had an excellent reputation for service and integrity. As Mr. Carnes has said, he did not spend money on advertising, but let CRS' reputation build by word of mouth, from satisfied patient to doctor, and from doctor to doctor. These events have gone a long way in strengthening the trademark of CRS in its marketplaces. CRS had the predominant market position in each of its markets and continually maintained and upgraded its position with diligent marketing efforts. These positive qualities provide value to a trademark and reduce the risk associated with it. As a result, we have selected a 20 percent discount rate.

This results in the value estimate of the trademark being calculated as follows:

Year	*Forecast Cash Flow*	×	*20% Present Value Factors*	=	*Present Value Future Cash Flow*
1996	$ 260,000		0.8333		$ 216,658
1997	293,800		0.6944		204,015
1998	331,994		0.5787		192,125
1999	375,153		0.4823		180,936
2000	420,172		0.4019		168,867
2001	445,382		0.3349		149,158
2002	472,105		0.2791		131,764
2003	500,431		0.2326		116,400
2004	530,457		0.1938		102,803
2005	562,284		0.1615		90,809
2006	596,021		0.1346		80,224
2007	631,783		0.1122		70,886
2008	669,690		0.0935		62,616
2009	709,871		0.0779		55,299
2010	752,463		0.0649		48,835
2011	797,611		0.0541		43,151
2012	845,468		0.0451		38,131
2013	896,196		0.0376		33,697
2014	949,968		0.0313		29,734
2015	1,006,966		0.0261		26,282
2016	1,067,384		0.0217		23,162
2017	1,131,427		0.0181		20,479
2018	1,199,312		0.0151		18,110
2019	1,271,271		0.0126		16,018
2020	1,347,547		0.0105		14,149
Total					**$2,134,308**

The indicated fair market value of CRS' trademark is $2,134,308, or $2,134,000 rounded.

Patient Records

One of the important intangible assets of a business like CRS is the patient records or customer list. These records are important to a potential purchaser because it is this very patient base that generates immediate cash flow to the company. This type of asset is generally valued by reviewing the expected life of the patient relationship, and applying some factor to the sales in order to estimate the cash flow that would be expected to be generated from this relationship. Before applying factors to the cash flow of the company, we must first determine the cash flow available from the patient records and the remaining assets. This is calculated in Table 8.

EXHIBIT 15.1 *(Continued)*

TABLE 8

Cash Flows Available to Patient Records

		Return on:				Cash Flow
Year	*Cash Flow*	*Accts. Rec.*	*Inventory*	*Fixed Assets*	*Trademark*	*to Other Intangibles*
1996	$ 1,011,916	36,300	2,880	59,808	260,000	652,928
1997	$ 1,257,349	36,300	2,880	59,808	293,800	864,561
1998	$ 1,544,677	36,300	2,880	59,808	331,994	1,113,695
1999	$ 1,869,357	36,300	2,880	59,808	375,153	1,395,216
2000	$ 2,233,003	36,300	2,880	59,808	420,172	1,713,843
2001	$ 2,366,983	36,300	2,880	59,808	445,382	1,822,613
2002	$ 2,509,002	36,300	2,880	59,808	472,105	1,937,909

Using Iowa curves, we have calculated the following survivorship rates for the life of the patient relationships:

Year	*Survivorship %*
1	83.88
2	62.43
3	47.22
4	34.57
5	23.13
6	12.32
7	1.87

Therefore, projected cash flows from the existing patient base are estimated in Table 9.

TABLE 9

Year	*Cash Flow to the Residual*	*Survivorship Rate*	*Cash Flow to Patient Records*
1996	$ 652,928	.8388	$ 547,676
1997	864,561	.6243	539,745
1998	1,113,695	.4722	525,887
1999	1,395,216	.3457	482,326
2000	1,713,843	.2313	396,412
2001	1,822,613	.1232	224,546
2002	1,937,909	.0187	36,236

After calculating the cash flow attributable to the patient records, the next step is to discount these amounts to their present values to determine an estimate of the value of the patient records. In our opinion, the least risky of the identified intangible assets are the patient records, as they are actual physical documents. Possessing these documents allows a buyer to continue servicing the existing patients. The remaining life of these records can and has been estimated. In addition, buyers such as Public Company Purchaser and other large companies in the industry have their own experiences with how long a patient will remain with the company. As these patients are currently availing themselves of CRS's services, they are generating cash flows and will generate a material and predictable portion of CRS' cash flows over the following months and years. This makes the risk of receiving these cash flows low. Therefore, we have applied a 14 percent discount rate to the patient records. This results in an estimate of value as calculated in Table 10.

(Continued)

EXHIBIT 15.1 *(Continued)*

TABLE 10

Cash Flows Allocable to Patient Records

Year	*Cash Flow to Patient Records*	*Present Value Factors*	*Present Value*
1996	$547,676	0.8782	$ 480,421
1997	539,745	0.7695	415,334
1998	525,887	0.6750	354,973
1999	482,326	0.5921	285,585
2000	396,412	0.5194	205,896
2001	224,546	0.4556	102,303
2002	36,239	0.3996	14,481
Total present value			**$1,858,995**

Therefore, based on our analysis, the value of the patient records is estimated to be $1,858,995, or $1,859,000 rounded.

Covenant Not to Compete

A covenant not to compete (non-compete agreement) is an intangible asset based on a contractual agreement. Typically, the seller of a business, the covenantor, agrees not to compete with the buyer of the business, the covenantee, in a defined industry or market for a specific period of time, in a geographically defined area. A non-compete agreement has value to the buyer to the degree that it protects the assets (tangible and intangible) from loss of value by restricting competitive actions of the seller. From an economic perspective, the value of a non-compete agreement is dependent on several factors, including the ability of the seller to compete, the derivation of the non-compete agreement, and the losses the company would suffer if the seller competed.

In the instance where the seller has the ability to compete, the relevant question becomes, what impact would competition from the seller have on the business? The answer to this question depends on a myriad of factors. Chief among them are: (1) the seller being in possession of relationships that could redirect business from the company to a new company established or invested into by the seller, and (2) the seller having either sufficient knowledge or technology to allow him or her to bring competitive services to market.

The single most important source document in determining the value of a covenant not-to-compete is the agreement in which the covenant is made. For this reason, we have performed a detailed review of the asset purchase agreement between Public Company Purchaser, CRS, and John W. Carnes, dated March 9, 1995 (the "Agreement"). The following discussion highlights items in the Agreement that impact the value of the covenant not to compete.

Article 1.1(b) defines business as it applies to the Agreement:

> "*Business*" shall mean the entire business of Company [CRS], including, but not limited to, the business of marketing, advertising, selling, leasing, renting, distributing or otherwise providing oxygen, oxygen equipment, aerosol inhalation therapy equipment and respiratory medications, nasal continuous positive airway pressure devices, infant monitoring equipment and services, home sleep studies and related therapy equipment, and other respiratory therapy and durable medical equipment, products, supplies and services to customers in their homes or other alternative site care facilities.

Article 1.1(f) defines territory as:

> [T]he State of State and a radius of one hundred fifty (150) miles from any of Company's current operating centers, regardless of which states such radius may include.

Section 3.4 of the Agreement pertains to the allocation of the purchase price and states:

> The parties agree to allocate the Purchase Price among the Assets as set forth in Addendum 3.4. The values assigned to the Assets as set forth Addendum 3.4 were separately established by the parties in good faith and each party agrees to report the transaction contemplated by this Agreement to the Internal Revenue Service as required by Section 1060 of the Internal Revenue Code in accordance with Addendum 3.4, subject to the approval of Public Company Purchaser's and Company's independent auditors.

An important statement in this section is the discussion of the values being "separately established by the parties in good faith." This indicates that the parties discussed each of the values and negotiated them separately, including the covenant not-to-compete. Addendum 3.4 has been attached to this report as Exhibit 3.

EXHIBIT 15.1 *(Continued)*

Article 8.2 contains a no-solicitation clause that states:

a. From and after the Closing, neither Company nor the Shareholder [John W. Carnes] shall:

   i. directly or indirectly, hire, offer to hire, or entice away, or in any other manner persuade or attempt to persuade, any officer, employee or agent of Public Company Purchaser (including, but not limited to, any former officer, employee or agent of Company), or in any manner persuade or attempt to persuade, any officer, employee or agent of Public Company Purchaser (including, but not limited to, any former officer, employee or agent of Company) to discontinue his or her relationship with Public Company Purchaser. It is understood and agreed that the prohibitions contained in this Section 8.2 (i) shall apply to all current and future officers, employees and agents of Public Company Purchaser (including, but not limited to, any former officer, employee or agent of Company), whether or not any such person is then currently an officer, employee or agent of Public Company Purchaser or whether any such prohibited activity is in connection with employment, an offer of employment or other action within or outside the Territory; or

   ii. directly or indirectly solicit, divert or take away, or attempt to solicit, divert or take away any business Company had enjoyed or solicited prior to the date hereof or which Public Company Purchaser may enjoy or solicit in the Territory after the date hereof.

b. It is expressly understood and agreed by the parties hereto that it shall be a breach hereof for Company or the Shareholder to assist in any way any member of his or her family, any business associate, or any other person, firm, corporation, partnership, joint venture, association, trust or other entity, to engage in any activity which is prohibited by this Section 8.2.

Notice that this article deals with the existing customers and employees being acquired at the time of the Agreement. This article acts as protection for Public Company Purchaser with respect to the customers and human capital it is acquiring.

Article 9 is the covenant not to compete and is presented in its entirety.

9.1 *Covenant.*

a. In consideration of the purchase by Public Company Purchaser of the Assets and the Business pursuant to the terms and conditions of this Agreement, and for other good and valuable consideration, the Company and Shareholder, (each hereinafter referred to individually as a "Covenantor" and collectively as the "Covenantors") hereby represent, warrant, covenant and agree, jointly and severally, that commencing on the date hereof and continuing for a period of five (5) years thereafter, none of the Covenantors will, directly or indirectly, engage in the business of marketing, advertising, selling, leasing, renting, distributing, or otherwise providing oxygen, oxygen equipment, aerosol inhalation therapy equipment and respiratory medications, nasal continuous positive airway pressure devices, infant monitoring equipment and services, home sleep studies and related therapy equipment, or any other respiratory therapy or durable medical equipment, products, supplies and services to customers in their homes or other alternative site care facilities within the Territory.

b. Without limiting the generality of the provisions of Section 9.1 (a) hereof, this Covenant Not-to-compete shall be construed so that Covenantors shall also be in breach hereof if any of them is an employee, officer, director, shareholder, investor, trustee, agent, principal or partner of, or a consultant or advisor to or for, or a subcontractor or manager for, a person, firm, corporation, partnership, joint venture, association, trust or other entity which is engaged in such business in the Territory, or if any of them receives any compensation or remuneration from or owns, directly or indirectly, any outstanding stock or shares or has a beneficial or other financial interest in the stock or assets of any such person, firm, corporation, partnership, joint venture, association, trust or other entity engaged in such business in the Territory. Notwithstanding anything to the contrary contained in this Section 9.1 (b), no Covenantor shall be deemed to be in breach of this Covenant Not-to-compete solely by reason of owning an interest of less than one percent (1%) of the shares of any company traded on a national securities exchange or in the over the counter market.

c. It is expressly understood and agreed by Covenantors that it shall be a breach of this Covenant Not-to-compete for any Covenantor to assist in any way any family member, any business associate, or any other person, firm, corporation, partnership, joint venture, association, trust or other entity, to engage in any activity which a Covenantor is prohibited from engaging in by this Covenant Not-to-compete.

9.2 *Remedies.*

d. Covenantors agree that the remedy at law for any breach of obligation under this Covenant Not-to-compete will be inadequate and that in addition to any other rights and remedies to which it may be entitled hereunder, at law or in equity, Public Company Purchaser shall be entitled to injunctive relief, and reimbursement for all reasonable attorneys' fees and other expenses incurred in connection with the enforcement hereof. It is the intention of Covenantors and Public Company Purchaser that this Covenant Not-to-compete be fully enforceable in accordance with its terms and that the provisions hereof be interpreted so as to be enforceable to the maximum extent permitted by applicable law. To the extent that any obligation to refrain from competing within an area for a period of time as provided in this Covenant Not-to-compete is held invalid or unenforceable, it shall, to the extent that it is invalid or unenforceable, be deemed void *ab initio*. The remaining obligations imposed by the provisions of this Covenant Not-to-compete shall be fully enforceable as if such invalid or unenforceable provisions had not been included herein and shall be construed to the extent possible, such that the purpose of this Covenant Not-to-compete, as intended by Covenantors and Public Company Purchaser, can be achieved in a lawful manner.

(Continued)

EXHIBIT 15.1 *(Continued)*

The key elements of the covenant not to compete are as follows:

- The covenant is for a term of five years.
- The covenant covers what the Agreement defines as "business."
- The covenant relates to the geographic region defined in the Agreement as the "territory."
- Prohibits partaking in the "business" in the "territory" for the five-year period.
- The covenant defines remedies for Public Company Purchaser if the covenant is violated.

The valuation of the covenant not to compete is highly dependent on the impact of the seller's ability to compete in the marketplace with the buyer. Therefore, in order to estimate the potential impact of CRS competing with Public Company Purchaser after the sale, we have performed a lost sales analysis.

A lost sales analysis entails estimating the potential losses to the covenantee from competition from the covenantor. The analysis is used as part of a residual method valuation of a non-compete. As part of a residual method of valuation, the lost sales analysis determines the cash flow that is allocable to the covenant not to compete. The cash flow is then valued directly in the residual valuation analysis.

Lost sales analysis can be used to value the subject business\' cash flow for the period of the covenant, first assuming the covenant is in place and then a second time without the covenant. The difference in the values in these two scenarios is the value of the non-compete agreement.

Regardless of how it is to be used, there are several steps involved in preparing a lost sales analysis. The first step is to prepare a forecast of the company's income statement and cash flow assuming the covenant is in place and the covenantor is not in violation of the agreement. This has previously been done to value the entire operating enterprise.

The next step is to ascertain what level of sales would be lost if the covenant were not in place. The impact of the lost sales on the company's income statement and cash flow must then be analyzed and forecast. Determining the likely level of lost sales is a highly intricate process that typically involves in-depth discussions with management of the acquiring company. The closest information we have to interviews in this case are the depositions of the Public Company Purchaser officials and of Mr. Carnes. Based on our review of the various deposition transcripts provided to us, we determined that the possible range of lost sales would be between 1 percent and 25 percent. Our analyses follows in Tables 11 and 12.

A general rule that is applied to these scenarios is that we have not reduced sales by more than 10 percent in any one year. This has been done to reflect that transferring revenues to a new entity would take Mr. Carnes time to accomplish.

Each of these tables has the same assumptions regarding to cost of sales, operating expenses and income taxes. They are:

1. Cost of sales is forecast at 14.1 percent of sales based on the historic cost of sales.
2. Operating expenses are forecast as 41.9 percent of sales.
3. We have assumed a combined federal and state tax rate of 40 percent.

Table 11 presents the forecast income statements of CRS for the years ended March 9, 1996, through 2000 assuming a 1 percent loss of revenues due to competition from Mr. Carnes.

TABLE 11

CRS's Forecast Income Statements Assuming a 1 Percent Loss in Revenues

	1996	*1997*	*1998*	*1999*	*2000*
Net sales[1]	$ 6,435,000	$ 7,271,550	$ 8,216,852	$ 9,285,042	$10,399,247
Less: Cost of sales	907,335	1,025,289	1,158,576	1,309,191	1,466,294
Equals: Gross profit	5,527,665	6,246,261	7,058,275	7,975,851	8,932,953
Less: Operating expenses	2,696,265	3,046,779	3,442,861	3,890,433	4,357,285
Equals: Net operating income	$ 2,831,400	$ 3,199,482	$ 3,615,415	$ 4,085,419	$ 4,575,669
Less: Taxes	1,132,560	1,279,793	1,446,166	1,634,167	1,830,268
Net income	**$1,698,840**	**$1,919,689**	**$2,169,249**	**$2,451,251**	**$2,745,401**

Note: Figures may be off due to rounding.

[1]Sales in 1996 have been multiplied by 99 percent of the $6,500,000 figure used in the non-competition forecast analysis ($6,500,000 × .99 = $6,435,000). Thereafter sales have been grown at the rates used in the non-competition forecast analysis.

EXHIBIT 15.1 *(Continued)*

[The next several tables have been omitted from this exhibit, but they were based on 5-, 10-, 15-, 20-, and 25-year analyses similar to this one.]

Having presented these analyses, the lost income calculated under each scenario is summarized in Table 12.

TABLE 12

Summary of Lost Income from Seller Competition

Lost Revenue	*1996*	*1997*	*1998*	*1999*	*2000*
1%	17,160	19,391	21,912	24,760	27,731
5%	85,800	96,964	109,558	123,801	138,657
10%	171,600	193,908	219,116	247,601	277,313
15%	171,600	281,167	317,718	359,022	402,104
20%	171,600	368,425	416,320	470,442	526,895
25%	171,600	368,425	505,062	570,721	639,207

As can be seen in Table 12, the greater the loss of sales, the greater the loss of income, and as a result, loss of cash flow. The question that needs to be answered after an analysis like this is, what is the most likely loss of revenue that would result from the competition of the seller? In order to answer this question, we reviewed numerous documents relating to this matter. We have highlighted that which we consider to be most relevant to our analysis.

The deposition of John Byrnes provided us with a significant amount of relevant information. Mr. Byrnes is, and was at the time of the CRS acquisition, Chief Operating Officer of Public Company Purchaser. From his deposition, it is clear that he is highly experienced in the respiratory therapy business as an industry insider.

On page 4 of his deposition, Mr. Byrnes explained his involvement in the acquisition of CRS by Public Company Purchaser. Mr. Byrnes indicated that he reviewed a "book" from Mr. Carnes's business brokers, and then attended a meeting with the brokers, John Carnes and Lori Rodgers. Mr. Byrnes indicated the reason he went to the meeting was "to see if Lori was capable of running the business herself." This is significant because it demonstrates that Public Company Purchaser believed Ms. Rodgers to be a key individual in the operations of CRS.

When asked if he knew of CRS and Mr. Carnes prior to their meeting in December 1994, he said, "We knew who they were and we knew that they're at four locations and were a good competitor." Later Mr. Byrnes was asked, "Why were you concerned about whether or not Ms. Rodgers would be able to run the company after the acquisition?" His response was, "Because the feeling I got was that Mr. Carnes wasn't coming in the acquisition." Mr. Byrnes was asked, "Did Public Company Purchaser have an interest in having Mr. Carnes continue on with the business in some capacity, if you recall?" Mr. Byrnes's reply was "No, we did not have an interest." This is a very clear statement that Public Company Purchaser's interest was in Lori Rodgers and not in John Carnes.

Mr. Byrnes was asked what Ms. Rodgers's role has been from the acquisition forward. His response was "Her title is an area manager. She runs the four Carnes locations. We opened up a City E office. She also runs several other locations for us now. She has several locations that report to her." Clearly Ms. Rodgers has shown the capabilities not only to effectively run what was CRS, but also the ability to take on these new locations.

When asked about the source of referrals that generate revenues for his company, Mr. Byrnes indicated that half come from doctors and half come from hospitals. Mr. Byrnes was asked how these referral relationships were maintained. He replied, "In Carnes's case, we continued to do exactly the same things that they were doing. They had four or five sales reps who called on hospitals, the doctors, the nursing agencies, who were willing to service their indigent patients who provided a high level of service." Mr. Byrnes was then asked, "Did you attempt to ascertain as part of the due diligence who had been responsible for generating the doctors, hospitals, and nurse referrals that Carnes Respiratory had?"

Mr. Byrnes responded that Public Company Purchaser had ascertained that information and "that it was the sales people who brought in the business." Mr. Byrnes was then asked, "Did you have any reason to believe that the relationships that existed with the doctors, nurses, and hospitals had been of long standing, namely initiated and started by Mr. Carnes himself?" Mr. Byrnes responded, "There's probably some in City A. But for the other locations outside of City A, I think it was the salespeople he hired." Mr. Byrnes was then asked a series of questions regarding the percentage of business CRS derived from each of its locations. His response indicated the following:

City A	25%
City D	15%
City B	40%
Total	80%

(Continued)

EXHIBIT 15.1 ***(Continued)***

In regard to the City B store, Mr. Byrnes was asked, "Did you attempt to ascertain or did you ascertain the role that Mr. Carnes individually had in initially establishing and having continuity in terms of the referral relationship?"

Mr. Byrnes answered, "It was Judy Clark that got the business there." Mr. Byrnes was asked how he was aware of this, and he responded "because when he opened in City B, I was the center manager there [for Public Company Purchaser]." Mr. Byrnes further commented that he "knew who was out calling on the docs."

From all of these questions and answers, it is clear that Mr. Byrnes is well versed in the local markets where CRS operated, and how the Company was generating its referrals. Mr. Byrnes's concerns were about the abilities of Lori Rodgers, as discussed above. Mr. Byrnes was later asked what his determination of Ms. Rodgers's abilities to run the locations was. He responded, "I thought she could." When asked why, Mr. Byrnes said, "She knew what was going on. She knew where the business was coming from. She knew what was going on in all four markets. And I just felt confident that she was on top of the business."

Another deposition that was helpful was that of Mr. Davidson, who was specifically asked about the non-compete agreement and how the value was derived. He responded as follows:

> As you know, we've been on a fairly active acquisition program for a number of years. From the beginning of 1991 through today, we've closed more than 70 acquisitions.
>
> Working with our independent auditors, we have determined that during 1995, we were basically allocating $50,000 per shareholder to the covenant. Because of the size of this transaction, which was—the business was larger than the normal business in the industry and larger than our normal acquisition, we felt it appropriate to increase that from 50,000 to 100,000 in terms of allocation of the purchase price to the covenant. So it was a standard calculation adjusted for the size of the business that we arrived at working with our outside auditors.

Although one could construe this statement as indicating that Public Company Purchaser applies a blind rule of thumb to the allocation of purchase price for a non-compete, we do not believe that is the case. As Mr. Davidson indicated, his company is very experienced in acquiring other companies. Their method of allocating to a non-compete is based on this experience, and as he mentioned, from working with Public Company Purchaser's independent auditors. At some point in this process, Public Company Purchaser, with its outside accountants' assistance, determined this to be an appropriate measure. This should also be held up against Public Company Purchaser's tax and accounting incentives. An allocation of purchase price to a non-compete agreement can be amortized over the life of the agreement. Goodwill on the other hand, is amortizable for financial statement purposes over 40 years. In prior years, goodwill was not at all deductible for income tax purposes. Now, it can be amortized over 15 years.

In addition, Public Company Purchaser is required by law to submit its financial statements to the Securities and Exchange Commission because of its status as a publicly traded company. These financial statements must fairly represent the financial condition of the company and have been audited by the company's outside accountant. In recording the allocation of purchase price, the company has a duty to fairly report it to its shareholders, and the independent accountant has opined to its fairness. Given these facts and circumstances, we do not believe that Public Company Purchaser's methodology is without merit.

The third Public Company Purchaser deponent was Robert G. Abbott, whose deposition pointed out two issues relevant to our analysis. The first issue is the importance of Lori Rodgers to Public Company Purchaser in the transaction.

Q. Now, in that regard, is that instrument or Ms. Rodgers's Employment Agreement with Public Company Purchaser pursuant to the terms of the agreement? Because I don't know why, but I was of the impression that Ms. Rodgers did not have a written Employment Agreement with Carnes Respiratory.

A. No. This is an Employment Agreement between Ms. Rodgers and Public Company Purchaser as a condition precedent to closing the acquisition.

The key is that her employment agreement with Public Company Purchaser was a precondition to the acquisition. Public Company Purchaser was concerned with locking her into the deal from the very beginning. The second issue is over the negotiation of the individual asset values.

Q. And did Mr. Gonzales or anyone on behalf of Mr. Carnes make any suggestion as to what the allocation should be or was the allocation something that was the product of Public Company Purchaser?

A. I do not believe anyone representing the seller or the seller himself made any suggestions as to what the allocation should be. I believe the process was we presented our good faith estimate of what the allocation should be and it was accepted by the seller after their review.

The importance of this response is that neither Mr. Carnes nor his representatives commented on the allocation of the asset values. This issue will be taken up again later in this report. The fourth and final Public Company Purchaser official deposed in this matter was Phillip Phillips. Mr. Phillips is Public Company Purchaser's controller. Mr. Phillips was deposed for the purposes of understanding more about Public Company Purchaser's acquisition process, and how Public Company Purchaser values individual assets, particularly covenants not to compete.

EXHIBIT 15.1 *(Continued)*

Mr. Phillips established that Public Company Purchaser does have a written policy as to how it allocates purchase prices. In establishing this, he stated:

> We have—using the term "protocol" or methodologies as to how we—how we come up with the end product of a purchase price allocation. That is, from the inception of the early—late 1990, '91 and '92 when we started acquiring businesses with our outside auditors, we developed that methodology.
>
> And it's been applied over that entire span of our acquisition program with very minor adjustments, very few in form and very few in substance. It's primarily the same methodologies from the time I started with the company in 1993.

The important points in this statement are that the methodology has been developed with Public Company Purchaser's outside auditor and that it has been applied over time with very little modification. Mr. Phillips goes on further to discuss how covenants are valued, and what the trend has been over time.

A. And the covenant, which is the second item—ready to go to the next one?—if you're in an asset and stock purchase, in each of those transactions, there is normally—with an asset purchase, there is one or more persons that are the influential persons in that business.

In a stock purchase, certainly there are shareholders that are oftentimes participants in the business in our industry, and they are the significant influencing persons involved in the business.

We value covenant based on the same methodology, the number of persons that are involved times an amount. And the amount in the case of March 9th of 1995 was $100,000 for the significant person involved in the Carnes Respiratory acquisition.

The methodology of using a number of persons involved times a dollar amount has been in place from 1994 through today. The only variation is that the dollar amount that we have assigned to each of those significant persons in the business has changed. It's continued to slide on a downward scale.

In 1994, we were valuing—when we were developing purchase price allocations, we were looking at businesses and saying—and we were buying from a different pool of sellers.

In this case, I don't think Mr. Carnes is a doctor. But in '94, we were buying many physician-owned practices. And you would often be buying for more than one person, and there's a—there's 12 shareholders. We were valuing those in that time frame from 50 to $100,000 per person.

Through the middle of '95, then we started to change the valuation to more in the $25,000 per person; in 1996, more in the 10,000, where today and for the last 12 to 18 months, we've been valuing each covenant based on the number of persons at $5,000 per person.

Q. Since that is truly the focus of our litigation, let me address that for a few moments.

A. Sure.

Q. The $100,000 number or $50,000 number, or whatever number may be used, where does that number come from?

A. It is purely an estimate based on management's ability to estimate what this covenant is valued to us internally.

There are two factors in this statement. First, that the dollar amount assigned to each shareholder has decreased through time. This indicates that Public Company Purchaser has seen what it believes to be trends in the value of non-compete agreements, and has adjusted its valuations accordingly. This further supports the notion that Public Company Purchaser's allocation is not arbitrary. Second, the value of the covenant is Public Company Purchaser's perception. This indicates that as an active participant in this market Public Company Purchaser does not believe that the owning individual is highly valuable to the success of the business.

A review of the deposition transcript of John Carnes also provides us with important information regarding the covenant not-to-compete. From reviewing Mr. Carnes's deposition transcript, we feel Mr. Carnes was very knowledgeable about his business and his industry. It appears that Mr. Carnes has good marketing skills and is a very effective teacher. These are both important skills in developing and growing a successful business in this industry. In addition, Mr. Carnes describes the importance of his employees and the level of service provided to customers in the success of CRS. The deposition covers topics from opening new locations, competition, and key employees, to marketing and referral development.

Mr. Carnes was asked about and discussed how CRS decided to open new locations. Key factors appeared to be a geographic area with an elderly population, and a sufficient potential referral base. In answering a question about how the actual decision process went, Mr. Carnes said:

> We'd take all my marketing people and I would think I'd see an area I thought would be good. I would visit it myself or I would have some kind of contact. And I would send all those marketing reps into the area, and they would talk with doctors about who they were using or how they were doing or how they could be, you know, handled better by a company. If we saw there was potential, then we would go there and open a facility.

(Continued)

EXHIBIT 15.1 ***(Continued)***

Mr. Carnes was asked why he opened the City D location. He responded:

> Carnes Respiratory continued to expand yearly looking for places that we thought we had potential business. And I had looked at purchasing a company down there one time and didn't. And then I thought it would be a good opportunity for Carnes to expand.
>
> So I expanded down there because I thought there would be some additional business, which, in that business, as always, you look for an older population of people that had some problems. That's why we moved there.

Mr. Carnes later discussed how City C differed in respect to why it was opened.

> No sir. We did that a little bit different than that. We had some doctors in City A that also covered City C. And so they were looking for some additional people. They wanted better coverage up there. So that helped make—there's more than just one reason you would decide to go there, but that was one of the major reasons to look at City C.
>
> And, again, it's an older population of people, which is what we were. We were government, Medicare—you needed older people—older sick people.

Training is a very important part of CRS' business. Employees who typically are not highly skilled when they began their employment at CRS must be trained to deliver a high level of service to CRS' patients. CRS' employees were trained in how to educate patients in using oxygen and other equipment. Mr. Carnes discussed the training of these individuals in-depth.

A. It would be delivered to the patient's home, and they would educate the patient in how the doctor prescribed the oxygen for him, and how the equipment worked.

Q. Okay. Would this be someone that had been trained in your operation to do this?

A. Yes, sir.

Q. This wouldn't be someone out of the labor pool—

A. No.

Q. —in City F or City B, would it?

A. No.

Q. This would be someone that you would recognize as having the degree of skill necessary to—

A. We had constant education programs at the company to educate everybody that came onboard. They all had to go through a training period or a training phase to do anything that was related to our company, whether it would be install a bedside commode or a walker. And we were governed by the joint commissions, which said that we were doing it in a proper safe manner for the patient.

Q. They were skilled people?

A. Well, you know, you don't hire them skilled. You hire them and then, you know, train them to do the job. So you weren't respiratory therapists or, you know, physical therapists or nurses, no, sir.

Q. Was there a difference between the truck driver and the person who actually took the tank to the patient?

A. No.

Q. Would that person that was trained by you—of course, he'd already know how to drive a truck, but, obviously, that person be trained by you, then, to take the tank inside and help the patient?

A. Yes, sir. Me or my staff trained them. Ninety percent of them I have trained myself.

Q. Was there some sort of formalized training you gave them? In other words, did you have some sort of brochure you followed or was it just based on your experience in the business?

A. Well, initially when we first did it, it was, you know, based around our experience the way—but when we became JCO certified or joint commissioned, then we had protocol that you had to follow, and it was a written procedure. We had a policy and procedure manual that we—Lori Rodgers, matter of fact, wrote our policy and procedure manual that joint commissions came in and inspected us and said, yes, we're following proper procedure with all the safety precautions and everything that should be done to maintain the health and safety for the patients with the equipment.

The quality of the services provided by CRS differentiated the Company from its competition. In discussing the quality of the services provided compared to its competition, Mr. Carnes felt that CRS was superior in all respects.

A. Not a chance.

Q. Is this because of the better training you provided your people?

EXHIBIT 15.1 ***(Continued)***

A. I think it was better training and just simply the way we maintained, you know, our equipment. And there was just never a question just from the physicians and the patients themselves and the referrals from social services workers at hospitals, nurses at hospitals. Your patients and word-of-mouth back to the physicians is what built Carnes Respiratory Services.

Q. And that's what I was going to ask you. Is it this quality of services that you—to which you attribute the obvious success of Carnes Respiratory Services in these areas?

A. I think we gave the best out there, yes, sir. Public Company Purchaser must think we gave pretty good, too, because they still carry our name in several of the locations. Even though they bought my company they still have my name on it.

Mr. Carnes answers a series of questions relating to competition from other companies in the oxygen business. Through his responses, he indicated that he did not believe any of the independent companies in his industry offered any significant competition to CRS. Mr. Carnes described CRS's competitive advantage as taking care of patients:

> And so you got business based around what your ability—the physician, he wanted his patients taken care of. I mean, that's what he was looking for. So whoever gave the best care to his patients is, you know, who he's normally going to use. And so it was a combination of a lot of things, and it was years. We didn't do it overnight. It took us, you know, 13 years to build that business.

In addition to providing high-quality service to patients, Mr. Carnes believed it was crucial to market these services to potential referral sources. When asked, Mr. Carnes discussed the importance of marketing and the marketing staff to CRS:

A. My marketing people met with me, not just—we had a meeting every week. There is no question about it. But it was daily that my marketing people would get on their radio or they had mobile phones in their car, that I talked to them constantly about, you know, this position, you need to do this. You need to do this. You need to do this hospital.

So my marketing people were in constant contact with me every day. My marketing people is the backbone and center of this whole thing. So did I spend the majority of my time with my marketing people? There is no question about that.

Q. How many marketing people did you meet with when you would meet weekly?

A. Whatever number we had. So what was it? Five maybe.

Q. That's what I'm asking. I don't know.

A. Yes, sir.

Q. Would that include Lori Rodgers or was she in addition to the marketing people that you're referring to?

A. Lori was a business director. That was her title. But it was not unusual for me to send Lori. If I had a big luncheon somewhere, if I had a special deal going on with a doctor, would I send Lori into one of the doctor's offices with the marketing person? Yes. That wasn't unusual for her to do that. It wasn't unusual for me to go to one myself.

The key to referrals is developing relationships with doctors, nurses, social workers, and certain hospital personnel. Mr. Carnes was asked about how significant referral sources were developed. His response to that question was:

> How you develop it was, it's a combination of a lot of things, but a lot of it depends on your reputation when you first did what you said you were going to do back in 1981, when Carnes Respiratory first started. You had to do what you said you were going to do.
>
> And one of the things that helped us more than anything is, we went out and we said, "We will have equipment in a patient's home within the hour." And so it was a reputation that you built over years of doing exactly what you said you were going to do and taking care of patients better than anybody else could take care of it. And that reputation rested, honest to God, with John Carnes, because it was Carnes Respiratory.

Referral development was discussed further with Mr. Carnes:

Q. When you—your sales personnel would call on a physician or a hospital, did you regard them as engaging in referral development at that point?

A. That was their job. So anything that they did—they might do a talk for a nursing service. They might go to a nursing service and put on a demonstration. They would take a driver with them and they would do, you know, a demonstration of how oxygen equipment would work, or if a nursing service, you know, wasn't sure where the low air loss mattress how it worked, we would use our marketing people to go put on a demonstration for a nursing service.

Mr. Carnes clearly believed that marketing was the key to his business, as he said, "Everything that you do is a marketing. Anything that you do good is going to be considered a marketing tool. So everything that we did is geared around making sure that we get referrals."

(Continued)

EXHIBIT 15.1 *(Continued)*

The discussion moved on to the subject of key personnel. One of the key individuals at CRS was Lori Rodgers. When asked to describe her role at CRS, Mr. Carnes responded:

A. Lori Rodgers started to work for me in City B for $5 an hour as a person to run the City B store. And from there she developed and was trained and aggressive about, and she ended up being the director for the business. She ran the businesses just like I would have done from years and years of training.

How good she is. She just was promoted this week to regional manager for Public Company Purchaser. She has the highest job, other than the CEO, here in State. She covers all of the State operations for them, which is their largest, by far, dollar volume dollarwise in their company. So how good is she? That's how good she is.

Q. What were her duties with CRS, Carnes Respiratory Services?

A. Yes, sir. Well, she started out, like I said, as a customer service person, and then, you know, from there, for different jobs, in charge of billing. And just finally, her title—I let her call herself whatever she wanted to—was director of business.

Q. Was that her title as of December of 1994?

A. Yes, sir.

Q. Okay. And what were her duties as of December 31, 1994?

A. She had, you know, combination of everything, to make sure that—you know, same as I would do. The drivers did what they were supposed to, the marketing people did what they were supposed to, billing, that we collected our money.

She met with—every time we had a marketing meeting, she was part of that. If I had a meeting with drivers, she was part of that. Many a times I would send her to—if I couldn't go to run one of the operations that I had problems, I would send her to City D or send her to City B or send her to City C to handle a situation that, you know, I didn't have time to get to.

So she did the same kind of things that I would have done if I couldn't get to them, or she was a part of what I wanted done. Like any CEO would do, that they would pass down to a president or someone under them to do things that, you know, needed to be done.

So did she—One of the biggest things she ever did for Carnes Respiratory, she wrote a manual—policies and procedures manual which was for joint commissions when we decided that we needed to be joint commissioned. Lori actually gathered the information and put this policy and procedure manual together that I would have had to spend $25,000 to get done. She did it for me in addition to her job. She did it on the weekends and at night and other times. So what did she do? She did everything.

Q. Did she have any responsibilities concerning the referral development?

A. Absolutely.

Q. What were those?

A. Again, you know, if we had a marketing—if one of the marketing people needed her to help support them in some way, did Lori go from the office into physicians' offices and take care of whatever needed to be done? Yes.

Q. What was—

A. That wasn't her major—that was not her major job, no.

Q. What was her major job?

A. All of it. But the marketing part would have just been one of the 10 other things that she did. Her job was to make sure that everything there—that she was part of everything that went on. Somebody that you can count on if you're not there, that you know is going to do everything that you would do, and make sure that if you did go on vacation or you did go skiing or you did something, that you knew it was going to get done right.

Mr. Carnes felt that there were several key people at CRS in addition to Ms. Rodgers, as indicated in the following discussion:

Q. Who did you regard as the management personnel of Carnes Respiratory Services in December of '94, other than yourself, obviously?

A. The key people?

Q. Yeah.

A. Key people at that point was Lori Rodgers, all of my marketing people. Judy Clark was really important. No question. She had tremendous—

EXHIBIT 15.1 *(Continued)*

Q. She is one of those four or five marketing people?

A. Yes. And Janie Wey; tremendously important.

Q. Another one of the marketing people?

A. Caroline Hanken; tremendously important. My other marketing person, Kathy Elston, at that time was fairly new. Wasn't near as effective, because she didn't have the time under her belt. She had a really tough territory.

God. Then, you know, my supervisor of my drivers was Johnie Goodson, my brother, a young lady by the name of Brenda Harrell, which ran my billing department for me, Cindy Jacobi.

From the deposition transcript, it is apparent that CRS's success is derived from the collaboration of several key individuals. As Mr. Carnes stated, the marketing representatives are the "backbone" of the Company. It also appears that Ms. Rodgers was very important to the business, as she worked in all facets of the business and was essentially interchangeable with Mr. Carnes. It appears that Mr. Carnes's skills lay in marketing and training. Mr. Carnes said that he performed over 90 percent of the training of all employees. This developed the skills of the employees, making them proficient at their jobs.

In addition to the Public Company Purchaser executives and John Carnes depositions, we also searched for other authoritative sources to assist in the valuation of the covenant not-to-compete. The value of non-compete agreements in the purchase and sale of a company has been the subject of numerous court cases involving the Internal Revenue Service ("IRS") and taxpayers. According to Neil C. Kelly, ASA, CFA, the IRS maintains a theory called the "mass asset" rule. Prior to tax reform, this theory held that certain intangible assets were "non-depreciable as a matter of law, because such intangible properties are part of a single mass asset, which, in the aggregate, has no determinable useful life and is either inextricably linked to goodwill or self-regenerating." According to Mr. Kelly, for a non-compete agreement to not fall under the mass asset rule, it must have the following components:

1. A recital to the effect that it is the intent of the parties that the covenant not to compete is separate and distinct from any goodwill the seller may be selling
2. That the subject covenant is not merely for the purpose of protecting the purchase goodwill
3. That the covenant has an independent basis-value
4. That the covenant was expressly bargained for—separate and distinct from the goodwill of the seller
5. That a specific monetary sum is being paid for the covenant
6. That the covenant is for a specified period of time—which goes to the permissible amortized period
7. That the covenant not to compete restrains a key individual from competing with the purchaser, and if same is not accomplished, that the purchaser will suffer an economic detriment because of the key person's ability and competitive activities
8. That even in the event of the death of the grantor of the covenant, such will not entitle the purchaser to depreciate or recover the cost of such covenant over a period shorter than the term of such a covenant
9. The amount the purchaser is paying for the covenant not to compete is depreciable over the life of the covenant regardless of whether the purchaser makes payments for such covenant over a period shorter than the life of the covenant
10. A recital to the effect that the value allocated to the covenant has economic reality or substance

In addition, guidance can be found in the four tests that the courts have historically applied to non-compete agreements in determining whether it could be amortized for federal income taxes. The four tests were summarized in *Forward Communications Corp. v. U.S.*, 78-2 USTC ¶ 9542, as follows:

1. Whether the compensation paid for the covenant is severable from the price paid for the acquired goodwill
2. Whether either party to the contract is attempting to repudiate an amount knowingly fixed by both the buyer and seller as allocable to the covenant
3. Whether there is proof that both parties actually intended, when they signed the sale agreement, that some portion of the price be assigned to the covenant
4. Whether the covenant is economically real and meaningful

The first test was effectively established in *Marsh & McLennan, Inc. v. Commissioner*, 51 T.C. 56 (1968), *aff'd on other grounds*, 420 F.2d 667 (3d Cir. 1969). In this case, the court looked at whether the compensation paid for the covenant is separable from the price for goodwill. Where goodwill and the covenant not to compete are closely related, the benefits of the elimination of competition may be permanent or of indefinite duration and, hence, the value of the covenant is not exhaustible or a wasting asset to be amortized over a limited period.

(Continued)

EXHIBIT 15.1 ***(Continued)***

In *Commissioner v. Danielson*, 378 F.2d 771 (3d. Cir.), *cert. denied* 389 U.S. 358 (1967), the courts looked at whether either party was attempting to repudiate an amount knowingly fixed by both as allocable to the covenant, the calculable tax benefit of which may fairly be assumed to have been a factor in determining the final price.

In *Annabelle Candy Co. v. Commissioner*, the courts looked at whether the covenant played a real part in the negotiations.

Although the valuation of a non-compete agreement is not concerned with whether or not the value is amortizable, these tests do provide meaningful guidance in the valuation process. In reviewing Mr. Kelly's points, we have determined the following:

1. Based on the asset purchase agreement, the parties intended for the covenant not to compete to have value separate and distinct from the value of goodwill.
2. It appears that Mr. Carnes was skilled in his business and would have the ability to compete with Public Company Purchaser. This does not indicate what level of competition Mr. Carnes might provide.
3. Based on our review, the covenant does have independent basis value as presented in Addendum 3.4 to the agreement.
4. The Agreement clearly lays out the allocation of purchase price. A series of documents dated between March 1 and March 9, 1995, between Robert G. Abbott, a member of Public Company Purchaser's acquisition group and Associate Corporate Counsel, and Mr. Carnes's attorney, Larry Gonzales, indicates that the asset purchase agreement and lease had been negotiated, as well as the value of the accounts receivable. In fact, Mr. Carnes appears to have been personally involved in this negotiation. In a fax transmittal dated March 1, 1995, from Rick Stevens of Richards & Associates, Inc. to Mr. Abbott, regarding the accounts receivable, Mr. Stevens writes "John believes a fair resolution would be additional consideration of $332,516. The excess over $600,000 as of stopping billing on February 28, 1995."

   Although there is no indication that Mr. Carnes or his representatives expressly bargained for the value of the covenant not to compete, they did negotiate the terms of the deal, as well as particular asset values. From this, we must conclude that Mr. Carnes and his advisors implicitly approved of the value of the covenant not to compete.
5. The agreement clearly states that $100,000 is being paid for the covenant not to compete.
6. The covenant is for a period of five years, after which it expires.
7. The covenant does constrain Mr. Carnes from competing and the same stated in 2 above holds here as well.
8. We are unaware of the impact the death of Mr. Carnes would have on Public Company Purchaser's ability to recover the cost over a shorter period of time.
9. The value of the covenant is depreciable over the life of the covenant even though payments for the covenant were made over a shorter period.
10. No recital of the economic reality of the covenant was found.

In reviewing the four tests put forth in *Forward Communications Corp. v. U.S.*, we found the following in regard to the Agreement:

1. The compensation paid is separable from goodwill, as it was expressly laid out in the Agreement.
2. We have found no evidence that Mr. Carnes repudiated or attempted to repudiate the allocation to the covenant offered by Public Company Purchaser.
3. Both parties clearly intended an allocation to be made to the covenant not to compete, as it is expressly laid out in the Agreement.
4. Based on Mr. Carnes's apparent skills and abilities, he appears to have an ability to compete. However, this is in no way an indication of the level of competition he could provide. Therefore, the covenant is economically real and meaningful.

Of particular importance, is whether the covenant was at issue in the negotiation process. This relates to the economic reality of the covenant and its economic significance. According to Kelly, the following are factors that are important in determining the economic reality of a non-compete agreement.

a. The presence of a grantor of the covenant not to compete having business expertise evidencing a formidable capability to compete
b. Grantor's ownership of technology and machinery necessary to compete
c. Grantor's possession of sufficient economic resources to compete
d. Legal enforceability of the covenant for the term of the particular covenant under state law
e. Grantor's legal capacity to compete
f. Covenant having sufficient scope to assure non-competition without overreaching
g. Not too advanced age of grantor

EXHIBIT 15.1 ***(Continued)***

h. Good health of grantor
i. Payments for covenant that are not pro rata to the grantor's stock ownership in the seller
j. Purchaser's policing of the covenant not to compete
k. Structuring payments under the covenant to occur over time and to cease upon breach of such covenant
l. Vigorous negotiations over the covenant and negotiations over its value should be recited in the agreement
m. A detailed, specific, and carefully drafted covenant not to compete
n. Independent appraisal of the value of the covenant not to compete
o. Some degree of reasonableness in the percentage of the considerations allocated to the covenant and other items

The importance of the covenant not to compete having economic substance was further delineated by a Bureau of National Affairs' paper on the subject published in 1992. The paper stated:

> The most important factor is whether the covenant is economically real, that is, whether the covenant is the product of bona fide bargaining rather than a sham. The economic reality theory is primarily concerned with business realities which would cause reasonable persons, genuinely concerned with their economic future, to bargain for the covenant not-to-compete.

Among the facts to be considered are whether the seller could actually compete with the purchaser. Where the seller is, objectively, likely to be a competitor, the paper states that courts have also looked at the actual contract negotiations to determine if the parties' intentions were for the covenant not to compete to have value:

> In addition, the amount allocated to the covenant not-to-compete may not reflect economic reality. The taxpayer has the burden of proving that he is entitled to the deduction. Welch v. Helvering, 290 U.S. 111 (1933). Courts have frequently found that covenants have no value or, at least, substantially less value than the purchaser attributes to them. The same factors as above have been considered for this purpose. Further, courts have looked at the actual contract negotiations to determine if the parties intended the covenant to have any value. For example, if the parties agreed to pay a certain amount for the assets of the seller and the purchase price is not altered when a covenant not-to-compete is later added, the covenant has no or minimal value.

Other guidance on determining the value of a covenant not to compete is given in Revenue Ruling 77-403. The ruling states that the relevant factors for determining the value of a non-compete agreement include:

> (1) Whether in the absence of the covenant the covenantor would desire to compete with the covenantee; (2) the ability of the covenantor to compete effectively with the covenantee in the activity in question; and (3) the feasibility, in view of the activity and market in question, of effective competition by the covenantor within the time and area specified in the covenant.

Based on the issues presented by Kelly in regard to the mass asset rule, the covenant is a distinguishable asset that can be valued separately from goodwill. Further, the covenant in the Public Company Purchaser-CRS deal appears to pass the four tests from *Forward Communication Corporation v. U.S.* Tests 2 and 3 are of particular importance here. The importance of test 2 is that after Public Company Purchaser proposed the allocation to the covenant, Mr. Carnes and his advisor did not attempt to repudiate or negotiate it, although they did negotiate several other items in the agreement. As a result, we believe the covenant is economically real. Test 3 is significant because the allocation to the covenant is clearly made in the agreement.

From the deposition of various Public Company Purchaser executives, we learned that Public Company Purchaser has developed a methodology for allocating a portion of the acquisition price to covenants with the assistance of its outside accountant. In addition, we know that Public Company Purchaser is a major player in the industry and has been undergoing a major acquisition program. Therefore, Public Company Purchaser's actions appear to be reflective of market conditions.

As Mr. Davidson states, "Public Company Purchaser's interest in CRS was due to its good locations, respiratory therapy control and good reputation." According to Mr. Byrnes, he did not believe that Mr. Carnes held many of the referral relationships personally. In fact, Mr. Byrnes knew first hand that in City B, Judy Clarke was generating the referrals. Mr. Byrnes believed that Mr. Carnes may have originally held some of the relationships in City A. This puts Mr. Carnes's control of the referral base at less than 25 percent.

As we know from Mr. Carnes, additional relationships were developed by the marketing representative in that territory. It was also the marketing person's responsibility to maintain existing relationships. In addition, from Mr. Carnes's deposition, we understand that the marketing people are critical to the success of CRS.

We also learned from Mr. Carnes that he was responsible for over 90 percent of the training of these individuals, as well as the other employees of the Company. Mr. Carnes has imparted a great deal of his knowledge and expertise to these individuals. It appears this has occurred to a large extent with Ms. Rodgers, who did everything Mr. Carnes did for the Company.

Ms. Rodgers's talents were recognized by Public Company Purchaser, who ensured that she was part of the acquisition by making an employment agreement with her a prerequisite to the acquisition closing. According to Mr. Byrnes, Public Company Purchaser's interest was always in Ms. Rodgers, and Public Company Purchaser had no interest in retaining the services of Mr. Carnes. We believe Mr. Byrnes to be credible on this issue because Public Company Purchaser did not offer Mr. Carnes an employment contract prior to the closing of the acquisition.

(Continued)

EXHIBIT 15.1 ***(Continued)***

If Public Company Purchaser felt that Mr. Carnes was essential to the business because he held many personal relationships, then it would be a prudent business decision to bring Mr. Carnes along with the acquisition, and lock him into an employment contract for a period of time that allows for a transfer of these relationships. In this type of a situation, a buyer needs to ensure the transferability of what it is purchasing. Relationships take time to develop. They cannot be transferred overnight.

An employment contract is typically used to retain the services of the seller as an employee of the acquirer for a specified period of time. Typical time periods range from six months to two years. During the term of the employment contract, the business seller assists the buyer in the transitioning of the business. Prudence dictates that such an agreement should be in place before closing, as was the agreement with Lori Rodgers. Yet Public Company Purchaser had no interest in such an arrangement with Mr. Carnes. From this position, one can reasonably infer that Public Company Purchaser did not believe that Mr. Carnes was important to the successful transition of the customers and referral sources to Public Company Purchaser.

Using all of this information, we have determined that Mr. Carnes would be able to provide a minimal loss of business to the CRS locations acquired by Public Company Purchaser. Mr. Carnes created a company of highly skilled individuals and significantly reduced CRS's reliance on himself. In addition, Lori Rodgers, the person who was most crucial to the deal taking place has been tied up in an employment contract by Public Company Purchaser. As a result, we believe that only a small portion of the sales could be diverted if CRS continued to compete with Public Company Purchaser. Therefore, we have selected 10 percent as the percentage of sales that CRS could divert from Public Company Purchaser.

Based on a lost sales analysis of 10 percent, we have determined that the lost income attributable to the covenant not-to-compete is as follows:

1996	*1997*	*1998*	*1999*	*2000*
$ 171,600	$ 193,908	$ 219,116	$ 247,601	$ 277,313

The estimated cash flows attributable to the lost income, calculated in a manner similar to what we calculated previously, are as follows:

1996	*1997*	*1998*	*1999*	*2000*
$ 22,471	$ 88,164	$ 116,897	$ 149,365	$ 185,730

The major difference between the lost net income and the cash flow is the level of capital expenditures, which far outpaces depreciation expense. These items were treated in a consistent manner when the valuation of CRS was previously performed. However, since management of the company can change the level of capital expenditures, we believe that it would be more prudent to discount the lost earnings, rather than cash flow, in valuing the covenant.

The value of the covenant not to compete is the present value of the lost income to the buyer. Using a discount rate of 24 percent, this equates to the value of the covenant being $578,766, or $579,000 rounded. The discount rate used is based on a discount rate applicable to cash flow of 18 percent, with a 6 percent premium due to the increased risk of earnings over cash flow.

The covenant not to compete is a less predictable asset and has several risk factors associated with it. In reviewing Kelly's factors pertaining to the economic reality of the covenant, we find the following:

1. Mr. Carnes has the expertise necessary to compete. Mr. Carnes has proven to be quite knowledgeable about his business, and by all accounts has been very successful.
2. Mr. Carnes has the financial resources necessary to compete. Given the low cost of doing business and Mr. Carnes's financial assets, Mr. Carnes reasonably has the economic capacity to compete.
3. Mr. Carnes is not advanced in age nor is he of diminished health that would keep him from competing.
4. Very little of the purchase price was structured over time. Only $500,000 was not paid at closing and this was for accounts receivable. Several of Kelly's factors also serve to reduce the risk associated with the covenant.
5. The covenant has sufficient scope to insure non-competition. This reduces the risks associated with violation of the covenant.
6. There is no technology or machinery that Mr. Carnes owns that would enable him to compete. In addition, CRS is a marketing-based business, and individuals other than Mr. Carnes are in control of many of the relationships.

As a result of these factors, we have selected an 18 percent discount rate for the covenant not to compete. It was increased by 6 percent to reflect the earnings premium. It should be noted that this rate does not reflect the level of competition that could be put forth by Mr. Carnes, but only the risk associated with Mr. Carnes competing.

As a test for reasonableness of the amount allocated to the covenant not to compete, we examined information available in the public domain. As a result of the respiratory therapy industry's current consolidation mode, we have reviewed the Securities and Exchange Commission's filings of publicly traded companies in the respiratory product and medical equipment sales and rental industry, to gain some insight into their acquisition practices and how they allocate purchase price to intangible assets, and non-compete agreements, in particular.

EXHIBIT 15.1 *(Continued)*

We reviewed the 1995 10-K filings for Apria Healthcare Group; American Home Patient, Inc.; Complete Management, Inc.; Interwest Home Medical, Inc.; Public Company Purchaser; Pediatric Services of America, Inc.; and Rotech Medical Corp. From these documents, we attempted to isolate information relating to how they allocated the purchase prices of their acquisitions. Although all of these companies discuss their acquisition in one form or another, only Public Company Purchaser and Pediatric Services of America ("PSA") provided enough detail to be meaningful to our analysis. As a result, we analyzed Public Company Purchaser's 10-Ks for 1993 through 1995, and PSA's 1995 filings.

In the notes to its consolidated financial statements, Public Company Purchaser discloses the purchase price of its acquisitions for the year and the allocation of the total purchase. Public Company Purchaser divides the allocation between current assets, fixed assets, identified intangibles, and goodwill. Table 13 presents this data for 1993 through 1995. Table 14 presents each item as a percentage of the year's total acquisition purchase price.

TABLE 13

Breakdown of Public Company Purchaser, Inc.'s Total Acquisitions by Year, 1993–1995

	1995	*1994*	*1993*	*Average*
Current assets	$ 8,097	$ 2,915	$ 1,704	$ 6,358
Property and equipment	4,731	4,024	2,828	3,861
Intangible assets	12,056	11,613	7,277	10,315
Goodwill	46,050	43,000	14,195	34,415
	$70,934	$61,552	$26,004	$54,949

TABLE 14

Breakdown of Public Company Purchaser, Inc.'s Total Acquisitions by Year as a Percentage of Total Acquisitions, 1993–1995

	1995	*1994*	*1993*	*Average*
Current assets	11.4%	4.7%	6.6%	11.6%
Property and equipment	6.7%	6.5%	10.9%	7.0%
Intangible assets	17.0%	18.9%	28.0%	18.8%
Goodwill	64.9%	69.9%	54.6%	62.6%
	100.0%	100.0%	100.0%	100.0%

From Table 13, it is clearly seen that the largest component of the acquisition costs for each year was goodwill, followed by identified intangibles. Of particular importance to this analysis is the allocation to identifiable intangible assets. Public Company Purchaser, as we will show later in this report, typically only identifies patient records and non-compete agreements. Therefore, we have made the assumption that the identified intangible assets line in Table 14 contains only these two types of assets. As can be seen in the data, these assets represented 17, 18.9, and 28 percent of the total purchase prices in 1995, 1994, and 1993, respectively.

As a major player in this industry, Public Company Purchaser's economic decisions are reflective of market conditions. Total acquisition purchase price for 1995 was $70,934,000. This represented the accumulation of 20 separate and distinct transactions. Each of these was negotiated with an arm's-length (nonrelated) party. Most of these businesses were much smaller than CRS, as total revenues for the acquired companies, excluding CRS, were $38.4 million, or an average of approximately $2 million. In 1993, Public Company Purchaser acquired 15 companies with revenues of $18 million or $1.2 million each. In 1994, Public Company Purchaser acquired 24 companies with $35 million in revenues, or $1.46 million each. As a result, the data taken from Public Company Purchaser's 10-Ks provide us with a guide from the marketplace for the combined values of a non-compete agreement and a customer list. This guide indicates that on a combined basis, these assets should constitute 17.0 to 18.8 percent of the purchase price, based on Public Company Purchaser's 1995 acquisitions and the three-year weighted average, respectively.

On October 3, 1994, PSA bought Oxygen Specialties, Inc. (OSI) for $4.9 million. OSI was a medical equipment company located in New Orleans. According to PSA's Form 10-K, $200,000 of the purchase price was paid for the non-compete agreement. This represents approximately 4.1 percent of the purchase price.

In our valuation, we determined the value of the covenant not to compete and the patient records (customer list) to be $2,450,000, and the covenant to be $579,000. Based on a total value of $13,500,000, the total of the covenant plus the patient records amounts to 18.06 percent of the total, and the covenant alone amounts to 4.3 percent of the total. This demonstrates the reasonableness of our calculations.

(Continued)

EXHIBIT 15.1 *(Continued)*

Allocation of the Covenant Not to Compete Between CRS and John Carnes, Individually

In addition to the issue of the economic reality of the covenant, the allocation of the covenant is significant in determining personal goodwill. A common practice in asset purchases is for the non-compete agreement to name the selling company, and its shareholders, as being subject to the non-compete. This is exactly the case in the sale of assets to Public Company Purchaser. The agreement was between Public Company Purchaser as the purchaser and CRS and John W. Carnes as the sellers. The issue becomes one of allocating the non-compete between the company, which results in corporate goodwill, and John Carnes, resulting in personal goodwill.

Carnes Respiratory Services developed an excellent reputation for the services it provided to clients. This reputation is, in large part, the corporation's, and not Mr. Carnes's. Mr. Carnes has done an excellent job, over the years, in training personnel, teaching his marketing people, and transferring his importance to other members of the company. Earlier in the business's formation, there can be no doubt that John Carnes was CRS. However, over the years there has been a clear transition to other members of the company. In fact, it was Lori Rodgers, and not John Carnes, who Public Company Purchaser insisted sign an employment contract with the firm as a prerequisite to a deal.

Recognizing the fact that Mr. Carnes is no longer required to provide a personal service to the patients, referral sources and others, we do not see there being any economic reason to allocate any of the covenant not to compete to Mr. Carnes personally. We further believe that the deposition transcripts reviewed and cited throughout our report justify our position.

Summary

The fair market value of Carnes Respiratory Services as of March 9, 1995, was $13,500,000. The allocation of the purchase price of the Company as of the same date is as follows:

Accounts receivable	$ 550,000
Inventory	40,000
Fixed assets	712,000
Trademark	2,134,000
Patient records	1,859,000
Covenant not to compete—CRS	579,000
Covenant not to compete—John W. Carnes	0
Goodwill	7,626,000
Fair market value	**$13,500,000**
Buyer's premium	1,535,000
Price paid by Public Company Purchaser	**$15,035,000**

The equitable distribution value of Carnes Respiratory Services, Inc. as of March 9, 1995, was $16,900,000, consisting of the following:

Price paid by Public Company Purchaser	$15,035,000
Retained assets	1,900,000
Total	$16,935,000
Rounded	$16,900,000

Valuation of Other Marital Assets

Over the past several years, new assets have joined the cadre of items being considered in the marital estate. Once again, the courts are trying to be fair to the non-professional spouse. Rather than treating certain items as an ability to pay additional support, the courts have found these items to be marital assets. Some of the items included in this group are professional licenses and celebrity goodwill.

Professional Licenses

The value of a professional license is frequently considered to be part of professional goodwill. In New York, the *O'Brien*[14] case provided that a professional license had value, even when there was no professional goodwill. In fact, the professional practice had not yet been started. In this case, Mrs. O'Brien worked so that Dr. O'Brien could attend medical school. About two months after Dr. O'Brien received his medical license and began serving a residency in general surgery, he filed for a divorce.

Clearly, there could be no professional goodwill in this case, since Dr. O'Brien has not started his practice yet. However, Mrs. O'Brien's expert valued the professional license on the basis that it had value due to the enhanced earning capacity provided to Dr. O'Brien. A comparison was made between the average income of a college graduate to the average income of a general surgeon. This difference was capitalized over Dr. O'Brien's expected working life adjusted for factors such as the time value of money and mortality.

Because New York started treating professional licenses as marital assets subject to distribution, additional issues have arisen. Arguments have now been raised that where the license holder has maintained a professional practice for a long period of time, the license has merged with the practice and no value should be given to the professional license. This concept was challenged in *McSparron v. McSparron.*[15]

In *McSparron*, the court stated:

> Application of the merger doctrine is particularly inimical to the statutory purposes because it generally favors the non-licensed spouse in a shorter marriage over the non-licensed spouse who is faced with rebuilding his or her economic life after the break-up of a long-term marriage. . . . In view of these logical and practical difficulties, we conclude that the letter and spirit of our holding in O'Brien is best served by eliminating the concept of "merger" from the inquiry. The merger doctrine should be discarded in favor of a common-sense approach that recognizes the ongoing independent vitality that a professional license may have and focuses solely on the problem of valuing that asset in a way that avoids duplicative awards. . . . Care must be taken to ensure that the monetary value assigned to the license does not overlap with the value assigned to other marital assets that are derived from the license such as the licensed spouse's professional practice.

Celebrity Goodwill

New Jersey was always famous for its turnpike. In fact, whenever I tell someone that I live in the Garden State, I am asked, "Near what exit on the turnpike?" Now we are on the map as the home of *The Sopranos*. But New Jersey also started a trend that may be nothing to be proud of. Joe Piscopo, comedian and entertainer, probably did not find it funny or entertaining when the New Jersey Superior Court found that he had a marital asset, with value, called *celebrity goodwill.*[16] The concept of celebrity goodwill is based on the premise that the enhanced earnings capacity of a celebrity is marital property. The determination of value in this case was made by applying a percentage to gross revenues of three of the last five years. New York, once again not wanting to be too far behind, ended up with two cases of its own, *Golub v. Golub*[17] and *Elkus v. Elkus.*[18] This craziness is catching on like wildfire.

[14]*O'Brien v. O'Brien*, 66 N.Y. 2d 576 (1985).

[15]*McSparron v. McSparron*, No. 260, 1995 WL 722880 (N.Y.App. Dec. 7, 1995).

[16]*Piscopo v. Piscopo*, 231 N.J. Super. 576.

[17]*Golub v. Golub*, 527 N.Y.S. 2d.

[18]*Elkus v. Elkus*, 572 N.Y.S. 2d 901 (App. Div. 1991), *review denied* 588 N.E.2d 99 (N.Y. 1992).

Conclusion

If you plan to do divorce valuations, make sure that you become familiar with the law of the land. Don't get caught up in the craziness of the litigation or the clients will most likely make you nuts. Do your valuation with the integrity and objectivity that is expected in any professional engagement.

If I did my job right, this chapter should have familiarized you with some of the nuances of the divorce valuation process. You should have even gotten a lesson on valuing a covenant not to compete. Remember that really long exhibit? It wasn't that long ago. Since we have had so much fun, let's move on.

16

Professional Practice Valuations

Chapter Goals

In this chapter, I will attempt to:

1. Discuss the reasons for valuing professional practices
2. Discuss the characteristics of a professional practice
3. Distinguish between valuations of professional practices and other types of businesses
4. Discuss engagement-specific matters

Overview

Valuations performed for professional practices frequently have unique aspects associated with them. Professional practices, by their very nature, are different from most businesses. Therefore, the appraiser must truly understand the attributes of each type of practice that may be valued. Professional practices, whether accounting practices, medical practices, engineering practices, or other practice, will all be similar but different. Yes, it is contradictory.

Before you can value a professional practice, a good starting point is to understand what is meant by a profession. The term *profession* means:

> A vocation or occupation requiring special, usually advanced, education, knowledge, and skill—e.g., law or medical professions. Also refers to whole body of such profession. The labor and skill involved in a profession is predominantly mental or intellectual, rather than physical or manual. The term originally contemplated only theology, law, and medicine, but as applications of science and learning are extended to other departments or affairs, other vocations also receive the name, which implies professed attainments in special knowledge as distinguished from mere skill.[1]

The valuation of professional practices will have many common aspects with the valuation of professional service firms. For example, the valuation techniques used to value a medical practice may be similar to the valuation of a tax preparation service business. Clearly, there will be differences between these two types of firms. Hopefully, by the end of this chapter, you will agree.

[1]Henry C. Black, *Black's Law Dictionary* (St. Paul, Minn.: West Publishing Co., 1997), 1210.

Why Are Professional Practices Valued?

A long time ago, back in Chapter 1, I provided you with a list that looked like this:

- Mergers and acquisitions
- Allocation of purchase price
- Estate and gift taxes
- Marital dissolution
- Employee stock ownership plans
- Liquidation or reorganization of a business
- Buy-sell agreements
- Stockholder disputes
- Financing
- Ad valorem taxes
- Incentive stock option considerations
- Initial public offerings
- Damages litigation
- Insurance claims
- Charitable contributions
- Eminent domain actions

Well, guess what? Most of these same reasons apply here. The reasons we see most often can be narrowed down to the following:

- Mergers and acquisitions
- Estate and gift taxes
- Marital dissolution
- Buy-sell agreements
- Stockholder/partner disputes
- Damages litigation

These are probably the major reasons for valuing professional practices. As with all valuations, the purpose and function of the valuation will impact the manner in which you will proceed.

Characteristics of the Professional Practice

The professional practice differs from other types of business because of its unique characteristics. These include the following:

- It is generally a service business where the tangible assets are considerably less than the intangible assets.
- There is a strong relationship between the professional and the client or patient that is based on the professional's reputation.
- The professional practice, more often than not, depends on a strong referral system to get new clients or patients.

- The professional is frequently licensed, regulated, or certified by a governmental or regulatory agency and/or professional organizations.
- In order to get licensed or accredited, most professionals are required to obtain an undergraduate degree as well as maintain some level of continuing education to keep their licenses or certifications.

Each of these aspects is pretty self-explanatory, so there is little need to expand on them.

Professional Practice Versus Other Business Valuations

Valuing professional practices will require the appraiser to follow the same general guidelines as with other types of business enterprises. Obviously, with most of the value being in the intangible assets, the professional practice will be much more oriented toward a market or income approach. An asset approach could be used, but you would have to find a suitable manner in which to value the intangible assets. There is the excess earnings method, but I said suitable! All kidding aside, the excess earnings method should result in the same value as in the income approach since the tangible assets are relatively small. Whether you are capitalizing the entire earnings stream or the majority of the earnings stream (the excess earnings), using the proper capitalization rates will get you to the same place. An example appears in Exhibit 16.1.

EXHIBIT 16.1
Capitalization of Earnings Versus Excess Earnings

Adjusted Book Value

As of September 22, 1999, the adjusted book value of the tangible assets of Dental Associates was as follows:

Total assets	$ 309,703
Total liabilities	51,118
Adjusted book value	$ 258,585
Rounded	$ 259,000

Goodwill—Excess Earnings Method

In addition to the value of the physical assets of Dental Associates, it is necessary to determine whether any goodwill exists and if so, what value to place on that goodwill.

Now that normalized earnings have been determined, a calculation must be performed to determine a reasonable return on the net assets of the practice. This must be subtracted from the economic net income to determine the excess earnings to be capitalized.

The adjusted tangible net assets of the practice have previously been determined to be approximately $259,000. If this amount was placed in an investment with risk similar to that of the components of these net assets, a certain amount of income would be generated, regardless of whether or not the business was operating. For this reason, the goodwill calculation requires the return on the net assets to be removed, as the income that would be generated from an alternative investment would not be part of the intangible value of the practice.

According to our research, in September 1999, corporate bonds (Aaa) were paying 7.96 percent, on average. A reasonable rate of return on the net assets would be 12 percent, in light of the fact that the net assets are not highly risky. This results in excess earnings being calculated as follows:

Normalized economic income	$ 148,135
Return on net assets ($259,000 × 12%)	31,080
Excess earnings	$ 117,055

Capitalizing excess earnings (pretax) at a rate of 30 percent results in an intangible value (goodwill) of $390,183 for this practice.

(Continued)

EXHIBIT 16.1 ***(Continued)***

Combining the tangible and intangible assets and liabilities yields the following result:

Assets other than goodwill	$ 309,703
Goodwill	390,183
Total assets	$ 699,886
Less: Liabilities	51,118
Estimate of value	$ 648,768
Rounded	$ 649,000

Capitalization of Historic Earnings

Another method of valuation, which places an emphasis on the earnings stream of the practice, is the capitalization of historic earnings method. This method capitalizes the entire income stream based on the earnings power of the net assets. Thus, an appropriate capitalization rate must be selected that would be appropriate for this income stream.

The normalized economic income for the practice was determined to be $148,135. Capitalizing this amount by 23 percent results in the value of this practice being $644,065, or $644,000 rounded.

The example in Exhibit 16.1 reflects the fact that there should not be a major difference between the estimates of value that you get when using the excess earnings method versus the capitalization of earnings method. You should already be familiar with that from Chapter 8. However, since most professional practices do not have substantial amounts of assets, most of the income stream will be attributable to the intangible assets of the practice. In these situations, the excess earnings will be very similar to the earnings stream being capitalized in a single-period capitalization model. This means that the capitalization rate for the income stream and the excess earnings should be relatively close. In fact, the capitalization rate must be high enough to reflect the risk associated with the income stream being predominantly derived from the intangible assets. They are clearly more risky than the tangible assets.

Buy-Sell Agreements

Many professional practices have buy-sell agreements in place to prevent fights over value in the event that a buyout must occur. Many of these agreements contain formulas that have nothing to do with the economic reality of the situation. This frequently causes fights among the owners. You should always read the agreement to determine if there is a mandatory provision regarding the determination of value. In certain circumstances, this will have to be the valuation methodology that the appraiser will follow. However, in other circumstances, that may not be the case. For example, in certain jurisdictions, these types of agreements may not be considered indicative of value for a marital dissolution case.

Sometimes, the buy-sell agreement may be the manner in which partners and/or stockholders come and go on a regular basis from a firm, thereby creating internal transactions or a market for the interest. Revenue Ruling 59-60 tells us to consider (factor number 7) the "sales of the stock and the size of the block of stock to be valued." Internal transactions may be the best indication of fair market value. However, be careful to properly understand the formula contained in these agreements. Many times, they are established to be punitive for owners who leave before retirement, disability, or death. The owners all agree that they do not want to finance each other if they choose to leave the practice and compete with the old firm.

Exhibit 16.2 demonstrates a simple calculation pursuant to a buy-sell agreement. In this example, three owners signed a stockholders' agreement that included a formula to calculate the value of the dental practice in the event one of the shareholders was to be bought out.

EXHIBIT 16.2
Buy-Sell Formula

Based on the formula, the value of Dental Associates would be:

50% gross receipts	$ 618,700
Plus:	
Fair market value of furniture & equipment	60,175
Inventory	3,500
95% of accounts receivable	186,909
Less:	
Liabilities	(51,118)
Value of Class A common stock	$ 818,166
Plus:	
Class B common stock[1]	3,500
Value of practice	**$ 821,666**
Rounded	**$ 822,000**

[1]According to the agreement, the Class B stock is to be valued at the price of $1,000 per share. At the date of the valuation, three and a half shares were outstanding.

Internal Transactions

The nature of professional practices is such that many times internal transactions can be used to determine the value of a fractional interest in the firm. Many firms have buy-sell agreements that outline how owners will come and go. In certain types of valuations, e.g., divorce, these may not be considered. Check with the attorney about the case law in the jurisdiction that you are working in. Sometimes, a review of prior transactions can also assist the appraiser in estimating the value of the firm, or at least the interest in the firm. Let's look at an example where there was a transaction. Exhibit 16.3 illustrates what happened.

Exhibit 16.3 contains a calculation of a one-third interest in the dental practice. The problem that the appraiser might face is using this information to estimate the value of a controlling interest in the practice. In theory, you could add a control premium to the minority result determined, but practically speaking, where would you get empirical evidence to support the size of the premium? Years ago, we went to *Mergerstat Review* as a basis of the premium. Today, I would not touch that with a 10-foot pole! Clearly, the public market strategic premiums cannot offer even a little assistance in determining the correct premium for a local dental practice. You do not have a choice but to be subjective, but be reasonable.

Another example is illustrated in Exhibit 16.4.

External Transactions

Sometimes, instead of there being an internal transaction, the practice may have acquired another practice, or a portion of one, that can be used to determine some formula that can be applied to the entire practice. The appraiser should obtain as much information about the acquisition as possible. At a minimum, get the contract, closing documents, financial disclosures made by the seller, and any due diligence performed by the acquirer or the acquirer's accountant. This can assist you in using this data. Exhibit 16.5 illustrates a small portion of a report where there was only limited data supplied by the doctor (non-client) in a divorce litigation.

EXHIBIT 16.3
Internal Transaction

Prior Transaction

As discussed in the "History of the Dental Practice," on January 1, 1989, Dr. Black signed an agreement with Drs. Brown and Green to purchase one-third of the dental practice. The terms of the purchase were that Dr. Black would receive a reduced salary ($85,000 in comparison to $160,000) for a seven-and-a-half-year period. At the end of this period, Dr. Black would own 50 shares of the Class A common stock, or one-third of the stock.

In order to determine the value of the dental practice at the time of the buy-in, it is necessary to discount the payments (the $75,000 salary differential) back to the date of the original transaction. At the time of the transaction, low-grade corporate bonds (Baa) were paying 10.73 percent (*Federal Reserve Bulletin*, April 1989). This transaction is considerably riskier than corporate bonds, so the discount rate used was 20 percent.

The value of a one-third interest in Dental Associates at January 1, 1989, is calculated as follows:

Year	*Amount*	*Discounted at 20%*
1989	$ 75,000	$ 62,500
1990	75,000	52,083
1991	75,000	43,403
1992	75,000	36,169
1993	75,000	30,141
1994	75,000	25,117
1995	75,000	20,931
1996	37,500	9,534
Value of one-third interest as of January 1, 1989		$279,898

EXHIBIT 16.4
Internal Transaction

Buyout of Shareholder

One method to use in determining the value of the practice is to consider past transactions in the practice itself. Pursuant to Revenue Ruling 59-60, the appraiser should consider as one factor in an appraisal "sale of stock and size of the block of the stock to be valued" of the subject company. One such transaction has taken place in this instance.

As previously discussed, the current shareholders of the practice bought out the interest of the former third shareholder, Timothy Gottfried, in July 2000 for a total consideration of $62,500. The amount of $25,000 was paid to Mr. Gottfried in July 2000, and the remaining $37,500 was paid in March 2001. Of the buyout $1,000 was allocated to the common stock held by Mr. Gottfried, resulting in the treasury stock on the practice's books. Mr. Gottfried was formerly a one-third owner in the practice; therefore, the total consideration paid to him represents the purchase of 33.33 percent of the practice's common stock.

Since no interest was paid on the deferred payment, the cash value of this payment must be calculated to determine the actual purchase price paid by the practice for Mr. Gottfried's shares. Calculating the present value of this payment at a discount rate of 8 percent results in a present value of $35,400, rounded. Therefore, the total purchase price paid for Mr. Gottfried's 33.33 percent interest in The Law Firm was $60,400 ($25,000 plus $35,400).

The value of Mr. Gottfried's 33.33 percent interest in The Law Firm represents a minority interest in the practice. Since a minority interest lacks the prerogatives of control, these interests tend to sell at a discount from the pro rata value of the entire entity. In order to estimate the control value of this interest, it is appropriate to add a control premium. Therefore, an estimate of the enterprise value on a control basis can be determined as follows:

Purchase price	$ 60,400
Interest purchased	33.33%
Minority value for 100 percent	$ 181,200
Control premium (30%)	54,360
Control value for 100 percent	$ 235,560
Rounded	$ 236,000

EXHIBIT 16.5
External Transaction

Purchase of Johnson Practice

In the history section of this report, we discussed Dr. Peters's purchase of Dr. Johnson's practice. Although Dr. Peters did not gain many new patients as a result of this transaction, the transaction itself can be used as a methodology for valuing Dr. Peter's practice.

Dr. Peters bought Dr. Johnson's patient list for $80 per patient. This did not include any of the other assets of the practice.

Utilizing this methodology results in a calculation of value as follows:

Patient list ($80 × 4,109)	$ 328,720
Other assets (net)	41,000
Value	$ 369,720
Rounded	$ 370,000

Subsequent Events

This section does not pertain only to professional practices. However, I put it here because I have an example of how it applied in the valuation of a professional practice. In reality, it could have been any kind of business. Although valuation, for the most part, is normally performed based on the events that were known or would have been knowable by the willing buyer and willing seller, there are many times that subsequent events can act as either your friend or your foe. The Tax Court has been known to look at transactions after the valuation date to test the reasonableness of what the appraiser has done. While I do not agree with the notion of playing Monday morning quarterback, sometimes it is necessary. For example, getting away from the pure standard of fair market value, sometimes the courts are concerned with doing what is *fair and equitable*. If a subsequent event will assist in that regard, the courts have taken advantage of the information. This does not mean that you can bend the rules to fit your valuation to the actual results. All I am saying is that in some circumstances, it may be appropriate to consider the subsequent event, and in other circumstances, while you may not choose to rely on it, you may want to present it to the court. Be prepared to discuss the factors that might have caused the subsequent event, such as a transaction, to be more or less because of other factors that may have impacted the subsequent price that was reached between the parties. Sometimes, we just don't know!

Exhibit 16.6 contains a section from a report where we were court appointed in a divorce case.

EXHIBIT 16.6
Subsequent Events

After the date of the filing of the divorce (the effective date of the valuation), Dr. Black decided to leave Dental Associates and open his own practice. The effective date of this dissolution was December 31, 1992.

Under the terms of the dissolution agreement, Dr. Black would open his own office by the end of June 1993. He was permitted to continue seeing his patients at Dental Associates' offices at no cost to him until May 15, 1993. When Dr. Black left, he took approximately 1,100 patient files with him, consisting of approximately $331,000 of annual revenues. In addition, his assistant followed him to his new offices, and he can pay the periodontist as an independent contractor to come to his office to treat patients, if he wishes.

In return, Dr. Black tendered his stock back to the corporation. No monies exchanged hands as a result of this transaction. Clearly, losing approximately one-third of the revenues will have an effect on the value of the practice. This is discussed in more detail below.

Adjusted Book Value

Per the terms of the dissolution agreement, Dr. Black will not take any of the assets of the practice with him. Therefore, the adjusted book value remains at $258,585, or $259,000 rounded.

(Continued)

EXHIBIT 16.6 *(Continued)*

Capitalization of Historic Earnings

An analysis was done showing the financial effect of Dr. Black's leaving the practice. This new income level was then normalized in a manner consistent with what was done in the "Valuation Calculations" section of this report. This analysis is shown below:

1992 taxable income	$ 3,031
Adjustments to 1992 taxable income	
Income generated by Dr. Black[1]	(330,810)
Dr. Black's salary	120,027
Assistant's salary	21,368
Supplies[2]	29,800
Lab fees[2]	43,453
Payroll taxes & benefits	14,140
Consulting services[2]	14,453
1992 income without Dr. Black	$ (84,538)
Normalization adjustments	
Interest & dividends	(718)
Insurance	8,675
Rent	7,520
Depreciation	8,294
Legal & accounting	10,624
Officers' compensation[3]	75,962
Contributions	263
Normalized net income	$ 26,082

[1]Income as reported on Dental Associates' internal Procedure Analysis Report.

[2]The assumption was made that Dr. Black accounted for approximately one-third of these expenses.

[3]Since Dr. Black's salary was added in above, only Dr. Brown's and Dr. Green's salaries were adjusted.

Using the same methodology as used previously in this report, capitalizing normalized net income results in a value of $113,400.

Value of the 50 Percent Interest Owned by Dr. Green

After Dr. Black's departure, Dr. Green owns 50 percent of the practice, rather than 44 percent. As a result, his interest in the practice is valued at $129,500 (one-half of $259,000).

Author's Note: The original report also contained a market approach which was ultimately used in the reconciliation of the values. By removing a chunk of the gross receipts of the practice, an asset approach ended up being the highest value. Go figure!

More About Professional Practice Versus Other Business Valuations

One of the key ingredients to a successful professional practice is the ability of the professional to service and keep the clients/patients happy. There tends to be much more dependence on the professional than in other types of businesses. In that regard, the professional is a *key* person. This does not necessarily mean that there should be a discount associated with that professional. During the valuation process, the attributes of the professional must be considered. Unusual skills, long work hours, a large referral base, and other, similar factors will certainly impact the valuation, whether it ends up as part of reasonable compensation or built into the discount or capitalization rates.

Another factor that differentiates the professional practice from other types of businesses is the fact the professional, and in some cases the firm, must be licensed or accredited. In most instances, the professional practice is subject to standards and possibly ethics that a normal business may not be subject to. For example, as accountants, we are subject to the rules promulgated by the Board of Accountancy in our state.

One other distinction between professional practices and other types of businesses immediately comes to mind—the method of accounting used to keep the books and records. Most smaller professional practices use the cash method of accounting. This will require the appraiser to obtain additional information that may normally be available for other types of businesses directly in the financial statements, e.g., accounts receivable.

The Valuation Process

In Chapter 2, I gave you some checklists that can be used to assist you in gathering information about different types of professional practices. In this chapter, I will demonstrate some of the unique aspects of professional practice reports by showing you sections of reports that contain different types of analyses. Before we get there, however, let's consider the questions that you probably want to ask at a management interview. Exhibit 16.7 includes a checklist that we have adapted from PPC's *Guide to Business Valuations*. Immediately following Exhibit 16.7 is a Medical Practice Profile and a Dental Practice Profile that we send out to the doctor or dentist before we interview him or her. This allows us to become more familiar with the practice before we do our site visit. Since they are related to Exhibit 16.7, I am numbering these Exhibit 16.7a and 16.7b.

EXHIBIT 16.7

Professional Practice Questionnaire

TRUGMAN VALUATION ASSOCIATES INC.
PROFESSIONAL PRACTICE COMPANY AND INDUSTRY BACKGROUND INFORMATION

Practice Name: ____________________

Completed by: ____________________ Date: __________

INSTRUCTIONS: This form is designed to be used in place of TVA-4 when valuing a professional practice. It covers the data typically needed to obtain an understanding of the professional practice being valued. This information should be obtained through reviewing practice documents and interviewing practice personnel. Many of these questions are general in nature and will not necessarily apply to all professional practices. Answer only the questions that apply to the practice being valued. Some of these questions may be duplicative if a medical or dental practice profile was filled out (see form TVA-5a).

Document the requested information in the space provided. Attach additional sheets if necessary. If the information is not relevant, write N/A in that space.

PRACTICE BACKGROUND

1. Describe the practice's legal structure.

   Practice's legal name: ____________________

   Type of entity (professional corporation, partnership, proprietorship):

   ____

   Date of incorporation or formation: ____________________

Source: Adapted with permission from *Guide to Business Valuations*, Twelfth Edition (January 2002), published by Practitioners Publishing Company, Fort Worth, Texas.

(Continued)

EXHIBIT 16.7 *(Continued)*

2. List the major stockholders, partners, or owners of the practice and their percentage of ownership or number of shares owned.

Name	% Ownership or Number of Shares Owned

3. List all known related parties (that is, subsidiaries, affiliates, or relatives) that the practice does business with.

Name	Relationship

4. List each location maintained by the practice and the primary activity at each, that is, executive office, practice office, laboratory, etc.

Location	Activity

5. Discuss evolution of:
   (a) Services

   (b) Customer Base

   (c) Locations

EXHIBIT 16.7 *(Continued)*

(d) Marketing Activities

(e) Employees

(f) Acquisitions

(g) Ownership

6. Other key dates or events in practice history:

7. Has the practice ever had any offers to merge with another practice?

(Continued)

EXHIBIT 16.7 *(Continued)*

SERVICE MIX

8. Description of the practice's service mix (i.e., types of engagements, or services performed):

9. Breakdown of revenue by service (major services):

Service	Percent of Revenue	% of Recurring Clients/Patients

10. How diversified is the service mix?

11. Do all revenues depend on the same factors?

12. Which service area is growing faster?

    The slowest?

13. Has the practice developed any proprietary products?

14. Does the practice have patents, technology, or expertise that prevents others from copying the services offered?

EXHIBIT 16.7 (Continued)

15. Discuss the practice's research and development efforts, the importance of new products or services, and the annual cost of research and development activities. ____________________

16. Are revenues cyclical? ____________________

17. What economic factors (inflation, interest rates, etc.) affect revenue? ____________________

18. Are revenues seasonal? ____________________

19. Describe the practice's client base. ____________________

20. How many clients/patients are seen per week, on average? ____________________

21. What percentage are seen in the practice office? ____________________

(Continued)

EXHIBIT 16.7 *(Continued)*

22. Describe the geographic area that client/patients come from (i.e., the approximate mile radius from the office).

23. How would the geographic area be described (i.e., urban or rural, growing or declining, affluent or blue collar, stable or transient)?

24. Are there any special demographic factors that should be considered, such as the age of clients/patients?

25. How does the practice obtain clients/patients?

26. What percentage of total clients/patients are the result of referrals?

27. Of this percentage, how many referrals were from other professionals?

28. How many referrals were from other clients/patients?

29. Are referrals to a specific professional/doctor, or to the firm in general?

30. Does any one referral source account for 10% or more of the practice revenue?

31. Does any referral source account for 5% or more?

EXHIBIT 16.7 ***(Continued)***

32. Are there any contractual relationships that provide the practice with access to facilities or client referrals?

33. Briefly describe the relationship and the percentage of revenues provided by the relationship.

34. Does the practice maintain records to track the source of client/patients?

35. Does the practice advertise? Describe marketing methods, if any.

36. What is the annual cost of marketing and practice development efforts, including travel and entertainment costs relating to entertaining referral sources or potential clients?

COMPETITION

37. Who are the practice's major competitor? Where are they located? How big are they? How diversified are they?

38. How does the practice compare in size to its competitors?

39. How easy is it to enter the profession? What are the barriers to entry?

(Continued)

EXHIBIT 16.7 ***(Continued)***

40. What are the practice's competitive strengths and weaknesses?

OPERATIONS

41. Describe the practice's organization structure. (Attach organization chart, if available.)

42. As of the valuation date, what are the weekly business hours for the practice?

43. How often does the practice bill? Describe the basis for fees, i.e., hourly charge, fixed fee, cost plus, fee schedule, etc. Provide a copy of the fee schedule, if available.

44. What is the balance of unbilled work in process? How much of this balance is collectible?

45. Does any of the work in process represent contingent fees? If so, what percentage?

46. Complete the following if the information is available:

Service	Gross Fees	Write Down	Net Fee	Paid by Insurance	Paid by Client/ Patient	Write Down
TOTAL						

EXHIBIT 16.7 ***(Continued)***

47. What is the practice's percentage of collectibility for accounts receivable?

48. How are fees paid (i.e., check, cash, credit cards)?

49. Are buildings and equipment owned or leased?

50. Provide details about the facilities. What is the square footage?

51. How many stories is the building?

52. Is the current facility adequate for the level of business being projected?

53. If leased, are the leases renewable and on what terms? Are leases between the practice and related parties?

54. What is the overall condition of the practice's equipment?

55. Is there any inefficient or obsolete equipment?

56. When is the equipment likely to be replaced?

(Continued)

EXHIBIT 16.7 *(Continued)*

57. What is the likelihood of major repairs?

58. Please provide a listing and approximate value of the drugs and/or supplies on hand.

59. Discuss technology trends that impact the profession.

60. Does the practice have any foreign clients?

61. If so, does the company have any problems with any foreign governments?

62. Discuss the effects of any federal or state regulation or subsidies on the practice's operations.

MANAGEMENT AND EMPLOYEES

63. List key members of management.

Name	Title

64. Discuss the practice's key management members (get curriculum vitae for each).

Member	Age	Health

EXHIBIT 16.7 *(Continued)*

65. List the primary administrative employees.

Employee	Age	Qualifications	Experience	Duties

66. Discuss basis of compensation. Also, describe employee benefits (insurance, profit sharing, etc.).

67. Discuss any employment contracts.

68. Briefly describe past and current employee relations (that is, contentious, harmonious). Also discuss employee turnover.

69. What is the number of employees on the payroll at the valuation date? Full-Time

Part-Time

70. How has the number of employees changed over the past five years?

71. What are the immediate needs of the company with respect to hiring additional personnel?

72. Are there any non-working relatives or friends on the payroll? If so, what are the names and levels of compensation for the years being analyzed?

(Continued)

EXHIBIT 16.7 *(Continued)*

73. How extensively are independent contractors used? ____________________

74. Discuss the current labor market. How easy is it to attract qualified employees? ____________________

75. As of the last firm fiscal year (or more recent 12-month period, if available) summarize the time spent by the key management personnel identified in question 60:

	HOURS			
Name	Charged to Clients/Patients	Administrative and Other	Vacations/ Holiday	Total

76. How easily can key employees be replaced (i.e., is there one or a few key officers on which the success of the company depends that cannot be easily replaced)? ____________________

77. Have the key employees executed noncompete agreements preventing them from taking practice clients without compensation?

MEDICAL PRACTICES

78. How many surgical procedures are performed each week? ____________________

79. Which hospitals are used for surgery? ____________________

80. How is the choice of hospitals determined? ____________________

EXHIBIT 16.7 *(Continued)*

81. Does any one type of surgery dominate the others?

82. Is a surgical diary maintained? If so, please provide a copy.

83. Are there any types of procedures that the practice will not perform? If so, what and why?

84. Does the practice maintain a statistical report that reflects the frequency of services provided by Current Procedural Terminology (CPT) code? If so, please provide a copy for the last 12 months of operations.

85. What are the top 10 outpatient procedures performed by the practice?

86. Is the amount of reimbursement received for those procedures declining because of recently negotiated managed care contracts?

87. Does the practice maintain a detailed appointment book for each physician? If so, please provide copies of the appointment books for the last 12 months.

88. What percentage of referrals are from patients?

89. What percentage are from other doctors?

90. Are patients referred to the practice or to a specific doctor?

(Continued)

EXHIBIT 16.7 ***(Continued)***

91. How many active patients are seen by the practice? ______

92. How many patients are seen in a day/week/month? ______

93. How many new patients are seen in a month? ______

94. Are patients seen by the practice once, or are follow-up visits regularly scheduled? ______

95. Does the practice primarily treat children, adults, or both? ______

96. For non-surgical procedures, are patients required to pay at the time the procedure is performed? ______

97. Is the practice affiliated with any insurance companies as a preferred provider? ______

98. Does the practice serve any HMOs? ______

99. List company names, describe the fee arrangements, and note the percentage of gross fees that comes from such arrangements.

100. What is the time frame for reimbursement from insurance companies, HMOs, PPOs, and Medicare and Medicaid?

101. What percentage of gross fees is received from Medicare or Medicaid? ______

EXHIBIT 16.7 (Continued)

102. Discuss the practice's payor mix and how that mix has changed in recent years. For example, has the practice been adversely affected by the shift from reimbursement on a fee-for-service basis to discounted managed care contracts with HMOs, PPOs, and others? ______

103. If so, is that adverse trend continuing, or has the practice negotiated contracts that increase both revenue and profits?

104. Does the practice have any global capitalization contracts with managed care companies? ______

105. If so, does the practice have the expertise to properly manage the risk of providing patient care in return for fixed monthly payments? ______

106. Does the practice have any "exclusive" contracts with the dominant managed care company in its market?

107. If so, has the practice received satisfactory patient survey results in connection with such contracts? ______

108. How many of the practice's managed care contracts are currently up for renewal? ______

109. How significant is the risk that the provider will be unable to renew those contracts? ______

110. Does the practice periodically update its patient fee schedule? ______

(Continued)

EXHIBIT 16.7 *(Continued)*

111. When was the last time the fee schedule was updated? Please provide a copy of the current fee schedule.

112. Has the practice entered into managed care contracts with HMOs, PPOs, or the Medicare program? If so, please provide copies of all managed care contracts.

113. Has the practice ever had any associates?

114. Were they offered the chance to buy into the practice?

115. If so, why didn't they buy in?

VETERINARY PRACTICES

116. What types of animals does the practice treat (e.g., small animal, large animal, mixed, or equine)? Give the estimated percentage of each type of animal treated.

117. Does the practice board animals?

118. Does the practice make house calls?

119. How many animals does the practice see in a day?

ACCOUNTING AND LEGAL PRACTICES

120. Have any new partners/owners been admitted in the last several years? If so, describe the admission process.

121. Will any of the staff be admitted into the partnership in the near future?

EXHIBIT 16.7 *(Continued)*

122. Has any partner or owner been bought out? ______

123. Describe the terms of any recent transactions involving partner/owner admissions or departures. ______

124. Describe the nature of any financial statement qualifications or unusual matters noted in reviewing the practice's financial statements that may affect the engagement. ______

125. Has there been any change in accounting principles during the past five years (e.g., cash to accrual) or similar changes that might affect the comparability of the financial statements? ______

126. What are the main discretionary expenses (such as bonus, profit sharing, advertising, and R&D)? ______

127. How have the levels of those expenses changed during the last five years? ______

128. Describe short-term sources of credit and how they were used during the last five years. ______

129. Describe long-term sources of credit and how they were used during the last five years. ______

130. Discuss plans for major capital expenditures, how they will be financed, and how much represents expansion versus replacement of existing assets. ______

(Continued)

EXHIBIT 16.7 *(Continued)*

131. Discuss any contingent liabilities, including lawsuits and pending or threatened litigation. ____

132. Describe any nonoperating assets, such as aircraft, boats, and real estate investments. ____

FUTURE EXPECTATIONS

133. Describe relevant past and expected future trends for the practice, such as growth patterns, expansion or cutbacks of business segments, possible spinoffs, mergers, or acquisitions. ____

134. Describe the practice's future expectations, goals, objectives, and long-range plans in the following areas:

Service mix. ____

Marketing and customers base. ____

R&D and technology. ____

135. Is there anything else that we should know in order to perform this valuation? ____

COMMENTS AND OBSERVATIONS

136. Describe any matters to be considered in applying the valuation methods selected. Factors to consider include:

- Growth expectations.
- Financial condition.
- Management depth and competence.
- Customer and service diversification.

EXHIBIT 16.7a
Medical Practice Profile

Practice Name: ______________________________

Office Address: ______________________________

____

Office Phone: ______________________________

Reason for Appraisal: ______________________________

____

Is the staff aware of this appraisal? ______________________________

If yes, do they know the reason? ______________________________

If no, shall this assignment remain confidential? ______________________________

Residency hospital ______________________________ Year __________

Internship hospital ______________________________ Year __________

Medical school degree at ______________________________ Year __________

Undergraduate degree at ______________________________ Year __________

Other degrees ______________________________ Year __________

____

Professional memberships ______________________________

____

The office is normally staffed during these hours:

M ______ T ______ W ______ Th ______ F ______ S ______

Doctor's normal hours in office. If same as above, leave blank.

M ______ T ______ W ______ Th ______ F ______ S ______

Typical hours patients are seen in office. If same as above, leave blank.

M ______ T ______ W ______ Th ______ F ______ S ______

Typical hours of hospital rounds.

M ______ T ______ W ______ Th ______ F ______ S ______

Years of practice in community? ____________ At this location? ______________________________

If less than five years at present location, address of previous location:

____

Where else have you practiced in the past? ______________________________

Dates ______________________________

(Continued)

EXHIBIT 16.7a ***(Continued)***

Form of practice ownership: Sole proprietorship? ____________ If yes, when began? ____________

Corporation? ____________ If yes, when began? ____________

Partnership? ____________ If yes, when began? ____________

Other? ____________ Describe: ____________

Provide a list of other practitioners and their percentage of ownership.

Associate practitioner(s) ____________

Terms of employment ____________

Terms of compensation ____________

Length of employment ____________

Future plans? ____________

Do you have a written contract? If so, enclose.

Do you own the office? ____________ If **NO**, go to the next section.

Form of ownership? ____________ Total sq. ft. in building: ____________

Your % of ownership: ____________

Amount of space occupied by your practice: ____________

Do you have an office lease? ________ If yes, please enclose.

Monthly rent paid by your practice: ____________

Original cost of your ownership: ____________

Mortgage balance ________ as of ________ Monthly payment ________

Potential rental price ____________ Option to buy? ________

Office Rental Information:

Landlord ____________

Square feet ____________ Monthly rent ____________

Lease expires ____________ Option to renew? ____________

Is the lease assumable? ____________

Services provided with lease: ____________

Tenant pays: ____________

Please enclose a copy of the lease.

Please describe your office location (office building or retail, area of town, type of structure, age, etc.): ____________

____

____

EXHIBIT 16.7a ***(Continued)***

Describe the community you practice in: ______________________________
____
____

Who are the major employers in the area? ______________________________
____
____

Describe the type of practice you have and the typical patient: ______________________________
____
____

Is your practice accepting new patients? ______________________________

If **NO**, where do you refer them? ______________________________

If **NO**, for accepting new patients, go to next section.

Approximate number of new patients per month: ______________

Do you note new patients in the appointment book? ______________

Do you acknowledge the referral source? ______________

In what manner? ______________

What percentage of new patients are from existing practice patients? ________

What percentage are from marketing? ______________

What percentage are from other sources? ______________

What is your typical new patient fee? ______________

Please break down the fee: ______________________

How many emergency patients do you see each month? ________ Existing patients? ______________

New patients? ______________

Are emergency patients included in new patient figures? ______________________

What percentage of services are paid for by:

Cash or check: ______

Credit card: ______

Insurance:

Patient carrier payments: ______

HMO or capitation: ______

PPO or other: ______

TOTAL 100 %

(Continued)

EXHIBIT 16.7a ***(Continued)***

Do you accept insurance assignments? ______________________________

Do you send statements? ______________________________

If yes, approximately how many per month? ______________________________

What percentage of your charges do you collect? ______________________________

What staff member is in charge of collections? ______________________________

What method is used for recording patient financial transactions?

Pegboard ______ Computer ______ Daily Log ______ Other ______

How many days a week do you employ a nurse? ______________________________

How many active patient files are in your practice? ______________________________

Are the files by family or individual? ______________________________

An active patient has received care (other than emergency) in the past twenty-four months. Was this figure obtained by:

Actual count? ________, Guesstimate? ________, Computer? ________, Other? ________

Describe any marketing or advertising currently being used and its cost: ______________________________

____

____

Do you consider it to be effective? ______________________________

Professional advisers to your practice:

Accountant: ______________ Phone: ______________

Address: ______________________________

Is this individual aware of this appraisal? ______________________________

Attorney: ______________ Phone: ______________

Address: ______________________________

Is this individual aware of this appraisal? ______________________________

Management consultant: ______________ Phone: ______________

Address: ______________________________

Is this individual aware of this appraisal? ______________________________

Are you or the practice currently involved in any litigation or threat of litigation? If **YES**, please explain: ______________

____

____

____

____

EXHIBIT 16.7a (Continued)

Have you ever been sued for professional malpractice or paid a claim? If **YES**, please explain: ______________________

____

____

____

Is there any other information that should be disclosed regarding your practice, i.e., board action, bankruptcy, liabilities, etc.?

If so, please explain: ____

____

____

EXHIBIT 16.7b

Dental Practice Profile

Practice Name: ____

Office Address: ____

____

Office Phone: ____

Reason for Appraisal: ____

____

Is the staff aware of this appraisal? ______________________________

If yes, do they know the reason? ______________________________

If no, shall this assignment remain confidential? ______________________________

Dental school degree at ______________________ Year __________

Undergraduate degree at ______________________ Year __________

Other degrees ______________________ Year __________

Professional memberships ____

____

____

The office is normally staffed during these hours:

M ______ T ______ W ______ Th ______ F ______ S ______

Doctor's normal hours in office. If same as above, leave blank.

M ______ T ______ W ______ Th ______ F ______ S ______

Typical hours patients are seen in office. If same as above, leave blank.

M ______ T ______ W ______ Th ______ F ______ S ______

(Continued)

EXHIBIT 16.7b ***(Continued)***

Years of practice in community? ____________ At this location? ____________

If less than five years at present location, address of previous location:

____

Where else have you practiced in the past? ____________

Dates ____________

Dates ____________

Form of practice ownership:

Sole proprietorship? ____________ If yes, when began? ____________

Corporation? ____________ If yes, when began? ____________

Partnership? ____________ If yes, when began? ____________

Other? ____________ Describe: ____________

Provide a list of other practitioners and their percentage of ownership.

Associate practitioner(s) ____________

Terms of employment ____________

Terms of compensation ____________

Length of employment ____________

Future plans? ____________

Do you have a written contract? If so, enclose.

Do you own the office? ______ If **NO**, go to the next section.

Form of ownership? ____________

Total sq. ft. in building: ______ Your % of ownership: ____________

Amount of space occupied by your practice:

Do you have an office lease? ______ If yes, please enclose.

Landlord ____________

Square feet ____________ Monthly rent ____________

Lease expires ____________ Option to renew? ____________

Is the lease assumable? ____________

Services provided with lease: ____________

Tenant pays: ____________

Please enclose a copy of the lease.

EXHIBIT 16.7b (*Continued*)

Please describe your office location (office building or retail, area of town, type of structure, age, etc): ____________

____

____

____

Describe the community you practice in: ____________

____

____

Who are the major employers in the area? ____________

____

____

Circle those that have dental insurance.

Describe the type of practice you have and the typical patient: ____________

____

____

Is your practice accepting new patients? ____________

If **NO**, where do you refer them? ____________

If **NO**, for accepting new patients, go to next section.

Monthly rent paid by your practice: ____________

Original cost of your ownership: ____________

Mortgage balance ____________ as of ________ Monthly payment ____________

Potential rental price ____________ Option to buy? ____________

Office Rental Information:

Approximate number of new patients per month: ____________

Do you note new patients in the appointment book? ____________

Do you acknowledge the referral source? ____________

In what manner? ____________

What percentage of new patients are from existing practice patients? ____________

What percentage are from marketing? ____________

What percentage are from other sources? ____________

What is your typical new patient fee? ____________

Please break down the fee: ____________

(Continued)

EXHIBIT 16.7b *(Continued)*

How many emergency patients do you see each month? Existing patients? ______________

Are emergency patients included in new patient figures? ______________

What percentage of services are paid for by:

Cash or check: ________

Credit card: ________

Insurance:

Patient carrier payments: ________

DMO or capitation: ________

PPO or other: ________

TOTAL 100 %

Do you accept insurance assignments? ______________

Do you send statements? ______________

If yes, approximately how many per month? ______________

What percentage of your charges do you collect? ______________

What staff member is in charge of collections? ______________

What method is used for recording patient financial transactions? ______________

Pegboard ________ Computer ________ Daily Log ________ Other ________

How many days a week do you employ a hygienist? ______________

What is your typical recall fee for adult and pedo?

Adult ________ Includes ______________

Pedo ________ Includes ______________

Describe your recall system and its effectiveness: ______________

____

Roughly what percentage of your fees are attributable to the following procedures?

Removable ______ % Perio ______ % Endo ______ %

Any other specialty work? ______________

What work do you refer out and how much?

Pedo ______ % Ortho ______ % Removable ______ %

Endo ______ % Perio ______ % Surgery ______ %

EXHIBIT 16.7b (*Continued*)

How many active patient files are in your practice? ______________________

Are the files by family or individual? ______________________

An active patient has received care (other than emergency) in the past twenty-four months. Was this figure obtained by:

Actual count? ________ Guesstimate? ________ Computer? ________

Other? ________

Describe any marketing or advertising currently being used and its cost: ______________________

____

____

Do you consider it to be effective? ______________________

Professional advisers to your practice:

Accountant: ______________________ Phone: ______________________

Address: ______________________

Is this individual aware of this appraisal? ______________________

Attorney: ______________________ Phone: ______________________

Address: ______________________

Is this individual aware of this appraisal? ______________________

Management consultant: ______________________ Phone: ______________________

Address: ______________________

Is this individual aware of this appraisal? ______________________

Are you or the practice currently involved in any litigation or threat of litigation? If **YES**, please explain: ________

____

____

____

Have you ever been sued for professional malpractice or paid a claim? If **YES**, please explain: ______________________

____

____

____

Is there any other information that should be disclosed regarding your practice, i.e., board action, bankruptcy, liabilities, etc.?

If so, please explain: ______________________

____

____

____

____

You can tell from Exhibit 16.7, 16.7a, and 16.7b that many questions asked in a professional practice valuation are similar, if not the same, as those asked in other types of business valuation assignments. However, there are some differences. The balance of this chapter is going to concentrate on those differences. Some of the issues that will be covered include:

- History of the practice
- Economy/industry analysis
- Cash versus accrual accounting
- Accounts receivable
- Work in process
- Prepaid insurance
- Supplies
- Library costs
- Reasonable compensation

History of the Practice

A well-written, comprehensive valuation report will generally contain a lot of information. Chapter 13 discussed the features that should be in a report. In a professional practice valuation assignment, there is frequently information about the type of profession that not only is important to demonstrate an understanding about the firm, but can also substantially impact the value conclusion. Let's highlight some history sections that would differ depending upon the type of practice being valued. The purpose of the following exhibits is to demonstrate some of the important information that the appraiser needs to be concerned about for various professional groups.

Let's start with an accounting practice. In addition to obtaining the normal stuff for inclusion in the history of the company section, accounting practices need to be distinguished from other types of businesses based on the types of services that they provide to their clients. A firm with traditional accounting work will more often be sold at a higher rate than a firm that does more management consulting or one-shot engagements. Exhibit 16.8 contains several excerpts from the history sections of various reports.

EXHIBIT 16.8

History Section—Accounting Practice

Excerpt 1

All of the clients of the firm came from relationships developed by the principals of John Smith & Company. Many times, the relationship was established long before any services were provided. Although the senior Mr. Smith was responsible for many of these personal relationships, both Mr. Jones and Mr. Smith, Jr. (Bob) had taken over client development and relationship building over the several years prior to the valuation date. Much of this relationship building has been through community affairs in which the firm's principals are involved.

By 1999, the firm's revenues were broken down as follows:

Audit	$ 450,971	44.2%
Tax	303,915	29.8%
Compilation & review	147,055	14.4%
Other services	117,539	11.6%
	$ 1,019,480	100.0%

A detailed analysis was conducted by the appraiser, on a client-by-client basis, indicating that approximately 70 percent of the firm's revenues came from 30 clients in 1999.

EXHIBIT 16.8 (Continued)

Many of these clients have been, and continue to be, served primarily by Bob Smith and Michael Jones. These relationships are key to the generation of revenues.

Author's Note: Not only did we address the breakdown of the services, but we also addressed who services the clients and how the relationships were built. We also looked at the risk of concentration of the client base. In another valuation, the same information looked like this:

Excerpt 2

The practice is a conventional accounting firm whose net revenues over the last three years have been derived from the following services:

	1990	%	*1991*	%	*1992*	%
Audit	$ 37,385	10.9	$ 27,956	8.0	$ 39,737	11.2
Review	4,866	1.4	5,129	1.5	4,982	1.4
Compilation	52,391	15.3	56,890	16.3	55,628	15.7
Tax	244,492	71.4	254,794	73.1	251,603	70.8
Other	3,372	1.0	3,732	1.1	3,268	0.9
Total	$342,506	100.0	$348,501	100.0	$355,218	100.0

The importance of the information contained in Exhibit 16.8 should be self-explanatory to accountants reading this book who have ever bought or sold an accounting practice. The types of services offered to clients make a big difference. Not only are different amounts paid for different types of clients, but the risk profile also needs to be considered regarding the transferability of the clients.

Just as the various types of services are important to the accounting practice, a medical practice has certain attributes that are important as well. Exhibit 16.9 describes some of them.

EXHIBIT 16.9
History Section—Medical Practice

Excerpt 1

One of the services historically offered by The Practice has been the taking of x-rays. However, in 1999, two events occurred that will eliminate this revenue stream. First, many of the insurance companies have stated that specialists other than approved radiologists will not be reimbursed for these services.[1] Second, the x-ray machine is located in a medical office down the hall from The Practice. This other medical practice has notified Dr. Smith that as of May 1999, it will no longer have space available for the x-ray equipment. Dr. Smith has determined that it does not make financial sense to attempt to relocate the x-ray machine in light of the lack of future reimbursements from the insurance company, and therefore is discontinuing this service. Collections from x-ray services were $74,145 and $67,593 in 1997 and 1998, respectively.

Author's Note: Another item of importance in a medical practice is the hours that the office is open, the hours that the doctor works, and the hours that the doctor sees patients. This information will allow the appraiser to compare this practice to other practices based on the studies published by the American Medical Association.

Excerpt 2

Dr. Smith typically sees patients during the following hours:

Monday	8:00 A.M.–5:00 P.M.
Tuesday	8:00 A.M.–7:00 P.M.
Wednesday	8:00 A.M.–5:00 P.M.
Thursday	8:00 A.M.–5:00 P.M.
Friday	8:00 A.M.–5:00 P.M.
Saturday	8:00 A.M.–12:00 P.M. (every third Saturday)

Dr. Smith's hours often start earlier than his patient hours for paperwork and other administrative activities.

[1]This was confirmed by the appraiser by making phone calls to various HMOs.

(Continued)

EXHIBIT 16.9 *(Continued)*

On average, Dr. Smith sees approximately 20 patients per day. However, the number of patients seen per day varies with respect to the type of patient (new vs. return). Appointments with new patients, on average, last approximately 45 to 60 minutes, while appointments with return patients last approximately 15 minutes. The fees for new patients range from approximately $100 to $150. According to an estimate by Dr. Smith, The Practice currently has between 750 and 800 active individual patient files.

Author's Note: No medical practice valuation would be considered complete without a discussion about health maintenance organizations (HMOs). Managed care is an important part of a medical practice valuation because it can severely impact the future cash flows. The appraiser should find out about the different types of contracts in place at the valuation date. Are they capitation plans (the doctor is paid so much per month per patient, whether or not the patients come in for an appointment) or are they fee for service (pay as you go type practice)? Let's look at what we found out.

Excerpt 3

According to Dr. Smith, The Practice maintains approximately 10 HMO contracts. Dr. Smith's practice consists primarily of Medicare patients, many in HMOs, with the balance consisting mostly of patients who are enrolled in HMOs. Given the nature of The Practice, Medicare and HMO reimbursement rates are a critical factor in its financial performance. According to Dr. Smith, these contracts can be canceled with 30 days notice, and most of The Practice's new patients come as a result of Dr. Smith's being listed as a specialist in the HMO provider books. This can be problematic, though, because many internists also provide rheumatology services, and they are generally listed as primary care providers in the HMO books. This makes The Practice reliant on referrals from these primary care physicians who can often treat these patients as well.

Author's Note: In another medical practice valuation, we were able to get more information about managed care. This is how it was presented:

Excerpt 4

We requested a list of the managed care companies that Dr. Peters had contracts with as of the valuation date, but this information was not available. Instead, we were provided with an assortment of lists and contracts for various times during 1999. We were informed that this information is not substantially different from what existed as of the valuation date. A summary of this data appears in Table 1.

TABLE 1
Managed Care Contracts

Company	*Date*	*Type of Contract*	*Number of Patients*	*Capitation Amount*
Blue Cross/Blue Shield of NJ	Oct. 1998	Fee for service	495	N/A
Mercy Health Plan	Nov. 1998	Capitation	57	$ 942.96
The Prudential	Oct. 1998	Capitation	233	3,122.45
Aetna U.S. Healthcare	Nov. 1998	Capitation	326	Not provided
NY/Care	Oct. 1998	Capitation	48	412.02
Keystone	Nov. 1998	Capitation	15	261.95
Amerihealth	Nov. 1998	Capitation	2	24.20
Cigna—NJ	Nov. 1998	Capitation	15	156.65
Cigna—NY	Nov. 1998	Capitation	140	1,571.58
Cigna	Nov. 1998	Capitation	53	731.55
Americaid	Nov. 1998	Capitation	33	293.00
Healthplans of America	Sept. 1998	Fee for service	21	N/A
Health Network America	Oct. 1998	Capitation	4	Not provided
American Preferred	Nov. 1998	Capitation	3	71.40
Physicians Healthcare	Oct. 1998	Unknown	4	N/A
Cannot Read	Nov. 1998	Capitation	44	413.27
United Healthcare	Nov. 1998	Both	71	Not provided
FPA Medical Management	May 1998	Capitation	372	5,033.61

EXHIBIT 16.9 *(Continued)*

In addition, Dr. Peters has submitted applications to the following companies over the last few years:

- First Option Health Plan of New Jersey
- Seton Health Network, Inc./Quality Pediatric Network
- Medichoice Network, Inc.
- First Option Health Plan/Medicaid
- Better Health Advantage
- Consumer Health Network
- Sanus Health Plan/New York Life
- Liberty Health Plan
- Metrahealth
- International Union of Operating Engineers
- QualCare
- Harmony Health Plan

The applications and/or contracts we reviewed for these companies do not provide enough detail to determine the type of contract it is, the reimbursement rates, the number of patients, or if Dr. Peters was participating in the plan as of the valuation date. What it shows is that the list provided in Table 1 is probably not complete.

Unfortunately, because of the litigation process, we do not always get all of the information that we ask for. The last excerpt in Exhibit 16.9 demonstrates that. In situations like this, the appraiser has to make a judgment call as to whether the missing information will have a material effect on the outcome of the valuation. If it does, **DO NOT ISSUE A REPORT!** Have I made my point? If you do not have enough information to give a reasonable indication of value, and if you do not care about your reputation, you can issue a report. If the information is not material, you can use your judgment by impacting the risk associated with the practice. In the case presented, we lowered the discount rate slightly to reflect the fact that the practice probably had contracts that we were not told about. This would have the impact of reducing the risk and raising the value (slightly).

Before we change topics, let's discuss a situation that appraisers face on a regular basis in preparing a valuation report for a divorce. (This could have gone in the divorce chapter, but since my example relates to a medical practice, it's here.) Imagine valuing an opthalmology practice where the doctor claims that his income has gone way down because Medicare cuts have eaten away at his ability to make a living. We call this RAIDS (Recently Acquired Income Deficiency Syndrome). Exhibit 16.10 contains a portion of the report of this poor doctor's practice.

EXHIBIT 16.10

The Poor Doctor Who Was Hurt by Medicare

Given the nature of The Practice, Medicare reimbursement rates are a critical factor in its financial performance. The following is Dr. Bassin's Medicare fee schedule for 1995 through 1999. Although it does not address all of the issues regarding Medicare reimbursements, it does give a general indication of the overall trends that may affect The Practice.

Table 1 shows a breakdown for all reimbursable Medicare activities. In an attempt to illustrate the overall changes in the Medicare fees over the period, the appraiser calculated year-to-year growth rates for each procedure as well as a compound annual growth rate for 1995 to 1999 for each procedure, and totals for each category. As the growth rates indicate, other than surgical procedures, most of the Medicare fees have increased over the last five years, indicating that overall revenues should be able to be maintained or increased.

(Continued)

EXHIBIT 16.10 (*Continued*)

TABLE 1

Medical Fee Schedule 1995–1999

		1995	*1996*	*% Change (95–96)*	*1997*	*% Change (96–97)*	*1998*	*% Change (97–98)*	*1999*	*% Change (98–99)*	CAGR (95–99)
NEW											
99205	LEVEL 5	$ 122.29	$ 125.37	2.52	$ 131.47	4.87	$ 139.34	5.99	$ 150.92	8.31	5.40
99204	LEVEL 4	100.73	100.73	—	105.05	4.29	111.82	6.44	121.46	8.62	4.79
99203	LEVEL 3	67.42	67.34	(0.12)	70.50	4.69	75.18	6.64	83.01	10.42	5.34
99203	LEVEL 2	48.50	49.36	1.77	51.31	3.95	55.09	7.37	59.98	8.88	5.45
92225	EXT RETINAL	43.21	43.21	—	31.25	(27.68)	33.69	7.81	40.93	21.49	(1.35)
92004	NEW COMPLETE	80.09	85.67	6.97	82.57	(3.62)	84.46	2.29	96.89	14.72	4.88
92002	NEW INTERMEDIATE	56.41	59.76	5.94	51.95	(13.07)	53.09	2.19	59.35	11.79	1.28
Total		**$ 518.65**	**$ 531.44**	**2.47**	**$ 524.10**	**(1.38)**	**$ 552.67**	**5.45**	**$ 612.54**	**10.83**	**4.25**
EST											
99215	LEVEL 5	$ 91.94	$ 91.96	0.02	$ 95.92	4.31	$ 102.45	6.81	$ 107.02	4.46	3.87
99214	LEVEL 4	58.23	58.29	0.10	60.67	4.08	65.08	7.27	69.77	7.21	4.62
99213	LEVEL 3	39.04	38.13	(2.33)	40.38	5.90	43.44	7.58	45.90	5.66	4.13
99212	LEVEL 2	26.99	27.08	0.33	28.17	4.03	30.53	8.38	33.20	8.75	5.31
92226	EXT RETINAL	34.82	35.96	3.27	27.60	(23.25)	29.76	7.83	37.79	26.98	2.07
92014	EST COMPLETE	58.67	62.38	6.32	58.35	(6.46)	63.03	8.02	71.85	13.99	5.20
92012	EST INTERMEDIATE	46.07	49.36	7.14	40.29	(18.38)	43.50	7.97	53.84	23.77	3.97
Total		**$ 355.76**	**$ 363.16**	**2.08**	**$ 351.38**	**(3.24)**	**$ 377.79**	**7.52**	**$ 419.37**	**11.01**	**4.20**
OFFICE CONSULTS											
99245	COMPLEX	$ 177.31	$ 185.49	4.61	$ 185.49	0.00	$ 200.48	8.08	$ 208.58	4.04	4.14
99244	COMPREHENSIVE	133.78	137.58	2.84	137.51	(0.05)	148.62	8.08	157.43	5.93	4.15
99243	INTERMEDIATE	95.67	98.40	2.85	98.64	0.24	106.59	8.06	113.21	6.21	4.30
Total		**$ 406.76**	**$ 421.47**	**3.62**	**$ 421.64**	**0.04**	**$ 455.69**	**8.08**	**$ 479.22**	**5.16**	**4.18**

EXHIBIT 16.10 (Continued)

		1995	1996	% Change (95–96)	1997	% Change (96–97)	1998	% Change (97–98)	1999	% Change (98–99)	CAGR (95–99)
SURGICAL PROCEDURES											
66984	CAT EXT&IOL	$ 893.67	$ 1,227.11	37.31	$ 1,047.75	(14.62)	$ 889.00	(15.15)	$ 858.49	(3.43)	(1.00)
66985	SECONDARY IMP	905.13	905.13	—	830.96	(8.19)	720.36	(13.31)	701.02	(2.68)	(6.19)
66170	TRABECULECT	1,071.32	1,120.73	4.61	1,064.12	(5.05)	980.16	(7.89)	972.60	(0.77)	(2.39)
66625	IRIDECTOMY	609.38	609.38	—	524.48	(13.93)	443.87	(15.37)	458.35	3.26	(6.87)
67917	ECTROPION	654.64	654.64	—	615.41	(5.99)	517.43	(15.92)	538.54	4.08	(4.76)
67923	ENTROPION	640.35	640.35	—	496.96	(22.39)	502.59	1.13	541.88	7.82	(4.09)
15823	BLEPH UP LID	808.27	808.27	—	664.35	(17.81)	606.36	(8.73)	623.14	2.77	(6.30)
15821	BLEPH LOW LID	564.46	602.76	6.79	575.65	(4.50)	500.44	(13.07)	528.27	5.56	(1.64)
67904	PTOSIS REPAIR	827.74	827.74	—	637.81	(22.95)	546.66	(14.29)	589.14	7.77	(8.15)
Total		**$ 6,974.96**	**$ 7,396.11**	**6.04**	**$ 6,457.49**	***(12.69)***	**$ 5,706.87**	***(11.62)***	**$ 5,811.43**	**1.83**	***(4.46)***
LASERS											
66761	IRIDOTOMY	$ 566.91	$ 566.91	0.00	$ 417.38	(26.38)	$ 355.75	(14.77)	$ 348.84	(1.94)	(11.43)
65855	TRABCUL (LTP)	649.07	649.07	0.00	478.92	(26.21)	432.11	(9.77)	418.22	(3.21)	(10.41)
67210	FOCAL FUNDUS	789.03	878.80	11.38	834.29	(5.06)	763.87	(8.44)	705.28	(7.67)	(2.77)
67228	PRP	912.51	1,023.08	12.12	967.56	(5.43)	875.31	(9.53)	886.62	1.29	(0.72)
66821	YAG	454.83	454.83	0.00	286.30	(37.05)	209.27	(26.91)	211.21	0.93	(17.45)
67145	RETINAL TEAR	560.52	563.67	0.56	537.94	(4.56)	490.02	(8.91)	475.13	(3.04)	(4.05)
66984	CAT EXT&IOL	$ 893.67	$ 1,227.11	37.31	$ 1,047.75	(14.62)	$ 889.00	(15.15)	$ 858.49	(3.43)	(1.00)
Total		**$ 3,932.87**	**$ 4,136.36**	**5.17**	**$ 3,522.39**	***(14.84)***	**$ 3,126.33**	***(11.24)***	**$ 3,045.30**	***(2.59)***	***(6.19)***
DIAGNOSTIC TESTING											
92020	GONIO	$ 25.67	$ 26.19	2.03	$ 24.12	(7.90)	$ 26.02	7.88	$ 28.80	10.68	2.92
92083	VISUAL FIELD	55.75	55.75	0.00	51.19	(8.18)	55.16	7.76	52.49	(4.84)	(1.50)
92060	MOTILITY EXAM	34.42	35.54	3.25	38.92	9.51	42.04	8.02	44.09	4.88	6.39
92235	FLUORESCEIN	103.93	103.93	0.00	93.30	(10.23)	100.52	7.74	99.23	(1.28)	(1.15)
92250	FUND/DIS PHOT	34.48	34.61	0.38	31.99	(7.57)	34.51	7.88	34.67	0.46	0.14
76519	ASCAN	81.63	85.04	4.18	79.86	(6.09)	86.04	7.74	86.56	0.60	1.48
76519	ASCAN SEC	81.63	85.04	4.18	35.00	(58.84)	35.00	0.00	35.00	0.00	(19.08)
92285	SCHIMER	14.47	15.15	4.70	14.01	(7.52)	15.06	7.49	15.38	2.12	1.54
92286	ENDO CELL	81.82	81.82	0.00	73.18	(10.56)	78.86	7.76	74.07	(6.07)	(2.46)
Total		**$ 513.80**	**$ 523.07**	**1.80**	**$ 441.57**	***(15.58)***	**$ 473.21**	**7.17**	**$ 470.29**	***(0.62)***	***(2.19)***

(Continued)

EXHIBIT 16.10 ***(Continued)***

The balance of The Practice's revenues comes primarily from patients affiliated with health maintenance organizations (HMOs). The Practice attempts to collect HMO co-payments from its patients as they are seen, but they are not always successful. Billing to insurance companies is done daily.

In order to more fully understand the declining performance of The Practice, the appraiser analyzed average monthly revenues for the years 1992 through 1998. Average monthly revenue is calculated by dividing total revenues (as reported on The Practice's tax returns) by 12. The result of this analysis is shown in Table 2.

TABLE 2

Historic Revenues

Year	*Annual Revenue*	***Average Monthly Revenue***
1992	$ 2,127,966	$ 177,331
1993	2,177,179	181,432
1994	2,413,674	201,140
1995	2,593,893	216,158
1996	2,084,128	173,677
1997	2,314,852	192,904
1998	1,886,458	157,205

As the data indicates, The Practice significantly underperformed in 1998 relative to preceding years. This decline corresponds closely to the date of the filing of the divorce complaint of February 6, 1998.

The appraiser also reviewed actual revenues for the monthly periods October 1998 through July 1999 based on the statement of Revenues and Expenses—Cash Basis, prepared by the firm's accountant. This is the period immediately following the date of the temporary support order of September 18, 1998. The results are shown in Table 3.

TABLE 3

Monthly Revenues
October 1998–July 1999

Month	*Revenue*
Oct 98	$ 162,118
Nov 98	146,325
Dec 98	82,753
Jan 99	90,846
Feb 99	99,469
Mar 99	105,659
Apr 99	134,903
May 99	135,211
Jun 99	116,479
Jul 99	130,143
Average	$ 120,391

Again, the data indicates a significant decline in monthly revenue compared to preceding years.

Author's Note: Although this is not a book on forensic accounting, take a look at the increases and decreases in the Medicare schedule. We compared this doctor's charges by billing code to the Medicare schedule and proved that his income decline was due to his working fewer hours. It had nothing to do with Medicare.

Economy/Industry Information

Besides the normal economy and industry stuff, there may be provisions in the state laws that are unique to a professional practice. Sometimes there may be regulatory issues that you would not even think about in the normal course of your research. Exhibit 16.11 illustrates one of those cases.

EXHIBIT 16.11
Economy/Industry Section—Accounting Practice

In the state of Arkansas, there are two major acts that affect an accounting practice. The Arkansas Professional Corporation Act, which was passed in 1963, provides regulations that are designed for those who provide "professional services," which includes certified public accountants. This act states that the officers, directors, and shareholders of a corporation must be licensed in their profession. In addition, the act includes regulations for the purchase of stock in a corporation. The act states,

> If the articles of incorporation or bylaws of a corporation subject to this subchapter fail to state a price or method of determining a fixed price at which the corporation or its shareholders may purchase the shares of a deceased shareholder or a shareholder no longer qualified to own shares in the corporation, then the price for the shares shall be the book value as of the end of the month immediately preceding the death or disqualification of the shareholder. Book value shall be determined from the books and records of the corporation in accordance with the regular method of accounting used by the corporation.

In addition, the Arkansas Public Accountancy Act of 1975 presents other regulations for the accounting industry. The purpose of this Act was to "promote the dependability of information" that is provided by the financial and accounting sectors regarding the financial condition of business enterprises. In other words, this Act is intended to set standards for those providing accounting and financial services to the public, and to assure the public that the information is fair and reliable and that the service was performed by a competent individual. This act also states,

> Each shareholder of the corporation must be a certified public accountant or a public accountant of this state in good standing and must be principally employed by the corporation or actively engaged in its business.

Author's Note: The importance of these provisions is that the law requires individuals to be licensed and *actively* engaged in the business. It also provides a formula to determine value under certain conditions. These are the types of provisions that an appraiser should locate, or the valuation may be performed in contradiction to the law.

Cash Versus Accrual Accounting

As an accountant, I would like to have all financial statements presented to me in accordance with GAAP. I would like to have these statements prepared on an accrual basis of accounting. I would also like to see Santa Claus come down my chimney! Life is not always that simple. Most professional practices report the financial results on a cash basis. If you are reading this book, I hope it is because you consider yourself to be an appraiser (or at least a wannabee). Having financial statements prepared on a cash basis, in many circumstances, should not be too upsetting. Be practical, and unless it is really called for, do not try to restate all of the prior years on an accrual basis. There is a good chance that the information does not exist to allow this to be done easily and in a cost-effective manner. Think about the impact of these statements.

Clearly, the balance sheet should be restated on an accrual basis as of the valuation date in order to capture all of the assets and liabilities of the practice. These will possibly be brought to fair market value in accordance with Chapter 8. The income statement may or may not be adjusted. If there is a consistent trend in the practice, cash basis probably is a good reflection of the cash-generating capabilities of the practice. This is the basis on which these practices are frequently sold. The accrual assets and liabilities may be above and beyond the value as determined in Chapter 7 using the transaction approach. Another alternative is to treat the accrual assets and liabilities as nonoperating assets and liabilities, and add or subtract the values from the income approach determination of value based on the cash basis figures.

Make sure that you review the billing records of the practice to ensure that the future cash flows will not suddenly change dramatically. The most current time period before the valuation date is most important. Let's say you are valuing an accounting practice. Look at billings and work in process to determine the future. In a mature practice, with a steady number of staff, these figures should not change materially from year to year. A staff person can only work so many hours each year. Therefore, the billing should be consistent, except for a possible change in the billing rate.

Since the balance sheet is probably more important than the income statement for these additional assets and liabilities, let's discuss what to do with several types of assets and liabilities for different types of professional practices.

Accounts Receivable. The nature of most professional practices is such that accounts receivable can be fairly high. The appraiser must spend an appropriate amount of time in this area because of its magnitude. In most smaller practices, the recordkeeping may require the appraiser to use some accounting skills to figure out how much is outstanding. Exhibit 16.12 reflects how we dealt with accounts receivable in the valuation of a psychology practice.

EXHIBIT 16.12
Accounts Receivable—Psychology Practice

Dr. Lewis submits insurance claims to insurance companies once each calendar quarter. By the time he submits these claims, it is not uncommon for an additional three to four weeks to go by, resulting in accounts receivable and unbilled work in process equaling four months of revenue.

In order to estimate the value of this asset as of October 29, 2000, a review of patient charts and appointment books indicated that billing for the period July 1, 2000, through September 30, 2000, was submitted to insurance companies in October 2000, and billing was not done for the period October 1, 2000, through October 29, 2000, until January 2001.

Accounts receivable and unbilled work in process has been estimated by the appraiser as follows:

Number of Patient Visits

July	177
August	194
September	182
October 1–29	191
Total visits	744
Average fee	× 85
Accounts receivable and unbilled work in process	$ 63,240

Most patients are billed at $100 per hour, but Dr. Lewis's practice has been to accept insurance assignment without pursuing the balance from most patients. A review of the patient files indicates some patients being billed as low as $45 per hour and others at $80 to $90 per hour. Most patients who have insurance (which is the majority of the patients) are covered after their deductible at 50 percent, 80 percent, or 100 percent, with the majority being 80 percent. Therefore, in order to compensate for the monies that will not be received by Dr. Lewis, the normal hourly rate of $100 was reduced by 15 percent.

Exhibit 16.12 shows the manner in which the records were used to estimate the accounts receivable. Under normal circumstances, this balance sheet item would have been tax-effected to recognize that upon receipt, the value is less because taxes would have to be paid. Exhibit 16.13 reflects the language in another valuation where we adjusted for taxes.

EXHIBIT 16.13
Accounts Receivable—Tax-Effecting

Accounts receivable, at the appraisal date, were $165,473. However, not all receivables are expected to be collected. Therefore, we have provided a 5 percent allowance for doubtful accounts, resulting in a net realizable value of $157,199. Since the firm reports its results of operations using the "cash method" of accounting, the actual amount that would be realized by the firm would be net of income taxes. Therefore, an adjustment has been made to reflect the anticipated taxes that would result from the collection of these receivables. Applying a 38 percent tax rate (34 percent federal and 6.5 percent Arkansas, or 4 percent effective state tax) results in a net accounts receivable value of $97,464.

Here is where being an accountant helps us do better appraisal work. Exhibit 16.14 includes an explanation of the accounting procedures that were employed and explained as part of our adjustments to the balance sheet of a law firm.

EXHIBIT 16.14
Accounts Receivable Procedures—Law Firm

Due to the nature in which the practice maintains its books and records, accounts receivable had not been included on the balance sheet as of April 30, 1993. We were provided with a list of accounts receivable as of this date, which indicated receivables of $69,341. We verified the reasonableness of this accounts receivable figure by reviewing subsequent cash receipts of the practice.

During our review of the firm's records, we discovered that one file was inadvertently omitted. A receivable should be included for file number 200563 (Adam Jones). This file was the subject of a lawsuit with a former employee who stole the settlement check. It was finally received by The Law Firm in August 1993. After deducting co-counsel fees, the receivable was $60,000.

Therefore, accounts receivable should be $129,341. We have been specifically requested by the court not to tax-effect this item.

Work in Process. Probably one of the most difficult assets to value on the balance sheet of a professional practice is work in process. Unless the firm keeps really good records, this can be pretty tricky. The worst type of practice in this regard is a contingency fee law firm. Many law firms that perform personal injury services or other services where they are paid a percentage of what they collect for the client, do not keep time records to support the number of hours worked. They feel that since their fee is based on a percentage instead of hourly billings, they do not have to account to the client for the hours spent on the client's matter.

If the law firm does not keep adequate records, the appraiser can estimate the work in process by using comparative data published by such companies as Altman Weil Pensa, which publishes the *Survey of Law Firm Economics*. The best that you can do in these circumstances is to use an industry average as a percent of revenues or billings. However, when records do exist, the appraiser may be able to take advantage to perform some detailed analysis. Sometimes, 20-20 hindsight may have to be used even though you are not supposed to use subsequent information. Sometimes the parties to a litigation will agree, for the sake of accuracy, to allow both sides to use data after the valuation date. The alternative would be to hire an experienced attorney to review all open cases and estimate the value of these files. This is impractical for a firm that has more than just a few cases.

Exhibit 16.15 illustrates part of the appraisal of a contingency fee law firm.

Exhibit 16.15 reflects an analysis that took a lot of hours to perform. This is anything but easy.

EXHIBIT 16.15
Work in Process—Contingency Fee Law Firm

One component that is normally part of the balance sheet of a law practice is work in process. Work in process is an estimate of the future profit (revenues less direct expenses) anticipated to be earned on cases that are pending but not completed as of the balance sheet date. Work in process was estimated to be $884,950. A detailed analysis of our estimate of work in process is provided later in this report in the section titled "Work in Process."

In order to value work in process, the services of an experienced personal injury attorney would normally be required so that each file could be reviewed to answer at least the following questions:

1. How much will the case be worth?
2. What stage of completion is the case in?
3. What expenses will be incurred to complete the case (direct and indirect)?
4. How long will the case take to go to trial?
5. If it is a large case, what is the probability of the judgment being appealed?

Fair market value generally requires the appraiser to consider only the information that would be available to the willing buyer at the appraisal date. This date is the assumed date of a transaction, and therefore, subsequent knowledge would not be available.

(Continued)

EXHIBIT 16.15 *(Continued)*

However, this valuation is being performed for a marital dissolution. As a result, the notion of fairness must enter into the appraiser's analysis so that the court can be assisted in effectuating equitable distribution. Since we have the benefit of 20-20 hindsight in this matter, the appraiser has reviewed subsequent information to get a more accurate value of the work in process. This procedure is not only more equitable, but it is also more cost-effective than bringing in a personal injury attorney to go through hundreds of files.

In order to determine the value of work in process, we were provided with records pertaining to the practice's clients, including case logs, case files, client ledger cards, closing statements, and records of trust account cash receipts and cash disbursements. The starting point was to review the case logs maintained by the practice. The Law Firm maintains a list of cases retained by the practice that includes, among other information, the client's name and case number. We obtained the case logs for all cases retained from 1993 through May 10, 1998. Since this case log includes all cases opened by the practice during this time period, it was necessary to determine which cases were closed as of May 10, 1998, and which cases remained open as of this date that need to be included as part of work in process. In order to determine the closing date of each individual case, we traced the client's name and case number to client ledger cards and case files. All cases remaining open as of May 10, 1998, were included in our schedule of work in process.

The next step was to trace all of the open cases to the corresponding closing statements. As cases are settled, a closing statement is prepared by the practice that indicates the date the gross settlement was received, the total costs to be reimbursed out of the settlement, and the attorney's fees to be deducted from the settlement, resulting in the net amount payable to the plaintiff. Closing statements are prepared for every case settled by the practice with the exception of worker's compensation and personal injury protection cases. As of the date of our field work, which was completed on February 29, 2001, many of the cases that were open as of May 10, 1998, had been closed. For each of the cases that was closed, and that had closing statements prepared, we traced the gross fee earned by the practice, the total costs reimbursed out of the gross settlement on the case, the date the gross settlement was received and the case closed, and the type of case. Recording the type of case enabled us to segregate work in process by major case type.

In several of the cases included in work in process, The Law Firm was required to split the gross fee earned with co-counsel. Since the actual fee earned by The Law Firm represents only a portion of the gross fee earned on a case, these co-counsel fees must be deducted in determining the fee that The Law Firm will ultimately collect. In addition, certain costs reimbursed to the practice were required to be split with co-counsel. Table 1 provides a summary of the co-counsel fees and costs that were deducted from the gross fees and costs in the calculation of gross fees and reimbursed costs of the practice.

TABLE 1
Co-counsel Fees and Costs Deducted from Work in Process

Case No.	*Party Name*	*Co-Counsel Fees and Costs*
200568	Singer, Z.	$ 12,422
200585	Jones-Gilmore, L.	1,727
200538	Carr, M.	693
200540	Iannou, P.	99,247
TOTAL		$ 114,089

The total fees earned by The Law Firm, and costs reimbursed to the practice, on cases open as of May 10, 1998, and closed as of February 29, 2001, are summarized in Table 2.

TABLE 2
Cases Closed as of February 29, 2001

		Actual		Average	
Case Type	*No. of Cases*	*Fees*	*Costs*	*Fees*	*Costs*
Auto	160	$ 1,492,745	$ 112,827	$ 9,330	$ 705
PIP	36	33,080	5,592	919	155
Premises	52	479,910	87,206	9,229	1,677
Worker's comp.	32	24,939	668	779	21
Environmental	2	290,055	100,500	145,028	50,250
Other	15	72,618	5,438	4,841	363
Total		**$ 2,393,347**	**$ 312,231**		

EXHIBIT 16.15 (Continued)

Table 2 indicates that the majority of the fees earned by the practice are from automobile liability cases. We have calculated the average fees and costs per case for each of the major categories of cases conducted by the practice. It can be seen that both automobile and premises cases[1] make up approximately two-thirds of the total cases in work in process and average approximately $9,000 per case in fees earned.

The next largest portion of cases handled by the practice are personal injury protection and worker's compensation cases. These cases are much less profitable, averaging under $1,000 per case. Environmental cases, by far, earn the largest fees; however, these cases generally take a much longer amount of time to complete.

Table 2 provides a starting point for valuing the work in process for cases that have been closed subsequent to May 10, 1998. However, there are additional factors that must be considered before the fair market value can be determined.

The more difficult part of the assignment is to value the cases that remain open as of the end of our field work on February 29, 2001. This was accomplished based on our analysis of the cases that have been closed, our review of open case files, and discussions with management. Table 3 provides a summary of the cases still open as of February 29, 2001.

TABLE 3

Cases Still Open as of February 29, 2001

			Estimated	
Case No.	*Party Name*	*Type*	*Fees*	*Costs*
200637	Brooks, J.	A	$ 9,330[1]	$ 705
200360	Rencevicz, D.	MISC	12,500[2]	—
200186	Anderson, L.	A	—[3]	—
200183	Hart, T.	A	—[3]	—
200335	Huff, S.	A	3,500	710
200428	McFadden, M.	A	4,000	710
200650	Ramsey, J.	A	9,330[1]	705
200659	Patrick, A.	WC	779[1]	21
200686	Earl, J.	A	3,750	705
200701	Rogers, L.	PRM	9,229[1]	1,677
200708	Best, N.	PRM	9,229[1]	1,677
E-999	Flood	ENV	—	—
E-343	Gormley	ENV	—	—
Totals			**$ 61,647**	**$ 6,910**

[1]For each of these cases, this appraiser has used the average fees earned per case type in order to determine an approximate fee that will be earned by the practice. Mr. Gravitz provided us with his estimate of the fees that could be earned on each of these cases. For each case, the expected fee was in line with the average fees indicated in Table 2.

[2]The average fee earned on a worker's compensation case is only $779. According to Mr. Gravitz, this case is likely to settle for an amount substantially more than the average. Mr. Gravitz has estimated that the fee earned on this case could be as high as $14,000. Of this amount, $1,500 is expected to be paid to co-counsel.

[3]According to Mr. Gravitz, both of these cases are likely to be limited by the lawsuit threshold. Since these cases are below the lawsuit threshold, it is highly unlikely that a fee will be earned.

[1]These cases are also referred to as "slip and fall" cases.

(Continued)

EXHIBIT 16.15 ***(Continued)***

These cases have been settled as of February 29, 2001; however, closing statements were unavailable. Based on our discussions with Mr. Gravitz and a review of correspondence pertaining to the cases, we believe that these fees will be earned by The Law Firm.

According to Mr. Gravitz, a tentative settlement has been reached in this case for $15,000, of which The Law Firm will get 25 percent.

This environmental case was substantially complete as of May 10, 1998; however, it remained open, pending further litigation. Per discussions with Michael Gravitz and a review of case documents, it appears unlikely that any additional fees will be earned. All other fees earned in this case were collected prior to May 10, 1998.

An inquiry was made to Michael Gravitz about this case in the beginning of 1998. It was eventually sent to another law firm. Per discussions with Michael Gravitz and a review of the case files, it appears likely that there may not be a fee earned on this case. It would be highly speculative to estimate a fee at this point in time.

The costs associated with each of the cases in Table 3 were estimated based on the average cost per case type provided in our analysis in Table 2.

In order to determine the completeness of work in process, we performed several additional procedures. The first procedure was to review the cash receipts and cash disbursements records from the practice's trust accounts to determine if any cases appeared on those records that were not included in the case logs. All cases appearing on the cash receipts and cash disbursements ledgers were found in the case logs. We also reviewed all of the 1998 through 2000 closing statements looking for cases that were closed after May 10, 1998, that may have been left off of work in process. Several cases were identified that were not included on our schedule; however, upon further review of case records, it was determined that all of these cases were not started until after May 10, 1998. Therefore, they were properly excluded from our schedule of work in process.

As a final test, we reviewed subsequent cash receipts records for the practice's trust account. On a test basis, we selected cash receipts subsequent to May 10, 1998, and traced the receipt amounts, case number, and client name to our work in process list in order to ensure that no receipts came into the practice for cases that were not included in our schedule. For all receipts that could not be traced to our schedule of work in process, we reviewed the corresponding closing statements to verify that the cases were not started until after May 10, 1998, and were therefore properly excluded from our schedule of work in process.

Once the preliminary work in process figures were derived, three additional steps were necessary to reach the fair market value. These steps were as follows:

1. *Apply an overhead factor.* Since ongoing overhead would be required after the appraisal date to allow the firm to generate the ultimate fees collected, consideration should be given to the costs associated with the collection process. This included direct out-of-pocket expenses for experts, salaries for lawyers to bring the case to trial, and other overhead costs associated with keeping the practice running.
2. *Tax-effect the work in process.* Since the work in process will ultimately turn into profit to the firm, taxes should be calculated since they will ultimately be paid (either by the firm or by the individuals in the form of extra compensation).
3. *Calculate the present value of the net profit after taxes.* Since the work in process will not be collected for a period of time after the valuation date, the time value of money should be considered.

In order to apply the preceding three steps to this assignment, we started with the determination of an appropriate overhead rate to apply to the work in process. Previously, we calculated the normalized net income before taxes for the practice. These figures were $52,187 and $103,216 for 1996 and 1997, respectively. To determine the value of work in process, we have to determine the total overhead that is attributable to work in process. Our review of Schedule 2, in the back of the report, indicates that only two items require further adjustment for this purpose. Eliminating advertising expense, which is a prospective type of expense, and meals and entertainment, which may or may not relate to the work in process, results in a revised normalized net income attributable to work in process of $106,320 and $147,577 for these two years.

Applying a weighted average to the most recent year indicates that The Law Firm's normalized overhead rate is approximately 88.7 percent. This means that for every $1 of revenue, it costs the firm 88.7 cents. Historically, The Law Firm has been considerably less profitable than other law firms. However, the reality is that the firm does not generate extraordinary profits.

The next consideration is the manner in which to apply the overhead factor. We have performed an analysis based on the amount of time that each file was open. Based not only on our discussions with Mr. Gravitz, but also our past experiences with other attorneys regarding similar matters, we have applied the overhead based on the allocation that 50 percent of the expenses are incurred in the last six months of the case, 25 percent of the expenses are incurred during the period between six months and one year of the end of the case, and the balance of the expenses are spread evenly during the remainder of the time that the case stayed open.

EXHIBIT 16.15 *(Continued)*

In order to perform the necessary calculations, we set up a computer model based on the parameters discussed above. The results appear as Schedule 3 at the back of the report. Using a burden rate of 88.7 percent results in an estimate of the expenses incurred after the valuation date to be $1,298,994. This results in the profit portion of work in process attributable after the business valuation date to be $975,301.

Applying a 35 percent tax rate and taking the present value of the net income from the date the file was closed to the valuation date results in the value of this portion of the work in process to be $592,993.

Another portion of the work in process are the reimbursed costs that The Law Firm received after the valuation date. These expenses had previously been considered in the overhead factor applied against the other work in process, so there is no need to apply another factor to it. However, since these expenses are deducted when paid by the practice, taxes will be paid when the reimbursements are received. These reimbursements must also be discounted back to the valuation date. Applying similar treatment to these expenses results in an addition to work in process of $285,328.

The final portion of work in process that needs to be added is the portion attributable to the open files. The gross estimates to be received by The Law Firm are $61,647 and $6,910 for fees and costs, respectively. With the exception of cases numbered 200360, 200335, and 200428, all of the other files were opened up in the beginning of 1998. In order to estimate the value of these cases, we followed similar procedures as were used for the cases that we knew were closed. In this instance, we assumed that these cases would remain open, on average, for four years. The value was estimated as follows:

Total fees	$ 61,647
Overhead factor (88.7%)	54,681
Profit	$ 6,966
Taxes (35%)	2,438
Net profit	$ 4,528
Present value	$ 3,328

The costs were estimated as follows:

Total	$ 6,910
Taxes (35%)	2,419
Net profit	$ 4,491
Present value	$ 3,301

As a result of our analysis, work in process is estimated to be:

Cases closed to date	$ 592,993
Reimbursed costs for cases closed to date	285,328
Cases still open	3,328
Reimbursed costs for cases still open	3,301
Total work in process	**884,950**

Prepaid Insurance. Certain types of professional practices, particularly medical practices, may be paying a significant amount in malpractice premiums. Typically, these items are expensed as they are paid. The appraiser needs to be aware of the policy period as this could turn out to be a large prepaid asset on the balance sheet at the appraisal date. Imagine a medical practice that pays $120,000 in malpractice premiums on February 1 and undergoes a valuation on March 1. Since 11 months' worth of the premium is prepaid, the practice value just increased (on the basis of its assets) by $110,000. Do not double-count this by adjusting the income statement. The entire premium should be reflected if you are performing an income or market approach. This asset may be considered as an additional item in fair market value appraisals as of a certain date subject to short-rating the policy. But since nothing in life is easy, the appraiser must also consider whether the practice would most likely have to purchase what is called a *tail* to protect against any malpractice claims that arise during the forward period for prior acts. This could turn out to be a liability rather than an asset. Medical surgical practices and possibly audit firms may need this type of coverage. Who said this stuff is a walk in the park?

Supplies. Certain types of professional practices maintain a supply inventory that could be material. For example, certain medical practices maintain an inventory of drugs that may have a very high price. The appraiser should inquire about supplies. Sometimes we find out how often supplies are ordered and prorate the supplies expense. We generally do this only when supplies are considered material to the value of the practice.

Library Costs. Law firms, accounting firms, appraisal firms (like ours), and other professional practices spend a considerable amount of money each year to keep their libraries current. In some cases the library may have significant value. In other cases the volumes and volumes of books sitting on shelves in the library have been replaced by a CD-ROM. In these instances, the value may not be substantial. In fact, it may be worth only pennies. The appraiser can make a few telephone calls to find out how much the major publications are worth in the used book market.

Reasonable Compensation. Probably the most important adjustment the appraiser makes during the valuation of the professional practice is reasonable compensation. This adjustment can literally make or break the valuation conclusion. The appraiser needs to be extremely careful to ensure that all reasonable considerations are made about the professional that would impact the amount of compensation required to be paid to an employee doing the same job as the individual currently in the practice. Many factors should be considered. Among them are:

1. Job description
2. Hours worked
3. Education
4. Age
5. Special skills
6. Rainmaking ability
7. Size of the practice
8. Profitability of the practice

Exhibit 16.16 illustrates various sections of different types of professional practice compensation considerations.

EXHIBIT 16.16

Reasonable Compensation

Dental Practice

In order to determine reasonable compensation for Drs. Brown, Green, and Black, several sources of information were used. There is much controversy over the issue of reasonable compensation, and generally it is determined based on numerous factors.

Appraisal theory has taught the appraiser to calculate reasonable compensation based on the norm within the industry. The hypothetical willing buyer will have the same qualifications and experience as the hypothetical willing seller, work the same number of hours as the hypothetical seller, and be in the same cost-of-living area of the country as the hypothetical seller.

EXHIBIT 16.16 *(Continued)*

In "Professional Practice Goodwill: An Abused Concept," published by the *Journal of the American Academy of Matrimonial Lawyers* (1986), James T. Friedman found that most lawyers and judges wrongfully equate high earnings and divisible goodwill, and that most highly salaried professionals do not enjoy any more compensation than highly salaried nonprofessionals.

Friedman attacks the excess earnings method and is highly critical of the methods used to determine reasonable compensation. He states,

> In calculating excess compensation you must first deduct fair compensation for the individual whose practice you are valuing. The more valuable that individual's contribution, the higher will be the compensation entitlement, or replacement costs.

Friedman goes further and states that "the hard working, highly skilled specialist probably earns his or her total compensation and derives little excess from the enterprise."

In *Valuing Small Businesses and Professional Practices*, published by Dow Jones–Irwin, Shannon P. Pratt, D.B.A., C.F.A., C.F.P., F.A.S.A., C.R.A., a renowned expert in the valuation field, states,

> The smaller the business or practice, the more important looms the role of the owner/manager. How much of the success of the operation is due to the talent and efforts of the owner/manager(s)? How much of that success can be transferred to new ownership?

Pratt continues by stating,

> There is no point in paying a sizable sum for a business or practice from which the customers will disappear as soon as the new owner takes over, or which is dependent on a seller's talent that will not be available to the new owner.

Pratt, in his discussion of goodwill, indicates that "several factors are dominant in determining the existence and value of practice and personal goodwill for professional practices:

1. Earnings levels that can be expected in the future.
2. The level of competition.
3. The referral base.
4. The types of patients or clients the practice serves.
5. Work habits of the practitioner.
6. The fees charged (compared to others in the same specialty).
7. Where the practice is located.
8. The practice's employees.
9. The general marketability of the type of practice being sold."

According to *Financial Studies of the Small Business*, 1992–1993, published by Financial Research Associates, officers' salaries in dental practices are approximately 29.71 percent of net sales. Using this information results in officers' compensation as follows:

	1992	*1991*	*1990*	*1989*
Sales	$ 1,237,400	$ 1,278,449	$ 1,257,051	$ 1,203,644
Refunds & allowances	(46,612)	(53,700)	(21,134)	(18,425)
Net sales	$ 1,190,788	$ 1,224,749	$ 1,235,917	$ 1,185,219
Salary percentage	× 29.71%	× 29.71%	× 29.71%	× 229.71%
Officers' compensation	$ 353,783	$ 363,873	$ 367,191	$ 352,129

(Continued)

EXHIBIT 16.16 *(Continued)*

Another source, *RMA Annual Statement Studies*, 1992, published by Robert Morris Associates, indicates that based on historical data, dentists in the upper quartile earn 32.9 percent of sales on average. The upper quartile was chosen to reflect the fact that salaries in the Mid-Atlantic/Northeast area tend to be higher than the national average.

Based on the Robert Morris Associates statistics, reasonable compensation for the officers of Dental Associates would be calculated as follows:

	1992	*1991*	*1990*	*1989*
Net sales	$ 1,190,788	$ 1,224,749	$ 1,235,917	$ 1,185,219
Salary percentage	× 32.9%	× 32.9%	× 32.9%	× 32.9%
Officers' compensation	$ 391,769	$ 402,942	$ 406,617	$ 389,937

In *The 1992 Survey of Dental Practice*, the American Dental Association breaks down dentists' incomes by other criteria. Table 1 shows net income of general practitioners who earn their money from the primary practice of dentistry.

TABLE 1
Net Income of Independent General Practitioners by Age and Source of Dental Income, 1991

Source of Net Income	*Mean*	*1st Q*	*Median*	*3rd Q*	*S.D.*	*n*
Primary Private Practice						
Age group						
Under 30[1]	$ —	$ —	$ —	$ —	$ —	18
30–34	82,000	45,000	69,500	100,000	53,120	166
35–39	98,820	64,500	90,000	124,500	58,740	272
40–44	97,270	60,990	88,700	122,000	52,870	239
45–49	109,090	70,000	100,000	140,060	59,870	204
50–54	102,670	70,000	90,700	125,000	57,550	133
55–59	83,500	50,000	75,630	110,000	44,490	115
60–64	74,580	46,870	66,000	91,000	41,880	100
65+	61,730	30,000	51,000	86,000	42,380	98

Source: American Dental Association, *The 1992 Survey of Dental Practice*.

[1]There were too few respondents in this category to allow for reliable statistical analysis.

According to Table 1, the doctors' salaries would be as follows:

	Median	*3rd Quartile*
Dr. Brown	$ 75,630	$ 110,000
Dr. Green	90,000	124,500
Dr. Black	69,500	100,000
Total	$ 235,130	$ 334,500

EXHIBIT 16.16 *(Continued)*

In Table 2 income is determined by the number of years since the doctor graduated from dental school.

TABLE 2

Net Income of Independent General Practitioners by Years Since Graduation and Source of Dental Income, 1991

Source of Net Income	*Mean*	*1st Q*	*Median*	*3rd Q*	*S.D.*	*n*
Primary Private Practice						
Years since graduation						
Under 5	$ 60,910	$ 28,500	$ 50,750	$ 73,750	$ 51,140	56
5–9	88,250	50,000	80,640	106,670	56,210	230
10–14	99,660	65,000	90,000	122,000	55,810	274
15–19	103,340	64,500	97,000	136,500	51,630	208
20–24	106,820	69,000	95,000	135,000	61,260	174
25–29	94,120	60,000	87,000	120,000	53,100	133
30–34	85,580	48,000	70,000	115,000	50,840	122
35+	65,690	35,000	60,660	87,720	41,390	148

Source: American Dental Association, *The 1992 Survey of Dental Practice.*

According to this data, the dentists would earn the following:

	Median	*3rd Quartile*
Dr. Brown	$ 70,000	$ 115,000
Dr. Green	97,000	136,500
Dr. Black	80,640	106,670
TOTAL	$ 247,640	$ 358,170

Table 3 indicates earnings by number of hours worked. Based on the office hours previously discussed, each doctor works 33 hours per week for two weeks, and 41 hours during the third week. Based on this, the data in Table 3 indicates income levels as follows:

	Median	*3rd Quartile*
More than 32 hours/week	$ 90,000	$ 122,000
More than 1,600 hours/year	87,000	120,000

TABLE 3

Net Income, Age, and Hours Worked of Independent General Practitioners by Hours Worked and Source of Dental Income, 1991

Hours per Week	*Mean*	*1st Q*	*Median*	*3rd Q*	*S.D.*	*n*
Less than 32 hours:						
Primary private practice	$ 62,570	$ 30,000	$ 51,000	$ 79,000	$ 49,030	201
Total from private practice	$ 63,560	$ 32,000	$ 51,000	$ 82,000	$ 49,050	201
Total from dentistry	$ 65,580	$ 36,000	$ 55,000	$ 82,000	$ 48,850	201
Dentist age	53.5	42.0	54.0	64.0	13.9	294
Hours worked per week	25.5	24.0	28.0	30.0	5.6	294

(Continued)

EXHIBIT 16.16 *(Continued)*

Hours per Week	*Mean*	*1st Q*	*Median*	*3rd Q*	*S.D.*	*n*
32 hours or more:						
Primary private practice	$ 97,200	$ 60,000	$ 90,000	$ 122,000	$ 54,670	1144
Total from private practice	$ 97,940	$ 60,000	$ 90,000	$ 124,000	$ 54,880	1144
Total from dentistry	$ 98,430	$ 61,000	$ 90,000	$ 124,000	$ 54,860	1144
Dentist age	45.1	37.0	43.0	52.0	10.2	1664
Hours worked per week	39.7	35.0	40.0	42.0	6.7	1664

Hours per Year	*Mean*	*1st Q*	*Median*	*3rd Q*	*S.D.*	*n*
Less than 1,600 hours:						
Primary private practice	$ 80,680	$ 41,800	$ 72,500	$ 106,500	$ 54,410	368
Total from private practice	$ 81,830	$ 42,970	$ 74,020	$ 108,000	$ 55,440	368
Total from dentistry	$ 83,360	$ 45,000	$ 75,000	$ 108,500	$ 55,300	368
Dentist age	51.5	42.0	51.0	61.0	12.6	511
Hours worked per year	1322.7	1215.0	1440.0	1536.0	293.7	511
1,600 hours or more:						
Primary private practice	$ 96,300	$ 60,000	$ 87,000	$ 120,000	$ 54,980	977
Total from private practice	$ 96,930	$ 60,000	$ 88,000	$ 120,000	$ 54,850	977
Total from dentistry	$ 97,350	$ 60,000	$ 90,000	$ 120,000	$ 54,760	977
Dentist age	44.5	37.0	43.0	51.0	10.1	1447
Hours worked per year	1995.1	1750.0	1920.0	2156.0	328.6	1447

Source: American Dental Association, *The 1992 Survey of Dental Practice.*

Table 4 shows the different earnings levels based on the dentist's employment status.

TABLE 4

Net Income, Age, and Hours Worked of Independent General Practitioners by Employment Status in the Primary Practice and Source of Dental Income, 1991

Source of Net Income	*Mean*	*1st Q*	*Median*	*3rd Q*	*S.D.*	*n*
Unincorporated Sole Proprietor						
Primary private practice	$ 82,920	$ 47,250	$ 76,000	$ 109,000	$ 49,560	804
Total from private practice	$ 83,530	$ 48,000	$ 77,000	$ 110,000	$ 49,410	804
Total from dentistry	$ 84,320	$ 50,000	$ 77,000	$ 110,000	$ 49,060	804
Dentist age	46.4	37.0	44.0	55.0	11.8	1175
Hours worked per year	1826.4	1568.0	1800.0	2040.0	450.6	1175
Unincorporated Partner						
Primary private practice	$ 91,070	$ 56,500	$ 76,500	$ 103,000	$ 52,910	88
Total from private practice	$ 93,390	$ 60,000	$ 82,000	$ 107,970	$ 52,500	88
Total from dentistry	$ 93,730	$ 60,000	$ 82,000	$ 107,970	$ 52,380	88
Dentist age	43.1	33.0	39.0	51.0	12.8	125
Hours worked per year	1789.2	1600.0	1800.0	2000.0	434.2	125

EXHIBIT 16.16 *(Continued)*

Source of Net Income	*Mean*	*1st Q*	*Median*	*3rd Q*	*S.D.*	*n*
Incorporated Sole Proprietor						
Primary private practice	$ 109,670	$ 66,000	$ 100,000	$ 138,000	$ 63,620	370
Total from private practice	$ 109,950	$ 66,000	$ 100,000	$ 140,000	$ 63,580	370
Total from dentistry	$ 110,320	$ 66,000	$ 100,000	$ 140,000	$ 63,610	370
Dentist age	47.6	41.0	47.0	54.0	9.3	533
Hours worked per year	1820.3	1600.0	1800.0	2000.0	397.8	533
Incorporated Partner						
Primary private practice	$ 102,630	$ 71,000	$ 95,000	$ 125,000	$ 49,460	83
Total from private practice	$ 105,510	$ 71,000	$ 95,000	$ 130,000	$ 54,370	83
Total from dentistry	$ 107,630	$ 72,000	$ 99,000	$ 135,000	$ 55,070	83
Dentist age	44.1	36.0	43.0	52.0	10.4	125
Hours worked per year	1784.0	1536.0	1800.0	2000.0	445.5	125

Source: American Dental Association, *The 1992 Survey of Dental Practice*.

Dental Associates is a professional corporation, so the dentists are considered incorporated partners. The median earnings level for an incorporated partner is $95,000, and the income in the third quartile is $125,000.

The ADA survey then broke its statistics down by region. Tables 5, 6, and 7 highlight some of the regional differences in income, age, and hours worked.

TABLE 5

Net Income of Independent General Practitioners by Region and Source of Dental Income, 1991

Source of Net Income	*Mean*	*1st Q*	*Median*	*3rd Q*	*S.D.*	*n*
Primary Private Practice						
Region						
New England	$ 105,350	$ 75,000	$ 90,000	$ 139,000	$ 67,570	89
Middle Atlantic	90,150	54,700	82,000	115,500	53,960	208
East North Central	90,050	52,000	85,000	115,000	51,350	246
West North Central	88,780	50,000	79,000	114,000	52,540	106
South Atlantic	98,140	56,000	90,000	130,000	53,650	179
East South Central	84,370	50,000	75,560	110,000	46,500	73
West South Central	81,720	45,000	75,000	97,000	49,050	129
Mountain	81,810	42,940	75,000	110,000	51,450	79
Pacific	100,280	60,000	85,000	126,000	62,570	230

Source: American Dental Association, *The 1992 Survey of Dental Practice*.

(Continued)

EXHIBIT 16.16 *(Continued)*

TABLE 6

Age of Independent General Practitioners by Region, 1991

Type of Dentist	*Mean*	*1st Q*	*Median*	*3rd Q*	*S.D.*	*n*
General Practitioner						
Region						
New England	47.1	38.0	45.0	54.0	11.5	120
Middle Atlantic	47.7	38.0	46.0	56.0	12.3	305
East North Central	46.1	37.0	45.0	54.0	11.7	371
West North Central	46.5	39.0	45.0	53.0	10.6	148
South Atlantic	46.2	37.0	44.0	53.0	11.5	277
East South Central	46.6	38.0	43.0	55.0	10.8	106
West South Central	45.7	36.0	44.0	55.0	10.8	195
Mountain	46.4	38.0	45.0	54.0	10.2	112
Pacific	45.8	38.0	45.0	52.0	10.1	314

Source: American Dental Association, *The 1992 Survey of Dental Practice.*

TABLE 7

Annual Hours Worked by Independent Dentists by Region, 1991

Type of Dentist	*Mean*	*1st Q*	*Median*	*3rd Q*	*S.D.*	*n*
General Practitioner						
Region						
New England	1833.8	1598.0	1836.0	2028.0	391.0	120
Middle Atlantic	1792.5	1560.0	1824.0	2009.0	486.0	305
East North Central	1830.8	1560.0	1764.0	2058.0	468.3	371
West North Central	1816.7	1673.0	1806.5	2000.0	372.5	148
South Atlantic	1885.1	1620.0	1840.0	2100.0	425.2	277
East South Central	1843.7	1620.0	1862.0	2000.0	330.9	106
West South Central	1802.4	1600.0	1750.0	1960.0	350.5	195
Mountain	1891.5	1584.0	1838.0	2067.0	468.9	112
Pacific	1741.4	1504.0	1728.0	1974.0	450.3	314

Source: American Dental Association, *The 1992 Survey of Dental Practice.*

The tables shown on the previous pages indicate that general dentists in the Middle Atlantic region earn a median salary of $82,000, are of average age 46, and work 1,800 hours per year.

Based on the various statistics shown, the appraiser has determined the following reasonable compensation amounts for 1992:

Dr. Brown	$ 115,000
Dr. Green	136,500
Dr. Black	106,670

EXHIBIT 16.16 (*Continued*)

The amounts are based on the salaries shown for years since graduation, because this approximately reflects the number of years each dentist has been practicing. In addition, the third quartile was chosen to reflect a fairly stable practice in the Middle Atlantic area, one that has been in existence for almost 30 years.

The salaries chosen approximately reflect the percentage of gross income earned by each doctor in 1992. Dental Associates maintains a Procedure Analysis Report, which is used to track each doctor's productivity. In 1992, the report showed the following breakdown of revenues:

Dr. Brown	$ 322,527
Dr. Green	410,381
Dr. Black	330,810

Although Dr. Black's revenues were higher than Dr. Brown's, Dr. Brown is responsible for most of the administrative work of the dental practice, and therefore should be compensated for those additional duties and responsibilities.

The total compensation determined above represents 30.1 percent of 1992 net sales. This percentage was used to determine reasonable compensation for the other years, and the normalization adjustment is calculated as follows:

	1992	*1991*	*1990*	*1989*
Net sales	$ 1,190,788	$ 1,224,729	$ 1,235,917	$ 1,185,219
Salary percentage	× 30.1%	× 30.1%	× 30.1%	× 30.1%
Reasonable compensation	$ 358,427	$ 368,643	$ 372,011	$ 356,751
Per tax return	468,873	594,376	538,742	515,825
Adjustment	$ 110,446	$ 225,733	$ 166,731	$ 159,074

Law Firm

One of the difficult components of a business valuation for a law practice is the determination of reasonable compensation for the owner of the practice. The purpose of reflecting reasonable compensation is so that a willing buyer, if purely an investor, would see what he or she would have to pay someone to perform the services that are done by the current owner.

Appraisal theory teaches the appraiser to calculate reasonable compensation based on the norm within the industry. The hypothetical willing buyer will have the same qualifications and experience as a hypothetical willing seller, work the same number of hours as the hypothetical seller, and be in the same cost-of-living area of the country as the hypothetical seller. In fact, case law has suggested that the appraiser examine the value of goodwill very carefully "for the individual practitioner will be forced to pay the ex-spouse 'tangible' dollars for an intangible asset at a value concededly arrived at on the basis of some uncertain elements."[1] Case law also suggests that the age, health, and professional reputation of the practitioner, the nature of the practice, the length of time the practice has been in existence, its past profits, its comparative professional success, and the value of its other assets should also be taken into consideration in the determination of goodwill.[2]

However, goodwill cannot be measured without properly considering the effort expended by the practitioner. A reasonable level of compensation cannot be determined by merely consulting a salary survey without considering the work habits of the professional. Shannon Pratt states,

> It's almost a cliché that professionals work long hours. However, some are willing to work longer hours than others. A practice that requires 80 hours a week of a practitioner's time will not be worth as much per dollar of income to a purchaser as one that requires only 50 hours per week.[3]

[1] *Dugan v. Dugan*, 92 N.J. Super. 435, 457 A.2d at 7.
[2] *In re marriage of Lopez*, 38 Cal. App. 3d 93, 113 Cal. Rptr. 58 (3d Dist. 1974).
[3] Shannon P. Pratt, *Valuing Small Businesses and Professional Practices*, 2nd ed. (Homewood, Ill.: Business One Irwin, 1993), 414.

(Continued)

EXHIBIT 16.16 ***(Continued)***

A review of the time and billing records of Donald Neal & Associates revealed the following billable hours per individual attorney over the past several years:

	1995	*1994*	*1993*	*1992*	*1991*
DAN	3486.25	3299.25	3284.00	3208.00	3576.00
KLJ	808.50				
MFS					1422.80
REG	973.40	2096.45	2135.50	629.00	
LJG					627.50
KEN		1191.00	2245.75	2105.75	738.75
AMC	317.75	2359.50	1690.25	1734.00	996.00
SCS	888.75				
BCS	2815.50	2753.50	2097.50		
DRR	2427.50	712.25			
LEC				1309.25	650.50

The billable hours worked by Mr. Neal far exceed those for all other attorneys in the firm. The nature of this practice requires exceptionally long hours. Turnover in associates has been a problem for this reason. However, as the owner, Mr. Neal does whatever it takes to get the job done. This is typical for a small professional practice.

What makes this practice somewhat unique is the "emergency room law" type of practice. If a client calls with a problem, it is not uncommon for the firm to dispatch at least one attorney immediately to investigate a situation. For example, if a call comes in about an alleged child molestation, a team of attorneys may be sent hours away to interview students, teachers, and the school administration. This can result in very long hours worked on a particular assignment. Also, school board meetings tend to be at night, and these types of jobs can also make for an exceptionally long day.

In order to determine a reasonable level of compensation for Mr. Neal, this appraiser consulted the *1996 Survey of Law Firm Economics*, published by Altman Weil Pensa (AWP). This survey gives the appraiser a benchmark of compensation levels. Various factors, besides the region in which the law practice operates, affect the amount of compensation earned by a practice's owners. These factors include the size of the practice, the type of law performed, and the year the owners were admitted to the bar. AWP provides a breakdown of the salaries for lawyers by each of these categories.

In order to use the survey, the appraiser considered several specialties within the legal profession to compare Donald Neal & Associates against. There are no statistics for education law, but there are enough similarities between insurance defense firms and labor/employment specialties that a meaningful comparison could be made.

The more meaningful data about the owners of the firms includes the following:

	Average	*Lower Quartile*	*Median*	*Upper Quartile*	*Ninth Decile*
Billable Hours					
All firms	1,722	1,471	1,707	1,948	2,216
South	1,759	1,512	1,747	1,976	2,245
Under nine lawyers	1,683	1,352	1,664	2,019	2,247
Insurance defense	1,943	1,693	1,916	2,164	2,540
Labor/employment	1,782	1,585	1,758	1,990	2,183
Admitted bar (1978)	1,728	1,479	1,691	1,950	2,246

EXHIBIT 16.16 *(Continued)*

	Average	*Lower Quartile*	*Median*	*Upper Quartile*	*Ninth Decile*
Total Compensation					
All firms	$ 194,966	$ 121,834	$ 168,751	$ 230,133	$ 320,411
South[1]	292,835	189,119	265,360	378,821	458,437
Under nine lawyers[2]	187,821	93,870	143,265	239,200	328,410
South	193,813	127,409	171,819	229,416	303,150
Under nine lawyers	170,174	96,617	134,294	216,399	318,170
Insurance defense	176,802	112,516	152,159	218,692	290,883
Labor/employment	173,284	115,804	157,091	199,227	280,210
Admitted bar (1978)	206,802	141,236	183,893	241,663	323,290
Admitted bar (1978)[3]	206,733	148,333	185,334	245,085	314,499
Admitted bar (1978)[4]	195,584	114,253	176,610	248,943	336,329

[1]Owners with significant management responsibilities.
[2]Owners with significant management responsibilities.
[3]South only.
[4]Firms with under nine lawyers.

A review of the above data indicates that the hours worked by Mr. Neal far exceed those of his peers. In fact, using 1995 as a comparison to the AWP data reflects the following:

				Percentage Over	
	Media AWP	*Ninth Decile*	*Billable Hours*	*Median*	*Ninth Decile*
All firms	1,707.00	2,216.00	3,486.25	+ 104.2%	+ 57.3%
South	1,747.00	2,245.00	3,486.25	+ 99.6%	+ 55.3%
Under nine lawyers	1,664.00	2,247.00	3,486.25	+ 109.5%	+ 55.2%
Insurance defense	1,916.00	2,540.00	3,486.25	+ 81.9%	+ 37.3%
Labor/employment	1,758.00	2,183.00	3,486.25	+ 98.3%	+ 59.7%
Admitted bar (1978)	1,691.00	2,246.00	3,486.25	+ 106.2%	+ 55.2%

Mr. Neal worked almost twice the number of hours of any of the attorneys, based on median hours worked. He also worked, on average, 53 percent more hours than the attorneys who made up the ninth decile of the survey. Clearly, the profitability of the firm is attributable, in large part, to the work habits of the owner.

A review of the total compensation for owners of firms reflects various levels, depending on the categorization within the survey. The median total compensation for firms in the south, where the owners have significant management responsibilities, was $265,360, while the ninth decile for this category was $458,437. It can only be assumed by this appraiser that there are larger firms reflected in these figures.

Firms with under nine lawyers for this same group had a median and ninth decile total compensation of $143,265 and $328,410, respectively. Total compensation for owners without significant management responsibilities ranged from a median of $134,294 to $183,893 and a ninth decile from $280,210 to $336,329.

(Continued)

EXHIBIT 16.16 *(Continued)*

Whether the median or the ninth decile compensation is used as a base compensation for Mr. Neal, these figures must be adjusted for the significant number of hours that he works. Based on the data presented above, a base amount, before this adjustment, appears to be approximately $175,000 for the median and $315,000 for the ninth decile. These figures can then be adjusted as follows:

	Median	*Ninth Decile*
Base amount	$ 175,000	$ 315,000
Excess billable hours percentage	× 100%	× 53%
Extra compensation	$ 175,000	$ 166,950
Total compensation	$ 350,000	$ 481,950

The next part of this analysis is the determination of which group of owners is considered to be applicable to Mr. Neal. Mr. Neal is the firm's "rainmaker." He is the reason that clients come back for more. While repeat patronage is an element of goodwill, the personal component of the goodwill will generally be reflected in the level of compensation that an individual can command. Being a rainmaker adds significant value to the firm. Part of that value is reflected in the salary.

The upper quartile of the survey is a more conservative level of compensation than the ninth decile. We feel that the median does not compensate Mr. Neal for his rainmaking or administrative responsibilities. The average billable hours for the upper quartile was about 2,000 hours, or about 74 percent less than Mr. Neal's billable hours. The survey compensation is about $230,000. After adjusting for hours worked, compensation is estimated as $400,200.

In our opinion, reasonable compensation appears to be about $400,000. This represents 26.8 percent of 1995 revenues. In order to check this amount for reasonableness, we consulted *RMA Annual Statement Studies 1996*, published by Robert Morris Associates, a banking organization that compiles financial information by Standard Industrial Classification Code. According to this publication, the percentage of officers', directors', or owners' compensation to sales was 28.7 percent for firms with $1–3 million in revenues.

Prior years' compensation has been calculated as 26.8 percent of revenues, to be consistent with our calculation in 1995.

Accounting Practice

In order to determine reasonable salaries for Messrs. Thomas and Lux we reviewed several sources of information. The first source was the survey from the Texas Society of CPAs, which indicates that owners of firms with revenues between $401,000 and $1,000,000 receive 52 percent of revenues as earnings. For firms with revenues over $1,000,000 this drops significantly to 38.2 percent of revenues. The second source we reviewed was Robert Morris Associates' *1997 Annual Statement Studies*. This data indicates salaries for partners of approximately 27.2 to 27.5 percent of revenues.

The third source of information we reviewed was the *1997 Accounting Finance and Information Technology Salary Guide*, published by Robert Half. While this survey does not discuss salaries at partner levels, it does report data for the manager level. According to the survey, managers' salaries could range as high as $76,000 in accounting firms with revenues under $15 million. This is based on Robert Half's placement experience. The fourth and final source of information we used was the firm itself. Brian Edwards, CPA, is the firm's manager, who at the valuation date was making $86,000 per year. Combined with the Robert Half data, this sets an absolute floor on the compensation of the firm's partners. Since the partners are the ones generating the accounts, they should naturally be more highly compensated than the individuals strictly servicing the accounts.

Since the Texas Society of CPAs survey deals with firms in New Jersey, it is more relevant than the RMA data. As discussed, the partners of firms with over $1,000,000 in revenues earn 38.2 percent of revenues. This is consistent with the RMA data when pretax profits are factored in; combining salaries and profits results in a 36.4 percent salary level of partners for firms with revenues between $1 million and $3 million. Based on this data, we have determined reasonable salaries for Mr. Thomas and Mr. Lux to be approximately 27 percent of revenues for 1997, or $285,000. We have assumed this to be the appropriate percentage for all years in our analysis to reflect their salaries based on fees generated. These figures are calculated as follows:

Year	*Revenues*	*%*	*Officers' Compensation*
1997	$ 1,055,627	27%	$ 285,019
1996	901,226	27%	243,331
1995	789,052	27%	213,044
1994	775,066	27%	209,268
1993	861,495	27%	232,604

Given the industry data and the number of hours worked by the two partners, the data appears reasonable.

EXHIBIT 16.16 *(Continued)*

Another Accounting Practice

According to The Firm's financial statements, none of The Firm's partners takes an annual salary. Therefore, the income statement must be normalized to account for the number of partners needed to maintain daily operations of The Firm, and for an appropriate level of compensation required to replace them. Based on information provided regarding partners' billable hours in the first nine months of 1993, on average each partner's total hours worked consisted of 42 percent billable hours and 58 percent nonbillable hours. In the first nine months of 1992, approximately 47 percent of partners' total hours were billable.

According to the Texas Society's *1994 Practice Management Survey,* 53 percent of total hours of active owners of large accounting practices are billable. Assuming that the 1992 and 1993 time analysis of the Jackson Greer partners' work is comparable to their billable hours worked as of October 1995, Jackson Greer's partner productivity is below the industry average. As of October 1995, The Firm has eight partners. We estimate that six partners would be the number of partners necessary to run the practice at an efficient level compared to its peer group.

Jackson Greer establishes hourly billing rates based on a .00225 multiple of the employee's annual salary. For partners of The Firm, the hourly billable rate is $250. Divided by the multiple, this results in an annual salary of approximately $110,000 per partner.

In order to verify the reasonableness of the level of salary, we performed research regarding salaries paid to partners of accounting in order to compare the Jackson Greer partner salary to industry statistics. Our findings are as follows:

Source	*Criterion*	*Salary*
CPA Newsletters	CPA Salaries—Partner Mid-Atlantic Region	$ 113,000
	CPA Salaries—Partner Firm Revenue over $1,700,000	120,000
Executive Compensation Survey Analysis[1]	CEO President—Median Sales Volume: $2.5–9.99 Mil.	110,815
Source Finance's *1994 Accounting & Finance Salary Survey*	Public Accounting Partner—Median	90,000

[1]Published by the National Institute of Business Management.

Utilizing these surveys, the average partner salary is approximately $108,000. Based on this research, we feel that $110,000 is a reasonable estimate for a partner's salary at Jackson Greer.

For 1995, a reasonable officers' compensation expense of $660,000 was added to Jackson Greer's operating expenses. This amount is composed of a $110,000 salary per partner, multiplied by six partners. In order to account for this expense in previous years, this amount was deflated at an annual rate of 6 percent based on the average of 6.5 percent and 5.4 percent reflected in *CPA Newsletters'* Annual Compensation Survey for 1994 and 1995, respectively. Before calculation of reasonable owner's compensation for 1990, two partner's salaries were removed (based on 1991 salary estimates) to accommodate the fact that two partners joined Jackson Greer in the November 1990 to January 1991 period.

Medical Practice

Since Dr. Peters operates as a sole proprietorship, he does not take a salary from the practice. Rather, he pays taxes on the net income from the practice.

A willing buyer might not operate the practice as a sole proprietorship, so in order to determine what a reasonable level of earnings will be from the practice, a reasonable level of salary must be factored in.

MGMA produces a second survey entitled *Physician Compensation and Production Survey: 1997 Report Based on 1996 Data.* According to this survey, some median compensation figures are as follows:

Pediatricians: single specialties	$ 137,994
Pediatricians: Eastern U.S.	128,177
Pediatricians: 51%–100% Managed Care	130,998
Primary care: Eastern U.S.	129,238
Primary care: 51%–100% managed care	135,598

(Continued)

EXHIBIT 16.16 *(Continued)*

According to the American Medical Association's publication *Physician Marketplace Statistics 1997/98*, some median compensation figures are:

Pediatricians: Self-employed (U.S.)	$ 149,000
Pediatricians: Self-employed (mid-Atlantic)	129,000

Some additional information provided in the AMA publication is:

Median office hours:	
Pediatricians	35
New Jersey	30
Self-employed	30

In addition, median hours spent in hospital rounds for all three categories are five.

The salary range provided above indicates that median salaries for pediatricians range from $129,000 to $149,000. Therefore, a salary of $135,000 appears to be reasonable.

According to the MGMA survey, median compensation rose 2.29 percent from 1995 to 1996, and 2.12 percent from 1994 to 1995. Therefore, these figures have been used to deflate the 1996 salaries for the prior years.

Another Medical Practice

Reasonable compensation must be deducted from the practice's net income to determine the economic return available to a purchaser after compensation for working the practice is considered. In order to determine a reasonable level of compensation, the work habits of the doctors were considered.

According to Dr. Dave, each doctor worked, on average, a 60-hour week. They rotated every fifth weekend with another medical group when they were "on call," but Dr. Dave had not performed night calls for the past two years as he is the senior doctor.

According to *Socioeconomic Characteristics of Medical Practice 1994*, published by the American Medical Association, the mean number of hours of direct patient care activities per week in 1993, for Internal Medicine Specialists, was 49.1 while the mean number of hours in all professional activities for this same group was 58.4. This places Dr. Dave and Dr. Arnold in line with their colleagues. *Medical Economics*, published by Medical Economics Company, Inc. and *Socioeconomic Characteristics of Medical Practice 1994* were consulted with respect to compensation. These sources reflect the following:

	1992	*1991*	*1990*	*1989*
Medical Economics				
All internists	115,140	111,970	110,860	110,500
Incorporated practices	132,190	123,290	N/A	122,000
Socioeconomic				
Mean—Internists	159,300	149,600	152,500	146,500
Median—Internists	130,000	125,000	120,000	120,000

Source: *Socioeconomic Characteristics of Medical Practice* 1994, American Medical Association, copy 1994.

The incorporated practices from *Medical Economics* and the median net income from *Socioeconomic Characteristics of Medical Practice 1994* are the best indications of compensation since Hypertension is incorporated and the median is generally a better statistical measure than the mean. Based on the 1992 figures of $132,190 and $130,000, respectively, reasonable compensation has been estimated at $135,000 each, or $270,000. Prior years have been estimated based on a similar rationale.

And Yet Another Medical Practice

Dr. Johnson works for The Practice and therefore is entitled to a salary for services rendered. As previously mentioned, Dr. Johnson has office hours 23 hours each week. Although he spends additional hours in professional activities each week, it is not equal to the 49.5 patient hours spent by the average OB-GYN.[1] According to the American Medical Association's (AMA) statistics, the average number of patients seen each week is 75.4, while Dr. Johnson sees approximately 35 patients each week. Clearly, Johnson P.C. is a part-time practice, and therefore, Dr. Johnson's salary should be commensurate with the amount of time spends.

[1]Marvin L. Gonzalez, ed., *Socioeconomic Characteristics of Medical Practice* (Chicago: American Medical Association, 1996).

EXHIBIT 16.16 *(Continued)*

An additional item to note in comparing Johnson P.C. to the industry statistics is The Practice's average fees. Johnson P.C. charges existing patients $35 for an office visit, while new patients are charged $58 per visit. The AMA statistics indicate that the average fee for existing patients in the Middle Atlantic region is $73.60, while new patients are charged $104.69. This is clearly related to the demographics of the area of practice. A comparison of various expense categories indicates that even on an adjusted basis, Johnson P.C.'s expenses are higher than the industry norms. These factors must be considered in determining a reasonable compensation level.

In order to determine a reasonable level of compensation for Dr. Johnson, we also utilized information located in *Physician Compensation and Production Survey: 1996 Report Based on 1995 Data*, published by the Medical Group Management Association (MGMA), which reports on compensation data for physicians in various specialties. According to the survey, medical specialists in the Southern region of the United States had the highest level of compensation, followed by the Midwest, Eastern, and Western regions of the United States.

According to the survey, the median compensation for an OB-GYN during 1995 was $215,000, while the mean compensation amounted to $235,500. In addition, OB-GYN salaries in the 25th percentile were $178,500.

Physician compensation was also broken down into geographic locations, as well as based on years of service. OB-GYNs in the Eastern region of the United States earned a median salary of $235,783, while the median salary for OB-GYNs with 8 to 17 years of experience was $232,009.

The salary levels do not include any benefits. According to MGMA, median retirement benefits for OB-GYNs are $18,750, while the 25th percentile amount was $12,000.

Based on the information provided in the MGMA survey, as well as considering the analysis performed, we have estimated reasonable compensation for Dr. Johnson to be $95,000 for 1995. This is based on approximately 50 percent of the salary and benefits of the 25th percentile. The 25th percentile was deemed to be appropriate, due to the analysis performed of Johnson P.C. We then considered the fact that Dr. Johnson only works approximately 50 percent of the hours of other OB-GYNs, based on industry statistics.

In addition to salary information, MGMA provided median salary increases for the last few years. Salaries for 1993 and 1994 were deflated using these percentages as follows:

	% Increase	*Compensation*
1995	8.17%	95,000
1994	3.29%	87,239
1993		84,369

Psychology Practice

In order to determine reasonable compensation for Dr. Lewis, several sources of information were used. There is much controversy over the issue of reasonable compensation, and it generally is determined based on numerous factors.

In *Valuing Professional Practices and Licenses: A Guide for the Matrimonial Practitioner*, published by Prentice Hall Law & Business, Ronald Klein, CPA, states that:

> capitalization techniques appear to be sound in theory, but they have many problems because they are subjective. For one, there is no industry source for determining average earnings for physicians. The AMA publication *Medical Economics*, and various other sources, all contain average earnings figures for physicians and break them down by specialty, by geographical location, by age, and so forth. Yet, there is no consensus on these figures and no consistency as to which average earnings figures should be used in the capitalization techniques.

Klein reminds us that "medical practices should be valued in the divorce based upon the same economic factors that are customarily considered in the sales process."

The work habits of the practitioner must also be considered in the determination of reasonable compensation. Pratt logically states that "a practice that requires 80 hours a week of a practitioner's time will not be worth as much per dollar of income to a purchaser as one that requires only 50 hours per week."

Finally, the American Psychological Association through their Office of Demographic Employment and Educational Research produces a salary survey every two years relating to salaries in psychology. The most recent survey published was in February 1990, entitled *Report of the 1989 Salary Survey*.

This survey breaks down the field of psychology into approximately 10 categories. Only that data which is applicable to Dr. Lewis's practice has been considered in this appraisal. According to the survey, the data represents salaries for individuals who are employed full-time and net income for full-time self-employed persons. Full-time is considered to be at least 32 to 35 hours per week. The survey also indicates that "the salary data in this report is based on a national sample. For locations where the cost of living differs significantly from the national average, the average salaries would be expected to vary accordingly."

(Continued)

EXHIBIT 16.16 ***(Continued)***

The survey indicates the following information for doctoral-level, licensed individuals with 20 to 24 years of experience:

11–12-Month Salary	*20–24 Years*
$150,000 or more	8
$100,000 to $149,000	37
$ 90,000 to $ 99,000	9
$ 80,000 to $ 89,000	21
$ 70,000 to $ 79,000	32
$ 60,000 to $ 69,000	29
$ 55,000 to $ 59,000	14
$ 50,000 to $ 54,000	43
$ 45,000 to $ 49,000	17
$ 40,000 to $ 44,000	18
$ 35,000 to $ 39,000	10
$ 30,000 to $ 34,000	9
$ 25,000 to $ 29,000	3
$ 20,000 to $ 24,000	3
$ 15,000 to $ 19,000	2
$ 10,000 to $ 14,000	0
Total	255
90th percentile	$ 120,000
75th percentile	$ 85,000
Median: 50th percentile	$ 60,000
25th percentile	$ 50,000
10th percentile	$ 38,600
Mean	$ 69,976
Standard deviation	$ 33,802

Another table in this survey indicates salary information by employment setting. Those practitioners in individual practice with 20 to 24 years of experience were reported as follows:

Median	*Q1*	*Q3*	*Mean*	*Std. Dev.*	*Number*
$ 72,000	$ 52,000	$ 96,000	$ 78,982	$ 41,334	135

A breakdown by region was provided in this survey where the median years of experience ranged from 13 to 15 years. Although the compensation levels cannot be used as presented, this data is useful to allow the appraiser to calculate the salary differential that is attributable to this part of the United States. Information provided in this table is as follows:

Region	*Salary—Indep. Practice*
New England	$ 60,000
Middle Atlantic	70,000
East North Central	65,000
West North Central	55,000
South Atlantic	70,000
East South Atlantic	63,000
West South Atlantic	70,000
Mountain	61,000
Pacific	72,000

EXHIBIT 16.16 *(Continued)*

New Jersey is categorized in the Middle Atlantic region and is approximately 7.5 percent higher than the national average.

Another source of financial information used was *SPBC Statistics, 1991,* based on a survey of medical and dental practices conducted by the Society of Professional Business Consultants and the PM Group.

According to this survey, psychologists in 1990 averaged gross charges of $162,973, receipts of $153,286, and a net profit before owner compensation of $97,045. This information must be used cautiously, however, because the sample size was relatively small and did not include the Middle Atlantic region. If the trend provided previously is correct, a 7.5 percent increase to these figures might be appropriate. This would result in the following:

Charges	$ 175,196
Receipts	$ 164,782
Profit before compensation	$ 104,323

Charges of $175,196 could be achieved by a practitioner that charges $100 per hour by working 1,752 contact hours with patients. A practitioner working more hours would be expected to see larger revenues charged and collected, resulting in a higher net income.

Another useful source of information is the *1991 Physician Starting Salary Survey,* published by The Health Care Group Inc. Selected data from this survey is presented below for psychology:

Year	*Location*	*1st Year*	*2nd Year*
1991	Urban D.C.	$ 75,000	$ 85,000
	Suburban Pa.	35% collections	same
1990	Washington	$ 125,000	ownership
1989	Sacramento, Calif.	$ 78,000	not given
1988	New Orleans, La.	$ 60,000	$ 75,000+ bonus
	Charlotte, N.C.	$ 90,000	$ 100,000

The information in this survey depicts starting salaries and does not indicate level of experience or employment setting. Therefore, this information must be used carefully.

Dr. Lewis's reasonable compensation must be based on the fact that he has approximately 22 years of experience, works 60 to 70 hours per week, and is located in New Jersey. Dr. Lewis's duties also include administrative functions that would normally be performed by a clerical person.

Dr. Lewis works almost twice the number of hours considered full-time by the American Psychological Association's survey (32 to 35 hours per week). The mean income for experienced practitioners was $69,976 with a standard deviation of $33,802. This means that the upper end of the salary scale within the range considered "normal" was $103,778 as a national average.

This must now be increased by 7.5 percent to compensate for being in New Jersey. This results in the average compensation being $111,561 without considering the long hours worked.

The other statistics presented above result in similar levels of compensation. The information by employment setting had a mean of $78,982 with a standard deviation of $41,334, yielding a normal distribution as high as $120,316 before applying a 7.5 percent increase for being in New Jersey. This results in compensation of $129,340.

The *SPBC Statistics, 1991* survey showed *starting* salaries of $75,000 to $125,000. Considering Dr. Lewis's experience, level of education, and long work hours, it would not be unreasonable to place Dr. Lewis at the higher end of this range, if not above it.

After weighing all of the factors discussed, a reasonable level of compensation for Dr. Lewis in 1990 would be as follows:

Psychologist	$ 125,000
Clerical duties	$ 12,000
Total	$ 137,000

Prior years will be reduced in the same proportion as hourly billing rates were charged. This results in the following:

Year	*Hourly Rate*	*Compensation*
1990	$ 100	$ 137,000
1989	$ 90	$ 123,300
1988	$ 80	$ 109,600
1987	$ 80	$ 109,600
1986	$ 70	$ 95,900

Valuation Calculations: Unique Aspects

Sometimes, professional practice valuations involve more than the typical calculations. All of the normal methodologies will be employed in the valuation process. However, many professional practices place a greater emphasis on the gross revenues of the practice. Obviously, you cannot ignore earnings, but the willing buyer, who may be a strategic or synergistic buyer, will frequently be purchasing the revenue stream. This may be the highest value for the practice. For control valuations, this may be the correct value even though it is higher than the other indications of value. Although not a professional practice valuation, read my analysis in Chapter 18 regarding the *Newhouse* case. Exhibit 16.17 contains an example of the market approach.

EXHIBIT 16.17
Market Approach

In order to determine the value of John Smith & Company using a market approach, an attempt was made by this appraiser to gather information regarding similar professional practices bought and sold in the open market. Due to the nature of closely held businesses, this information is difficult to obtain. The only information that was located was the data that is maintained in a market data file by The Institute of Business Appraisers, Inc. The Institute of Business Appraisers is a professional appraisal organization that, among other things, maintains a computer database of transactions of closely held businesses. There are approximately 18,000 entries in the database. The information contained in the database is submitted by members of the organization who have been involved in actual transactions. Some data is purchased from outside sources that are deemed reliable. We have analyzed this data and determined that annual sales of bookkeeping, accounting, and tax practices ranged from $12,000 to $455,000, with sales prices varying from $4,000 to $468,000.

Most of the transactions in the database took place in California, which generally has the same multiples as the East Coast of the United States, slightly higher than other parts of the country. The appraisal subject is in Some Town. Although this is one factor to consider in selecting a pricing multiple, the impact of the location is relatively immaterial.

Considering the fees generated by John Smith & Company, only firms with revenues in excess of $100,000 are considered in this analysis. This leaves 35 transactions from which pricing multiples can possibly be calculated.

Annual earnings are defined in the database as reported earnings before owner's compensation, interest, and taxes. The ratios for firms with revenues greater than $100,000 are reflected as follows:

	Sales Price to Gross Revenues	*Sales Price to Annual Earnings*
Mean	1.10	2.25
Median	1.07	2.10

Statistically, whether the mean or median is used, the results will be close in this case. Using the median ratio, which is more statistically correct than the mean, as a benchmark for beginning further analysis results in an indication of value of John Smith & Company as explained in the following sections of this report.

Sales Price to Gross Revenues

John Smith & Company's revenues for 1991 were $1,019,644 on a cash basis. The question that a willing buyer would raise in an acquisition of the firm is how much of this revenue would I keep? Accounting practices are generally sold on the basis of client retention. An earnout is the most common method, but in the case of an appraisal, the value must be estimated, in order to determine a cash-equivalent price for the practice. For example, a typical transaction may be for the buyer to pay the seller $0.xx for every $1 collected from the existing client base for the next number of years. In this manner, the buyer would make payments only if the client is retained. This creates a solid reason for the seller to assist in a smooth transition to the buyer.

In order to estimate that portion of the client base that may be retained by the purchaser, this appraiser made a thorough review of the client relationships and potential for transferability of these clients. We had lengthy discussions with management about their clients and the services that are rendered for them.

As indicated previously, about 70 percent of the firm's 1991 revenues came from only 30 clients. We analyzed each of the client relationships with the firm, the services that were provided by the firm to the client, and other such matters that may affect the transferability of the client revenues to another firm. Our workpapers contain our detailed analysis. The result of this analysis is that a purchaser of John Smith & Company could expect to keep approximately $602,238 in revenues. We do not believe that a prudent purchaser would pay for this practice without considering client retention.

EXHIBIT 16.17 *(Continued)*

Another consideration is the appropriate multiple to be used, based on the quality of the practice, its clients, and its revenue base, particularly its expected stability and the firm's profitability. Furthermore, a review of the firm's revenues shows a reasonable growth from year to year. The firm also reflects a modest level of profitability, which once again makes John Smith & Company a plausible acquisition candidate.

This means that John Smith & Company would be valued, for sale, before considering certain assets and liabilities that would not be sold with the practice, as follows:

Gross revenues (forecast)	$ 602,238
Multiple	× 1.25
Indicated value	$ 752,798

The value of the practice must now be adjusted for those assets and liabilities that would not ordinarily be sold in this type of transaction. In this instance, all assets and liabilities, other than the leasehold, fixed assets, and work in progress of the practice, would remain with the sellers. The net value of these assets was negative $418,417 (see the section of this report entitled "The Asset-Based Approach" for a discussion of the company's assets and liabilities).

The value of the equity of the firm would, therefore, be derived as follows:

Indicated sales price	$ 752,798
Net retained assets	(418,417)
Enterprise value	$ 334,381
Rounded	$ 334,000

The detailed analysis that is referred to in Exhibit 16.17 included discussing every client with the partners to determine the likelihood of that client staying with a new owner if the firm were sold. We looked at one-time events, personal relationships, location of the clients (out-of-town clients are frequently the first to go if there has been a long-distance relationship between the accountant and the client), as well as the client's involvement in the community. Certain clients belonged to the local country club and played golf with individuals who were partners in other accounting firms. There was a good possibility that in the event of a sale that client would be lost. Once we synthesized all of this data, we assigned weights to them based on the likelihood of losing the client. Although somewhat arbitrary (the weights, I mean), we determined what was the most likely percentage of retention for the client base. From my own experience, you generally keep only 65 percent to 80 percent of the clients during the first three to five years.

This firm also had a large deferred pension liability that impacted its balance sheet. Usually the liabilities are not greater than the assets that are retained.

Although the previous illustration involved an accounting practice, let's take this opportunity to discuss a useful source for market data for medical practices. The *Irving Levin Associates' Health Care Acquisition Report* is possibly the most up-to-date resource for medical practice transactions. If you value medical practices, visit www.irvinglevin.com for more information about this resource.

Rules of Thumb

A very popular, but often abused method of valuation for professional practices is the multiple-of-revenue method. This method is also referred to as the "industry rule of thumb" method. There are many disadvantages to this method. The major disadvantage is the number of different multiples that are used for the same type of practice. A classic example of the danger in applying this method is one of the historical rules of thumb for an accounting practice. Over the years, accounting practices have been sold for a range between

50 percent and 150 percent of gross billings. This means that an accounting practice with gross billings of $1 million could be valued anywhere from $500,000 to $1,500,000. This is clearly too wide a spread to be meaningful. Disparities such as this take place all of the time and must be considered before applying *unsupported* rules of thumb.

Sometimes we will put a rule-of-thumb section into a report to act as a sanity check on the other, real methods of valuation. When we do this, we usually start off our report with the discussion that started off this section of the book. Exhibit 16.18 illustrates a section of a report.

EXHIBIT 16.18
Rules of Thumb

There were several "rules of thumb" located for accounting practices. In *Handbook of Small Business Valuation Formulas and Rules of Thumb*, published by Valuation Press, Glenn M. Desmond, A.S.A., M.A.I., suggests two methods:

1. A monthly net revenue multiplier of 9 to 15.

   As a result of this multiplier, the value of the practice, without considering the retained assets, would be as follows:

	Low	*High*
Annual Forecast revenues	$ 602,238	$ 602,238
	÷ 12	÷ 12
Monthly revenues	$ 50,187	$ 50,187
	× 9	× 15
Indicated value	$ 451,683	$ 752,805
Retained assets	(418,417)	(418,417)
Enterprise value	$ 33,266	$ 334,388
Rounded	$ 33,000	$ 334,000

2. Annual owner's cash flow multiplier, with a multiplier between 2 and 5.

   The value range under this method is calculated as follows:

Normalized owner's cash flow	$ 420,289	$ 420,289
Multiplier	× 2.0	× 5.0
Indicated value	$ 840,578	$ 2,101,445
Add retained assets	(418,417)	(418,417)
Enterprise value	$ 422,161	$ 1,683,028
Rounded	$ 422,000	$ 1,683,000

The problems with using rules of thumb are apparent from reviewing the wide divergence of values that are calculated, with little data supporting the conclusions. Although rules of thumb can sometimes be used as a sanity check on other methodologies employed by an appraiser, they should never be considered as a stand-alone, viable appraisal method. In Exhibit 16.18, the rules of thumb create values ranging from $33,000 to $1,683,000—a 5,000 percent swing in values. Very meaningful, isn't it?

Statutory Rule Value

Once in a while, the appraiser will find a provision built into a professional licensing law that requires a particular methodology to be used in certain circumstances. If there is a statutory valuation method required, use it. Even if it is not required, it may give you one more indication to consider. Exhibit 16.19 contains a section of a report dealing with a statutory methodology.

EXHIBIT 16.19
Statutory Valuation Method

The State of Arkansas has passed laws governing business formation and conduct within Arkansas. The Arkansas Professional Corporation Act, in particular, governs the formation; corporate names; limitations on officers, directors, and shareholders; employees; certification; and price of shares of deceased or disqualified shareholders.

Although this valuation does not deal with a deceased or disqualified shareholder, the statute does provide guidance in determining value. The statute states,

> 4-29-213. Shares of deceased or disqualified shareholder—Price.
> If the articles of incorporation or bylaws of a corporation subject to this subchapter fail to state a price or method of determining a fixed price at which the corporation or its shareholders may purchase the shares of a deceased shareholder or a shareholder no longer qualified to own shares in the corporation, then the price for the shares shall be the book value as of the end of the month immediately preceding the death or disqualification of the shareholder. Book value shall be determined from the books and records of the corporation in accordance with the regular method of accounting used by the corporation.

In accordance with this statute, the value of John Smith & Company is determined as $125,186, as stated in the balance sheet dated December 31, 1991, located in Schedule 1 at the end of this report.

While the statutory method discussed in Exhibit 16.19 did not provide us with anything even remotely close to the values that we derived (other than the low end of the rule of thumb), it turned out to be pretty useful. In this valuation, the IRS was challenging the buyout of the senior partner from this accounting practice. In fact, the IRS agent claimed that the practice was worth a fortune. Unfortunately, he used the high end of a rule of thumb. Even the statutory method showed that it was not worth anywhere near what the agent came up with.

Asset-Based Approach

More often than not, an adjusted balance sheet may be created for the purpose of figuring out the value of the assets and liabilities that may be retained by the owners if a market approach (transaction method) valuation is performed. In other cases, it is done to allow an excess earnings methodology to be used in the valuation. Use of the asset-based approach will really depend on the composition of the asset base of the practice. Since so many practices get the majority of their value from the intangible assets, going through the tedious exercise of reviewing each balance sheet item and valuing it separately may make little sense. However, some assets that we discussed earlier may need to be valued even if a full balance sheet valuation is not performed. You need to use your head. Hopefully, you won't need the next exhibit. But in case you do, Exhibit 16.20 demonstrates the result of an adjusted book value methodology being applied to a professional practice (tangible assets only); we have omitted the explanation of each adjustment because you have seen many of them before. This book is already thick enough without repeating this stuff.

EXHIBIT 16.20
Adjusted Book Value Presentation:
Tangible Assets Only

The firm's balance sheet was prepared as of December 31, 1999, a couple of days prior to the valuation date. Book value rarely reflects the fair market value of the company's balance sheet, and therefore, certain adjustments were deemed necessary by the appraiser. Table 1 reflects this analysis.

(Continued)

EXHIBIT 16.20 *(Continued)*

TABLE 1

Balance Sheet

	Book Value	*Adjustments*	*Adjusted Book Value*
Current assets			
Cash	$ 74,365	—	$ 74,365
Accounts receivable	—	97,464	97,464
Advances	(14,719)	—	(14,719)
Work in progress	—	51,305	51,305
Prepaid insurance	—	8,481	8,481
Other investments	6,875	—	6,875
Total current assets	$ 66,521	$ 157,250	$ 223,771
Gross fixed assets	$ 47,969	(7,739)	$ 30,230
Accumulated depreciation	(42,966)	42,966	—
Net fixed assets	$ 5,003	$ 25,227	$ 30,230
Other assets			
Cash surrender value of officer's life insurance	75,000	—	75,000
Total assets	**$ 146,524**	**$ 182,477**	**$ 329,001**
Current liabilities			
Mortgages & notes payable (current)	$ 6,519	$ —	$ 6,519
Unfunded deferred compensation payable	—	39,059	39,059
Funded compensation payable	—	75,000	75,000
Taxes payable	6,968	—	6,968
Total current liabilities	$ 13,487	$ 114,059	$ 127,546
Long-term liabilities			
Unfunded deferred compensation payable	—	$ 530,486	$ 30,486
Loans from stockholders	$ 7,851	—	7,851
Total long-term liabilities	$ 7,851	$ 530,486	$ 538,337
Total liabilities	$ 21,338	$ 644,545	$ 665,883
Stockholders' equity			
Common stock	$ 200	$ —	$ 200
Paid-in capital	8,910	—	8,910
Retained earnings	116,076	(462,068)	(345,992)
Total stockholders' equity	$ 125,186	$ (462,068)	$ (336,882)
Total liabilities and stockholders' equity	$ 146,524	$ 182,477	$ 329,001

Conclusion

Valuing a professional practice is not too terribly different from valuing other types of businesses. However, the appraiser must understand the unique aspects of each type of practice if a reasonable value is to be determined. Hopefully, this chapter gave you some things to think about the next time (or the first time) you value a professional practice.

17

Shareholder Disputes

Chapter Goals

In this chapter, I will attempt to explain the following:

1. What causes shareholder disputes
2. The difference between dissenting and oppression cases
3. The impact of case law on the standard of value
4. Valuation methodologies accepted by the courts
5. Anything else that comes to me (by now, you should know me)

Overview

Before I begin, let me start off with some attribution for the materials that are summarized by me in this chapter. In addition to my own stuff, valuable information came from *Valuing A Business*[1] and *The Handbook of Advanced Business Valuation*.[2] (I told you earlier, if it ain't broke, don't fix it.) These books, in addition to so many other materials, have allowed me to organize this chapter.

I probably should not have to state this up front, but I want to play it safe. Shareholder disputes typically result from a minority owner who feels that he or she (or they) has not been treated fairly by those who have control over the company. A controlling shareholder would probably not have to file a lawsuit against himself or herself. Therefore, individuals who own minority interests in closely held corporations are subject to an additional element of risk solely because they have a minority position in the corporation. The major risk factor is that they cannot exercise the prerogatives of control that were discussed in Chapter 11. As a result, they are in a pretty vulnerable position. This significant lack of control also causes them to have a lack of liquidity because who in their right mind wants to buy minority shares in a closely held company? As such, a minority shareholder is a prisoner in the company.

---

[1]Shannon Pratt, Robert Reilly, and Robert Schweihs, *Valuing A Business*, 4th ed. (New York: McGraw-Hill, 2000) has some excellent materials throughout the book.

[2]*The Handbook of Advanced Business Valuation*, edited by Robert Reilly and Robert Schweihs (New York: McGraw-Hill, 2000), particularly Chapter 15, authored by Anne C. Singer and Jay E. Fishman.

The minority shareholder lacks control and, therefore, cannot do the following:

- Appoint or change operational management
- Appoint or change members of the board of directors
- Determine management compensation and perquisites
- Set operational and strategic policy and change the course of the business
- Acquire, lease, or liquidate business assets, including plant, property, and equipment
- Select suppliers, vendors, and subcontractors to do business with and award contracts to
- Negotiate and consummate mergers and acquisitions
- Liquidate, dissolve, sell out, or recapitalize the company
- Sell or acquire treasury shares
- Register the company's debt or equity securities for an initial or secondary public offering
- Declare and pay cash and/or stock dividends
- Change the articles of incorporation or bylaws
- Select joint ventures and enter into joint venture and partnership agreements
- Determine business policy
- Enter into license or sharing agreements regarding intellectual properties
- Block any of the above actions

These items are the prerogatives of control that were previously discussed. These are also the reasons for many shareholder lawsuits. When the minority shareholder feels that the controlling shareholder is taking advantage or mismanaging the company, a lawsuit frequently takes place. There are also times when the shareholder may be squeezed out of the company, which may trigger a lawsuit. I will attempt to explain this stuff soon.

Many times, in a closely held company, the minority shareholder is an officer or employee of the company, rather than purely an investor. Disputes also arise when the controlling shareholder decides to:

- Terminate the minority shareholder as an employee, director, or officer of the corporation
- Change his or her salary
- Completely *freeze out* minority shareholders
- Otherwise abuse him or her (this abuse is called *oppression*)

In order to avoid allowing controlling shareholders to take advantage of the minority shareholders, most jurisdictions have passed laws to protect the underprivileged. These laws provide minority shareholders with remedies for actions regarding fraud, abusive behavior, and mismanagement by the controlling shareholder. These laws are frequently referred to as *oppressed shareholders' statutes* or *dissolution statutes*.

Every jurisdiction has enacted dissenters' rights statutes. These statutes provide an appraisal remedy for the minority shareholder who does not agree with certain types of transactions approved by the controlling shareholders that have a financial impact on the value of their shares. In these instances, the statutes generally provide the remedy of allowing the shares to be sold.

Despite the different reasons for dissenting and oppressed shareholder suits, the standard of value in most of these cases is *fair value*. For dissenting shareholders, the purchase of their stock for fair value is usually the only remedy. For minority shareholders seeking a remedy for oppression, fraud, mismanagement, or similar problems, the courts frequently have more latitude as to the remedy. In most instances, the minority shareholder will be allowed to sell his or her shares back to the corporation at fair value. In some instances, the shareholder may be entitled to compensation as a measure of damages; but for the mismanagement of the company, the shares would have been worth this much. In one very rare situation the minority shareholder was allowed to buy out the controlling shareholders by the court.[3] Our firm was actually involved in that case! Justice was truly served when our client was allowed to purchase the shares of the controlling shareholders and keep the company that he had worked so hard to build. Once in a while, there really is justice in our legal system.

Since oppressed and dissenting shareholders rarely, if ever, have a ready market for their stock on the open market, as do stockholders in publicly traded companies, fair value is an important standard of value to ensure that they receive adequate consideration for their investment.

As discussed in Chapter 3, *fair value* is not clearly defined, but it is used in the vast majority of dissenters' rights[4] and oppressed shareholders' statutes. Unlike the term *fair market value,* this term is rarely, if ever, defined in a statute. Therefore, the definition has been left to judicial interpretation. You must check with your client's attorney for the interpretation of the jurisdiction in which the litigation takes place. This stuff can get very tricky when it comes to control versus minority issues, as well as marketable versus nonmarketable issues.

Dissenting Shareholder Matters

Minority shareholders who believe that the value of their shares in a company undergoing some form of transaction, recapitalization, or merger, for example, is greater than the proposed consideration to be received by them, are entitled, by statute, to dissent from the transaction, recapitalization, or merger. This generally means that they have to file a lawsuit. The lawsuit usually says something like "I'm not getting what I believe to be the fair value of my shares, and I want more." Most of the time, these matters come about because of a merger; however, dissenting shareholders' rights may also come into play when a corporation sells substantially all of its corporate assets or makes certain changes in its basic organizational structure that result in its shareholders being compelled to sell their shares for what is perceived to be an unfair price. Notice the use of the word "compelled." They usually do not have a choice. Remember the definition of fair market value—neither party is compelled. Here the seller is compelled. In most cases, the dissenting shareholder's only remedy is to seek an independent appraisal as the basis for an alternative cash settlement.

In dissenting shareholder actions the appropriate standard or definition of value is "fair value." In states that have adopted the Uniform Business Corporation Act, the definition of fair value is "the value of the shares immediately before the effectuation of the corporate action to which the dissenter objects, excluding any appreciation or depreciation in anticipation of the corporate action unless exclusion would be inequitable." However, even in those states that have accepted this definition, there is little guidance as to what this truly means. What is somewhat clear, and actually seems to be agreed upon by most courts, is that fair value is not synonymous with fair market value.

Since the definition of fair market value involves the hypothetical willing buyer and the hypothetical willing seller, where neither party is under any compulsion to buy or sell, there should be little doubt that a minority stockholder of a company involved in a statutory merger is a specific seller (not hypothetical) and is compelled to sell for a unilaterally determined price. In the absence of the right to refuse the "offer," a dissenting shareholder has no choice but to seek fair value with the court's help.

Under the principle of alternatives, discussed in Chapter 3, the hypothetical willing seller, in a free and open market, has the option of rejecting a tender offer. As a result, the hypothetical buyers are typically motivated to pay a (control) premium in order to entice sellers to forgo future participation or ownership. Distinctions between fair market value and fair value notwithstanding, guidance concerning the

[3]*Muellenberg v. Bikon Corp.*, 143 N.J. 167, 182, 669 A.2d 1382, 1389 (1996).

[4]Not all states have adopted the fair value standard in dissenters' cases.

interpretation and application of fair value as evidenced by case law varies considerably between the jurisdictions.

One of the most important determinations impacting the calculation of fair value is the appropriate level of value—minority or controlling interest, marketable or nonmarketable basis. The case law is literally all over the place. In *Valuing A Business*, the authors discuss various interpretations of the courts. I am not going to repeat the discussion here. For the most part, my interpretation of the case law is that in dissenting shareholder suits, typically the shares are valued as a pro rata share of the whole company. Logically, if the entire company were sold, the minority shareholder would get a proportionate share of the transaction. Minority discounts are a concept applicable to fair market value. Since each shareholder should have the same value per share, minority discounts in fair value cases do not make sense.

Case law for dissenting shareholder actions also seems to discourage the use of marketability discounts in the calculation of fair value. This is primarily due to the fact that there is some sort of transaction being proposed. This makes a market for the shares. Accordingly, the use of a marketability discount in calculating the fair value of the subject shares is not warranted. However, considering the complexity and contradictory nature of the case law regarding this stuff, you should always rely on the advice of counsel on this issue.

Minority shareholders who believe that certain fundamental or extraordinary corporate changes voted by the controlling shareholders will adversely affect the value of their interest in the company have available statutory rights as dissenters. Currently, the statutes of all states permit such shareholders to dissent from the controlling shareholders' action, compelling the corporation to purchase their stock.

In Delaware, the jurisdiction that sees an awful lot of this type of litigation, only a merger or consolidation triggers dissenters' rights. However, under the statutes of most states, dissenters' rights are triggered by a variety of actions, such as a merger, sale, lease, exchange, or other disposition of all or substantially all of the corporate stock.

Under normal circumstances, shareholders who wish to exercise their rights must give notice in advance of the vote to the corporation that they intend to demand payment for their shares if the proposed action is approved. The stockholder must then make a written demand for payment within some time period of the mailing of notice, advising that the corporate action was approved. In some jurisdictions, once the demand for payment is made, the dissenting shareholder no longer continues "to have any rights of a shareholder, except the right to be paid the fair value of his shares. . . ."[5]

For example, in my home state, New Jersey, the applicable statute provides that the corporation must mail to each dissenting shareholder the financial statements of the corporation as of the latest available date, and profit and loss statements for a 12-month period ending on the date of the balance sheet. The corporation may, at the time of this mailing, make a written offer to purchase the dissenting shareholders' shares at a specified price, deemed to be the fair value. If no agreement as to fair value is reached within the statutory time period, the dissenting shareholder may serve a demand on the corporation that it commence an action to determine fair value. Once the action is initiated, the court may appoint an appraiser to estimate the fair value of the dissenter's shares.

Oppressed Shareholder Matters

An oppressed shareholder case is, in effect, the "War of the Roses" between shareholders instead of husband and wife. These types of cases provide relief to a non-controlling shareholder in a closely held business who seeks such relief for the controlling shareholder's fraud, oppression, mismanagement, etc. Courts

[5]This is the language that appears in N.J.S.A. §14A:11-3(2).

have recognized that relief is frequently necessary for shareholders in closely held corporations because of the unique nature of a closely held entity. In a closely held company:

- Shareholders who are employed by the company often expect to be active participants in management.
- When disagreements occur, the controlling shareholder usually has the ability to use his or her power to unfairly take advantage of the minority shareholder, preventing the minority shareholder from obtaining a fair return on his or her investment.
- The illiquidity associated with the minority shareholder's stock means that he or she may not be able to get out of the investment that he or she no longer wants.

Although courts usually have a number of equitable remedies available, including corporate dissolution, the most common remedy afforded minority shareholders is an award of fair value for their stock.

The buyout remedy provides the minority shareholder with the ability to liquidate an otherwise relatively illiquid investment. If the system works properly, it provides the minority shareholder with a fair return on his or her investment, and it divorces people that do not want to stay married in business.

Under most of the state statutes, the minority shareholder cannot just waltz into court and get the fair value for his or her stock. The shareholder usually has to prove oppression, fraud, or mismanagement before the court will order a buyout at fair value. In certain jurisdictions, once a minority shareholder files a lawsuit requesting dissolution of the corporation on the basis of oppression or related grounds, the controlling shareholder can automatically elect to purchase the shares of the minority shareholder for fair value.[6] This turns the case into nothing more than a simple stock purchase, eliminating the allegations of oppression or wrongdoing. In some jurisdictions, the alternative of purchasing a minority shareholder's stock is irrevocable, absent court approval. In other states, the corporation may elect not to proceed with the purchase if it is dissatisfied with the value eventually set by the court for the stock. Once again, good, consistent laws make our job difficult.

The payment of fair value to an oppressed shareholder has been recognized as a complete and just remedy for oppression. The Delaware Supreme Court has said that fair value "measures that which has been taken from [the shareholder], viz., his proportionate interest in a going concern."[7]

Fair Value

A proper understanding and definition of the applicable standard of value is a key to achieving a proper opinion of value. The failure to stick to the correct standard of value can cause otherwise qualified business appraisers to greatly differ in their conclusions.

As mentioned previously, fair value is rarely legislatively defined. As a business valuer, this often leads to confusion about the meaning of fair value in the context of these assignments. Moreover, even when the courts have addressed this issue, legal precedents can be vague or contradictory and therefore offer inadequate guidance as to the application of the fair value standard. The dissenters' rights section of the Model Act does not provide any direction as to how fair value is to be determined, although it contains a definition. This definition states:

> "Fair value," with respect to a dissenter's shares, means the value of the shares immediately before the effectuation of the corporate action to which the dissenter objects, excluding any appreciation or depreciation in anticipation of the corporate action unless exclusion would be inequitable.[8]

---

[6]For example, Rev. Model Act, § 14.34 (1995 Supp.); Alaska Stat. § 10.06.628(b) (1998); N.Y. Bus. Corp. Law § 1104-a, 1118 (McKinney's 1998 Supp.); and Cal. Corp. Code § 2000 (West 1995).

[7]*Matter of Shell Oil Co.*, 607 A.2d 1213, 1218 (Del. 1992) (citations omitted), quoting *Tri-Continental Corp. v. Battye*, 74 A.2d 71, 72 (Del. 1950); see also *Beerly v. Dept. of Treasury*, 768 F.2d 942 (7th Cir. 1985).

[8]Model Act, § 13.01(3).

The definition contained in the Model Act has varied at the state level. Although some states have adopted the identical definition, other states use the definition without the final phrase "unless exclusion would be inequitable."[9] Some states use terms such as "fair cash value,"[10] "value,"[11] or even "fair market value."[12] This is why you must know the rules of the jurisdiction.

Fair value will usually be different from fair market value. Since fair market value refers to the price at which stock would be bought and sold in the marketplace, the estimation of the value of a minority shareholder's stock under this standard may include a discount for lack of marketability and a discount for minority ownership interest. The methodology used in a fair value appraisal may also be different than in a fair market value appraisal. This could be the case where the *market* price of stocks is not reflective of the *true* value of the guideline companies, resulting in a market value but not a fair value of the subject interest.

Shareholder disputes often include a battle as to which discounts, if any, should be applied in a fair value context. While it is the intention of the court to be equitable, these discounts are the cause of extremely contentious litigation.

The New Jersey Supreme Court decided two separate cases on the same day, one dealing with a dissenting shareholder issue and the other dealing with an oppressed shareholder issue. The contrasting issues of which discounts, if any, should be considered by the court were addressed in these two rulings, which were explained in our firm's newsletter as follows:

> In July 1999, the Supreme Court of New Jersey ruled on two fair value cases. One of these cases was filed as a dissenting shareholder action, while the other was filed under the New Jersey Oppressed Shareholder Statute. Although there were several issues on appeal in each case, the commonality between them was the issue of a Discount for Lack of Marketability (DLOM). While we recognize that all of our readers are not from New Jersey, we felt that these two cases are a good follow-up to the last issue's article. These cases highlight the differences that can arise under the same standard of value.
>
> The *Lawson Mardon Wheaton, Inc. v. Smith* (A-63/64-98) case deals with a family owned business. After a number of shares of this family owned business were sold or conditionally sold to a British company, the Board of Directors approved a plan to restructure the corporation. The reason for this restructuring was to keep the stock in the family by restricting future public sales of the company's stock. When the plan was approved in 1991, those stockholders who did not approve were notified of their right to demand payment of the fair value of their shares under N.J.S.A. 14A:11-1 to -11, also known as The Appraisal Statute. Twenty-six shareholders owning approximately 15 percent of the shares dissented and demanded payment for their shares. The corporation offered $41.50 per share, which included the deduction of a 25 percent DLOM. This discount was based on the belief that there was a limited market of potential buyers for this stock. When the dissenters rejected this offer, this action was instituted.
>
> Both the trial court and the appellate court determined the price of the stock after considering a DLOM finding that there were "extraordinary circumstances" in this situation giving applicability to this discount. The Supreme Court disagreed.
>
> The Supreme Court's opinion stresses the nature of the term "fair value," and states "courts must take fairness and equity in account in deciding to apply a discount to the value of the dissenting shareholders' stock in an appraisal action." The court goes on to say,
>
>> Indeed, equitable considerations have led the majority of states and commentators to conclude that marketability and minority discounts should not be applied when determining fair value of dissenting shareholders' stock in an appraisal action. Although there is no clear consensus, the use of a *fair value* standard, combined with application of equitable principles, has resulted in a majority of jurisdictions holding that a

[9]The statutes of approximately 27 states contain the same definition of fair value. Approximately 14 other states, including New Jersey (N.J.S.A. § 14A:11-3), use the same general concept of fair value without the final phrase "unless exclusion would be inequitable."

[10]Ohio Rev. Code Ann. § 1701.85(C) (Page's 1997 Supp.) (defined in the same way as fair market value); La. Rev. Stat. Ann. § 12:131C(2) (West 1998 Supp.).

[11]Kan. Stat. Ann. § 17-6712 (1997 Supp.).

[12]Cal. Corp. Code § 1300(a) (West 1998 Supp.).

> dissenting shareholder is entitled to her proportional share of the fair market value of the corporation. The value of the shares will not be discounted on the ground that the shares are a minority interest or on the related grounds of a lack of liquidity or marketability.

In addressing the issue of extraordinary circumstances, the Supreme Court disagreed with the lower courts. According to the decision, extraordinary circumstances exist when a dissenting shareholder holds out in order to benefit him or herself by doing so. In this case, the court felt that disagreeing (dissenting) to a corporate change was not extraordinary, but rather an ordinary business matter.

In light of the issue of fairness, and the fact that extraordinary circumstances did not appear to exist, the Supreme Court overturned the lower court on these issues, and held that a Discount for Lack of Marketability was not applicable in this case.

On the same date, the court ruled in the opposite direction in *Emanuel Balsamides, Sr., et al. v. Protameen Chemicals, Inc., et al.* (A-27-1998), which was an action brought under the New Jersey Oppressed Shareholder Statute (N.J.S.A. 14A:12-7).

In this case, Messrs. Balsamides and Perle were equal partners in a manufacturing business. After many years of jointly running the business, the partners began having trouble working together, and over a number of years, this relationship deteriorated. Mr. Balsamides sought relief as an oppressed shareholder. Under this statute, if the court finds the plaintiff to be oppressed, the court "may appoint a custodian, appoint a provisional director, order a sale of the corporation's stock [as provided below], or enter a judgment dissolving the corporation." After a 19-day trial, the court found that Mr. Balsamides was oppressed, that Mr. Perle had conducted himself in such a way as to harm the business, and concluded that Mr. Balsamides should purchase Mr. Perle's share of the business. The trial court determined the purchase price of these shares of stock after the deduction of a 35 percent DLOM.

The case was appealed to the Appellate Division, which overturned the trial court's decision relating to this discount. The Appellate Court "concluded that such a discount was not appropriate in this case because there was no sale of Perle's stock to the public, nor was Balsamides buying an interest that might result in the later sale of that interest to the public."

The case was then appealed to the Supreme Court, which overturned the Appellate Division on the issue of the Discount for Lack of Marketability. The decision stated,

> The position of the Appellate Division ignores the reality that Balsamides is buying a company that will remain illiquid because it is not publicly traded and public information about it is not widely disseminated. Protameen will continue to have a small base of available purchasers. If it is resold in the future, Balsamides will receive a lower purchase price because of the company's closely held nature.
>
> If Perle and Balsamides sold Protameen together, the price they received would reflect Protameen's illiquidity. They would split the price and also share that detriment. Similarly, if Balsamides pays Perle a discounted price, Perle suffers half the lack-of-marketability now; Balsamides suffers the other half when he eventually sells his closely held business. Conversely, if Perle is not required to sell his shares at a price that reflects Protameen's lack of marketability, Balsamides will suffer the full effect of Protameen's lack of marketability at the time he sells.

In the *Balsamides* decision, the Supreme Court distinguishes the two cases. In summary, the cases are distinct based on the facts and the different statutes under which these cases arise. Regarding *Wheaton*, the court states, "it would be unfair and inequitable to apply a marketability discount. To allow the major shareholders to buy out the minority dissenters at a discount would penalize the minority for exercising their statutory rights. Moreover, it would create the wrong incentives for shareholders." Regarding the *Balsamides* decision, the court states, "In cases where the oppressing shareholder instigates the problems, as in this case, fairness dictates that the oppressing shareholder should not benefit at the expense of the oppressed. The statute does not allow the oppressor to harm his partner and the company and be rewarded with the right to buy out that partner at a discount. We do not want to afford a shareholder any incentive to oppress other shareholders."

Despite the differences that appear to exist in the cases, the bottom line appears to be that the court is looking for all shareholders to be treated fairly, regardless of the circumstances.[13]

---

[13]Trugman Valuation Associates Inc. Newsletter, *Valuation Trends* (Winter 2000), available online at http://www.trugmanvaluation.com/Archive/Winter2000.html#Anchor_Fair_60059

The Valuation Date

An appraisal is an estimate of value at a given point in time. The date of the appraisal, whether statutorily mandated or otherwise, is of great importance. And by now, you know that. Most state statutes provide that when a dissenting shareholder's stock is to be purchased, fair value is determined as of the day prior to the meeting of shareholders at which the action dissented from was opposed. You must get a copy of the statute and read it. For example, the New Jersey statute provides, "In all cases, fair value shall exclude any appreciation or depreciation resulting from the proposed action."[14] This means that the dissenting shareholder does not get credit for any gain nor is he or she penalized for any loss that results from the action from which he or she dissented. This actually makes sense when you think about it.

Under the fair market value concept, the appraiser uses only information known or knowable as of the date of the valuation. Under the fair value concept, some courts have allowed subsequent information to be used as well. For example, the Delaware Supreme Court has ruled that the language limiting consideration of some post-merger changes in value eliminates the consideration of the speculative elements of value created by the merger. It does not rule out consideration of elements of future value, including the nature of the enterprise, "that are known or susceptible of proof as of the date of the merger and not the product of speculation."[15]

In reading the statutes, pay close attention to the wording. For example, under the New Jersey statute applicable to oppressed shareholders, the purchase price of any shares sold "shall be their fair value as of the date of the commencement of the action plus or minus any adjustments deemed equitable by the court."[16] Notice the "plus or minus any adjustments deemed equitable by the court." This gives the court latitude to do the fair thing. Many times, equitable adjustments will be made by the court. In some instances, it will be the role of the appraiser to provide these adjustments to the judge or jury. Exhibit 17.1 demonstrates a section of a valuation report in a fair value litigation. This section was at the end of the valuation. Our client was going to be bought out. The valuation date was determined by the court to be January 31, 1996. However, our client continued to be active in the business as a shareholder and employee until December 31, 2000. Significant dividends and distributions were made to the client subsequent to the valuation date, and the issue of double counting came up. Since the valuation was based on the anticipated future income stream and the shareholder received part of that income stream, the court wanted each side to address the issue of double counting. We performed our analysis in accordance with the case law that the judge and our client's attorney referred us to.

EXHIBIT 17.1
Equitable Adjustment Analysis

At the request of Tom Sawyer, Esq., Trugman Valuation Associates Inc. has performed an analysis that is intended to assist the court regarding the issues raised in *William C. Musto v. Vincent G. Vidas, John S. Degnan, and Semcor, Inc.* (333 N.J. Super. 52 (App. Div. 2000), particularly the issues of interest and double recovery. Interest is considered under N.J.S.A. 14A:12-7(8)(d).

Interest

N.J.S.A. 14A:12-7(8)(d) provides that:

> Interest may be allowed at the rate and from the date determined by the court to be equitable, and if the court finds that the refusal of the shareholder to accept any offer of payment was arbitrary, vexatious, or otherwise not in good faith, no interest shall be allowed.

The court selected January 1996 as the valuation date, but the monies will not be paid to Susan Littleton until sometime in the future, many years after the valuation date. The statute compensates for the time lag through a consideration of interest. We must determine an appropriate interest rate.

---

[14] N.J.S.A. § 14A:11-3(3)(c).

[15] *Weinberger v. UOP, Inc.*, 457 A.2d 701 (Del. 1983); see also *Cede & Co. v. Technicolor, Inc.*, 684 A.2d 289 (Del. 1996).

[16] N.J.S.A. § 14A:12-7(8).

EXHIBIT 17.1 *(Continued)*

In *Musto*, an argument was made regarding the use of an "equitable interest rate."

The court determined that the interest rate to be used should be a rate that pertains to a creditor/lender as opposed to an equity owner. In fact, Judge Gottlieb used the prime lending rate, compounding the interest annually. He stated:

> Now interest. Defendants urge that it be not available but realistically as—a cutoff as of March 1992. This is when the several motions were made which memorialized a buy-out offer of the other. I'm not going to go on with that because then that overlooks the ultimate fact and that is that defendant had the use of plaintiff's money. . . .
>
> What I have selected for the use of an interest rate payable here is the prime rate and why I have selected the prime rate is, it is most analogous to a corporate borrower and in light of Semcor's solid financial position. . . .
>
> I am not going to use the risk free rates, and by that I refer to the treasury notes, treasury bills, CDs, that sort of thing, since that would be intellectually inconsistent with my earlier determination of fair value where I said the cap rate which I have to apply . . . to the income stream or reasonable income in order to arrive at the formulation of value, put a certain amount in there additional for Semcor not being, "risk free."
>
> I have thought about . . . whether it should be compound or simple. . . . What I've done is try, since I'm using the prima [sic] rate . . . to figure out if it were going to ABC Bank what it would be doing in borrowing X dollars for two years, four years, whatever it is, some period longer than one year.
>
> In that marketplace, to my knowledge, it would be compounded on an annual basis at best, maybe compounded at a shorter period of time. That's why I have chosen compounding as opposed to simple. I have chosen annual as opposed to quarterly compounding only because it seems to me that in the light of the events that occurred if it had been the equivalent circumstance the lending of money to Semcor would have been on probably not a quarterly compounding basis but on an annual.

In this instance, the fair value of Susan Littleton's interest in The Littleton Entities was determined to be $44,100,000 as of January 31, 1996. Interest should be added from that date.

In *Musto*, the court used the prime rate because "it is most analogous to a corporate borrower and in light of Semcor's solid financial position." According to the 1995 financial statements for the operating Littleton entities, the interest rates being paid by these companies were as follows:

> Notes payable to banks due in installments through December 2002 at interest rates of 8.75 percent to 9.48 percent.
>
> Notes payable to financial institutions due in installments through August 2002 at interest rates of 7.5 percent to 13.2 percent.

On a weighted average basis, The Littleton Entities were paying about 10.35 percent.[1] Since this is the rate of interest being paid by The Littleton Entities, we have applied this rate, with annual compounding through July 31, 2001. This calculation is included in Table 1.

TABLE 1
Pro Rata Valuation Plus Interest

Pro rata 1/3 ownership	$44,100,000
Interest (10.35%)	
1/31/96–1/31/97	4,564,350
	$48,664,350
1/31/97–1/31/98	5,036,760
	$53,701,110
1/31/98–1/31/99	5,558,065
	$59,259,175
1/31/99–1/31/00	6,133,325
	$65,392,500
1/31/00–1/31/01	6,768,124
	$72,160,623
1/31/01–7/31/01	3,734,312
Total	$75,894,936

[1] It is important to note that these rates represent collateralized loans that are secured. Any interest calculated for unsecured loans would normally be at a higher rate of interest to account for the additional risk to the lender.

(Continued)

EXHIBIT 17.1 *(Continued)*

Double Recovery

After interest, the next item to consider is whether any adjustment should be made for the monies received by Susan Littleton after the buyout date to avoid a double recovery. The issue raised in *Musto* was whether the court should have permitted an equitable adjustment of account for the post-valuation growth until the stockholder's interest was actually redeemed. The facts in *Musto* are different from the litigation at hand. In *Musto*, the plaintiff filed his complaint in December 1990. Shortly before the complaint was filed, the plaintiff was terminated from the company. The plaintiff received his year-end 1990 distribution, but received no other bimonthly distributions or paychecks from the company after that. He actually left in February 1991. In July 1991, he received a distribution from the company in the amount of $200,000 and received an additional $550,000 in deferred compensation. Value was determined in 1996, although Musto was out of the company for more than five years, earning his living elsewhere.

In the most recent appellate decision, Judge Wallace stated:

> Defendants maintain the trial judge was correct in not deviating from the presumptive valuation date set forth in the statute (the date of the filing of the complaint) because an award of post-1990 profits under any rationale would constitute an illegal double recovery since the determination of fair value is actually based upon a company's future income stream. Defendants further assert that plaintiff would not have sought a post-1990 valuation date if Semcor's value had decreased after 1990. *Musto*, 333 N.J. Super. at 58–59.

The valuation date was set by the judge in this case as January 31, 1996. This is the date that has been used in our report. However, unlike *Musto*, Susan Littleton continued to work for The Littleton Entities after the valuation date. She continued to assist in creating value for the entities that she is being bought out of. The statute requires the court to consider whether any equitable adjustments should be made to reach a fair and just result for *all* of the parties to this litigation. N.J.S.A. 14A:12-7(8)(a) provides:

> The purchase price of any shares so sold shall be their fair value as of the date of the commencement of the action or such earlier or later date deemed equitable by the court, plus or minus any adjustments deemed equitable by the court if the action was brought in whole or in part under paragraph 14A:12-7(1)(c).

In the *Musto* decision, Judge Gottlieb subsequently decided against an equitable adjustment for post-complaint corporate profits. Discussing the trial court's use of discretion, the appellate court stated:

Thus, if the judge had allowed an equitable adjustment to account for a company's actual growth in the years following the valuation date, he might as well have accorded plaintiff a double recovery. Consequently, we find no abuse of discretion in the trial judge's denial of plaintiff's request for equitable adjustments to fair value. *Musto*, 333 N.J. Super. at 64.

To prevent any such double recovery, after applying interest, we must examine the money that Susan Littleton received after the valuation date to see what portion represents compensation for the work that she continued to perform as an employee of The Company and what portion represents payment for her equity interest.

In order to respond to this issue, we reviewed the various entities' tax returns and financial information after 1995 (although January 1996 should be excluded from this analysis, we did not have the detail that would allow us to exclude it). Susan Littleton received the following monies from The Littleton Entities:

	Salaries	*Commissions*	*Distributions*
1996	$ 498,429	$1,425,000	$ 38,400
1997	898,429	3,510,000	1,000,000
1998	1,172,927	3,380,000	2,638,477
1999	488,726	3,182,500	3,019,607
2000	500,000	1,000,000	1,314,500

In addition to the above, Susan Littleton was allocated profits and losses from The Littleton Entities as follows:

	1996	*1997*	*1998*	*1999*	*2000*
Company A	$ (8,333)	$ (9,657)	$ (150)	$ 2,506	N/A
Company B	7,979	6,710	10,495	9,637	
Company C	(320,522)	(568,217)	(133,044)	94,539	
Company D	17,807	(920,139)	(818,995)	(483,770)	
Company E	221,592	322,836	358,188	372,000	
Company F	159,756	189,150	177,225	176,206	
Company G	77,251	54,321	40,676	72,657	

EXHIBIT 17.1 *(Continued)*

	1996	*1997*	*1998*	*1999*	*2000*
Company H	22,813	46,068	12,733	50,844	N/A
Company I	1,225,024	474,501	2,585,351	1,289,664	
Company J	(171)	—	(200)	15,728	
Company K	22,370	5,138	(200)	94,643	
Company L	673,539	(746,437)	110,909	242,849	
Company M	—	—	1,299,385	1,687,856	
Total	$2,099,105	$(1,145,726)	$3,642,373	$3,625,359	

Some of the monies received by Susan Littleton may create a problem similar to the one that had to be addressed in *Musto*, namely, the court's treatment of the deferred compensation received after the valuation date.

In disallowing the adjustment sought by the defendants, Judge Gottlieb stated:

> [I]t was characterized by the defendants as deferred compensation. It has been argued to me that . . . that characterization was just a fiction in order to be able to take out of the corporation monies that year and still meet the equal compensation requirements.
>
> [I]t was called deferred compensation . . . to avoid taxes which would otherwise have had to have been paid to the State of New Jersey as a then subchapter S corporation. . . .
>
> So, the first concern that I have is the defendants have selected to go that route . . . in order to gain a tax advantage and now having obtained that tax advantage wish to disavow it. I will not permit that. I find that they are estopped from characterizing it as anything other than deferred compensation for efforts before January 1, 1991.
>
> The second basis is . . . that it was paid pursuant to the equal compensation agreement and not for reasons of distributing to plaintiff a share of the corporation.

The appellate court, once again, supported Judge Gottlieb's opinion in stating:

> As noted above, N.J.S.A. 14A:12-7 (8)(a) authorizes a trial judge to make adjustments to fair value, either plus or minus, which the trial Judge finds equitable. The fact that Semcor was not obligated to make a payment to plaintiff, but did so voluntarily, does not mean the trial judge was obligated to make an equitable adjustment to fair value to account for the payment, or that his failure to do so constitutes an abuse of discretion. *Musto*, 333 N.J. Super. at 76.

In this litigation, Susan Littleton received current compensation (salaries and commissions), as opposed to deferred compensation. She also received some cash distributions. Here also, allocated profits and losses were reflected on the partnership and S corporation tax returns filed by the various companies.

The difficulties in trying to create an equitable adjustment would be determining which of the monies paid to Susan Littleton (salary, commission, or distributions) should be considered as a double recovery and how the offsetting credit will be applied against these monies for all of the income taxes that have been paid on these items, including the allocated profits and losses.

Using an estimated 45 percent combined personal income tax rate, the net result of all of these items is as follows:

	1996	*1997*	*1998*	*1999*
Salary	$ 498,429	$ 898,429	$ 1,172,927	$ 488,726
Commissions	1,425,000	3,510,000	3,380,000	3,182,500
Allocations	2,099,105	(1,145,726)	3,642,373	3,625,359
Subtotal	$ 4,022,534	$ 3,262,703	$ 8,195,300	$ 7,296,585
Tax cost (45%)	1,810,140	1,468,216	3,687,885	3,283,463
Subtotal	$ 2,212,394	$ 1,794,487	$ 4,507,415	$ 4,013,122
Distributions	38,400	1,000,000	2,638,477	3,019,607
Net after tax	$ 2,250,794	$ 2,794,487	$ 7,145,892	$ 7,032,729
Non-cash allocation	(2,099,105)	1,145,726	(3,642,373)	(3,625,359)
Net cash benefit	$ 151,689	$ 3,940,213	$ 3,503,519	$ 3,407,370

(Continued)

EXHIBIT 17.1 *(Continued)*

In addition to the preceding, the year 2000 figures have been estimated as follows:

Salary	$ 500,000
Commissions	1,000,000
Allocations[a]	3,625,359
Subtotal	$ 5,125,359
Tax cost (45%)	2,306,412
Subtotal	$ 2,818,947
Distributions	1,314,500
Net after tax	$ 4,133,447
Non-cash allocation	(3,625,359)
Net cash benefit	$ 508,088

[a]At the time of the preparation of this report, the year 2000 figures were unknown. Since 1998 and 1999 were similar, we have estimated the year 2000 to be the same as 1999.

Assuming that the court wants to offset a portion of Susan Littleton's entitlement to avoid a "double recovery," the most that should be offset is the net cash benefit that has been received by her. The problem with adding back the entire amount is that Susan Littleton would also be giving back her compensation as an employee. The net cash benefit received by Susan Littleton should be reduced by whatever amount the court deems to be reasonable to compensate her for her efforts as an employee during these years. This salary amount should be reduced by 45 percent to be consistent with our calculations.

Reconciliation of Interest and Equitable Adjustments

In the valuation analysis previously presented, a reasonable allowance for officers' compensation was estimated to be 2 percent of sales. This was unallocated between the officers, but if we assume that it was to be split evenly between Joan and Susan Littleton, each would be entitled to the following amounts:

1996	$1,207,932
1997	1,328,725
1998	1,461,598
1999	1,607,757

The most equitable way to adjust the award to Susan Littleton would be to use the same level of compensation that was used in the valuation. This would avoid a "double recovery" and both value and compensation would be determined in a consistent fashion. We believe the following calculation to be consistent with the intent of *Musto*.

Pro rata 1/3 ownership	$ 44,100,000
1996 equitable adjustment	512,674
Subtotal	$ 44,612,674
Interest 1/31/96–1/31/97	4,617,412
Subtotal	$ 49,230,085
1997 equitable adjustment	(3,209,414)
Subtotal	$ 46,020,671
Interest 1/31/97–1/31/98	4,763,139
Subtotal	$ 50,783,811
1998 equitable adjustment	(2,699,640)

EXHIBIT 17.1 (*Continued*)

Subtotal	$ 48,084,170
Interest 1/31/98–1/31/99	4,976,712
Subtotal	$ 53,060,882
1999 equitable adjustment	(2,523,104)
Subtotal	$ 50,537,778
Interest 1/31/99–1/31/00	5,230,660
Subtotal	$ 55,768,438
2000 equitable adjustment	456,566
Subtotal	$ 56,225,005
Interest 1/31/00–1/31/01	5,819,288
Subtotal	$ 62,044,293
Interest 1/31/01–7/31/01	3,210,792
Total due Susan Littleton	$ 65,255,085

The determination of a valuation date, whether in a dissenters' rights case or an oppressed shareholder case (or any valuation case) is of considerable importance. This is because only those facts known or knowable on the valuation date should generally be considered. Courts have bought into this principle. It has been said that "valuation of securities is 'in essence a prophecy as to the future,' but this prophecy must be based upon facts available at the critical [valuation] date."[17] The Seventh Circuit Court of Appeals has stated that investors would be entitled to the future value "when 'known or susceptible of proof as of the [valuation] date.'" The court continued:

> Here the subsequent events . . . were no more than speculation as of the time of the merger. . . . We, like the district court, therefore exclude from consideration the fact that Mobil paid in 1980 more than twice the value implied by the merger in 1979. Only facts known in 1979 count. . . . Any increment of value attributable to changes after August 1979 [the valuation date] in the market for oil and gas, or to Mobil's willingness to make changes or bear special risks, belongs to [the purchasing] shareholders rather than [the selling shareholders]. The investors in a firm are entitled only to what it is worth as it exists, not as it could become in other hands.[18]

Therefore, the choice of a valuation date is essential because it acts as a cutoff date for the information that the appraiser may consider in performing the business valuation.

Fair Value Methodology

Although business valuation contains many methods for an appraiser to use in estimating the value of a business, the valuation methods employed to estimate fair value have been heavily influenced by judicial precedents emerging from the Delaware courts. Delaware is the state where many large companies incorporate, and as such, this jurisdiction sees more litigation in this area than many other jurisdictions. As a result of the case law that has come from these courts, Delaware's holdings have been followed in other jurisdictions. Although Delaware case law suggests that "all factors and elements which reasonably might enter

[17] Rev. Rul. 59-60, quoted in *Blass v. United States*, 344 F. Supp. 669, 670 (E.D. Ark. 1972).

[18] *Metlyn Realty Corp. v. Esmart Inc.*, 763 R.2d 826, 838 (7th Cir. 1985) at 838. See also *Kastenbaum v. Falstaff Brewing Corp.*, 514 F. Supp. 690, 698 (5th Cir.1976) (elements to be considered in determining the value of a business are the prospects that profits will continue into the future, "considering all circumstances existing and known as of the date of the valuation"); *Gratto v. Gratto*, 272 N.J. Super. 140, 639 A.2d 390 (App. Div. 1994); *Bogosian v. Woloohojian Realty Corp.*, 923 E.2d 898 (1st Cir. 1991).

into the fixing of value"[19] are relevant, until 1983 Delaware courts relied heavily on a fairly mechanical method known as the "Delaware Block Method." This method was adopted by a number of other states.

The Delaware Block Method had the valuer do the following:

- Derive separate values using methods under the income (based on earnings or dividends), asset-based, and market approaches
- Apply weights to each of the methods depending upon the type of business being valued
- Add the results to determine the final estimate of value

In the application of this method, the appraiser used pricing multiples derived from publicly traded guideline companies for the earnings or dividend methods. For public companies, the market approach would be based on some measure of the market price of the company's stock.

In 1983, the Delaware Supreme Court decided the case of *Weinberger v. UOP, Inc.*[20] In this case, a minority shareholder objected to a freeze-out merger, and the shares had to be valued. A *freeze-out merger* is where a minority shareholder's interest in a corporation is involuntarily eliminated when controlling shareholders create a dummy corporation, transfer their stock to that corporation, and then agree to merge the old corporation with the new one. The new corporation acquires the assets and liabilities of the original corporation, with the controlling shareholders of the old corporation owning the stock of the surviving corporation. The minority shareholders no longer have any equity interest in the new business and have the right to receive only cash for their shares in the original company.

Although freeze-out mergers may be thought to create special valuation problems, because minority shareholders subject to a freeze-out merger do not have a choice as to whether to sell their stock, this is not the case. Although the valuation does not take into account any increased value or synergies that may result from the merger, an ousted shareholder bears no costs or risks of the future enterprise and so should not share in its possible rewards. However, in *Mills v. Electric Auto-Lite Co.*,[21] it was determined that an undervaluation can occur in a freeze-out situation.[22]

Weinberger became an important case because the Delaware Supreme Court held that the Delaware Block Method was "clearly outmoded" because it "excludes other generally accepted techniques used in the financial community."[23] Although this case did not totally eliminate the use of this method, it seems to have relaxed its exclusivity as a valuation method. Other valuation methods are much more common today. Thus, in most states, courts may base their valuation determination on any method accepted in the financial community. The discounted cash flow method has become considerably more prevalent in the recent past.

The general interpretation by most courts in both dissenters' cases and oppression cases has held that fair value means valuing the business as a going concern rather than as if in liquidation. This recognizes the fact that the business should be valued based on its status in the hands of the shareholders whose shares have been taken away from them. According to the Delaware Supreme Court, "The basic concept for value under the appraisal statute is that the stockholder is entitled to what has been taken from him, viz., *his proportionate interest in a going concern.*"[24]

---

[19] *Tri-Continental Corp. v. Battye*, 74 A.2d 71, 72 (Del. 1980).

[20] *Weinberger v. UOP, Inc.*, 457 A.2d 701 (Del. 1983).

[21] *Mills v. Electric Auto-Lite Co.*, 552 F.2d 1239, 1248 (7th Cir. 1977).

[22] *The Handbook of Advanced Business Valuation*, p. 306.

[23] 547 A.2d at 713. See also *Stringer v. Car Data Systems, Inc.*, 314 Or. 576, 841 P.2d 1183, 1189 (1992) (fair value includes "all relevant factors"); *Schechter v. Watkins*, 395 Pa. Super. 363, 577 A.2d 585, 592 (1990) (in a forced buyout, the jury is instructed to consider any factor deemed appropriate).

[24] *In re McLoon Oil Co.*, 565 A.2d at 997, 1003 (emphasis in original).

The battles that you may find yourself involved in can be truly challenging. You really have to know your appraisal theory if you are going to compete in this business. Exhibit 17.2 is a critique of a very large firm's appraisal report in a shareholder dispute. It has been edited to demonstrate only the points that have been discussed in this chapter (with a few other educational items thrown in). This firm used only the guideline company method, whereas we used the guideline company method and the discounted cash flow method. In this instance the value derived using the discounted cash flow method was substantially greater than the guideline company method value because the guideline companies have a lower market value than intrinsic value.

EXHIBIT 17.2
Partial Critique of Fair Value Report

Page 1

In the first paragraph of the executive summary, ABC Appraisal Co. says "Judge Harris directed that the purchase price be determined based on the fair value of John's interest as of January 31, 1996, or the end of the proceeding year December 31, 1995 (valuation date), provided that the value not be materially different." This statement is incorrect. According to the November 1, 2000, order, Judge Harris specifically determined that the value was to be as of January 31, 1996. There is nothing in that order to indicate a different valuation date. The month does not materially change the value, but it allowed ABC Appraisal Co. to heavily rely on XYZ Appraisal Co., since their report was as of December 31, 1995. Practically speaking, we used December 31, 1995, financial data, however, the multiples and prices from the public market, as well as any known information to be considered in this appraisal, should have included through January 31,1996.

In the last paragraph on this page, ABC Appraisal Co. mentions reading the XYZ Appraisal Co. report, and they concur with XYZ Appraisal Co. that the market approach is the most reliable methodology to determine "the fair value of the interest." XYZ Appraisal Co. did not determine fair value, nor did they ever say that they were determining fair value. XYZ Appraisal Co. very clearly in their report determined fair market value, and any reliance by ABC Appraisal Co. on the XYZ Appraisal Co. report for fair value is incorrect.

ABC Appraisal Co. also states "because the Littleton Company did not prepare financial forecasts, we could not perform a discounted cash flow (DCF) analysis, a form of the income approach." This statement is nonsense, since ABC Appraisal Co. knew that the value would be considerably greater using a DCF because this company was a very profitable company and postured for substantial growth. The fact that the Littleton Company did not prepare financial forecasts is not a reason for the appraiser not to perform a discounted cash flow analysis. We run into this situation 90 out of 100 times in valuation, when the company does not prepare its own forecasts. Part of being an appraiser is working with management to prepare a forecast and/or preparing your own since valuation is a prophecy of the future. Reliance on history, which the market approach does, will frequently undervalue the company unless the appraiser is lucky enough to guess at the growth rate of the subject company and have guideline companies that are so comparable that little subjectivity has to be applied in the valuation process. This is rarely the case.

ABC Appraisal Co. also says "our valuation was based on all information that was known or should have been known as of the valuation date." This is clearly not true, because they should have been able to determine, based on the financial information, that there was a ramping up of fixed assets, that the customer base was growing, that Littleton was coming out of their refinancing mode, and that growth was clearly going to happen. All of this was known at the valuation date. They chose to ignore it.

ABC Appraisal Co. also said, "if such company forecasts had existed as of the valuation date, the value derived from a DCF analysis would be consistent with our determination of value." This is not true if fair market value understates the true value of the company. Clearly, we are dealing with an industry whose companies are undervalued by the market. Even reading the Alex Brown Report attached to ABC Appraisal Co.'s report (which I will discuss later), the intrinsic value of most of these companies was considerably higher than fair market value. Since market perception is undervaluing these companies, a DCF analysis would not be consistent; if anything, the DCF analysis would tend to be considerably higher than the market approach. The DCF analysis actually values Littleton, as opposed to trying to make believe that the various publicly traded companies are a "good fit" in an industry that went through tough times in 1995.

Page 2

ABC Appraisal Co. indicates "an analysis of the guideline companies as of the valuation date indicates the market did not forecast any material future earnings growth." While their statement may be correct regarding investors, and the prices that they are willing to pay for trucking company stocks, clearly growth was being forecast. Morgan Keegan was forecasting anywhere from 18 percent to 35 percent growth, and the analyst expectations regarding growth of guideline companies were substantial. Alex Brown was forecasting 15 percent to 30 percent growth. ABC Appraisal Co. should have read its own attachment.

(Continued)

EXHIBIT 17.2 *(Continued)*

ABC Appraisal Co. also discusses at the bottom of the page that it determined a 35 percent discount for lack of marketability in this valuation. The 35 percent, which will be discussed in more detail later, is appropriate for a minority interest in a fair market value appraisal under certain circumstances. This discount is punitive if applied in a fair value context if the determination of value is to provide a pro rata interest in the company to the shareholder who is forced to sell shares.

Page 3

At the top of the page, ABC Appraisal Co. indicates "John was found by the court to be the oppressor, and should not gain disproportionally from the forced buyout." While this may be true, he should also not be punished. The November 1, 2000, order of Judge Harris clearly indicates this.

Page 5

ABC Appraisal Co. indicates "we consider fair value to be based on the price that is 'fair and equitable' to both parties that would effectuate a transaction in the interest in The Littleton Company on the open market." This definition is problematic for a number of reasons. First, by treating a partial interest as being sold on the open market, they are clearly indicating that their valuation will be on a minority basis. I do not believe that that is the intent of the New Jersey Statute, as it appears that case law tends to disfavor a minority discount in fair value oppression cases. Therefore, treating an *interest* in The Littleton Company on the open market is very different from treating *The Littleton Company* on the open market. For this reason, I believe the premise that ABC Appraisal Co. is operating under violates the intent of the New Jersey Statute.

According to Pratt (*Valuing a Business*, page 352) "certain precedents—including those pursuant to California Corporation Code, Section 2000—have suggested that fair value may be interpreted to mean fair market value without a non-controlling ownership interest discount (i.e., a proportionate share of the overall business enterprise value)."

In discussing the difference between fair value and fair market value, Pratt includes a discussion in his book (page 801) on dissenting stockholder and minority oppression court cases. He states, "In most states, the standard value for dissenting stockholder suits and for minority oppression suits is fair value." Several state statutes indicate that either "fair cash value" or simply "value" is the appropriate standard. While the various states interpret fair value quite differently from one another, and sometimes differently under differing facts and circumstances, they do *not* strictly equate fair value with fair market value.

This point is illustrated well by a New York court's rejection of an expert's valuation report based on fair market value in a dissenting stockholder case. The court stated:

> Because the petitioner's expert . . . in its valuation report (on title page) and on 15 occasions refers to its valuation to be based on Fair Market Value, and the Business Corporation Law only uses the term Fair Value. . . . The court considers it a threshold question as to whether fair value and fair market value are synonymous.
>
> The standard upon which (the company's experts') valuation was based, was market value. . . the statutory standard is much broader. . . . The court may give *no weight* (emphasis supplied) to market value if the facts of the case are required. [1]

Pratt indicates that the court ultimately rejected the fair market value of $52 per share and awarded the dissenting shareholders $99 per share. This illustrates the potential range of difference between fair market value and fair value. Another case cited by Pratt is *LeBeau v. N.G. Bancorporation, Inc.* (No. Civ. A. 13414, 1998 WL 44993 (Del. Ch. Jan. 29, 1998)). In this case, when fair market value is used rather than fair value, the Delaware Court of Chancery stated that this was "legally flawed" as evidence regarding fair value.

ABC Appraisal Co. also says "pursuant to Judge Harris's order, we have used December 31, 1995 as the valuation date." What order are they talking about? The November 1, 2000, order clearly indicates January 31, 1996, to be the valuation date. At the bottom of that same paragraph, ABC Appraisal Co., in discussing using only items that were foreseeable as of the valuation date, feels that this is consistent with Musto, which stated "equitable adjustments to fair value to reflect corporations' growth in the years following the valuation date would have been improper." However, equitable adjustments are very different from excluding anticipated growth. If something happens after the valuation date that caused the company to change, I would agree that this should be excluded if the foundation had not been set prior to the valuation date. In this instance, the economic, industry, and company data all point to the company being positioned for growth, including a substantial investment in rolling stock in the most recent year. This rolling stock was added for new business, as opposed to replacement of existing assets.

Footnote 5 at the bottom of the page refers to the "Zukin book"; however, ABC Appraisal Co. does not discuss the context in which this quote is probably made. I have subsequent editions of this book as opposed to the 1990 book, but Zukin discusses dissenters' rights cases, and not oppression cases. Their underlying quote in the footnote would be true, except the New Jersey Statute also provides the court with the ability to make any equitable adjustments deemed necessary.

Rather than guessing at certain instances, actual information can be used as a sanity check on what might have been known or was knowable at that time. Based on our analysis of the actual 1996 to 1999 results, as compared to our forecasts for that same time period, it was reasonably predictable that this company should have been able to accomplish what it actually did. In fact, I believe it could have done better, had management not been distracted by this litigation.

---

[1]*Matter of Slant/Fin. Corp. v. The Chicago Corp.* (N.Y. Sup. Ct Oct. 5, 1995), *aff'd* 236 A.D. 2d 547, 654 N.Y.S. 2d 627 (N.Y. App. Div. Feb. 18, 1997).

EXHIBIT 17.2 *(Continued)*

As a side note, getting back to the concept of being "fair and equitable," ABC Appraisal Co. wants the court to accept that John gives up the income that he has received historically out of this business for $8 million. Joe and Jane get to split what John gives up. If we discuss what would have actually been given up during 1996 to 2000, John received salaries, commissions, and distributions totaling $24,066,995.

Even if we were to buy into the concept that ABC Appraisal Co.'s reasonable compensation for John of $250,000 per year is appropriate, five years of compensation, or $1,250,000 being subtracted from the $24 million + would result in John receiving excess distributions of $22,816,995. On average, this is $4.56 million per year. ABC Appraisal Co. wants the court to believe that someone receiving $4.56 million per year should give this up for $8 million. This defies common sense and logic.

What it also excludes is any rights in the future to receive this level of income. If we assume a simple capitalization of $4.56 million at 20 percent, it results in a $22.8 million value for the terminal period beyond the year 2000. Adding $22.8 million to the other $22.8 million that I have come up with indicates a value of about $45.6 million without any discounting being taken into consideration. This in itself indicates the serious flaw in the $8 million value that ABC Appraisal Co. derives. It is anything but "fair and equitable" to give up a stream of income averaging $4.56 million per year for only $8 million.

Page 9

Once again, ABC Appraisal Co. indicates that they read pages 21 through 23 of the XYZ Appraisal Co. report and that they believe that the XYZ Appraisal Co. discussion depicts an accurate portrayal of the general economic environment as of the valuation date. They also indicate that they agree with XYZ Appraisal Co.'s findings. First, did they do any independent analysis, or did they read only XYZ Appraisal Co.'s report?

Second, despite the quote appearing at the top of this page, they ignore the fact that on page 23 of the XYZ Appraisal Co. report, it discusses stock market increases, particularly the Dow being up 33.5 percent and the Nasdaq almost 40 percent up in that year. What they also ignore is on page 23 of the XYZ Appraisal Co. report, where XYZ Appraisal Co. discusses the Federal Reserve Board lowering interest rates in December 1995 "to recharge the stalled economy." This would have a positive effect on the value of The Littleton Companies.

ABC Appraisal Co. also states "the slowing economy led to a slowing within the trucking sector as retail sales and manufacturing production had been declining. These economic factors led to a decline in the demand for trucking services and a resulting over-capacity of trucks and service." While this statement is true for 1995, they totally ignore the fact that it is expected to turn around in 1996 and forward. In fact, according to the Alex Brown report attached to the ABC Appraisal Co. report (on page 6), revenue growth is expected to be anywhere from 15 to 30 percent for this industry. The growth prospects for the industry look pretty good. ABC Appraisal Co., however, decides to only pick and choose that which serves their purpose in low-balling this valuation.

Page 10

According to ABC Appraisal Co., "market multiples in the trucking industry in 1995 were reflective of the economic outlook and other factors specific to the trucking industry." This statement appears to be absolutely false when reading the Alex Brown report attached to the ABC Appraisal Co. report. In fact, Alex Brown is talking about many trucking stocks looking attractively valued to them, and they even indicated "stock valuations reflect diminished expectations and are at cyclically low levels." They also indicate "we are 12-month bulls on trucking stocks, as we believe multiples are likely to expand on the prospect of yr/yr earnings growth in 2H 1996."

Ironically, ABC Appraisal Co. also quotes from the Alex Brown report stating, "(Trucking) stocks with market capitalizations of less than $100 million were penalized for their illiquidity and are trading at what we consider to be private company valuations (3–5× EBITDA, vs. 6–10× for larger stock)." First of all, we used a multiple of six in our report. What is also interesting is that ABC Appraisal Co. uses this to help try to support their lower EBITDA multiple, but they ignore the fact that Alex Brown is also talking about the public companies being penalized for their illiquidity and that they are also trading at what looked like "private company valuations." Despite all of this, ABC Appraisal Co. still wants to apply a 35 percent discount for lack of marketability (illiquidity). This is a clear case of double counting.

Page 11

Once again, ABC Appraisal Co. refers to the XYZ Appraisal Co. report as the basis for the business description. They also acknowledge the breakdown of the company revenues being one-third for each of the following categories: less-than-truckload, truckload, and fleet management. This point becomes important in the search for guideline (comparable) companies because, as XYZ Appraisal Co. pointed out in their report, comparability is frequently difficult to achieve.

XYZ Appraisal Co. valued the Littleton entities separately and used different guideline companies for each because these companies did different types of trucking services. Now we are comparing a broader category of company to a combined Littleton entity, which actually makes them a bit less comparable. If anything, because of Littleton's diversification and the mix of business, they are probably less risky regarding any one aspect of the business, compared to the guideline companies. However, it makes comparability that much more of a problem. This is one more reason for questioning the validity of the outcome of the market approach.

(Continued)

EXHIBIT 17.2 *(Continued)*

Page 12

In discussing all of the nonconsolidated entities that were made part of this report, ABC Appraisal Co. lists Company A as being one of the companies included. One of the major differences between their report and our report is that we treated this valuation of Company A as a non-operating asset, which added $12.5 million to the value of the operating entity. It is my understanding from the real estate appraiser that this property was not legally zoned for the use, nor would it be necessary to use a $12.5 million piece of property as a parking lot for trailers.

All of the other entities were combined in our report as well, but here also there is a significant difference in value because of the treatment of these entities. At the bottom of the page, ABC Appraisal Co. indicates "We conducted a functional review and benchmarking analysis of the nonconsolidating entities' contribution to the consolidating entities. This review indicated they were all functional components of the primary business." ABC Appraisal Co. should be questioned regarding the functional use of Company A.

Page 13

ABC Appraisal Co. also presents net fixed assets to sales and intangible assets to sales to indicate that the guideline companies have much greater levels of assets to sales than The Littleton Companies. Once again, this is not necessarily a deficiency on the part of The Littleton Companies. In reality, closely held companies have a lower ratio because they utilize their assets for a longer period of time, as they do not necessarily have the asset replacement policy of the public companies. Once again, this is not necessarily a weakness. If the assets are in good working order, and if the assets do not require extraordinary repairs, what the private company effectively is doing is becoming more profitable by utilizing their assets for a longer period of time. ABC Appraisal Co. wants to turn this into a negative.

ABC Appraisal Co. also indicates "this analysis further confirms Judge Harris's conclusions that The Littleton Company represented a single, unified entity." This analysis did not confirm that at all. Quite frankly, the judge is absolutely correct, but it is common sense that dictates that these entities have been operated as a single unified entity. The ABC Appraisal Co. analysis in no way confirms the unification of these companies.

Getting back to ABC Appraisal Co.'s assessment that The Littleton Company was undercapitalized, nowhere does ABC Appraisal Co. recognize the fact that the officers of the company have been withdrawing extraordinary amounts of money, clearly indicating, as with most closely held companies, that they can operate the company as they wish to. Now, ABC Appraisal Co. wants to penalize the value of The Littleton Companies for this reason. In reality, this company is not undercapitalized; it has had an extraordinary dividend-paying capacity that the shareholders have taken advantage of.

It is important for the judge to understand that there is a very big difference between the operation of a public company, and the operation of a closely held business. The public company has a board of directors that is charged with maximizing shareholder value. That is typically not the manner in which a private company is operated. A private company operates to not only minimize income taxes, but also to maximize the benefits to the current shareholders. In this instance, while ABC Appraisal Co. talks about The Littleton Company needing a capital infusion of $19 million, they fail to recognize the fact that the excess compensation from 1993 to 1995 alone amounts to almost $10 million. This is not taking into consideration any other cash distributions that were made to the shareholders during this period of time that were not considered to be compensation.

Clearly, the Littleton family as a unified group has elected to operate this company as a cash cow for the owners rather than reinvesting these monies into the company. This does not necessarily mean that the company is weak. It shows that the company has the ability to operate in this fashion. In 1995, the company purchased and/or leased a significant amount of rolling stock to get ready for the next influx of business that was foreseeable in the upcoming year(s).

Overall, the analysis included on this page is extremely misleading and, in my opinion, is intended to deceive the court rather than provide an independent analysis.

Page 15

In the discussion of valuation methods, ABC Appraisal Co. provides a brief description of the three basic approaches to valuation. I agree with them regarding not using a net asset approach. However, I clearly disagree with them regarding their lack of using the income approach. In the middle of the page they state "we agree with XYZ Appraisal Co. that the market approach is the most appropriate methodology to determine the fair value of the interest. The income approach was considered, but not used due to the lack of any contemporaneous projections prepared by The Littleton Company during the general time frame of, or anytime prior to the valuation date."

There are several problems with this statement. First, while they agree with XYZ Appraisal Co., XYZ Appraisal Co. nowhere in their report refers to the standard of value as fair value. XYZ Appraisal Co. strictly performed a fair market value analysis. Fair market value is very different from fair value. Also, ABC Appraisal Co.'s rejection of the income approach because The Littleton Company did not have contemporaneous projections is utter nonsense. As appraisers, we prepare projections in valuation reports on a regular basis. I find it hard to believe that ABC Appraisal Co. does not do the same. In fact, it would be interesting to get information from some of their old valuation reports, particularly the smaller, privately held companies because more often than not, only the large companies have the internal staff to make projections. Valuation in itself is a prophecy of the future, and I find it hard to believe that ABC Appraisal Co. never uses the income approach.

EXHIBIT 17.2 *(Continued)*

ABC Appraisal Co. indicates, "inherent in the market approach are assumptions related to the future growth in cash flows and the associated risks in obtaining that growth." However, they fail to further indicate that the growth inherent in the market approach is typically considered to be short-term growth, as opposed to long-term growth, which is considered in the income approach.

The public market is extremely short-term oriented, and more often than not the multiples will reflect short-term growth. In fact, if a company has experienced substantial growth over the past several years, there is a good possibility that their multiples will be even lower than you would expect, because the marketplace will have perceived that a lot of the growth has taken place, and that future growth will slow down. This is one of the misleading factors in comparing public companies to privately held companies, particularly where the public company has a track record of growing through acquisition.

Pratt discusses the various approaches to value in the context of dissenting rights and oppression suits. He indicates that "most Courts embrace all three broad approaches to value (income, market, and asset-based approaches) in dissenting stockholder and judicial dissolution cases. The Chancery Court of Delaware has repeatedly expressed a preference for the discounted cash flow method. . . . However, reliance on the DCF method is dependent on reasonable projections, which are not always available." In discussing a Supreme Court of Utah case, *Oakridge Energy v. Clifton*, No. 960049, 1997 WL 191487 (Utah, April 18, 1997), Pratt indicates:

> The court noted that the consensus of the cases cited is that the component elements to be relied on in estimating fair value are market value, net asset value, and investment value, and the courts have traditionally favored investment value[2] rather than asset value, as the most important of the three elements.

In this instance, Pratt quotes the case that stated "we conclude that the trial court erred in using the stock market price . . . as the sole criterion for determining the fair value."

Market Approach

There are a number of cases, however, where the market approach was accepted. For example, Pratt states in *Borruso v. Communications Telesystems International*[3] that "both experts used only the guideline publicly traded company method, both relying primarily on multiples of revenue, because the financial history was insufficient to provide a basis for a DCF analysis, or even multiples of economic income variables, such as EBITDA." Once again, although the market approach was accepted, in this instance, a DCF could not be performed due to insufficient history. That is certainly not the case regarding the Littleton valuation. All of the cases cited by Pratt relate to dissenting shareholder cases as opposed to oppression cases. This creates a distinction between the court's considering a minority value versus a pro rata share of the entire company.

Discounted Cash Flow Method

In discussing the DCF method, Pratt indicates in *Grimes v. Vitalink*[4] that the Delaware Court of Chancery characterized the DCF method as "increasingly the model of choice for valuations in this Court." Another case where the court favored a DCF method over the guideline company method is *Gilbert v. M.P.M. Enterprises.*[5]

Excess Earnings Method

Although neither of us used the excess earnings method in the Littleton valuation, Pratt discusses *Balsamides* in the context of this method being accepted because the expert could not obtain all of the information needed to perform better valuation methods, but it should be noted that the excess earnings method is considered to be a control valuation. This means that the entire enterprise is valued without consideration of any minority discounts. You may wish to advance this argument as another reason why the use of the guideline company method in the ABC Appraisal Co. report without a control premium effectively penalizes John by valuing his interest on a minority basis as opposed to a pro rata share of the whole.

ABC Appraisal Co. is relying on the XYZ Appraisal Co. report to support the sole use of the market approach. Not only does the XYZ Appraisal Co. report not discuss their lack of use of the income approach, but XYZ Appraisal Co. states:

> As a practical matter, it became obvious early in our search that it would be impossible to find an adequate number of publicly held businesses corresponding precisely to these definitions. (These definitions relate to the description of the type of business that Company B, Company C, and Company D are engaged in.) It thus became necessary for us to broaden our criteria enough to select a group large enough for valuation purposes but not so much as to impair valuation results by inclusion of companies only little or remotely analogous to Company B, Company C, and Company D." (Parenthetical remark added for explanation.)

[2]Investment value, as used here, is as defined in the previous chapter (a value based on earnings), as opposed to the definition of investment value in a context other than fair value determinations—that is, the value to a particular buyer or seller.

[3]*Karl Borruso and William Lee v. Communications Telesystems International*, C.A. No.16316-NC, 999 LEXIS 197 (Del. Ch. September 24, 1999).

[4]*Charles M. Grimes v. Vitalink Communications Corp.*, C.A. No. 12334, 1997 WL 538676 (Del. Ch. August 28,1997), *aff'd* No. 425, 1997 (Del. April 1, 1998).

[5]*Gilbert v. M.P. Enterprises Inc.*, C.A. No. 14416-NC, 1998 LEXIS 60 (Del. Ch. April 24, 1998), *aff'd M.P. Enterprises Inc. v. Jeffrey D. Gilbert*, 731 A.2d 790 (Del. June 24, 1999).

(Continued)

EXHIBIT 17.2 *(Continued)*

Even XYZ Appraisal Co. recognizes that they had to reach in order to meet a good definition of comparability. Now, ABC Appraisal Co. wants to solely rely on this method, despite the fact that there are potential problems with its application due to the subjectivity of comparability. Clearly, we ran into the same issue when we applied our market approach, but that is a reason to continue beyond the market approach. In fact, ABC Appraisal Co. talks about the market approach taking into consideration future growth and the associated risks in getting to the growth, but they once again fail to discuss the impact if the market undervalues stocks in the public marketplace.

Substantial support exists for our position on this issue in Pratt's *Valuing A Business*, 4th edition. In a discussion involving standards of value, Pratt discusses the different standards regarding the definition of intrinsic or fundamental value. On page 31, he indicates the following:

> **Intrinsic or Fundamental Value**
>
> *Intrinsic value* (sometimes called *fundamental value*) differs from *investment value* in that it represents an analytical judgment of value based on the perceived characteristics inherent in the investment, not tempered by characteristics peculiar to any one investor, but rather tempered by how these perceived characteristics are interpreted by one analyst versus another.
>
> In the analysis of stocks, *intrinsic value* is generally considered the appropriate price for a stock according to a security analyst who has completed a *fundamental analysis* of the company's assets, earning power, and other factors.
>
> *Intrinsic Value*. The amount that an investor considers, on the basis of an evaluation of available fact, to be the "true" or "real" worth of an item, usually an *equity security*. It is the value that will become the market value when other investors reach the same conclusions. The various approaches to determining intrinsic value in the *finance* literature are based on expectations and discounted cash flows. See *expected value; fundamental analysis; discounted cash flow method*.[6]
>
> *Fundamental Analysis*. An approach in security analysis which assumes that a security has an "intrinsic value" that can be determined through a rigorous evaluation of relevant variables. Expected earnings is usually the most important variable in this analysis, but many other variables, such as dividends, capital structure, management quality, and so on, may also be studied. An analyst estimates the "intrinsic value" of a security on the basis of those fundamental variables and compares this value with the current market price of this security to arrive at an investment decision.[7]
>
> The purpose of security analysis is to detect differences between the value of a security as determined by the market and a security's "intrinsic value"—that is, the value that the security *ought* to have and will have when other investors have the same insight and knowledge as the analyst.[8]
>
> If the market value is below what the analyst concludes is the intrinsic value, the analyst considers the stock a "buy." If the market value is above the assumed intrinsic value, the analyst suggests selling the stock. (Some analysts also factor market expectations into their fundamental analysis.)
>
> It is important to note that the concept of intrinsic value cannot be entirely divorced from the concept of fair market value because the actions of buyers and sellers based on their *specific* perceptions of intrinsic value eventually lead to the general consensus market value and to the constant and dynamic changes in market value over time.
>
> Case law often refers to the term *intrinsic value*. However, almost universally such references do not define the term other than by reference to the language in the context in which it appears. Such references to *intrinsic value* can be found both in cases where there is no statutory standard of value and in cases where the statutory standard of value is specified as *fair value* or even *fair market value*. When references to *intrinsic value* appear in the relevant case law, the analyst should heed the notions ascribed to that term as discussed in this section.

As you can see from the above definition, Pratt indicates that "the various approaches to determining intrinsic value in the finance literature are based on expectations and discounted cash flows." Clearly, expected earnings are of critical importance, but other variables, such as dividends, capital structure, management quality, and so on, are also considered in a fundamental analysis. What is striking is that Pratt indicates that "if the market value is below what the analyst concludes is the intrinsic value, the analyst considers the stock a "buy." This is exactly what is taking place in the Alex Brown report attached to the ABC Appraisal Co. report. In fact, not only does Alex Brown consider certain stocks to be a "buy," they in fact suggest that certain of these stocks are considered to be a "strong buy."

On the front page of the December 1995 Transportation Report, Alex Brown lists a number of truckload, and less-than-truckload, public companies that are considered to be strong buys and buys. In fact, we used eight of these companies as guideline companies, whereas three of the seven of ABC Appraisal Co.'s guideline companies are also listed in this category.

---

[6]W.W. Cooper and Yuri Ijiri, eds., *Kohler's Dictionary for Accountants*, 6th ed. (Englewood Cliffs, N.J.: Prentice Hall, 1983), 285. Reprinted by permission of Prentice Hall, Inc., Englewood Cliffs, New Jersey.

[7]Ibid., 228.

[8]James H. Lorie and Mary T. Hamilton, *The Stock Market: Theories and Evidence* (Burr Ridge, Ill.: Irwin, 1973), 114.

EXHIBIT 17.2 *(Continued)*

ABC Appraisal Co. says, "Hence the market approach is a fair proxy for the income approach." Besides the fact that this assumes that the market comparable companies are properly priced, it is also not the case in this situation. We point out at the top of page 166 in our report that our correlation analysis indicates that there is no direct correlation between earnings growth and the pricing multiples. We say "it appears that the companies with the lowest three-year compound growth rate in earnings have the highest earnings estimates, but this is not translating directly into high multiples." Clearly, there are many factors that impact the prices of stocks in the public market, and in this instance we have an industry that does not necessarily behave as analysts would expect. Therefore, the results can be extremely misleading and caution must be exercised by an appraiser in using this information, particularly as the sole source of deriving a valuation conclusion for a closely held company. This is one of the reasons that it is suggested that appraisers use as many approaches and methods as may be applicable in any given situation, not only to serve as checks and balances upon ourselves, but also because there is a subjective element to the valuation process. Using a single approach can bias the result, and that is not necessarily the intention of the valuation process.

Page 16

At the bottom of this page, ABC Appraisal Co. discusses excess compensation. Their analysis refers to a Court Trial Exhibit Number 1707, indicating the total salary and commissions for Joe and John to be approximately $2.75 million each. We have no problem with the use of this figure, as it is the same amount that we reflect in our report. However, at the very bottom of the page, carrying over to the next page, is a discussion about Judge Harris's perception of Joe being the dominant person in the business.

ABC Appraisal Co. uses the court's findings as a basis of determining reasonable compensation for Joe to be what he was actually paid and substantially reducing John's salary. There is no empirical basis to support the level of replacement compensation based upon the court's statement. Regardless of who the dominant person is, the issue becomes what would be the cost of replacing this person with someone of equal ability to run this company if the company was to be sold? In order to support their conclusion, ABC Appraisal Co. refers to a return on equity analysis that they performed, which showed that investors would be content paying Joe this huge amount of money because they would continue to get their return. However, what ABC Appraisal Co. has done is an extremely misleading and incorrect analysis.

The return on equity analysis is used as one of the factors to consider in the reasonableness for the deductibility of compensation paid to an officer of a company. There is a large distinction between reasonable compensation from an income tax standpoint and reasonable compensation in an appraisal situation. The partial analysis that ABC Appraisal Co. has included is used frequently to support deductions under Section 162 of the Internal Revenue Code relating to deductibility of ordinary and necessary business expenses.

Two cases that describe the use of a return on equity analysis are *Mad Auto Wrecking Inc. v. The Commissioner* (T.C. Memo 1995-153) and *Elliotts, Inc. v. Commissioner* (52 AFTR 2d 83-5976). These are both income tax cases dealing with reasonable compensation.

In a valuation context, the issue that we address is, what is the replacement cost of the officer, and not, what is a reasonable amount for past efforts that may be tax deductible? According to Pratt (page 79), "in order to make the appropriate adjustments regarding executive compensation of the closely held business, the appraiser identifies the total compensation from all sources being paid to the existing executive and compares that to the total compensation required to attract an executive of similar skills." If public company executives are the appropriate basis for comparison, then total compensation from all sources paid to the public company executive (including stock options, bonus plans, pension plans, prerequisites, etc.) should be evaluated along with the contribution to the company provided by the executive. ABC Appraisal Co. did not do this analysis as part of their report.

Page 18

Continuing with the excess compensation analysis, discussing The Littleton Company's compound annual growth rates, ABC Appraisal Co. indicates at the top of the page that The Littleton Companies exceeded several market indices over the same period. This indicates that Littleton outperformed the market. Once again, while attempting to justify a higher salary for Joe, ABC Appraisal Co. supports the notion that The Littleton Companies are considerably stronger, which should positively impact its value.

In the first full paragraph on the top of page 18, ABC Appraisal Co. states "it seems from the CAGR, since Joe took over the business and the level of dividends received by the shareholders, that all shareholders (particularly John) have been well compensated for their association with this successful business." One of the ethical provisions of the appraisal profession is that we are only supposed to be advocates for our opinion, and we are not supposed to advocate on behalf of a client. ABC Appraisal Co.'s parenthetical remark, as well as numerous remarks throughout this report, borderlines advocacy.

Ironically, when it comes to John's compensation, they pull out a study and support his salary as being $250,000. The real issue becomes, would it take $3 million to compensate management in this company if the company were sold? ABC Appraisal Co. tries to use an "independent investor test" to further support Joe's $2.75 million. They indicate " . . . this comparison shows that an independent investor would be willing to pay the level of compensation that we have deemed appropriate for Joe ($2.75 million)." The question isn't would they have been willing to pay this, but would they have to pay this? In our report we performed an analysis of reasonable compensation.

(Continued)

EXHIBIT 17.2 *(Continued)*

Furthermore, we have taken information from the 1995 proxy statements of the public companies, which are shown next.

Company	*Position*	*Salary and Bonus*	*Options Granted*	*Sales*	*Salary/ Sales*
American Freightways	President and CEO	$ 266,191	50,000	$ 572,100,000	0.05%
Arkansas Best	Executive V.P.	945,821		1,437,279,000	0.07%
Arnold	President and Chairman	635,140		330,136	0.19%
Builders Transport	CEO	327,014		289,527,000	0.11%
Heartland Transport	Chairman and President	300,000		191,507,000	0.16%
MS Carriers	Chairman and CEO	389,484		333,070,000	0.12%
Old Dominion	Chairman and CEO	474,103		248,079,000	0.19%
OTR Express	President and CEO	142,086	7,455	49,211,000	0.29%
PAM Transportation	President and CEO	294,875	50,000	91,595,000	0.32%
Swift Transportation	Chairman and President	801,303		458,165,000	0.17%
Transportation Corp. of America	CEO	299,890		144,254,000	0.21%
USA Truck	Chairman	380,984		102,400,000	0.37%
US Xpress	Co-Chairman	1,210,127		254,331,000	0.48%
Werner Enterprises	CEO	738,185		576,002,000	0.13%
Anuhco (Transfinancial Holdings)	President	188,264	10,000	97,444,000	0.19%

It should be noted that the options granted in the schedule were under water at the time of the grant, so looking at these public company executives, the highest paid executive earned $1.2 million for a company that was twice the size of The Littleton Entities. Clearly, Joe could be replaced by the president, chairman, or CEO of one of these public companies for less than $2.75 million. This shows the unreasonableness of the unsubstantiated compensation amount.

Table 2 of the ABC Appraisal Co. report, once again, indicates that The Littleton Companies were stronger than the guideline companies, because they have a stronger EBIT margin. This further substantiates the fact that Littleton should be valued higher than ABC Appraisal Co. concluded.

Pages 26–27

The discussion for the adjustment for lack of marketability is flawed. Pratt includes a brief discussion about the fact that lack of control discounts are rejected in several instances. I am not going to elaborate on these cases because neither appraiser in the Littleton valuations actually took a minority discount. However, Pratt also highlights the fact that a control premium was accepted by the Delaware Chancery Court under two specific circumstances. He lists these as:

1. When the base value is a publicly traded equivalent value derived by the guideline publicly traded company method
2. When valuing a controlling ownership position in this subsidiary company

In Borruso, both experts agreed that a control premium should be applied. In fact, in *Rapid American Corporation v. Harris*,[9] the Delaware Supreme Court concluded that a control premium was appropriate, explaining "the exclusion of a control premium artificially and unrealistically treated Rapid as a minority shareholder." In LeBeau, the Delaware Court of Chancery implicitly allowed a control premium by allowing the guideline merger and acquisition method to be used.

[9]*Rapid American Corporation v. Harris*, 603 A.2d 796 (Del.1992).

EXHIBIT 17.2 (Continued)

In *Quantifying Marketability Discounts* written by Z. Christopher Mercer, ASA, CFA, the author discusses various levels of value that are used in the appraisal process. Mercer states:

> *The controlling interest value* represents the value of the enterprise as a whole. The controlling interest appraisal should, therefore, encompass the rights, risks, and rewards of having controlling power in a business. In the context of this discussion, controlling interests and enterprises are considered to be marketable, and a marketability discount is not used. Some appraisers, however, do apply a marketability discount, which may reflect the costs of brokerage or transactions costs, to control values.

Basically, Mercer's position is that since a controlling interest can readily be sold, there should not be a discount taken for lack of marketability. This would further suggest that if there is a discount to be taken, it would be no more than a brokerage cost, which for a company the size of Littleton would probably not exceed about 5 percent. Certainly, the discount for marketability taken by ABC Appraisal Co. represents a discount for a minority value, and as such, we believe that it unfairly penalizes John since we believe he should be entitled to a pro rata share of the entire business.

After reading Exhibit 17.2 you probably realize that even the big firms don't always do good work. Part of the problem in the litigation of Exhibit 17.2 was that the lead appraiser was clearly advocating for his client rather than providing a fair appraisal.

Conclusion

If I did my job, you now have a better understanding of valuations to be used in shareholder disputes. If I did not do my job, or if you just want more information on this subject, see Pratt's *Valuing A Business* or *The Handbook of Advanced Business Valuation*. Both are dandy resources.

18

My Favorite Court Cases

Chapter Goals

In this chapter, I am going to discuss some of my favorite court cases. These include:

1. *Estate of Joyce C. Hall v. Commissioner*
2. *Estate of Samuel I. Newhouse v. IRS Commissioner*
3. *Charles S. Foltz et al. v. U.S. News & World Report, Inc., et al.*
4. *Bernard Mandelbaum v. IRS Commissioner*
5. *Mad Auto Wrecking v. IRS Commissioner*

Overview

If you are anything like me, you probably are starving for guidance in the stuff we do for a living. I keep reading everything that I can get my hands on in the hopes that I will get better at it. The one lesson that I have learned over the past 20 years of doing business valuations is that on occasion a court ruling gets issued that is well thought out and well written. I'm not being critical of the courts, but most opinions do not really help me understand what the court did to reach its opinion.

In all fairness to the courts, many expert reports, and much of the expert testimony rendered before the court, quite frankly, stinks. These poor judges are being asked to rule, in many cases, using expert testimony and expert reports that are *anything but* expert work. I give the judges a lot of credit (no cash, but a lot of credit) for doing their jobs as well as they do. As appraisers, we read court cases and do not fully appreciate how little good information was presented to the court for it to rule on.

In this chapter, I am going to discuss some of the court cases that I have found to be very helpful in doing my job. These are the cases I have found to be very instructional, and I find that I keep going back to them in order to get some really good guidance.

Although I am only going to cover certain aspects of these cases, you really should read the entire court opinion. Enough of the introduction, let's do it!

Estate of Joyce C. Hall v. Commissioner[1]

This case involves a well-known company, Hallmark Cards, Inc. (the greeting card company) and the determination of the decedent's holdings within that privately held company. The main issue that I

[1] *Estate of Joyce C. Hall v. Commissioner*, 92 T.C. 312(RIA) (1989).

want to discuss is the treatment given to the guideline company method, in particular the search for guideline companies. Revenue Ruling 59-60 states as number 8 on the hit parade that the appraiser should consider:

> The market price of stocks of corporations engaged in the same or similar line of business and having their stocks actively traded in a free and open market, either on an exchange or over the counter.[2]

If you reread this statement, the guideline companies are supposed to be in the *same or similar* line of business as the subject company. Notice the word "similar." That's what this case is all about.

In the battle between the experts, all of the experts agreed on one thing: there was only one good publicly traded "comparable" company, American Greetings Corporation. The Petitioner's experts selected additional guideline companies from other industries because they believed that using only one guideline company could be misleading—sort of like taking a poll and asking only one person who will win an election. Not a very meaningful result!

The IRS's expert made his determination based only on American Greetings (surprise, surprise!). He also ended up with values per share of the three classes of stock at more than two times those from the other two experts.

The taxpayer's initial expert, from First Boston, selected five companies as guidelines in addition to American Greetings. They were:

- A.T. Cross Co. (the pen and pencil people)
- Avon Products, Inc. (the world's largest manufacturer of cosmetics, fragrances, and fashion jewelry)
- Coca-Cola Co. (the soda people)
- Lenox, Inc. (the fine china folks)
- Papercraft Corp. (a manufacturer of gift wrap items)

These companies did not sell greeting cards. However, First Boston felt that these would be good guideline companies because they:

1. Produced brand-name consumer goods
2. Were leading companies in their respective industries
3. Had publicly traded stocks
4. Had business and financial characteristics similar to Hallmark

The lesson to be learned from this is if you look for an exact fit, you will probably never find one. However, to apply the guideline company method, you need to use some imagination to set parameters for a search other than the subject company's SIC code. Sometimes better guideline companies may exist in different industries.

The second expert for the estate, Shearson Lehman, believed that considering several guideline companies reduced the probability that individual characteristics, temporary market inefficiencies, or aberrations relating to one company might bias the valuation analysis.

Despite American Greetings being Hallmark's closest publicly held competitor, Shearson looked for a broad group of companies that shared one or more of the following traits with Hallmark:

[2]Revenue Ruling 59-60 (1959-1 C.B. 237).

1. Sold low-cost consumer, nondurable goods through channels similar to those used by greeting card companies
2. Had a stable, high-profile, quality reputation with the consumer and a leading brand name
3. Sold products in which the images of both the product and the company, and the product's function, were differentiable from those of its competitors
4. Sold products that involved some element of social expression

In addition to companies that met the above criteria (the opinion does not tell us which companies), Shearson picked four other companies that they considered comparable to Hallmark in that they were leaders in their industries. They were:

- McDonald's
- Anheuser Busch
- IBM
- Coca-Cola

Hamburgers, beer, computers, and soda! Many individuals could argue that these companies are not *comparable* to Hallmark. This is the reason that we now call them *guideline companies*. The idea is to get guidance from the market as to the investing public's perception of companies that have similar investment characteristics. These companies were highly regarded by the investment community for their quality management, leading market position, and excellent financial condition. Shearson Lehman also believed that if Hallmark were a public company, it would enjoy a similar reputation.

The lesson that comes out of this case can be highlighted through some of the sections of the Court's ruling. These are as follows:

- Moreover, it is inconceivable to us that a potential buyer of Hallmark stock would consider only one alternative "comparable," i.e., American Greetings stock.
- Respondent argues that it is "simply wrong as a matter of law" to look beyond the single, publicly held company engaged in the sale of greeting cards to other companies engaged in the sale of other types of consumer nondurable goods or having similar financial characteristics. Respondent's argument too narrowly construes the concept of comparability and ignores the use of "similar" as well as "same" in section 2031(b). Respondent relies on *Northern Trust Co., Transferee v. Commissioner*, 87 T.C. 349, 376 (1986), aff'd sub nom. *Citizens Bank & Trust Co., Transferee v. Commissioner*, 87 T.C. 349, 376 1249 (7th Cir. 1988). That case, however, rejected expert opinions based on companies that were found to be noncomparable and concluded that "the market comparable approach is not available in this case." 87 T.C. at 377. That opinion does not justify using a market comparable approach based on a single competitor.
- Overall, we can only conclude that PCA (the IRS expert) was instructed to prepare and did prepare an analysis that led to an artificial and excessive value for the Hallmark stock. In contrast to PCA, petitioner's experts acted reasonably in selecting comparable companies in the similar business of consumer nondurable goods, in drawing conclusions based upon careful comparisons of Hallmark with individual comparables.

So what does this tell us? Similar does not mean an exact fit. Using the guideline company method requires the appraiser to look beyond the obvious in the search for companies that can provide guidance from the market. This case is excellent in reiterating the very essence of the market approach.

Estate of Samuel I. Newhouse v. Commissioner[3]

This case is another excellent learning tool. The theme that I am going to highlight is only a small, but important, part of the case. Valuations that are performed for estate tax purposes must use the *fair market value* standard of value. Valuation theory tells us that fair market value assumes a hypothetical transaction between a hypothetical willing buyer and a hypothetical willing seller. This case addresses the issue of fair market value "to whom."

Fair market value deals with the hypothetical willing buyer and willing seller. This case addressed the issue of which class of willing buyer should be considered in the determination of fair market value. Appraisers frequently use terms such as strategic or synergistic buyer. We immediately respond by stating that if there were a strategic or synergistic buyer involved, the value determined would represent investment value and not fair market value. This is not always correct.

Part of the determination of fair market value requires the appraiser to determine the likely market for the property. Clearly, the willing seller, if prudent, will look to sell the property in the market that would bring him or her the greatest price.

The *Newhouse* case examined four classes of potential investors. They were:

- The passive investor
- The active investor
- The control investor
- The public investor

Goldman Sachs analyzed these four categories of investors as all being valid "willing buyers" in the definition of fair market value. The Court's opinion discusses the different types of investor. The subject company of the appraisal is referred to as "Advance." Important descriptions from the opinion are excerpted below.

- A *passive investor* would not be interested in managing Advance and would not attempt to wrest control from management. Expecting to realize value from dividends and private resale, the passive investor would not expect to extract value from Advance through liquidation, merger, or public offering. The passive investor would consider that Advance's stock was not publicly traded, which would depress expectations of resale value. Due to this illiquidity, lack of control, and the uncertainties and constraints affecting the purchase, Goldman Sachs concluded that the passive investor would have offered 30 percent less than the public trading market value of the common stock and thus only $141 million for the common stock.
- The *active investor* would be inclined to pursue action, short of seeking control, that would quickly maximize the return on his investment. One course of action would be to declare a dividend of Advance's excess cash and any funds that could be obtained through borrowing. Because of the high prevailing interest rate and planned capital expenditures, the common shareholder could extract no more than $74 million of excess cash plus loan proceeds. Advance also had $145 million of excess cash, which could be distributed with the loan proceeds. Because of the time and uncertainty involved in this plan of action, the active investor would pay no more than 85 percent of the amount he hoped to extract. This figure would be far less than the $141 million the passive investor would be willing to pay.

  Alternatively, the active investor might cause the excess cash to be distributed immediately and then cause Advance to pay dividends at the highest possible level. Assuming that the active investor

[3]*Estate of Samuel I. Newhouse v. Commissioner*, 94 T.C. 193(RIA) (1990).

would insist on an after-tax yield on his investment of about 13 or 14 percent, Goldman Sachs concluded that the active investor would be willing to pay $150 million for the Advance common stock.

- A *control investor* would have purchased the Advance common stock with the goal of acquiring 100 percent of the equity ownership and control of the company. A control investor would hope to realize value from his purchase by dividend distributions, by liquidation, or by merger, but Advance's unusual capital structure would prevent the latter two courses of action without eliminating the preferred stock or securing their consent. The preferred had the right to block liquidation. Because the common's power to effect a merger adverse to the preferred's interests was so uncertain, Goldman Sachs concluded that any willing buyer, as a matter of sound business judgment, would analyze the value of the common as if that option were foreclosed. Goldman Sachs' analysis is persuasive.

  Goldman Sachs concluded that only another media company would be interested in acquiring Advance and that none of the major media companies would have considered buying the common stock without first eliminating the claims of the preferred shareholders. Because the control investor would assume that he could not receive anything except 22 percent of the highest level of dividends declared, he would be in the same position as the active investor and would pay no more than what the active investor would pay, viz, $150 million.

- Goldman Sachs concluded that an underwritten *public offering* would be the best way to sell the Advance common stock, requiring the three different types of stock to be recapitalized into a single class. Goldman Sachs' research indicated that in approximately half of the transactions in which voting control was transferred, the buyers paid a premium for control. Goldman Sachs concluded that no control premium was warranted. Goldman Sachs then determined that, after exchanging the class A common stock one-for-three, and the class B common and the preferred stock one-for-one, the offering price would be $25 per share subject to a 7 percent discount. The price for all of the shares would be $778 million, and for petitioner's shares it would be $176 million.

  Because the benchmark value for a public offering, $176 million, was the highest value, Goldman Sachs concluded that the value of petitioner's Advance common stock was $176 million on February 29, 1980.

In the AICPA's self-study program *Business Valuation Methods*, Alan Zipp discusses the categories of investor. He states:

The Passive Investor

A passive investor would not be interested in managing the business. He would expect to realize value from dividends and resale and not from liquidation, merger, or public offering. Although the passive investor neither controls management, business operations, nor cash flow, he would expect to have some influence on management to increase dividends in the future. The passive investor would consider a depressed resale value since a closely held company is not publicly traded. Due to this illiquidity, lack of control, the uncertainties of future dividends, and constraints affecting a resale, a passive investor would be willing to purchase the business only at a substantial discount, of perhaps 30 percent or more.

The Active Investor

The active investor would be inclined to pursue action, short of seeking control, that would quickly maximize the return on his investment. One course of action would be to pressure the control interest to declare a dividend. Continuous pressure on management to promote business growth and to distribute dividends would be the role of the active investor. Because of the time and uncertainty involved in this plan of action, the active investor would pay no more than 85 percent of the amount he hoped to extract as dividend distributions.

The Control Investor

The control investor would purchase an interest in a business with the goal of acquiring 100 percent of the equity ownership and control of the company. A control investor would hope to realize value from his purchase through excess salary and fringe benefits, dividend distributions, liquidation, merger, or perhaps a public offering. A control investor, being in a position to determine the timing and amount of dividend distributions, salary and fringe benefits, and liquidation or sale prospects, would be willing to pay about 90 percent of the amount he expects to receive.

The Public Investor

The public investor would purchase a business interest with the full acceptance of being a minority stockholder and having no influence over business operations. The public investor would hope to realize value from his purchase in the appreciation in value of the investment, along with dividends received. The public investor would only consider historical dividends, even though the company had the ability to pay higher dividends, since the public investor is not inclined to seek larger distributions. The public investor, unlike the passive investor, would make the investment only if the company planned to make a public or private offering creating a market for the shares. Therefore, in addition to a substantial discount for the lack of control and influence, illiquidity, uncertainty of future dividends, and risk of liquidation, the public investor would want a discount for the costs associated with the underwriting of a public or private offering, from 5 percent to 20 percent. Hence, the public investor in a closely held business would expect a discount from 35 percent to 55 percent or more.

The importance of this case is that it explicitly contends that the willing buyer of a company can be any number of possible buyers with varying intentions and return on investment requirements. The result of such a conclusion is the creation of an awareness that one type of buyer, based on his or her intentions, will pay a much different price from that of another buyer. As displayed in this analysis, there are many different traits and factors that must be considered. The review of such issues is not relegated only to those mentioned within this case summary. The motivations for investment for the different classes of willing buyers can vary greatly. The difficult part of this exercise is to identify as many of the different classes of buyers as possible. Identifying the numerous reasons why one investor differs from another will support the existence of a difference in value even for the same company.

Although this portion of the willing buyer analysis is rational and sound, it is frequently overlooked. The process of valuation must consider all factors, regardless of whether they are used in the final conclusions of the report. Ensuring that all variables have been analyzed will justify conclusions better than by ignoring them.

The appraiser is faced with the challenge of defining the market for the subject interest being valued. Just keep in mind that the market should represent a rational, knowledgeable buyer and not the biggest sucker who will pay the most for the property. Suckers don't count!

Charles S. Foltz v. U.S. News & World Report, Inc.[4]

These lawsuits are oldies but goodies. They were brought by retirees of U.S. News & World Report who felt they were underpaid at retirement because the stock of U.S. News & World Report, Inc., a closely held company, was undervalued by the independent appraisers for the nine-year period 1973 through 1981. I wonder why they woke up after nine years?

[4]*Charles S. Foltz et al. v. U.S. News & World Report, Inc., et al., and David B. Richardson et al. v. U.S. News & World Report, Inc., et al.* U.S. District Court, District of Columbia, Civil Actions No. 84-0447 and 85-2195, June 22, 1987. (The *Foltz* case, a class action, dealt with the years 1973 through 1980; the *Richardson* case, not a class action, covered 1981.)

Well, this case got everyone sued—the company, certain directors, the profit-sharing plan that held the stock, and the appraiser. Are you sure you really want to do this stuff?

Some quick background: U.S. News had a profit-sharing plan that worked like an ESOP. When employees retired, they got paid for their shares at fair market value. As time went by, the company purchased real estate near its headquarters located in Washington, D.C. The value of this real estate started to climb during the 1970s. There were discussions about developing the real estate for alternative uses, but nothing was done about it until 1981.

In the Court's opinion, Judge Barrington D. Parker stated that "the central issue requiring resolution in this litigation has always been the propriety of the methodology employed in appraising the U.S. News stock." The primary valuation issues in the case were as follows.

- *Control versus minority valuation basis*. The annual appraisals valued the stock on a minority basis. Plaintiffs contended that the stock should have been valued on a control basis.
- *Discounts for lack of marketability*. Almost all of the annual appraisals applied a 10 percent discount for lack of marketability (DLOM). The plaintiffs contended that no DLOM should have been applied. Unlike today's ESOPs, the stock had no put option. The company had a call option at the appraised value, which it exercised consistently to retire stock from the stock bonus plan when employees left. Most of the calls were for cash, but on occasion the company exercised its option to purchase the stock on extended terms, at a low interest rate, which the call option permitted.
- *Importance of real estate and other assets*. The annual appraisals placed various weights on the real estate values in different years, depending on the facts and circumstances at that time. In all valuations, the primary emphasis in the appraisals was on the earning power of the company. Plaintiffs contended that more weight should have been given to the analysis and values of the real estate and other assets.
- *Subsequent events*. The annual appraisals valued the stock on a going-concern basis, taking into consideration only facts and circumstances that were known or knowable as of the valuation date. Plaintiffs contended that prospects for future changes, such as a synergistic buyer of the company who might be willing to pay more for the company, should have been considered and reflected in the annual appraisals. The company was sold in 1984 for a lot more than the appraised value.

Judge Parker's decision is good reading as a learning tool. The Court concluded, "After consideration of the expert testimony presented, the Court is not persuaded that the per-share price arrived at each year by American Appraisal did not fall within a reasonable range of acceptable values." Let's hear it for the appraisers!

Control Versus Minority

On this point, the Court stated:

> Since the terms of the U.S. News plan did not contemplate anything other than a series of minority-interest transactions , . . . the valuation of its stock on a minority basis does not offend ERISA.
>
> Various individuals concurrently held undivided, minority interests in a control block of stock. . . . The mere fact that Plan members' interests, if added together, amounted to a majority of the outstanding shares in the company, does not, standing alone, entitle them to a pro rata control value.

The judge not only discussed the control versus minority issue, but he also strongly supported the acceptance of appraisers' judgment when reasonable alternatives were available. He said:

> Clearly, in the absence of any statutory, administrative, or judicial authority for the proposition that a control value might have been indicated, defendants cannot be faulted for employing a minority valuation. . . . ERISA

> does not require plan fiduciaries to maximize the benefits of departing employees . . . ; it only requires them to make a reasonable choice from among possible alternatives.

The Court also noted that the minority-interest valuation was consistent with the appraisal methodology used when the plan purchased its stock in 1962 and 1966. Consistency is the key in this business.

With respect to the voting trust that was part of the profit-sharing plan, the Court noted:

> It is well recognized that, not only does the existence of a voting trust fail to make the underlying stock more valuable, it most often decreases the value of those shares. . . . Defendants would have been justified in reducing the value of the company's stock to reflect the impediment that the trust placed against the full enjoyment of the rights that would ordinarily have attached to the stock.

DLOM

Here, the Court noted:

> The Company was under no obligation to repurchase the stock. It had, rather, an option to *call* the stock . . . . Moreover, . . . the Company could—and from time to time did—exercise its option . . . to pay for the stock on terms that would not have been accepted gladly by an outside investor. . . . The modest 10 percent marketability discount that American Appraisal applied generally to the U.S. News stock in the aggregate was perfectly appropriate.

Real Estate and Other Assets

Judge Parker said:

> In a minority valuation, . . . assets may or may not play an important part in arriving at a per-share figure, because a minority shareholder cannot reach those assets. . . . Generally speaking, if the valuation being undertaken is of a business, such as U.S. News, that produces goods or services, primary consideration will be given to the earnings of the company and the resultant return on a shareholder's investment.

Subsequent Events

In this regard, the Court found that:

> The approach to be used is not retrospective, but prospective. One must look at the situation as of the time that each employee separated from the Company. Therefore, the appropriate inquiry is whether the Company was properly valued during the class period, not whether former employees become eligible for a greater share of benefits upon the contingency of a subsequent sale.

With respect to possible future development of the real estate holdings, Judge Parker cited testimony that:

> Any realizable value should be attributed to the real estate only "if it was evident that the controlling interest had a firm and clear intent to dispose of the real estate within a very short or reasonable period of time [, that is,] absolute evidence . . . not mere development plans."

Several valuable lessons can be learned from this case. One of the most important lessons is the concept that since a minority stockholder does not have the ability to reach the underlying assets of the corporation, only a minor amount of weight, if any, should be given to the value of these assets. Modern appraisal theory addresses this as one of the prerogatives of control.

Another lesson is that valuation is a prospective process and not a retrospective process. I strongly urge you to read the entire case. We cite a portion of the opinion when we value minority interests. See Exhibit 18.1.

EXHIBIT 18.1
Partial Discussion—Minority Interest Report

Description of the Assignment

Trugman Valuation Associates Inc. was retained by Howard Bros., Inc. to determine the fair market value of Howard Bros., Inc., a New Jersey Corporation, on a minority basis as of December 19, 2000. The purpose of this valuation is to determine the value of the shares for potential gifts that will be made.

The Asset-Based Approach

The asset-based approach, sometimes referred to as the cost approach, is an asset-oriented approach rather than a market-oriented approach. Each component of a business is valued separately and then summed up to derive the total value of the enterprise.

The appraiser estimates value using this approach by estimating the cost of duplicating or replacing the individual elements of the business property being appraised, item by item, asset by asset.

The tangible assets of the business are valued using this approach, although it cannot be used alone, as many businesses have intangible value as well, to which this approach cannot be applied.

This approach is generally inappropriate for a minority interest unless the shareholder has the right to liquidate or sell off the assets and liabilities of the company. Since minority shareholders cannot realize the value of the net assets, regardless of the amount of appreciation that may have taken place, it is inappropriate for the appraiser to apply this methodology for most minority stock valuations. This concept was discussed by the Court in *U.S. News & World Report, Inc.*,[1] where the plaintiffs claimed that they were underpaid for the value of their shares of stock in the company.

The essence of the case was the fact that there was significantly appreciated real estate that had not been considered by the appraiser when the shares of stock were valued on a minority basis. In this matter, the Court cited testimony that

> Any realizable value should be attributed to the real estate only if it was evident that the controlling interest had a firm and clear intent to dispose of the real estate within a very short or reasonable period of time.

This same process applies to all balance sheet items since the minority shareholder cannot realize proceeds from an event that he or she cannot control.

[1]*Charles S. Foltz et al. v. U.S. News & World Report, Inc., et al., and David B. Richardson et al. v. U.S. News & World Report, Inc., et al.*, U.S. District Court, District of Columbia, Civil Actions No. 84-0447 and 85-2195, June 22,1987 .

Bernard Mandelbaum et al. v. Commissioner[5]

Many court cases involve multiple issues. However, *Bernard Mandelbaum et al. v. Commissioner* relates to only one aspect of the valuation universe, namely, the DLOM.

In discussing the DLOM and how it fits in with this case, let's first discuss some of the background regarding the opposing arguments. There were six dates in which shares of the appraisal subject (Big M) were gifted from shareholders to other parties. These gifts required the filing of gift tax returns covering dates from 1986 to 1990.

One issue needs to be mentioned here. The Big M stock was subject to two shareholder agreements. The first agreement required that any positions on the board that became vacant be filled by current members and that the new directors be either current shareholders or their spouses. Upon death, the shares were to be sold to Big M, and the company had sole discretion over what period of time they would pay for the shares. The company also had a right of first refusal for live shareholders (as opposed to dead ones) and, again, could determine that time period for the purchase. The company had 90 days to decide whether it would exercise its purchase option.

The second agreement was pretty similar to the first, but it stated that those who wanted out had to offer their shares to family members before they could sell to outsiders. These types of agreements are not terribly unusual except for the provision that allows the company to have sole discretion over the time period for the payout.

[5]*Bernard Mandelbaum et al. v. IRS Commissioner*, T.C. Memo. 1995-255 (RIA).

To support its determination of value, and therefore calculation of the taxpayers' deficiency, the respondent, the IRS Commissioner, employed an expert by the name of Paul Mallarkey. Mallarkey concluded an applicable DLOM of 30 percent for the gifted shares on the six dates in question. This discount level was calculated relying on three of the restricted stock studies discussed in Chapter 11. These studies provided a range of DLOMs between 30 percent and 35 percent.

On the other side, the petitioner, Bernard Mandelbaum and family, utilized the services of Roger Grabowski to support the values reported on their gift tax returns for the specified dates. To find an applicable DLOM, Grabowski employed a similar analysis to that of Mallarkey. However, Grabowski used 10 studies, including the 3 used by Mallarkey, to determine an acceptable range of DLOMs. Furthermore, Grabowski also took into account the details of Big M's shareholder agreements and prior events involving The Company and shareholders. Based upon these considerations, and the 10 studies that included 7 restricted stock studies and 3 IPO studies, Grabowski concluded that a 75 percent DLOM applied for the valuation dates in 1986 through 1989, and a 70 percent DLOM was applicable for the dates in 1990.

The discounts that were concluded were substantially higher than the discounts included in the 10 studies analyzed because of Grabowski's analysis of the restrictions placed upon The Company's shares by the shareholders' agreements. Also, he interviewed employees of investment firms to determine the required rate of return of potential investors. These returns ranged from 25 percent to 40 percent. As a result of this, Grabowski determined that a rate between 35 percent and 40 percent would be appropriate for Big M.

After listening to both experts, Judge David Laro gave no weight to either side's expert. First, the Court discussed the respondent's expert, Mallarkey, his determination of a DLOM, and the resulting value of the gifted shares for the subject dates. The Court basically felt that this expert was full of malarkey (I know, another bad joke). Judge Laro did not like the fact that Mallarkey compared this private company to restricted stocks of public companies while choosing to ignore the shareholders' agreements.

Also, the Court found additional fault with Mallarkey's conclusions because of his use of such a limited number of restricted stock studies when several others existed. Using the studies for a basis of a range without considering the inherent differences between the subject company and the companies included in the analyses did not conform to what the Court felt was a reasonable and justified comparison. To say the least, the judge did not seem impressed.

Analyzing the petitioner's expert, the Court found several faults with the basis of his conclusions. He was less impressed with Grabowski. The shareholders' agreement was deemed as having too much weight within Grabowski's conclusion of the DLOM. Whereas Judge Laro stated that Mallarkey's conclusions mistakenly left out the effect of the agreements, he felt that Grabowski placed too much emphasis upon them.

The biggest problem that the Court found with Grabowski's opinion was that his analysis did not look at both a willing seller and a willing buyer; it only considered the hypothetical buyer. Judge Laro felt that no shareholder would be willing to sell Big M stock at such a large discount. He was probably correct! The Court also was not too thrilled with Grabowski's analysis that indicated that the shareholders would be stuck holding the stock for a 10- to 20-year period.

The second theme that Judge Laro discusses in his opinion is how closely the experts followed the valuation guidelines set forth by the definition of fair market value. In critiquing Grabowski, the Court stated that his analysis lacked the consideration of a willing seller. The judge did not believe that a willing seller would have accepted such a large discount. Also, when trying to reflect the characteristics of a willing buyer, Grabowski erred in developing a comparable group of possible investors. According to the Court, the group of investors that Grabowski attempted to use as a surrogate did not reflect a good sample of willing buyers. For these reasons, Judge Laro did not hold either analysis in high regard and, for the most part, left them out of his resolution of the correct DLOM value.

Since Judge Laro did not find any value in either expert's analysis, he took on the responsibility of concluding a DLOM for application to the value of Big M's share price on each of the valuation dates. This is where I take my hat off to Judge Laro. Although I may not agree with all of the factors that he discusses in his opinion, it is clear that he gave more thought to getting at a reasonable DLOM than either expert did. When you read this opinion, think of the 11 factors from the Moroney article that I discussed in Chapter 11. Judge Laro attempted to do a similar analysis with some slightly different factors.

The reason that I like this opinion is not because of the conclusion. Reading this opinion provides me with a great idea of what the judge was thinking when pure mathematics would not allow him (or an appraiser) to quantify the DLOM. He looked at qualitative factors and elaborated on each as to the impact on the DLOM. This is exactly what I suggest you do to support your opinion.

Before I tell you what I don't agree with (and why), let's look at the factors considered by Judge Laro. They were:

1. Private versus public sales of stock
2. Financial statement analysis
3. Company's dividend policy
4. Nature of the company, its history, its position in the industry, and its economic outlook
5. Company's management
6. Amount of control in transferred shares
7. Restrictions on transferability of stock
8. Holding period for stock
9. Company's redemption policy
10. Costs associated with making a public offering

Let's discuss each item.

Private Versus Public Sales of the Stock

This factor was used by the Court because the studies reflect transactions of securities with similar attributes to those of privately held stock. Restricted stock is stock of a public corporation that, in order to avoid dilution and registration costs, is not registered for trading within the public market. However, these shares of stock can be traded privately, mirroring the transaction characteristics of a closely held company. Since these transactions were required to be registered with the SEC until 1990, analysis was permitted, resulting in the creation of the studies. As a result, Judge Laro started his analysis by using the 35 percent to 45 percent discounts from these studies as a benchmark.

Financial Statement Analysis

The purpose of including this factor in the analysis was to reflect the notion that a company with favorable financial characteristics is attractive to willing investors. This attractiveness will result in added marketability. On the other hand, if the company's financial position is weak, it is less marketable.

Since companies are involved in their own respective industries, this analysis should be done according to publicly traded industry competitors that share similar operating characteristics so that the subject company can be rated accordingly. The purpose of using this factor is to rate and highlight the financial characteristics of a firm according to such items as income, liquidity, and debt. This sounds like a guideline company analysis.

Company's Dividend Policy

In determining a company's attractiveness, most investors will look to see what type of dividend-paying history the company has. Investors purchase a company's stock for one of three reasons:

1. To realize capital appreciation in the stock's price
2. To receive dividend payments over the course of owning the security
3. To realize a combination of factors 1 and 2

The company's dividend policy, either payment history or capacity for payment, as in this case, will increase the attractiveness and therefore the marketability of a firm's stock. If an investor can receive dividend payments on top of potential appreciation, there will be additional individuals who may want to purchase the stock. This has the potential of increasing marketability, resulting in a decreasing effect on a DLOM for a privately held stock.

Nature of the Company, Its History, Its Position in the Industry, and Its Economic Outlook

In general, business performance varies in relationship to the economy. Businesses can be affected by global, national, and local events. For industry purposes, changes in regulatory environments and market forces will also have an impact on the attractiveness of a company.

Investors will analyze a company's background, industry, and the economic factors that affect it so that they will have a better idea of what to base future expectations on. This is done to determine where the company is heading and how that will affect its attractiveness to potential investors.

Company's Management

Because the operations and goals of a company are determined by management, their experience and involvement is fundamental in assessing attractiveness. The management team is responsible for the company's performance. If investors lack confidence in a company's management, the organization will lose marketability because some investors will not be interested in stock ownership. Based on the conclusion of the management team's effect on operations and financial performance, according to Judge Laro, this factor's effect on the DLOM can be determined.

Amount of Control in Transferred Shares

When a company's stock is transferred in blocks, a block that represents control will have additional appeal over a block without such control. This is true because, as a block of stock has more control, a potential investor will have the ability to direct and run a company by his or her procedures and guidelines (or whims!).

This will affect the attractiveness of a company's stock, depending on the type of investor. In some but not all occasions, investors will not address this factor when determining the attractiveness of a company, because control is not an issue.

Restrictions on Transferability of Stock

The more restrictive it is to transfer shares, the less marketable the shares will be. This is why we see so many attorneys who draft family limited partnership agreements put in these really stringent restrictions—for example, you cannot sell your shares unless the sky becomes pink with yellow polka dots. In this case, the judge felt that since the shareholder agreements did not fix a price, there was less of a restriction in selling to an outsider.

Holding Period for Stock

In some instances, a company's stock may have to be held for a period of time so that the benefits of ownership can accumulate to create a sufficient profit for the investor. Such an event would cause the security to lose some of its marketability because of the need to maintain ownership. This increases market risk while marketability decreases. The holding period is essential for calculating marketability levels and the resulting DLOM, since it is a direct determinant of how quickly an individual can purchase a stock and turn around and sell it in the future.

Company's Redemption Policy

This factor is important because it determines if the company can purchase shares from shareholders so that they can gain access to cash. This analysis will display how the company can aid in, or detract from, its stock's liquidity. This is especially important for privately held firms because of the nonexistence of a ready market. If a company readily buys back shares, this will increase the liquidity of those shares, thereby increasing marketability. However, if the opposite is true, then the stock of the company is less marketable because another option for sale is removed.

Costs Associated With Making a Public Offering

In determining the value of a privately held stock, the cost to make a public offering is typically incorporated in the analysis. This is due to the need for determining which party is required to realize the costs of registering the security. In the case where the buyer must bear the expense, marketability will decrease because some investors will not consider such a transaction as an option because of the cost. This event causes the pool of potential investors to decrease. If the investor does not have to absorb this cost when making the purchase, the marketability of the stock will be greater. This factor is directly related to economics because as the expense of purchases go up, demand will decrease and vice versa.

I told you before that I do not agree with everything in this case. In my humble opinion, I believe that Judge Laro mixed up some issues that affect risk and those that affect liquidity. While there may be a fine line, and possibly an overlap, I think that many of the factors discussed by Judge Laro impact the freely traded value of the stock, and impact liquidity to a much lesser degree. The factors that bother me the most are:

1. Financial statement analysis
2. Dividend capacity and growth prospects
3. Nature of the company, its history, its position in the industry, and its economic outlook
4. Management

If you read Revenue Ruling 59-60, the eight factors cited there assist us in the valuation of the closely held stock. The four factors that I have listed above impact the underlying valuation. They should not impact both value as freely traded and liquidity. While I fully agree that dividends will lower the DLOM due to the mitigation of the holding period risk, dividend-paying capacity is considered in valuing an interest in a company.

Overall, I still think that this is a great case to read.

Mad Auto Wrecking Inc. v. Commissioner[6]

The case of *MAD Auto Wrecking Inc. v. Commissioner* deals with the subject of reasonable compensation for key personnel within a privately held business. Although this is not a business valuation case, I really like this one because as appraisers, we are always dealing with reasonable compensation. Before we begin, let me make one comment. Reasonable compensation issues arise in a different context for income tax purposes as compared to valuation matters. Income tax cases generally address the reasonableness of the

[6]*Mad Auto Wrecking Inc. v. Commissioner*, T.C. Memo. 1995-153 (RIA).

compensation based on the requirements for deductibility under IRC Section 162. The issue becomes one of an historic nature. Valuation, on the other hand, is prospective in nature. The issue that we generally deal with is what *will* be the cost of replacing the officers rather than what they *should* have received in the past.

Despite it being an income tax case, *Mad Auto Wrecking* is a really good case because it gives appraisers great guidance about the factors to consider in assessing reasonable compensation. Just remember the context of the case. By the way, you may even find a new area of service to offer your clients.

Mad Auto Wrecking is a high-volume, wholesale scrap business that purchases automobiles, removes usable parts, and offers the frames for sale as scrap metal. The company then takes the reusable parts and sells them at wholesale prices.

As with the vast majority of small businesses, the owners must put in a lot of time to ensure that the business remains productive and profitable. This situation was no different. The two equal owners worked between 60 and 70 hours per week, 52 weeks per year.

The issue in this case involved the reasonableness of the officers' compensation for the years 1989, 1990, and 1991. During these years, Mad's figures were as follows:

Year	*Gross Receipts*	*Taxable Net Income*	*Officer's Compensation*
1989	$ 2,554,942	$ 67,690	$ 856,000
1990	2,169,125	56,974	606,000
1991	1,884,853	(22,199)	711,000

As you can see, officers' compensation was a pretty high percentage of gross receipts. The IRS was not happy with this and felt that less should be allowed, with the excess treated as a dividend. We accountants call that double taxation.

The concept of reasonable compensation is something that depends on the facts and circumstances. Judge Laro (the Mandelbaum judge) wrote another really good opinion in this case. The judge was very methodical in formulating the opinion and cited other good case law, and eventually concluded that the compensation paid was reasonable. The elements considered by the Court were as follows:

- The employee's qualifications
- The nature, extent, and scope of the employee's work
- The size and complexities of the employer's business
- A comparison of salaries paid with the employer's gross and net income
- The prevailing general economic conditions
- A comparison of salaries with distributions to shareholders and retained earnings
- The prevailing rates of compensation for comparable positions in comparable concerns
- The salary policy of the employer as to all employees
- The amount of compensation paid to the particular employee in previous years
- The employer's financial condition
- Whether the employer and employee dealt at arm's length
- Whether the employee guaranteed the employer's debt
- Whether the employer offered a pension plan or profit-sharing plan to its employees
- Whether the employee was reimbursed by the employer for business expenses that the employee paid personally

To effectively understand how each of these factors aided the Court in its decision, and how it helps appraisers, we will look at summaries of each below.

Employee's Qualifications

The first pertinent factor that requires analysis is to determine whether an employee's background is applicable to the fiscal status of the company he or she works for. This background includes several aspects of an employee's familiarity with various components of the type of business in which he or she is involved. These essential items include experience, training, and education in a field related to the operations at hand. As with the vast majority of business and organizational positions, these three fundamentals are the basis for a conclusion as to the degree to which a worker is qualified for the function with which he or she is delegated. This preliminary detail in the reasonableness of compensation analysis allows an appraiser to locate a foundation on which to create an opinion of an employee's value to the organization.

Nature, Extent, and Scope of the Employee's Work

This factor is analyzed so that it can be seen how important and involved an employee is in relation to the operations of the business. To analyze this factor, the position(s) and responsibilities of the position(s) are studied to determine the number and depth of tasks completed by the employee.

In addition to viewing the position(s) held by the employee and the resulting obligations inherent in the position(s), one must also look at the effects of the employee's activities on the business' bottom line, as well as the consequences if the worker were to leave the organization. By completing these examinations, an analyst will be able to better estimate the employee's impact upon the company, both positive and negative. This will allow the forecast of various scenarios of the employee's employment status so that a clear explanation of the value of the employee can be given.

Size and Complexities of the Employer's Business

This element of the overall inspection of reasonable compensation is utilized to further understand the previous two factors. A small, simple operation will require a less-experienced, less-involved employee than one on the opposite side of the spectrum. The degree of an employee's specialization is also affected by this element. The replaceability of an employee can be resolved through the analysis of this factor in relation to the earlier ones.

Also of note within this section of the analysis is how the employee, using his or her qualifications in tandem with the comprehensiveness of the employee's position, affected the actual procedures of the business. With regard to key employees, the skills and abilities they hold are typically not shared by those under their control. Therefore, it is advisable for one doing this analysis to consider how the employee has worked to implement his or her knowledge in creating efficient and simplified procedures so that other, lower-level employees can be quickly replaced to ensure minimal interruptions of operations.

Comparison of Salaries Paid to Net and Gross Income

This factor is included to determine whether these values can be considered excessive in light of the concluded status of the previously discussed elements of reasonable compensation. Had those factors necessitated the conclusion that a key employee was not as vital as specified by the company, the values seen in this portion of the analysis would be expected to be low. However, had the employee been favored by inspection of the prior factors, these percentages would be expected to be somewhat higher. Again, as with the previous factor, this analyzed component is based on the conclusions reached earlier.

General Economic Conditions

In order to complete the examination of whether the employee's involvement affected the operation, the company's performance is reviewed during varying economic conditions. Analyzing the results of the business processes will determine whether, based upon his or her degree of involvement, a key employee has important skills to buoy financial results.

This factor is important within the analysis because it enables an analyst to find out how the existence of the employee within the organization can direct and dictate the success of a firm's operations during times of uncertainty.

Comparison of Salaries With Distributions to Shareholders and Retained Earnings

This part of the reasonable compensation analysis is done to conclude whether some of the compensation paid actually consists of dividends. This may be done especially when the key employee(s) are the only shareholder(s).

This analysis must be done keeping in mind the importance of the key employee(s) in relation to the level of growth realized by the company. Its dividends are paid out of funds that could be kept for reinvestment and expansion. If growth of operations is absent, the conclusion that parts of compensation are really dividend payments may be viable when no dividend history exists.

Prevailing Rates of Compensation for Comparable Positions in Comparable Companies

Over the course of this analysis, some weight must be given to the activities of competing comparable companies. This is done to resolve whether, in the specific situation at hand, the levels of compensation of the key employee are normal for the specific industry.

In completing this segment, one should look to find companies that are closest to the subject company in terms of several business characteristics deemed important in the operations, such as organizational traits, product type, and customers.

Once this comparison is completed, it can be determined if the levels of compensation for the key employee(s) are reasonable. However, adjustments to this comparison must be made to assess the differing characteristics between the guideline firms and the subject company. After these individual adjustments are completed, a final conclusion can be made. This almost sounds like valuation, doesn't it?

Employer's Salary Policy as to All Employees

Regardless of the employee's involvement, qualifications, or ownership status, he or she should be compensated on the same basis as other workers. It is expected that because of the employee's key importance, he or she will be given a greater amount of compensation. However, the basis should be relatively the same for all workers. Employees overcompensated in relation to the provision of their services and the salaries of other employees will be identified upon completion of this analysis.

These individuals and their respective compensation should be viewed within a framework of substitution. This analysis requires estimation of the reasonableness of the compensation in the event the position were filled by another individual with more generic attributes. Also, some consideration should be given to the determination of compensation if the employee in question is an owner and decides his or her salary. This characteristic should be removed to conclude whether a hypothetical owner would act in the same way.

Compensation Paid in Prior Years

Analyzing the levels realized in previous time periods will allow for the development of a trend analysis. This is done to determine if any of the subject periods show up as exceptions to a developed pattern. If one does exist, it must be somehow related to the performance of the company, as this will almost always affect a key employee's level of compensation. Also to be viewed is a change in any of the employee's responsibilities, as this will also adversely affect the subject year's compensation value in relation to any developed trend.

Don't overlook whether payments for services are accrued according to services performed in the past or expected to be done in the future. This event would constitute a normalization of compensation to correctly match the payment with the initiation and completion of the services.

Employer's Past and Present Financial Condition

The company's fiscal performance will generally be attributable to the actions of a key employee. This consideration is important because the financial condition of the company will allow greater or lesser amounts of compensation to be paid.

Basically, as the performance and profitability of the subject company varies, so should the level of the key employee's salary and bonus. It is rather obvious if a poorly performing company is paying an exorbitant amount of money to a key employee that reasonable compensation is not being paid.

Whether Employer and Employee Deal at Arm's Length

This factor is not always pertinent, as it usually applies only if the key employee is also a shareholder who determines his or her own level of compensation. If that is the case, an appraiser must use a substitute to determine if an independent owner would do the same for the same employee. This portion of the analysis can take into consideration levels seen in comparable companies, as well as the overall effect on the financial standing of the organization of making these payments.

Whether Employee Guaranteed Employer's Debt

If an employee assesses the risk of personally guaranteeing his or her employer's debt, it is the general opinion of the courts that this employee does deserve compensation above what would normally be paid. I certainly could not get my employees to guarantee my debt. If they would, I would pay them more.

Absence of Pension Plan/Profit-Sharing Plan

Since World War II, benefits outside of normal salary and bonus considerations have become expected. Because of this, courts have typically opined that the absence of such benefits as pension or profit-sharing plans constitute a certain level of additional payments within normal compensation.

Again, like the previous factor, this element of the analysis will allow for some slack when such plans are nonexistent. This is allowed by the courts primarily because it is understood that such measures must be taken by organizations to keep employees because competitors probably will offer similar or alternative benefits.

Lack of Reimbursement of Business Expenses

In the course of performing services for an employer, employees are sometimes required to pay expenses out of their own pockets. In such instances, it is normal for the employer to require a receipt and the employee to be reimbursed for the amount upon presentation of the documentation of payment. However, in some situations, employees and employers may have an agreement for the worker to receive a fixed amount of additional compensation instead of dealing with expense reimbursements. This is typical when the key employee is also an owner of the company.

As a result of using these factors to develop an analysis of whether a key employee's compensation is reasonable, a logical conclusion can be reached. The early steps form the basis for elements later in the analysis.

Exhibit 18.2 contains a reasonable compensation analysis we performed that addresses these issues.

EXHIBIT 18.2
Reasonable Compensation

Description of Assignment

Trugman Valuation Associates Inc. was retained by Decorative Stone Co., Inc. (hereafter referred to as Decorative Stone or The Company) to determine if the level of compensation paid to Bob Richardson, President of The Company, for the fiscal years ended December 31, 1996, 1997, and 1998, is reasonable. It is our understanding that this report will be used in regard to an audit of The Company by the state taxing authority.

Section 162(a)(1) of the IRC allows a corporation to deduct "a reasonable allowance for salaries or other compensation for personal services actually rendered." In order for compensation to be deductible under Section 162(a)(1), a two-pronged test must be met. The first part is that the amount of compensation must be reasonable. The second part of the test, which is more subjective in nature, is that the payment must be purely for services. This means that it cannot be disguised as a return on equity or some other type of payment.

Many court cases have arisen in the area of reasonable compensation. Guidance can be obtained from the opinions in many of these cases. One of the best cases that can be used for guidance in the determination of reasonable compensation is *Mad Auto Wrecking, Inc. v. Commissioner*, T.C. Memo. 1995-153. This well-thought-out opinion by Judge Laro of the United States Tax Court provides the necessary guidance for factors to consider in the assessment of reasonable compensation. This case cited numerous other cases that support the judge's opinion. In particular, *Elliotts, Inc. v. Commissioner*, 52 AFTR 2d 83-5976, is cited in this opinion, another excellent case to be used for guidance in this area. In order to allow this report to follow in a logical sequence, the factors outlined in these cases will be addressed.

Factual History

Decorative Stone Co., Inc. began business in about 1952. The Company was incorporated in the state on June 25, 1956, and was started by Charles Brown and Bob Richardson. Messrs. Brown and Richardson were stonemason contractors. They installed stone at schools, churches, and other such structures. At the inception of the business, and for several years thereafter, The Company used to store materials at Mr. Richardson's home. After a while, these materials became too voluminous to store at Mr. Richardson's home, and as a result, the business was moved to its present location. At that time, Messrs. Brown and Richardson began bringing in more materials and started to stock a greater amount of inventory. By the early 1960s, they needed trucks, forklifts, and other personnel in order to carry on the business.

For years, The Company operated with no accounts receivable. Once they moved to their current location and began selling inventory, they started billing for their materials. The Company got into financial trouble because of the slow collection of accounts receivable. In fact, The Company almost went out of business. The only reason The Company survived is that Messrs. Brown and Richardson barely took any salary. Mr. Brown was single and took only enough money each week to survive. This included food money and money for rent, but not much more than that. Mr. Richardson remembers taking as little as $100 per week for his compensation, since he had no mortgage. He basically took enough at that time to cover groceries, taxes, etc. Mr. Richardson remembers the lean years lasting well into the 1970s. In the early 1980s, Mr. Brown retired at age 65, leaving Mr. Richardson to take over his responsibilities, as well as continuing with his own. Mr. Brown had responsibility for being the yard supervisor, assisting with customer sales, and providing some dispatching. Mr. Richardson continues to operate The Company today at age 79, working more than full time. Decorative Stone, by his own admission, has been his passion in life. He has worked countless hours toward building this business and creating an exceptionally profitable company.

During the late 1980s and into the early 1990s, business was down, but through Mr. Richardson's efforts of making displays, having seminars, and opening up longer hours, he managed to keep the business going. Mr. Richardson's duties generally remained the same for a considerable number of years. Besides being the Chief Executive Officer and President of The Company, he acts as the General Manager, Sales Manager, Purchasing Manager, Dispatcher, and Foreman. Mr. Richardson opens the doors of the business at the start of the day and closes the doors at the end of the day. In addition, he performs all required paperwork and analysis at home in the evenings. Store hours are generally from 7:00 A.M. to 4:30 P.M., Monday through Friday, with Saturday hours in the winter months from 7:00 A.M. to 12:00 noon, and during the summer months from 7:00 A.M. to 3:00 P.M. During other times, store hours are frequently expanded to 8:00 or 9:00 P.M. during the week. On average, during the period under examination, store hours were approximately 52 hours per week. Besides the store hours, Mr. Richardson works at least one extra hour at the business each day, and approximately two hours at home in the evenings. Since Mr. Richardson dispatches the trucks, he generally arrives prior to the actual retail store opening.

EXHIBIT 18.2 *(Continued)*

Mr. Richardson's commitment and management style has benefited The Company in that The Company maintains long-term employees who work long hours resulting from the dedication of Mr. Richardson to his employees. Including Mr. Richardson, the employee count for the years under examination was as follows:

1996	23
1997	24
1998	26

Mr. Richardson works 70 hours per week on average. The Company's growth has exceeded industry growth, and the level of profitability is far beyond that for the industry. This will be discussed later in the report.

During the tax years in question, Mr. Richardson received the following levels of compensation from Decorative Stone:

1996	$1,042,713
1997	1,243,912
1998	1,414,200

During the years in question, Mr. Richardson received compensation as follows:

	1996	*1997*	*1998*
Base salary (paid weekly)	$ 42,713	$ 43,912	$ 44,200
Bonus—May	300,000	200,000	300,000
Bonus—July	0	300,000	300,000
Bonus—September	300,000	300,000	300,000
Bonus—October	0	250,000	0
Bonus—November	400,000	125,000	350,000
Bonus—December	0	25,000	120,000
Total	$1,042,713	$1,243,912	$1,414,200

In addition to salary, Mr. Richardson receives the same health insurance coverage as all other employees of Decorative Stone. He also receives the same three weeks vacation as every other employee. He receives no pension benefits, life insurance, disability insurance, travel and entertainment allowances, or automobile allowances. Basically, his compensation is intended to include all forms of compensation that would customarily be paid to an executive of a company.

There are no other employees that have any managerial responsibilities for The Company. As such, Mr. Richardson constitutes the entire management team, while continuing to also perform many of the functions in the daily operations of The Company. At our visit to the business establishment, we observed the fact that Mr. Richardson does not have a private office and he conducts his sales, purchasing, dispatching, and other functions from a front counter in the retail storefront. In fact, when entering the business establishment, the first person visible from the entrance is Mr. Richardson.

Using a Judge's Methodology

Judge Laro begins his opinion in *Mad Auto Salvage* with the following:

> This is another case pertaining to whether amounts paid by a closely held corporation to its shareholders/employees are deductible compensation under section 162(a)(1). Inherently, there is a natural tension between: (1) Shareholders/employees who feel that they are entitled to be paid from a corporation's profits, even to the exhaustion thereof, of an amount that reflects their skills and efforts, and (2) a provision in the tax law that conditions the deductibility of compensation on the concept of reasonableness. What is reasonable to the entrepreneur/employee often may not be to the tax collector. Accordingly, this and other courts are repeatedly asked to examine the relevant facts and circumstances of the business and the underlying employment relationship in order to render an opinion as to whether the compensation paid was reasonable. *In so doing, we must be careful not to define the term "reasonable" too narrowly. The dynamic nature of business, the entrepreneurial spirit, and the dedication of purpose all play a role in the composition of reasonable compensation. We must not rigidly apply form over substance when we measure one's contribution to the success of his or her business.* Of course, it may be argued that when an individual chooses to conduct business in the corporate form, he or she is obligated to observe all of the corporate formalities inherent in that form, including the standard that to be deductible, the compensation paid must be reasonable. The term "reasonable," however, must reflect the intrinsic value of employees in the broadest and most comprehensive sense [emphasis added].

(Continued)

EXHIBIT 18.2 *(Continued)*

Citing the tax law, Judge Laro points out that "Section 162(a)(1) allows a corporation to deduct 'a reasonable allowance for salaries or other compensation for personal services actually rendered' as an ordinary and necessary business expense. To be deductible under section 162(a)(1), compensation must be both: (1) Reasonable and, (2) paid purely for services rendered to the corporation."

1. *Was the Compensation Paid Reasonable?*

According to the judge, "Reasonable compensation is determined by comparing the compensation paid to an employee with the value of the services that he or she performed in return. Such a determination is made with respect to employees individually, rather than with respect to the compensation paid to all employees collectively. Such a determination is a question of fact."

In discussing the various cases concerning reasonable compensation, the judge indicates that there are many factors to be considered in making this factual determination:

> The factors which may be considered, none of which is controlling in itself, include: (a) The employee's qualifications; (b) the nature, extent, and scope of the employee's work; (c) the size and complexities of the employer's business; (d) a comparison of salaries paid with the employer's gross and net income; (e) the prevailing general economic conditions; (f) a comparison of salaries with distributions to shareholders and retained earnings; (g) the prevailing rates of compensation for comparable positions in comparable concerns; (h) the salary policy of the employer as to all employees; (i) the amount of compensation paid to the particular employee in previous years; (j) the employer's financial condition; (k) whether the employer and employee dealt at arm's length; (l) whether the employee guaranteed the employer's debt; (m) whether the employer offered a pension plan or profit-sharing plan to its employees; and (n) whether the employee was reimbursed by the employer for business expenses that the employee paid personally.

a. Employee's Qualifications. Mr. Richardson is exceptionally qualified for Decorative Stone's business by virtue of his experience and dedication, as well as his understanding and control of every aspect of the operations. He is highly motivated and extremely productive as an employee and is clearly the primary reason for The Company's success. His outstanding qualifications justify high compensation. Decorative Stone's profitability rests upon its sales, and Mr. Richardson's ambition, inventiveness during slow times, and energy (as opposed to his investment in capital) are the primary reasons for Decorative Stone's sales, growth, and success.

b. Nature, Extent, and Scope of the Employee's Work. The nature, extent, and scope of the work performed by Mr. Richardson are fundamental, substantial, and all-encompassing. He performs all of The Company's executive and managerial functions and formerly performed, but now oversees, all of its manual labor. Mr. Richardson also supervises the daily operations, including supervising and directing the other employees, and makes all of the business decisions. Given the vital role played by Mr. Richardson in Decorative Stone's operations and success, and the long hours that he has dedicated to the business, he is indispensable to the business. Decorative Stone's growth and prosperity are due directly to his skills, dedication, and creativity. If the business were to lose him, it would be in a rough situation until a suitable replacement (if any) could be found.

c. Size and Complexities of the Employer's Business. Decorative Stone is not necessarily the most complex business around, but because it primarily involves building and/or construction-type materials, its operations demand expertise to compensate for changing economies. The success and growth of the business even during poor economic periods demonstrates the value that has been added by Mr. Richardson. Based on data extracted from Integra Information's *Business Profiler* product for companies in the same Standard Industrial Classification code as Decorative Stone, The Company has grown to be one of the larger businesses of this type. Integra data includes 3,501 companies broken down as follows:

Sales Range	*Business Count*	*Percent of Total*
All sales ranges	3,501	100.00%
Less than $250,000	1,115	31.85%
$250,000–$499,999	728	20.79%
$500,000–$999,999	346	9.88%
$1,000,000–$2,499,999	540	15.42%
$2,500,000–$4,999,999	429	12.25%
$5,000,000–$9,999,999	207	5.91%
$10,000,000–$24,999,999	84	2.40%
$25,000,000–$49,999,999	27	0.78%
$50,000,000–$99,999,999	17	0.49%
$100,000,000–$249,999,999	1	0.03%
$250,000,000–$499,999,999	7	0.20%
More than $500,000,000	0	0.00%

According to the Integra data, Decorative Stone, based on revenues, falls in the top 9.81 percent of its peer group.

EXHIBIT 18.2 *(Continued)*

d. Comparison of Salaries Paid to Net and Gross Income. The percentage of officers' salaries to gross receipts for 1996, 1997, and 1998 was 15.2, 17.0, and 17.5, respectively. The percentage of officers' salaries to book net income (before deducting officers' compensation) for 1996, 1997, and 1998 was 94.7, 100.65, and 92.08, respectively.

Based on the state tax returns reviewed, the entire net income before net operating loss deductions was $58,218, –$7,236, and $122,295, despite the deduction of officer's compensation. This means that The Company would have been subject to tax and would have paid taxes based on net income had it not been for the net operating loss deduction that it used as an offset to the income. In addition, Mr. Richardson reported his compensation on his tax returns and paid taxes on these amounts.

e. General Economic Conditions. During the years under audit, the economy was reasonably strong. Part of The Company's growth during this period could be attributable to the economy. However, a good part of the success is also attributable to the solid foundation that Mr. Richardson has created for the business over the years. Mr. Richardson's financial commitment to this business has also allowed a substantial amount of inventory to be stocked by The Company, assisting in the production of sales. If the product were not in inventory, the customer may have gone elsewhere.

f. Comparison of Salaries With Distributions to Shareholders and Retained Earnings. In another case, Judge Laro points out, "The absence of a dividend history is a significant factor that may suggest that some of the amounts paid as compensation to a shareholder/employee is really a dividend," although he also said, "Such an absence (and inference), however, does not automatically convert compensation that would otherwise be reasonable into a dividend. Corporations are not required to pay dividends."

Judge Laro went on to state:

> Instead, an individual shareholder may participate in the success of a corporation through the appreciation in the value of his or her stock brought on by retained earnings and the possibility of a future return. Thus, a corporate employer with little or no dividend history may be able to pay and deduct large amounts of compensation if the Court is convinced that a reasonable person would still have invested in the corporation. Courts sometimes apply a hypothetical investor test to determine whether a reasonable person would have invested in the corporation. Critical to this test is whether the shareholders of the corporation received a fair rate of return (without taking into account any compensation) from the total of their initial and subsequent investments.

This analysis was also discussed in detail in *Elliott, Inc. v. Commissioner*, which was referenced by Judge Laro. A financial analysis will be presented later in this report addressing the issue of a hypothetical investor. We believe that this further substantiates the level of compensation that should be deemed reasonable for Mr. Richardson.

g. Prevailing Rates of Compensation for Comparable Positions in Comparable Companies. In a perfect world, we could look at other companies that are similar to Decorative Stone to determine what rate of compensation is paid for comparable positions in these "comparable" companies. However, we do not believe that this is possible in this instance. First and foremost, closely held companies do not readily volunteer this information. Second, in order for a company to be comparable to Decorative Stone, we believe that consideration must also be given to the level of growth and profitability exhibited by The Company. There can be no doubt that management is frequently compensated for success. Stock option plans and bonuses are regularly made available to key executives. In fact, there are many industries where the stock option compensation or the bonuses are much greater than the executive's base pay.

Our review of the Integra industry composite data will be discussed in more detail as part of our financial analysis. It will become obvious that Decorative Stone is not really comparable to its industry peer group. We believe that it is unreasonable to try to compare Mr. Richardson's compensation to another executive in a privately owned company that either brings a different skill set, work ethic, level of expertise, or proven track record for success to that company. We do not believe that composite industry data adequately allows a meaningful analysis to be performed.

h. Employer's Salary Policy as to All Employees. There is no written salary policy as to all of The Company's employees. Since there are also no other employees besides Mr. Richardson who participate in management, we could not determine whether Mr. Richardson was compensated differently than the other employees merely because of his status as a shareholder.

i. Compensation Paid in Prior Years. The compensation (including bonuses) paid by Decorative Stone to Mr. Richardson prior to the years in issue ranged from $825,797 to $1,192,713 from 1990 to 1995, with 1991 and 1992 dipping to $649,203 and $675,798, respectively. As The Company has been growing, Mr. Richardson's compensation has been adjusted to compensate him for his success. During the downturn of the early 1990s, Mr. Richardson took less salary.

j. Employer's Past and Present Financial Condition. Decorative Stone has grown and is very profitable. Its shareholder's equity has grown from $1,457,497 in 1995 to $1,628,841 in 1998. This will be discussed in the financial analysis later in this report.

(Continued)

EXHIBIT 18.2 *(Continued)*

k. Whether Employer and Employee Dealt at Arm's Length. Mr. Richardson was paid high compensation as The Company's principal employee. Given his relationship to The Company as its only shareholder, consideration should be given to whether an independent investor would have paid Mr. Richardson the amount of compensation that he received during the years in issue. This will be addressed as part of the financial analysis.

An interesting quote from *Mad Auto Salvage* that was referenced by Judge Laro in his opinion was one of the shareholders discussing the work habits of the other shareholder. The quote was:

> Dick [Andrews] is more like a workaholic. And anybody that works that hard has got to be compensated for the work that they do. If you don't do that, your business is going to suffer because the guy that is putting in more hours and not receiving any money—he is definitely going to reject the idea, not work as hard.

Substituting Mr. Richardson in the above quote accurately describes this situation as well.

l. Whether Employee Guaranteed Employer's Debt. According to Judge Laro, "Courts have considered whether an employee personally guaranteed his or her employer's debt, in determining whether the employee's compensation was reasonable. In certain situations, an employee's personal guarantee of his or her employer's debt may entitle the employer to pay a greater salary to the employee than the employer would otherwise have paid."

In this instance, Mr. Richardson does not guarantee any corporate debt. However, instead of using borrowed funds to provide an extraordinary balance sheet and financial condition, Mr. Richardson has actually loaned The Company over $3 million, interest free, which The Company has used to take advantage of buying opportunities, favorable vendor pricing, and other such items that have significantly contributed to the success of Decorative Stone.

Over the past several years, had interest been paid to Mr. Richardson, his compensation would have been lower, since he would have received interest expense instead. In fact, Mr. Richardson has forgone the following interest to the benefit of The Company:

Year	*Value of Stockholder Loan*	*Two-Year Average Balance*	*Prime Rate*	*Prime Rate +2%*	*Interest Saved*
1995	1,905,074				
1996	2,375,739	2,140,407	8.27%	10.27%	219,820
1997	2,681,945	2,528,842	8.44%	10.44%	264,011
1998	3,135,147	2,908,546	8.35%	10.35%	301,035

This illustrates the fact that Mr. Richardson's compensation should be considered to include at least these amounts since he has loaned this money to The Company without interest being paid to him.

m. Absence of Pension Plan/Profit-Sharing Plan. Mr. Richardson was not a participant in any pension plan or profit-sharing plan offered by The Company. Courts have considered the absence of a pension plan or a profit-sharing plan in determining reasonable compensation. These same court cases have indicated that "Such an absence may allow the employer to pay the employee more compensation than the employer would have paid had the employer offered the employee a pension plan or a profit-sharing plan."

n. Lack of Reimbursement of Business Expenses. Mr. Richardson does not really incur any material out-of-pocket expenses on behalf of Decorative Stone. This point is insignificant.

2. *Was Compensation Paid for Services Rendered?*

There can be no doubt that Mr. Richardson works long hours for The Company. All of his services are rendered on behalf of Decorative Stone and no other entity.

Financial Analysis

In order to determine whether a hypothetical investor could have received a comparable return on investment from Decorative Stone Co., Inc., a financial analysis of The Company was performed. Since specific financial data could not be obtained about similar closely held companies, due to the privacy of the financial data, we turned to the *Business Profiler* CD-ROM product produced by Integra Information for comparative composite data.

Decorative Stone falls into Standard Industrial Classification (SIC) code 5032, described as Wholesale Trade—Brick, Stone, and Related Materials. Using the *Business Profiler* software, we searched for data for companies located in SIC code 5032 with sales between $5,000,000 and $9,999,999 for use in our comparison. There were 207 companies included in this data.

Historically, Decorative Stone's reported profitability has been as shown in Table 1.

EXHIBIT 18.2 *(Continued)*

TABLE 1

Historic Income Statement for the Years Ended December 31,

	1990	1991	1992	1993	1994	1995	1996	1997	1998
Total revenues	$4,435,719	$4,041,345	$4,748,289	$5,420,974	$6,243,002	$6,260,609	$6,849,980	$7,324,031	$8,090,785
Total cost of sales	2,557,828	2,453,132	3,199,281	3,433,818	4,105,862	3,943,259	4,761,688	5,219,165	5,571,673
Gross profit	$1,877,891	$1,588,213	$1,549,008	$1,987,156	$2,137,140	$2,317,350	$2,088,292	$2,104,866	$2,519,112
Total operating expenses	1,905,125	1,637,241	1,698,665	2,078,653	2,241,108	2,391,839	2,120,739	2,252,688	2,570,892
Operating income (loss)	$ (27,234)	$ (49,028)	$ (149,657)	$ (91,497)	$ (103,968)	$ (74,489)	$ (32,447)	$ (147,822)	$ (51,780)
Total other income	$ 113,065	$ 86,275	$ 103,422	$ 91,555	$ $28,230	$ 42,046	$ 90,229	$ 139,772	$ 173,392
Income (loss) before taxes	**$ 85,831**	**$ 37,247**	**$ (46,235)**	**$ 58**	**$ (75,738)**	**$ (32,443)**	**$ 57,782**	**$ (8,050)**	**$ 121,612**

Table 1 reflects the figures reported in The Company's tax returns, adjusted for those items that were either reported on Schedule K (directly to the stockholder) or Schedule M-1 (reconciling adjustments). These figures are now comparable to the *Business Profiler* (Integra) figures.

TABLE 2

Historic Common-Size Income Statement for the Years Ended December 31,

	1990	1991	1992	1993	1994	1995	1996	1997	1998	Integra
Total revenues	100.00%	100.00%	100.00%	100.00%	100.00%	100.00%	100.00%	100.00%	100.00%	100.00%
Total cost of sales	57.66%	60.70%	67.38%	63.34%	65.77%	62.99%	69.51%	71.26%	68.86%	82.79%
Gross profit	42.34%	39.30%	32.62%	36.66%	34.23%	37.01%	30.49%	28.74%	31.14%	17.20%
Total operating expenses	42.95%	40.51%	35.77%	38.34%	35.90%	38.20%	30.96%	30.76%	31.78%	15.10%
Operating income (loss)	-0.61%	-1.21%	-3.15%	-1.69%	-1.67%	-1.19%	-0.47%	-2.02%	-0.64%	2.10%
Interest expense	0.00%	0.00%	0.00%	0.00%	0.00%	0.00%	0.00%	0.00%	0.00%	0.82%
Total other income	2.55%	2.13%	2.18%	1.69%	0.45%	0.67%	1.32%	1.91%	2.14%	0.16%
Income before taxes	1.93%	0.92%	-0.97%	0.00%	-1.21%	-0.52%	0.84%	-0.11%	1.50%	1.46%

Note: Figures may not add due to rounding.

Based on the reported figures, Decorative Stone was slightly less profitable before taxes than the peer group. During the years under audit, Decorative Stone was weaker in 1996 and 1997 but stronger in 1998.

(Continued)

EXHIBIT 18.2 *(Continued)*

However, further analysis is required to properly determine the investment attributes of The Company. Officer's compensation has been reported as follows:

		Growth
1995	$ 1,192,713	
1996	1,042,713	−12.58%
1997	1,243,912	+19.30%
1998	1,414,200	+13.69%

During this same time period, stockholder's equity grew as follows:

		Growth
1995	$ 1,457,497	
1996	1,515,279	+3.96%
1997	1,507,229	−0.53%
1998	1,628,841	+8.07%

Revenue growth for Decorative Stone surpassed the industry group during this same period as depicted in the following table:

	1996	*1997*	*1998*
Decorative Stone	9.41%	6.92%	10.47%
Integra	8.93%	2.38%	6.30%

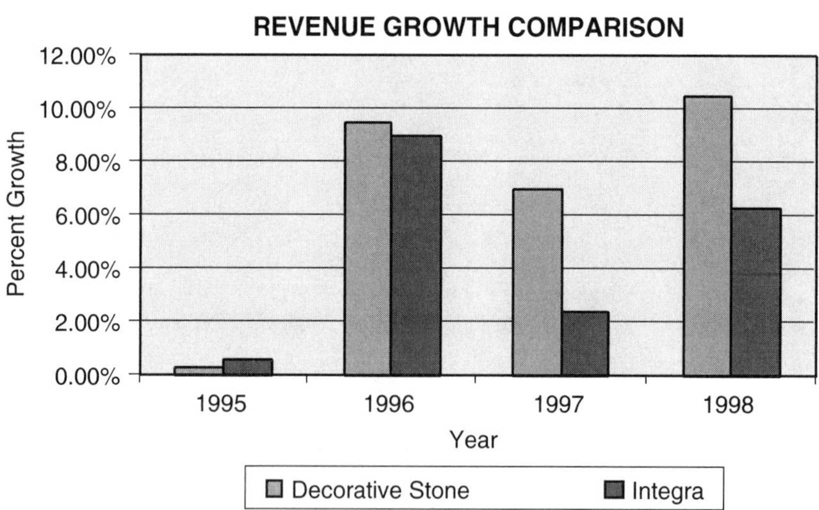

On an unadjusted basis, Decorative Stone was compared to the Integra data in terms of key financial ratios. This is presented in Table 3.

EXHIBIT 18.2 *(Continued)*

TABLE 3

Historic Financial Ratios

	1996	*1997*	*1998*
Liquidity/solvency			
Quick ratio	14.31	16.81	15.49
Quick ratio—Integra	0.95	0.96	0.97
Current ratio	21.52	23.90	21.46
Current ratio—Integra	1.72	1.76	1.76
Turnover			
Fixed asset turnover	51.44	45.03	41.53
Fixed asset turnover—Integra	17.82	18.06	18.51
Payables turnover	29.55	29.21	28.03
Payables turnover—Integra	12.71	12.57	13.22
Debt			
Times interest earned	N/A	N/A	N/A
Times interest earned—Integra	2.71	2.65	2.58
Total liabilities to total assets	0.63	0.65	0.67
Total liabilities to total assets—Integra	0.64	0.64	0.64
Short-term debt to equity	0.00	0.00	0.00
Short-term debt to equity—Integra	0.43	0.42	0.43
Profitability			
Pretax return on assets	0.01	0.00	0.02
Pretax return on assets—Integra	0.03	0.03	0.03
Pretax return on equity	0.04	–0.01	0.07
Pretax return on equity—Integra	0.09	0.08	0.08
Pretax return on net sales	0.01	0.00	0.02
Pretax return on net sales—Integra	0.01	0.01	0.01

As demonstrated above, Decorative Stone reflects substantially higher liquidity than its peer group. The Company is turning over its fixed assets and payables much faster than the industry as well. The debt ratios are solid, particularly since the only debt is financed interest free by Mr. Richardson. Profitability is relatively in line with the industry *even after* Mr. Richardson's compensation.

In order to provide a more meaningful analysis, or what we believe to be more helpful in the assessment of reasonable compensation, we have added back the officer's compensation in its entirety. Table 4 reflects the adjusted common-size income statements for 1996 through 1998 for Decorative Stone.

TABLE 4

Common-Size Income Statement With Officer's Compensation Removed

	1996	*1997*	*1998*
Total revenues	100.00%	100.00%	100.00%
Total cost of sales	69.51%	71.26%	68.86%
Gross profit	30.49%	28.74%	31.14%
Total operating expenses	15.74%	13.77%	14.30%
Operating income	14.75%	14.97%	16.84%
Total other income	1.32%	1.91%	2.14%
Income before taxes	16.07%	16.87%	18.98%

(Continued)

EXHIBIT 18.2 *(Continued)*

In order to compare these figures with the Integra data, we have also added back the officer's compensation reflected by Integra. This appears in Table 5.

TABLE 5

Common-Size Addback of Officer's Compensation

	Decorative Stone	*Integra*
1998		
Pretax income	1.50%	1.40%
Add: Officer's compensation	17.48%	1.60%
Adjusted pretax income	**18.98%**	**3.00%**
1997		
Pretax income	−0.11%	1.50%
Add: Officer's compensation	16.98%	1.70%
Adjusted pretax income	**16.87%**	**3.20%**
1996		
Pretax income	0.84%	1.50%
Add: Officer's compensation	15.22%	1.70%
Adjusted pretax income	**16.06%**	**3.20%**

Officer's compensation, as a percentage, has been added back to both Decorative Stone and Integra. The Integra data provides a percentage for officer's compensation but cannot be used by itself to properly assess reasonable compensation. The reported data does not allow the analyst to answer many important questions about this percentage. For example, What part of the country are these businesses located in? Are there other individuals who performed various duties that may be reflected in other expense categories (e.g., cost of sales or general and administrative) that should be added to officer's salary to be comparable?

After making the adjustment to both sets of data, it becomes obvious that Decorative Stone is substantially more profitable than the industry group. This demonstrates, in part, the effectiveness of Mr. Richardson in running this company.

One test for reasonableness of compensation would be to determine how much compensation The Company could afford to pay the officer, rewarding him for his efforts and performance, while continuing to produce a return on equity that would be consistent with the industry. This test is illustrated in Table 6.

TABLE 6

Income of Decorative Stone With Adjustments to Officers' Compensation, Which Will Bring the Return on Equity of the Company in Line With the Integra Industry Estimate

	1996	*1997*	*1998*
Historic net income (Table 1)	$ 57,782	$ (8,050)	$ 121,612
Adjustments			
Officers' compensation—addback	$ 1,042,713	$ 1,243,912	$ 1,414,200
Officers' compensation—reasonable	(971,696)	(1,110,762)	(1,403,876)
Adjusted pretax net income	**$ 128,799**	**$ 125,100**	**$ 131,936**
Decorative Stone historic return on equity	3.81%	−0.53%	7.47%
Integra return on equity	8.50%	8.30%	8.10%
Decorative Stone return on equity with compensation adjustment	8.50%	8.30%	8.10%

EXHIBIT 18.2 *(Continued)*

Table 6 illustrates that an investor could get a comparable return on equity to the industry while compensating Mr. Richardson as follows:

1996	$ 971,696
1997	1,110,762
1998	1,403,876

This would bring Decorative Stone's comparison to the industry as illustrated in Table 7. Table 7 reflects the common size comparison to Integra after adjusting Decorative Stone's earnings for the level of officer's compensation that would allow a shareholder to receive a return on equity in line with the industry. After making this adjustment, Decorative Stone becomes more profitable than the industry group in all three years.

TABLE 7

Adjusted Common-Size Income Statement With Compensation Adjusted to Match Company Return on Equity to Industry Figures

	1996	*1997*	*1998*	*Integra*
Total revenues	100.00%	100.00%	100.00%	100.00%
Total cost of sales	69.51%	71.26%	68.86%	82.79%
Gross profit	30.49%	28.74%	31.14%	17.20%
Total operating expenses	29.92%	28.94%	31.65%	15.10%
Operating income (loss)	0.56%	–0.20%	–0.51%	2.10%
Interest expense	0.00%	0.00%	0.00%	0.82%
Total other income	1.32%	1.91%	2.14%	0.16%
Income before taxes	**1.88%**	**1.71%**	**1.63%**	**1.46%**

Conclusion

After considering the facts and circumstances of Decorative Stone, using guidance from the United States Tax Court, we believe that reasonable compensation for Mr. Richardson is as follows:

1996	$ 971,696
1997	1,110,762
1998	1,403,876

These levels of compensation would provide the shareholder of The Company with the same return on equity as other shareholders in the industry, while compensating Mr. Richardson for his long hours, significant contribution to the growth and profitability of The Company, as well as the $200,000 to $300,000 of forgone interest expense on the substantial loans made to The Company over the years.

As you can see from Exhibit 18.2, the court case gave great guidance in analyzing reasonable compensation. By the way—the taxing authority accepted our figures!

Conclusion

There are great lessons to be learned from reading court cases. A well-written judicial opinion can provide the appraiser with significant guidance on many topics, even when they are not necessarily valuation cases. While it is not our intention to perform legal research, particularly for the purpose of taking a position in a litigation, the well-seasoned appraiser will be aware of how the Court thinks. These are clearly a few of my favorite court cases.

19

Economic Damages

Chapter Goals

In this chapter, I will attempt to explain the following:

- The similarities of an economic damages analysis to a business valuation assignment
- Types of economic damage claims
- How to perform a lost profits analysis
- Methodologies available to perform a lost profits analysis

Introduction

Business damages can arise from many different situations, and it would be nearly impossible to cover every variation that the CPA, economist, or appraiser will encounter. Some damages may relate to lost profits, whereas others may relate to the diminution in value of the business enterprise. This chapter is intended to address some of the principles of business damages from the perspective of the CPA. In many instances, the services offered in this area of practice are similar to the application of business valuation techniques. For example, in a lost profits analysis, the expert may need to project the future income that might have occurred "but for" the actions of the defendant in the litigation. These lost profits are then discounted to present value. This should sound like the same process I discussed in the application of a multi-period discounting model.

This type of service may also involve the valuation of the business enterprise if it was completely destroyed. Sometimes, both lost profits and lost business value may be applicable in the same assignment. You must be careful not to double-count the elements of damages when doing this stuff. I will explain more about this in a little while.

While this book is certainly not intended to cover all aspects of economic damages, I decided to add this chapter because many of us who offer business valuation services, particularly in a litigation setting, are also requested, from time to time, to address economic damages. As an expert, you are, once again, faced with finding out about the case law in the jurisdiction of the litigation. Work with your client's attorney to get the most relevant cases. Enough of the introduction stuff—let's get on to the meat and potatoes.

Lost Profits

A business enterprise may suffer lost profits when, as a result of the act of someone, any of the following takes place:

- Revenues are lower than they would have been.
- Costs are higher than they would have been.
- There exists some combination of lower revenues and higher costs.

Elements of a Lost Profits Claim

I'm no lawyer, but let me give you some background on this stuff from my perspective. You can, and probably should, check with a lawyer about this stuff. To be allowed a claim for lost profits, a plaintiff must generally prove the following:

- The defendant breached a legal duty to the plaintiff.
- The defendant's actions or failures to act damaged the plaintiff.
- The plaintiff's damages are directly related to the defendant's actions or failures to act.

Breach of a Legal Duty. A claim for lost profits can arise from either a broken contract between two parties or a tort (that's tort and not tart—a tart is something you eat!). A breach of contract claim involves the alleged breach of an agreement between the parties. For example, a company might sue a general contractor for its profits lost due to the contractor's delay in completing renovations on the company's facility. A sales person may sue a manufacturer for breaching its exclusive marketing agreement in the designated territory. A doctor's group might sue a former doctor for violating a non-compete agreement. Table 19.1 lists the most common types of contractual disputes that lead to lost profit claims.

TABLE 19.1

Breaches of Contract That May Lead to Lost Profit Claims

- Agency agreements, such as with manufacturer's sales representatives
- Breaches of express or implied warranties
- Construction contracts
- Covenants not to compete
- Employment contracts
- Failures to pay or to provide services
- Franchise agreements
- Insurance contracts
- Real estate transactions
- Sales of businesses
- Sales of goods (to which the Uniform Commercial Code may apply)
- Sales of stock

In a tort claim, the plaintiff accuses the defendant of owing a legal duty to the plaintiff and claims that the defendant breached that duty. For example, a self-employed individual might sue a gas company for the profits lost as a result of an explosion caused by the gas company's negligent repair that destroyed the plaintiff's business. I did a job once for a pizza joint that got blown up because the gas company goofed. A movie studio might sue a movie critic for its lost profits resulting from the critic's malicious attempt to damage the movie studio by printing false allegations rather than honest opinions. If the movie really stinks, it is okay to say it. Honesty is a defense. However, you cannot just say the movie was horrible if the intent is to keep others from seeing it. Table 19.2 lists the most common types of torts that lead to lost profit claims.

TABLE 19.2

Torts That May Lead to Lost Profit Claims

- Acts of simple or gross negligence
- Conversion or theft of funds
- Damage to income-producing property
- Defamation
- Fraud (for example, when a supplier pays kickbacks to a company's employees resulting in higher costs)
- Intentional interference with business or contractual relationships
- Malicious prosecution
- Patent/trademark infringement
- Professional malpractice
- Unfair trade practices

Causation. The second element of a lost profits claim is causation. Whether a claim relates to a tort or a breach of contract, the plaintiff must prove that the defendant's actions caused the damage to the plaintiff. While causation may seem obvious, proving this element of damage can frequently be challenging. For example, assume a defendant admits responsibility for the fire that closed the plaintiff's hardware store for six months. Also assume, however, that a Home Depot opened across the street from the plaintiff's business six weeks before the fire. Although the plaintiff can demonstrate that it was closed for six months and lost profits during this period of time, the amount of profits lost due to the fire, and the amount of profits that would have been lost in any event due to the increased competition, is a matter of great uncertainty. At least three or four times in my career someone has called me to claim that the telephone company left an ad out of the telephone book. Think about how to prove that there is a direct link between the ad being left out and the lost earnings of the business. Unless really good records are maintained by the business as to where the customers come from, this is not easy.

Damages Must Be Directly Related to the Defendant's Actions. The third element of proof that must be demonstrated by the plaintiff is the amount of damages that are directly related to the defendant's actions. This causal relationship is sometimes referred to as the "but for" rule. In other words, "but for" the actions of the defendant, the plaintiff would have made an additional $2,000,000 in profits. "But for" the defendant's negligence, the plaintiff would not have incurred $650,000 in replacement costs and property damage. "But for" the breach of the contract, the plaintiff would have earned royalties of $300,000. "But for" writing this book, I would be spending more time on vacation (only kidding!).

In theory, a well-prepared "but for" analysis of the plaintiff's claim calculates the limit of damages related to the defendant's actions. However, even though we may think the client got royally shafted, the law rarely allows the plaintiff's recovery to go that far. For example, assume a dairy farmer intentionally pollutes a competing dairy farmer's land in hopes of driving him out of business. The polluter does not know, however, that the competing farmer has a heart condition and as a result, upon seeing hundreds of his cows laying in the field, he has a heart attack and drops dead. There is probably no question that the polluter breached a legal duty to the poor guy that died, and his actions are what caused the decedent's loss of profits on the sale of dairy products, as well as his death. However, the law generally allows the decedent's estate to recover only for his loss of profits because the decedent's death was not a foreseeable consequence of polluting the field. Therefore, it can be said that damages are directly related to an act when they are foreseeable. You have to love this legal stuff to do these assignments. Some guy causes another guy to croak and the jury has to worry about his lost profits because of dead cows. So what if he had a heart attack along the way!

Types of Damages

A typical lawsuit has many types of damages. Some damages that might be awarded are classified as compensatory or punitive. Damages can be compensatory or punitive in nature, depending on whether they are awarded as a measure of actual loss suffered or to punish for the behavior of the defendant. Let's hang the guy that killed the cows. Compensatory damages consist of general and special damages.

Consequential damages represent a type of special compensatory damages. Consequential damages do not flow directly and immediately from the act of the party, but only from some of the consequences or results of the act. Lost profits as discussed in this chapter are consequential damages.

The Lost Profits Analysis

Experts will frequently participate in many types of lost profits cases. Since the rules of recovery vary from one jurisdiction to the next, and from one type of case to the next, the specific procedures that the expert will apply will also vary from case to case. Make sure that you are working with a lawyer when you do this stuff. Many similarities are common to all lost profits engagements. In fact, the procedures that should be applied are basically the same, regardless of the facts of the case (dead cows, lost sheep, who cares!). Let's discuss the procedures for a lost profits analysis.

Meet With the Client and Client's Attorney to Determine the Objectives of the Assignment

A good place to start is always at the beginning. Sometimes, I start in the middle, but I get confused and lose track of what I am doing. You do not have to be a genius to realize that the plaintiff and the defendant have different objectives in the case. The plaintiff seeks to maximize the damages claim (wants lots of money or maybe revenge), while the defendant seeks to minimize or deny damages (the cows would have died from foot and mouth disease, so I did that farmer a favor). The expert's job in working with the plaintiff's attorney is to develop a carefully reasoned, well-justified damages estimate using accepted methodology in the field that will withstand pointed cross-examination and potential challenge by the other side. In other words—no "junk science" type of stuff.

In working with the defendant's attorney, the expert's job is to challenge the estimate prepared by the plaintiff's expert when it does not meet these objectives. For example, suppose a four-month-old business gets destroyed in an explosion of the business next door. The owners of the destroyed business purchased the assets of the business four months ago for about $200,000. The expert for the plaintiff comes up with damages for this four-month-old business of $7 million. If you were working for the defendant's attorney, your job would be to show how absurd the other expert's opinion is. Think about it: a four-month-old business, with no history, an investment of about $200,000, and damages of $7 million. What is wrong with this picture?

Determine the Known Facts and Assumptions of the Case

The client will usually have a pretty good idea of what is going on in the case, including details of the contract that was breached (or the nature of the tort that was committed) and the extent of financial damages that have been incurred. Therefore, you should discuss the known facts of the case with the client and the client's attorney as a means of gaining an overview of the situation.

If you end up testifying to this stuff, you will probably have to make a series of assumptions. It is really important for the client's attorney to know all of the key assumptions, as well as the basis for those assumptions. I like to lay them out in my report so that it is clear to the reader of my report what I did. This is not too different from including assumptions when you do a forecast. Common assumptions that you may rely on include the following.

Assumptions About the Facts. Depending on the case, the expert will obtain certain information that is purported to be factual and be asked to assume it is correct. Generally, the attorney will give this stuff to you or you may pick it up by reading the complaint that alleges what happened. Sometimes, the information will be presented during a deposition or trial testimony. Some of the facts may need to be verified. You will have to use judgment to decide which to verify.

Assumptions Involving the Opinions of Other Experts. Additional experts may be employed to analyze different aspects of the damage claim. Other experts may include appraisers, industry experts, engineering experts, etc. You may need to consolidate all of these other opinions into an overall conclusion of the amount of damages.

Economic and Financial Assumptions. You may also find yourself having to make general economic and financial assumptions during your analyses. This is the same stuff that we do in a business valuation assignment. Research and support your assumptions.

Plaster Your Files With Support

Documentary evidence is a critical element of all litigation services, including those involving lost profits. Make sure your work papers are loaded with support. The primary source of the documentation may be the plaintiff's business records. If you are representing the plaintiff, getting these records will generally not be a problem—unless, of course, the job is like the one for the pizza joint that I did, where the records all got blown up in the explosion. If, however, you are engaged to represent the defendant, your client's attorney may need to use a request for production of documents or a subpoena to get this stuff. There should be some documentation that is available to everybody and that may be useful in a lost profits case, including:

- The plaintiff's verified complaint, the defendant's answer, all counterclaims, and all third-party demands.
- The answers to all interrogatories and requests for production of documents of all parties to the proceeding.
- Transcripts of the deposition testimony of all parties and witnesses.
- The plaintiff's financial and tax information for a period of years before the breach or tort occurred and for all subsequent periods through the present. This information would include income tax returns, sales tax returns, payroll tax returns, quarterly and annual financial statements, adjusted trial balances and detailed general ledgers (including adjusting journal entries), accounts receivable and payable subsidiary ledgers, depreciation schedules and other fixed asset reports, business plans and financial forecasts, loan documents and agreements, contracts involving the sales of assets, lease agreements, employment contracts, and all of the other stuff that we discussed in the valuation checklist in Chapter 2.

Usually, you will only get this type of financial information for the plaintiff. You don't really need this stuff for the defendant's business because the claim relates to the plaintiff's loss of profits. However, sometimes you may be able to measure the plaintiff's lost profits by the defendant's results of operations. For example, the defendant may have breached an agreement not to compete against the plaintiff for a period of time in a specified area. The easiest way for the plaintiff to prove its loss of profits may be to determine the amount of profits made by the defendant during the prohibited time in the prohibited location. Obviously, in this case, the plaintiff must have access to the defendant's records in order to prove the amount of the defendant's profits. This usually requires the lawyers to do their thing. No one seems to voluntarily turn over these records.

Obtaining Documents and Records From the Opposing Side

Ask for the records that you think you need from the other side of the litigation. Documents and records may be obtained from the other side by having the attorney send out a request for production of documents. This is really no different from using an information request in a business valuation assignment. You may need some different types of records because of the nature of the case.

Sometimes, the other side will object to the production of the information on the grounds that it contains proprietary or trade secret information. For example, you may request the source code from a rival software company to prove the rival copied your client's source code. Disclosure of the source code will require the disclosure of proprietary and trade secret information. When this kind of information is involved, do not be surprised if you are requested to sign a confidentiality agreement, or you may also find yourself subject to a court-imposed protective order limiting the use of the materials to the disputed issue. The protective order usually provides that the parties (including their attorneys and/or experts) will return all information produced subject to the order to the producing party at the conclusion of the litigation. In addition, you cannot blab about the substance of the information in any manner other than in using it to prove the claim or defense in your assignment. Be careful not to violate a protective order. That's not a good thing.

Should You Work With Original Documents or Copies?

Courts do not always require original documents to be presented as evidence. Generally, photocopies may serve as evidence unless the authenticity of a document is challenged. Your client's attorney has to guide you on this one. For example, in a lost profits case involving an alleged breach of contract, the defense may assert that the contract presented by the plaintiff has been forged or altered in some way. When one side to a dispute doubts the authenticity of a document that the opposing side presents as evidence, the court will usually insist that the original document, rather than a photocopy, be presented as evidence.

Get Information From the Client and the Other Side

In addition to the written documentation, you can use your interview skills to conduct management interviews aimed at getting more information needed to do your job. This stuff begins to look like a business valuation assignment. As I told you before, it really is similar in many respects.

Interviewing Client and Opposing Personnel. Rarely will you be able to draw accurate conclusions if you only look at a bunch of documents. You really want to interview client personnel. These are the folks who can explain the documents to you and answer any questions that you might have about the documents. Client interviews are especially important when you represent the plaintiff. Be careful, however, because your client may provide you with information that needs to be reviewed for reasonableness. For example, your client tells you that "but for" the actions of the defendant, the business could have achieved $10 million in sales in the next two years. When you look at the history of the business, the best year reflected sales of $1.5 million. How realistic is the growth being forecast if you find out that the industry is expecting a downturn because of a change in a regulation affecting the use of its product?

In some cases, you may also be able to interview officers and employees of the other side. These interviews may help you to understand the positions taken by them. The interviews may enable you to uncover important information that should be considered in your analysis. If you can't interview officers or employees of the other side, don't give up. You may have to depend on interrogatories and depositions to obtain needed information. Get the information with the help of the attorney.

Performing the Lost Profits Computation

Once you receive the documentation that has been requested (or at least once you realize that you are not going to get any more documentation) and all of your interviews are completed, you should be in a position to start your number crunching. The assignment will probably require you to estimate the lost revenues and relevant costs and determine if there is any appropriate mitigation of the damages. This process will require you to also determine these items by estimating the appropriate period of loss, possibly an appropriate discounting method, and the appropriate discount rate.

The specific components of the lost profits computation will vary somewhat from one engagement to the next, but you will almost always be dealing with a pretrial component and an after-trial portion. The first step in computing lost profits is to determine the amount of lost revenues before the trial. This process can also be described as determining the revenues that the plaintiff could have earned "but for" the defendant's actions. There are three generally accepted ways to estimate lost revenues:

- The "before and after" method
- The "yardstick" method
- The "but for" method

The "Before and After" Method. The simplest way to estimate revenues lost by the plaintiff as a result of the defendant's actions is to conduct a "before and after" analysis. Just as the name implies, the expert compares the plaintiff's revenues before the alleged breach or tort to the revenues after the event. Any reduction in revenues after the alleged breach or tort is presumed to be caused by the event. This, of course, assumes that the plaintiff's operations before and after the event were comparable. The expert will usually analyze the business before and after the event to ensure comparability. Important differences (such as an owner who worked 60 hours per week in the business before the event and only works 20 hours per week after the event) should be considered in estimating the amount of lost revenues that relate to the event. You should also make sure that the business results are reported in a consistent manner.

To illustrate the use of the before and after method, assume John Smith is a salesman for ABC Electronics and he breaches his employment contract to establish a competing business on January 1, 1999. Mr. Smith's contract required him to provide services to the company through December 31, 2000. The contract also contained a three-year non-compete clause. Therefore, under the terms of the contract, Mr. Smith was not supposed to compete with ABC Electronics through December 31, 2003. Mr. Smith is liable to the company for any damages from the breach. Assume the company's gross revenues were $14 million in 1998 (the year before Mr. Smith began competing with the company) and dropped to $10 million in 1999. Further assume that the company recruited and hired a new salesman on January 1, 2000, to take Mr. Smith's place, and revenues returned to $14 million in 2000.

Before Mr. Smith's breach, the company had revenues of $14 million. After Mr. Smith's breach, the company had revenues of $10 million. Under this fact pattern, it appears that Mr. Smith's actions caused the company to lose $4 million of revenues in 1999. Damages in subsequent years were mitigated by the fact that the company hired a replacement for Mr. Smith in 2000, resulting in revenues returning to $14 million in 2000. The "before and after" approach gives a quick and easy approximation of the amount of revenues lost by the company as a result of Mr. Smith's breach of contract. This, of course, assumes that all else remained constant during this time.

The Yardstick Method. Another common approach to estimating revenues lost in this type of litigation assignment is known as the yardstick method. This method compares the plaintiff's earnings against those of a similar business, product, or other measure. Let's assume from the previous example that the company demonstrated that Mr. Smith's 1999 and 2000 revenues were derived from former customers of the business. These revenues may approximate the amount of revenues the business lost as a result of Mr. Smith's breach of contract.

The best "yardstick" for a closely held business is a business of similar size and nature in the same geographic area as the plaintiff. If the plaintiff has multiple locations, the expert can compare a related entity's results of operations to the plaintiff's. The plaintiff's competitors are also a good source of comparative information, but they will not usually disclose confidential financial information. If the competitors are public companies, you can use the great skills that were discussed in Chapter 6 to find good guideline companies. This can also be a perfect time to use Integra Information's *Business Profiler* software. Gee, we can really get our money's worth from this product if we use it for all of the different types of engagements that we perform (and no, I still do not own a piece of Integra).

The "But for" Method. These other methods can be used when the facts are fairly straightforward and the amount in controversy does not justify a more precise estimation of the revenues lost by the plaintiff "but for" the actions of the defendant. The problem with those methods is that they don't always consider other factors that might increase or decrease the amount of the plaintiff's lost earnings. To illustrate this using the same example, if Mr. Smith had not breached his employment contract, the revenue of the company could have far exceeded $14 million in 1999 and 2000. Mr. Smith's efforts could have increased the company's customer base, leading to new referral business. What might really happen is that the other salespeople's attention may be diverted from the business to help the attorney make the case for the lawsuit against Mr. Smith. On the other hand, other factors that reduced the company's revenues may have nothing to do with Mr. Smith's departure. For example, a change in the economy could have reduced sales.

In a perfect world, a good "but for" analysis will consider as many of the potential factors working in concert that affect the plaintiff's earnings during the period under consideration and will, in turn, segregate those that were caused by the defendant from those that were not. This sometimes is easier said than done.

Mitigation of Damages

The plaintiff has a duty to mitigate its damages. This means that the plaintiff has a responsibility to do whatever it takes to reasonably overcome the damage caused by the defendant's breach or tort. In determining the plaintiff's lost earnings, the amount of earnings lost as a result of the plaintiff's failure to mitigate its own damages are not recoverable. You probably should speak to the client's attorney about this.

Returning to the ABC Electronics example previously discussed, the company mitigated its damages by replacing Mr. Smith on January 1, 2000. Had the company not replaced Mr. Smith, its claim for lost earnings might be reduced by the amount of money the replacement salesman could have generated over and above his or her salary and other benefits.

Period of Recovery

Because the plaintiff has a duty to mitigate damages, the plaintiff cannot expect to be awarded lost profits from the date of the harmful event until the end of time—although I have seen some experts forecast damages until the plaintiff's great grandchildren might be born and become president. Somehow projections of lost earnings for the next 62 years may be hard to swallow. The plaintiff is entitled to recover earnings lost as a result of the defendant's actions for that period of time directly related to those actions. The shorter the period, the easier it is to demonstrate a direct link to the defendant's acts. As the period increases, other factors may be responsible for the plaintiff's losses. These may include general economic conditions, increased competition, poor business judgment, or the plaintiff's failure to mitigate its damages. Other than in special circumstances, a direct link is usually difficult to establish between current earnings and the actions of a defendant for more than only a few years into the past. Likewise, lost earnings are equally difficult to project more than a few years into the future without losing a direct link. There are just too many variables that can impact the projections.

Variable Cost of Lost Revenues

Once the lost revenues have been determined, the next step is to estimate the variable costs that would have been incurred had the revenues not been lost. For example, assume that a plumbing distributor lost $350,000 in gross revenues as a result of a breach of an exclusive distribution agreement by one of its major suppliers. Under the agreement, the distributor was to be the exclusive source for the supplier's merchandise in a particular market area. When the agreement was breached, the distributor didn't suffer $350,000 in damages. Instead, the distributor really lost revenues of $350,000, less whatever variable costs (including cost of goods sold) it would have incurred to sell the $350,000 of merchandise.

For the non-accountants reading this book, a company's costs are usually divided into fixed and variable categories. Sometimes costs may also be semi-fixed or semi-variable. Fixed costs remain the same regardless of how much revenue a company generates. Rent is an example of a fixed cost. You sign a lease and pay the rent whether you produce one widget or 200 widgets. Variable costs, on the other hand, vary with the company's revenues. The higher the company's sales, the higher the variable costs. Cost of goods sold, for example, is a variable cost.

In reality, many costs have both a fixed and a variable component and are referred to as "mixed" costs (semi-fixed or semi-variable—it's like saying, is the glass half full or half empty?). For example, business rent may be a fixed cost assuming the current level of production. Once the level of production increases to a certain point, the existing facility may need to be expanded, thereby raising the rent expense.

Usually, mixed costs tend to be fixed when the damage period is short, but exhibit mixed characteristics when the damage period is long. For example, if the defendant failed to supply goods to the plaintiff, which caused a 30-day shutdown of the plaintiff's production line, the rent paid by the plaintiff on its physical plant would probably remain fixed during this 30-day period. Rent, therefore, would not be a variable cost saved by the plaintiff as a result of the defendant's actions. On the other hand, if the defendant's failure to supply goods prevented the plaintiff from opening a new production line in a new manufacturing plant, the rent saved by the plaintiff would be a variable cost, which must be netted against the plaintiff's lost revenues.

Determining whether an expense will vary with the level of revenues takes a great deal of judgment. You need to analyze each expense item during the damage period and carefully assess whether the expense is fixed or variable. For those that are variable (or are "mixed" with a variable component), try to estimate the amount of the expense that would have been incurred during the damage period if the lost revenues had actually been generated. In many cases, the estimate can be based on historical ratios or percentages. For example, if a company's gross profit percentage has traditionally been 35 percent, it may be reasonable for the expert to estimate that cost of goods sold will be 65 percent (100 percent – 35 percent) of lost revenues.

Should Lost Net Earnings Be Reduced for Income Taxes?

Remember the discussion that we had before in the conventional business valuation chapters about pretax and after-tax stuff? Here, it matters. Although income tax is considered to be a variable expense, it is usually not subtracted from lost revenues to arrive at lost net earnings. Most lost profits calculations are based on pretax amounts because damage awards are usually taxable to the plaintiff. You now have the extent of the tax stuff that I plan to discuss. Make sure that you find out how the jurisdiction of the litigation handles taxes, and don't forget Uncle Sam. Ask your client's attorney!

Prejudgment Interest

Once the lost profits are calculated, you may need to calculate prejudgment interest. This is intended to compensate the plaintiff for not having the use of the lost profits from the time that the damages were sustained until the recovery of the damages (usually the trial) is made. However, prejudgment interest is not allowed in all jurisdictions. In addition, many attorneys would rather keep the interest out of the calculations, even though they expect the courts to award it. Before computing prejudgment interest, find out from the attorney if you should calculate it. You may also want to find out if there is a statutory percentage that is required to be used. I had one case where the statutory rate was 9 percent at a time when interest rates were at about 4 percent. The damage recovery was a good investment once the client got past the aggravation of the litigation. Other items that you probably should talk to the attorney about include when the interest begins to run and if the interest is compound or simple.

Projected Lost Revenues After Trial

Many times the damages will extend to after the trial date. This component of the damages involves obtaining estimated future revenue and expense amounts from the plaintiff and reviewing the estimates for reasonableness. In some cases, if financial forecasts are not available from the plaintiff, you may have to prepare them. Because such estimates are based on events that have not yet occurred, you better be careful. This is like doing a discounted cash flow analysis under the income approach. Make sure that the assumptions that enter into the forecast are reasonable. If they are too speculative, the judge may throw them out.

When you estimate future damages, a two-step approach can be used. First, project the future gross revenues, assuming the breach of contract or tort had never occurred. This projection should reflect gross revenues "but for" the defendant's acts. Second, a forecast of the future gross revenues actually expected to be realized should be prepared. This forecast should reflect the reduced gross revenues that result from the defendant's acts.

AICPA Standards Relating to Forecasts and Projections

This is probably a good time to throw this in. The AICPA's Statement on Standards for Accountants' Services on Prospective Financial Information entitled *Financial Forecasts and Projections* defines a "financial projection" as follows:

> Prospective financial statements that present, to the best of the responsible party's knowledge and belief, given one or more hypothetical assumptions, an entity's expected financial position, results of operations, and cash flows.

The AICPA standard defines a "financial forecast" in exactly the same way, except that the definition of a forecast leaves out the words "given one or more hypothetical assumptions." This AICPA standard typically *does not* have to be followed by CPAs in a litigation engagement. However, it provides excellent guidance relating to preparing and reviewing financial forecasts and projections and should be used for guidance by the CPA/expert.

Factors to Consider in Preparing Financial Forecasts and Projections. The preparation of financial forecasts and projections is beyond the scope of this book. Certain factors to consider, however, are summarized below.

- *Inflation.* Inflation should be considered in estimating future gross revenues. When current rates are extreme relative to historical ranges, the expert should usually reflect gradual increases or decreases toward more normal rates during the forecast period.
- *Product demand.* Products typically go through a life cycle that includes four distinct phases: introduction, growth, maturity, and decline. In estimating future revenues, the CPA should consider the life cycle stage of the plaintiff's primary products. This is the same as the business valuation stuff that we discussed before.
- *Competition.* Within each industry, many companies usually compete for a share of the market, and such competitive pressures must be considered in estimating future revenues. Some factors to consider in estimating the effect of competition are the following:
  - The plaintiff's current market share.
  - The plaintiff's trend in market share (is it increasing or decreasing?).
  - The plaintiff's business plan. This should specifically address how the company proposes to keep or increase market share through such means as reduced prices, increased promotional expenditures, and product improvements supported by increased R&D expenditures.

Revenue Factors for Certain Industries. In estimating future revenues, it is always helpful to understand the key drivers for the particular industry that you are working in. This allows you to formulate numbers that make sense and test the reasonableness of the result. Here are some of the factors to consider for certain industries:

- Professional service businesses, such as engineering, accounting, and law firms—chargeable hours and average billable rates
- Nursing homes and hospitals—beds available, occupancy rates, and average charge per patient
- Home builders—number of home sales closed and average closing prices
- Apartment lessors—units available, expected occupancy rates, and average rent per unit
- Restaurants—tables turned per day and average charge per table
- Commercial real estate lessors—net rentable area and average annual rent per square foot
- Manufacturers—units shipped and average selling prices
- Retail stores—floor space and sales per square foot
- Agricultural producers—acres planted, yield per acre, and selling price
- Associations—number of members and annual dues

Go to a book on rules of thumb for business valuation and you can generally figure out the driver for that type of business. It really is a big help. If the plaintiff has several major product lines or several locations, it may be necessary to develop assumptions by product line or location.

Discounting Projected Lost Profits After Trial to Present Value. After estimating the amount of future lost revenues and variable expenses that relate to the defendant's actions, you will probably have to discount the projected lost net earnings to present value as of the trial date. This can be done in a number of ways.

There is a great deal of controversy as to what discount rate should be used in a lost profits case. Some practitioners prefer to apply a risk-free rate of return (that is, a personal injury type model). Others prefer to include business risk in their calculations (that is, use a business valuation model). Use the guidance from Chapter 10 to help you develop the appropriate discount rate. The only decision that I cannot help you with is if you should be using a risk-free rate or an equity discount rate. This will depend on the jurisdiction, as well as the facts and circumstances of the case.

Don't Forget to Check the Lost Profits Computation for Reasonableness

After completing the last step, you should have an idea of the damages involved in the case. Before reporting the results to the client and the client's attorney, however, you must review the results of the computations and make sure that the results are reasonable. After all, you may have to defend the computations and their underlying assumptions under aggressive cross-examination from the opposing attorney if the case goes to trial.

Other Situations

Sometimes you may be faced with more than just a lost profits calculation. The entire business may have been destroyed. Other times, you may have a relatively new business that has been impacted by a defendant. Here are some tips about those situations.

Destruction of a Business. If the business has been completely destroyed, most courts have ruled that the proper measure of damages is the fair market value of the business on the day of the loss. The theory behind this rule is that the plaintiff who recovers damages equal to the value of the business has, in effect, sold the business to the defendant. The plaintiff should not be able to recover future lost profits after the imputed sales as well.

In this instance, you will most likely be asked to value the business. Use all of the stuff that you learned in the earlier chapters of this book to get you there. If you have already forgotten what you read, reread it!

Startup Businesses. In a lost profits case, the plaintiff's damages must be proved to a reasonable certainty, and may not be based merely on speculation or conjecture. Most new business ventures fail. Accordingly, the *new business rule* generally precludes a startup business from recovering lost profits because there is usually no evidence that the business would have been able to generate a profit but for the defendant's actions.

The new business rule does, however, have some exceptions. Some of the more common exceptions include:

- If the new business has begun operations, it may be able to demonstrate that it is capable of producing revenues and profits. If this is the case, its projection of lost revenues and profits may be based on more than mere speculation.
- If the new business is a franchise operation or a new location of an existing business, it may be able to demonstrate the historical revenue and profit results of similar franchises or locations. If the plaintiff has a demonstrated track record of success with similar endeavors, its projection of profits lost from the new business may rise to the level of a reasonable certainty.
- If the new business would have enjoyed a competitive advantage over existing businesses in the industry, projecting this advantage in terms of lost profits over and above existing competitors' results of operations may be accepted as reasonable. Any such projection should be limited to the period of time it would have taken the competition to "catch up" to the new business.

If you represent the plaintiff, you must be extremely creative to overcome the new business rule. All financial data implying that the plaintiff's new business could have made a profit should be referred to and relied upon in projecting the lost profits of a startup business.

Plaintiff or Defense?

You may be called upon to work for the plaintiff or the defense in a damages litigation. Obviously, as stated earlier, the objectives of each side are very different. If you represent the plaintiff, your job is to help establish how much the damages really are. You are not the liability expert, so keep your analysis to the economics of the situation (unless your role is also as a liability expert). It is always a good idea to state early in your report that your report assumes that there is liability, but you are not offering an opinion in that regard. If there is no liability found, your numbers are meaningless.

When you work for the defense, your job will frequently be to shoot holes in the plaintiff's expert's report, and sometimes, conclude your own estimate of damages. You can use your skills and resources as a business valuer to your advantage if you really try.

Exhibits 19.1, 19.2, and 19.3 provide you with some sample analyses that were performed in actual assignments. In all instances, the identities of the parties and the locations have been changed to protect the guilty. If there are inconsistencies because of locational changes, they only exist because of the changes made in the exhibits to protect the identity of the players. The last exhibit is a critique of the plaintiff's expert's work when we worked for the defense team. These should at least provide you with a starting point if you have never done this stuff before.

EXHIBIT 19.1

This case deals with the issues of lost profits and lost business value arising out of a litigation where the plaintiff, a physical therapy operation, sued several insurers and related entities for not making timely payments for monies due them.

Description of the Assignment

Trugman Valuation Associates Inc. was retained by Haverstraw Physical Therapy Services, P.A., to calculate the economic damages that have been incurred as a result of the actions of the defendants in this matter. These damages are calculated as part of the litigation entitled *Haverstraw Physical Therapy Services v. The Johnson Plan Corporation, The Johnson Plan of Any State Corporation, National Insurance Corporation (NCIC), Material Damage Adjusters (MDA) et al.*, filed in the Superior Court of Any State, Law Division: Haverstraw County, Docket No. HVS-L-1234-95.

Company History

Haverstraw Physical Therapy Services, P.A. (HPT or The Company) purchased the assets of Haverstraw Physical Therapy Services, Inc. (HPTSI) in April 1992 from the original owner, Howard Tarten. At the time, HPT's sole location was in City One. The Company provides outpatient physical therapy services to individuals with injuries requiring rehabilitation, exercise, and/or massage therapy. The management of HPT saw significant growth potential in the physical therapy business due to the expanding demand for these services and the changing health care environment that would favor larger service providers over smaller ones.

HPT establishes referral networks by marketing and developing relationships with physicians, hospital administrators, and attorneys. In purchasing the assets of HPTSI, HPT acquired 35 years of individual and corporate relationships that had already been established by HPTSI. Management believed The Company could experience significant growth by actively advertising and marketing The Company's services. To enhance its professional community marketing, HPT developed an information kit to provide to potential referral sources, and advertised in medical journals and newsletters serving the Any State medical community.

The Company's fees are received from several sources, including health maintenance organizations, preferred provider organizations, medical insurance companies, worker's compensation claims, Medicare, automobile insurance claims, and attorney litigation. A significant portion of HPT's clients are persons who have been injured in automobile accidents, seeking services under automobile insurance claims.

In February 1994, HPT acquired its second location in City Two. The facility had previously been unable to operate very successfully, never being able to generate more than 100 patient visits in a single week. The prior owner had invested more than $100,000 in the center and was reluctant to invest further. HPT had no money to invest in the center as a result of its cash flow difficulties. HPT convinced the owner to invest an additional $60,000 so that, with HPT as a partner, they might be able to turn the facility into a profitable business. A joint venture arrangement was completed in February and HPT began operating in the facility. HPT achieved great success with the facility and averaged 295 patient visits per week in 1997. This is the second largest volume for a HPT facility, behind the 393 patient visits per week average of the City One facility.

(Continued)

EXHIBIT 19.1 ***(Continued)***

In 1995, cash flow had improved slightly from 1994 and HPT opened two additional centers in City Three and City Four. The two facilities were opened in April and May, respectively. According to Mr. Gerber, the Company felt that in 1995 there was an excellent opportunity to open four additional facilities, but the lack of sufficient capital prohibited HPT from opening more than the City Three and City Four facilities. Both of these facilities became profitable in a very short period of time. In addition to physical therapy services, the City Three facility provides occupational therapy services for people who require rehabilitation to allow them to perform work-related tasks after an accident or injury. During 1997, City Three averaged 277 patient visits per week and City Four averaged 141 visits per week. Of City Three's 277 visit per week average, approximately 210 were physical therapy patients.

By the end of 1995, HPT had developed a strong reputation for providing excellent service to clients. In addition, HPT had developed its accounting, billing, collection, marketing, advertising, and other support and administrative systems to a level where they would easily facilitate further growth. The combined effect of reputation and systems strategically positioned The Company to further expand its operations into other parts of Smith and Haverstraw counties. At this point, growth would provide two significant advantages: access to HMOs and insurers attempting to limit the number of service providers with which they contract; and increased referrals from HPT's existing referral base resulting from the convenience that additional locations would create for prospective clients for whom the locations of existing facilities were not convenient.

During 1996, The Company did not expand its operations because of insufficient capital, but it began to identify opportunities for new facilities that could be opened in 1997. The first facility established in 1997 was in City Five, where The Company took over an existing physical therapy center that had a full complement of the necessary physical therapy equipment. The acquisition was attractive to HPT because of the location and the minimal startup capital required to open the center.

In March 1997, HPT opened a new center in City Six with $35,000 in capital contributions from limited partners. The Company acquired equipment and leasehold improvements of approximately $70,000, of which $25,000 were leased.

In May 1997, The Company opened a center in City Seven, taking over an existing facility that had most of the necessary equipment. The operating expenses were funded by a limited partner, Dr. Linder, during the initial months of HPT ownership.

The last facility opened was a startup facility in City Eight. This took place in November 1997. HPT acquired approximately $75,000 in equipment, with $35,000 through leases and $40,000 financed through a loan from Statewide Savings Bank.

As a result of this recent activity, HPT now has eight locations. During 1997, The Company averaged 1,275 patient visits per week or 66,300 visits annually in all of its facilities.

HPT has identified several geographical locations that it believes present opportunities to open successful centers, including City Nine, City Ten, City Eleven, and City Twelve. HPT is also exploring the potential for centers in other locations and found City Thirteen, City Fourteen, City Fifteen, and City Sixteen as areas that also would provide good growth opportunities. Through its marketing efforts, HPT has established relationships with a significant number of physicians, including physicians who practice in all of these areas, except City Eleven, and feels confident that a solid referral base would readily be established if centers could be opened. In the case of City Eleven, HPT believes the area to be underserved.

Damage Calculations

The damages calculated in this report have been calculated through December 31, 1997, and consist of several components, including:

- Claims unpaid by NCIC and MDA
- Lost reinvestment opportunities by HPT
- Lost interest [omitted from this exhibit]
- Lost business value
- Expert fees [omitted from this exhibit]
- Contingent legal fees [omitted from this exhibit]

Each of these items (except the ones noted) is explained in the following sections of the report.

Claims Unpaid by NCIC and MDA

The basis of this action was damage done to HPT by Johnson Plan Corporation (JPC) and its subsidiaries through the denial of payment for services rendered to individuals under their auto insurance personal injury protection (PIP) coverage; JPC was responsible for either authorizing payment to HPT or making payment to HPT. In the initial years contained in the complaint, JPC acted as a servicing agent for the Joint Automobile Insurance Underwriting Association (JUA) and its successor organization, Market Transition Facility (MTF), which were the two statutory automobile insurance funds in Any State. HPT would treat insured motorists who were injured in automobile accidents. The company would bill JUA and MTF under the PIP sections of the individual's automobile insurance policy.

EXHIBIT 19.1 *(Continued)*

The insurance companies did not pay the claims directly but, rather, had their claims serviced by several private insurance servicing agencies, including JPC, through the servicing subsidiary, Material Damage Adjusters (MDA). After submitting a claim, HPT would be paid based on the statutory Any State PIP fee schedule. All of the insurance servicing agents were obligated to remit to service providers based on the PIP schedule after determining that the claim had been filed properly.

By late 1993, Any State had decided to withdraw from the insurance industry, and private insurers began writing auto insurance policies that had previously been written by the state-run funds. JPC quickly became a major player in the urban auto insurance market through its subsidiary National Insurance Company (NCIC). After performing services for clients covered by NCIC insurance policies, HPT would submit claims to NCIC for payment for services rendered to NCIC clients. NCIC paid very few of these claims through 1994. At December 31, 1997, the unpaid claim balance was $1,224,459. This balance represents total damages for unpaid claims.

Lost Reinvestment Opportunities by HPT

The claims unpaid by NCIC and MDA left HPT with significantly reduced cash flow. The lack of cash flow inhibited HPT from investing in additional physical therapy centers and generating further profits and cash flow. The Company's historic cash flow for 1992 through 1997 is presented in Table 1.

TABLE 1

Calculation of Historic Cash Flow

	1992	*1993*	*1994*	*1995*	*1996*	*1997*
Net income after dividends and distributions	$ 487,581	$ 770,041	$ 34,830	$ 222,353	$ 115,109	$ 498,684
Plus: Depreciation and amortization	173,119	384,703	521,471	450,469	208,005	183,300
Gross cash flow	$ 660,700	$1,154,744	$ 556,301	$ 672,822	$ 323,114	$ 681,984
Change in working capital	31,400	548,947	(648,428)	(403,977)	2,012,801	(2,795,274)
Fixed asset additions	(168,700)	(14,154)	(13,979)	(234,218)	(14,926)	(152,257)
Principal repayments/ (new borrowings)	(317,024)	(842,898)	(43,568)	4,898	(94,010)	66,431
Change in other assets/ liabilities	2,414	(992,612)	295,320	(29,793)	(2,167,645)	2,137,494
Net cash flow	$ 208,790	$ (145,973)	$ 145,646	$ 9,732	$ 59,334	$ (61,622)

Had claims been paid in a timely manner, HPT's cash flow position would have been significantly different from that in Table 1. Table 2 shows the net claims made and outstanding to HPT annually from 1991 to 1997.

TABLE 2

Net Claims Made by HPT Outstanding at December 31, 1997

Year	*Net Claims Made*
1991	$ 10,530
1992	120,852
1993	700,116
1994	482,490
1995	173,001
1996	(140,523)
1997	(122,006)
Total	**$ 1,224,459**

(Continued)

EXHIBIT 19.1 *(Continued)*

According to the Any State law, NCIC and MDA had 60 days to pay lawfully submitted claims by service providers after receiving written notice of the covered loss and the amount. Based on the amounts reflected in Table 2, we calculated the amount of each claim that should have been paid to HPT in Table 3. This calculation assumes that billing and collection is spread evenly throughout the year. Therefore, the amount reflected in Table 3 is assumed to have been collected during the years.

TABLE 3
Claims That Should Have Been Paid

Year	*Net Claims Made*	*Net Claims Assumed Paid*
1991	$ 10,530	$ 8,775
1992	120,852	102,465
1993	700,116	603,572
1994	482,490	518,761
1995	173,001	224,583
1996	(140,523)	(88,269)
1997	(122,006)	(125,092)
1998	—	(20,334)
Total	**$ 1,224,459**	**$ 1,224,459**

Had NCIC and MDA made these payments to HPT, The Company's cash flow position would have looked very different. Adding these payments to the cash flow figures reflected in Table 1 results in an adjusted cash flow that is reflected in Table 4.

TABLE 4
Calculation of Adjusted Cash Flow

	1992	*1993*	*1994*	*1995*	*1996*	*1997*
Net cash flow (from Table 1)	$ 208,790	$ (145,973)	$ 145,646	$ 9,732	$ 59,334	$ (61,622)
Adjustment for receivables assumed collected	102,465	603,572	518,761	224,583	(88,269)	(125,092)
Adjusted net cash flow	$ 311,255	$ 457,599	$ 664,407	$ 234,315	$ (28,935)	$ (186,714)

If HPT had been paid these monies, its ability to invest in itself would have been greatly enhanced, allowing HPT to grow its business by opening additional physical therapy centers throughout the various counties. To determine the growth potential for HPT, we analyzed each of The Company's existing facilities from its inception through December 31, 1997, for the purpose of estimating what an average or "typical" new center looks like from a financial perspective. We have assumed that all new centers would be startups, rather than existing facilities that HPT would take over. This required us to determine the maximum investment The Company would have to make in equipment and other startup costs to open each additional new facility. This would also allow us to calculate the payback period and the contribution to The Company's cash flow after the payback of startup capital was completed.

To accomplish this, we reviewed the patient visits, revenues, collections, and expenses related to each facility, ascertaining the trend from the startup of operations to maturity of each center's operations.

HPT currently has eight facilities. For the purposes of estimating the financial profile of a "typical" facility, we analyzed five of these facilities: City Two, City Three, City Four, City Five, and City Six. These facilities were either started by HPT or were very immature when taken over, allowing an analysis of how a facility grows from startup through its first three years.

EXHIBIT 19.1 *(Continued)*

The remaining three facilities were not used for various reasons. City One was not used because it was a mature operation when purchased by HPT and does not provide any information on the growth pattern of immature facilities. Although City Eight is an HPT startup, it only began operations in November 1997. Having only two months of operational data in 1997, we did not consider it a good indication of what a facility would look like after a full year of operations. The City Seven facility was taken over in May 1997. HPT has a joint venture partner in this operation that pays the operating expenses. As a result, the financial information kept by HPT does not include the operating expense data that is necessary to establish what the financial profile of the facility was at December 31, 1997.

Using the remaining five facilities, we determined the financial profile of the "average" facility for its first three years of operations. To accomplish this, we analyzed income statements for each of the facilities for its first, and where available, its second and third years of operations. All periods ended December 31. The specific calendar years analyzed depend on when each facility was opened. Table 5 shows each facility and which calendar years represent its first, second, and third year of operations.

TABLE 5

Year of Operation by Facility

Location	*Year 1*	*Year 2*	*Year 3*
City Two	1994	1995	1996
City Three	1995	1996	1997
City Four	1995	1996	1997
City Five	1997	N/A	N/A
City Six	1997	N/A	N/A

The first item we estimated was revenues. Revenues are based on collectible charges per patient visit. For the facilities we analyzed, we computed an average number of visits per year. Table 6 shows the number of visits each facility had during its first three years of operations.

TABLE 6

Visits by Location

Location	*Year 1*[1]	*Year 2*	*Year 3*
City Two	7,864	9,305	15,635
City Three	5,392	9,232	12,477
City Four	3,363	6,152	7,432
City Five	2,268	—	—
City Six	5,969	—	—
Average	4,971	8,230	11,848

[1]Visits in the first year of operations have been annualized to reflect a full year of operation.

To calculate revenues, the average visits were then multiplied by HPT's historic net realized collection per visit for each year. For example, we have estimated that a facility in its first year of operations will have 4,971 patient visits. If this facility opened in 1994, those visits are multiplied by $98.48, HTP's net collection per patient in 1994. If the facility is opened in 1996, then the same number of visits are multiplied by $102.41, HPT's net collection per patient in 1996. This was done to reflect the changing environment that HPT has operated in over the last five years. Changes in the health care industry, the insurance industry, and the regulations governing both had a significant impact on the money that HPT was able to collect. Therefore we felt it was important to capture this feature of estimating the financial performance of additional facilities. Net collections per patient are summarized in Table 7.

(Continued)

EXHIBIT 19.1 *(Continued)*

TABLE 7

Net Collection per Visit
1992–1997

	1992	*1993*	*1994*	*1995*	*1996*	*1997*
Revenue	$ 2,938,598	$ 3,700,882	$ 3,028,148	$ 3,967,376	$ 5,429,830	$ 6,639,012
Number of visits	25,747	35,390	30,748	37,740	53,022	66,035
Net collection per visit	$ 114.13	$ 104.57	$ 98.48	$ 105.12	$ 102.41	$ 100.54

In analyzing the financial statements for each facility, all general and administrative expenses were eliminated, leaving only the direct costs associated with the operations of the facility. Direct costs in The Company's financial statements consist of salaries for physical therapists, assistants, aids, receptionists, and secretaries, along with the related benefits and taxes; medical supplies; linens; patient parking; equipment repairs and maintenance; equipment leases; insurance; and utilities. This was done because general and administrative expenses are incurred at the corporate level, not at the facility level, and they are mostly fixed in nature. To use the allocations present in the facility income statements would not enable us to capture the incremental overhead expense associated with a new facility, only the historic allocation of general and administrative expense over the facilities existing at each particular point in time. As The Company opens more facilities, general and administrative expense per facility should decrease. This is not to say that HTP would not incur any additional overhead with each new facility it opens, but it would be a reduced level from the historic averages. As a result, an allowance for general and administrative expenses was made and is discussed later in this report.

Expense for equipment leases was also eliminated from the direct expenses, because not all facilities leased equipment. In addition, our analysis assumes that all equipment is purchased outright, rather than financed, in order to calculate the maximum capital outlay HPT would need to make to open a new facility. Rent expense was also eliminated to make the income statements consistent. Facilities are of different sizes and pay different rents based on their locations. We analyzed the leases for each facility and estimated rental expense for the typical facility. The results of our analysis are presented later in this section.

For each facility, the first period of operations ending December 31 was less than a full year. To compute a full period, we annualized the data based on the number of months that the facility was open. After annualizing the results for each facility, the average of the five facilities was taken. We used this average to represent the first year's performance for a typical facility. This data is presented in Table 8. Tables 9 and 10 reflect the second and third year of operations for these facilities, respectively.

TABLE 8

Income Statement by Location
First Year of Operations—Annualized

	City Two	*City Five*	*City Six*	*City Three*	*City Four*	*Annualized Average*
Revenues	$ 619,560	$176,931	$ 431,628	$ 388,856	$ 256,962	$ 464,591
Cost of operations						
Salaries	$ 170,900	$ 78,218	$ 165,460	$ 153,849	$ 90,071	$ 163,887
Payroll taxes	15,303	2,445	17,069	13,827	9,028	14,523
Employee benefits	6,424	2,242	1,144	3,568	1,441	3,616
Medical supplies	11,880	4,607	8,397	9,969	5,856	10,151
Linen, towels, and uniforms	581	608	189	—	459	449
Equipment repairs and maintenance	968	615	2,748	1,337	920	1,647
Insurance	318	1,454	2,529	202	20	1,057
Utilities	4,178	—	—	3,892	958	2,280
Total cost of operations	$ 210,552	$ 90,189	$ 197,536	$ 186,644	$ 108,753	$ 197,611
Contribution	**$409,000**	**$ 86,742**	**$234,092**	**$202,212**	**$148,209**	**$ 266,980**

EXHIBIT 19.1 *(Continued)*

TABLE 9

Income Statement by Location Second Year of Operations

	City Two	*City Three*	*City Four*	*Average*
Revenues	$1,066,425	$ 995,661	$ 546,399	$ 869,495
Cost of operations				
Salaries	$ 253,047	$ 324,670	$ 191,742	$ 256,486
Payroll taxes	25,382	28,043	17,632	23,686
Employee benefits	6,773	12,412	6,932	8,706
Medical supplies	14,854	34,088	9,767	19,570
Linen, towels, and uniforms	108	1,070	1,178	785
Patient parking	—	—	2,249	750
Equipment repairs and maintenance	1,969	2,285	3,782	2,679
Insurance	434	1,777	798	1,003
Utilities	5,292	8,340	4,298	5,977
Total cost of operations	$ 307,859	$ 412,685	$ 238,378	$ 319,642
Facility contribution	**$ 758,566**	**$ 582,976**	**$ 308,021**	**$ 549,854**

TABLE 10

Income Statement by Location Third Year of Operations

	City Two	*City Three*	*City Four*	*Average*
Revenues	$ 1,807,124	$ 1,191,004	$ 704,870	$ 1,234,333
Cost of operations				
Salaries	$ 507,251	$ 333,664	$ 237,582	$ 359,499
Payroll taxes	43,356	34,050	21,570	32,992
Employee benefits	14,669	4,406	7,073	8,716
Medical supplies	43,498	16,600	7,884	22,661
Linen, towels, and uniforms	2,285	5,788	1,397	3,157
Patient parking	—	3,003	—	1,001
Equipment repairs and maintenance	8,914	459	4,176	4,516
Insurance	1,932	3,012	2,690	2,545
Utilities	4,056	4,026	4,399	4,160
Total cost of operations	$ 625,961	$ 405,008	$ 286,771	$ 439,247
Facility Contribution	**$ 1,181,163**	**$ 785,996**	**$ 418,099**	**$ 795,086**

City Six and City Five were opened in 1997 and only have one year of operations, leaving three facilities with two and three years of operations. For years 2 and 3 the same expense adjustments were made as described earlier in this section. As each period represents a full year of operations, no annualization was required. The average for years 2 and 3 were taken as was described for year 1.

(Continued)

EXHIBIT 19.1 *(Continued)*

HPT provided us with copies of leases for each of its facilities where they were available. We used the leases to estimate average rent expense for 1997. Table 11 summarizes this data.

TABLE 11

Calculation of Average Rent Expense

Location	*Square Feet*	*Annual Rent*
City Two	4,256	$ 68,096
City Three	2,500	54,405
City Four	2,100	25,200
City Six	3,600	79,200
City One	2,684	68,268
Total	15,140	$ 295,169
Average square feet per facility	3,028	
Average rent per square feet		$ 19.50

Rent for typical facility = 3,028 × $19.50 = $59,046

We estimated the average square footage of the facilities to be 3,028 and the average cost per square foot to be $19.50. Multiplying these two numbers together results in an estimated rental expense of $59,046. Four of the leases had escalator clauses to increase the rental payments from year to year. Three of these leases had a 4 percent escalator clause. We have used 4 percent to deflate rental expense for 1996 through 1993. In addition, we have assumed a security deposit of $10,000 for the facility, which is approximately two months of 1997 rent and was typical of the leases used in this analysis. Three of HPT's current facilities, City Four, City Six, and City Eight were HPT startups. Table 12 shows the costs that HPT incurred in setting up the facilities.

TABLE 12

Facility Startup Costs

	City Eight	*City Six*	*City Four*
PT equipment & gym equipment	$ 49,423	$ 46,621	$ 29,824
OT equipment	2,469	N/A	N/A
Treatment room curtains	1,500	1,867	1,500
Phone system/computer cabling	3,021	2,318	1,500
Washer/dryer	1,661	1,896	1,200
Office/waiting room furniture	3,519	5,778	3,000
Burglar/fire alarm/sound system	3,510	2,878	1,500
Countertops/wall paper/paint	11,577	5,446	N/A
Miscellaneous	3,000	3,859	2,000
	$ 79,680	$ 70,663	$ 40,524

City Four understates the requirements for a new facility because it opened with the bare minimum equipment necessary and added equipment and improvements in later years. Taking the average of the City Eight and City Six facilities reveals that $75,000 of startup costs (rounded) is required to open a new facility.

The results of the above analysis indicate that HPT would need $85,000 (equipment $75,000 and security deposit $10,000) to open a new physical therapy center. Based on the adjusted cash flow (Table 4) and the cash balances presented, HPT should have been able to open additional facilities.

As each additional facility is opened, a certain level of general and administrative expenses is incurred at the corporate level to support the facility operations. General and administrative expenses reported on the combined HPT and PMB financial statements for 1992 through 1997 were as shown in Table 13.

EXHIBIT 19.1 *(Continued)*

TABLE 13

General and Administrative Expense

1992	*1993*	*1994*	*1995*	*1996*	*1997*
$ 1,185,321	$ 1,490,478	$ 1,244,258	$ 1,548,566	$ 1,746,113	$ 1,357,400

To derive additional general and administrative expense for each facility, we used the historic expense for 1993 through 1996. 1992 was excluded because it is not a full year and does not allow a true comparison to full year periods. 1997 was excluded from this analysis because the recorded general and administrative expenses were classified inconsistently with the presentation from 1992 to 1996.

In analyzing this data, we noted general and administrative expenses increased to $1,746,113 in 1996 from $1,498,478 in 1993, or $255,635. During that same period, three additional facilities were added. This means that the three additional locations can be assumed to have added $255,635 to the general and administrative expenses of The Company, or $85,212 per facility. Since inflation was relatively low during this time frame, we have excluded it from our calculations.

To complete the profile of a new facility, we needed to estimate a fourth and fifth year of operations. Out of the five facilities we used to estimate years 1 through 3, only City Two had existed for four years. We felt that using this facility as a proxy for the fourth year of operations of a typical facility was not appropriate. Instead we analyzed the rates of growth in all facilities with two or more years of operations. Table 14 presents these rates of growth.

TABLE 14

Growth Rate in Annual Patient Visits by Facility
Annualized for First Year of Operations

	1993	*1994*	*1995*	*1996*	*1997*
City One	1.7%	–32.6%	–8.4%	–0.3%	–6.0%
City Two			18.3%	68.0%	10.7%
City Three				71.2%	35.1%
City Four				83.0%	20.8%

The City Two, City Three, and City Four locations have all experienced high rates of growth in the number of visits. Those rates decrease after two to three years of operations. City Three and City Four experienced 35.1 and 20.8 percent growth, respectively, in visits in their third year of operations. It should be noted that had we not annualized the first year's visits for each facility before computing the growth rates, these figures would have been overstated. In its third year, City Two experienced 68 percent growth followed by 10.7 percent in its fourth year. After analyzing this data, we assumed that the typical facility would grow 10 percent in its fourth year, and 5 percent in its fifth year of operation. Cost of sales for year four was grown by an inflationary factor taken from the Consumer Price Index for 1996 and the eleven months of 1997 and annualized. The rates of inflation were 3.3 and 2.0 percent, respectively.

To generate cash flow from the income statement profiles, we needed to make an assumption about the timing of the collection of receivables and the payment of accounts payable. To analyze accounts receivable, we looked at the same five facilities and calculated their days receivable. This is summarized in Table 15.

TABLE 15

Average Days Receivables

	Year One		Year Two		Year Three	
	Sales	*Receivables*	*Sales*	*Receivables*	*Sales*	*Receivables*
City Two	$ 619,560	$ 148,263	$ 1,066,425	$ 359,142	$ 1,807,124	$ 685,678
City Three	388,856	171,668	995,661	353,169	1,191,004	613,294
City Four	256,962	167,438	546,399	300,648	704,870	542,568
City Five	176,931	79,279	—	—	—	—
City Six	431,628	187,789	—	—	—	—
Total	$ 1,873,937	$ 754,437	$ 2,608,485	$ 1,012,959	$ 3,702,998	$ 1,841,540
Days receivable	365/(1,873,937/754,437) = 147		365/(2,608,485/1,012,959) = 142		365/(3,702,998/1,841,540) = 182	

(Continued)

EXHIBIT 19.1 *(Continued)*

The receivable assumption used for the typical facility is the average for each year of operations. We assumed that days receivable for years 4 and 5 are the same as for year 3. We considered, but did not use, HPT's overall days receivable because it is not typical of what would be experienced in new facilities. This is because there are several categories of clients that distort overall accounts receivable aging and collection. Specifically, these are accounts HPT refers to as "Bill Attorney." These are accounts where HPT provides services to a client and then bills the client's attorney, who will pay HPT for its services after collecting in litigation on behalf of the client. Many of these accounts can go uncollected for over a year, possibly two. Most of this work has been done in the City One facility and is not significant in the other facilities. In addition, HPT has several litigations ongoing, including one for which this analysis is being done, that pertain to the collection of accounts receivable. Again, most of these accounts are held at City One and do not significantly affect other facilities.

Based on the adjusted cash flow from Table 4, we determined that HPT would have been able to open at least two facilities in 1993, four more in 1994, and two in 1995. The income statements for an individual facility opening in each of these years are presented in Tables 16 through 18.

TABLE 16

1993 Startup Facility Income Statement

	1993	*1994*	*1995*	*1996*	*1997*
Revenues	$ 519,838	$ 810,458	$ 1,245,462	$ 1,334,689	$ 1,375,834
Cost of sales	194,611	319,641	439,247	453,742	462,817
Gross margin	$ 325,227	$ 490,817	$ 806,215	$ 880,947	$ 913,017
Rent	$ 50,473	$ 52,492	$ 54,591	$ 56,775	$ 59,046
General and administration	85,212	85,212	85,212	85,212	85,212
Depreciation	15,000	15,000	15,000	15,000	15,000
Period costs	$ 150,685	$ 152,704	$ 154,803	$ 156,987	$ 159,258
Profit before taxes	$ 174,542	$ 338,114	$ 651,412	$ 723,960	$ 753,759
Taxes	69,817	135,245	260,565	289,584	301,503
Profit after taxes	$ 104,725	$ 202,869	$ 390,847	$ 434,376	$ 452,256

TABLE 17

1994 Startup Facility Income Statement

	1994	*1995*	*1996*	*1997*
Revenues	$ 489,564	$ 865,103	$ 1,213,354	$ 1,310,318
Cost of sales	194,611	319,641	439,247	453,742
Gross margin	$ 294,953	$ 545,462	$ 774,107	$ 856,576
Rent	$ 52,492	$ 54,591	$ 56,775	$ 59,046
General and administration	85,212	85,212	85,212	85,212
Depreciation	15,000	15,000	15,000	15,000
Period costs	$ 152,704	$ 154,803	$ 156,987	$ 159,258
Profit before taxes	$ 142,249	$ 390,659	$ 617,120	$ 697,318
Taxes	56,900	156,263	246,848	278,926
Profit after taxes	$ 85,349	$ 234,396	$ 370,272	$ 418,392

EXHIBIT 19.1 *(Continued)*

TABLE 18

1995 Startup Facility Income Statement

	1995	*1996*	*1997*
Revenues	$ 522,573	$ 842,800	$ 1,191,198
Cost of sales	194,611	319,641	439,247
Gross margin	$ 327,962	$ 523,159	$ 751,951
Rent	$ 54,591	$ 56,775	$ 59,046
General and administration	85,212	85,212	85,212
Depreciation	15,000	15,000	15,000
Period costs	$ 154,803	$ 156,987	$ 159,258
Profit before taxes	173,159	366,172	592,693
Taxes	69,263	146,469	237,077
Profit after taxes	$ 103,896	$ 219,703	$ 355,616

Table 19 illustrates the profit contribution of the additional facilities that would have resulted if HPT had the cash flow resulting from the NCIC and MDA claims.

TABLE 19

Rollout of Additional Facilities
Combined Income Statement for the Years Ended December 31,

	1993	*1994*	*1995*	*1996*	*1997*
Revenues	$ 519,838	$ 3,089,608	$ 6,996,482	$ 9,208,394	$ 10,375,336
Cost of sales	194,611	1,223,115	2,546,280	3,303,754	3,619,096
Gross margin	$ 325,227	$ 1,866,493	$ 4,450,202	$ 5,904,640	$ 6,756,240
Rent	$ 50,473	$ 262,460	$ 436,728	$ 454,200	$ 472,368
General and administration	85,212	255,636	681,696	681,696	681,696
Depreciation	15,000	75,000	120,000	120,000	120,000
Period costs	$ 150,685	$ 593,096	$ 1,238,424	$ 1,255,896	$ 1,274,064
Profit before taxes	$ 174,542	$ 1,273,397	$ 3,211,778	$ 4,648,744	$ 5,482,176
Taxes	69,817	509,359	1,284,711	1,859,496	2,192,870
Profit after taxes	$ 104,725	$ 764,038	$ 1,927,067	$ 2,789,248	$ 3,289,306
Facilities opened	2	4	2	0	0

The figures reflected in Table 19 assume that the first new facility would have been opened in approximately March 1993, about one full year after HPT acquired HPTSI; the second 1993 startup would occur six months later. Therefore, one full facility is reflected in 1993. In addition, it is assumed that two facilities will be opened every six months thereafter. Despite the cash flow availability, we did not provide for more than two locations to be opened simultaneously based on HPT's actual experience. Therefore, the figures in 1994 reflect three facilities as opposed to the four that would have been opened up (computed as two facilities on January 1 and two facilities on July 1).

In performing the cash flow calculations, we reviewed the resulting figures to make certain that HPT would have had the startup capital of $85,000 available, plus an additional $65,000, which would be required for working capital for the new facility. Therefore, $150,000 was needed before a new location could be opened up.

In order to calculate the revised cash flow from the new facilities, a similar calculation had to be performed for the days receivables, as previously discussed. Since the revenues changed due to the opening of new facilities, the average days receivable is expected to change as well. This is calculated in Table 20.

(Continued)

EXHIBIT 19.1 (Continued)

TABLE 20
Calculation of Days Receivables

	1993		1994		1995		1996		1997	
Facility	*Sales*	*Receivables*	*Sales*	*Receivables*	*Sales*	*Receivables*	*Sales*	*Receivables*	*Sales*	*Receivables*
1	$ 259,919	$ 104,680	$ 810,458	$ 315,301	$ 1,245,462	$ 621,025	$ 1,334,689	$ 665,516	$ 1,375,834	$ 686,032
2	259,919	104,680	810,458	315,301	1,245,462	621,025	1,334,689	665,516	1,375,834	686,032
3	—	—	489,564	197,167	865,103	336,561	1,213,354	605,015	1,310,318	653,364
4	—	—	489,564	197,167	865,103	336,561	1,213,354	605,015	1,310,318	653,364
5	—	—	244,782	98,583	865,103	336,561	1,213,354	605,015	1,310,318	653,364
6	—	—	244,782	98,583	865,103	336,561	1,213,354	605,015	1,310,318	653,364
7	—	—	—	—	522,573	210,461	842,800	327,884	1,191,198	593,967
8	—	—	—	—	522,573	210,461	842,800	327,884	1,191,198	593,967
Total	$519,838	$ 209,360	$3,089,608	$1,222,104	$6,996,482	$3,009,214	$9,208,394	$4,406,859	$10,375,336	$5,173,455
Days receiv.	365(519,838/209,360) = 147		365(3,089,608/1,222,100) = 144		365(6,996,482/3,009,214) = 157		365(9,208,394/4,406,859) = 175		365(10,375,336/5,173,455) = 182	

EXHIBIT 19.1 *(Continued)*

In addition to accounts receivable, an assumption regarding the days payable must also be made. HPT experienced cash flow problems in its earlier years, resulting in slower payments to its vendors. By 1997, the days payable were down to 70 days, which we have used in this analysis. The resulting cash flows from the new facilities are calculated in Table 21.

TABLE 21

Calculation of Additional Cash Flow

	1993	1994	1995	1996	1997
Net income (Table 19)	$ 104,725	$ 764,038	$ 1,927,067	$ 2,789,246	$ 3,289,306
Plus: Depreciation and amortization	15,000	75,000	120,000	120,000	120,000
Gross cash flow	$ 119,725	$ 839,038	$ 2,047,067	$ 2,909,246	$ 3,409,306
Change in working capital	(194,426)	(866,823)	(1,574,649)	(1,269,771)	(715,926)
Fixed asset additions	(150,000)	(300,000)	(150,000)	—	—
Net cash flow	**$ (224,701)**	**$ (327,785)**	**$ 322,417**	**$1,639,475**	**$2,693,379**

Based on the net cash flow illustrated in Table 21, the damages for HPT's lost investment opportunities amount to:

1993	$ (224,701)
1994	(327,785)
1995	322,417
1996	1,639,476
1997	2,693,379
Total	$ 4,102,786

Lost Business Value

One of the elements of damage sustained by HPT is the lost value of the enterprise as a result of not being able to reinvest into itself. The cash flow that was lost is an element of actual historical damages, but at December 31, 1997, the business is considerably smaller than it should have been.

Because of the growth of the physical therapy business over the last several years, HPT missed a window of opportunity that will probably not be recaptured. Therefore, the value of The Company has been diminished.

Had HPT been able to reinvest into the new facilities estimated previously, The Company would most likely have an increased value based on a multiple of additional earnings. The question becomes, what is a reasonable multiple for this business?

In order to determine an appropriate multiple, we considered several sources. The first is our general knowledge of valuation multiples for businesses of this size. The next consideration is that HPT purchased the assets of HPTSI in 1982 for a multiple of cash flow for a single facility at 3.85 times the historical cash flow. Finally, we reviewed transactions from the public domain.

We searched Securities Data Corporation's *Domestic Mergers and Acquisitions Database* for acquisitions of physical therapy centers and similar allied health profession businesses. Our search produced three transactions, which are summarized in Table 22.

TABLE 22

Acquisition Multiples

Target Name	*Acquirer Name*	*Value to Sales*	*Value to Net Income*
Arthritis Trauma Sports	Pacific Rehab & Sports Medicine	2.470	5.682
Professional Sports Care Management	Health South Corp.	2.577	28.516
Total Rehabilitation, Inc.	Horizon Healthcare Corp.	0.694	N/A
Average		1.914	17.099

(Continued)

EXHIBIT 19.1 *(Continued)*

The above transactions indicate that companies that were purchased in the public domain with net income were purchased at wide multiples of net income. However, the value-to-sales multiple for the companies with net income sold at about 2.5 times sales. The third multiple was much lower, but this company did not have net income.

In our opinion, a multiple of five times income before taxes is reasonable for HPT. First, larger companies generally sell at higher multiples than smaller businesses, and the HPT acquisition, at a 3.85 multiple, is a "floor" for the multiple selection. Second, HPT maintains about a 40 percent profit margin, which would result in a multiple of two times sales (.40 × 5 = 2.00), a reasonable estimate when reviewing the first two transactions above.

Additional support for the position that larger businesses sell for larger multiples of earnings can be found in at least the following three sources:

- *Stocks, Bonds, Bills & Inflation*[1]
- *Business Valuation Review*[2]
- The Institute of Business Appraisers, Inc.

According to *Stocks, Bonds, Bills & Inflation*, the annual returns from 1926 to 1996, based on size-decile portfolios of the New York Stock Exchange have been as follows:

Decile	*Arithmetic Mean*
1—largest	11.6%
2	13.5
3	14.1
4	14.8
5	15.6
6	15.6
7	16.1
8	17.3
9	18.0
10—smallest	21.9

Higher rates of return have been available in the marketplace for smaller companies. The data presented above represents companies in the public stock market.

In a series of articles written by Jerry Peters, CPA, CBA, AM, in *Business Valuation Review*, the author analyzes acquisitions of private companies versus public companies, and demonstrates that the price-to-earnings ratio paid is higher for the larger companies.

Further support, more closely related to smaller companies, comes from a market data file maintained by The Institute of Business Appraisers, Inc., a professional business appraisal organization. The Institute of Business Appraisers, Inc., maintains a database of approximately 10,000 transactions involving the sale of closely held companies. Statistical data regarding the price-to-earnings ratios relative to company size appears below.

Range of Company Size ($ Thousands)	*Mean P/E*
0 to 49	1.66
50 to 99	2.11
100 to 149	2.44
150 to 199	2.74
200 to 249	3.06
250 to 499	3.44
500 to 1,000	4.26

[1]Published by Ibbotson Associates, Chicago, Illinois.

[2]A series of articles published by Jerry Peters, CPA, CBA, AM.

EXHIBIT 19.1 (Continued)

Despite proof in the marketplace that HPT could have received a higher multiple, we are only using a multiple of five times the adjusted net income before interest and taxes to perform the damage calculation. Table 23 illustrates this calculation.

TABLE 23

Lost Business Value From New Facilities

1997 Net income before taxes	$ 5,482,176
Multiple	× 5
Damages	**$27,410,880**

Summary of Damages

Several elements of damages were discussed in this report. They are summarized as follows:

Claims unpaid by NCIC and MDA	$ 1,224,459
Lost reinvestment opportunities by HPT	4,102,786
Lost interest	144,618
Lost business value	27,410,880
Expert fees	20,000
Contingent legal fees	13,161,097
Total damages	**$46,063,840**

EXHIBIT 19.2

This case involved a substance abuse clinic that was unable to open due to the difficulties that it had with a municipality. The essence of the damages was that the company incurred expenses to set up this clinic and had to forgo the profits that it would have generated had it opened.

Description of the Assignment

Trugman Valuation Associates Inc. was retained by Nature Home, Inc. (NHI or The Company) to calculate the economic damages that have been incurred as a result of the actions of the defendants in this matter. These damages are calculated as part of the litigation entitled *Nature Home v. Metropolitan Board of Zoning Appeals at Some County, State; Westend Community Organization, Inc.; Health Care Center, Inc.; East Healthcare Center et al.*, filed in the Some County Superior Court sitting at State, Docket No. 12D06-1234-LS-1123.

In order to perform this assignment, numerous documents were reviewed and relied on. These items include the following:

1. Tax returns for an S corporation for several Nature Home, Inc.'s clinics including (years of tax returns in parentheses):
   a. Vermont Substance Abuse Treatment (1989–1997)
   b. Center For Health—PA (1990–1997)
   c. Center For Health—VT (1987–1991, 1993, 1997)
   d. Center For Health—ME (1992–1997)
   e. Center For Health—HA (1993–1997)
   f. Nature Home, Inc.—Bucks County (1995–1997)
   g. Nature Home, Inc.—Burlington, VT (1995–1997)
   h. Nature Home Utah, Inc. (1995–1997)
2. Annual Reports for Nature Home clinics including:
   a. Nature Home Midwest Business Plan, Fourth Quarter 1995
   b. Nature Home, Inc., 1997 Annual Report

(Continued)

EXHIBIT 19.2 *(Continued)*

c. Nature Home—Vermont and Northern Vermont, 1996 Annual Report
d. Nature Home—Bucks County, Lake County, and State, 1996 Annual Report
e. Nature Home—Pittsburgh and Butler, 1996 Annual Report
f. Nature Home—Maine and Utah, 1996 Annual Report
g. Nature Home Inc., 1995 Annual Report
h. Nature Home Inc., 1994 Annual Report

3. A Nature Home general ledger that details the costs incurred for the unopened State clinic.
4. Documentation such as invoices and bills supporting the incurred costs detailed in #3
5. Legal documents pertaining to the case of *Nature Home, Inc. vs. the City of State; and the Metropolitan Board of Zoning Appeals at Some County, State.*
6. Income statements for the following Nature Home, Inc. clinics:

a. Nature Home, PA (for years ended 1995–1998)
b. Nature Home, Butler (for years ended 1995–1998)
c. Nature Home, Inc. (for year ended 1998)
d. Nature Home, Bucks County (for year ended 1998)
e. Vermont Substance Abuse Treatment, Burlington (for years ended 1997–1998)
f. Vermont Substance Abuse Treatment, Wheaton (for years ended 1997–1998)
g. Center For Health, Maine (for year ended 1998)
h. Nature Home, Utah (for year ended 1998)
i. Center For Health, HA (for year ended 1998)
j. Nature Home Central Maine (for year ended 1998)

7. A leasing agreement for the unopened State property.

Damages Calculations

The damages calculated in this report have been adjusted for a present value date of October 31, 1999. The damages sustained by NHI because of the actions of the City of State are as follows:

- Lost profits
- Clinic costs including capital expenditures and operating expenses
- Legal and expert fees
- Statutory interest

Each of these items is explained in the following sections of the report.

Damages From Lost Profits

The calculation of lost profits involves the estimation of the period over which profits have been and will be lost and the amount of profits lost in each period. Based on our discussions with management, a facility is typically open to service patients six months after the signing of a lease and/or three months after U.S. Drug Enforcement Agency (DEA) inspection. NHI signed a lease for the facility in State on November 9, 1995, and had already ascertained that the zoning regulations permitted the establishment of a methadone clinic at the location.

Due to the difficulties that NHI had with the City of State, the DEA did not come in to inspect the facility. According to management, DEA wanted to wait until the community and political issues were resolved. Therefore, since an inspection never occurred, we used the lease signing date as a trigger date for the opening of the clinic. Consequently, we have assumed NHI would have opened on June 1, 1996 (six months after the lease signing, rounded to the beginning of the next month).

The calculation of lost profits is based on the estimation of two factors: expected profits and mitigation of damages. To estimate expected profits, we reviewed the financial information for 12 clinics owned, operated, and/or managed by Dart Management, Inc. (DMI), NHI's management company. The clinics reviewed include:

- Nature Home CBH—Pennsylvania
- Nature Home CBH—Butler, Pennsylvania

EXHIBIT 19.2 *(Continued)*

- VT Substance Abuse Treatment—Burlington, VT
- VT Substance Abuse Treatment—Wheaton, VT
- Nature Home, Inc.—Utah
- Nature Home, Inc.—Bucks County, Pennsylvania
- Center for Health—Harrisburg, Pennsylvania
- Center for Health—Maine
- Nature Home Inc.—Lake County, State
- Center for Health—Vermont
- Center for Health—NPA
- Nature Home—Central Maine

Financial information was compiled through tax returns and internal financial documents provided to us by NHI. We reviewed the financial statements for each clinic since its inception to understand the growth pattern of a typical methadone clinic under management similar to that which State would have had. While we cannot predict the actual growth pattern for NHI, we can estimate the typical growth pattern for clinics under similar management. Tables 1 through 11 present historical income statements for the 11 clinics reviewed by us in order to estimate expected profits. The Nature Home of Central Maine, which opened in August 1998, is not presented due to the fact that it does not have enough history of operations to be meaningful in this analysis.

TABLE 1

Nature Home CBH—PA Income Statement

	1990	*1991*	*1992*	*1993*	*1994*	*1995*	*1996*	*1997*	*1998*
	1	*2*	*3*	*4*	*5*	*6*	*7*	*8*	*9*
Revenues	$213,048	$548,249	$744,130	$825,745	$1,035,102	$1,027,653	$1,135,822	$1,312,382	$1,455,434
Cost of sales	12,133	42,121	67,016	72,151	77,138	72,687	71,854	79,947	95,866
Gross profit	$200,915	$506,128	$677,114	$753,594	$ 957,964	$ 954,966	$1,063,968	$1,232,435	$1,359,568
Operating expenses:									
Salaries & wages	$ 84,113	$154,105	$188,026	$191,246	$ 289,474	$ 230,440	$ 280,882	$ 341,906	$ 381,720
Security	—	1,232	4,100	2,904	1,049	3,045	1,722	7,432	12,322
Payroll taxes	—	—	—	—	—	32,770	43,714	34,395	34,270
Insurance	3,354	6,899	9,575	18,805	28,260	29,226	33,160	41,279	32,853
Medical director fees	—	—	—	57,415	—	55,869	82,392	92,138	96,286
Consultant fees	13,183	53,407	71,113	12,988	8,017	1,040	2,600	827	1,294
Administrative expense	—	—	14,089	9,370	3,291	4,676	9,629	4,676	11,522
Dart management	6,300	16,000	22,000	49,557	62,106	61,648	68,307	78,743	87,327
Rent	24,851	27,566	28,344	26,088	26,647	26,088	28,107	28,759	28,759
Utilities	4,235	6,860	9,569	7,893	8,120	9,153	9,951	9,939	9,682
Telephone	3,920	5,824	—	—	—	9,304	12,747	12,563	11,144
Repairs and maintenance	1,003	1,599	2,537	3,535	3,382	3,271	6,793	4,515	5,399
Software/hardware expense	—	—	—	—	—	2,231	4,458	5,526	3,830
Supplies	8,451	13,827	6,921	7,804	47	9,838	10,902	12,536	10,726
Freight	1,615	3,413	4,817	2,571	9,211	1,067	1,379	1,970	1,881
Postage	—	—	—	—	—	646	1,134	421	701
Credit card charges	—	—	—	—	—	1,848	2,229	2,893	3,927

(Continued)

EXHIBIT 19.2 *(Continued)*

	1990 1	*1991* 2	*1992* 3	*1993* 4	*1994* 5	*1995* 6	*1996* 7	*1997* 8	*1998* 9
Patient refunds	—	—	—	—	—	888	148	544	28
Property & other taxes	12,710	38,160	41,629	35,693	68,305	4,908	3,585	1,969	1,978
Printing costs	1,490	1,883	1,160	351	878	952	2,204	2,960	4,428
Legal & professional fees	4,683	4,935	42,674	20,950	17,548	799	2,512	3,631	7,840
Dues & subscriptions	250	265	—	—	480	511	397	304	883
Education & seminars	—	735	1,683	495	1,261	972	3,272	2,557	2,592
Royalty fees	10,849	26,798	37,346	41,297	51,755	51,373	56,923	65,619	72,773
Accounting/ bookkeeping	—	—	—	—	—	13,530	21,811	21,440	18,265
Auto expense	28	—	—	673	—	282	936	1,257	1,834
Travel & entertainment	3,733	8,747	15,132	4,899	2,581	1,764	8,135	4,254	9,755
Bank service charge	461	720	1,531	971	1,863	326	909	1,083	925
Licenses & fees	—	60	—	—	—	535	335	292	250
Advertising & promotion	1,405	1,041	706	3,166	448	694	2,080	3,802	7,286
Contributions/ donations	—	—	—	—	—	—	100	—	500
Janitorial services	664	2,511	5,679	5,769	6,086	6,858	9,139	10,438	10,917
Depreciation expense	1,392	6,561	19,434	19,433	12,798	8,940	23,296	15,944	2,287
Bad debts expense	955	10,532	16,483	8,006	8,826	20,233	33,551	33,408	43,969
Interest expense	1,481	1,410	1,003	953	340	330	239	—	431
Equipment rental	—	—	1,751	994	1,528	4,861	1,719	—	—
Penalties/late charges	—	—	—	—	—	—	—	18	—
Vacation/sick pay expense	—	—	—	—	—	19,129	28,123	—	—
Employee benefits	—	11,106	8,481	—	—	1,085	1,727	—	—
Miscellaneous	143	109	914	733	8,092	—	—	—	—
Communications	—	—	7,139	8,267	9,296	—	—	—	—
Subcontractor	—	1,773	—	—	—	—	—	—	—
Total operating expenses	$191,269	$408,078	$563,836	$542,826	$ 631,689	$ 621,129	$ 801,244	$ 850,039	$ 920,581
Net income from operations	$ 9,646	$ 98,050	$113,278	$210,768	$ 326,275	$ 333,838	$ 262,724	$ 382,397	$ 438,987
Other income/expenses	475	270	—	—	20,032	(56,935)	(46,617)	(61,181)	(26,236)
Earnings before income tax	$ 10,121	$ 98,320	$113,278	$210,768	$ 346,307	$ 276,903	$ 216,107	$ 321,216	$ 412,752

TABLE 2

Nature Home CBH—Butler Income Statement

	1995 1	*1996* 2	*1997* 3	*1998* 4
Revenues	$ 168,423	$ 378,125	$ 484,741	$ 466,633
Cost of sales	10,816	26,896	34,543	29,692
Gross profit	$ 157,607	$ 351,229	$ 450,197	$ 436,941

EXHIBIT 19.2 ***(Continued)***

	1995 1	1996 2	1997 3	1998 4
Operating expenses:				
Salaries & wages	$ 37,310	$ 100,658	$ 148,268	$ 129,604
Security	335	90	469	985
Payroll taxes	—	—	17,634	17,459
Insurance	—	12	1,899	16,493
Medical director fees	3,306	27,182	63,111	33,736
Consultant fees	—	—	253	225
Administrative expense	548	130	855	3,286
Dart management	16,964	37,813	48,474	46,664
Rent	14,675	14,625	14,625	14,625
Utilities	797	1,339	1,488	1,360
Telephone	3,562	4,828	6,466	7,494
Repairs and maintenance	1,098	391	366	227
Software/hardware expense	38	2,292	2,827	3,057
Supplies	771	1,771	2,113	3,938
Freight	234	822	717	926
Postage	195	137	189	746
Credit card charges	8	—	245	2,383
Patient refunds	290	40	59	—
Property & other taxes	—	47	—	—
Printing costs	726	460	635	1,723
Legal & professional fees	—	416	3,093	7,498
Dues & subscriptions	—	—	222	303
Education & seminars	26	1,165	1,781	3,317
Royalty fees	8,482	18,906	24,233	23,332
Accounting/bookkeeping	329	248	—	8,180
Auto expense	2,933	1,549	657	940
Travel & entertainment	766	1,775	1,009	1,871
Licenses & fees	70	—	170	150
Advertising & promotion	200	416	1,323	1,589
Contributions/donations	—	100	—	525
Janitorial services	60	543	1,843	2,235
Depreciation expense	—	—	—	2,837
Bad debts expense	1,910	10,713	13,312	9,773
Equipment rental	—	501	1,371	1,312
Total operating expenses	$ 95,633	$ 228,968	$ 359,707	$ 348,792
Net income from operations	$ 61,974	$ 122,261	$ 90,490	$ 88,149
Other income/expenses	—	—	—	—
Earnings before income tax	$ 61,974	$ 122,261	$ 90,490	$ 88,149

(Continued)

EXHIBIT 19.2 (Continued)

TABLE 3

VT Substance Abuse Treatment—Burlington Income Statement

	1989 1	*1990* 2	*1991* 3	*1992* 4	*1993* 5	*1994* 6	*1995* 7	*1996* 8	*1997* 9	*1998* 10
Revenues	$ 129,514	$ 393,261	$ 624,909	$ 798,533	$ 956,442	$ 918,795	$ 990,335	$ 1,057,991	$ 1,294,308	$ 1,429,228
Cost of sales	57,544	280,779	57,329	104,406	99,517	102,069	86,120	71,918	81,719	76,056
Gross profit	$ 71,970	$ 112,482	$ 567,580	$ 694,127	$ 856,925	$ 816,726	$ 904,215	$ 986,073	$ 1,212,589	$ 1,353,172
Operating expenses:										
Salaries & wages	$ 9,861	$ 105,875	$ 155,868	$ 171,358	$ 226,711	$ 232,237	$ 299,516	$ 330,724	$ 358,315	$ 425,756
Security	1,316	21,989	18,013	25,746	24,237	2,637	2,077	26,765	24,556	24,822
Payroll taxes	5,031	—	24,956	—	—	—	—	37,700	43,923	50,205
Insurance	4,251	4,303	5,505	11,682	15,987	25,986	27,595	34,676	37,617	46,263
Medical director fees	—	10,057	20,500	32,965	33,608	38,970	34,463	52,104	75,112	79,883
Consultant fees	8,949	6,900	23,522	50,957	65,179	—	9,991	67,660	172,034	11,815
Administrative expense	—	—	—	5,036	24,028	4,667	5,977	5,796	4,584	12,451
Management expense	—	—	—	—	—	58,480	61,113	—	88,662	85,754
Rent	10,900	21,900	21,600	23,700	27,300	28,800	44,200	53,846	38,919	42,059
Utilities	200	2,432	600	500	600	600	2,156	7,683	8,459	6,992
Telephone	2,003	—	6,883	—	—	—	—	8,808	9,688	10,296
Repairs and maintenance	1,752	808	2,230	7,479	10,536	8,009	9,129	24,736	5,536	13,032
Software/hardware	—	—	—	—	—	—	—	—	3,324	5,274
Supplies	3,519	4,895	10,589	8,182	4,290	3,955	7,284	7,507	10,601	10,453
Freight	—	183	541	—	306	282	681	740	1,065	1,893
Postage	352	—	—	—	—	—	—	—	—	—
Credit card charges	—	—	—	—	—	—	—	626	362	812
Patient refunds	—	—	—	—	—	—	—	490	1,867	718
Property & other taxes	—	18,263	701	19,987	30,716	31,827	43,603	8,361	15,176	8,385
Printing costs	—	1,537	1,247	3,995	3,295	2,385	2,107	2,287	4,241	7,850
Legal & professional fees	7,246	15,069	24,491	50,276	23,854	23,501	28,464	17,613	7,817	8,223
Dues & subscriptions	100	50	72	—	—	1,389	1,078	7,287	3,468	1,452
Education & seminars	—	224	1,180	—	—	988	513	2,806	493	3,513

EXHIBIT 19.2 (Continued)

	1989 1	1990 2	1991 3	1992 4	1993 5	1994 6	1995 7	1996 8	1997 9	1998 10
Royalty fees	—	19,836	31,295	40,064	47,830	48,735	50,927	53,225	64,715	71,461
Accounting/bookkeeping	—	—	—	—	—	—	—	19,135	19,446	20,692
Auto expense	—	—	—	—	—	—	—	174	314	329
Travel & entertainment	67	70	887	639	724	935	1,186	258	469	3,864
Bank service charge	138	214	259	—	333	587	607	237	494	167
Licenses & fees	—	70	70	—	—	—	—	1,805	791	234
Advertising & promotion	591	1,021	1,607	4,150	4,252	5,450	4,543	5,777	6,647	20,179
Contributions/donations	—	—	—	—	—	—	—	—	—	2,168
Janitorial services	—	4,148	5,108	7,760	7,929	8,461	11,727	9,659	9,498	12,387
Depreciation expense	3,528	12,852	12,690	23,824	25,488	17,923	38,897	12,971	28,367	26,470
Bad debts expense	615	9,770	2,937	16,038	20,762	16,986	13,028	36,746	33,419	26,094
Interest expense	2,639	3,942	3,632	382	34	114	3,860	9,223	26,356	19,046
Equipment rental	144	3,460	1,560	—	—	879	5,114	10	553	2,756
Contract labor	—	—	—	—	6,521	23,690	47,511	10,704	10,426	406
Penalties/late charges	—	—	—	—	—	—	—	—	684	—
Miscellaneous	88	—	88	1,808	3,878	905	28,064	3,237	—	—
Communications	—	—	—	7,728	6,034	6,654	6,598	—	—	—
Employee benefits	—	—	—	—	1,181	4,002	1,424	—	—	—
Total operating expenses	63,290	269,868	378,631	514,256	615,613	600,034	793,433	861,376	1,117,999	1,064,154
Net income from operations	$ 8,680	$ (157,386)	$ 188,949	$ 179,871	$ 241,312	$ 216,692	$ 110,782	$ 124,697	$ 94,590	$ 289,018
Other income/expenses	—	1,199	742	—	—	—	29,459	10,243	754	1,286
Earnings before income tax	$ 8,680	$ (156,187)	$ 189,691	$ 179,871	$ 241,312	$ 216,692	$ 140,241	$ 134,940	$ 95,344	$ 290,304

(Continued)

EXHIBIT 19.2 *(Continued)*

TABLE 4

VT Substance Abuse Treatment—Wheaton
Income Statement

	1997	*1998*
	1	*2*
Revenues	$ 137,529	$ 234,027
Cost of sales	9,480	14,672
Gross profit	$ 128,049	$ 219,355
Operating expenses:		
Salaries & wages	$ 61,052	$ 88,432
Security	3,514	3,524
Payroll taxes	8,221	11,326
Insurance	—	4,931
Medical director fees	9,371	15,740
Consultant fees	8,694	1,776
Administrative expense	3,959	3,579
Management expense	13,277	14,042
Rent	15,877	16,232
Utilities	4,373	3,470
Telephone	4,423	5,527
Repairs and maintenance	145	387
Software/hardware expense	2,511	4,535
Supplies	1,357	3,406
Freight	23	76
Property & other taxes	—	345
Printing costs	793	1,207
Legal & professional fees	—	2,609
Dues & subscriptions	1,534	2,416
Education & seminars	157	940
Royalty fees	6,876	11,701
Accounting/bookkeeping	5,040	7,183
Auto expense	312	282
Travel & entertainment	197	1,391
Licenses & fees	145	120
Advertising & promotion	1,094	3,213
Contributions/donations	—	500
Janitorial services	1,442	1,277
Depreciation expense	—	4,872
Bad debts expense	5,208	12,070
Equipment rental	906	867
Contract labor	2,707	39
Penalties/late charges	—	—
Total operating expenses	$ 163,208	$ 228,015
Net income from operations	$ (35,160)	$ (8,660)
Other income/expenses	—	—
Earnings before income tax	$ (35,160)	$ (8,660)

EXHIBIT 19.2 *(Continued)*

TABLE 5

Nature Home, Inc.—Utah Income Statement

	1995 1	1996 2	1997 3	1998 4
Revenues	$ 12,130	$ 196,565	$ 308,454	$ 269,086
Cost of sales	1,171	21,309	25,735	20,820
Gross profit	$ 10,959	$ 175,256	$ 282,719	$ 248,266
Operating expenses:				
Salaries & wages	$ 9,787	$ 93,969	$ 111,174	$ 113,450
Security	149	265	602	889
Payroll taxes	—	7,991	10,587	9,153
Insurance	1,655	7,388	10,894	11,212
Medical director fees	4,726	26,836	26,497	23,315
Consultant fees	1,006	4,468	2,407	16,725
Administrative expense	—	—	—	590
Management expense	—	—	25,000	—
Rent	10,048	15,072	15,313	15,485
Utilities	—	—	—	—
Telephone	—	8,092	5,341	7,334
Repairs and maintenance	—	489	475	1,884
Software/hardware expense	—	171	—	3,734
Supplies	1,937	3,972	2,750	4,373
Freight	1,312	1,318	1,208	871
Postage	—	173	198	263
Credit card charges	—	—	697	2,415
Patient refunds	—	56	569	1,050
Property & other taxes	1,458	498	2,407	241
Printing costs	719	1,574	1,771	1,501
Legal & professional fees	5,659	3,141	355	733
Dues & subscriptions	38	195	395	507
Education & seminars	—	746	144	712
Royalty fees	—	—	—	3,523
Accounting/bookkeeping	—	1,300	1,324	939
Auto expense	—	611	643	3,718
Travel & entertainment	11,009	5,597	7,766	18,996
Bank service charge	34	138	390	203
Licenses & fees	—	484	452	400
Advertising & promotion	3,796	3,271	6,891	5,705
Contributions/donations	—	—	—	100
Janitorial services	—	—	—	47
Depreciation expense	2,759	5,073	3,915	3,262
Bad debts expense	12	24,015	15,698	15,990
Interest expense	87	5,026	235	98
Equipment rental	—	221	862	1,123

(Continued)

EXHIBIT 19.2 *(Continued)*

	1995	*1996*	*1997*	*1998*
	1	*2*	*3*	*4*
Contract labor	274	3,530	190	3,537
Penalties/late charges	—	—	—	—
Communications	1,654	—	—	—
Total operating expenses	$ 58,119	$225,680	$ 257,150	$274,076
Net income from operations	$ (47,160)	$ (50,424)	$ 25,569	$ (25,811)
Other income/expenses	—	11	21	27
Earnings before income tax	$ (47,160)	$ (50,413)	$ 25,590	$ (25,784)

TABLE 6

Nature Home, Inc.—Bucks County
Income Statement

	1995	*1996*	*1997*	*1998*
	1	*2*	*3*	*4*
Revenues	$ 6,403	$ 72,142	$ 241,163	$ 337,960
Cost of sales	661	7,361	17,057	16,347
Gross profit	$ 5,742	$ 64,781	$ 224,106	$ 321,613
Operating expenses:				
Salaries & wages	$ 14,132	$ 62,270	$ 96,918	$ 146,254
Security	—	545	793	450
Payroll taxes	—	5,960	8,410	(7,798)
Insurance	942	4,502	5,532	10,950
Medical director fees	1,900	17,625	37,060	40,688
Consultant fees	—	—	—	7,000
Administrative expense	15,888	—	—	—
Management expense	—	—	—	—
Rent	8,925	13,000	13,900	14,260
Utilities	647	3,019	3,266	4,067
Telephone	—	5,430	8,393	8,439
Repairs and maintenance	1,928	2,234	2,223	2,796
Software/hardware expense	—	—	—	2,868
Supplies	2,101	3,134	3,828	6,274
Freight	1,023	—	—	382
Postage	—	1,046	905	478
Credit card charges	—	—	—	—
Patient refunds	—	—	1,675	418
Property & other taxes	1,647	600	1,266	322
Printing costs	1,329	542	950	879
Legal & professional fees	4,691	715	926	3,137
Dues & subscriptions	350	341	288	372
Education & seminars	290	128	288	1,391
Royalty fees	—	—	—	3,085
Accounting/bookkeeping	—	2,575	1,272	1,997
Auto expense	—	4,503	5,091	6,928

EXHIBIT 19.2 *(Continued)*

	1995 1	1996 2	1997 3	1998 4
Travel & entertainment	9,864	5,359	7,125	12,703
Bank service charge	81	1,012	766	502
Licenses & fees	—	599	154	199
Advertising & promotion	14,085	2,796	3,150	10,272
Contributions/donations	—	—	—	100
Janitorial services	317	1,105	1,381	980
Depreciation expense	1,559	8,392	11,802	8,136
Bad debts expense	161	4,185	5,628	6,557
Interest expense	34	141	154	79
Equipment rental	—	—	159	1,094
Contract labor	658	731	202	—
Penalties/late charges	—	—	—	—
Miscellaneous expense	101	222	45	—
Communication	2,555	—	—	—
Total operating expenses	$ 85,208	$ 152,711	$ 223,550	$ 296,258
Net income from operations	$ (79,466)	$ (87,930)	$ 556	$ 25,355
Other income/expenses	—	—	82	104
Earnings before income tax	$ (79,466)	$ (87,930)	$ 638	$ 25,459

TABLE 7

Center for Health—HA Income Statement

	1993 1	1994 2	1995 3	1996 4	1997 5	1998 6
Revenues	$ 75,407	$ 189,712	$ 224,794	$ 309,657	$ 489,186	$ 476,131
Cost of sales	8,458	14,049	22,139	22,679	31,975	28,545
Gross profit	$ 66,949	$ 175,663	$ 202,655	$ 286,978	$ 457,211	$ 447,586
Operating expenses:						
Salaries & wages	$ 26,147	$ 79,639	$ 85,451	$ 112,613	$ 182,741	$ 163,630
Security	—	184	216	280	3,249	3,818
Payroll taxes	—	—	—	10,291	14,863	16,583
Insurance	5,660	5,375	6,608	8,538	10,889	7,231
Medical director fees	6,888	10,960	15,228	35,081	47,465	38,738
Consultant fees	—	10,241	22,479	31,278	100	47,882
Administrative expense	6,439	1,703	2,083	—	5,512	10,249
Management expense	—	—	1,541	—	39,639	—
Rent	14,384	11,400	11,919	14,382	27,193	18,256
Utilities	20	—	—	—	643	—
Telephone	4,680	5,654	4,615	9,297	15,633	16,175
Repairs and maintenance	360	121	—	2,575	3,518	2,699
Software/hardware expense	769	—	—	—	2,613	4,396

(Continued)

EXHIBIT 19.2 *(Continued)*

	1993	*1994*	*1995*	*1996*	*1997*	*1998*
	1	*2*	*3*	*4*	*5*	*6*
Supplies	1,391	2,517	2,760	10,328	9,498	7,823
Freight	655	1,349	2,476	2,413	3,033	1,384
Postage	—	—	—	—	—	—
Credit card charges	—	—	—	—	—	—
Patient refunds	—	—	—	—	731	351
Property & other taxes	4,748	9,359	8,705	2,455	1,322	61
Printing costs	1,582	1,101	837	1,341	2,581	2,406
Legal & professional fees	—	—	250	1,812	9,227	4,046
Dues & subscriptions	—	115	208	455	853	409
Education & seminars	295	958	429	925	573	420
Royalty fees	—	—	—	—	—	23,807
Accounting/bookkeeping	7,694	7,998	7,074	13,627	8,839	15,371
Auto expense	599	279	—	1,007	4,300	1,630
Travel & entertainment	5,208	2,520	2,206	4,323	3,168	7,127
Bank service charge	786	565	61	206	591	186
Licenses & fees	192	—	—	380	780	220
Advertising & promotion	14,001	1,154	677	2,225	4,829	6,628
Contributions/donations	—	—	—	—	—	100
Janitorial services	—	—	35	76	503	22
Depreciation expense	3,013	4,064	4,955	5,278	8,747	3,564
Bad debts expense	1,808	5,585	5,146	5,077	3,291	8,706
Interest expense	—	—	160	236	328	1,547
Equipment rental	—	5,172	8,031	8,031	4,773	2,465
Contract labor	—	899	—	1,648	3,376	9,197
Penalties/late charges	—	—	—	—	—	—
Miscellaneous	—	—	335	123	5	22,942
Employee benefits	—	—	125	—	—	—
Total operating expenses	$ 107,319	$ 168,912	$ 194,610	$ 286,301	$ 425,406	$ 450,067
Net income from operations	$ (40,370)	$ 6,751	$ 8,045	$ 677	$ 31,805	$ (2,482)
Other income/expenses	—	636	—	615	170	—
Earnings before income tax	$ (40,370)	$ 7,387	$ 8,045	$ 1,292	$ 31,975	$ (2,482)

TABLE 8

Center for Health—ME
Income Statement

	1994	*1995*	*1996*	*1997*	*1998*
	1	*2*	*3*	*4*	*5*
Revenues	$70,276	$260,985	$737,447	$917,219	$1,099,345
Cost of sales	$ 8,124	$ 19,341	$ 52,265	$ 64,238	$ 69,410
Gross profit	$62,152	$241,644	$685,182	$852,981	$1,029,936
Operating expenses:					
Salaries & wages	$ 24,983	$ 89,817	$190,167	$ 239,568	$ 249,556
Security	1,117	304	569	1,756	15,300

EXHIBIT 19.2 *(Continued)*

	1994 1	1995 2	1996 3	1997 4	1998 5
Payroll taxes	—	—	19,978	24,768	25,889
Insurance	1,952	5,450	11,752	14,088	35,930
Medical director fees	10,400	24,960	20,280	26,921	49,966
Consultant fees	870	3,050	13,115	6,020	125,607
Administrative expense	445	7,010	—	4,201	10,770
Management expense	—	26,098	81,700	91,722	—
Rent	—	20,400	31,500	28,800	32,400
Utilities	—	—	—	4,193	4,434
Telephone	4,236	6,323	9,271	10,906	11,670
Repairs and maintenance	1,257	261	12,155	5,053	11,575
Software/hardware expense	—	—	—	2,556	—
Supplies	47	4,174	12,658	5,430	6,283
Freight	475	840	—	—	—
Postage	—	—	1,387	1,288	1,961
Credit card charges	—	—	—	—	—
Patient refunds	—	—	—	12,868	364
Property & other taxes	3,699	10,231	256	3,036	3,483
Printing costs	1,398	1,245	2,197	2,151	3,658
Legal & professional fees	12,513	30,290	37,732	37,027	11,809
Dues & subscriptions	613	52	1,105	70	441
Education & seminars	584	454	1,917	529	1,401
Royalty fees	—	—	53,721	45,861	54,967
Accounting/bookkeeping	2,399	8,273	14,642	12,988	16,118
Auto expense	1,074	683	4,011	4,933	999
Travel & entertainment	4,021	2,463	1,835	2,930	2,737
Bank service charge	70	178	172	220	212
Licenses & fees	—	—	1,279	1,240	1,069
Advertising & promotion	7,095	1,971	2,137	2,431	9,844
Contributions/donations	—	—	—	—	200
Janitorial services	—	1,480	3,038	13,678	13,854
Depreciation expense	9,428	10,279	10,288	10,267	6,187
Bad debts expense	709	15,739	21,886	12,155	8,447
Interest expense	53	119	1,040	92	868
Equipment rental	61	12,128	11,418	12,191	1,238
Contract labor	973	1,370	15,259	11,077	2,795
Penalties/late charges	—	—	—	—	—
Consolidated expense	—	—	—	—	39,910
Miscellaneous	—	96	201	240	—
Total operating expenses	$ 90,472	$ 285,738	$ 588,666	$ 653,254	$ 761,942
Net income from operations	$ (28,320)	$ (44,094)	$ 96,516	$ (199,727)	$ 267,994
Other income/expenses	—	85	416	75	645
Earnings before income tax	$ (28,320)	$ (44,009)	$ 96,932	$ (199,802)	$ 268,639

(Continued)

EXHIBIT 19.2 *(Continued)*

TABLE 9

Nature Home Inc.—Lake County
Income Statement

	1996	*1997*	*1998*
	1	*2*	*3*
Revenues	$ 18,396	$ 170,026	$ 177,881
Cost of sales	3,359	14,607	14,082
Gross profit	$ 15,037	$ 155,419	$ 163,800
Operating expenses:			
Salaries & wages	$ 35,331	$ 83,871	$ 89,657
Security	1,722	1,195	840
Payroll taxes	2,844	8,861	8,616
Insurance	2,404	4,555	4,936
Medical director fees	4,600	15,750	15,664
Consultant fees	—	29	6,090
Administrative expense	—	—	85
Dart management	—	—	—
Rent	28,805	22,112	11,885
Utilities	2,398	3,915	2,801
Telephone	6,564	9,681	5,481
Repairs and maintenance	3,491	1,939	596
Software/hardware expense	—	617	3,589
Supplies	3,260	5,617	3,834
Freight	—	—	811
Postage	1,391	1,578	354
Credit card charges	—	—	—
Patient refunds	—	29	65
Property & other taxes	—	427	154
Printing costs	1,302	1,131	1,247
Legal & professional fees	8,852	10,254	28,733
Dues & subscriptions	31	32	44
Education & seminars	624	257	1,157
Royalty fees	—	—	2,373
Accounting/bookkeeping	1,300	1,220	1,334
Auto expense	2,011	3,705	623
Travel & entertainment	4,279	13,984	3,745
Bank service charge	610	1,248	57
Licenses & fees	47	259	160
Advertising & promotion	4,474	3,829	3,681
Contributions/donations	—	—	100
Janitorial services	464	1,045	2,804
Depreciation expense	3,426	5,244	3,910
Bad debts expense	7,441	10,712	10,068
Interest expense	562	173	77

EXHIBIT 19.2 (Continued)

	1996 1	1997 2	1998 3
Equipment expense	—	—	—
Penalties/late charges	—	—	—
Vacation/sick pay expense	—	—	—
Employee benefits	—	—	—
Contract labor	1,343	4,134	75
Total operating expenses	$ 129,576	$217,403	$215,646
Net income from operations	$(114,539)	$ (61,984)	$ (51,846)
Other income/expenses	—	11	371
Earnings before income tax	$(114,539)	$ (61,973)	$ (51,476)

TABLE 10

Center for Health—VT
Income Statement

	1987 1	1988 2	1989 3	1990 4	1991 5
Revenues	$ 489,705	$ 906,476	$ 943,254	$ 723,465	$ 730,471
Cost of sales	—	73,123	138,780	316,770	62,794
Gross profit	$ 489,705	$ 833,353	$ 804,474	$ 406,695	$ 667,677
Operating expenses:					
Salaries & wages	$ 104,461	$ 263,049	$ 278,412	$ —	$ 161,675
Security	7,316	24,545	29,273	19,376	16,999
Payroll taxes	—	—	29,737	—	19,930
Insurance	582	23,644	31,902	7,809	13,668
Medical director fees	14,709	—	—	—	—
Medical supplies	21,929	—	—	—	—
Consultant fees	14,653	40,892	500	—	—
Compensation of officers	36,815	26,742	—	—	—
Management fees	—	19,985	—	34,433	43,266
Rent	16,312	29,422	22,788	19,460	25,800
Utilities	—	—	890	4,112	10,813
Telephone	8,574	9,126	9,906	5,872	—
Repairs and maintenance	—	4,370	573	1,512	3,862
Software/hardware expense	—	684	4,830	4,719	—
Supplies	12,177	15,383	8,278	8,548	12,008
Freight	—	—	—	1,346	2,103
Postage	—	—	2,523	—	—
Property & other taxes	17,959	32,146	665	—	3,298
Printing costs	—	—	857	1,486	—
Legal & professional fees	9,550	17,865	32,107	23,782	46,783
Dues & subscriptions	2,312	2,632	1,767	2,940	—

(Continued)

EXHIBIT 19.2 *(Continued)*

	1987 *1*	*1988* *2*	*1989* *3*	*1990* *4*	*1991* *5*
Education & seminars	339	4,724	1,455	25	1,252
Accounting/bookkeeping	—	—	1,409	—	—
Auto expense	—	—	—	7,299	7,467
Travel & entertainment	5,159	7,758	3,036	1,999	1,700
Bank service charge	—	256	268	212	215
Licenses & fees	1,258	185	883	809	—
Advertising & promotion	994	15,663	6,521	2,428	1,338
Janitorial services	—	—	4,619	4,429	9,375
Depreciation expense	23,343	25,238	61,368	27,791	30,717
Bad debts expense	—	15,692	20,936	33,872	3,796
Interest expense	—	—	15,014	7,441	270
Equipment rental	697	1,706	1,697	4,110	—
Penalties/late charges	—	351	—	—	—
Employee benefits	4,698	—	—	—	—
Miscellaneous	750	6,177	5,123	—	451
Bonus	3,450	200	—	—	—
Communications	—	—	—	—	—
Subcontractor	—	16,346	33,653	—	—
Lab fees	23,861	—	—	—	—
Total operating expenses	$ 331,898	$ 604,781	$ 610,990	$ 225,810	$ 416,786
Net income from operations	$ 157,807	$ 228,572	$ 193,484	$ 180,885	$ 250,891
Other income/expenses	2,079	894	8,421	3,309	2,802
Earnings before income tax	$ 159,886	$ 229,466	$ 201,905	$ 184,194	$ 253,693

TABLE 11

Center for Health—NPA
Income Statement

	1998 *1*
Revenues	$ 392,924
Cost of sales	25,422
Gross profit	$ 367,502
Operating expenses:	
Salaries & wages	$ 133,912
Security	437
Payroll taxes	8,151
Insurance	7,795
Medical director fees	33,301
Consultant fees	39,483
Administrative expense	5,880
Rent	19,980
Telephone	7,674

EXHIBIT 19.2 (Continued)

	1998
	1
Utilities	1,507
Repairs and maintenance	6,031
Software/hardware expense	3,162
Supplies	7,658
Freight	2,203
Patient refunds	65
Property & other taxes	200
Printing costs	1,942
Legal & professional fees	318
Dues & subscriptions	314
Education & seminars	1,255
Royalty fees	19,632
Accounting/bookkeeping	8,859
Auto expense	7,626
Travel & entertainment	8,605
Bank service charge	16
Licenses & fees	93
Advertising & promotion	3,153
Contributions/donations	100
Janitorial services	4,838
Bad debts expense	17,926
Interest expense	36
Equipment rental	716
Contract labor	398
Total operating expenses	$ 353,264
Net income from operations	$ 14,239
Other income/expenses	—
Earnings before income tax	$ 14,239

Each of these clinics was discussed with management to determine its applicability to this analysis. We excluded several clinics from this analysis based on factors that make them markedly different from the clinic planned for State. The clinics excluded, and the reasons for each, are as follows:

- Nature Home—Bucks County. This clinic is located in Pennsylvania. The state has the ability to strictly regulate methadone clinics. In the case of Bucks County, the state limited the facility's capacity to 35 patients and subsequently raised it to 105. This limitation is not consistent with the planned State clinic and most of the other clinics. We excluded Bucks County because it distorts the growth pattern of a clinic free of severe operating restrictions. Even at 105 patients, it has 50 to 100 fewer patients than many of the operating capacities of other Dart Management clinics.
- Center for Health—Harrisburg. This clinic is also located in Pennsylvania and has had operating restrictions imposed on it by the state. Although the initial location of the clinic was determined to be poor, we eliminated the clinic due to the state-imposed restrictions.

(Continued)

EXHIBIT 19.2 *(Continued)*

- Nature Home, Inc. This entity operated a clinic in Lake County, State, similar to the location (state) of the clinic that is the subject of this analysis. However, DMI designed the Lake County facility to be a feeder clinic, designed to enhance the performance of State. As a result of the State clinic not opening, Lake County has suffered significantly. Therefore, we excluded Lake County, and thus Nature Home, Inc., from our analysis.
- Nature Home—Utah. This clinic does not have a long enough history of operations to be meaningful in this analysis.

After eliminating these locations from our analysis, we then compared the remaining seven clinics by year of operations (i.e., first year, second year, etc., as opposed to calendar year, 1995, 1996, etc.). This information was used to create an average income statement for each of the first four years of operations. The result is a four-year profile of an "average" clinic.

Before we could utilize this data to analyze the expected profits from NHI, several adjustments were necessary. The first set of adjustments deals with creating the average for the first year of operations. As will be shown in Table 15, we annualized the clinics' income statements so that each represented 12 months of operations. This was necessary because the clinics opened at different times during the year. However, this procedure could not be performed on Nature Home—NPA and Nature Home—Maine because they were only open for less than three and four months, respectively. These short periods do not allow annualization to be meaningful. For these clinics, we used their second fiscal year in our first-year calculations. This gave us a much more meaningful presentation of how the clinics progressed and did not detract from the analysis of startup. This is especially true in the case of Nature Home—Maine, as the startup costs were minimal because the clinic initially used staff from another Dart Management clinic, thereby minimizing startup costs.

The second set of adjustments pertains to expenses that we can calculate directly for State. These expenses are management fees, depreciation, consulting fees, rent, royalties, medical director's fees, and interest expense. We removed these expenses from the four-year profile of a typical clinic.

We elected to end our analysis after four years of operations for two reasons. First, our sample of clinics included only three that had been in operation for five years (there were five in the fourth year). Data becomes less reliable as the sample size decreases. Second, after its third year of operations, Nature Home—Vermont experienced a decrease in revenues as the result of competition from another Dart Management clinic. While this affected the fourth year of operations, it did not have as much effect on the fourth year average, because there were five clinics in the fourth year sample. Taking these two factors in combination, we did not have enough data to create a meaningful fifth year average. Instead, we assumed that the fourth year represented stability for the average clinic and continued our projections thereafter based on a long-term rate of growth. We believe that this assumption is reasonable in light of the fifth year of operations projection that DMI developed and presented in the Nature Home—Midwest offering document. The result of this projection for year 5 is very similar to what we have developed for year 4.

The clinics in the sample are of various sizes. To simply average their revenues and ascribe this to State would be improper. To make the data usable we performed two additional analyses. The first was to create common-size income statements from the four-year profile to make the cost of sales and expenses a percentage of revenues. This allowed us to scale the profile to the size of the planned State clinic. The second analysis was to estimate revenues for each clinic as a percentage of maximum capacity revenues. Maximum capacity revenues can be defined as the maximum annual revenue a clinic can achieve based on its clinic capacity to treat clients. Comparing average clinic capacity for each profile year to the maximum average clinic capacity resulted in the average capacity utilization for the "typical" clinic. This allowed us to determine how a clinic develops, regardless of actual size. The following presents our forecast income statements for an average clinic, including common size, by year of operation.

TABLE 12

Nature Home First Year of Company Operations Income Statement

	Nature Home—PA	*CBH—Butler*	*VTSAT Burlington*	*VTSAT—Wheaton*	*CBH—Maine*	*CBH—NPA*	*CBH—Vermont*	*Average*
Revenues	$ 213,048	$ 168,423	$ 129,514	$ 137,529	$ 260,985	$ 392,924	$ 489,705	$ 256,018
Cost of sales	12,133	10,816	57,544	9,480	19,341	25,422	—	19,248
Gross profit	$ 200,915	$ 157,607	$ 71,970	$ 128,049	$ 241,644	$ 367,502	$ 489,705	$ 236,770
Total operating expenses	191,269	95,633	63,290	163,208	285,738	353,264	331,898	212,043
Net income from operations	$ 9,646	$ 61,974	$ 8,680	$ (35,160)	$ (44,094)	$ 14,239	$ 157,807	$ 24,727
Other income/expenses	475	—	—	—	85	—	2,079	377
Pretax income	$ 10,121	$ 61,974	$ 8,680	$ (35,160)	$ (44,009)	$ 14,239	$ 159,886	$ 25,104

EXHIBIT 19.2 (Continued)

	Nature Home—PA	CBH—Butler	VTSAT Burlington	VTSAT—Wheaton	CBH—Maine	CBH—NPA	CBH—Vermont	Average
Addbacks								
Management fees	$ 6,300	$ 16,964	$ —	$ 13,277	$ 26,098	$ —	$ —	$ 8,948
Depreciation	1,392	—	3,528	—	10,279	—	23,343	5,506
Consulting fees	13,183	—	8,949	8,694	3,050	39,483	14,653	12,573
Rent	24,851	14,675	10,900	15,877	20,400	33,301	16,312	19,474
Royalties	10,849	8,482	—	6,876	—	19,980	—	6,598
Medical director's fees	—	3,306	—	9,371	24,960	19,632	14,709	10,283
Interest expense	1,481	—	2,639	—	119	36	—	611
Other income/expense	(475)	—	—	—	(85)	—	(2,079)	(377)
Total addback expenses	$ 57,581	$ 43,427	$ 26,016	$ 54,095	$ 84,821	$ 112,432	$ 66,938	$ 63,616
Adjusted pretax income	$ 67,702	$ 105,401	$ 34,696	$ 18,935	$ 40,812	$ 126,670	$ 226,824	$ 88,720

TABLE 13

Nature Home
First Year of Company Operations
Common-Size Income Statement

	Nature Home—PA	CBH—Butler	VTSAT—Burlington	VTSAT—Wheaton	CBH—Maine	CBH—NPA	CBH—Vermont	Average
Revenues	100.00%	100.00%	100.00%	100.00%	100.00%	100.00%	100.00%	100.00%
Cost of sales	5.69%	6.42%	44.43%	6.89%	7.41%	6.47%	0.00%	7.52%
Gross profit	94.31%	93.58%	55.57%	93.11%	92.59%	93.53%	100.00%	92.48%
Total operating expenses	89.78%	56.78%	48.87%	118.67%	109.48%	89.91%	67.78%	82.82%
Net income from operations	4.53%	36.80%	6.70%	−25.57%	−16.90%	3.62%	32.22%	9.66%
Other income/expenses	0.22%	0.00%	0.00%	0.00%	0.03%	0.00%	0.42%	0.15%
Pretax income	4.75%	36.80%	6.70%	−25.57%	−16.86%	3.62%	32.65%	9.81%
Total expense addbacks	27.03%	25.78%	20.09%	39.33%	32.50%	28.61%	13.67%	24.85%
Adjusted pretax income	31.78%	62.58%	26.79%	13.77%	15.64%	32.24%	46.32%	34.65%

TABLE 14

Nature Home
First Year of Company Operations
Number of Visits and Capacity Utilization

	Nature Home—PA	CBH—Butler	VTSAT—Burlington	VTSAT—Wheaton	CBH—Maine	CBH—NPA	CBH—Vermont	Average
Revenues	$ 213,048	$ 168,423	$ 129,514	$ 137,529	$ 260,985	$ 392,924	$ 489,705	$ 256,018
Fee per visit	77	70	60	63	76	80	60	—
Number of visits	2,767	2,406	2,159	2,183	3,434	4,912	8,162	3,717
Visit capacity	10,920	3,900	7,800	7,800	7,800	7,280	7,800	7,614
Capacity utilization	25.3%	61.7%	27.67%	27.99%	44.03%	67.47%	104.64%	51.3%
Adjusted capacity	25.34%	61.69%	27.67%	27.99%	44.03%	67.47%	100.00%	50.6%

(Continued)

EXHIBIT 19.2 *(Continued)*

TABLE 15

Nature Home
First Year of Company Operations—Annualized[1]
Income Statement

	Nature Home—PA	*CBH—Butler*	*VTSAT—Burlington*	*VTSAT—Wheaton*	*CBH—Maine*	*CBH—NPA*	*CBH—Vermont*	*Average*
Revenues	$ 213,048	$ 224,564	$ 310,834	$ 137,529	$ 260,985	$ 392,924	$ 489,705	$ 289,941
Cost of sales	12,133	14,422	138,106	9,480	19,341	25,422	—	31,272
Gross profit	$ 200,915	$ 210,142	$ 172,728	$ 128,049	$ 241,644	$ 367,502	$ 489,705	$ 258,669
Total operating expenses	191,269	127,511	151,896	163,208	285,738	353,264	331,898	229,255
Net income from operations	$ 9,646	$ 82,631	$ 20,832	$ (35,160)	$ (44,094)	$ 14,239	$ 157,807	$ 29,415
Other income/expenses	475	—	—	—	85	—	2,079	377
Pretax income	$ 10,121	$ 82,631	$ 20,832	$ (35,160)	$ (44,009)	$ 14,239	$ 159,886	$ 29,792
Addbacks								
Management fees	$ 6,300	$ 22,618	$ —	$ 13,277	$ 26,098	$ —	$ —	$ 9,756
Depreciation	1,392	—	8,467	—	10,279	—	23,343	6,212
Consulting fees	13,183	—	21,478	8,694	3,050	39,483	14,653	14,363
Rent	24,851	19,567	26,160	15,877	20,400	33,301	16,312	22,353
Royalties	10,849	11,309	—	6,876	—	19,980	—	7,002
Medical director's fees	—	4,408	—	9,371	24,960	19,632	14,709	10,440
Interest expense	1,481	—	6,334	—	119	36	—	1,139
Other income/expense	(475)	—	—	—	(85)	—	(2,079)	(377)
Total addback expenses	$ 57,581	$ 57,903	$ 62,438	$ 54,095	$ 84,821	$ 112,432	$ 66,938	$ 70,887
Adjusted pretax income	$ 67,702	$ 140,534	$ 83,270	$ 18,935	$ 40,812	$ 126,670	$ 226,824	$ 100,678

[1]The following annualization factors were used:
CBH—Butler 4/3
VTSAT—Burlington 12/5

TABLE 16

Nature Home
First Year of Company Operations—Annualized[1]
Common-Size Income Statement

	Nature Home—PA	*CBH—Butler*	*VTSAT—Burlington*	*VTSAT—Wheaton*	*CBH—Maine*	*CBH—NPA*	*CBH—Vermont*	*Average*
Revenues	100.00%	100.00%	100.00%	100.00%	100.00%	100.00%	100.00%	100.00%
Cost of sales	5.69%	6.42%	44.43%	6.89%	7.41%	6.47%	0.00%	10.79%
Gross profit	94.31%	93.58%	55.57%	93.11%	92.59%	93.53%	100.00%	89.21%
Total operating expenses	89.78%	56.78%	48.87%	118.67%	109.48%	89.91%	67.78%	79.07%
Net income from operations	4.53%	36.80%	6.70%	–25.57%	–16.90%	3.62%	32.22%	10.14%
Other income/expenses	0.22%	0.00%	0.00%	0.00%	0.03%	0.00%	0.42%	0.13%

EXHIBIT 19.2 *(Continued)*

	Nature Home—PA	CBH—Butler	VTSAT—Burlington	VTSAT—Wheaton	CBH—Maine	CBH—NPA	CBH—Vermont	Average
Pretax income	4.75%	36.80%	6.70%	−25.57%	−16.86%	3.62%	32.65%	10.28%
Total expense addbacks	27.03%	25.78%	20.09%	39.33%	32.50%	28.61%	13.67%	24.45%
Adjusted pretax income	31.78%	62.58%	26.79%	13.77%	15.64%	32.24%	46.32%	34.72%

[1]The following annualization factors were used:
CBH— Butler 4/3
VTSAT— Burlington 12/5

TABLE 17

Nature Home
First Year of Company Operations—Annualized
Number of Visits and Capacity Utilization

	Nature Home—PA	CBH—Butler	VTSAT—Burlington	VTAT—Wheaton	CBH—Maine	CBH—NPA	CBH—Vermont	Average
Revenues	$ 213,048	$ 224,564	$ 310,834	$ 137,529	$ 260,985	$ 392,924	$ 489,705	$ 289,941
Fee per visit	77	77	60	63	76	80	60	—
Number of visits	2,767	2,916	5,181	2,183	3,434	4,912	8,162	4,222
Visit capacity	10,920	5,460	7,800	7,800	7,800	7,280	7,800	7,837
Capacity utilization	25.3%	53.4%	66.4%	28.0%	44.0%	67.5%	104.6%	55.6%
Adjusted capacity utilization	25.34%	53.41%	66.42%	27.99%	44.03%	67.47%	100.00%	54.9%

TABLE 18

Nature Home
Second Year of Company Operations
Income Statement

	Nature Home—PA	CBH—Butler	VTSAT—Burlington	VTSAT—Wheaton	CBH—Maine	CBH—Vermont	Average
Revenues	$ 548,249	$ 378,125	$ 393,261	$ 234,027	$ 737,447	$ 906,476	$ 532,931
Cost of sales	42,121	26,896	280,779	14,672	52,265	73,123	81,643
Gross profit	$ 506,128	$ 351,229	$ 112,482	$ 219,355	$ 685,182	$ 833,353	$ 451,288
Total operating expenses	408,078	228,968	29,868	228,015	588,666	604,781	388,063
Net income from operations	$ 98,050	$ 122,261	$(157,386)	$ (8,660)	$ 96,516	$ 228,572	$ 63,226
Other income/expenses	270	—	1,199	—	416	894	463
Pretax income	$ 98,320	$ 122,261	$(156,187)	$ (8,660)	$ 96,932	$ 229,466	$ 63,689
Addbacks							
Management fees	$ 16,000	$ 37,813	$ —	$ 14,042	$ 81,700	$ 19,985	$ 28,257
Depreciation	6,561	—	12,852	4,872	10,288	25,238	9,968
Consulting fees	53,407	—	6,900	1,776	13,115	40,892	19,348

(Continued)

EXHIBIT 19.2 (Continued)

	Nature Home—PA	*CBH—Butler*	*VTSAT—Burlington*	*VTSAT—Wheaton*	*CBH—Maine*	*CBH—Vermont*	*Average*
Rent	27,566	14,625	21,900	16,232	31,500	29,422	23,541
Royalties	26,798	18,906	19,836	11,701	53,721	—	21,827
Medical director's fees	—	27,182	10,057	15,740	20,280	—	12,210
Interest expense	1,410	—	3,942	—	1,040	—	1065
Other income/expense	(270)	—	(1,199)	—	(416)	(894)	(463)
Total addback expenses	$ 131,472	$ 98,526	$ 74,288	$ 64,362	$ 211,228	$ 114,643	$ 115,753
Adjusted pretax income	$ 229,792	$ 220,787	$ (81,899)	$ 55,703	$ 308,160	$ 344,109	$ 179,442

TABLE 19

Nature Home
Second Year of Company Operations
Common Size Income Statement

	Nature Home—PA	*CH—Butler*	*VTSAT—Burlington*	*VTSAT—Wheaton*	*CH—Maine*	*CH—Vermont*	*Average*
Revenues	100.00%	100.00%	100.00%	100.00%	100.00%	100.00%	100.00%
Cost of sales	7.68%	7.11%	71.40%	6.27%	7.09%	8.07%	15.32%
Gross profit	92.32%	92.89%	28.60%	93.73%	92.91%	91.93%	84.68%
Total operating expenses	74.43%	60.55%	68.62%	97.43%	79.82%	66.72%	72.82%
Net income from operations	17.88%	32.33%	–40.02%	–3.70%	13.09%	25.22%	11.86%
Other income/expenses	0.05%	0.00%	0.30%	0.00%	0.06%	0.10%	0.09%
Pretax income	17.93%	32.33%	–39.72%	–3.70%	13.14%	25.31%	11.95%
Total expense addbacks	23.98%	26.06%	18.89%	27.50%	28.64%	12.65%	21.72%
Adjusted pretax income	41.91%	58.39%	–20.83%	23.80%	41.79%	37.96%	33.67%

TABLE 20

Nature Home
Second Year of Company Operations
Number of Visits and Capacity Utilization

	Nature Home—PA	*CH—Butler*	*VTSAT—Burlington*	*VTSAT—Wheaton*	*CH—Maine*	*CH—Vermont*	*Average*
Revenues	$ 548,249	$ 378,125	$ 393,261	$ 234,027	$ 737,447	$ 906,476	$ 532,931
Fee per visit	77	77	60	60	76	60	—
Number of visits	7,120	4,911	6,554	3,900	9,703	15,108	7,883
Visit capacity	10,920	5,460	7,800	7,800	10,400	10,400	8,797
Capacity utilization	65.2%	89.9%	84.0%	50.0%	93.3%	145.3%	88.0%
Adjusted capacity utilization	65.20%	89.94%	84.03%	50.01%	93.30%	100.00%	80.4%

EXHIBIT 19.2 *(Continued)*

TABLE 21

Nature Home
Third Year of Company Operations
Income Statement

	Nature Home—PA	*CH—Butler*	*VTSAT—Burlington*	*CH—Maine*	*CH—Vermont*	*Average*
Revenues	$ 744,130	$ 484,741	$ 624,909	$ 917,219	$ 943,254	$ 742,851
Cost of sales	67,016	34,543	57,329	64,238	138,780	72,381
Gross profit	$ 677,114	$ 450,197	$ 567,580	$ 852,981	$ 804,474	$ 670,469
Total operating expenses	563,836	359,707	378,631	653,254	610,990	513,284
Net income from operations	$ 113,278	$ 90,490	$ 188,949	$ 199,727	$ 193,484	$ 157,186
Other income/expenses	—	—	742	75	8,421	1,848
Pretax income	$ 113,278	$ 90,490	$ 189,691	$ 199,802	$ 201,905	$ 159,033
Addbacks						
Management fees	$ 22,000	$ 48,474	$ —	$ 91,722	$ —	$ 32,439
Depreciation	19,434	—	12,690	10,267	61,368	20,752
Consulting fees	71,113	253	23,522	6,020	500	20,282
Rent	28,344	14,625	21,600	28,800	22,788	23,231
Royalties	37,346	24,233	31,295	45,861	—	27,747
Medical director's fees	—	63,111	20,500	26,921	—	22,106
Interest expense	1,003	—	3,632	92	15,014	3,948
Other income/expense	—	—	(742)	(75)	(8,421)	(1,848)
Total addback expenses	$ 179,240	$ 150,697	$ 112,497	$ 209,608	$ 91,249	$ 148,658
Adjusted pretax income	$ 292,518	$ 241,187	$ 302,188	$ 409,410	$ 293,154	$ 307,691

TABLE 22

Nature Home
Third Year of Company Operations
Common-Size Income Statement

	Nature Home—PA	*CH—Butler*	*VTSAT—Burlington*	*CH—Maine*	*CH—Vermont*	*Average*
Revenues	100.00%	100.00%	100.00%	100.00%	100.00%	100.00%
Cost of sales	9.01%	7.13%	9.17%	7.00%	14.71%	9.74%
Gross profit	90.99%	92.87%	90.83%	93.00%	85.29%	90.26%
Total operating expenses	75.77%	74.21%	60.59%	71.22%	64.77%	69.10%
Net income from operations	15.22%	18.67%	30.24%	21.78%	20.51%	21.16%
Other income/expenses	0.00%	0.00%	0.12%	0.01%	0.89%	0.25%
Pretax income	15.22%	18.67%	30.35%	21.78%	21.41%	21.41%
Total expense addbacks	24.09%	31.09%	18.00%	22.85%	9.67%	20.01%
Adjusted pretax income	39.31%	49.76%	48.36%	44.64%	31.08%	41.42%

(Continued)

EXHIBIT 19.2 *(Continued)*

TABLE 23

Nature Home
Third Year of Company Operations
Number of Visits and Capacity Utilization

	Nature Home—PA	*CH—Butler*	*VTSAT—Burlington*	*CH—Maine*	*CH—Vermont*	*Average*
Revenues	$ 744,130	$ 484,741	$ 624,909	$ 917,219	$ 943,254	$ 742,851
Fee per visit	77	77	60	76	60	—
Number of visits	9,664	6,295	10,415	12,069	15,721	54,164
Visit capacity	10,920	7,280	10,400	14,300	10,400	53,300
Capacity utilization	88.5%	86.5%	100.1%	84.4%	151.2%	102.1%
Adjusted capacity utilization	88.50%	86.47%	100.00%	84.40%	100.00%	91.9%

TABLE 24

Nature Home
Fourth Year of Company Operations
Income Statement

	Nature Home—PA	*CH—Butler*	*VTSAT—Burlington*	*CH—Maine*	*CH—Vermont*	*Average*
Revenues	$ 825,745	$ 466,633	$ 798,533	$1,099,345	$ 723,465	$ 782,744
Cost of sales	72,151	29,692	104,406	69,410	316,770	118,486
Gross profit	$ 735,594	$ 436,941	$ 694,127	$1,029,936	$ 406,695	$ 664,259
Total operating expenses	542,826	348,792	514,256	761,942	225,810	478,725
Net income from operations	$ 210,768	$ 88,149	$ 179,871	$ 267,994	$ 180,885	$ 185,533
Other income/expenses	—	—	—	645	3,309	791
Pretax income	$ 210,768	$ 88,149	$ 179,871	$ 268,639	$ 184,194	$ 186,324
Addbacks						
Management fees	$ 49,557	$ 46,664	$ —	$ —	$ 34,433	$ 26,131
Depreciation	19,433	2,837	23,824	6,187	27,791	16,014
Consulting fees	12,988	225	50,957	125,607	—	37,955
Rent	26,088	14,625	23,700	32,400	19,460	23,255
Royalties	41,297	23,332	40,064	54,967	—	31,932
Medical director's fees	57,415	33,736	32,965	49,966	—	34,816
Interest expense	953	—	382	868	7,441	1,929
Other income/expense	—	—	—	(645)	(3,309)	(791)
Total addback expenses	$ 207,731	$ 121,419	$ 171,892	$ 269,351	$ 85,816	$ 171,242
Adjusted pretax income	$ 418,499	$ 209,567	$ 351,763	$ 537,989	$ 270,010	$ 357,566

EXHIBIT 19.2 *(Continued)*

TABLE 25

Nature Home
Fourth Year of Company Operations
Common-Size Income Statement

	Nature Home—PA	CH—Butler	VTSAT—Burlington	CH—Maine	CH—Vermont	Average
Revenues	100.00%	100.00%	100.00%	100.00%	100.00%	100.00%
Cost of sales	8.74%	6.36%	13.07%	6.31%	43.79%	15.14%
Gross profit	91.26%	93.64%	86.93%	93.69%	56.21%	84.86%
Total operating expenses	65.74%	74.75%	64.40%	69.31%	31.21%	61.16%
Net income from operations	25.52%	18.89%	22.53%	24.38%	25.00%	23.70%
Other income/expenses	0.00%	0.00%	0.00%	0.06%	0.46%	0.10%
Pretax income	25.52%	18.89%	22.53%	24.44%	25.46%	23.80%
Total expense addbacks	25.16%	26.02%	21.53%	24.50%	11.86%	21.88%
Adjusted pretax income	50.68%	44.91%	44.05%	48.94%	37.32%	45.68%

TABLE 26

Nature Home
Fourth Year of Company Operations
Number of Visits and Capacity Utilization

	Nature Home—PA	CH—Butler	VTSAT—Burlington	CH—Maine	CH—Vermont	Average
Revenues	$ 825,745	$ 466,633	$ 798,533	$ 1,099,345	$ 723,465	$ 782,744
Fee per visit	77	77	60	76	60	—
Number of visits	10,724	6,060	13,309	14,465	12,058	56,616
Visit capacity	10,920	7,280	13,000	14,300	10,400	55,900
Capacity utilization	98.2%	83.2%	102.4%	101.2%	115.9%	100.2%
Adjusted capacity utilization	98.20%	83.24%	100.00%	100.00%	100.00%	96.3%

TABLE 27

Nature Home
Profile of Company Operations
Income Statements

	First Year Average	Second Year Average	Third Year Average	Fourth Year Average
Revenues	$ 289,941	$ 532,931	$ 742,851	$ 782,744
Cost of sales	31,272	81,643	72,381	118,486
Gross profit	$ 258,669	$ 451,288	$ 670,469	$ 664,259
Total operating expenses	229,255	388,063	513,284	478,725
Net income from operations	$ 29,415	$ 63,226	$ 157,186	$ 185,533
Other income/expenses	377	463	1,848	791

(Continued)

EXHIBIT 19.2 *(Continued)*

	First Year Average	*Second Year Average*	*Third Year Average*	*Fourth Year Average*
Pretax income	$ 29,792	$ 63,689	$ 159,033	$ 186,324
Addbacks				
Management fees	$ 9,756	$ 28,257	$ 32,439	$ 26,131
Depreciation	6,212	9,968	20,752	16,014
Consulting fees	14,363	19,348	20,282	37,955
Rent	22,353	23,541	23,231	23,255
Royalties	7,002	21,827	27,747	31,932
Medical director's fees	10,440	12,210	22,106	34,816
Interest expense	1,139	1,065	3,948	1,929
Other income/expense	(377)	(463)	(1,848)	(791)
Total addback expenses	$ 70,887	$ 115,753	$ 148,658	$ 171,242
Adjusted pretax income	$ 100,678	$ 179,442	$ 307,691	$ 357,566

TABLE 28

Nature Home
Profile of Company Operations
Common-Size Income Statement

	First Year Average	*Second Year Average*	*Third Year Average*	*Fourth Year Average*
Revenues	100.00%	100.00%	100.00%	100.00%
Cost of sales	10.79%	15.32%	9.74%	15.14%
Gross profit	89.21%	84.68%	90.26%	84.86%
Total operating expenses	79.07%	72.82%	69.10%	61.16%
Net income from operations	10.14%	11.86%	21.16%	23.70%
Other income/expenses	0.13%	0.09%	0.25%	0.10%
Pretax income	10.28%	11.95%	21.41%	23.80%
Depreciation addback	2.14%	1.87%	2.79%	2.05%
Total expense addbacks	24.45%	21.72%	20.01%	21.88%
Adjusted pretax income	34.72%	33.67%	41.42%	45.68%

TABLE 29

Nature Home
Profile of Company Operations
Number of Visits and Capacity Utilization

	First Year Average	*Second Year Average*	*Third Year Average*	*Fourth Year Average*
Revenues	$ 289,941	$ 532,931	$ 742,851	$ 782,744
Capacity utilization	55.6%	88.0%	102.1%	100.2%
Adjusted capacity utilization	54.9%	80.4%	91.9%	96.3%

EXHIBIT 19.2 *(Continued)*

Using the average profile of company operations displayed in Tables 28 and 29, an operations profile for the unopened State clinic can be created. In order to accomplish this, we needed to identify the maximum client capacity of the clinic and apply the capacity utilization percentages to this capacity. This provided the estimated number of patient weeks the clinic would have had per year. In the case of State, the weekly client capacity was 300 clients. Multiplying 300 clients times 52 weeks results in 15,600 client weeks per year. This is the maximum number of weeks the clinic could have received weekly fees for in one year. By taking the maximum clinic capacity per year and multiplying that figure by the estimated capacity utilization, the estimated number of patient weeks per year can be obtained. Multiplying this estimate by the average weekly fee, $74, gives the estimated annual projected clinic revenue. For 1997, revenues at the clinic would have been $616,790 (8,335 estimated patient weeks times $74). The following tables present our income forecast for the State clinic through 2000, had the opening of the clinic not been interrupted.

TABLE 30

Nature Home
Profile of State Operations
Income Statement

	1997	*1998*	*1999*	*2000*
Maximum capacity	15,600	15,600	15,600	15,600
Estimated capacity utilization	54.90%	80.41%	91.87%	96.29%
Estimated patients	8,564	12,544	14,332	15,021
Fees per patient	$ 74	$ 74	$ 74	$ 74
Revenues	$ 633,766	$ 928,256	$ 1,060,568	$ 1,111,554
Common-size expenses	65.41%	66.42%	58.83%	54.42%
Typical expenses	$ 414,546	$ 616,548	$ 623,932	$ 604,908
State expenses				
Rent	18,509	18,509	18,509	21,600
Depreciation	4,018	8,035	8,035	8,035
Management fees	63,377	92,826	106,057	111,155
Royalties	31,688	46,413	53,028	55,578
Medical directors fees	26,000	26,780	27,583	28,410
Consulting fees	26,000	26,780	27,583	28,410
Total state expenses	$ 169,592	$ 219,343	$ 240,795	$ 253,188
Total expenses	$ 584,138	$ 835,891	$ 864,727	$ 858,096
Net income before taxes	$ 49,628	$ 92,365	$ 195,841	$ 253,458

TABLE 31

Nature Home
Profile of State Operations
Common-Size Income Statement

	1997	*1998*	*1999*	*2000*
Revenues	100.00%	100.00%	100.00%	100.00%
Common-size expenses	65.41%	66.42%	58.83%	54.42%
State expenses				
Rent	2.92%	1.99%	1.75%	1.94%
Depreciation	0.63%	0.87%	0.76%	0.72%
Management fees	10.00%	10.00%	10.00%	10.00%

(Continued)

EXHIBIT 19.2 *(Continued)*

	1997	*1998*	*1999*	*2000*
Royalties	5.00%	5.00%	5.00%	5.00%
Medical directors fees	4.10%	2.88%	2.60%	2.56%
Consulting fees	4.10%	2.88%	2.60%	2.56%
Total state expenses	26.76%	23.63%	22.70%	22.78%
Total expenses	92.17%	90.05%	81.53%	77.20%
Net income before taxes	7.83%	9.95%	18.47%	22.80%

To derive lost profits for the State clinic, we subtracted expenses and costs of sales from the revenues. The first step in this process was to multiply revenues by the common-size expense percentages developed in the profile. For a given year, this resulted in income before the directly estimated expenses for State. We have calculated each of these expenses as follows:

- NHI pays management fees to Dart Management, Inc., based on 10 percent of revenues.
- The clinic pays royalty fees to David Smith, Sr., based on 5 percent of revenues.
- We based depreciation on actual capital expenditures that included:

Telephone system	$ 1,200
Copier/fax	$ 3,000
Software/hardware	$ 50,000
Furniture & fixtures	$ 5,000

The useful life for the telephone system and furniture and fixtures was determined to be 10 years. The copier/fax and software/hardware were estimated to have a useful life of six years.

- We determined rents based on the lease signed by Nature Home, Inc. In 1996, the lease calls for payments of $1,545.42 per month for the first three years of the lease. An amendment was added that gives the option to extend the lease an additional six years. Rent per month in the extension period would be $1,800 in the first year, $1,900 in the second year, $2,000 in the third year, and an applicable market rate for the other three years.
- The clinic pays Medical Director's fees to a doctor who oversees the clinic. Fees are calculated as $100 per hour for five hours per week, or $26,000 for the first year. They have been grown 3 percent per year thereafter.
- The clinic pays consulting fees to nurses who are contracted to perform services at the clinics. Fees are estimated at $25 per hour for 20 hours per week, or $26,000 for the first year. They have been grown 3 percent per year thereafter.
- We did not forecast interest expense, as there was no expectation for The Company to borrow funds. In addition, we have not seen any indication that The Company would need to do so.

Projecting and subtracting each of these expenses from the income statement projections for State results in pretax income, which is expected profits.

The next step in the process is to determine NHI's mitigation of lost expected profits. We have based the mitigation on the same four-year forecast for NHI. To use the forecast, the date that NHI may begin operations needs to be determined. Based on discussions with management and counsel, we have assumed that Nature Home, Inc., will be able to open a clinic in State after the completion of this litigation. We have estimated damages based on a trial date of October 31, 1999. Therefore, we have assumed that Nature Home could begin developing a new location at that time. According to management, The Company most likely will be in a position to sign a lease shortly after the litigation is completed. Therefore, we have assumed that the clinic will open on May 1, 2000. This assumes that the trial is completed and Nature Home signs a lease by December 1, 1999.

Lost profits are the difference between what The Company would have made if it were not harmed (expected profits) and what it will make after suffering the damage (mitigation). Since NHI could not operate from June 1, 1996, to May 1, 2000, lost profits over that period equal total expected profits. Thereafter, lost profits become the difference between expected profits and mitigation. We have extended the projections of expected profits beyond four years to allow the mitigation earnings stream to stabilize. We have done this by growing revenues and expenses at a stable growth rate of 3 percent.

We have forecast lost profits based on periods ending on June 30. Due to the timing of events, we have forecast the mitigation based on periods ending on April 30. This creates a mismatch of periods in subtracting mitigation from the expected profits. To compensate for this, we have adjusted the mitigation for the overlapping periods as follows:

- 1999's mitigation represents two months of the first forecast year of operations (May and June).
- 2000's mitigation represents 10 months of the first forecast year of operations and 2 months of the second year.

EXHIBIT 19.2 *(Continued)*

- 2001's mitigation represents 10 months of the second forecast year of operations and 2 months of the third year.
- 2002's mitigation represents 10 months of the third forecast year of operations and 2 months of the fourth year.
- 2003's mitigation represents 10 months of the fourth forecast year of operations and 2 months of the fourth year as well. We also used year 4's figures for the last 2 months since stabilization has been reached after four years.

We calculated damages from lost profits as of October 31, 1999. Table 32 reflects these computations. The discount rate used in the present and future value calculations is 8 percent, the statutory rate of interest provided to us by legal counsel.

TABLE 32

Nature Home
Calculation of Lost Profits

	1997	*1998*	*1999*	*2000*	*2001*	*2002*	*2003*
Estimated profits	$ 49,628	$ 92,365	$ 195,841	$ 253,458	$ 273,735	$ 295,633	$ 319,284
Estimated mitigated profits	—	—	8,271	56,751	109,611	205,444	256,837
Estimated lost profits	$ 49,628	$ 92,365	$ 187,570	$ 196,707	$ 164,124	$ 90,190	$ 62,447
Present value factor	1.1664	1.0800	1.0000	0.9259	0.8573	0.7938	0.7350
Present value of lost profits	$ 57,886	$ 99,754	$ 187,570	$ 182,131	$ 140,703	$ 71,592	$ 45,898
Total damages from lost profits	$ 785,535						

Lost profits, after mitigation, amount to $785,535. This includes statutory interest through October 31, 1999.

Damages From Clinic Costs

In preparing to open a clinic in State, NHI began making necessary expenditures and, therefore, incurred costs to prepare and build their facility. Due to the actions of the City, NHI lost its capital equipment and incurred significant operating expenses.

To calculate damages from these sources, we reviewed internal accounting records and detailed invoices to support the expenses. Costs incurred from each type of capital expenditure or operating expense are detailed separately. We calculated interest on each expense at the statutory rate of 8 percent to bring the damages forward to a present value. The trial date of October 31, 1999, was used as a present value date. Table 33 presents costs incurred by Nature Home.

TABLE 33

Nature Home
Costs Incurred

	Date	*Amount*	*Days*	*Daily Interest Factor*	*Interest*	*Damage*
Capital expenditures						
Furniture and fixtures						
Al Carroll	2/15/96	253.00	1,336	0.022%	75.11	328.11
Al Carroll	2/23/96	294.99	1,328	0.022%	87.05	382.04
New England Surgical	5/15/96	332.85	1,246	0.022%	92.16	425.01
D Pico Interior Design	5/30/96	1423.00	1,230	0.022%	388.95	1811.95
D Pico Interior Design	5/30/96	409.00	1,230	0.022%	111.79	520.79

(Continued)

EXHIBIT 19.2 ***(Continued)***

	Date	*Amount*	*Days*	*Daily Interest Factor*	*Interest*	*Damage*
Office equipment						
William Jones & Assoc.	2/29/96	1645.00	1,320	0.022%	482.53	2127.53
Security system						
Jameson Alarm Co.	2/14/96	1927.50	1,337	0.022%	572.68	2500.18
Jameson Alarm Co.	2/29/96	1927.50	1,320	0.022%	565.40	2492.90
Leasehold improvements						
Thurman Jones	2/12/96	1061.50	1,339	0.022%	315.86	1377.36
Thurman Jones	4/15/96	1061.50	1,276	0.022%	300.99	1362.49
Deposits						
Allen Equipment	11/9/95	3084.90	1,432	0.022%	981.68	4066.58
Rent						
Grandview One	1/30/96	1542.45	1,350	0.022%	462.74	2005.19
Grandview One	2/15/96	1542.45	1,336	0.022%	457.94	2000.39
Grandview One	3/15/96	1542.45	1,306	0.022%	447.65	1990.10
Grandview One	4/15/96	1542.45	1,276	0.022%	437.37	1979.82
Grandview One	5/15/96	1542.45	1,246	0.022%	427.09	1969.54
Grandview One	6/15/96	1542.45	1,216	0.022%	416.80	1959.25
Grandview One	7/15/96	1542.45	1,186	0.022%	406.52	1948.97
Grandview One	8/15/96	1542.45	1,156	0.022%	396.24	1938.69
Grandview One	9/15/96	1542.45	1,126	0.022%	385.96	1928.41
Grandview One	10/15/96	1542.45	1,096	0.022%	375.67	1918.12
Grandview One	11/15/96	1542.45	1,066	0.022%	365.39	1907.84
Grandview One	12/15/96	1542.45	1,036	0.022%	355.11	1897.56
Grandview One	1/15/97	1542.45	1,006	0.022%	344.82	1887.27
Grandview One	2/15/97	1542.45	976	0.022%	334.54	1876.99
Grandview One	3/15/97	1542.45	946	0.022%	324.26	1866.71
Grandview One	4/15/97	1542.45	916	0.022%	313.97	1856.42
Grandview One	5/15/97	1542.45	886	0.022%	303.69	1846.14
Grandview One	6/15/97	1542.45	856	0.022%	293.41	1835.86
Grandview One	7/15/97	1542.45	826	0.022%	283.13	1825.58
Utilities						
State Power & Light	4/2/96	31.62	1,289	0.022%	9.06	40.68
State Power & Light	5/30/96	39.35	1,230	0.022%	10.76	50.11
State Power & Light	5/30/96	16.33	1,230	0.022%	4.46	20.79
State Power & Light	5/30/96	–1.30	1,230	0.022%	–0.36	–1.66
State Power & Light	6/15/96	31.30	1,216	0.022%	8.46	39.76
State Power & Light	6/15/96	–1.04	1,216	0.022%	–0.28	–1.32
State Power & Light	7/30/96	29.19	1,170	0.022%	7.59	36.78
State Power & Light	8/30/96	30.23	1,140	0.022%	7.66	37.89
State Power & Light	9/15/96	26.47	1,126	0.022%	6.62	33.09
State Power & Light	10/30/96	26.34	1,080	0.022%	6.32	32.66

EXHIBIT 19.2 *(Continued)*

	Date	*Amount*	*Days*	*Daily Interest Factor*	*Interest*	*Damage*
State Power & Light	11/30/96	26.48	1,050	0.022%	6.18	32.66
State Power & Light	12/15/96	30.03	1,036	0.022%	6.91	36.94
State Power & Light	1/30/97	33.16	990	0.022%	7.30	40.46
State Power & Light	2/28/97	30.64	960	0.022%	6.54	37.18
State Power & Light	3/30/97	30.88	930	0.022%	6.38	37.26
State Power & Light	4/30/97	31.73	900	0.022%	6.35	38.08
State Power & Light	5/30/97	35.93	870	0.022%	6.95	42.88
State Power & Light	6/15/97	31.64	856	0.022%	6.02	37.66
State Power & Light	7/30/97	30.40	810	0.022%	5.47	35.87
State Power & Light	8/20/97	31.41	791	0.022%	5.52	36.93
State Power & Light	9/20/97	30.24	761	0.022%	5.11	35.35
State Power & Light	10/20/97	21.16	731	0.022%	3.44	24.60
Telephone						
Ameritech	1/30/96	219.46	1,350	0.022%	65.84	285.30
Ameritech	2/29/96	122.65	1,320	0.022%	35.98	158.63
Ameritech	3/29/96	18.14	1,292	0.022%	5.21	23.35
AT&T	3/29/96	5.15	1,292	0.022%	1.48	6.63
AT&T	3/29/96	5.15	1,292	0.022%	1.48	6.63
Ameritech	3/30/96	131.84	1,290	0.022%	37.79	169.63
Ameritech	4/30/96	17.38	1,260	0.022%	4.87	22.25
AT&T	4/30/96	5.15	1,260	0.022%	1.44	6.59
AT&T	4/30/96	5.15	1,260	0.022%	1.44	6.59
Ameritech	4/30/96	128.27	1,260	0.022%	35.92	164.19
Ameritech	5/30/96	17.38	1,230	0.022%	4.75	22.13
AT&T	5/30/96	5.15	1,230	0.022%	1.41	6.56
Ameritech	5/30/96	116.68	1,230	0.022%	31.89	148.57
AT&T	5/30/96	5.15	1,230	0.022%	1.41	6.56
Ameritech	6/30/96	17.23	1,200	0.022%	4.59	21.82
AT&T	6/30/96	5.15	1,200	0.022%	1.37	6.52
Ameritech	6/30/96	125.88	1,200	0.022%	33.57	159.45
Ameritech	7/30/96	17.23	1,170	0.022%	4.48	21.71
AT&T	7/30/96	5.15	1,170	0.022%	1.34	6.49
Ameritech	7/30/96	127.35	1,170	0.022%	33.11	160.46
AT&T	8/30/96	5.15	1,140	0.022%	1.30	6.45
Ameritech	8/30/96	17.23	1,140	0.022%	4.36	21.59
Ameritech	8/30/96	127.17	1,140	0.022%	32.22	159.39
Ameritech	9/30/96	17.23	1,110	0.022%	4.25	21.48
Ameritech	9/30/96	126.54	1,110	0.022%	31.21	157.75
AT&T	9/30/96	5.15	1,110	0.022%	1.27	6.42
Ameritech	10/8/96	14.49	1,103	0.022%	3.55	18.04
Ameritech	10/30/96	17.23	1,080	0.022%	4.14	21.37

(Continued)

EXHIBIT 19.2 (Continued)

	Date	Amount	Days	Daily Interest Factor	Interest	Damage
AT&T	10/30/96	5.15	1,080	0.022%	1.24	6.39
Ameritech	10/30/96	130.72	1,080	0.022%	31.37	162.09
Ameritech	11/30/96	17.23	1,050	0.022%	4.02	21.25
AT&T	11/30/96	5.15	1,050	0.022%	1.20	6.35
Ameritech	11/30/96	123.36	1,050	0.022%	28.78	152.14
Ameritech	12/30/96	17.50	1,020	0.022%	3.97	21.47
Ameritech	12/30/96	130.61	1,020	0.022%	29.60	160.21
AT&T	12/30/96	5.15	1,020	0.022%	1.17	6.32
Ameritech	1/30/97	17.50	990	0.022%	3.85	21.35
AT&T	1/30/97	5.15	990	0.022%	1.13	6.28
Ameritech	1/30/97	127.04	990	0.022%	27.95	154.99
Ameritech	2/28/97	17.23	960	0.022%	3.68	20.91
AT&T	2/28/97	5.15	960	0.022%	1.10	6.25
Ameritech	2/28/97	130.72	960	0.022%	27.89	158.61
Ameritech	2/28/97	130.72	960	0.022%	27.89	158.61
Ameritech	3/30/97	17.50	930	0.022%	3.62	21.12
AT&T	3/30/97	5.15	930	0.022%	1.06	6.21
Ameritech	3/30/97	127.04	930	0.022%	26.25	153.29
Ameritech	4/30/97	17.23	900	0.022%	3.45	20.68
Ameritech	4/30/97	130.72	900	0.022%	26.14	156.86
AT&T	4/30/97	5.15	900	0.022%	1.03	6.18
Ameritech	5/30/97	17.50	870	0.022%	3.38	20.88
AT&T	5/30/97	5.15	870	0.022%	1.00	6.15
Ameritech	5/30/97	127.04	870	0.022%	24.56	151.60
Ameritech	6/30/97	17.23	840	0.022%	3.22	20.45
Ameritech	6/30/97	127.04	840	0.022%	23.71	150.75
AT&T	6/30/97	5.15	840	0.022%	0.96	6.11
Ameritech	7/30/97	17.50	810	0.022%	3.15	20.65
AT&T	7/30/97	5.15	810	0.022%	0.93	6.08
Ameritech	7/30/97	121.96	810	0.022%	21.95	143.91
Ameritech	8/30/97	17.23	780	0.022%	2.99	20.22
AT&T	8/30/97	5.15	780	0.022%	0.89	6.04
Ameritech	8/30/97	124.22	780	0.022%	21.53	145.75
Ameritech	9/30/97	17.23	750	0.022%	2.87	20.10
AT&T	9/30/97	5.15	750	0.022%	0.86	6.01
Ameritech	10/20/97	124.22	731	0.022%	20.18	144.40
Ameritech	10/30/97	17.23	720	0.022%	2.76	19.99
Ameritech	11/30/97	17.50	690	0.022%	2.68	20.18
Ameritech	12/30/97	17.23	660	0.022%	2.53	19.76
Ameritech	1/30/98	17.23	630	0.022%	2.41	19.64
Ameritech	2/28/98	17.23	600	0.022%	2.30	19.53
Ameritech	3/30/98	18.20	570	0.022%	2.31	20.51

EXHIBIT 19.2 (Continued)

	Date	Amount	Days	Daily Interest Factor	Interest	Damage
Ameritech	4/20/98	17.93	551	0.022%	2.20	20.13
Ameritech	5/30/98	19.34	510	0.022%	2.19	21.53
Ameritech	6/30/98	18.58	480	0.022%	1.98	20.56
Ameritech	7/30/98	18.58	450	0.022%	1.86	20.44
Professional fees						
Alan A. Wartenberg, MD	1/15/96	218.75	1,366	0.022%	66.40	285.15
Alan A. Wartenberg, MD	1/30/96	125.00	1,350	0.022%	37.50	162.50
Alan A. Wartenberg, MD	1/30/96	62.50	1,350	0.022%	18.75	81.25
Alan A. Wartenberg, MD	4/15/96	125.00	1,276	0.022%	35.44	160.44
Alan A. Wartenberg, MD	4/30/96	125.00	1,260	0.022%	35.00	160.00
Alan A. Wartenberg, MD	6/30/97	187.50	840	0.022%	35.00	222.50
Auto expense						
Paul Alexander	10/8/96	81.61	1,103	0.022%	20.00	101.61
Paul Alexander	10/8/96	74.96	1,103	0.022%	18.37	93.33
Paul Alexander	10/8/96	70.96	1,103	0.022%	17.39	88.35
Paul Alexander	11/8/96	68.96	1,073	0.022%	16.44	85.40
Travel						
Nationsbank of Delaware	9/15/96	733.00	1,126	0.022%	183.41	916.41
Paul Alexander	10/8/96	80.69	1,103	0.022%	19.78	100.47
Paul Alexander	11/8/96	194.70	1,073	0.022%	46.43	241.13
American Express	2/20/98	139.00	611	0.022%	18.87	157.87
Meals and entertainment						
Nationsbank of Delaware	10/8/96	20.68	1,103	0.022%	5.07	25.75
Nationsbank of Delaware	10/8/96	22.93	1,103	0.022%	5.62	28.55
Nationsbank of Delaware	11/8/96	31.27	1,073	0.022%	7.46	38.73
Nationsbank of Delaware	2/20/98	6.44	611	0.022%	0.87	7.31
Advertising & promotion						
State Newspapers	4/15/96	451.80	1,276	0.022%	128.11	579.91
State Newspapers	4/30/96	117.00	1,260	0.022%	32.76	149.76
State Newspapers	4/30/96	110.50	1,260	0.022%	30.94	141.44
State Newspapers	4/30/96	97.50	1,260	0.022%	27.30	124.80
State Newspapers	4/30/96	34.35	1,260	0.022%	9.62	43.97
State Newspapers	4/30/96	38.93	1,260	0.022%	10.90	49.83
State Newspapers	3/30/97	230.00	930	0.022%	47.53	277.53
State Newspapers	6/15/97	303.28	856	0.022%	57.69	360.97
Legal and expert costs						
Johnson, Jones	11/30/97	1039.77	690	0.022%	159.43	1199.20
Smith, Brown	11/30/97	500.00	690	0.022%	76.67	576.67
Smith, Brown	11/30/97	2793.00	690	0.022%	428.26	3221.26

(Continued)

EXHIBIT 19.2 *(Continued)*

	Date	*Amount*	*Days*	*Daily Interest Factor*	*Interest*	*Damage*
Smith, Brown	12/15/97	500.00	676	0.022%	75.11	575.11
Smith, Brown	1/15/98	500.00	646	0.022%	71.78	571.78
Smith, Brown	2/15/98	500.00	616	0.022%	68.44	568.44
Smith, Brown	2/20/98	2883.75	611	0.022%	391.55	3275.30
Smith, Brown	3/20/98	500.00	581	0.022%	64.56	564.56
Smith, Brown	4/20/98	500.00	551	0.022%	61.22	561.22
Smith, Brown	5/20/98	500.00	521	0.022%	57.89	557.89
Smith, Brown	6/20/98	500.00	491	0.022%	54.56	554.56
Smith, Brown	7/20/98	500.00	461	0.022%	51.22	551.22
Stephen Wright	7/30/98	458.50	450	0.022%	45.85	504.35
Smith, Brown	7/30/98	4422.22	450	0.022%	442.22	4864.44
Stephen Wright	8/10/98	475.00	441	0.022%	46.55	521.55
Smith, Brown	8/20/98	500.00	431	0.022%	47.89	547.89
Johnson, Jones	9/20/98	192.25	401	0.022%	17.13	209.38
Johnson, Jones	9/20/98	154.00	401	0.022%	13.72	167.72
Smith, Brown	9/20/98	500.00	401	0.022%	44.56	544.56
Smith, Brown	9/30/98	3517.70	390	0.022%	304.87	3822.57
Smith, Brown	10/20/98	500.00	371	0.022%	41.22	541.22
Smith, Brown	10/30/98	8033.77	360	0.022%	642.70	8676.47
Smith, Brown	11/20/98	575.00	341	0.022%	43.57	618.57
Smith, Brown	12/20/98	1316.30	311	0.022%	90.97	1407.27
Stephen Wright	12/31/98	525.00	300	0.022%	35.00	560.00
Trugman Valuation	1/6/99	10000.00	295	0.022%	655.56	10655.56
Stephen Wright	3/10/99	625.00	231	0.022%	32.08	657.08
Smith, Brown	3/30/99	2553.10	210	0.022%	119.14	2672.24
Wright & Reilly	8/30/96	275.00	1,140	0.022%	69.67	344.67
Wright & Reilly	11/30/96	1292.25	1,050	0.022%	301.53	1593.78
Smith, Brown	12/31/96	5000.00	1,020	0.022%	1133.33	6133.33
Wright & Reilly	1/30/97	499.25	990	0.022%	109.84	609.09
Smith, Brown	5/30/97	4219.94	870	0.022%	815.86	5035.80
Wright & Reilly	4/20/98	150.00	551	0.022%	18.37	168.37
Smith, Brown	4/20/99	3202.46	191	0.022%	135.93	3338.39
United Parcel Service	4/20/99	12.50	191	0.022%	0.53	13.03
Grand total		**110,805.57**			**19,743.85**	**130,549.42**

Summary of Damages

Several elements of damages were discussed in this report. They are summarized as follows and include adjustments for lost interest.

Lost profits	$ 785,535
Damages from costs incurred	130,549
Total damages	$ 916,084

We reserve the right to adjust our damage calculations as additional information becomes available.

EXHIBIT 19.3

The following is a critique of a plaintiff's expert report. Obviously, we were working with the defense in this assignment. Our client's business had a major explosion that caused damage to many of the surrounding businesses in the area. There was little question about liability in this case, but quantifying the damages was an interesting experience. Although you do not have the benefit of seeing the other side's report, this critique should give you a good lesson in using your business valuation skills in this type of assignment.

September 29, 2000

John Smith, Esquire
Dewey, Cheathum & Howe P.C.
123 Main Avenue
City, State 00000

Re: *Cups Plus, Inc. v Ajax Chemical Company*

Dear Mr. Smith:

Pursuant to your request, Trugman Valuation Associates Inc. has performed a critique of the economic damages report issued by Carl Lewis, Ph.D., and Robert Reed, CPA, (hereafter referred to as "the authors") on behalf of the Econ Group, LLP, entitled "An Appraisal of Economic Loss Suffered by Cups Plus, Inc." (hereafter referred to as "The Econ Report") dated July 25, 2000. This critique is not intended to be a personal attack on the authors, but rather a critique of the underlying work product and assumptions used in deriving their conclusion.

In order to make this critique easy to follow, we will be following the sequence of The Econ Report. All page references are to that document.

General Comments

The Econ Report contains numerous technical errors and unsupported assumptions, lacks independent verification of many critical components of the underlying data, and generally defies logic regarding the conclusion of damages. We find that the underlying assumptions are so full of unsupported speculation that the authors cannot meet their burden to opine in this matter about the damages with any reasonable degree of accounting or economic certainty. Furthermore, the technical errors made throughout the report render the results unusable.

Although the purpose of The Econ Report is to estimate economic damages, the authors have attempted to rely on business valuation concepts and theory to reach their conclusion. While we agree with the use of business valuation concepts in a situation where an entire business is destroyed, The Econ Report has misapplied these concepts and commingled them in an attempt to perform a lost profits analysis. We believe that this is not only inappropriate for this matter, but because of the many errors made throughout the analysis, an incorrect conclusion has been reached.

One of the most well-known business valuation references that provides guidance on the valuation of closely held businesses is Internal Revenue Ruling 59-60, promulgated by the United States Treasury Department. According to Section 3.01 of this frequently cited document:

> A sound valuation will be based upon all relevant facts, but the elements of common sense, informed judgment, and reasonableness must enter into the process of weighing those facts and determining their aggregate significance.

This statement lays the foundation for much of the critique presented herein. One of the most critical aspects of business valuation, as well as economic damages analysis, is that the appraiser/economist approaches the assignment objectively and uses common sense and sound judgment. As the remainder of this critique will demonstrate, this does not appear to be the case in The Econ Report.

An experienced damages expert must consider those methodologies and procedures that are normal and customary in the field of damages and/or valuation. Part of the obligation of being an expert is to be familiar with issues that are regularly raised in the case law affecting the manner in which the expert will be guided. While we are not expected to practice law, certain legal concepts should be considered by the expert, and if the expert deviates from the norm, that position should be explained and well justified.

An important concept that should have been considered within the context of the analysis presented but was ignored by the authors is "The New-Business Rule." This is especially pertinent considering that Cups Plus, Inc. (hereafter referred to as "Cups Plus" or "The Company") was a new company when the accident occurred (The Company was approximately four months old).

According to the *Recovery of Damages For Lost Profits*, "a substantial body of older case law stated that lost profits of an unestablished business cannot be recovered."[1] Discussing more modern rulings, Robert Dunn states:

> Most recent cases reject the once generally accepted rule that lost profits damages for a new business are not recoverable. The development of the law has been to find damages for lost profits of an unestablished business recoverable *when they can be adequately proved with reasonable certainty* [emphasis added].[2]

---

[1]Robert L. Dunn, *Recovery of Damages for Lost Profits*, 5th ed. (Westport, Conn.: Lawpress Corporation), vol. 1, 342.

[2]Ibid., 345–346.

(Continued)

EXHIBIT 19.3 *(Continued)*

Dunn later adds:

> A number of cases have held that a business established for only a short period of time falls within the definition of an unestablished business, and that damages for lost profits of the business are not recoverable. The rationale appears to be that *the operating history of the business must be long enough to provide a basis to forecast future lost profits with confidence. A brief operating history, these cases say, does not establish that the results are typical* [emphasis added].[3]

At the time of the economic loss, Cups Plus, Inc. was a four-month-old company. In accordance with the theory discussed in Dunn's treatise, a lost profits analysis for The Company cannot be performed due to Cups Plus, Inc.'s limited operating history. As will be explained shortly, such a lack of operating history for Cups Plus has resulted in unsupportable conclusions being reached in The Econ Report.

In addition to the New-Business Rule, The Econ Report has also ignored other written treatises on this subject. Section 303.62 of the *Guide to Litigation Support Services*, in the discussion about the "Destruction of a Business," states:

> However if the business has been completely destroyed, most courts have ruled that *the proper measure of damages is the market value of the business on the day of the loss*. The theory behind this rule is that the plaintiff who recovers damages equal to the value of the business has, in effect, sold the business to the defendant. *The plaintiff should not also be able to recover future lost profits after the imputed sale* [emphasis added].[4]

Dunn provides similar analysis when he states:

> If a business has not been just injured, but has been destroyed, almost all of the few cases in point hold that lost profits damages are not recoverable at all. *The measure of damages is said to be the market value of the business on the date of destruction* [emphasis added].[5]

The Econ Report indicates that the business was destroyed. For example, on pages 5–6, the authors write:

> In order to fulfill existing in-house orders Cups Plus attempted immediately to continue its business from other locations and even was in the process of negotiating leased space at another location (15,000 square feet). However, the nature of the business and the type of specialized equipment needed to apply the decals and artwork to the cups and glassware (specifically the high temperature oven), made the continuation of the business at other locations not feasible. *The business of Cups Plus was thus lost as well* [emphasis added].

Also, on page 11, The Econ report states, "The loss of tangible assets, trained employees, sales reps, customers, and associated business opportunities for Cups Plus, Inc. *is deemed to be definite and permanent*" (emphasis added). Based on the authors' own statements, the Cups Plus business had been destroyed.

Therefore, the appropriate measure of damages would be the market value of the business at the time of the loss. While The Econ Report attempts to determine the "market value" of the business using the anticipated future benefits that the owners of this company wished they would have achieved, the analysis is really nothing more than a lost profits calculation. In fact, the lost profits calculation was performed for a 25-year period based on four months of history.

As stated in more detail later, at pages 12–13, the market value of the business as of the date of the explosion is no more than $317,500 at best. The available documentation, however, supports a valuation of only $97,500. Because of both the New-Business Rule and the destruction of the business, the market value of Cups Plus is the only legitimate way to calculate damages. Nonetheless, The Econ Report erroneously uses other methods to attempt a calculation of Cups Plus's damages, and this report will provide additional criticism in the discussion that follows.

Page 5

Under the section of "Background Facts and Assumptions, the authors have stated that the source of their information was the "Cups Plus, Inc. Business Plan and Request for Mediation documents." In fact, it is obvious that the authors have relied on these documents throughout their report. These documents are loaded with unsupportable pie-in-the-sky innuendo that does not provide any reasonable basis for reliance on this information. The business plan contains a sales pitch made by the owners of Cups Plus that was created to induce investors into making an investment in The Company. This document does not even attempt to quantify the rhetoric that was included in the business plan. We will point out many of these problems areas as we proceed with this critique.

Much of the analysis that was provided in The Econ Report is based on the comparison of the expected performance and profitability of Cups Plus to other companies in the same industry as Cups Plus. According to the authors, Cups Plus, Inc., is categorized under several Standard Industrial Classification (SIC) codes. These SIC codes include 3231, 3999, 5190, and 5199. These codes are used to obtain comparative industry data, such as sales growth rates and profit margins, which are used later in The Econ Report. Therefore, these figures are also being used as benchmark data to calculate damages.

---

[3]Ibid., 365.

[4]Brian P. Brinig, Douglas R. Carmichael, Raymond P. Ladouceur, Jay E. Fishman, J. Clifford Griffith, Meryl L. Reed, and Cherie W. Shipp, *Guide to Litigation Support Service*, 5th ed. (Fort Worth, Tex.: Practitioners Publishing Company), vol. 1, 3–21.

[5]*Recovery of Damages for Lost Profits*, vol. 1, 500.

EXHIBIT 19.3 *(Continued)*

Using this type of benchmark data is a common method to estimate the expected performance of a company "but for" an incident occurring that prevented the company from achieving certain results. However, the use of benchmark data is only effective if the benchmark data closely resembles the company whose performance is being estimated. In this instance, the use of these four SIC codes can result in a margin of error that cannot be quantified by the authors or anyone else. A description[6] of these four SIC codes follows:

3231 Glass Products, Made of Purchased Glass
Establishments primarily engaged in manufacturing glass products from purchased glass.

- Aquariums and reflectors, made from purchased glass
- Art glass, made from purchased glass
- Christmas tree ornaments, made from purchased glass
- Cut and engraved glassware, made from purchased glass
- Decorated glassware: e.g., chipped, engraved, etched
- Doors, made from purchased glass
- Enameled glass, made from purchased glass
- Encrusting gold, silver, or other metals on glass products
- Flowers, foliage, fruits and vines: artificial glass-made from
- Fruit, artificial: made from purchased glass
- Furniture tops, glass: cut, beveled, and polished
- Glass, scientific apparatus: for druggists, hospitals, laboratories-made
- Glass, sheet: bent-made from purchased glass
- Grasses, artificial: made from purchased glass
- Ground glass, made from purchased glass
- Industrial glassware, made from purchased glass
- Laboratory glassware, made from purchased glass
- Laminated glass, made from purchased glass
- Leaded glass, made from purchased glass
- Medicine droppers, made from purchased glass
- Mirrors, framed or unframed: made from purchased glass
- Mirrors, transportation equipment: made from purchased glass
- Multiple-glazed insulating units, made from purchased glass
- Novelties, glass: e.g., fruit, foliage, flowers, animals, made from purchased glass
- Ornamented glass, made from purchased glass
- Plants and foliage, artificial: made from purchased glass
- Reflector glass beads, for highway signs and other reflectors: made from purchased glass
- Slivered glass, made from purchased glass
- Stained glass, made from purchased glass
- Table tops made from purchased glass
- Technical glassware, made from purchased glass
- Tempered glass, made from purchased glass

[6]All descriptions have been obtained from Occupational Safety and Health Administration, U.S. Department of Labor, from the Web site http://www.osha.gov/cgi-bin/sic/sicser2.

(Continued)

EXHIBIT 19.3 *(Continued)*

- Test tubes, made from purchased glass
- Vials, made from purchased glass
- Watch crystals, made from purchased glass
- Windows, stained glass: made from purchased glass
- Windshields, made from purchased glass

3999 Manufacturing Industries, Not Elsewhere Classified
Establishments primarily engaged in manufacturing miscellaneous fabricated products, including beauty shop and barber shop equipment; hair work; tobacco pipes and cigarette holders; coin-operated amusement machines; matches; candles; lamp shades; feathers; artificial trees and flowers made from all materials, except glass; dressed and dyed furs; umbrellas, parasols, and canes; and other articles not elsewhere classified.

- Advertising curtains
- Amusement machines. Coin-operated: except coin-operated
- Artificial and preserved flowers, foliage, fruits and vines: except glass
- Artificial flower arrangements
- Atomizers, other than medical
- Badges for policemen and firemen-metal
- Barber shop equipment
- Barbers' clippers, hand and electric
- Beach umbrellas
- Beaded novelties
- Beads, unassembled
- Beauty shop equipment
- Beekeeping supplies, except wood
- Bone novelties
- Book matches
- Boutiquing: for the trade (decorating gift items)
- Bric-a-brac
- Bristles, dressing of
- Burnt wood articles
- Buttons: Red Cross, union, and identification
- Calendars, framed
- Candles
- Canes and cane trimmings, except precious metal
- Chairs, hydraulic: barber and beauty shop
- Christmas tree ornaments, except electrical and glass
- Christmas trees, artificial
- Cigar and cigarette holders
- Cigarette filters, not made in chemical plants
- Cigarette lighter flints
- Cleaners, pipe and cigarette holder
- Combs, except hard rubber

EXHIBIT 19.3 *(Continued)*

- Curlers, hair: designed for beauty parlors
- Curls, artificial (hair)
- Decalcomania work, except on china or glass: for the trade
- Desk pads, except paper
- Doll wigs
- Down (feathers)
- Dressing of furs: bleaching, blending, currying, scraping, and tanning
- Driers, hair: designed for beauty parlors
- Dusters, feather
- Embroidery kits
- Feathers: curling, dyeing, and renovating for the trade
- Figures, wax: mannequins
- Fingerprint equipment, except cameras and optical equipment
- Fire extinguishers, portable
- Flocking metal products for the trade
- Fly swatters
- Forms: display, dress, and show except shore display forms
- Frames and handles, handbag and luggage: except precious metal
- Fruits, artificial, except glass
- Fur stripping
- Furniture, beauty shop and barber shop
- Furs, dressed: bleached, curried, scraped, tanned, and dyed
- Games, coin-operated: pinball and other
- Globes, geographical
- Gold stamping for the trade, except books
- Glass
- Grenades, hand (fire extinguishers)
- Grinding purchased nut shells
- Hair clippers for human use, hand and electric
- Hair goods: braids, nets, switches, toupees, and wigs
- Hair, dressing of, for the trade
- Hairpin mountings
- Hat blocks and display forms
- Honeycomb foundations (beekeepers' supplies)
- Hosiery kits, sewing and mending
- Identification plates
- Identification tags, except paper
- Lamp shade frames
- Lamp shades: except metal and glass
- Lighters, cigar and cigarette: except precious metal and electric

(Continued)

EXHIBIT 19.3 *(Continued)*

- Mannequins and display forms
- Marionettes (puppets)
- Massage machines, electric: designed for beauty and barber shops
- Matches and match books
- Military insignia, except textile
- Models, except toy and hobby
- Mosaics: ivory, shell, horn, and bone
- Mountings, comb and hairpin: except precious metal
- Music boxes
- Musical chests
- Novelties: bone, beaded, and shell
- Pads, permanent waving
- Painting instrument dials, for the trade
- Parasols and frames: handles, parts, and trimmings, except precious
- Pelts: scraping, currying, tanning, bleaching, and dyeing
- Permanent wave equipment and machines
- Picture plaques, laminated
- Pipes, pipe stems, and bib: tobacco, except hard rubber
- Plaques, picture: laminated
- Plumes, feather
- Preparation of slides and exhibits, for classroom use
- Printing eyeglass frames for the trade
- Puppets
- Scenery for theaters, opera houses, halls and schools
- Sewing kits, novelty: other than sewing cases and cabinets
- Shades, lamp and candle: except glass and metal
- Shell novelties
- Shoe patterns
- Slot machines
- Smokers, bee (beekeepers' supplies)
- Soap dispensers
- Sponges, bleaching and dyeing of
- Stage hardware and equipment, except lighting equipment
- Stereographs, photographic
- Sterilizers, beauty and barber shop
- Straw goods
- Stringing beads for the trade
- Tape measures
- Tear gas devices and equipment
- Tinsel

EXHIBIT 19.3 *(Continued)*

- Transformations, hair
- Treating clock and watch dials with luminous material
- Trees, Christmas, artificial
- Trimmings, feather
- Umbrellas and parts, except precious metal
- Umbrellas: beach, garden and wagon
- Veils made of hair
- Vibrators, electric: designed for beauty and barber shops
- Walnut shell flour
- Wigs, including doll wigs, toupees, or wiglets, except custom made
- Wind chimes
- Wool pulling
- Wreaths, artificial

5199 Non-durable Goods, Not Elsewhere Classified
Establishments primarily engaged in the wholesale distribution of non-durable goods, not elsewhere classified, such as art goods, industrial yarns, textile bags, and bagging and burlap.

- Advertising specialties—wholesale
- Art goods—wholesale
- Artists' materials—wholesale
- Bags, textile—wholesale
- Baskets: reed, rattan, willow, and wood—wholesale
- Broom, mop, and paint handles—wholesale
- Burlap—wholesale
- Candles—wholesale
- Canvas products—wholesale
- Cats—wholesale
- Chamois leather—wholesale
- Charcoal—wholesale
- Christmas trees, including artificial—wholesale
- Clothes hampers—wholesale
- Cotton yarns—wholesale
- Curios—wholesale
- Dogs—wholesale
- Felt—wholesale
- Fish, tropical—wholesale
- Foam rubber—wholesale
- Furs, dressed—wholesale
- Gifts and novelties—wholesale
- Glassware, novelty—wholesale

(Continued)

EXHIBIT 19.3 ***(Continued)***

- Greases, animal and vegetable—wholesale
- Hairbrushes—wholesale
- Ice, manufactured or natural—wholesale
- Industrial yarn—wholesale
- Jewelry boxes—wholesale
- Leather and cut stock—wholesale
- Leather goods, except footware, gloves, luggage, and belting—wholesale
- Lighters, cigar and cigarette—wholesale
- Linseed oil—wholesale
- Matches—wholesale
- Novelties, paper—wholesale
- Oils, except cooking: animal and vegetable—wholesale
- Oilseed cake and meal—wholesale
- Pet supplies, except pet food—wholesale
- Pipes, smokers'—wholesale
- Plant food—wholesale
- Plastics foam—wholesale
- Rayon yarns—wholesale
- Rennet—wholesale
- Rubber, crude—wholesale
- Sawdust—wholesale
- Sheet music—wholesale
- Silk yarns—wholesale
- Smokers' supplies—wholesale
- Sponges—wholesale
- Statuary—wholesale
- Vegetable cake and meal—wholesale
- Wigs—Wholesale
- Wood carvings—wholesale
- Woolen and worsted yarns—wholesale
- Worms—wholesale
- Yarns—wholesale

As illustrated above, these industry categories are very general and are used to classify a long list of miscellaneous manufacturing and wholesaling businesses. For example, SIC code 3231 contains businesses that manufacture glass products, such as doors, flowers, fruit, furniture tops, mirrors, and watch crystals. These businesses can have very different cost structures and profit margins than a company that makes and/or decorates cups. SIC code 3999 is a miscellaneous catch-all of all manufacturing entities that do not fit into another category. The companies manufacture amusement machines, book matches, candles, cigarette lighter flints, down feathers, pelts, puppets, and vibrators. These too, are very different from a company that makes and/or decorates cups.

There really is no SIC code 5190, as the three-digit code 519 is a major grouping. SIC codes do not end in a zero. The SIC code grouping 519 represents Wholesale Trade—Nondurable Goods. We even reviewed the *Standard Industrial Classification Manual*, published by the United States government, but could not find this classification (5190) as a stand-alone category. SIC code 5199 includes the distribution of cats, fish, plant food, and wigs. This is also not similar to a maker and/or decorator of cups.

EXHIBIT 19.3 *(Continued)*

Based on the types of companies included in these SIC codes, it would be impossible to know what the mix of companies is that is included in the benchmark data used by the authors. We do not understand how the authors can have any reliance on the data included in these categories. Clearly, there are times when the use of this type of benchmark data can be deemed appropriate. However, this data is being used in this instance to assist in creating benchmarks for a four-month-old company with primarily one product line of business and no track record, and it is being used to estimate lost profits for the next 25 years.

The authors state that Cups Plus, Inc. purchased the business of Delphi for $237,500 and that this price "represented a deep discount below the fair market value of the firm because the seller was not looking to continue manufacturing, but rather found an opportunity to sell to an entity (Cups Plus) which would serve seller's own business of wholesale distribution on an ongoing basis at a discounted price."

According to The Econ Report, the $237,500 was composed of "$52,500 for equipment, + $45,000 for inventory + $70,000 for artwork + $70,000 for decals." There does not appear to be any support for some of these figures. The documentation provided reflects the purchase of equipment for $52,500 from Best Corp. (Delphi) in December 1994. We also saw documentation for the $45,000 of inventory. However, our review of the documentation does not reflect substantiation of the payment for artwork or decals. A letter dated July 11, 1995, approximately three months after the accident, from Best to Cups Plus discusses the supposed purchase of $70,000 worth of transparencies and artwork. It seems ironic that these items were not part of the original purchase. However, this letter also seems to indicate that because Best sold these transparencies at a "discount," Cups Plus would provide a 15 cents rebate "on all items decorated by you (Cups) for me (Best) after August 1, 1995." We have not seen documentation to show that the $70,000 was ever paid to Best.

Also, Cups Plus filed a tax return for the year 1995 that does not reflect any depreciable assets being acquired other than $52,000, the original acquisition. Furthermore, the underlying contention in The Econ Report is that the $237,500 was a "bargain purchase" because of the deal with Best to decorate their cups with a rebate. The original agreement of sale of the equipment is silent about any bargain purchase.

The July 11, 1995, letter provides that Best estimated the value of the transparencies to be $100 each and discusses that 1,500 units were sold to Cups Plus. Even if one buys into the concept that this purchase was legitimate, the maximum consideration for these 1,500 units would be $150,000 (1,500 units @ $100) assuming that $100 per unit is the correct value. The bargain purchase theory used in The Econ Report to argue why the purchase price of the business should not be used as a representative market value for The Company is therefore flawed.

Even if we accept The Econ Report's contention that a bargain purchase of $237,500 does not represent fair market value of this business at the time of the acquisition because of the side deal with Best, the maximum value based on the documentation seems to be $317,500 ($237,000 + $150,000 for the transparencies – $70,000 listed for the transparencies by the authors). If you accept all of the other components of the purchase price (and we still have not seen proof of payment for the transparencies or the decals), the fair market value of the negotiated transaction between the willing buyer and willing seller with both parties having knowledge of the relevant facts about the property and neither party being under duress is $317,500. If you remove those items that have not been paid for, the purchase price would be $97,500. This is not even remotely close to the $6.6 million of damages opined by the authors.

In addition, even if it is considered that the Best assets were sold at a discount, the authors do not discuss any additional expense or the effect on the profit margins of the side deal with Best. They seem to have forgotten about this in their profit projections.

According to The Econ Report, at the time of the acquisition, the ownership interests were "Russell Jones—45%, Larry Graham—45%, Alice Carlson—10%." According to a document entitled "Draft 2 Agreement," a shareholder agreement between all of the stockholders, Alice Carlson was to contribute $100,000 for her interest in the company. In simple mathematical terms, The Econ Report wants the court to award damages that would equate to approximately $660,000 for a 10 percent interest in the company. This would provide Ms. Carlson with a return of 660 percent for four months, or 1,980 percent annualized.

Furthermore, the same shareholders' agreement reflects life insurance to be purchased on the owners, for buyout purposes, at $100,000 each. That would indicate that they thought the business was worth $300,000 at that time.

Page 6

According to The Econ Report, the Delphi business purchased by Cups Plus "had been in existence for a number of years at the same location. It was operating as an Ad Specialty firm decorating customer's glassware and ceramics with annual gross sales of four to five (4–5) million dollars." First of all, the purchase documents reflect the purchase of some equipment and not an ongoing business. Second, we were provided with Delphi financial statements that appear to be the basis for the statement that the company was doing 4 to 5 million dollars in sales. We have no idea what Delphi's sales were at the time of the acquisition, and we have no idea as to how the company's product line differed from that of Cups Plus. The financial statements that were provided reflect the following information:

	1987	*1986*	*1984*	*1983*
Sales	$ 4,036,362	$ 4,211,626	$ 3,612,640	$ 4,034,598
Net income	$ (159,635)	$ (206,622)	$ 86,330	$ 45,864

(Continued)

EXHIBIT 19.3 *(Continued)*

What is apparently left out of the discussion in The Econ Report is that the financial information was at least eight years old. They also ignored that fact that the compound annual growth rate over the five years (1983 through 1987) was 0 percent, and Delphi was showing large losses. This should have raised serious doubts as to the reliability of the financial information that their clients provided them with since they had never owned this type of business before. Furthermore, it would seem that the Delphi data may have been better benchmark data than relying on SIC codes that included so many unrelated types of businesses as to render the comparison meaningless.

Presenting the limited information to the reader suggests an attempt by the author to convince the reader that Cups Plus, Inc., would have instantly achieved 4 to 5 million dollars in sales in its first year of operations. The authors do not present to the reader the fact that Cups Plus, Inc. would have a different operating structure, management team, and financial condition than Delphi.

Page 7

The Econ Report includes a list of companies that Mr. Jones has indicated are contacts from his previous employment. However, there is no support to indicate any of the following:

- Would any of these customers follow Jones?
- What would be the size of the orders placed with Cups Plus?
- Could Cups Plus handle the volume of business without making a substantial investment to meet customer demands?
- How much would such an investment be?
- Could Cups Plus raise the necessary capital?
- Are there any written contracts that Cups Plus had with any of these contacts to indicate that they would be a continuing source of business in the future?

There are many more questions that need to be answered as well, but The Econ Report does not address any of them. The authors merely accepted their clients' word for what they would achieve. This is highly speculative since there is no track record to support this type of success. Although the authors discuss Mr. Jones's success at Star Giftware, bringing the company from $9.0 million to $28.0 million in sales in a span of five to seven years, no proof has been furnished that this was due solely to his efforts. Once again, the authors attribute the success of Star to the fact that Mr. Jones was sent to manage the company. Mr. Jones may have done a good job for the company, but there is no independent proof that the company's success was solely, or even more than a little bit, due to Mr. Jones's effort. What is omitted from The Econ Report is the fact that Star, as a subsidiary of XYZ Company, was part of a publicly traded company with sales revenues of approximately $348 million (in 1995 per Form 10K filed with the Securities and Exchange Commission) and a book value of about $223 million. Having these resources behind a company like Star, and having a parent company like XYZ Company, may have impacted the growth a little bit more than merely bringing in Mr. Jones to manage the company. Actually, XYZ Company decided to sell Star in the early part of 1996 because it did not fit within the company's strategic plan. If the projections for this industry were so spectacular, XYZ Company may have wanted to keep its subsidiary.

Page 8

At the top of this page, The Econ Report indicates, "These customers were bringing in over two (2) million dollars a year in sales of Cups and giftware for Star." Besides not providing documentation to support this amount, the authors are implying that this business would be transferred to Cups Plus. It is more than conceivable to think that many of these large customers are dealing with Star and have deals and relationships with Star due to XYZ Company. For example, if XYZ Company makes stuffed animals for The Disney Company, Disney may purchase other products from the company and its subsidiaries because of the ongoing relationship. There is more of an ongoing trend for a large company to consolidate its vendors. No proof has been furnished to support the "dreams" of a salesman that ended up in these projections.

According to The Econ Report, "as a result of the explosion and the ensuing business interruption, plaintiff lost the opportunity at hand to sell Cups to millions of Olympic games visitors not only at the 1996 Olympics in Atlanta but at all future Olympic games as well." This is another highly speculative statement. There is no proof to suggest that Cups Plus, Inc. would have continuing revenue from future Olympic games. In fact, the apparent relationship was with the Atlanta Visitors Bureau and not the Olympics.

Page 10

According to The Econ Report, "Cups Plus's strategy to dominate the competition was by offering high quality 12 ounce ceramic cups and glassware, exceptional design, decorated by their designers, and pricing less than their competitors." The report continues with "Their estimated cost of a decorated ceramic mug was $0.80. Their wholesale price was $2.50 per mug. The result was a gross profit of $1.70 per mug (68% gross profit). The plan was to maintain a minimum gross profit margin of 60% on all Cups and glassware." The authors cite the business plan as their source for this information. The documentation supplied to us does not contain any cost sheets demonstrating where these figures came from.

EXHIBIT 19.3 *(Continued)*

Delphi's financial statements reflect gross margins of 30.7 percent and 21.9 percent, respectively, for 1987 and 1986. Furthermore, the authors have repeatedly indicated that the original purchase was at a bargain price because of future discounts being provided to Delphi (Best), but there is no discussion of how this fits into the figures cited above. How does anyone know whether the projected gross profits could be achieved? Are management's estimates calculated by an experienced cost accountant with knowledge about the production facilities that were purchased? It appears that it was older equipment worth $52,500. How much money would have to be invested to make the production facility modern enough and efficient enough to allow this level of profitability to be achieved? Could The Company find a labor force that would work at a low enough wage to keep these profit margins? One of the very substantial reasons why so much of the manufacturing in this country has left is due to the high cost of labor. Why would Cups Plus achieve what the rest of the country cannot?

Page 11

According to the authors, their firm was retained in this matter "to evaluate, within a reasonable degree of economic certainty, the economic loss sustained by the 'closely held' business of Cups Plus, Inc. as a result of its permanent business interruption caused by the defendant."

The only apparent measure of the economic loss suffered by The Company, since its loss is permanent, was the fair market value of the business at the time of the accident. Without reiterating all of the reasons that we have previously raised about the speculation and unsupported information presented and used in The Econ Report, we must once again raise the commonsense issue, can a four-month-old closely held company that is in the glassware business, purchased for about $300,000 (maybe), be sold to a willing buyer for $6.6 million? This defies logic. Cups Plus was not an Internet company, nor was it going to go public in April 1995.

Page 12

In discussing the theory of calculating damages, the authors discuss the yardstick approach. We agree with the theory and especially agree with them when they say that "one of the key issues in applying the yardstick method is the issue of comparability." It is obvious from the SIC codes previously discussed that the issue of comparability is highly questionable.

The authors then continue and discuss different valuation approaches. They state, "*The Cost Approach* is based on the business's underlying value of net assets at the valuation date." What they omitted was that this approach is frequently used for businesses that do not have a great deal of intangible value. A four-month-old company that bought equipment for $52,500 probably has little, if any, intangible value. But then, they reject the cost approach and use other methods of valuation that result in a very large amount of intangible value.

The next problem, because there is not much intangible value after only four months, is that there is no proven track record of continued patronage to Cups Plus. Unfortunately, the accident put them out of business. If they had continued in business, without the accident, would a willing buyer have paid $6.6 million for the business at that time? Clearly not. Therefore, the cost approach is probably the most applicable approach to use to value this new business.

Under the heading, "Earning-Based Models," the author states that "the discounted future earnings model, capitalization of earnings, and the excess earnings method, also known as the formula approach, are considered in this report." The *Guide to Business Valuations* notes conditions regarding the use of these methodologies. This publication states:

> Preconditions for Using the Capitalized Returns or the Discounted Future Returns Methods
>
> Before beginning this discussion, it should be noted that two important conditions should be present when any of these methods are used. First, *the valuation consultant must be able to estimate future returns* (either net cash flow or net earnings) *with a reasonable degree of probability. Second, there generally should be a reasonable likelihood that future operations will continue at a predictable rate. If the company is too volatile to predict future operations, the consultant should seriously question whether any of these methods are appropriate. If this latter situation exists, other methods, including the net asset value method or the liquidation value method may be appropriate* [emphasis added].[7]

Clearly, The Econ Report does not follow the above concept in its analysis. It is unlikely that the authors could estimate the future returns of a four-month-old company for 25 years with a "reasonable degree of probability." Also, there is no basis presented within the report for the authors to expect that there is "a reasonable likelihood that future operations will continue at a predictable rate."

Since a new company's results would be too volatile to predict, The Econ Report should have used "other methods, including the net asset value method or the liquidation value method (as) may be appropriate."

[7] Jay E. Fishman, Shannon P. Pratt, J. Clifford Griffith, and D. Keith Wilson, *Guide to Business Valuations*, 10th ed. (Fort Worth, Tex: Practitioner's Publishing Co., 2000), vol. 1, 5-1.

(Continued)

EXHIBIT 19.3 *(Continued)*

The Econ Report also violated proper appraisal theory in its use of both the capitalization and discounted future earnings methods. Section 500.4 of the *PPC Guide* states:

> A capitalized returns method tends to be more appropriate when it appears that a company's *current operations are indicative of its future operations* (assuming a normal growth rate). On the other hand, a discounted future returns method tends to be more appropriate when *future returns are expected to be "substantially different" from current operations*. ("Substantially different" means materially greater or less than a normal growth rate.) In some cases, it may be desirable to use both types of methods to estimate a company's value [emphasis added].[8]

Valuation theory dictates the proper use of each method with respect to expected volatility in future growth. The use of both methodologies to obtain the lost business value in The Econ Report is not only improper through its implication that estimating future growth for Cups Plus can be performed with reasonable probability, but also that both stable and volatile growth is expected by the authors. Using both methods for the same earnings stream is contradictory. While capitalization methods are frequently used in the calculation of the residual value in a discounted cash flow model, the proper time to use this method is at the point of stabilization. The authors stabilize earnings, albeit wrong earnings, after the year 2000 and not 2020.

Page 13

The Econ Report states:

> The methods adopted in this appraisal report are that of applying accepted financial models to the financial characteristics of a firm in order to estimate a fair market value for the firm as though an active market for its shares existed.

However, the documentation provided to us is totally inadequate for a prospective purchaser to properly analyze Cups Plus. In addition, there is no basis to assume that an active market exists for this four-month-old company with inadequate records.

Similarly, there is no basis for the statement in The Econ Report that "for many manufacturing and service firms, the intangible assets produce more value to a business than do tangible assets." Capital-intensive manufacturing firms are very different from labor-intensive service firms. Combining these two groups in the same statement is misleading. What is even worse is the footnote that the authors use to provide an example of what they mean. The authors give an example of Microsoft to support their claim. Although the statement holds true in the case of Microsoft, the use of one of the nation's largest technology companies as a comparison example to Cups Plus is wrong on many levels, including company size, age, type of business, and financial history. This would be like saying that the local hardware store is worth a tremendous amount of money because it is in the same industry as Home Depot.

The authors discuss the need to value the tangible and intangible assets of the business, but they make no attempt to value any of the intangible assets that may exist. The cost approach could have been used to value the net assets that were on the balance sheet at the time of the accident and they could have added to that amount the value of any additional assets that may exist. This would have required more work on their part. Instead, they chose to use methods of valuation that normally capture the tangible and intangible value of the business enterprise. Unfortunately, the manner in which they applied these methodologies is fatally flawed.

Page 14

The authors discuss the three approaches to valuing intangible assets and the related models based on the Smith and Parr treatise. However, they never value these assets using these models. In fact, they have not provided a complete discussion about the valuation of intangible assets. Had they performed additional research, they would have also found out that:

> For an intangible asset to have a quantifiable value from an economic analysis or appraisal perspective, it must possess certain additional attributes. Some of these additional requisite attributes include the following:
>
> - It must generate some measurable amount of economic benefit to its owner; this economic benefit could be in the form of an income increment or of a cost decrement
> - This economic benefit may be measured in any of several ways, including net income or net operating income or net cash flow, etc.
> - It must enhance the value of other assets with which it is associated; the other assets may include tangible personal property and tangible real estate
>
> Clearly there may be a substantial distinction between the legal existence of an intangible asset and the economic value of an intangible asset. An example of this situation would be the new registration of a legally binding and enforceable patent that, upon creation, is immediately and permanently locked in the corporate vault. If the patent is never used in the production of, or in the protection of, income, then it has no economic value—even though it has legal existence.[9]

[8]Ibid., 5-2.1

[9]Shannon P. Pratt, Robert E. Reilly, and Robert P. Schweihs, *Valuing a Business: The Analysis and Appraisal of Closely Held Companies*, 3rd ed. (Homewood, Ill.:Irwin Professional Publishing), 537.

EXHIBIT 19.3 *(Continued)*

Basically, the important distinction that Pratt makes is that you can have an intangible asset but it may not have value. All of these supposed contacts that Mr. Jones would have brought to the company are similar to the patent that has not had an opportunity to be tested in the market. Initially, it has no value. Value may have come in time, but certainly not after four months when there is no proven track record of what a willing buyer would be purchasing. If John Smith bought Cups Plus in April 1995, these possible intangible assets would not have been worth much, if anything, at all. In fact, there is no guarantee that they ever would have had value. Without history, this cannot be substantiated with any reasonable degree of certainty.

Pages 15–16

The Econ Report identifies lost customers "who have bought products of Cups Plus, Inc. before the business interruption." The table at the top of page 16 is intended to reflect the lost value of the sales. The sales in this table total $5,700,000. According to the 1995 corporation tax return for Cups Plus (Cups 001404-00001414), sales were $36,476. No documentation has been furnished to determine how these figures were derived. The note in The Econ Report indicates that the $5.7 million comes from purchase orders per Messrs. Graham and Jones. On page 10 of their report, the authors state, "After only a few months in operation, Cups Plus booked sales of over seven hundred fifty thousand dollars ($750,000)." This is a vastly different figure from $5.7 million. It is also contradictory to their previous statement.

Our review of the documentation provided reflects sales and purchase orders of $992,338. A comparison was made to the table at the top of this page. The results are as follows:

Customer Name	*Per Econ*	*Documented*
Bob Anderson	$ 1,000,000	$ 259,200
Best	200,000	—
Raleys Drug	500,000	4,116
Uptons Department Stores	250,000	21,751
Canner & Hirsh	2,000,000	493,632
Target Stores	250,000	1,800
Bellcrest	250,000	13,141
Consumer Promotion	100,000	3,049
Atlanta Visitors Bureau (Atlanta Olympics)	1,000,000	10,000
Dandee Creations	50,000	—
Cardinal	100,000	1,144
Total	$ 5,700,000	$ 807,833

In addition to these sales and/or orders, we also found the following:

Company	*Sales*	*Bates #*
Ace Hardware	$ 3,600	Cups 001316
Big Apple & Beer Co.	1,807	Cups 002126
Logo's & Promotions	2,143	Cups 002126
OH NUTS, Inc.	125	Cups 002126
QED Communications	538	Cups 002126
Riedys	59	Cups 002187
The Hass Company	226	Cups 002126
Touch of Georgia	345	Cups 002126
Westchester Restaurant Supply	270	Cups 002126
Food 4 Less Supermarkets	137,376	Cups 001672
Hughes Family Markets	38,016	Cups 001671
Total	$ 184,505	

This further demonstrates that the authors have relied on incorrect and unsubstantiated figures.

(Continued)

EXHIBIT 19.3 *(Continued)*

Even if purchase orders had been received, more questions would have to be answered before any of this information is usable. For example, what are the delivery dates for the product; can the orders be canceled by the customer? These figures are as unsupported as many of the other statements that appear in The Econ Report. It would appear prudent for the damage expert to have quantified these figures and not merely accept them from the client. There is no evidence in The Econ Report that this was done.

Also on this page, The Econ Report lists contacts of Mr. Jones as "potential customers" from which over $2,500,000 in future sales are projected. These contacts are just that, contacts, and it is unsupported to assume that these "potential customers" would become customers in the first year since there is no basis for this assumption. Not only does this inflate the first year's sales estimate, but it inflates the next 24 years as well since the first year is used as the starting point to project results well into the new millennium.

Page 17

A list of lost sales representatives with projected first year sales figures attained from each is presented on this page. As mentioned about the previous page, at the time of loss, the sales to be made through these representatives is purely speculative. Projected sales from these representatives should not be considered in estimating future annual sales unless actual purchase orders were obtained, and even then, with serious reservation. There is no support for these figures.

Based on the speculative nature of the entire first year sales projection for Cups Plus, we find that the total first year sales volume of $10,900,000 anticipated by the authors, used to estimate future earnings and damages in The Econ Report, is totally unreasonable, unsupported, and arbitrary. There has not been any support using benchmark data to show that a new company in this business could grow to almost $11 million in its first year. Delphi was doing about $4 million based on the last known financial data that even the authors reviewed. The authors have accepted the statements of their clients as to all of the sales that would have been generated without performing any due diligence as to the reasonableness of the probability of occurrence. The basis of damage calculations should be based on supportable information. Not having a track record is the very reason that The Courts have not allowed damages in these cases.

It would have been reasonable to assume that if the authors had verified the $750,000 of supposed purchase orders that were previously discussed, an annualized sales figure of about $4 million might have occurred. However, not only did they not verify the information (at least there is no evidence in their report that they did), but accepting their clients' assertions without verification renders their opinion without any factual support.

Pages 18–19

In their discussion of the length of the loss period, the authors are mixing concepts relating to lost profits and the complete loss of the business. Since the business was completely lost, calculating lost profits to the year 2020 is not the correct manner in which to calculate damages. First of all, there are very few businesses that can forecast next year's results with any degree of certainty, let alone to go out 25 years. A discounted cash flow analysis will typically go out to the period at which time growth stabilizes and then a terminal value is calculated. More often than not, the financial community is very reluctant to go out much further than five years since the further out you go, the more speculative the projections become. Second, the methodology used by the authors makes no sense.

The authors have treated this case as if it were a personal injury case and the projections were being made of an individual's lost wages. This methodology is not correct for calculating the lost business value in April 1995 of Cups Plus. If the willing buyer placed him or herself at April 1995, how would they project the impact of the Internet on this company? Could they have guessed at what the economy would be like in the year 2000 or 2010?

The concept of fair market value is supposed to be based on what information is known or knowable at the date of the valuation. In April 1995, all that was known is that there was a four-month-old acquisition of $52,500 of equipment and $45,000 of inventory and a dream. A willing buyer would not attempt to project to the year 2020 with "any reasonable degree of economic certainty."

Pages 19–22

The authors go through an explanation of macroeconomics but fail to get down to the real issues surrounding Cups Plus. Although all of the items discussed in The Econ Report are valid, they fail to specifically discuss how these economic issues pertain to The Company. Using national economic figures makes sense but fails to recognize the tight labor market in the State. Their discussion also fails to discuss how inflation relating to materials and labor would have impacted The Company. Could they have maintained management's expected gross profit margins?

Pages 22–26

The authors perform what they call an "Industry Analysis." First, they start off with an analysis of "All Manufacturing Industries." Their contention is that "the core of the plaintiff's business was manufacturing." Comparing all manufacturing industries with Cups Plus is a meaningless analysis. Companies that manufacture hand grenades, horseshoes, and computers are being compared to Cups Plus.

EXHIBIT 19.3 *(Continued)*

Next, they continue with an analysis of "Miscellaneous Manufacturing Industries SIC 39." We previously discussed the poor choice of yardstick data because of the lack of comparability of the companies that are included in this SIC code. The same argument exists here as well.

The Econ Report then gets a little more specific by looking at SIC code 32. How much of this data is from manufacturers of pots, dishes, and other types of glassware as opposed to "cheap" cups? The same problems are also incurred for the wholesale categories.

While there is no doubt that an economic analysis is important, we do not believe that the information that has been included in The Econ Report is meaningful enough to provide the authors with the ability to opine within a reasonable degree of certainty. What would have been much more meaningful, but was not included in this report, would have been an extensive analysis of the "ceramic cups" industry. Industry data from 1995 should have been obtained to provide support for many of the unsupported figures that were used to make a 25-year forecast. Even with good industry data, a 25-year forecast is unreasonable and unsupportable.

In order to obtain industry growth rates for use in their damages analysis, the authors performed two arbitrary tasks. First, they took the average of four SIC code industry growth rate averages to obtain another average growth rate. Averaging a series of averages is a meaningless mathematical exercise. Further, the decision to grow the hypothetical business of Cups Plus by 7.94 percent through 2000 and 5.67 percent through 2020 also has no basis. Besides using four SIC codes that may not truly have enough comparable data to be meaningful, the authors used data from 1988 through 1997, a period that for the most part had a booming economy, as a basis to justify using a 5.67 percent growth rate from the year 2001 through 2020. This means that the authors are forecasting a continuing booming economy.

Pages 27–28

The authors attempt to perform a "firm-specific analysis" by quoting information from one article that appeared in *Giftware News*. There is little information in this section that can assist in the quantification of the future for Cups Plus. We all have coffee cups with cute sayings on them, but that does not provide enough data to allow a forecast to be relied upon. There really was no firm-specific analysis performed here, despite what the authors called it.

At the bottom of page 28, the authors indicate, "For purposes of this report, it is assumed, very conservatively, that the growth rate of the sales of Cups Plus, Inc. is 7.94%." How do they know that the rate that they are using is conservative? They do not have any empirical data to compare this against that is in any way reliable. They have taken averages of averages, which has resulted in large standard deviations, and then tried to justify their conclusions by running a correlation analysis showing good correlation among the variables. Other than attempting to use statistics for the sake of the presentation, the authors have yet to present good empirical data that supports their self-serving statement about how "conservative" they are being. For a new company without a proven track record, forecasting growth based on a group of mature businesses that are not necessarily similar, and very possibly considerably larger and better capitalized, is not conservative; it is foolish.

The reality is that even though the growth rate matters, the figures being applied to are so unsupported that the results are meaningless. The fact is that The Econ Report includes sales for 1995 of $10,900,000 for a company that recorded actual sales from January 1, 1995, to April 21, 1995, of $36,476. So the authors want us to accept that sales from April 21, 1995, to December 31, 1995, would have been $10,863,524. This would have been achieved by a company that bought $52,500 worth of used equipment. How would they have produced this level of sales?

Page 29

In the "Measurement of Economic Loss" section of their report, the authors once again cite documents from this litigation as support. The profit margins discussed, as if accurate, come from Exhibit B of the Request for Mediation. Exhibit B is a self-serving letter "To whom it may concern" from Mr. Jones. He says, "*Based upon my experience in the industry*, I know that an unboxed mug costs forty-five cents to purchase" (emphasis added).

The authors then take this statement and turn it around as if factual that "*For Cups Plus*, an unboxed mug costs forty-five cent to purchase" (emphasis added). The authors have represented the cost of an unboxed mug as if it is factual, when it is anything but.

Mr. Jones has worked for many large companies that have tremendous buying power, and as a result, can obtain all types of discounts on the purchase of goods. Documentation supplied in this matter reflects a purchase price based on large quantities varying from 25 cents to 85 cents. The authors cannot state with certainty that cups cost 45 cents. We have not been provided with a written contract guaranteeing this price for Cups Plus.

The authors also refer to Arthur Bylin, a business owner who tells of his companies' gross profit margins. Again, how comparable is Cups Plus to Mr. Bylin's businesses? If this is good benchmark data, why didn't the authors obtain financial data from Mr. Bylin to use as a yardstick? Then at least a true comparison could be done to determine similarities. Let's see what Mr. Bylin's balance sheet looks like, and his income statements and the type of equipment and number of personnel employed in his businesses. Otherwise, this information does not tell us anything. We also cannot tell what the mix of product is between manufacturing (decorating) at a 15 to 20 percent margin versus general gift items at 50 to 70 percent. Without knowing the mix, The Econ Report again states that "very conservatively" they will use 30 percent on total sales. Further justification is then used in the report that shows average gross margins for the poorly comparative SIC code information ranging from 20.18 percent to 36.35 percent. The average of the averages is 29.5 percent. Therefore, how can the authors say that they were conservative?

(Continued)

EXHIBIT 19.3 *(Continued)*

Page 30

At the top of the page, average profit margins before taxes are averaged again to derive a figure to apply to Cups Plus. The same problem exists here as before. Besides poor comparability, the profit percentages are being applied against a number that makes no sense. Applying the 2.99 percent profit against different sales levels would throw off the calculation of profits as follows:

Sales	$ 10,900,000.00	$ 4,000,000.00
Pretax profit percentage	× 2.99%	× 2.99%
Forecast pretax profit	$ 325,910.00	$ 119,600.00

Using the sales forecast of $10,900,000 results in an overstatement of pretax profits by $206,310, or 272.5 percent, in the very first year of the forecast and this gets compounded for 24 more years. Furthermore if Cups Plus had this type of profit, the company would pay approximately 40 percent in taxes.

In the middle of this page, the authors discuss the "Lost Tangible Assets." The values listed in The Econ Report do not represent the fair market value of the assets that were destroyed. Our review of the documentation attached to the request for mediation leads us to believe that the figures used were "replacement costs" for these assets as if purchased new. Machinery and equipment is generally not appraised at replacement cost new. The concept that should be used for these assets is "depreciated replacement cost." What is the value of the *used* equipment, not *new* equipment? Four months earlier, The Company's assets were bought for $52,500. The artwork and the decals do not appear to have been on the books of the company since they apparently had not been paid for. The lost tangible asset value is not the $827,228 claimed in The Econ Report.

Pages 31–32

A discussion about the methodology used to derive the discount and capitalization rates used by the authors begins on page 31. On page 32, the authors illustrate how they derived a discount rate of 22 percent and a capitalization rate for earnings of 16.33 percent.

First, let's address the most obvious technical error made by the authors. They point out that the source used for their equity risk premium data is *Stocks, Bonds, Bills and Inflation*, published by Ibbotson Associates. This is a well-regarded source. However, this source provides information for a discount rate to be derived for net cash flow and not earnings. The 22 percent discount rate derived on page 32 should be applied to net cash flow. Subtracting growth from this figure provides a capitalization rate to be applied to net cash flow and not earnings.

Ibbotson data calculates the cash returns in the marketplace. Therefore it is applicable to net cash flow. The model for the build up method presented in the *Guide to Business Valuation*[10] illustrates the steps as follows:

Step 1		Risk-free rate
Step 2	+	Equity risk premium
	=	Average market return at valuation date
Step 3		Increments for risk differentials of the company being valued
Step 3a	+	a. Risk premium for size
Step 3b	+ or −	b. Other risk factors
	=	**Net cash flow discount rate**
Step 4	+	Additional increment by which the net earnings discount rate exceeds the net cash flow discount rate
	=	**Net earnings discount rate**

An additional incremental adjustment should have been reflected in the build-up of the discount rate if the authors intended to apply the discount rate to net income instead of net cash flow. Certainly, even the authors would have to admit that in a growing company, such as they projected, cash flow would be considerably less than net income when factoring in such items as needed working capital and capital expenditures.

Also, despite stating in The Econ Report that "additional risk may be due to specific risks associated with the industry or the company as compared to the entire market place," the authors have not accounted for any company-specific risk within their build-up model for a discount rate. That is represented in Step 3b above. Understating the discount rate increases the value that they derive.

[10]*Guide to Business Valuations*, 5-14

EXHIBIT 19.3 *(Continued)*

According to Pratt:

> Broken down into its simplest components, the discount rate, or the rate of return that investors require, incorporates the following elements:
>
> - A "risk-free rate" (the amount that an investor feels certain of realizing over the holding period). This includes:
>   - A "rental rate" for forgoing the use of funds over the holding period.
>   - The expected rate of inflation over the holding period.
> - A premium for risk. This includes:
>   - Systematic risk (that risk that relates to movements in returns on the investment market in general).
>   - Unsystematic risk (that risk that is specific to the subject investment).[11]

The Econ Report has ignored part 2b of the above reference. Within the model, no effort is made to account for the risk of Cups Plus being a small private business with financial and economic risks that are specific to it alone. Specific risks pertaining to Cups Plus that have been ignored by the authors include, but are not limited to: The Company is not a public company, it does not have the capital base of a public company, it has only been in business for four months, it lacks depth in management, it does not have the ability to raise capital, and in this instance, the forecast has significant risk of never being achieved. Failure to add a premium has resulted, once again, in the understatement of the discount rate by the authors. This has also caused the value to be overstated.

Another error in the use of the discount rate derived by the authors is that the authors have applied these rates to the pretax income derived in their unsupported projections. We previously demonstrated that this should have been applied to net cash flow. Net cash flow is also calculated after income taxes. Applying the discount rate to pretax income would have warranted an additional adjustment to the build-up of the discount rate. This error, on behalf of the authors, also overstated the damages.

Discussing common errors made in business valuation, Pratt discusses the mismatching of the discount rate with the economic income measure. He states:

> **Applying a Discount Rate to an Income Variable Defined Differently Than That to Which the Discount Rate Is Applicable**
>
> This general error in itself has many variations. As discussed earlier, most of the methods and sources for developing discount rates used in the practical application of contemporary financial theory and discussed in this book produce a rate to discount net cash flow, as defined in the earlier section. The *SBBI: Valuation Edition 1999 Yearbook* makes the following point: "It is implicit that the market return data represents returns after corporate taxes but before personal taxes" [footnote omitted].[12]

Page 32

At the bottom of this page, The Econ Report discusses the valuation going to the year 2020 because that is when the principals would sell the business. They discuss using three different approaches and methodologies and employing the incorrectly calculated discount and capitalization rates as well as some others in each direction. None of these rates is appropriate for this brand new company. Not only did they calculate the discount rate improperly, they attempt to perform a sensitivity analysis by arbitrarily picking two other discount rates, one higher and one lower. Since the main discount rate is terribly understated, the other two rates follow as well.

Page 33

The first method used by the authors is the "Price-Earnings Method." What the authors have attempted to do is use multiples from actual transactions from the marketplace to determine the multiples that should be applied to Cups Plus in 2020 when the business will ultimately be sold. The authors used data from 1995 to 1999 (a very hot market) to apply to Cups Plus in 2020 (an unknown market).

The authors used *Mergerstat Review* to identify transactions in the marketplace. *Mergerstat Review* reports the purchase of fairly large companies by public companies. The authors calculate a weighted average price-to-earnings multiple for companies sold in the miscellaneous manufacturing and wholesale and distribution categories in 1995 through 1999. The authors indicate in their report that they are attempting to "find out the P/E ratios at which other companies in the same or similar industries are selling," but the data in *Mergerstat* did not meet their purpose, and should not have been used.

The authors demonstrate the lack of business valuation experience by blindly applying price-to-earnings multiples based on an SIC code rather than looking at the true comparability of the transactions. For example, a review of the wholesale and distribution category in the 1999 *Mergerstat* data would have revealed transactions involving companies in the voice, video, and data equipment business; a wholesale pharmaceutical distributor; a grocery wholesaler; and others that do not in any manner resemble Cups Plus.

[11] *Valuing A Business*, 4th ed., 160.

[12] Ibid., 195.

(Continued)

EXHIBIT 19.3 *(Continued)*

The concept behind the market approach is to use information for comparability in the valuation process. The authors have failed in this area. Furthermore, the use of the *Mergerstat* data without any consideration of the differences between large and small companies, or public and private companies, is also troublesome. The P/E ratios used in The Econ Report are a mix of those from public and private companies.

To illustrate the vast differences between the multiples for public and private companies, we have included some of the data presented in *Mergerstat*. This information cuts across all SIC codes and cannot be used to calculate damages in this case without considerable analysis and research.

Median P/E Offered:
Public vs. Private 1990–1999

	Acquisitions of Public Companies		*Acquisitions of Private Companies*	
1990	17.1	(117)	13.2	(36)
1991	15.9	(93)	8.5	(23)
1992	18.1	(89)	17.6	(15)
1993	19.7	(113)	22.0	(14)
1994	19.8	(194)	22.0	(18)
1995	19.4	(239)	15.5	(16)
1996	21.7	(288)	17.7	(31)
1997	25.0	(389)	17.0	(83)
1998	24.0	(362)	16.0	(207)
1999	21.7	(434)	18.4	(174)

( ) Denotes number of transactions reporting P/E.

As shown above, in 8 out of 10 years, the P/E ratio for private companies has been significantly lower than that for public companies. In addition, notice the number of transactions of public companies as opposed to private companies in this data. The usage of the P/E ratios from *Mergerstat Review* is a meaningless exercise without an appropriate analysis to accompany the process.

According to the *1996 Business Reference Guide*, the suggested rule of thumb to value a small manufacturing business is 1.25 to 1.75 times annual adjusted earnings. This ratio is well below the authors' suggested P/E ratio of 8.28 for Cups Plus. Furthermore, we contacted The Institute of Business Appraisers, a professional appraisal organization, for possible transaction data that this organization maintains in its market database of small private business transactions. This is what we received:

Business Type	*Annual Earnings ($000)*	*Sales Price ($000)*	*Price/Earnings*
SIC Code: 3231			
Glass etcher	15	22	1.47
SIC Code: 5199			
Distribution biz	132	158	1.20
Housewares, import	147	150	1.02
Import glassware	101	284	2.81
Artwork, wholesale	57	106	1.86
Ice delivery	42	175	4.17
Product distribution	48	65	1.35
Import housewares	200	740	3.70
Gifts, wholesale	28	35	1.25
Tropical fish, whsle	102	225	2.21
Advert specialty—dist.	38	17	0.45
Graphic arts, export	100	218	2.18
Whsle—video tapes	89	100	1.12

EXHIBIT 19.3 *(Continued)*

Business Type	*Annual Earnings ($000)*	*Sales Price ($000)*	*Price/Earnings*
SIC Code: 3999			
Silk flowers—mfg.	50	105	2.10
Traffic contrl device mfg.	126	370	2.94
Mfg.—giftware product	336	1350	4.02
Mfg.—flowers, artificial	24	185	7.71
Windchime, mfg.	34	61	1.79
Badge mfg.	12	23	1.92
Candle/lamps, mfg.	21	40	1.90
Flowers—mfg. silk	91	135	1.48
Hair color	85	130	1.53
Mfg.—stained glass gifts	61	120	1.97
Windchime, mfg.	55	61	1.11

Not only do these sample transactions show the varied type of industries within the SIC codes used by the authors to obtain their industry data, but they also show more reasonable P/E ratio figures for industry transactions. All of these transactions have a P/E ratio below the authors' suggested P/E ratio of 8.28.

Also, the 30 percent reduction in the weighted average P/E ratio in order to create the company-specific ratio is arbitrary and unsupported. The authors have made no effort to explain why the pretax P/E ratio of 11.83 is reduced by 30 percent to 8.28. The evidence above suggests that the business value of Cups Plus, Inc. obtained through the P/E method is greatly overstated, as is the damages estimate for loss of increased market value to Cups Plus that is put forth by the authors.

Page 35

The calculation of economic losses in Scenario 1 is incorrect because the values are unsupported. The use of replacement costs is inappropriate since the damages should be based on the fair market value of the business and not what it would cost to replace it brand new.

The calculation of damages from prior lost sales is inappropriate because the sales forecast is unsupported, the profit is calculated on a pretax basis, and the determination of damages should be based on the lost value of the business and not lost profits.

Page 36

The calculation of lost future sales is also inappropriate due to unsupported forecasts, incorrectly calculated profits, and the incorrect method of determining damages.

Pages 37–38

The calculation of the value of the business in the year 2020 using incorrect price-earnings multiples based on unsupported forecasts results in a meaningless number. The entire exercise on this page makes no sense, defies proper valuation practice, and is discounted improperly.

Another problem with the business values calculated by the authors is the failure to consider appropriate valuation discounts. For all calculations of value for the Cups Plus business on this page and after, the authors value The Company as if it were a freely traded public company. Even if they performed their calculations correctly, which they did not, they should have applied an appropriate discount for lack of marketability. According to Pratt:

> Since interests in closely held businesses do not, by definition, enjoy the ready market of a publicly traded stock, a share in a privately held company usually is worth less than an otherwise comparable share in a publicly traded one. Many factors affect the relative marketability of different business interests. Sometimes size of the interest is a factor; a smaller block may be easier to market than a larger block, and in other cases the reverse is true. In most cases, the lack of marketability factor harshly impacts minority interests. However, even controlling interests in closely held businesses obviously are not as readily marketable as shares of publicly traded stock.[13]

[13]Ibid., 49–50.

(Continued)

EXHIBIT 19.3 *(Continued)*

Failure to consider a lack of marketability discount in all business valuation calculations for Cups Plus greatly overstates the value of the business in all scenarios. Based on studies involving restricted stock, lack of marketability discounts range from 25 to 45 percent. This would also have the impact of overvaluing the company.

For all scenarios, under the "Discounted Future Earnings Methodology Summary" the authors state that earnings at 2020 (they incorrectly referred to 2040) are being capitalized at 18.34 percent. There are mathematical calculation errors in these schedules.

Page 39

Besides the fact that the authors have incorrect figures in their report, they have also left out a digit from most of their final calculations for damages within this scenario. Furthermore, the authors have double-counted the damages. When an income or market approach is used to calculate value, the value of the tangible assets is included in the result. It is inappropriate to add the value of the assets to the total value derived.

Pages 40–43

Scenario 2 contains all of the same errors as Scenario 1.

Page 44

Once again, the authors have left out a digit from most of their final calculations for damages within this scenario.

Pages 45–49

Scenario 3 is plagued with the same errors as Scenarios 1 and 2.

Final Comments

The conclusions reached in The Econ Report have been demonstrated to lack support, violate proper theory, and represent anything but reality. The damages sustained by Cups Plus is no more than the purchase price of the assets plus any additional items that may have increased the value from December 1994 to April 1995. This value had certainly not grown to $6.6 million.

Two items that were not discussed in The Econ Report include the reliability of their clients' information and mitigation of damages. All one has to do is look at the business plan that was prepared by an apparently over-optimistic salesman who thought he could set the world on fire. The business plan states, "to implement our plans we require an investment of $24,876,000." Where did they think they were going to get that kind of capital to grow the business?

Another concept ignored by the authors is that if they were correct in calculating damages to the year 2020, why didn't they consider the obligation of the damaged parties to mitigate their damages? The authors started their report by claiming that they were calculating damages to The Company, but they end their report by calculating damages to the shareholders. Without mitigation, the shareholders get a windfall.

According to the *Guide to Litigation Support Services*:

> **Mitigation of Damages**
>
> The plaintiff has a duty to mitigate its damages. This means that the plaintiff has a responsibility to take whatever actions are appropriate to overcome the damage caused by the defendant's breach or tort. Generally, if a plaintiff loses an income-producing asset, for example, it cannot recover lost profits the asset would have produced beyond the reasonable period of time it should have taken the plaintiff to replace the asset. Lack of adequate resources to replace the asset would generally not be a sufficient legal excuse to justify the failure to mitigate one's damages. In determining the plaintiff's lost earnings, the amount of earnings lost as a result of the plaintiff's failure to mitigate its own damages are not recoverable.[14]

The authors of the report have made no attempt to offset the plaintiff's loss from the time of loss through the year 2020. The authors have written off the loss of business as permanent, citing various excuses including loss of resources and ability. As this treatise indicates "lack of adequate resources to replace the asset would generally not be a sufficient legal excuse to justify the failure to mitigate one's damages."

Clearly there is an obligation to mitigate on the part of the plaintiffs. The *Guide to Litigation Support Services* discusses how refusing to mitigate damages impacts the period of recovery for an economic loss. This treatise states:

> **303.36 Period of Recovery.** Because the plaintiff has a duty to mitigate damages, the plaintiff cannot expect to be awarded lost profits from the date of the harmful event until the end of time. As one court ruled, a plaintiff cannot expect to retire for life from the taking of his business.

[14] *Guide to Litigation Support Services*, 3-14 and 3-15.

EXHIBIT 19.3 *(Continued)*

303.37 The plaintiff is entitled to recover earnings lost as a result of the defendant's actions for that period of time "proximately" related to those actions. The shorter the period, the easier it is to demonstrate a proximate link to the defendant's acts. As the period increases, other factors may be responsible for the plaintiff's losses. These may include general economic conditions, increased competition, poor business judgment, or the plaintiff's failure to mitigate its damages. Except for special circumstances, a proximate link is usually difficult to establish between current earnings and the actions of a defendant three or more years into the past. Likewise, as discussed beginning in Paragraph 303.46, lost earnings are equally difficult to project three or more years into the future without losing a proximate link to the cause of the future losses.[15]

Overall, The Econ Report fails to support its value of damages to Cups Plus. Revenue, and therefore, profit projections for the business are highly speculative and include careless errors. In addition, the authors have ignored numerous business valuation and economic damages concepts and theory including the proper use of valuation methodology and the mitigation of damages.

Cups Plus, Inc.'s being a new business is a fact. According to the *Guide to Litigation Support Services*:

In a lost profits case, the plaintiff's damages must be proved to a reasonable certainty and may not be based merely on speculation or conjecture. Most new business ventures fail. Accordingly, the "new business" rule generally precludes a startup business from recovering lost profits because there is usually no evidence that the business would have been able to generate a profit but for the defendant's actions.

The plaintiff's expert must be very creative to overcome the new business rule.[16]

We believe that we have sufficiently pointed out the many flaws in The Econ Report. Clearly, their calculations are based on speculation and conjecture. Cups Plus was a new business, and the New-Business Rule should be considered. We do not believe that the plaintiff's experts were very creative, nor did they overcome the New-Business Rule.

I have attached my professional qualifications and a list of the documents that we reviewed in this matter as appendices to this letter. Should it become necessary, I will be ready to testify about our findings in this matter.

Very truly yours,
TRUGMAN VALUATION ASSOCIATES INC.

Gary R. Trugman
CPA/ABV, MCBA, ASA, MVS

[15]Ibid., 3-15.

[16]Ibid., 3-22.

Conclusion

If I did my job, you should feel a little bit better informed about economic damages. Hopefully, you now realize that if you can perform business valuation assignments, you can also perform economic damage assignments. You certainly can do better than the individuals I ripped apart in Exhibit 19.3. Although this chapter is not going to make you an expert (you probably need two more chapters for that), you can begin to think about performing these assignments by using the same skill set that you have gained in the first 18 chapters of this book. Good luck!

Appendix 1 *AICPA Statement on Consulting Services Standards I*

Consulting Services: Definitions and Standards

Introduction

1. Consulting services that CPAs provide to their clients have evolved from advice on accounting-related matters to a wide range of services involving diverse technical disciplines, industry knowledge, and consulting skills. Most practitioners, including those who provide audit and tax services, also provide business and management consulting services to their clients.
2. Consulting services differ fundamentally from the CPA's function of attesting to the assertions of other parties. In an attest service, the practitioner expresses a conclusion about the reliability of a written assertion that is the responsibility of another party, the asserter. In a consulting service, the practitioner develops the findings, conclusions, and recommendations presented. The nature and scope of work is determined solely by the agreement between the practitioner and the client. Generally, the work is performed only for the use and benefit of the client.
3. Historically, CPA consulting services have been commonly referred to as management consulting services, management advisory services, business advisory services, or management services. A series of Statements on Standards for Management Advisory Services (SSMASs) previously issued by the AICPA contained guidance on certain types of consulting services provided by members. This Statement on Standards for Consulting Services (SSCS) supersedes the SSMASs and provides standards of practice for a broader range of professional services, as described in paragraph 5.
4. This SSCS and any subsequent SSCSs apply to any AICPA member holding out as a CPA while providing consulting services as defined herein.

Definitions

5. Terms established for the purpose of SSCS are as follows:

Consulting Services Practitioner. Any AICPA member holding out as a CPA while engaged in the performance of a consulting service for a client, or any other individual who is carrying out a Consulting Service for a client on behalf of any Institute member or member's firm holding out as a CPA.

Consulting Process. The analytical approach and process applied in a consulting service. It typically involves some combination of activities relating to determination of client objectives, fact-finding, definition of the problems or opportunities, evaluation of alternatives, formulation of proposed action, communication of results, implementation, and follow-up.

Consulting Services. Professional services that employ the practitioner's technical skills, education, observations, experiences, and knowledge of the consulting process.[1] Consulting services may include one or more of the following:

1. *Consultations*, in which the practitioner's function is to provide counsel in a short time-frame, based mostly, if not entirely, on existing personal knowledge about the client, the circumstances, the technical matters involved, client representations, and the mutual intent of the parties. Examples of consultations are reviewing and commenting on a client-prepared business plan and suggesting computer software for further client investigation.
2. *Advisory services*, in which the practitioner's function is to develop findings, conclusions, and recommendations for client consideration and decision-making. Examples of advisory services are an operational review and improvement study, analysis of an accounting system, assistance with strategic planning, and definition of requirements for an information system.
3. *Implementation services*, in which the practitioner's function is to put an action plan into effect. Client personnel and resources may be pooled with the practitioner's to accomplish the implementation objectives. The practitioner is responsible to the client for the conduct and management of engagement activities. Examples of implementation services are providing computer system installation and support, executing steps to improve productivity, and assisting with the merger of organizations.
4. *Transaction services*, in which the practitioner's function is to provide services related to a specific client transaction, generally with a third party. Examples of transaction services are insolvency services, valuation services, preparation of information for obtaining financing, analysis of a potential merger or acquisition, and litigation services.
5. *Staff and other support services*, in which the practitioner's function is to provide appropriate staff and possibly other support to perform tasks specified by the client. The staff provided will be directed by the client as circumstances require. Examples of staff and other support services are data processing facilities management, computer programming, bankruptcy trusteeship, and controllership activities.
6. *Product services*, in which the practitioner's function is to provide the client with a product and associated professional services in support of the installation, use, or maintenance of the product. Examples of product services are the sale and delivery of packaged training programs, the sale and implementation of computer software, and the sale and installation of systems development methodologies.

Standards for Consulting Services

6. The general standards of the profession are contained in Rule 201 of the AICPA Code of Professional Conduct [ET section 201.01] and apply to all services performed by members. They are as follows:

Professional competence. Undertake only those professional services that the member or the member's firm can reasonably expect to be completed with professional competence.

Due professional care. Exercise due professional care in the performance of professional services.

---

[1]The definition of consulting services excludes the following:

1. Services subject to other AICPA Technical Standards such as Statements on Auditing Standards (SASs), Statements on Standards for Attestation Engagements (SSAEs), or Statements on Standards for Accounting and Review Services (SSARSs). (These excluded services may be performed in conjunction with consulting services, but only the consulting services are subject to the SSCS.)
2. Engagements specifically to perform tax return preparation, tax planning/advice, tax representation, personal financial planning, or bookkeeping services, or situations involving the preparation of written reports or the provision of oral advice on the application of accounting principles to specified transactions or events, either completed or proposed, and the reporting thereof.
3. Recommendations and comments prepared during the same engagement as a direct result of observations made while performing the excluded services.

Planning and supervision. Adequately plan and supervise the performance of professional services.

Sufficient relevant data. Obtain sufficient relevant data to afford a reasonable basis for conclusions or recommendations in relation to any professional services performed.

7. The following additional general standards for all consulting services are promulgated to address the distinctive nature of consulting services in which the understanding with the client may establish valid limitations on the practitioner's performance of services. These standards are established under Rule 202 of the AICPA Code of Professional Conduct [ET section 202.01].

Client interest. Serve the client interest by seeking to accomplish the objectives established by the understanding with the client while maintaining integrity and objectivity.[2]

Understanding with client. Establish with the client a written or oral understanding about the responsibilities of the parties and the nature, scope, and limitations of services to be performed, and modify the understanding if circumstances require a significant change during the engagement.

Communication with client. Inform the client of (a) conflicts of interest that may occur pursuant to interpretations of Rule 102[3] of the Code of Professional Conduct [ET section 102.03],[3] (b) significant reservations concerning the scope or benefits of the engagement, and (c) significant engagement findings or events.

8. Professional judgment must be used in applying Statements on Standards for Consulting Services in a specific instance since the oral or written understanding with the client may establish constraints within which services are to be provided. For example, the understanding with the client may limit the practitioner's effort with regard to gathering relevant data. The practitioner is not required to decline or withdraw from a consulting engagement when the agreed-upon scope of' services includes such limitations.

Consulting Services for Attest Clients

9. The performance of consulting services for an attest client does not, in and of itself, impair independence.[4] However, members and their firms performing attest services for a client should comply with applicable independence standards, rules and regulations issued by the AICPA, the state boards of accountancy, state CPA societies, and other regulatory agencies.

Effective Date

10. This statement is effective for engagements accepted on or after January 1, 1992. Early application of the provisions of this statement is permissible.

---

[2]Article III of the Code of Professional Conduct describes *integrity* as follows:

> Integrity requires a member to be, among other things, honest and candid within the constraints of client confidentiality. Service and the public trust should not be subordinated to personal gain and advantage. Integrity can accommodate the inadvertent error and the honest difference of opinion; it cannot accommodate deceit or subordination of principle.

Article IV of the Code of Professional Conduct differentiates between *objectivity* and *independence* as follows:

> Objectivity is a state of mind, a quality that lends value to a member's services. It is a distinguishing feature of the profession. The principle of objectivity imposes the obligation to be impartial, intellectually honest, and free of conflicts of interest. Independence precludes relationships that may appear to impair a member's objectivity in rendering attestation services.

[3]Rule 102-2 on Conflicts of Interest states, in part, the following:

> A conflict of interest may occur if a member performs a professional service for a client or employer and the member or his or her firm has a significant relationship with another person, entity, product, or service that could be viewed as impairing the member's objectivity. If this significant relationship is disclosed to and consent is obtained from such client, employer, or other appropriate parties, the rule shall not operate or prohibit the performance of the professional service.

[4]AICPA independence standards relate only to the performance of attestation services; objectivity standa'rds apply to all services. See footnote 2.

Appendix 2 *IBA Standards*

Business Appraisal Standards
As Promulgated by
The Institute of Business Appraisers, Inc.
May 6, 1998
Publication P-311b

NOTICE

This publication supersedes and replaces the following IBA publications:
P-243 Standards of Business Appraisal Practice
P-244 Standards for Business Appraisal Reports
P-311a Business Appraisal Standards

Foreword

Only a small percentage of individuals representing themselves as business appraisers have been tested and certified by a professional business appraisal institute or society.

Those considering employing a business appraiser are undoubtedly doing so in relation to a matter which can have far reaching financial or legal ramifications. Beyond the obvious caution that a proper valuation cannot be done without adequate preparation, competency, and documentation, we suggest verification that the individual is certified as a business appraiser and intends to prepare the appraisal in compliance with these standards.

The Institute of Business Appraisers would like to thank those associated with The Appraisal Foundation and the American Society of Appraisers whose efforts toward developing business appraisal standards and ethics have contributed greatly to the product of this Committee.

Founding Standards Committee

David M. Bishop, CBA, Chairman
Larry R. Cook, CBA, CPA
James M. Hansen, CBA, CRA
Steven F. Schroeder, CBA, ASA
Raymond C. Miles, CBA, ASA Ex-Officio

Preamble

1. Certain professions, by their nature, and by the way they are perceived by the public, are capable of exerting substantial influence on the public welfare. It is our firm conviction that the practice of business appraisal falls in a similar category.
2. The performance of business appraisal/valuation requires a high degree of skill, imposes upon the appraiser a duty of non-advocacy to the client and an obligation to the general public as a third party beneficiary of the work. It is our purpose here to articulate standards by which those who aspire to participation, and those already established, in business appraisal practice may be guided in the ethical and skillful execution of their tasks, and report the results and conclusions of their work in the most effective manner.
3. It is also our purpose to state these standards in such a clear and unequivocal way that the world at large, and especially those who may engage the services of a business appraiser, will know the parameters by which professional competence is to be measured, and by which its professional practitioners wish to be judged.
4. Each standard is qualified as: (i) should, (ii) must, or (iii) shall. *Should* and *must* standards are guidelines. While an appraiser may depart from a *should* standard without a statement of departure, such departure should be made knowingly. In those instances where the appraiser feels a departure from a *must* standard is warranted, the report *shall* include a statement of departure. It is the position of the IBA that standards designated *shall* are those from which departure is not justified.
5. These standards have been developed to provide guidance to appraisers who are members of the Institute of Business Appraisers (IBA) and others performing appraisals of closely held businesses, business ownership interests, or securities. They have also been developed to assist in the evaluation and regulation of members of the IBA through creating uniform practices and procedures. Departures from the standards are not intended to provide a basis for civil liability, and should not be presumed to create evidence that any legal duty has been breached, or to imply the creation of any additional relationships or duties other than those specified herein.

Format

These standards are presented in a naturally progressive format beginning with overall professional conduct and ethics, followed by specific standards applicable to oral reports, expert testimony, letter reports, formal reports, and preliminary reports.

No attempt is made to anticipate every possible scenario or unique circumstance and create standards specific thereto. Conversely, these standards were developed under the premise that the professional business appraiser practicing within the proper standard of care can, on a case-by-case basis, adequately apply these standards in such a manner to result in a competent report while still permitting the flexibility necessary to meet the reasonable requests of the client and the vicissitudes of the assignment.

Within this publication, reference to all individuals has been in the masculine. This is done in the interest of simplicity, and is not intended as a gender bias. Terms should be assumed to be in the singular or plural as appropriate to the context in which they are used.

Standard One: Professional Conduct & Ethics

1.1 Competence. The achievement of certification as a business appraiser (CBA) is a result of specialized training, study, practice, the successful completion of a proctored examination, and a favorable review of the candidate's actual appraisal reports by The Institute of Business Appraisers' Qualifications Review Committee.

To maintain certification, a CBA will adhere to continuing education requirements and periodic recertification as required by IBA.

Prior to accepting an engagement to perform a business appraisal, the appraiser *must* judge his competence to complete the assignment. Should the appraiser have a meaningful lack of knowledge and experience, the appraiser *must* immediately disclose that fact to the client. If the client desires the appraiser to continue with the assignment, the appraiser *shall* take those steps necessary to perform the appraisal in a competent manner, or take those steps necessary to complete the assignment under the supervision of an appraiser who has the requisite skill, or, with the permission of the client, refer the engagement to a qualified business appraiser.

It is essential that a business appraiser communicate the research and thought processes which led to his opinions and conclusions in a manner that is clear, meaningful, and not misleading. Said communication, whether oral or written, *shall* not be rendered in a careless or negligent manner.

The appraiser as an individual *must* be competent. Software valuation programs and/or excessive reliance on rules of thumb are not surrogates for individual competence.

The professional business appraiser recognizes and understands that compliance with these standards and ethics is an essential part of competence.

1.2 Confidentiality. The very fact an appraiser has been retained to value all or a portion of a business enterprise, or its securities, is in itself confidential. Consequently, it is considered unethical for a business appraiser to disclose either the assignment itself or any of the reasonably identifiable contents of an appraisal report without the client's express permission.

1.3 Disinterestedness. It is unethical for a business appraiser to accept any assignment when the appraiser has a present or contemplated interest in the property being appraised or a bias for or against any person associated therewith, either directly or indirectly. Such interests include, but are not limited to, present, contemplated, or prospective activity with the business enterprise, its officers, directors, or owners, including possible acquirers or investors.

However, if a prospective client, after full disclosure by the appraiser of said interest or bias, still elects to engage the appraiser, the appraiser may accept the assignment. When accepting such an assignment, the business appraiser *shall* include a Statement of Departure as required by Standard 1.21(b). The Statement of Departure *shall* include a complete disclosure of the interest or bias.

1.4 Nonadvocacy vs. Advocacy. Nonadvocacy is considered to be a mandatory standard of appraisal. The appraiser's obligation to serve the public interest assures that the integrity of valuations will be preserved. Hence, the appraiser may only be an advocate for his unbiased process and conclusions. The appraiser *must* be guided by nothing other than his informed judgment, the dictates of the client (as permitted under these standards), applicable administrative rulings, and the law.

In the event the appraiser is engaged to function not as an appraiser but as an advisor or consultant, he may serve as an advocate. In such instances the appraiser *shall* include a statement of departure which states that any positions taken were taken as an advocate for the client.

1.5 Engagement. Prior to performing an appraisal assignment, a business appraiser *should* obtain a written agreement signed by the client or his agent. At the very least, the engagement agreement *should* specify what the appraiser is being engaged to appraise, the function (use) of the appraisal, the purpose (standard of value) including the definition thereof, the effective date of the appraisal, the scope of the appraisal, that the appraisal will be performed on a nonadvocacy basis (see Standard 1.4), the amount of or method for calculating the appraiser's fee, together with the method for payment of same, and an indication of when the client may expect the report.

1.6 Coherence and Production. Appraisal reports must have logical organization. Readers' questions that can reasonably be anticipated should be answered. Data in one part of the report should not contradict other portions without reconciliation.

The appraiser should develop contributing conclusions from the various components of the appraisal process, drawing them together in a cross-supporting manner that logically brings the reader to the appraiser's conclusion.

The report should be produced in a manner and style which brings credit to the appraiser and the profession. Typographical errors and the like *shall* be eliminated. In formal reports, page and exhibit numbers *should* be used together with a table of contents or index to enhance readability.

1.7 Supportable Opinion. The essence of business appraisal is a supportable opinion. While it is intuitively logical that on a case-by-case basis certain opinions will be based on the informed, but subjective, judgment of the appraiser to a greater degree than others, the appraiser's goal is to have a supportable opinion. The reader should not be expected to accept critical elements such as adjustments to financial statements, the selected capitalization or discount rates, or weightings, without support—even in those instances where the vicissitudes of the assignment dictate that support be primarily based on the informed judgment of the appraiser.

1.8 Replicability. The appraiser's procedures and conclusions in the formal report *must* be presented in sufficient detail to permit the reader to replicate the appraisal process.

1.9 Appropriateness. The standard of value, the type of report, and the valuation approaches/methods utilized should be appropriate to the assignment. The material included in the report should be relevant, clear, and cogent.

1.10 Jurisdictional Exception. If any part of these standards is contrary to the law or public policy of any jurisdiction, only that part shall be void and of no force and effect in that jurisdiction.

1.11 Fiduciary Duty to Clients, and Other Duties

- *Client:* The one employing the business appraiser.
- *Third Parties:* Others who could be expected to review the report, e.g., attorneys, accountants, lenders, buyers, investors, regulatory agencies, courts, etc.
- *Public:* Society at large.

a. *Specialized Character of Business Appraisal.* Seldom are others intimately familiar with the process of business appraisal. Therefore, it is anticipated the business appraiser will use his professional abilities properly, as more fully described throughout these standards.

b. *Loyalty, Obedience, and Reasonable Skill and Care.* Agents have such duties to clients. While no fiduciary or other affirmative duty is owed to others, services provided in accordance with these standards should be clear as to meaning and not be misleading to others.

1.12 Duty to Profession

a. *Professional Cooperation and Courtesy.* It is unethical to damage or attempt to damage the professional reputations or interfere with the performance of other business appraisers practicing within the scope of these standards through false or malicious statement or innuendo.

b. *Conduct.* Every member is reminded that his demeanor and general conduct represents his profession and fellow practitioners, and unprofessional conduct damages more than his individual reputation.

c. *Cooperation.* Each member *shall* cooperate fully with the efforts of the Institute and/or its Ethics and Discipline Committee when investigating possible activities which are contrary to these standards.

1.13 *Substance vs. Form.* The form of an appraisal report can be oral or written with variations of each. However, it is only the form of the report that varies. The appraiser's responsibilities to gather data, analyze the data, and draw supportable conclusions as applicable to the type of assignment undertaken does not change. Regardless of whether the final valuation is reported orally, in a summarizing letter report, or a formal report, the appraiser *must* have first completed an appropriate valuation determination process.

A preliminary report is an exception to the above requirement for a thorough, complete work process. By its nature, a preliminary report results from a more cursory evaluation. (See Standard Six, Preliminary Reports.)

1.14 *Professional Fees.* The fees charged for the services of an appraiser are a product of the marketplace; however, a business appraiser is ethically denied the selection of a fee that could in itself call to question the objectivity of the appraiser.

a. *Finder's Fees.* No appraiser will pay fees, or offer gain in any form, to others to promote the appraiser's work in such a way, or under any circumstances, that will diminish the dignity of, or reflect discredit or disrepute upon, the appraisal profession.
b. *Referral Fees.* It is the right of an appraiser and, therefore, not unethical to pay a referral fee to another professional for the referral of appraisal assignments.
c. *Percentage Fees.* To accept any engagement for which the compensation is based on a percentage of the valuation conclusion impairs independence and is thus unethical.

1.15 *Access to Requisite Data.* The business appraiser *must* decide what documents and/or information are requisite to a competent appraisal.

a. *Reliability of Data.* An appraiser may rely upon documents and/or information provided by the client and/or his agents without further corroboration, provided the report clearly states he has done so. This right, however, does not abrogate the appraiser's duty to ask or otherwise inquire regarding information which on its surface clearly appears to be incomplete or otherwise inaccurate.
b. *Pertinent Data.* In situations where access to "pertinent" data is denied to the appraiser, the appraiser may, at his option, withdraw from completing the assignment. However, should the appraiser elect to complete the assignment, the report *must* include a Statement of Departure as required under Standard 1.21Co). Such Statement of Departure *must* describe the limitation and/or restriction and its potential effect on the appraiser's conclusion.
c. *Essential Data.* When the business appraiser is denied access to data considered essential to a proper appraisal, the business appraiser *should* not proceed with the assignment.

1.16 *Valuation Approaches/Methods.* The approaches/methods used within a given assignment are a matter that must be determined by the business appraiser's professional judgment. The task is generally decided through consideration of the approaches/methods that are conceptually most appropriate and those for which the most reliable data is available.

1.17 *Definitions*

a. *Terms.* The appraiser should be careful in the use of ambiguous or esoteric terms. Such terms require definition to prevent the reader from applying a different definition.

b. *Computations*. All computations, particularly those used to compute ratios and weightings, should be clearly defined.

1.18 Principal Sources and References

a. *Formal Report*. A formal report *must* include a list of the principal sources of non-confidential information and references whenever their inclusion will materially contribute to the clarity and understanding of the report.
b. *Oral and Informal Reports*. The appraiser's workpapers *must* include a general description of the principal sources of information and references.

1.19 Site Tours and Interviews

a. *Tour*. Familiarity with an appraisal subject is a compelling necessity to a credible valuation. For this reason, it is desirable that a business appraiser make personal inspections or tours of appraisal subject sites whenever possible. When such activities are not performed, the appraiser's report *shall* disclose that the appraisal process did not include a site tour.
b. *Interview*. An appraiser *should* not perform an appraisal without interviewing the management and other parties considered appropriate in the circumstances.

1.20 Eligibility of Data. An appraisal shall be based upon what a reasonably informed person would have knowledge of as of a certain date. This shall be known as the appraisal's "date of valuation" or "effective date" and accordingly reflect the appraiser's supportable conclusion as of that date. Information unavailable or unknown on the date of valuation *must* not influence the appraiser or contribute to the concluding opinion of value.

a. *Imminent Change*. The appraiser is sometimes faced with the knowledge of a material imminent change in the business; a change not known of on the "date of valuation," but known as of the appraisal's "report" date. In such an event, the imminent change (positive or negative) *should* not affect the valuation conclusion unless a reasonably informed person could have anticipated the imminent change. However, it is not uncommon for an appraiser to disclose such a change within the narrative portion of the report.
b. *Data on Guideline Companies*. When an appraiser selects guideline companies, the data on the companies judged sufficiently similar should be information knowable, although perhaps not yet compiled, on or before the appraisal's date of valuation. Additionally, the data on the guideline companies should be for the same accounting period; however, if it is as of a different period, said different period *must* be on or before the appraisal's date of valuation.

   This restriction should apply whether the guideline companies are specific companies or aggregate industry statistics or ratios.

1.21 Departure. A business appraiser may be engaged to perform an appraisal assignment that calls for something different from the work that would routinely result from the appraiser's compliance with all *must* standards, provided that prior to entering into an agreement to perform such an assignment:

a. The appraiser is of the opinion that the assignment is not so limited in scope that the resulting report would tend to mislead or confuse the client or other anticipated readers; and
b. The appraiser has advised the client that the assignment calls for something different than that which would normally result from compliance with applicable standards and, therefore, the report shall include a statement of departure.

1.22 Hypothetical Reports. An analysis or appraisal may be prepared under a hypothetical assumption, or series thereof, even though they may appear improbable. However, such a report must clearly state (i) the hypothetical assumption and (ii) the purpose of the analysis or appraisal, and any opinion of value *must* clearly be identified as resulting from a hypothetical assumption.

1.23 Dissenting Opinion

a. *Dissenting Opinion With Other Appraisers.* Collaborating appraisers and review appraisers *must* sign the report. When a signing appraiser disagrees in whole or in part with any or all of the findings of other appraisers, said dissenting opinion *must* be included in the report, signed by the dissenting appraiser.

b. *Dissenting Opinion With Case Law and/or Administrative Regulation.* As any other member of society, appraisers are required to comply with statutory law and statutory definitions as they may exist from time to time and from jurisdiction to jurisdiction. However, case law and/or administrative regulations do not have the same force as statutory law. Therefore, the business appraiser may, when he believes it is warranted, express within the appraisal report a dissenting opinion to case law and/or an administrative regulation.

1.24 Membership Designations. It is considered unethical conduct for any individual to explicitly or implicitly indicate he is a Certified Business Appraiser (CBA) when he has not been awarded the designation.

a. *Certified Business Appraisal Reports.* An appraisal report may be considered a "Certified Report" when it is signed by a Certified Business Appraiser who is taking technical responsibilities for its content.

b. *Certification of Firms.* The designation Certified Business Appraiser (CBA) is awarded to individuals, not business enterprises; therefore, it is unethical for an appraiser to explicitly or implicitly indicate that the firm is certified.

c. *Misuse of Certification.* Each Certified Business Appraiser is honor-bound to refrain from any use of his professional designation in connection with any form of activity that may reflect discredit upon his designation, or the organization that conferred it, or deceive his client or the public. As with actual appraisal conclusions, this has been left as a matter of individual judgment and conscience; those who abuse this privilege could be subject to disciplinary action by IBA's Ethics and Discipline Committee.

1.25 Certification. Each written report *must* contain a certification signed by the appraiser. Additional appraisers signing the report *must* accept responsibility for the full contents of the report. [In the event of a dissenting opinion, see Standard 1.23(a).] The certificate must be similar in content to the following:

a. That to the best of the appraiser's knowledge, the statements of fact contained in the report are true and correct.

b. That the reported analyses, opinions, and conclusions are limited only by the reported assumptions and limiting conditions and are the appraiser's personal, unbiased professional analyses, opinions, and conclusions.

c. That the appraisal was performed on a basis of nonadvocacy, including a statement that the appraiser has no present or contemplated interest in the property appraised and has no personal bias with respect to the parties involved, or a complete disclosure of any such interest or bias.

d. That the appraiser's compensation is not contingent on an action or event resulting from the analyses, opinions, or conclusions in, or the use of, the report.

e. That the appraiser's analyses, opinions, and conclusions were developed and that the report has been prepared in conformity with the Business Appraisal Standards of The Institute of Business Appraisers.

f. That no one provided significant professional assistance to the person signing the report. However, if there are exceptions to this, then the name of each individual providing significant professional assistance must be disclosed.

1.26 Qualifications of the Appraiser. The reader cannot fully judge the quality of the appraisal report without being given the opportunity to judge the appraiser's qualifications. Therefore, each appraisal report *must* include the appraiser's qualifications in a manner the appraiser believes accurately presents his appraisal experience, certification, professional activities, and other qualifications.

1.27 Force and Effect. These standards shall be in full force and effect on the date of their issuance. (Earlier compliance is encouraged.) Any and all prior standards regarding business appraisal practices, reports, conduct, or ethics are superseded. Future amendments, to be effective, *shall* be initiated and passed in accordance with Standard 1.29.

1.28 Enforcement. The enforcement of these standards, including amendments or modifications as may occur in accordance with Standard 1.29, *shall* be the responsibility and duty of all members as to their own performance, and otherwise by the standing Ethics and Discipline Committee of The Institute of Business Appraisers and/or such other individuals or committees as are designated from time to time by the governing body of The Institute of Business Appraisers.

1.29 Amendments to Standards. The Standards Committee of The Institute of Business Appraisers is a standing committee. Certified members desiring to propose amendments, additions, or deletions to these standards should submit a clear expression of the proposed change to The Institute of Business Appraisers, Attention: Chairperson, Standards Committee. The chairperson reserves the right to return any submitted change for further clarification as to the precise change proposed. The chairperson shall distribute copies of the proposed change to the members of the Standards Committee for their opinions on the proposed change. Should two-thirds or more of the Committee support the change, it shall be endorsed by the Committee and an exposure draft be provided to all CBAs. The exposure draft shall provide for a thirty-day period for the vote of all CBAs. In the event that those certified members who vote "No" exceeds 50% of all CBAs (those voting plus those not voting), the Committee's vote will be overruled and the proposed change will die for lack of support. Otherwise, the change will be adopted as of the first day of the month following the date copies of the amendments are provided to all members.

1.30 Signing Reports. Each written report *must* be signed by the appraiser and any other appraisers, including those signing as a "Review Appraiser" or "Collaborating Appraiser," shall accept responsibility for the full content of the report. [In the event of a dissenting opinion, see Standard 1.23(a).]

a. *Exception*. Should the policy of a given firm be that all reports are to be signed by a person authorized to sign reports on behalf of the firm, an exception to Standards 1.30 and 1.25 is permitted. However, in this event:

    (i) The designated signer *shall* take technical responsibility for the full content of the report; and
    (ii) The report may not be considered a "Certified Appraisal Report" unless a Certified Business Appraiser taking technical responsibility signs the report.
    (iii) The fact that a given appraisal report is signed under 1.30(a) is not intended in any way to justify or excuse deviation from any standard that would otherwise apply.

Standard Two: Oral Appraisal Reports

2.1 Usage. In general, written reports are preferred; however, oral appraisal reports are permitted when ordered by the client.

2.2 Mandatory Content. When presenting an oral report, the business appraiser *shall* in a manner that is clear and not misleading communicate the following:

a. *Introduction.* Identify the client, and set forth the property being appraised, the purpose and function of the appraisal, the definition of the standard of value, and the effective date of the appraisal.
b. *Assumptions and Limiting Conditions.* Disclose any extraordinary assumptions or limiting conditions that in the appraiser's judgment affected the value.
c. *Disinterestedness.* That the appraisal was performed on a basis of nonadvocacy, including a statement that the appraiser has no present or contemplated interest in the property appraised and has no personal bias with respect to the parties involved, or a complete disclosure of any such interest or bias. [See Standard 1.3.]
d. *Valuation Conclusion.* Represents a concluding opinion of value expressed as:
   (i) statement of a specific opinion of value; or
   (ii) range of values; or
   (iii) a preliminary estimate which *must* include a statement that an opinion of value resulting from a formal report might be different and that difference might be material. (See also Standard Six, Preliminary Reports.)

2.3 Conformity. Oral appraisal reports should comply with all applicable sections of Standard One, Professional Conduct and Ethics.

2.4 Written Follow-up. By its nature, the oral report is less detailed than the written report. Therefore, whenever feasible, it is suggested that oral reports be followed by a written presentation of the salient features of the oral report. In general, the written follow-up *should* include:

a. *Assumptions and Limiting Conditions.* All applicable assumptions and limiting conditions.
b. *Support.* In general, a brief presentation of the information considered, the appraisal approaches used, and the research and thought processes that support the appraiser's analyses, opinions, and conclusions.
c. *Appraiser's Certification* as specified in section 1.25.

2.5 Recordkeeping. An appraiser *should* retain written records of appraisal reports for a period of at least five (5) years after preparation or at least two (2) years after final disposition of any judicial proceeding in which the appraiser gave testimony, whichever period expires last.

Standard Three: Expert Testimony

3.1 Definition. Expert testimony is an oral report given in the form of testimony in a deposition and/or on the witness stand before a court of proper jurisdiction or other trier of fact.

3.2 Mandatory Content. The appraiser shall answer all questions put to him in a manner that is clear and not misleading. When giving testimony, the appraiser *shall* not advocate any position that is incompatible with the appraiser's obligation of nonadvocacy; i.e., it is unethical for the appraiser to suppress any facts, data, or opinions which are adverse to the case his client is trying to establish, or to overemphasize any facts, data, or opinions which are favorable to his client's case, or in any other particulars become an advocate. The expert witness *must* at least comply in a manner that is clear and not misleading with the following:

a. *Introduction*. Identify the client, and set forth the property being appraised, the purpose and function of the appraisal, the definition of the standard of value, and the effective date of the appraisal.
b. *Assumptions and Limiting Conditions*. Disclose any extraordinary assumptions or limiting conditions that in the appraiser's judgment affected the value.
c. *Disinterestedness*. That the appraisal was performed on a basis of nonadvocacy, including a statement that the appraiser has no present or contemplated interest in the property appraised and has no personal bias with respect to the parties involved, or a complete disclosure of any such interest or bias. (See Standard 1.3.)
d. *Valuation Conclusion*. Any concluding opinion of value may be expressed as:
    (i) a statement of a specific opinion of value; or
    (ii) a range of values; or
    (iii) a preliminary estimate which *must* include a statement that an opinion of value resulting from a formal report may be different and that difference may be material. (See also Standard Six, Preliminary Reports.)

3.3 Conformity. Expert testimony reports *should* comply with all applicable sections of Standard One, Professional Conduct and Ethics.

3.4 Recordkeeping. An appraiser *should* retain written records of appraisal reports for a period of at least five (5) years after preparation or at least two (2) years after final disposition of any judicial proceeding in which the appraiser gave testimony, whichever period expires last.

Standard Four: Letter Form Written Appraisal Reports

4.1 Definition. An appraiser's written report can be in the form of a letter report or a formal report. The letter report, which is shorter than the formal report, presents conclusions together with brief generalized comments. This type of report is often referred to as a short-form report, letter opinion, or an informal report.

By its nature, the letter form report is an instrument of brevity. It should contain at least a summary of the material factors that led to its conclusions, but it is usually intended by the parties to reduce the normal appraisal burden of writing a comprehensive report and thereby allow the client to realize some economic benefit. However, the appraiser is still required to perform materially the same investigation and analysis as would be required for a comprehensive formal report and maintain in his file the workpapers necessary to support the conclusions stated in the letter report.

4.2 Conformity. The letter form written report *must* comply with all applicable provisions of Business Appraisal Standards, Standard One, Professional Conduct and Ethics.

4.3 Mandatory Content. All letter form written appraisal reports *shall* minimally set forth in a manner that is clear and not misleading:

a. Identify the client, and set forth a description of the business enterprise, security, or other tangible and/or intangible property being appraised.

b. Form of the organization and, if incorporated, the state of incorporation, together with a description, adequate to the assignment, of all classes of securities outstanding and a list of shareholders whose interest should, in the appraiser's judgment, be specified. If a partnership, the type and the state of filing, together with a list of those partners, whether general or limited, whose interest should, in the appraiser's judgment, be specified.
c. The purpose (standard of value) of the appraisal.
d. The function (use) of the appraisal.
e. The definition of the standard of value that is the purpose of the appraisal.
f. The effective ("as of") date of the appraisal.
g. The date the appraisal report was prepared.
h. The report's assumptions and limiting conditions.
i. Any special factors that affected the opinion of value. Such factors include, but are not limited to, buy-sell agreements, restrictive stock agreements, corporate articles, bylaws and resolutions, partnership agreements, litigation, regulatory compliance, or environmental hazards.
j. Applicable discounts and premiums such as minority interest, control, marketability, or lack thereof.
k. A certification consistent with the intent of section 1.25.

4.4 Distribution of Report. The letter report *should* include a clear statement of the expected distribution of the report.

4.5 Valuation Conclusion. The letter report *must* include a clear statement of the appraiser's concluding opinion of value expressed as appropriate to the assignment:

a. a statement of a specific opinion of value; or
b. a range of values; or
c. a preliminary estimate which *must* include a statement that an opinion of value resulting from a formal report might be different and that difference might be material. (See also Standard Six, Preliminary Reports.)

4.6 Transmittal Letter. If a transmittal letter is used, it *should* include a summary of the engagement. It may be structured in the form of a letter, an executive summary, or a similar rendering. However, regardless of the structure used, if a transmittal is used, it *shall* refer to the report in a manner sufficient to discourage any attempt to remove and use the transmittal without the report.

4.7 Recordkeeping. An appraiser should retain written records of appraisal reports for a period of at least five (5) years after preparation or at least two (2) years after final disposition of any judicial proceeding in which the appraiser gave testimony, whichever period expires last.

Standard Five: Formal Written Appraisal Reports

5.1 Definition. The formal appraisal report is a comprehensive business appraisal report prepared to contain, at a minimum, the requirements described within this standard. It is sometimes called the long form, narrative, or comprehensive report.

5.2 Conformity. The formal written report *must* comply with all applicable provisions of Business Appraisal Standards, Standard One, Professional Conduct and Ethics.

5.3 Mandatory Content. All formal appraisal reports shall minimally set forth the following items in a manner that is clear and not misleading, including detail sufficient to permit the reader to reasonably replicate the appraiser's procedures:

a. Identify the client, and set forth a description of the business enterprise, security, or other tangible and/or intangible property being appraised.
b. Form of the organization and, if incorporated, the state of incorporation, together with a description, adequate to the assignment, of all classes of securities outstanding and a list of shareholders whose interest should, in the appraiser's judgment, be specified. If a partnership, the type and the state of filing, together with a list of those partners, whether general or limited, whose interest should, in the appraiser's judgment, be specified.
c. The purpose (standard of value) of the appraisal.
d. The function (use) of the appraisal.
e. The definition of the standard of value that is the purpose of the appraisal.
f. The effective ("as of") date of the appraisal.
g. The date the appraisal report was prepared.
h. The report's assumptions and limiting conditions.
i. The principal sources and references used by the appraiser.
j. The consideration of relevant data regarding:
    (i) The nature and history of the business.
    (ii) The present economic conditions and the outlook affecting the business, its industry, and the general economy.
    (iii) Past results, current operations, and future prospects of the business.
    (iv) Past sales of interests in the business enterprise bring appraised.
    (v) Sales of similar businesses or interests therein, whether closely held or publicly held.
    (vi) The valuation approaches/methods considered and rejected, the approaches/methods utilized, and the research, sources, computations, and reasoning that supports the appraiser's analyses, opinions, and conclusions.
    (vii) Any special factors that affected the opinion of value. Such factors include, but are not limited to, buy-sell agreements, restrictive stock agreements, corporate articles, bylaws and resolutions, partnership agreements, litigation, regulatory compliance, or environmental hazards.
    (viii) Applicable discounts and premiums, such as minority interest, control, marketability or lack thereof.
    (ix) When valuing a majority interest in a business on a "going concern" basis, consider whether the business' highest value may be achieved on a liquidation basis.
    (x) A Certification consistent with the intent of section 1.25.

5.4 Distribution of Report. The formal report *should* include a clear statement of the expected distribution of the report.

5.5 Valuation Conclusion. The formal report *must* include a clear statement of the appraiser's concluding opinion of value expressed as appropriate to the assignment:

a. a statement of a specific opinion of value; or
b. a range of values.

5.6 Transmittal Letter. If a transmittal letter is used, it *should* include a summary of the engagement. It may be structured in the form of a letter, an executive summary, or a similar rendering. However, regardless of the structure, if used, the transmittal *shall* refer to the report in a manner sufficient to discourage any attempt to remove and use the transmittal without the report.

5.7 Recordkeeping. An appraiser *should* retain written records of appraisal reports for a period of at least five (5) years after preparation or at least two (2) years after final disposition of any judicial proceeding in which the appraiser gave testimony, whichever period expires last.

Standard Six: Preliminary Reports

6.1 Definition. A brief oral or written report reflecting the appraiser's limited opinion.

A preliminary report *must* clearly identify any valuation as a "limited" opinion of value as the appraiser has not performed the detailed investigation and analysis essential to a cogent appraisal. [See Standard 6.5.]

6.2 Conformity. The preliminary report *must* comply with all applicable provisions of Business Appraisal Standards, Standard One, Professional Conduct and Ethics.

6.3 Usage. The preliminary report has use when a client desires the appraiser's limited opinion.

6.4 Disclosure. The presentation of a preliminary opinion without disclosing its limitations is unethical.

6.5 Departure. If an appraiser makes a preliminary report without including a clear statement that it is preliminary, there is the possibility a user of the report could accord the report and its limited opinion of value a greater degree of accuracy and reliability than is inherent in the preliminary report process. Therefore, all preliminary reports *shall* include a Statement of Departure in accordance with Standard 1.21(b). The Statement of Departure *shall* include a statement that the report is preliminary and the conclusion subject to change following a proper appraisal and that said change could be material.

6.6 Oral vs. Written. All preliminary reports, whether oral or written, are subject to Standard Six.

6.7 Recordkeeping. An appraiser *should* retain written records of appraisal reports for a period of at least five (5) years after preparation or at least two (2) years after final disposition of any judicial proceeding in which the appraiser gave testimony, whichever period expires last.

Appendix 3 *ASA Standards*

American Society of Appraisers Business Valuation Standards Preamble Approved by the ASA Board of Governors, September 1992

I. To enhance and maintain the quality of business valuations for the benefit of the business valuation profession and users of business valuations, the American Society of Appraisers, through its Business Valuation Committee, has adopted these standards.

II. The American Society of Appraisers (in its Principles of Appraisal Practice and Code of Ethics) and the Appraisal Foundation (in its Uniform Standards of Professional Appraisal Practice) have established authoritative principles and a code of professional ethics. These standards include these requirements, either explicitly or by reference, and are designed to clarify and provide additional requirements specifically applicable to the valuation of businesses, business ownership interests, or securities.

III. These standards incorporate, where appropriate, all relevant business valuation standards adopted by the American Society of Appraisers through its Business Valuation Committee.

IV. These standards provide minimum criteria to be followed by business appraisers in the valuation of businesses, business ownership interests, or securities.

V. If, in the opinion of the appraiser, circumstances of a specific business valuation assignment dictate a departure from any provisions of any Standard, such departure must be disclosed and will apply only to the specific departure.

VI. These Standards are designed to provide guidance to ASA Appraisers conducting business valuations and to provide a structure for regulating conduct of members of the ASA through Uniform Practices and Procedures. Deviations from the Standards are not designed or intended to be the basis of any civil liability and should not create any presumption or evidence that a legal duty has been breached or create any special relationship between the appraiser and any other person.

BVS-I. General Requirements for Developing a Business Valuation

I. Preamble

A. This standard is required to be followed in all valuations of businesses, business ownership interests, and securities by all members of the American Society of Appraisers, be they Candidates, Accredited Members (AM), Accredited Senior Appraisers (ASA), or Fellows (FASA).

B. The purpose of this standard is to define and describe the general requirements for developing the valuation of businesses, business ownership interests, or securities.

C. This standard incorporates the general preamble to the Business Valuation Standards of the American Society of Appraisers.

II. The Valuation Assignment Shall Be Appropriately Defined

A. In developing a business valuation, an appraiser must identify and define the following:

1. The business, business ownership interest, or security to be valued
2. The effective date of the appraisal
3. The standard of value
4. The purpose and use of the valuation

B. The nature and scope of the assignment must be defined. Acceptable scopes of work would generally be of three types as delineated below. Other scopes of work should be explained and described.

1. Appraisal

   a. The objective of an appraisal is to express an unambiguous opinion as to the value of the business, business ownership interest, or security, which is supported by all procedures that the appraiser deemed to be relevant to the valuation.

   b. An appraisal has the following qualities:

      (1) It is expressed as a single dollar amount or as a range.

      (2) It considers all relevant information as of the appraisal date available to the appraiser at the time of performance of the valuation.

      (3) The appraiser conducts appropriate procedures to collect and analyze all information expected to be relevant to the valuation.

      (4) The valuation is based upon consideration of all conceptual approaches deemed to be relevant by the appraiser.

2. Limited Appraisal

   a. The objective of a limited appraisal is to express an estimate as to the value of a business, business ownership interest, or security, which lacks the performance of additional procedures that are required in an appraisal.

   b. A limited appraisal has the following qualities:

      (1) It is expressed as a single dollar amount or as a range.

      (2) It is based upon consideration of limited relevant information.

      (3) The appraiser conducts only limited procedures to collect and analyze the information which such appraiser considers necessary to support the conclusion presented.

      (4) The valuation is based upon the conceptual approach(es) deemed by the appraiser to be most appropriate.

3. Calculations

   a. The objective of calculations is to provide an approximate indication of value based upon the performance of limited procedures agreed upon by the appraiser and the client.

   b. Calculations have the following qualities:

      (1) They may be expressed as a single dollar amount or as a range.

      (2) They may be based upon consideration of only limited relevant information.

      (3) The appraiser performs limited information collection and analysis procedures.

      (4) The calculations may be based upon conceptual approaches as agreed upon with the client.

III. Information Collection and Analysis

The appraiser shall gather, analyze, and adjust relevant information to perform the valuation as appropriate to the scope of work. Such information shall include the following:

A. Characteristics of the business, business ownership interest, or security to be valued including rights, privileges and conditions, quantity, factors affecting control, and agreements restricting sale or transfer.

B. Nature, history, and outlook of the business.

C. Historical financial information for the business.

D. Assets and liabilities of the business.

E. Nature and conditions of the relevant industries which have an impact on the business.

F. Economic factors affecting the business.

G. Capital markets providing relevant information, e.g., available rates of return on alternative investments, relevant public stock transactions, and relevant mergers and acquisitions.

H. Prior transactions involving the subject business, interest in the subject business, or its securities.

I. Other information deemed by the appraiser to be relevant.

IV. Approaches, Methods, and Procedures

A. The appraiser shall select and apply appropriate valuation approaches, methods, and procedures.

B. The appraiser shall develop a conclusion of value pursuant to the valuation assignment as defined, considering the relevant valuation approaches, methods, and procedures, and appropriate premiums and discounts, if any.

V. Documentation and Retention

The appraiser shall appropriately document and retain all information and work product that were relied on in reaching the conclusion.

VI. Reporting

The appraiser shall report to the client the conclusion of value in an appropriate written or oral format. The report must meet the requirements of Standard 10 of The Uniform Standards of Professional Appraisal Practice. In the event the assignment results in a comprehensive written report, the report shall meet the requirements of BVS-VII.

BVS-II. Financial Statement Adjustments

I. Preamble

A. This standard is required to be followed in all valuations of businesses, business ownership interests, and securities by all members of the American Society of Appraisers, be they Candidates, Accredited Members (AM), Accredited Senior Appraisers (ASA), or Fellows (FASA).

B. The purpose of this standard is to define and describe the requirements for making financial statement adjustments in valuation of businesses, business ownership interests, and securities.

C. This present standard is applicable to appraisals and may not necessarily be applicable to limited appraisals and calculations as defined in BVS-I, Section II.B.

D. This standard incorporates the general preamble to the Business Valuation Standards of the American Society of Appraisers.

II. Conceptual Framework

A. Financial statements should be analyzed and, if appropriate, adjusted as a procedure in the valuation process. Financial statements to be analyzed include those of the subject entity and any entities used as guideline companies.

B. Financial statement adjustments are modifications to reported financial information that are relevant and significant to the appraisal process. Adjustments may be necessary in order to make the financial statements more meaningful for the appraisal process. Adjustments may be *appropriate* for the following reasons, among others: (1) To present financial data of the subject and guideline companies on a consistent basis; (2) To adjust from reported values to current values; (3) To adjust revenues and expenses to levels which are reasonably representative of continuing results; and (4) To adjust for non-operating assets and liabilities and the related revenue and expenses.

C. Financial statement adjustments are made for the purpose of assisting the appraiser in reaching a valuation conclusion and for no other purpose.

III. Documentation of Adjustments

Adjustments made should be fully described and supported.

BVS-III. Asset-Based Approach to Business Valuation

I. Preamble

A. This standard is required to be followed in all valuations of businesses, business ownership interests, and securities by all members of the American Society of Appraisers, be they Candidates, Accredited Members (AM), Accredited Senior Appraisers (ASA), or Fellows (FASA).

B. The purpose of this standard is to define and describe the requirements for the use of the Asset-Based Approach to business valuation and the circumstances in which it is appropriate.

C. This present standard is applicable to appraisals and may not necessarily be applicable to limited appraisals and calculations as defined in BVS-1, Section II.B.

D. This standard incorporates the general preamble to the Business Valuation Standards of the American Society of Appraisers.

II. The Asset-Based Approach

A. In business valuation the Asset-Based Approach may be analogous to the Cost Approach of other disciplines.

B. Assets, liabilities, and equity relate to a business that is an operating company, a holding company, or a combination thereof (mixed business).

1. An operating company is a business which conducts an economic activity by generating and selling, or trading, in a product or service.
2. A holding company is a business which derives its revenues by receiving returns on its assets, which may include operating companies and/or other businesses.

C. The Asset-Based Approach should be considered in valuations conducted at the *total entity level* and involving the following:

1. An investment or real estate holding company.
2. A business appraised on a basis other than as a going concern.

Valuations of particular *ownership interests* in an entity may or may not require the use of the Asset-Based Approach.

D. The Asset-Based Approach should not be the sole appraisal approach used in assignments relating to operating companies appraised as going concerns unless it is customarily used by sellers and buyers. In such cases, the appraiser must support the selection of this approach.

BVS-IV. Income Approach to Business Valuation

I. Preamble

A. This standard is required to be followed in all valuations of businesses, business ownership interests, and securities by all members of the American Society of Appraisers, be they Candidates, Accredited Members (AM), Accredited Senior Appraisers (ASA), or Fellows (FASA).

B. The purpose of this standard is to define and describe the requirements for use of the income approach in valuation of businesses, business ownership interests, and securities, but not the reporting thereof.

C. This present standard is applicable to appraisals and may not necessarily be applicable to limited appraisals and calculations as defined in BVS-I, Section II.B.

D. This standard incorporates the general preamble to the Business Valuation Standards of the American Society of Appraisers.

II. The Income Approach

A. The income approach is a general way of determining a value indication of a business, business ownership interest, or security using one or more methods wherein a value is determined by convening anticipated benefits.

B. Both capitalization of benefits methods and discounted future benefits methods are acceptable. In capitalization of benefits methods, a representative benefit level is divided or multiplied by a capitalization factor to convert the benefit to value. In discounted future benefits methods, benefits are estimated for each of several future periods. These benefits are converted to value by the application of a discount rate using present value techniques.

III. Anticipated Benefits

A. Anticipated benefits, as used in the income approach, are expressed in monetary terms. Depending on the nature of the business, business ownership interest, or security being appraised and other relevant factors, anticipated benefits may be reasonably represented by such items as net cash flow, dividends, and various forms of earnings.

B. Anticipated benefits should be estimated considering such items as the nature, capital structure, and historical performance of the related business entity, expected future outlook for the business entity and relevant industries, and relevant economic factors.

IV. Conversion of Anticipated Benefit

A. Anticipated benefits are convened to value using procedures which consider the expected growth and timing of the benefits, the risk profile of the benefits stream, and the time value of money.

B. The conversion of anticipated benefits to value normally requires the determination of a capitalization rate or discount rate. In determining the appropriate rate, the appraiser should consider such factors as the level of interest rates, rates of return expected by investors on relevant investments, and the risk characteristics of the anticipated benefits.

C. In discounted future benefits methods, expected growth is considered in estimating the future stream of benefits. In capitalization of benefits methods, expected growth is incorporated in the capitalization rate.

D. The rate of return used (capitalization rate or discount rate) should be consistent with the type of anticipated benefits used. For example, pre-tax rates of return should be used with pre-tax benefits, common equity rates of return should be used with common equity benefits, and net cash flow rates should be used with net cash flow benefits.

BVS-V. Market Approach to Business Valuation

I. Preamble

A. This standard is required to be followed in all valuations of businesses, business ownership interests, and securities by all members of the American Society of Appraisers, be they Candidates, Accredited Members (AM), Accredited Senior Appraisers (ASA), or Fellows (FASA).

B. The purpose of this standard is to define and describe the requirements for use of the market approach in valuation of businesses, business ownership interests, and securities, but not the reporting therefor.

C. This present standard is applicable to appraisals and may not necessarily be applicable to limited appraisals and calculations as defined in BVS-I, Section II.B.

D. This standard incorporates the general preamble to the Business Valuation Standards of the American Society of Appraisers.

II. The Market Approach

A. The market approach is a general way of determining a value indication of a business, business ownership interest, or security using one or more methods that compare the subject to similar businesses, business ownership interests, and securities that have been sold.

B. Examples of market approach methods include the Guideline Company Method and analysis of prior transactions in the ownership of the subject company.

III. Reasonable Basis for Comparison

A. The investment used for comparison must provide a reasonable basis for the comparison.

B. Factors to be considered in judging whether a reasonable basis for comparison exists include:

1. Sufficient similarity of qualitative and quantitative investment characteristics.
2. Amount and verifiability of data known about the similar investment.
3. Whether or not the price of the similar investment was obtained in an arm's length transaction, or a forced or distress sale.

IV. Manner of Comparison

A. The comparison must be made in a meaningful manner and must not be misleading. Such comparisons are normally made through the use of valuation ratios. The computation and use of such ratios should provide meaningful insight about the pricing of the subject considering all relevant factors. Accordingly, care should be exercised in the following:

1. Selection of underlying data used for the ratio.
2. Selection of the time period and/or averaging method used for the underlying data.
3. Manner of computing and comparing the subject's underlying data.
4. The timing of the price data used in the ratio.

B. In general, comparisons should be made using comparable definitions of the components of the valuation ratios. However, where appropriate, valuation ratios based on components which are reasonably representative of continuing results may be used.

V. Rules of Thumb

A. Rules of thumb may provide insight on the value of a business, business ownership interest, or security. However, value indications derived from the use of rules of thumb should not be given substantial weight unless supported by other valuation methods and it can be established that knowledgeable buyers and sellers place substantial reliance on them.

BVS-VI. Reaching a Conclusion of Value

I. Preamble

A. This standard is required to be followed in all valuations of businesses, business ownership interests, and securities by all members of the American Society of Appraisers, be they Candidates, Accredited Members (AM), Accredited Senior Appraisers (ASA), or Fellows (FASA).

B. The purpose of this standard is to define and describe the requirements for reaching a final conclusion of value in valuation of businesses, business ownership interests, or securities.

C. This present standard is applicable to appraisals and may not necessarily be applicable to limited appraisals and calculations as defined in BVS-I, Section II.B.

D. This standard incorporates the general preamble to the Business Valuation Standards of the American Society of Appraisers.

II. General

A. The conclusion of value reached by the appraiser shall be based upon the applicable standard of value, the purpose and intended use of the valuation, and all relevant information obtained as of the appraisal date in carrying out the scope of the assignment.

B. The conclusion of value reached by the appraiser will be based on value indications resulting from one or more methods performed under one or more appraisal approaches.

III. Selection and Weighing of Methods

A. The selection of and reliance on the appropriate method and procedures depends on the judgment of the appraiser and not on the basis of any prescribed formula. One or more approaches may not be relevant to the particular situation. More than one method under an approach may be relevant to a particular situation.

B. The appraiser must use informed judgment when determining the relative weight to be accorded to indications of value reached on the basis of various methods or whether an indication of value from a single method should dominate. The appraiser's judgment may be presented either in general terms or in terms of mathematical weighting of the indicated values reflected in the conclusion. In any case, the appraiser should provide the rationale for the selection or weighing of the method or methods relied on in reaching the conclusion.

C. In formulating a judgment about the relative weights to be accorded to indications of value determined under each method or whether an indication of value from a single method should dominate, the appraiser should consider factors such as:

1. The applicable standard of value;
2. The purpose and intended use of the valuation;
3. Whether the subject is an operating company, a real estate or investment holding company, or a company with substantial non-operating or excess assets;
4. Quality and reliability of data underlying the indication of value;
5. Such other factors which, in the opinion of the appraiser, are appropriate for consideration.

IV. Additional Factors to Consider

As appropriate for the valuation assignment as defined, and if not considered in the process of determining and weighting the indications of value provided by various procedures, the appraiser should separately consider the following factors in reaching a final conclusion of value:

A. Marketability, or lack thereof, considering the nature of the business, business ownership interest or security, the effect of relevant contractual and legal restrictions, and the condition of the markets.

B. Ability of the appraised interest to control the operation, sale, or liquidation of the relevant business.

C. Such other factors which, in the opinion of the appraiser, are appropriate for consideration.

BVS-VII. Comprehensive Written Business Valuation Report

I. Preamble

A. This standard is required to be followed in the preparation of comprehensive, written business valuation reports by all members of the American Society of Appraisers, be they Candidates, Accredited Members (AM), Accredited Senior Appraisers (ASA), or Fellows (FASA).

B. The purpose of this standard is to define and describe the requirements for the written communication of the results of a business valuation, analysis, or opinion, but not the conduct thereof.

C. This standard incorporates the general preamble to the Business Valuation Standards of the American Society of Appraisers.

II. Signature and Certification

A. An appraiser assumes responsibility for the statements made in the comprehensive, written report and indicates the acceptance of that responsibility by signing the report. To comply with this standard, a comprehensive, written report must be signed by the appraiser. For the purpose of this standard, the appraiser is the individual or entity undertaking the appraisal assignment under a contract with the client.

B. Clearly, at least one individual is responsible for the valuation conclusion(s) expressed in the report. A report must contain a certification, as required by Standard 10 of the *Uniform Standards of Professional Appraisal Practice* of The Appraisal Foundation, in which the individuals responsible for the valuation conclusion(s) must be identified.

III. Assumptions and Limiting Conditions

The following assumptions and/or limiting conditions must be stated:

A. Pertaining to bias—a report must contain a statement that the appraiser has no interest in the asset appraised, or other conflict, which could cause a question as to the appraiser's independence or objectivity, or if such an interest or conflict exists, it must be disclosed.

B. Pertaining to data used—where appropriate, a report must indicate that an appraiser relied on data supplied by others, without further verification by the appraiser, as well as the sources which were relied on.

C. Pertaining to validity of the valuation—a report must contain a statement that a valuation is valid only for the valuation date indicated and for the purpose stated.

IV. Definition of the Valuation Assignment

The precise definition of the valuation assignment is a key aspect of communication with users of the report. The following are key components of such a definition and must be included in the report:

A. The business interest valued must be clearly defined, such as "100 shares of the Class A common stock of the XYZ Corporation" or "a 20% limited partnership interest in the ABC Limited Partnership." The existence, rights, and/or restrictions of other classes of ownership in the business appraised must also be adequately described if they are relevant to the conclusion of value.

B. The purpose and use of the valuation must be clearly stated, such as "a determination of fair market value for ESOP purposes" or "a determination of fair value for dissenter's fight purposes." If a valuation is being done pursuant to a particular statute, the particular statute must be referenced.

   1. The standard of value used in the valuation must be stated and defined. The premise of value, such as a valuation on a minority interest or a control basis, must be stated.
   2. The appraisal date must be clearly defined. The date of the preparation of the report must be indicated.

V. Business Description

A comprehensive, written business valuation report must include a business description which covers all relevant factual areas, such as:

1. Form of organization (corporation, partnership, etc.)
2. History

3. Products and/or services and markets and customers
4. Management
5. Major assets, both tangible and intangible
6. Outlook for the economy, industry, and company
7. Past transactional evidence of value
8. Sensitivity to seasonal or cyclical factors
9. Competition
10. Sources of information used

VI. Financial Analysis

A. An analysis and discussion of a firm's financial statements is an integral part of a business valuation and must be included. Exhibits summarizing balance sheets and income statements for a period of years sufficient to the purpose of the valuation and the nature of the subject company must be included in the valuation report.

B. Any adjustments made to the reported financial data must be fully explained.

C. If projections of balance sheets or income statements were utilized in the valuation, key assumptions underlying the projections must be included and discussed.

D. If appropriate, the company's financial results relative to those of its industry must be discussed.

VII. Valuation Methodology

A. The valuation method or methods selected, and the reasons for their selection, must be discussed. The steps followed in the application of the method or methods selected must be described and must lead to the valuation conclusion.

B. The report must include an explanation of how any variables, such as discount rates, capitalization rates, or valuation multiples, were determined and used. The rationale and/or supporting data for any premiums or discounts must be clearly presented.

VIII. Comprehensive, Written Report Format

The comprehensive, written report format must provide a logical progression for clear communication of pertinent information, valuation methods, and conclusions and must incorporate the other specific requirements of this standard, including the signature and certification provisions.

IX. Confidentiality of Report

No copies of the report will be furnished to persons other than the client without the client's specific permission or direction unless ordered by a court of competent jurisdiction.

Definitions

ADJUSTED BOOK VALUE	The book value which results after one or more asset or liability amounts are added, deleted, or changed from the respective book amounts.

APPRAISAL	The act or process of determining value. It is synonymous with valuation.
APPRAISAL APPROACH	A general way of determining value using one or more specific appraisal methods. (See ASSET-BASED APPROACH, MARKET APPROACH, and INCOME APPROACH definitions.)
APPRAISAL METHOD	Within approaches, a specific way to determine value.
APPRAISAL PROCEDURE	The act, manner, and technique of performing the steps of an appraisal method.
APPRAISED VALUE	The appraiser's opinion or determination of value.
ASSET-BASED APPROACH	A general way of determining a value indication of a business's assets and/or equity interest using one or more methods based directly on the value of the assets of the business less liabilities.
BOOK VALUE	1. With respect to assets, the capitalized cost of an asset less accumulated depreciation, depletion, or amortization as it appears on the books of account of the enterprise. 2. With respect to a business enterprise, the difference between total assets (net of depreciation, depletion, and amortization) and total liabilities of an enterprise as they appear on the balance sheet. It is synonymous with net book value, net worth, and shareholder's equity.
BUSINESS APPRAISER	A person, who by education, training, and experience is qualified to make an appraisal of a business enterprise and/or its intangible assets.
BUSINESS ENTERPRISE	A commercial, industrial, or service organization pursuing an economic activity.
BUSINESS VALUATION	The act or process of arriving at an opinion or determination of the value of a business or enterprise or an interest therein.
CAPITALIZATION	1. The conversion of income into value. 2. The capital structure of a business enterprise. 3. The recognition of an expenditure as a capital asset rather than a period expense.
CAPITALIZATION FACTOR	Any multiple or divisor used to convert income into value.
CAPITALIZATION RATE	Any divisor (usually expressed as a percentage) that is used to convert income into value.
CAPITAL STRUCTURE	The composition of the invested capital.
CASH FLOW	Net income plus depreciation and other non-cash charges.
CONTROL	The power to direct the management and policies of an enterprise.
CONTROL PREMIUM	The additional value inherent in the control interest, as contrasted to a minority interest, that reflects its power of control.
DISCOUNT FOR LACK OF CONTROL	An amount or percentage deducted from a pro rata share of the value of 100 percent of an equity interest in a business to reflect the absence of some or all of the powers of control.
DISCOUNT RATE	A rate of return used to convert a monetary sum, payable or receivable in the future, into present value.
ECONOMIC LIFE	The period over which property may be profitably used.

EFFECTIVE DATE — The date as of which the appraiser's opinion of value applies (also referred to as Appraisal Date, Valuation Date, or "As of" Date).

ENTERPRISE — See BUSINESS ENTERPRISE.

EQUITY — The owner's interest in property after deduction of all liabilities.

FAIR MARKET VALUE — The amount at which property would change hands between a willing seller and a willing buyer when neither is under compulsion and when both have reasonable knowledge of the relevant facts.

GOING CONCERN — An operating business enterprise.

GOING-CONCERN VALUE —

1. The value of an enterprise, or an interest therein, as a going concern.
2. Intangible elements of value in a business enterprise resulting from factors such as having a trained work force; an operational plant; and the necessary licenses, systems, and procedures in place.

GOODWILL — That intangible asset which arises as a result of name, reputation, customer patronage, location, products, and similar factors that have not been separately identified and/or valued but which generate economic benefits.

INCOME APPROACH — A general way of determining a value indication of a business, business ownership interest, or security using one or more methods wherein a value is determined by converting anticipated benefits.

INVESTED CAPITAL — The sum of the debt and equity in an enterprise on a long-term basis.

MAJORITY CONTROL —

1. Ownership position greater than 50% of the voting interest in an enterprise.
2. The degree of control provided by a majority position.

MARKET APPROACH — A general way of determining a value indication of a business, business ownership interest, or security using one or more methods that compare the subject to similar businesses, business ownership interests, or securities that have been sold.

MARKETABILITY DISCOUNT — An amount or percentage deducted from an equity interest to reflect lack of marketability.

MINORITY INTEREST — Ownership position less than 50% of the voting interest in an enterprise.

MINORITY DISCOUNT — A DISCOUNT FOR LACK OF CONTROL applicable to a minority interest.

NET ASSETS — Total assets less total liabilities.

NET INCOME — Revenue less expenses, including taxes.

RATE OF RETURN — An amount of income (loss) and/or change in value realized or anticipated on an investment, expressed as a percentage of that investment.

REPLACEMENT COST NEW — The current cost of a similar new item having the nearest equivalent utility as item being appraised.

REPORT DATE — The date of the report. May be the same as or different from the APPRAISAL DATE.

REPRODUCTION COST NEW	The current cost of an identical new item.
RULE OF THUMB	A mathematical relationship between or among a number of variables based on experience, observation, hearsay, or a combination of these, usually applicable to a specific industry.
VALUATION	See APPRAISAL.
VALUATION RATIO	A factor wherein a value or price serves as the numerator and financial, operating, or physical data serve as the denominator.
WORKING CAPITAL	The amount by which current assets exceed current liabilities.

SBVS-1. The Guideline Company Valuation Method

I. Preamble

A. This statement is required to be followed in all valuations of businesses, business ownership interests, and securities by all members of the American Society of Appraisers, be they Candidates, Accredited Members (AM), Accredited Senior Appraisers (ASA), or Fellows (FASA).

B. The purpose of this statement is to define and describe the requirements for the use of guideline companies in the valuation of businesses, business ownership interests, or securities.

C. This statement incorporates the general preamble to the Business Valuation Standards of the American Society of Appraisers.

II. Conceptual Framework

A. Market transactions in businesses, business ownership interests, or securities can provide objective, empirical data for developing valuation ratios to apply in business valuation.

B. The development of valuation ratios from guideline companies should be considered for use in the valuation of businesses, business ownership interests, or securities, to the extent that adequate information is available.

C. Guideline companies are companies that provide a reasonable basis for comparison to the investment characteristics of the company being valued. Ideal guideline companies are in the *same* industry as the company being valued; but if there is insufficient transaction evidence available in the same industry it may be necessary to select companies with an underlying similarity of relevant investment characteristics, such as markets, products, growth, cyclical variability, and other salient factors.

III. Search for and Selection of Guideline Companies

A. A thorough, objective search for guideline companies is required to establish the credibility of the valuation analysis. The procedure must include criteria for screening and selecting guideline companies.

B. Empirical data from guideline companies can be found in transactions involving either minority or controlling interests in either publicly traded or closely held companies.

IV. Financial Data of the Guideline Companies

A. It is necessary to obtain and analyze financial and operating data on the guideline companies, as available.

B. Consideration should be given to adjustments to the financial data of the subject company and the guideline companies to minimize the difference in accounting treatments when such differences are significant. Unusual or nonrecurring items should be analyzed and adjusted as appropriate.

V. Comparative Analysis of Qualitative and Quantitative Factors

A comparative analysis of qualitative and quantitative similarities and differences between guideline companies and the subject company must be made to assess the investment attributes of the guideline companies relative to the subject company.

VI. Valuation Ratios Derived from Guideline Companies

A. Price information of the guideline companies must be related to the appropriate underlying financial data of each guideline company in order to compute appropriate valuation ratios.

B. The valuation ratios for the guideline companies and comparative analysis of qualitative and quantitative factors should be used together to determine appropriate valuation ratios for application to the subject company.

C. Several valuation ratios may be selected for application to the subject company and several value indications may be obtained. The appraiser should consider the relative importance accorded to each of the value indications utilized in arriving at the valuation conclusion.

D. To the extent that adjustments for dissimilarities with respect to minority and control, or marketability, have not been made earlier, appropriate adjustments for these factors must be made, if applicable.

Appendix 4 NACVA *Professional Standards*

Contents

PREAMBLE
- *General*
- *Conclusions of Value*
- *Other Valuation Services*
- *Litigation Engagements*
- *Purpose of Standards*

GENERAL STANDARDS
- *AICPA Code of Professional Conduct*
- *AICPA Statement on Standards for Consulting Services*
- *Independence*

DEVELOPMENT STANDARDS
- *Identification*
- *Fundamental Analysis*
- *Scope Limitations*
- *Valuation Approaches and Methods*
- *Financial Statement Adjustments*
- *Earnings Determination*
- *Capitalization/Discount Rate*
- *Premiums and Discounts*
- *Documentation*

REPORTING STANDARDS
- *Overview*
- *Opinion of Value Reporting Standards*
- *Estimate of Value Reporting Standards*
- *Litigation Engagements Reporting Standards*

OTHER GUIDELINES AND REQUIREMENTS
- *Other Requirements*
- *Department of Labor*
- *Internal Revenue Service*

Federal and State Laws
Uniform Standards of Professional Appraisal Practice
International Glossary of Business Valuation Terms
EFFECTIVE DATE
APPENDICES
APPENDIX 1: AICPA CODE OF PROFESSIONAL CONDUCT RULES
Rule 102—Integrity and Objectivity
Rule 201—General Standards
Rule 202—Compliance with Standards
Rule 301—Confidential Client Information
Rule 302—Contingent Fees
Rule 501—Acts Discreditable
APPENDIX 2: AICPA STATEMENT ON STANDARDS FOR CONSULTING SERVICES NO. 1
Definitions
Standards for Consulting Services
Consulting Services for Attest Clients
Effective Date
APPENDIX 3: INTERNATIONAL GLOSSARY OF BUSINESS VALUATION TERMS

Preamble

1.1 General. All members of the National Association of Certified Valuation Analysts (NACVA), an association of Certified Public Accountants and other business valuation professionals who perform valuation services, will comply with the standards and definitions of the AICPA's Code of Professional Conduct and Statement on Standards for Consulting Services (SSCS). Under the SSCS, litigation support and valuation services are considered "transaction" consulting services when the practitioner's function is to provide services related to a specific client transaction, generally in conjunction with a third party. NACVA members will comply with the business valuation standards as promulgated by the AICPA and NACVA. NACVA will adopt changes and interpretations of the standards when necessary to avoid conflicts and ambiguities between the Standards of Practice issued by the AICPA and NACVA.

1.2 Conclusions of Value. Conclusions of value can be expressed as an *Opinion of Value*, as a single number, or an *Estimate of Value*, as a single number or a range of values. Where, in the professional judgment of the Valuation Analyst, an Opinion of Value cannot be expressed, the valuation analyst may report an Estimate of Value.

1.3 Other Valuation Services. Any other services provided by a valuation analyst are not subject to NACVA standards. Such services may, however, be subject to other standards, such as the SSCS.

1.4 Litigation Engagements. Generally, opinions of expert witnesses in litigation engagements are subject to discovery and/or cross-examination. In such engagements, when a valuation analyst is expressing an Opinion or Estimate of Value, all NACVA standards apply, except for the Reporting Standards.

1.5 Purpose of Standards. These standards have been developed to provide guidelines to the members of NACVA.

General Standards

2.1 The Following Rules from the AICPA *Code of Professional Conduct* Shall Apply (see Appendix):

2.1.1 Rule 102—Integrity and Objectivity, as modified by SSCS No. 1.

2.1.2 Rule 201—General Standards.

2.1.3 Rule 202—Compliance with Standards.

2.1.4 Rule 301—Confidential Client Information.

2.1.5 Rule 302—Contingent Fees.

2.1.6 Rule 501—Acts Discreditable.

2.2 The following Standards from the AICPA *Statement on Standards for Consulting Services* (SSCS) shall apply [see Appendix 1 of this book]:

2.2.1 Statement on Standards for Consulting Services No. 1—Consulting Services: Definitions and Standards (SSCS No. 1).

2.3 Independence. A valuation analyst shall not express an Opinion of Value or Estimate of Value unless the valuation analyst and the valuation analyst's firm state either of the following:

a. *"I (We) have no financial interest or contemplated financial interest in the property that is the subject of this report."*; or
b. *"I (We) have a (specified) financial interest or contemplated financial interest in the property that is the subject of this report."*

A valuation analyst or the valuation analyst's firm may only state a conclusion of value associated with independence statement 2.3b above with the written consent of the client and full disclosure of the financial interest, present or contemplated, in the valuation analyst's report.

Development Standards

3.1 Identification. In developing a conclusion of value, a valuation analyst must define the assignment and determine the scope of work necessary by identifying the following:

a. Subject to be valued;
b. Interest to be valued;
c. Valuation date;
d. Purpose of the valuation;
e. Standard of value;

f. Premise of value;
g. Assumptions, limiting conditions, and scope limitations; and
h. Ownership size, nature, restrictions, and agreements.

3.2 Fundamental Analysis. In developing a conclusion of value, the valuation analyst must consider and, when applicable, perform research and analysis of the following factors:

a. The nature of the business and the history of the enterprise;
b. The economic outlook in general and the condition and outlook of the specific industry in particular;
c. The book value of the interest to be valued and the financial condition of the business;
d. The earning capacity of the enterprise;
e. The dividend-paying capacity of the enterprise;
f. Whether or not the enterprise has goodwill or other intangible value;
g. Sales of interests and the size of the block of interest to be valued; and
h. The market price of interests of enterprises engaged in the same or a similar line of business having interests actively traded in a free and open market.

3.3 Scope Limitations. In developing a conclusion of value, the valuation analyst must identify and evaluate limitations on the scope of work which affect the research, analysis, and/or level of reliance the valuation analyst places on the valuation results.

3.4 Valuation Approaches and Methods. Valuation methods are commonly categorized into the asset-based approach, the market approach, the income approach, or a combination of the foregoing. Professional judgment must be used to select the methods to consider and the methodology that best indicates the value of the business interest.

3.5 Financial Statement Adjustments. The historical financial statements should be analyzed and, if appropriate, adjusted to reflect the hypothetically transferable asset value, income, cash flows, and/or benefit stream, as applicable, to be consistent with the valuation methodologies selected by the valuation analyst.

3.6 Earnings Determination. The valuation analyst should select the appropriate benefit stream, such as pretax or after-tax income and/or cash flows, and select appropriate projection models to be consistent with the valuation methodologies selected by the valuation analyst.

3.7 Capitalization/Discount Rate. The valuation analyst must consider appropriate capitalization/discount rates, if applicable. Capitalization/discount rates are used to convert a benefit stream to an indicated present value. Incorporated in these rates are components which reflect the risk associated with the subject to be valued, such as an investment in a privately held entity, and the likelihood of realizing the benefit stream.

3.8 Premiums and Discounts. The valuation analyst must consider appropriate premiums and discounts, if applicable. These are factors that can impact value, such as the value of a specific business versus the value of a partial interest in a specific business. If applied, the base upon which the premiums and/or discounts are applied should be clearly defined.

3.9 Documentation. Documentation must be retained for all information relied upon in the valuation process. Inclusion of such information in the report satisfies this standard.

Reporting Standards

4.1 Overview. One of the final stages in the valuation process is the communication of the results of the valuation to the client or other user of the report. The form of any particular report will depend on the nature of the engagement, its purpose, its findings, and the needs of the decision makers who receive and rely upon it. NACVA has adopted the following standards for reporting on valuations. The purpose of these standards is to establish minimum reporting criteria. The objective of these standards is to ensure consistency and quality of valuation reports issued by members of NACVA.

4.2 Opinion of Value Reporting Standards.

4.2.1 A written report expressing an Opinion of Value should be well written, communicate the results, and identify the information relied upon in the valuation process. The wording used in the report should effectively communicate important thoughts, methods, and reasoning, as well as identify the supporting documentation in a simple and concise manner, so that the user of the report can replicate the process followed by the valuation analyst.

4.2.2 Any reporting of an Opinion of Value must be in writing and set forth the following information concerning the valuation engagement and its results:

- Identification of the subject being valued;
- Description of the interest being valued;
- Valuation date;
- Report date;
- Purpose of the valuation;
- Identification of the standard of value;
- Identification of the premise of value;
- Identification of the assumptions, limiting conditions, and scope limitations;
- Conclusion as to Opinion of Value;
- Limitations on use of the report;
- Responsible valuation analyst signature;
- A statement of independence;
- Enterprise background and description;
- Ownership size, nature, restrictions, and agreements;
- A description of the fundamental analysis;
- Valuation approaches and methodologies;
- Historical financial statement summaries, when applicable;
- Adjustments to historical financial statements, when applicable;
- Adjusted financial statement summaries, when applicable; and

- Projected/forecasted financial statements including the underlying assumptions, when applicable.

4.2.3 *Assumptions, Limiting Conditions, and Scope Limitations:* All valuation cases vary as to specific assumptions, limiting conditions, and scope. The valuation analyst must identify material matters considered.

4.2.4 *Responsible Valuation Analyst Signature:* The valuation analyst who has primary responsibility for the conclusion of value must sign the report. If an individual does not sign the report, the individual or individuals who have primary responsibility for the Conclusion of Value must be identified in the report.

4.2.5 *Statement That the Report Is in Accordance with NACVA Standards:* A statement similar to the following should be included in the valuation analyst's report:

> This valuation and report were completed in accordance with the National Association of Certified Valuation Analysts standards for conducting and reporting on business valuations.

4.3 Estimate of Value Reporting Standards. Valuation analysts may be requested to report a valuation conclusion where, in the professional judgment of the valuation analyst, an Opinion of Value cannot be expressed. In such instances, the valuation analyst may conclude that value can be expressed as a range of values or a single number and label the value conclusion "Estimate of Value." Such a report must be in writing and include all the information required in a report on Opinion of Value plus the following statement:

> An Estimate of Value is not an Opinion of Value and such difference may be material.

4.4 Litigation Engagements Reporting Standards. Generally, reporting as an expert witness in the litigation engagement is subject to discovery and/or cross-examination. When in a litigation engagement and when the valuation analyst's expression of a conclusion of value is subject to discovery and/or cross-examination, NACVA's Reporting Standards do not apply.

Other Guidelines and Requirements

5.1 Besides NACVA's Professional Standards, valuation analysts may also find it necessary to consider guidelines and/or other requirements established by other organizations, such as:

- Department of Labor (DOL);
- Internal Revenue Service (IRS);
- Federal and State laws; and
- The Appraisal Foundation (USPAP).

5.2 Department of Labor. The DOL has developed guidelines and other requirements that apply to business valuations for ESOPs. Accordingly, a report for the valuation of an ESOP should discuss applicable DOL guidelines and requirements.

5.3 Internal Revenue Service. The IRS has guidelines and other requirements regarding business valuations. Accordingly, a report for a tax-related valuation should discuss applicable IRS guidelines and other requirements.

5.4 Federal and State Laws. The valuation analyst must be aware of applicable federal and state law and judicial requirements.

5.5 Uniform Standards of Professional Appraisal Practice. The Appraisal Foundation has issued standards (USPAP) for appraisals. These standards are required to be followed for certain federally related transactions.

5.6 International Glossary of Business Valuation Terms. Developed jointly by the AICPA, ASA, CICBV, IBA, and NACVA, the glossary definitions should be used by the analyst (see Appendix 3).

Effective Date

6.1 These Professional Standards are effective for engagements accepted on or after May 31, 1998.

6.2 Amended May 31, 2000, to include the International Glossary of Business Valuation Terms.

Appendix I: AICPA Code of Professional Conduct Rules

Rule 102: Integrity and Objectivity

.01 Rule 102—Integrity and Objectivity. In the performance of any professional service, a member shall maintain objectivity and integrity, shall be free of conflicts of interest, and shall not knowingly misrepresent facts or subordinate his or her judgment to others.

[As adopted January 12, 1988.]

Interpretations Under Rule 102—Integrity and Objectivity

.02 102-1—Knowing misrepresentations in the preparation of financial statements or records. A member shall be considered to have knowingly misrepresented facts in violation of rule 102 [*section 102.01*] when he or she knowingly:

a. Makes, or permits or directs another to make, materially false and misleading entries in an entity's financial statements or records; or
b. Fails to correct an entity's financial statements or records that are materially false and misleading when he or she has the authority to record an entry; or
c. Signs, or permits or directs another to sign, a document containing materially false and misleading information.

[Revised, effective May 31, 1999, by the Professional Ethics Executive Committee.]

.03 102-2—Conflicts of interest. A conflict of interest may occur if a member performs a professional service for a client or employer and the member or his or her firm has a relationship with another person, entity, product, or service that could, in the member's professional judgment, be viewed by the client, employer, or other appropriate parties as impairing the member's objectivity. If the member believes that the professional service can be performed with objectivity, and the relationship is disclosed to and consent is obtained from such client, employer, or other appropriate parties, the rule shall not operate to prohibit the performance of the professional service. When making the disclosure, the member should consider Rule 301, *Confidential Client Information* [ET *section 301.01*].

Certain professional engagements, such as audits, reviews, and other attest services, require independence. Independence impairments under rule 101 [ET *section 101.01*], its interpretations, and rulings cannot be eliminated by such disclosure and consent.

The following are examples, not all-inclusive, of situations that should cause a member to consider whether or not the client, employer, or other appropriate parties could view the relationship as impairing the member's objectivity:

- A member has been asked to perform litigation services for the plaintiff in connection with a lawsuit filed against a client of the member's firm.
- A member has provided tax or personal financial planning (PFP) services for a married couple who are undergoing a divorce, and the member has been asked to provide the services for both parties during the divorce proceedings.
- In connection with a PFP engagement, a member plans to suggest that the client invest in a business in which he or she has a financial interest.
- A member provides tax or PFP services for several members of a family who may have opposing interests.
- A member has a significant financial interest, is a member of management, or is in a position of influence in a company that is a major competitor of a client for which the member performs consulting services.
- A member serves on a city's board of tax appeals, which considers matters involving several of the member's tax clients.
- A member has been approached to provide services in connection with the purchase of real estate from a client of the member's firm.
- A member refers a PFP or tax client to an insurance broker or other service provider, which refers clients to the member under an exclusive arrangement to do so.
- A member recommends or refers a client to a service bureau in which the member or partner(s) in the member's firm hold material financial interest(s).

The above examples are not intended to be all-inclusive.

[Replaces previous interpretation 102-2, *Conflicts of Interest*, August 1995, effective August 31, 1995.]

.04 102-3—Obligations of a member to his or her employer's external accountant. Under rule 102 [ET *section 102.01*], a member must maintain objectivity and integrity in the performance of a professional service. In dealing with his or her employer's external accountant, a member must be candid and not knowingly misrepresent facts or knowingly fail to disclose material facts. This would include, for example, responding to specific inquiries for which his or her employer's external accountant requests written representation.

[Effective November 30, 1993.]

.05 102-4—Subordination of judgment by a member. Rule 102 [ET *section 102.01*] prohibits a member from knowingly misrepresenting facts or subordinating his or her judgment when performing professional services. Under this rule, if a member and his or her supervisor have a disagreement or dispute relating to the preparation of financial statements or the recording of transactions, the member should take the following steps to ensure that the situation does not constitute a subordination of judgment:

1. The member should consider whether (a) the entry or the failure to record a transaction in the records, or (b) the financial statement presentation or the nature or omission of disclosure in the financial statements, as proposed by the supervisor, represents the use of an acceptable alternative and does not

materially misrepresent the facts. If, after appropriate research or consultation, the member concludes that the matter has authoritative support and/or does not result in a material misrepresentation, the member need do nothing further.

2. If the member concludes that the financial statements or records could be materially misstated, the member should make his or her concerns known to the appropriate higher level(s) of management within the organization (for example, the supervisor's immediate superior, senior management, the audit committee or equivalent, the board of directors, the company's owners). The member should consider documenting his or her understanding of the facts, the accounting principles involved, the application of those principles to the facts, and the parties with whom these matters were discussed.
3. If, after discussing his or her concerns with the appropriate person(s) in the organization, the member concludes that appropriate action was not taken, he or she should consider his or her continuing relationship with the employer. The member also should consider any responsibility that may exist to communicate to third parties, such as regulatory authorities or the employer's (former employer's) external accountant. In this connection, the member may wish to consult with his or her legal counsel.
4. The member should at all times be cognizant of his or her obligations under interpretation 102-3 [ET *section 102.04*].

[Effective November 30, 1993.]

.06 102-5—Applicability of Rule 102 to members performing educational services. Educational services (for example, teaching full- or part-time at a university, teaching a continuing professional education course, or engaging in research and scholarship) are professional services as defined in ET *section 92.10* and are therefore subject to rule 102 [ET *section 102.01*]. Rule 102 [ET *section 102.01*] provides that the member shall maintain objectivity and integrity, shall be free of conflicts of interest, and shall not knowingly misrepresent facts or subordinate his or her judgment to others.

[Effective March 31, 1995.]

.07 102-6—Professional services involving client advocacy. A member or a member's firm may be requested by a client:

1. To perform tax or consulting services engagements that involve acting as an advocate for the client.
2. To act as an advocate in support of the client's position on accounting or financial reporting issues, either within the firm or outside the firm with standard setters, regulators, or others.

Services provided or actions taken pursuant to such types of client requests are professional services [ET *section 92.10*] governed by the Code of Professional Conduct and shall be performed in compliance with Rule 201, *General Standards* [ET *section 201.01*], Rule 202, *Compliance With Standards* [ET *section 202.01*], and Rule 203, *Accounting Principles* [ET *section 203.01*], and interpretations thereof, as applicable. Furthermore, in the performance of any professional service, a member shall comply with rule 102 [ET *section 102.01*], which requires maintaining objectivity and integrity and prohibits subordination of judgment to others. When performing professional services requiring independence, a member shall also comply with rule 101 [ET *section 101.01*] of the Code of Professional Conduct.

Moreover, there is a possibility that some requested professional services involving client advocacy may appear to stretch the bounds of performance standards, may go beyond sound and reasonable professional practice, or may compromise credibility, and thereby pose an unacceptable risk of impairing the reputation of the member and his or her firm with respect to independence, integrity, and objectivity. In such circumstances, the member and the member's firm should consider whether it is appropriate to perform the service.

[Effective August 31, 1995.]

A member in the practice of public accounting should refer to the Statements on Auditing Standards. For example, see SAS No. 22, *Planning and Supervision* [AU *section 311*], which discusses what the auditor should do when there are differences of opinion concerning accounting and auditing standards.

AICPA Rule 102, Effective August 31, 1995; reprinted by permission.

Rule 201: General Standards

.01 Rule 201 General Standards. A member shall comply with the following standards and with any interpretations thereof by bodies designated by Council.

A. *Professional Competence.* Undertake only those professional services that the member or the member's firm can reasonably expect to be completed with professional competence.

B. *Due Professional Care.* Exercise due professional care in the performance of professional services.

C. *Planning and Supervision.* Adequately plan and supervise the performance of professional services.

D. *Sufficient Relevant Data.* Obtain sufficient relevant data to afford a reasonable basis for conclusions or recommendations in relation to any professional services performed.

[As adopted January 12, 1988.]

(See Appendix A.)

Interpretations Under Rule 201—General Standards

.02 201—Incompetence. A member's agreement to perform professional services implies that the member has the necessary competence to complete those professional services according to professional standards, applying his or her knowledge and skill with reasonable care and diligence, but the member does not assume a responsibility for infallibility of knowledge or judgment.

Competence to perform professional services involves both the technical qualifications of the member and the member's staff and the ability to supervise and evaluate the quality of the work performed. Competence relates both to knowledge of the profession's standards, techniques, and the technical subject matter involved and to the capability to exercise sound judgment in applying such knowledge in the performance of professional services.

The member may have the knowledge required to complete the services in accordance with professional standards prior to performance. In some cases, however, additional research or consultation with others may be necessary during the performance of the professional services. This does not ordinarily represent a lack of competence but rather is a normal part of the performance of professional services.

However, if a member is unable to gain sufficient competence through these means, the member should suggest, in fairness to the client and the public, the engagement of someone competent to perform the needed professional service, either independently or as an associate.

AICPA Rule 201; reprinted by permission.

Rule 202: Compliance With Standards

.01 Rule 202 Compliance With Standards. A member who performs auditing, review, compilation, management consulting, tax, or other professional services shall comply with standards promulgated by bodies designated by Council.

[As adopted January 12, 1988.]

AICPA Rule 202; reprinted by permission.

Rule 301: Confidential Client Information

.01 Rule 301 Confidential Client Information. A member in public practice shall not disclose any confidential client information without the specific consent of the client.

This rule shall not be construed (1) to relieve a member of his or her professional obligations under rules 202 [ET *section 202.01*] and 203 [ET *section 203.01*], (2) to affect in any way the member's obligation to comply with a validly issued and enforceable subpoena or summons or to prohibit a member's compliance with applicable laws and government regulations, (3) to prohibit review of a member's professional practice under AICPA or state CPA society or Board of Accountancy authorization, or (4) to preclude a member from initiating a complaint with, or responding to any inquiry made by, the professional ethics division or trial board of the Institute or a duly constituted investigative or disciplinary body of a state CPA society or Board of Accountancy.

Members of any of the bodies identified in (4) above and members involved with professional practice reviews identified in (3) above shall not use to their own advantage or disclose any member's confidential client information that comes to their attention in carrying out those activities. This prohibition shall not restrict members' exchange of information in connection with the investigative or disciplinary proceedings described in (4) above or the professional practice reviews described in (3) above.

[As amended January 14, 1992.]

Interpretations Under Rule 301—Confidential Client Information

[.02] [301-1]. [Deleted]

[.03] [301-2]. [Deleted]

.04 301-3. Confidential information and the purchase, sale, or merger of a practice. Rule 301 [ET *section 301.01*] prohibits a member in public practice from disclosing any confidential client information without the specific consent of the client. The rule provides that it shall not be construed to prohibit the review of a member's professional practice under AICPA or state CPA society authorization.

For purposes of rule 301 [ET *section 301.01*], a review of a member's professional practice is hereby authorized to include a review in conjunction with a prospective purchase, sale, or merger of all or part of a member's practice. The member must take appropriate precautions (for example, through a written confidentiality agreement) so that the prospective purchaser does not disclose any information obtained in the course of the review since such information is deemed to be confidential client information.

Members reviewing a practice in connection with a prospective purchase or merger shall not use to their advantage nor disclose any member's confidential client information that comes to their attention.

[Effective February 28, 1990.]

AICPA Rule 301; reprinted by permission.

Rule 302: Contingent Fees

.01 Rule 302—Contingent Fees. A member in public practice shall not:

1. Perform for a contingent fee any professional services for, or receive such a fee from a client for whom the member or the member's firm performs,

a. an audit or review of a financial statement; or

b. a compilation of a financial statement when the member expects, or reasonably might expect, that a third party will use the financial statement and the member's compilation report does not disclose a lack of independence; or

c. an examination of prospective financial information;

or

2. Prepare an original or amended tax return or claim for a tax refund for a contingent fee for any client.

The prohibition in (1) above applies during the period in which the member or the member's firm is engaged to perform any of the services listed above and the period covered by any historical financial statements involved in any such listed services.

Except as stated in the next sentence, a contingent fee is a fee established for the performance of any service pursuant to an arrangement in which no fee will be charged unless a specified finding or result is attained, or in which the amount of the fee is otherwise dependent upon the finding or result of such service. Solely for purposes of this rule, fees are not regarded as being contingent if fixed by courts or other public authorities, or, in tax matters, if determined based on the results of judicial proceedings or the findings of governmental agencies.

A member's fees may vary depending, for example, on the complexity of services rendered. [As adopted May 20, 1991.]

Interpretation Under Rule 302—Contingent Fees

.02 302-1—Contingent Fees in Tax Matters. This interpretation defines certain terms in Rule 302 [*section 302.01*] and provides examples of the application of the rule.

Definition of Terms

a. Preparation of an original or amended tax return or claim for tax refund includes giving advice on events which have occurred at the time the advice is given if such advice is directly relevant to determining the existence, character, or amount of a schedule, entry, or other portion of a return or claim for refund.

b. A fee is considered determined based on the findings of governmental agencies if the member can demonstrate a reasonable expectation, at the time of a fee arrangement, of substantive consideration by an agency with respect to the member's client. Such an expectation is deemed not reasonable in the case of preparation of original tax returns.

Examples. The following are examples, not all-inclusive, of circumstances where a contingent fee would be permitted:

a. Representing a client in an examination by a revenue agent of the client's federal or state income tax return.

b. Filing an amended federal or state income tax return claiming a tax refund based on a tax issue that is either the subject of a test case (involving a different taxpayer) or with respect to which the taxing authority is developing a position.

c. Filing an amended federal or state income tax return (or refund claim) claiming a tax refund in an amount greater than the threshold for review by the Joint Committee on Internal Revenue Taxation ($1 million at March 1991) or state taxing authority.

d. Requesting a refund of either overpayments of interest or penalties charged to a client's account or deposits of taxes improperly accounted for by the federal or state taxing authority in circumstances where the taxing authority has established procedures for the substantive review of such refund requests.
e. Requesting, by means of "protest" or similar document, consideration by the state or local taxing authority of a reduction in the "assessed value" of property under an established taxing authority review process for hearing all taxpayer arguments relating to assessed value.
f. Representing a client in connection with obtaining a private letter ruling or influencing the drafting of a regulation or statute.

The following is an example of a circumstance where a contingent fee would not be permitted:

a. Preparing an amended federal or state income tax return for a client claiming a refund of taxes because a deduction was inadvertently omitted from the return originally filed. There is no question as to the propriety of the deduction; rather the claim is filed to correct an omission.

AICPA Rule 302; reprinted by permission.

Rule 501: Acts Discreditable

.01 Rule 501—Acts Discreditable. A member shall not commit an act discreditable to the profession. [As adopted January 12, 1988.]

Interpretations Under Rule 501—Acts Discreditable

.02 501-1—Retention of Client Records. Retention of client records after a demand is made for them is an act discreditable to the profession in violation of rule 501 [ET *section 501.01*]. The fact that the statutes of the state in which a member practices may grant the member a lien on certain records in his or her possession does not change this ethical standard.

A client's records are any accounting or other records belonging to the client that were provided to the member by or on behalf of the client. If an engagement is terminated prior to completion, the member is required to return only client records.

A member's workpapers, including, but not limited to analyses and schedules prepared by the client at the request of the member, are the member's property, not client records, and need not be made available.

In some instances a member's workpapers contain information that is not reflected in the client's books and records, with the result that the client's financial information is incomplete. This would include, for example, (1) adjusting, closing, combining, or consolidating journal entries, (2) information normally contained in books of original entry and general ledgers or subsidiary ledgers, and (3) tax and depreciation carry-forward information. In those instances when an engagement has been completed, such information should also be made available to the client upon request. The information should be provided in the medium in which it is requested, provided it exists in that medium. The member is not required to convert information that is not in electronic format to an electronic form. The member may require that all fees due the member, including the fees for the above services, be paid before such information is provided.

Once the member has complied with the foregoing requirements, he or she need not comply with any subsequent requests to again provide such information.

.03 501-2—Discrimination and Harassment in Employment Practices. Whenever a member is finally determined by a court of competent jurisdiction to have violated any of the anti-discrimination laws of the United States or any state or municipality thereof, including those related to sexual and other forms of harassment, or has waived or lost his or her right of appeal after a hearing by an administrative agency, the member will be presumed to have committed an act discreditable to the profession in violation of rule 501 [ET *section 501.01*].

[Revised, effective November 30, 1997, by the Professional Ethics Executive Committee.]

.04 501-3—Failure to follow standards and/or procedures or other requirements in governmental audits. Engagements for audits of government grants, government units, or other recipients of government monies typically require that such audits be in compliance with government audit standards, guides, procedures, statutes, rules, and regulations in addition to generally accepted auditing standards. If a member has accepted such an engagement and undertakes an obligation to follow specified government audit standards, guides, procedures, statutes, rules, and regulations, in addition to generally accepted auditing standards, he is obligated to follow such requirements. Failure to do so is an act discreditable to the profession in violation of rule 501 [ET *section 501.01*], unless the member discloses in his report the fact that such requirements were not followed and the reasons therefore.

.05 501-4—Negligence in the Preparation of Financial Statements or Records. A member shall be considered to have committed an act discreditable to the profession in violation of rule 501 [ET *section 501.01*] when, by virtue of his or her negligence, such member:

1. Makes, or permits or directs another to make, materially false and misleading entries in the financial statements or records of an entity; or
2. Fails to correct an entity's financial statements that are materially false and misleading when the member has the authority to record an entry; or
3. Signs, or permits or directs another to sign, a document containing materially false and misleading information.

[Revised, effective May 31, 1999, by the Professional Ethics Executive Committee.]

.06 501-5—Failure to Follow Requirements of Governmental Bodies, Commissions, or Other Regulatory Agencies in Performing Attest or Similar Services. Many governmental bodies, commissions, or other regulatory agencies have established requirements such as audit standards, guides, rules, and regulations that members are required to follow in performing attest or similar services for clients subject to their jurisdiction. For example, the Securities and Exchange Commission, Federal Communications Commission, state insurance commissions, and other regulatory agencies have established such requirements.

When a member agrees to perform an attest or similar service for the purpose of reporting to such bodies, commissions, or regulatory agencies, the member should follow such requirements, in addition to generally accepted auditing standards (where applicable). Failure to substantially follow such requirements is an act discreditable to the profession, unless the member discloses in his or her report that such requirements were not followed and the reasons therefore. Not following such requirements could require the member to modify his or her report.

If the agency requires additional disclosures of the auditor, they must be made in accordance with the disclosure requirements established by the governmental body, commission, or other regulatory agency. Failure to substantially follow such requirements is an act discreditable to the profession.

[Effective August 31, 1989.]

.07 501-6—Solicitation or Disclosure of CPA Examination Questions and Answers. A member who solicits or knowingly discloses the May 1996 or later Uniform CPA Examination question(s) and/or answer(s) without the written authorization of the AICPA shall be considered to have committed an act discreditable to the profession in violation of rule 501 [ET *section 501.01*].

[Effective January 31, 1996. Revised, effective May 31, 1996, by the Professional Ethics Executive Committee.]

.08 501-7—Failure to File Tax Return or Pay Tax Liability. A member who fails to comply with applicable federal, state, or local laws or regulations regarding the timely filing of his or her personal tax returns or tax returns of the member's firm, or the timely remittance of all payroll and other taxes collected on behalf of others, may be considered to have committed an act discreditable to the profession in violation of rule 501 [ET *section 501.01*].

[Effective May 31, 1999]

AICPA Rule 501; reprinted by permission.

Appendix 2: AICPA Statement on Standards for Consulting Services No. 1

[This item has been omitted from this appendix and can be found in Appendix 1 of this book.]

Appendix 3: International Glossary of Business Valuation Terms

[See Appendix 5 of this book for this item.]

Appendix 5 *International Glossary of Business Valuation Terms*

To enhance and sustain the quality of business valuations for the benefit of the profession and its clientele, the below identified societies and organizations have adopted the definitions for the terms included in this glossary.

The performance of business valuation services requires a high degree of skill and imposes upon the valuation professional a duty to communicate the valuation process and conclusion in a manner that is clear and not misleading. This duty is advanced through the use of terms whose meanings are clearly established and consistently applied throughout the profession.

If, in the opinion of the business valuation professional, one or more of these terms needs to be used in a manner that materially departs from the enclosed definitions, it is recommended that the term be defined as used within that valuation engagement.

This glossary has been developed to provide guidance to business valuation practitioners by further memorializing the body of knowledge that constitutes the competent and careful determination of value and, more particularly, the communication of how that value was determined.

Departure from this glossary is not intended to provide a basis for civil liability and should not be presumed to create evidence that any duty has been breached.

American Institute of Certified Public Accountants
American Society of Appraisers
Canadian Institute of Chartered Business Valuators
National Association of Certified Valuation Analysts
The Institute of Business Appraisers

Adjusted Book Value Method A method within the asset approach whereby all assets and liabilities (including off-balance-sheet, intangible, and contingent) are adjusted to their fair market values (*Note*: In Canada on a going-concern basis).

Adjusted Net Asset Method See **Adjusted Book Value Method.**

Appraisal See **Valuation.**

Appraisal Approach See **Valuation Approach.**

Appraisal Date See **Valuation Date.**

Appraisal Method See **Valuation Method.**

Appraisal Procedure See **Valuation Procedure.**

Arbitrage Pricing Theory A multivariate model for estimating the cost of equity capital, which incorporates several systematic risk factors.

Asset (Asset-Based) Approach A general way of determining a value indication of a business, business ownership interest, or security using one or more methods based on the value of the assets net of liabilities.

Beta A measure of systematic risk of a stock; the tendency of a stock's price to correlate with changes in a specific index.

Blockage Discount An amount or percentage deducted from the current market price of a publicly traded stock to reflect the decrease in the per-share value of a block of stock that is of a size that could not be sold in a reasonable period of time given normal trading volume.

Book Value See **Net Book Value**.

Business See **Business Enterprise**.

Business Enterprise A commercial, industrial, service, or investment entity (or a combination thereof) pursuing an economic activity.

Business Risk The degree of uncertainty of realizing expected future returns of the business resulting from factors other than financial leverage. See **Financial Risk**.

Business Valuation The act or process of determining the value of a business enterprise or ownership interest therein.

Capital Asset Pricing Model (CAPM) A model in which the cost of capital for any stock or portfolio of stocks equals a risk-free rate plus a risk premium that is proportionate to the systematic risk of the stock or portfolio.

Capitalization A conversion of a single period of economic benefits into value.

Capitalization Factor Any multiple or divisor used to convert anticipated economic benefits of a single period into value.

Capitalization of Earnings Method A method within the income approach whereby economic benefits for a representative single period are converted to value through division by a capitalization rate.

Capitalization Rate Any divisor (usually expressed as a percentage) used to convert anticipated economic benefits of a single period into value.

Capital Structure The composition of the invested capital of a business enterprise; the mix of debt and equity financing.

Cash Flow Cash that is generated over a period of time by an asset, group of assets, or business enterprise. It may be used in a general sense to encompass various levels of specifically defined cash flows. When the term is used, it should be supplemented by a qualifier (for example, "discretionary" or "operating") and a specific definition in the given valuation context.

Common-Size Statements Financial statements in which each line is expressed as a percentage of the total. On the balance sheet, each line item is shown as a percentage of total assets, and on the income statement, each item is expressed as a percentage of sales.

Control The power to direct the management and policies of a business enterprise.

Control Premium An amount or a percentage by which the pro rata value of a controlling interest exceeds the pro rata value of a non-controlling interest in a business enterprise to reflect the power of control.

Cost Approach A general way of determining a value indication of an individual asset by quantifying the amount of money required to replace the future service capability of that asset.

Cost of Capital The expected rate of return that the market requires in order to attract funds to a particular investment.

Debt-Free ***We discourage the use of this term***. See **Invested Capital**.

Discount for Lack of Control An amount or percentage deducted from the pro rata share of value of 100% of an equity interest in a business to reflect the absence of some or all of the powers of control.

Discount for Lack of Marketability An amount or percentage deducted from the value of an ownership interest to reflect the relative absence of marketability.

Discount for Lack of Voting Rights An amount or percentage deducted from the per-share value of a minority interest voting share to reflect the absence of voting rights.

Discount Rate A rate of return used to convert a future monetary sum into present value.

Discounted Cash Flow Method A method within the income approach whereby the present value of future expected net cash flows is calculated using a discount rate.

Discounted Future Earnings Method A method within the income approach whereby the present value of future expected economic benefits is calculated using a discount rate.

Economic Benefits Inflows such as revenues, net income, net cash flows, etc.

Economic Life The period of time over which property may generate economic benefits.

Effective Date See **Valuation Date**.

Enterprise See **Business Enterprise**.

Equity The owner's interest in property after deduction of all liabilities.

Equity Net Cash Flows Those cash flows available to pay out to equity holders (in the form of dividends) after funding operations of the business enterprise, making necessary capital investments, and increasing or decreasing debt financing.

Equity Risk Premium A rate of return added to a risk-free rate to reflect the additional risk of equity instruments over risk-free instruments (a component of the cost of equity capital or equity discount rate).

Excess Earnings That amount of anticipated economic benefits that exceeds an appropriate rate of return on the value of a selected asset base (often net tangible assets) used to generate those anticipated economic benefits.

Excess Earnings Method A specific way of determining a value indication of a business, business ownership interest, or security determined as the sum of (a) the value of the assets derived by capitalizing excess earnings and (b) the value of the selected asset base. Also frequently used to value intangible assets. See **Excess Earnings**.

Fair Market Value The price, expressed in terms of cash equivalents, at which property would change hands between a hypothetical willing and able buyer and a hypothetical willing and able seller, acting at arm's length in an open and unrestricted market, when neither is under compulsion to buy or sell and when both have reasonable knowledge of the relevant facts. (*Note:* In Canada, the term "price" should be replaced with the term "highest price.")

Fairness Opinion An opinion as to whether or not the consideration in a transaction is fair from a financial point of view.

Financial Risk The degree of uncertainty of realizing expected future returns of the business resulting from financial leverage. See **Business Risk**.

Forced Liquidation Value Liquidation value, at which the asset or assets are sold as quickly as possible, such as at an auction.

Free Cash Flow ***We discourage the use of this term***. See **Net Cash Flow**.

Going Concern An ongoing operating business enterprise.

Going-Concern Value The value of a business enterprise that is expected to continue to operate into the future. The intangible elements of Going-Concern Value result from factors such as having a trained work force, an operational plant, and the necessary licenses, systems, and procedures in place.

Goodwill That intangible asset arising as a result of name, reputation, customer loyalty, location, products, and similar factors not separately identified.

Goodwill Value The value attributable to goodwill.

Guideline Public Company Method A method within the market approach whereby market multiples are derived from market prices of stocks of companies that are engaged in the same or similar lines of business, and that are actively traded on a free and open market.

Income (Income-Based) Approach A general way of determining a value indication of a business, business ownership interest, security, or intangible asset using one or more methods that convert anticipated economic benefits into a present single amount.

Intangible Assets Non-physical assets such as franchises, trademarks, patents, copyrights, goodwill, equities, mineral rights, securities and contracts (as distinguished from physical assets) that grant rights and privileges, and have value for the owner.

Internal Rate of Return A discount rate at which the present value of the future cash flows of the investment equals the cost of the investment.

Intrinsic Value The value that an investor considers, on the basis of an evaluation or available facts, to be the "true" or "real" value that will become the market value when other investors reach the same conclusion. When the term applies to options, it is the difference between the exercise price or strike price of an option and the market value of the underlying security.

Invested Capital The sum of equity and debt in a business enterprise. Debt is typically (a) all interest-bearing debt or (b) long-term interest-bearing debt. When the term is used, it should be supplemented by a specific definition in the given valuation context.

Invested Capital Net Cash Flows Those cash flows available to pay out to equity holders (in the form of dividends) and debt investors (in the form of principal and interest) after funding operations of the business enterprise and making necessary capital investments.

Investment Risk The degree of uncertainty as to the realization of expected returns.

Investment Value The value to a particular investor based on individual investment requirements and expectations. (*Note:* In Canada, the term used is "Value to the Owner.")

Key Person Discount An amount or percentage deducted from the value of an ownership interest to reflect the reduction in value resulting from the actual or potential loss of a key person in a business enterprise.

Levered Beta The beta reflecting a capital structure that includes debt.

Limited Appraisal The act or process of determining the value of a business, business ownership interest, security, or intangible asset with limitations in analyses, procedures, or scope.

Liquidity The ability to quickly convert property to cash or pay a liability.

Liquidation Value The net amount that would be realized if the business is terminated and the assets are sold piecemeal. Liquidation can be either "orderly" or "forced."

Majority Control The degree of control provided by a majority position.

Majority Interest An ownership interest greater than 50% of the voting interest in a business enterprise.

Market (Market-Based) Approach A general way of determining a value indication of a business, business ownership interest, security, or intangible asset by using one or more methods that compare the subject to similar businesses, business ownership interests, securities, or intangible assets that have been sold.

Market Capitalization of Equity The share price of a publicly traded stock multiplied by the number of shares outstanding.

Market Capitalization of Invested Capital The market capitalization of equity plus the market value of the debt component of invested capital.

Market Multiple The market value of a company's stock or invested capital divided by a company measure (such as economic benefits, number of customers).

Marketability The ability to quickly convert property to cash at minimal cost.

Marketability Discount See **Discount for Lack of Marketability**.

Merger and Acquisition Method A method within the market approach whereby pricing multiples are derived from transactions of significant interests in companies engaged in the same or similar lines of business.

Mid-Year Discounting A convention used in the Discounted Future Earnings Method that reflects economic benefits being generated at midyear, approximating the effect of economic benefits being generated evenly throughout the year.

Minority Discount A discount for lack of control applicable to a minority interest.

Minority Interest An ownership interest less than 50% of the voting interest in a business enterprise.

Multiple The inverse of the capitalization rate.

Net Book Value With respect to a business enterprise, the difference between total assets (net of accumulated depreciation, depletion, and amortization) and total liabilities as they appear on the balance sheet (synonymous with Shareholder's Equity). With respect to a specific asset, the capitalized cost less accumulated amortization or depreciation as it appears on the books of account of the business enterprise.

Net Cash Flows When the term is used, it should be supplemented by a qualifier. See **Equity Net Cash Flows** and **Invested Capital Net Cash Flows**.

Net Present Value The value, as of a specified date, of future cash inflows less all cash outflows (including the cost of investment) calculated using an appropriate discount rate.

Net Tangible Asset Value The value of the business enterprise's tangible assets (excluding excess assets and non-operating assets) minus the value of its liabilities.

Non-Operating Assets Assets not necessary to ongoing operations of the business enterprise. (*Note*: In Canada, the term used is "Redundant Assets.")

Normalized Earnings Economic benefits adjusted for nonrecurring, noneconomic, or other unusual items to eliminate anomalies and/or facilitate comparisons.

Normalized Financial Statements Financial statements adjusted for non-operating assets and liabilities and/or for nonrecurring, noneconomic, or other unusual items to eliminate anomalies and/or facilitate comparisons.

Orderly Liquidation Value Liquidation value at which the asset or assets are sold over a reasonable period of time to maximize proceeds received.

Premise of Value An assumption regarding the most likely set of transactional circumstances that may be applicable to the subject valuation (e.g., going concern, liquidation).

Present Value The value, as of a specified date, of future economic benefits and/or proceeds from sale, calculated using an appropriate discount rate.

Portfolio Discount An amount or percentage deducted from the value of a business enterprise to reflect the fact that it owns dissimilar operations or assets that do not fit well together.

Price/Earnings Multiple The price of a share of stock divided by its earnings per share.

Rate of Return An amount of income (loss) and/or change in value realized or anticipated on an investment, expressed as a percentage of that investment.

Redundant Assets See **Non-Operating Assets**.

Report Date The date conclusions are transmitted to the client.

Replacement Cost New The current cost of a similar new property having the nearest equivalent utility to the property being valued.

Reproduction Cost New The current cost of an identical new property.

Required Rate of Return The minimum rate of return acceptable by investors before they will commit money to an investment at a given level of risk.

Residual Value The value as of the end of the discrete projection period in a discounted future earnings model.

Return on Equity The amount, expressed as a percentage, earned on a company's common equity for a given period.

Return on Investment See **Return on Invested Capital** and **Return on Equity**.

Return on Invested Capital The amount, expressed as a percentage, earned on a company's total capital for a given period.

Risk-Free Rate The rate of return available in the market on an investment free of default risk.

Risk Premium A rate of return added to a risk-free rate to reflect risk.

Rule of Thumb A mathematical formula developed from the relationship between price and certain variables based on experience, observation, hearsay, or a combination of these; usually industry specific.

Special Interest Purchasers Acquirers who believe they can enjoy post-acquisition economies of scale, synergies, or strategic advantages by combining the acquired business interest with their own.

Standard of Value The identification of the type of value being used in a specific engagement (e.g., fair market value, fair value, investment value).

Sustaining Capital Reinvestment The periodic capital outlay required to maintain operations at existing levels, net of the tax shield available from such outlays.

Systematic Risk The risk that is common to all risky securities and cannot be eliminated through diversification. The measure of systematic risk in stocks is the beta coefficient.

Tangible Assets Physical assets (such as cash, accounts receivable, inventory, property, plant and equipment, etc.).

Terminal Value See **Residual Value**.

Transaction Method See **Merger and Acquisition Method**.

Unlevered Beta The beta reflecting a capital structure without debt.

Unsystematic Risk The risk specific to an individual security that can be avoided through diversification.

Valuation The act or process of determining the value of a business, business ownership interest, security, or intangible asset.

Valuation Approach A general way of determining a value indication of a business, business ownership interest, security, or intangible asset using one or more valuation methods.

Valuation Date The specific point in time as of which the valuator's opinion of value applies (also referred to as "Effective Date" or "Appraisal Date").

Valuation Method Within approaches, a specific way to determine value.

Valuation Procedure The act, manner, and technique of performing the steps of an appraisal method.

Valuation Ratio A fraction in which a value or price serves as the numerator and financial, operating, or physical data serves as the denominator.

Value to the Owner See **Investment Value**.

Voting Control *De jure* control of a business enterprise.

Weighted Average Cost of Capital (WACC) The cost of capital (discount rate) determined by the weighted average, at market value, of the cost of all financing sources in the business enterprise's capital structure.

Appendix 6 *Revenue Ruling 59-60*

Rev. Rul. 59-60, 1959-1 C.B. 237 IRC Sec. 2031

Sec. 2031—DEFINITION OF GROSS ESTATE
26 CFR 20.2031-2: Valuation of stocks and bonds.
(Also Section 2512.)
(Also Part II, Sections 811(k), 1005, Regulations 105, Section 81.10.)

Headnote

In valuing the stock of closely held corporations, or the stock of corporations where market quotations are not available, all other available financial data, as well as all relevant factors affecting the fair market value must be considered for estate tax and gift tax purposes. No general formula may be given that is applicable to the many different valuation situations arising in the valuation of such stock. However, the general approach, methods, and factors which must be considered in valuing such securities are outlined. Revenue Ruling 54-77, C.B. 1954-1, 187, superseded.

Text

Sec. 1. Purpose

The purpose of this Revenue Ruling is to outline and review in general the approach, methods, and factors to be considered in valuing shares of the capital stock of closely held corporations for estate tax and gift tax purposes. The methods discussed herein will apply likewise to the valuation of corporate stocks on which market quotations are either unavailable or are of such scarcity that they do not reflect the fair market value.

Sec. 2. Background and Definitions

.01 All valuations must be made in accordance with the applicable provisions of the Internal Revenue Code of 1954 and the Federal Estate Tax and Gift Tax Regulations. Sections 2031(a), 2032, and 2512(a) of the 1954 Code (sections 811 and 1005 of the 1939 Code) require that the property to be included in the gross estate, or made the subject of a gift, shall be taxed on the basis of the value of the property at the time of death of the decedent, the alternate date if so elected, or the date of gift.

.02 Section 20.2031-1(b) of the Estate Tax Regulations (section 81.10 of the Estate Tax Regulations 105) and section 25.2512-1 of the Gift Tax Regulations (section 86.19 of Gift Tax Regulations 108) define fair market value, in effect, as the price at which the property would change hands between a willing buyer and a willing seller when the former is not under any compulsion to buy and the latter is not under any compulsion to sell, both parties having reasonable knowledge of relevant facts. Court decisions frequently state in addition that the hypothetical buyer and seller are assumed to be able, as well as willing, to trade and to be well informed about the property and concerning the market for such property.

.03 Closely held corporations are those corporations the shares of which are owned by a relatively limited number of stockholders. Often the entire stock issue is held by one family. The result of this situation is that little, if any, trading in the shares takes place. There is, therefore, no established market for the stock and such sales as occur at irregular intervals seldom reflect all of the elements of a representative transaction as defined by the term "fair market value."

Sec. 3. Approach to Valuation

.01 A determination of fair market value, being a question of fact, will depend upon the circumstances in each case. No formula can be devised that will be generally applicable to the multitude of different valuation issues arising in estate and gift tax cases. Often, an appraiser will find wide differences of opinion as to the fair market value of a particular stock. In resolving such differences, he should maintain a reasonable attitude in recognition of the fact that valuation is not an exact science. A sound valuation will be based upon all the relevant facts, but the elements of common sense, informed judgment and reasonableness must enter into the process of weighing those facts and determining their aggregate significance.

.02 The fair market value of specific shares of stock will vary as general economic conditions change from "normal" to "boom" or "depression," that is, according to the degree of optimism or pessimism with which the investing public regards the future at the required date of appraisal. Uncertainty as to the stability or continuity of the future income from a property decreases its value by increasing the risk of loss of earnings and value in the future. The value of shares of stock of a company with very uncertain future prospects is highly speculative. The appraiser must exercise his judgment as to the degree of risk attaching to the business of the corporation which issued the stock, but that judgment must be related to all of the other factors affecting value.

.03 Valuation of securities is, in essence, a prophecy as to the future and must be based on facts available at the required date of appraisal. As a generalization, the prices of stocks which are traded in volume in a free and active market by informed persons best reflect the consensus of the investing public as to what the future holds for the corporations and industries represented. When a stock is closely held, is traded infrequently, or is traded in an erratic market, some other measure of value must be used. In many instances, the next best measure may be found in the prices at which the stocks of companies engaged in the same or a similar line of business are selling in a free and open market.

Sec. 4. Factors to Consider

.01 It is advisable to emphasize that in the valuation of the stock of closely held corporations or the stock of corporations where market quotations are either lacking or too scarce to be recognized, all available financial data, as well as all relevant factors affecting the fair market value, should be considered. The following factors, although not all-inclusive, are fundamental and require careful analysis in each case:

a. The nature of the business and the history of the enterprise from its inception
b. The economic outlook in general and the condition and outlook of the specific industry in particular
c. The book value of the stock and the financial condition of the business
d. The earning capacity of the company
e. The dividend-paying capacity

f. Whether or not the enterprise has goodwill or other intangible value
g. Sales of the stock and the size of the block of stock to be valued
h. The market price of stocks of corporations engaged in the same or a similar line of business having their stocks actively traded in a free and open market, either on an exchange or over-the-counter

.02 The following is a brief discussion of each of the foregoing factors:

a. The history of a corporate enterprise will show its past stability or instability, its growth or lack of growth, the diversity or lack of diversity of its operations, and other facts needed to form an opinion of the degree of risk involved in the business. For an enterprise which changed its form of organization but carried on the same or closely similar operations of its predecessor, the history of the former enterprise should be considered. The detail to be considered should increase with approach to the required date of appraisal since recent events are of greatest help in predicting the future; but a study of gross and net income, and of dividends covering a long prior period, is highly desirable. The history to be studied should include, but need not be limited to, the nature of the business, its products or services, its operating and investment assets, capital structure, plant facilities, sales records, and management, all of which should be considered as of the date of the appraisal, with due regard for recent significant changes. Events of the past that are unlikely to recur in the future should be discounted, since value has a close relation to future expectancy.
b. A sound appraisal of a closely held stock must consider current and prospective economic conditions as of the date of appraisal, both in the national economy and in the industry or industries with which the corporation is allied. It is important to know that the company is more or less successful than its competitors in the same industry, or that it is maintaining a stable position with respect to competitors. Equal or even greater significance may attach to the ability of the industry with which the company is allied to compete with other industries. Prospective competition which has not been a factor in prior years should be given careful attention. For example, high profits due to the novelty of its product and the lack of competition often lead to increasing competition. The public's appraisal of the future prospects of competitive industries or of competitors within an industry may be indicated by price trends in the markets for commodities and for securities. The loss of the manager of a so-called "one-man" business may have a depressing effect upon the value of the stock of such business, particularly if there is a lack of trained personnel capable of succeeding to the management of the enterprise. In valuing the stock of this type of business, therefore, the effect of the loss of the manager on the future expectancy of the business and the absence of management-succession potentialities are pertinent factors to be taken into consideration. On the other hand, there may be factors which offset, in whole or in part, the loss of the manager's services. For instance, the nature of the business and of its assets may be such that they will not be impaired by the loss of the manager. Furthermore, the loss may be adequately covered by life insurance, or competent management might be employed on the basis of the consideration paid for the former manager's services. These, or other offsetting factors, if found to exist, should be carefully weighed against the loss of the manager's services in valuing the stock of the enterprise.
c. Balance sheets should be obtained, preferably in the form of comparative annual statements for two or more years immediately preceding the date of appraisal, together with a balance sheet at the end of the month preceding that date, if corporate accounting will permit. Any balance sheet descriptions that are not self-explanatory, and balance sheet items comprehending diverse assets or liabilities, should be clarified in essential detail by supporting supplemental schedules. These statements usually will disclose to the appraiser (1) liquid position (ratio of current assets to current liabilities); (2) gross and net book value of principal classes of fixed assets; (3) working capital; (4) long-term

indebtedness; (5) capital structure; and (6) net worth. Consideration also should be given to any assets not essential to the operation of the business, such as investments in securities, real estate, etc. In general, such non-operating assets will command a lower rate of return than do the operating assets, although in exceptional cases the reverse may be true. In computing the book value per share of stock, assets of the investment type should be revalued on the basis of their market price and the book value adjusted accordingly. Comparison of the company's balance sheets over several years may reveal, among other facts, such developments as the acquisition of additional production facilities or subsidiary companies, improvement in financial position, and details as to recapitalizations and other changes in the capital structure of the corporation. If the corporation has more than one class of stock outstanding, the charter or certificate of incorporation should be examined to ascertain the explicit rights and privileges of the various stock issues including: (1) voting powers, (2) preference as to dividends, and (3) preference as to assets in the event of liquidation.

d. Detailed profit-and-loss statements should be obtained and considered for a representative period immediately prior to the required date of appraisal, preferably five or more years. Such statements should show (1) gross income by principal items; (2) principal deductions from gross income including major prior items of operating expenses, interest and other expense on each item of long-term debt, depreciation and depletion if such deductions are made, officers' salaries, in total if they appear to be reasonable or in detail if they seem to be excessive, contributions (whether or not deductible for tax purposes) that the nature of its business and its community position require the corporation to make, and taxes by principal items, including income and excess profits taxes; (3) net income available for dividends; (4) rates and amounts of dividends paid on each class of stock; (5) remaining amount carried to surplus; and (6) adjustments to, and reconciliation with, surplus as stated on the balance sheet. With profit and loss statements of this character available, the appraiser should be able to separate recurrent from nonrecurrent items of income and expense, to distinguish between operating income and investment income, and to ascertain whether or not any line of business in which the company is engaged is operated consistently at a loss and might be abandoned with benefit to the company. The percentage of earnings retained for business expansion should be noted when dividend-paying capacity is considered. Potential future income is a major factor in many valuations of closely held stocks, and all information concerning past income which will be helpful in predicting the future should be secured. Prior earnings records usually are the most reliable guide as to the future expectancy, but resort to arbitrary five- or ten-year averages without regard to current trends or future prospects will not produce a realistic valuation. If, for instance, a record of progressively increasing or decreasing net income is found, then greater weight may be accorded the most recent years' profits in estimating earning power. It will be helpful, in judging risk and the extent to which a business is a marginal operator, to consider deductions from income and net income in terms of percentage of sales. Major categories of cost and expense to be so analyzed include the consumption of raw materials and supplies in the case of manufacturers, processors, and fabricators; the cost of purchased merchandise in the case of merchants; utility services; insurance; taxes; depletion or depreciation; and interest.

e. Primary consideration should be given to the dividend-paying capacity of the company rather than to dividends actually paid in the past. Recognition must be given to the necessity of retaining a reasonable portion of profits in a company to meet competition. Dividend-paying capacity is a factor that must be considered in an appraisal, but dividends actually paid in the past may not have any relation to dividend-paying capacity. Specifically, the dividends paid by a closely held family company may be measured by the income needs of the stockholders or by their desire to avoid taxes on dividend receipts, instead of by the ability of the company to pay dividends. Where an actual or effective controlling interest in a corporation is to be valued, the dividend factor is not a material element, since the payment of such dividends is discretionary with the controlling stockholders. The individual or group in control can substitute salaries and bonuses for dividends, thus reducing net income and understating the dividend-paying capacity of the company. It follows, therefore, that dividends are less reliable criteria of fair market value than other applicable factors.

f. In the final analysis, goodwill is based upon earning capacity. The presence of goodwill and its value, therefore, rests upon the excess of net earnings over and above a fair return on the net tangible assets. While the element of goodwill may be based primarily on earnings, such factors as the prestige and renown of the business, the ownership of a trade or brand name, and a record of successful operation over a prolonged period in a particular locality also may furnish support for the inclusion of intangible value. In some instances it may not be possible to make a separate appraisal of the tangible and intangible assets of the business. The enterprise has a value as an entity. Whatever intangible value there is, which is supportable by the facts, may be measured by the amount by which the appraised value of the tangible assets exceeds the net book value of such assets.

g. Sales of stock of a closely held corporation should be carefully investigated to determine whether they represent transactions at arm's length. Forced or distress sales do not ordinarily reflect fair market value nor do isolated sales in small amounts necessarily control as the measure of value. This is especially true in the valuation of a controlling interest in a corporation. Since, in the case of closely held stocks, no prevailing market prices are available, there is no basis for making an adjustment for blockage. It follows, therefore, that such stocks should be valued upon a consideration of all the evidence affecting the fair market value. The size of the block of stock itself is a relevant factor to be considered. Although it is true that a minority interest in an unlisted corporation's stock is more difficult to sell than a similar block of listed stock, it is equally true that control of a corporation, either actual or in effect, representing as it does an added element of value, may justify a higher value for a specific block of stock.

h. Section 2031(b) of the Code states, in effect, that in valuing unlisted securities the value of stock or securities of corporations engaged in the same or a similar line of business which are listed on an exchange should be taken into consideration along with all other factors. An important consideration is that the corporations to be used for comparisons have capital stocks which are actively traded by the public. In accordance with section 2031(b) of the Code, stocks listed on an exchange are to be considered first. However, if sufficient comparable companies whose stocks are listed on an exchange cannot be found, other comparable companies which have stocks actively traded on the over-the-counter market also may be used. The essential factor is that whether the stocks are sold on an exchange or over-the-counter there is evidence of an active, free public market for the stock as of the valuation date. In selecting corporations for comparative purposes, care should be taken to use only comparable companies. Although the only restrictive requirement as to comparable corporations specified in the statute is that their lines of business be the same or similar, yet it is obvious that consideration must be given to other relevant factors in order that the most valid comparison possible will be obtained. For illustration, a corporation having one or more issues of preferred stock, bonds, or debentures in addition to its common stock should not be considered to be directly comparable to one having only common stock outstanding. In like manner, a company with a declining business and decreasing markets is not comparable to one with a record of current progress and market expansion.

Sec. 5. Weight to Be Accorded Various Factors

The valuation of closely held corporate stock entails the consideration of all relevant factors as stated in Section 4. Depending upon the circumstances in each case, certain factors may carry more weight than others because of the nature of the company's business. To illustrate:

1. Earnings may be the most important criterion of value in some cases, whereas asset value will receive primary consideration in others. In general, the appraiser will accord primary consideration to earnings when valuing stocks of companies which sell products or services to the public; conversely, in the investment or holding type of company, the appraiser may accord the greatest weight to the assets underlying the security to be valued.
2. The value of the stock of a closely held investment or real estate holding company, whether or not family owned, is closely related to the value of the assets underlying the stock. For companies of this type the appraiser should determine the fair market values of the assets of the company. Operating expenses of such a company and the cost of liquidating it, if any, merit consideration when appraising the relative values of the stock and the underlying assets. The market values of the underlying assets give due weight to potential earnings and dividends of the particular items of property underlying the stock, capitalized at rates deemed proper by the investing public at the date of appraisal. A current appraisal by the investing public should be superior to the retrospective opinion of an individual. For these reasons, adjusted net worth should be accorded greater weight in valuing the stock of a closely held investment or real estate holding company, whether or not family owned, than any of the other customary yardsticks of appraisal, such as earnings and dividend paying capacity.

Sec. 6. Capitalization Rates

In the application of certain fundamental valuation factors, such as earnings and dividends, it is necessary to capitalize the average or current results at some appropriate rate. A determination of the proper capitalization rate presents one of the most difficult problems in valuation. That there is no ready or simple solution will become apparent by a cursory check of the rates of return and dividend yields in terms of the selling prices of corporate shares listed on the major exchanges of the country. Wide variations will be found even for companies in the same industry. Moreover, the ratio will fluctuate from year to year depending upon economic conditions. Thus, no standard tables of capitalization rates applicable to closely held corporations can be formulated. Among the more important factors to be taken into consideration in deciding upon a capitalization rate in a particular case are: (1) the nature of the business; (2) the risk involved; and (3) the stability or irregularity of earnings.

Sec. 7. Average of Factors

Because valuations cannot be made on the basis of a prescribed formula, there is no means whereby the various applicable factors in a particular case can be assigned mathematical weights in deriving the fair market value. For this reason, no useful purpose is served by taking an average of several factors (for example, book value, capitalized earnings, and capitalized dividends) and basing the valuation on the result. Such a process excludes active consideration of other pertinent factors, and the end result cannot be supported by a realistic application of the significant facts in the case except by mere chance.

Sec. 8. Restrictive Agreements

Frequently, in the valuation of closely held stock for estate and gift tax purposes, it will be found that the stock is subject to an agreement restricting its sale or transfer. Where shares of stock were acquired by a decedent subject to an option reserved by the issuing corporation to repurchase at a certain price, the option price is usually accepted as the fair market value for estate tax purposes. See Rev. Rul. 54-76, C.B. 1954-1, 194. However, in such case the option price is not determinative of fair market value for gift tax purposes. Where the option, or buy and sell agreement, is the result of voluntary action by the stockholders and is binding during the life as well as at the death of the stockholders, such agreement may or may not, depending upon the circumstances of each case, fix the value for estate tax purposes. However, such agreement is a factor to be considered, with other relevant factors, in determining fair market value. Where the stockholder is free to dispose of his shares during life and the option is to become effective only upon his death, the fair market value is not limited to the option price. It is always necessary to consider the relationship of the parties, the relative number of shares held by the decedent, and other material facts to determine whether the agreement represents a bona fide business arrangement or is a device to pass the decedent's shares to the natural objects of his bounty for less than an adequate and full consideration in money or money's worth. In this connection see Rev. Rul. 157 C.B. 1953-2, 255, and Rev. Rul. 189, C.B. 1953-2, 294.

Sec. 9. Effect on Other Documents

Revenue Ruling 54-77, C.B. 1954-1, 187, is hereby superseded.

Appendix 7 *Revenue Ruling 65-192*

Rev. Rul. 65-192

The general approach, methods, and factors outlined in Revenue Ruling 59-60, C.B. 1959-1, 237, for use in valuing closely held corporate stocks for estate and gift tax purposes are equally applicable to valuations thereof for income and other tax purposes and also in determinations of the fair market values of business interests of any type and of intangible assets for all tax purposes.

The formula approach set forth in A.R.M. 34, C.B. 2, 31 (1920), and A.R.M. 68, C.B. 3, 43 (1920), has no valid application in determinations of the fair market values of corporate stocks or of business interests, unless it is necessary to value the intangible assets of the corporation or the intangible assets included in the business interest. The formula approach may be used in determining the fair market values of intangible assets only if there is no better basis therefor available. In applying the formula, the average earnings period and the capitalization rates are dependent upon the facts and circumstances pertinent thereto in such case.

Full Text

Sec. 1. Purpose

The purpose of this Revenue Ruling is to furnish information and guidance as to the usage to be made of suggested methods for determining the value as of March 1, 1913, or of any other date, of intangible assets and to identify those areas where a valuation formula set forth in A.R.M. 34, C.B. 2, 31 (1920), as modified by A.R.M. 68, C.B. 3, 43 (1920), both quoted in full below should and should not be applied. Since it appears that such formula has been applied to many valuation issues for which it was never intended, the Internal Revenue Service reindicates its limited application.

Sec. 2. Background

A.R.M. 34 was issued in 1920 for the purpose of providing suggested formulas for determining the amount of March 1, 1913, intangible asset value lost by breweries and other businesses connected with the distilling industry, as a result of the passage of the 18th Amendment to the Constitution of the United States. A.R.M. 68 was issued later in the same year and contained a minor revision of the original ruling so that its third formula would be applied in accordance with its purpose and intent.

Sec. 3. Statement of Position

.01 Although the formulas and approach contained in A.R.M. 34 were specifically aimed at the valuation of intangible assets of distilling and related companies as of March 1, 1913, the last two paragraphs of the ruling seemingly broaden it to make its third formula applicable to almost any kind of enterprise. The final sentences, however, limit the purpose of such formula by stating that "In . . . all of the cases the effort should be to determine what net earnings a purchaser of a business on March 1, 1913, might reasonably have expected to receive from it" and by providing certain checks and alternatives. Also, both A.R.M. 34 and A.R.M. 68 expressly stated that such formula was merely a rule for guidance and not controlling in the presence of "better evidence" in determining the value of intangible assets. Furthermore, T.B.R. 57, C.B. 1, 40 (1919), relating to the meaning of "fair market value" of property received in exchange for other property, which was published before A.R.M. 34 and A.R.M. 68 and has not been revoked, set forth general principles of valuation that are consistent with Revenue Ruling 59-60, C.B. 1959-1, 237. Moreover, in S.M. 1609, C.B. III-1, 48 (1924) it was stated that "the method suggested in A.R.M. 34 for determining the value of intangibles is . . . controlling only in the absence of better evidence." As said in *North American Service Co., Inc. v. Commissioner*, 33 T.C. 677, 694 (1960), *acq*., C.B. 1960-2, 6, "an A.R.M. 34 computation would not be conclusive of the existence and value of good will if better evidence were available."

.02 Revenue Ruling 59-60 sets forth the proper approach to use in the valuation of closely held corporate stocks for estate and gift tax purposes. That ruling contains the statement that no formula can be devised that will be generally applicable to the multitude of different valuation issues. It also contains a discussion of intangible value in closely held corporations and some of the elements which may support such value in a given business.

Sec. 4. Delineation of Areas in Which Suggested Methods Will Be Effective

.01 The general approach, methods, and factors outlined in Revenue Ruling 59-60 are equally applicable to valuations of corporate stocks for income and other tax purposes as well as for estate and gift tax purposes. They apply also to problems involving the determination of the fair market value of business interests of any type, including partnerships, proprietorships, etc., and of intangible assets for all tax purposes.

.02 Valuation, especially where earning power is an important factor, is in essence a process requiring the exercise of informed judgment and common sense. Thus, the suggested formula approach set forth in A.R.M. 34 has no valid application in determinations of the fair market value of corporate stocks or of business interests unless it is necessary to value the intangible assets of the corporation or the intangible assets included in the business interest. The formula approach may be used in determining the fair market values of intangible assets only if there is no better basis therefor available. In applying the formula, the average earnings period and the capitalization rates are dependent upon the facts and circumstances pertinent thereto in each case. See *John Q. Shunk et al. v. Commissioner*, 10 T.C. 293, 304-5 (1948), *acq*., C.B. 1948-1, 3, *aff'd* 173 Fed. (2d) 747 (1949); *USHCO Manufacturing Co., Inc. v. Commissioner*, Tax Court Memorandum Opinion entered March 10, 1945, *aff'd* 175 Fed. (2d) 821 (1945); and *White & Wells Co. v. Commissioner*, 19 B.T.A. 416, *nonacq*., C.B. IX-2, 87 (1930), *rev'd and remanded*, 50 Fed. (2d) 120 (1931).

Sec. 5. Quotation of A.R.M. 34

For convenience, A.R.M. 34 reads as follows:

The Committee has considered the question of providing some practical formula for determining value as of March 1, 1913, or of any other date, which might be considered as applying to intangible assets, but finds itself unable to lay down any specific rule of guidance for determining the value of intangibles which would be applicable in all cases and under all circumstances. Where there is no established market to serve as a guide, the question of value, even of tangible assets, is one largely of judgment and opinion, and the same thing is even more true of intangible assets such as goodwill, trademarks, trade brands, etc. However, there are several methods of reaching a conclusion as to the value of intangibles which the Committee suggests may be utilized broadly in passing upon questions of valuation, not to be regarded as controlling, however, if better evidence is presented in any specific case.

Where deduction is claimed for obsolescence or loss of goodwill or trademarks, the burden of proof is primarily upon the taxpayer to show the value of such goodwill or trademarks on March 1, 1913. Of course, if goodwill or trademarks have been acquired for cash or other valuable considerations subsequent to March 1, 1913, the measure of loss will be determined by the amount of cash or value of other considerations paid therefor, and no deduction will be allowed for the value of goodwill or trademarks built up by the taxpayer since March 1, 1913. The following suggestions are made, therefore, merely as suggestions for checks upon the soundness and validity of the taxpayers' claims. No obsolescence or loss with respect to goodwill should be allowed except in cases of actual disposition of the asset or abandonment of the business.

In the first place, it is recognized that in numerous instances it has been the practice of distillers and wholesale liquor dealers to put out under well-known and popular brands only so much goods as could be marketed without affecting the established market price therefor and to sell other goods of the same identical manufacture, age, and character under other brands, or under no brand at all, at figures very much below those which the well-known brands commanded. In such cases the difference between the price at which whisky was sold under a given brand name and also under another brand name, or under no brand, multiplied by the number of units sold during a given year gives an accurate determination of the amount of profit attributable to that brand during that year, and where this practice is continued for a long enough period to show that this amount was fairly constant and regular and might be expected to yield annually that average profit, by capitalizing this earning at the rate, say, of 20 percent, the value of the brand is fairly well established.

Another method is to compare the volume of business done under the trademark or brand under consideration and profits made, or by the business whose goodwill is under consideration, with the similar volume of business and profit made in other cases where goodwill or trademarks have been actually sold for cash, recognizing as the value of the first the same proportion of the selling price of the second, as the profits of the first attributable to brands or goodwill, is of the similar profits of the second.

The third method and possibly the one which will most frequently have to be applied as a check in the absence of data necessary for the application of the preceding ones, is to allow out of average earnings over a period of years prior to March 1, 1913, preferably not less than five years, a return of 10 percent upon the average tangible assets for the period. The surplus earnings will then be the average amount available for return upon the value of the intangible assets, and it is the opinion of the Committee that this return should be capitalized upon the basis of not more than five years' purchase that is to say, five times the amount available as return from intangibles should be the value of the intangibles.

In view of the hazards of the business, the changes in popular tastes, and the difficulties in preventing limitation or counterfeiting of popular brands affecting the sales of the genuine goods, the Committee is of the opinion that the figure given of 20 percent return on intangibles is not unreasonable, and it recommends that no higher figure than that be attached in any case to intangibles without a very clear and adequate showing that the value of the intangibles was in fact greater than would be reached by applying this formula.

The foregoing is intended to apply particularly to businesses put out of existence by the prohibition law, but will be equally applicable so far as the third formula is concerned, to other businesses of a more or less hazardous nature. In the case, however, of valuation of goodwill of a business which consists of the manufacture or sale of standard articles of everyday necessity not subject to violent fluctuations and where the hazard is not so great, the Committee is of the opinion that the figure for determination of the return on tangible assets might be reduced from 10 to 8 or 9 percent, and that the percentage for capitalization of the return upon intangibles might be reduced from 20 to 15 percent.

In any or all of the cases the effort should be to determine what net earnings a purchaser of a business on March 1, 1913, might reasonably have expected to receive from it, and therefore a representative period should be used for averaging actual earnings, eliminating any year in which there were extraordinary factors affecting earnings either way. Also, in the case of the sale of goodwill of a going business the percentage rate of capitalization of earnings applicable to goodwill shown by the amount actually paid for the business should be used as a check against the determination of goodwill value as of March 1, 1913, and if the goodwill is sold upon the basis of capitalization of earnings less than the figures above indicated as the ones ordinarily to be adopted, the same percentage should be used in figuring value as of March 1, 1913.

Sec. 6. Quotation of A.R.M. 68

Also for convenience, A.R.M. 68 reads as follows:

The Committee is in receipt of a request for advice as to whether under A.R.M. 34 the 10 percent upon tangible assets is to be applied only to the net tangible assets or to all tangible assets on the books of the corporation, regardless of any outstanding obligations.

The Committee, in the memorandum in question, undertook to lay down a rule for guidance in the absence of better evidence in determining the value as of March 1, 1913, of goodwill, and held that in determining such value, income over an average period in excess of an amount sufficient to return 10 percent upon tangible assets should be capitalized at 20 percent. Manifestly, since the effort is to determine the value of the goodwill, and therefore the true net worth of the taxpayer as of March 1, 1913, the 10 percent should be applied only to the tangible assets entering into net worth, including accounts and bills receivable in excess of accounts and bills payable.

In other words, the purpose and intent are to provide for a return to the taxpayer of 10 percent upon so much of his investment as is represented by tangible assets and to capitalize the excess of earnings over the amount necessary to provide such return, at 20 percent.

Sec. 7. Effect on Other Documents

Although the limited application of A.R.M. 34 and A.R.M. 68 is reindicated in this Revenue Ruling, the principles enunciated in those rulings are not thereby affected.

Appendix 8 *Revenue Ruling 65-193*

Rev. Rul. 65-193, 1965-2 C.B. 370, IRC Sec. 2031

Sec. 2031—DEFINITION OF GROSS ESTATE
26 CFR 20.2031-2: Valuation of stocks and bonds.
(Also Sections 1001, 2512; 1.1001-1, 25.2512-2.)

Text

Revenue Ruling 59-60, C.B. 1959-1, 237, is hereby modified to delete the statements, contained therein at section 4.02(f), that "In some instances it may not be possible to make a separate appraisal of the tangible and intangible assets of the business. The enterprise has a value as an entity. Whatever intangible value there is, which is supportable by the facts, may be measured by the amount by which the appraised value of the tangible assets exceeds the net book value of such assets."

The instances where it is not possible to make a separate appraisal of the tangible and intangible assets of a business are rare and each case varies from the other. No rule can be devised which will be generally applicable to such cases.

Other than this modification, Revenue Ruling 59-60 continues in full force and effect. See Rev. Rul. 65-192, page 259, this Bulletin.

Appendix 9 *Revenue Procedure 66-49*

Rev. Proc. 66-49

Section 170

Headnote

Rev. Proc. 66-49. A procedure to be used as a guideline by all persons making appraisals of donated property for Federal income tax purposes.

Full Text

Sec. 1. Purpose

The purpose of this procedure is to provide information and guidelines for taxpayers, individual appraisers, and valuation groups relative to appraisals of contributed property for Federal income tax purposes. The procedures outlined are applicable to all types of non-cash property for which an appraisal is required, such as real property, tangible or intangible personal property, and securities. These procedures are also appropriate for unique properties, such as art objects, literary manuscripts, antiques, etc., with respect to which the determination of value often is more difficult.

Sec. 2. Law and Regulations

.01 Numerous sections of the Internal Revenue Code of 1954, as amended, give rise to a determination of value for Federal tax purposes; however, the significant section for purposes of this Revenue Procedure is section 170, Charitable, Etc., Contributions and Gifts.

.02 Value is defined in section 1.170-1(c) of the Income Tax Regulations as follows:

> The fair market value is the price at which the property would change hands between a willing buyer and a willing seller, neither being under any compulsion to buy or sell and both having reasonable knowledge of relevant facts.

.03 This section further provides that:

> If the contribution is made in property of a type which the taxpayer sells in the course of his business, the fair market value is the price which the taxpayer would have received if he had sold the contributed property in the lowest usual market in which he customarily sells, at the time and place of contribution (and in the case of a contribution of goods in quantity, in the quantity contributed).

.04 As to the measure of Proof in determining the fair market value, all factors bearing on value are relevant including, where pertinent, the cost, or selling price of the item, sales of comparable properties, cost of reproduction, opinion evidence, and appraisals. Fair market value depends upon value in the market and not on intrinsic worth.

.05 The cost or actual selling price of an item within a reasonable time before or after the valuation date may be the best evidence of its fair market value. Before such information is taken into account, it must be ascertained that the transaction was at arm's length and that the parties were fully informed as to all relevant facts. Absent such evidence, even the sales price of the item in question will not be persuasive.

.06 Sales of similar properties are often given probative weight by the courts in establishing fair market value. The weight to be given such evidence will be affected by the degree of similarity to the property under appraisal and the proximity of the date of sale to the valuation date.

.07 With respect to reproductive cost as a measure of fair market value, it must be shown that there is a probative correlation between the cost of reproduction and fair market value. Frequently, reproductive cost will be in excess of the fair market value.

.08 Generally, the weight to be given to opinion evidence depends on its origin and the thoroughness with which it is supported by experience and facts. It is only where expert opinion is supported by facts having strong probative value that the opinion testimony will in itself be given appropriate weight. The underlying facts must corroborate the opinion; otherwise such opinion will be discounted or disregarded.

.09 The weight to be accorded any appraisal made either at or after the valuation date will depend largely upon the competence and knowledge of the appraiser with respect to the property and the market for such property.

Sec. 3. Appraisal Format

.01 When it becomes necessary to secure an appraisal in order to determine the values of items for Federal income tax purposes, such appraisals should be obtained from qualified and reputable sources, and the appraisal report should accompany the return when it is filed. The more complete the information filed with a tax return the more unlikely it will be that the Internal Revenue Service will find it necessary to question items on it. Thus, when reporting deduction for charitable contributions on an income tax return, it will facilitate the review and the acceptance of the returned values if any appraisals which have been secured are furnished. The above-mentioned regulations prescribe that support of values claimed should be submitted and a properly prepared appraisal by a person qualified to make such an appraisal may well constitute the necessary substantiation. In this respect, it is not intended that all value determinations be supported by formal written appraisals as outlined in detail below. This is particularly applicable to minor items of property or where the value of the property is easily ascertainable by methods other than appraisal.

.02 In general, an appraisal report should contain at least the following:

a. A summary of the appraiser's qualifications
b. A statement of the value and the appraiser's definition of the value he has obtained
c. The bases upon which the appraisal was made, including any restrictions, understandings, or covenants limiting the use or disposition of the property

d. The date as of which the property was valued
e. The signature of the appraiser and the date the appraisal was made

.03 An example of the kind of data which should be contained in a typical appraisal is included below. This relates to the valuation of art objects, but a similar detailed breakdown can be outlined for any type of property. Appraisals of art objects, paintings in particular, should include:

a. A complete description of the object, indicating the size, the subject matter, the medium, the name of the artist, approximate date created, the interest transferred, etc.
b. The cost, date, and manner of acquisition
c. A history of the item including proof of authenticity such as a certificate of authentication if such exists
d. A photograph of a size and quality fully identifying the subject matter, preferably a 10", 12", or larger print
e. A statement of the factors upon which the appraisal was based, such as:

    1. Sales of other works by the same artist particularly on or around the valuation date
    2. Quoted prices in dealers' catalogs of the artist's works or of other artists of comparable statute
    3. The economic state of the art market at or around the time of valuation, particularly with respect to the specific property
    4. A record of any exhibitions at which the particular art object had been displayed
    5. A statement as to the standing of the artist in his profession and in the particular school or time period

.04 Although an appraisal report meets these requirements, the Internal Revenue Service is not relieved of the responsibility of reviewing appraisals to the extent deemed necessary.

Sec. 4. Review of Valuation Appraisals

.01 While the Service is responsible for reviewing appraisals, it is not responsible for making appraisals; the burden of supporting the fair market value listed on a return is the taxpayer's. The Internal Revenue Service cannot accord recognition to any appraiser or group of appraisers from the standpoint of unquestioned acceptance of their appraisals. Furthermore, the Service cannot approve valuations or appraisals prior to the actual filing of the tax return to which the appraisal pertains and cannot issue advance rulings approving or disapproving such appraisals.

.02 In determining the acceptability of the claimed value of the donated property, the Service may either accept the value claimed based on information or appraisals submitted with the return or make its own determination as to the fair market value. In either instance, the Service may find it necessary to:

1. Contact the taxpayer and ask for additional information.
2. Refer the valuation problem to a Service appraiser or valuation specialist.
3. Recommend that an independent appraiser be employed by the Service to appraise the asset in question. (This latter course is frequently used by the Service when objects requiring appraisers of highly specialized experience and knowledge are involved.)

Appendix 10 *Revenue Ruling 68-609*

Rev. Rul. 68-609, 1968-2 C.B. 327 IRC Sec. 1001

Sec. 1001—DETERMINATION OF AMOUNT OF AND RECOGNITION OF GAIN OR LOSS
26 CFR 1.1001-1: Computation of gain or loss
(Also Section 167; 1.167(a)-3.)

Headnote

The "formula" approach may be used in determining the fair market value of intangible assets of a business only if there is no better basis available for making the determination; A.R.M. 34, A.R.M. 68, O.D. 937, and Revenue Ruling 65-192 superseded.

Text

The purpose of this Revenue Ruling is to update and restate, under the current statute and regulations, the currently outstanding portions of A.R.M. 34, C.B. 2, 31 (1920), A.R.M. 68, C.B. 3, 43 (1920), and O.D. 937, C.B. 4, 43 (1921).

Prepared pursuant to Rev. Proc. 67-6, C.B. 1967-1, 576.

The question presented is whether the "formula" approach, the capitalization of earnings in excess of a fair rate of return on net tangible assets, may be used to determine the fair market value of the intangible assets of a business.

The "formula" approach may be stated as follows:

> A percentage return on the average annual value of the tangible assets used in a business is determined, using a period of years (preferably not less than five) immediately prior to the valuation date. The amount of the percentage return on tangible assets, thus determined, is deducted from the average earnings of the business for such period and the remainder, if any, is considered to be the amount of the average annual earnings from the intangible assets of the business for the period. This amount (considered as the average annual earnings from intangibles), capitalized at a percentage of, say, 15 to 20 percent, is the value of the intangible assets of the business determined under the "formula" approach.
>
> The percentage of return on the average annual value of the tangible assets used should be the percentage prevailing in the industry involved at the date of valuation, or (when the industry percentage is not available) a percentage of 8 to 10 percent may be used.
>
> The 8 percent rate of return and the 15 percent rate of capitalization are applied to tangibles and intangibles, respectively, of businesses with a small risk factor and stable and regular earnings; the 10 percent rate of return and 20 percent rate of capitalization are applied to businesses in which the hazards of business are relatively high.
>
> The above rates are used as examples and are not appropriate in all cases. In applying the "formula" approach, the average earnings period and the capitalization rates are dependent upon the facts pertinent thereto in each case.
>
> The past earnings to which the formula is applied should fairly reflect the probable future earnings. Ordinarily, the period should not be less than five years, and abnormal years, whether above or below the average, should be eliminated. If the business is a sole proprietorship or partnership, there should be deducted from the earnings of the business a reasonable amount for services performed by the owner or partners engaged in the business.

See *Lloyd B. Sanderson Estate v. Commissioner*, 42 F.2d 160 (1930). Further, only the tangible assets entering into net worth, including accounts and bills receivable in excess of accounts and bills payable, are used for determining earnings on the tangible assets. Factors that influence the capitalization rate include (1) the nature of the business, (2) the risk involved, and (3) the stability or irregularity of earnings.

The "formula" approach should not be used if there is better evidence available from which the value of intangibles can be determined. If the assets of a going business are sold upon the basis of a rate of capitalization that can be substantiated as being realistic, though it is not within the range of figures indicated here as the ones ordinarily to be adopted, the same rate of capitalization should be used in determining the value of intangibles.

Accordingly, the "formula" approach may be used for determining the fair market value of intangible assets of a business only if there is no better basis therefor available.

See also Revenue Ruling 59-60, C.B. 1959-1, 237, as modified by Revenue Ruling 65-193, C.B. 1965-2, 370, which sets forth the proper approach to use in the valuation of closely held corporate stocks for estate and gift tax purposes. The general approach, methods, and factors, outlined in Revenue Ruling 59-60, as modified, are equally applicable to valuations of corporate stocks for income and other tax purposes as well as for estate and gift tax purposes. They apply also to problems involving the determination of the fair market value of business interests of any type, including partnerships and proprietorships, and of intangible assets for all tax purposes.

A.R.M. 34, A.R.M. 68, and O.D. 937 are superseded, since the positions set forth therein are restated to the extent applicable under current law in this Revenue Ruling. Revenue Ruling 65-192, C.B. 1965-2, 259, which contained restatements of A.R.M. 34 and A.R.M. 68, is also superseded.

Appendix 11 *Revenue Procedure 77-12*

Rev. Proc. 77-12, 1977-1 C.B. 569

Sec. 7805—RULES AND REGULATIONS
26 CFR 601.105: Examination of returns and claims for refund, credit, or abatement; determination of correct tax liability
(Also Part I, Section 334; 1.334-1.)

Text

Sec. 1. Purpose

The purpose of this Revenue Procedure is to set forth guidelines for use by taxpayers and Service personnel in making fair market value determinations in situations where a corporation purchases the assets of a business containing inventory items for a lump sum or where a corporation acquires assets including inventory items by the liquidation of a subsidiary pursuant to the provisions of section 332 of the Internal Revenue Code of 1954 and the basis of the inventory received in liquidation is determined under section 334(b)(2). These guidelines are designed to assist taxpayers and Service personnel in assigning a fair market value to such assets.

Sec. 2. Background

If the assets of a business are purchased for a lump sum, or if the stock of a corporation is purchased and that corporation is liquidated under section 332 of the Code and the basis is determined under section 334(b)(2), the purchase price must be allocated among the assets acquired to determine the basis of each of such assets. In making such determinations, it is necessary to determine the fair market value of any inventory items involved. This Revenue Procedure describes methods that may be used to determine the fair market value of inventory items.

In determining the fair market value of inventory under the situations set forth in this Revenue Procedure, the amount of inventory generally would be different from the amounts usually purchased. In addition, the goods in process and finished goods on hand must be considered in light of what a willing purchaser would pay and a willing seller would accept for the inventory at the various stages of completion, when the former is not under any compulsion to buy and the latter is not under any compulsion to sell, both parties having reasonable knowledge of relevant facts.

Sec. 3. Procedures for Determination of Fair Market Value

Three basic methods an appraiser may use to determine the fair market value of inventory are the *cost of reproduction method*, the *comparative sales method*, and the *income method*. All methods of valuation are based on one or a combination of these three methods.

.01 The cost of reproduction method generally provides a good indication of fair market value if inventory is readily replaceable in a wholesale or retail business but generally should not be used in establishing the fair market value of the finished goods of a manufacturing concern. In valuing a particular inventory under this method, however, other factors may be relevant. For example, a well-balanced inventory available to fill customers' orders in the ordinary course of business may have a fair market value in excess of its cost of reproduction because it provides a continuity of business, whereas an inventory containing obsolete merchandise unsuitable for customers might have a fair market value of less than the cost of reproduction.

.02 The comparative sales method utilizes the actual or expected selling prices of finished goods to customers as a basis of determining fair market values of those finished goods. When the expected selling price is used as a basis for valuing finished goods inventory, consideration should be given to the time that would be required to dispose of this inventory, the expenses that would be expected to be incurred in such disposition—for example, all costs of disposition, applicable discounts (including those for quantity), sales commissions, and freight and shipping charges—and a profit commensurate with the amount of investment and degree of risk. It should also be recognized that the inventory to be valued may represent a larger quantity than the normal trading volume and the expected selling price can be a valid starting point only if customers' orders are filled in the ordinary course of business.

.03 The income method, when applied to fair market value determinations for finished goods, recognizes that finished goods must generally be valued in a profit-motivated business. Since the amount of inventory may be large in relation to normal trading volume, the highest and best use of the inventory will be to provide for a continuity of the marketing operation of the going business. Additionally, the finished goods inventory will usually provide the only source of revenue of an acquired business during the period it is being used to fill customers' orders. The historical financial data of an acquired company can be used to determine the amount that could be attributed to finished goods in order to pay all costs of disposition and provide a return on the investment during the period of disposition.

.04 The fair market value of work in process should be based on the same factors used to determine the fair market value of finished goods reduced by the expected costs of completion, including a reasonable profit allowance for the completion and selling effort of the acquiring corporation. In determining the fair market value of raw materials, the current costs of replacing the inventory in the quantities to be valued generally provides the most reliable standard.

Sec. 4. Conclusion

Because valuing inventory is an inherently factual determination, no rigid formulas can be applied. Consequently, the methods outlined above can only serve as guidelines for determining the fair market value of inventories.

Appendix 12 *Revenue Ruling 77-287*

Rev. Rul. 77-287, 1977-2 C.B. 319 IRC Sec. 2031

Sec. 2031—DEFINITION OF GROSS ESTATE
26 CFR 20.2031-2: Valuation of stocks and bonds
(Also Sections 170, 2032, 2512; 1.170A-1, 20.2032-1, 25.2512-2.)

Headnote

Valuation of securities restricted from immediate resale. Guidelines are set forth for the valuation, for Federal tax purposes, of securities that cannot be immediately resold because they are restricted from resale pursuant to Federal securities laws; Rev. Rul. 59-60 amplified.

Text

Sec. 1. Purpose

The purpose of this Revenue Ruling is to amplify Rev. Rul. 59-60, 1959-1 C.B. 237, as modified by Rev. Rul. 65-193, 1965-2 C.B. 370, and to provide information and guidance to taxpayers, Internal Revenue Service personnel, and others concerned with the valuation, for Federal tax purposes, of securities that cannot be immediately resold because they are restricted from resale pursuant to Federal securities laws. This guidance is applicable only in cases where it is not inconsistent with valuation requirements of the Internal Revenue Code of 1954 or the regulations thereunder. Further, this ruling does not establish the time at which property shall be valued.

Sec. 2. Nature of the Problem

It frequently becomes necessary to establish the fair market value of stock that has not been registered for public trading when the issuing company has stock of the same class that is actively traded in one or more securities markets. The problem is to determine the difference in fair market value between the registered shares that are actively traded and the unregistered shares. This problem is often encountered in estate and gift tax cases. However, it is sometimes encountered when unregistered shares are issued in exchange for assets or the stock of an acquired company.

Sec. 3. Background and Definitions

.01 The Service outlined and reviewed in general the approach, methods, and factors to be considered in valuing shares of closely held corporate stock for estate and gift tax purposes in Rev. Rul. 59-60, as modified by Rev. Rul. 65-193. The provisions of Rev. Rul. 59-60, as modified, were extended to the valuation of corporate securities for income and other tax purposes by Rev. Rul. 68-609, 1968-2 C.B. 327.

.02 There are several terms currently in use in the securities industry that denote restrictions imposed on the resale and transfer of certain securities. The term frequently used to describe these securities is "restricted securities," but they are sometimes referred to as "unregistered securities," "investment letter stock," "control stock," or "private placement stock." Frequently these terms are used interchangeably. They all indicate that these particular securities cannot lawfully be distributed to the general public until a registration statement relating to the corporation underlying the securities has been filed, and has also become effective under the rules promulgated and enforced by the United States Securities & Exchange Commission (SEC) pursuant to the Federal securities laws. The following represents a more refined definition of each of the following terms along with two other terms—"exempted securities" and "exempted transactions."

1. The term "restricted securities" is defined in Rule 144 adopted by the SEC as "securities acquired directly or indirectly from the issuer thereof, or from an affiliate of such issuer, in a transaction or chain of transactions not involving any public offering."
2. The term "unregistered securities" refers to those securities with respect to which a registration statement, providing full disclosure by the issuing corporation, has not been filed with the SEC pursuant to the Securities Act of 1933. The registration statement is a condition precedent to a public distribution of securities in interstate commerce and is aimed at providing the prospective investor with a factual basis for sound judgment in making investment decisions.
3. The terms "investment letter stock" and "letter stock" denote shares of stock that have been issued by a corporation without the benefit of filing a registration statement with the SEC. Such stock is subject to resale and transfer restrictions set forth in a letter agreement requested by the issuer and signed by the buyer of the stock when the stock is delivered. Such stock may be found in the hands of either individual investors or institutional investors.
4. The term "control stock" indicates that the shares of stock have been held or are being held by an officer, director, or other person close to the management of the corporation. These persons are subject to certain requirements pursuant to SEC rules upon resale of shares they own in such corporations.
5. The term "private placement stock" indicates that the stock has been placed with an institution or other investor who will presumably hold it for a long period and ultimately arrange to have the stock registered if it is to be offered to the general public. Such stock may or may not be subject to a letter agreement. Private placements of stock are exempted from the registration and prospectus provisions of the Securities Act of 1933.
6. The term "exempted securities" refers to those classes of securities that are expressly excluded from the registration provisions of the Securities Act of 1933 and the distribution provisions of the Securities Exchange Act of 1934.
7. The term "exempted transactions" refers to certain sales or distributions of securities that do not involve a public offering and are excluded from the registration and prospectus provisions of the Securities Act of 1933 and distribution provisions of the Securities Exchange Act of 1934. The exempted status makes it unnecessary for issuers of securities to go through the registration process.

Sec. 4. Securities Industry Practice in Valuing Restricted Securities

.01 Investment Company Valuation Practices. The Investment Company Act of 1940 requires open-end investment companies to publish the valuation of their portfolio securities daily. Some of these companies have portfolios containing restricted securities, but also have unrestricted securities of the same class traded on a securities exchange. In recent years the number of restricted securities in such portfolios has increased. The following methods have been used by investment companies in the valuation of such restricted securities:

a. Current market price of the unrestricted stock less a constant percentage discount based on purchase discount;
b. Current market price of unrestricted stock less a constant percentage discount different from purchase discount;
c. Current market price of the unrestricted stock less a discount amortized over a fixed period;
d. Current market price of the unrestricted stock; and
e. Cost of the restricted stock until it is registered.

The SEC ruled in its Investment Company Act Release No. 5847, dated October 21, 1969, that there can be no automatic formula by which an investment company can value the restricted securities in its portfolios. Rather, the SEC has determined that it is the responsibility of the board of directors of the particular investment company to determine the "fair value" of each issue of restricted securities in good faith.

.02 Institutional Investors Study. Pursuant to Congressional direction, the SEC undertook an analysis of the purchases, sales, and holding of securities by financial institutions, in order to determine the effect of institutional activity upon the securities market. The study report was published in eight volumes in March 1971. The fifth volume provides an analysis of restricted securities and deals with such items as the characteristics of the restricted securities purchasers and issuers, the size of transactions (dollars and shares), the marketability discounts on different trading markets, and the resale provisions. This research project provides some guidance for measuring the discount in that it contains information, based on the actual experience of the marketplace, showing that, during the period surveyed (January 1, 1966, through June 30, 1969), the amount of discount allowed for restricted securities from the trading price of the unrestricted securities was generally related to the following four factors.

1. **Earnings.** Earnings and sales consistently have a significant influence on the size of restricted securities discounts according to the study. Earnings played the major part in establishing the ultimate discounts at which these stocks were sold from the current market price. Apparently earnings patterns, rather than sales patterns, determine the degree of risk of an investment.
2. **Sales.** The dollar amount of sales of issuers' securities also has a major influence on the amount of discount at which restricted securities sell from the current market price. The results of the study generally indicate that the companies with the lowest dollar amount of sales during the test period accounted for most of the transactions involving the highest discount rates, while they accounted for only a small portion of all transactions involving the lowest discount rates.
3. **Trading Market.** The market in which publicly held securities are traded also reflects variances in the amount of discount that is applied to restricted securities purchases. According to the study, discount rates were greatest on restricted stocks with unrestricted counterparts traded over-the-counter, followed by those with unrestricted counterparts listed on the American Stock Exchange, while the discount rates for those stocks with unrestricted counterparts listed on the New York Stock Exchange were the smallest.
4. **Resale Agreement Provisions.** Resale agreement provisions often affect the size of the discount. The discount from the market price provides the main incentive for a potential buyer to acquire restricted securities. In judging the opportunity cost of freezing funds, the purchaser is analyzing two separate factors. The first factor is the risk that underlying value of the stock will change in a way that, absent the restrictive provisions, would have prompted a decision to sell. The second factor is the risk that the contemplated means of legally disposing of the stock may not materialize. From the seller's point of view, a discount is justified where the seller is relieved of the expenses of registration

and public distribution, as well as of the risk that the market will adversely change before the offering is completed. The ultimate agreement between buyer and seller is a reflection of these and other considerations. Relative bargaining strengths of the parties to the agreement are major considerations that influence the resale terms and consequently the size of discounts in restricted securities transactions. Certain provisions are often found in agreements between buyers and sellers that affect the size of discounts at which restricted stocks are sold. Several such provisions follow, all of which, other than number (3), would tend to reduce the size of the discount:

(1) A provision giving the buyer an option to "piggyback," that is, to register restricted stock with the next registration statement, if any, filed by the issuer with the SEC;
(2) A provision giving the buyer an option to require registration at the seller's expense;
(3) A provision giving the buyer an option to require registration, but only at the buyer's own expense;
(4) A provision giving the buyer a right to receive continuous disclosure of information about the issuer from the seller;
(5) A provision giving the buyer a right to select one or more directors of the issuer,
(6) A provision giving the buyer an option to purchase additional shares of the issuer's stock; and
(7) A provision giving the buyer the right to have a greater voice in operations of the issuer, if the issuer does not meet previously agreed upon operating standards.

Institutional buyers can and often do obtain many of these rights and options from the sellers of restricted securities, and naturally, the more rights the buyer can acquire, the lower the buyer's risk is going to be, thereby reducing the buyer's discount as well. Smaller buyers may not be able to negotiate the large discounts or the rights and options that volume buyers are able to negotiate.

.03 Summary. A variety of methods have been used by the securities industry to value restricted securities. The SEC rejects all automatic or mechanical solutions to the valuation of restricted securities, and prefers, in the case of the valuation of investment company portfolio stocks, to rely upon good faith valuations by the board of directors of each company. The study made by the SEC found that restricted securities generally are issued at a discount from the market value of freely tradable securities.

Sec. 5. Facts and Circumstances Material to Valuation of Restricted Securities

.01 Frequently, a company has a class of stock that cannot be traded publicly. The reason such stock cannot be traded may arise from the securities statutes, as in the case of an "investment letter" restriction; it may arise from a corporate charter restriction, or perhaps from a trust agreement restriction. In such cases, certain documents and facts should be obtained for analysis.

.02 The following documents and facts, when used in conjunction with those discussed in Section 4 of Rev. Rul. 59-60, will be useful in the valuation of restricted securities:

1. A copy of any declaration of trust, trust agreement, and any other agreements relating to the shares of restricted stock;
2. A copy of any document showing any offers to buy or sell or indications of interest in buying or selling the restricted shares;
3. The latest prospectus of the company;
4. Annual reports of the company for 3 to 5 years preceding the valuation date;

5. The trading prices and trading volume of the related class of traded securities 1 month preceding the valuation date, if they are traded on a stock exchange (if traded over-the-counter, prices may be obtained from the National Quotations Bureau, the National Association of Securities Dealers Automated Quotations (NASDAQ), or sometimes from broker-dealers making markets in the shares);
6. The relationship of the parties to the agreements concerning the restricted stock, such as whether they are members of the immediate family or perhaps whether they are officers or directors of the company; and
7. Whether the interest being valued represents a majority or minority ownership.

Sec. 6. Weighing Facts and Circumstances Material to Restricted Stock Valuation

All relevant facts and circumstances that bear upon the worth of restricted stock, including those set forth above in the preceding Sections 4 and 5, and those set forth in Section 4 of Rev. Rul. 59-60, must be taken into account in arriving at the fair market value of such securities. Depending on the circumstances of each case, certain factors may carry more weight than others. To illustrate:

.01 Earnings, net assets, and net sales must be given primary consideration in arriving at an appropriate discount for restricted securities from the freely traded shares. These are the elements of value that are always used by investors in making investment decisions. In some cases, one element may be more important than in other cases. In the case of manufacturing, producing, or distributing companies, primary weight must be accorded earnings and net sales; but in the case of investment or holding companies, primary weight must be given to the net assets of the company underlying the stock. In the former type of company, value is more closely linked to past, present, and future earnings while in the latter type of company, value is more closely linked to the existing net assets of the company. See the discussion in Section 5 of Rev. Rul. 59-60.

.02 Resale provisions found in the restriction agreements must be scrutinized and weighed to determine the amount of discount to apply to the preliminary fair market value of the company. The two elements of time and expense bear upon this discount; the longer the buyer of the shares must wait to liquidate the shares, the greater the discount. Moreover, if the provisions make it necessary for the buyer to bear the expense of registration, the greater the discount. However, if the provisions of the restricted stock agreement make it possible for the buyer to "piggyback" shares at the next offering, the discount would be smaller.

.03 The relative negotiation strengths of the buyer and seller of restricted stock may have a profound effect on the amount of discount. For example, a tight money situation may cause the buyer to have the greater balance of negotiation strength in a transaction. However, in some cases the relative strengths may tend to cancel each other out.

.04 The market experience of freely tradable securities of the same class as the restricted securities is also significant in determining the amount of discount. Whether the shares are privately held or publicly traded affects the worth of the shares to the holder. Securities traded on a public market generally are worth more to investors than those that are not traded on a public market. Moreover, the type of public market in which the unrestricted securities are traded is to be given consideration.

Sec. 7. Effect on Other Documents

Rev. Rul. 59-60, as modified by Rev. Rul. 65-193, is amplified.

Appendix 13 *Revenue Ruling 83-120*

Rev. Rul. 83-120, 1983-2 C.B. 170 IRC Sec. 2512

Sec. 2512 VALUATION OF GIFTS
26 CFR 25.2512-2: Stocks and bonds
(Also Sections 305, 351, 354, 368, 2031; 1.305-5, 1.351-1, 1.354-1, 1.368-1, 20.2031-2.)

Headnote

Valuation; stock; closely held business. The significant factors in deriving the fair market value of preferred and common stock received in certain corporate reorganizations are discussed. Rev. Rul. 59-60 amplified.

Text

Sec. 1. Purpose

The purpose of this Revenue Ruling is to amplify Rev. Rul. 59-60, 1959-1 C.B. 237, by specifying additional factors to be considered in valuing common and preferred stock of a closely held corporation for gift tax and other purposes in a recapitalization of closely held businesses. This type of valuation problem frequently arises with respect to estate planning transactions wherein an individual receives preferred stock with a stated par value equal to all or a large portion of the fair market value of the individual's former stock interest in a corporation. The individual also receives common stock, which is then transferred, usually as a gift, to a relative.

Sec. 2. Background

.01 One of the frequent objectives of the type of transaction mentioned above is the transfer of the potential appreciation of an individual's stock interest in a corporation to relatives at a nominal or small gift tax cost. Achievement of this objective requires preferred stock having a fair market value equal to a large part of the fair market value of the individual's former stock interest and common stock having a nominal or small fair market value. The approach and factors described in this Revenue Ruling are directed toward ascertaining the true fair market value of the common and preferred stock and will usually result in the determination of a substantial fair market value for the common stock and a fair market value for the preferred stock which is substantially less than its par value.

.02 The type of transaction referred to above can arise in many different contexts. Some examples are:

a. A owns 100% of the common stock (the only outstanding stock) of Z Corporation, which has a fair market value of 10,500×. In a recapitalization described in section 368(a)(1)(E), A receives preferred stock with a par value of 10,000× and new common stock, which A then transfers to A's son B.

b. A owns some of the common stock of Z Corporation (or the stock of several corporations), the fair market value of which stock is 10,500×. A transfers this stock to a new corporation X in exchange for preferred stock of X Corporation with a par value of 10,000× and common stock of corporation, which A then transfers to A's son B.

c. A owns 80 shares and his son B owns 20 shares of the common stock (the only stock outstanding) of Z Corporation. In a recapitalization described in section 368(a)(1)(E), A exchanges his 80 shares of common stock for 80 shares of new preferred stock of Z Corporation with a par value of 10,000×. A's common stock had a fair market value of 10,000×.

Sec. 3. General Approach to Valuation

Under section 25.2512-2(f)(2) of the Gift Tax Regulations, the fair market value of stock in a closely held corporation depends upon numerous factors, including the corporation's net worth, its prospective earning power, and its capacity to pay dividends. In addition, other relevant factors must be taken into account. See Rev. Rul. 59-60. The weight to be accorded any evidentiary factor depends on the circumstances of each case. See section 25.2512-2(f) of the Gift Tax Regulations.

Sec. 4. Approach to Valuation Preferred Stock

.01 In general the most important factors to be considered in determining the value of preferred stock are its yield, dividend coverage, and protection of its liquidation preference.

.02 Whether the yield of the preferred stock supports a valuation of the stock at par value depends in part on the adequacy of the dividend rate. The adequacy of the dividend rate should be determined by comparing its dividend rate with the dividend rate of high-grade publicly traded preferred stock. A lower yield than that of high-grade preferred stock indicates a preferred stock value of less than par. If the rate of interest charged by independent creditors to the corporation on loans is higher than the rate such independent creditors charge their most credit-worthy borrowers, then the yield on the preferred stock should be correspondingly higher than the yield on high-quality preferred stock. A yield which is not correspondingly higher reduces the value of the preferred stock. In addition, whether the preferred stock has a fixed dividend rate and is nonparticipating influences the value of the preferred stock. A publicly traded preferred stock for a company having a similar business and similar assets with similar liquidation preferences, voting rights, and other similar terms would be the ideal comparable for determining yield required in arm's-length transactions for closely held stock. Such ideal comparables will frequently not exist. In such circumstances, the most comparable publicly traded issues should be selected for comparison and appropriate adjustments made for differing factors.

.03 The actual dividend rate on a preferred stock can be assumed to be its stated rate if the issuing corporation will be able to pay its stated dividends in a timely manner and will, in fact, pay such dividends. The risk that the corporation may be unable to timely pay the stated dividends on the preferred stock can be measured by the coverage of such stated dividends by the corporation's earnings. Coverage of the dividend is measured by the ratio of the sum of pretax and pre-interest earnings to the sum of the total interest to be paid and the pretax earnings needed to pay the after-tax dividends. Standard & Poor's Ratings Guide, 58 (1979). Inadequate coverage exists where a decline in corporate profits would be likely to jeopardize the corporation's ability to pay dividends on the preferred stock. The ratio for the preferred stock in question should be compared with the ratios for high quality preferred stock to determine whether the preferred stock has adequate coverage. Prior earnings history is important in this determination. Inadequate coverage indicates that the value of preferred stock is lower than its par value. Moreover, the absence of a provision that preferred dividends are cumulative raises substantial questions concerning whether the stated dividend rate will, in fact, be paid. Accordingly, preferred stock with noncumulative dividend features will normally have a value substantially lower than a cumulative preferred stock with the same yield, liquidation preference, and dividend coverage.

.04 Whether the issuing corporation will be able to pay the full liquidation preference at liquidation must be taken into account in determining fair market value. This risk can be measured by the protection afforded by the corporation's net assets. Such protection can be measured by the ratio of the excess of the current market value of the corporation's assets over its liabilities to the aggregate liquidation preference. The protection ratio should be compared with the ratios for high quality preferred stock to determine adequacy of coverage. Inadequate asset protection exists where any unforeseen business reverses would be likely to jeopardize the corporation's ability to pay the full liquidation preference to the holders of the preferred stock.

.05 Another factor to be considered in valuing the preferred stock is whether it has voting rights and, if so, whether the preferred stock has voting control. See, however, Section 5.02 below.

.06 Peculiar covenants or provisions of the preferred stock of a type not ordinarily found in publicly traded preferred stock should be carefully evaluated to determine the effects of such covenants on the value of the preferred stock. In general, if covenants would inhibit the marketability of the stock or the power of the holder to enforce dividend or liquidation rights, such provisions will reduce the value of the preferred stock by comparison to the value of preferred stock not containing such covenants or provisions.

.07 Whether the preferred stock contains a redemption privilege is another factor to be considered in determining the value of the preferred stock. The value of a redemption privilege triggered by death of the preferred shareholder will not exceed the present value of the redemption premium payable at the preferred shareholder's death (i.e., the present value of the excess of the redemption price over the fair market value of the preferred stock upon its issuance). The value of the redemption privilege should be reduced to reflect any risk that the corporation may not possess sufficient assets to redeem its preferred stock at the stated redemption price. See .03 above.

Sec. 5. Approach to Valuation Common Stock

.01 If the preferred stock has a fixed rate of dividend and is nonparticipating, the common stock has the exclusive right to the benefits of future appreciation of the value of the corporation. This right is valuable and usually warrants a determination that the common stock has substantial value. The actual value of this right depends upon the corporation's past growth experience, the economic condition of the industry in which the corporation operates, and general economic conditions. The factor to be used in capitalizing the corporation's prospective earnings must be determined after an analysis of numerous factors concerning the corporation and the economy as a whole. See Rev. Rul. 59-60, page 243. In addition, after-tax earnings of the corporation at the time the preferred stock is issued in excess of the stated dividends on the preferred stock will increase the value of the common stock. Furthermore, a corporate policy of reinvesting earnings will also increase the value of the common stock.

.02 A factor to be considered in determining the value of the common stock is whether the preferred stock also has voting rights. Voting rights of the preferred stock, especially if the preferred stock has voting control, could under certain circumstances increase the value of the preferred stock and reduce the value of the common stock. This factor may be reduced in significance where the rights of common stockholders as a class are protected under state law from actions by another class of shareholders, see *Singer v. Magnavox Co.*, 380 A.2d 969 (Del. 1977), particularly where the common shareholders, as a class, are given the power to disapprove a proposal to allow preferred stock to be converted into common stock. See ABA-ALI Model Bus. Corp. Act, Section 60 (1969).

Sec. 6. Effect on Other Revenue Rulings

Rev. Rul. 59-60, as modified by Rev. Rul. 65-193, 1965-2 C.B. 370, and as amplified by Rev. Rul. 77-287, 1977-2 C.B. 319, and Rev. Rul. 80-213, 1980-2 C.B. 101, is further amplified.

Appendix 14 *Revenue Ruling 85-75*

Rev. Rul. 85-75, 1985-1 C.B. 376 IRC Sec. 6659

Sec. 6659 ADDITION TO TAX IN THE CASE OF VALUATION OVERSTATEMENTS FOR PURPOSES OF THE INCOME TAX

Headnote

Penalties; valuation overstatement; basis of property acquired from a decedent. The penalty for overvaluation under section 6659 of the Code may apply when a beneficiary of an estate adopts an overstated amount shown on an estate tax return as the beneficiary's adjusted basis under section 1014.

Text

Issue

May the addition to tax under section 6659 of the Internal Revenue Code apply to an income tax return if a beneficiary of an estate adopts an overstated amount shown on an estate tax return as the beneficiary's adjusted basis under section 10147?

Facts

H and W were married at the time of W's death on December 31, 1982. W's will left all property to H. Included in the property was a building with a fair market value of 2,000× dollars. The executor filed Form 706, United States Estate Tax Return, valuing the property at 3,500× dollars. Because the entire estate qualified for the marital deduction under section 2056 of the Code, no estate tax was due.

H filed an income tax return for 1983 claiming an Accelerated Cost Recovery System deduction under section 168 of the Code for the building in question, using a basis under section 1014 of 3,500× dollars. The Internal Revenue Service examined H's 1983 income tax return and determined that the value of the building at the time of W's death was 2,000× dollars. This resulted in an underpayment of $1,000.

Law and Analysis

Section 6659(a) of the Code imposes an addition to tax if an individual or closely held corporation or a personal service corporation has an underpayment of income tax attributable to a valuation overstatement.

Section 6659(c) of the Code provides that there is a valuation overstatement if the value of any property, or the adjusted basis of any property, claimed on any return is 150 percent or more of the amount determined to be the correct amount of such valuation or adjusted basis.

Under section 6659(d) of the Code, the addition to tax is limited to situations in which there is an underpayment attributable to valuation overstatements of at least $1,000.

Section 6659(e) of the Code provides that the Service may waive all or part of the addition to tax on a showing by the taxpayer that there was a reasonable basis for the valuation or adjusted basis claimed on the return and that the claim was made in good faith.

Section 1014 of the Code generally provides that the basis of property in the hands of a person to whom the property passed from a decedent shall be its fair market value at the date of the decedent's death.

The underpayment of H's income tax for 1983 was attributable to a valuation overstatement of 150 percent or more and was at least $1,000. Accordingly, the addition to tax applies, if not waived by the Service. The fact that the adjusted basis of the building on H's income tax return is the same as the value on W's estate tax return does not of itself show the H had a reasonable basis to claim the valuation.

Holding

The addition to tax under section 6659 of the Code applies to an income tax return, absent a waiver by the Service, if a taxpayer adopts an overstated amount shown on an estate tax return as the taxpayer's adjusted basis under section 1014.

Appendix 15 *Revenue Ruling 93-12*

Rev. Rul. 93-12, 1993-7 I.R.B. 13, 1/26/93

January 26, 1993
Section 2512 VALUATION OF GIFTS
Family's Degree of Control Not Considered in Valuing Stock Transferred to Family Members

Headnote

In Revenue Ruling 93-12, the Service has addressed whether, for gift tax purposes, "corporate control" is a factor that should be considered in determining the value of stock transferred from one family member to another.

Facts. A parent, who owned all of the outstanding stock in a corporation with a single class of stock, transferred his entire interest to his five children, giving each child 20 percent of his shares.

Issue. At issue is how the transferred shares should be valued for purposes of section 2512—in particular, whether the extent of the family's control over the corporation should be considered in determining the value of the transferred interests.

Holding. The Service has ruled that, for gift tax purposes, when a donor transfers to his children shares in a corporation having only a single class of stock, the extent of the family's control over the corporation will not be considered in determining the value of the transferred interests.

Analysis. Basically, the Service decided to acquiesce in the Tax Court's decision in *Estate of Lee v. Commissioner*, 69 T.C. 860 (1978). Consequently, it will no longer assume that all voting power held by family members must be aggregated for purposes of determining whether the transferred interests should be valued as part of a controlling interest. Likewise, a minority discount will not be disallowed simply because a transferred interest, when aggregated with the interests held by other family members, would be part of a controlling interest. Because this position conflicts with the position the Service took in Rev. Rul. 81-253, 1981-1 C.B. 187, that ruling has been revoked.

Full Text

Part I

Section 2512.—Valuation of Gifts
26 CFR 25.2512-1: Valuation of property; in general.

Issue. If a donor transfers shares in a corporation to each of the donor's children, is the factor of corporate control in the family to be considered in valuing each transferred interest, for purposes of section 2512 of the Internal Revenue Code?

Facts. P owned all of the single outstanding class of stock of X corporation. P transferred all of P's shares by making simultaneous gifts of 20 percent of the shares to each of P's five children, A, B, C, D, and E.

Law and Analysis. Section 2512(a) of the Code provides that the value of the property at the date of the gift shall be considered the amount of the gift.

Section 25.2512-1 of the Gift Tax Regulations provides that, if a gift is made in property, its value at the date of the gift shall be considered the amount of the gift. The value of the property is the price at which the property would change hands between a willing buyer and a willing seller, neither being under any compulsion to buy or to sell, and both having reasonable knowledge of relevant facts.

Section 25.2512-2(a) of the regulations provides that the value of stocks and bonds is the fair market value per share or bond on the date of the gift. Section 25.2512-2(f) provides that the degree of control of the business represented by the block of stock to be valued is among the factors to be considered in valuing stock where there are no sales prices or bona fide bid or asked prices.

Rev. Rul. 81-253, 1981-1 C.B. 187, holds that, ordinarily, no minority shareholder discount is allowed with respect to transfers of shares of stock between family members if, based upon a composite of the family members' interests at the time of the transfer, control (either majority voting control or de facto control through family relationships) of the corporation exists in the family unit. The ruling also states that the Service will not follow the decision of the Fifth Circuit in *Estate of Bright v. United States*, 658 F.2d 999 (5th Cir. 1981).

In *Bright*, the decedent's undivided community property interest in shares of stock, together with the corresponding undivided community property interest of the decedent's surviving spouse, constituted a control block of 55 percent of the shares of a corporation. The court held that, because the community-held shares were subject to a right of partition, the decedent's own interest was equivalent to 27.5 percent of the outstanding shares and, therefore, should be valued as a minority interest, even though the shares were to be held by the decedent's surviving spouse as trustee of a testamentary trust. See also *Propstra v. United States*, 680 F.2d 1248 (9th Cir. 1982). In addition, *Estate of Andrews v. Commissioner*, 79 T.C. 938 (1982), and *Estate of Lee v. Commissioner*, 69 T.C. 860 (1978), *nonacq.*, 1980-2 C.B. 2, held that the corporation shares owned by other family members cannot be attributed to an individual family member for determining whether the individual family member's shares should be valued as the controlling interest of the corporation.

After further consideration of the position taken in Rev. Rul. 81-253, and in light of the cases noted above, the Service has concluded that, in the case of a corporation with a single class of stock, notwithstanding the family relationship of the donor, the donee, and other shareholders, the shares of other family members will not be aggregated with the transferred shares to determine whether the transferred shares should be valued as part of a controlling interest.

In the present case, the minority interests transferred to A, B, C, D, and E should be valued for gift tax purposes without regard to the family relationship of the parties.

Holding. If a donor transfers shares in a corporation to each of the donor's children, the factor of corporate control in the family is not considered in valuing each transferred interest for purposes of section 2512 of the Code. For estate and gift tax valuation purposes, the Service will follow *Bright*, *Propstra*, *Andrews*, and *Lee* in not assuming that all voting power held by family members may be aggregated for purposes of determining whether the transferred shares should be valued as part of a controlling interest. Consequently, a minority discount will not be disallowed solely because a transferred interest, when aggregated with interests held by family members, would be a part of a controlling interest. This would be the case whether the donor held 100 percent or some lesser percentage of the stock immediately before the gift.

Effect on Other Documents. Rev. Rul. 81-253 is revoked. Acquiescence is substituted for the nonacquiescence in issue one of *Lee*, 1980-2 C.B. 2.

Drafting Information

The principal author of this Revenue Ruling is Deborah Ryan of the Office of Assistant Chief Counsel (Passthroughs and Special Industries). For further information regarding this Revenue Ruling, contact Ms. Ryan at (202) 622-3090 (not a toll-free call).

Appendix 16 *Technical Advice Memorandum 94-36005*

Full Text

Date: May 26, 1994

Issue

Should the fact that each of three 30 percent blocks of stock transferred has "swing vote" attributes be taken into account as a factor in determining the fair market value of the stock?

Facts

The donor owned all of outstanding common stock of Corporation, totaling 28,975 shares. On December 18, 1989, the donor transferred 8,592 shares (approximately 30 percent of the outstanding common stock in Corporation) to each of three children. The donor also transferred 1,509 shares (approximately 5 percent of the stock) to his spouse. The donor retained 1,510 shares or approximately 5 percent of the stock. The transfers to the children were reported on a timely filed federal Gift Tax Return, Form 709. The donor's spouse consented to the gift-splitting provisions of section 2513 of the Internal Revenue Code.

Corporation was authorized 100,000 shares of common stock, of which 36,955 were issued. Of the shares issued, 8,160 were held as Treasury stock and the balance was owned by the donor.

The ownership of the stock before and after the transfer may be summarized as follows:

Summary of Stock Holdings

	Donor	*Child 1*	*Child 2*	*Child 3*	*Spouse*
Before	100%	0%	0%	0%	0%
After	5%	30%	30%	30%	5%

With respect to each gift, the stock was valued at approximately $50 per share, representing the net asset value of Corporation, less a 25 percent discount characterized as a discount for "minority interest and marketability."

Applicable Law and Analysis

Section 2501 provides that a gift tax is imposed for each calendar year on the transfer of property by gift.

Section 2511 provides that the gift tax shall apply whether the transfer is in trust or otherwise, whether the gift is direct or indirect, and whether the property is real or personal, tangible or intangible.

Section 2512(a) provides that the value of the property at the date of the gift shall be considered the amount of the gift.

Section 25.2512-1 of the Gift Tax Regulations provides that, if a gift is made in property, its value at the date of the gift shall be considered the amount of the gift. The value of the property is the price at which the property would change hands between a willing buyer and a willing seller, neither being under any compulsion to buy or sell, and both having reasonable knowledge of relevant facts.

Section 25.2512-2(a) provides that the value of stocks and bonds is the fair market value per share or bond on the date of the gift. Section 25.2512-2(f) provides that all relevant factors are to be taken into account in determining fair market value, including the degree of control of the business represented by the block of stock to be valued.

Rev. Rul. 59-60, 1959-1 C.B. 237, provides guidelines for valuing closely held stock. Rev. Rul. 59-60 specifically states that the size of a block of stock is a factor to be considered in determining fair market value. The Revenue Ruling also holds that all relevant factors must be considered and that no general formula may be used that is applicable to different valuation situations.

In general, in determining the value of shares of stock that represent a minority interest, a discount may be allowed in appropriate circumstances to reflect the fact that the holder of a minority interest lacks control over corporate policy and thus, for example, cannot compel the payment of dividends or the liquidation of the corporation. *Ward v. Commissioner*, 87 T.C. 78, 106 (1986). Where a donor makes simultaneous gifts of multiple shares of securities to different donees, each gift is valued separately in determining fair market value for gift tax purposes. See, e.g., *Whittemore v. Fitzpatrick*, 127 F. Supp. 710 [47 AFTR 77] (D.C. Conn. 1954); *Avery v. Commissioner*, 3 T.C. 963 (1944); section 25.2512-2(e).

In Rev. Rul. 93-12, 1993-1 C.B. 202, a donor transferred 20 percent of the outstanding shares of a closely held corporation to each of his five children. The ruling concludes that, if a donor transfers shares in a corporation to each of the donor's children, the factor of corporate control in the family is not considered in valuing each transferred interest for purposes of section 2512. Thus, in valuing the shares, a minority discount will not be disallowed *solely* because a transferred interest, when aggregated with interests held by other family members, would be a part of a controlling interest.

In *Estate of Winkler v. Commissioner*, T.C.M. 1989-232 [¶89,232 PH Memo T.C.], the decedent, Clara Winkler, owned 10 percent of the voting stock of a closely held corporation. Of the balance of the voting stock, 40 percent was owned by other members of the Winkler family and 50 percent was owned by members of the Simmons family. The court recognized that the decedent's block constituted a minority interest in the corporation. However, the court found that, in view of the fact that neither family possessed a controlling interest in the corporation, the decedent's minority block had special characteristics that enhanced its value. The court described these "swing vote" characteristics as follows:

> This 10 percent voting stock could become pivotal in this closely held corporation where members of one family held 50 percent and members of another family held 40 percent. By joining with the Simmons family a minority shareholder could effect control over the corporation and by joining the Winkler family, such a minority shareholder could block action. . . . Looking at this even split between the two families, the 10 percent block of voting stock, in the hands of a third party unrelated to either family, could indeed become critical. While it is difficult to put a value on this factor, we think it increases the value of the Class A voting stock by at least the 10 percent that [respondent's appraiser] found.

The court went on to find that, under the facts presented, the increased value attributable to the swing vote characteristics of the stock offset any minority discount otherwise available. See also, Glenn Desmond and Richard Kelley, *Business Valuation Handbook*, section 11.01 (1991) ("Likewise, if a minority block would enable another minority holder to achieve a majority with control or if the minority were needed to reach the percentage ownership needed to merge or file consolidated statements, the stock would have added value."); Shannon P. Pratt, *Valuing Small Businesses and Professional Practices*, 527 (2d ed. 1994) ("[I]f two stockholders own 49 percent [of the stock] and a third owns 2 percent, the 49 percent stockholders may be on a par with each other. . . . The 2 percent stockholder may be able to command a considerable premium over the pro-rata value for that particular block because of the swing vote power."); *Estate of Bright v. United States*, 658 F.2d 999 [48 AFTR 2d 81-6292], 1007 and 1009 n.9 (5th Cir. 1981), where the court discussed swing vote analysis in detail.

In the instant case, immediately before the transfers, the donor owned 100 percent of the outstanding stock of Corporation. The donor simultaneously transferred 3 blocks of stock, each constituting 30 percent of the outstanding stock, to each of his three children. As discussed above, the three transfers are valued separately for gift tax purposes. As is evident, each gift, viewed separately, possesses the same swing vote characteristics described by the court in *Estate of Winkler*. That is, as a result of the simultaneous transfer, three individuals each owned a 30 percent block of stock. The owner of any one of the transferred blocks could join with the owner of any of the other transferred blocks and control the corporation. Thus, any one of these 30 percent blocks, whether owned by an individual related or unrelated to the family, could be critical in controlling the corporation. As the court concluded in *Estate of Winkler*, this swing vote attribute of each of the transferred blocks enhances the value of each block and is properly taken into account in determining the fair market value of each block transferred.

For valuation purposes, the focus is on shares actually transferred by the donor, notwithstanding that the transfers were treated as made one-half by the donor's spouse under section 2513.

The donor argues that attributing a swing vote value to each transferred block in this case produces an arbitrary result.

That is, if the donor had not made a simultaneous transfer, but rather had transferred each 30 percent block at different times, the valuation of each block would be different. For example, the first 30 percent block transferred might have no swing vote attributes, since after the initial transfer, the donor would continue to possess control of the corporation through his ownership of the retained 70 percent block.

However, the objection raised by the donor is inapposite. First, donor's assumption that the value of none of the three seriatim gifts would reflect swing vote attributes is incorrect. We agree that the value of the first 30 percent transfer would not reflect any swing vote value. However, the second transfer of 30 percent of the stock would possess swing vote value. Further, as a result of this second transfer, the value of the 30 percent interest held by the first transferee would increase, because that block would acquire enhanced voting control in the form of swing vote value as a result of the second transfer. After that transfer, the value of each of the three blocks would have been equalized, because no one stockholder would possess control of the corporation. This enhancement of value with respect to the first transferee's block at the time of the second transfer would constitute an indirect gift to that transferee at the time of the second transfer. Finally, the third 30 percent block would also have swing vote value both before and after the third transfer. Thus, we believe that, even if the three transfers were made at different times, the total value of the gifts would ultimately be the same as if the three transfers were made simultaneously.

Further, under established case law, gift tax valuation results are often dependent on the nature and timing of the gift. For example, a single transfer of a large block of stock to an individual might be valued differently for gift tax purposes than several independent transfers of smaller blocks at different times. On the other hand, the result might not differ with respect to the swing value approach, or any other valuation principles, in the case of an integrated series of transfers. See, e.g., *Citizens Bank and Trust Co. v. Commissioner*, 839 F.2d 1249 [61 AFTR 2d 88-1335] (7th Cir. 1988); *Estate of Murphy v. Commissioner*, T.C.M. 1990-472 [¶90,472 PH Memo T.C.]. Accordingly, we do not believe the donor's objections in any way mitigate against applying swing vote analysis to the facts presented here.

As discussed above, all relevant factors are to be considered when valuing closely held stock. As the court concluded in *Estate of Winkler*, swing block potential is one such factor. In this case, each 30 percent block of stock has swing vote characteristics. The extent to which the swing vote potential enhances the value of each block transferred is a factual determination. However, all relevant factors, including the minority nature of each block, any marketability concerns, and swing vote potential, should be taken into account in valuing each block.

Conclusion

In determining the fair market value of three 30 percent blocks of stock transferred by the donor, the swing vote attributes of each block are factors to be taken into consideration in determining the value of each block.

A copy of this Technical Advice Memorandum is to be given to the taxpayer. Section 6110(j)(3) of the Code provides that it may not be used or cited as precedent.

Appendix 17 *Private Letter Ruling 91-50001*

Full Text

UIL Number(s) 2031.00-00
Date:August 20, 1991
Control No.:TR-32-41-91

Issue

In determining the estate tax value of the decedent's stock in a subchapter C corporation based on net asset value, should a discount be allowed for potential capital gains taxes that would be incurred if the corporation was liquidated if no liquidation is planned?

Facts

At her death, Decedent owned 779 shares of stock in Company X, a closely held corporation, subject to taxation under subchapter C of the Internal Revenue Code. Decedent owned 69.4 percent of the stock, which gave Decedent voting control of the corporation. The remaining shares were owned by relatives.

Company X was a real estate holding company. Its real estate holdings consisted of residential and commercial rental properties. The properties were depreciated and have a low basis. As a result of amendments to sections 337 and 336 of the Internal Revenue Code enacted by the Tax Reform Act of 1986, if Company X is liquidated, the corporation would incur a capital gains tax upon the disposition of the assets. A transitional rule was available under which the estate could have liquidated Company X prior to 1989 at a phased-in tax rate.

Decedent's estate contends that in determining the net asset value of the decedent's stock under section 2031 of the Code, a discount should be permitted for the potential capital gains tax that would be payable if the estate beneficiaries or a purchaser of the stock liquidated the corporation. Decedent's estate contends that a willing buyer would not pay the full value of the underlying assets for the stock, but would consider the capital gains tax payable upon disposition of the assets and adjust the price he would be willing to pay for the company accordingly. Decedent's estate has represented that no liquidation is planned.

Law and Analysis

Section 2031 of the Code provides that the value of the gross estate shall be determined by including the value at the time of death of all property, real or personal, tangible or intangible, wherever situated. Section 20.2031-1(b) of the Estate Tax Regulations provides that the value of property includible in the decedent's gross estate is its fair market value on the appropriate valuation date. The fair market value is the price at which the property would change hands between a willing buyer and a willing seller, neither being under any compulsion to buy or sell and both having a reasonable knowledge of the relevant facts.

Prior to amendment by the Tax Reform Act of 1986, sections 336 and 337 of the Code provided rules allowing the liquidation of a subchapter C corporation without incurring capital gains tax at the corporate level (commonly known as the General Utilities doctrine). However, section 631 of the Act amended these Code sections to eliminate the nonrecognition provisions. Section 336 now provides that gain or loss shall be recognized to a liquidating corporation on the distribution of property in complete liquidation as if such property were sold to the distributee at its fair market value.

In analogous situations involving similar valuation issues, several cases considered the effect of potential corporate level capital gains taxes on the estate tax valuation of closely held stock in circumstances arising prior to the 1986 amendments to sections 336 and 337. In *Estate of Cruikshank v. Commissioner*, 9 T.C. 162 (1947), for example, the decedent held stock in a closely held corporation that was an investment holding company. The parties agreed that the corporation should be valued based on the value of its underlying assets. The issue presented was whether the value of the underlying assets should be reduced by amounts of commissions and stamp and capital gains taxes that would become payable if the assets were sold.

The court held that the nature of the corporate business (investment to produce income) was such that the continued retention of the assets in corporate form would be consistent with the corporate purpose and there was otherwise no indication that the corporation would be liquidated or the assets sold. Thus, the court declined to allow a discount or reduction for any possible brokerage commissions and taxes, describing these items as "a hypothetical and supposititious liability . . . on sales not made nor projected" that should not be taken into account.

In addition, the court found that the underlying assets should be valued in the same manner as if the assets were owned outright, that is, based on what a willing buyer would pay a willing seller. Such a methodology focuses on the price the buyer would pay and precludes any reduction for potential income taxes the seller might incur on the sale.[1]

More recent cases have adopted the court's reasoning in *Estate of Cruikshank* that no discount should be allowed where the potential sales expenses and tax liability are speculative, either because there is no evidence that the corporation will be liquidated or because the tax could be avoided through the operation of sections 336 and 337. See, e.g., *Ward v. Commissioner*, 87 T.C. 78, 103–104 (1986); *Estate of Andrews v. Commissioner*, 79 T.C. 938, 942 (1982); *Estate of Piper v. Commissioner*, 72 T.C. 1062, 1086–1087 (1979); *Estate of McTighe v. Commissioner*, T.C. Memo 1977-410; *Gallun v. Commissioner*, T.C. Memo 1974-284.

In *Ward*, the court summarized its position as follows:

> The petitioner's contend that, in arriving at the corporation's net asset value, adjustments should be made to reflect costs that would be incurred if its assets were liquidated. They seek adjustments for the expenses of selling the real estate (including sales commissions) and the income taxes that would be recognized by the corporation or its shareholders upon liquidation. We disagree with this argument. J-Seven is not in the business of selling its assets piecemeal, and as petitioners themselves have argued, there is no evidence that the liquidation of the entire corporation is imminent or even contemplated. Under such circumstances, "We need not assume that conversion into cash is the only use available to an owner, for property which we know would cost market to replace." *Estate of Cruikshank v. Commissioner*, 9 T.C. 162, 165 (1947). A hypothetical willing buyer of the shares in an arm's-length sale could expect no reduction in price for sales expenses and taxes that he might incur in a subsequent sale of either the shares or the corporations underlying assets. When liquidation is only speculative, such costs are not to be taken into account[citations omitted].
>
> (*Ward v. Commissioner*, 87 T.C. at 103–104)

Taxpayer argues that in view of the amendments to sections 336 and 337, it is now a virtual certainty that if the corporation is liquidated, a capital gains tax will be imposed at the corporate level. Thus, they argue that this change in the law justifies the allowance of a discount for potential taxes. The cases discussed above were decided based on the law as it existed prior to the 1986 amendments to sections 336 and 337 and, therefore, are no longer pertinent.

---

[1]See *Estate of Robinson v. Commissioner*, 69 T.C. 199, 225 (1977), where the court held that in valuing installment notes owned outright by the decedent, no discount was allowable for potential income tax that the estate or beneficiary might incur if the notes were sold. The court held that the price a willing buyer would pay for the notes would be determined without regard to the seller's potential income tax liability.

We disagree. In the cases discussed above, the courts disallowed the discounts because the tax liability was speculative. That is, there was no assurance that the estate beneficiaries would liquidate the corporation or sell the underlying assets and incur the tax and other expenses. Further, there was no indication that the hypothetical willing buyer would desire to purchase the stock only with a view toward liquidating the corporation or selling the assets, such that the potential tax liability would be of any concern.

As the above quoted discussion in *Ward* as well as the decision in *Estate of Cruikshank* indicate, a discount for any potential costs of sale or liquidation, whether in the nature of selling expenses or income taxes that might be incurred, is not appropriate simply because the sale or liquidation is itself speculative. The court drew no distinction between potential sales expenses that have always been an unavoidable cost of sale or liquidation and potential income taxes. Both potential expenses are not taken into account because the event generating these expenses (a sale or liquidation) is speculative. See also *Estate of Andrews v. Commissioner*, 79 T.C. at 942. Thus, although in some cases the courts did note that the nonrecognition provisions of sections 336 and 337 added to the speculative nature of the tax liability, we believe the decisions were primarily grounded on the speculative nature of the liquidation itself.[2] Accordingly, we conclude that the amendments to section 336 and 337 should have no impact on the decisions discussed above disallowing a discount for potential income tax liability.

In this case, the estate does not anticipate that the corporation will be liquidated. Therefore, the liquidation in this case is speculative at best. In view of the case law cited above, no discount should be allowed for potential capital gains tax.

Conclusion

In determining the value of the decedent's stock in a subchapter C corporation based on net asset value, no discount should be allowed for potential capital gains taxes that would be incurred if the corporation was liquidated since there is no indication that a liquidation is contemplated.

A copy of this Technical Advice Memorandum is to be given to the taxpayers. Section 6110(j)(3) of the Code provides that it may not be used or cited as precedent.

[2]See, e.g., *Estate of Piper*, supra, 72 T.C. at 1087, n.27. In this regard, we note that in appropriate circumstances, the corporation could liquidate and avoid a tax at the corporate level. A subchapter C corporation that converts to a corporation described in subchapter S (section 1361, et seq.) can avoid recognition of any gain if the corporation retains the assets for a period of ten years from the date of conversion to an S corporation. See section 1374(d)(7) of the Code. If the corporation is eligible for a subchapter S election, a technique would exist for avoiding recognition of gain.

Appendix 18 *Equitable Distribution Value of Small, Closely Held Businesses and Professional Practices**

Gary R. Trugman, CPA, CBA, ASA, MVS

Culminating project presented to the Faculty of the Graduate School of Lindenwood College in partial fulfillment of the requirements for the degree of Master of Valuation Sciences.

Abstract

The valuation of small, closely held businesses and professional practices that are used to determine equitable distribution of a marital estate in New Jersey has been the subject of much controversy over the past two decades. The State of New Jersey, in an attempt to arrive at an equitable splitting of the marital assets, passed legislation to provide guidance to the courts as to the factors to be considered in a matrimonial litigation. The courts have failed to fulfill the legislative intent of fairness due to the imposition of a value concept of appraisal that is inappropriate under the circumstances for which it is applied. There is little doubt that a better, more equitable method of appraisal exists for these types of businesses.

Contents

Chapter 1 Introduction
- 1.1 Equitable Distribution
- 1.2 Value Concept Used in New Jersey
- 1.3 Types of Businesses
- 1.4 Statement of Purpose

Chapter 2 History and Review of the Literature
- 2.1 Legislative History
- 2.2 Definition of Equitable Distribution
- 2.3 Valuation Literature
- 2.4 Literature Search

Chapter 3 Theory and Methods
- 3.1 Value Concept
- 3.2 Appraisal Principles

3.3 Marital Property
3.4 Leading Cases Affecting Valuation
3.4a *Stern v. Stern*
3.4b *Lavene v. Lavene*
3.4c *Levy v. Levy*
3.4d *Dugan v. Dugan*
3.5 Valuation Methods Allowed by the Court
Chapter 4 Argument
4.1 Fair Market Value Is Incorrect
4.2 Appraisal Principles Are Ignored
4.3 *Stern v. Stern*
4.4 Potential Earning Capacity
4.5 Excess Earnings
4.6 The Excess Earnings Method
4.7 Double Counting
4.8 Reasonable Compensation
4.9 Divorce Value—A Better Approach
Chapter 5 Replies to Opposition
Chapter 6 Summary and Conclusion

1 Introduction

Divorce has become a major social issue in the United States. As a result, legislation has been passed throughout the country addressing issues such as alimony, child support, and how to divide the marital estate.

1.1 Equitable Distribution

In the State of New Jersey, the division of the marital estate is called equitable distribution. New Jersey Statute 2A:34-23 provides that the court may make an award to parties going through a divorce "to effectuate an equitable distribution of the property, both real and personal, which was legally and beneficially acquired by them or either of them during the marriage."

1.2 Value Concept Used in New Jersey

The New Jersey courts have made a serious error with respect to the manner in which they have allowed small, closely held businesses and professional practices to be valued for equitable distribution purposes. The courts require the value concept of "fair market value" to be used for valuing these businesses without fully understanding the many factors that enter into the determination of this value. This problem will be reviewed later.

1.3 Types of Businesses

The majority of businesses today are small, closely held businesses or professional practices. The primary focus of this paper will be on these types of businesses.

A closely held business is one that is not traded on a stock exchange. This is the opposite of an entity that is "publicly held" and whose shares are generally freely traded on the open market. The closely held business is not always a corporation; it can also be a sole proprietorship or a partnership.

What is meant by small? Many interpretations exist as to what is considered small. Some definitions address asset size while others look at gross income of the business. These are not the only factors to be considered regarding size.

There are primarily two types of closely held businesses. They are "the personal business" and "the professionally managed business." Glenn Desmond and Richard Kelley point out that:

> [t]he most common type of closely held venture can be characterized as a very personal business operated primarily by and for the benefit of a single individual or a partnership of relatively few individuals. It is tied closely to the personality of the owners who are directly involved in all aspects of the enterprise (5–6).

This type differs from the professionally managed business, which has "grown to the point where the individual owner is unable to personally control a significant number of its activities" (6).

Desmond and Kelly elaborate further by stating that:

> for purposes of appraisal, the degree of personal control is more important than a determination of whether it is truly large or small. The personally controlled business tends to be valued in the marketplace on the basis of its tangible assets plus an arbitrary amount for goodwill, or on the basis of a formula acceptable within the industry. The formula is usually related to gross income and net profits, including provision for the owner's salaries (ibid.).

The professional practice can be large or small. The major difference between the closely held company and the professional practice is the education required by the profession in order to provide the services that it renders.

This paper will concentrate on the personal business and professional practice rather than the professionally managed one. Throughout this paper, the terms "closely held business" and "professional practice" will be used interchangeably. The same characteristics are often found in these businesses, and the same problems relating to valuation exist for each.

1.4 Statement of Purpose

As stated previously, the New Jersey courts use the standard of fair market value for valuing these types of businesses in divorce litigation. The purpose of this paper is to explain why the New Jersey courts should use a different value concept in order to comply with the intent of N.J.S.A. 2A:34-23 and to help in the selection of the appropriate value concept when an appraisal is for equitable distribution purposes. It is my intention to determine a new value concept to apply to closely held businesses that I will call "divorce value."

2 History and Review of the Literature

2.1 Legislative History

I performed a review of the literature in order to determine the origin of the concept of equitable distribution in the State of New Jersey.

The Divorce Reform Act of 1971 is the source of the judicial authority to divide property for equitable distribution purposes. This legislation failed to provide any criteria or guidelines and, as a result, trial judges were left to determine the manner in which the statute was to be interpreted. Subsequent case law supports the discretion allowed to the trial judge, evidenced by the wide divergence of opinions that have resulted.

The first amendment to the Act, in 1980, listed several items that were not subject to equitable distribution. Other amendments followed, primarily in response to the litigations that followed.

The most recent amendment, in 1988, identified numerous criteria for the courts to consider relating to equitable distribution. These issues are discussed in N.J.S.A. 2A:34-1 et seq., most notably section 23, addressing support and equitable distribution. These issues will not be discussed within this paper. They are not specific to valuation issues but rather pertain to the guidelines for the Court to follow in dividing the actual property.

2.2 Definition of Equitable Distribution

Equitable distribution relates to the division of marital property. This is not to be confused with the concept of alimony or support. The courts have found that although there may be similarities between alimony and the division of property, they are, in fact, different.

In *Mendell v. Mendell*, the Court concluded that alimony is awarded as a measurement of the postmarital duty of support, representing an income stream, whereas equitable distribution is an award of property relative to the contributions of each spouse, during the marriage, toward the accumulation of the marital assets, otherwise considered to be a "reversion" (475–476).

Justice Pashman stated in *Kikkert v. Kikkert* that:

> [t]he purposes of equitable distribution differ from those of alimony and child support. Alimony and child support can help maintain the income of both parties at a certain level over time by using one party's income to support the other. However, the primary purpose of marital property distribution laws is not to compensate for changes in the parties' fortunes after they have separated, but to achieve a fair distribution of what the parties 'lawfully and beneficially acquired' while they were together (9).

In *Stout v. Stout*, the court found that the division of marital assets was much more complex than merely creating an equal distribution to the parties. "Equitable" does not mean "equal," as "the word 'equitable' itself implies the weighing of the many considerations and circumstances that are present in each case" (205).

Numerous other cases acknowledged that while equitable distribution is not a substitute for alimony, it is a complement to it. Nonetheless, there is a relationship between alimony and equitable distribution (N.J. Family Law Practice 751). This becomes apparent in *Painter v. Painter*, *Rothman v. Rothman*, *Stern v. Stern*, *Daly v. Daly*, *Smith v. Smith*, and others.

Determination of which assets are subject to equitable distribution and how they are to be valued are addressed in *Dugan v. Dugan*, *Lavene v. Lavene*, *Stern v. Stern*, *Levy v. Levy*, and *Piscopo v. Piscopo*. These will be discussed in the next chapter, to further clarify the meaning of "equitable distribution."

2.3 Valuation Literature

The issue of valuing a small, closely held business has created numerous problems. Books such as *Valuing Professional Practices and Licenses*, *Basic Business Appraisal*, *Valuation of Divorce Assets*, *Valuing a Business*, *Valuing Small Businesses and Professional Practices*, *When a Lawyer Divorces*, and *Business Valuation Handbook* address valuation techniques in general, but none addresses the special problems that are encountered relating to the divorce.

Internal Revenue Ruling 59-60 and Internal Revenue Ruling 68-609 provide guidelines as to how closely held businesses should be valued for estate and gift tax purposes. Unfortunately, the New Jersey courts have built a foundation for valuing closely held businesses in matrimonial litigations on these overused and much-abused rulings.

2.4 Literature Search

The literature search has been conducted by using the online service "Westlaw," a product of West Publishing Co. This search was limited to New Jersey cases through April 1990. The book and article review was conducted by using the extensive bibliographical services of the Institute of Business Appraisers, Inc. through December 1989. The final search was made possible by provision with the sixth edition of *New Jersey Family Law Practice* prior to its release to the general public in July 1990. This treatise includes all major New Jersey case law and is updated regularly by the Institute of Continuing Legal Education, its publisher.

3 Theory and Methods

3.1 Value Concept

The valuation of closely held businesses for equitable distribution purposes requires the appraiser to derive the fair market value of the subject business. In *Lavene v. Lavene*, the court employed the most frequently used definition of fair market value. This is found in Internal Revenue Ruling 59-60. Section 2, paragraph .02 defines this as:

> the price at which the property would change hands between a willing buyer and a willing seller when the former is not under any compulsion to buy and the latter is not under any compulsion to sell, both parties having reasonable knowledge of relevant facts. Court decisions frequently state in addition that the hypothetical buyer and seller are assumed to be able, as well as willing, to trade and to be well informed about the property and concerning the market for such property.

A similar definition can be found in *Basic Business Appraisal*, by Raymond C. Miles, Executive Director of the Institute of Business Appraisers Inc. Miles states that:

> fair market value is the price, in cash or equivalent, that a buyer could reasonably be expected to pay and a seller could reasonably be expected to accept, if the property were exposed for sale on the open market for a reasonable period of time with buyer and seller being in possession of the pertinent facts, and neither being under any compulsion to act (19).

Both of these definitions are regularly accepted by the appraisal profession and are used interchangeably.

3.2 Appraisal Principles

There are three appraisal principles that comprise the foundation of valuation theory used to determine fair market value. They are:

1. The Principle of Alternatives
2. The Principle of Substitution
3. The Principle of Future Benefits

In *Basic Business Appraisal*, Miles discusses these appraisal principles. The Principle of Alternatives states that "in any contemplated transaction, each party has alternatives to consummating the transaction" (22). This indicates that there are generally alternatives to the investment.

This concept can be illustrated by the following scenario. Assume that I wish to sell my record collection. I have alternatives as to whether or not I sell the collection, how much I sell it for, and to whom I will sell it.

This principle is apparent and does not need to be belabored. Miles points out that:

> because it is one of the fundamental principles that form the basis of almost all appraisals, including those under circumstances that do not actually involve a contemplated sale or other transaction, the appraiser needs to be aware of its existence (ibid.).

On the other hand, the Principle of Substitution is a presupposition of appraisal practice, expressing a generalized prediction concerned with behavior related to an event involving economic choices and values. It "predicts how people will normally choose among comparable properties when prices vary" (*Appraisal and Valuation: An Interdisciplinary Approach*, 5).

To illustrate how the Principle of Substitution operates to determine value, assume that a new record has been released and due to what I have heard about it, I wish to buy it. Let us further assume that the record is available as a cassette tape selling for $7.95 and as a compact disc selling for $12.95.

If my only concern is to be able to listen to this music, that is, if I am not concerned about the quality differential in the sound, then from my standpoint these two recorded media are equally desirable. Therefore, I would place the same use value on the compact disc as I would place on the cassette tape. Therefore, *all other things being equal*, their exchange value *to me* would be equal.

Valuation theory emphasizes the use of market data to help the appraiser determine value. The sales comparison or market value approach emphasizes the Principle of Substitution.

The sales comparison approach estimates market value "by comparing the subject property to similar properties that have been sold recently or for which offers to purchase have been made" (*The Appraisal of Real Estate*, 311).

Regardless of whether the appraisal subject is real estate or a business, market comparable approaches are highly recommended in valuation theory.

The Principle of Future Benefits is the third appraisal principle that is fundamental to the valuation process. This principle states that "economic value reflects anticipated future benefits" (*Basic Business Appraisal*, 27). This appraisal principle can best be illustrated by assuming that you want to buy a particular business. Would historic earnings be as important to use in determining value as prospective earnings? Probably not. You would not care what the business did for the prior owner as much as what it can do for you, the purchaser.

It should always be remembered that valuation is based on the future outlook of the business. Internal Revenue Ruling 59-60 included the statement that valuation is a "prophecy as to the future."

3.3 Marital Property

The word "property" in the equitable distribution statute, N.J.S.A. 2A:34-23, denotes many forms of ownership. For equitable distribution purposes, "property" includes tangible assets, intangible assets, future interests, pensions, and many different forms of ownership, whether they be absolute, beneficial, defeasible, joint, or subject to a reversion (*New Jersey Family Law Practice*, 767). The New Jersey case law includes a considerable number of matters determining those assets that are subject to equitable distribution.

The issue of fairness is one that the courts consider in determining equitable distribution as evidenced by the previous discussion of *Kikkert* and *Stout*. The term "fair" is used frequently throughout the case law as well as in the appraisal literature and must be explained to avoid misunderstanding.

"Fair," as used for equitable distribution purposes, refers to splitting the marital estate in a manner that is just to both parties. The notion of fairness is not intended to split assets equally but rather in a manner consistent with the contributions of each spouse.

In order to achieve this fairness, N.J.S.A. 2A:34-23.1 states that:

> [i]n making an equitable distribution of property, the court shall consider, but not be limited to, the following factors:

> a. The duration of the marriage;
> b. The age and physical and emotional health of the parties;
> c. The income or property brought to the marriage by each party;
> d. The standard of living established during the marriage;
> e. Any written agreement made by the parties before or during the marriage concerning an arrangement of property distribution;
> f. The economic circumstances of each party at the time the division of property becomes effective;
> g. The income and earning capacity of each party, including educational background, training, employment skills, work experience, length of absence from the job market, custodial responsibilities for children, and the time and expense necessary to acquire sufficient education or training to enable the party to become self-supporting at a standard of living reasonably comparable to that enjoyed during the marriage;
> h. The contribution by each party to the education, training, or earning power of the other;
> i. The contribution of each party to the acquisition, dissipation, preservation, depreciation, or appreciation in the amount or value of the marital property, as well as the contribution of a party as a homemaker;
> j. The tax consequences of the proposed distribution to each party;
> k. The present value of the property;
> l. The need of a parent who has physical custody of a child to own or occupy the marital residence and to use or own the household effects;
> m. The debts and liabilities of the parties;
> n. The need for creation, now or in the future, of a trust fund to secure reasonably foreseeable medical or educational costs for a spouse or children; and
> o. Any other factors which the court may deem relevant.
>
> In every case, the court shall make specific findings of fact on the evidence relative to all issues pertaining to asset eligibility or ineligibility, asset valuation, and equitable distribution, including specifically, but not limited to, the factors set forth in this section.
>
> It shall be a rebuttable presumption that each party made a substantial financial or nonfinancial contribution to the acquisition of income and property while the party was married.

Article 6 of this same statute addresses the issue of alimony and maintenance and provides that the court consider 10 cited factors and others if deemed relevant in awarding permanent or rehabilitative alimony. Factor 9 that the court should consider is:

> The equitable distribution of property ordered and any payout on equitable distribution, directly or indirectly, out of current income, to the extent this consideration is reasonable, just, and fair [2A:34-23(b)(9)].

"Fair" is used by the appraisal profession as part of the value concept "fair market value." This definition has been previously discussed and does not need to be repeated. It is essential to understand that the use of the word "fair" has two distinct meanings that are not interchangeable.

The court has rendered opinions as to which assets should be included for equitable distribution under the statute. The purpose of this inclusion of certain assets and not others is to be fair to the parties. Business interests have clearly been included as marital property subject to equitable distribution. These interests may include both tangible and intangible attributes. The tangible assets have not presented the difficulty to the courts that the intangible assets have, in particular goodwill.

The ethics of the legal profession prohibit the sale of goodwill, and as a result, the value of goodwill as a marital asset was challenged. Once it was determined that a law firm's goodwill was includable in the marital estate (see *Dugan*), the next step was to determine its value.

Four New Jersey cases have had a significant impact on the valuation issues that are brought before the court. They have been cited over and over in subsequent cases and have clearly established precedent.

These four cases are summarized in the following pages with respect to the business valuation issues only. These cases are:

1. *Stern v. Stern*
2. *Lavene v. Lavene*
3. *Levy v. Levy*
4. *Dugan v. Dugan*

3.4a *Stern v. Stern.* This case was decided by the Supreme Court of New Jersey on January 23, 1975. The husband was a partner in a law firm. The issues were:

1. Should Mr. Stern's earning capacity be considered a marital asset if its development has been aided and enhanced by his spouse?
2. How should Mr. Stern's partnership interest be valued?

Addressing these issues, the court held that "potential earning capacity" should have been considered by the lower court judge in determining the fairness of a particular distribution and its correlation to alimony, but it should not be deemed "property" within the meaning of the statute, even where its development has been aided and enhanced by the other spouse (345).

Relating to the valuation issues, the Supreme Court felt that the trial court would have been justified in combining the value stated in the partnership agreement that would be payable to Stern's personal representative upon his death, the value of Stern's capital account, and Stern's percentage of the accounts receivable of the firm.

According to the partnership agreement, Stern's estate would receive his capital account and a fixed sum appearing after his name on a schedule appended to the agreement. The schedule was revised quarterly. The court found that it was the intent of the partnership to reflect each partner's true worth rather than the amount in his capital account. This was considered to be the presumptive value of his interest in the firm.

The result of *Stern v. Stern* is that appraisers must now consider a partnership agreement to be presumptive of value if the books and records of the partnership are well maintained, the value stipulated in the agreement is updated regularly, and there is some underlying basis for the value as stated.

3.4b *Lavene v. Lavene.* This case was appealed by both parties. On remand, the court decided the case on July 31, 1978. The valuation issue for the court to decide was the appropriate valuation method to be used to value the 42.8 percent interest owned by the husband in a closely held corporation.

In the court's opinion, it was stated that "[t]he valuation of the stock of a closely held corporation calls for an attempt to fix a fair market value for the stock that is . . ." (*Lavene*, 192). The definition given is that which appears in Internal Revenue Ruling 59-60.

Justice Arnone proceeded with an elaborate discussion of the eight attributes of Internal Revenue Ruling 59-60. He then continued by stating that "[o]nce the appraiser has obtained, if possible, the above information [eight attributes], he can then proceed to the actual evaluation" (ibid. at 197).

The judge further opined that there are three principal methods of valuing a closely held company. These methods are:

a. Capitalization of indicated earnings at a reasonable return on investment based on relative risk and current interest rates . . . (ibid.),

b. Comparison with price earnings ratios of publicly traded companies in the same or comparable industry . . . (ibid. at 198), and
c. Appraisal of all underlying assets, tangible and intangible, with adjustment for existing liabilities (ibid.).

The significance of this case is the importance the courts have placed on the eight attributes of Internal Revenue Ruling 59-60 in valuing closely held businesses. These attributes are to be used by appraisers to determine the fair market value of a business. They may not necessarily result in a "fair" value for equitable distribution purposes.

3.4c *Levy v. Levy.* This case was decided December 6, 1978. The husband was a self-employed attorney with over 20 years of experience.

The valuation issue was the determination of the value of goodwill to be included in the overall appraisal of the law practice. In this case, the wife's expert calculated goodwill based on a factor equal to one to one-and-a-half times the gross annual earnings based on no supportable evidence. The court stated that "goodwill is found in measuring neither the gross nor unadjusted net income of the business, but rather its excess net earnings" (ibid. at 547).

In order to calculate goodwill, the court-appointed expert raised the issue of using the "formula approach," otherwise known as the excess earnings method, promulgated in Internal Revenue Ruling 68-609. Justice O'Neil quoted from Internal Revenue Ruling 68-609, stating that "[t]he past earnings to which the formula is applied should fairly reflect the probable future earnings" (ibid. at 551). The findings in this case were that after deducting reasonable compensation for the attorney, there were no excess earnings and, therefore, no goodwill.

3.4d *Dugan v. Dugan.* This case was decided by the Supreme Court of New Jersey on February 28, 1983. Once again, the husband was an attorney. The valuation issues were:

1. Was Dugan's goodwill in his wholly owned professional corporation subject to equitable distribution?
2. How should the law practice be valued?

The court found that Dugan's goodwill was subject to equitable distribution. Justice Schreiber stated that "[t]here can be no doubt that goodwill exists" (*Dugan*, 429).

Addressing the valuation issue, Justice Schreiber cited Internal Revenue Ruling 68-609, *Lavene v. Lavene*, *Stern v. Stern*, and *Levy v. Levy*. The judge stated that:

> [f]uture earning capacity per se is not goodwill. However, when the future earning capacity has been enhanced because reputation leads to probable future patronage from existing and potential clients, goodwill may exist and have value (ibid. at 433).

The court then continued with "[g]oodwill is to be differentiated from earning capacity. It reflects not simply a *possibility* of future earnings, but a *probability* based on existing circumstances" [emphasis added] (ibid).

Clarifying that the enhanced earnings that are part of goodwill must be differentiated from a professional license or educational degree, the judge then proceeded by acknowledging that "[g]oodwill should be valued with great care, for the individual practitioner will be forced to pay the ex-spouse 'tangible' dollars for an intangible asset at a value concededly arrived at on the basis of some uncertain elements" (ibid. at 435).

The methodology used by the court was to compare the attorney's earnings with that which he would have earned as an employee based on his qualifications, experience, and capabilities. As the court distinguished this, "The effort that the practitioner expends on his law practice should not be overlooked when comparing his income to that of the hypothetical employee," stated the judge (ibid. at 439).

The next step was to average the attorney's net income before income taxes for a period of five years. This average would then be compared with what he would have earned as an employee. Justice Schreiber continued: "If the attorney's actual average realistically exceeds the total of (1) the employee norm and (2) a return on the investment in the physical assets, the excess would be the basis for evaluating goodwill" (ibid. at 439–440).

3.5 Valuation Methods Allowed by the Court

The leading cases, discussed above, indicate the valuation methodology accepted by the courts.

The findings in *Stern v. Stern* relied on the terms of the partnership agreement plus adjustments, since the books were well kept and the value stipulated in the partnership agreement was updated regularly.

All of the other cases show a judicial trend that relies on Internal Revenue Ruling 59-60 and Internal Revenue Ruling 68-609. These rulings have introduced the formula approach, otherwise known as the excess earnings method, which has become widely accepted by the court.

4 Argument

A fair division of the marital estate is the motivation behind the equitable distribution statute. The court's inconsistent treatment of the issues has created a voluminous amount of litigation over the years. This is clearly evidenced by following the number of cases that have transpired regarding issues involving equitable distribution.

4.1 Fair Market Value Is Incorrect

The value concept repeatedly used in the case law is fair market value (see Section 3.1 for definition), but in a matrimonial proceeding, fair market value is the wrong value concept to be used. Not only has case law resulted in the use of an incorrect value concept, but the manner in which it is derived is flawed.

The use of Internal Revenue Ruling 59-60 to define fair market value presents its own set of problems, as even this ruling, when defining closely held corporations, states:

> Closely held corporations are those corporations, the shares of which are owned by a relatively limited number of stockholders. Often the entire stock issue is held by one family. The result of this situation is that little, if any, trading takes place. There is, therefore, no established market for the stock, and such sales as occur at irregular intervals seldom reflect all of the elements of a representative transaction, as defined by the term "fair market value" (237).

In *Valuation of Divorce Assets*, Barth Goldberg discusses this point by stating:

> In essence, then, what Revenue Ruling 59-60 does is to ask the expert to hypothesize a situation at or around the date of valuation. Thereafter, the appraiser is asked to imagine himself to be playing two parts, that of the prospective buyer and that of the prospective seller and to deduce that essentially dichotomized position at which price the company should actually be sold considering all of the "motivational" factors involved. The reasons why the buyer wants to buy the company and the reasons why the seller chooses to sell it, always keeping in mind the opportunity for alternate or comparative forms of investment (136).

Every business appraiser is aware of the difficulties presented in determining the fair market value of an interest in a closely held corporation. This is because:

> valuation of stock of a closely held company is an attempt to determine the fair market value of an asset which by definition does not have a fair market value since a market wherein a willing buyer will meet a willing seller, neither under any compulsion, generally does not exist. The stock of a closely held corporation is, as a rule, offered for sale only under unusual circumstances. The number of prospects is usually extremely limited (*Journal of Taxation*, 14).

Dissecting the definition of fair market value will demonstrate the many flaws that exist. The appraiser's assignment of determining the equivalent of cash that would be paid for the business being appraised is difficult. Frequently, small, closely held businesses are sold for a price that is created around the terms that were negotiated between the buyer and seller. Very often, the seller holds a mortgage or note at a rate of interest that is below the market rate to induce the buyer to consummate the transaction.

Shannon Pratt correctly points out that:

> most small businesses and professional practices do not sell for cash or cash equivalents. The majority of small business and professional practice sales include a cash down payment, typically 20–35 percent of what we will call the transaction price, with the balance on a contract to be paid over some period of time, usually a few years (*Valuing Small Businesses and Professional Practices*, 13).

He continues by stating:

> I know of no other class of transactions whose prices diverge as far from a cash equivalent value or fair market value as the values of contracts arising from sales of small businesses and professional practices. It is not at all uncommon for the terms of the contract to be such that the cash equivalent value is 20 percent or more below the face value of the transaction (ibid.).

The business appraiser's assignment is to determine the equivalent of cash that would be paid for the business being appraised as of the valuation date. Often, a business may be sold with the seller holding a mortgage at a rate of interest below the market rate, to induce the buyer to enter into the transaction. This situation requires a present value calculation, because some of the value will not be received until a future date. Indeed, appraisal theory is founded on the "Principle of Future Benefits," with the value of any property constituted by the sum of the benefits that will be obtained by its owner in the future. No one will buy property if there will be no future benefits, whether in the form of income or the appreciation to be realized upon subsequent resale of the property.

Present value theory can be illustrated by comparing the sale of two businesses, each for $100,000, one with a five-year payout, and the other a seven-year payout. The value of these businesses can be determined using the present value formula

$$PV = \frac{FV}{(1 + r)^n}$$

where

PV = Present value
FV = Future value
r = Rate of return (sometimes called the discount rate)
n = Number of periods into the future for which the compounding is being computed

A discount rate of 10 percent would yield the following present values:

Business 1	*Business 2*
$PV = \frac{FV}{(1 + r)^n}$	$PV = \frac{FV}{(1 + r)^n}$
$PV = \frac{100{,}000}{(1 + .10)^5}$	$PV = \frac{100{,}000}{(1 + .10)^7}$
PV = $62,092.13	PV = $51,315.81

The example illustrates that the cash equivalents of these two businesses are quite different in today's dollars.

The appraiser is to assume that the value is that which a buyer could reasonably be expected to pay and a seller could reasonably be expected to accept. This part of the definition of fair market value is frequently overlooked. For a value to be representative of fair market value, it must be reasonable. Pratt points out that:

> the willing buyer and willing seller are hypothetical persons dealing at arm's length rather than any "particular" buyer or seller. In other words, a price would not be considered representative of fair market value if influenced by motivations not characteristic of a typical buyer or seller (*Valuing a Business*, 23).

This concept also assumes a willing buyer and a willing seller, each being competent. All too often the court overlooks the fact that the excess earnings may be attributable to the owner's skill in running the business. Depending on the business, there may be very few, if any, buyers of equal ability. In reality, the value of the business would be different for the buyer and the seller. The earnings would probably change due to the "key man" leaving the business. In some instances, consulting agreements and employment agreements become part of a change of ownership of a business, but frequently they are not. Small businesses generally change hands with a short management transition, if any, and for that reason should not be considered a normal occurrence. Furthermore, in a divorce this will not happen. The business owner will remain with the business, and it should, therefore, be expected that the business will continue into perpetuity and should be valued accordingly. This should generally create a higher value than fair market value.

Fair market value assumes that the business has been placed on the open market, and that there are similar businesses available in the open market. This also assumes the Principle of Substitution, namely, that no person will pay more for a property than he or she would have to pay for an equally desirable substitute.

In matters involving equitable distribution, however, there is not going to be a sale on the open market. To make the assumption that the owner of a business is going to sell his or her only form of livelihood is clearly without merit. Furthermore, if he or she were to sell this business, the selling price necessary to motivate such a sale would be expected to be greater than the fair market value, which violates the very definition of fair market value. On the other hand, the purchaser of a closely held business often buys such a business due to the entrepreneurial attributes of the purchaser, the intrinsic value of owning such a business, or to purchase employment for him- or herself.

In the real world, there are few transactions, if any, where buyer and seller are in possession of all pertinent facts. In an appraisal assignment, however, the determination of fair market value must assume that buyers and sellers are on equal ground.

Another piece of the definition of fair market value is that the parties are not to be under compulsion to act. Small businesses are generally sold for specific reasons. They are frequently bought for other reasons. Although neither party may act under duress, there are motivational factors that cause the buyer and seller to ultimately come together.

The concept of fair market value requires the appraiser to make so many assumptions about the hypothetical transaction that the value estimate derived may be based on nothing more than assumptions so far removed from reality that the conclusion is irrelevant. Using fair market value to determine the value of the small, closely held business or professional practice results in a value that is not representative of that which the New Jersey statute intended to accomplish in its effort "to effectuate an equitable distribution of the property" (N.J.S.A. 2A:34-23).

4.2 Appraisal Principles Are Ignored

The three fundamental appraisal principles discussed in Section 3.2 were:

1. The Principle of Alternatives
2. The Principle of Substitution
3. The Principle of Future Benefits

The importance of these principles cannot be overemphasized. They are as important to appraisal theory as the law of supply and demand is to economics. In being compelled to perform matrimonial valuations using fair market value as the value concept, the appraiser is forced to ignore these three important principles.

The Principle of Alternatives is ignored because very often the owner of a closely held business does not have an alternative. He or she cannot sell the business because it is his or her livelihood, the debt structure is such that he or she would not have the cash flow from the sale to pay the capital gains taxes, or he or she must continue to earn enough to pay the required alimony and/or child support that will result from the divorce or separation.

The Principle of Substitution is misapplied by assuming that an equally desirable substitute exists for the business being appraised. Due to the personal nature of a closely held business, no two businesses are alike. There is generally a major problem in finding comparable market data for a closely held business. Frequently, the owner of such a business is a "key man" who cannot be easily replaced. As Pratt puts it, "The smaller the company, the more important the role of one or a few owner(s)/manager(s)" (*Valuing Small Businesses and Professional Practices*, 29).

Market comparable approaches are emphasized in valuation theory. The last attribute of Internal Revenue Ruling 59-60 emphasizes this technique. In *Valuation and Distribution of Marital Property*, the discussion on market value states:

> Market valuation is so unexceptionable that no court has balked at its application. Some courts believe that it is the only acceptable method of valuation.
>
> In many instances, however, market valuation may undervalue excess earnings or may be entirely incapable of establishing any value. The latter problem occurs when there is no market. The absence of a market may result from legal constraints or economic conditions. For example, an attorney's goodwill may not be legally saleable. Alternatively, a business may be economically valuable, but there may be no market by which to estimate the value of that business (23-66).

The author continues by stating:

> The most pervasive problem presented by market valuation is systematic undervaluation. This is particularly a problem with professional practices. Sale of professional goodwill may be lawful and there may be a market for such goodwill, but the sale price will not fully reflect the excess earnings of the practice. This occurs because most professional goodwill, and in small businesses much business goodwill, is personal to the holder. It will not or may not survive transfer, which makes a buyer unwilling to pay what it is worth in the seller's hands. Market valuation effectively measures that portion and only that portion of excess earnings that will or may survive transfer to a buyer. Insofar as no sale or transfer is contemplated, market valuation understates the value of the business or practice (ibid. at 23-67).

The Principle of Future Benefits is ignored if "potential earning capacity" is not considered in the business valuation.

The courts have allowed the use of the five periods prior to the valuation date as suggested by the Revenue Ruling. Many experts have ignored the fact that valuation is a "prophecy as to the future" (Internal Revenue Ruling 59-60) and should be treated as such.

One of the most theoretically correct methods of appraisal is the Discounted Future Earnings Method. In applying this method, future earnings are projected and discounted back to the valuation date using present value techniques. Since potential future earnings are not to be considered as a marital asset, this method of valuation, although theoretically sound, cannot be considered in valuing a closely held business. The courts have found that "potential future earnings" is not an asset subject to equitable distribution (see *Stern*) and that the projections associated with small businesses are frequently so speculative that their inclusion is afforded no weight in the valuation process.

In reality, good appraisal practice dictates that it is "potential earning capacity" that the appraiser should be valuing. The Principle of Future Benefits is founded on this thought. Future value is at the very heart of the appraisal process, and by the court's refusal to allow its use, the appraiser is not being permitted to determine the true value of the business in question.

4.3 *Stern v. Stern*

In addition to ignoring appraisal principles, the courts have allowed valuation methodology to be used that has no foundation in determining value. In the matter of *Stern v. Stern*, the court addressed the issue of equitable distribution of a partnership interest in a law practice. In this instance, the court found that resorting to fair market value of the partnership interest would be inappropriate since Stern would continue as a partner in the firm.

Instead, the court looked to the terms of the partnership agreement in order to establish the methodology that the partnership would use to pay partners who withdraw from the firm, become disabled, die, or retire. In this case, the court determined that the provisions containing the formula for the calculation and payment of a partner's interest to a personal representative upon death were the most appropriate indication of value for equitable distribution purposes.

The formula that existed in the partnership agreement was updated on a regular basis, which became one of the decisive factors in allowing this methodology to be applied. Since the court determined that the value stated in the partnership agreement was presumptive of the value of the husband's partnership interest in the firm, it would be up to the parties to the litigation "to challenge the figure so determined as not being reflective of the true value" (*Stern* 346).

Insofar as the partner had not and probably would not withdraw from the partnership, the value of his interest, that is, his capacity to produce further income, might bear no relation to the withdrawal figure set in the agreement. Withdrawal provisions are drawn up for various reasons, many of which bear no relation to accurate valuation.

Attorneys have argued that a partner going through a divorce should have this type of agreement used to set an upper limit in the valuation of the interest. Those partners taking such a position assert that the interest cannot be worth more as a marital asset than could be realized at death or withdrawal from the partnership.

Partnership agreements are rarely drawn up in anticipation of a divorce. The partners are generally motivated by other factors such as maintaining continuity of the partnership, protection of a partner or his or her heirs in the event of disability or death, and in the event of retirement. Many partnership agreements penalize the partners for a voluntary withdrawal and, as such, require a very low value to be placed on the interest, whereas the death provisions protect the decedent's heirs with an overstated value. For that reason, partnership agreements should not be used to determine the value of an interest in a divorce proceeding.

Although the *Stern* decision allowed the use of a partnership agreement formula, the courts have generally accepted capitalization of excess earnings as the measure of value and have quite properly rejected the partnership agreement value argument.

4.4 Potential Earning Capacity

Potential earning capacity has been considered by the court in several cases. Although a distinction was made between possible earnings and probable earnings, an inconsistency has been created in the case law due to the difficulties related to determining the difference of when an event is possible versus probable.

In *Stern v. Stern*, the Supreme Court held that "potential earning capacity" should be considered by the trial judge in determining the fairness of a particular distribution and its correlation to alimony, but it should not be deemed "property" within the meaning of N.J.S.A. 2A:34-23, even where its development has been aided and enhanced by the other spouse (345).

Approximately eight years subsequent to the *Stern* decision, the Supreme Court rendered its decision in *Dugan v. Dugan*. In *Dugan*, the Court addressed the issue of "future earning capacity."

The Court changed the terminology slightly and now considered that if "future earnings capacity has been enhanced because reputation . . . goodwill may exist and have value" (*Dugan*, 433).

Potential earning capacity, which was not property under the statute, became future earning capacity, which is a component of goodwill and is now property to be included in equitable distribution.

To make matters worse, the findings in *Piscopo v. Piscopo* consider the concept of "celebrity" goodwill. This concept relates to an entertainer's future income stream. The findings in *Piscopo* were that since the entertainer would *probably* continue to have earnings in the future, the goodwill associated with these future earnings was a marital asset subject to equitable distribution. This concept "pushes equitable distribution of one's endeavors close to the extreme outer limits" (*New Jersey Family Law Practice*, 869). A new question has been raised in response to the Court's findings: "Is there a 'value' to a high-ranking, corporate executive's achievements and ability to trade on his or her reputation?" (ibid.).

4.5 Excess Earnings

In *Levy v. Levy* the Court determined that in order for there to be goodwill in an attorney's law practice, excess earnings were required. The Court stated:

> In an enterprise where earnings are principally the product of invested capital, the question of whether they are excess requires comparison of the rate of return on its own capital with the average or ordinary rate of return being realized in other businesses of the same type. Where the business is a service organization, then the question of excess requires comparison of the net earnings with the reasonable value of the personal services which produced them. In either case, testimony is needed (*Levy*, 547).

The rationale applied to this case, requiring excess earnings to be necessary to establish value, is troublesome. Considering the fact that most small, closely held businesses and professional practices are generally bought and sold for a particular purpose, usually of a different nature to the seller and purchaser, excess earnings frequently are not important.

In the valuation of a professional practice, one must look at the facts and circumstances surrounding such a transaction. If one accounting firm were to purchase another accounting firm, is excess earnings really essential for the acquirer who may already have an ongoing entity consisting of an office, equipment, personnel, and other such factors? Taking over the seller's accounts may be nothing more than adding gross revenue to the existing practice. Due to the economies of scale of having an existing entity, many of the operating expenses that were part of the old practice will not be repeated as part of the new. In this instance, excess earnings is irrelevant.

On the other hand, excess earnings may be a consideration if the purchaser has never been in practice and must now acquire the ongoing expenses of conducting a professional practice in addition to servicing the client base. Excess earnings become more of a consideration in this instance because the purchaser must be concerned with how much will be available to cover debt service and other matters relating to the purchase. Depending upon the facts and circumstances of a particular situation, the method used will provide a result that is quite different. The court's reliance on excess earnings is fallacious due to the imposition of a hypothetical buyer and seller in a utopian transaction.

4.6 The Excess Earnings Method

In its attempt to use excess earnings in order to calculate goodwill value, the New Jersey Courts have allowed and now basically require appraisers to use Internal Revenue Ruling 68-609, which has been called the "formula approach" or the "excess earnings method."

The formula approach may be stated as follows:

> A percentage return on the average annual value of the tangible assets used in a business is determined using a period of years (preferably not less than five) immediately prior to the valuation date. The amount of the percentage return on tangible assets, thus determined, is deducted from the average earnings of the business for such period and the remainder, if any, is considered the amount of the average annual earnings from the intangible assets for the business for the period. This amount 'considered as the average annual earnings from intangibles,' capitalized at a percentage of, say, 15 to 20 percent, is the value of the intangible assets of the business determined under the 'formula approach' (Internal Revenue Ruling 68-609).

The potential problems that exist in applying the formula approach are many. Where possible, appraisers are generally encouraged to use other valuation methods to determine the value of the intangibles rather than the formula approach. Even the Internal Revenue Service has stated that "[a]ccordingly, the 'formula' approach may be used for determining the fair market value of intangible assets of a business only if there is no better basis therefore available" (Internal Revenue Ruling 68-609). Unfortunately, this is very often the only approach that can be used.

One of the problems that exists in using the excess earnings method in a professional practice valuation is the question of the degree of earnings that constitutes excess earnings. In *Levy*, the court had no trouble with the determination that if the professional had been employed by a firm as opposed to being a single practitioner:

> the salary he could command would not be less than the average earnings of his practice . . . for goodwill to be found in a case of this sort, competent, informed and expert testimony should be offered to establish that the value of the personal services is less than the net income of the practice. The difference would then be what the revenue ruling refers to as the earnings of the intangible assets of goodwill (*Levy*, 554).

In order to illustrate the deficiencies of the excess earnings method, let's examine a typical valuation using this technique. Since *Dugan*, *Stern*, and *Levy* involved law firms, let's appraise a law practice.

Assume the following facts: Mr. Lawyer is a professional corporation. He has been in practice for 19 years and practices all areas of law. He is the only professional in the practice and bases his salary on whatever is required to bring profit to $0 for income tax purposes. Comparative financial statements prepared by the firm's accountants for the five years prior to the valuation appear in Tables 4.1 and 4.2.

TABLE 4.1

Mr. Lawyer, P.C.
Comparative Income Statement
for the Year Ended December 31,

	1989	*1988*	*1987*	*1986*	*1985*
Fee income	$975,000	$845,000	$ 902,000	$766,000	$500,000
Operating expenses					
Officer's salary	$450,000	$325,000	$ 400,000	$300,000	$200,000
Pension	30,000	30,000	30,000	30,000	30,000
Auto expenses	17,250	16,975	15,910	13,425	10,000
Entertainment expenses	38,410	29,815	32,450	27,960	24,950
Other expenses	439,340	443,210	423,640	394,615	235,050
Total operating expenses	$975,000	$845,000	$ 902,000	$766,000	$500,000
Net income before taxes	$ 0	$ 0	$ 0	$ 0	$ 0
Income taxes	0	0	0	0	0
Net income	$ 0	$ 0	$ 0	$ 0	$ 0

The first step in the valuation process is to determine the fair market value of the assets and liabilities of the subject company ignoring goodwill or other intangible value, if such value exists.

TABLE 4.2
Mr. Lawyer, P.C.
Comparative Balance Sheet
December 31,

	1989	*1988*	*1987*	*1986*	*1985*
Assets					
Current assets					
Cash	$ 1,000	$ 1,000	$ 1,000	$ 1,000	$ 1,000
Accounts receivable	100,000	90,000	100,000	70,000	60,000
Work in progress	10,000	10,000	10,000	10,000	5,000
Prepaid expenses	1,000	1,000	1,000	1,000	1,000
Total current assets	$ 112,000	$ 102,000	$ 112,000	$ 82,000	$ 67,000
Fixed assets (net)	20,000	22,000	24,000	26,000	28,000
Total assets	**$132,000**	**$124,000**	**$136,000**	**$108,000**	**$95,000**
Liabilities and stockholder's equity					
Current liabilities					
Notes payable	$ 113,500	$ 106,300	$ 117,400	$ 90,350	$ 77,900
Accounts payable	1,900	1,300	2,100	1,400	1,000
Payroll taxes	600	400	500	250	100
Total current liabilities	$ 116,000	$ 108,000	$ 120,000	$ 92,000	$ 79,000
Long-term debt	0	0	0	0	0
Total liabilities	$ 116,000	$ 108,000	$ 120,000	$ 92,000	$ 79,000
Stockholder's equity					
Common stock	$ 10,000	$ 10,000	$ 10,000	$ 10,000	$ 10,000
Retained earnings	6,000	6,000	6,000	6,000	6,000
Total stockholder's equity	$ 16,000	$ 16,000	$ 16,000	$ 16,000	$ 16,000
Total liabilities and stockholder's equity	**$132,000**	**$124,000**	**$136,000**	**$108,000**	**$95,000**

After reviewing the balance sheet at December 31, 1989 (the appraisal date), the following has been determined to be the fair market value of the tangible net assets:

Current assets	$112,000
Fixed assets	35,000
Total assets	$147,000
Total liabilities	116,000
Net assets	$ 31,000

Fixed assets were adjusted to reflect an equipment appraisal that was performed as of the valuation date. The other assets and liabilities did not require adjustment.

The next step in the valuation process is to determine whether or not there is goodwill or other intangible value (this illustration will consider all intangible value to be attributable to goodwill).

In order to determine if there is goodwill value under the excess earnings method, we must first determine the economic income of the law practice. This process is sometimes referred to as "normalizing" the income statement.

During the normalization process, the appraiser reviews the accounting or tax income statement and makes adjustments that are designed to bring this statement in line with what a prospective purchaser might expect the economic income of the business to be.

In *Valuing of the Professional Practice*, William Shulman, CPA, states that it is important to identify perquisites not only because of their effect on the value of the practice but also because they "have a very important impact on the amount of alimony and child support available to the other spouse" (3).

Table 4.3 reflects the normalization process by adjusting those items that this appraiser deemed necessary.

TABLE 4.3

Normalization of Income

	1989	*1988*	*1987*	*1986*	*1985*
Net income (from Table 4-2)	$ 0	$ 0	$ 0	$ 0	$ 0
Adjustments					
Officer's salary[1]	250,000	145,000	235,000	170,000	100,000
Pension[2]	30,000	30,000	30,000	30,000	30,000
Auto expenses[3]	10,250	9,975	9,910	8,425	6,000
Entertainment expenses[4]	30,000	22,000	25,000	22,000	19,000
Adjusted net income	**$320,250**	**$206,975**	**$299,910**	**$230,425**	**$155,000**

[1]Officer's salary was adjusted to remove excessive compensation based on the appraiser's research of salaries in surveys published by the Bar Association. These surveys consider Mr. Lawyer's experience, type of practice, size of firm, and hours worked.

Since Mr. Lawyer paid himself so much more than other attorneys, this adjustment is required. This issue was cited in *Dugan v. Dugan*.

[2]Since pension payments are discretionary and considered part of Mr. Lawyer's compensation, they are added back to reflect normalized net income.

[3]Included in the auto expenses deducted by Mr. Lawyer, PC, are expenses paid for Mr. Lawyer's personal automobiles. These expenses have been added back as an unnecessary and unrelated business expense.

[4]Entertainment was deemed to be excessive by the appraiser and a careful review of these expenses determined that most of these expenses were not client related but rather involved Mr. Lawyer entertaining his secretary.

Now that an adjusted net income has been derived, the next step is to compute the average net income for these years. Generally, a weighted average is calculated that gives a heavier weight to the years closest to the valuation date. Table 4.4 illustrates this calculation.

TABLE 4.4

Calculation of Weighted Average Adjusted Net Income

Year	*Adjusted Net Income*		*Factor*	=	*Extension*
1989	$ 320,250	×	5		$1,601,250
1988	206,975	×	4		827,900
1987	299,910	×	3		899,730
1986	230,425	×	2		460,850
1985	155,000	×	1		155,000
			15		$3,944,730
					÷ 15
Weighted average adjusted net income					$ 262,982

Prior to the capitalization process, the excess earnings approach requires the weighted average adjusted net income to be reduced by a reasonable return on the net tangible assets of the business. The purpose of this step is to allow for the fact that if Mr. Lawyer invested his money in a different type of investment, rather than the net assets of the law firm, he would receive a return. This return should not be considered attributable to goodwill.

The December 31, 1989, balance sheet shows net assets of $16,000. The appraiser has determined that fifteen percent is a reasonable rate of return in this circumstance.

Excess earnings is therefore calculated as follows:

Weighted average adjusted net income	$262,982
Less: Reasonable return on net assets	
$16,000 × 15%	2,400
Excess earnings	$260,582

The final step in the appraisal is the capitalization of excess earnings that determines goodwill value. (Some appraisers also subtract income taxes from the weighted average adjusted net income to determine excess earnings. This would affect the capitalization rate but would not have an effect on the final value.)

In *Dugan v. Dugan*, a multiplier of 3, which equates to a capitalization rate of 33⅓ percent, was used. Using this same capitalization rate, goodwill is calculated as:

$$\$260{,}582 / 33\tfrac{1}{3}\% = \$781{,}746$$

The total value of Mr. Lawyer, PC, can therefore be summarized as follows:

Total assets other than goodwill	$147,000
Goodwill	781,746
Total assets	$928,746
Total liabilities	116,000
Value of law practice	$812,746
Rounded	$800,000

The appraiser has now completed his assignment in accordance with Internal Revenue Ruling 59-60, Internal Revenue Ruling 68-609, and case law.

Now, in accordance with New Jersey Statute 2A:34-23, the judge includes an $800,000 asset with the other marital assets available for equitable distribution.

What is wrong with this scenario? Plenty! The court now determines equitable distribution using the $800,000 value, as well as using the same information to determine alimony and child support. The salary component added back to derive adjusted net income in Table 4-3 is used not only to calculate goodwill, as illustrated above, but it will also be used to determine alimony and/or child support. This double counting is explained below.

4.7 Double Counting

Mrs. Lawyer was involved with the law practice throughout the years and the judge determines that she is entitled to 35 percent of this asset, or $280,000 ($800,000 × 35%). Mrs. Lawyer does not get 35 percent of the corporation's stock; she receives other assets of equal value.

Next, the judge must consider alimony and child support. First he summarizes Mr. Lawyer's income as follows:

Salary (1989)	$450,000
Pension	30,000
Personal auto	10,250
Personal entertainment	30,000
Total	$520,250
Less: Income taxes paid	112,500
Available for support	$407,750

The judge then determines the support that Mr. Lawyer will pay based on income of $407,750.

Depicted above is a slightly overdramatized version of "double counting." This is typical of what takes place in the New Jersey courts. Double counting treats goodwill as marital property subject to equitable distribution and then considers it again as a source of spousal or child support.

These calculations reflect an increased value of a marital asset that the spouse would be entitled to share, as well as receive support from the same income stream that created the asset.

Double counting is improper only if no immediate property division is made and one spouse is ordered to satisfy the other's marital property interest in that property from future receipts. In this case, only the business or professional spouse's remaining interest in those future receipts should be used for support purposes.

Unfortunately, the New Jersey courts have failed to compensate for this double counting, which allows distribution of the marital estate to become terribly inequitable. As previously stated, N.J.S.A. 2A:34-23(b)(9) addresses this issue and states that this point should be considered when awarding alimony and support. More often than not, the business is divided with other assets and the support is added on. This disregards the fact that the business owner has already paid for his "excess earnings."

In order to compensate for this inequity, the courts should consider only the amount of compensation that was allowed as reasonable compensation in the appraisal process. This would eliminate the double counting. The alternative approach would be to allow the full amount of compensation as part of the excess earning computation. This would lower the intangible value of the practice, but could then be considered for support.

In a recent New Jersey Supreme Court case, *Innes v. Innes*, it was found that if a portion of a pension is distributed for equitable distribution, then support cannot be paid from the income stream once the pension reaches pay status.

In essence, court decisions should be the same whether the asset is a pension or a business. This is an inconsistency that penalizes the business owner.

4.8 Determination of Reasonable Compensation

The next problem relates to the determination of reasonable compensation. The appraiser must estimate reasonable compensation for the owner of the business so that a "normal" earnings level is achieved. The courts have required this step as evidenced in *Dugan* and *Levy*. A salary survey was used to determine reasonable compensation for Mr. Lawyer based on his experience, age, etc. If Mr. Lawyer operates his law practice more efficiently and more profitably than his colleagues, shouldn't he be entitled to more compensation?

If a business owner is able to take a salary of $750,000 per year when the norm in the industry is $250,000, he is obviously doing something that makes him worth considerably more. Needless to say, this assumes that he is not bleeding the company just for the sake of being able to draw this big salary.

James Friedman found that most lawyers and judges wrongfully equate high earnings and divisible goodwill and that most highly salaried professionals do not enjoy any more excess compensation than highly salaried non-professionals do (*Journal of the American Academy of Matrimonial Lawyer*, 25–26).

Friedman attacks the excess earnings method and is highly critical of the methods used to determine reasonable compensation. He states:

> In calculating excess compensation, you must first deduct fair compensation for the individual whose practice you are valuing. The more valuable that individual's contribution, the higher will be the compensation entitlement, or "replacement costs" (ibid.).

Reasonable compensation has continuously presented difficulties for the appraiser and is a much-disputed issue. Pratt points out that "larger companies are more likely to remunerate owners at something near a market rate of compensation, while small companies tend to pay owners what they can afford, which may be above or below a market rate" (*Valuing Small Businesses and Professional Practices*, 29). Friedman goes as far as to state that "the hard working, highly skilled specialist probably earns his or her total compensation and derives little excess from the enterprise" (*Journal of the American Academy of Matrimonial Lawyer*, 25–26).

4.9 Divorce Value—A Better Approach

Since small, closely held businesses are unlike most other marital assets, a new valuation concept should be considered for equitable distribution purposes. I call this "divorce value."

The divorce value of a small, closely held business is determined by how much that business is worth to the existing owner. This must be based on the performance of the business as operated by the owner, including such factors as current compensation, perquisites, cash flow, and ability to have the business support debt service. It does not assume a hypothetical buyer or seller, nor does it consider a hypothetical transfer using an investment value approach. When using this approach, the owner of the business is compensated in the manner which the historical results of the business reflect. The rationale employed is that a small business owner will compensate him- or herself similarly to another small business owner. This compensation may be higher or lower than the average compensation found in surveys, but the entrepreneur does not generally concern him- or herself with this type of detail.

Small businesses are generally sold as an asset sale rather than a stock sale. Specific assets are sold that are essential to the conduct of the business and those assets that are unrelated to the actual business activity are kept by the seller (e.g., cash, marketable securities).

The determination of value between the buyer and the seller is generally based on how much debt the business can service after deducting normal compensation. The purchaser of the business will generally use the cash flow of the business to pay off this newly acquired debt with the attitude that he or she is sacrificing additional compensation during the payback period.

Although the payback period has been known to vary, a period of two to five years is commonly used. This has been supported by many citings within the case law as well as in published materials such as *The Capital Budgeting Decision* (34) and "What Do Venture Capital 'Pricing' Methods Tell About Valuation of Closely Held Firms?" (*Business Valuation Review*, 73–79).

Another manner in which payback can be measured is by the required rate of return that a purchaser requires. Generally, the higher the rate of return, the shorter the payback period required by the purchaser.

Summarizing a report prepared by QED Research Inc., Bradley Fowler provides a table indicating a range from 30 percent to 75 percent as the required rate of return for closely held businesses depending on the status of the company, ranging from the well-seasoned company about to go public to the company in its startup stage (ibid.).

Although businesses dealing with venture capital firms tend to be larger than the small, closely held business, the required rate of return would be indicative of the excess risk associated with the small business and would, therefore, be higher. Even a well-seasoned small company can be risky due to its size, marketplace, and inability to raise capital needed for expansion.

Divorce value is intended to remove the inequities from the valuation process relative to the appraisal. This will be demonstrated shortly by illustrating how divorce value compares to the value derived under the traditional approach. It is not meant to create a new appraisal technique but merely to assist the courts to derive a value that is more equitable to both parties to the divorce.

Previously, a one-sided example of a law practice was used to exaggerate the problems that exist with the court-accepted excess earnings method. Now, let's illustrate how the tables may be turned against the non-owner spouse in the valuation of a small business. Using the excess earnings method will result in an inequity to the non-owner spouse, whereas divorce value will result in the achievement of fairness. In order to demonstrate how divorce value works, we will use the example of Mark's Hardware Store.

This business has been in existence for 17 years. Mark is presently going through a divorce. The New Jersey court understands the excess earnings method of appraisal, and as a result the appraiser uses this method. The company's balance sheet for the last five years is presented in Table 4.5.

TABLE 4.5
Mark's Hardware Store
Balance Sheet Comparison
December 31,

	1989	*1988*	*1987*	*1986*	*1985*
Assets					
Current assets					
Cash & equivalents	$ 3,200	$ 5,000	$ 800	$ 1,200	$ 1,000
Net accounts receivable	19,000	16,000	27,000	12,000	6,700
Notes receivable	8,000	5,000	1,000	1,000	1,000
Prepaid expenses	1,400	1,825	1,575	1,550	1,200
Inventory	87,000	84,000	75,000	90,000	88,000
Total current assets	$ 118,600	$ 111,825	$ 105,375	$ 105,750	$ 97,900
Fixed assets					
Furniture & fixtures	$ 17,500	$ 15,000	$ 15,000	$ 14,000	$ 14,000
M & E	3,000	3,000	3,000	3,000	3,000
Leasehold improvements	18,500	18,500	18,500	18,500	18,500
Accumulated depreciation	(36,600)	(35,500)	(34,900)	(34,300)	(33,900)
Net fixed assets	$ 2,400	$ 1,000	$ 1,600	$ 1,200	$ 1,600
Other non-current assets					
Deposits	$ 1,000	$ 1,000	$ 1,000	$ 1,000	$ 1,000
Non-operating assets					
Cash value life insurance	55,000	52,000	49,500	48,000	47,000
Total other assets	$ 56,000	$ 53,000	$ 50,500	$ 49,000	$ 48,000
Total assets	**$ 177,000**	**$ 165,825**	**$ 157,475**	**$ 155,950**	**$ 147,500**

	1989	1988	1987	1986	1985
Liabilities & equity					
Current liabilities					
Accounts payable	$ 84,875	$ 74,360	$ 78,350	$ 67,130	$ 63,500
Notes payable	6,700	5,800	5,000	4,200	3,400
Payroll tax payable	1,800	3,000	900	1,200	1,000
Sales tax payable	2,950	2,890	2,450	2,345	2,225
Total current liabilities	$ 96,325	$ 86,050	$ 86,700	$ 74,875	$ 70,125
Long-term liabilities					
Notes payable	$ 43,300	$ 49,200	$ 55,000	$ 63,300	$ 71,600
Non-operating liabilities	35,000	35,000	35,000	35,000	35,000
Total long-term liabilities	$ 78,300	$ 84,200	$ 90,000	$ 98,300	$ 106,600
Total liabilities	$ 174,625	$ 170,250	$ 176,700	$ 173,175	$ 176,725
Equity					
Common stock	$ 1,000	$ 1,000	$ 1,000	$ 1,000	$ 1,000
Retained earnings	1,375	(5,425)	(20,225)	(18,225)	(30,225)
Total equity	$ 2,375	$ (4,425)	$ (19,225)	$ (17,225)	$ (29,225)
Total liabilities and stockholder's equity	**$ 177,000**	**$ 165,825**	**$ 157,475**	**$ 155,950**	**$ 147,500**

Income statements for the same five-year period are presented in Table 4.6.

TABLE 4.6

Mark's Hardware Store
Income Statement Comparison
for the Years Ended December 31,

	1989	1988	1987	1986	1985
Sales	$ 508,000	$ 490,000	$ 487,000	$ 510,000	$ 500,000
Less: Cost of sales	320,830	310,687	310,735	340,680	336,825
Gross profit	$ 187,170	$ 179,313	$ 176,265	$ 169,320	$ 163,175
Expenses					
Advertising	$ 4,175	$ 4,300	$ 3,200	$ 3,825	$ 3,600
Auto and truck	2,800	3,000	2,475	2,200	1,980
Depreciation	1,100	600	600	400	400
Dues and subscriptions	600	575	525	480	500
Fees—professional	3,000	2,500	2,000	1,500	1,000
Insurance—life	2,500	2,000	2,000	2,000	2,000
Insurance—other	4,200	4,500	4,000	3,600	2,500
Interest	4,900	5,800	6,325	6,800	190
Office expense	4,300	4,225	2,725	2,000	3,000
Rent	22,725	21,438	20,225	19,080	18,000
Salary—officer	28,000	25,000	24,000	22,000	25,000
Salary—others	80,500	78,800	76,890	80,225	78,500
Taxes—payroll	12,570	13,125	10,500	11,225	10,655
Utilities	9,000	8,450	6,000	7,500	3,850
Miscellaneous	.0	0	0	8,485	0
Total operating expenses	$ 180,370	$ 174,313	$ 161,465	$ 171,320	$ 151,175
Net income	$ 6,800	$ 5,000	$ 14,800	$ (2,000)	$ 12,000

A typical excess earnings valuation is illustrated in Tables 4.7 through 4.9.

TABLE 4.7

Mark's Hardware Store
Tangible Asset Analysis

	Book Value 12/89	Adjustments and Elimination	Adjusted Book Value 12/89	Liquidation Discount	Liquidation Value 12/89
Assets					
Current assets					
Cash & equivalents	$ 3,200	$ 0	$ 3,200	0%	$ 3,200
Net accounts receivable	19,000	(1,500)	17,500	10%	15,750
Notes receivable	8,000	(8,000)	0	0%	0
Prepaid expenses	1,400	0	1,400	0%	1,400
Inventory	87,000	10,000	97,000	25%	72,750
Total current assets	$ 118,600	$ 500	$ 119,100		$ 93,100
Fixed assets					
Furniture & fixtures	$ 17,500	$ (10,000)	$ 7,500	40%	$ 4,500
M & E	3,000	(2,000)	1,000	30%	700
Leasehold	18,500	(18,500)	0	0%	0
Accumulated depreciation	(36,600)	36,600	0	0%	0
Net fixed assets	$ 2,400	$ 6,100	$ 8,500		$ 5,200
Other non-current assets					
Deposits	$ 1,000	$ 0	$ 1,000	0%	$ 1,000
Non-operating assets					
Cash value life insurance	55,000	0	55,000	0%	55,000
Total other assets	$ 56,000	$ 0	$ 56,000		$ 56,000
Total assets	**$ 177,000**	**$ 6,600**	**$ 183,600**		**$ 154,300**
Liabilities and equity					
Current liabilities					
Accounts payable	$ 84,875	$ 0	$ 84,875	0%	$ 84,875
Notes payable	6,700	0	6,700	0%	6,700
Payroll tax payable	1,800	0	1,800	0%	1,800
Sales tax payable	2,950	0	2,950	0%	2,950
Total current liabilities	$ 96,325	$ 0	$ 96,325		$ 96,325
Long-term liabilities					
Notes payable	$ 43,300	$ 0	$ 43,300	0%	$ 43,300
Non-operating liabilities	35,000	0	35,000	0%	35,000
Total long-term liabilities	$ 78,300	$ 0	$ 78,300		$ 78,300
Total liabilities	$ 174,625	$ 0	$ 174,625		$ 174,625
Equity					
Adjusted for valuation	$ 0	$ 6,600	$ 6,600		$ (20,325)
Common stock	1,000	0	1,000		0
Retained earnings	1,375	0	1,375		0
Total equity	$ 2,375	$ 6,600	$ 8,975		$ (20,325)
Total liabilities and stockholder's equity	**$ 177,000**	**$ 6,600**	**$ 183,600**		**$ 154,300**

In Table 4.7, the appraiser has performed two important steps in the valuation process. The first step was to adjust the historical balance sheet at the valuation date to current value. These values are reflected in the column titled "Adjusted Book Value." This analysis results in the current value of the net tangible assets being reflected as $8,975.

The second step in the valuation process was to determine the liquidation value of Mark's Hardware Store. All valuations should include a test of the liquidation value of the business (Institute of Business Appraisers, Inc.). This value is generally used by the appraiser to determine the lowest value of the business. Mark's Hardware Store has a liquidation value of ($20,325). This means that if the business is liquidated, there are not enough assets to satisfy the debts of the business.

Table 4.8 illustrates the normalization of earnings used to derive the economic income of the business. The historical income statements are adjusted to reflect reasonable compensation for Mark. Mark's salary was based on what he felt he could afford rather than the normal level of compensation reported in the annual survey from his trade association. This is quite common for these types of businesses. Since Mark's salary was below the amount considered reasonable, an adjustment is made by the appraiser deducting the unpaid compensation. Since life insurance premiums are considered to be a perquisite, the amounts deducted have been added back to derive the adjusted net income.

TABLE 4.8

Mark's Hardware Store
Adjusted Net Income
for the Years Ended December 31,

	1989	*1988*	*1987*	*1986*	*1985*
Total revenue	$ 508,000	$ 490,000	$ 487,000	$ 510,000	$ 500,000
Cost of sales	320,830	310,687	310,735	340,680	336,825
Gross profit	$ 187,170	$ 179,313	$ 176,265	$ 169,320	$ 163,175
Operating expenses	$ 174,370	$ 167,913	$ 154,540	$ 164,120	$ 150,585
Depreciation	1,100	600	600	400	400
Interest	4,900	5,800	6,325	6,800	190
Total expenses	$ 180,370	$ 174,313	$ 161,465	$ 171,320	$ 151,175
Net income	$ 6,800	$ 5,000	$ 14,800	$ (2,000)	$ 12,000
Adjustments					
Officers' compensation	$ (7,000)	$ (10,000)	$ (9,000)	$ (8,000)	$ (2,000)
Life insurance	2,500	2,000	2,000	2,000	2,000
Total adjustments	$ (4,500)	$ (8,000)	$ (7,000)	$ (6,000)	$ 0
Adjusted net income	**$ 2,300**	**$ (3,000)**	**$ 7,800**	**$ (8,000)**	**$ 12,000**

In accordance with Internal Revenue Ruling 68-609, the appraiser must now deduct a return on the net assets of the business in order to determine the excess earnings available for capitalization. This is reflected in Table 4.9.

TABLE 4.9

Mark's Hardware Store
Capitalization of Earnings
for the Years Ended December 31,

	1989	1988	1987	1986	1985
Adjusted net income	$2,300	$(3,000)	$7,800	$(8,000)	$12,000
Less: Return on net assets*	0	0	0	0	0
Excess earnings	$2,000	$(3,000)	$7,800	$(8,000)	$12,000

*Net assets are negative for each year. This computation excludes the non-operating assets and liabilities of the business.

Weighting:

	Earnings	×	Factor	=	Extension
December 1989	$ 2,300	×	1		$ 2,300
December 1988	(3,000)	×	1		(3,000)
December 1987	7,800	×	1		7,800
December 1986	(8,000)	×	1		(8,000)
December 1985	12,000	×	1		12,000
			5		
Aggregate extension					$ 11,100
Divided by total factor					÷ 5
Weighted average earnings					$ 2,220
Capitalization rate (divided by)					33.33%
Intangible value					$ 6,660
Adjusted book value					8,975
Total fair market value					$ 15,635

The appraiser found that the return on the net assets of the business would be $0 since Mark's Hardware Store has more liabilities than assets. A negative return would be meaningless.

The average excess earnings is calculated in Table 4.9 by using a simple average since the annual excess earnings are unstable. This average is capitalized by a rate determined by the appraiser after performing a thorough risk analysis with ratios and graphs.

The intangible value of Mark's Hardware Store was determined to be $6,660. The adjusted book value of $8,975 is added to the intangible value of the business, resulting in the total value of Mark's Hardware Store being $15,635. The judge then uses this amount to award equitable distribution to Mark's wife. This award is normally between 25 percent and 40 percent of $15,635.

Now that the excess earnings calculation has been computed, additional computations need to be performed to reflect the divorce value of this business: the value of the business to the owner.

What is the likelihood of Mark selling his business for almost half of his annual earnings? This probably would not happen. Mark's salary in 1989 was $28,000 while the resulting value was only $15,635. He might as well continue to work the business, as he would see more of a financial benefit and would not have to work for someone else.

What is the value of the business to Mark? It is the amount that he could actually sell the business for under the terms and conditions that are typical for a small business. Although in concept this appears to be fair market value, it is not. This value would not be representative of a cash equivalent since terms will create the deal. Other elements of fair market value would also be missing.

Assuming that Mark was going to sell his business, he would require a down payment of approximately 25 percent and would be required to hold paper in order to consummate the transaction. The buyer, on the other hand, not only requires Mark to finance the transaction, but also requires the business cash flow to cover this debt. This is illustrated in Table 4.10.

The calculations performed in Table 4.10 represent a reasonable transaction. This business would be worth $66,640 to a potential purchaser. This would also be more reflective of the true value of the business to the owner.

TABLE 4.10

Sale of Mark's Hardware Store

	1989	*1988*	*1987*	*1986*	*1985*
Net income	$ 6,800	$ 5,000	$ 14,800	$(2,000)	$ 12,000
Add: Interest expense	4,900	5,800	6,325	6,800	190
Debt-free net income	$ 11,700	$ 10,800	$ 21,125	$ 4,800	$ 12,190
Add: Depreciation	1,100	600	600	400	400
Cash flow	$ 12,800	$ 11,400	$ 21,725	$ 5,200	$ 12,590

Weighting:

	Cash Flow	*3*	*Factor*	=	*Extension*	
1989	$12,800	×	1		$ 12,800	
1988	11,400	×	1		11,400	
1987	21,725	×	1		21,725	
1986	5,200	×	1		5,200	
1985	12,590	×	1		12,590	
			5			
Aggregate extension					$ 63,715	
Divided by total factor					÷ 5	
Weighted average cash flow					$ 12,743	
Monthly cash flow					$ 1,061.92	
Debt 5 years 10% per annum					$ 49,980	(75%)
Down payment					$ 16,660	(25%)
Total Sales Price					$ 66,640	

The divorce value of this business would be $49,980, the total debt service that is available as a result of the business cash flow. Since a transaction will not take place, the down payment should not be included.

The non-business owner spouse would then be entitled to 50 percent of the $49,980 or $24,990. This equates to 37.5 percent of the total sale price.

New Jersey case law has generally provided the non-business owner spouse with anywhere from 25 percent to 40 percent of the fair market value as determined by the experts. Of course, there have also been awards under equitable distribution of more or less than this amount.

The divorce value award of 50 percent would fix the amount that the non-business owner spouse would be entitled to and remove the arbitrary allocations that currently take place. While many judges are concerned with the notion of fairness, the allocation used by the courts is frequently subjective. It is not uncommon to see a judge allocate a percentage of the business that will equal the equity in the marital home. The divorce value approach would eliminate this subjectivity.

In addition to the value of the income stream, Mark's Hardware Store also owns assets and liabilities that would not be part of a sales transaction, such as cash, receivables, payables, etc. The furniture and fixtures, machinery and equipment, and leasehold improvements would be sold since these assets are necessary to generate the income stream. All other assets and liabilities must now be added to the divorce value in order to determine the final amount subject to equitable distribution. In this case, the following items would be added:

Current assets	$119,000
Other assets	56,000
Total assets	$175,000
Total liabilities	174,625
Net assets	$ 375

Unless other marital assets could be used to offset this additional value, the payout time would have to be extended to allow these net assets to be paid for from the business cash flow.

Now that the "divorce value" technique has been demonstrated, we can look back at Mr. Lawyer's practice, which would have an insignificant cash flow amounting to the depreciation expense included in the computation of net income. This would result in a negligible amount of value. The net assets of $31,000 would approximate the value of the practice. Since Mr. Lawyer would not be required to pay much equitable distribution, he will have a great ability to pay alimony or support. This situation is the opposite of Mark's Hardware Store, where support would be lower but equitable distribution would be greater.

After the proper amount is determined for equitable distribution, the judge could then award alimony and/or child support based on the actual compensation of the business owner, eliminating double counting. This would result in a more "equitable" division of the marital estate. This is not a new idea, however, since N.J.S.A. 2A:34-23(b)(9) tells the court to consider these facts.

The value derived does not have the elements of fair market value since an adjustment for reasonable compensation is not made. The market value of the business would generally consider the amount of compensation a new owner could draw from the business, as well as the ability to service debt that would result from the acquisition. Instead, the result is the achievement of the value of the business to its owner. This value will have an effect on ability to pay alimony and/or child support. If fair market value was the value concept used, alimony and child support would be less dependent on the computation of the value of the business.

5 Replies to Opposition

There is no doubt that the "divorce value" concept will experience opposition. The New Jersey courts have relied upon the United States Treasury Department as demonstrated by its strong adaptation of the use of Internal Revenue Ruling 59-60 and Internal Revenue Ruling 68-609.

The judicial process is one that does not change quickly or easily. The trial judge knows that when a decision is reached that violates precedent, one side to the litigation will take the matter to the appellate court. Even if the new concept finds its way through the appellate court, it is conceivable that the party that feels that they have been wronged will request that the New Jersey Supreme Court rule on the issue.

The judicial system has been provided with a formula that can be used to value the subject business, and after years of applying this formula, there appears to be little reason to change, but precedent must be overcome. Many judicial opinions recognize that there are other appraisal methods available. Since judges are not appraisers, they rely on experts to provide them with the facts necessary for them to decide upon the issues. Most of the experts used in divorce proceedings are accountants and not appraisers. The accountants are tax oriented with very little training or experience with appraisal theory. The accountant is trained to understand the tax laws. Since the Internal Revenue Service is related to the Revenue Rulings cited, change will be resisted.

The double-counting issue may be opposed by those advocates who primarily represent non-business owner spouses in matrimonial litigation. Their argument will be that the ability of the business owner to earn large sums of money is an integral part of the value of the business. Equitable distribution only takes place once. Spousal or dependent support, on the other hand, is required in order to provide for the displaced family unit.

The opponent will argue that since alimony and equitable distribution are so interrelated, a separation cannot be adequately performed without having an effect on the other item. This will most likely force the court to compensate by adjusting these items up or down as required to obtain the end result.

Reasonable compensation certainly has an effect on the calculation of fair market value, and opponents of divorce value would be expected to argue that too much room for manipulation exists if reasonable compensation is not used in the determination of value. The owner of a small, closely held business or professional practice has the ability to set the level of compensation at an amount that could negate profits and substantially reduce the value of the business.

Fair market value is the value concept most often used in the field of appraisal. It is supposed to reflect that which exists in the market. Appraisals are market driven, and opponents could argue that this is the value concept that has been used since the inception of the appraisal process. Valuing some assets at fair market value and others at divorce value would be inconsistent and as a result should not be done.

The final argument that I would anticipate is that using cash flow to determine the amount of debt that the business could support does not take into consideration other forms of debt, capital expenditures, and future working capital required by the business.

6 Summary and Conclusion

The previous chapters of this paper have taken us through the creation of the New Jersey equitable distribution case law and the valuation precedent that has transpired over the years. You now know that the small, closely held businesses discussed are marital assets that need to be valued. By now, you should also be aware of the problems that have been created by the results of the leading cases.

Reiterating the points made in this paper:

1. Fair market value is the incorrect value concept to be used for valuing small, closely held businesses for divorce purposes.
2. The imprecision of the language of N.J.S.A. 2A:34-23, as well as the business valuation practice of appraisers allowed to testify in the courts, have created precedent using incorrect appraisal methodology, resulting in an unfair equitable distribution of business assets.
3. Appraisal principles are being ignored in matrimonial appraisals of these businesses.
4. The excess earnings method of appraisal, although convenient, should not be used because the result frequently is unfair to one of the parties to the divorce.
5. Double counting can be eliminated if the same compensation is used to value the business and determine support.
6. Reasonable compensation is unique to the business owner based on his or her abilities and should not be adjusted due to a survey.
7. Divorce value more appropriately reflects the value of the business in the hands of the current owner regardless of what the business is worth to someone else.

Divorce value is defined as the value of the business to the current owner when the elements of fair market value are not present and when equitable distribution is to be effectuated in accordance with New Jersey

Statute 2A:34-23. Implicit in this definition is that the value will be based on the actual benefits derived by the owner and that those benefits will be used to determine the amount of alimony and child support.

Over the years, the New Jersey courts have allowed case law to develop that has and continues to create controversy and much litigation. Valuation techniques that result in what has been called the fair market value of a business have then been used by the court to manipulate equitable distribution and support. The courts have become too comfortable with the excess earnings approach, and due to the lack of understanding of not only the attorneys and judges but also the "experts" using this technique, poor precedent has evolved.

Valuing a business for equitable distribution is unlike valuing a business for most other purposes. Since market information is limited, these small, closely held businesses and professional practices have been valued without regard to the ability to pay the required sums that result from the enterprise. This frequently creates undue strain on the business owner to make these payments.

The New Jersey courts must redirect their thinking to help compensate for the many deficiencies that exist in the application of a formula approach that includes double counting, questionable determination of reasonable compensation, and a value that is based on so many assumptions that it would be impossible to achieve.

I feel that the courts must allow small businesses and professional practices to be valued using an approach that is more appropriate for divorce litigation. Based on the inequities that can be circumvented, I believe the value concept should be changed to "divorce value."

Works Cited and Consulted

American Institute of Real Estate Appraisers, *The Appraisal of Real Estate*, 9th ed., Chicago, 1987.

Amling, Frederick, *Investments, An Introduction to Analysis and Management*, 6th ed., Prentice Hall, Englewood Cliffs, N.J., 1989.

Brown, Ronald L., editor, *Valuing Professional Practices and Licenses: A Guide for the Matrimonial Practitioner*, Prentice Hall Law & Business, Clifton, N.J., 1987.

Daly v. Daly, 179 N.J. Super. 1981.

Desmond, Glenn M., and Kelley, Richard E., *Business Valuation Handbook*, Valuation Press, Los Angeles, 1977.

Dugan v. Dugan, 92 N.J. 423 (N.J. Supreme Court 1983).

Friedman, James T., "Professional Practice Goodwill: An Abused Concept," *Journal of the American Academy of Matrimonial Lawyers*, 1986.

Goldberg, Barth H., *Valuation of Divorce Assets*, West Publishing Co., St. Paul, Minn., 1988.

The Institute of Business Appraisers, Seminar, "Business Valuation for Accountants," 1986.

Kikkert v. Kikkert, 88 N.J. 4, 1981.

Lavene v. Lavene, 162 N.J. Super. 1987 (App. Div. 1978).

Levy v. Levy, 164 N.J. Super. 1978.

Mendell v. Mendell, 162 N.J. Super. 469, 475–476 (App. Div. 1978).

Miles, Raymond C., *Basic Business Appraisal*, John Wiley & Sons, New York, 1984.

Office of the Clerk, "The Supreme Court of New Jersey." *Judicial Opinion of Justice Garibaldi in Innes v. Innes*, decided January 17, 1990.

Painter v. Painter, 65 N.J. Supreme Court 1974.

Piscopo v. Piscopo, 231 N.J. Super. 576 (Ch. Div. 1988).

Piscopo v. Piscopo, 232 N.J. Super. 559 (App. Div. 1989).

Pratt, Shannon, *Valuing a Business*, 2nd ed., Dow Jones–Irwin, Homewood, Ill., 1989.

Pratt, Shannon, *Valuing Small Businesses and Professional Practices*. Dow Jones–Irwin, Homewood, Ill., 1986.

Rickert, Richard, *Appraisal and Valuation: An Interdisciplinary Approach*, American Society of Appraisers, Washington, D.C., 1987, Chapter 3.

Rothman v. Rothman, 65 N.J. Supreme Court 1974.

Rutken, Arnold H., "Valuation of a Closely Held Corporation, Small Business or Professional Practice," in *Valuation and Distribution of Marital Property*, Matthew Bender & Co., New York, 1990, vol 2.

Skoloff, Gary N., and Cutler, Lawrence J., *New Jersey Family Law Practice*, 6th ed., New Jersey Institute for Continuing Legal Education, New Brunswick, 1990.

Skoloff, Gary N., and Orenstein, Theodore P., *When a Lawyer Divorces: How to Value a Professional Practice, How to Get Extraordinary Remedies*, American Bar Association, Chicago, 1986.

Smith v. Smith, 72 N.J. Supreme Court 1977.

Stern v. Stern, 66 N.J. Super. 1975.

Stout v. Stout, 155 N.J. Super. 1977.

Tierney, Joseph E., Jr., "A New Approach to the Valuation of Common Stock of Closely Held Companies," *Journal of Taxation*, July 1962.

United States Treasury Department, Internal Revenue Ruling 59-60, C.B. 1959-1, 237, Washington, D.C.

United States Treasury Department, Internal Revenue Ruling 68-609, C.B. 1968-2, 327–328, Washington, D.C.

Appendix 19 *Business Valuation Resources*

Books, Periodicals, and More

Abrams, Jay B. "Discount for Lack of Marketability: A Theoretical Model." *Business Valuation Review* (September 1994), 132–139.

Agiato, Joseph A., and Thomas L. Johnston. "The Relationship Between the Earnings Yield and the Cash Flow Yield." *CPA Expert* (Winter 1996), 6–9.

Alerding, James R. *Valuation of a Closely Held Business*. New York: Research Institute of America, 1996.

Alico, John, ed. *Appraising Machinery and Equipment*. Herndon, Va.: American Society of Appraisers, 1989.

Almanac of Business and Industrial Financial Ratios. Englewood Cliffs, N.J.: Prentice Hall, annual.

Annin, Michael. "Using Ibbotson Associates' Data to Develop Minority Discount Rates." *CPA Expert* (Winter 1997), 1–4.

Annin, Michael E., and Dominic A. Falaschetti. "Equity Risk Premium Still Produces Debate." *Valuation Strategies* (January/February 1998), 17–19, 44.

The Appraisal of Real Estate, 11th ed. Chicago: Appraisal Institute, 1996.

Arneson, George S. "Nonmarketability Discounts Should Exceed Fifty Percent." *Taxes* (January 1981), 25–31.

Aschwald, Kathryn. "Restricted Stock Discounts Decline as a Result of 1-Year Holding Period." *Shannon Pratt's Business Valuation Update* (May 2000), 1–3.

Asset Business Appraisal. *BizComps*. San Diego: Asset Business Appraisal, annual (four separate editions: Western, Eastern, Central, and National Industrial).

Barron, Michael S. "When Will the Tax Court Allow a Discount for Lack of Marketability?" *Journal of Taxation* (January 1997), 46–50.

Bernstein, Leopold A. *Analysis of Financial Statements*, 5th ed. New York: McGraw-Hill, 1999.

Bernstein, Leopold A. *Financial Statement Analysis: Theory, Application, and Interpretation*, 6th ed. New York: McGraw-Hill, 1997.

Bishop, David M. "Excess Earnings Cap Rate: Six Market Influences." *Business Appraisal Practice* (Winter 1999), 409.

Blackman, Irwin L. *Valuing the Privately-Held Business: The Art & Science of Establishing a Company's Worth*. Chicago: Probus Publishing Co., 1992.

Bolotsky, Michael J. "Adjustments for Differences in Ownership Rights, Liquidity, Information Access, and Information Reliability: An Assessment of 'Prevailing Wisdom' Versus the 'Nath Hypotheses.'" *Business Valuation Review* (September 1991), 94–110.

Brealey, Richard A., and Stewart C. Myers. *Principles of Corporate Finance*, 5th ed. New York: McGraw-Hill, 1996.

Business Valuation Review. Denver: American Society of Appraisers, quarterly.

Chaffe, David B.H., III. "Option Pricing as a Proxy for Discount for Lack of Marketability in Private Company Valuations." *Business Valuation Review* (December 1993), 182–188.

Copeland, Tom, Tim Killer, and Jack Murrin. *Valuation: Measuring and Managing the Value of Companies*, 2nd ed. New York: John Wiley & Sons, 1994.

Cornell, Bradford. *Corporate Valuation: Tools for Effective Appraisal and Decision Making*. Burr Ridge, Ill.: Irwin Professional Publishing, 1993.

CPA Expert. Jersey City, N.J.: AICPA, quarterly.

Crow, Matthew R. "Discounts and Family Limited Partnerships Holding Only Marketable Securities." *CPA Litigation Service Counselor* (May 1999), 9–12.

Damodaran, Aswath. *Damodaran on Valuation: Security Analysis for Investment and Corporate Finance*. New York: John Wiley & Sons, 1994.

Desmond, Glenn M. *Handbook of Small Business Valuation Formulas*. Los Angeles: Valuation Press, 1993.

Desmond, Glenn M., and Richard E. Kelley. *Business Valuation Handbook*. Marina Del Ray, Calif.: Valuation Press, 1977.

Dewing, A.S. *The Financial Policy of Corporations*. New York: Ronald Press Co., 1953.

Emory, John D. "The Value of Marketability as Illustrated in Initial Public Offerings of Common Stock—January 1994 through June 1995." *Business Valuation Review* (December 1995), 155–160.

Emory, John D. "The Value of Marketability as Illustrated in Initial Public Offerings of Common Stock—November 1995 through April 1997." *Business Valuation Review* (September 1997), 3–7.

Emory, John D., Sr., F.R. Dengel III, and John D. Emory, Jr. "The Value of Marketability as Illustrated in Initial Public Offerings of Common Stock—May 1997 through December 2000," *Business Valuation Review* (September 2001), 15–19.

Encyclopedia of Associations. Detroit: Gale Research, annual.

Evans, Frank C. "Making Sense of Rates of Return and Multiples." *Business Valuation Review* (June 1999), 51–57.

Executive Compensation Assessor. Redmond, Wash.: Economic Research Institute, quarterly (www.erieri.com).

Executive Compensation: Survey Results. New York: National Association of Business Management, annual.

Fair$hare: The Matrimonial Law Monthly, monthly. Aspen Law & Business, 7201 McKinney Circle, Frederick, MD 21704, (800) 638-8437 (www.aspenpublishers.com).

Family Advocate, quarterly. American Bar Association, P.O. Box 10892, Chicago, IL 60610-0892, (312) 988-5522 (www.abanet.org/family/advocate/home.html).

Feder, Robert D. *Valuation Strategies in Divorce*. New York: Aspen Law & Business, annual.

Federal Reserve Bulletin. Washington, D.C.: Board of Governors of the Federal Reserve System, monthly.

Financial Research Associates. *Financial Studies of the Small Business*. Winter Haven, Fla.: Financial Research Associates, annual.

Fishman, Jay E., Shannon P. Pratt, J. Clifford Griffiths, and D. Keith Wilson. *Guide to Business Valuations*. Fort Worth, Tex: Practitioners Publishing Co., annual.

Gale Research. *Business Organizations, Agencies, and Publications Directory*, 8th ed. Detroit: Gale Research, 1996.

Gale Research. *Encyclopedia of Business Information Sources, 1997–98*. Detroit: Gale Research, 1996.

Goldberg, Barth H. *Valuation of Divorce Assets*. St. Paul: West Publishing Company, 1984.

Goldberg, Barth H., and Joseph N. DuCanto. *Valuation of Divorce Assets*, 1994 supplement. St. Paul: West Publishing Company, 1994.

Grabowski, Roger, and David King. "New Evidence on Equity Returns and Company Risk." *Business Valuation Review* (September 1999), 112–130.

Grabowski, Roger, and David King. "New Evidence on Equity Returns and Company Risk: A Revision." *Business Valuation Review* (March 2000), 32–43.

Grabowski, Roger, and David King. "New Evidence on Size Effects and Rates of Return." *Business Valuation Review* (September 1996), 103–114.

Hall, Lance S., and Timothy C. Polacek. "Strategies for Obtaining the Largest Valuation Discounts." *Estate Planning* (January/February 1994), 38–44.

Hamilton, Janet. "Marketability Discounts in the Courts, 1991–1996." *Shannon Pratt's Business Valuation Update* (March 1997), special report.

Hawkins, George B., and Michael A. Paschall. *CCH Business Valuation Guide*. Chicago: CCH, Inc., 1999.

The Hay Report: Compensation & Benefits. Philadelphia: Center for Management Research, annual.

Hayes, John W., and Scott D. Miller. "Marketability Issues in the Valuation of ESOPs." *CPA Expert* (Summer 1996), 7–11.

Hillstrom, Kevin, ed. *Encyclopedia of American Industries* (2 vols.), 2nd ed. Detroit: Gale Research, 1998.

Hitchner, James R. "Tax Court Reviews Nine Factors for Selecting Marketability Discounts." *CPA Expert*, (Winter 1996), 11–13.

Horvath, James L. *Valuing Professional Practices*. Don Mills, Ontario: CCH International, 1990.

Houlihan Howard Lokey & Zukin. *Mergerstat Review*. Los Angeles: annual.

Howitt, Idelle A., and Susan E. Schechter. *Federal Tax Valuation Digest*. Boston: Warren Gorham & Lamont, annual.

Ibbotson Associates. *Cost of Capital Quarterly*. Chicago: Ibbotson Associates, annual.

Ibbotson Associates. *Stocks, Bonds, Bills and Inflation*. Chicago: Ibbotson Associates, annual.

Industry Norms and Key Business Ratios. New York: Dun & Bradstreet, annual.

Internal Revenue Service. *Corporation Source Book: Statistics of Income*; *Partnership Source Book: Statistics of Income*; and *Sole Proprietorship Source Book: Statistics of Income*. Washington, D.C.: Government Printing Office, annual.

Internal Revenue Service. *Source Book Statistics of Income*. Washington, D.C.: Internal Revenue Service, annual.

IRS Valuation Guide For Income, Estate and Gift Taxes. Chicago: Commerce Clearing House, 1994.

IRS Valuation Training for Appeals Officers. Chicago: Commerce Clearing House, 1998.

Johnson, Bruce A., and Jeffferies, Spencer J., *Comprehensive Guide for the Valuation of Family Limited Partnerships*, Dallas, Tex.: Partnership Profiles, 2001.

Julius, J. Michael. "Market Returns in Rolling Multi-year Holding Periods: An Alternative Interpretation of the Ibbotson Data." *Business Valuation Review* (June 1996), 57–71.

Kaplan, Paul D. "Why the Expected Rate of Return Is an Arithmetic Mean." *Business Valuation Review* (September 1995), 126–129.

Kenny, Thomas J. "Closely Held Corporation Valuation: Determining a Proper Discount Rate." *Business Valuation Review* (March 1992), 22–30.

King, David W. "Recent Evidence on Discount Rates." *Proceedings of the AICPA 1995 National Business Valuation Conference*, New Orleans. December 1995, 12-i–12-13.

Kleeman, Robert E., Jr., ed. *Valuation Strategies in Divorce*, 2nd ed. New York: John Wiley & Sons, 1992.

Kleeman, Robert E., Jr., R. James Alerding, and Benjamin D. Miller. *The Handbook for Divorce Valuations*. New York: John Wiley & Sons, 1999.

Lang, Eva M., and Tudor, Jan D. *The Best Websites for Financial Professionals, Business Appraisers and Accountants*. New York: John Wiley & Sons, 2001.

Lerch, Mary Ann. "Discount for Key Man Loss: A Quantitative Analysis." *Business Valuation Review* (December 1992), 183–194.

Leung, Tony T.S. "Myths About Capitalization Rate and Risk Premium." *Business Valuation News* (March 1986), 6–10.

Lippitt, Jeffrey W., and Nicholas J. Mastriacchio. "Developing Capitalization Rates for Valuing a Business." *CPA Journal* (November 1995), 24–28.

Maher, J. Michael. "Discounts for Lack of Marketability for Closely Held Business Interests." *Taxes* (September 1976), 562–571.

Mard, Michael J., and James S. Rigby. "New Research to Estimate Cost of Capital." *CPA Expert* (Fall 1995), 9–12.

Marren, Joseph H. *Mergers & Acquisitions*. Burr Ridge, Ill.: Irwin Professional Publishing, 1993.

The Matrimonial Strategist, monthly. Leader Publications, 345 Park Avenue South, New York, NY 10010, (800) 537-2128 (www.lawcatalog.com).

McMullin, Scott G. "Discount Rate Selection." *Business Valuation News* (September 1986), 16–19.

Mercer, Capital. *Valuation for Impairment Testing*. Memphis: Peabody Publishing, L.P., 2002.

Mercer, Z. Christopher. "Are Marketability Discounts Applicable to Controlling Interests in Private Companies?" *Valuation Strategies* (November/December 1997), 31–36.

Mercer, Z. Christopher. *Qualifying Marketability Discounts*. Memphis, Tenn.: Peabody Publishing, 1997.

Mercer, Z. Christopher. "Should 'Marketability Discounts' Be Applied to Controlling Interests of Private Companies?" *Business Valuation Review* (June 1994), 55–65.

Mercer, Z. Christopher. *Valuing Financial Institutions*. Burr Ridge, Ill.: Irwin Professional Publishing, 1992.

Mercer, Z. Christopher, and Terry S. Brown. "Fair Market Value vs. the Real World." *Valuation Strategies* (March/April 1999), 6–15.

Mergers & Acquisitions Magazine. Philadelphia: MLR Publishing Co., bimonthly.

Mezzullo, Louis A. "Buy-Sell Agreements after Chapter 14." *Trusts & Estates* (June 1994), 49–59.

Mezzullo, Louis A. *Valuation Rules Under Chapter 14*. Chicago: American Bar Association, 1995.

Miles, Raymond C. *Basic Business Appraisal*. Plantation, Fla.: Institute of Business Appraisers, 1984.

Miller, Warren D. "Assessing Unsystematic Risk." *CPA Expert* (Summer 1999), 1–5.

Moroney, Robert E. "Why 25 Percent Discount for Nonmarketability in One Valuation, 100 Percent in Another?" *Taxes* (May 1977), 316–320.

Nath, Eric W. "Control Premiums and Minority Interest Discounts in Private Companies." *Business Valuation Review* (June 1990), 39–46.

Nath, Eric W. "How Public Guideline Companies Represent a 'Control' Value for a Private Company." *Business Valuation Review* (December 1997), 167–171.

Nath, Eric W. "Tale of Two Markets." *Business Valuation Review* (September 1994), 107–112.

National Association of Business Management. *Executive Compensation Survey Results*. New York: National Association of Business Management, annual.

National Litigation Consultants' Review, Litigation Consultants, LLC, P.O. Box 161873, Altamonte Springs, FL 32716, monthly.

National Trade and Professional Associations of the United States. Washington, D.C.: Columbia Books, Inc., annual.

Nevers, Thomas J. "Capitalization Rates." *Business Valuation News* (June 1985), 3–6.

Officer Compensation Report. Greenvale, N.Y.: Panel Publishers, annual.

Oldham, J. Thomas. *Divorce, Separation and the Distribution of Property*. New York: Law Journal Seminars Press, annual.

Orenstein, Theodore P., and Gary N. Skoloff. *When a Professional Divorces: Strategies for Valuing Practices, Licenses, and Degrees*, 2nd ed. Chicago: American Bar Association, 1994.

Pack, Steven M. *Family Limited Partnerships: Practical Strategies & Solutions*. California: Steven M. Pack, JD, 2001.

Peters, Jerry O. "Adjusting Price/Earnings Ratios for Differences in Company Size." *Business Valuation Review* (June 1999), 71–85.

Peters, Jerry O. "Lack of Marketability Discounts for Controlling Interests: An Analysis of Public vs. Private Transactions." *Business Valuation Review* (June 1995), 59–61.

Pratt, Shannon P. *Business Valuation Body of Knowledge: Exam Review and Professional Reference*. New York: John Wiley & Sons, 1998.

Pratt, Shannon P. *Business Valuation Discounts and Premiums*. New York: John Wiley & Sons, 2001.

Pratt, Shannon P. "Control Premiums? Maybe, Maybe Not—34% of 3rd Quarter Buyouts at Discounts." *Shannon Pratt's Business Valuation Update* (January 1999), 1–2.

Pratt, Shannon P. *Cost of Capital: Estimation and Applications*. New York: John Wiley & Sons, 1998.

Pratt, Shannon P., ed. "Evidence Suggests Equity Risk Premium Lower Than Conventional Wisdom Thinks." *Shannon Pratt's Business Valuation Update* (July 1996), 1–5 (Part 1); (August 1996), 1–2 (Part 2).

Pratt, Shannon P. *The Market Approach to Valuing Businesses*. New York: John Wiley & Sons, 2001.

Pratt, Shannon P., Robert F. Reilly, and Robert P. Schweihs. *Valuing Small Businesses and Professional Practices*. New York: McGraw-Hill, 1998.

Pratt, Shannon P., Robert F. Reilly, and Robert P. Schweihs. *Valuing a Business*, 4th ed. New York: McGraw-Hill, 2000.

Reeves, James F., Linda A. Markwood, and Suzanne Scrivan. *Guide to Family Partnerships*, Forth Worth, Tex.: Practitioners Publishing Company, annual.

Reilly, Robert F., and Robert P. Schweihs, eds. *The Handbook of Advanced Business Valuation*. New York: McGraw-Hill, 2000.

Reilly, Robert F., and Robert P. Schweihs. *Valuing Accounting Practices*. New York: John Wiley & Sons, 1997.

Reilly, Robert F., and Robert P. Schweihs. *Valuing Intangible Assets*. New York: McGraw-Hill, 1999.

Rigby, Jim, and Michael J. Mattson. "Capitalization and Discount Rates: Mathematically Related, but Conceptually Different." *CPA Expert* (Fall 1996), 1–3.

Robert Morris Associates. *Annual Statement Studies*. Philadelphia: Robert Morris Associates, annual.

Schilt, James H. "Selection of Capitalization Rates for Valuing." *Business Valuation News* (June 1982), 2–6.

Schilt, James H. "Selection of Capitalization Rates—Revisited." *Business Valuation Review* (June 1991), 51–52.

Shannon Pratt's Business Valuation Update. Portland, Ore.: Business Valuation Resources, monthly.

Shiffrin, Daniel. "Tax Court Determines Weight of Asset-Based and Earnings-Based Valuation Approaches." *CPA Litigation Counselor* (February 2000), 3, 12.

Silber, William L. "Discounts on Restricted Stock: The Impact of Illiquidity on Stock Prices." *Financial Analysts Journal* (July–August 1991), 60–64.

Skoloff, Gary N., and Theodore P. Orenstein. *When a Lawyer Divorces: How to Value a Professional Practice*. Chicago: American Bar Association Press, 1986.

Sliwoski, Leonard J. "Built-in-Gains Tax, Discounts for Lack of Marketability, and *Eisenberg v. Commissioner*." *Business Valuation Review* (March 1998), 3–6.

Smith, Gordon V. *Corporate Valuation: A Business and Professional Guide*. New York: John Wiley & Sons, 1988.

Smith, Gordon V., and Russell L. Parr. *Valuation of Intellectual Property and Intangible Assets*, 2nd ed. New York: John Wiley & Sons, 1994.

Standard & Poor's Analyst's Handbook. New York: Standard & Poor's, annual.

Standard & Poor's Execucomp. New York: Standard & Poor's, quarterly (www.umi.compustat.com/cgi-mi-auth/mihome.cgi).

Standard & Poor's Industry Surveys. New York: Standard & Poor's, biannnual.

Standard & Poor's Statistical Service. New York: Standard & Poor's DRI, monthly, with cumulations (www.dri.mcgraw-hill.com).

Standard & Poor's Trends and Projections. New York: Standard & Poor's DRI, monthly (www.dri.mcgraw-hill.com).

Statistical Abstract of the United States. Washington, D.C.: Government Printing Office, annual (www.census.gov/statab).

Survey of Current Business. Washington, D.C.: Government Printing Office, monthly (www.bea.doc.gov/bea/pubs.htm).

Swad, Randy. "Discount and Capitalization Rates in Business Valuations." *CPA Journal* (October 1994), 40–46.

Taub, Maxwell J. "Valuing a Minority Interest: Whether to Adjust Elements of a Financial Statement Over Which the Minority Shareholder Has No Control." *Business Valuation Review* (March 1998), 7–9.

Troy, Leo. *Almanac of Business and Industrial Ratios*. Englewood Cliffs, N.J.: Prentice Hall, annual.

Trugman, Gary R. *Conducting a Valuation of a Closely Held Business* (Management Consulting Services Practice Aid 93-3). Jersey City, N.J.: AICPA, 1993.

Trugman, Gary R. *A CPA's Guide to Valuing a Closely Held Business*. Jersey City, N.J.: AICPA, 2001.

Trugman, Gary R., Stanton L. Meltzer, David A. Rooney, et al. *Guide to Divorce Engagements*. Fort Worth, Tex.: Practitioners Publishing Co., annual.

Tudor, Jan Davis, "Industry Information on the Internet: A Case Study." *CPA Expert* (Fall 1998), 10–12.

Tudor, Jan Davis, "The Internet as Librarian: Online General Info Sources." *CPA Litigation Service Counselor* (January 2000), 5–6.

Uniform Standards of Appraisal Practice. Washington, D.C.: Appraisal Foundation, annual.

U.S. Industry & Trade Outlook. DRI/McGraw-Hill, Standard & Poor's, and U.S. Department of Commerce/International Trade Administration, annual.

The Value Line Investment Survey. New York: Value Line Publishing, weekly.

Vander Linden, Eric. "Cost of Capital Derived from Ibbotson Data Equals Minority Value." *Business Valuation Review* (December 1998), 123–127.

Vignocchi, Roger, ed. *Merger and Acquisition Sourcebook*. Santa Barbara, Calif.: Quality Services Co., updated annually.

West, Thomas L., ed. *Business Reference Guide*, Concord, Mass.: Business Brokerage Press, annual.

West, Thomas L., and Jeffrey D. Jones, eds. *Handbook of Business Valuation*. New York: John Wiley & Sons, 1999.

Zukin, James H., ed. *Financial Valuation: Business and Business Interests*. New York: Warren Gorham & Lamont, 1990, updated annually.

Government Regulatory Material

Appeals and Review

Memoranda (ARMs)	*Review Procedures*
34	66-49
68	77-12

Internal Revenue Code (IRC)

Revenue Rulings	*Sections*
59-60	338
65-192	341
65-193	1060
68-609	2031
77-287	2036
83-120	2501
85-75	2701
93-12	2702
	2703
	2704
	6659
	6660

Technical Advice Memoranda	*Private Letter Rulings*
9436005	91-50001

Organizations

American Institute of Certified Public Accountants, Harborside Financial Center, 201 Plaza III, Jersey City, NJ 07311, (800) 862-4272, www.aicpa.org

American Society of Appraisers, P.O. Box 17265, Washington, DC 20041, (703) 478-2228, www.appraisers.org

The Appraisal Foundation, 1029 Vermont Avenue, NW, Suite 900, Washington, DC 20005, (202) 347-7722, www.appraisalfoundation.org

Association for Investment Management and Research, 5 Boar's Head Lane, P.O. Box 3668, Charlottesville, VA 22903, (804) 977-6600, www.aimr.org

The ESOP Association, 1100 17th Street, NW Suite 210, Washington, DC 20036, (202) 293-2971, www.the-esop-emplowner.org

Institute of Business Appraisers, P.O. Box 17410, Plantation, FL 33418, (954) 584-1144, www.go-iba.org

National Association of Certified Valuation Analysts, 1111 East Brickyard Road, Suite 200, Salt Lake City, UT 84106, (801) 486-0600, www.nacva.com

Sources of Data

American Institute of Certified Public Accountants NAARS, 1211 Avenue of the Americas, New York, NY 10036-8775, (800) 862-4272

Appraisal Profession Online, P.O. Box 17265, Washington, DC 20041, (703) 478-5500

Asset Business Appraisal BizComps, P.O. Box 711777, San Diego, CA 92171, (858) 457-0366, www.bizcomps.com

Business Valuation Resources, 7412 S.W. Beaverton-Hillsdale Highway, Suite 106, Portland, OR 97225, (888) BUS-VALU, www.bvlibrary.com

CCH Inc. 4025 West Peterson Ave., Chicago, IL 60646, (800) TELL-CCH

CompuServe Information Service, 500 Arlington Center Blvd., Columbus, OH 43220-0742, (800) 524-3388, www.compuserve.com

Datatimes, 14000 Quaff Springs Pkwy., Oklahoma City, OK 73134, (405) 751-6400

The Dialog Corporation, 11000 Regency Parkway, Suite 10, Cary, NC 27512-8004, (800) 334-2564, www.dialog.com/homepage.shtml

Dialog on Disc, Knight-Ridder Information, (800) 334-2564, www.dialog.com

Disclosure, Inc. 888 Seventh Avenue, 44th Floor, New York, NY 10106, (800) 846-0365

Dow Jones News Retrieval, Dow Jones Business Information Services, P.O. Box 300, Princeton, NJ 08543-0300, (800) 369-7466, www.djinteractive.com

Economic Bulletin Board STAT-USA, U.S. Department of Commerce, HCHB Room 4885, Washington, DC 20230, (202) 482-1986

Economic Census. Washington, DC: Government Printing Office, www.census.gov

EDGAR Database, Securities and Exchange Commission, www.sec.gov/cgi-gin/srch-edgar

Houlihan, Lokey, Howard & Zukin, *Mergerstat* and *The Control Premium Study*, 1930 Century Park West, Los Angeles, CA 90067, (310) 553-8871

Ibbotson Associates, 225 North Michigan Ave., Suite 700, Chicago, IL 60601-7676, (312) 616-1620, www.ibbotson.com

Integra Information, Inc., 245 Main Street, Suite 101, Chester, NJ 07930, 800-780-2660. www.integrainfo.com

Kleinrock Publishing, Inc., 7094 Peachtree Industrial Blvd., Suite 150, Norcross, GA 30071, (800) 678-2315

Knight-Ridder Information Dialog, 343 Sansome St., Suite 825, San Francisco, CA 94140, (800) 3DIALOG

Lexis-Nexis, 9393 Springboro Pike, P.O. Box 933-NR, Dayton, OH 45401, (800) 346-9759, www.lexis-nexis.com

Lotus OneSource, 150 Cambridge Park Drive, Cambridge, MA 02140, (800) 554-5501

Mercer Capital Management National Economic Review, 5860 Ridgeway Center Pkwy., Suite 410, Memphis, TN 38120, (901) 685-2120

Moody's Investors Service, 1 Sansome St., Suite 3100, San Francisco, CA 94104 (800) 700-1709, www.moodys.com

Newsnet, 945 Haverford Rd., Bryn Mawr, PA 19010, (800) 952-0122

PRS, SI: Special Issues, 9597 Jones Road #118, Houston, TX 77065, (713) 469-6004

Research Institute of America, 117 East Stevens Ave., Valhalla, NY 10595-1264, (800) 431-9025

Securities Data Publishing Company, Thompson Financial Securities Data, 40 West 57th Street, Suite 1000, New York, NY 10019, (212) 765-5311, www.securitiesdata.com

Sheshunoff Information Services, 900 East Las Colinas Blvd., Suite 1150, Irving, TX 75039, (800) 929-8277

Standard & Poor's Corp., 25 Broadway, 16th Floor, New York, NY 10004, (800) 523-4534, www.standardpoor.com

Tax Analysts, 6830 N. Fairfax Drive, Arlington, VA 22213, (800) 955-2444

Thomson Corporation, One Station Place, Stamford, CT 06902, (203) 969-8700, www.thomson.com

Thomson Securities Data Company, 40 W. 57th Street, New York, NY 10019, (201) 622-3100

UMI–ABI Inform, 300 North Zeeb Road, Ann Arbor, MI, (800) 521-0600, ext. 2705

U.S. Bureau of Economic Analysis, Department of Commerce. Washington, DC, (202) 377-1986, www.bea.doc.gov

U.S. Government Printing Office, Superintendent of Documents, Washington, DC 20402, (202) 783-3238

Value Line Publishing, Inc., 220 East 42nd Street, 6th Floor, New York, NY 10017, (212) 907-1500, www.valueline.com

Wiley-ValuSource, 7222 Commerce Center Drive, Suite 210, Colorado Springs, CO 80919, (800) 825-8763

Index

A

About.com, 104
Accountants (CPAs), as business appraisers, 10
Accounting practice
  economy/industry section, 591
  history section, 584–585
  reasonable compensation, 608–609
Accounting Principle Bulletins (APBs)
  No. 16, 5
  No. 17, 5
Accounts payable
  adjustment for balance sheet, 262
  payout period, 129
Accounts payable to inventory, 129
Accounts receivable
  adjustment for balance sheet, 260
  for law firm, 593
  for professional practices, 592–593
  for psychology practice, 592
  tax-effecting, 592
Accrual accounting, versus cash basis, 591–613
Acquisition
  and business valuation, 4
  data on, 88
Active investor, 648–649
Active trading, 173
Additional productive capacity, adjustments due to, 303
Adjusted book value method, 259–276, 617–618
  illustration of, 274–275
Adjustments, after calculation of, 273
Ad valorem taxes, 7
After-tax information, 285–286
  advantages, 285
After-tax rates, 350
Agreement of Partnership, 452
AICPA. *See* American Institute of Certified Public Accountants
AICPA standards
  business valuation, 15
  and the client, 16
  code of professional conduct, 15
  consulting services, 14–15
  due professional care, 15
  planning and supervision, 15
  professional competence, 15
  sufficient relevant data, 16
AJR NewsLink, 102
Alimony, 871
AllTheWeb, 103
Almanac of Business and Industrial Financial Ratios, 83
Alpha, 339
AltaVista, 104
Alternative cost of capital, 325
Alternatives, Principle of. *See* Principle of Alternatives
American Institute of Certified Public Accountants (AICPA), 2, 21
  ABV designation, 3, 12
  Certificate of Educational Achievement (CEA) program, 13
  consulting services (CS), 12
  role in business valuation, 12
  standards, 297, 682–684
  statement on consulting services standards, 755–757
American Society of Appraisers (ASA), 2
  accreditation, 12–13
  AM designation, 12–13
  ASA designation, 13
  designation for appraisers, 279–280
  standards, 16–17, 39–40, 771–784
Annual Report of the Council of Economic Advisers, 80–81
Annual Statement Studies, 313
Appeals and Review Memorandums (ARMs)
  No. 34, 2, 65, 66, 314, 319–320
  No. 68, 65, 66
Appendixes, 425
Applicable restriction, 455
Application of Professional Standards in the Performance of Litigation Services, 15, 16
Appraisal. *See also* Valuation
  and benefit stream, 284
  defined, 40
  function, 284
  IRS influence on, 64–68
  limited, 40–43
  literature, 846–847
  minority, 284–285
  principles of, 55–56, 847–848, 854–856
  purpose, 284
  questions, 108–113
  standards, 14–19
Appraisal assignment, 45
Appraisal Foundation, 2, 17–18
  need for, 14
  USPAP. See Uniform Standards of Professional Appraisal Practice

Appraisal Institute, designations for appraisers, 280
Appraisal method, choice of, 444
Appraisal organizations, 12–14
  American Institute of Certified Public Accountants (AICPA), 12, 21
  American Society of Appraisers (ASA), 12
  Appraisal Foundation, 14
  Association for Investment Management and Research, 14
  Institute of Business Appraisers, Inc. (IBA), 13
  National Association of Certified Valuation Analysts (NACVA), 13
Appraisal principles, 847–848, 854–856
Appraisal report. *See also* Valuation report
  economy section, 116–118
  industry section, 119–124
  samples, CD-1–CD-128
Appraisal subject, 43
Appraisers, 9–11
  accountants, 10
  business, 10
  business brokers, 10–11
  collaboration with, 279
  college professors, 11
  commercial real estate appraisers, 11
  communication among, 273–274
  investment bankers, 11
  role of, 406–509
  self-protection, 442
Appraiser's reputation, 28, 35, 45
Arm's length, 661
ASA. *See* American Society of Appraisers
Ask Jeeves, 104
Asset-based approach, 257–280
  advantages and disadvantages, 259
  common applications of, 257–259
  and partnerships, 459
  for professional practices, 617–618
Asset risk, 192
Asset sales, 27–28, 43, 223
Assignee interest, 459
Assignment
  nature of, 452
  objectives of, 676
Association for Investment Management and Research, CFA designation, 14
Associations on the Net, 100–101
Assumptions, 423, 676–677
  economic and financial, 677
  about the facts, 677
  involving the opinions of other experts, 677
  in valuation report, 44
Automobile expenses, 149
Average collection period, 129

B

Balance sheets
  adjustment, 260–263, 303–309
  analysis of, 141
  tax-effecting, 263–272
Ballpark, 35
Bankruptcy, 4
Bardahl analysis, 142–143
Bardahl Manufacturing Corp., 142
Beasley v. Beasley, 518
Beerly v. Dept. of Treasury, 625
"Before and after" method, 679–680
"Beige Book," 96
Benefit streams, 284
  adjustments, 303
  after-debt, 286
  debt-free, 286
  factors in selecting, 284–285
  matching with capitalization rates, 301–302
  projecting, 288–293
Best fit, 196
Betas, 107, 336–339
  levered, 338–339
Bigger fool theory, 249
BizComps, 107, 226–229, 250, 347
  difference with IBA, 229
  transaction, 227, 230, 233, 234
  2001 field definitions, 226
Blass v. United States, 633
Blockage discount, 402–405, 417
Bloomberg Financial Markets, 106
Bogosian v. Woloohojian Realty Corp., 633
Bonds, data on, 99
Breach of a legal duty, 674–675
Brown v. Brown, 508
Buildings, adjustment for balance sheet, 261
Build up method, 334–335, 347
Bureau of Economic Analysis (BEA), 93, 97–98
Bureau of Labor Statistics (BLS), 94
Bureau of the Census, 94
Business, size and complexities of, 659
Business appraisers, 10
Business brokers, 236–238
  as business appraisers, 10–11
Business description, 171
Business expenses, lack of reimbursement of, 661
Business goodwill. *See* Practice goodwill
Business location, 333
Business Profiler, 104, 132–137, 313
Business risk, 191

"But for" method, 680
"But for" rule, 675
Buy-sell agreement, 552
  use of formulas in, 6
Buy-sell formula, 553

C
Calculation of value, 35
Calculation of value report, sample, CD-119–CD-128
Calculations, defined, 40
Capital asset pricing model (CAPM), 329, 335–340
  valuation of a closely held company, 339–340
Capital gains tax, built-in, 464
Capitalization, 281–282
  of earnings versus excess earnings, 551–552
Capitalization method, 319
Capitalization of benefits method, 299–304
  adjustments, 302
  example, 301
  with minority interests, 302
  with service businesses, 303
  single-period model, 301, 304
Capitalization rates, 323–324, 326, 344–356, 419, 444
  deriving directly from the market, 348
  dividend yield, 353–354
  example, 349
  factors affecting the selection of, 345
  mixed holdings, 352–353
  real estate holdings, 351
  sources of data on, 346–347
Capital structure, and benefit streams, 284
CAPM. *See* Capital asset pricing model
Cash basis, versus accrual accounting, 591–613
Cash flow, 286–288
  definition of, 287–288
  and dividends, 287
  gross, 287
  net, 287–288
  short-term, 288
Cash flow discount rate, 347
Cash or equivalent, 58–59
  adjusting for balance sheet, 260
Cash or income tax basis, conversion to GAAP, 139–140
Cash to current liabilities, 128–129
Causation, 675
C corporation, 286
Cede and Co. v. Technicolor, Inc., 628
Celebrity goodwill, 547
Census Information Center (CIC), 94
Central Intelligence Agency, 100
Central Trust v. United States, 293
Certificate of Limited Partnership, 452
Certified business appraiser (CBA), 13
Chapter 14, 68, 450, 453–455
  Section 2701, 454
  Section 2703, 454
  Section 2704, 454–455
Charitable contributions, 8
Church v. United States, 456
Citizens Bank and Trust Co., Transferee v. Commissioner, 647
Client responsibilities, 44
Closely held businesses, 283, 411
  adapting CAPM for, 339–340
  equitable distribution value, 843–872
  non-operating debt, 190
Closely held market, data from, 222
College professors, as business appraisers, 11
Columbia Financial Advisors study, 379
Commercial goodwill. *See* Practice goodwill
Common-size financial analysis, 126–128
Common-size financial statements, 125–128
Company size, 171–173
Comparability adjustments, 143–144
Comparables, 70, 84, 159. *See also* Guideline companies
Comparative companies. *See* Guideline companies
Comparative company analysis, 125
Comparative industry analysis, 131–137
Compensation
  for family members, 150
  prevailing rates of, 660
  in prior years, 660–661
  reasonable. *See* Reasonable compensation
Compensation surveys, 104
Competency standards, 21
Competition, 333, 683
Compound growth rate, 130
Compulsion to act, 60
CompuServe, 102, 104, 105
Compustat, 105, 107
Conclusion, illogical, 445
Conducting a Valuation of a Closely Held Business, 15
Conference Board, 96
Conflict of interest, 22–27
  and deductible compensation for income tax purposes, 24
  in divorce suits, 24
  protection against, 24–27
  representing an existing client, 23–24
  and retainer agreements, 24–27
  verification form, 22–23
Consulting agreement, 36
Contract
  adjustment for balance sheet, 262
  breach of, 674–675
Control, nonmarketable, 222

Control basis, 651
Control investor, 649–650
Control premium, 359–366
Corporation, liquidation of, 4
Cost approach. *See* Asset-based approach
Cost of capital, 107
Cost of Capital Quarterly, 82
Cost of money, 326
Costs of flotation, 381–383
Cost to create method, 279
Covenant not to compete, 518–546
CPAs, 17–18
  level of service, 39
Critiquing opposing reports, 35
Current ratio, 128
Cyclical industries, 116, 118

D
Daly v. Daly, 846
Damages
  compensatory, 676
  consequential, 676
  mitigation of, 680–681
  relation to defendant's actions, 675–676
  types of, 676
Damages litigation, 8
Data analysis, 115–155
Data gathering, 69–114
  electronic, 90–108
Data providers and vendors, 91
Daubert, William, et al. v. Merrell Dow Pharmaceuticals, Inc., 8
Debt to equity, 129
Deemed transfers, 454
Deferred taxes, adjustment for balance sheet, 262–263
Definitions, 780–783, 800–805
Delaware block method, 634
Dental practice
  profile, 579–583
  reasonable compensation, 598–605
Depreciated replacement cost new, 273
Depreciation deduction, 319
Describe, meaning of, 425
Description of the assignment, 422
Destruction of a business, 684
Dialog, 105
Dialog Corporation, 101–102
Dialog Select, 106
DialogWeb, 101–112
Disclosure, 105
Discounted future benefits method, 304–309
  applications of, 305
  example, 306
  with mid-year convention, 306–307
  report, 308
  terminal value, 305–309
Discounted future earnings method, 855
Discount for lack of marketability, 370–391
Discounting, 282
Discount rates, 323–344, 354–356, 444
  components of, 326–332
  deriving directly from the market, 348
  example, 349
  factors affecting the selection of, 325–326
  methods for estimating, 334–344
Discounts, 357–407, 445
  application of, 401
  blockage, 402–405
  key person, 400–401
  lack of control, 366–370, 459–460
  marketability, 624
  from net asset value, 392–400
  small company, 391–392
  summary of, 380
  for uncertainty litigation, 405–407
Discounts for lack of marketability (DLOM), 461–462, 651
  application of, 401
  application to controlling interests, 385–390
Discretionary adjustments, 146–150
Discretionary costs, 139
Dismal Scientist, 96, 101
Dispute resolution, 38
Dissenters' rights, 623
Dissolution statutes, 622
Distress sale, 60
Dividend-paying capacity, 416
Dividend policy, 656
Dividend yield, 353–354
Divorce, 24
Divorce Reform Act of 1971, 845–846
Divorce valuations, 505–548, 587–590
  versus the market, 515–516
  of professional practices, 514–518
  valuation dates, 509–510
Divorce value, 863–871
  opposition replies to, 870–871
DLOM. *See* Discounts for lack of marketability
Document checklist
  accounting practice, 52–53
  law practice, 50–51
  medical practice, 48–50
Document request, 45–53
Documents and records
  from opposition, 678
  original versus copies, 678
Donations, 8

Done Deals, 234–236, 347
  search results, 235
Double counting, 861–862, 871
Dow Jones averages, 99
Dow Jones Interactive, 102
Dugan v. Dugan, 346, 515, 518, 846, 849, 851–852, 857, 861, 862
Dupont analysis, 130

E
Earnings
  versus excess earnings, 551–552
  lost, 681–682
Earnings base, method of calculating, 193–194
Earnings capacity, 286
  defined, 281
EBIT to total assets, 129
Economagic, 96
Economic Abstract of the United States, 80
Economic analysis, 115–118
Economic conditions, 333, 660
Economic damages, 673–753
Economic data, global approach, 78
Economic indicators, 117
Economic outlook, 656
Economic Report of the President, 80–81
Economic risk, 191
Economy, 77–80
  information on, 92–100, 423
  state and local, 97
  U.S., 92–97
Economy.com, 96–97
Economy/industry section
  for accounting practice, 591
  example, 290–292
Economy section, 116–118
EDGAR, 106, 168
Electronic data gathering, 90–108
  definition of, 90–91
Electronic Data Gathering Analysts and Retrieval. *See* EDGAR
Elkus v. Elkus, 547
Embassies, 100
Eminent domain actions, 9
Employee qualifications, 659
Employee Stock Ownership Plans (ESOPs), 6, 72
Employee work, nature, extent, and scope of, 659
Employer debt, guaranteed by employee, 661
Encyclopedia Britannica, 101
Engagement
  conflict of interest, 22–27
  factors in accepting, 22–32
  initial document request, 45–53
  learning about, 21–22
  letters, 32–45
  purpose and function of, 27–28
  and scope of assignment, 28
  time required, 28
  type of report, 32
Engagement acceptance form, 28–32
Engagement letters. *See also* Retainer agreement
  "as of" date, 35, 44
  and "ballparks," 35
  with calculation of value services, 35–38
  client responsibilities, 44
  critiquing opposing reports, 35
  description of, 39, 43
  dispute resolution, 38
  effective date(s) of valuation, 35, 44
  and forensic accounting, 35
  form of, 38
  indemnification, 38
  list of assumptions and limiting conditions, 44
  litigation reports, 45
  payment terms, 38
  sample, 32–34, 36–38, 40–43
  standard of value, 38, 43
  terms of payment, 44–45
  types of report, 44
Entertainment expenses, 149
Equipment, 71
Equitable adjustment analysis, 628–633
Equitable distribution, 843–872
  definition, 844, 846
  determining reasonable compensation, 862–863
  differences from alimony, 846
  divorce value, 863–871
  and fair market value, 852–854
  and fairness, 848–849
  value concept, 847
  value concept used in New Jersey, 844
Equity
  in net cash flow, 287–288
  valuation of, 27
Equity risk premium, 327–331, 337–338
ESOPs. *See* Employee Stock Ownership Plans
Estate of Albert Strangi v. Commissioner, 455–456
Estate of Beatrice Ellen Jones Dunn v. Commissioner, 491–492
Estate of Chas. A. Borgatello et al. v. Commissioner, 498–499
Estate of Eileen K. Brocato v. Commissioner, 491
Estate of Emily F. Klauss v. Commissioner, 494–495
Estate of Etta H. Weinberg, et al. v. Commissioner, 458, 493–494
Estate of Frank M. DiSanto et al. v. Commissioner, 489–490
Estate of James J. Renier et al. v. Commissioner, 499–501
Estate of Joyce C. Hall v. Commissioner, 160, 645–647

Estate of Kirkpatrick, 293
Estate of Mary T. Maggos et ux. v. Commissioner, 497–498
Estate of Morton B. Harper v. Commissioner, 495–496
Estate of Pauline Welch, et al. v. Commissioner, 496–497
Estate of Piper v. Commissioner, 464
Estate of Samuel I. Newhouse v. Commissioner, 60, 648–650
Estate of William Luton, 263
Estate planning, 452
Estates, 5
Estate tax, repeal of, 5, 449
Estate valuations, 449–503
Ethics, 22
Evidence, 677–678
Excess earnings, 857
  capitalization, 311
Excess earnings method, 857–861
  advantages, 315
  appropriateness of, 311–312
  disadvantages, 313–321
  as discussed in Revenue Ruling 68-609, 320–321
  errors, 314
  guidelines for use, 310–311
  as hybrid approach, 310
  and intangible value, 310
  as last resort, 315, 321
  problematic result, 315
  rates of return comparison, 313
Executive Compensation Assessor, 104
Exhibits, 425
Expert testimony, 28
Exposure for open market sale, 59
External transactions, 553, 555

F

Factor rating method, 341
Fair cash value, 626
Fair market value, 6, 57–60, 506–508, 623, 626, 648, 871
  defined, 410–411, 452, 847
  in exchange, 274
  versus fair value, 61
  in place in use, 274
  use in equitable distribution, 852–854
Fairness, meaning of, 848–849
Fairness opinions, 9
Fair value, 60, 622–627
  versus fair market value, 61
  methodology, 633–643
  report, 635–643
Family limited partnership (FLP), 392–399
  advantages of, 451
  definition of, 450–451
  documents needed to prepare the appraisal, 452–453
  report, 450–489
  valuation adjustments, 459
  valuation issues, 451–452
  valuation methodology, 458
Family members, definition of, 451
FASB. *See* Financial Accounting Standards Board
Federal Reserve Board, 95–96
Federal Reserve Bulletin, 81
Federal Rules of Civil Procedure (FRCP), 426–427
Fedstats, 92–93
Fees, 44–45
FIFO, 176
Financial Accounting Standards Board (FASB), 5, 287
Financial analysis, 125–139, 444
Financial condition of employer, 661
Financial forecasts, factors in preparing, 682–683
Financial information, adjustments to, 516
Financial Institutions Reform, Recovery, and Enforcement Act of 1989 (FIRREA), 2, 17, 421
  requirements, 14
Financial projection, 682
Financial ratio analysis, of guideline companies, 179–186
Financial ratios, 128–131
  accounts payable payout period, 129
  accounts payable to inventory, 129
  average collection period, 129
  cash to current liabilities, 128–129
  compound growth rate, 130
  current ratio, 128
  debt to equity, 129
  EBIT to total assets, 129
  inventory holding period, 129
  inventory turnover, 129
  quick ratio, 128
  return on equity, 130
  times interest earned, 129
Financial risk, 191–192
Financial statements
  adjustments, 139–155
  analysis, 424, 655
  consistency, 139
  normalizing, 150–151, 512–514
Financial Statement Studies of the Small Business, 83
Financing, 7
FIRREA. *See* Financial Institutions Reform, Recovery, and Enforcement Act of 1989
FirstGov, 94, 98
Flotation, cost of, 381–383
FLP. *See* Family limited partnership
FMV study, 376
Foltz, Charles S., et al. v. U.S. News & World Report, Inc., et al., 260, 650–653
Forecast financial data, 88

Forecasts, 293, 682–684. *See also* Projections
Forecast section, 294–297
Formal reports, 425
Forms, 23
Formula approach. *See* Excess earnings method
Fraction interest adjustment, 463–464
Fraud, 24
FreeEDGAR, 168, 169
FreeLunch.com, 96
Fundamental value. *See* Intrinsic value
Future benefits, 412
  principle of. *See* Principle of Future Benefits

G
Gelman study, 373
Generally accepted accounting principles (GAAP), 5, 7, 139–140
General risk premium. *See* Equity risk premium
General Utilities Doctrine, 263, 418
Gift valuations, 449–503
Glossary, 800–805
Golub v. Golub, 547
Goodwill, 319, 416–417
  allocation of purchase price and, 4–5
  celebrity, 547, 857
  and divorce valuation, 516–518
  and equitable distribution, 849–852
  excess earnings, 857
  excess earnings method, 857–861
  practice, 515–516
  professional, 515–516, 547
Google, 103, 172
Graphs, 428
Gratto v. Gratto, 633
Gross, Walter L., Jr., et al. v. Commissioner, 286
Gross profit analysis, 137–138
Growth
  and inflation, 307
  volatile, 191
Growth rate, 344–345, 347
Guideline companies, 70, 84, 159, 332
  acquired or merged, 107
  actively traded, 173
  adjustments to, 176–177
  checklist, 160–162
  creating a list of, 166–170
  financial and operating data, 175–186
  financial ratio analysis with, 179–186
  financial statement information, 106
  finding, 105, 107
  publicly traded, 105, 106
  selection of, 444
  size criteria, 171–173
  stock quotes, 106–107
  valuation considerations, 192–194
Guideline public companies, comparison worksheet, 162–164
Guideline public company method, 158–186
  advantages of, 201
  disadvantages of, 201–202
  example of, 198
  illustration, 202–219
  report, 202–219
  using invested capital, 200
Guide to Business Valuations, 23

H
Historical Market Data Center, 103
History and nature of the business, 72–76, 656
History section
  accounting practice, 584–585
  medical practice, 585–587
HLHZ Premium for Control Study. See *Mergerstat Control Premium Study*
Hoover's Company Database, 105
Hoover's Online, 170, 171

I
IBA. *See* Institute of Business Appraisers, Inc.
Ibbotson Associates, 327–331
I/B/E/S, 106
Identifiable intangible assets, adjustment for balance sheet, 262
Incentive stock option, 7
Income
  comparison of salaries paid to, 659
  defined, 281
Income approach, 281–321
  advantages, 283
  with after-tax information, 285–286
  capitalization, 281–282
  and cash flow, 286
  disadvantages, 283–284
  discounting, 282
  and earnings capacity, 286
  fundamental theory behind, 282
  methods, 299–321
  and partnerships, 459
  with pretax information, 285–286
Income discount rate premium, 347
Income section, normalization of, 151–155
Income statements
  adjustments, 288–289, 303
  analysis of, 141
Income taxes, 514
Indemnification, 38

Industry, data on, 82–84, 100, 423
Industry analysis, 118–124, 170
Industry conditions, 333
Industry method, 255–256
Industry Norms & Key Business Ratios, 84
Industry ratio and compensation data sources, 104
Industry research, 170
Industry rule of thumb method. *See* Industry method
Industry section, 119–124
Inexperience, 22
Inflation, 307, 683
Informal reports, 425–426
Information
  analysis, 511–512
  from business brokers, 236–238
  from client and opposition, 678–679
  economic, 77–80, 92–100, 423
  economy/industry, 591
  external, 77
  financial, 77, 512, 516
  gathering, 69–114, 511–512
  guideline company, 84
  industry, 82–84, 423
  industry and company, 100
  internal, 69–77
  nonfinancial, 69–72
  publicly traded, 175–186
  state and local, 97–100
  subject company, 424
  United States, 92–97
Initial document request
  appraisal assignment, 45–53
  multiple checklist, 48–53
  standard checklist, 46–48
Initial public offering (IPO), stock valuation, 8
Innes v. Innes, 862
Insiders, 174
InSite, 103
Institute of Business Appraisers, Inc. (IBA), 2, 250, 347
  AIBA designation, 13
  business description analysis, 239–242
  CBA designation, 13
  data and definitions, 224
  difference with BizComps, 229
  market database, 223–226, 234
  MCBA designation, 13
  standards, 16, 758–770
  transaction, 230, 233
Insufficient skills or capacity, adjustments due to, 303
Insurance claims, 8
Intangible assets, 262
Intangibles, 319–321
Integra Information, 313
Integra Information's Business Profiler, 83
Interest expense, 150
Internal Revenue Code (IRC)
  Chapter 14, 68, 450, 453–455
  Section 162, 658
  Section 303, 5
  Section 754, 453, 457, 462
  Section 1031, 4
  Section 1060, 4
  Section 2036(c), 5
  Sections 2701 to 2704, 5
  Section 2702, 6
  Section 6662, 451
  Section 6701, 451–452
Internal Revenue Service (IRS), 318–319
  adequate disclosure rules, 465–468
Internal transactions, 255, 553, 554
International data, 100
International Trade Administration, 100
Internet, 91–92, 244
Internet Public Library, 102
Interview, on-site, 108
Intrinsic value, 62–64, 507–508
Inventory, adjusting for balance sheet, 261
Inventory accounting method, 289
Inventory holding period, 129
Inventory turnover, 129
Invested capital, 27
  in net cash flow, 287–288
  valuing, versus equity, 189–201
Investext, 104
Investment bankers, as business appraisers, 11
Investment value, 60, 62
IPO. *See* Initial public offering
IRC. *See* Internal Revenue Code
IRS. *See* Internal Revenue Service

J
Justification for purchase test, 446–448

K
Kerr, Baine P., et ux. v. Commissioner, 455
Key person discount, 400–401, 556
Kikkert v. Kikkert, 846, 848
Knight, Ina F., v. Commissioner, et vir v. Commissioner, 456, 502
Known facts, 676–677
Kumho Tire company, Ltd., et al. v. Patrick Carmichael, et al., 8

L
Lack of control discount, 366–370
  calculating, 367
Land, adjustment for balance sheet, 261

Lavene v. Lavene, 846, 847, 850–851
Law firm
  accounts receivable, 593
  reasonable compensation, 605–608
  work in process, 593–597
Leasehold improvements, adjustment for balance sheet, 261
Leasehold interests, adjustment for balance sheet, 261–262
Least squares, 247
Legal risk, 192
Letter of transmittal, 422
Letter reports, 426
Letter stock. *See* Restricted stock
Levy v. Levy, 846, 851, 857, 858, 862
Library costs, in professional practices, 598
LIFO, 176
Limited appraisal valuation, 40
Limited approach, 40
Limited liability companies, 285
Limited Partnership Act, 455
Limiting conditions, 423
  in valuation report, 44
Linear regression, 246–248
Liquidation value method, 276–279
Litigation, uncertainty of, 405–407
Lone Star Industries, Inc., 172
Lopez v. Lopez, 507, 517
Lost profits, 673–676
  analysis, 676–753
  computation, 679–680, 684
  discounting, 683–684
  elements of, 674–676
  to present value, 683
  sample analysis, 685–753
Lost revenues
  projected, after trial, 682, 683–684
  variable cost of, 681

M

Machinery and equipment, adjustment for balance sheet, 261
McSparron v. McSparron, 547
Mad Auto Wrecking, Inc. v. Commissioner, 147, 657–671
Maher study, 374–375
Management, 656
  depth of, 333
  interview with, 166
  quality of, 333
Management Planning study, 376–377
Mandelbaum, Bernard, et al. v. Commissioner, 383, 653–657
Marital assets, valuation of, 546–547
Marital dissolution, and asset valuation, 5–6
Marital property, 848–852
Marketability
  discounts, 463, 624
  provisions affecting, 462
  value of, 379
Marketable securities, adjusting for balance sheet, 260
Market absorption adjustment, 464
Market approach, 157–219, 221–256, 412, 614–615
  and partnerships, 459
Market data, 99, 444
Market entry, barriers to, 333
Market risk, 192
Markets and marketing, 71
Market value of invested capital (MVIC), 187, 199
Master document checklist, 48
Matter of Shell Oil Co., 625
Mean, 245, 246, 248
Measures of central tendency, 245, 246
Measures of dispersion, 246
Measures of location, 246
Measures of relative position, 246, 248, 249
Media General Plus, 105
Median, 245, 246, 248
Medical practice
  history section, 585–587
  profile, 575–579
  reasonable compensation, 609–611
Medicare, and professional practice valuation, 587
Mendell v. Mendell, 846
Mercer Capital, 96–99
Merger and acquisition method. *See* Transaction method
Mergers
  and business valuation, 4
  data on, 88
Mergerstat Control Premium Study, 89, 368
Mergerstat Review, 89, 368
Merger Yearbook, The, 89
Metlyn Realty Corp. v. Esmart Inc., 633
Mills v. Electric Auto-Life Co., 634
Minority basis, 651
Minority interest, 366–370, 392–399
  report, 653
Mixed holdings, 352–353
Model Act, 625–626
Monaghan v. Monaghan, 518–519
Moody's Investors Services, 105
Moody's Manuals, 87
Moroney study, 373–374
Mosaic, 91
Multiple document checklist, samples, 48–53
Multiple-of-revenue method. *See* Industry method
Multiples. *See* Valuation multiples
MVIC. *See* Market value of invested capital

N

NACVA. *See* National Association of Certified Valuation Analysts
Nasdaq Web site, 99, 105, 107
National Association of Certified Valuation Analysts (NACVA), 2
  AVA designation, 13
  CVA designation, 13
  GVA designation, 13
  professional standards, 785–799
  standards, 18
National Association of Independent Fee Appraisers, designations for appraisers, 280
National Income and Products Account (NIPA), 81
Nature of the business, 284, 656
NAVs. *See* Net asset values
NEBEDISM, 65–66
Nelson's Directory of Investment Research, 106
Nelson's Earnings Outlook, 106
Net asset values (NAVs), 460
Net cash flow model, 416
Net tangible assets, required rate of return on, 312–313
Net working capital, adjustments due to, 303
Neuman v. Neuman, 508
Newspapers, 102
Newspapers.com, 102
Non-compete agreements, 518–546
Non-operating assets, adjustments due to, 303
Non-operating/non-recurring adjustments, 144
Normalization adjustments, 143
Normalization process, 413
North American Industry Classification System Manual, 86–87
Northern Trust Co., Transferee v. Commissioner, 647
Notes payable, adjustment for balance sheet, 262

O

O'Brien v. O'Brien, 547
Officer's and owner's compensation, 147
Online database, 170
On-site interview, 108
Operating results, analysis of, 289
Operating risk, 191
Operational analysis, 137–139
Opportunity cost of capital, 325
Oppressed shareholders' statutes, 622
Oppression, 189
Oral reports, 426
Organizational form, 70–71
Organization for Economic Cooperation and Development (OECD), 100
OSHA Web site, 167, 168
Ownership of business, 70–71
Owner's perquisites, 149

P

Painter v. Painter, 846
Partnership Agreement, 462
Partnership Spectrum, 461
Passive investor, 648–649
Pass-through entities
  tax-effecting, 286
  valuation of, 285
Payment terms, 38
Penny stocks, 173
Pension plan, absence of, 661
Period of recovery for lost profits, 680
Personal goodwill. *See* Professional goodwill
Personnel, 71–72
Physical facilities, 71
Piscopo v. Piscopo, 508, 547, 846, 857
Portfolio adjustment, 464
Potential earning capacity, 856–857
Practice goodwill, 515
  versus professional goodwill, 516–518
Pratt's Stats, 229–234, 347
  analysis, 250–253
  field definitions, 231–233
  transaction, 234
  transaction report, 229–230
Predicast's Forecasts, 89
Prejudgment interest, 682
Premise of value, 39
Premium, 357–407, 445
  application of, 401
  control, 359–366
  percent paid over market price, 369
Prepaid expenses, adjustment for balance sheet, 261
Prepaid insurance, in professional practices, 597–598
Present value, adjustment to, 464
Present value theory, 853
Pretax information, 285–286
  advantages, 285
Pretax rates, 350
Price/earnings reciprocal plus growth, 340–341
Price to book value, 189
Price to cash flow, 188
Price to dividend or dividend-paying capacity, 188–189
Price to earnings, 225
Price to gross revenues, 225
Price to net earnings, 187–188
Price to pretax earnings, 188
Price to revenues to return on sales, 250
Price to sales, 188
Pricewaterhouse Coopers, 328–330
Principle of Alternatives, 55, 623, 847–848, 855
Principle of Future Benefits, 56, 848, 853, 855
Principle of Substitution, 55–56, 848, 855

Private Letter Ruling 91-50001, 263, 418, 840–842
Private versus public sales of stock, 655
Product demand, 683
Product risk, 192
Products and services, 71
Profession, defined, 549
Professional goodwill, 515, 547
  versus practice goodwill, 516–518
Professional license, valuation of, 547
Professional practices, 843–872
  characteristics, 550–551
  and divorce valuation, 514–518
  history of, 584
  market approach, 614–615
  versus other business, 551–557
  questionnaire, 557–574
  reasons for valuation of, 550
  versus regular business enterprises, 515
  valuation, 549–619
  valuation calculations, 614–618
  valuation process, 557–574
Profit-sharing plan, absence of, 661
Profound, 101
Projections, 682–684
  acceptance of, 293–299
  from company's management, 298–299
  difficulty of, 297
  factors in preparing, 682–683
  range of, 292–293
  sample, 294–297
Property, 456
  as defined in Section 2703, 454
  definition, 848
Psychology practice
  accounts receivable, 592
  reasonable compensation, 611–613
Public company
  adjusting multiples for risk, 190–192
  guideline, 158–186
Public investor, 650
Public market, data from, 222
Public offering, 649
  costs associated with, 657
Purchase price
  goodwill and, 4–5
  tax treatment of, 4

Q
Qualitative analysis, 239–244
  Pratt's Stats, 243
  transaction data, 243–244
Quantitative analysis, 245–252
Quick ratio, 128

R
Rate of return, 324
Real estate appraisers, as business appraisers, 11
Real estate holding company, valuation of, 264–266
Real estate holdings, 351–352
Real estate limited partnerships (RELPs), 461
Reasonable compensation, 662–671, 862–863, 870, 871
  accounting practice, 608–609
  dental practice, 598–605
  law firm, 605–608
  medical practice, 609–611
  in professional practices, 598–613
  psychology practice, 611–613
Reconciliation process, 445
Redemption policy, 657
Regression
  least squares, 247
  linear, 247, 248
Regression analysis, 194
Regulation Section 301.6501, 465
Regulatory risk, 192
Relative position, measures of, 246, 248, 249
Rent expense, 150
Replacement-cost approach. *See* Asset-based approach
Replacement cost new, 273
Reproduction cost new, 273–274
Required rate of return, on net tangible assets, 312–313
Research@Economy.com, 96, 101
Resources, 874–882
Restricted securities adjustment, 464
Restricted stock, 371
  as a form of payment, 4
Restrictive agreements, 419
Retained earnings, comparison of salaries with, 660
Retainer agreement. *See* Engagement letters
Return on equity, 130
Revenue factors, 683
Revenue Procedure 66-49, 66, 818–820
Revenue Procedure 77-12, 67, 823–824
Revenue Ruling 59-60, 2, 57, 65–66, 67, 77, 115, 124, 158–159, 173, 189, 191, 193, 221, 255, 258, 281, 293, 304, 318, 333, 409–420, 424, 444, 449, 453, 464, 506, 552, 646, 657, 806–812, 846, 847, 849, 851, 852, 855, 870
  for appraising FLPs, 453
  approach to valuation, 411–412
  background, 410–411
  balance sheets, 414–415
  blockage discount, 417
  capitalization rates, 419
  definitions, 410–411
  factors to consider in valuation, 412–413
  goodwill, 416–417
  profit-and-loss statements, 415–416

Revenue Ruling 59-60 (*Cont.*)
purpose, 409
restrictive agreements, 419
Section 4, 453, 458
using comparable companies, 417–418
Revenue Ruling 65-192, 66, 410, 813–816
Revenue Ruling 65-193, 66, 817
Revenue Ruling 68-609, 2, 66, 193, 273, 293, 310, 314, 411, 444, 821–822, 846, 851, 852, 857–861, 870
excess earnings method, 320–321
Revenue Ruling 77-287, 67, 370–371, 383, 411, 825–829
Revenue Ruling 81-253, 67
Revenue Ruling 83-120, 67, 830–832
Revenue Ruling 85-75, 67, 833–834
Revenue Ruling 93-12, 67–68, 835–836
Revenues, unreported, 513
Revised Uniform Limited Partnership Act (RULPA), 450
Richardson, David B., et al. v. U.S. News & World Report, Inc., et al., 260
Risk, 324–325
systematic, 336–339
Risk factors, 190–192
Risk-free rate of return, 326–327
Risk Management Association, 84, 313
RMA Annual Statement Studies, 83–84
Rothman v. Rothman, 846
R^2, 196, 247
Rule 144, 4, 371
Rules of thumb, 11, 255–256, 615–616

S
Safe rate, 326
Salary Assessor, 104
Salary policy, 660
S&P500, 99
S&P Register of Corporations, 87
Schecher v. Watkins, 634
Schedules, 425
Scope of assignment, 28–32
and appraisers' reputation, 28
description of, 39
engagement acceptance form, 28–32
level of service, 39
premise of value, 39
S corporations, 285–286
valuation of, 5
Search engines, 103–104
Securities, marketable, 460
Securities Act of 1933, 371
Securities Data Company (SDC), 107. *See also* Thomson Financial Securities Data (TFSD)
Securities Exchange Commission (SEC), 234, 371, 460
Institutional Investor Study, 372–373
Self-contained reports. *See* Formal reports
Separability, 319
SGLPTL, 186, 196–201, 249–250
analysis, 197
Shareholder
dissenting, 623–624
oppressed, 624–625
Shareholder disputes, 621–643
Shareholder distributions, comparison of salaries with, 660
Shepherd, J. C., v. Commissioner, 501–502
SIC code. *See* Standard Industrial Classification code
Silber study, 376
Small company discount, 391–392
Small company risk premium, 339–340
Smith v. Smith, 846
Specialists, locating, 279–280
Specific company adjustment, 339–340
Specific company risk premium, 331–332
Spinoffs, 4
Standard and Poor's (S&P), 105
Standard & Poor's Earnings Guide, 106
Standard & Poor's Register of Corporations, 87
Standard & Poor's Stock Reports, 107
Standard document checklist
alternatives to, 48
in litigation, 48
sample, 46–47
Standard Industrial Classification code (SIC code), 84–86
searching, 166–170
Standard Industrial Classification Manual, 84–85
sample, 85–86
Standard of value, 38, 43, 57, 64
incorrect, 61–62
marital dissolution and, 6
Standard Research Consultants study, 375
Standards
AICPA, 1, 14, 755–757. *See also* AICPA standards
ASA, 16–17, 39–40, 771–784
IBA, 16, 758–770
NACVA, 18, 785–799
Startup businesses, 684
State, meaning of, 425
State and local government on the Net, 98
State and local Web sites, 98
State Data Center (SDC), 97
State Data Center (SDC) program, 97
Statistical Resources on the Web, 95
Statistical techniques, 194–196
Statistics
definition of, 245
terms and definitions, 245–246
Stat-USA/Internet, 95

Statutory valuation method, 616–617
Stern v. Stern, 518, 846, 849, 850, 852, 856
Stock
  data on, 99
  holding period for, 656
  Rule 144, 4
Stockholder dispute, 6–7
Stockholder loans, 513–514
  adjustment for balance sheet, 263
Stock option, 7
Stock price volatility, 173
Stock pricing reports, 173–174
Stock sales, 27–28, 223
Stocks, Bonds, Bills, and Inflation Yearbook, 81, 327–331
Stout v. Stout, 846, 848
Stringer v. Car Data Systems, Inc., 634
Subject companies
  comparing, 332–334
  information on, 424
Subject company analysis, 124–125
Subject of valuation, and benefit streams, 284
Subsequent events, 555–556
Substitution, principle of. *See* Principle of Substitution
Summarize, meaning of, 425
Summary reports. *See* Informal reports
Supplies, in professional practices, 598
Survey of Current Business, 81
Systematic risk, 336

T
Tables and charts, 429
Tax-effecting
  accounts receivable, 592
  balance sheet, 263–272
  pass-through entities, 286
Tax Reform Act of 1986, 4, 263, 331, 418
Tax return adjustments, 140–141
Technical Advice Memorandum 94-36005, 68, 837–839
Technological risk, 192
10K Wizard, 168, 170
Terminal value, 305–309
  calculation of, 307
  discounting of, 307
Terms of payment, 44–45
Thelien v. Thelien, 508
Thinly traded public companies, 70
Thomson Financial Securities Data (TFSD), 236, 347
Time periods, in the application of pricing multiples, 193
Times interest earned, 129
Tort, 674–675
Trade association Web sites, 100
Tradeline, 106–107
Trading activity analysis, 174–175
Transaction analysis, qualitative versus quantitative, 238–253
Transaction method, 221–238
  advantages of, 253–254
  advice, 254–255
  disadvantages of, 254
Transactions
  external, 553, 555
  internal, 255, 553, 554
  tax-free under IRC § 1031, 4
  terms of, for mergers and acquisitions, 4
Transferability of stock, restrictions on, 656
Transferred shares, amount of control in, 656
Treasury bonds, 326–327
Treasury Regulations
  20.2031-1(b), 452
  25.2512-1, 452
  25.2512-2(e), 464
  60.2031-2(e), 464
Trend analysis, 137
Tri-Continental Corp. vs. Battye, 625, 634
Trout study, 375
Typographical errors, 445

U
Underutilized capacity, adjustments due to, 303
Uniform Business Corporation Act, 623
Uniform Partnership Act, 70
Uniform Standards of Professional Appraisal Practice (USPAP), 2, 14, 15, 16–18, 21, 39–40, 45, 421
  importance of, 17–18
  Standard 10, 421–422, 425
U.S. Census Bureau, 97
U.S. Industry & Trade Outlook, 83
USPAP. See *Uniform Standards of Professional Appraisal Practice*

V
Valuation. *See also* Appraisal
  "as of" date, 35, 510–511
  considerations, 192–194
  effective date(s) of, 44
  history of, 1–3
  of marital assets, 546–547
  methods. *See* Valuation methods
  overview, 1–19
  pass-through entities, 285
  providers, 9–11
  purpose of, 3, 64
  of real estate holding company, 264–266
  reasons for, 3–9
  subject of, 284–285

Valuation (*Cont.*)
terminology, 18–19
weight to be assigned to different approaches, 418–419
Valuation date, 628–633
Valuation Guide for Income, Estate and Gift Taxes, 318–319
Valuation methods, 259–279, 510–511, 514
in equitable distributions, 852
Valuation multiples, 186–189
adjusting, based on SGLPTL, 196–201
adjusting for risk, 190–192
invested capital, 200–201
price used in, 194
selection of, 199
Valuation process, 512
weaknesses in, 441–442
Valuation report, 421–448, 450. *See also* Appraisal report
common errors in, 443–445
components of, 421–425
defending, 443
formal, CD-1–CD-99
informal, CD-100–CD-119
opposition's, 430–437
preparing, 426
responding to opposition's, 437–441
as a selling tool, 427–429
types of, 425–426
Valuation section, 424
Value, 626
of closely held businesses, 283
control, 358
controlling interest, 624
intrinsic, 62–64, 507–508
investment, 62
from investor's viewpoint, 283
items affecting, 69, 72
marketable, 358, 624
minority, 358, 624
nonmarketable, 358, 624
types of, 358
Value, definition of, 57–64, 444, 506–509
fair market value, 57. *See also* Fair market value
fair value, 60–62
intrinsic value, 62–64
investment value, 62
Value Line Investment Survey, 87, 106
Value multiple, computation worksheet, 164–166
Value of marketability, 379

W
WACC. *See* Weighted average cost of capital
Weighted average, danger of, 193–194
Weighted average cost of capital (WACC), 325, 341–343
application, 342
formula, 342
Weinberger v. UOP, Inc., 627, 634
Willamette Management Associates, Inc. study, 375–376
criticisms of, 381
Williams v. Williams, 517–518
Willing buyer, 410, 508, 623
Willing seller, 410, 623
Work in process
for contingency fee law firm, 593–597
for a professional practice, 593–597
World Wide Web (WWW), 91

Y
Yahoo!, 103
Yardstick method, 680

Z
Zack's Earnings Forecaster, 106

About the Author

Gary R. Trugman, CPA/ABV, MCBA, ASA, MVS

Gary R. Trugman is a certified public accountant licensed in the states of New Jersey, New York, and Florida. He is accredited in business valuation by the AICPA and is a Master Certified Business Appraiser as designated by The Institute of Business Appraisers, Inc. He is also designated as an Accredited Senior Appraiser in Business Valuation by the American Society of Appraisers. Gary is regularly court appointed and has served as an expert witness in federal court and state courts in several jurisdictions, testifying on business valuation, matrimonial matters, business and economic damages, and other litigation matters.

Gary is currently on the AICPA subcommittee working with the judiciary. He is a former member of the Executive Committee of the Management Consulting Services Division of the AICPA, the Litigation Services Committee of the New Jersey Society of CPAs, the Business Valuation Subcommittee (past chairman) of the New Jersey Society of CPAs, the Matrimonial Committee of the New Jersey Society of CPAs, and the Business Valuation and Appraisal Subcommittee of the AICPA.

Gary is chairman of the Ethics and Discipline Committee, serves on the Qualification Review Committee, and is the former regional governor of the mid-Atlantic region of The Institute of Business Appraisers, Inc. He has received a Fellow Award from The Institute of Business Appraisers, Inc. for his many years of volunteer work in the profession. Gary has also received an AICPA Hall of Fame Award for his service to the accounting profession in assisting in the accreditation process in business valuation. Gary serves on the Business Valuation Education Subcommittee and the International Board of Examiners of the American Society of Appraisers. He is also a faculty member of the National Judicial College.

Gary lectures nationally on business valuation topics. In addition to authoring this text, he has written *A CPA's Guide to Valuing a Closely Held Business*, published by the AICPA. He has also developed numerous education courses, including a six-day business valuation educational series and a seminar titled "Understanding Business Valuation for the Practice of Law" for the Institute of Continuing Legal Education. Gary also serves as an editorial advisor for *The Journal of Accountancy*, *The CPA Expert*, and *The CPA Litigation Service Counselor*. He has lectured before numerous groups and has been published in *The Journal of Accountancy*, *FairShare*, and *The CPA Litigation Service Counselor*.

Gary was born in New York and received his undergraduate degree from the Bernard M. Baruch College of the City University of New York. He was the first business appraiser in the United States to earn a master's in valuation sciences from Lindenwood College. His master's thesis topic was "Equitable Distribution Value of Closely Held Businesses and Professional Practices." Gary's appraisal education also includes various courses offered by The Institute of Business Appraisers, Inc., the American Society of Appraisers, the AICPA, and other organizations. He has taught federal income taxation at Centenary College, financial statement analysis in the master's degree program at Lindenwood College, and several topics at the AICPA National Tax School in Champaign, Illinois. He is a member of The Institute of Business Appraisers, Inc., the American Society of Appraisers, the American Institute of Certified Public Accountants, the New Jersey Society of Certified Public Accountants, and the New York State Society of Certified Public Accountants.